STREET ATLAS

Devon

First published in 2003 by

Philip's, a division of
Octopus Publishing Group Ltd
2–4 Heron Quays, London E14 4JP

First edition 2003
Second impression 2003

ISBN 0-540-08130-2 (spiral)

Printed and bound in Spain
by Cayfosa-Quebecor

Contents

III **Key to map symbols**

IV **Key to map pages**

VI **Route planning**

X **Administrative and Postcode boundaries**

1 **Street maps** at 1¾ inches to 1 mile

150 **Street maps** at 3½ inches to 1 mile

261 **Street maps of Exeter and Plymouth city centres** at 7 inches to 1 mile

264 **Index** of towns and villages

266 **Index** of streets, hospitals, industrial estates, railway stations, schools, shopping centres, universities and places of interest

Digital Data

The exceptionally high-quality mapping found in this atlas is available as digital data in TIFF format, which is easily convertible to other bitmapped (raster) image formats.

The index is also available in digital form as a standard database table. It contains all the details found in the printed index together with the National Grid reference for the map square in which each entry is named.

For further information and to discuss your requirements, please contact Philip's on 020 7531 8438 or james.mann@philips-maps.co.uk

Key to map symbols

22a
Motorway with junction number
Primary route – dual/single carriageway
A road – dual/single carriageway
B road – dual/single carriageway
Minor road – dual/single carriageway
Other minor road – dual/single carriageway
Road under construction
Tunnel, covered road
Rural track, private road or narrow road in urban area
Gate or obstruction to traffic (restrictions may not apply at all times or to all vehicles)
Path, bridleway, byway open to all traffic, road used as a public path
Pedestrianised area
DY7
Postcode boundaries
County and unitary authority boundaries
Railway, tunnel, railway under construction
Tramway, tramway under construction
Miniature railway
Walsall
Railway station
Private railway station
South Shields
Metro station
Tram stop, tram stop under construction
Bus, coach station
Ambulance station
Coastguard station
Fire station
Police station
Accident and Emergency entrance to hospital
H
Hospital
Place of worship
i
Information Centre (open all year)
P
Parking
P&R
Park and Ride
PO
Post Office
Camping site
Caravan site
Golf course
Picnic site
Prim Sch
Important buildings, schools, colleges, universities and hospitals
River Medway
Water name
River, weir, stream
Canal, lock, tunnel
Water
Tidal water
Woods
Built up area
Church
Non-Roman antiquity
ROMAN FORT
Roman antiquity
87
228
Adjoining page indicators and overlap bands
The colour of the arrow and the band indicates the scale of the adjoining or overlapping page (see scales below)
Acad Academy
Allot Gdns Allotments
Cemy Cemetery
C Ctr Civic Centre
CH Club House
Coll College
Crem Crematorium
Ent Enterprise
Ex H Exhibition Hall
Ind Est Industrial Estate
IRB Sta Inshore Rescue Boat Station
Inst Institute
Ct Law Court
L Ctr Leisure Centre
LC Level Crossing
Liby Library
Mkt Market
Meml Memorial
Mon Monument
Mus Museum
Obsy Observatory
Pal Royal Palace
PH Public House
Recn Gd Recreation Ground
Resr Reservoir
Ret Pk Retail Park
Sch School
Sh Ctr Shopping Centre
TH Town Hall/House
Trad Est Trading Estate
Univ University
Wks Works
YH Youth Hostel
■ The small numbers around the edges of the maps identify the 1 kilometre National Grid lines
■ The dark grey border on the inside edge of some pages indicates that the mapping does not continue onto the adjacent page
The scale of the maps on the pages numbered in blue is 5.52 cm to 1 km • 3½ inches to 1 mile • 1: 18103
0 ¼ ½ ¾ 1 mile
0 250 m 500 m 750 m 1 kilometre
The scale of the maps on pages numbered in green is 2.76 cm to 1 km • 1¾ inches to 1 mile • 1: 36206
0 ¼ ½ ¾ 1 mile
0 250m 500m 750m 1kilometre
The scale of the maps on pages numbered in red is 11.04 cm to 1 km • 7 inches to 1 mile • 1: 9051.4
0 220 yards 440 yards 660 yards ½ mile
0 125m 250m 375m ½ kilometre

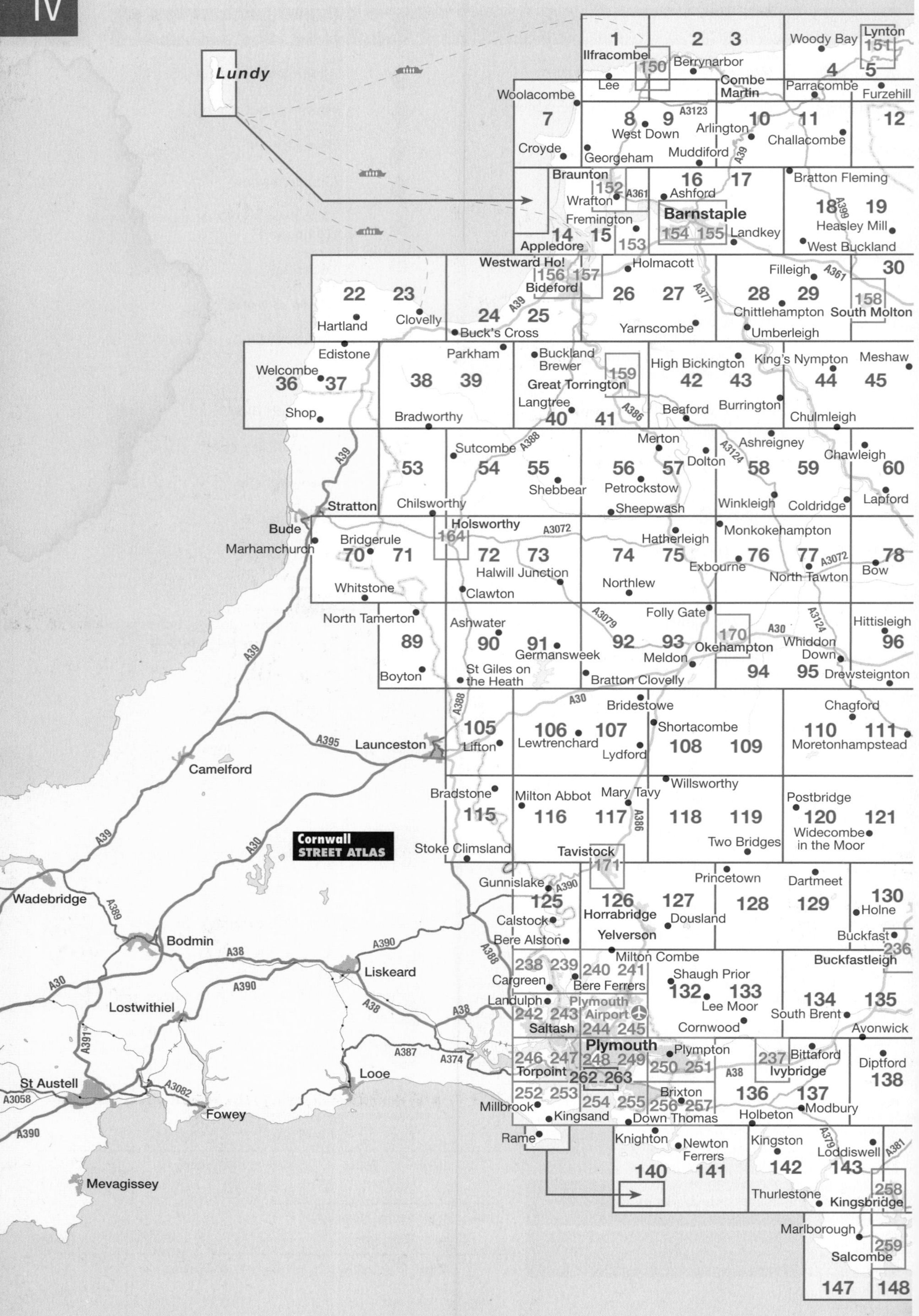

Lundy
1
Ilfracombe
150
2
3
Berrynarbor
Woody Bay
Lynton
151
4
5
Lee
Combe Martin
Parracombe
Furzehill
Woolacombe
7
8
9
A3123
West Down
Arlington
10
11
Challacombe
12
Croyde
Georgeham
Muddiford
A39
Braunton
152
A361
16
Ashford
17
Bratton Fleming
Wrafton
Barnstaple
18
A399
19
Fremington
Heasley Mill
14
15
153
154
155
Landkey
West Buckland
Appledore
Westward Ho!
156
157
Holmacott
Filleigh
A361
30
Bideford
22
23
26
27
A377
28
29
158
A39
Chittlehampton
South Molton
Hartland
Clovelly
24
25
Buck's Cross
Yarnscombe
Umberleigh
Edistone
Parkham
Buckland Brewer
High Bickington
King's Nympton
Meshaw
Welcombe
36
37
38
39
159
Great Torrington
42
43
44
45
Langtree
Burrington
Shop
Bradworthy
40
41
A386
Beaford
Chulmleigh
Merton
Ashreigney
Sutcombe
A388
A3124
Chawleigh
A39
53
54
55
56
57
Dolton
58
59
60
Shebbear
Petrockstow
Lapford
Stratton
Chilsworthy
Sheepwash
Winkleigh
Coldridge
Bude
Holsworthy
A3072
Hatherleigh
Monkokehampton
164
Bridgerule
Marhamchurch
70
71
72
73
74
75
76
77
A3072
78
Halwill Junction
Exbourne
Bow
Whitstone
Northlew
North Tawton
Clawton
North Tamerton
A3079
Folly Gate
A3124
Hittisleigh
Ashwater
170
A30
89
90
91
92
93
Okehampton
Whiddon Down
96
A39
Germansweek
Meldon
St Giles on the Heath
94
95
Drewsteignton
Boyton
Bratton Clovelly
A388
A30
Bridestowe
Chagford
105
106
107
Shortacombe
110
111
108
109
A395
Launceston
Lifton
Lewtrenchard
Moretonhampstead
Lydford
Camelford
Willsworthy
Bradstone
Milton Abbot
Mary Tavy
Postbridge
115
116
117
A386
118
119
120
121
Widecombe in the Moor
Two Bridges
A39
A30
Cornwall
STREET ATLAS
Stoke Climsland
Tavistock
171
Princetown
Dartmeet
130
Gunnislake
A390
126
127
128
129
Holne
Wadebridge
125
Horrabridge
A389
Calstock
Dousland
Buckfast
Yelverton
236
Bodmin
Bere Alston
A388
A390
A38
238
239
240
241
Milton Combe
Buckfastleigh
Liskeard
Shaugh Prior
A30
Cargreen
Bere Ferrers
A390
132
133
134
135
Landulph
Plymouth Airport
Lee Moor
Lostwithiel
A38
A38
242
243
244
245
South Brent
Saltash
Cornwood
Avonwick
Plymouth
Plympton
A391
A387
A374
246
247
248
249
250
251
237
Bittaford
Diptford
Torpoint
262
263
A38
Ivybridge
St Austell
Looe
138
A3058
A3082
252
253
254
255
256
257
Brixton
136
137
Millbrook
Kingsand
Down Thomas
Holbeton
Modbury
Fowey
A390
Rame
Knighton
Newton Ferrers
Kingston
A379
Loddiswell
A381
140
141
142
143
Mevagissey
258
Thurlestone
Kingsbridge
Marlborough
259
Salcombe
147
148

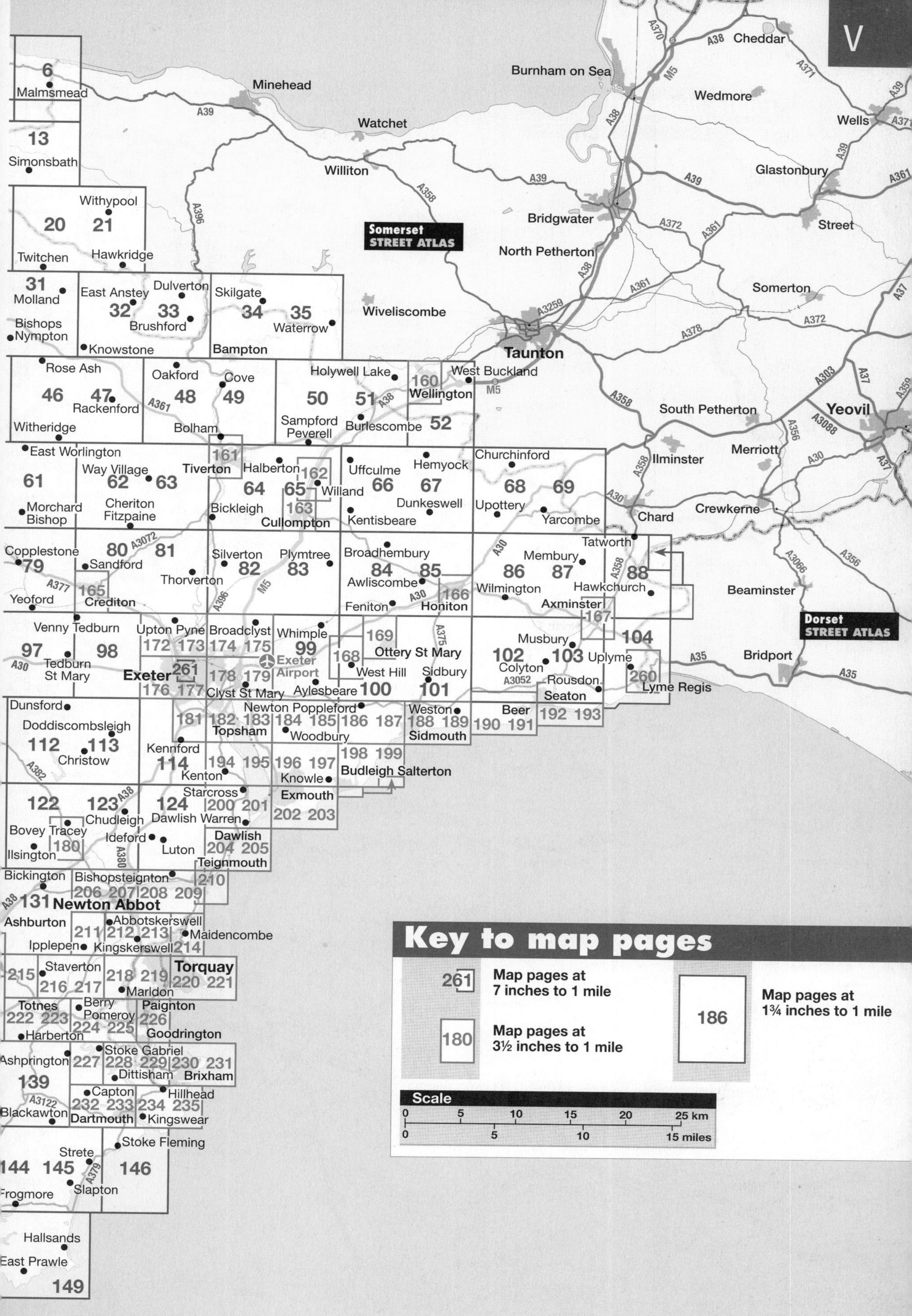

Cheddar
Burnham on Sea
Wedmore
Wells
Minehead
Watchet
Williton
Glastonbury
Bridgwater
Street
North Petherton
Somerset
STREET ATLAS
Somerton
Wiveliscombe
Taunton
South Petherton
Yeovil
Ilminster
Merriott
Chard
Crewkerne
Beaminster
Dorset
STREET ATLAS
Bridport
Lyme Regis
6
Malmsmead
13
Simonsbath
20
21
Withypool
Twitchen
Hawkridge
31
Molland
East Anstey
32
Dulverton
33
Brushford
Skilgate
34
35
Waterrow
Bampton
Bishops Nympton
Knowstone
Rose Ash
46
47
Rackenford
Witheridge
Oakford
48
Cove
49
Bolham
Holywell Lake
50
51
Sampford Peverell
Burlescombe
160
Wellington
West Buckland
52
East Worlington
61
Way Village
62
63
Tiverton
161
Halberton
64
162
65
163
Willand
Uffculme
66
Hemyock
67
Dunkeswell
Kentisbeare
Cullompton
Churchinford
68
69
Upottery
Yarcombe
Morchard Bishop
Cheriton Fitzpaine
Bickleigh
Copplestone
79
80
81
Sandford
Silverton
82
Plymtree
83
Broadhembury
84
85
Awliscombe
Feniton
166
Honiton
86
Membury
87
Tatworth
88
Wilmington
Hawkchurch
Axminster
167
Yeoford
165
Crediton
Thorverton
Venny Tedburn
97
98
Tedburn St Mary
Upton Pyne
172
173
Broadclyst
174
175
Whimple
99
Exeter
261
Exeter Airport
178
179
176
177
Clyst St Mary
169
168
Ottery St Mary
West Hill
Aylesbeare
100
Sidbury
101
Musbury
102
103
Colyton
Uplyme
104
260
Rousdon
Seaton
Dunsford
Doddiscombsleigh
112
113
Christow
Kennford
114
181
182
183
Topsham
Newton Poppleford
184
185
186
187
Woodbury
Weston
188
189
Sidmouth
Beer
190
191
192
193
194
195
Kenton
196
197
Knowle
198
199
Budleigh Salterton
Exmouth
202
203
122
123
Chudleigh
124
Starcross
200
201
Dawlish Warren
Bovey Tracey
180
Ilsington
Ideford
Luton
Dawlish
204
205
Teignmouth
Bickington
Bishopsteignton
210
206
207
208
209
131
Newton Abbot
Ashburton
Abbotskerswell
211
212
213
Maidencombe
Ipplepen
Kingskerswell
214
215
Staverton
216
217
218
219
Marldon
Torquay
220
221
Totnes
222
223
Berry Pomeroy
224
225
Paignton
226
Goodrington
Harberton
Stoke Gabriel
Ashprington
227
228
229
230
231
139
Dittisham
Brixham
Capton
Hillhead
Blackawton
232
233
Dartmouth
234
235
Kingswear
Stoke Fleming
Strete
144
145
146
Frogmore
Slapton
Hallsands
East Prawle
149
A39
A38
A370
M5
A371
A358
A396
A361
A372
A3259
A378
A303
A37
A3088
A356
A30
A3066
A35
A3052
A3072
A377
A375
A382
A380
A379
A3122
Key to map pages
261
Map pages at 7 inches to 1 mile
180
Map pages at 3½ inches to 1 mile
186
Map pages at 1¾ inches to 1 mile
Scale
0
5
10
15
20
25 km
0
5
10
15 miles

Route planning

Scale

0 1 2 3 4 5 6 7 8 km

0 1 2 3 4 5 miles

BARNSTAPLE OR BIDEFORD BAY

DARTMOOR FOREST

DARTMOOR

ILFRACOMBE
BARNSTAPLE
BIDEFORD
GREAT TORRINGTON
BUDE
STRATTON
OKEHAMPTON
LAUNCESTON

Heddon's Mouth
Woody Bay
Trentishoe
Martinhoe
Combe Martin Bay
Combe Martin
Hele
Berrynarbor
Kentisbury
Parracombe
Blackmoor Gate
Heale
Kemacott
Toll
Bull Point
Rockham Bay
Lee
Mortehoe
Morte Point
Slade
Woolacombe
Trimstone
West Down
Morte Bay
Patchole
East Down
Arlington
Wistlandpound Reservoir
Challacombe
Baggy Point
Pickwell
North Buckland
Georgeham
Bittadon
Milltown
Muddiford
Loxhore
Knightacott
Lyworthy
Croyde Bay
Croyde
Knowle
Halsinger
Marwood
Bratton Fleming
Saunton
Pippacott
Braunton
Heanton Punchardon
Prixford
Shirwell
Lydcott
Braunton Burrows
Wrafton
Ashford
Chivenor
Goodleigh
Stoke Rivers
Brayford
Bideford Bar
River Taw
Fremington
Bickington
Newport
Gunn
Charles
Yelland
Landkey
West Buckland
East Buckland
Appledore
Instow
Bickleton
Bishop's Tawton
HARTLAND POINT
Westward Ho!
Westleigh
Tawstock
Swimbridge
Filleigh
Northam
Windbury Point
Titchberry
Abbotsham
Horwood
Newton Tracey
Ensis
Chapelton
Herner
Cobbaton
Woodtown
Hiscott
Chittlehampton
Hartland Quay
Stoke
Hartland
Clovelly
Higher Clovelly
Clovelly Dykes
Buck's Mills
Fairy Cross
East-the-Water
Littleham
Landcross
Alverdiscott
Yarnscombe
Atherington
Umberleigh
Clapworthy
George Nympton
Milford
Philham
Horns Cross
Buck's Cross
Parkham
Weare Giffard
Monkleigh
Warkleigh
Chittlehamholt
Satterleigh
Elmscott
Buckland Brewer
Sherwood Green
High Bickington
Portsmouth Arms Station
South Hole
Woolfardisworthy or Woolsery
Alminstone Cross
Frithelstock
St Giles in the Wood
King's Nympton
Knaps Longpeak
Welcombe
Ashmansworthy
Kingscott
Northcote Manor
Little Torrington
Roborough
Meddon
Gooseham
Eastcott
East Putford
Burrington
King's Nympton Station
Cadbury Barton
Elstone
Morwenstow
Dipworthy
West Putford
Stibb Cross
Langtree
Beaford
Shop
Youlstone
Colscott
Bradworthy
Haytown
Peters Marland
Riddlecombe
Ashreigney
Chulmleigh
Woodford
Bulkworthy
Winswell
Upper Tamar Lake
Abbots Bickington
Newton St Petrock
Coombe
Merton
Huish
Dolton
Eggesford Station
Kilkhampton
Thurdon
Sutcombe
Alfardisworthy
Lower Tamar Lake
River Waldon
Stibb
Soldon Cross
Milton Damerel
Hollocombe
Dowland
River Torridge
Shebbear
Petrockstowe
Wembworthy
Buckland Filleigh
Poughill
Holsworthy Beacon
Thornbury
Meeth
Iddesleigh
Winkleigh
Coldridge
Flexbury
Lana
Bradford
Brushford
Grimscott
Beechworthy
Cookbury
Sheepwash
Pancrasweek
Launcells
Holemoor
Black Torrington
Monkokehampton
Broadwoodkelly
East Leigh
Bondleigh
Highampton
Holsworthy
Hatherleigh
North Tawton
Bridgerule
Marhamchurch
Pyworthy
Whimble
Hollacombe
Graddon Moor
Honeychurch
Jacobstowe
Exbourne
Coppathorne
Sampford Courtenay
Poundstock
Halwill Junction
River Lew
River Okement
River Deer
Halwill
Beaworthy
Northlew
Inwardleigh
Itton
Whitstone
Clawton
River Tamar
River Claw
Treskinnick Cross
Ashbury
Folly Gate
Sampford Courtenay Station
Week St Mary
North Tamerton
Quoditch
Broadbury
Penhallam Manor House
Jacobstow
Tetcott
Lana
Ashwater
Taw Green
South Tawton
Spreyton
West Curry
Luffincott
Germansweek
Eworthy
Sticklepath
Finch Foundry
South Zeal
South Wheatley
Maxworthy
Chapmans Well
Boasley Cross
Thorndon Cross
Belstone
Okehampton Camp
Clubworthy
Northcott
Virginstow
Roadford Lake (reservoir)
Bratton Clovelly
Sourton Cross Services
Meldon
Okehampton Common
Cosdon Hill
Whiddon Down
Canworthy Water
East Panson
Bennacott
Brazacott
Boyton
River Thrushel
Meldon Reservoir
Yes Tor
High Willhays
Throwleigh
Warbstow
St Giles on the Heath
Sourton
Wonson
Gidleigh
Tremaine
North Petherwin
Bridgetown
Cross Green
Broadwoodwidger
Bridestowe
Bridestowe and Sourton Common
Treneglos
River Ottery
Yeolmbridge
Werrington
Combebow
Thrushelton
Tresmeer
Egloskerry
Langore
River Carey
Stowford
Lewdown
Shortacombe
Hangingstone Hill
Chagford
Tregeare
Red Down
St Stephens
River Wolf
Portgate
Lewtrenchard
Lydford
Amicombe Hill
Frenchbeer
Tregadillett
Lifton
Tinhay
River Lyd
Castle
Laneast
St Clether
River Inny
Trewen
Coryton
Cut Hill
Sittaford Tor
Fernworthy Reservoir
Leftaford
Lawhitton
Marystow
North Brentor
Black Down
River Tavy
Polyphant
Kelly
Chillaton
South Petherwin
Altarnun
Lewannick
Bradstone
Milton Abbot
Mary Tavy
Cocks Hill
Rough Tor
Postbridge
Lezant
Dunterton
Cudlipptown
Peter Tavy
Larrick
Endsleigh House
Great Mis Tor
Bellever
Cator Court
Trebartha
Coad's Green
Treburley
Lamerton
North Hill
Sydenham Damerel
Polventor

A39
A361
A399
A3123
B3343
B3230
B3231
B3233
A377
B3227
B3226
B3232
B3237
B3248
B3217
A386
A388
A3124
B3220
B3254
A3072
B3216
A3079
B3215
A30
A395
B3362
B3212
B3357

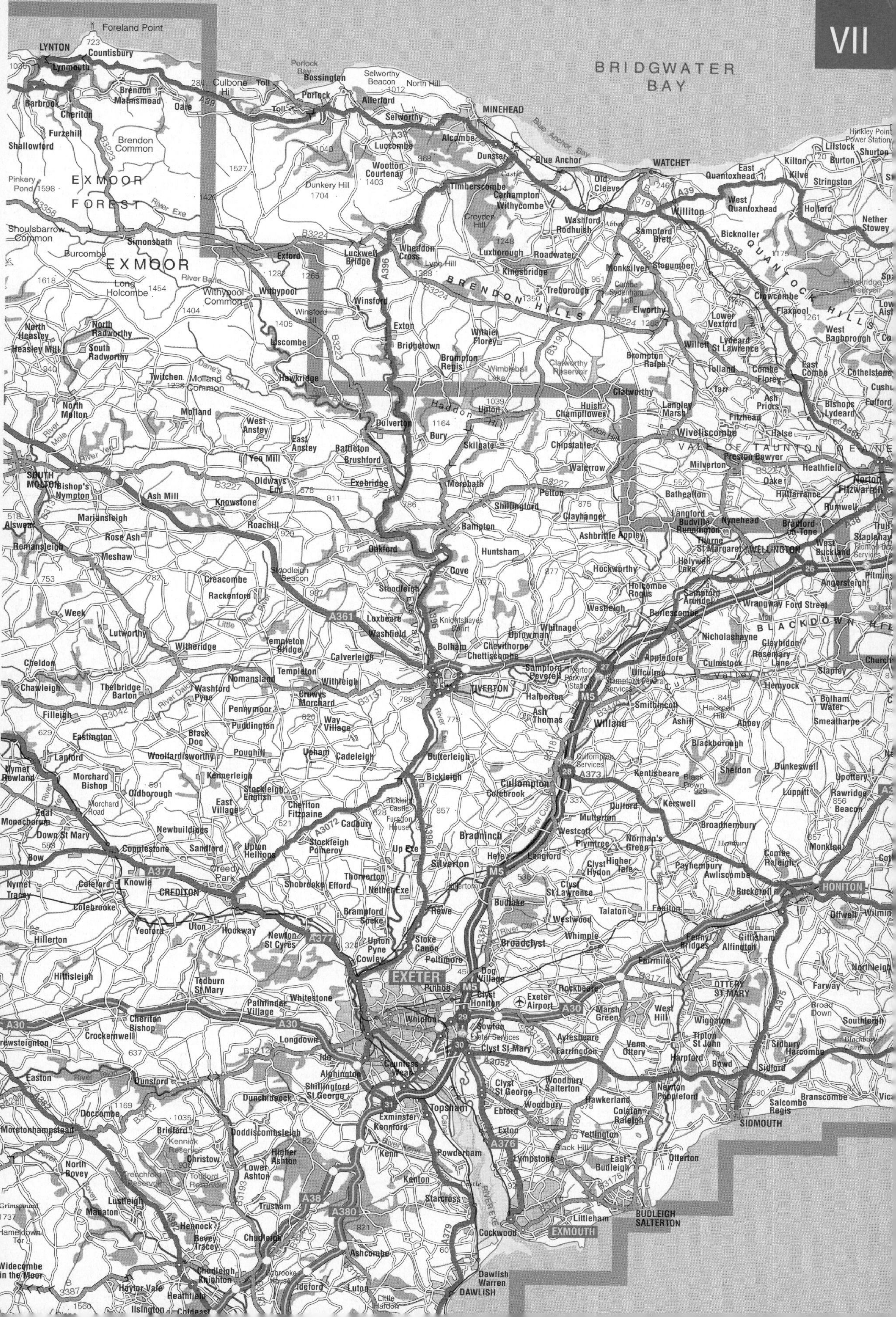

BRIDGWATER BAY

Foreland Point
LYNTON
Countisbury
Lynmouth
Porlock Bay
Bossington
Selworthy Beacon
North Hill
Culbone Hill
Brendon
Malmsmead
Oare
Porlock
Allerford
Barbrook
Cheriton
Selworthy
MINEHEAD
Furzehill
Shallowford
Brendon Common
Alcombe
Luccombe
Dunster
Blue Anchor Bay
Blue Anchor
WATCHET
Hinkley Point Power Station
Lilstock
Kilton
Burton
Shurton
EXMOOR FOREST
Pinkery Pond
Wootton Courtenay
Dunkery Hill
Timberscombe
Carhampton
Withycombe
Old Cleeve
East Quantoxhead
Kilve
Stringston
Williton
West Quantoxhead
Holford
Nether Stowey
River Exe
Shoulsbarrow Common
Simonsbath
Croydon Hill
Washford
Rodhuish
Sampford Brett
Bicknoller
QUANTOCK HILLS
Burcombe
EXMOOR
Exford
Luckwell Bridge
Wheddon Cross
Lype Hill
Luxborough
Roadwater
Kingsbridge
Monksilver
Stogumber
River Barle
Long Holcombe
Withypool
Withypool Common
Winsford Hill
Winsford
BRENDON HILLS
Treborough
Combe Sydenham Hall
Elworthy
Crowcombe
Flaxpool
Hawkridge Reservoir
North Heasley
North Radworthy
Heasley Mill
South Radworthy
Liscombe
Exton
Bridgetown
Withiel Florey
Brompton Regis
Wimbleball Lake
Clatworthy Reservoir
Brompton Ralph
Lower Vexford
Willett
Lydeard St Lawrence
West Bagborough
Tolland
Combe Florey
East Combe
Cothelstone
Twitchen
Molland Common
Dane's Brook
Hawkridge
Clatworthy
Tarr
Ash Priors
Bishops Lydeard
North Molton
Molland
West Anstey
Haddon Hill
Upton
Huish Champflower
Langley Marsh
Fitzhead
Dulverton
Bury
Heydon Hill
Wiveliscombe
Halse
East Anstey
Battleton
Brushford
Skilgate
Chipstable
VALE OF TAUNTON DEANE
River Mole
River Yeo
Yeo Mill
Waterrow
Milverton
Preston Bowyer
Heathfield
SOUTH MOLTON
Bishop's Nympton
Oldways End
Exebridge
Morebath
Oake
Norton Fitzwarren
Ash Mill
Knowstone
Petton
Bathealton
Hillfarrance
Mariansleigh
Shillingford
Clayhanger
Langford Budville
Nynehead
Rumwell
Alswear
Roachill
Bampton
Ashbrittle
Appley
Runnington
Bradford-on-Tone
Trull
Romansleigh
Rose Ash
Oakford
Thorne St Margaret
WELLINGTON
West Buckland
Staplehay
Meshaw
Huntsham
Holywell Lake
Taunton Deane Services
Stoodleigh Beacon
Cove
Hockworthy
Angersleigh
Pitminster
Creacombe
Stoodleigh
Holcombe Rogus
Sampford Arundel
Rackenford
Wrangway
Ford Street
Week
Little Dart River
A361
Loxbeare
Exe Valley
Knightshayes Court
Westleigh
Burlescombe
BLACKDOWN HILLS
Lutworthy
Washfield
Uplowman
Whitnage
Canal
Nicholashayne
Templeton Bridge
Bolham
Chevithorne
Chettiscombe
Clayhidon
Witheridge
Cheldon
Calverleigh
Appledore
Culmstock
Rosemary Lane
Churchstanton
Templeton
Sampford Peverell
Tiverton Parkway Station
Stapley
Uffculme
Culm Valley
Chawleigh
Thelbridge Barton
Nomansland
Withleigh
TIVERTON
Halberton
Stamford Peverell Services
Hemyock
Washford Pyne
River Dalch
Cruwys Morchard
M5
Bolham Water
Smithincott
Pennymoor
Ash Thomas
Hackpen Hill
Filleigh
Way Village
Willand
Ashill
Abbey
Smeatharpe
Puddington
River Exe
Eastington
Black Dog
Blackborough
Poughill
Upham
Cadeleigh
Cullompton Services
Lapford
Woolfardisworthy
Butterleigh
Kentisbeare
Nymet Rowland
Sheldon
Dunkeswell
Morchard Bishop
Kennerleigh
Bickleigh
Cullompton
Black Down
Upottery
Oldborough
Stockleigh English
Colebrook
Luppitt
Rawridge
Morchard Road
East Village
Cheriton Fitzpaine
Bickleigh Castle
Dulford
Kerswell
Beacon
Zeal Monachorum
Fursdon House
Mutterton
Broadhembury
Cadbury
Down St Mary
Newbuildings
Stockleigh Pomeroy
Bradninch
Westcott
Plymtree
Norman's Green
Monkton
Copplestone
Sandford
Upton Hellions
Up Exe
Bow
Creedy Park
Hele
Langford
Higher Tale
Combe Raleigh
Clyst Hydon
Payhembury
Awliscombe
Silverton
Knowle
Nymet Tracey
Coleford
CREDITON
Shobrooke
Efford
Thorverton
Nether Exe
Killerton
Clyst St Lawrence
Buckerell
HONITON
Colebrooke
Budlake
Talaton
Feniton
Offwell
Wilmington
Brampford Speke
Rewe
Westwood
Yeoford
Uton
Hookway
River Clyst
Whimple
Gittisham
Hillerton
Newton St Cyres
Upton Pyne
Stoke Canon
Broadclyst
Fenny Bridges
Alfington
Cowley
Poltimore
Fairmile
Northleigh
Hittisleigh
EXETER
Pinhoe
Dog Village
Rockbeare
OTTERY ST MARY
Farway
Tedburn St Mary
Clyst Honiton
Exeter Airport
Whitestone
Pathfinder Village
Marsh Green
West Hill
Wiggaton
Broad Down
Cheriton Bishop
Whipton
Sowton
Southleigh
Drewsteignton
Crockernwell
Longdown
Exeter Services
Aylesbeare
Venn Ottery
Tipton St John
Sidbury
Harcombe
Blackbury Camp
Clyst St Mary
Farringdon
Harpford
Bowd
Ide
Countess Wear
Alphington
Sidford
Easton
River Teign
Dunsford
Clyst St George
Woodbury Salterton
Newton Poppleford
Salcombe Regis
Branscombe
Shillingford St George
Dunchideock
Topsham
Ebford
Woodbury
Hawkerland
Colaton Raleigh
SIDMOUTH
Doccombe
Exminster
Kenford
Canal
Exton
Moretonhampstead
Bridford
Doddiscombsleigh
Yettington
Kennick Reservoir
Higher Ashton
Kenn
Powderham
Black Hill
Lympstone
East Budleigh
Otterton
North Bovey
Christow
Trenchford Reservoir
Tottiford Reservoir
Lower Ashton
Kenton
Castle
RIVER EXE
Starcross
Lustleigh
Trusham
Grimspound
Manaton
Littleham
BUDLEIGH SALTERTON
Hameldown Tor
Hennock
Chudleigh
Cockwood
EXMOUTH
Bovey Tracey
Ashcombe
Widecombe in the Moor
Chudleigh Knighton
Ugbrooke House
Dawlish Warren
Haytor Vale
Heathfield
Ideford
Luton
DAWLISH
Little Haldon
Ilsington
Coldeast

Newton St Petrock
Merton
Huish
Dolton
Hollocombe
Eggesford Station
Chawleigh
Thelbridge Barton
Washford Pyne
Cruwys Morchard
Pennymoor
Puddington
Sheepbear
Petrockstowe
Dowland
River Torridge
Wembworthy
Filleigh
Eastington
Black Dog
Poughill
Thornbury
Buckland Filleigh
Meeth
Iddesleigh
Winkleigh
Brushford
Coldridge
Nymet Rowland
Lapford
Woolfardisworthy
Morchard Bishop
Kennerleigh
Cheriton Fitzpaine
Bradford
Oldborough
Morchard Road
East Village
Stockleigh English
Cookbury
Sheepwash
Monkokehampton
Broadwoodkelly
Bondleigh
East Leigh
Holemoor
Black Torrington
Newbuildings
Highampton
Hatherleigh
Honeychurch
Down St Mary
North Tawton
Zeal Monachorum
Copplestone
Sandford
Upton Hellions
Hollacombe
Graddon Moor
Jacobstowe
Exbourne
Bow
Creedy Park
Shobrooke
Halwill Junction
Sampford Courtenay
Nymet Tracey
Coleford
Knowle
CREDITON
Halwill
Beaworthy
Northlew
Inwardleigh
Itton
Colebrooke
Yeoford
Uton
Hookway
Newton St Cyres
Quoditch
Ashbury
Folly Gate
Sampford Courtenay Sta
Spreyton
Hillerton
Broadbury
OKEHAMPTON
Taw Green
South Tawton
Hittisleigh
Tedburn St Mary
Germansweek
Eworthy
Sticklepath
Finch Foundry
South Zeal
Pathfinder Village
Virginstow
Boasley Cross
Thorndon Cross
Castle
Belstone
Okehampton Camp
Whiddon Down
Cheriton Bishop
Roadford Lake
Bratton Clovelly
Meldon
Cosdon Hill
Drewsteignton
Crockernwell
Longdown
Okehampton Common
Meldon Reservoir
Yes Tor
High Willhays
Sourton
Throwleigh
River Thrushel
Sourton Cross Services
Cross Green
Broadwoodwidger
Bridestowe
Wonson
Easton
River Teign
Dunsford
Gidleigh
Combebow
Bridestowe and Sourton Common
Dunchideock
Thrushelton
Lewdown
Stowford
Shortacombe
Hangingstone Hill
Chagford
Doccombe
Bridford
Doddiscombsleigh
Portgate
Lewtrenchard
Amicombe Hill
Frenchbeer
Moretonhampstead
Kennick Reservoir
Higher Ashton
Lifton
Tinhay
Lydford
Christow
Coryton
North Bovey
Lettaford
Tottiford Reservoir
Trenchford Reservoir
Lower Ashton
Cut Hill
Sittaford Tor
Fernworthy Reservoir
Marystow
North Brentor
Black Down
River Tavy
Lustleigh
Trusham
Chillaton
Kelly
DARTMOOR FOREST
Grimspound
Hameldown Tor
Manaton
Bradstone
Hennock
Chudleigh
Bovey Tracey
Milton Abbot
Mary Tavy
Cocks Hill
Rough Tor
Postbridge
Cudlipptown
Endsleigh House
Peter Tavy
Great Mis Tor
Bellever
Cator Court
Widecombe in the Moor
Chudleigh Knighton
Lamerton
Haytor Vale
Heathfield
Sydenham Damerel
DARTMOOR
Settlement
Two Bridges
Rippon Tor
Babeny
Ilsington
Coldeast
Teigngrace
Kingsteignton
TAVISTOCK
Merrivale
HM Prison
Ponsworthy
Luckett
Latchley
Chilsworthy
Sampford Spiney
Princetown
West Dart River
Buckland in the Moor
Sigford
Dartmeet
Poundsgate
Hexworthy
Higher Walreddon
Whitchurch
Bickington
NEWTON ABBOT
St Ann's Chapel
Gunnislake
Horrabridge
Whiteworks
Venford Reservoir
West Ogwell
Albaston
Harrowbarrow
Cotehele House
Walkhampton
Burrator Reservoir
ASHBURTON
Woodland
East Ogwell
Abbotskerswell
Buckland Monachorum
Yelverton
Cater's Beam
Ryder's Hill
Holne
Scorriton
Denbury
Kingskerswell
St Dominick
Calstock
Bere Alston
Dousland
Sheepstor
Buckfast
Forder Green
Torbryan
North Whilborough
Buckland Abbey
Crapstone
Meavy
BUCKFASTLEIGH
Landscove
Broadhempston
Ipplepen
Milton Combe
River Plym
Avon Dam Reservoir
Woolston Green
Mellion
Dean
Castle
Compton
Pillaton
Lopwell
Shell Top
Dean Prior
Staverton
Littlehempston
Marldon
Cargreen
Bere Ferrers
Shaugh Prior
Dartington
Dartington Hall
Landulph
Tamerton Foliot
Bickleigh
Ugborough Moor
Didworthy
Berry Pomeroy
Hatt
Wotter
Lee Moor
Rattery
Tigley
Totnes
Blagdon
Botusfleming
Plymouth City Airport
Cornwood
South Brent
Collaton St Mary
Trematon
Drakeland Corner
Lutton
Harford
Ugborough Beacon
Belsford
SALTASH
Toll
Crownhill
Sparkwell
Bittaford
Lincombe
Harberton
Stoke Gabriel
St Stephens
St Budeaux
PLYMOUTH
Plympton
IVYBRIDGE
Avonwick
Harbertonford
Ashprington
Antony House
Devonport
Lee Mill
Smithaleigh Services
River Erme
North Huish
Diptford
Tuckenhay
Cornworthy
Sheviock
Saltram House
Ugborough
Washbourne
Antony
TORPOINT
St John
Westlake
Curtisknowle
Dittisham
Capton
Halwell
Ashleigh
Britannia RN College
Millbrook
Cremyll
Drake's Island
Elburton
Ermington
Brownston
Freathy
The Sound
Hooe
Plymstock
Brixton
Modbury
Moreleigh
Woodford
DARTMOUTH
WHITSAND BAY
Kingsand
Staddiscombe
Yealmpton
Cawsand
Plymouth Breakwater
Knighton
Holbeton
Woodleigh
Blackawton
Rame
Hutcherleigh
Penlee Point
Heybrook Bay
Wembury
Newton Ferrers
Noss Mayo
Loddiswell
Bowden
Rame Head
Great Mew Stone
Wembury Bay
St Ann's Chapel
Aveton Gifford
East Allington
Stoke Fleming
Kingston
Strete
Ringmore
Bigbury
Goveton
Churchstow
Harleston
Stoke Point
Bigbury-on-Sea
West Alvington
Sherford
Slapton
Burgh Island
Bantham
KINGSBRIDGE
Stokenham
START BAY
Thurlestone
South Milton
Chillington
Memorial
Woolston
West Charleton
Frogmore
Torcross
Bigbury Bay
Beeson
Galmpton
South Pool
Ford
Beesands
Malborough
Bolt Tail
Bolberry
Kellaton
Hallsands
SALCOMBE
East Portlemouth
South Allington
START POINT
East Prawle
Bolt
A30
A386
A3072
A3079
A377
A3124
B3220
B3217
B3215
B3212
B3357
B3387
A38
A382
A383
A385
A381
A380
A388
A390
A374
A379
A3121
A3122
B3213
B3392
B3186
B3193
B3362

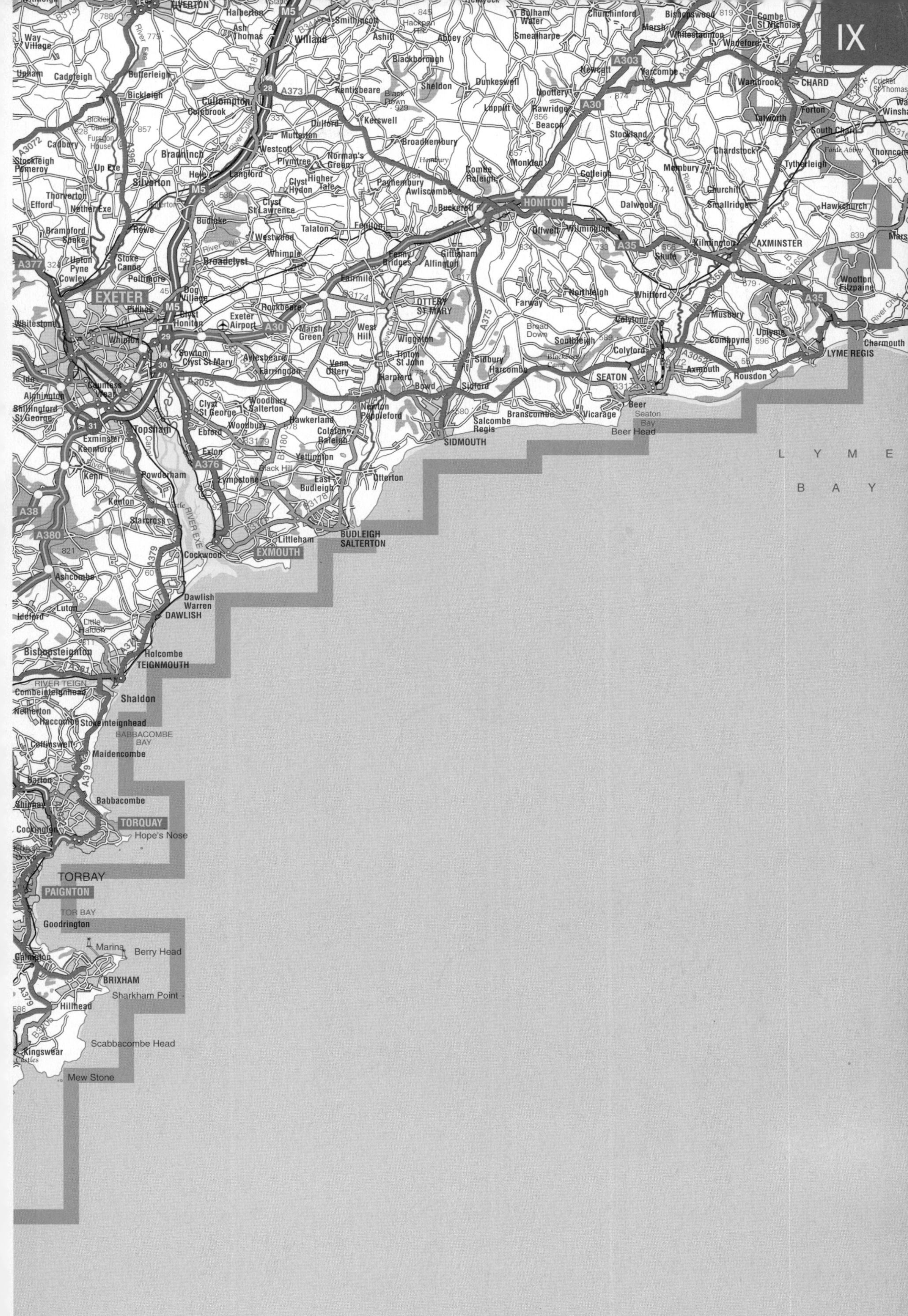
TIVERTON
Halberton
M5
Smithincott
Bolham Water
Churchinford
Marsh
Bishopswood
Combe St Nicholas
Way Village
Ash Thomas
Willand
Ashill
Hackpen Hill
Abbey
Smeatharpe
Whitestaunton
Wadeford
Upham
Cadeleigh
Butterleigh
Blackborough
Newcott
A303
Yarcombe
Wambrook
CHARD
Bickleigh
Kentisbeare
Sheldon
Dunkeswell
Upottery
A373
Cullompton
Colebrook
Black Down
Luppitt
Rawridge
A30
Tatworth
Forton
Beacon
Dulford
Kerswell
South Chard
Cadbury
Mutterton
Stockland
Bradninch
Westcott
Broadhembury
Chardstock
Forde Abbey
Thorncombe
Stockleigh Pomeroy
Up Exe
Hele
Plymtree
Norman's Green
Combe Raleigh
Monkton
Membury
Tytherleigh
Langford
Silverton
Clyst Hydon
Higher Tale
Payhembury
Awliscombe
Cotleigh
Thorverton
Efford
Nether Exe
Clyst St Lawrence
Buckerell
HONITON
Dalwood
Churchill
Smallridge
Hawkchurch
Budlake
Brampford Speke
Rewe
Westwood
Talaton
Feniton
Offwell
Wilmington
A35
Kilmington
AXMINSTER
Whimple
Fenny Bridges
Gittisham
Alfington
Shute
A377
Upton Pyne
Stoke Canon
Cowley
Poltimore
Broadclyst
Fairmile
OTTERY ST MARY
Northleigh
Whitford
Wootton Fitzpaine
EXETER
Dog Village
Pinhoe
Clyst Honiton
Exeter Airport
Rockbeare
A30
Farway
Musbury
Whitestone
Whipton
Marsh Green
West Hill
Wiggaton
Broad Down
Southleigh
Colyton
Uplyme
Combpyne
Sowton
Clyst St Mary
Aylesbeare
Farringdon
Venn Ottery
Tipton St John
Sidbury
Harcombe
Colyford
A3052
Axmouth
Rousdon
Charmouth
LYME REGIS
Ide
Countess Wear
Harpford
Bowd
Sidford
SEATON
Alphington
Shillingford St George
Clyst St George
Woodbury Salterton
Newton Poppleford
Salcombe Regis
Branscombe
Vicarage
Beer
Seaton Bay
Beer Head
Topsham
Woodbury
Hawkerland
Colaton Raleigh
SIDMOUTH
Exminster
Kennford
Ebford
Exton
Yettington
LYME BAY
A376
Kenn
Powderham
Lympstone
Black Hill
East Budleigh
Otterton
A38
Kenton
Starcross
A380
Littleham
BUDLEIGH SALTERTON
Cockwood
EXMOUTH
RIVER EXE
Ashcombe
A379
Dawlish Warren
Luton
DAWLISH
Ideford
Little Haldon
Bishopsteignton
Holcombe
TEIGNMOUTH
RIVER TEIGN
Combeinteignhead
Shaldon
Netherton
Haccombe
Stokeinteignhead
BABBACOMBE BAY
Coffinswell
Maidencombe
Barton
Babbacombe
Shiphay
TORQUAY
Hope's Nose
Cockington
TORBAY
PAIGNTON
TOR BAY
Goodrington
Marina
Berry Head
Galmpton
BRIXHAM
Sharkham Point
Hillhead
Scabbacombe Head
Kingswear
Mew Stone

Major administrative and Postcode boundaries

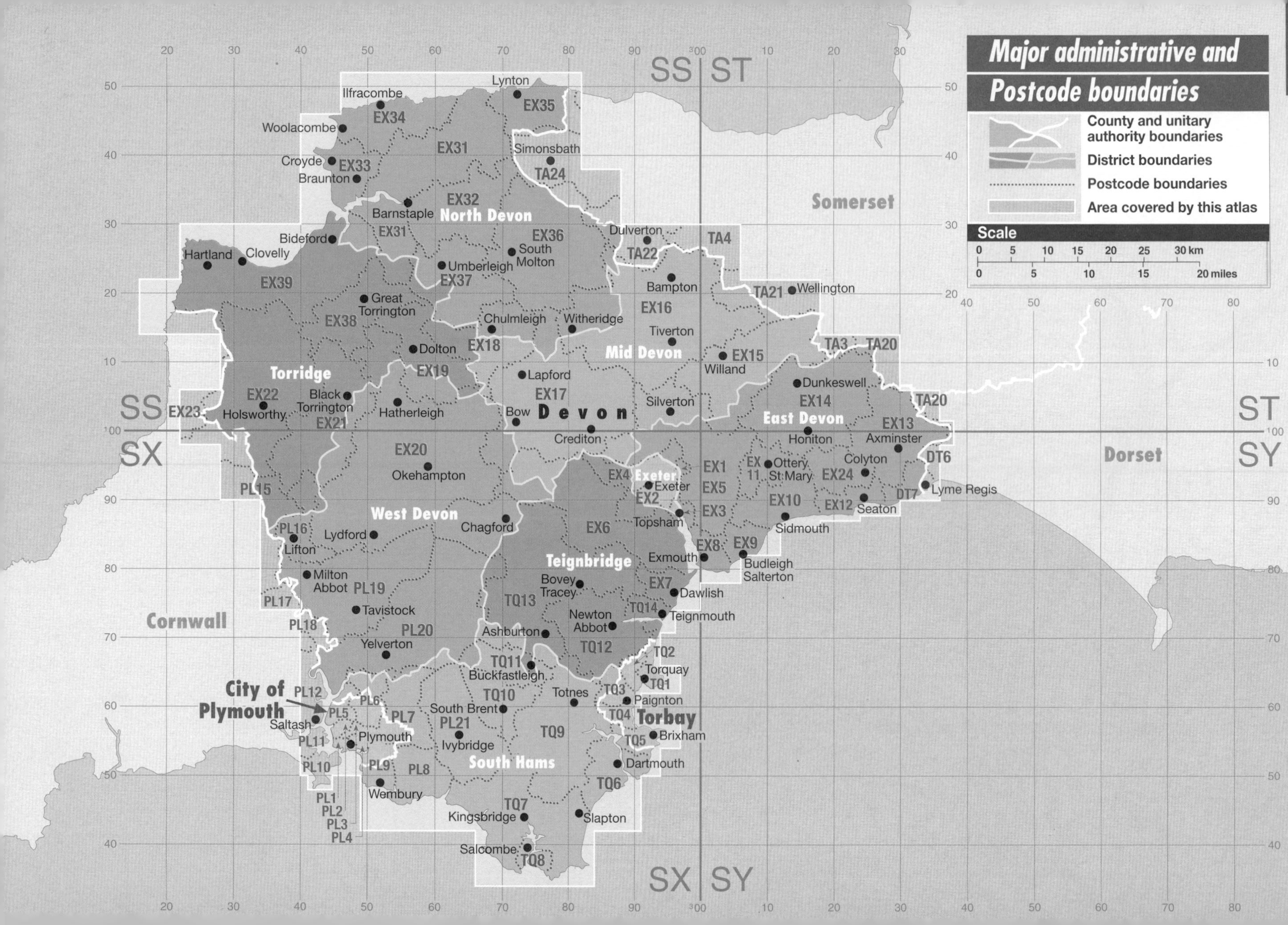

County and unitary authority boundaries
District boundaries
Postcode boundaries
Area covered by this atlas

Scale
0 5 10 15 20 25 30 km
0 5 10 15 20 miles

SS ST
SX SY

Somerset
Dorset
Cornwall
Devon
North Devon
Mid Devon
East Devon
Torridge
West Devon
Exeter
Teignbridge
Torbay
South Hams
City of Plymouth

Lynton
Ilfracombe
Woolacombe
Croyde
Braunton
Barnstaple
Simonsbath
Bideford
Hartland
Clovelly
Dulverton
South Molton
Umberleigh
Bampton
Wellington
Great Torrington
Chulmleigh
Witheridge
Tiverton
Dolton
Willand
Lapford
Dunkeswell
Black Torrington
Holsworthy
Hatherleigh
Bow
Crediton
Silverton
Honiton
Axminster
Okehampton
Exeter
Ottery St Mary
Colyton
Lyme Regis
Topsham
Sidmouth
Seaton
Chagford
Lydford
Lifton
Exmouth
Budleigh Salterton
Milton Abbot
Bovey Tracey
Dawlish
Tavistock
Newton Abbot
Teignmouth
Ashburton
Yelverton
Buckfastleigh
Torquay
Totnes
Paignton
South Brent
Saltash
Plymouth
Ivybridge
Brixham
Dartmouth
Wembury
Kingsbridge
Slapton
Salcombe

EX1 EX2 EX3 EX4 EX5 EX6 EX7 EX8 EX9 EX10 EX11 EX12 EX13 EX14 EX15 EX16 EX17 EX18 EX19 EX20 EX21 EX22 EX23 EX24 EX31 EX32 EX33 EX34 EX35 EX36 EX37 EX38 EX39
TA3 TA4 TA20 TA21 TA22 TA24
DT6 DT7
TQ1 TQ2 TQ3 TQ4 TQ5 TQ6 TQ7 TQ8 TQ9 TQ10 TQ11 TQ12 TQ13 TQ14
PL1 PL2 PL3 PL4 PL5 PL6 PL7 PL8 PL9 PL10 PL11 PL12 PL15 PL16 PL17 PL18 PL19 PL20 PL21

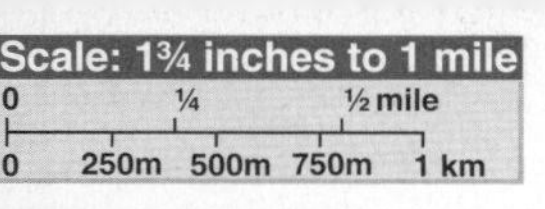

2

A B C D E F

8
51
7
50
6
49
150
5
ILFRACOMBE
Ferry P
Lundy (summer only)
48
The Outfalls
Mus
Liby
GRANVILLE RD
WILDER RD
HIGH ST A399
A361
Sch
HIGHFIELD RD
MARLBOROUGH RD
Brandy Cove Point
4
TORRS PK
TORRS WALK AVE
UPPER TORRS
LANGLEIGH RD
Torrs Park
Flat Point
Shag Point
Pensport Rock
Lee Bay
SOUTH VIEW
LANGLEIGH LA
LANGLEIGH PK
BROAD PARK AVE
HORNE PARK RD
FURZE HILL RD
47
Tarka Trail
South West Coast Path
Langleigh
Mast
Lee
HOME LA
PO
PH
Hotel
Whitestone Farm
Higher Slade
SLADE VALLEY RD
SLADE RD
CAIRN RD
ST BRANNOCK'S RD
BICCLESCOMBE PARK RD
3
Lincombe
Higher Warcombe
Pludd
DOGGIE LA
HIGHER SLADE RD
SALTMER CL
Lower Slade
46
NORTH MORTE RD
CHANNEL VIEW
Easewell Farm
Mortehoe
Damage Barton
Borough Valley
WARCOMBE LA
Windcutter Hill
Lower Campscott
DIBBON'S LA
Shaftsboro Farm
Middle Campscott
Slade Resrs
Mullacott
2
EX34
SHAFTSBOROUGH LA
Shire Horse Ctr
150
45
Twitchen House
MORTEHOE STATION RD
Higher Campscott
Borough Farm
BOROUGH CROSS
Bickenbridge
Little Shelfin Farm
PH
A361
A3123
1
SEYMOUR BGLWS 1
SEYMOUR VILLAS 2
SANDY LA
POOL LA
Pool Farm
HEADLANDS VIEW AVE
HARTLAND VIEW RD
LEE CROSS
B3343
B3343
MULLACOTT CROSS
Ind Est
44

46 A 47 B 48 C 49 D 50 E 51 F

8
2
For full street detail of the highlighted area see page 150.

1

Scale: 1¾ inches to 1 mile
0 ¼ ½ mile
0 250m 500m 750m 1 km

A B C D E F

8
51
7
50
6
49
5
48
4
47
3
46
2
45
1
44

52 53 54 55 56 57

150

Rillage Point
Samson's Bay
Widmouth Head
Burrow Nose
Water Mouth
Ferry P
Lundy (summer only)
ILFRACOMBE
Beacon Point
Hele Bay
Capstone Point
Chapel
Briery Cave
Widmouth
CH
Lydford Farm
Watermouth Castle
South West Coast Path
Combe Martin Bay
Wild Pear Beach
Lester Point
PO
LB Sta
Hillsborough
WATERMOUTH RD
Widmouth Hill
Hole Farm
PORTLAND ST
A399
B3230
HIGHFIELD RD
Sch
Hele Mill
Hele
Goosewell
Hotel
BARTON HILL
OLD COAST RD
BARTON LA
NEWBERRY CL
SANDAWAY LA
NEWBERRY HILL
WOODLANDS
BOROUGH RD
A399
Sch
Coll
WORTH RD
CHAMBERCOMBE LA
FOXBEARE RD
COOVEDALE CL
CAT LA
OLD BERRYNARBOR RD
PIT HILL
MILL LA
Beara Farm
Chambercombe
Chambercombe Manor
Hagginton Hill
BIRDSWELL LA
Mast
Home Barton
The Castle
Berrynarbor
Cemy
Lee
Sch
DOONE WAY
West Haggington
Lee Hills
PIT HILL
PH
SILVER ST
CASTLE HILL
EASTER LA
PO
P
RIDGE HILL
CROSS LA
WOOLHANGER'S LA
SALT WOOD LA
NEW BARNSTAPLE RD
Trayne Hills
Shield Tor
Kitstone Hill
OXENPARK LA
RECTORY HILL
ROCK HILL
CROFTS LEA
Channe Farm
Trayne
EX34
Hill Barton
WOOD PARK LA
OLD BARNSTAPLE RD
SLEW HILL
9
Sterridge Valley
RUGGATON LA
RIDGE HILL
Warmscombe Farm
Cockhill
Ruggaton Farm
Hodges
Oakridge Farm
Keypitts Farm
Shelfin Farm
150
Bowden Farm
Bodstone Barton
Yetland Farm
Francis Farm
OXENPARK LA
Woolscott Barton
BOUNTICE LA
Smythen Farm
WHEEL CROSS
RIDGE HILL
Two Pots
Mast
Mast
Hempster Farm
WHEEL LA
Works
IRON LETTERS CROSS
BERRYDOWN CROSS
A3123
B3230
Ettiford Farm
A3123
LONG LA
A3123

BERRY LA 1
NEWBERRY LA 2
NEWBERRY RD 3
THE GABLES 4
WHITE GATES 5
SEASIDE 6
HANGMAN PATH 7
CROSS ST 8
MOORY MDW 9
REW'S CL 10
LIBRA GDNS 11
KING ST 12
UMBER CL 13
TRENODE AVE 14
BELMONT AVE 15

For full street detail of the highlighted area see page 150

1

9

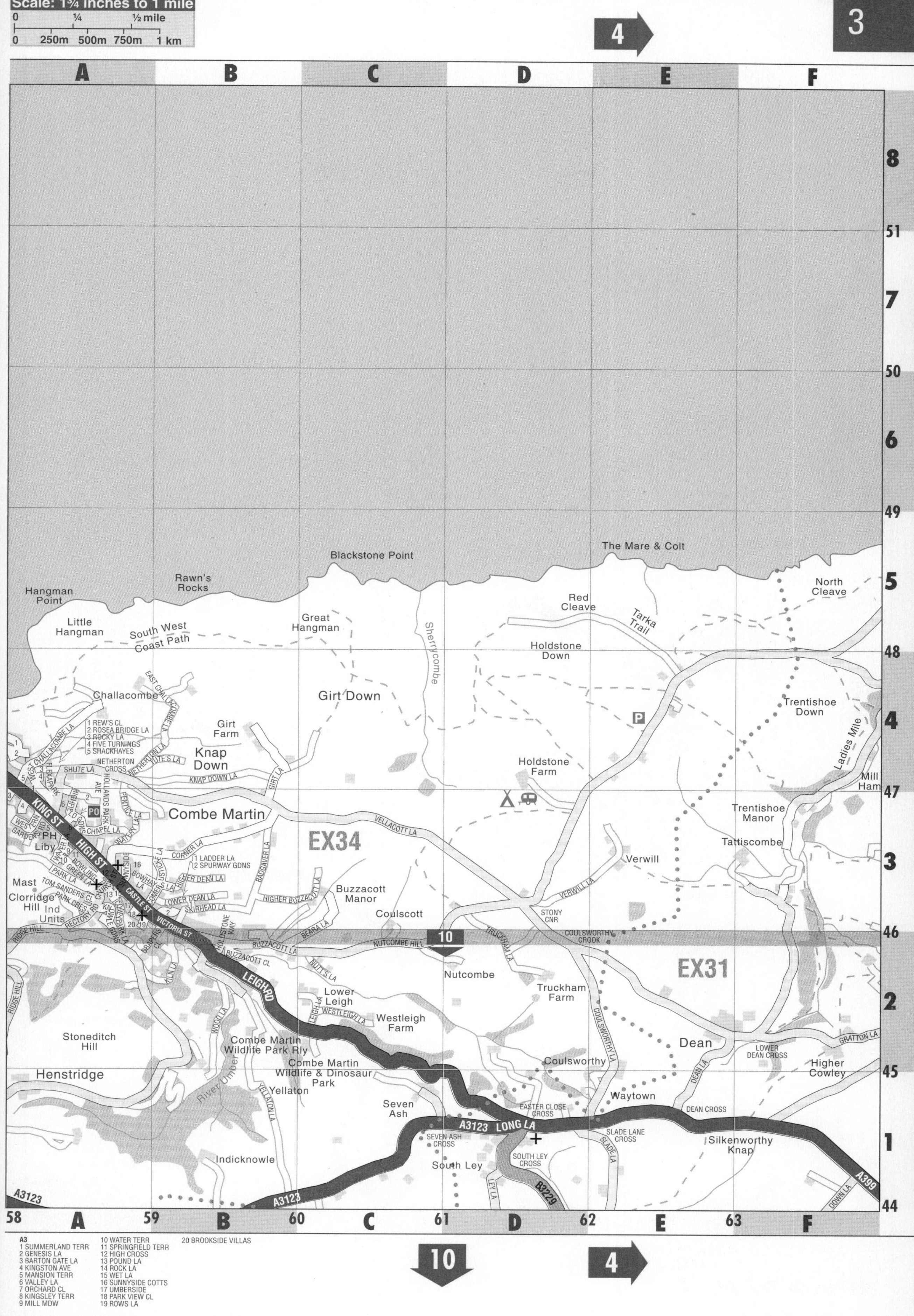

Scale: 1¾ inches to 1 mile
0 ¼ ½ mile
0 250m 500m 750m 1 km
4
3
A B C D E F
8
51
7
50
6
49
5
48
4
47
3
46
2
45
1
44
58 A 59 B 60 C 61 D 62 E 63 F
Hangman Point
Rawn's Rocks
Blackstone Point
The Mare & Colt
Little Hangman
South West Coast Path
Great Hangman
Sherrycombe
Red Cleave
Tarka Trail
North Cleave
Holdstone Down
Challacombe
Girt Down
Trentishoe Down
Ladies Mile
Girt Farm
Knap Down
Holdstone Farm
Mill Ham
1 REW'S CL
2 ROSEA BRIDGE LA
3 ROCKY LA
4 FIVE TURNINGS
5 SHACKHAYES
NETHERTON CROSS
SHUTE LA
KNAP DOWN LA
GIRT LA
Combe Martin
KING ST
HIGH ST
PO
PH
Liby
EX34
VELLACOTT LA
Trentishoe Manor
Tattiscombe
Verwill
CORNER LA
1 LADDER LA
2 SPURWAY GDNS
HIGHER DEAN LA
LOWER DEAN LA
SKIRHEAD LA
Mast
Clorridge Hill
Ind Units
TOM SANDERS CL
PARK LA
RECTORY RD
CASTLE ST
VICTORIA ST
Buzzacott Manor
Coulscott
HIGHER BUZZACOTT LA
VERWILL LA
STONY CNR
RIDGE HILL
HOLDSTONE WAY
BEARA LA
BUZZACOTT LA
NUTCOMBE HILL
10
TRUCKHAM LA
COULSWORTHY CROOK
BUZZACOTT CL
Nutcombe
EX31
NUTT'S LA
LEIGH RD
Lower Leigh
Truckham Farm
WESTLEIGH LA
Westleigh Farm
COULSWORTHY LA
Stoneditch Hill
WOOD LA
Combe Martin Wildlife Park Rly
Dean
GRATTON LA
LOWER DEAN CROSS
Combe Martin Wildlife & Dinosaur Park
Coulsworthy
Higher Cowley
Henstridge
River Umber
Yellaton
YELLATON LA
Seven Ash
Waytown
EASTER CLOSE CROSS
DEAN LA
DEAN CROSS
A3123 LONG LA
SEVEN ASH CROSS
SLADE LANE CROSS
SLADE LA
Silkenworthy Knap
SOUTH LEY CROSS
Indicknowle
South Ley
LEY LA
B3229
A399
A3123
DOWN LA
A3
1 SUMMERLAND TERR
2 GENESIS LA
3 BARTON GATE LA
4 KINGSTON AVE
5 MANSION TERR
6 VALLEY LA
7 ORCHARD CL
8 KINGSLEY TERR
9 MILL MDW
10 WATER TERR
11 SPRINGFIELD TERR
12 HIGH CROSS
13 POUND LA
14 ROCK LA
15 WET LA
16 SUNNYSIDE COTTS
17 UMBERSIDE
18 PARK VIEW CL
19 ROWS LA
20 BROOKSIDE VILLAS
10
4

3

Scale: 1¾ inches to 1 mile
0 ¼ ½ mile
0 250m 500m 750m 1 km

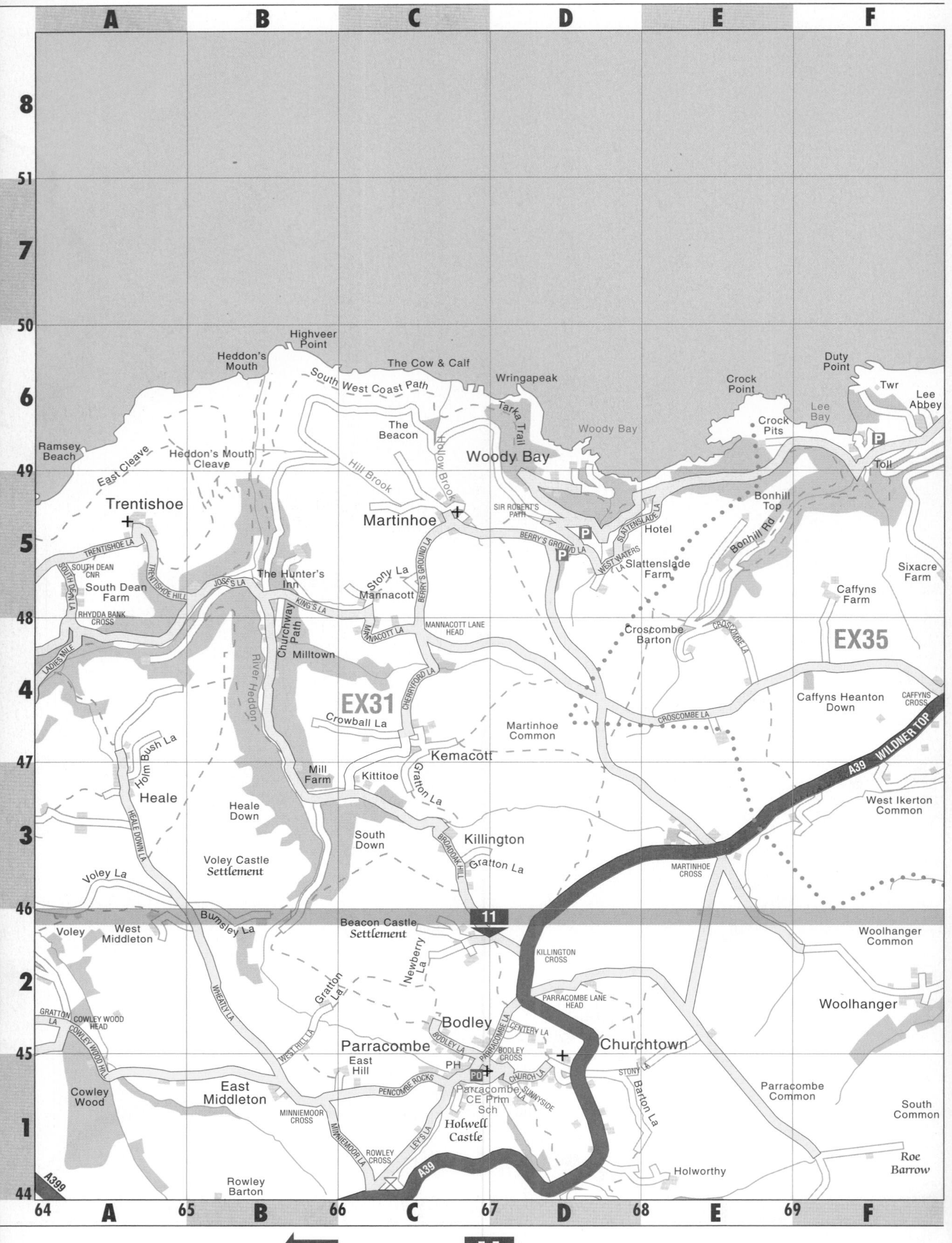

3

11

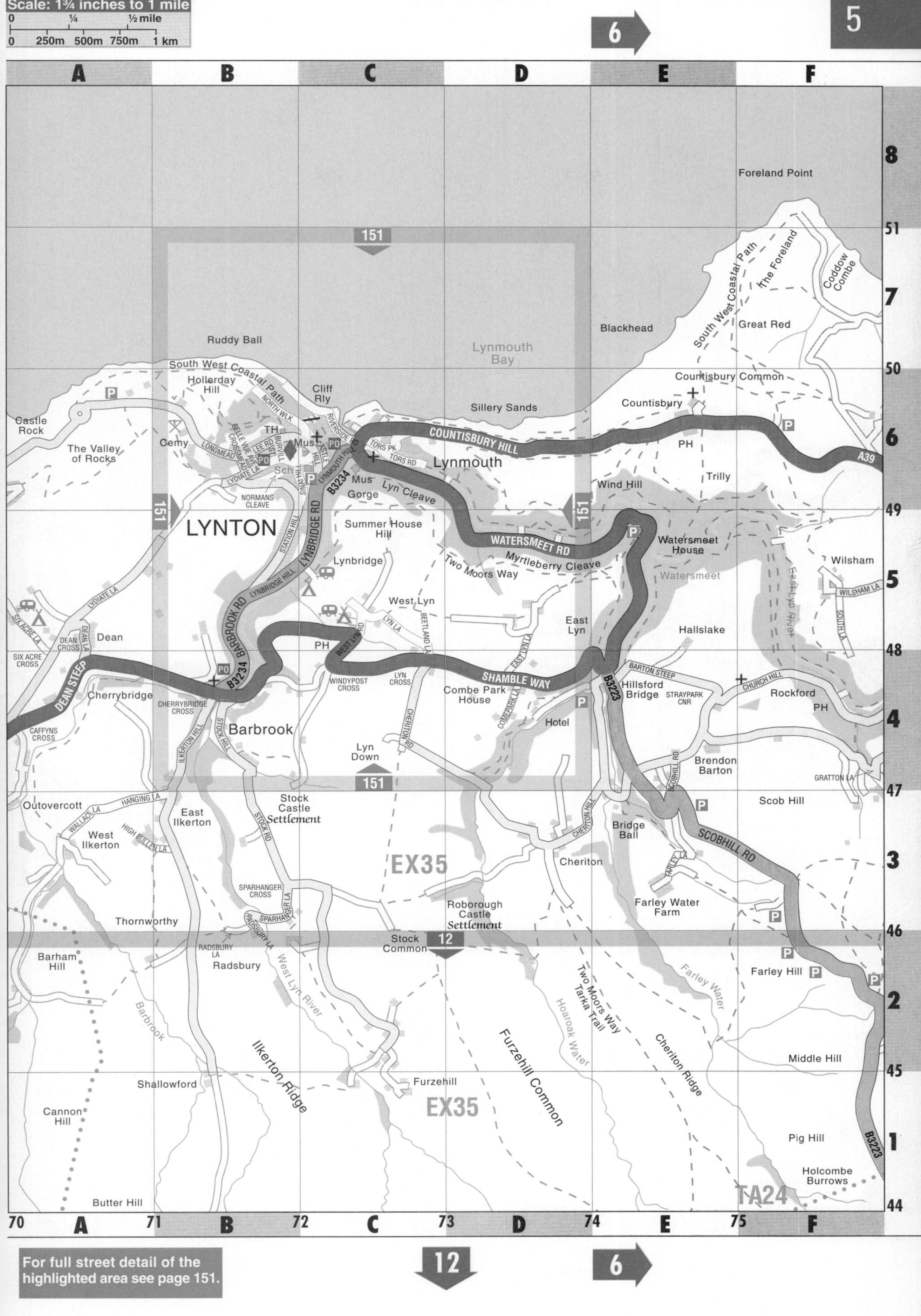

12
6
For full street detail of the highlighted area see page 151.

Scale: 1¾ inches to 1 mile
0 ¼ ½ mile
0 250m 500m 750m 1 km

A B C D E F

8
51
7
50
6
49
5
48
4
47
3
46
2
45
1
44

Countisbury Cove
Desolate
South West Coast Path
Glenthorne
Kipscombe Hill
KIPSCOMBE CROSS
A39
Old Burrow Hill
Wingate Farm
Embelle Wood
Sugarloaf Hill
SEVEN THORNS
WILSHAM CROSS
Coombe Farm
Visitor Ctr
COSGATES FEET OR COUNTY GATE
Ashton
Yenworthy Farm
HALL HILL
Hall Farm
WILSHAM LA
Leeford
Southern Wood
Broomstreet Farm
Yenworthy Common
YEARNOR MILL
LEEFORD LA
East Lyn River
PH
WOOD WAY
TA24
Brendon
Malmsmead
NEW RD
CROSS LA
Oare
A39
Deddy Combe
Deercombe
Fellingscott
EX35
Lower Tippacott
GRATTON LA
POST LA
Oare Water
TIPPACOTT LA
EASTER LA
BAZE LA
Slocombeslade
North Common
Shilstone
Cloud Farm
Badgworthy Water
Tippacott Ridge
Malmsmead Hill
Oareford
Meml
Shilstone Hill
Little Black Hill
Oare Common
Great Black Hill
Chalk Water
Dry Bridge
Lank Combe
Stowey Ridge
Doone Country
EX35
Withycombe Ridge
Badgworthy Water
Black Hill
Badgworthy Lees
Brendon Common
Hoccombe Combe
B3223
South Common
TA24
Badgworthy Hill

76 A 77 B 78 C 79 D 80 E 81 F

A39 Minehead

13

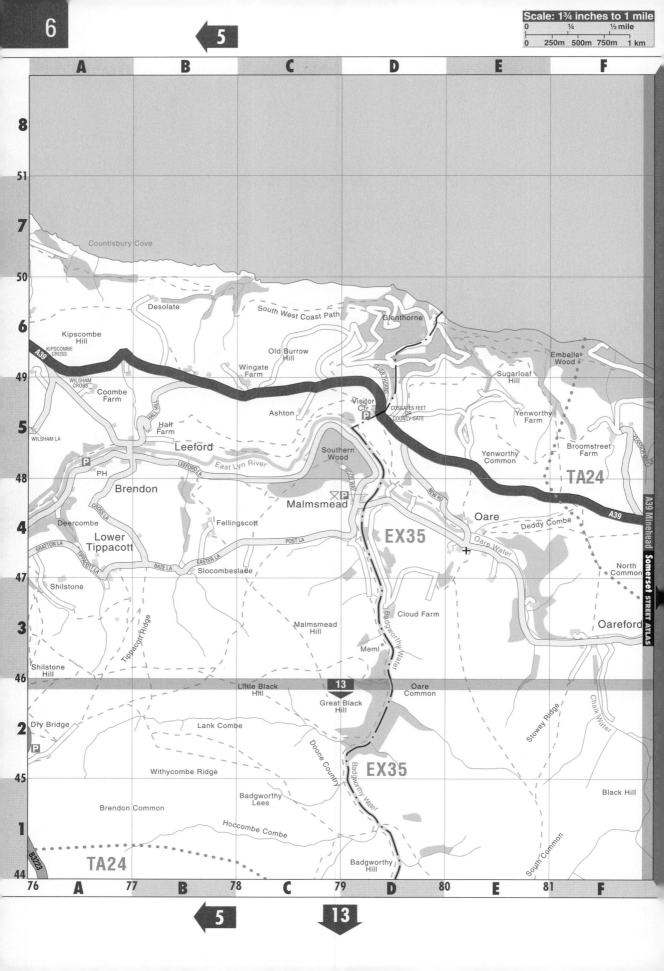

Scale: 1¾ inches to 1 mile

7
1

Scale: 1¾ inches to 1 mile

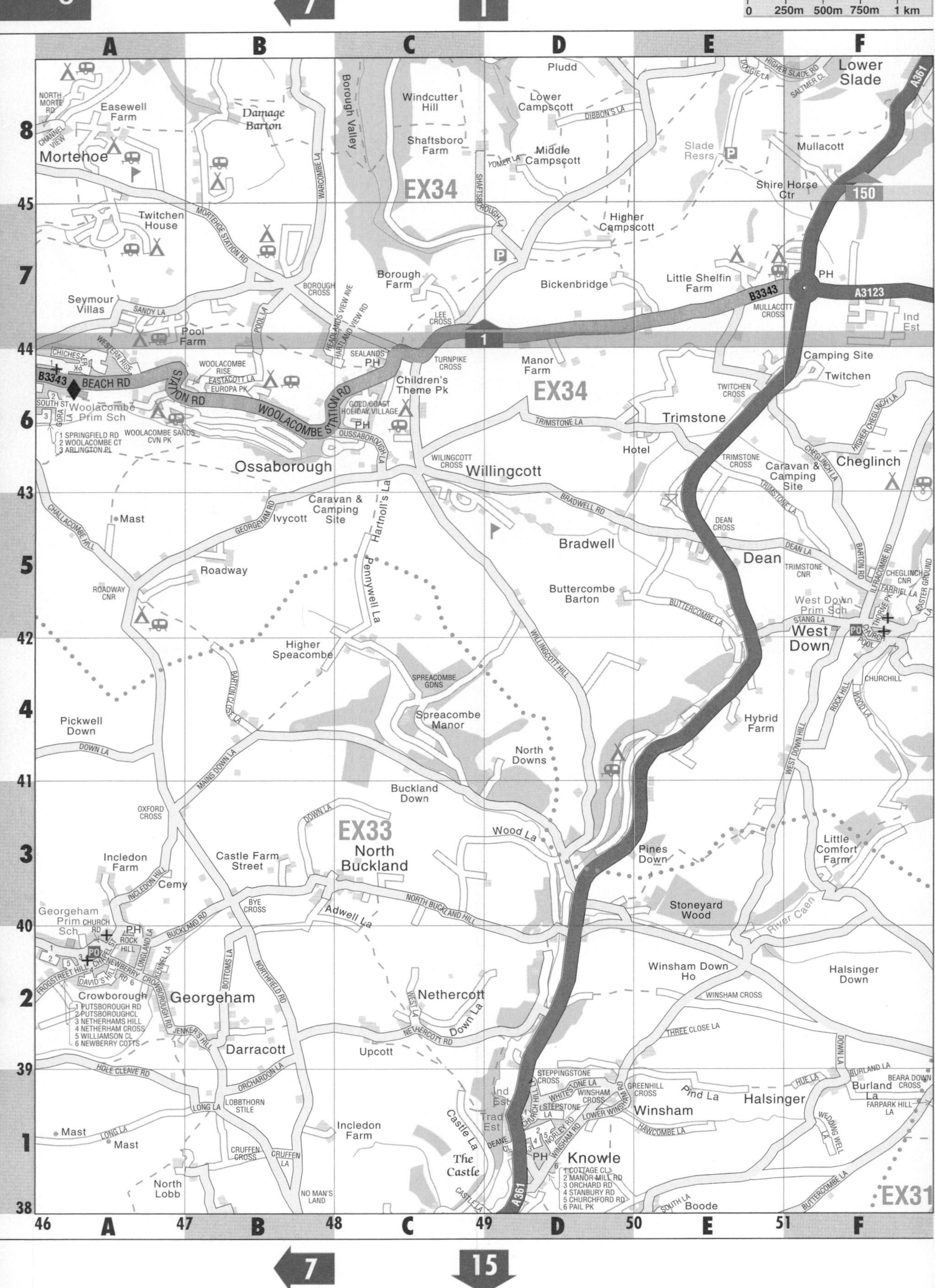

7
15

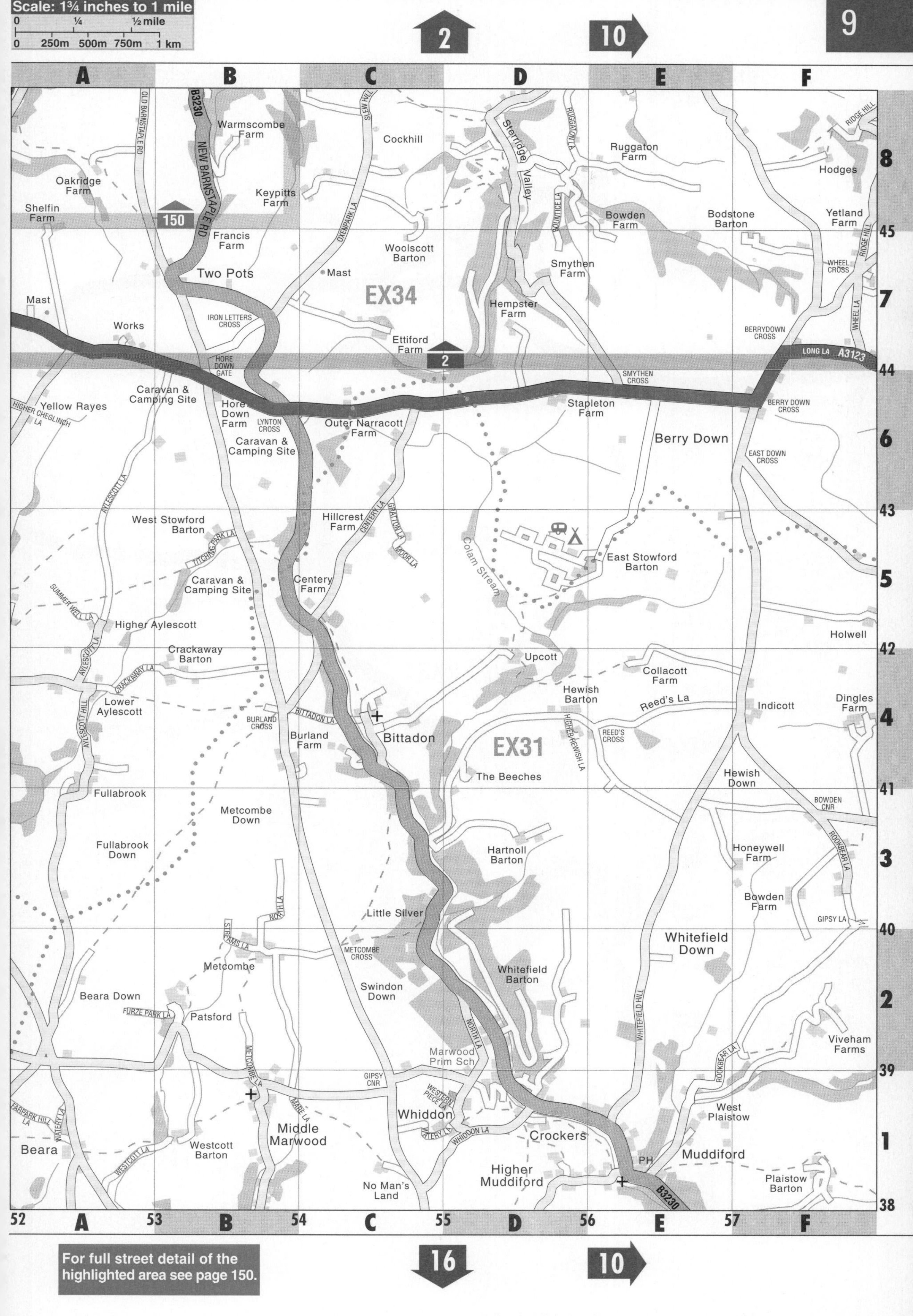
Scale: 1¾ inches to 1 mile
0 ¼ ½ mile
0 250m 500m 750m 1 km
2
10
9
A B C D E F
8 45 7 44 6 43 5 42 4 41 3 40 2 39 1 38
52 53 54 55 56 57
B3230
OLD BARNSTAPLE RD
NEW BARNSTAPLE RD
Warmscombe Farm
Cockhill
SLEW HILL
Sterridge Valley
RUGGATON LA
Ruggaton Farm
RIDGE HILL
Hodges
Oakridge Farm
Shelfin Farm
150
Keypitts Farm
Francis Farm
OXENPARK LA
Woolscott Barton
BOUNTICE LA
Bowden Farm
Bodstone Barton
Yetland Farm
RIDGE HILL
WHEEL CROSS
Smythen Farm
Two Pots
Mast
EX34
Mast
Hempster Farm
WHEEL LA
IRON LETTERS CROSS
Works
Ettiford Farm
BERRYDOWN CROSS
HORE DOWN GATE
LONG LA
A3123
SMYTHEN CROSS
Caravan & Camping Site
HIGHER CHEGLINCH LA
Yellow Rayes
Hore Down Farm
LYNTON CROSS
Outer Narracott Farm
Stapleton Farm
BERRY DOWN CROSS
Berry Down
Caravan & Camping Site
EAST DOWN CROSS
AYLESCOTT LA
West Stowford Barton
Hillcrest Farm
CENTERY LA
GRATTON LA
MOOR LA
Colam Stream
TITCHING PARK LA
East Stowford Barton
Caravan & Camping Site
Centery Farm
SUMMER WELL LA
Higher Aylescott
Holwell
Crackaway Barton
AYLESCOTT LA
CRACKAWAY LA
Upcott
Collacott Farm
Hewish Barton
Reed's La
Lower Aylescott
Indicott
Dingles Farm
BURLAND CROSS
BITTADON LA
Bittadon
REED'S CROSS
HIGHER HEWISH LA
EX31
AYLESCOTT HILL
Burland Farm
The Beeches
Hewish Down
Fullabrook
BOWDEN CNR
Metcombe Down
Fullabrook Down
Hartnoll Barton
Honeywell Farm
ROOKBEAR LA
Bowden Farm
NORTH LA
Little Silver
GIPSY LA
STREAMS LA
Whitefield Down
METCOMBE CROSS
Metcombe
Whitefield Barton
Swindon Down
Beara Down
FURZE PARK LA
Patsford
NORTH LA
WHITEFIELD HILL
Viveham Farms
METCOMBE LA
Marwood Prim Sch
ROOKBEAR LA
GIPSY CNR
WESTERN PIECE
FARPARK HILL LA
WATERY LA
Whiddon
West Plaistow
MARE LA
WATERY LA
WHIDDON LA
Crockers
Middle Marwood
Beara
Westcott Barton
WESTCOTT LA
PH
Muddiford
Higher Muddiford
Plaistow Barton
No Man's Land
B3230
16
10
For full street detail of the highlighted area see page 150.

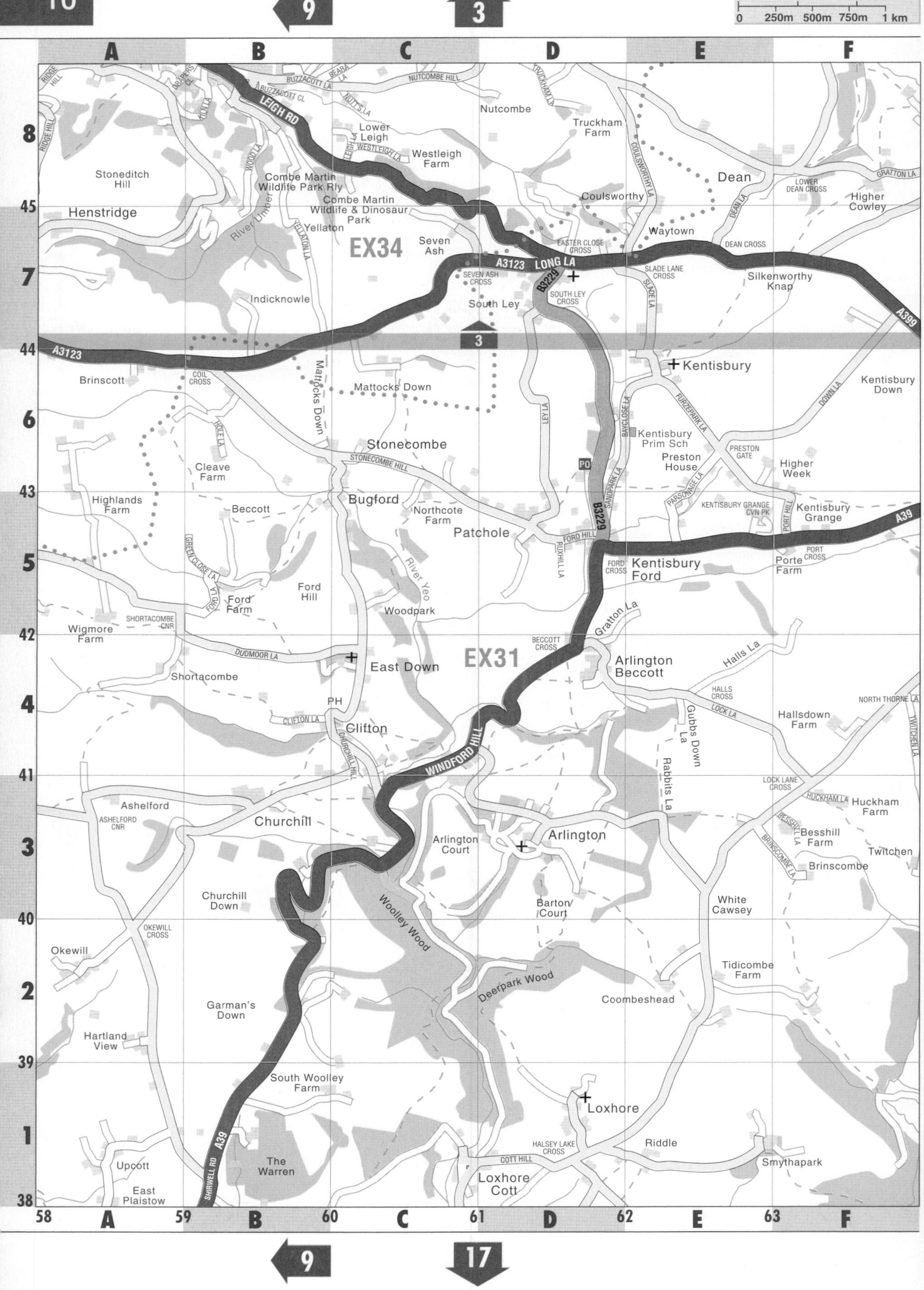

Scale: 1¾ inches to 1 mile
0 ¼ ½ mile
0 250m 500m 750m 1 km
9
3
17
A B C D E F
58 59 60 61 62 63
8 7 6 5 4 3 2 1
45 44 43 42 41 40 39 38
Nutcombe
Truckham Farm
Lower Leigh
Westleigh Farm
Stoneditch Hill
Combe Martin Wildlife Park Rly
Combe Martin Wildlife & Dinosaur Park
Dean
Coulsworthy
Higher Cowley
Henstridge
Yellaton
EX34
Seven Ash
Waytown
LONG LA
A3123
Silkenworthy Knap
Indicknowle
South Ley
A399
Kentisbury
Kentisbury Down
Brinscott
Mattocks Down
Stonecombe
Kentisbury Prim Sch
Preston House
Higher Week
Cleave Farm
Highlands Farm
Beccott
Bugford
Northcote Farm
Patchole
Kentisbury Grange
A39
Kentisbury Ford
Porte Farm
Ford Farm
Ford Hill
River Yeo
Woodpark
Wigmore Farm
Shortacombe
East Down
EX31
Arlington Beccott
Halls La
Gratton La
Clifton
Hallsdown Farm
Gubbs Down La
Rabbits La
WINDFORD HILL
Ashelford
Churchill
Arlington Court
Arlington
Huckham Farm
Besshill Farm
Twitchen
Brinscombe
Churchill Down
Woolley Wood
Barton Court
White Cawsey
Okewill
Tidicombe Farm
Deerpark Wood
Coombeshead
Garman's Down
Hartland View
South Woolley Farm
Loxhore
The Warren
Riddle
Smythapark
Upcott
East Plaistow
Loxhore Cott
B3229
LEIGH RD
SHIRWELL RD

Scale: 1¾ inches to 1 mile

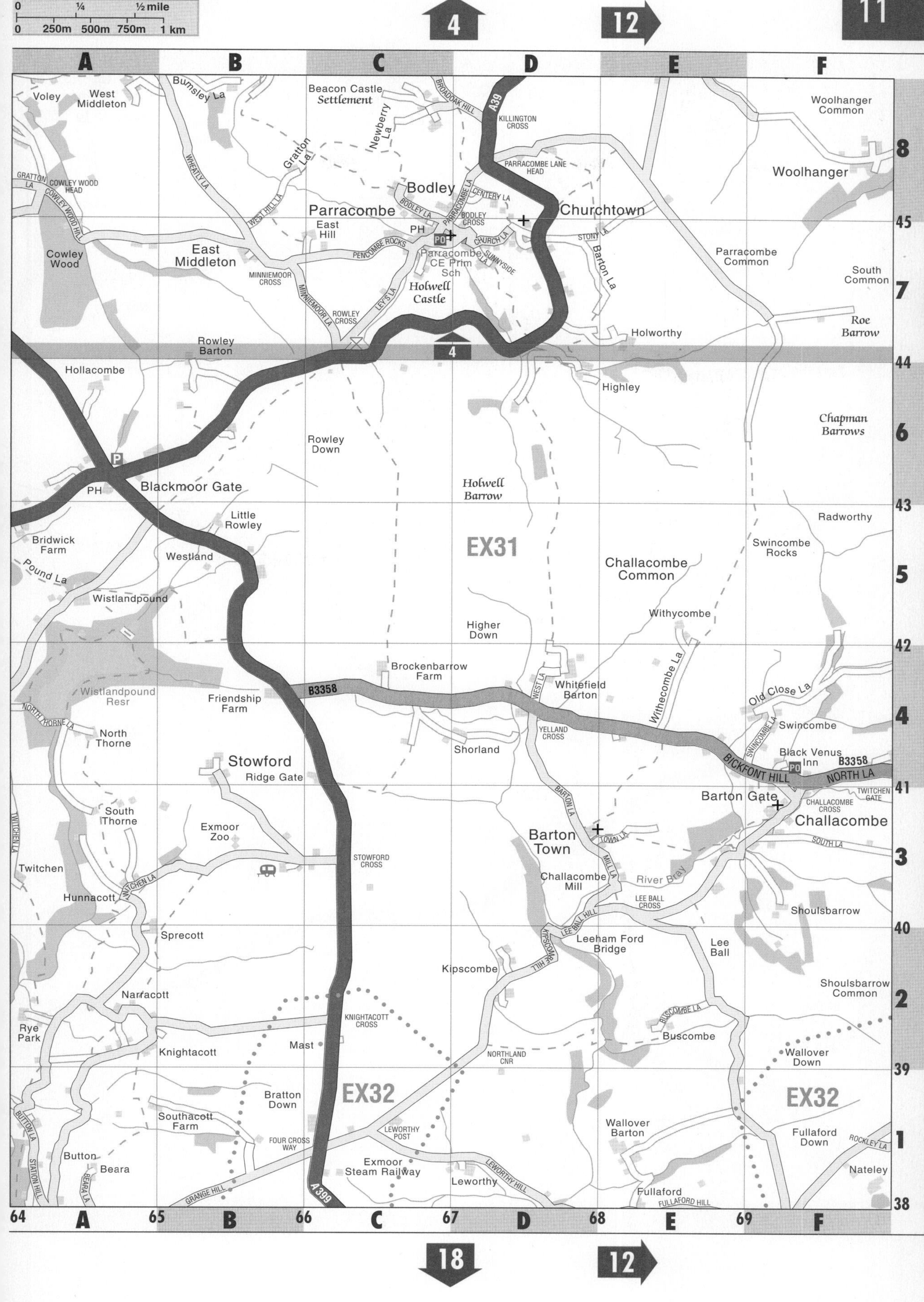

11
5

Scale: 1¾ inches to 1 mile
0 ¼ ½ mile
0 250m 500m 750m 1 km

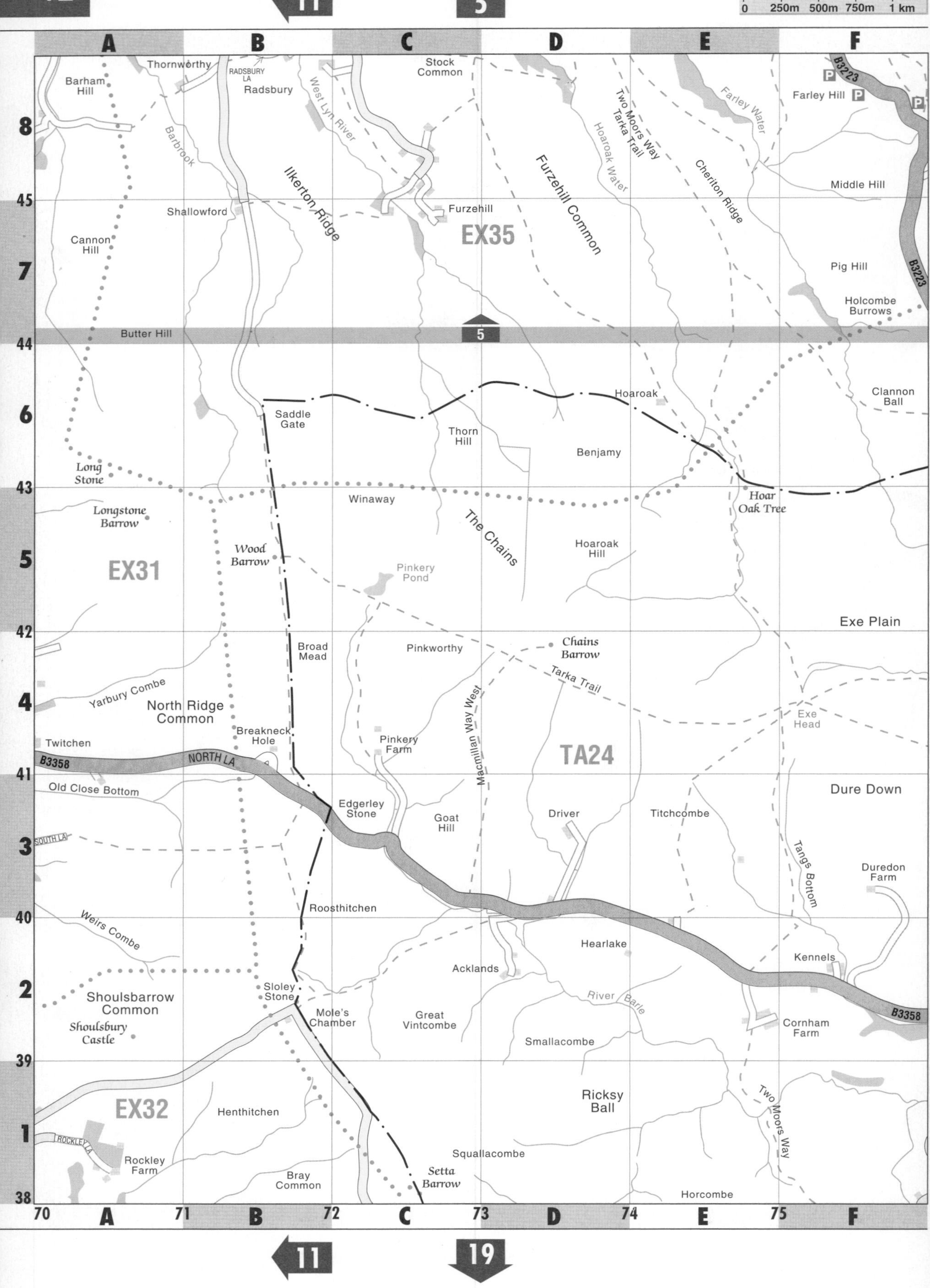

11
19

Scale: 1¾ inches to 1 mile

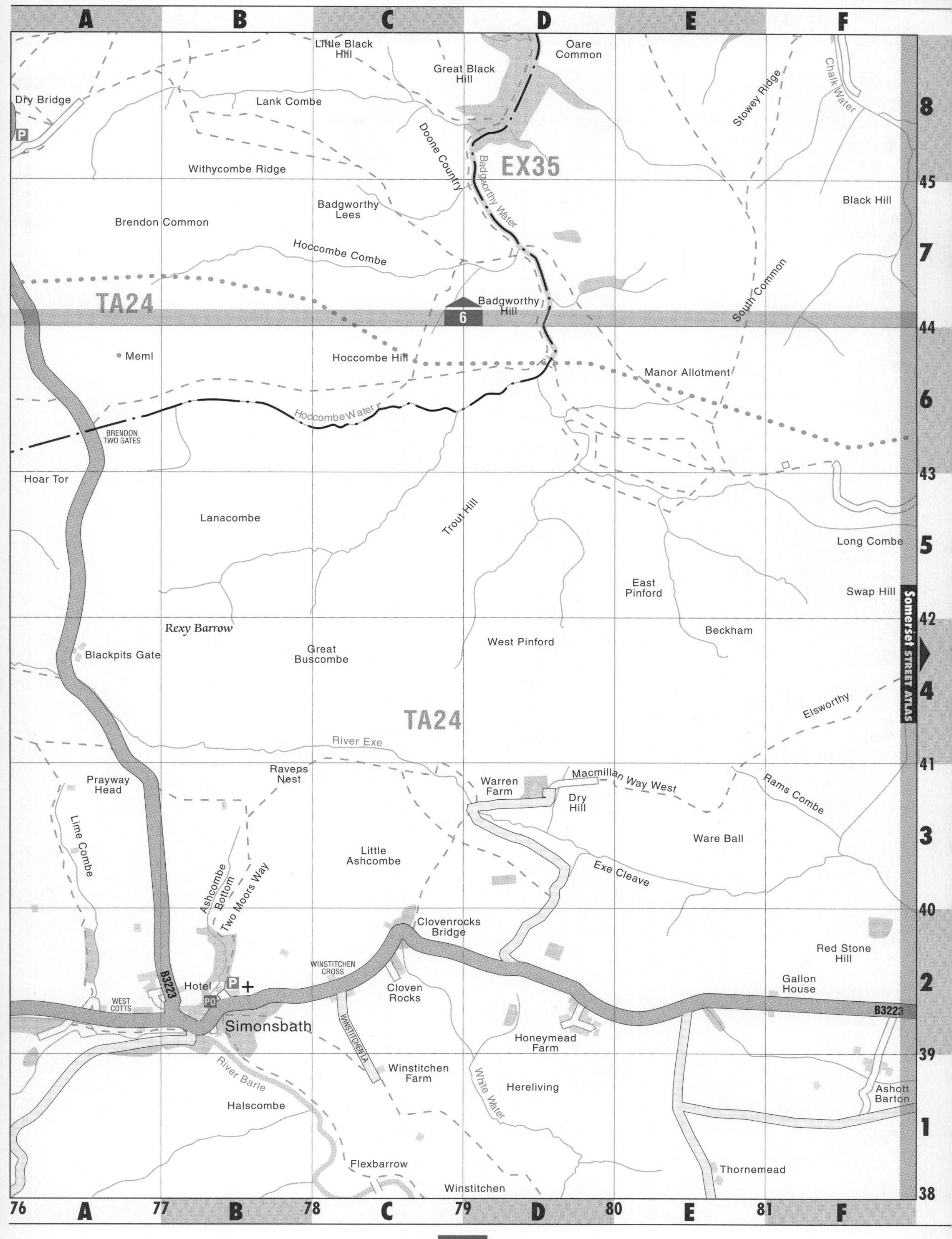

7

Scale: 1¾ inches to 1 mile

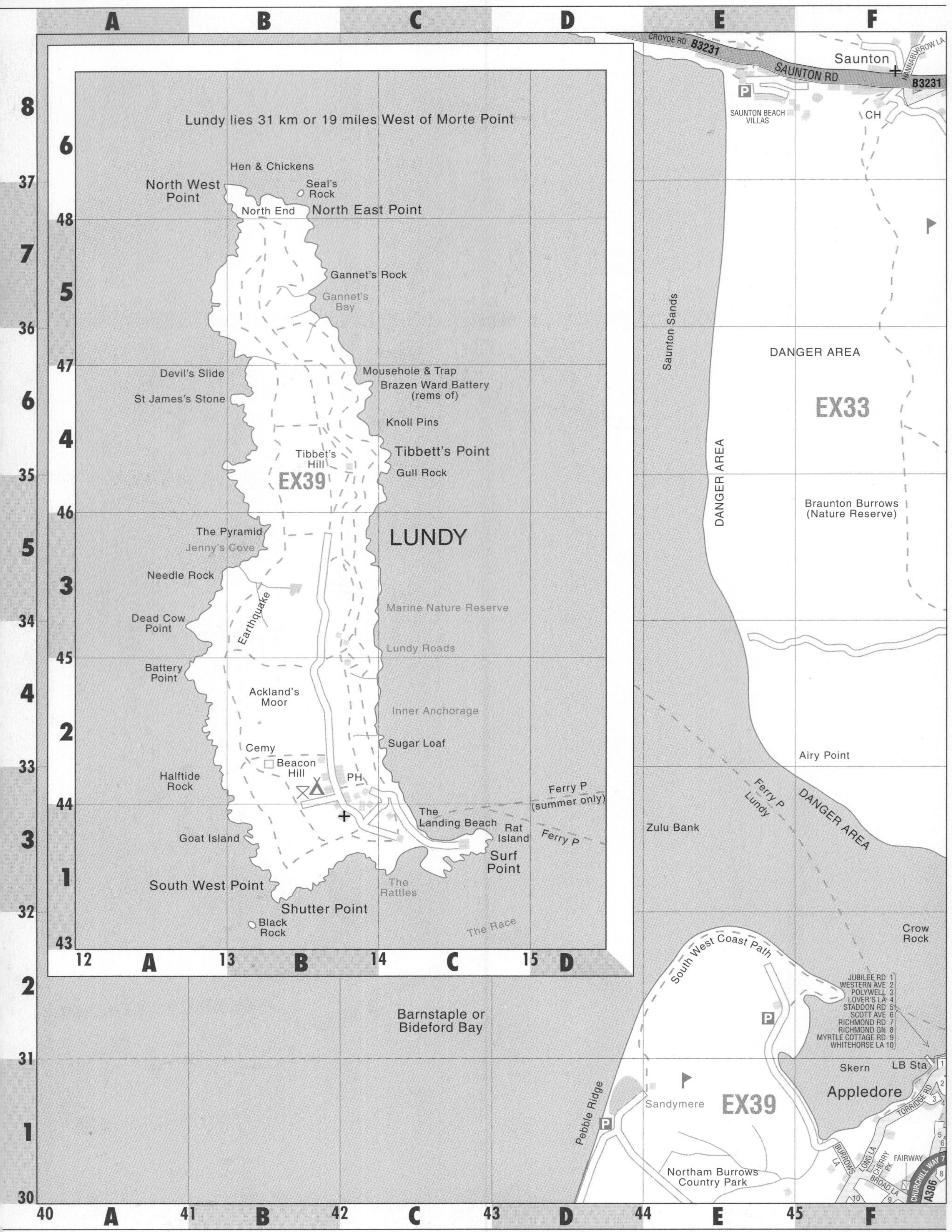

25

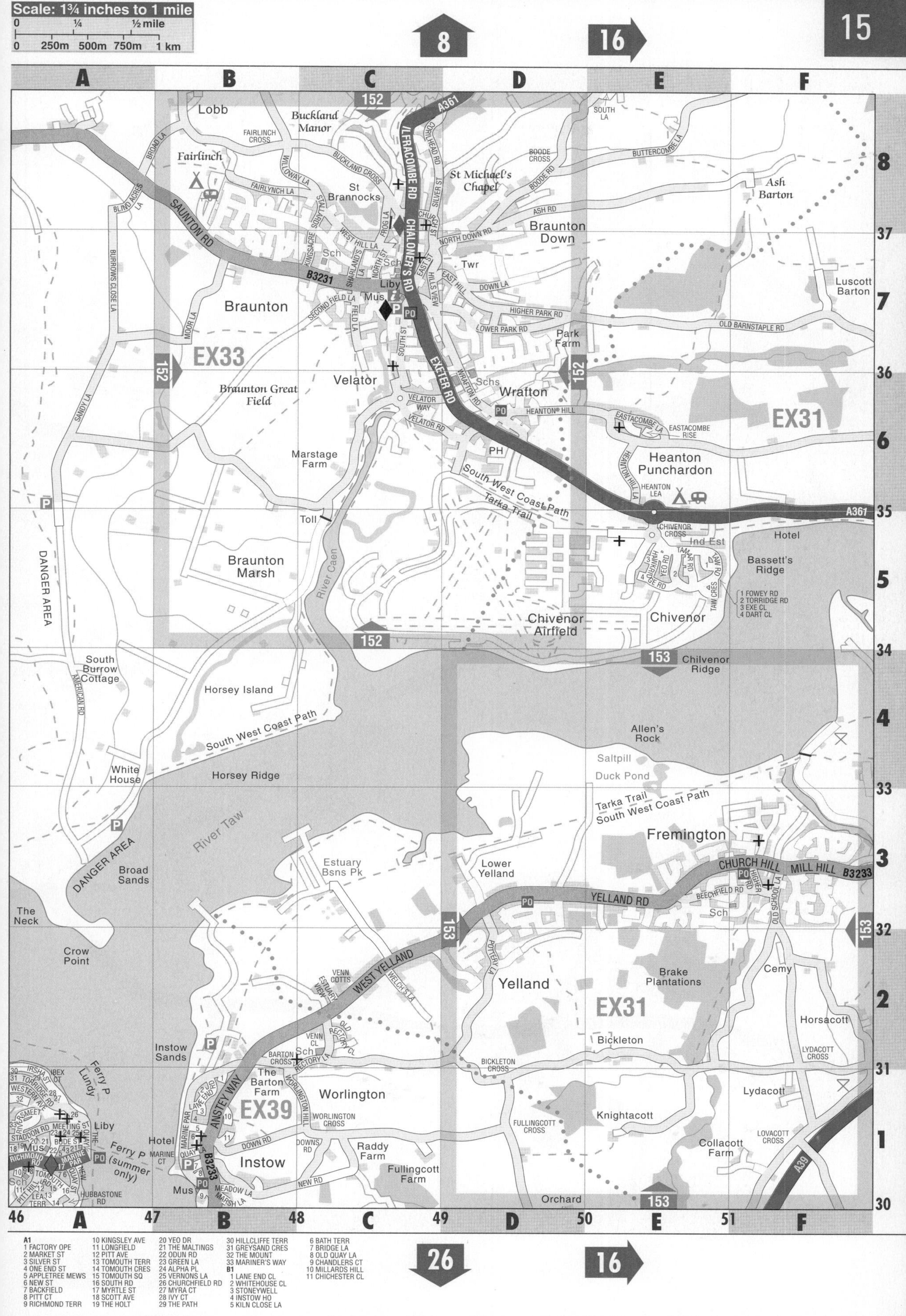

Scale: 1¾ inches to 1 mile
0 ¼ ½ mile
0 250m 500m 750m 1 km
8
16
A B C D E F
152
Lobb
Buckland Manor
FAIRLINCH CROSS
Fairlinch
A361
ILFRACOMBE RD
CHALONER'S RD
St Brannocks
St Michael's Chapel
BOODE CROSS
BUTTERCOMBE LA
SOUTH LA
Ash Barton
SAUNTON RD
B3231
Braunton Down
ASH RD
NORTH DOWN RD
Twr
DOWN LA
Luscott Barton
Braunton
Liby
Mus
PO
HIGHER PARK RD
LOWER PARK RD
OLD BARNSTAPLE RD
Park Farm
EX33
Velator
Braunton Great Field
EXETER RD
Schs
Wrafton
HEANTON HILL
EASTACOMBE LA
EASTACOMBE RISE
EX31
Marstage Farm
PH
Heanton Punchardon
HEANTON LEA
South West Coast Path
Tarka Trail
A361
Toll
CHIVENOR CROSS
Ind Est
Hotel
Bassett's Ridge
Braunton Marsh
River Caen
DANGER AREA
1 FOWEY RD
2 TORRIDGE RD
3 EXE CL
4 DART CL
Chivenor Airfield
Chivenor
153
Chilvenor Ridge
South Burrow Cottage
AMERICAN RD
Horsey Island
South West Coast Path
Allen's Rock
White House
Horsey Ridge
Saltpill
Duck Pond
Tarka Trail
South West Coast Path
River Taw
Fremington
DANGER AREA
Broad Sands
Estuary Bsns Pk
Lower Yelland
CHURCH HILL
MILL HILL
B3233
YELLAND RD
BEECHFIELD RD
The Neck
Sch
Crow Point
WEST YELLAND
VENN COTTS
Yelland
Brake Plantations
Cemy
EX31
Horsacott
Instow Sands
BARTON CROSS
Bickleton
BICKLETON CROSS
LYDACOTT CROSS
The Barton Farm
Worlington
Lydacott
Ferry P Lundy
EX39
WORLINGTON CROSS
Knightacott
Liby
Hotel
FULLINGCOTT CROSS
LOVACOTT CROSS
Ferry P (summer only)
Instow
Raddy Farm
Collacott Farm
A39
Fullingcott Farm
Mus
B3233
MEADOW LA
MARSH LA
NEW RD
HUBBASTONE RD
Orchard
153
46 A 47 B 48 C 49 D 50 E 51 F
8 37 7 36 6 35 5 34 4 33 3 32 2 31 1 30
A1
1 FACTORY OPE
2 MARKET ST
3 SILVER ST
4 ONE END ST
5 APPLETREE MEWS
6 NEW ST
7 BACKFIELD
8 PITT CT
9 RICHMOND TERR
10 KINGSLEY AVE
11 LONGFIELD
12 PITT AVE
13 TOMOUTH TERR
14 TOMOUTH CRES
15 TOMOUTH SQ
16 SOUTH RD
17 MYRTLE ST
18 SCOTT AVE
19 THE HOLT
20 YEO DR
21 THE MALTINGS
22 ODUN RD
23 GREEN LA
24 ALPHA PL
25 VERNONS LA
26 CHURCHFIELD RD
27 MYRA CT
28 IVY CT
29 THE PATH
30 HILLCLIFFE TERR
31 GREYSAND CRES
32 THE MOUNT
33 MARINER'S WAY
B1
1 LANE END CL
2 WHITEHOUSE CL
3 STONEYWELL
4 INSTOW HO
5 KILN CLOSE LA
6 BATH TERR
7 BRIDGE LA
8 OLD QUAY LA
9 CHANDLERS CT
10 MILLARDS HILL
11 CHICHESTER CL
26
16

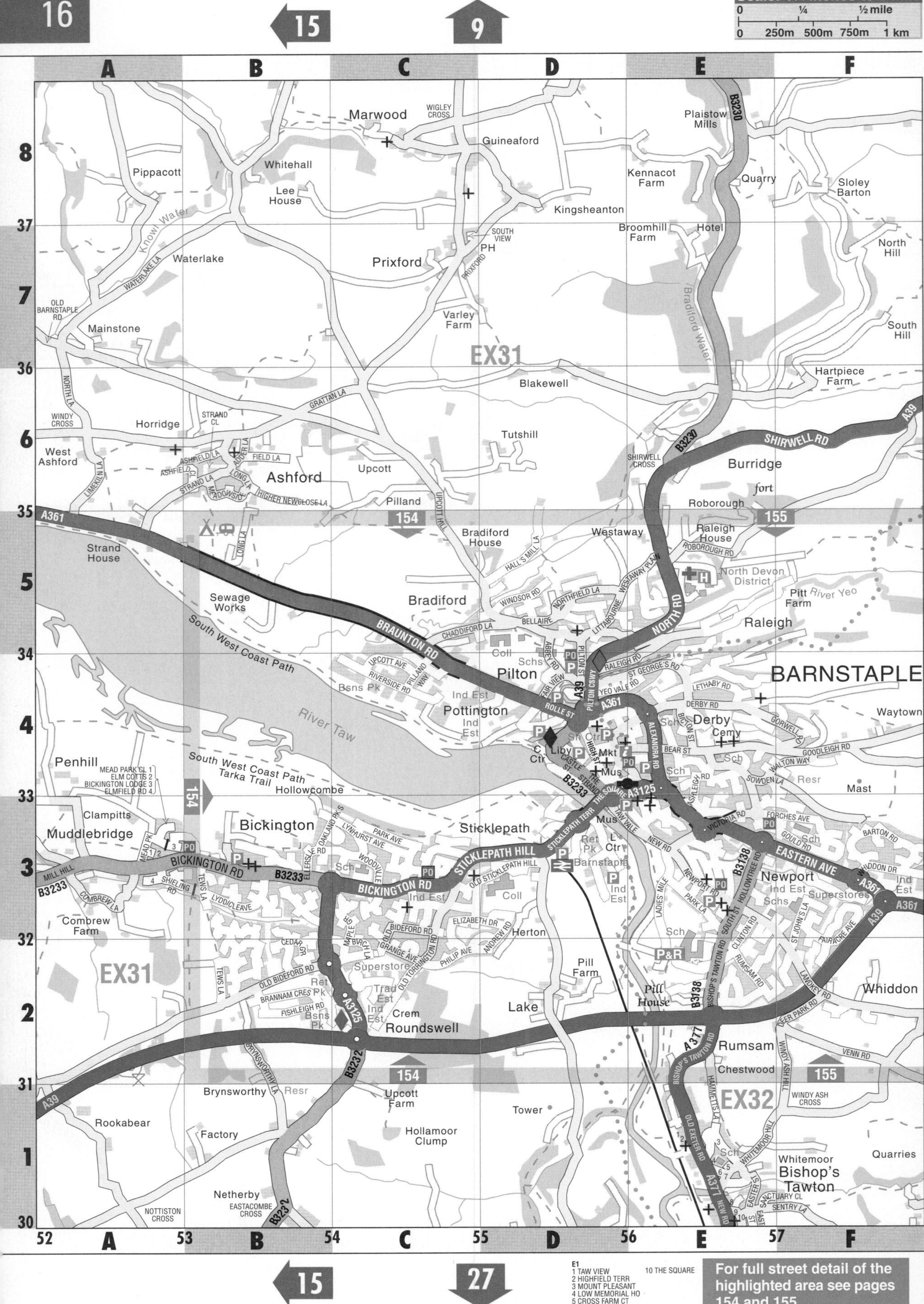

15
27

E1
1 TAW VIEW
2 HIGHFIELD TERR
3 MOUNT PLEASANT
4 LOW MEMORIAL HO
5 CROSS FARM CT
6 SCHOOL LA
7 SANDERS LA
8 ROSE COTTS
9 VILLAGE ST
10 THE SQUARE

For full street detail of the highlighted area see pages 154 and 155.

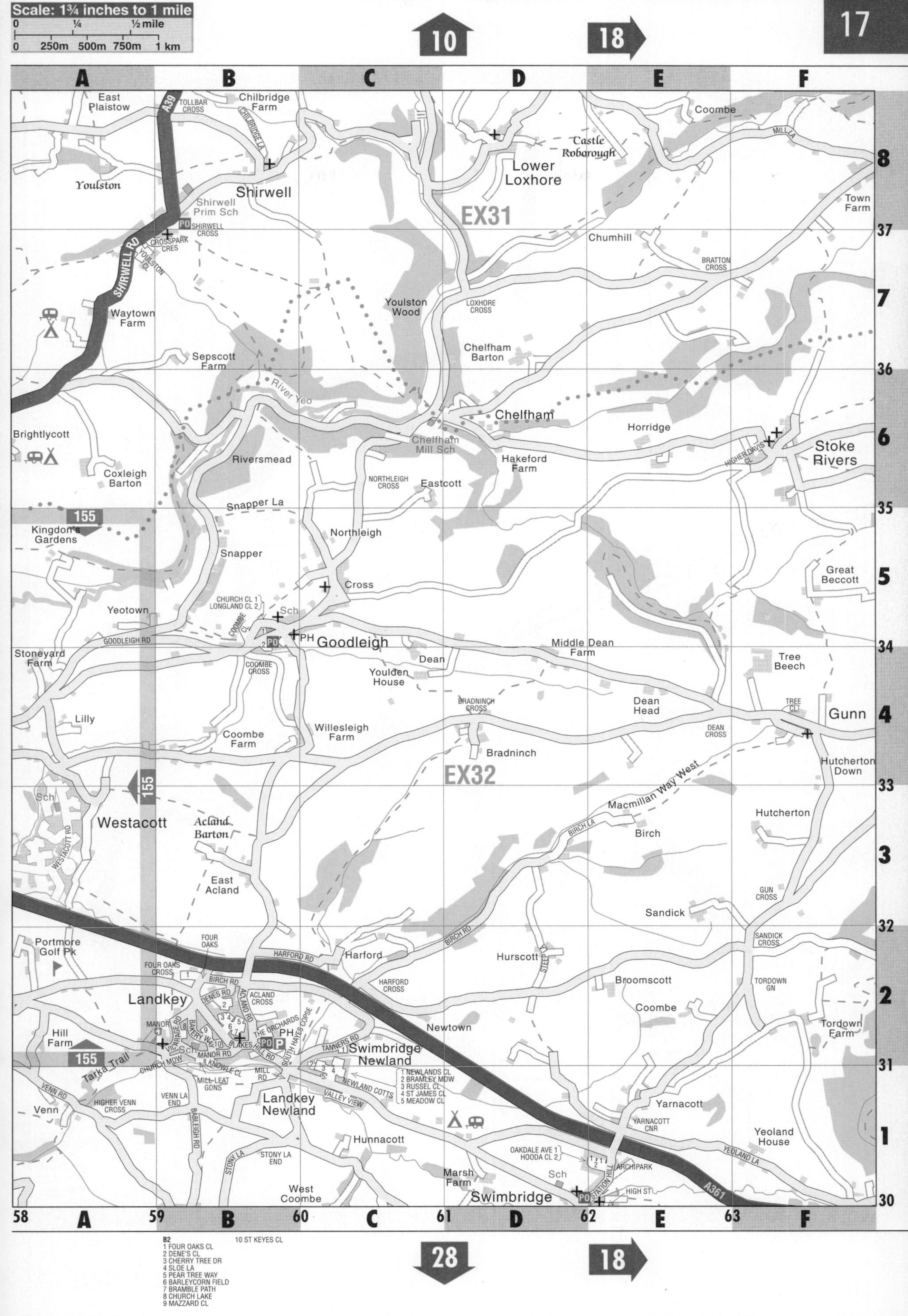
Scale: 1¾ inches to 1 mile
0 ¼ ½ mile
0 250m 500m 750m 1 km
10
18
A B C D E F
East Plaistow
A39
TOLLBAR CROSS
Chilbridge Farm
CHILBRIDGE LA
Coombe
MILL LA
Castle Roborough
Lower Loxhore
Youlston
Shirwell
Shirwell Prim Sch
PO
SHIRWELL CROSS
EX31
Town Farm
CROSSPARK CRES
YOULSTON CL
Chumhill
BRATTON CROSS
SHIRWELL RD
Youlston Wood
LOXHORE CROSS
Waytown Farm
Chelfham Barton
Sepscott Farm
River Yeo
Chelfham
Chelfham Mill Sch
Horridge
Brightlycott
Riversmead
Hakeford Farm
HIGHER DAVIS CL
Stoke Rivers
Coxleigh Barton
NORTHLEIGH CROSS
Eastcott
Snapper La
155
Kingdon's Gardens
Northleigh
Snapper
Great Beccott
Cross
CHURCH CL 1
LONGLAND CL 2
Sch
Yeotown
COOMBE CL
GOODLEIGH RD
PH
Goodleigh
Middle Dean Farm
Stoneyard Farm
COOMBE CROSS
Dean
Youlden House
Tree Beech
BRADNINCH CROSS
Dean Head
TREE CL
Gunn
Lilly
Willesleigh Farm
DEAN CROSS
Coombe Farm
Bradninch
Hutcherton Down
EX32
Macmillan Way West
Sch
Westacott
Acland Barton
BIRCH LA
Hutcherton
Birch
WESTACOTT RD
East Acland
GUN CROSS
Sandick
Portmore Golf Pk
FOUR OAKS
SANDICK CROSS
HARFORD RD
Harford
BIRCH RD
Hurscott
STEEP LA
FOUR OAKS CROSS
BIRCH RD
HARFORD CROSS
Broomscott
TORDOWN GN
Landkey
DENES RD
ACLAND RD
ACLAND CROSS
Coombe
MANOR CL
VICARAGE RD
BAKERY WAY
THE ORCHARDS
SOUTH HAYES COPSE
Newtown
Tordown Farm
Hill Farm
PH
P
TANNERS RD
Swimbridge Newland
MANOR RD
BLAKES HILL RD
Tarka Trail
CHURCH MDW
KNOWLE CL
MILL RD
MILL LEAT GDNS
1 NEWLANDS CL
2 BRAMLEY MDW
3 RUSSEL CL
4 ST JAMES CL
5 MEADOW CL
NEWLAND COTTS
VALLEY VIEW
VENN RD
HIGHER VENN CROSS
VENN LA END
Landkey Newland
Yarnacott
Venn
BABLEIGH RD
YARNACOTT CNR
Hunnacott
Yeoland House
OAKDALE AVE 1
HOODA CL 2
YEOLAND LA
STONY LA
STONY LA END
ARCHIPARK
Marsh Farm
Sch
West Coombe
Swimbridge
STATION HILL
HIGH ST
A361
58 59 60 61 62 63
30 31 32 33 34 35 36 37
1 2 3 4 5 6 7 8
B2
1 FOUR OAKS CL
2 DENE'S CL
3 CHERRY TREE DR
4 SLOE LA
5 PEAR TREE WAY
6 BARLEYCORN FIELD
7 BRAMBLE PATH
8 CHURCH LAKE
9 MAZZARD CL
10 ST KEYES CL
28
18

17
11

Scale: 1¾ inches to 1 mile
0 ¼ ½ mile
0 250m 500m 750m 1 km

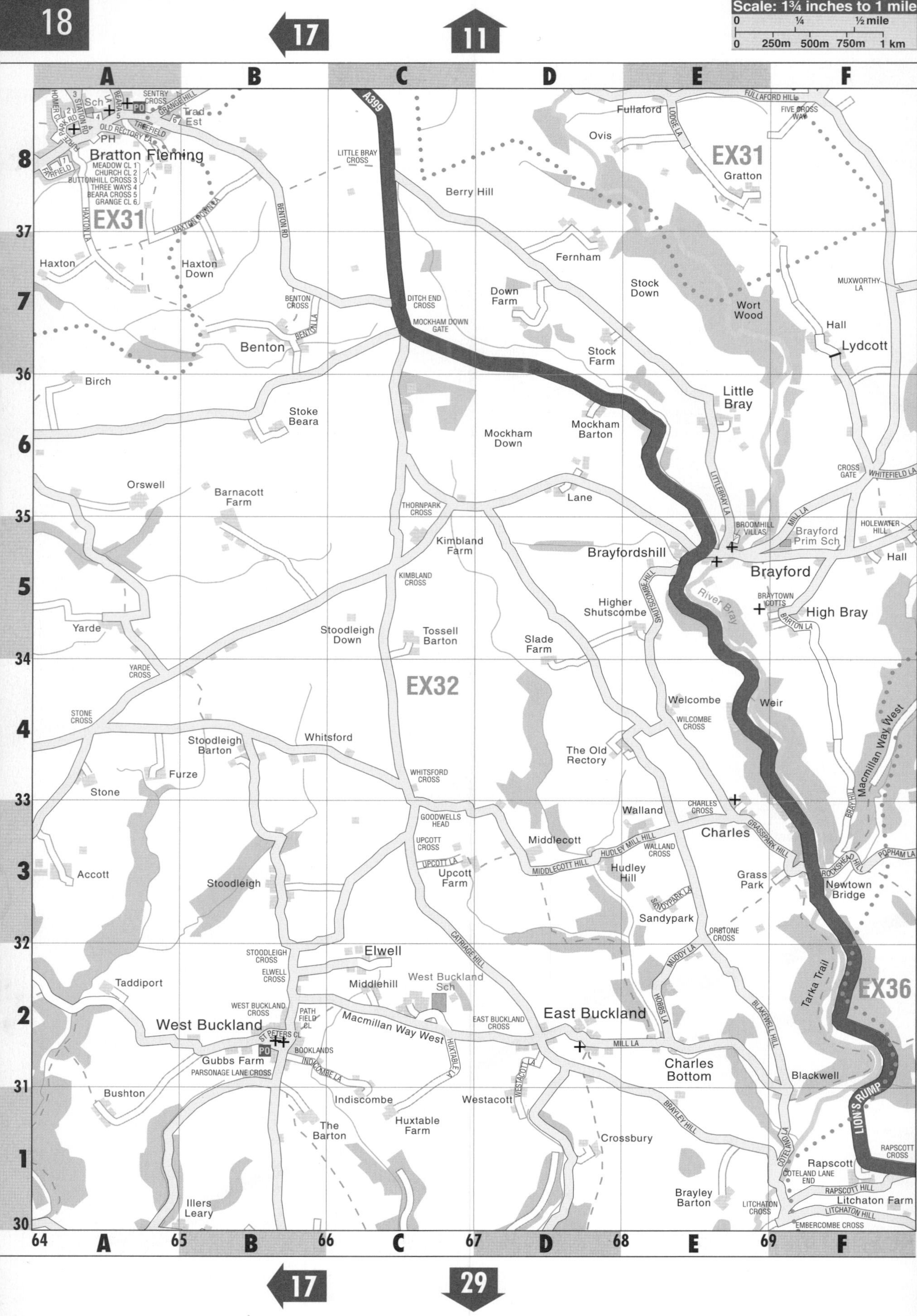

17
29

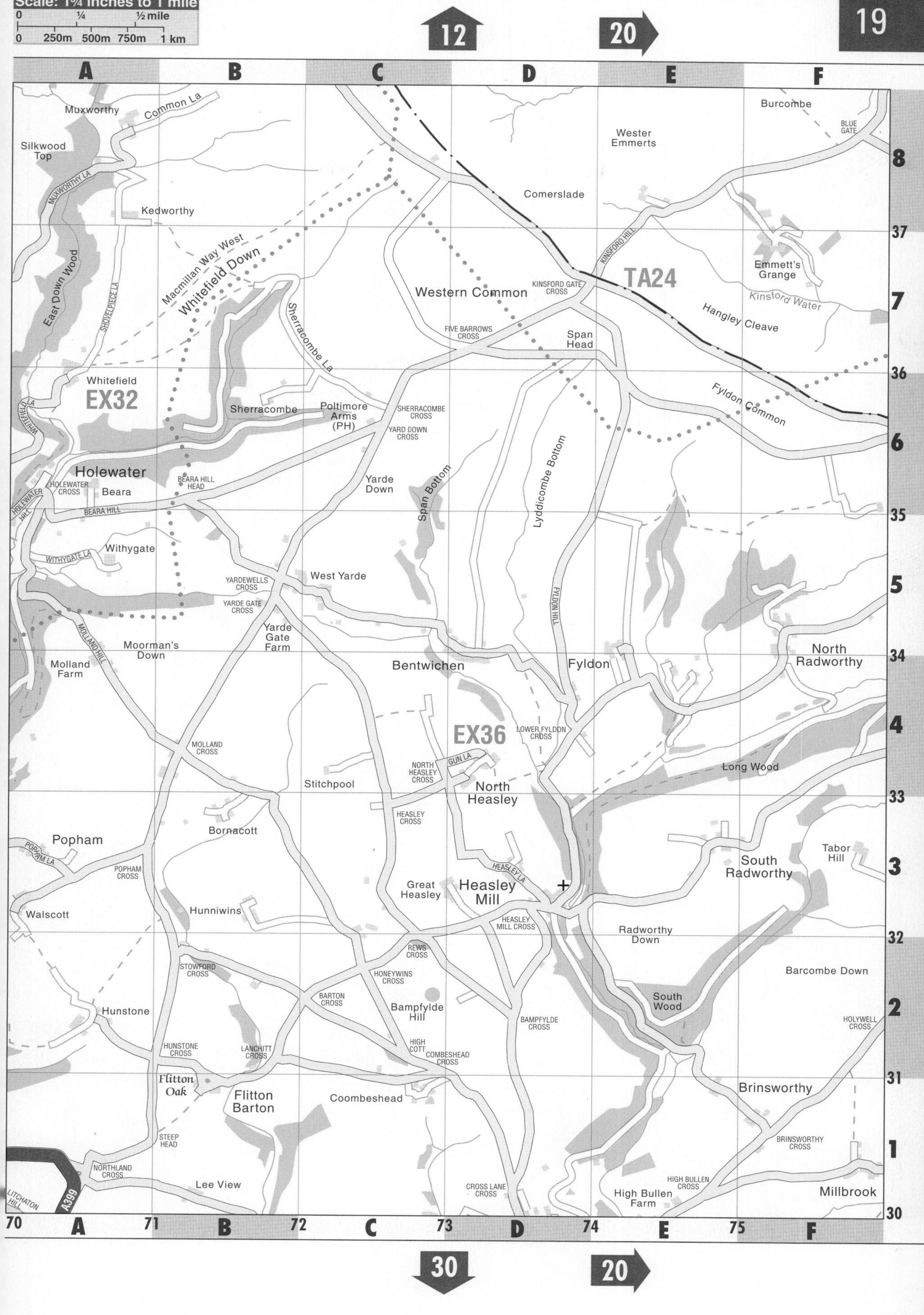
Scale: 1¾ inches to 1 mile
0 ¼ ½ mile
0 250m 500m 750m 1 km
12
20
A B C D E F
Muxworthy
Common La
Silkwood Top
Burcombe
BLUE GATE
Wester Emmerts
Comerslade
Kedworthy
MUXWORTHY LA
East Down Wood
SHOVELPIECE LA
Macmillan Way West
Whitefield Down
Sherracombe La
Western Common
KINSFORD GATE CROSS
KINSFORD HILL
TA24
Emmett's Grange
Kinsford Water
Hangley Cleave
FIVE BARROWS CROSS
Span Head
Whitefield
EX32
WHITEFIELD LA
Sherracombe
Poltimore Arms (PH)
SHERRACOMBE CROSS
YARD DOWN CROSS
Fyldon Common
Holewater
HOLEWATER CROSS
HOLEWATER HILL
Beara
BEARA HILL HEAD
BEARA HILL
Yarde Down
Span Bottom
Lyddicombe Bottom
Withygate
WITHYGATE LA
YARDEWELLS CROSS
West Yarde
YARDE GATE CROSS
FYLDON HILL
MOLLAND HILL
Moorman's Down
Yarde Gate Farm
Molland Farm
Bentwichen
Fyldon
North Radworthy
EX36
LOWER FYLDON CROSS
MOLLAND CROSS
NORTH HEASLEY CROSS
GUN LA
Long Wood
Stitchpool
North Heasley
Popham
POPHAM LA
Bornacott
HEASLEY CROSS
South Radworthy
Tabor Hill
POPHAM CROSS
HEASLEY LA
Great Heasley
Heasley Mill
Walscott
Hunniwins
HEASLEY MILL CROSS
Radworthy Down
REWS CROSS
STOWFORD CROSS
HONEYWINS CROSS
Barcombe Down
BARTON CROSS
Bampfylde Hill
South Wood
Hunstone
BAMPFYLDE CROSS
HOLYWELL CROSS
HUNSTONE CROSS
LANCHITT CROSS
HIGH COTT
COMBESHEAD CROSS
Flitton Oak
Flitton Barton
Coombeshead
Brinsworthy
STEEP HEAD
BRINSWORTHY CROSS
NORTHLAND CROSS
Lee View
CROSS LANE CROSS
HIGH BULLEN CROSS
High Bullen Farm
Millbrook
LITCHATON HILL
A399
8
37
7
36
6
35
5
34
4
33
3
32
2
31
1
30
70 71 72 73 74 75
30
20

19
13

Scale: 1¾ inches to 1 mile
0 ¼ ½ mile
0 250m 500m 750m 1 km

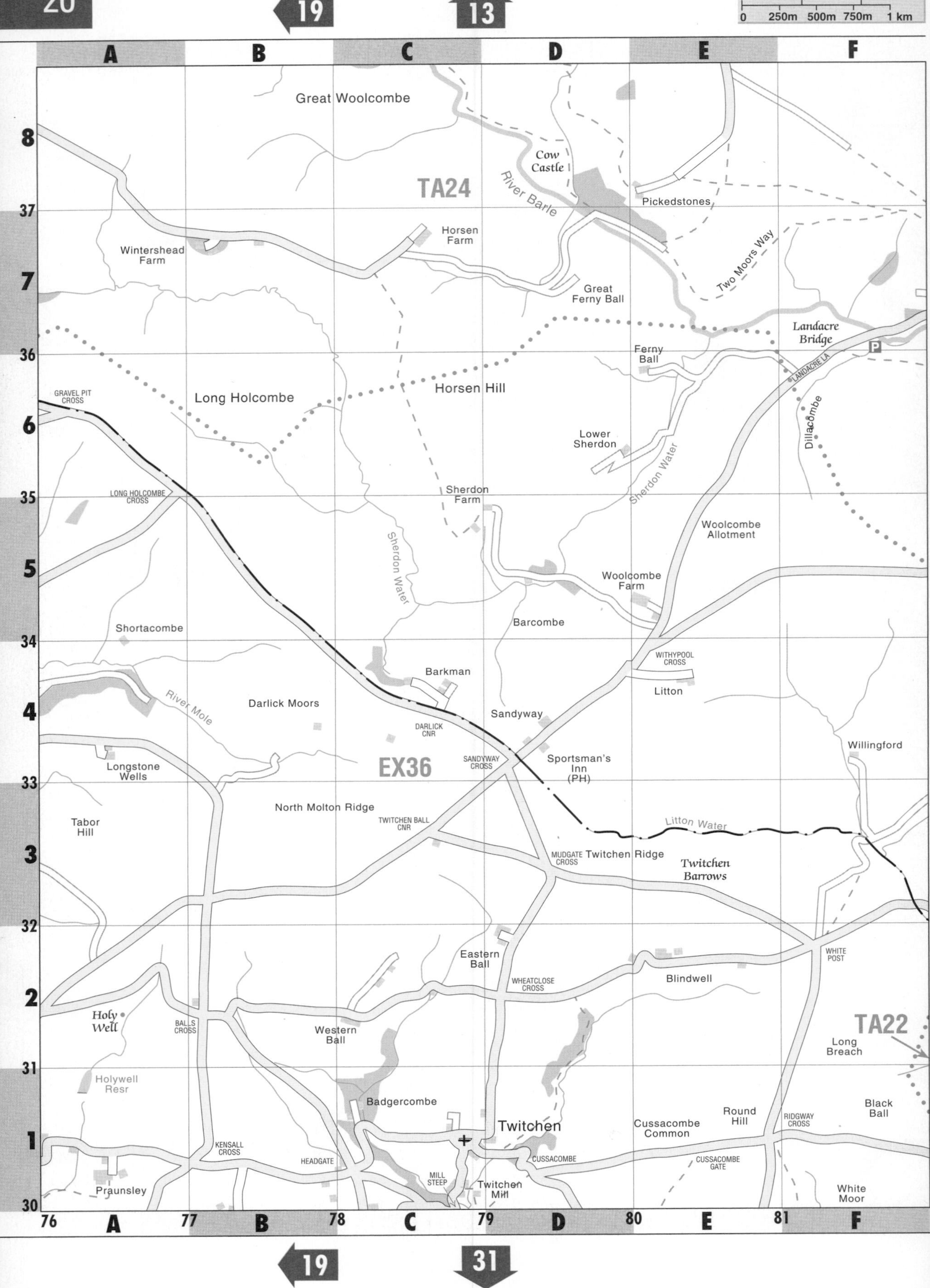

19
31

Scale: 1¾ inches to 1 mile
0 ¼ ½ mile
0 250m 500m 750m 1 km

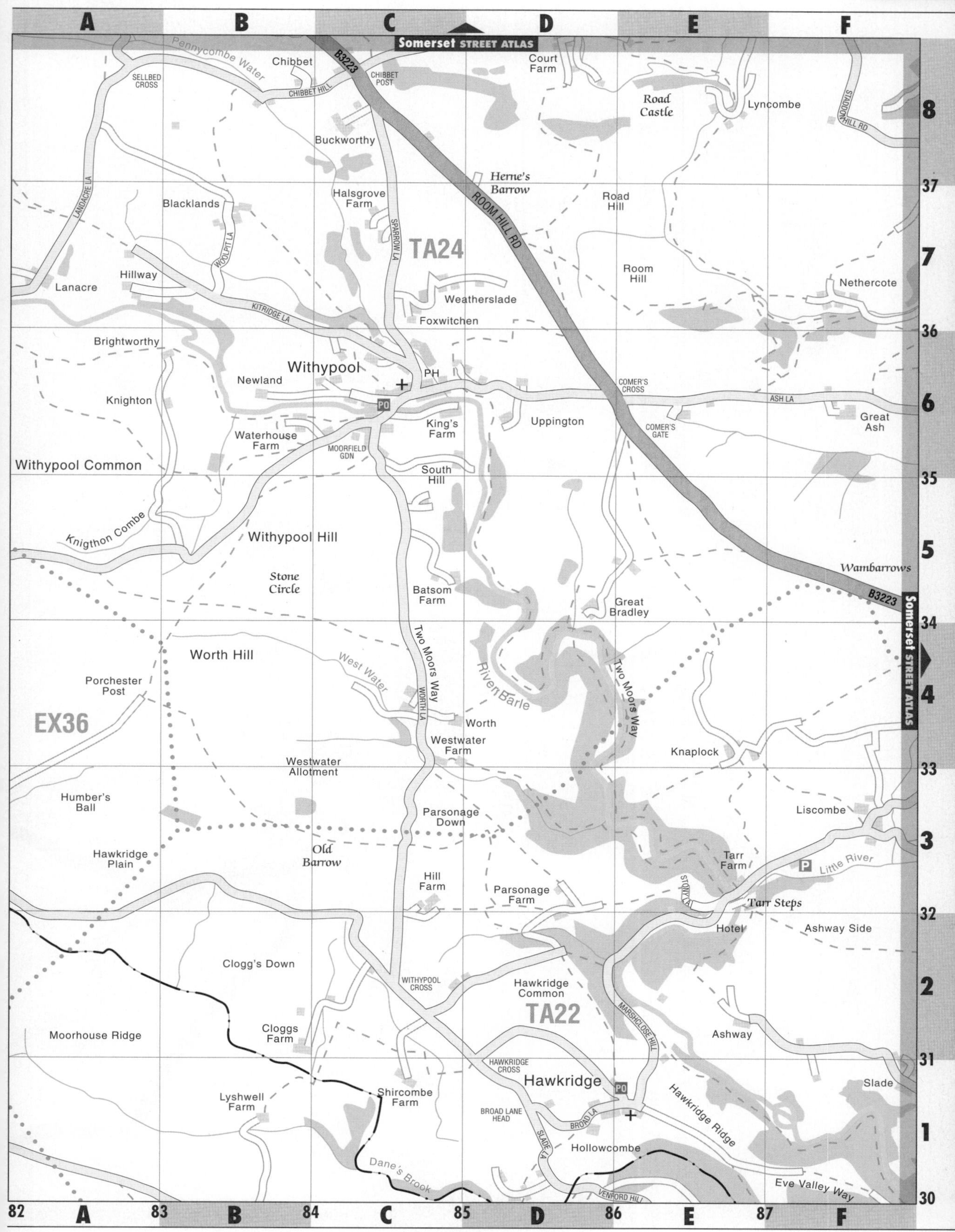

32

Scale: 1¾ inches to 1 mile

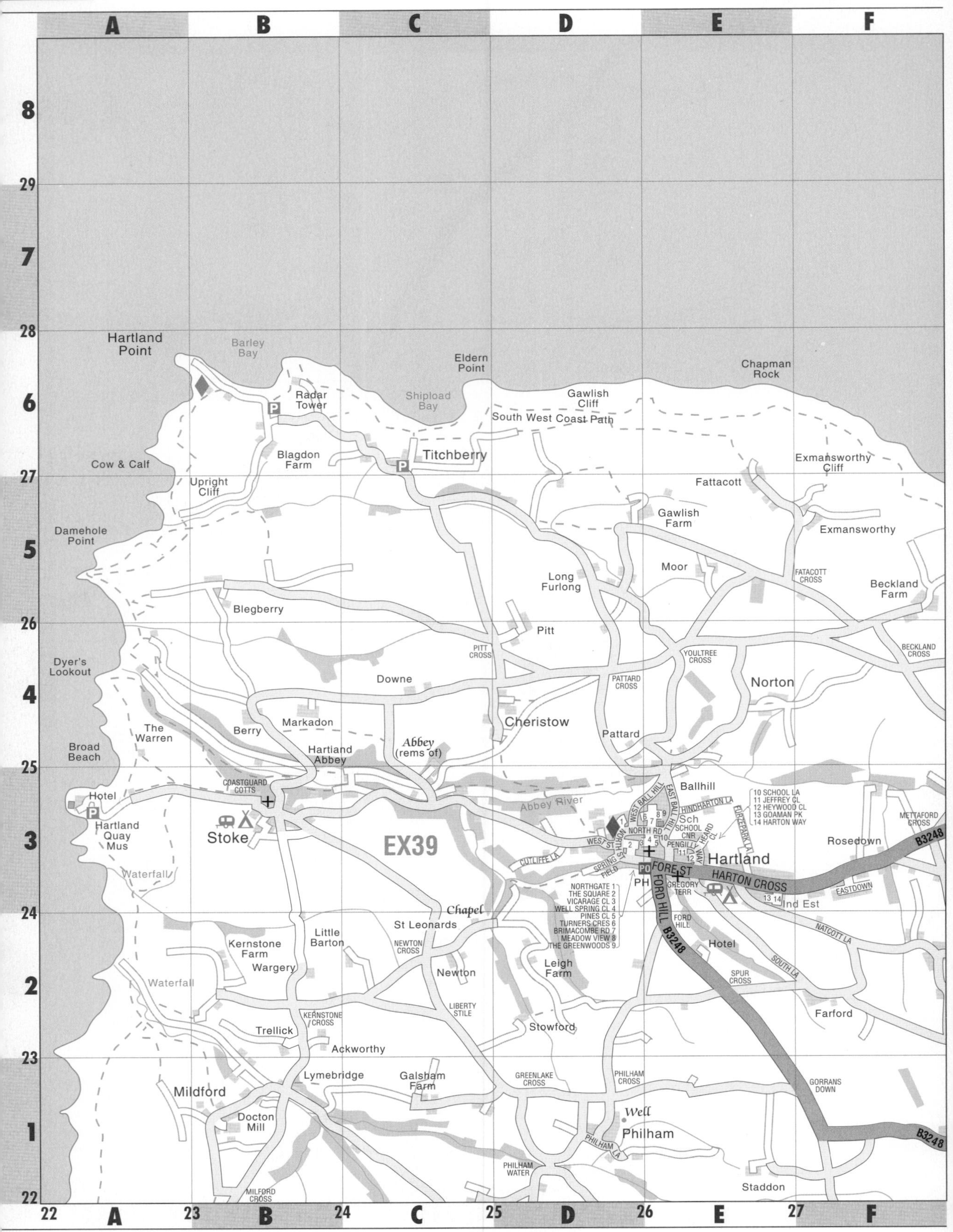

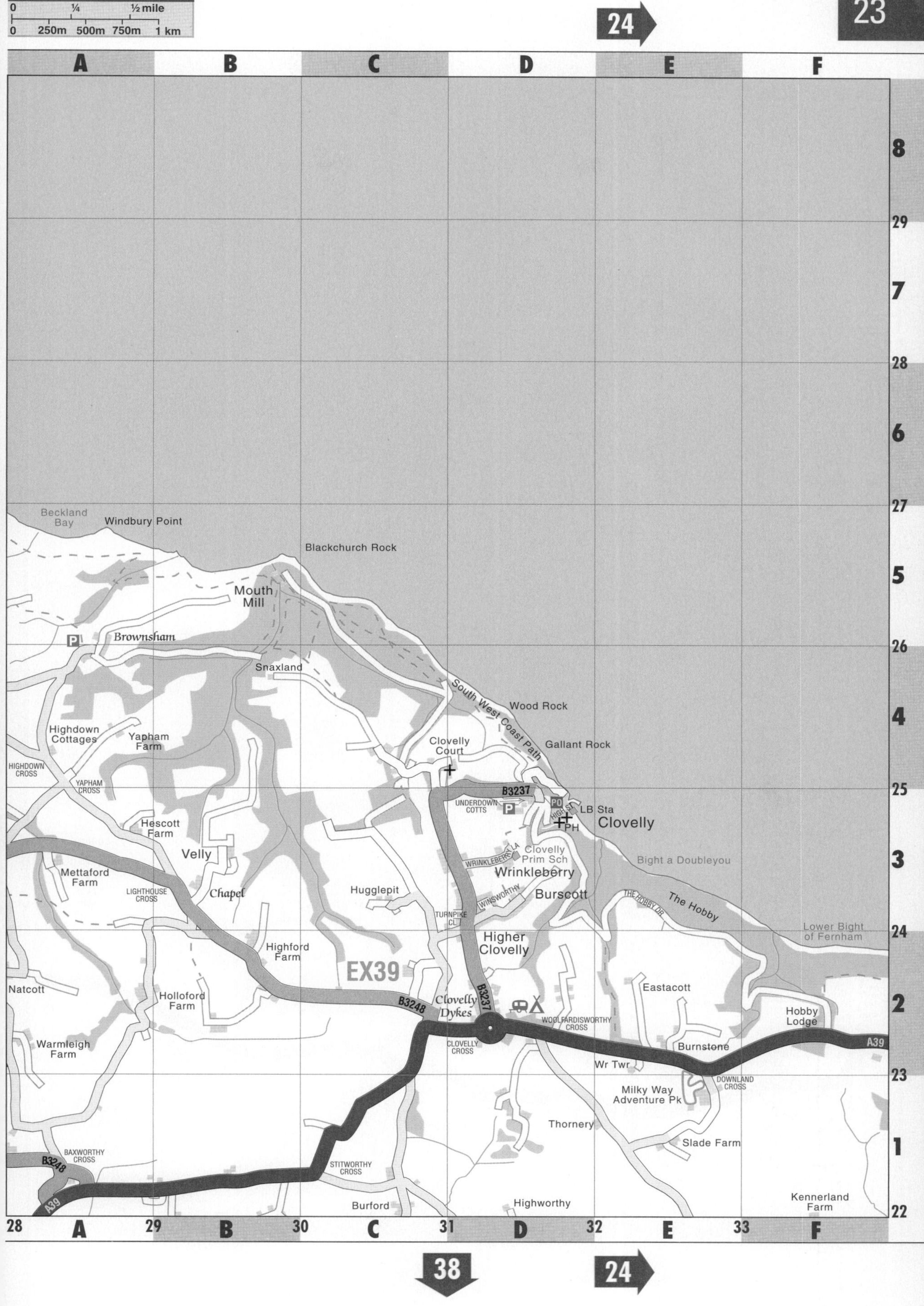
Scale: 1¾ inches to 1 mile
0 ¼ ½ mile
0 250m 500m 750m 1 km
24
A B C D E F
8
29
7
28
6
27
5
26
4
25
3
24
2
23
1
22
28 A 29 B 30 C 31 D 32 E 33 F
Beckland Bay
Windbury Point
Blackchurch Rock
Mouth Mill
Brownsham
Snaxland
South West Coast Path
Wood Rock
Gallant Rock
Highdown Cottages
Yapham Farm
HIGHDOWN CROSS
YAPHAM CROSS
Clovelly Court
B3237
UNDERDOWN COTTS
HIGH ST
LB Sta
PH
Clovelly
Hescott Farm
Velly
Clovelly Prim Sch
WRINKLEBERRY LA
Wrinkleberry
Bight a Doubleyou
Mettaford Farm
LIGHTHOUSE CROSS
Chapel
Hugglepit
WINSWORTHY
Burscott
THE HOBBY DR
The Hobby
TURNPIKE CL
Higher Clovelly
Lower Bight of Fernham
Highford Farm
EX39
Natcott
Holloford Farm
B3248
Clovelly Dykes
Eastacott
Hobby Lodge
WOOLFARDISWORTHY CROSS
Warmleigh Farm
CLOVELLY CROSS
Burnstone
A39
Wr Twr
DOWNLAND CROSS
Milky Way Adventure Pk
Thornery
Slade Farm
BAXWORTHY CROSS
STITWORTHY CROSS
Burford
Highworthy
Kennerland Farm

38
24

23

Scale: 1¾ inches to 1 mile

23

39

A B C D E F

Northam Burrows Ctry Pk
Westward Ho!
Diddywell
CH
Sch
Rock Nose
Mermaid's Pool
South West Coast Path
Nelson Rd
Atlantic Way
Stanwell Hill
Merley Rd
Golf Links Rd
Beach Rd
Avon La
Pebbleridge Rd
Kingsley Rd
Tadworthy Rd
Lakenham Hill
Sandymere Rd
Jackets La
Highbury Hill
Diddywell Rd
Lily Cl
Long La
Churchill Way
Bidna La
Pitt Hill
Wooda Rd
Taylor Dr
Daneshay
Tower St
North St
Cross St
Fore St
Windmill La
Bay View Rd
Mast
Buckleigh
Cornborough Rd
Cludden Rd
Chope Rd
Daddon Hill
Heywood Rd
Cleveland Pk
Goats Hill Rd
Northam
Durrant La
Lower Cleave
Limers La
Port Hill
Silford Rd
Lenwood Rd
Raleigh Hill
Buckleigh Rd
B3236
Cornborough Range
Cornborough
PH
Pusehill
Pusehill Rd
Silford
A39
Orchard Hill
Orchard Hill
Torridge Bridge
Greencliff Rock
Abbotsham Court
Kenwith
Raleigh Hill
First Raleigh
Northam Rd
Kingsley Rd
Chanters Rd
Park La
Park Ave
Ferry P
Rickard's Down
Combe Walter
Rock La
Combe
Shamland
Greencliff
Rixlade
Abbotsham
Back La
Plump La
BIDEFORD
Coll
Northdown Rd
Slade
Osborne La
Water Park Rd
Lane Field Rd
North Rd
Lime Gr
Belvoir Rd
Pitt La
Mill St
High St
The Quay
A386
Mus
Barnstaple St
Winsford
Abbotsham Rd
Old Town
Meddon St
Liby
Royston Rd
Sch
Farm Pk
Moreton Park
Laurel Ave
Moreton Park Rd
Stucley Rd
Pynes La
Capern Rd
Schs
Torrington La
Clifton St
New Rd
Westacott
Gipsy La
Bowood
Abbotsham Cross
Meadow Pk
Hamilton Cl
Brookfield
Kingdon Ent Pk
Ind Est
Clovelly Rd
Cemy
Oldford House
Marlen Ct
Ford Rise
Kynock Ind Est
Nuttaberry Bglws
River Torridge
Cockington Farm
Babbacombe Farm
Atlantic Village
Caddsdown Ind Pk
Caddsdown
1 Grenville Estate Cres
2 Richard Cl
3 Pynes Wlk
4 The Grenville Est
5 Bowden Gn
1 Chestnut Dr
2 Willow Gr
3 Cedar Way
4 Lombard Cl
5 Beech Bank
6 Brennacott Rd
7 High Park Cl
Adjavin Farm
Scratchface La
Upcott Farm
Upcott Hill
Forest Hill
Coach Dr
Tarka Trail
Knotty Corner
High Park
Ford
EX39
Jennetts Resr
Hallsannery
Fairy Cross
Winscott
Littleham Court
Ashridge
Pork Edge Pl
Church Pk
Yeo Vale
Moorhead
Dunn La
Woodtown
Mount Pleasant
Altamira Cotts
App's La
Scratchface La
Heale House
Church La
A388
Littleham
Alwington
Rollstone
Crealock Arms (PH)
Hooper's Water Farm
Edge Mill
Dotheridge La
River Yeo
Bulland
South Yeo
Annery
Tuckingmill
Howley
Orleigh Ct
Orleigh Mills
Beara Farm
Halsbury
Saltrens
Lee Ave

29 28 27 26 25 24 23 22
8 7 6 5 4 3 2 1
40 41 42 43 44 45

156
157
40
26
For full street detail of the highlighted area see pages 156 and 157.

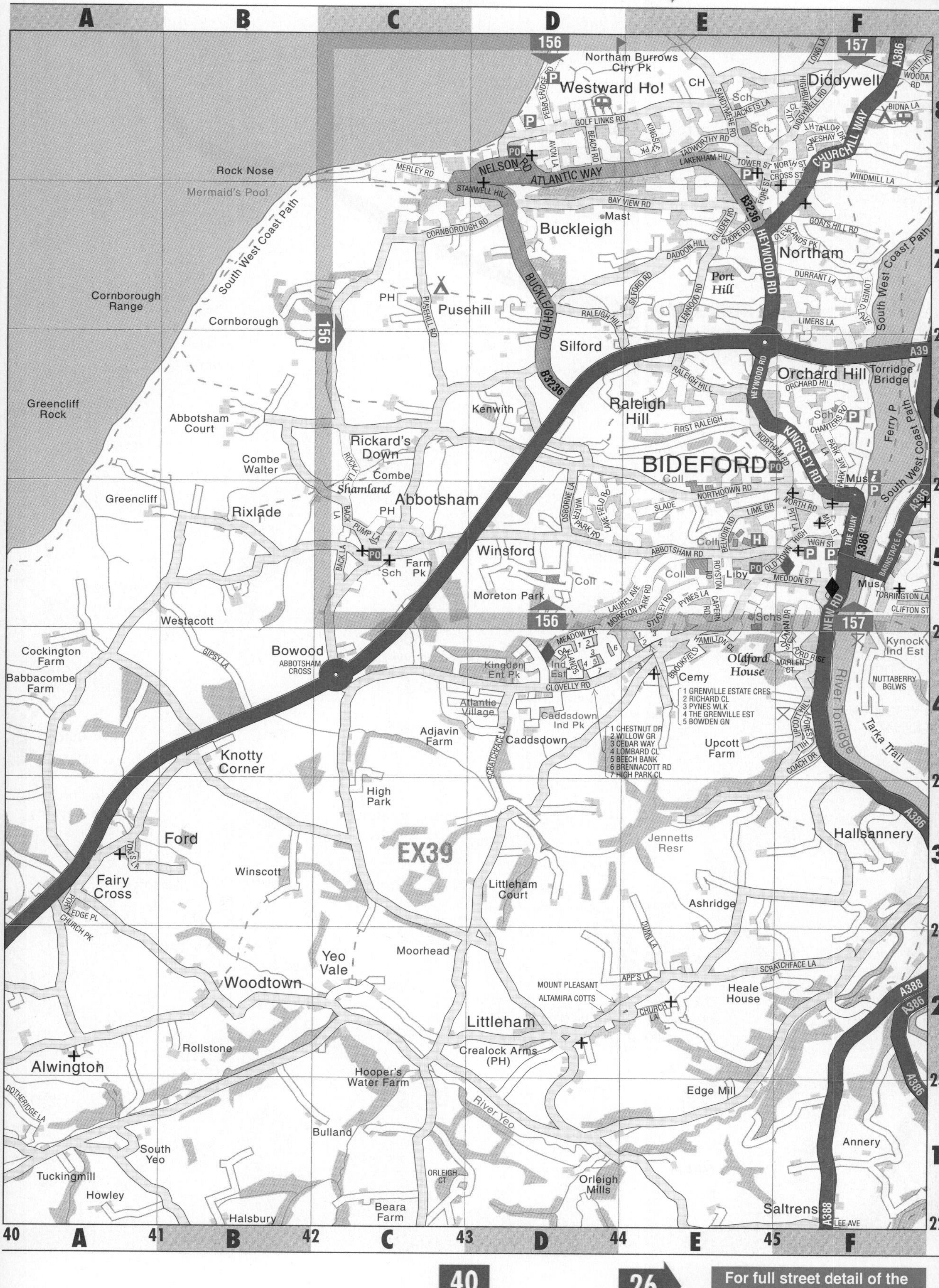

25
15

Scale: 1¾ inches to 1 mile
0 ¼ ½ mile
0 250m 500m 750m 1 km

For full street detail of the highlighted area see page 157.
25
41

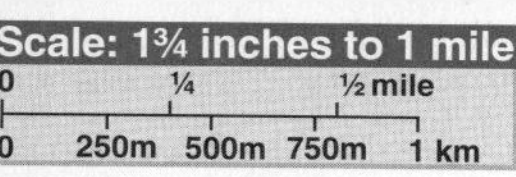

16
28

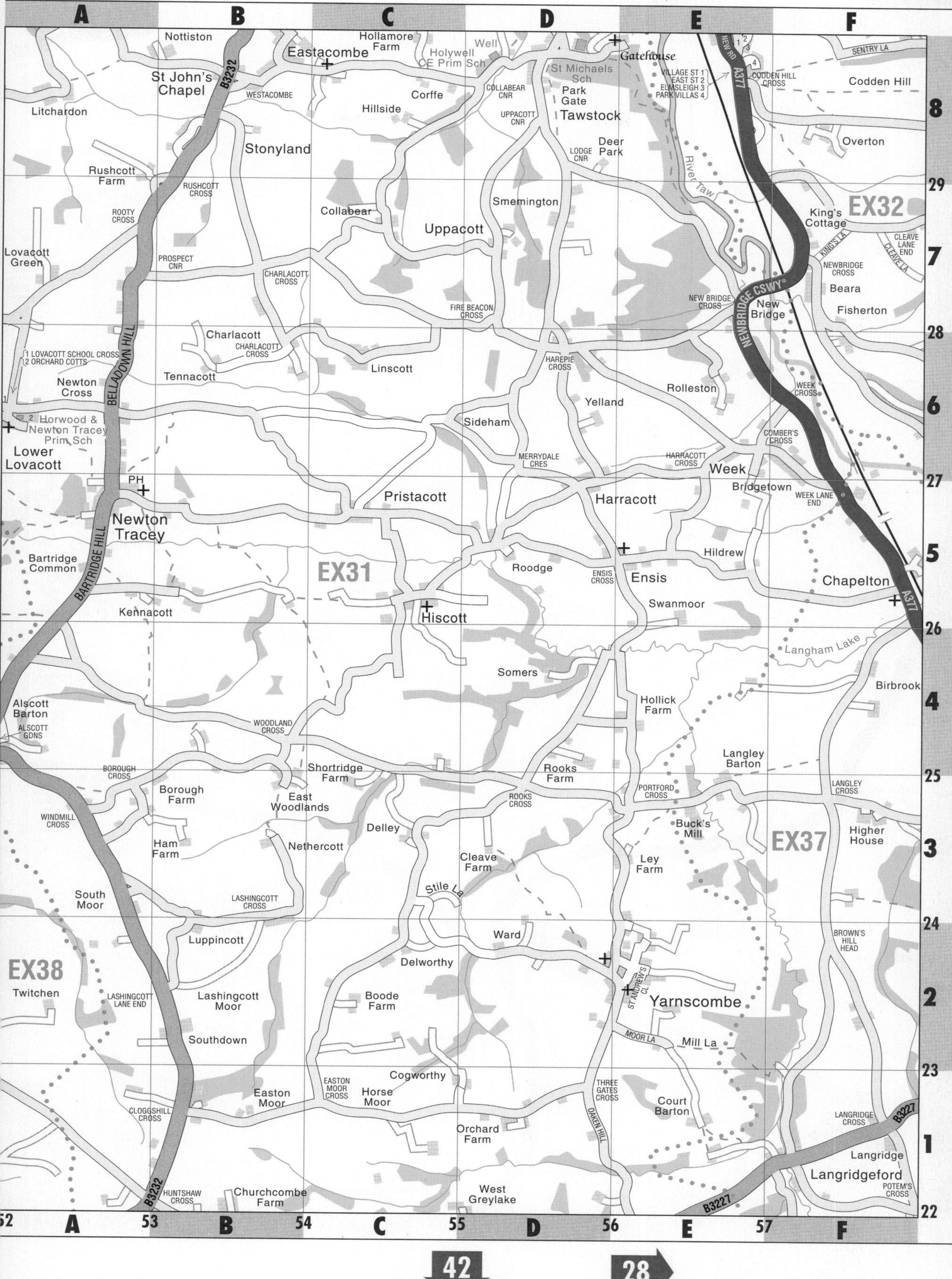

A B C D E F

Nottiston
Hollamore Farm
Well
Gatehouse
Eastacombe
Holywell CE Prim Sch
St Michaels Sch
NEW RD
VILLAGE ST 1
EAST ST 2
ELMSLEIGH 3
PARK VILLAS 4
SENTRY LA
CODDEN HILL CROSS
Codden Hill
St John's Chapel
B3232
WESTACOMBE
Corffe
COLLABEAR CNR
Park Gate
A377
Litchardon
Hillside
UPPACOTT CNR
Tawstock
8
Overton
Stonyland
LODGE CNR
Deer Park
River Taw
Rushcott Farm
RUSHCOTT CROSS
29
ROOTY CROSS
Smemington
Collabear
King's Cottage
EX32
Uppacott
CLEAVE LANE END
KING'S LA
CLEAVE LA
Lovacott Green
PROSPECT CNR
CHARLACOTT CROSS
7
NEWBRIDGE CROSS
Beara
NEW BRIDGE CROSS
NEWBRIDGE CSWY
New Bridge
Fisherton
FIRE BEACON CROSS
28
Charlacott
CHARLACOTT CROSS
1 LOVACOTT SCHOOL CROSS
2 ORCHARD COTTS
Linscott
HAREPIE CROSS
Tennacott
BELLADOWN HILL
Newton Cross
Rolleston
Yelland
WEEK CROSS
6
Horwood & Newton Tracey Prim Sch
Sideham
COMBER'S CROSS
Lower Lovacott
MERRYDALE CRES
HARRACOTT CROSS
Week
27
PH
Bridgetown
Pristacott
Harracott
WEEK LANE END
Newton Tracey
BARTRIDGE HILL
5
Bartridge Common
Hildrew
Roodge
EX31
ENSIS CROSS
Ensis
Chapelton
Kennacott
Hiscott
Swanmoor
26
Langham Lake
Somers
Birbrook
Hollick Farm
4
Alscott Barton
ALSCOTT GDNS
WOODLAND CROSS
Langley Barton
BOROUGH CROSS
Shortridge Farm
Rooks Farm
25
Borough Farm
East Woodlands
ROOKS CROSS
PORTFORD CROSS
LANGLEY CROSS
WINDMILL CROSS
Delley
Buck's Mill
Higher House
EX37
3
Ham Farm
Nethercott
Cleave Farm
Ley Farm
South Moor
Stile La
LASHINGCOTT CROSS
24
BROWN'S HILL HEAD
Luppincott
Ward
Delworthy
EX38
Twitchen
LASHINGCOTT LANE END
Lashingcott Moor
Boode Farm
ST ANDREW'S CL
Yarnscombe
2
Southdown
MOOR LA
Mill La
23
Cogworthy
EASTON MOOR CROSS
Horse Moor
Easton Moor
THREE GATES CROSS
Court Barton
CLOGGSHILL CROSS
OAKEN HILL
LANGRIDGE CROSS
B3227
Orchard Farm
1
Langridge
Langridgeford
HUNTSHAW CROSS
Churchcombe Farm
West Greylake
POTEM'S CROSS
22

52 A 53 B 54 C 55 D 56 E 57 F

27
17

Scale: 1¾ inches to 1 mile
0 ¼ ½ mile
0 250m 500m 750m 1 km

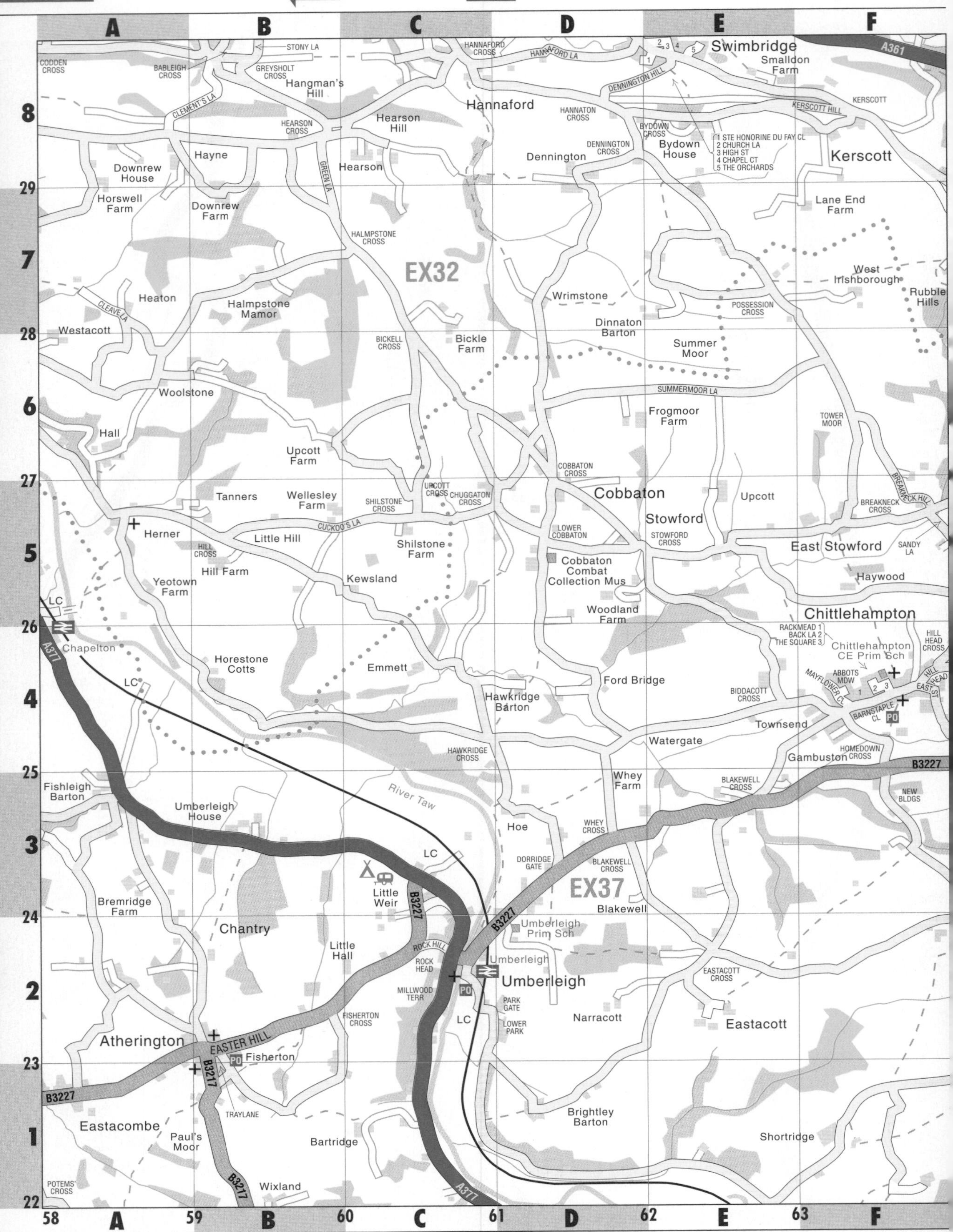

27
43

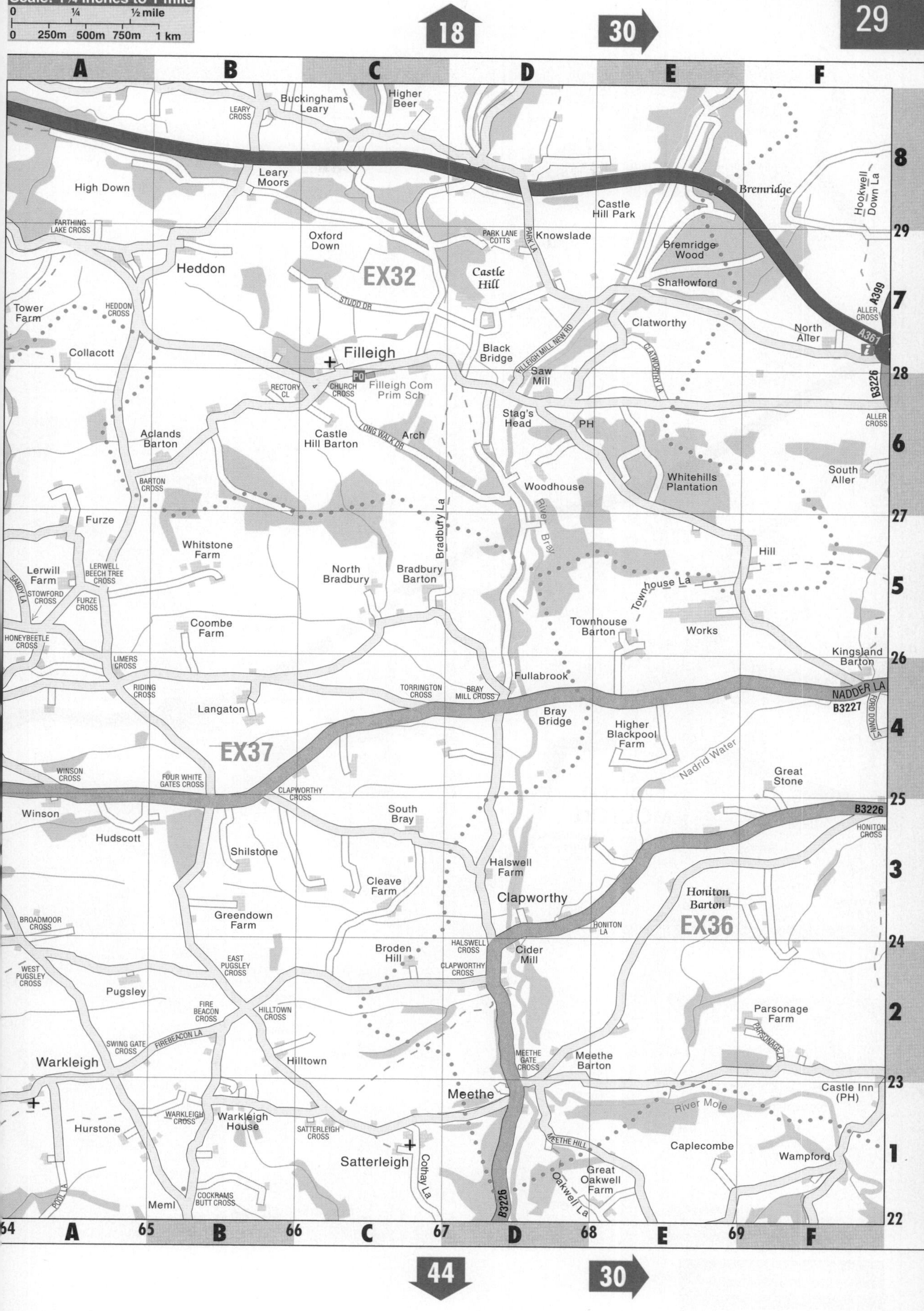
Scale: 1¾ inches to 1 mile
0 ¼ ½ mile
0 250m 500m 750m 1 km
18
30
A B C D E F
Buckinghams Leary
Higher Beer
LEARY CROSS
Leary Moors
High Down
Bremridge
Castle Hill Park
Hookwell Down La
FARTHING LAKE CROSS
Oxford Down
PARK LANE COTTS
PARK LA
Knowslade
Bremridge Wood
Heddon
EX32
Castle Hill
Shallowford
A399
STUDD DR
HEDDON CROSS
Tower Farm
Clatworthy
ALLER CROSS
North Aller
A361
Collacott
Filleigh
Black Bridge
FILLEIGH MILL NEW RD
Saw Mill
CLATWORTHY LA
B3226
RECTORY CL
CHURCH CROSS
PO
Filleigh Com Prim Sch
LONG WALK DR
Stag's Head
PH
ALLER CROSS
Aclands Barton
Castle Hill Barton
Arch
BARTON CROSS
Woodhouse
Whitehills Plantation
South Aller
River Bray
Furze
Bradbury La
Whitstone Farm
Hill
Lerwill Farm
LERWELL BEECH TREE CROSS
North Bradbury
Bradbury Barton
Townhouse La
SANDY LA
STOWFORD CROSS
FURZE CROSS
Townhouse Barton
Works
Coombe Farm
HONEYBEETLE CROSS
Kingsland Barton
LIMERS CROSS
Fullabrook
RIDING CROSS
TORRINGTON CROSS
BRAY MILL CROSS
NADDER LA
B3227
FORD DOWN LA
Langaton
Bray Bridge
Higher Blackpool Farm
EX37
Nadrid Water
WINSON CROSS
FOUR WHITE GATES CROSS
Great Stone
CLAPWORTHY CROSS
B3226
Winson
South Bray
HONITON CROSS
Hudscott
Shilstone
Halswell Farm
Cleave Farm
Honiton Barton
Clapworthy
BROADMOOR CROSS
Greendown Farm
HONITON LA
EX36
Broden Hill
HALSWELL CROSS
Cider Mill
WEST PUGSLEY CROSS
EAST PUGSLEY CROSS
CLAPWORTHY CROSS
Pugsley
FIRE BEACON CROSS
HILLTOWN CROSS
Parsonage Farm
PARSONAGE LA
FIREBEACON LA
SWING GATE CROSS
Warkleigh
Hilltown
MEETHE GATE CROSS
Meethe Barton
Meethe
Castle Inn (PH)
River Mole
Hurstone
WARKLEIGH CROSS
Warkleigh House
SATTERLEIGH CROSS
MEETHE HILL
Caplecombe
Wampford
Satterleigh
Cothay La
Great Oakwell Farm
Oakwell La
POOL LA
COCKRAMS BUTT CROSS
Meml
B3226
8 29 7 28 6 27 5 26 4 25 3 24 2 23 1 22
64 65 66 67 68 69
44
30

29
19

Scale: 1¾ inches to 1 mile
0 ¼ ½ mile
0 250m 500m 750m 1 km

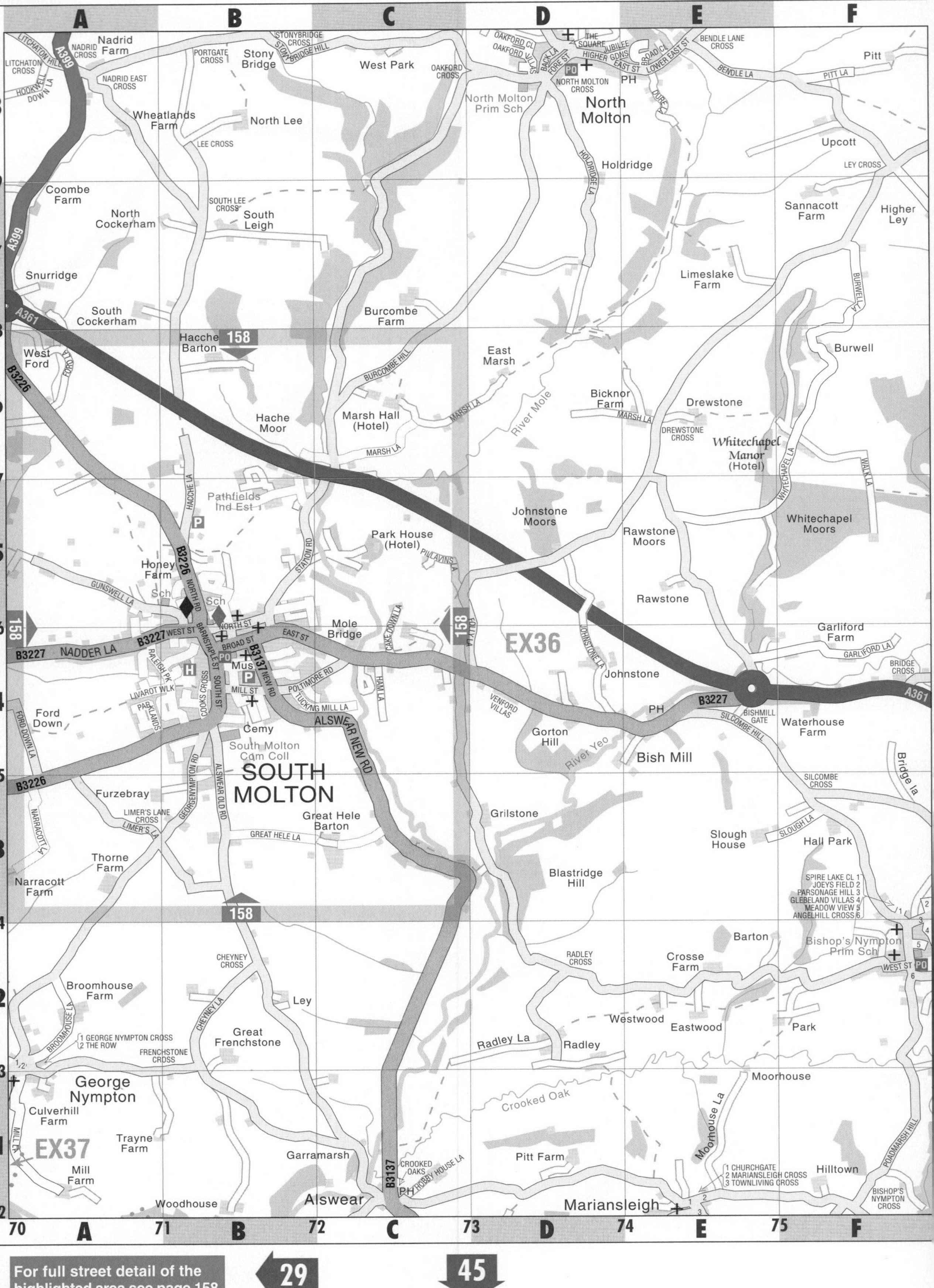

A B C D E F

Nadrid Farm
NADRID CROSS
LITCHATON HILL
LITCHATON CROSS
HOOKWELL DOWN LA
NADRID EAST CROSS
PORTGATE CROSS
Stony Bridge
STONYBRIDGE CROSS
STONYBRIDGE HILL
West Park
OAKFORD CROSS
OAKFORD CL
OAKFORD VILLAS
BACK LA
FORE ST
THE SQUARE
JUBILEE
HIGHER GDNS
BROAD CL
EAST ST
LOWER EAST ST
BENDLE LANE CROSS
BENDLE LA
Pitt
PITT LA
PO
PH
NORTH MOLTON CROSS
North Molton Prim Sch
North Molton
DURE LA
Wheatlands Farm
North Lee
LEE CROSS
Upcott
Holdridge
HOLDRIDGE LA
LEY CROSS
Coombe Farm
North Cockerham
SOUTH LEE CROSS
South Leigh
Sannacott Farm
Higher Ley
A399
Snurridge
Limeslake Farm
BURWELL LA
South Cockerham
Burcombe Farm
A361
Hacche Barton
158
West Ford
FORD LA
B3226
East Marsh
Burwell
BURCOMBE HILL
Hache Moor
Marsh Hall (Hotel)
MARSH LA
Bicknor Farm
River Mole
Drewstone
DREWSTONE CROSS
Whitechapel Manor (Hotel)
WHITECHAPEL LA
WALK LA
HACCHE LA
Pathfields Ind Est
P
Johnstone Moors
Rawstone Moors
Whitechapel Moors
Park House (Hotel)
PILLAVINS LA
STATION RD
Honey Farm
B3226
NORTH RD
GUNSWELL LA
Sch
Rawstone
CAKE DOWN LA
WEST ST
NORTH ST
EAST ST
Mole Bridge
158
FOLLY LA
EX36
JOHNSTONE LA
Garliford Farm
GARLIFORD LA
BRIDGE CROSS
B3227
NADDER LA
B3227
BARNSTAPLE ST
BROAD ST
B3137
NEW RD
PO
Mus
RALEIGH PK
H
SOUTH ST
POLTIMORE RD
HAM LA
Johnstone
LIVAROT WLK
PARKLANDS
COOKS CROSS
MILL ST
P
TUCKING MILL LA
VENFORD VILLAS
PH
B3227
BISHMILL GATE
SILCOMBE HILL
A361
Ford Down
FORD DOWN LA
ALSWEAR NEW RD
Cemy
Gorton Hill
Waterhouse Farm
South Molton Com Coll
River Yeo
Bish Mill
Bridge la
SOUTH MOLTON
B3226
GEORGENYMPTON RD
ALSWEAR OLD RD
Furzebray
SILCOMBE CROSS
NARRACOTT LA
LIMER'S LANE CROSS
LIMER'S LA
Great Hele Barton
Grilstone
GREAT HELE LA
Slough House
SLOUGH LA
Hall Park
Thorne Farm
Narracott Farm
Blastridge Hill
SPIRE LAKE CL 1
JOEYS FIELD 2
PARSONAGE HILL 3
GLEBELAND VILLAS 4
MEADOW VIEW 5
ANGELHILL CROSS 6
158
Barton
Bishop's Nympton Prim Sch
CHEYNEY CROSS
RADLEY CROSS
Crosse Farm
WEST ST
PO
Broomhouse Farm
Ley
BROOMHOUSE LA
CHEYNEY LA
Great Frenchstone
Westwood
Eastwood
Park
1 GEORGE NYMPTON CROSS
2 THE ROW
FRENCHSTONE CROSS
Radley La
Radley
George Nympton
Moorhouse
Culverhill Farm
Crooked Oak
Moorhouse La
MILL LA
EX37
Trayne Farm
Pitt Farm
POADMARSH HILL
Mill Farm
Garramarsh
B3137
CROOKED OAKS
HOBBY HOUSE LA
PH
1 CHURCHGATE
2 MARIANSLEIGH CROSS
3 TOWNLIVING CROSS
Hilltown
BISHOP'S NYMPTON CROSS
Woodhouse
Alswear
Mariansleigh

70 A 71 B 72 C 73 D 74 E 75 F

8 29 7 28 6 27 5 26 4 25 3 24 2 23 1 22

For full street detail of the highlighted area see page 158.
29
45

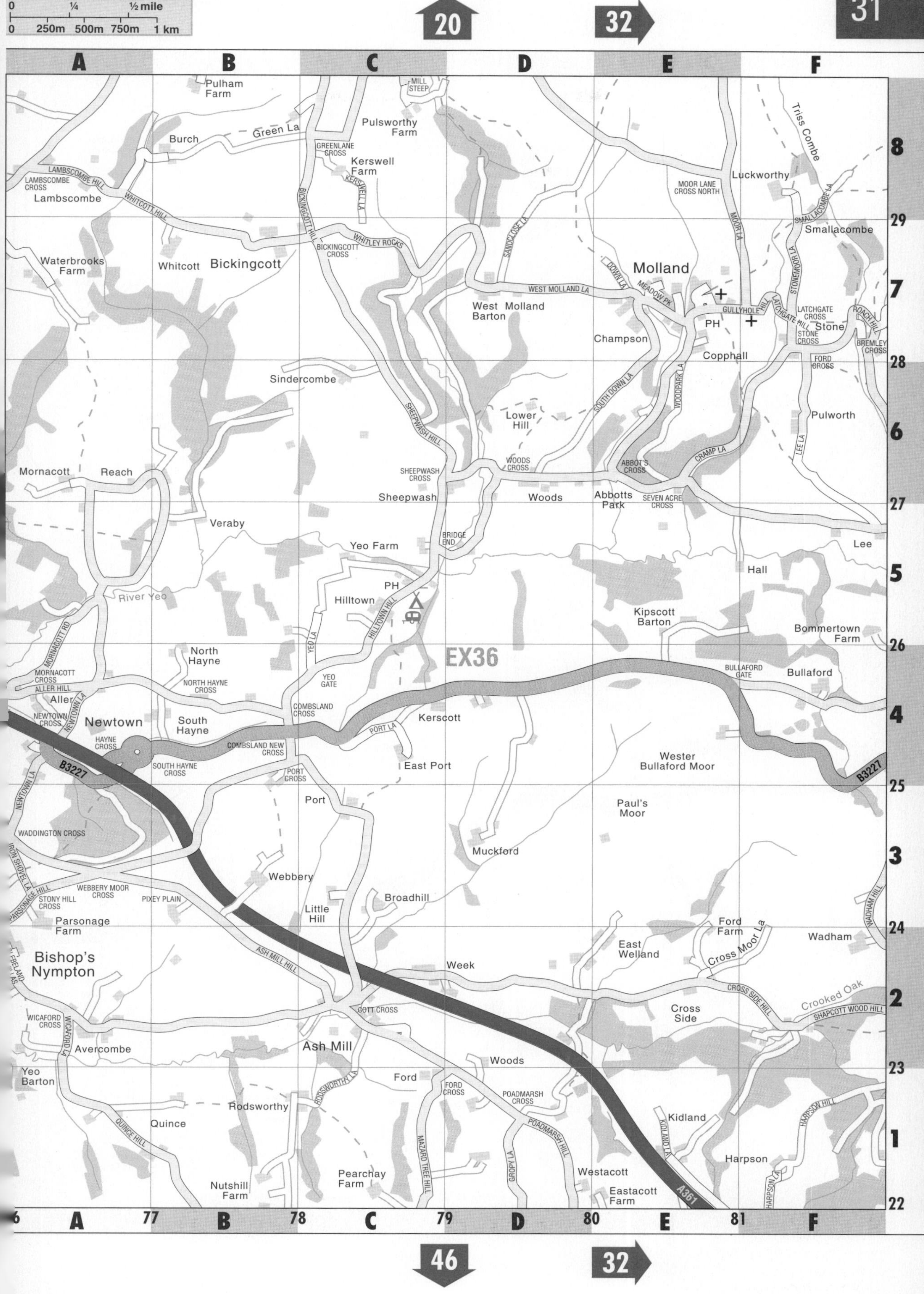

Scale: 1¾ inches to 1 mile
0
¼
½ mile
0
250m
500m
750m
1 km
20
32
A
B
C
D
E
F
Pulham Farm
MILL STEEP
Pulsworthy Farm
Triss Combe
Burch
Green La
GREENLANE CROSS
Kerswell Farm
KERSWELL LA
8
LAMBSCOMBE HILL
LAMBSCOMBE CROSS
Lambscombe
WHITCOTT HILL
BICKINGCOTT HILL
MOOR LANE CROSS NORTH
Luckworthy
MOOR LA
SMALLACOMBE LA
Smallacombe
29
BICKINGCOTT CROSS
WHITLEY ROCKS
SANDCLOSE LA
Waterbrooks Farm
Whitcott
Bickingcott
Molland
DOWN LA
MEADOW PK
WEST MOLLAND LA
7
STONEMOOR LA
GULLYHOLE
LATCHGATE HILL
LATCHGATE CROSS
ROACH HILL
West Molland Barton
PH
Stone
STONE CROSS
Champson
BREMLEY CROSS
Copphall
28
FORD CROSS
Sindercombe
SOUTH DOWN LA
WOODPARK LA
Lower Hill
Pulworth
SHEEPWASH HILL
6
LEE LA
CRAMP LA
WOODS CROSS
ABBOT'S CROSS
Mornacott
Reach
SHEEPWASH CROSS
Sheepwash
Woods
Abbotts Park
SEVEN ACRE CROSS
27
Veraby
BRIDGE END
Yeo Farm
Lee
Hall
5
River Yeo
PH
Hilltown
HILLTOWN HILL
Kipscott Barton
Bommertown Farm
MORNACOTT RD
YEO LA
26
North Hayne
EX36
BULLAFORD GATE
Bullaford
MORNACOTT CROSS
ALLER HILL
NORTH HAYNE CROSS
YEO GATE
Aller
NEWTOWN LA
COMBSLAND CROSS
4
NEWTOWN CROSS
Newtown
South Hayne
Kerscott
PORT LA
HAYNE CROSS
COMBSLAND NEW CROSS
B3227
SOUTH HAYNE CROSS
East Port
Wester Bullaford Moor
B3227
NEWTOWN LA
PORT CROSS
25
Port
Paul's Moor
WADDINGTON CROSS
Muckford
3
IRON SHOVEL LA
Webbery
PARSONAGE HILL
WEBBERY MOOR CROSS
STONY HILL CROSS
PIXEY PLAIN
Broadhill
Little Hill
WADHAM HILL
Parsonage Farm
Ford Farm
24
Bishop's Nympton
ASH MILL HILL
East Welland
Cross Moor La
Wadham
Week
2
CROSS SIDE HILL
Crooked Oak
WICAFORD CROSS
COTT CROSS
Cross Side
SHAPCOTT WOOD HILL
WICAFORD LA
Avercombe
Ash Mill
Woods
23
Yeo Barton
Ford
FORD CROSS
POADMARSH CROSS
RODSWORTHY LA
Rodsworthy
Kidland
HARPSON HILL
QUINCE HILL
Quince
POADMARSH HILL
KIDLAND LA
1
GROPY LA
MAZARD TREE HILL
Harpson
Pearchay Farm
Westacott
Nutshill Farm
Eastacott Farm
A361
HARPSON LA
22
A
77
B
78
C
79
D
80
E
81
F
46
32

31
21

Scale: 1¾ inches to 1 mile
0 ¼ ½ mile
0 250m 500m 750m 1 km

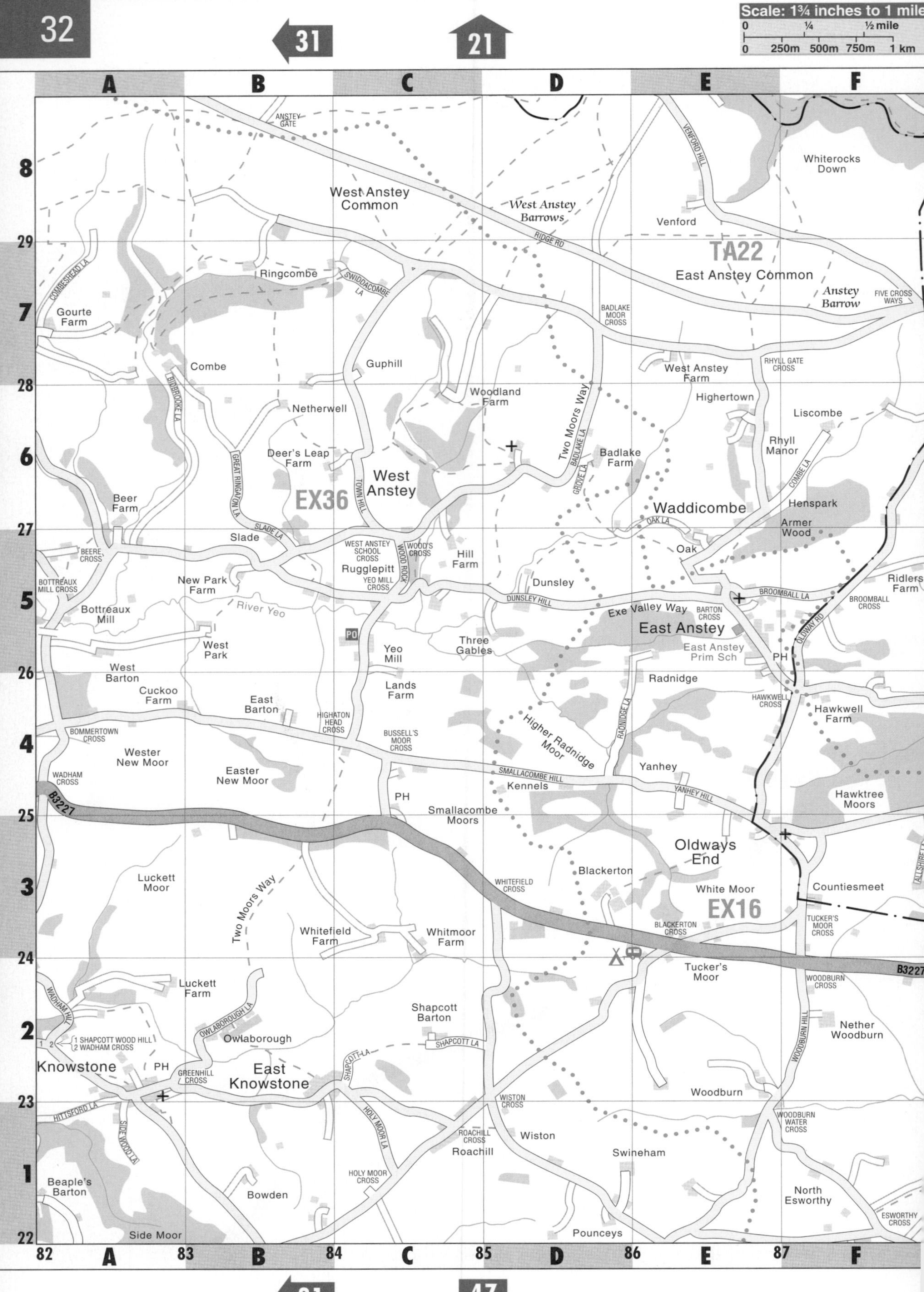

31
47

Scale: 1¾ inches to 1 mile
0 ¼ ½ mile
0 250m 500m 750m 1 km

34

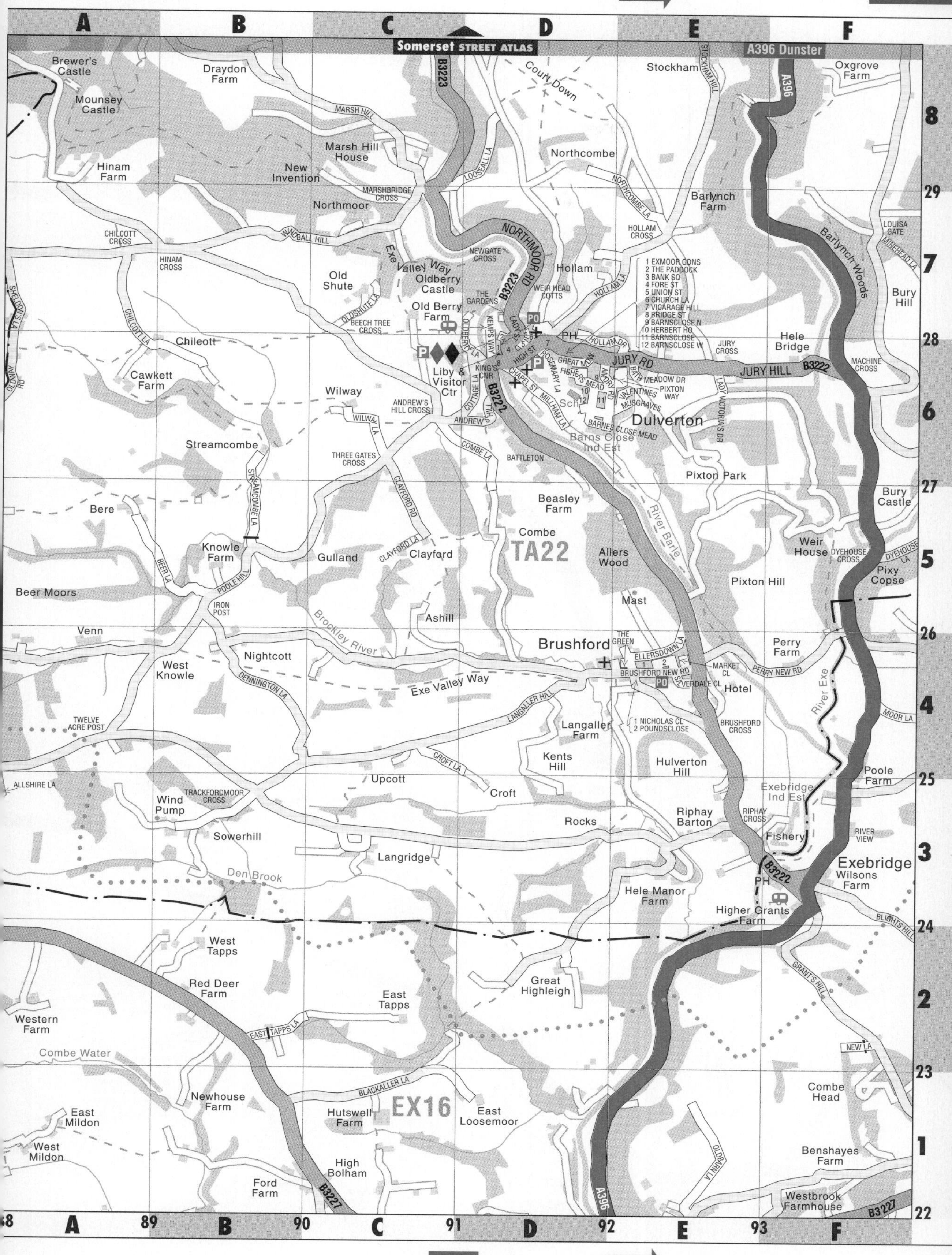

A 89 B 90 C 91 D 92 E 93 F

48
34

33

B1
1 WINIFRED CLIFF CT
2 MEADOW VIEW
3 BALLHILL LA
4 MARKET CL
5 LORDS MEADOW LA
6 BARNHAY
7 CHURCH TERR
8 NEWTON SQ
9 FORE ST
10 MARY LA
11 SILVER ST
12 BOURCHIER DR
13 BOURCHIER CL

C1
1 TIVERTON RD
2 BRITON ST
3 NEW BLDGS

33
49

Scale: 1¾ inches to 1 mile
0 ¼ ½ mile
0 250m 500m 750m 1 km

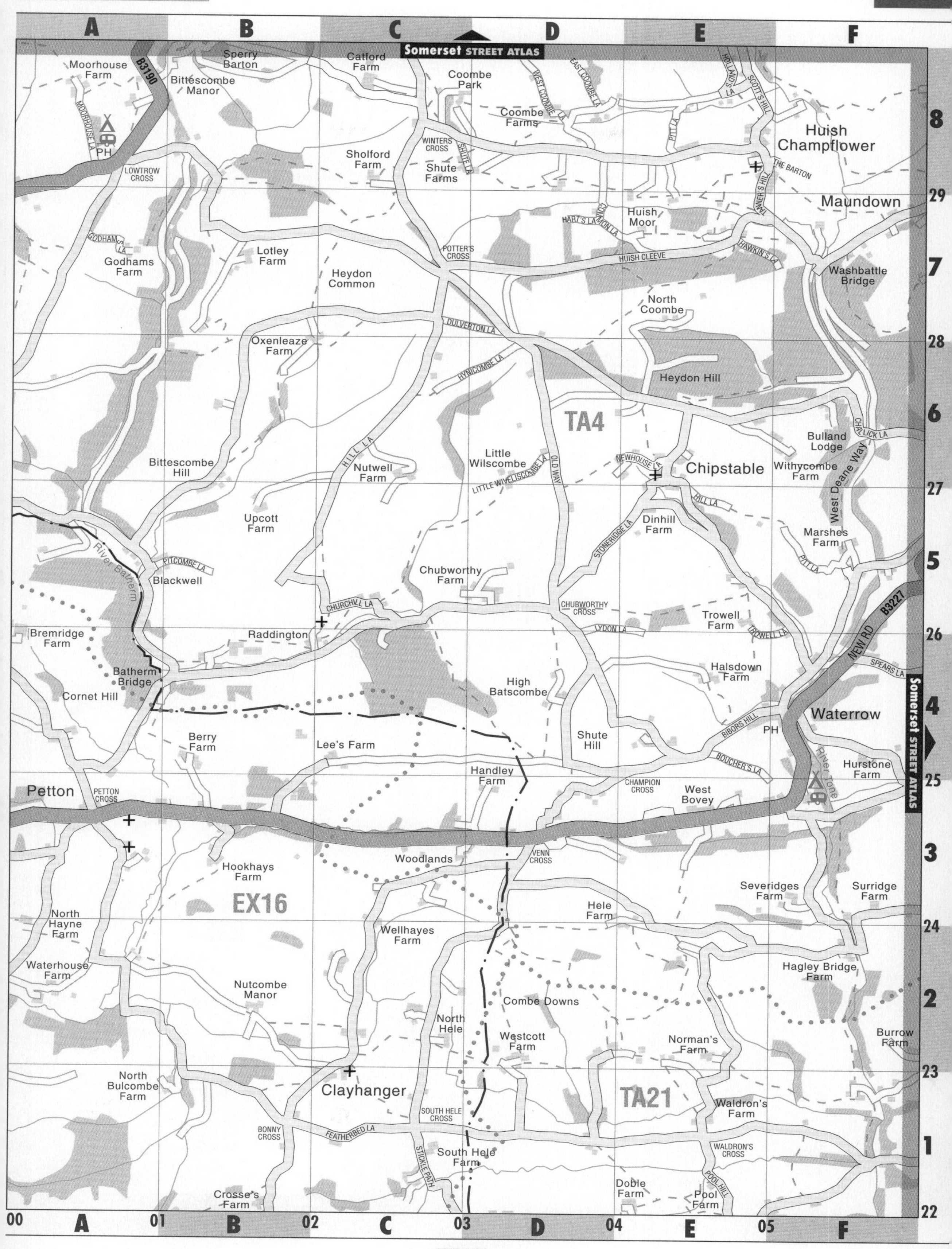

Scale: 1¾ inches to 1 mile
0 ¼ ½ mile
0 250m 500m 750m 1 km

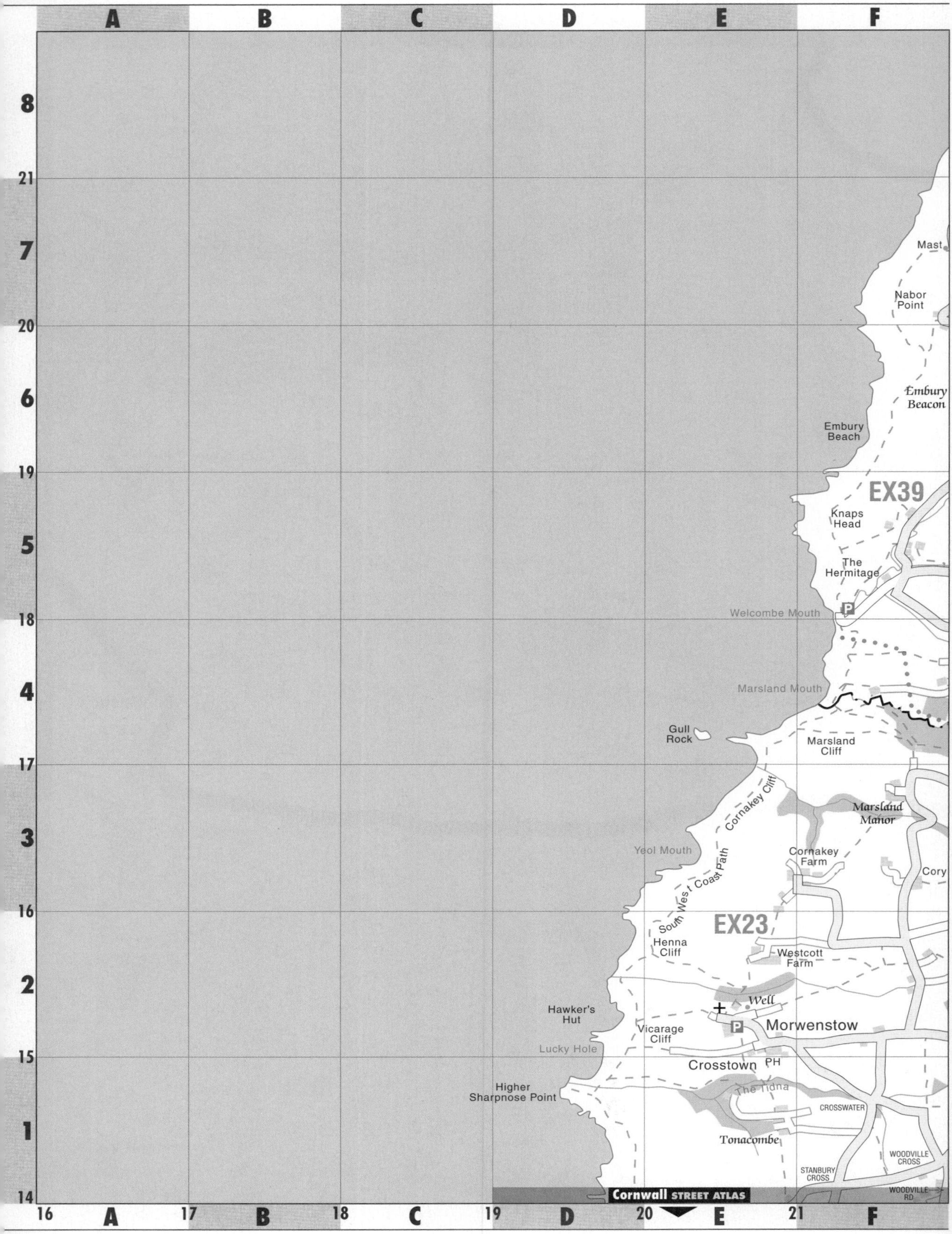

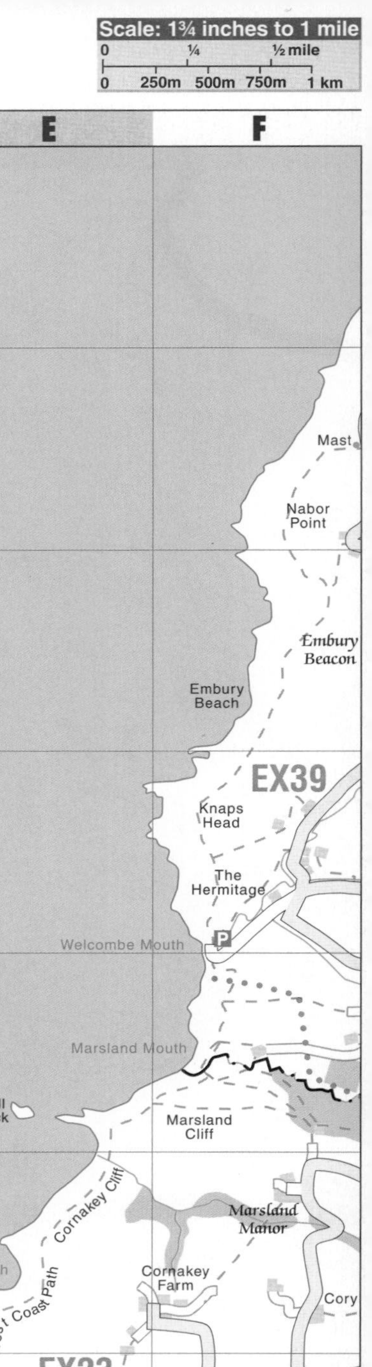

A B C D E F

8 21 7 20 6 19 5 18 4 17 3 16 2 15 1 14

16 17 18 19 20 21

Cornwall STREET ATLAS

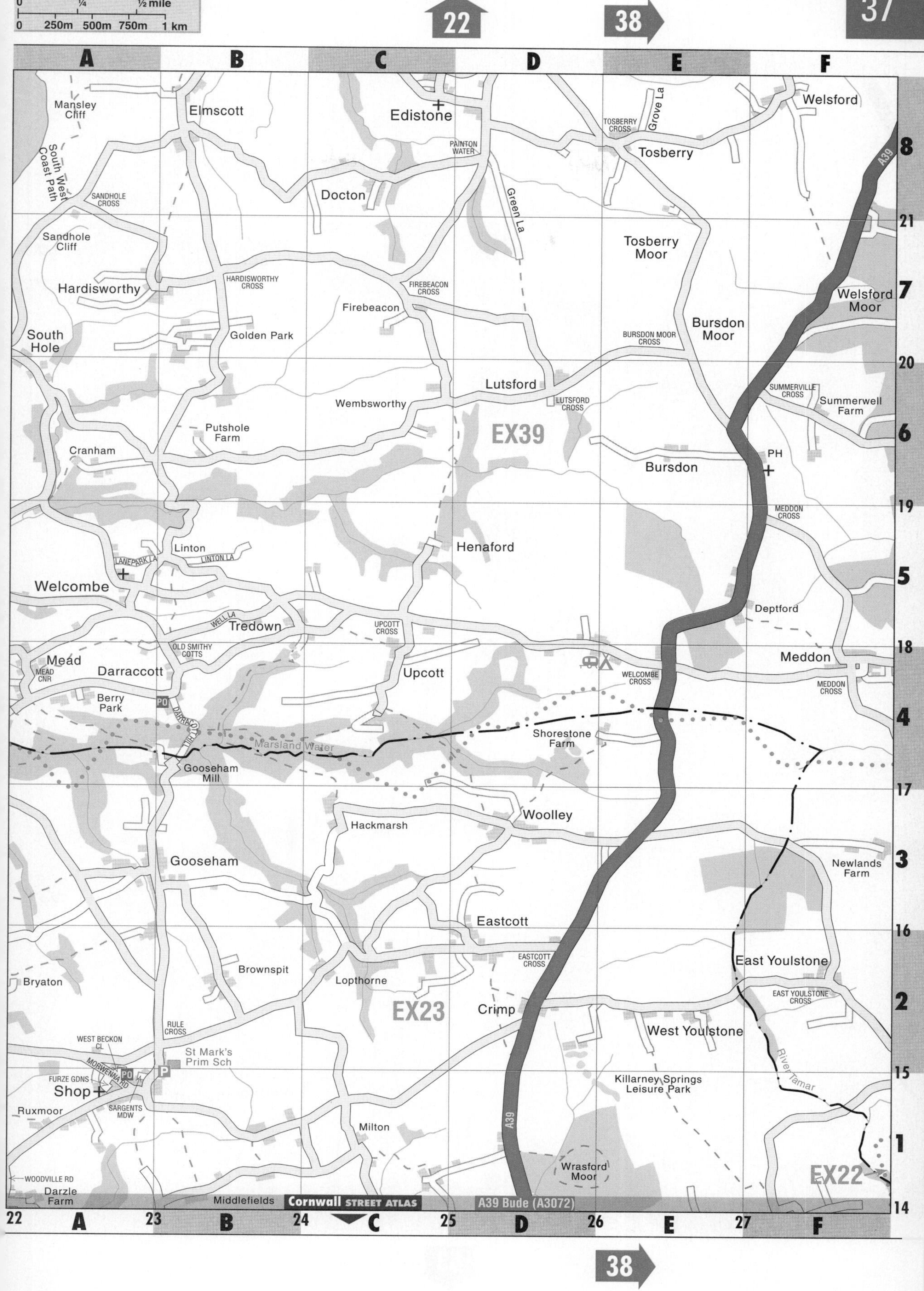
Scale: 1¾ inches to 1 mile
0 ¼ ½ mile
0 250m 500m 750m 1 km
22
38
A B C D E F
Mansley Cliff
Elmscott
Edistone
Welsford
Tosberry Cross
Grove La
Painton Water
Tosberry
South West Coast Path
Sandhole Cross
Docton
Green La
Sandhole Cliff
Tosberry Moor
Hardisworthy
Hardisworthy Cross
Firebeacon Cross
Welsford Moor
Firebeacon
Bursdon Moor
South Hole
Golden Park
Bursdon Moor Cross
Lutsford
Summerville Cross
Summerwell Farm
Wembsworthy
Lutsford Cross
Putshole Farm
EX39
Cranham
Bursdon
PH
Meddon Cross
Henaford
Linton
Lanepark La
Linton La
Welcombe
Deptford
Well La
Tredown
Upcott Cross
Old Smithy Cotts
Mead
Mead Cnr
Darracott
Upcott
Meddon
Welcombe Cross
Meddon Cross
Berry Park
PO
Darracott Hill
Shorestone Farm
Marsland Water
Gooseham Mill
Woolley
Hackmarsh
Gooseham
Newlands Farm
Eastcott
Eastcott Cross
East Youlstone
Brownspit
Lopthorne
Bryaton
East Youlstone Cross
EX23
Crimp
Rule Cross
West Youlstone
West Beckon Cl
St Mark's Prim Sch
River Tamar
Furze Gdns
Morwenna Rd
PO
P
Shop
Killarney Springs Leisure Park
Ruxmoor
Sargents Mdw
A39
Milton
Wrasford Moor
Woodville Rd
EX22
Darzle Farm
Middlefields
Cornwall STREET ATLAS
A39 Bude (A3072)
8 21 7 20 6 19 5 18 4 17 3 16 2 15 1 14
22 23 24 25 26 27

38

37
23
Scale: 1¾ inches to 1 mile
0 ¼ ½ mile
0 250m 500m 750m 1 km
A
B
C
D
E
F
A39
Stitworthy Farm
Seckington Farm
Trew Farm
Blagdon
Clifford
HARRIS CROSS
West Town
WEST TOWN CROSS
KENNERLAND CROSS
Kennerland Farm
1 TOWN MDWS
2 AUCTION WAY
3 COPPER CL
4 THE BEECHES
ABBOTS CL
BELVIRON CL
PARK MANOR
Sch
OLD MARKET DR
LOWER TOWN
EAST PK
SOUTH PK
5 BACK ST
6 SUNNYSIDE
7 CHAPEL ST
Woolfardisworthy or Woolsery
Seckington Water
Clifford Water
HUDDISFORD CROSS
Maid's Moor
EX39
Gorvin Farm
GORVIN CROSS
Huddisford
CH
Venn
DUERDON CROSS
STROXWORTHY CROSS
Duerdon
West Moor
LOWER BITEFORD CROSS
Gorrel Farm
CLAW CROSS
Biteford
Runland Farm
Horton Bridge
Marshall Farm
River Torridge
Greadon
Horton Farm
Fordmill Farm
Hole
Atworthy
Brimford Bridge
BRIMFORD CROSS
HELE CROSS
Lower Hele
Dural
DURAL CROSS
HORTON CROSS
Holyrood House
Northmoor
NORTH MOOR CROSS
ATWORTHY CROSS
West Ash
East Ash
Loatmead
Hardsworthy
LOATMEAD CROSS
EX22
QUOITGATE CROSS
EAST ASH CROSS
ASHDOWN CROSS
East Youlstone
MADDOCKS CROSS
Whiteley
Redmonsford
Dinworthy
Heath Farm
EX23
SILWORTHY CROSS
TRENTWORTHY CROSS
Ryall Farm
River Waldon
Trentworthy Farm
Bradworthy Common
Bradworthy
HORSE HILL CROSS
West Down
Berridon
NORTH RD
CROSSPARK CROSS
THREE LANE END
BLATCHBOROUGH CROSS
HIGHER TUCKERS PK
ELIZABETH
LEA CL
LANGDON RD
TUCKERS PK
Ind Est
Bradworthy Com Prim Sch
MILL RD
PO
LOWER TERR
Blatchborough
8
21
7
20
6
19
5
18
4
17
3
16
2
15
1
14
28
29
30
31
32
33
37
53

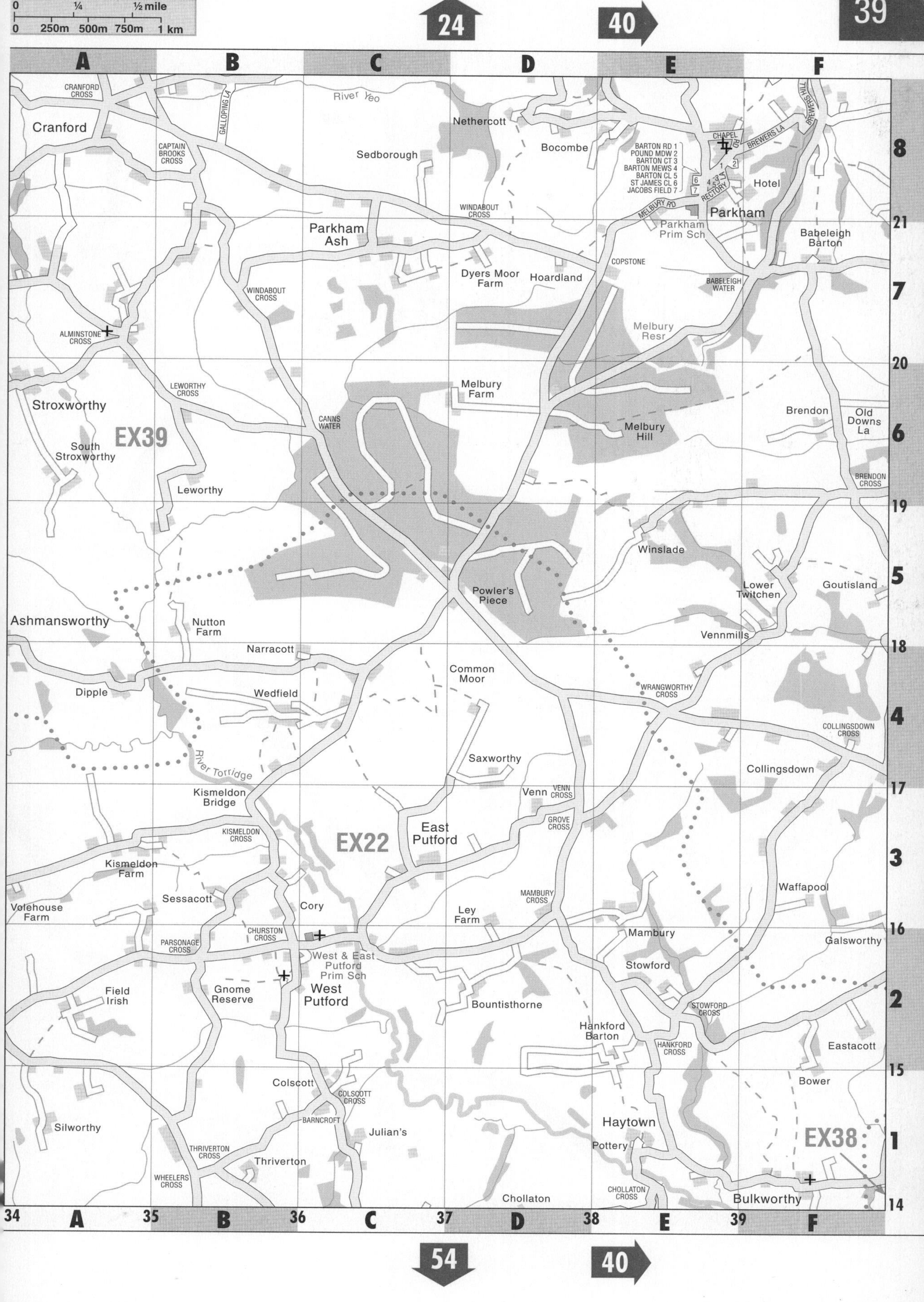
Scale: 1¾ inches to 1 mile
0 ¼ ½ mile
0 250m 500m 750m 1 km
24
40
A B C D E F
CRANFORD CROSS
Cranford
GALLOPING LA
River Yeo
Nethercott
CAPTAIN BROOKS CROSS
Sedborough
Bocombe
CHAPEL
BREWERS LA
BREWERS HILL
BARTON RD 1
POUND MDW 2
BARTON CT 3
BARTON MEWS 4
BARTON CL 5
ST JAMES CL 6
JACOBS FIELD 7
RECTORY
Hotel
8
WINDABOUT CROSS
MELBURY RD
Parkham
Parkham Ash
Parkham Prim Sch
21
Babeleigh Barton
COPSTONE
Dyers Moor Farm
Hoardland
BABELEIGH WATER
WINDABOUT CROSS
7
ALMINSTONE CROSS
Melbury Resr
20
LEWORTHY CROSS
Melbury Farm
Stroxworthy
CANNS WATER
Brendon
Old Downs La
EX39
Melbury Hill
6
South Stroxworthy
BRENDON CROSS
Leworthy
19
Winslade
5
Lower Twitchen
Goutisland
Powler's Piece
Ashmansworthy
Nutton Farm
Vennmills
Narracott
18
Common Moor
Dipple
Wedfield
WRANGWORTHY CROSS
4
COLLINGSDOWN CROSS
River Torridge
Saxworthy
Collingsdown
Kismeldon Bridge
Venn
VENN CROSS
17
GROVE CROSS
KISMELDON CROSS
East Putford
EX22
3
Kismeldon Farm
Sessacott
MAMBURY CROSS
Waffapool
Volehouse Farm
Cory
Ley Farm
CHURSTON CROSS
16
Mambury
Galsworthy
PARSONAGE CROSS
West & East Putford Prim Sch
Stowford
Field Irish
Gnome Reserve
West Putford
2
Bountisthorne
STOWFORD CROSS
Hankford Barton
Eastacott
HANKFORD CROSS
15
Colscott
Bower
COLSCOTT CROSS
Silworthy
BARNCROFT
Julian's
Haytown
EX38
1
THRIVERTON CROSS
Pottery
Thriverton
WHEELERS CROSS
Chollaton
CHOLLATON CROSS
Bulkworthy
14
34 A 35 B 36 C 37 D 38 E 39 F
54
40

39
25

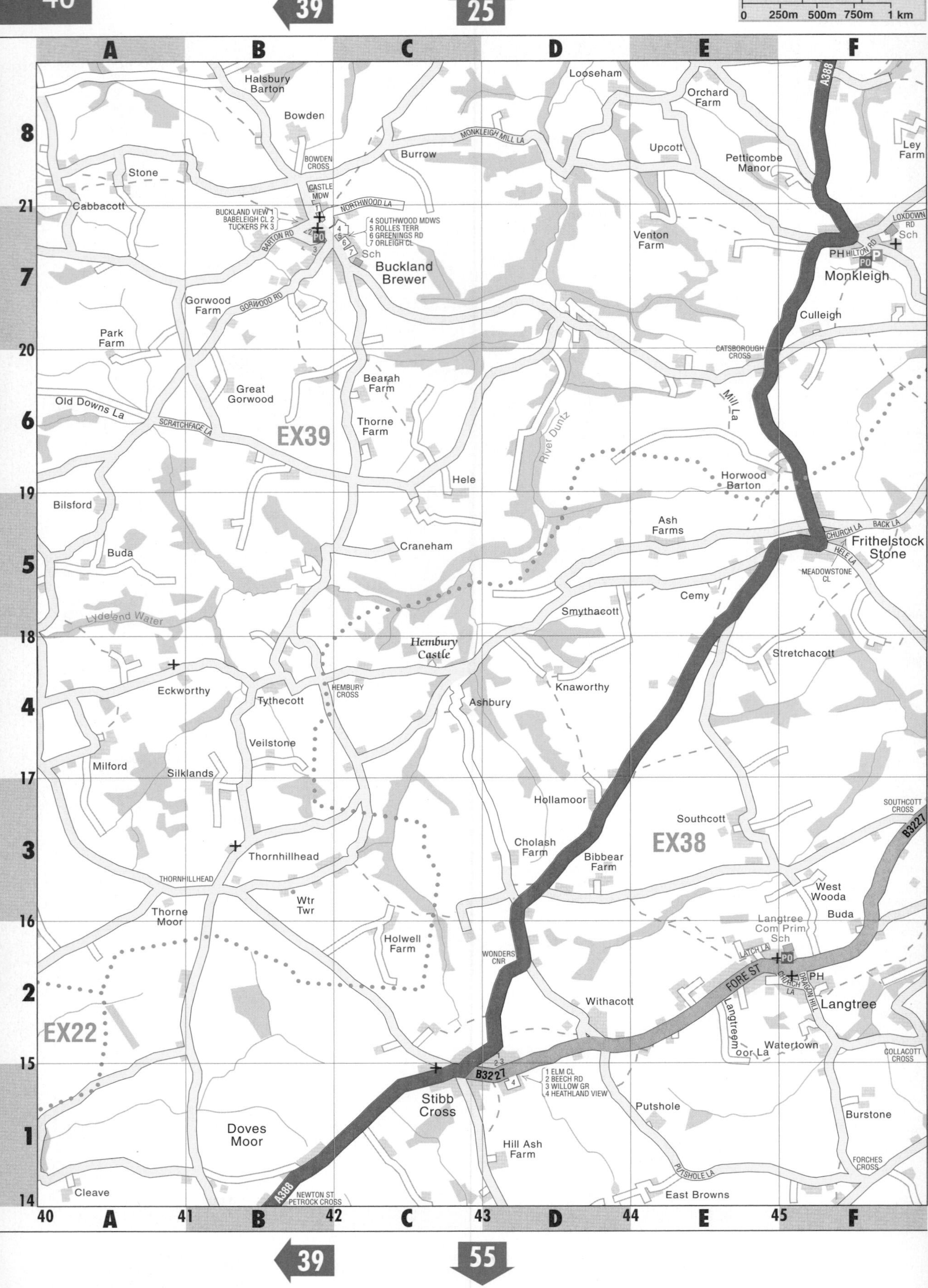
Scale: 1¾ inches to 1 mile
0 ¼ ½ mile
0 250m 500m 750m 1 km
A B C D E F
8 21 7 20 6 19 5 18 4 17 3 16 2 15 1 14
40 41 42 43 44 45
Halsbury Barton
Bowden
Looseham
Orchard Farm
A388
Upcott
Petticombe Manor
Ley Farm
MONKLEIGH MILL LA
Burrow
BOWDEN CROSS
Stone
CASTLE MDW
Cabbacott
NORTHWOOD LA
BUCKLAND VIEW 1
BABELEIGH CL 2
TUCKERS PK 3
4 SOUTHWOOD MDWS
5 ROLLES TERR
6 GREENINGS RD
7 ORLEIGH CL
BARTON RD
PO
Sch
Buckland Brewer
Venton Farm
LOXDOWN RD
Sch
PH
HILTON RD
P
Monkleigh
Gorwood Farm
GORWOOD RD
Culleigh
Park Farm
CATSBOROUGH CROSS
Bearah Farm
Great Gorwood
Mill La
Old Downs La
SCRATCHFACE LA
EX39
Thorne Farm
River Duntz
Hele
Horwood Barton
Bilsford
Ash Farms
CHURCH LA
BACK LA
Frithelstock Stone
HELE LA
Craneham
Buda
MEADOWSTONE CL
Cemy
Smythacott
Lydeland Water
Hembury Castle
Stretchacott
Eckworthy
HEMBURY CROSS
Knaworthy
Tythecott
Ashbury
Veilstone
Milford
Silklands
Hollamoor
SOUTHCOTT CROSS
Southcott
B3227
Cholash Farm
EX38
Thornhillhead
Bibbear Farm
THORNHILLHEAD
West Wooda
Wtr Twr
Thorne Moor
Buda
Langtree Com Prim Sch
Holwell Farm
WONDERS CNR
LATCH LA
PO
FORE ST
CHURCH LA
DRAGON HILL
PH
Withacott
Langtree
EX22
Langtreemoor La
Watertown
COLLACOTT CROSS
B3227
1 ELM CL
2 BEECH RD
3 WILLOW GR
4 HEATHLAND VIEW
Stibb Cross
Putshole
Burstone
Doves Moor
Hill Ash Farm
FORCHES CROSS
PUTSHOLE LA
Cleave
NEWTON ST PETROCK CROSS
East Browns

39
55

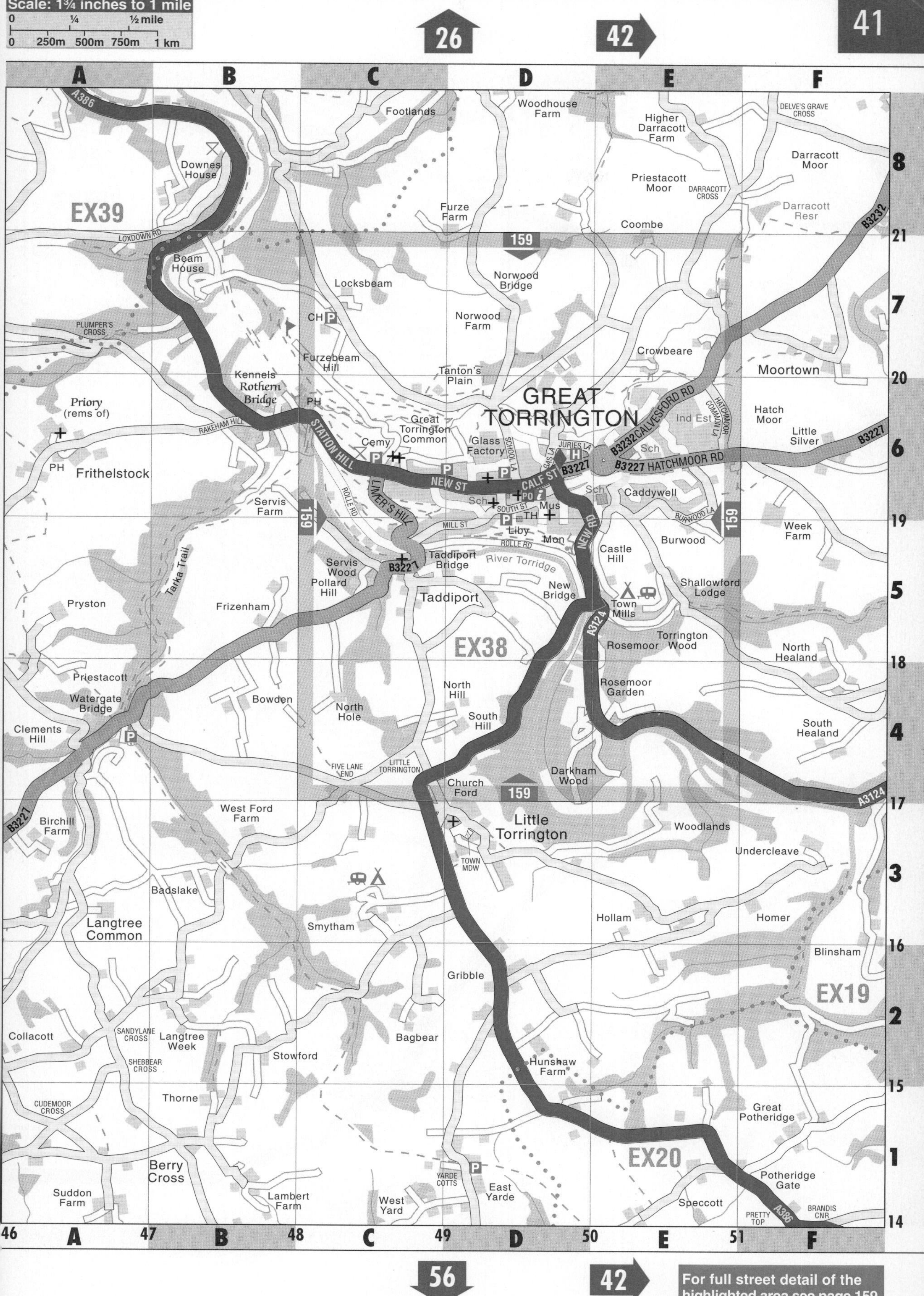

For full street detail of the highlighted area see page 159.

Scale: 1¾ inches to 1 mile
0 ¼ ½ mile
0 250m 500m 750m 1 km

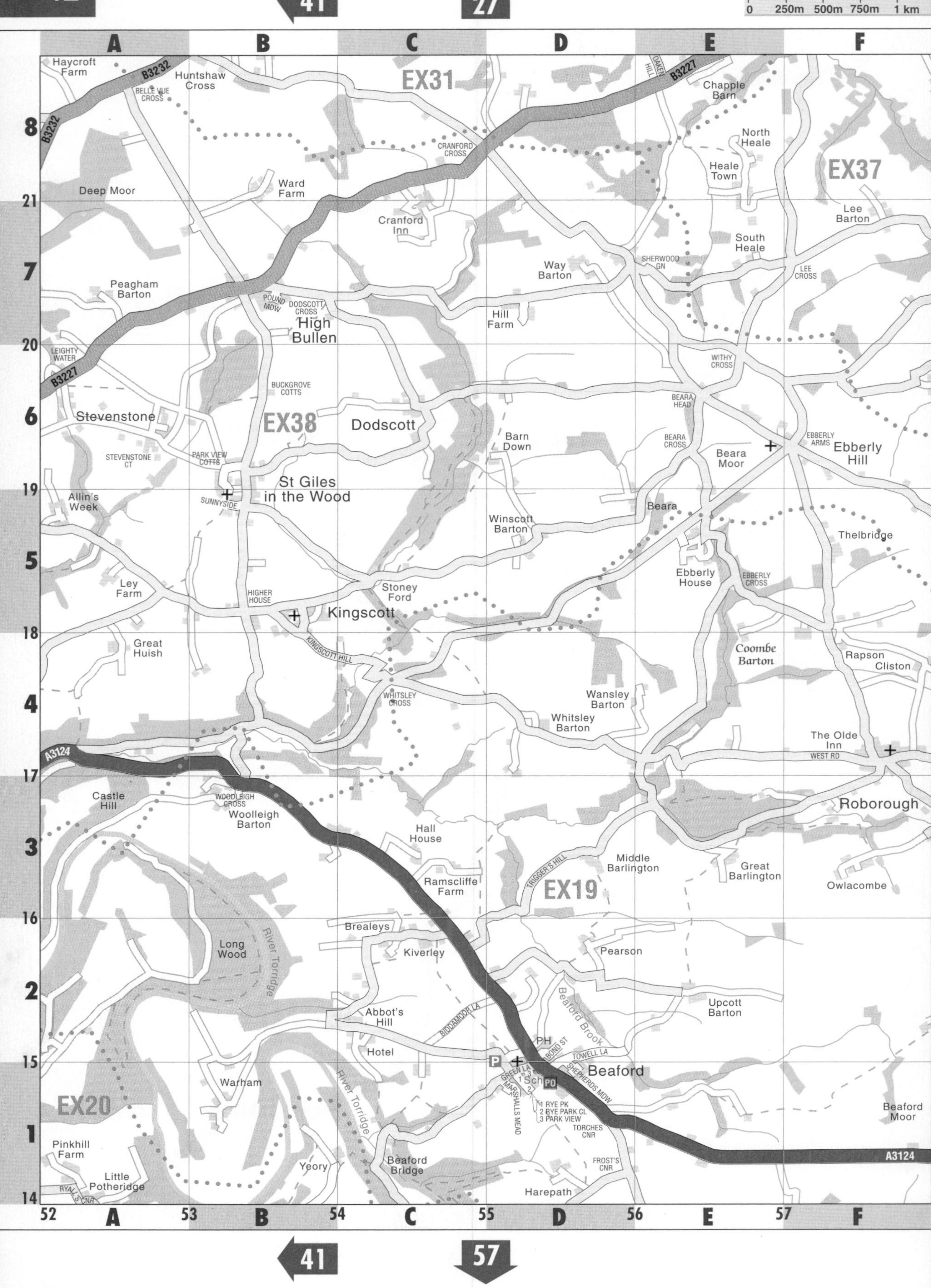

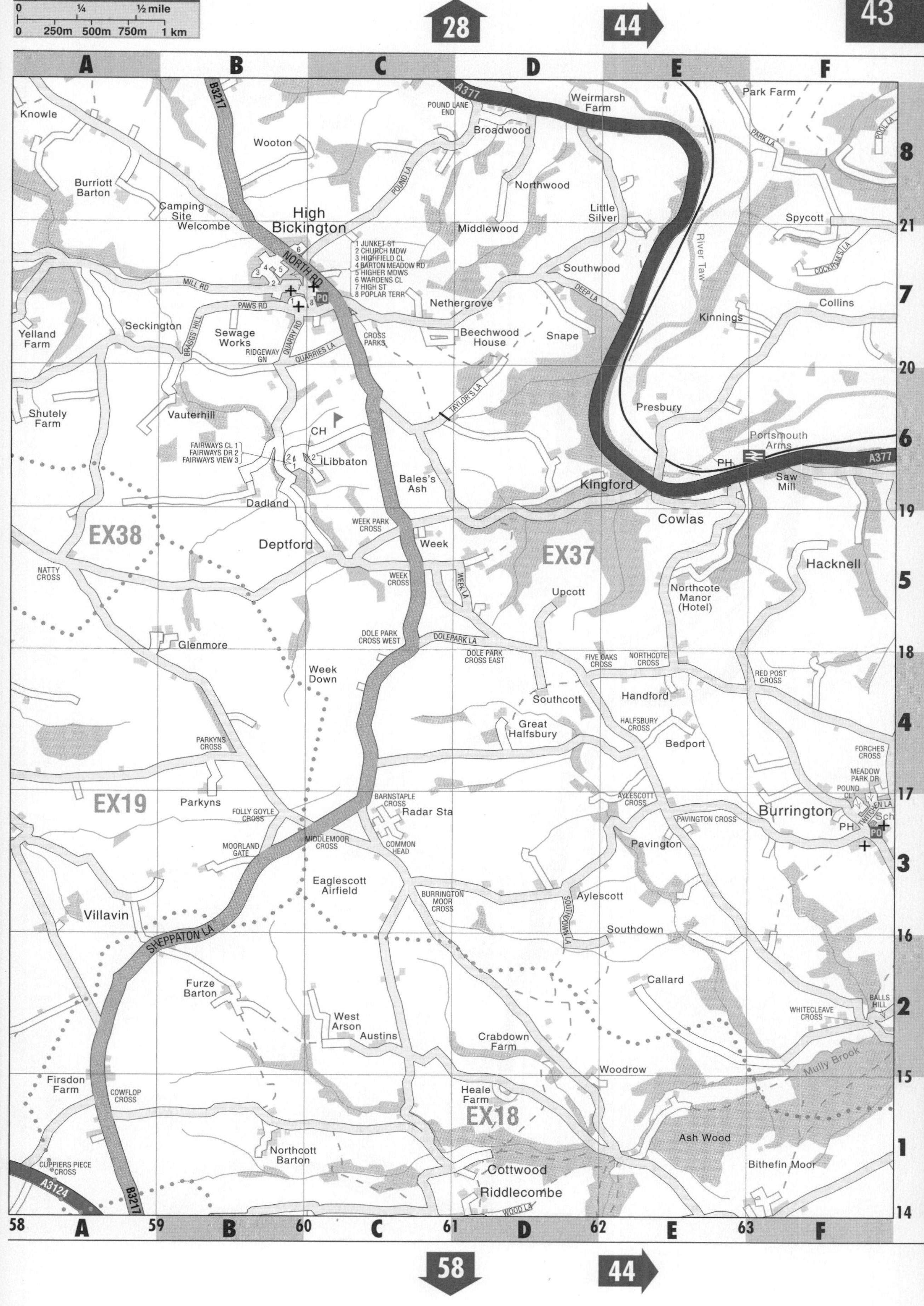
Scale: 1¾ inches to 1 mile
0 ¼ ½ mile
0 250m 500m 750m 1 km
28
44
A B C D E F
Knowle
Wooton
Burriott Barton
Camping Site
Welcombe
High Bickington
NORTH RD
MILL RD
PAWS RD
BRAGGS' HILL
QUARRY RD
QUARRIES LA
RIDGEWAY GN
1 JUNKET ST
2 CHURCH MDW
3 HIGHFIELD CL
4 BARTON MEADOW RD
5 HIGHER MDWS
6 WARDENS CL
7 HIGH ST
8 POPLAR TERR
PO
Seckington
Sewage Works
Yelland Farm
Shutely Farm
Vauterhill
CH
FAIRWAYS CL 1
FAIRWAYS DR 2
FAIRWAYS VIEW 3
Libbaton
Dadland
EX38
NATTY CROSS
Deptford
Glenmore
Week Down
PARKYNS CROSS
EX19
Parkyns
FOLLY GOYLE CROSS
MOORLAND GATE
Villavin
SHEPPATON LA
Furze Barton
Firsdon Farm
COWFLOP CROSS
CUPPIERS PIECE CROSS
A3124
B3217
POUND LANE END
Broadwood
POUND LA
Northwood
Middlewood
Nethergrove
CROSS PARKS
Beechwood House
TAYLOR'S LA
Bales's Ash
WEEK PARK CROSS
Week
WEEK CROSS
WEEK LA
DOLE PARK CROSS WEST
DOLEPARK LA
DOLE PARK CROSS EAST
BARNSTAPLE CROSS
Radar Sta
MIDDLEMOOR CROSS
COMMON HEAD
Eaglescott Airfield
BURRINGTON MOOR CROSS
West Arson
Austins
Crabdown Farm
Heale Farm
EX18
Northcott Barton
Cottwood
Riddlecombe
WOOD LA
A377
Weirmarsh Farm
Little Silver
Southwood
DEEP LA
Snape
River Taw
Kinnings
Presbury
Kingford
Cowlas
EX37
Upcott
Northcote Manor (Hotel)
FIVE OAKS CROSS
NORTHCOTE CROSS
Southcott
Handford
Great Halfsbury
HALFSBURY CROSS
Bedport
AYLESCOTT CROSS
PAVINGTON CROSS
Pavington
Aylescott
SOUTHDOWN LA
Southdown
Callard
Woodrow
Ash Wood
Park Farm
PARK LA
POOL LA
Spycott
COCKRAMS LA
Collins
Portsmouth Arms
PH
Saw Mill
Hacknell
RED POST CROSS
FORCHES CROSS
MEADOW PARK DR
POUND CL
TWITCHEN LA
Burrington
Sch
WHITECLEAVE CROSS
BALLS HILL
Mully Brook
Bithefin Moor
8 21 7 20 6 19 5 18 4 17 3 16 2 15 1 14
58 59 60 61 62 63
58
44

43
29

Scale: 1¾ inches to 1 mile
0 ¼ ½ mile
0 250m 500m 750m 1 km

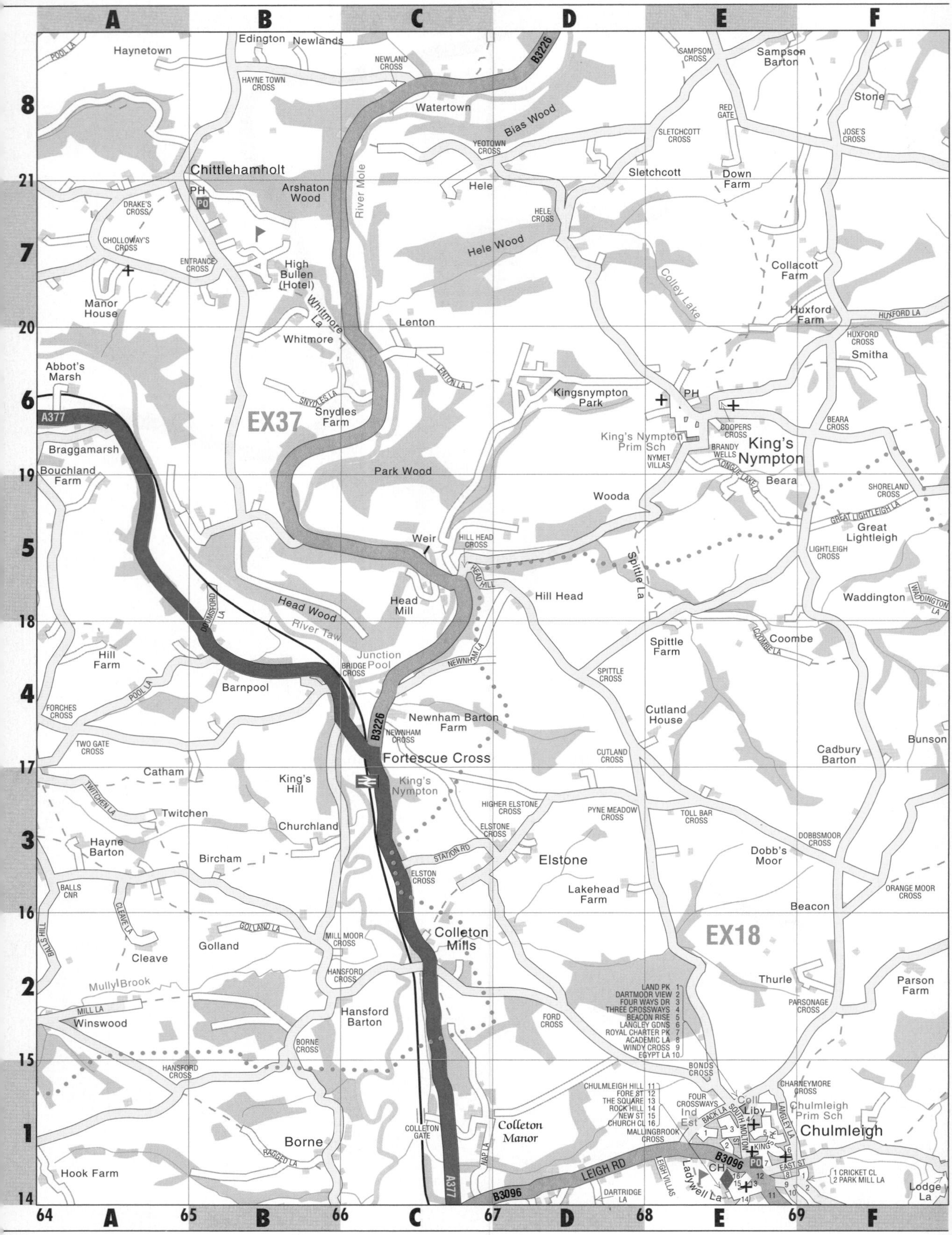

A B C D E F

8
21
7
20
6
19
5
18
4
17
3
16
2
15
1
14

Pool La
Haynetown
Edington
Newlands
Haynetown Cross
Newland Cross
B3226
Sampson Cross
Sampson Barton
Stone
Watertown
Bias Wood
Red Gate
Sletchcott Cross
Jose's Cross
Yeotown Cross
Chittlehamholt
PH
PO
Arshaton Wood
River Mole
Hele
Sletchcott
Down Farm
Drake's Cross
Hele Cross
Cholloway's Cross
Hele Wood
Entrance Cross
High Bullen (Hotel)
Collacott Farm
Colley Lake
Manor House
Whitmore La
Huxford Farm
Huxford La
Lenton
Whitmore
Huxford Cross
Smitha
Abbot's Marsh
Lenton La
Snydles La
Kingsnympton Park
PH
A377
EX37
Snydles Farm
King's Nympton Prim Sch
Coopers Cross
Beara Cross
Braggamarsh
Brandy Wells
Nymet Villas
King's Nympton
Bouchland Farm
Park Wood
Longue Lake La
Beara
Shoreland Cross
Wooda
Great Lightleigh La
Great Lightleigh
Weir
Hill Head Cross
Spittle La
Lightleigh Cross
Head Hill
Hill Head
Waddington
Waddington La
Drumsford La
Head Wood
Head Mill
River Taw
Coombe
Coombe La
Hill Farm
Junction Pool
Bridge Cross
Newnham La
Spittle Farm
Spittle Cross
Pool La
Barnpool
Forches Cross
Newnham Barton Farm
Cutland House
B3226
Newnham Cross
Bunson
Two Gate Cross
Fortescue Cross
Cutland Cross
Cadbury Barton
Catham
King's Hill
King's Nympton
Twitchen La
Higher Elstone Cross
Pyne Meadow Cross
Toll Bar Cross
Twitchen
Elstone Cross
Churchland
Hayne Barton
Dobbsmoor Cross
Station Rd
Dobb's Moor
Bircham
Elstone
Balls Cnr
Elston Cross
Lakehead Farm
Orange Moor Cross
Cleave La
Beacon
Balls Hill
Golland La
Mill Moor Cross
Colleton Mills
EX18
Golland
Cleave
Hansford Cross
Thurle
Parson Farm
Mully Brook
Mill La
Hansford Barton
Parsonage Cross
Winswood
Ford Cross
Borne Cross
Hansford Cross
Bonds Cross
Charneymore Cross
Four Crossways
Coll
Ind Est
Liby
Chulmleigh Prim Sch
Back La
South Molton St
Langley La
Colleton Gate
Colleton Manor
Nap La
Chulmleigh
Borne
Ragged La
Mallingbrook Cross
King's Pk
Leigh Rd
B3096
East St
Hook Farm
A377
Leigh Villas
Ladywell La
CH
PO
Dartridge La
Lodge La
B3096

LAND PK 1
DARTMOOR VIEW 2
FOUR WAYS DR 3
THREE CROSSWAYS 4
BEACON RISE 5
LANGLEY GDNS 6
ROYAL CHARTER PK 7
ACADEMIC LA 8
WINDY CROSS 9
EGYPT LA 10

CHULMLEIGH HILL 11
FORE ST 12
THE SQUARE 13
ROCK HILL 14
NEW ST 15
CHURCH CL 16

1 CRICKET CL
2 PARK MILL LA

64 A 65 B 66 C 67 D 68 E 69 F

43
59

Scale: 1¾ inches to 1 mile
0 ¼ ½ mile
0 250m 500m 750m 1 km
30
46
A B C D E F
Tidlake
B3137
TIDLAKE LA
Littlewood Farm
Yelmacott
Broomham
Cleave Farm
Westacott Farm
Uppacott
Trittencott
UPPACOTT CROSS
Rowcliffe Farm
OXHAM CROSS
WESTACOTT CROSS
EX36
TONGUE GATE
TONGUE GATE HILL
BROOMHAM CROSS
HIGHRIDGE CROSS
Highridge Farm
Romansleigh
Odam Bridge
Notcliffe
MILLTOWN HILL
Milltown
HUXFORD LA
ROMANSLEIGH CROSS
BUCKHAM CROSS
PARTRIDGE H/L
ODAM CROSS
BUCKHAM HILL
MILL LA
DRYMUMP HILL
Broomham Moor
NORTHDOWN LA
EX37
Odam Barton
Beara
Kingstree
Higher Kitcott
KITCOTT CROSS
KITCOTT HILL
Meshaw
Hummacott
Horridge
SOUTHDOWN HILL
Rowley
Langley
EAST ROWLEY LA
GARLAND CROSS
THREE CORNER CROSS
BEACON CROSS
ODAM MOOR CROSS
HILL SIDE CROSS
ROMANSLEIGH RIDGE
MEASBURY MOOR CROSS
West Garland Moor
Measbury Moor
Great Odam Moor Plantation
Middle Garland
Waterloo
Batney Farm
Thornham
WADDINGTON LA
Bourne Park
West Garland Farm
BYCOTT LA
Broads Moor Farm
BUNSON GATE
Bycott Farm
Beara
EX18
Week
WIXON CROSS
WIXON LA
HOLE LA
Wixon
WEEK CROSS
Molland
Hole Farm
Huntacott Water
Horridge Moor
MOLLAND CROSS
CHALLACOMBE CROSS
Challacombe
Sheepsbyre
KEMPLAND LA
Kempland
BEALEY COURT CROSS
Bealy Court
BENLEY CROSS
Brookland Farm
Holland Farm
CHELDON CROSS
EDGIFORD CROSS
STONE MOOR CROSS
Winswood Moor
EX17
Huntacott
MOUNTICOMBE CROSS
Philham
MOUNTICOMBE LA
Mounticombe
LODGE CROSS
8
21
7
20
6
19
5
18
4
17
3
16
2
15
1
14
70 71 72 73 74 75
60
46

45
31

Scale: 1¾ inches to 1 mile
0 ¼ ½ mile
0 250m 500m 750m 1 km

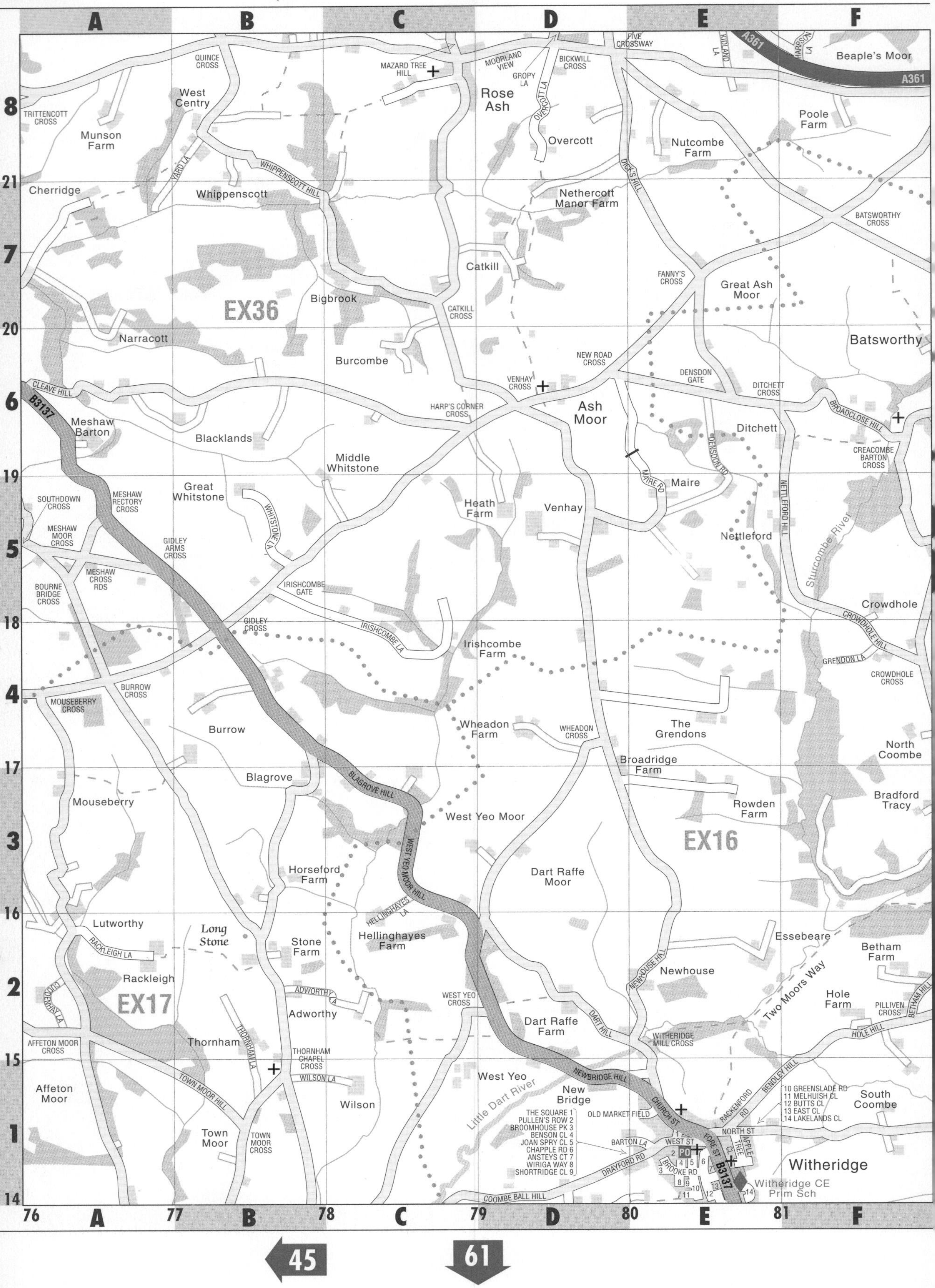

45
61

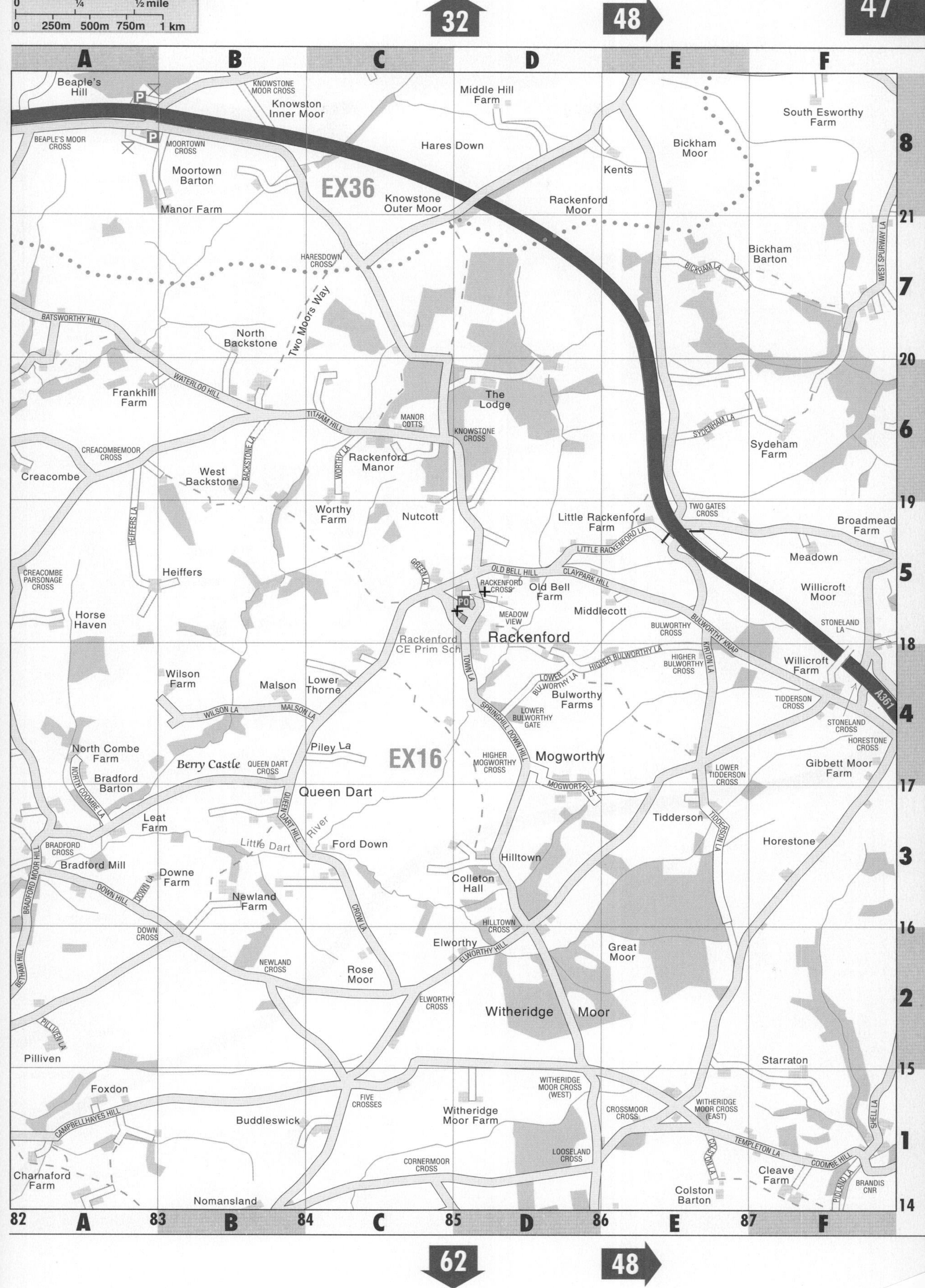
Scale: 1¾ inches to 1 mile
0 ¼ ½ mile
0 250m 500m 750m 1 km
32
48
A
B
C
D
E
F
Beaple's Hill
KNOWSTONE MOOR CROSS
Knowston Inner Moor
Middle Hill Farm
South Esworthy Farm
BEAPLE'S MOOR CROSS
MOORTOWN CROSS
Hares Down
Bickham Moor
Moortown Barton
EX36
Kents
Knowstone Outer Moor
Rackenford Moor
Manor Farm
HARESDOWN CROSS
BICKHAM LA
Bickham Barton
WEST SPURWAY LA
Two Moors Way
BATSWORTHY HILL
North Backstone
WATERLOO HILL
Frankhill Farm
The Lodge
MANOR COTTS
TITHAM HILL
KNOWSTONE CROSS
SYDENHAM LA
Sydeham Farm
CREACOMBEMOOR CROSS
Rackenford Manor
WORTHY LA
BACKSTONE LA
Creacombe
West Backstone
HEIFFERS LA
Worthy Farm
Nutcott
Little Rackenford Farm
TWO GATES CROSS
Broadmead Farm
LITTLE RACKENFORD LA
Meadown
GREEN LA
OLD BELL HILL
CLAYPARK HILL
CREACOMBE PARSONAGE CROSS
Heiffers
RACKENFORD CROSS
Old Bell Farm
Willicroft Moor
PO
Middlecott
Horse Haven
MEADOW VIEW
BULWORTHY CROSS
BULWORTHY KNAP
STONELAND LA
Rackenford CE Prim Sch
Rackenford
HIGHER BULWORTHY LA
HIGHER BULWORTHY CROSS
KIRTON LA
Willicroft Farm
TOWN LA
Wilson Farm
Lower Thorne
LOWER BULWORTHY LA
Bulworthy Farms
Malson
TIDDERSON CROSS
A361
WILSON LA
MALSON LA
SPRINGHILL DOWN HILL
LOWER BULWORTHY GATE
STONELAND CROSS
HORESTONE CROSS
North Combe Farm
Piley La
EX16
HIGHER MOGWORTHY CROSS
Mogworthy
Gibbett Moor Farm
Berry Castle
QUEEN DART CROSS
LOWER TIDDERSON CROSS
Bradford Barton
NORTH COOMBE LA
Queen Dart
MOGWORTHY LA
Leat Farm
QUEEN DART HILL
River
Tidderson
TIDDERSON LA
Horestone
BRADFORD CROSS
Little Dart
Ford Down
Bradford Mill
BRADFORD MOOR HILL
Downe Farm
Hilltown
Colleton Hall
DOWN HILL
DOWN LA
Newland Farm
CROW LA
HILLTOWN CROSS
DOWN CROSS
Elworthy
Great Moor
ELWORTHY HILL
BETHAM HILL
NEWLAND CROSS
Rose Moor
ELWORTHY CROSS
Witheridge
Moor
PILLIVEN LA
Pilliven
Starraton
Foxdon
WITHERIDGE MOOR CROSS (WEST)
FIVE CROSSES
CROSSMOOR CROSS
WITHERIDGE MOOR CROSS (EAST)
CAMPBELLHAYES HILL
Witheridge Moor Farm
Buddleswick
SHELL LA
TEMPLETON LA
COLSTON LA
LOOSELAND CROSS
COOMBE HILL
CORNERMOOR CROSS
Charnaford Farm
Cleave Farm
PIDLAND LA
BRANDIS CNR
Colston Barton
Nomansland
8
21
7
20
6
19
5
18
4
17
3
16
2
15
1
14
82
83
84
85
86
87
62
48

Scale: 1¾ inches to 1 mile
0 ¼ ½ mile
0 250m 500m 750m 1 km

For full street detail of the highlighted area see page 161.

49
35

Scale: 1¾ inches to 1 mile

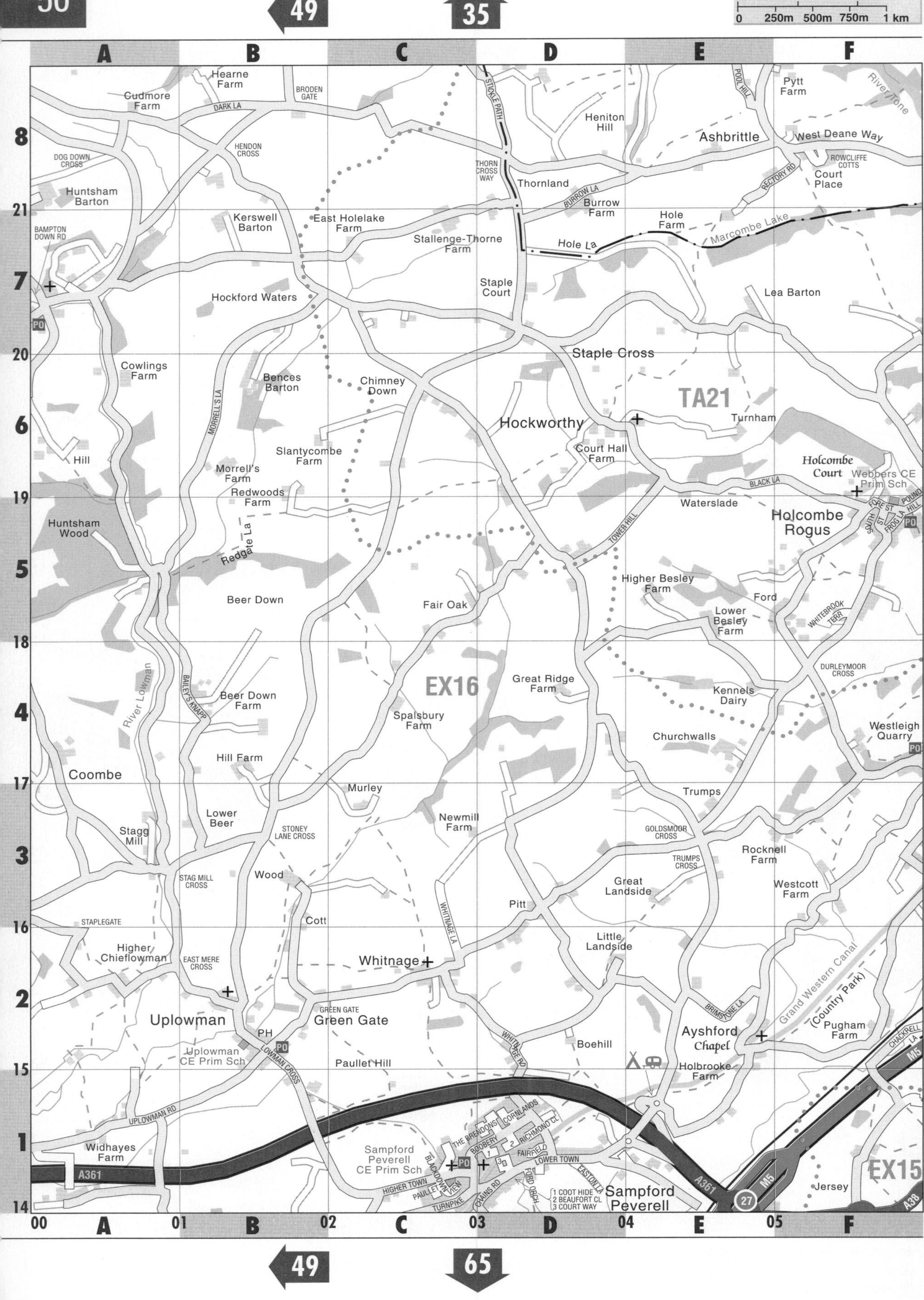

49
65

Scale: 1¾ inches to 1 mile

52

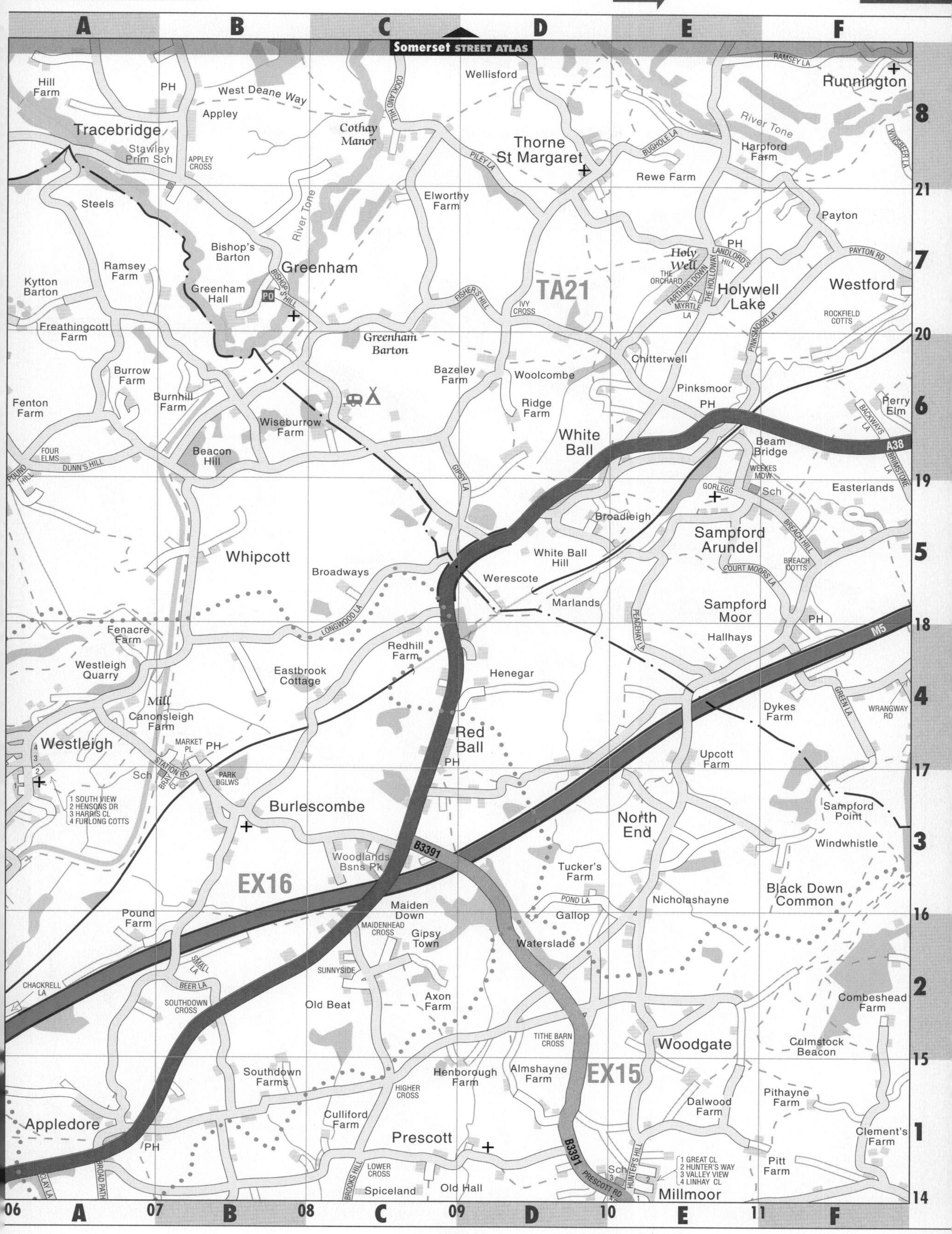

Scale: 1¾ inches to 1 mile
0 ¼ ½ mile
0 250m 500m 750m 1 km

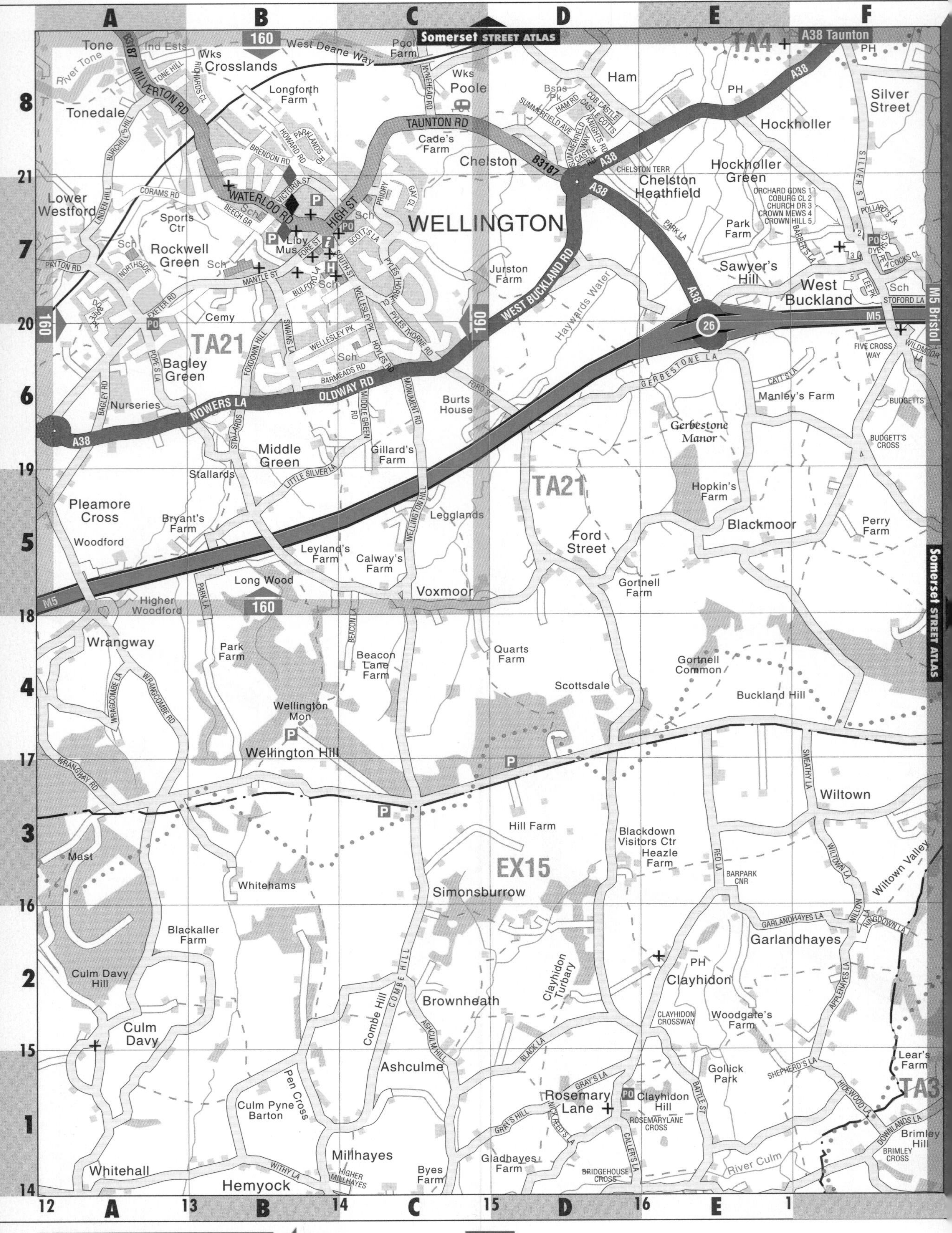

For full street detail of the highlighted area see page 160

Scale: 1¾ inches to 1 mile
0 ¼ ½ mile
0 250m 500m 750m 1 km

38
54

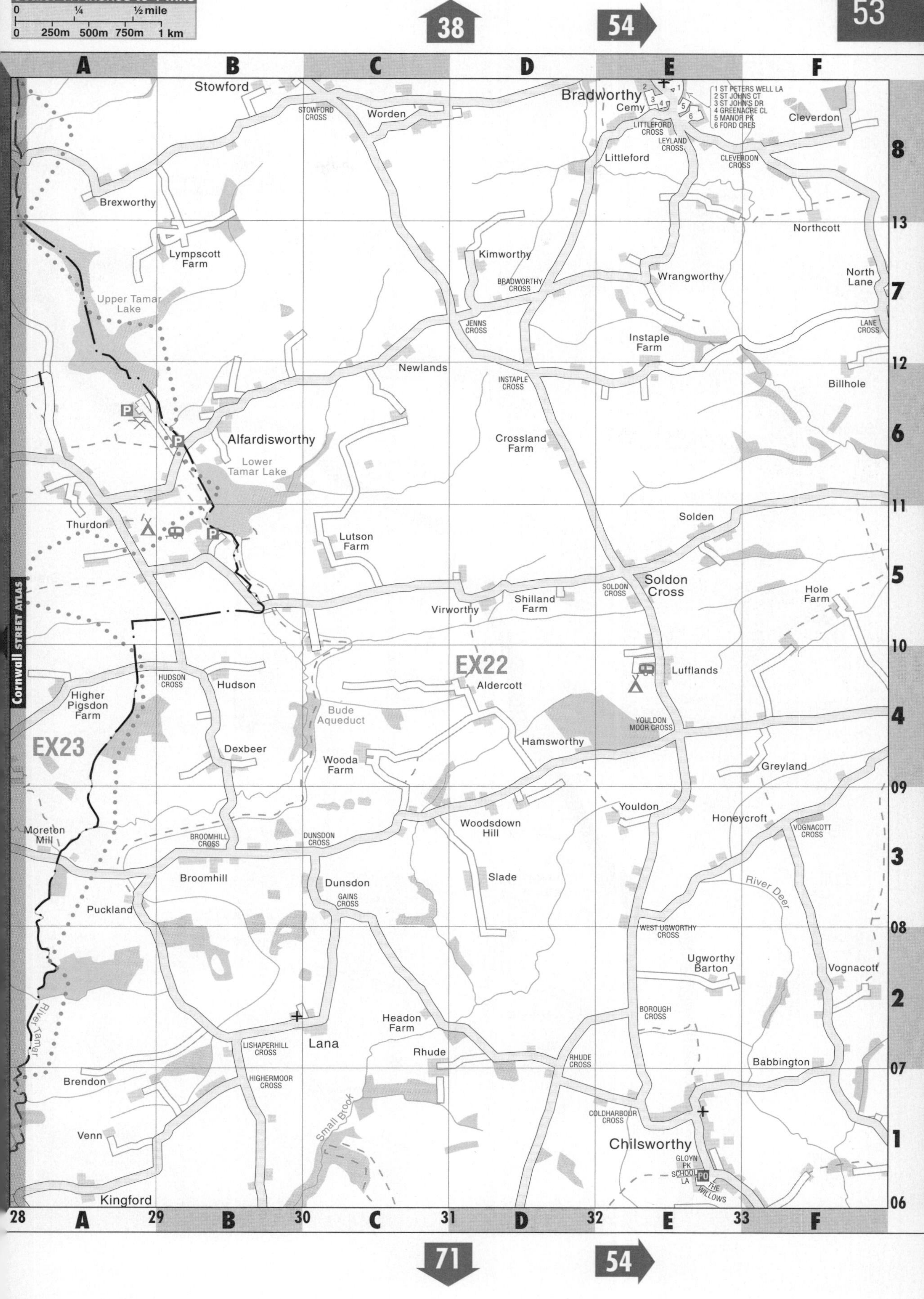

71
54

53
39

Scale: 1¾ inches to 1 mile

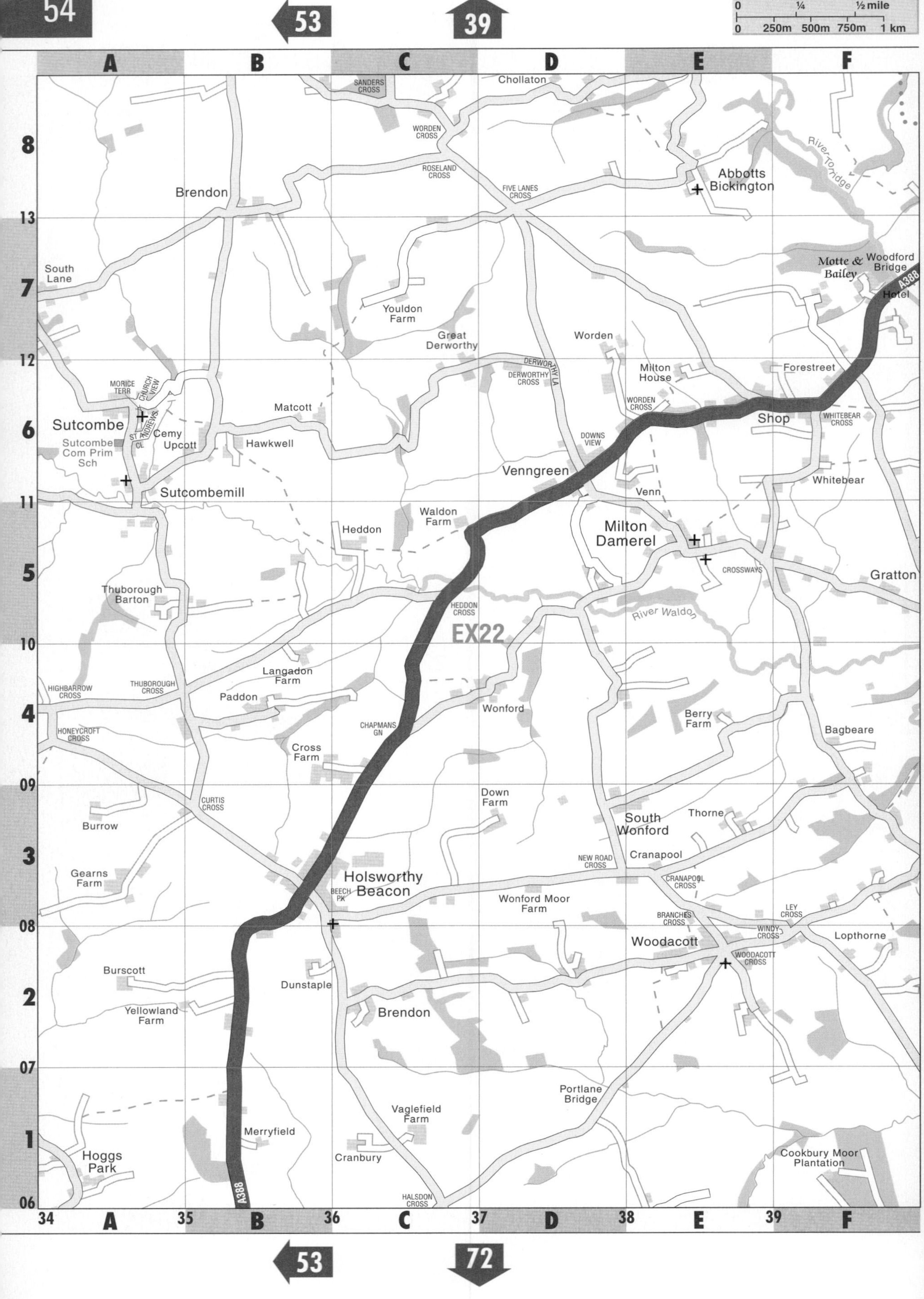

53
72

40
56

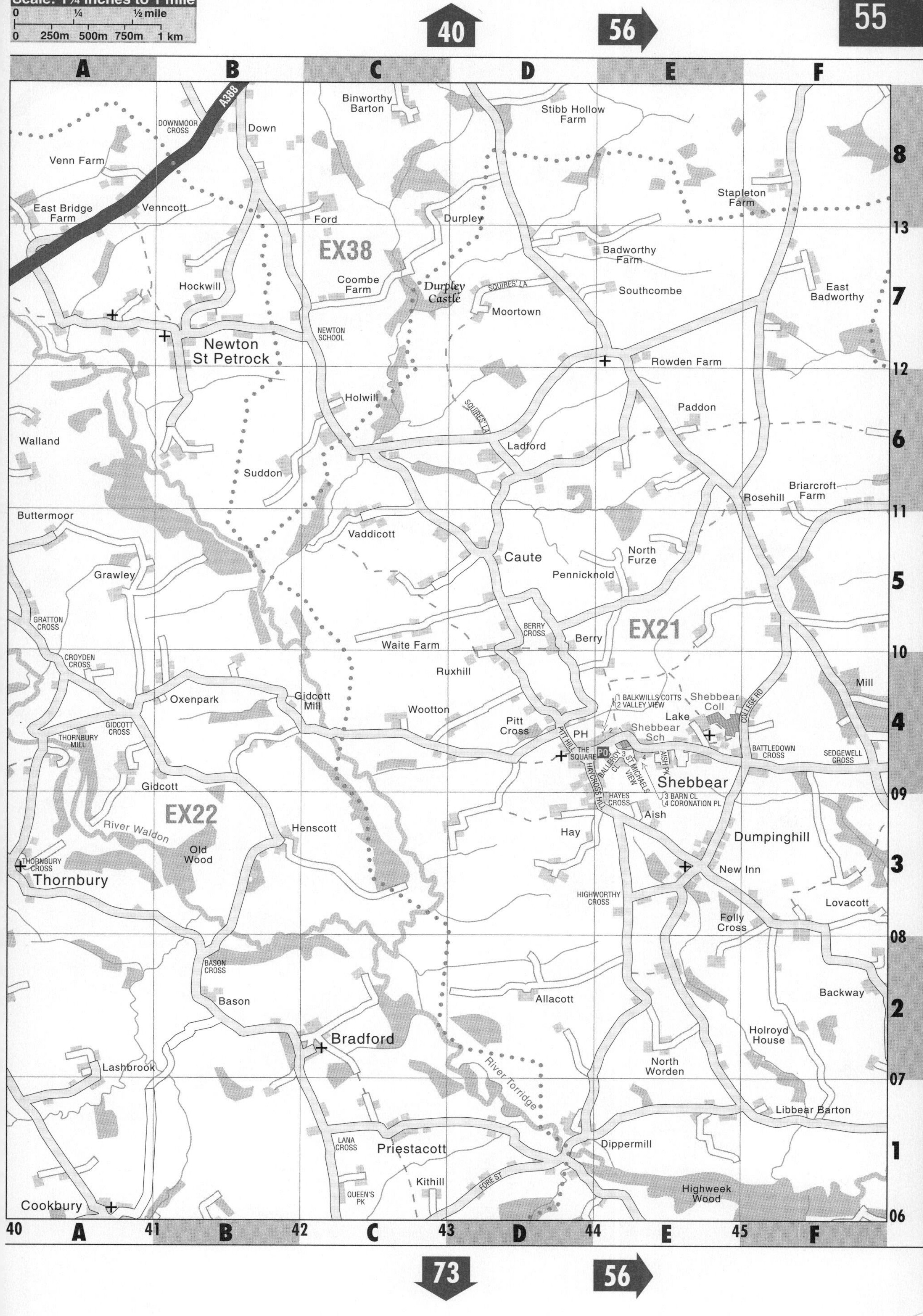
Scale: 1¾ inches to 1 mile
0 ¼ ½ mile
0 250m 500m 750m 1 km
A
B
C
D
E
F
A388
DOWNMOOR CROSS
Down
Binworthy Barton
Stibb Hollow Farm
Venn Farm
Stapleton Farm
East Bridge Farm
Venncott
Ford
Durpley
EX38
Badworthy Farm
Hockwill
Coombe Farm
Durpley Castle
SQUIRES' LA
Moortown
Southcombe
East Badworthy
NEWTON SCHOOL
Newton St Petrock
Rowden Farm
Holwill
SQUIRES' LA
Paddon
Walland
Ladford
Suddon
Rosehill
Briarcroft Farm
Buttermoor
Vaddicott
Caute
North Furze
Pennicknold
Grawley
GRATTON CROSS
BERRY CROSS
Berry
EX21
CROYDEN CROSS
Waite Farm
Ruxhill
Oxenpark
Gidcott Mill
Wootton
Pitt Cross
1 BALKWILLS COTTS
2 VALLEY VIEW
Shebbear Coll
Lake
COLLEGE RD
Mill
GIDCOTT CROSS
THORNBURY MILL
PH
Shebbear Sch
PITT HILL
THE SQUARE
PO
BALLEROY CL
ST MICHAELS VIEW
AISH PK
BATTLEDOWN CROSS
SEDGEWELL CROSS
Gidcott
HAYCROSS HILL
Shebbear
3 BARN CL
4 CORONATION PL
HAYES CROSS
Aish
EX22
River Waldon
Henscott
Hay
Dumpinghill
THORNBURY CROSS
Old Wood
New Inn
Thornbury
HIGHWORTHY CROSS
Lovacott
Folly Cross
BASON CROSS
Allacott
Backway
Bason
Bradford
Holroyd House
Lashbrook
River Torridge
North Worden
Libbear Barton
LANA CROSS
Priestacott
Dippermill
Kithill
FORE ST
Highweek Wood
QUEEN'S PK
Cookbury
8
13
7
12
6
11
5
10
4
09
3
08
2
07
1
06
40
41
42
43
44
45

73
56

55
41

Scale: 1¾ inches to 1 mile

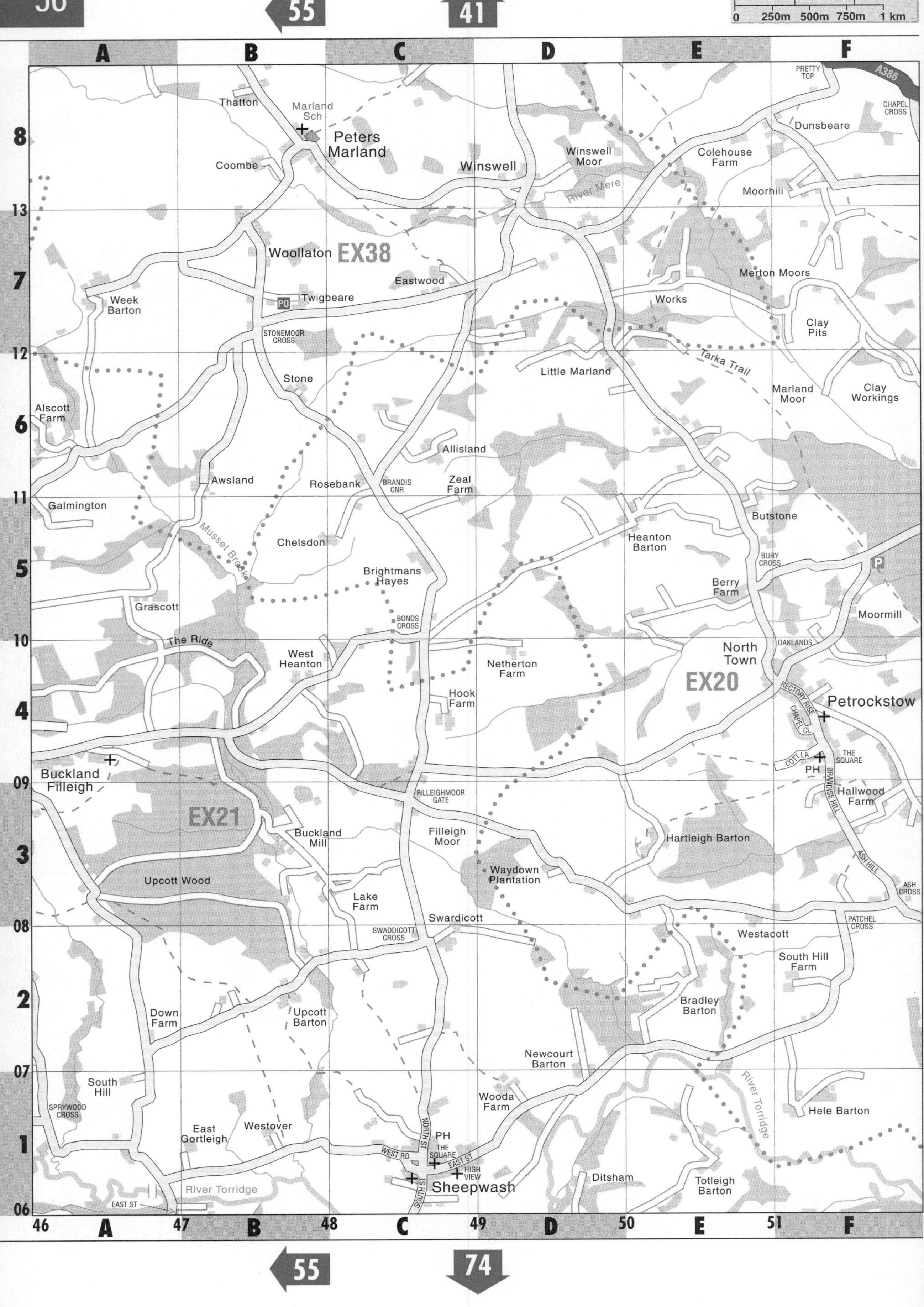

55
74

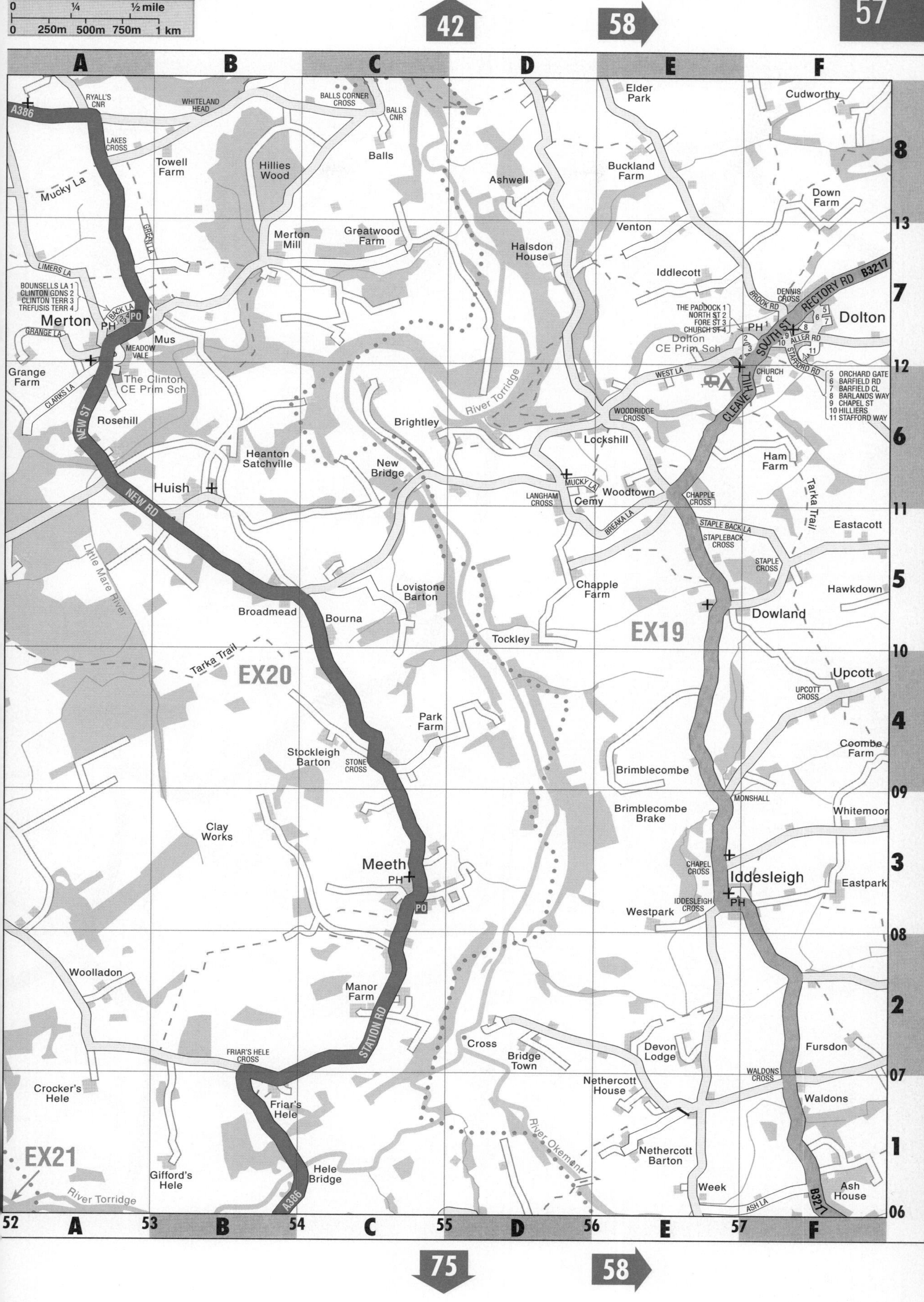
Scale: 1¾ inches to 1 mile
0 ¼ ½ mile
0 250m 500m 750m 1 km
42
58
A B C D E F
8
13
7
12
6
11
5
10
4
09
3
08
2
07
1
06
52 53 54 55 56 57
Merton
Mucky La
Towell Farm
Hillies Wood
Balls
Ashwell
Buckland Farm
Elder Park
Cudworthy
Down Farm
Venton
Merton Mill
Greatwood Farm
Halsdon House
Iddlecott
Dolton
Dolton CE Prim Sch
Grange Farm
Mus
The Clinton CE Prim Sch
Rosehill
River Torridge
Brightley
Lockshill
Ham Farm
Heanton Satchville
New Bridge
Huish
Woodtown
Cemy
Eastacott
Tarka Trail
Little Mare River
Chapple Farm
Lovistone Barton
Broadmead
Bourna
Dowland
Hawkdown
Tockley
EX19
EX20
Upcott
Park Farm
Stockleigh Barton
Coombe Farm
Brimblecombe
Clay Works
Brimblecombe Brake
Whitemoor
Meeth
Iddesleigh
Eastpark
Westpark
Woolladon
Manor Farm
Fursdon
Cross
Bridge Town
Devon Lodge
Nethercott House
Crocker's Hele
Friar's Hele
Waldons
River Okement
Nethercott Barton
EX21
Gifford's Hele
Hele Bridge
Week
Ash House
A386
B3217
NEW ST
NEW RD
STATION RD
CLEAVE HILL
SOUTH ST
RECTORY RD
BROOK RD
WEST LA
ALLER RD
STAFFORD RD
STAPLE BACK LA
BREAKA LA
MUCKY LA
GREAT LA
LIMERS LA
GRANGE LA
CLARKS LA
BACK LA
ASH LA
RYALL'S CNR
WHITELAND HEAD
BALLS CORNER CROSS
BALLS CNR
LAKES CROSS
MEADOW VALE
DENNIS CROSS
WOODRIDGE CROSS
LANGHAM CROSS
CHAPPLE CROSS
STAPLEBACK CROSS
STAPLE CROSS
UPCOTT CROSS
STONE CROSS
MONSHALL
CHAPEL CROSS
IDDESLEIGH CROSS
FRIAR'S HELE CROSS
WALDONS CROSS
CHURCH CL
BOUNSELLS LA 1
CLINTON GDNS 2
CLINTON TERR 3
TREFUSIS TERR 4
THE PADDOCK 1
NORTH ST 2
FORE ST 3
CHURCH ST 4
5 ORCHARD GATE
6 BARFIELD RD
7 BARFIELD CL
8 BARLANDS WAY
9 CHAPEL ST
10 HILLIERS
11 STAFFORD WAY
PH
PO
75
58

57
43

Scale: 1¾ inches to 1 mile
0 ¼ ½ mile
0 250m 500m 750m 1 km

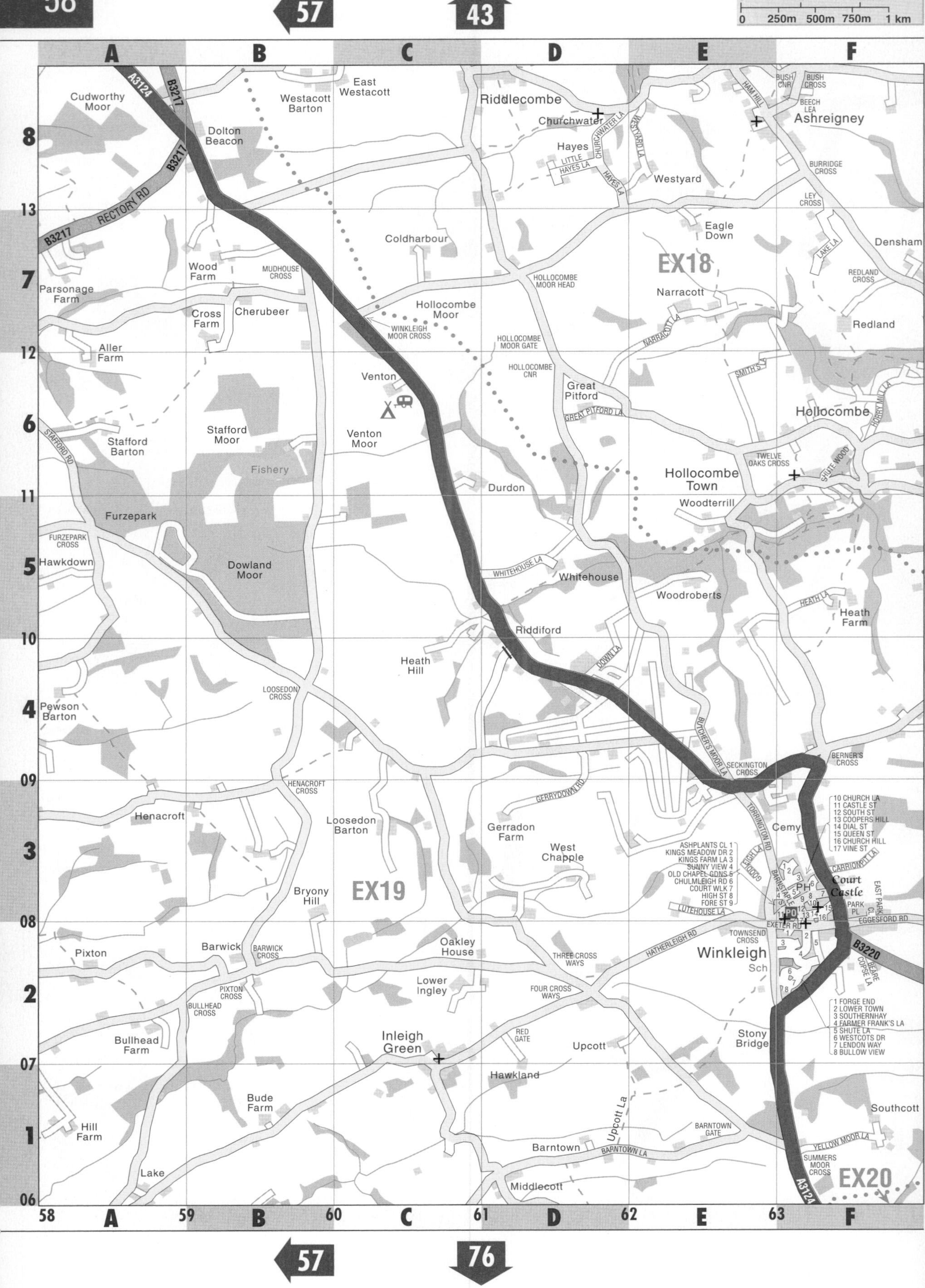

57
76

Scale: 1¾ inches to 1 mile

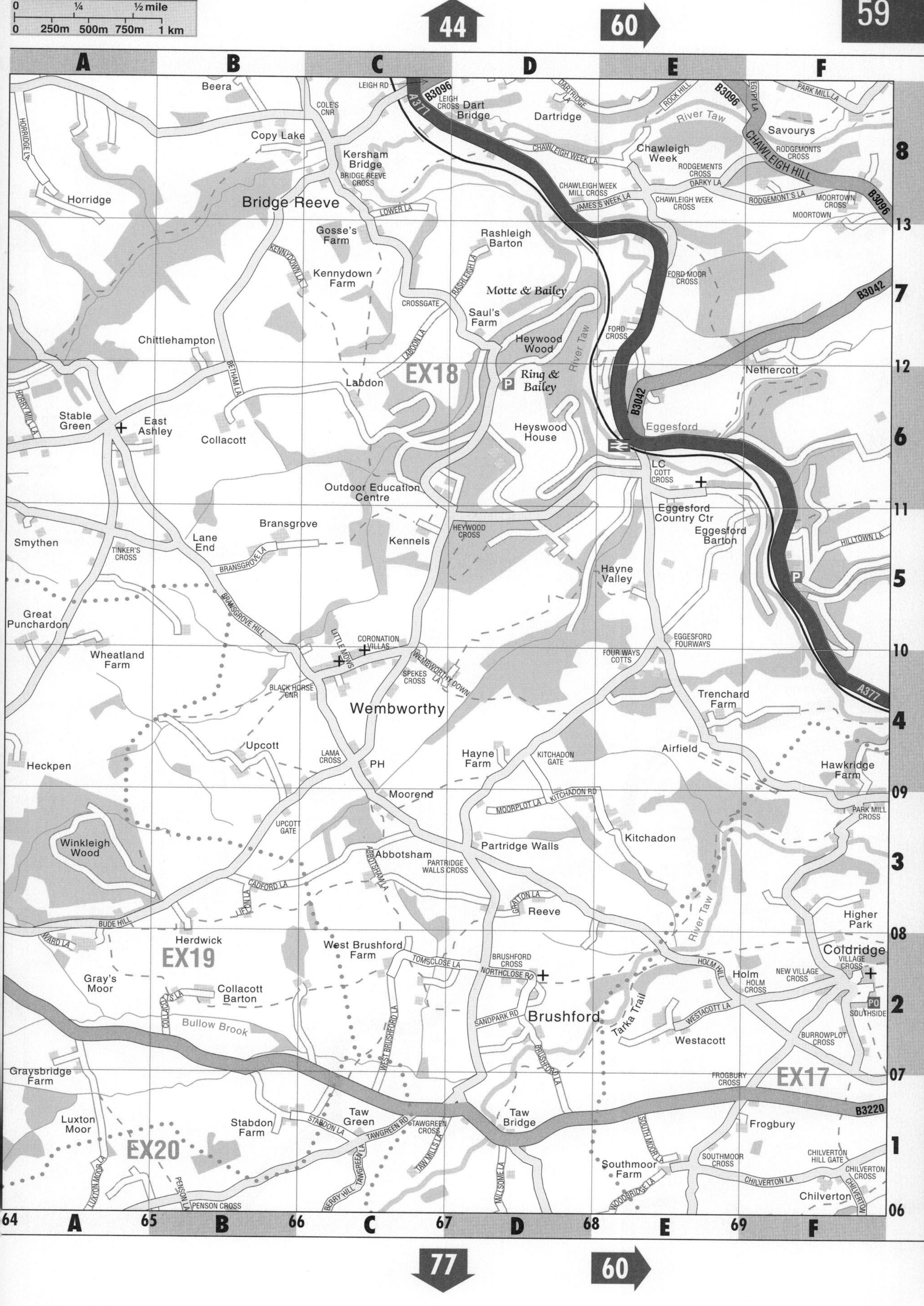

59
45

Scale: 1¾ inches to 1 mile

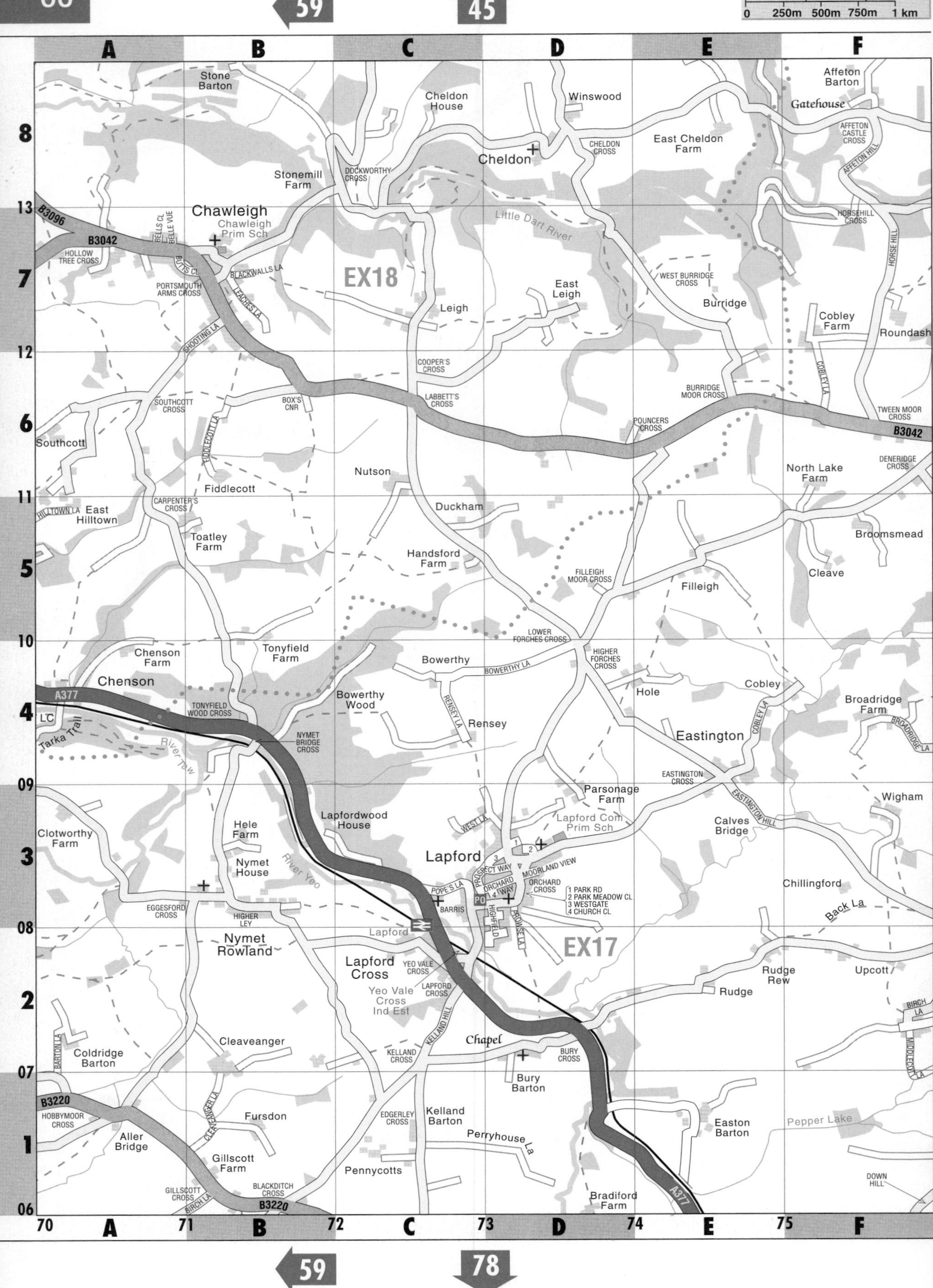

59
78

Scale: 1¾ inches to 1 mile

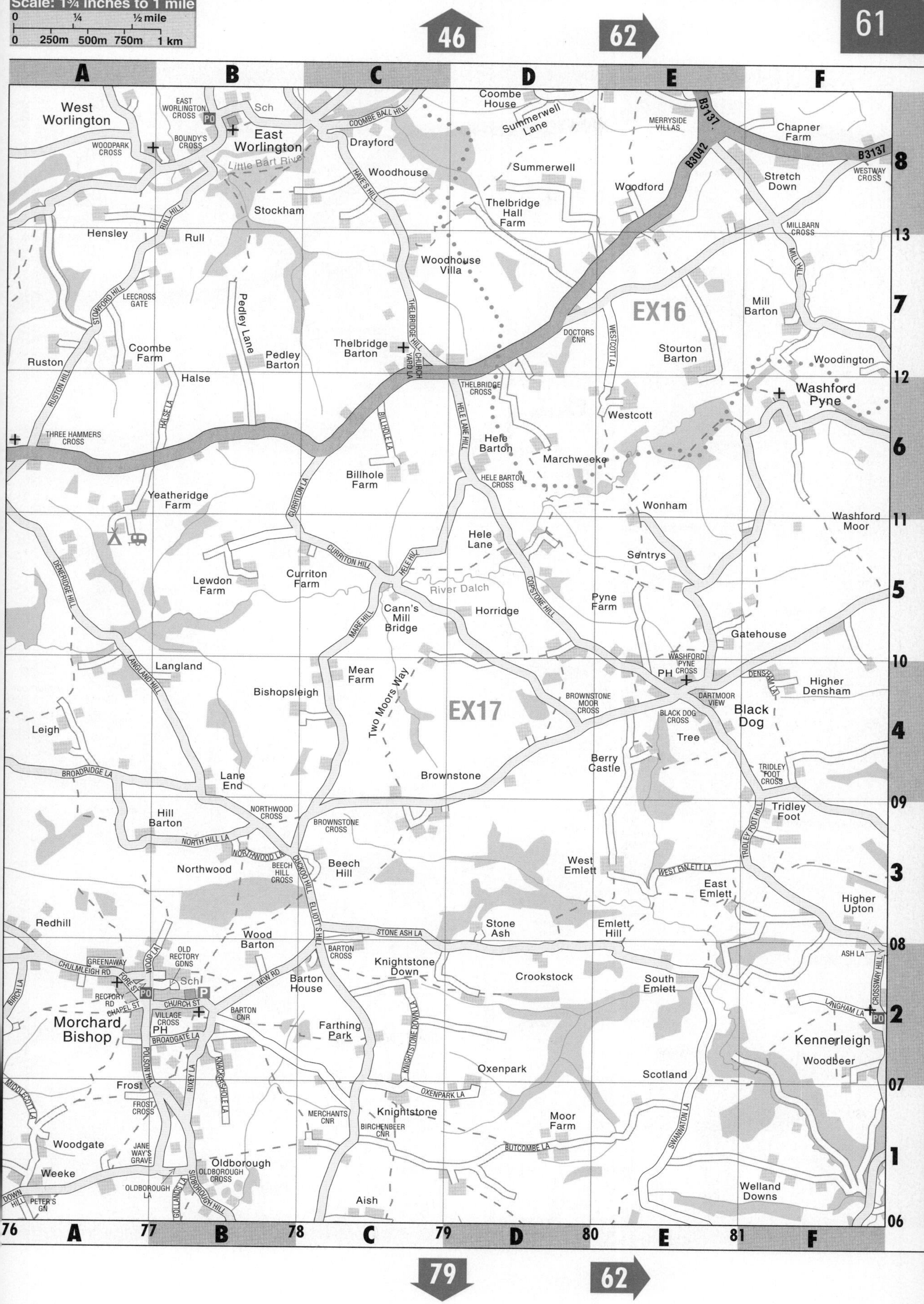

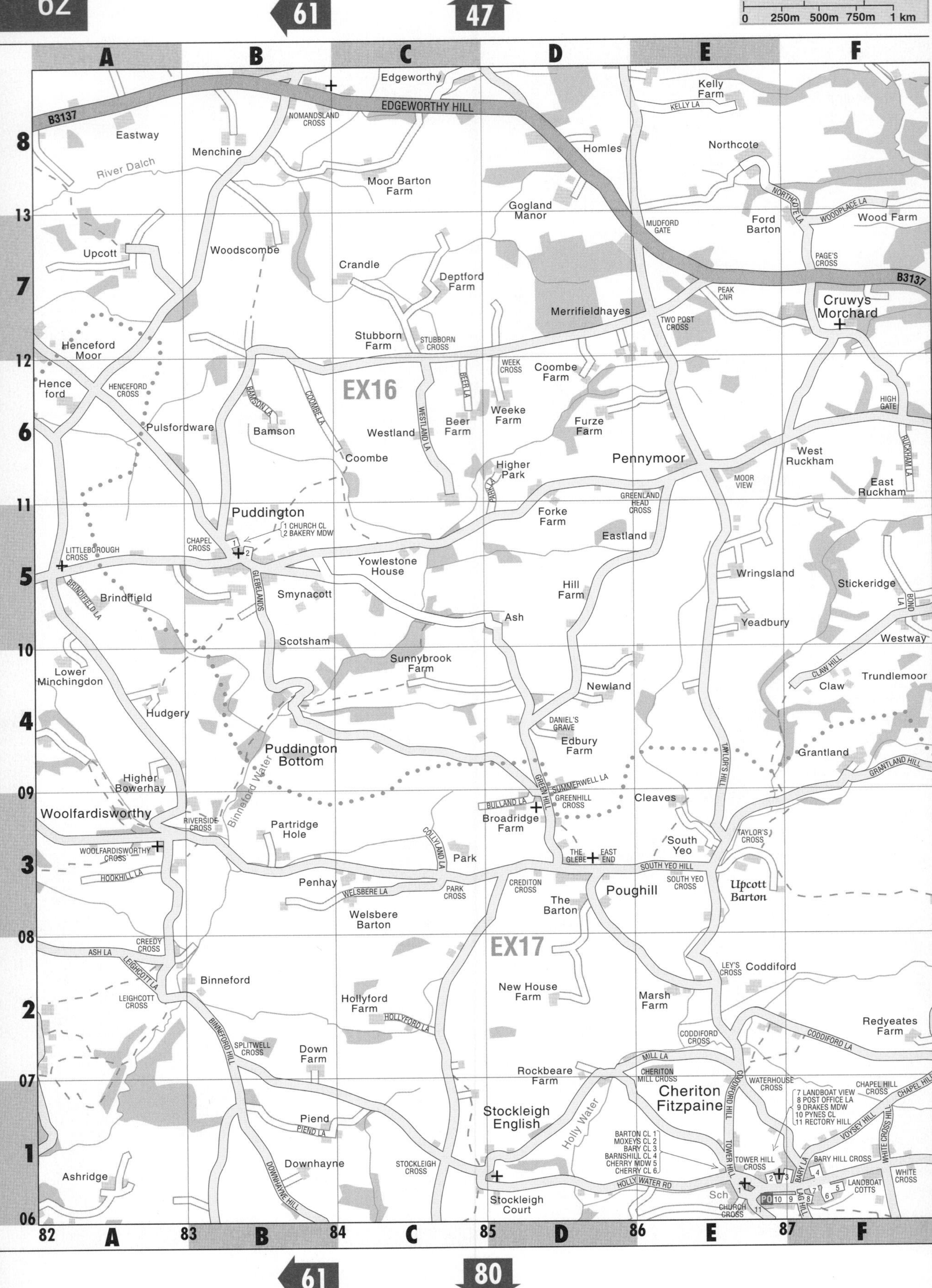
61
47
Scale: 1¾ inches to 1 mile
0 ¼ ½ mile
0 250m 500m 750m 1 km
A
B
C
D
E
F
8
13
7
12
6
11
5
10
4
09
3
08
2
07
1
06
B3137
EDGEWORTHY HILL
Edgeworthy
Kelly Farm
KELLY LA
NOMANDSLAND CROSS
Eastway
Menchine
Homles
Northcote
River Dalch
Moor Barton Farm
Gogland Manor
NORTHCOTE LA
WOODPLACE LA
Wood Farm
MUDFORD GATE
Ford Barton
Upcott
Woodscombe
Crandle
PAGE'S CROSS
Deptford Farm
B3137
PEAK CNR
Cruwys Morchard
Merrifieldhayes
TWO POST CROSS
Henceford Moor
Stubborn Farm
STUBBORN CROSS
WEEK CROSS
Coombe Farm
Hence ford
HENCEFORD CROSS
EX16
BAMSON LA
COOMBE LA
BEER LA
HIGH GATE
WESTLAND LA
Weeke Farm
Beer Farm
Furze Farm
Pulsfordware
Bamson
Westland
RUCKHAM LA
West Ruckham
Coombe
Pennymoor
Higher Park
MOOR VIEW
East Ruckham
PARK LA
GREENLAND HEAD CROSS
Puddington
Forke Farm
1 CHURCH CL
2 BAKERY MDW
CHAPEL CROSS
Eastland
LITTLEBOROUGH CROSS
Yowlestone House
Wringsland
Stickeridge
BRINDIFIELD LA
Hill Farm
Brindifield
Smynacott
BOND LA
GLEBELANDS
Ash
Yeadbury
Westway
Scotsham
Lower Minchingdon
Sunnybrook Farm
CLAW HILL
Trundlemoor
Newland
Claw
Hudgery
DANIEL'S GRAVE
Edbury Farm
Puddington Bottom
Grantland
TAYLOR'S HILL
GRANTLAND HILL
Higher Bowerhay
Binneford Water
SUMMERWELL LA
GREEN HILL
BULLAND LA
GREENHILL CROSS
Cleaves
Woolfardisworthy
RIVERSIDE CROSS
Partridge Hole
Broadridge Farm
South Yeo
TAYLOR'S CROSS
COLLYLAND LA
WOOLFARDISWORTHY CROSS
Park
THE GLEBE
EAST END
SOUTH YEO HILL
HOOKHILL LA
Penhay
CREDITON CROSS
SOUTH YEO CROSS
Upcott Barton
PARK CROSS
Poughill
WELSBERE LA
The Barton
Welsbere Barton
CREEDY CROSS
ASH LA
EX17
LEIGHCOTT LA
LEY'S CROSS
Coddiford
Binneford
New House Farm
LEIGHCOTT CROSS
Hollyford Farm
Marsh Farm
HOLLYFORD LA
Redyeates Farm
BINNEFORD HILL
CODDIFORD CROSS
CODDIFORD LA
SPLITWELL CROSS
Down Farm
MILL LA
Rockbeare Farm
CHERITON MILL CROSS
WATERHOUSE CROSS
CHAPEL HILL CROSS
CHAPEL HILL
Cheriton Fitzpaine
7 LANDBOAT VIEW
8 POST OFFICE LA
9 DRAKES MDW
10 PYNES CL
11 RECTORY HILL
CODDIFORD HILL
Stockleigh English
Holly Water
Piend
PIEND LA
VOYSEY HILL
WHITE CROSS HILL
BARTON CL 1
MOXEYS CL 2
BARY CL 3
BARNSHILL CL 4
CHERRY MDW 5
CHERRY CL 6
TOWER HILL
TOWER HILL CROSS
BARY LA
BARY HILL CROSS
Downhayne
Ashridge
STOCKLEIGH CROSS
WHITE CROSS
DOWNHAYNE HILL
HOLLY WATER RD
Sch
LANDBOAT COTTS
PO
LAG HILL
CHURCH CROSS
Stockleigh Court
82
A
83
B
84
C
85
D
86
E
87
F
61
80

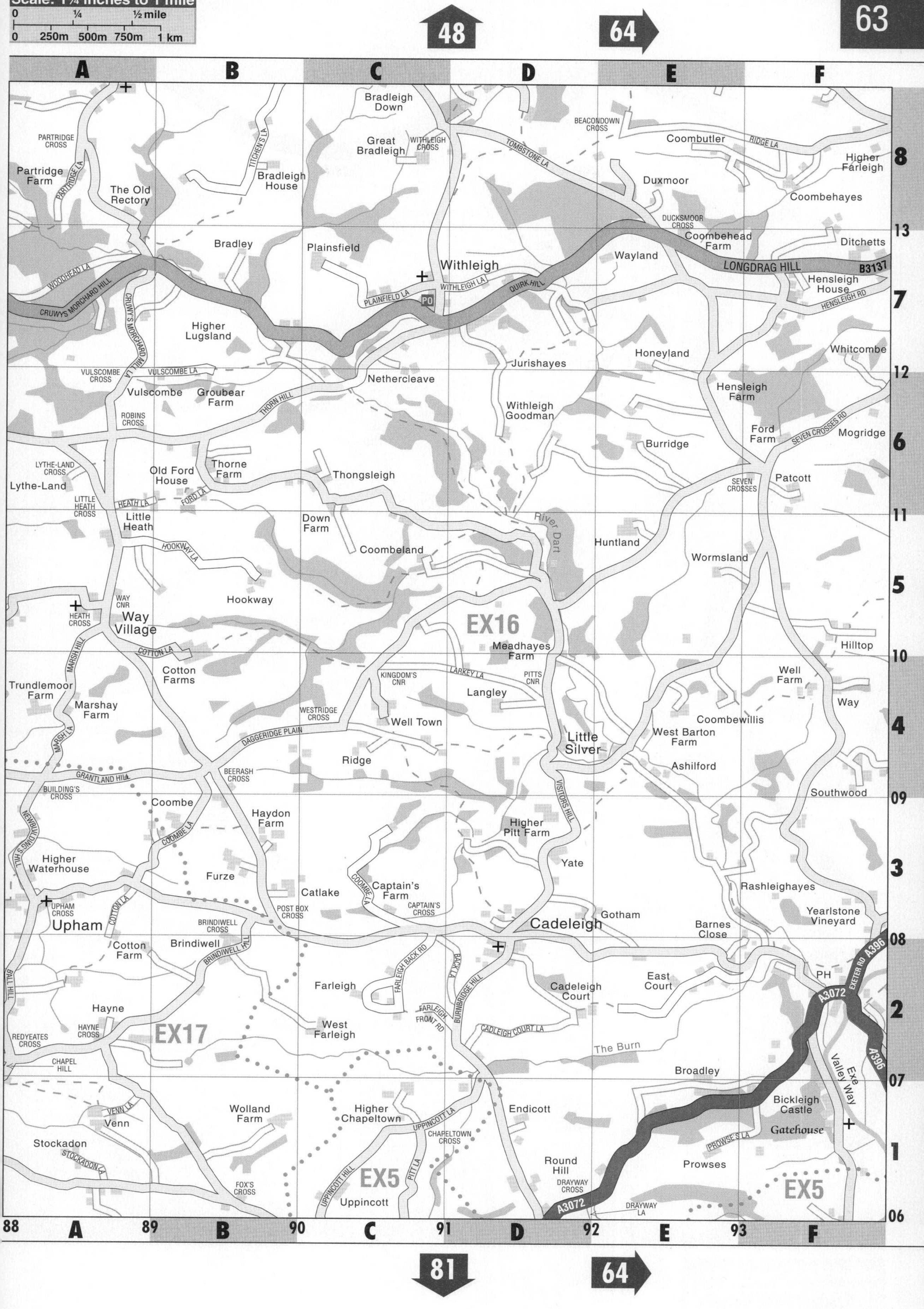
Scale: 1¾ inches to 1 mile
0 ¼ ½ mile
0 250m 500m 750m 1 km
48
64
A B C D E F
8
13
7
12
6
11
5
10
4
09
3
08
2
07
1
06
88 89 90 91 92 93
81
64
Bradleigh Down
Great Bradleigh
WITHLEIGH CROSS
BEACONDOWN CROSS
Coombutler
RIDGE LA
Higher Farleigh
PARTRIDGE CROSS
Partridge Farm
PARTRIDGE LA
The Old Rectory
TITCHEN'S LA
Bradleigh House
TOMBSTONE LA
Duxmoor
Coombehayes
DUCKSMOOR CROSS
Coombehead Farm
Ditchetts
Bradley
Plainsfield
Withleigh
Wayland
LONGDRAG HILL
B3137
WOODHEAD LA
CRUWYS MORCHARD HILL
CRUWY'S MORCHARD MILL LA
PLAINFIELD LA
WITHLEIGH LA
QUIRK HILL
PO
Hensleigh House
HENSLEIGH RD
Higher Lugsland
Honeyland
Whitcombe
Jurishayes
VULSCOMBE CROSS
VULSCOMBE LA
Nethercleave
Vulscombe
Groubear Farm
Hensleigh Farm
THORN HILL
Withleigh Goodman
ROBINS CROSS
Ford Farm
Mogridge
SEVEN CROSSES RD
Burridge
LYTHE-LAND CROSS
Lythe-Land
Old Ford House
Thorne Farm
Thongsleigh
SEVEN CROSSES
Patcott
LITTLE HEATH CROSS
HEATH LA
FORD LA
Little Heath
Down Farm
River Dart
Huntland
HOOKWAY LA
Coombeland
Wormsland
WAY CNR
HEATH CROSS
Way Village
Hookway
EX16
Meadhayes Farm
Hilltop
COTTON LA
MARSH HILL
KINGDOM'S CNR
LARKEY LA
PITTS CNR
Well Farm
Trundlemoor Farm
Cotton Farms
Langley
Way
Marshay Farm
WESTRIDGE CROSS
Well Town
Coombewillis
MARSH LA
DAGGERIDGE PLAIN
Little Silver
West Barton Farm
Ridge
Ashilford
GRANTLAND HILL
BEERASH CROSS
BUILDING'S CROSS
Southwood
Coombe
Haydon Farm
VISITORS HILL
NEWBUILDING'S HILL
Higher Pitt Farm
COOMBE LA
Higher Waterhouse
Furze
Yate
Rashleighayes
Captain's Farm
COOMBE LA
Catlake
Yearlstone Vineyard
UPHAM CROSS
Upham
COTTON LA
POST BOX CROSS
CAPTAIN'S CROSS
Gotham
BRINDIWELL CROSS
Cadeleigh
Barnes Close
Brindiwell
Cotton Farm
BRINDIWELL HILL
FARLEIGH BACK RD
BACK LA
A396
EXETER RD
BALL HILL
Farleigh
East Court
PH
Cadeleigh Court
A3072
BURNBRIDGE HILL
FARLEIGH FRONT RD
Hayne
HAYNE CROSS
West Farleigh
CADLEIGH COURT LA
REDYEATES CROSS
EX17
The Burn
A396
CHAPEL HILL
Broadley
Exe Valley Way
VENN LA
Venn
Wolland Farm
Higher Chapeltown
Endicott
Bickleigh Castle
Gatehouse
UPPINCOTT LA
CHAPELTOWN CROSS
PROWSE'S LA
Stockadon
STOCKADON LA
Round Hill
Prowses
UPPINCOTT HILL
EX5
PITT LA
FOX'S CROSS
DRAYWAY CROSS
EX5
Uppincott
A3072
DRAYWAY LA

63

49

D7
1 LIME TREE MEAD
2 RENNIE RD
3 WESLEY CL
4 FRANCIS CRES
5 CHILCOTT CL
6 MARINA WAY
7 CHICHESTER PL
8 COLERIDGE RD
9 PUGSLEY RD
10 STARKEY CL
11 TIDCOMBE CL
12 ST LAWRENCE CL
13 RAYER RD
14 POLWHELE RD
15 WESTCOTT RD
16 RYDER CL
17 RIPPON CL

Scale: 1¾ inches to 1 mile

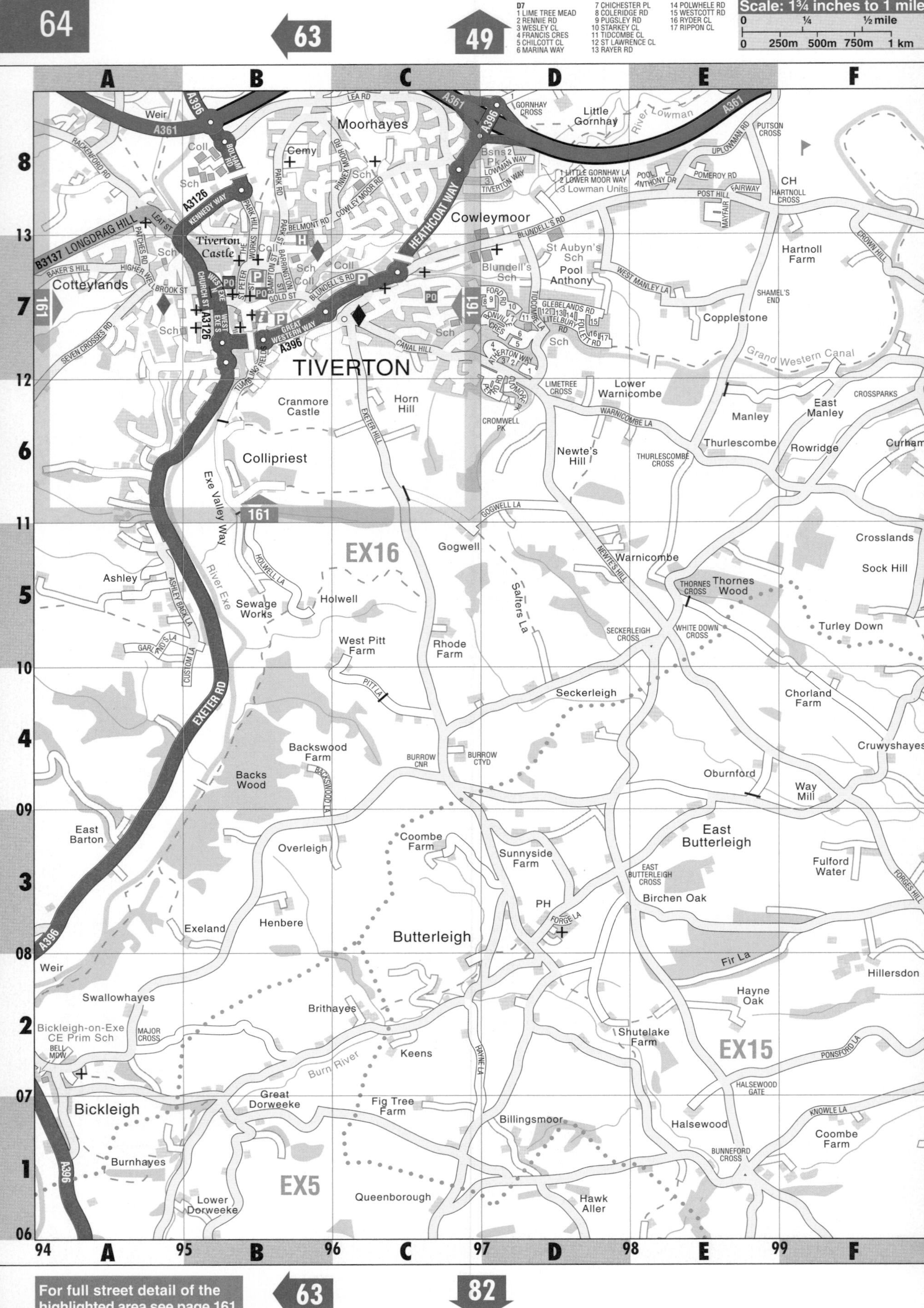

94 95 96 97 98 99

For full street detail of the highlighted area see page 161.

63

82

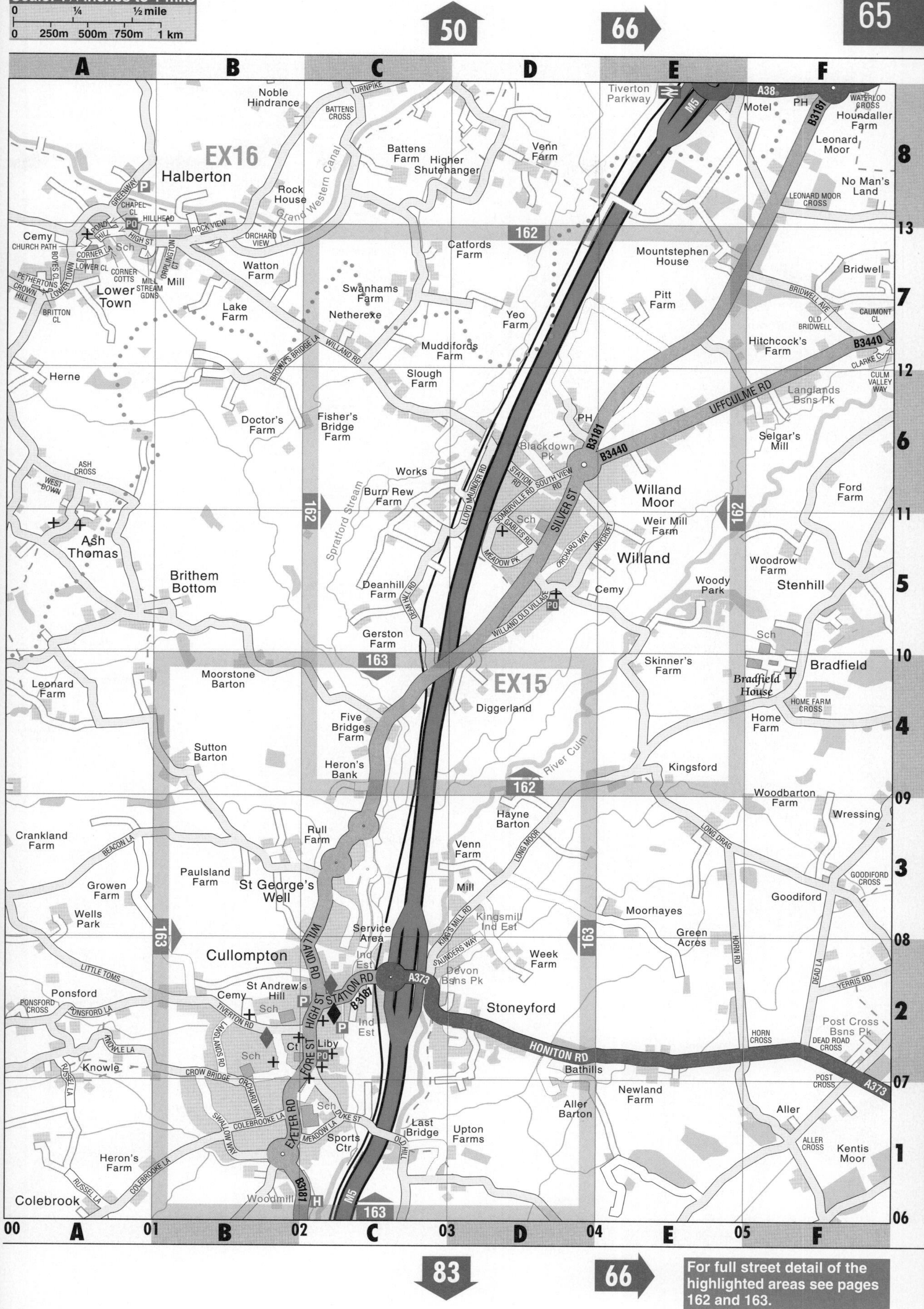
Scale: 1¾ inches to 1 mile
0 ¼ ½ mile
0 250m 500m 750m 1 km
50
66
A B C D E F
EX16
Halberton
Noble Hindrance
Battens Cross
Turnpike
Battens Farm
Higher Shutehanger
Venn Farm
Tiverton Parkway
M5
A38
Motel
PH
B3181
Waterloo Cross
Houndaller Farm
Leonard Moor
No Man's Land
Leonard Moor Cross
Rock House
Grand Western Canal
Greenway
Chapel Cl
Hillhead
Rock View
Orchard View
Pond Hill
High St
Cemy
Church Path
Corner La
Sch
Boyes Cl
Lower Town
Lower Cl
Corner Cotts
Mill Stream Gdns
Orplington Ct
Pethertons
Crown Hill
Britton Cl
Watton Farm
Mill
Lower Town
Lake Farm
Catfords Farm
Swanhams Farm
Netherexe
Mountstephen House
Pitt Farm
Bridwell
Bridwell Ave
Old Bridwell
Caumont Cl
Yeo Farm
Muddifords Farm
Hitchcock's Farm
B3440
Clarke Cl
Culm Valley Way
Herne
Brown's Bridge La
Willand Rd
Slough Farm
Langlands Bsns Pk
Uffculme Rd
Doctor's Farm
Fisher's Bridge Farm
PH
Blackdown Pk
Selgar's Mill
Ash Cross
West Down
Works
Lloyd Maunder Rd
Station Rd
South View Rd
Somerville Rd
Burn Rew Farm
Silver St
Willand Moor
Ford Farm
Spratford Stream
Sch
Gables Rd
Meadow Pk
Orchard Way
Jaycroft
Weir Mill Farm
Ash Thomas
Brithem Bottom
Willand
Woodrow Farm
Stenhill
Woody Park
Deanhill Farm
Dean Hill Rd
Cemy
Willand Old Village
PO
Gerston Farm
Sch
Leonard Farm
Moorstone Barton
EX15
Skinner's Farm
Bradfield
Bradfield House
Home Farm Cross
Home Farm
Diggerland
Five Bridges Farm
Sutton Barton
Heron's Bank
River Culm
Kingsford
Woodbarton Farm
Wressing
Hayne Barton
Crankland Farm
Beacon La
Rull Farm
Long Drag
Venn Farm
Long Moor
Paulsland Farm
Growen Farm
St George's Well
Mill
Goodiford Cross
Goodiford
Wells Park
Moorhayes
Kingsmill Ind Est
King's Mill Rd
Saunders Way
Service Area
Green Acres
Horn Rd
Willand Rd
Cullompton
Ind Est
Week Farm
Dead La
Little Toms
A373
Devon Bsns Pk
Yerris Rd
Ponsford
St Andrew's Hill
Station Rd
B3187
Cemy
Ponsford Cross
Ponsford La
Tiverton Rd
Sch
High St
Stoneyford
Post Cross Bsns Pk
Langlands Rd
Ind Est
Horn Cross
Dead Road Cross
Knowle La
Ct
Liby
Fore St
PO
Honiton Rd
Knowle
Crow Bridge
Orchard Way
Bathills
Post Cross
Newland Farm
Aller Barton
Russel La
Swallow Way
Colebrooke La
Exeter Rd
Sch
Duke St
Aller
Meadow La
Last Bridge
Upton Farms
Sports Ctr
Old Hill
Aller Cross
Kentis Moor
Heron's Farm
Colebrooke La
Russel La
Woodmill
B3181
H
Colebrook
162
163
8 13 7 12 6 11 5 10 4 09 3 08 2 07 1 06
00 01 02 03 04 05
83
66
For full street detail of the highlighted areas see pages 162 and 163.

65
51

Scale: 1¾ inches to 1 mile

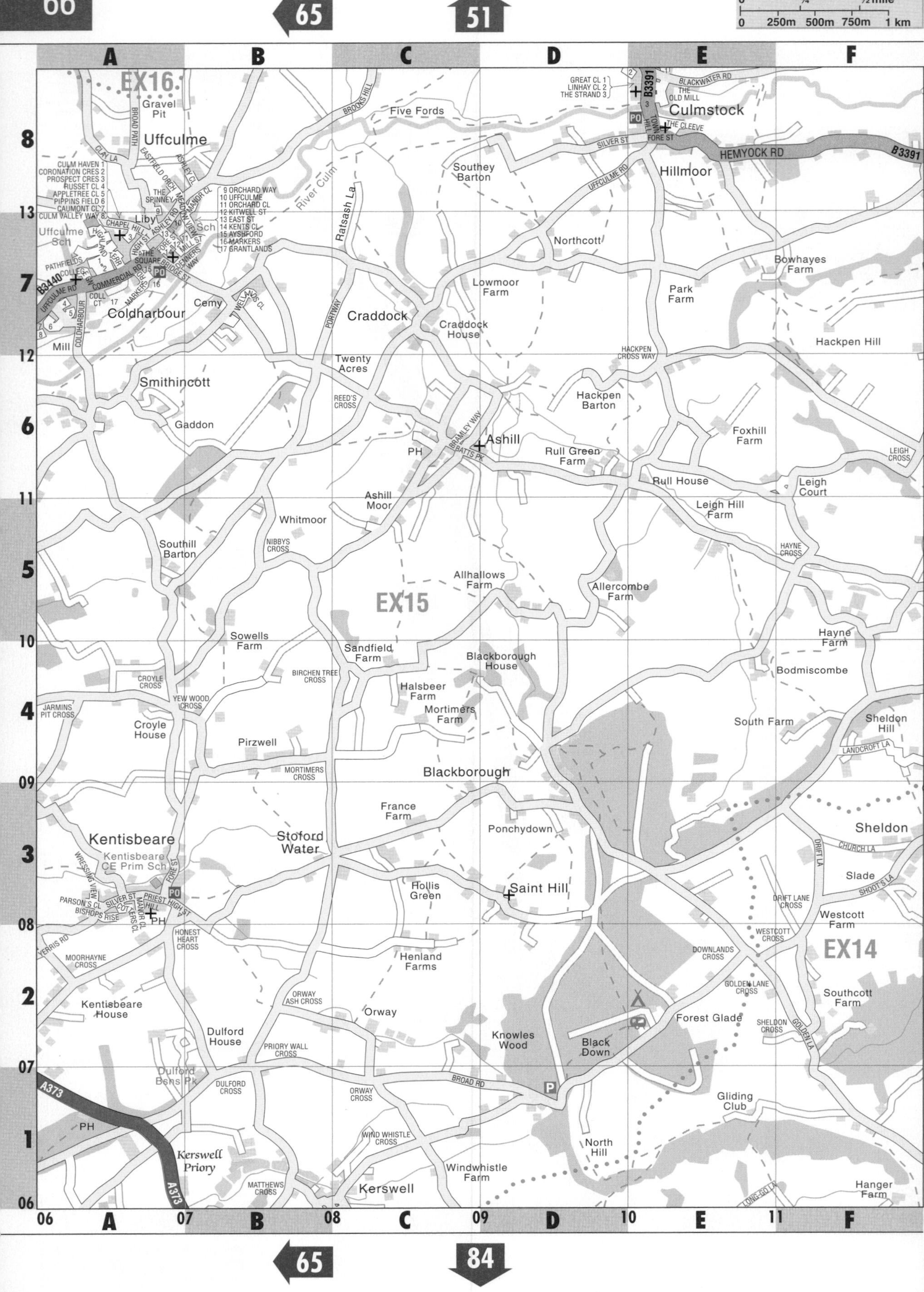

65
84

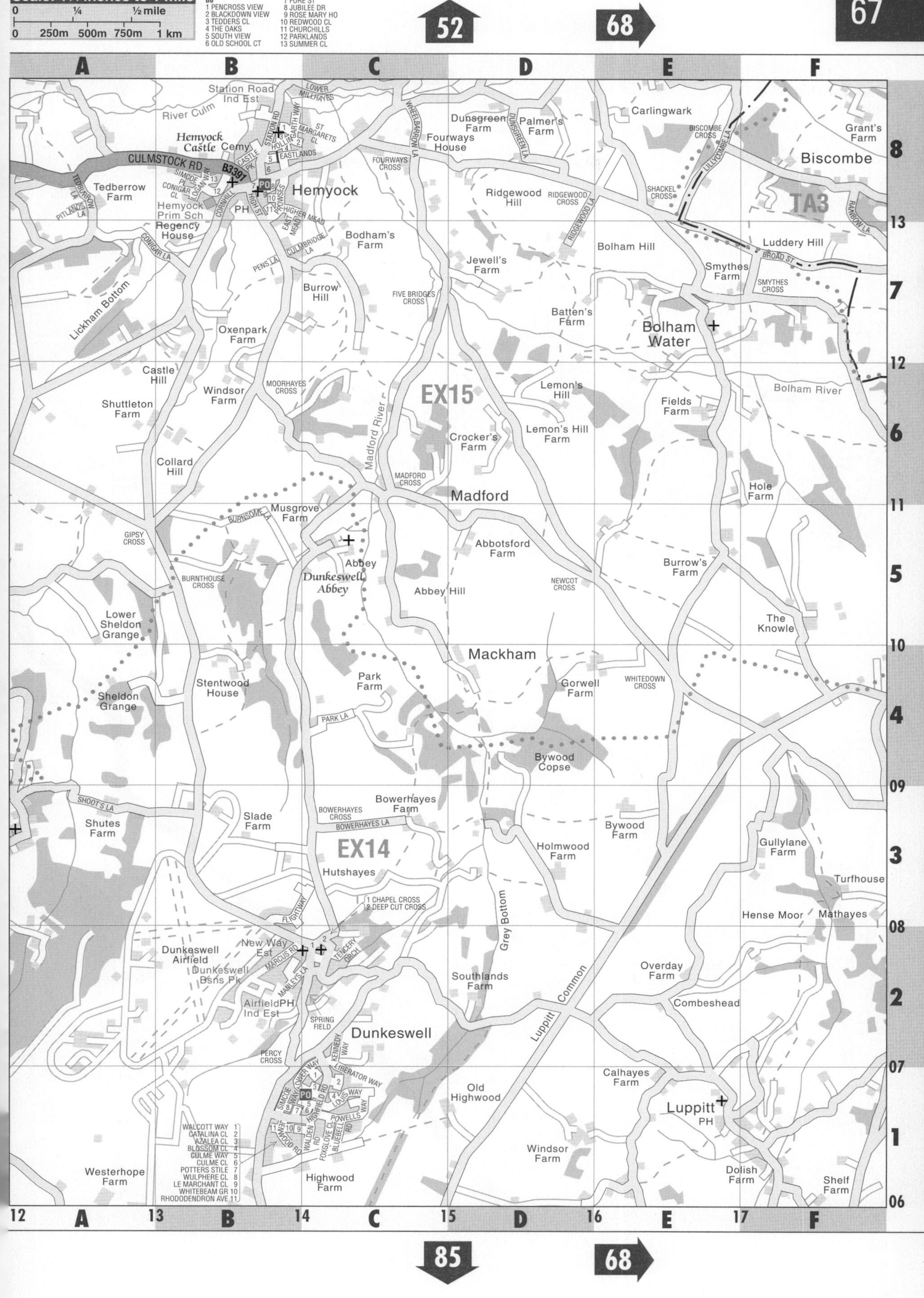

Scale: 1¾ inches to 1 mile
0 ¼ ½ mile
0 250m 500m 750m 1 km
B8
1 PENCROSS VIEW
2 BLACKDOWN VIEW
3 TEDDERS CL
4 THE OAKS
5 SOUTH VIEW
6 OLD SCHOOL CT
7 FORE ST
8 JUBILEE DR
9 ROSE MARY HO
10 REDWOOD CL
11 CHURCHILLS
12 PARKLANDS
13 SUMMER CL
52
68
A B C D E F
Station Road Ind Est
LOWER MILLHAYES
River Culm
Hemyock Castle
Cemy
STATION RD
GARTH WAY
ST MARGARETS CL
HOLLIS
EASTLANDS
CASTLE PK
WHEELBARROW LA
Dunsgreen Farm
DUNSGREEN LA
Palmer's Farm
Fourways House
FOURWAYS CROSS
Carlingwark
BISCOMBE CROSS
LILLYCOMBE LA
Grant's Farm
Biscombe
8
CULMSTOCK RD
B3391
TEDBURROW LA
Tedberrow Farm
SIMCOE PL
LOGAN WAY
CONIGAR CL
PO
POWSES
Hemyock
Ridgewood Hill
RIDGEWOOD CROSS
RIDGEWOOD LA
SHACKEL CROSS
TA3
RAINBOW LA
13
PITLANDS LA
Hemyock Prim Sch
PH
CORNHILL
HIGH ST
HIGHER MEAD
EAST MEAD
Regency House
CONIGAR LA
CULMBRIDGE LA
PENS LA
Bodham's Farm
Jewell's Farm
Bolham Hill
Luddery Hill
BROAD ST
Smythes Farm
SMYTHES CROSS
Lickham Bottom
Burrow Hill
FIVE BRIDGES CROSS
7
Batten's Farm
Bolham Water
Oxenpark Farm
12
Castle Hill
Windsor Farm
MOORHAYES CROSS
EX15
Lemon's Hill
Fields Farm
Bolham River
Shuttleton Farm
Madford River
Crocker's Farm
Lemon's Hill Farm
6
Collard Hill
MADFORD CROSS
Madford
Hole Farm
11
Musgrove Farm
BURNSOME LA
GIPSY CROSS
Abbotsford Farm
Burrow's Farm
Abbey
Dunkeswell Abbey
BURNTHOUSE CROSS
NEWCOT CROSS
Abbey Hill
5
Lower Sheldon Grange
The Knowle
10
Mackham
Stentwood House
Park Farm
Gorwell Farm
WHITEDOWN CROSS
Sheldon Grange
PARK LA
4
Bywood Copse
09
SHOOT'S LA
Shutes Farm
Slade Farm
BOWERHAYES CROSS
Bowerhayes Farm
BOWERHAYES LA
Bywood Farm
Holmwood Farm
Gullylane Farm
EX14
3
Hutshayes
Turfhouse
FLIGHTWAY
1 CHAPEL CROSS
2 DEEP CUT CROSS
Hense Moor
Mathayes
08
Grey Bottom
Dunkeswell Airfield
New Way Est
MARCUS RD
TENCERY ORCH
Dunkeswell Bsns Pk
MANLEYS LA
Overday Farm
Southlands Farm
Luppitt Common
Airfield Ind Est
PH
2
Combeshead
SPRING FIELD
Dunkeswell
KENNEDY WAY
PERCY CROSS
07
LIBERATOR WAY
SIMCOE WAY
SILVER WAY
HIGHFIELD RD
LOUIS WAY
Old Highwood
Calhayes Farm
Luppitt
PH
POWELLS RD
WALCOTT WAY 1
CATALINA CL 2
AZALEA CL 3
BLOSSOM CL 4
CULME WAY 5
CULME CL 6
POTTERS STILE 7
WULPHERE CL 8
LE MARCHANT CL 9
WHITEBEAM GR 10
RHODODENDRON AVE 11
JUNIPER RD
WALDEN RD
FOXGLOVE CL
BLUEBELL RD
Windsor Farm
1
Westerhope Farm
Highwood Farm
Dolish Farm
Shelf Farm
06
12 A 13 B 14 C 15 D 16 E 17 F
85
68

67

Scale: 1¾ inches to 1 mile
0 ¼ ½ mile
0 250m 500m 750m 1 km

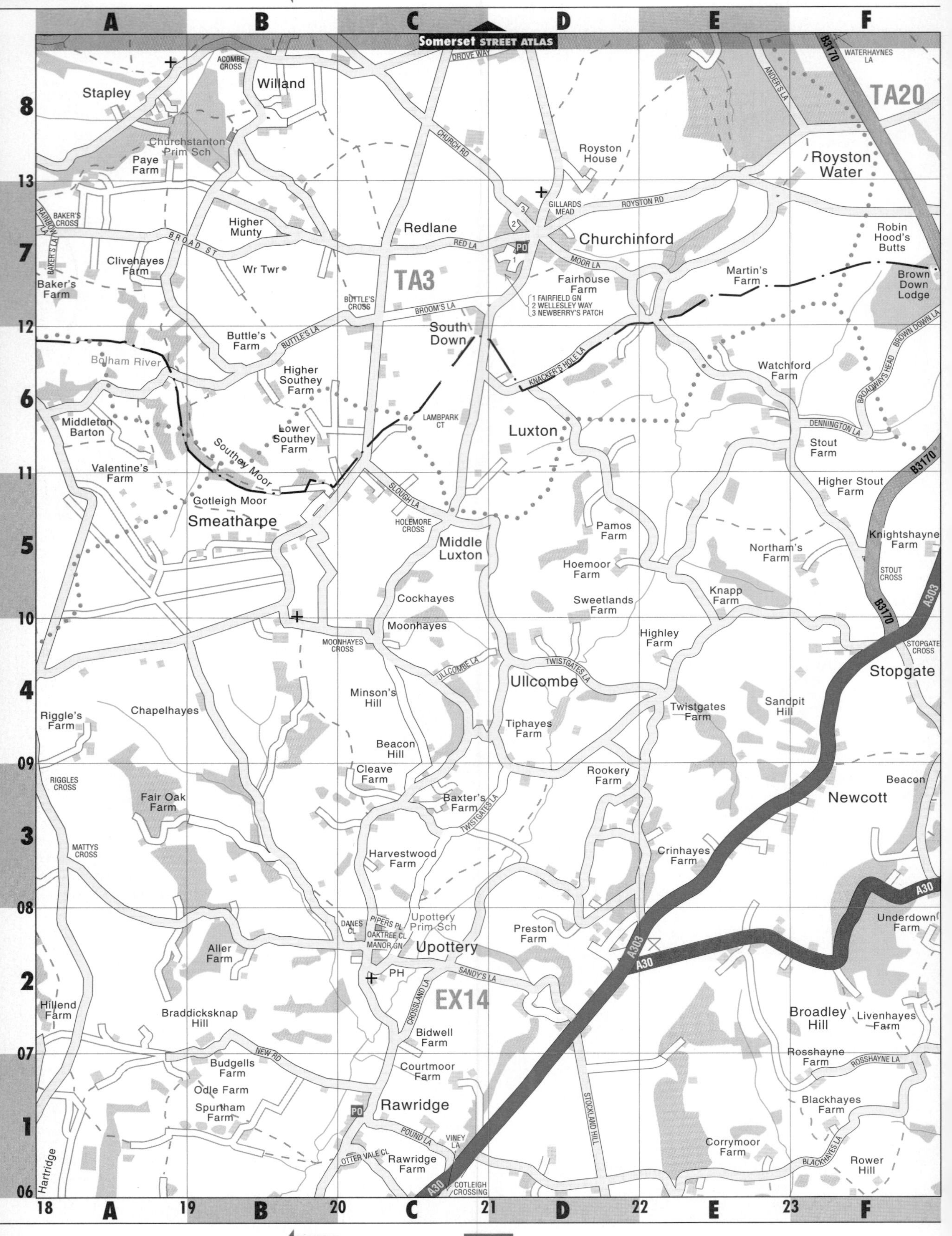

67
86

Scale: 1¾ inches to 1 mile
0 ¼ ½ mile
0 250m 500m 750m 1 km

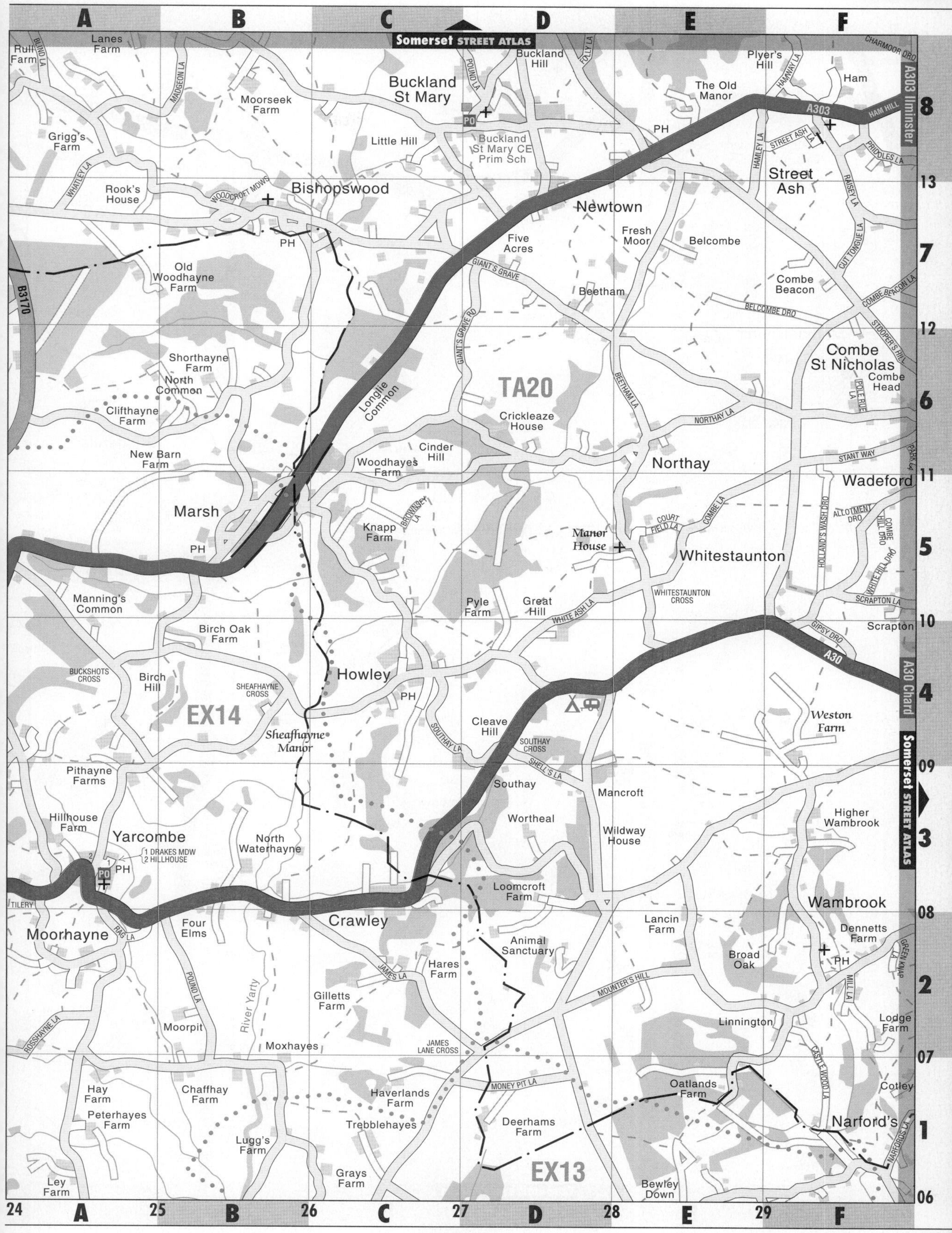

Scale: 1¾ inches to 1 mile
0 ¼ ½ mile
0 250m 500m 750m 1 km

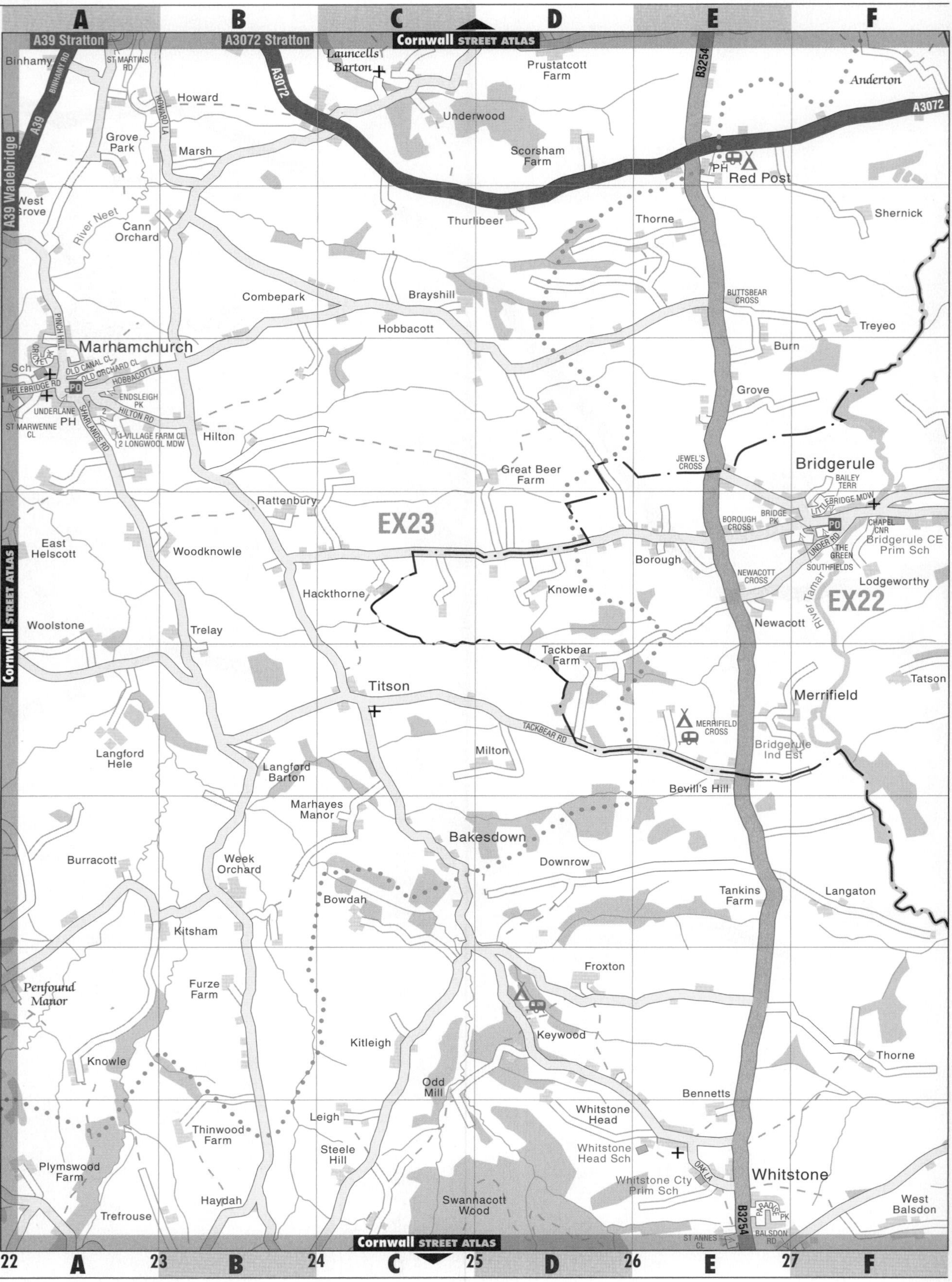

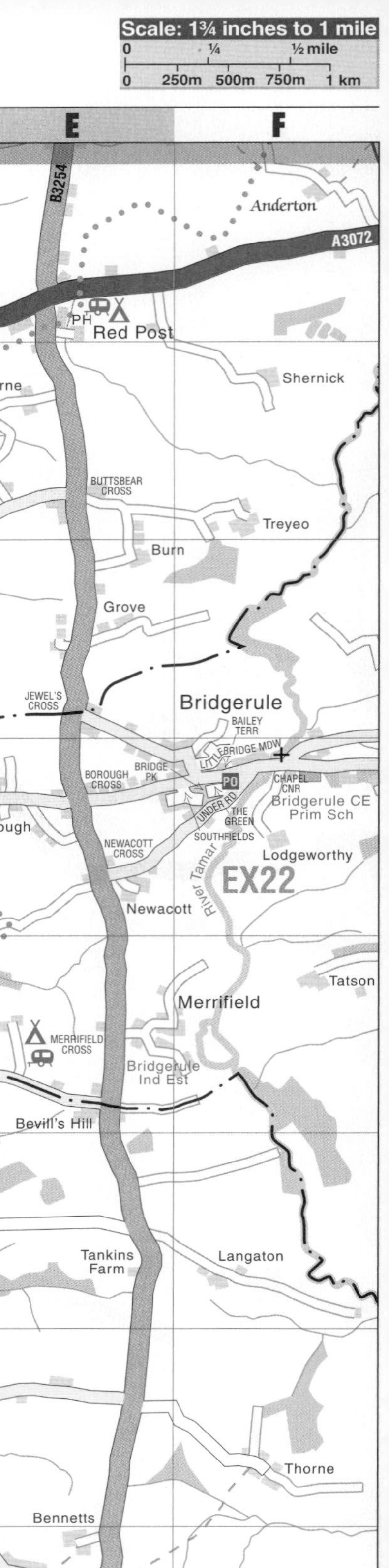

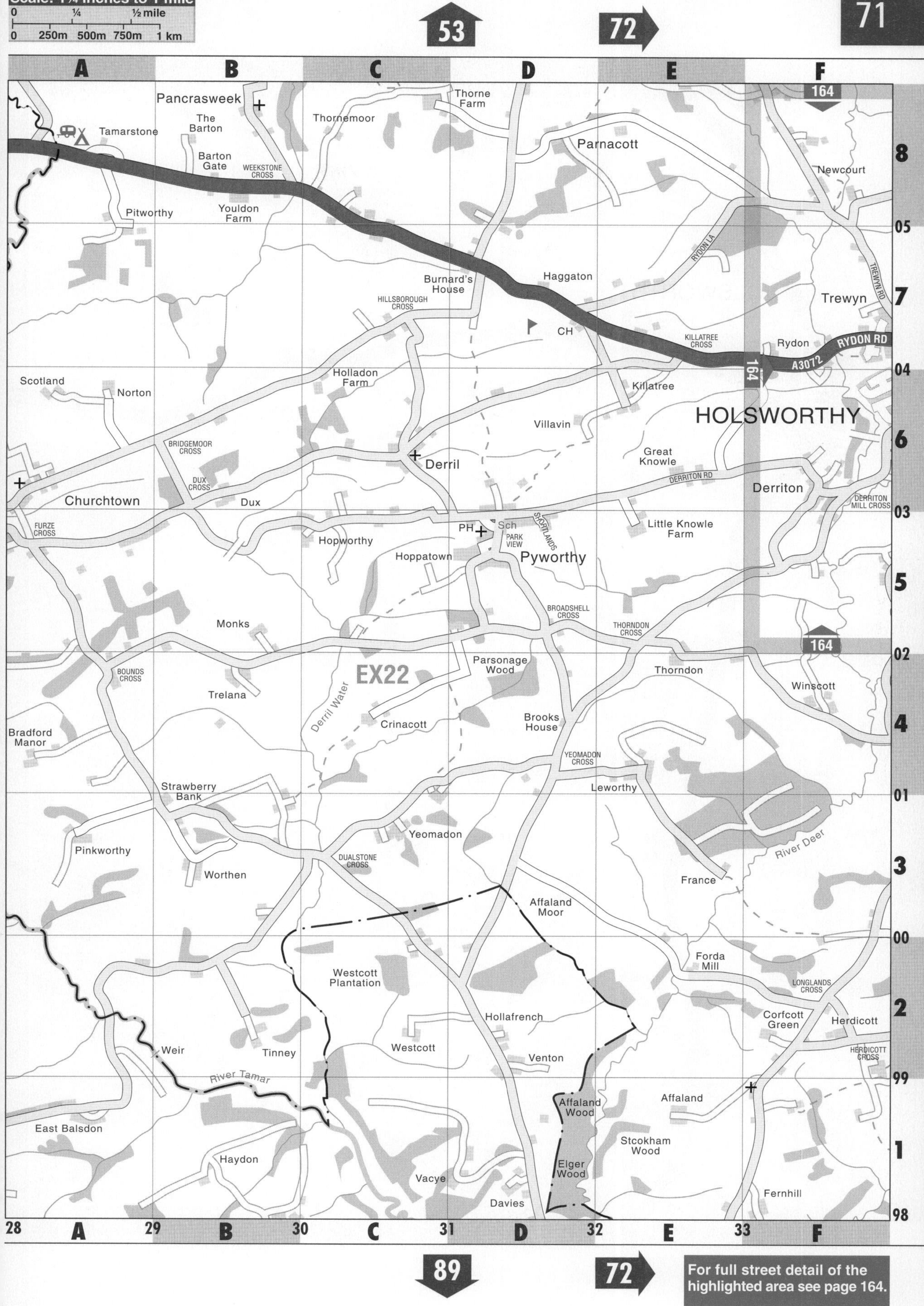
Scale: 1¾ inches to 1 mile
0 ¼ ½ mile
0 250m 500m 750m 1 km
53
72
164
Pancrasweek
The Barton
Tamarstone
Barton Gate
WEEKSTONE CROSS
Thornemoor
Thorne Farm
Parnacott
Newcourt
Pitworthy
Youldon Farm
RYDON LA
TREWYN RD
Trewyn
Haggaton
Burnard's House
HILLSBOROUGH CROSS
CH
KILLATREE CROSS
Rydon
RYDON RD
A3072
Killatree
Scotland
Norton
Holladon Farm
HOLSWORTHY
Villavin
BRIDGEMOOR CROSS
Derril
Great Knowle
DUX CROSS
DERRITON RD
Derriton
Churchtown
Dux
DERRITON MILL CROSS
FURZE CROSS
Hopworthy
PH
Sch
SHORTLANDS
PARK VIEW
Little Knowle Farm
Hoppatown
Pyworthy
Monks
BROADSHELL CROSS
THORNDON CROSS
Parsonage Wood
EX22
Thorndon
Winscott
BOUNDS CROSS
Trelana
Derril Water
Crinacott
Brooks House
Bradford Manor
YEOMADON CROSS
Leworthy
Strawberry Bank
Pinkworthy
Yeomadon
River Deer
DUALSTONE CROSS
Worthen
France
Affaland Moor
Forda Mill
Westcott Plantation
LONGLANDS CROSS
Corfcott Green
Herdicott
Hollafrench
Weir
Tinney
Westcott
Venton
HERDICOTT CROSS
River Tamar
Affaland Wood
Affaland
East Balsdon
Stcokham Wood
Haydon
Elger Wood
Vacye
Davies
Fernhill
8
05
7
04
6
03
5
02
4
01
3
00
2
99
1
98
A B C D E F
28 29 30 31 32 33
89
72
For full street detail of the highlighted area see page 164.

For full street detail of the highlighted area see page 164.

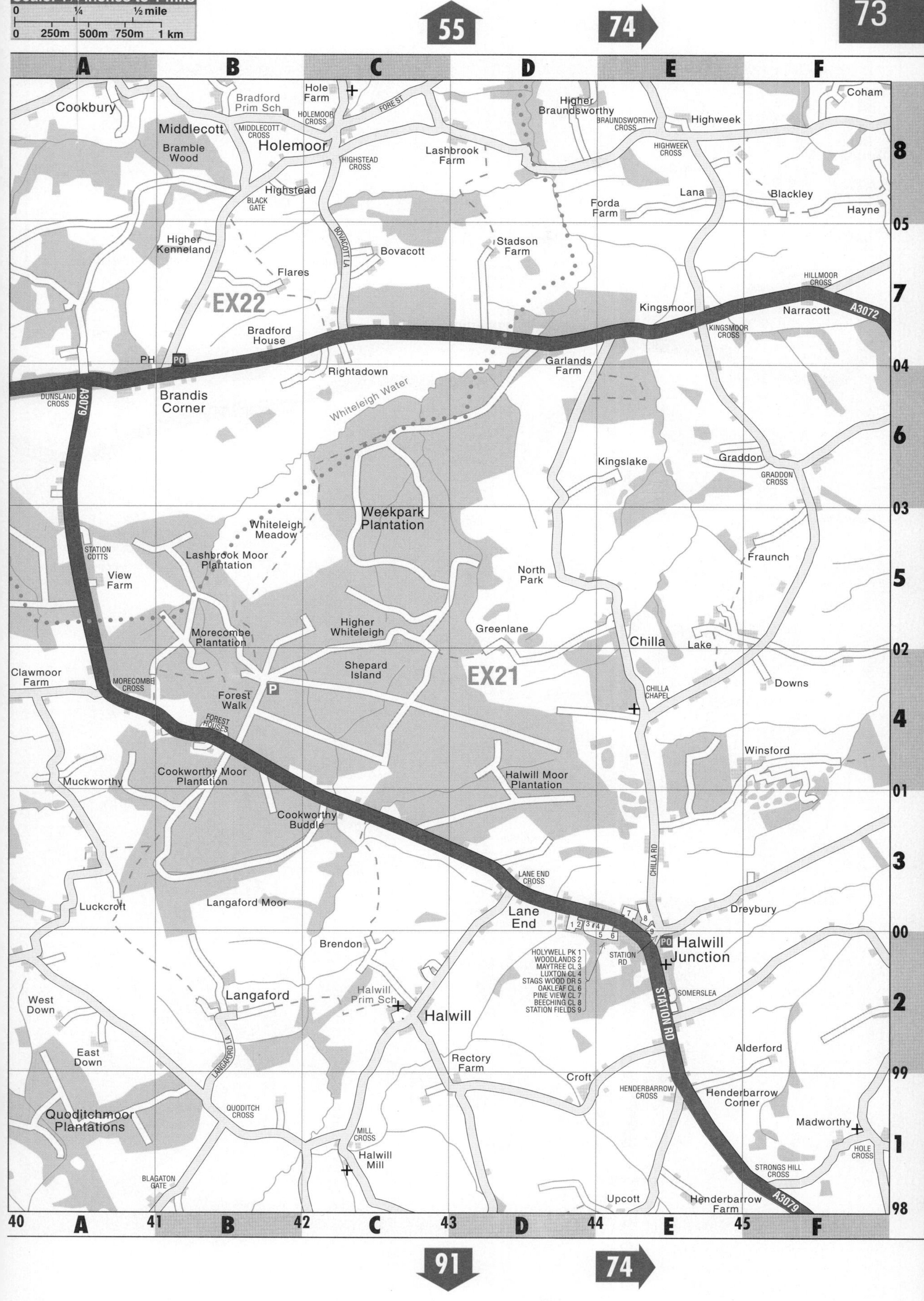
Scale: 1¾ inches to 1 mile
0
¼
½ mile
0
250m
500m
750m
1 km
55
74
73
A
B
C
D
E
F
Cookbury
Bradford Prim Sch
Hole Farm
FORE ST
HOLEMOOR CROSS
Higher Braundsworthy
BRAUNDSWORTHY CROSS
Highweek
Coham
Middlecott
MIDDLECOTT CROSS
Holemoor
Bramble Wood
HIGHSTEAD CROSS
Lashbrook Farm
HIGHWEEK CROSS
8
Highstead
BLACK GATE
Lana
Blackley
Forda Farm
Hayne
05
Higher Kenneland
BOVACOTT LA
Bovacott
Stadson Farm
Flares
HILLMOOR CROSS
EX22
7
Kingsmoor
Narracott
A3072
Bradford House
KINGSMOOR CROSS
PH
PO
Garlands Farm
Rightadown
04
DUNSLAND CROSS
A3079
Brandis Corner
Whiteleigh Water
6
Kingslake
Graddon
GRADDON CROSS
Weekpark Plantation
03
Whiteleigh Meadow
STATION COTTS
Lashbrook Moor Plantation
Fraunch
View Farm
North Park
5
Higher Whiteleigh
Greenlane
Morecombe Plantation
Chilla
Lake
02
Clawmoor Farm
Shepard Island
EX21
Downs
MORECOMBE CROSS
P
CHILLA CHAPEL
Forest Walk
FOREST HOUSES
4
Winsford
Cookworthy Moor Plantation
Halwill Moor Plantation
Muckworthy
01
Cookworthy Buddle
3
CHILLA RD
LANE END CROSS
Luckcroft
Langaford Moor
Lane End
Dreybury
00
Brendon
PO
Halwill Junction
HOLYWELL PK 1
WOODLANDS 2
MAYTREE CL 3
LUXTON CL 4
STAGS WOOD DR 5
OAKLEAF CL 6
PINE VIEW CL 7
BEECHING CL 8
STATION FIELDS 9
STATION RD
SOMERSLEA
West Down
Langaford
Halwill Prim Sch
Halwill
2
STATION RD
East Down
LANGAFORD LA
Rectory Farm
Alderford
Croft
99
HENDERBARROW CROSS
Henderbarrow Corner
Quoditchmoor Plantations
QUODITCH CROSS
Madworthy
MILL CROSS
1
Halwill Mill
HOLE CROSS
STRONGS HILL CROSS
BLAGATON GATE
Upcott
Henderbarrow Farm
A3079
98
40
41
42
43
44
45
91
74

73
56

Scale: 1¾ inches to 1 mile

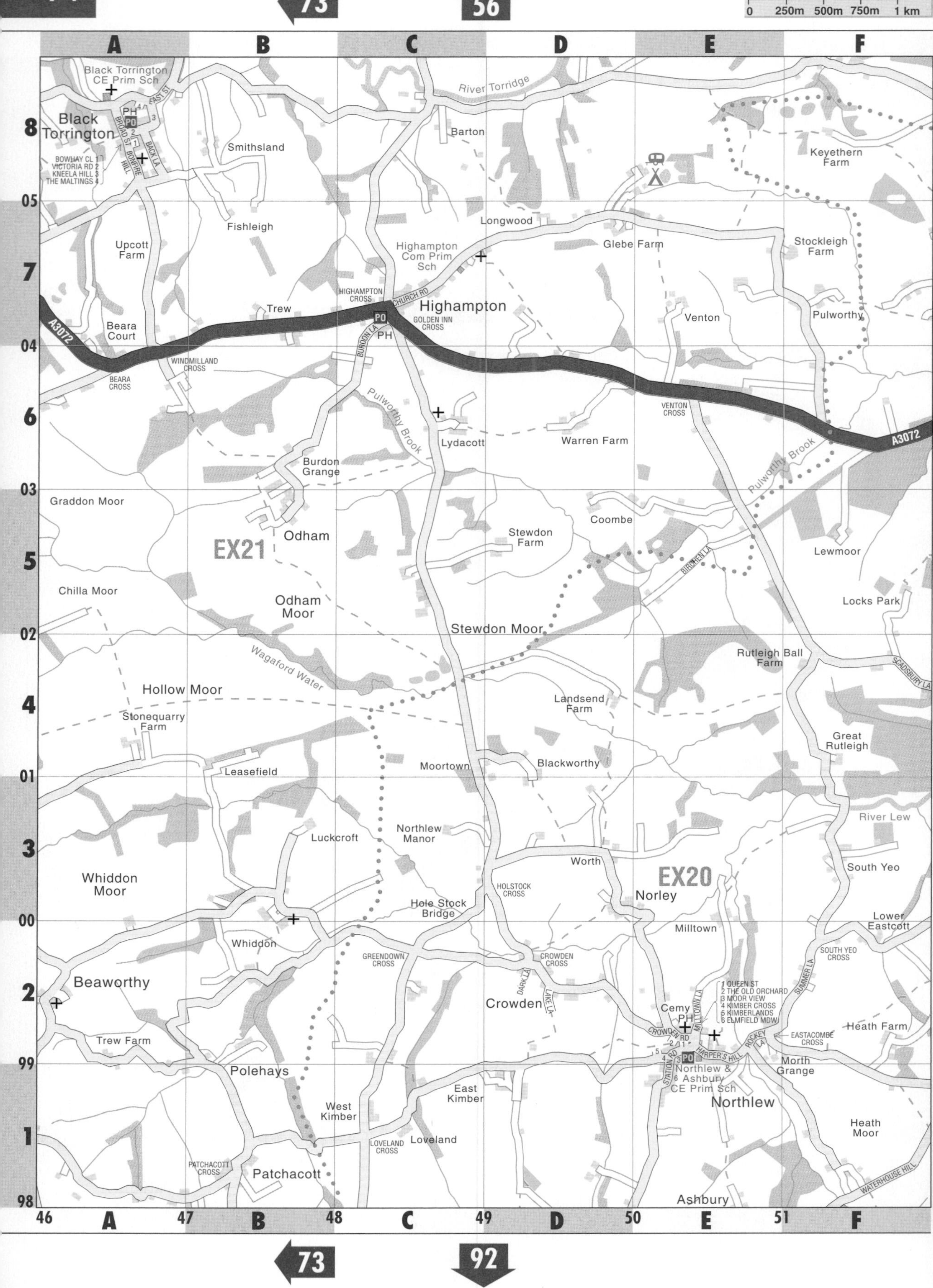

73
92

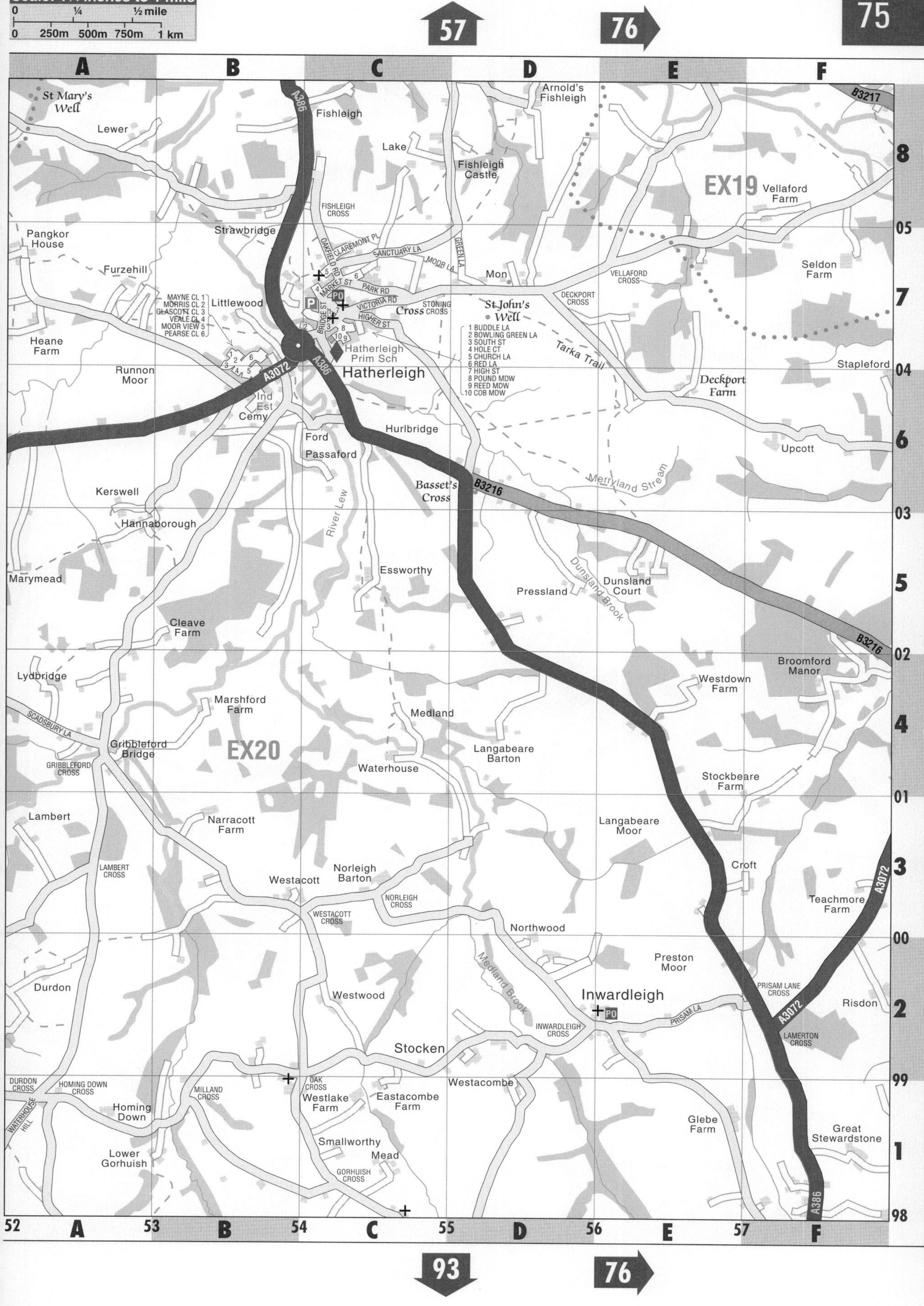
Scale: 1¾ inches to 1 mile
0 ¼ ½ mile
0 250m 500m 750m 1 km
57
76
A B C D E F
8 05 7 04 6 03 5 02 4 01 3 00 2 99 1 98
52 53 54 55 56 57
St Mary's Well
Lewer
Fishleigh
Lake
Arnold's Fishleigh
Fishleigh Castle
EX19
Vellaford Farm
B3217
FISHLEIGH CROSS
Pangkor House
Strawbridge
Furzehill
OAKFIELD RD
CLAREMONT PL
SANCTUARY LA
MOOR LA
GREEN LA
MARKET ST
PARK RD
VICTORIA RD
BRIDGE ST
HIGHER ST
Mon
VELLAFORD CROSS
Seldon Farm
DECKPORT CROSS
MAYNE CL 1
MORRIS CL 2
GLASCOTT CL 3
VEALE CL 4
MOOR VIEW 5
PEARSE CL 6
Littlewood
STONING CROSS
Cross
St John's Well
Tarka Trail
Heane Farm
1 BUDDLE LA
2 BOWLING GREEN LA
3 SOUTH ST
4 HOLE CT
5 CHURCH LA
6 RED LA
7 HIGH ST
8 POUND MDW
9 REED MDW
10 COB MDW
Hatherleigh Prim Sch
Hatherleigh
Runnon Moor
A3072
A386
Ind Est
Cemy
Deckport Farm
Stapleford
Ford
Hurlbridge
Passaford
Upcott
Basset's Cross
B3216
Merryland Stream
Kerswell
Hannaborough
River Lew
Marymead
Essworthy
Dunsland Brook
Pressland
Dunsland Court
Cleave Farm
B3216
Broomford Manor
Lydbridge
Westdown Farm
Marshford Farm
Medland
SCADSBURY LA
Gribbleford Bridge
EX20
Langabeare Barton
GRIBBLEFORD CROSS
Waterhouse
Stockbeare Farm
Lambert
Narracott Farm
Langabeare Moor
LAMBERT CROSS
Norleigh Barton
Westacott
Croft
A3072
NORLEIGH CROSS
Teachmore Farm
WESTACOTT CROSS
Northwood
Preston Moor
Medland Brook
Durdon
Westwood
Inwardleigh
PO
PRISAM LANE CROSS
PRISAM LA
Risdon
A3072
INWARDLEIGH CROSS
LAMERTON CROSS
Stocken
DURDON CROSS
HOMING DOWN CROSS
MILLAND CROSS
OAK CROSS
Westacombe
Westlake Farm
Eastacombe Farm
WATERHOUSE HILL
Homing Down
Glebe Farm
Great Stewardstone
Smallworthy
Lower Gorhuish
Mead
GORHUISH CROSS
A386
93
76

75
58

Scale: 1¾ inches to 1 mile
0 ¼ ½ mile
0 250m 500m 750m 1 km

A B C D E F

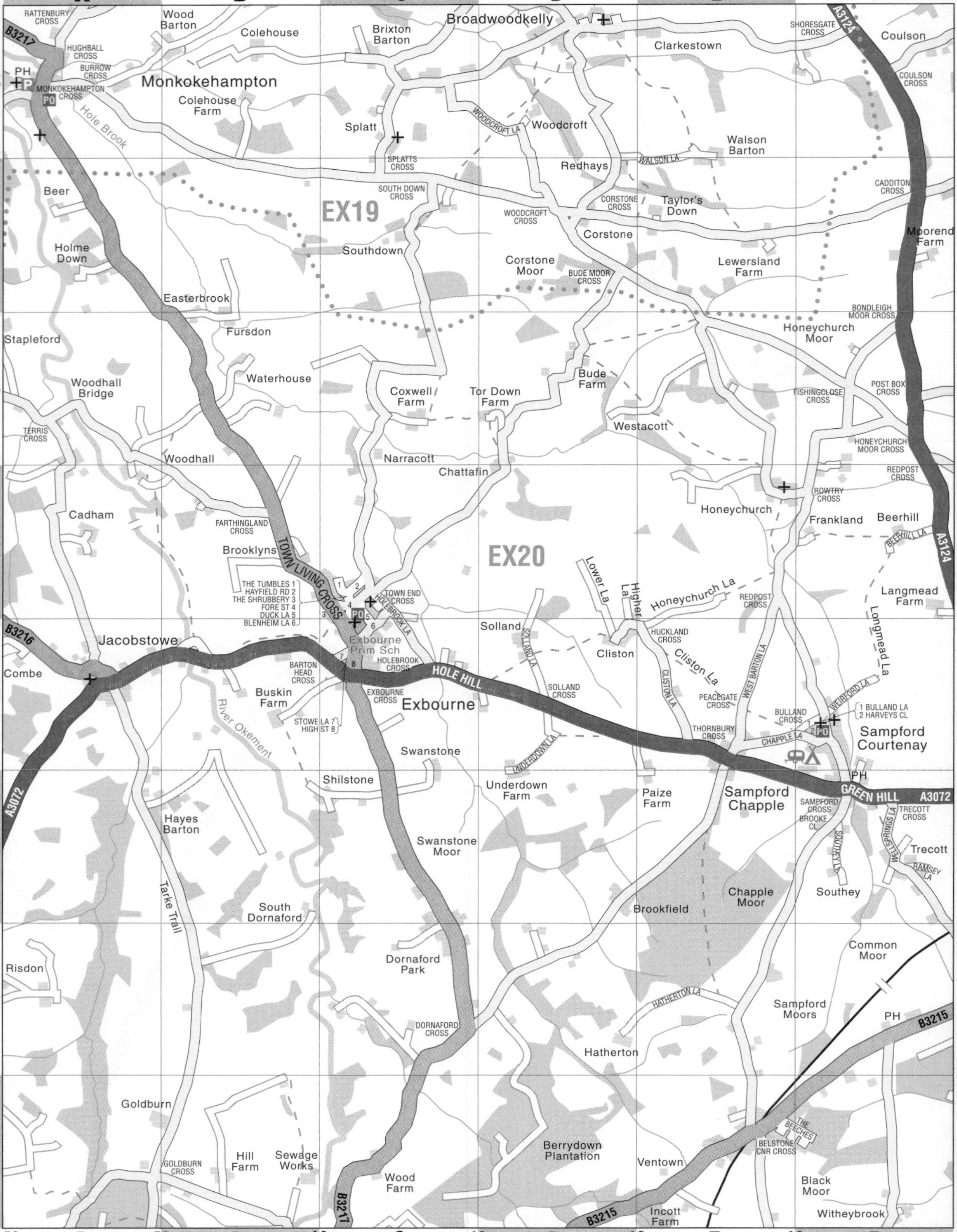

A B C D E F

75
94

Scale: 1¾ inches to 1 mile

59
78
95
78

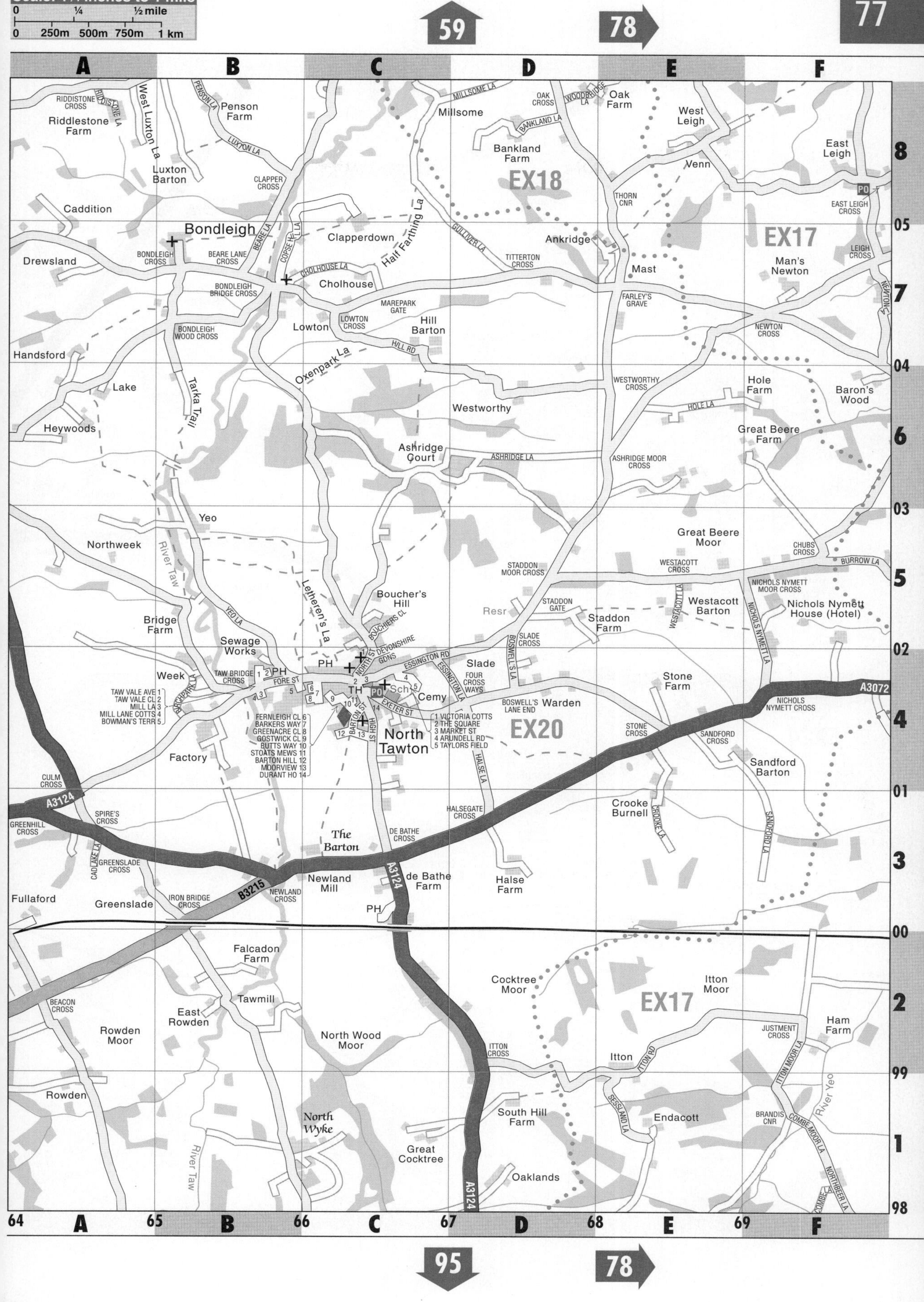

77
60

Scale: 1¾ inches to 1 mile
0 ¼ ½ mile
0 250m 500m 750m 1 km

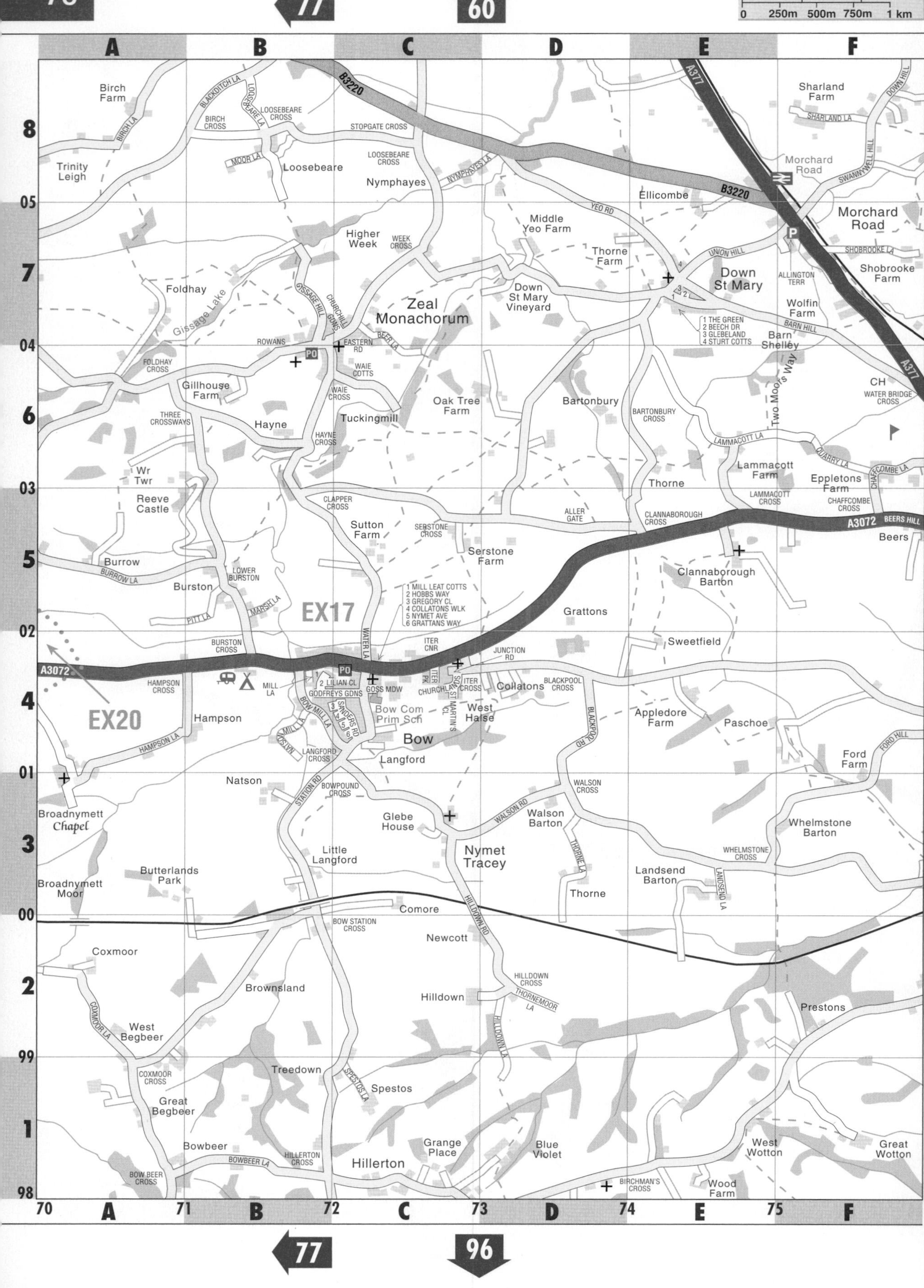

77
96

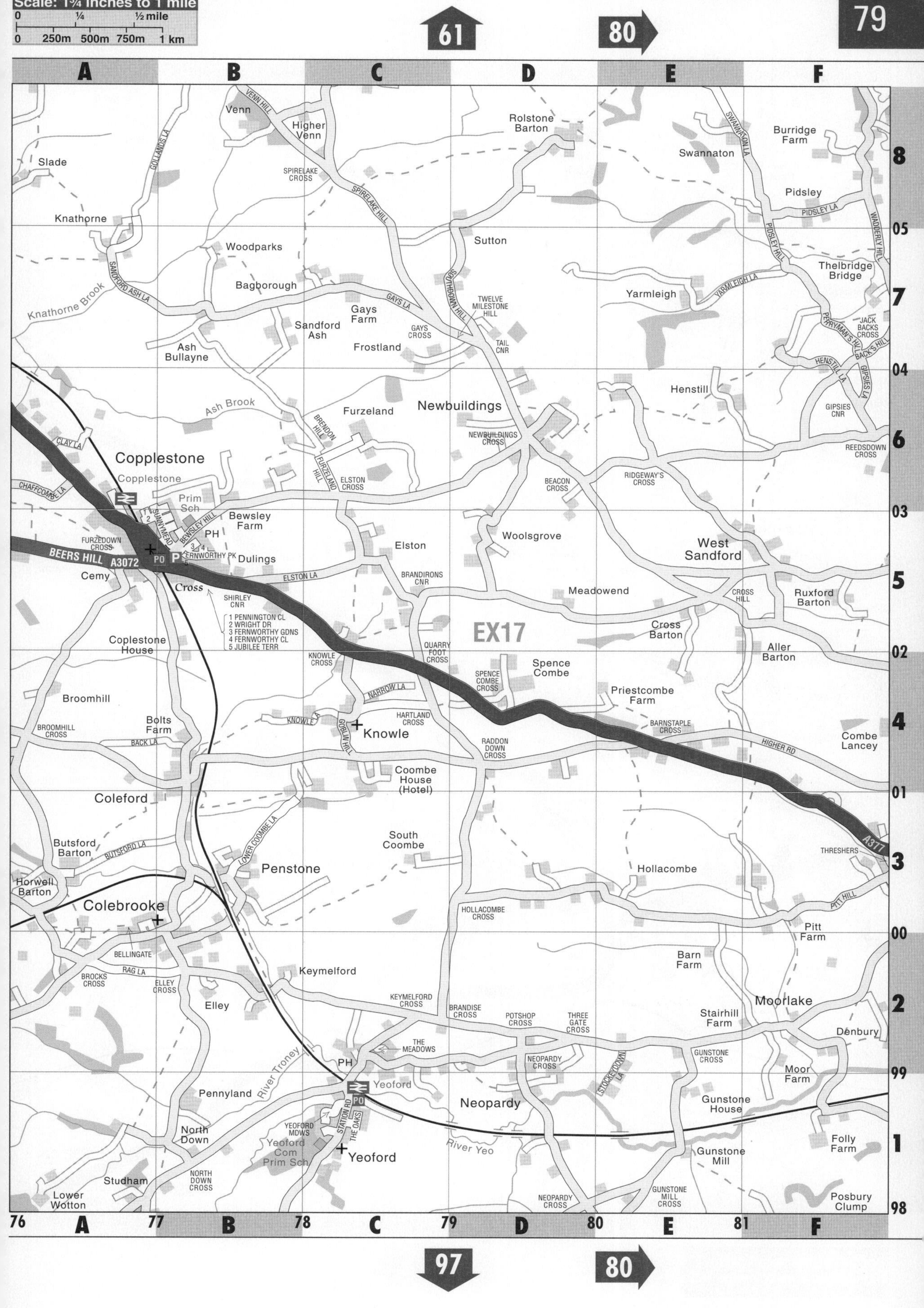
Scale: 1¾ inches to 1 mile
0 ¼ ½ mile
0 250m 500m 750m 1 km
61
80
97
80
Venn
Higher Venn
Rolstone Barton
Burridge Farm
Slade
Swannaton
Pidsley
Knathorne
Woodparks
Sutton
Thelbridge Bridge
Bagborough
Yarmleigh
Knathorne Brook
Gays Farm
Sandford Ash
Ash Bullayne
Frostland
Henstill
Ash Brook
Furzeland
Newbuildings
Copplestone
Bewsley Farm
Woolsgrove
West Sandford
Dulings
Elston
Cemy
Meadowend
Ruxford Barton
EX17
Coplestone House
Cross Barton
Aller Barton
Spence Combe
Broomhill
Priestcombe Farm
Bolts Farm
Knowle
Combe Lancey
Coombe House (Hotel)
Coleford
Butsford Barton
South Coombe
Penstone
Hollacombe
Horwell Barton
Colebrooke
Pitt Farm
Barn Farm
Keymelford
Elley
Moorlake
Stairhill Farm
Denbury
Pennyland
River Troney
Yeoford
Neopardy
Moor Farm
Gunstone House
North Down
Yeoford Com Prim Sch
River Yeo
Gunstone Mill
Folly Farm
Studham
Lower Wotton
Posbury Clump
BEERS HILL A3072
A377
CLAY LA
CHAFFCOMBE LA
SUNNYMEAD
BEWSLEY HILL
FERNWORTHY PK
FURZEDOWN CROSS
ELSTON LA
SHIRLEY CNR
1 PENNINGTON CL
2 WRIGHT DR
3 FERNWORTHY GDNS
4 FERNWORTHY CL
5 JUBILEE TERR
GOLLANDS LA
VENN HILL
SPIRELAKE CROSS
SPIRELAKE HILL
SANDFORD ASH LA
GAYS LA
GAYS CROSS
SOUTHDOWN HILL
TWELVE MILESTONE HILL
TAIL CNR
BRENDON HILL
FURZELAND HILL
ELSTON CROSS
NEWBUILDINGS CROSS
BEACON CROSS
RIDGEWAY'S CROSS
SWANNATON LA
PIDSLEY LA
PIDSLEY HILL
WADDERLY HILL
YARMLEIGH LA
PERRYMAN'S HILL
JACK BACKS CROSS
BACK'S HILL
HENSTILL LA
GIPSIES LA
GIPSIES CNR
REEDSDOWN CROSS
BRANDIRONS CNR
CROSS HILL
KNOWLE CROSS
QUARRY FOOT CROSS
SPENCE COMBE CROSS
NARROW LA
KNOWLE LA
GOBLIN HILL
HARTLAND CROSS
BARNSTAPLE CROSS
RADDON DOWN CROSS
HIGHER RD
BROOMHILL CROSS
BACK LA
LOWER COOMBE LA
BUTSFORD LA
THRESHERS
HOLLACOMBE CROSS
PITT HILL
BELLINGATE
RAG LA
BROCKS CROSS
ELLEY CROSS
KEYMELFORD CROSS
BRANDISE CROSS
POTSHOP CROSS
THREE GATE CROSS
THE MEADOWS
NEOPARDY CROSS
STOCKEYDOWN LA
GUNSTONE CROSS
YEOFORD MDWS
STATION RD
THE OAKS
NORTH DOWN CROSS
GUNSTONE MILL CROSS
PH
PO
P
Prim Sch

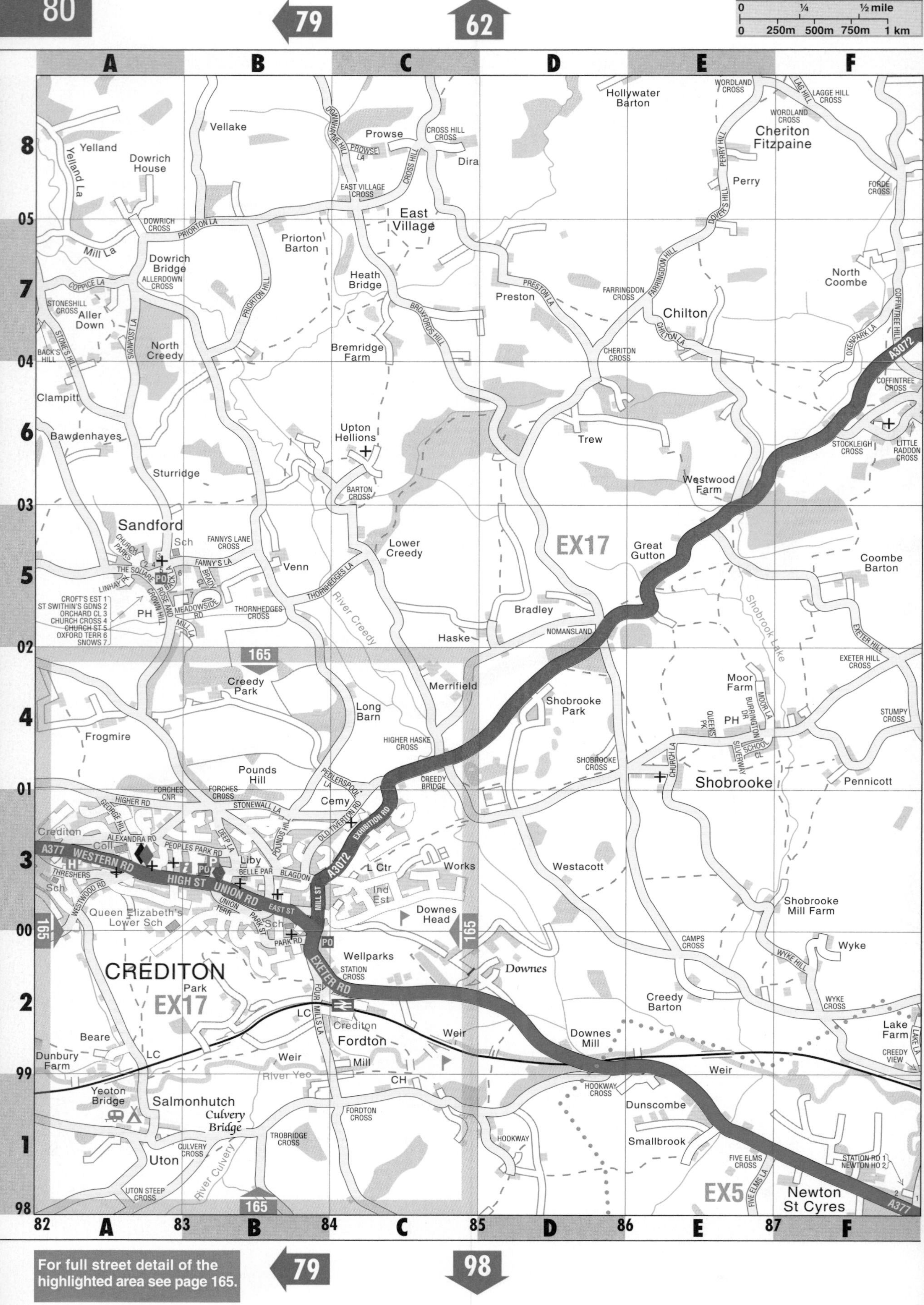

For full street detail of the highlighted area see page 165.

Scale: 1¾ inches to 1 mile

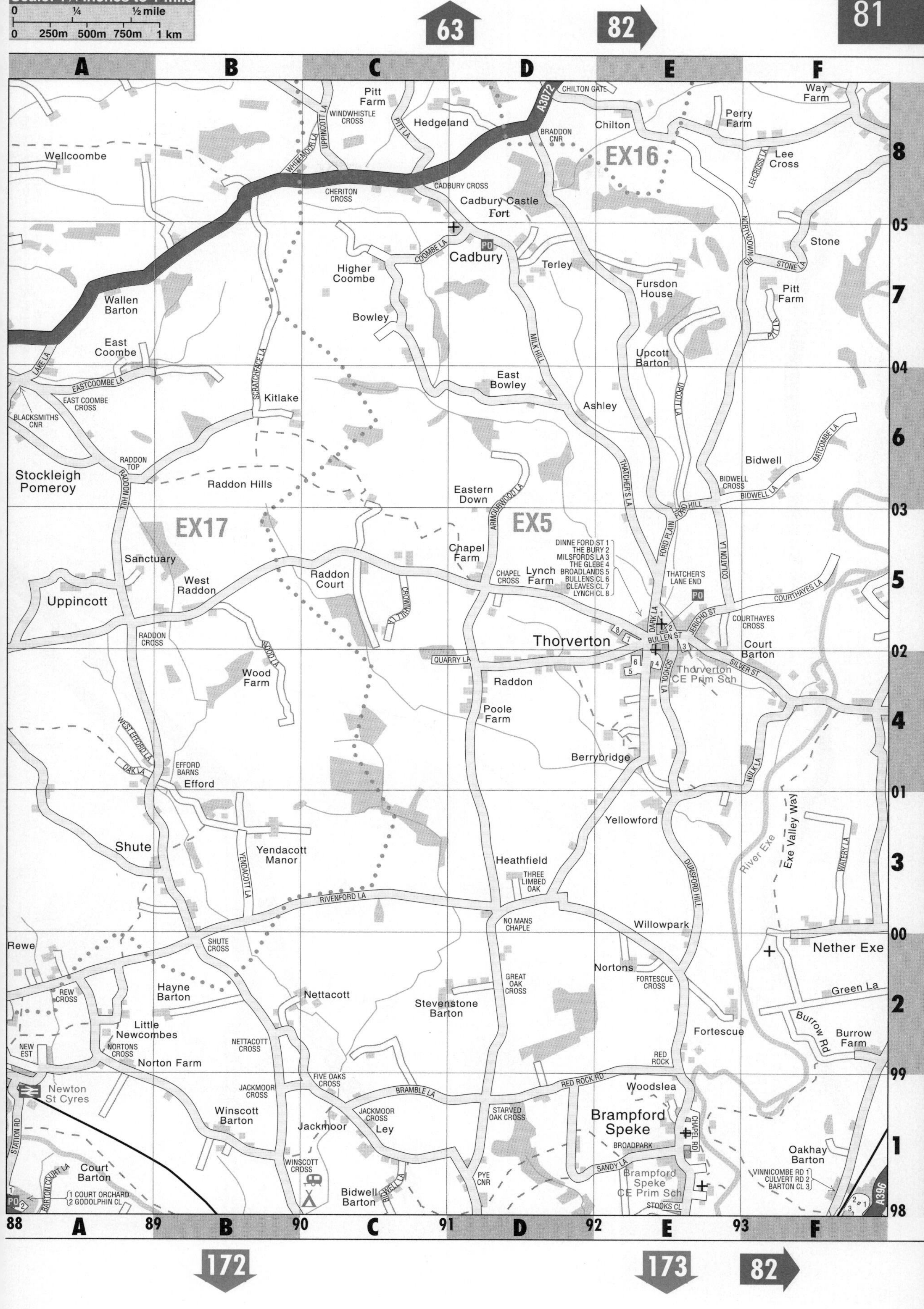

81
64

Scale: 1¾ inches to 1 mile

81
174
175

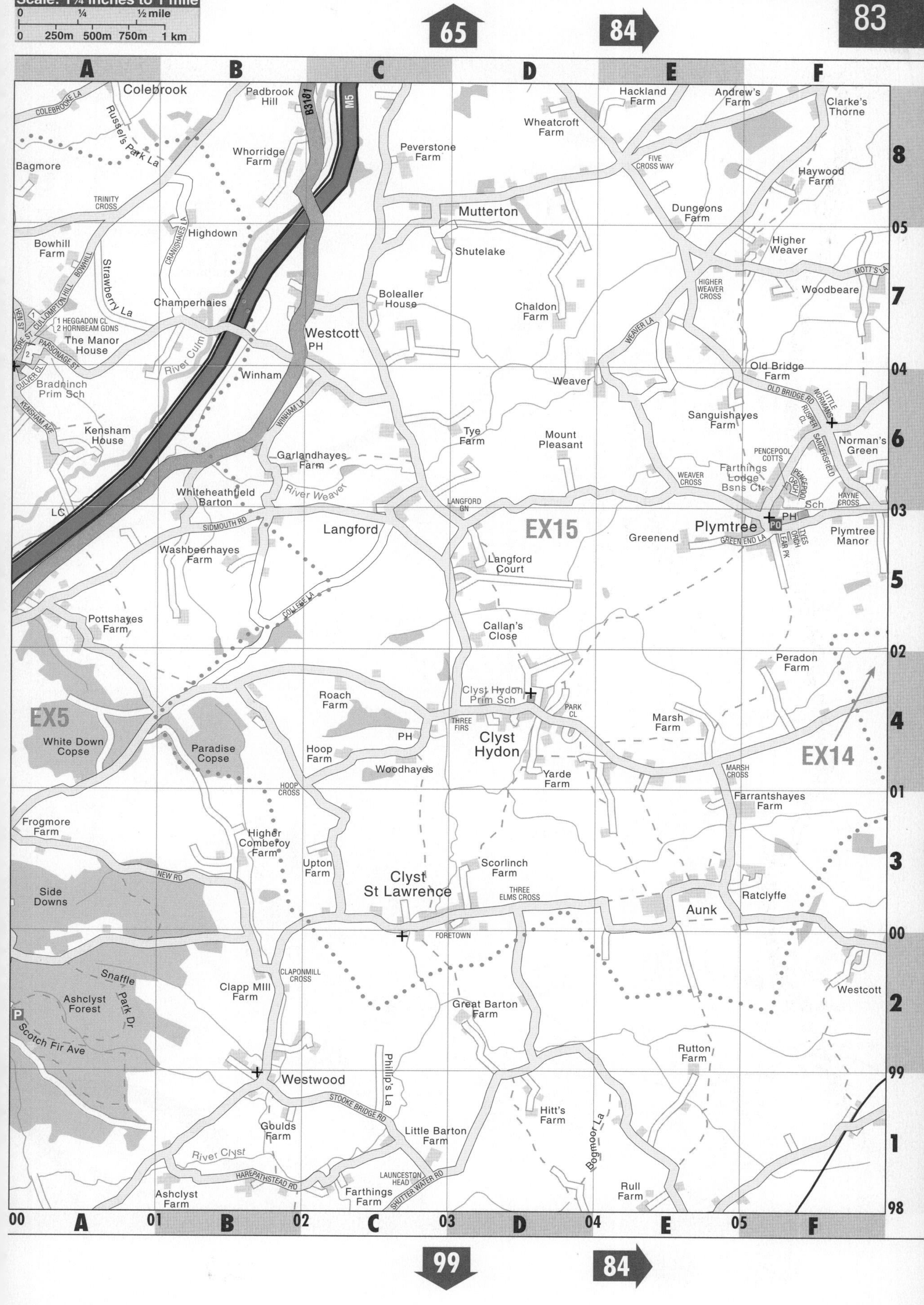
Scale: 1¾ inches to 1 mile
0 ¼ ½ mile
0 250m 500m 750m 1 km
65
84
A B C D E F
8
05
7
04
6
03
5
02
4
01
3
00
2
99
1
98
00 A 01 B 02 C 03 D 04 E 05 F
Colebrook
Colebrooke La
Russel's Park La
Padbrook Hill
B3181
M5
Bagmore
Whorridge Farm
Peverstone Farm
Wheatcroft Farm
Hackland Farm
Andrew's Farm
Clarke's Thorne
Five Cross Way
Haywood Farm
Trinity Cross
Mutterton
Dungeons Farm
Bowhill Farm
Highdown
Cranishaies La
Shutelake
Higher Weaver
Bowhill
Cullompton Hill
Strawberry La
Mott's La
Woodbeare
Higher Weaver Cross
Champerhaies
Bolealler House
Chaldon Farm
Hen St
Fore St
1 Heggadon Cl
2 Hornbeam Gdns
Parsonage St
The Manor House
Westcott
PH
Weaver La
Culver Cl
River Culm
Bradninch Prim Sch
Winham
Weaver
Old Bridge Farm
Old Bridge Rd
Little Normans
Kensham Ave
Winham La
Sanguishayes Farm
Rusper Cl
Kensham House
Tye Farm
Mount Pleasant
Norman's Green
Sandersfield
Garlandhayes Farm
Pencepool Cotts
Farthings Lodge Bsns Ctr
Pencepool Orch
River Weaver
Weaver Cross
Whiteheathfield Barton
Langford Gn
Hayne Cross
Sch
LC
Sidmouth Rd
Langford
EX15
Plymtree
Greenend
Green End La
Lear Pk
Tyes Orch
PO
Plymtree Manor
Washbeerhayes Farm
Langford Court
College La
Pottshayes Farm
Callan's Close
Peradon Farm
Roach Farm
Clyst Hydon Prim Sch
Park Cl
EX5
Three Firs
Marsh Farm
White Down Copse
Paradise Copse
Clyst Hydon
Hoop Farm
EX14
Woodhayes
Yarde Farm
Marsh Cross
Hoop Cross
Farrantshayes Farm
Frogmore Farm
Higher Comberoy Farm
New Rd
Upton Farm
Scorlinch Farm
Clyst St Lawrence
Side Downs
Three Elms Cross
Ratclyffe
Aunk
Foretown
Snaffle
Claponmill Cross
Clapp Mill Farm
Ashclyst Forest
Park Dr
Great Barton Farm
Westcott
P
Scotch Fir Ave
Rutton Farm
Phillip's La
Westwood
Stooke Bridge Rd
Hitt's Farm
Goulds Farm
Little Barton Farm
Bogmoor La
River Clyst
Harepathstead Rd
Launceston Head
Shutter Water Rd
Rull Farm
Ashclyst Farm
Farthings Farm
99
84

83
66

Scale: 1¾ inches to 1 mile
0 ¼ ½ mile
0 250m 500m 750m 1 km

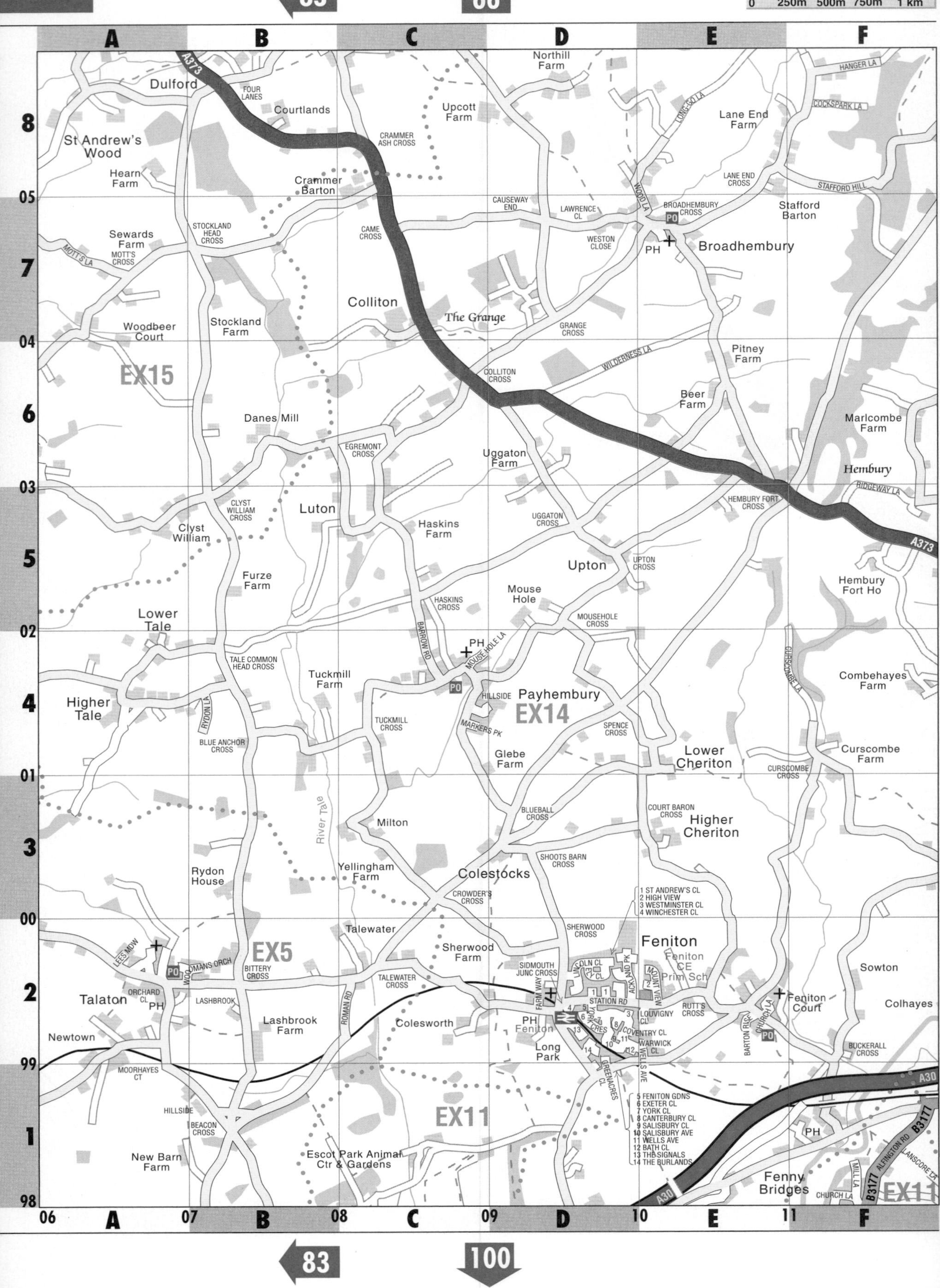

83
100

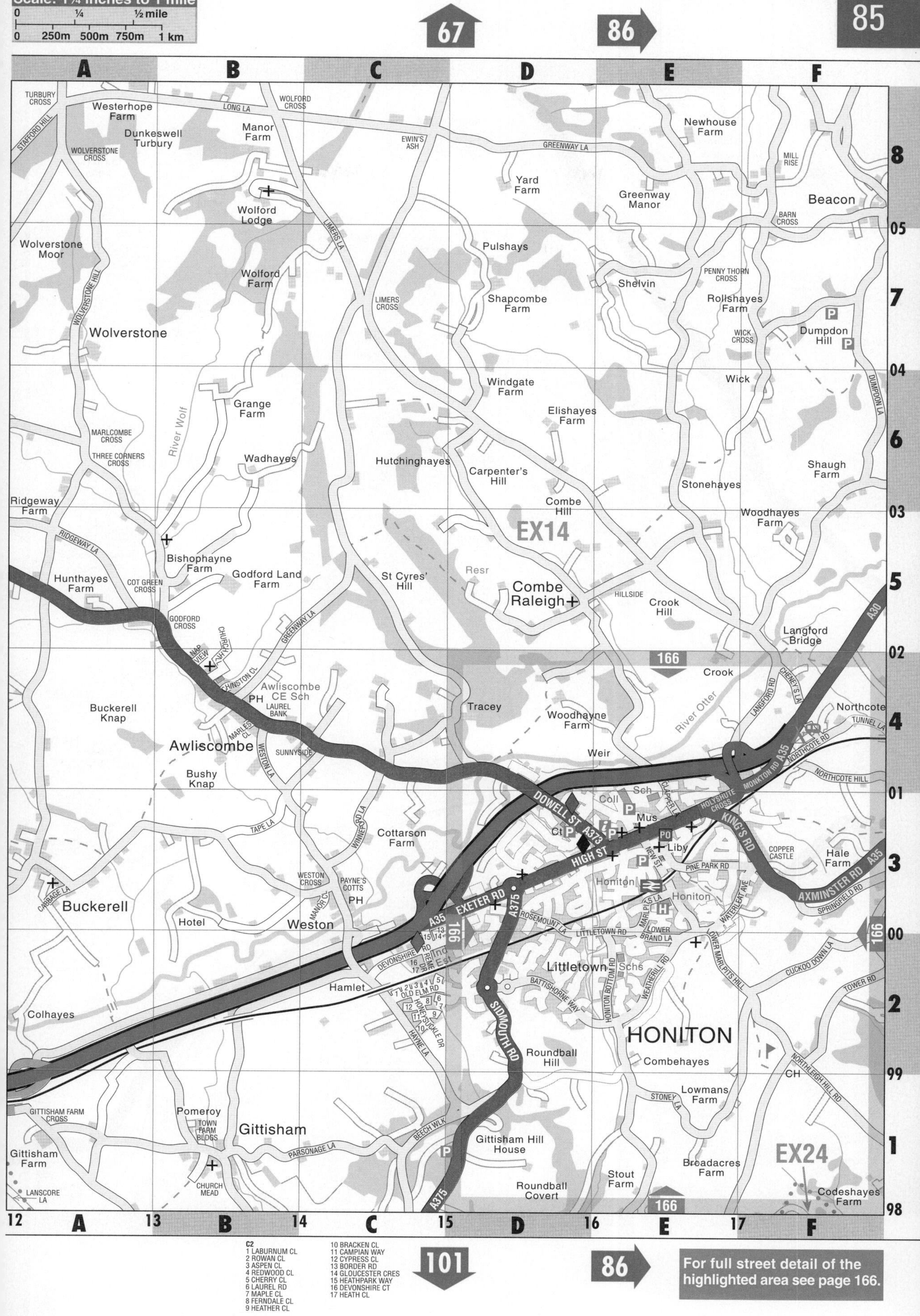

C2
1 LABURNUM CL
2 ROWAN CL
3 ASPEN CL
4 REDWOOD CL
5 CHERRY CL
6 LAUREL RD
7 MAPLE CL
8 FERNDALE CL
9 HEATHER CL
10 BRACKEN CL
11 CAMPIAN WAY
12 CYPRESS CL
13 BORDER RD
14 GLOUCESTER CRES
15 HEATHPARK WAY
16 DEVONSHIRE CT
17 HEATH CL

101

86

For full street detail of the highlighted area see page 166.

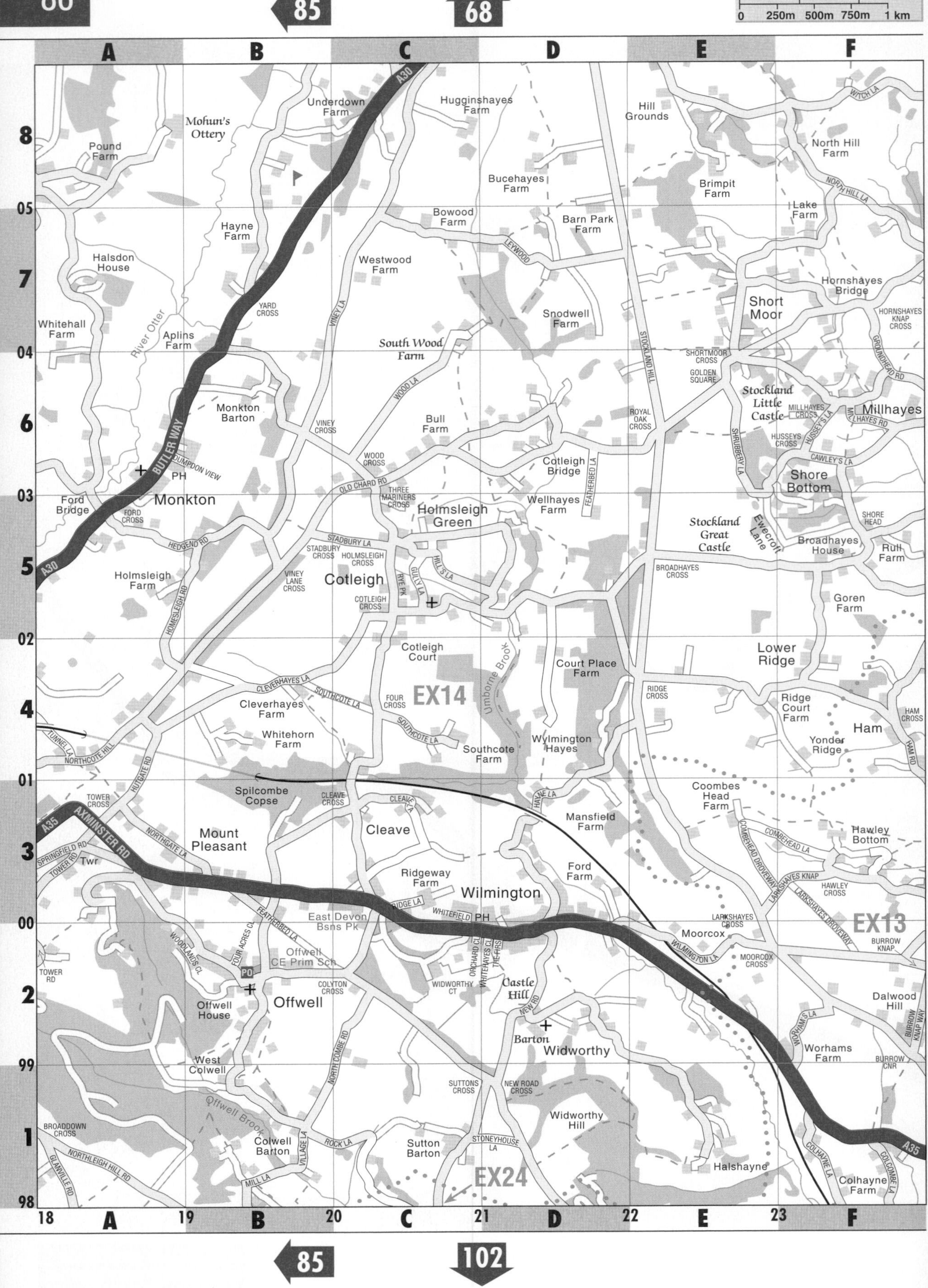

85
68
Scale: 1¾ inches to 1 mile
0 ¼ ½ mile
0 250m 500m 750m 1 km
A B C D E F
8 05 7 04 6 03 5 02 4 01 3 00 2 99 1 98
18 19 20 21 22 23
Pound Farm
Mohun's Ottery
Underdown Farm
A30
Hugginshayes Farm
Hill Grounds
North Hill Farm
WITCH LA
Bucehayes Farm
Brimpit Farm
NORTH HILL LA
Lake Farm
Bowood Farm
Barn Park Farm
Hayne Farm
Halsdon House
Westwood Farm
LEYWOOD
Hornshayes Bridge
Short Moor
HORNSHAYES KNAP CROSS
YARD CROSS
VINEY LA
Snodwell Farm
Whitehall Farm
River Otter
Aplins Farm
South Wood Farm
STOCKLAND HILL
SHORTMOOR CROSS
GOLDEN SQUARE
GROUNDHEAD RD
WOOD LA
Stockland Little Castle
MILLHAYES CROSS
Millhayes
MILLHAYES RD
HUSSEYS LA
Monkton Barton
VINEY CROSS
Bull Farm
ROYAL OAK CROSS
SHRUBBERY LA
HUSSEYS CROSS
CAWLEY'S LA
BUTLER WAY
DUMPDON VIEW
PH
WOOD CROSS
Cotleigh Bridge
FEATHERBED LA
Shore Bottom
Ford Bridge
Monkton
OLD CHARD RD
THREE MARINERS CROSS
Holmsleigh Green
Wellhayes Farm
Stockland Great Castle
Ewecroft Lane
SHORE HEAD
FORD CROSS
HEDGEND RD
STADBURY LA
STADBURY CROSS
HOLMSLEIGH CROSS
Broadhayes House
Rull Farm
HILL'S LA
BROADHAYES CROSS
Holmsleigh Farm
VINEY LANE CROSS
Cotleigh
GULLY LA
RYE PK
HOMESLEIGH RD
COTLEIGH CROSS
Goren Farm
Cotleigh Court
Court Place Farm
Lower Ridge
CLEVERHAYES LA
SOUTHCOTE LA
EX14
Umborne Brook
RIDGE CROSS
Ridge Court Farm
Cleverhayes Farm
FOUR CROSS
HAM CROSS
Ham
HAM RD
Yonder Ridge
Whitehorn Farm
Wylmington Hayes
TUNNEL LA
NORTHCOTE HILL
Southcote Farm
HUTGATE RD
Coombes Head Farm
Spilcombe Copse
CLEAVE CROSS
CLEAVE LA
HAYNE LA
TOWER CROSS
Mansfield Farm
A35
AXMINSTER RD
NORTHGATE LA
Mount Pleasant
Cleave
COMBEHEAD LA
COMBEHEAD DROVEWAY
Hawley Bottom
SPRINGFIELD RD
TOWER RD
Twr
Ford Farm
Ridgeway Farm
LARKSHAYES KNAP
HAWLEY CROSS
LARKSHAYES DROVEWAY
Wilmington
RIDGE LA
WHITEFIELD
East Devon Bsns Pk
FEATHERBED LA
LARKSHAYES CROSS
EX13
Moorcox
WALMINGTON LA
MOORCOX CROSS
BURROW KNAP
WOODLANDS CL
FOUR ACRES CL
Offwell CE Prim Sch
ORCHARD CL
WHITEHAYES CL
THE FIRS
TOWER RD
PO
COLYTON CROSS
WIDWORTHY CT
Castle Hill
Offwell House
Offwell
NEW RD
Dalwood Hill
WORHAMS LA
BURROW KNAP WAY
Barton
Widworthy
Worhams Farm
West Colwell
NORTH COMBE RD
BURROW CNR
SUTTONS CROSS
NEW ROAD CROSS
Offwell Brook
Widworthy Hill
BROADDOWN CROSS
Colwell Barton
VILLAGE LA
ROCK LA
Sutton Barton
STONEYHOUSE LA
COLHAYNE LA
COLCOMBE LA
NORTHLEIGH HILL RD
GLANVILLE RD
MILL LA
EX24
Halshayne
Colhayne Farm
85
102

Scale: 1¾ inches to 1 mile

69
88

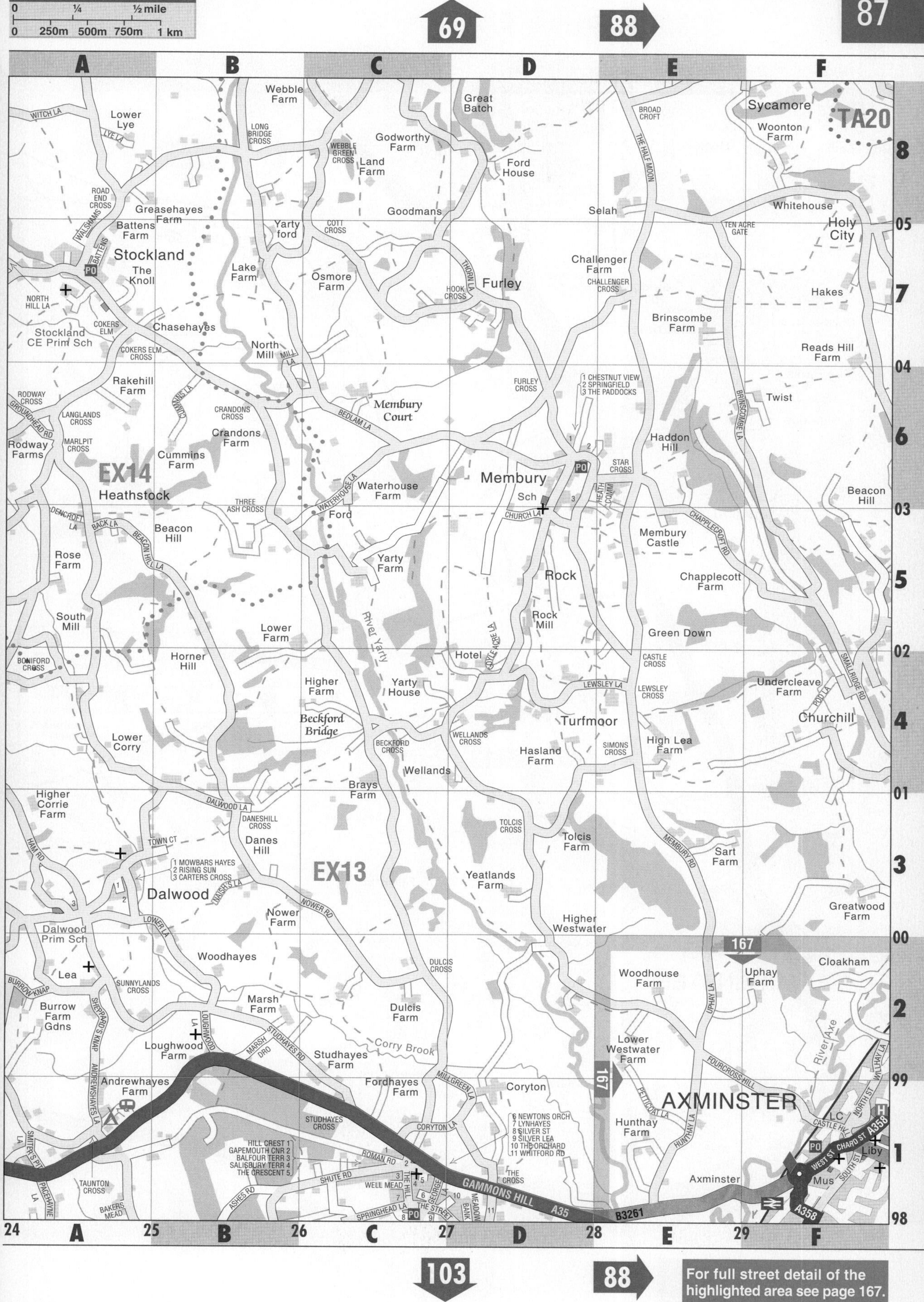

103
88
For full street detail of the highlighted area see page 167.

87

Scale: 1¾ inches to 1 mile
0 ¼ ½ mile
0 250m 500m 750m 1 km

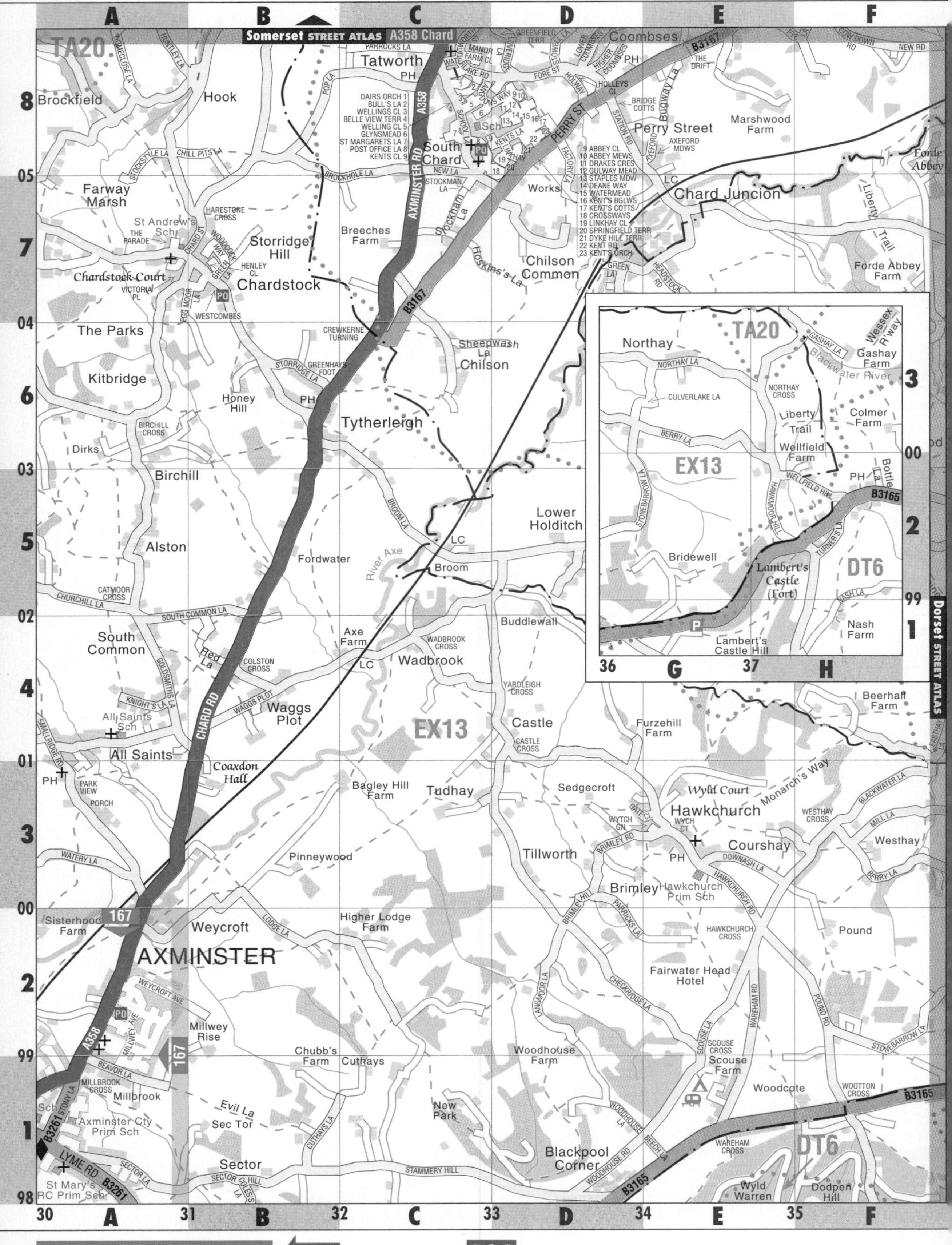

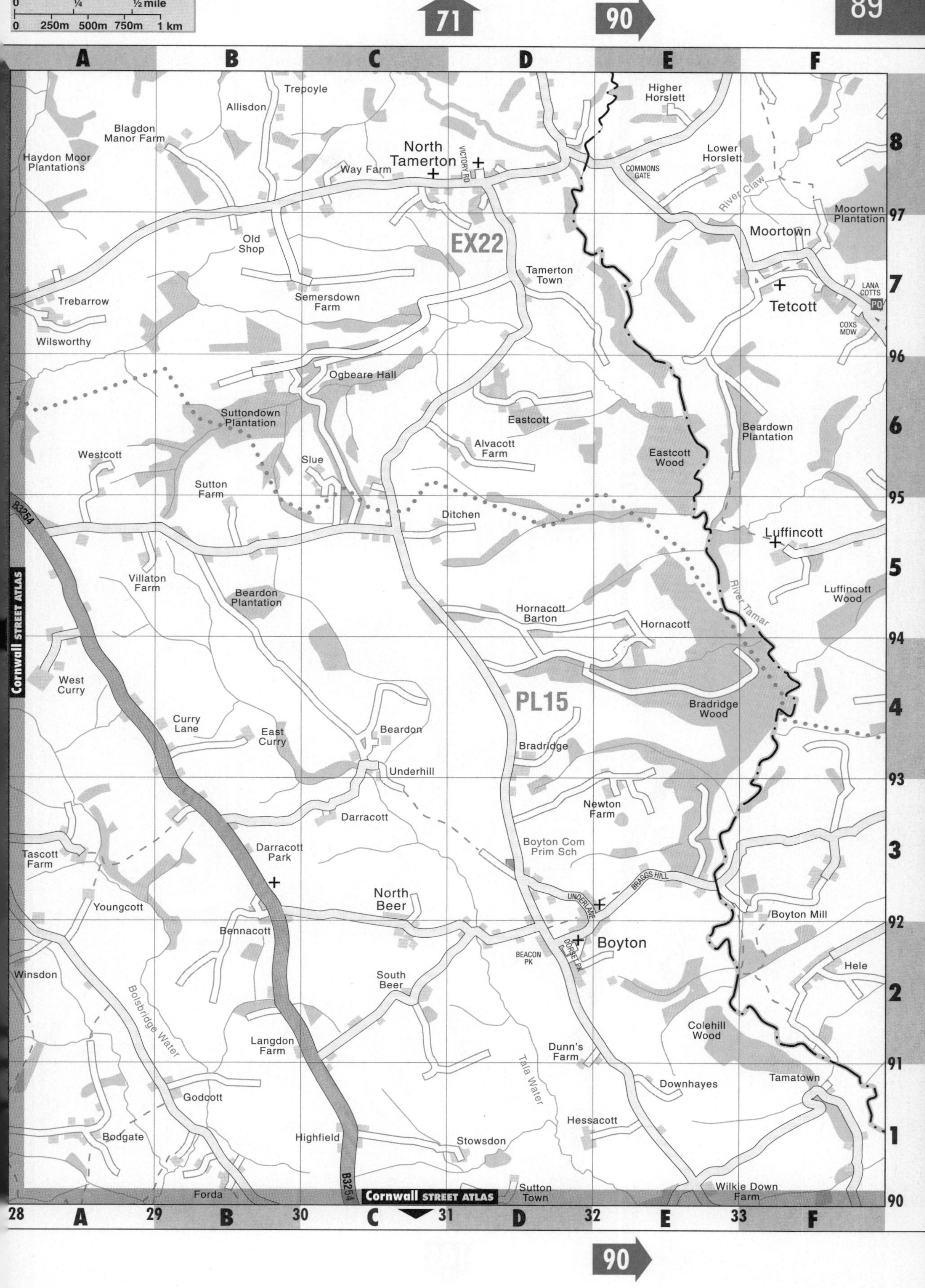
A
B
C
D
E
F
Trepoyle
Allisdon
Higher Horslett
Blagdon Manor Farm
Haydon Moor Plantations
North Tamerton
VICTORY RD
Way Farm
COMMONS GATE
Lower Horslett
River Claw
Moortown Plantation
Moortown
Old Shop
EX22
Tamerton Town
Trebarrow
Semersdown Farm
Tetcott
LANA COTTS
PO
COXS MDW
Wilsworthy
Ogbeare Hall
Suttondown Plantation
Eastcott
Beardown Plantation
Westcott
Alvacott Farm
Eastcott Wood
Slue
Sutton Farm
B3254
Ditchen
Luffincott
Villaton Farm
Luffincott Wood
Beardon Plantation
Hornacott Barton
Hornacott
River Tamar
Cornwall STREET ATLAS
West Curry
PL15
Bradridge Wood
Curry Lane
East Curry
Beardon
Bradridge
Underhill
Newton Farm
Darracott
Tascott Farm
Boyton Com Prim Sch
Darracott Park
BRAGGS HILL
North Beer
UNDERLANE
Youngcott
Boyton Mill
Bennacott
BEACON PK
DORSE PK
Boyton
Winsdon
Hele
South Beer
Bolsbridge Water
Colehill Wood
Langdon Farm
Dunn's Farm
Tala Water
Downhayes
Tamatown
Godcott
Hessacott
Bodgate
Highfield
Stowsdon
Forda
Sutton Town
Wilkie Down Farm
8
97
7
96
6
95
5
94
4
93
3
92
2
91
1
90
28
29
30
31
32
33

89
72

Scale: 1¾ inches to 1 mile
0 ¼ ½ mile
0 250m 500m 750m 1 km

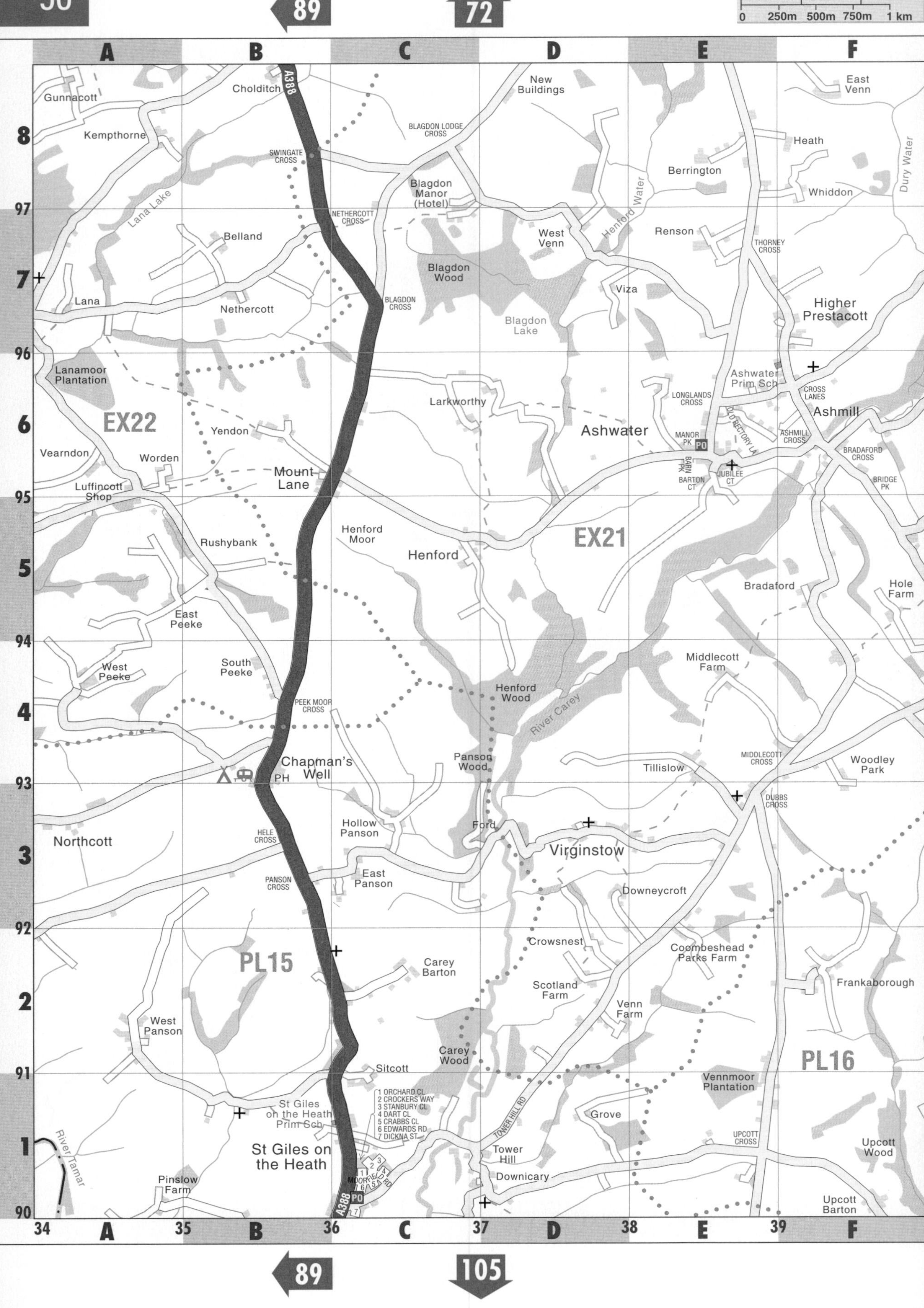

89
105

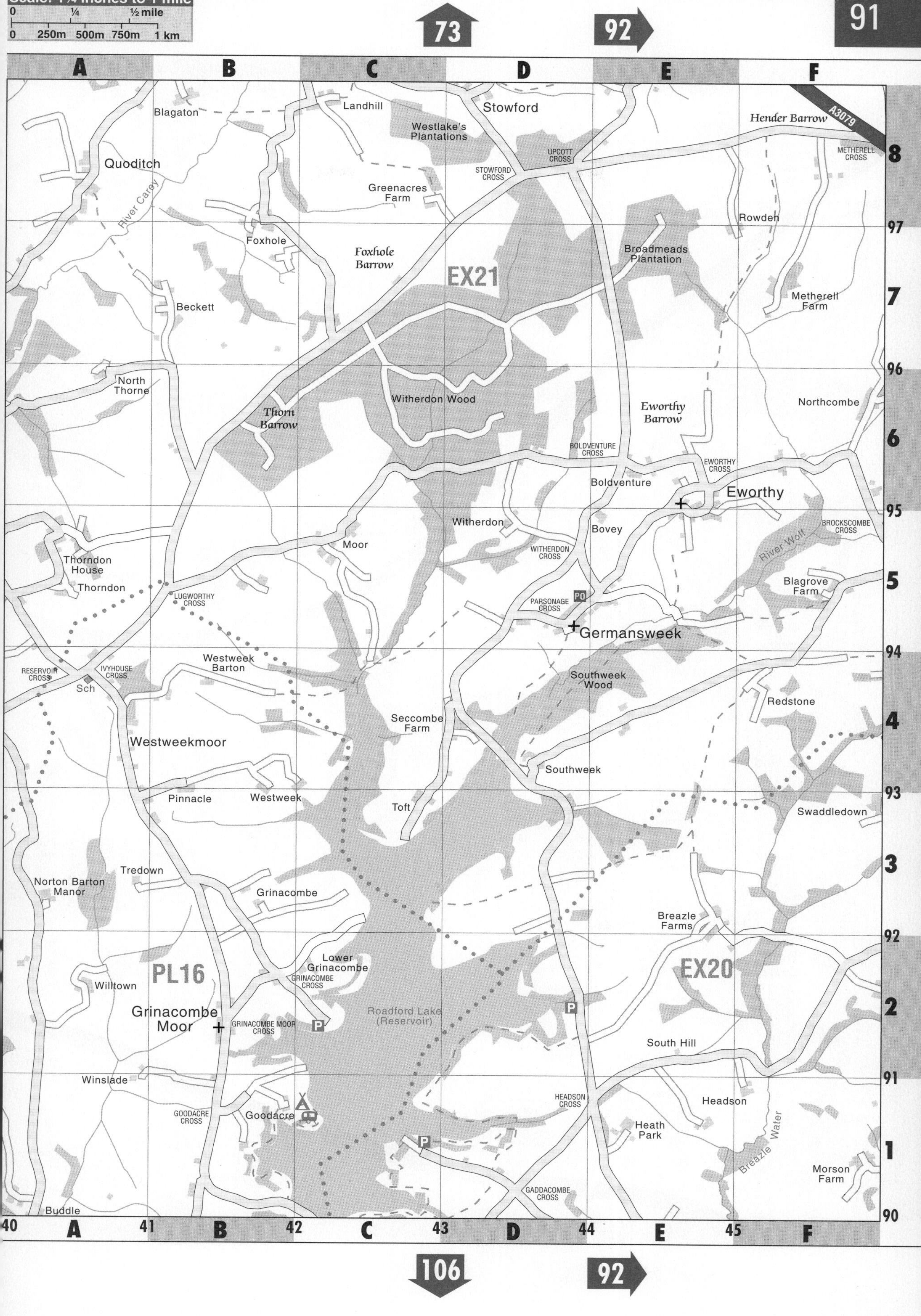
Scale: 1¾ inches to 1 mile
0 ¼ ½ mile
0 250m 500m 750m 1 km
73
92
A B C D E F
Blagaton
Landhill
Stowford
Westlake's Plantations
Hender Barrow
A3079
Quoditch
UPCOTT CROSS
STOWFORD CROSS
METHERELL CROSS
Greenacres Farm
River Carey
Rowden
Foxhole
Foxhole Barrow
Broadmeads Plantation
EX21
Beckett
Metherell Farm
North Thorne
Witherdon Wood
Eworthy Barrow
Northcombe
Thorn Barrow
BOLDVENTURE CROSS
EWORTHY CROSS
Boldventure
Eworthy
Witherdon
Bovey
BROCKSCOMBE CROSS
Moor
WITHERDON CROSS
River Wolf
Thorndon House
Thorndon
Blagrove Farm
LUGWORTHY CROSS
PARSONAGE CROSS
PO
Germansweek
Westweek Barton
RESERVOIR CROSS
IVYHOUSE CROSS
Sch
Southweek Wood
Redstone
Seccombe Farm
Westweekmoor
Southweek
Pinnacle
Westweek
Toft
Swaddledown
Tredown
Norton Barton Manor
Grinacombe
Breazle Farms
EX20
Lower Grinacombe
PL16
Willtown
GRINACOMBE CROSS
Roadford Lake (Reservoir)
Grinacombe Moor
GRINACOMBE MOOR CROSS
P
South Hill
Winslade
HEADSON CROSS
Headson
Goodacre
GOODACRE CROSS
Heath Park
Breazle Water
Morson Farm
GADDACOMBE CROSS
Buddle
8
97
7
96
6
95
5
94
4
93
3
92
2
91
1
90
40 41 42 43 44 45
106
92

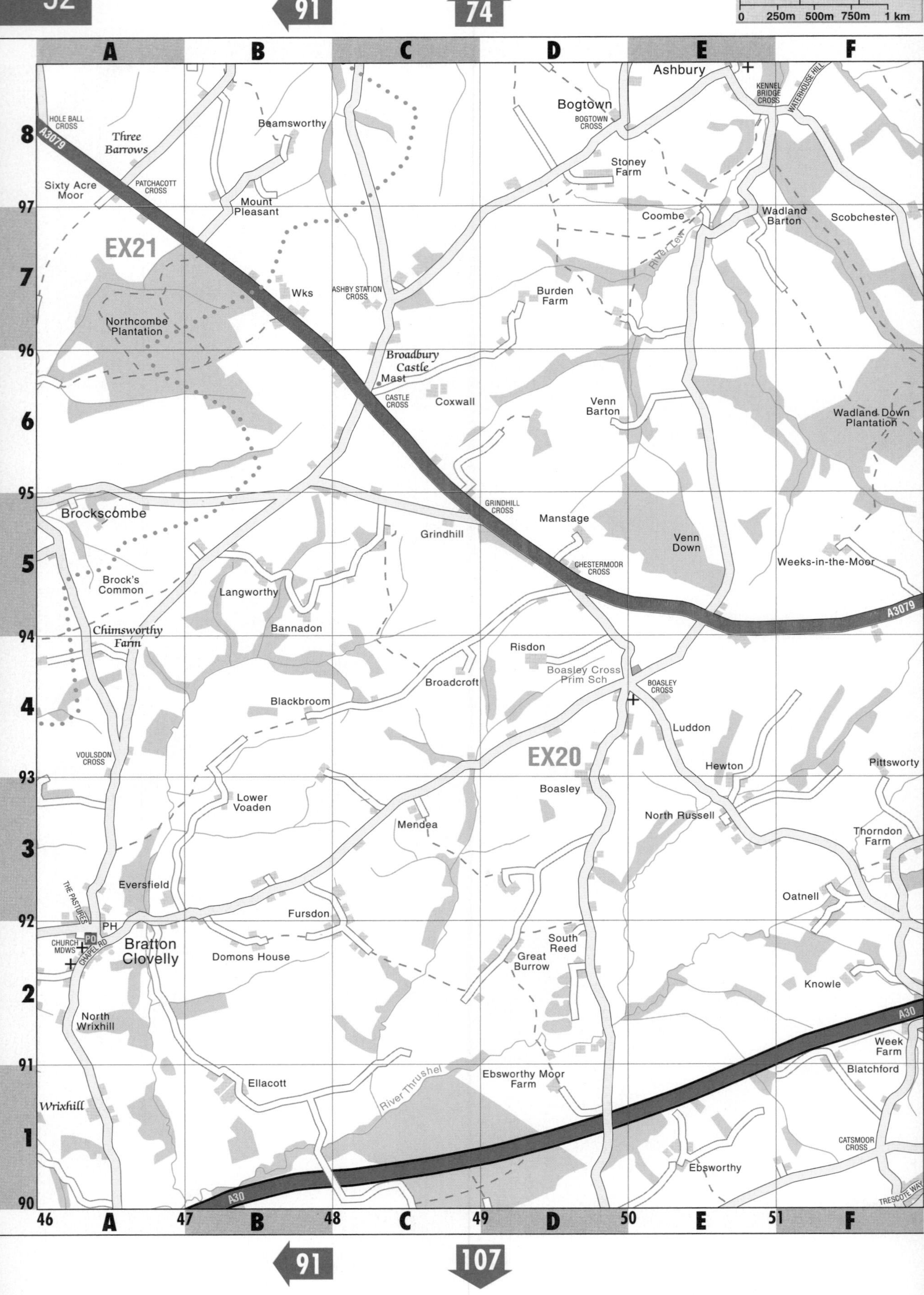
91
74
Scale: 1¾ inches to 1 mile
0 ¼ ½ mile
0 250m 500m 750m 1 km
A B C D E F
Ashbury
KENNEL BRIDGE CROSS
WATERHOUSE HILL
Bogtown
BOGTOWN CROSS
HOLE BALL CROSS
Three Barrows
A3079
Beamsworthy
Stoney Farm
Sixty Acre Moor
PATCHACOTT CROSS
Mount Pleasant
Coombe
Wadland Barton
Scobchester
River Lew
EX21
Wks
ASHBY STATION CROSS
Burden Farm
Northcombe Plantation
Broadbury Castle
Mast
CASTLE CROSS
Coxwall
Venn Barton
Wadland Down Plantation
GRINDHILL CROSS
Brockscombe
Manstage
Grindhill
Venn Down
Weeks-in-the-Moor
CHESTERMOOR CROSS
Brock's Common
Langworthy
Chimsworthy Farm
Bannadon
Risdon
Boasley Cross Prim Sch
Broadcroft
BOASLEY CROSS
Blackbroom
Luddon
EX20
VOULSDON CROSS
Hewton
Pittsworty
Boasley
Lower Voaden
North Russell
Mendea
Thorndon Farm
Eversfield
THE PASTURES
Oatnell
Fursdon
PH
CHURCH MDWS
PO
CHAPEL RD
Bratton Clovelly
Domons House
South Reed
Great Burrow
Knowle
North Wrixhill
A30
Week Farm
Blatchford
Ellacott
River Thrushel
Ebsworthy Moor Farm
Wrixhill
CATSMOOR CROSS
Ebsworthy
TRESCOTE WAY
8 97 7 96 6 95 5 94 4 93 3 92 2 91 1 90
46 47 48 49 50 51
91
107

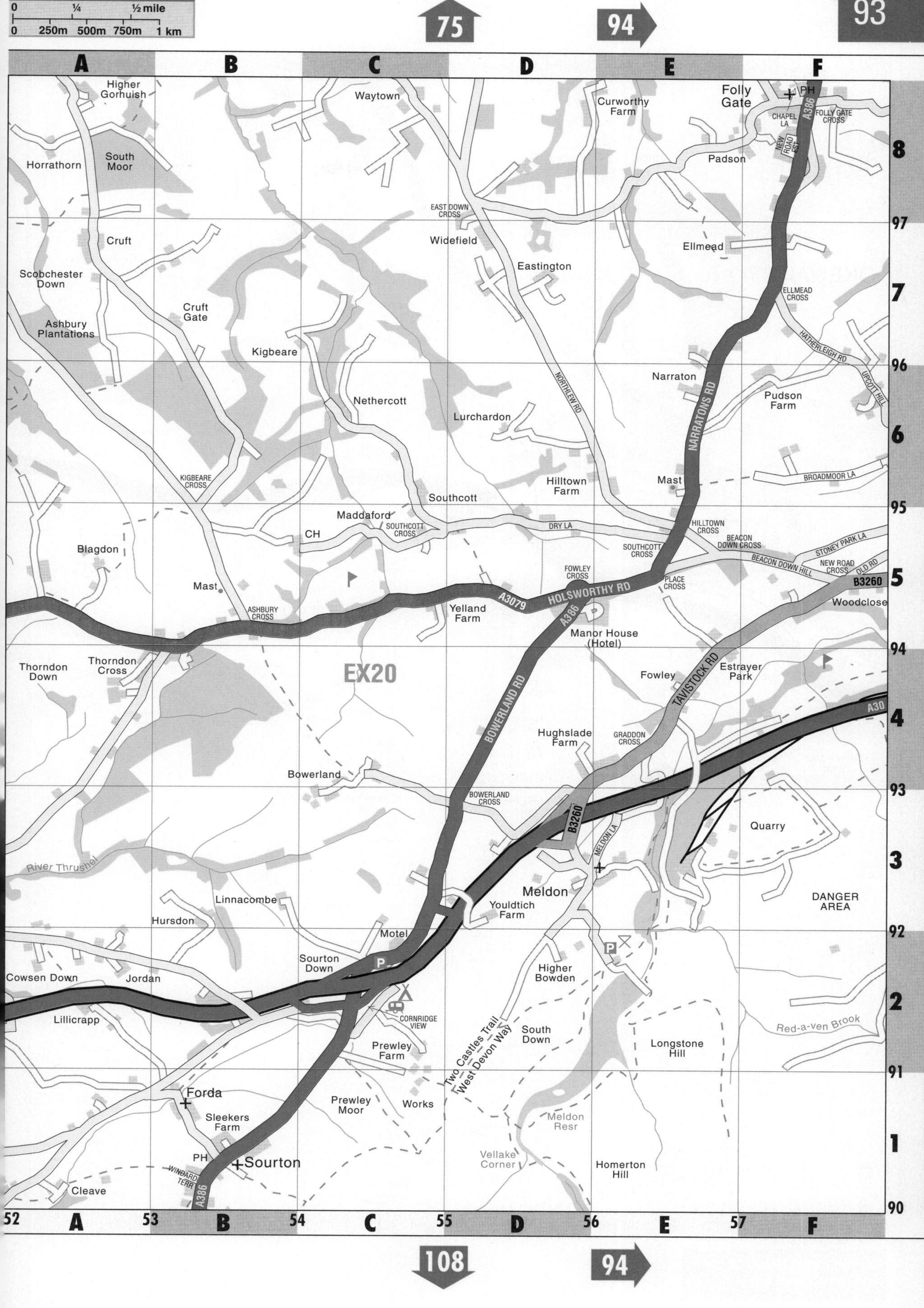
Scale: 1¾ inches to 1 mile
0 ¼ ½ mile
0 250m 500m 750m 1 km
75
94
108
94
Higher Gorhuish
South Moor
Horrathorn
Waytown
Curworthy Farm
Folly Gate
PH
CHAPEL LA
FOLLY GATE CROSS
NEW ROAD EST
Padson
EAST DOWN CROSS
Widefield
Cruft
Scobchester Down
Eastington
Ellmead
ELLMEAD CROSS
Cruft Gate
Ashbury Plantations
Kigbeare
HATHERLEIGH RD
UPCOTT HILL
Narraton
Pudson Farm
NORTHLEW RD
NARRATONS RD
Nethercott
Lurchardon
KIGBEARE CROSS
Hilltown Farm
Mast
BROADMOOR LA
Southcott
Maddaford
SOUTHCOTT CROSS
DRY LA
HILLTOWN CROSS
BEACON DOWN CROSS
STONEY PARK LA
Blagdon
CH
SOUTHCOTT CROSS
BEACON DOWN HILL
NEW ROAD CROSS
OLD RD
FOWLEY CROSS
PLACE CROSS
B3260
Mast
HOLSWORTHY RD
A3079
A386
Woodclose
ASHBURY CROSS
Yelland Farm
Manor House (Hotel)
Thorndon Down
Thorndon Cross
EX20
Fowley
TAVISTOCK RD
Estrayer Park
BOWERLAND RD
A30
Hughslade Farm
GRADDON CROSS
Bowerland
BOWERLAND CROSS
B3260
Quarry
MELDON LA
River Thrushel
Meldon
DANGER AREA
Linnacombe
Youldtich Farm
Hursdon
Motel
Sourton Down
P
Higher Bowden
Cowsen Down
Jordan
Lillicrapp
CORNRIDGE VIEW
Prewley Farm
South Down
Two Castles Trail
West Devon Way
Longstone Hill
Red-a-ven Brook
Forda
Prewley Moor
Works
Sleekers Farm
Meldon Resr
PH
Sourton
WINDARD TERR
Vellake Corner
Homerton Hill
Cleave
A B C D E F
8 97 7 96 6 95 5 94 4 93 3 92 2 91 1 90
52 53 54 55 56 57

93
76

Scale: 1¾ inches to 1 mile
0 ¼ ½ mile
0 250m 500m 750m 1 km

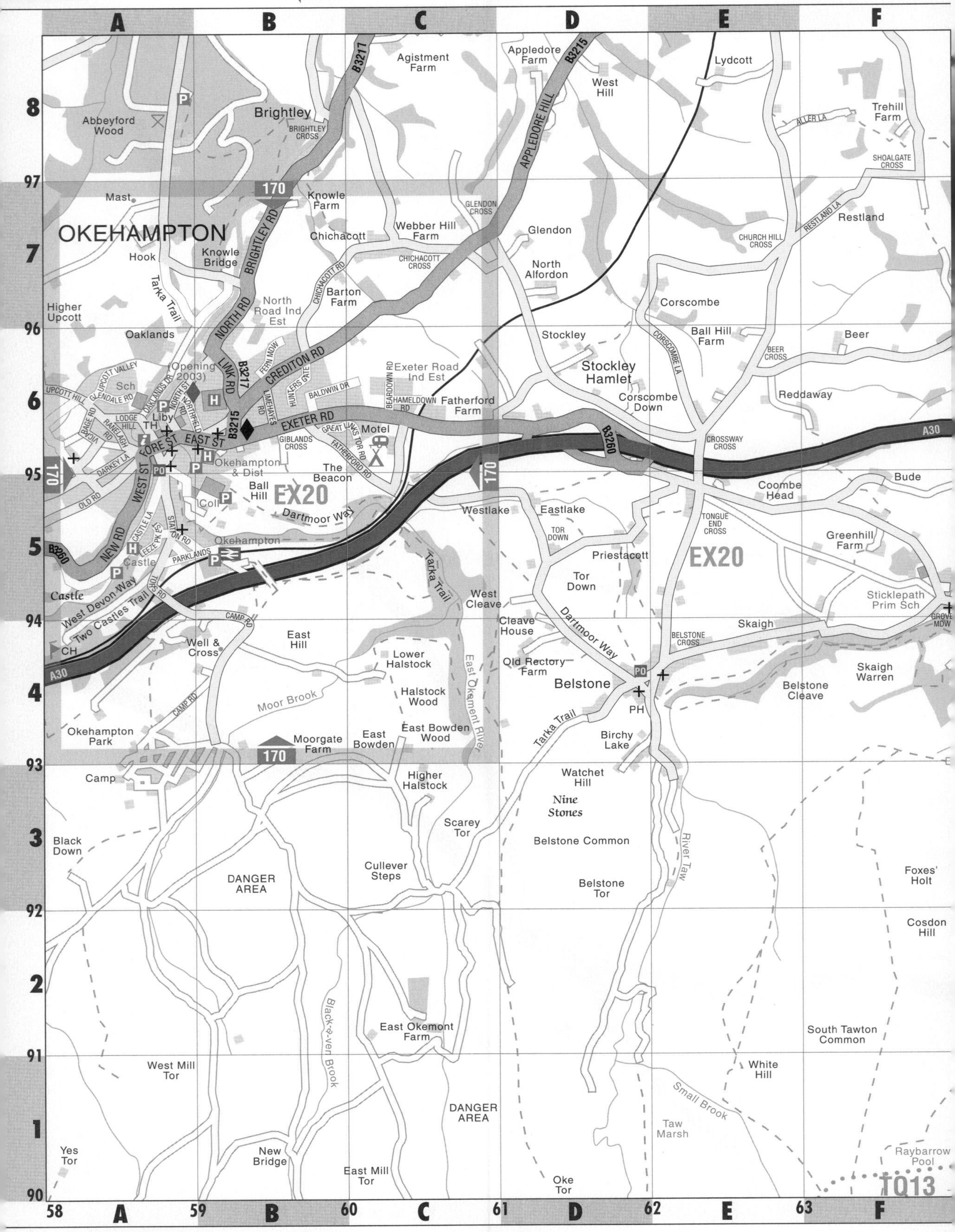

A B C D E F

OKEHAMPTON
Abbeyford Wood
Brightley
BRIGHTLEY CROSS
Agistment Farm
Appledore Farm
West Hill
Lydcott
Trehill Farm
ALLER LA
SHOALGATE CROSS
Mast
Knowle Farm
Chichacott
Webber Hill Farm
GLENDON CROSS
Glendon
North Alfordon
Restland
RESTLAND LA
CHURCH HILL CROSS
Hook
Knowle Bridge
Tarka Trail
CHICHACOTT CROSS
Barton Farm
North Road Ind Est
Corscombe
Higher Upcott
Oaklands
Stockley
Ball Hill Farm
Beer
BEER CROSS
CORSCOMBE LA
Stockley Hamlet
Reddaway
Corscombe Down
(Opening 2003)
Exeter Road Ind Est
Fatherford Farm
HAMELDOWN RD
BEARDOWN RD
BALDWIN DR
HUNTERS GATE
LIMEHAYES RD
FERN MDW
CREDITON RD
EXETER RD
NORTH RD
LINK RD
BRIGHTLEY RD
APPLEDORE HILL
B3217
B3215
B3260
A30
UPCOTT HILL
UPCOTT VALLEY
GLENDALE RD
OAKLANDS DR
NORTH ST
NORTHFIELD RD
Sch
Liby
TH
LODGE HILL
RAMELAGH RD
VICARAGE RD
DARKEY LA
FORE ST
EAST ST
WEST ST
OLD RD
NEW RD
GIBLANDS CROSS
GREAT LINKS TOR RD
FATHERFORD RD
Motel
CROSSWAY CROSS
Okehampton & Dist
The Beacon
Ball Hill
EX20
Coll
Dartmoor Way
Westlake
Eastlake
TOR DOWN
Coombe Head
Bude
TONGUE END CROSS
Greenhill Farm
Okehampton
Priestacott
EX20
CASTLE LA
LEEZE PK ES
STATION RD
PARKLANDS
Castle
Tor Down
Castle
West Devon Way
Two Castles Trail
HOLT RD
CAMP RD
West Cleave
Sticklepath Prim Sch
GROVE MDW
Cleave House
Skaigh
BELSTONE CROSS
CH
Well & Cross
East Hill
Lower Halstock
Old Rectory Farm
Skaigh Warren
Halstock Wood
East Okement River
Belstone
PO
PH
Belstone Cleave
Moor Brook
Tarka Trail
Okehampton Park
East Bowden
East Bowden Wood
Birchy Lake
Moorgate Farm
170
Camp
Higher Halstock
Watchet Hill
Nine Stones
Black Down
Scarey Tor
Belstone Common
River Taw
Cullever Steps
DANGER AREA
Belstone Tor
Foxes' Holt
Cosdon Hill
Black-a-ven Brook
East Okemont Farm
South Tawton Common
West Mill Tor
White Hill
Small Brook
DANGER AREA
Taw Marsh
Yes Tor
New Bridge
East Mill Tor
Oke Tor
Raybarrow Pool
TQ13

8 97 7 96 6 95 5 94 4 93 3 92 2 91 1 90
58 A 59 B 60 C 61 D 62 E 63 F

For full street detail of the highlighted area see page 170.
93
109

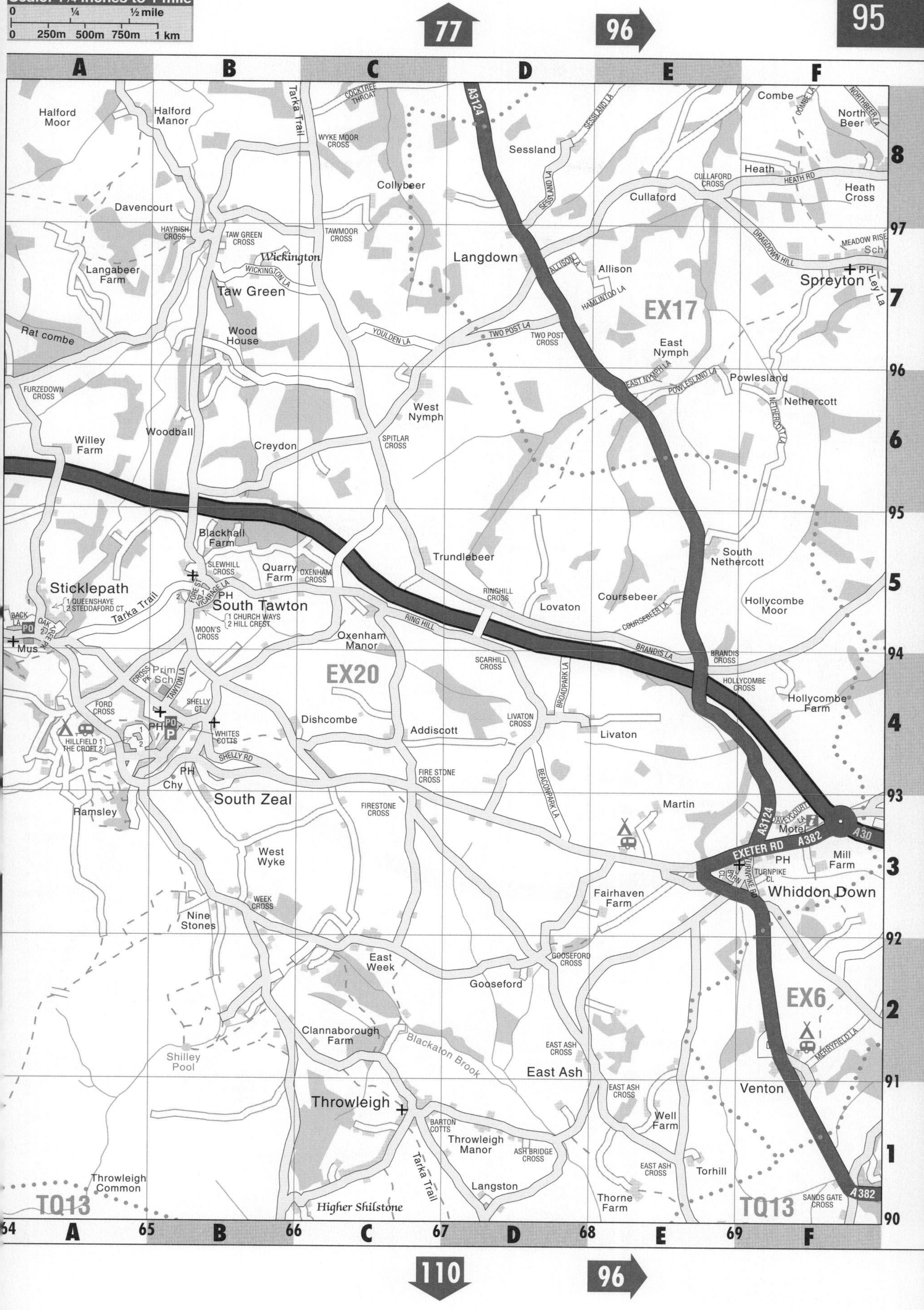
Scale: 1¾ inches to 1 mile
0 ¼ ½ mile
0 250m 500m 750m 1 km
77
96
110
96
Halford Moor
Halford Manor
Tarka Trail
Cocktree Throat
A3124
Sessland La
Combe
Combe La
Northbeer La
North Beer
Wyke Moor Cross
Sessland
Collybeer
Heath
Cullaford Cross
Heath Rd
Heath Cross
Cullaford
Davencourt
Hayrish Cross
Taw Green Cross
Tawmoor Cross
Wickington
Wickington La
Langdown
Allison La
Allison
Dragdown Hill
Meadow Rise
Sch
PH
Spreyton
Ley La
Langabeer Farm
Taw Green
Hamlintoo La
EX17
Rat combe
Wood House
Youlden La
Two Post La
Two Post Cross
East Nymph
Furzedown Cross
East Nymph La
Powlesland La
Powlesland
Nethercott La
Nethercott
West Nymph
Willey Farm
Woodball
Creydon
Spitlar Cross
Blackhall Farm
Trundlebeer
South Nethercott
Sticklepath
Slewhill Cross
Quarry Farm
Oxenham Cross
1 Queenshaye
2 Steddaford Ct
Tarka Trail
Fore St
Vicarage La
PH
South Tawton
Ringhill Cross
Lovaton
Coursebeer
Hollycombe Moor
Back La
PO
Oak Tree Pk
Mus
1 Church Ways
2 Hill Crest
Moon's Cross
Oxenham Manor
Ring Hill
Coursebeer La
Brandis La
Brandis Cross
Scarhill Cross
EX20
Cross Pk
Prim Sch
Tawton La
Hollycombe Cross
Hollycombe Farm
Broadpark La
Ford Cross
Shelly Ct
Dishcombe
Livaton Cross
PH
PO
P
Whites Cotts
Addiscott
Livaton
Hillfield 1
The Croft 2
Shelly Rd
Fire Stone Cross
Beaconpark La
PH
Chy
South Zeal
Ramsley
Firestone Cross
Martin
Davey Court La
Motel
A3124
A30
Exeter Rd
A382
PH
Mill Farm
West Wyke
Barn Cl
Turnpike Rd
Turnpike Cl
Whiddon Down
Week Cross
Fairhaven Farm
Nine Stones
East Week
Gooseford Cross
Gooseford
EX6
Clannaborough Farm
Blackaton Brook
Merryfield La
Shilley Pool
East Ash Cross
East Ash
East Ash Cross
Venton
Throwleigh
Barton Cotts
Well Farm
Throwleigh Manor
Ash Bridge Cross
Tarka Trail
Throwleigh Common
Langston
East Ash Cross
Torhill
TQ13
Higher Shilstone
Thorne Farm
Sands Gate Cross
A382
TQ13
A B C D E F
64 65 66 67 68 69
90 91 92 93 94 95 96 97
1 2 3 4 5 6 7 8

95 78

Scale: 1¾ inches to 1 mile

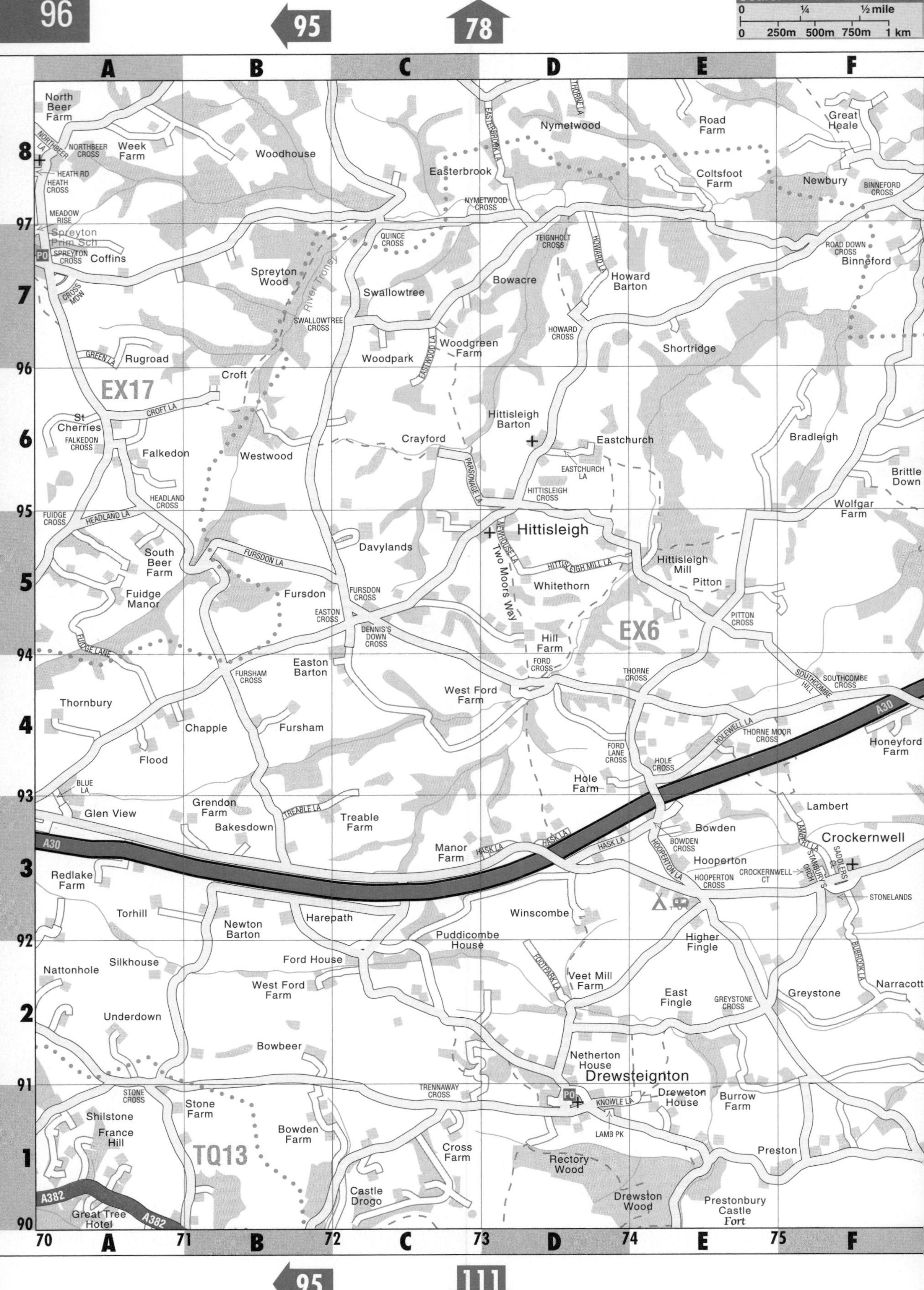

95 111

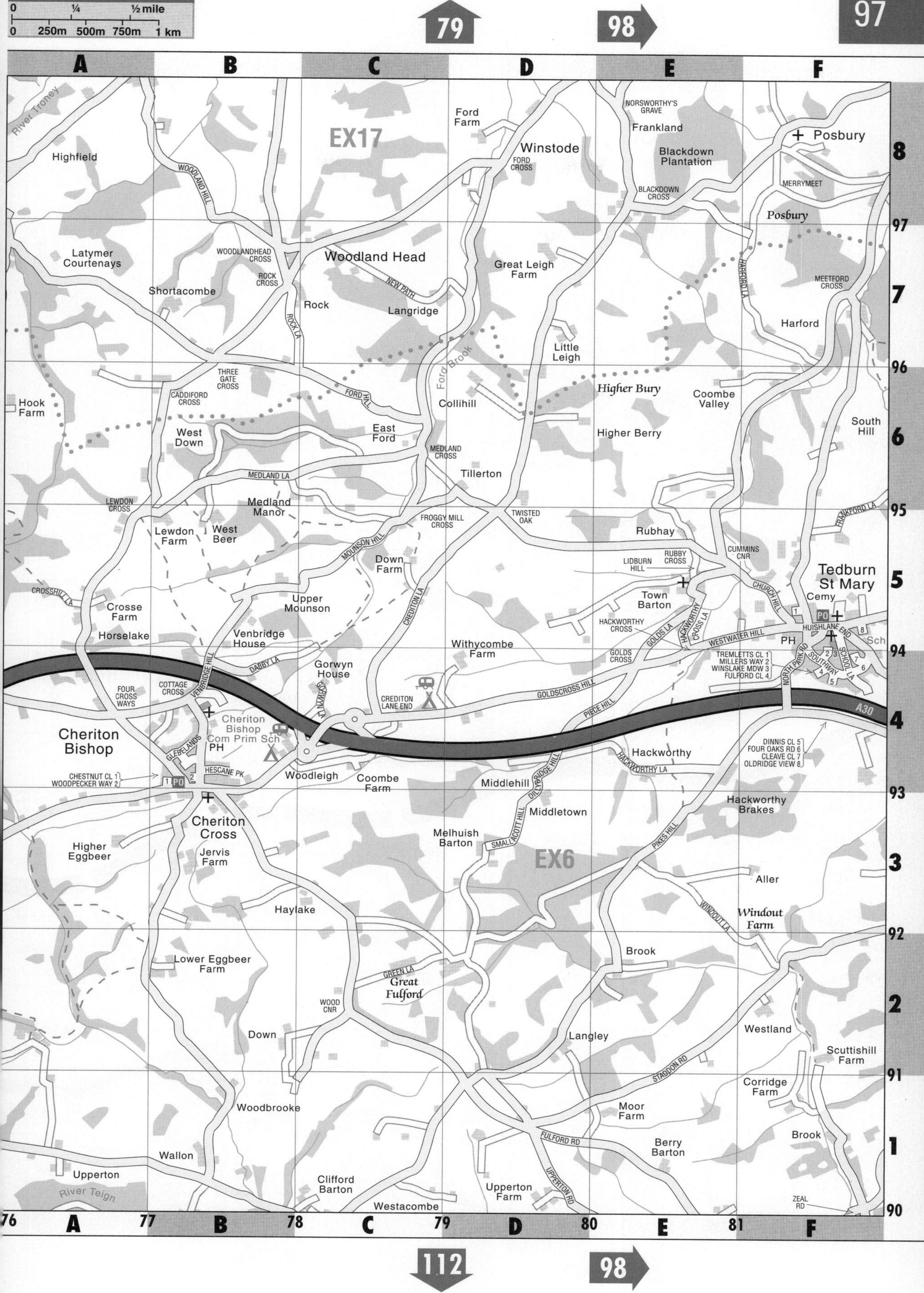
Scale: 1¾ inches to 1 mile
0 ¼ ½ mile
0 250m 500m 750m 1 km
79
98
EX17
Highfield
Latymer Courtenays
Shortacombe
Woodland Head
Rock
Langridge
Ford Farm
Winstode
Frankland
Blackdown Plantation
Posbury
Harford
Hook Farm
West Down
Medland Manor
Lewdon Farm
West Beer
Crosse Farm
Horselake
Upper Mounson
Venbridge House
Gorwyn House
Down Farm
East Ford
Collihill
Tillerton
Great Leigh Farm
Little Leigh
Higher Bury
Higher Berry
Coombe Valley
South Hill
Rubhay
Town Barton
Tedburn St Mary
Withycombe Farm
Cheriton Bishop
Cheriton Bishop Com Prim Sch
Woodleigh
Coombe Farm
Middlehill
Middletown
Hackworthy
Hackworthy Brakes
Cheriton Cross
Higher Eggbeer
Jervis Farm
Melhuish Barton
EX6
Aller
Windout Farm
Haylake
Lower Eggbeer Farm
Great Fulford
Brook
Down
Langley
Westland
Scuttishill Farm
Woodbrooke
Corridge Farm
Moor Farm
Wallon
Upperton
River Teign
Clifford Barton
Westacombe
Upperton Farm
Berry Barton
Brook
River Troney
Ford Brook
A30
112
98

97 80 172

Scale: 1¾ inches to 1 mile

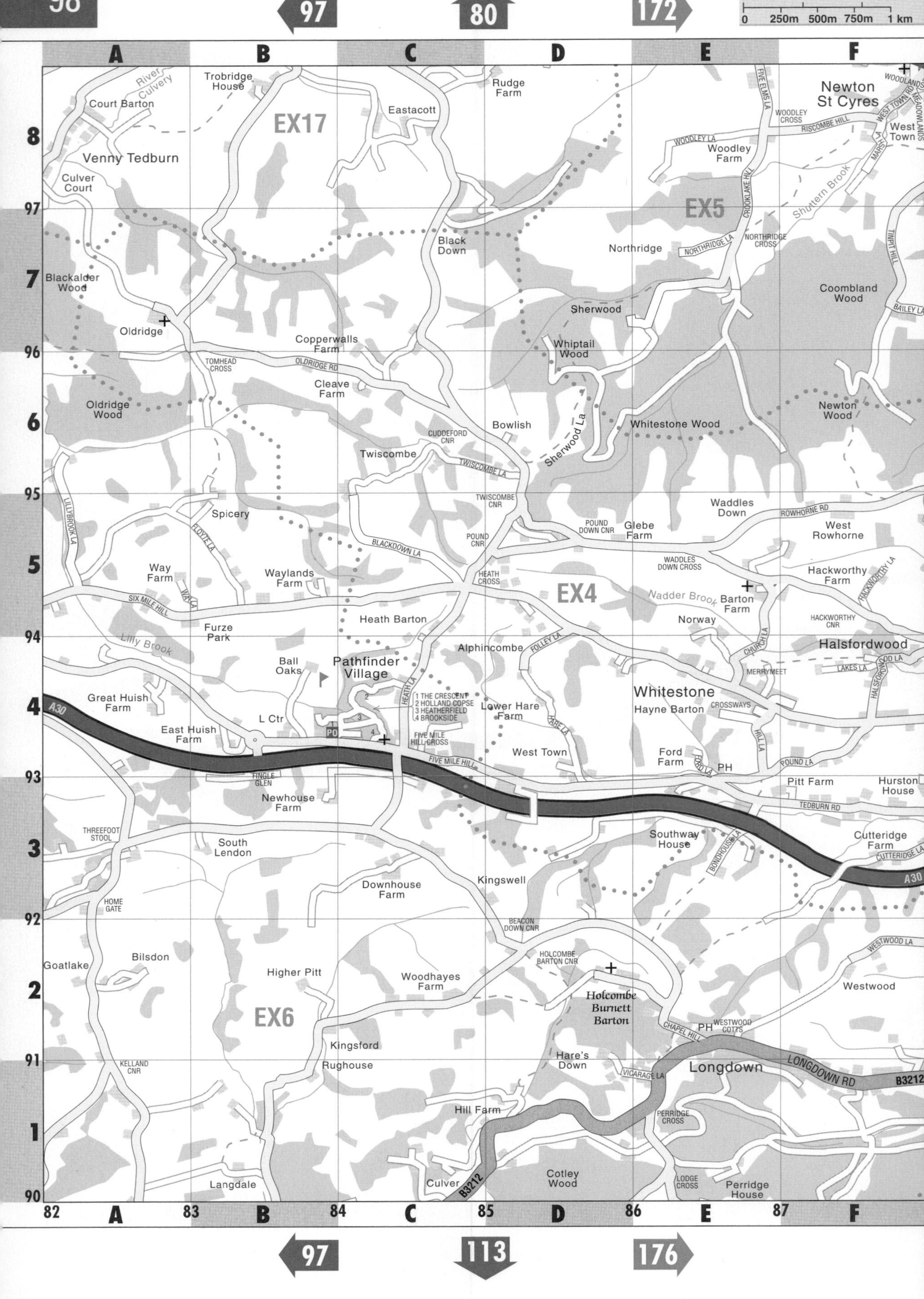

97 113 176

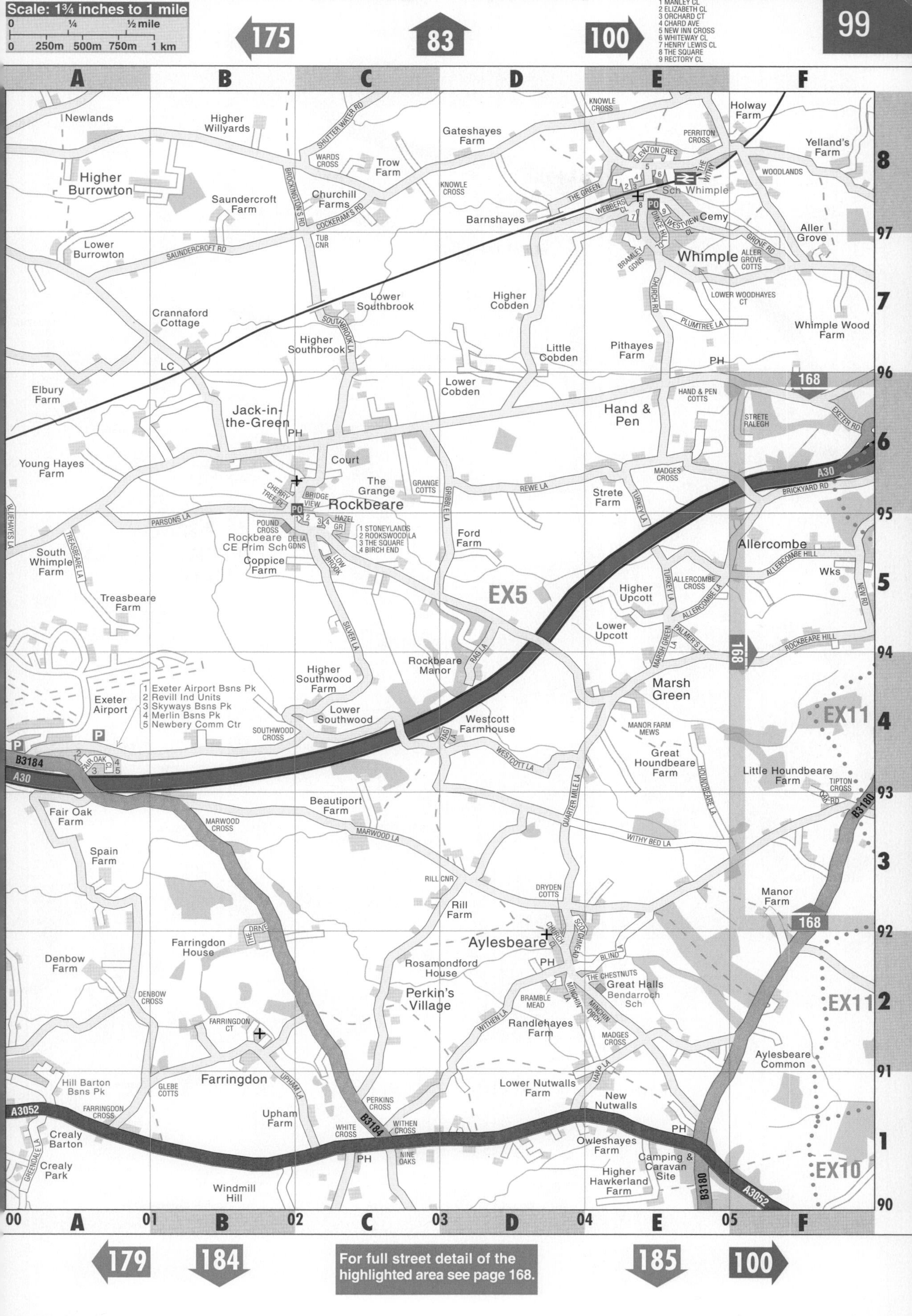
Scale: 1¾ inches to 1 mile
0
¼
½ mile
0
250m
500m
750m
1 km
175
83
100
E8
1 MANLEY CL
2 ELIZABETH CL
3 ORCHARD CT
4 CHARD AVE
5 NEW INN CROSS
6 WHITEWAY CL
7 HENRY LEWIS CL
8 THE SQUARE
9 RECTORY CL
99
A
B
C
D
E
F
Newlands
Higher Willyards
SHUTTER WATER RD
Gateshayes Farm
KNOWLE CROSS
Holway Farm
PERRITON CROSS
Yelland's Farm
WARDS CROSS
Trow Farm
SLEWTON CRES
THE WITHY
WOODLANDS
8
Higher Burrowton
BROCKINGTON'S RD
Churchill Farms
KNOWLE CROSS
THE GREEN
Sch Whimple
Saundercroft Farm
COCKERAM'S RD
Barnshayes
WEBBERS CL
PO
DINCE HILL
WESTVIEW CL
Cemy
Aller Grove
97
TUB CNR
GRONE RD
Lower Burrowton
SAUNDERCROFT RD
BRAMLEY GDNS
Whimple
ALLER GROVE COTTS
LOWER WOODHAYES CT
Lower Southbrook
Higher Cobden
CHURCH RD
7
Crannaford Cottage
SOUTHBROOK LA
PLUMTREE LA
Whimple Wood Farm
Higher Southbrook
Little Cobden
Pithayes Farm
LC
PH
96
168
Elbury Farm
Lower Cobden
HAND & PEN COTTS
Jack-in-the-Green
Hand & Pen
STRETE RALEGH
EXETER RD
PH
6
Young Hayes Farm
Court
MADGES CROSS
A30
The Grange
GRANGE COTTS
REWE LA
CHERRY TREE CL
BRIDGE VIEW
Rockbeare
Strete Farm
BRICKYARD RD
PO
TURKEY LA
PARSONS LA
POUND CROSS
HAZEL GR
GRIBBLE LA
95
1 STONEYLANDS
2 ROOKSWOOD LA
3 THE SQUARE
4 BIRCH END
Ford Farm
Rockbeare CE Prim Sch
DELIA GDNS
Allercombe
South Whimple Farm
TREASBEARE LA
Coppice Farm
LOW BROOK
ALLERCOMBE HILL
Wks
ALLERCOMBE CROSS
TURKEY LA
NEW RD
EX5
Higher Upcott
5
Treasbeare Farm
ALLERCOMBE LA
Lower Upcott
SILVER LA
PALMER'S LA
MARSH GREEN LA
Rockbeare Manor
RAG LA
168
ROCKBEARE HILL
94
Higher Southwood Farm
Marsh Green
Exeter Airport
1 Exeter Airport Bsns Pk
2 Revill Ind Units
3 Skyways Bsns Pk
4 Merlin Bsns Pk
5 Newbery Comm Ctr
Lower Southwood
Westcott Farmhouse
EX11
4
MANOR FARM MEWS
P
SOUTHWOOD CROSS
RAG LA
P
WESTCOTT LA
Great Houndbeare Farm
HOUNDBEARE LA
B3184
FAIR OAK CL
Little Houndbeare Farm
TIPTON CROSS
A30
QUARTER MILE LA
OAK RD
93
Fair Oak Farm
Beautiport Farm
MARWOOD CROSS
B3180
MARWOOD LA
WITHY BED LA
Spain Farm
3
RILL CNR
DRYDEN COTTS
Manor Farm
Rill Farm
168
92
THE DRIVE
CHURCH CL
SCOTCHMEAD
Farringdon House
Aylesbeare
BLIND LA
Denbow Farm
Rosamondford House
PH
THE CHESTNUTS
Great Halls
Bendarroch Sch
Perkin's Village
BRAMBLE MEAD
MINCHIN LA
EX11
2
DENBOW CROSS
WITHEN LA
MINCHIN ORCH
Randlehayes Farm
FARRINGDON CT
MADGES CROSS
Aylesbeare Common
91
Hill Barton Bsns Pk
Farringdon
UPHAM LA
Lower Nutwalls Farm
HARP LA
GLEBE COTTS
New Nutwalls
A3052
FARRINGDON CROSS
PERKINS CROSS
Upham Farm
Crealy Barton
WHITE CROSS
B3184
WITHEN CROSS
PH
1
Owleshayes Farm
GREENDALE LA
Crealy Park
PH
NINE OAKS
Camping & Caravan Site
Higher Hawkerland Farm
EX10
Windmill Hill
B3180
A3052
90
00
01
02
03
04
05
179
184
For full street detail of the highlighted area see page 168.
185
100

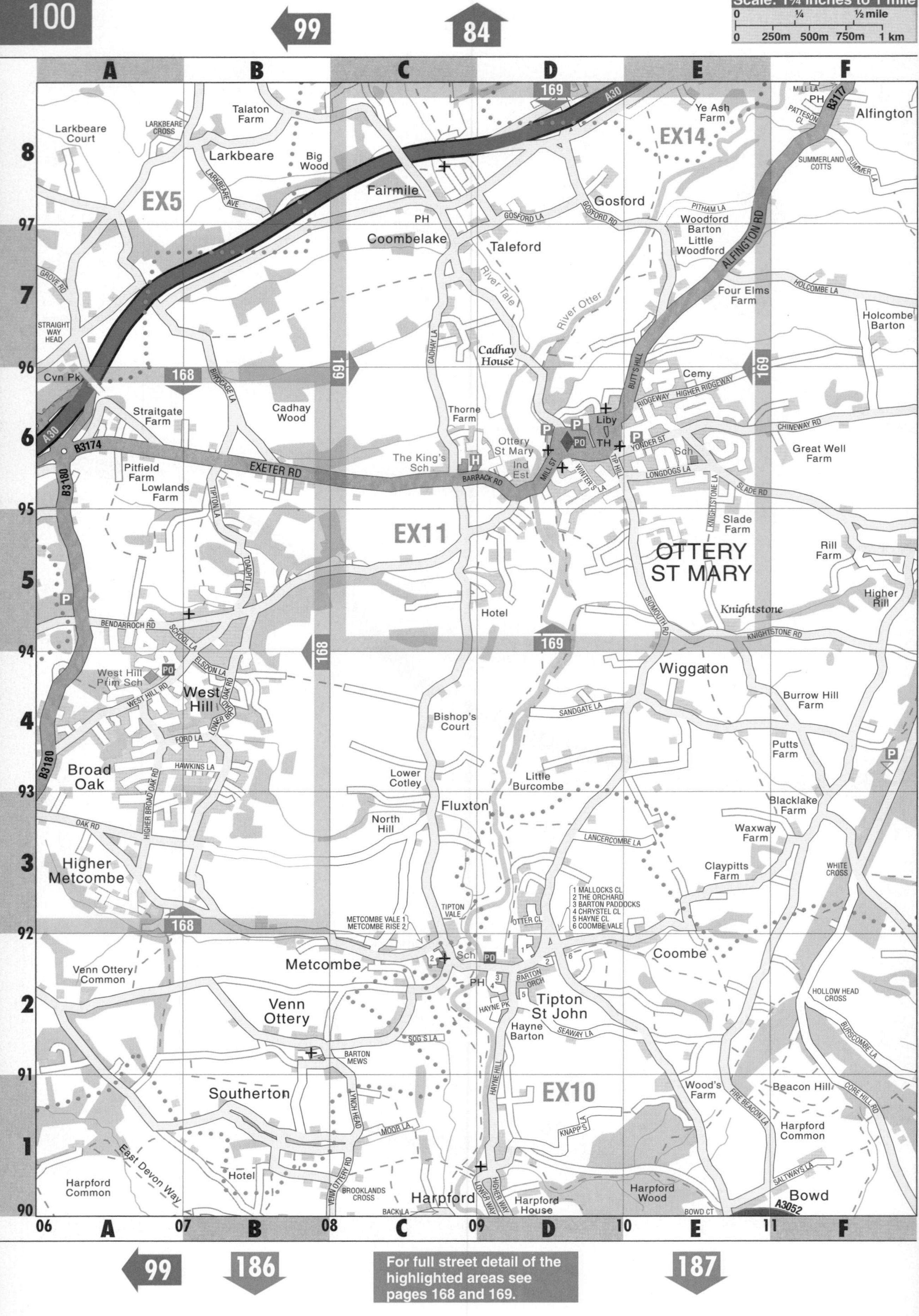

100
99
84
Scale: 1¾ inches to 1 mile
0 ¼ ½ mile
0 250m 500m 750m 1 km
A B C D E F
8 97 7 96 6 95 5 94 4 93 3 92 2 91 1 90
06 07 08 09 10 11
Larkbeare Court
Larkbeare Cross
Talaton Farm
Larkbeare
Big Wood
EX5
Larkbeare Ave
A30
169
Fairmile
PH
Coombelake
Taleford
Gosford La
Gosford Rd
Gosford
Ye Ash Farm
EX14
Mill La
PH
Patteson Cl
B3177
Alfington
Summerland Cotts
Summer La
Pitham La
Woodford Barton
Little Woodford
Alfington Rd
Grove Rd
Straight Way Head
River Tale
River Otter
Four Elms Farm
Holcombe La
Holcombe Barton
Cadhay La
Cadhay House
Cvn Pk
168
Birdcage La
Straitgate Farm
Cadhay Wood
Thorne Farm
Butts Hill
Cemy
Ridgeway
Higher Ridgeway
Liby
Chineway Rd
B3174
Pitfield Farm
Lowlands Farm
B3180
Tipton La
Exeter Rd
The King's Sch
H
Ottery St Mary
Ind Est
Barrack Rd
Mill St
P
PO
TH
Yonder St
Sch
Winter's La
Tip Hill
Longdogs La
Great Well Farm
Slade Rd
Knightstone La
EX11
Toadpit La
Slade Farm
OTTERY ST MARY
Rill Farm
Higher Rill
Knightstone
Hotel
Sidmouth Rd
Bendarroch Rd
School La
Knightstone Rd
Elsdon La
West Hill Prim Sch
West Hill Rd
West Hill
Oak Rd
Lower Broad Oak Rd
Wiggaton
Burrow Hill Farm
Sandgate La
Bishop's Court
Ford La
Hawkins La
Broad Oak
Higher Broad Oak Rd
Putts Farm
Lower Cotley
Little Burcombe
Fluxton
North Hill
Blacklake Farm
Waxway Farm
Lancercombe La
Higher Metcombe
Claypitts Farm
White Cross
1 Mallocks Cl
2 The Orchard
3 Barton Paddocks
4 Chrystel Cl
5 Hayne Cl
6 Coombe Vale
Tipton Vale
Metcombe Vale 1
Metcombe Rise 2
Otter Cl
Venn Ottery Common
Metcombe
Coombe
Barton Orch
Hayne Pk
Tipton St John
Hollow Head Cross
Venn Ottery
Hayne Barton
Seaway La
Sog's La
Burscombe La
Barton Mews
Hayne Hill
Southerton
EX10
Wood's Farm
Beacon Hill
Fire Beacon La
Core Hill Rd
Lynch Head
Moor La
Knapp's La
East Devon Way
Harpford Common
Hotel
Venn Ottery Rd
Brooklands Cross
Back La
Harpford
Lower Way
Higher Way
Harpford House
Harpford Wood
Bowd Ct
Saltways La
Bowd
A3052
99
186
For full street detail of the highlighted areas see pages 168 and 169.
187

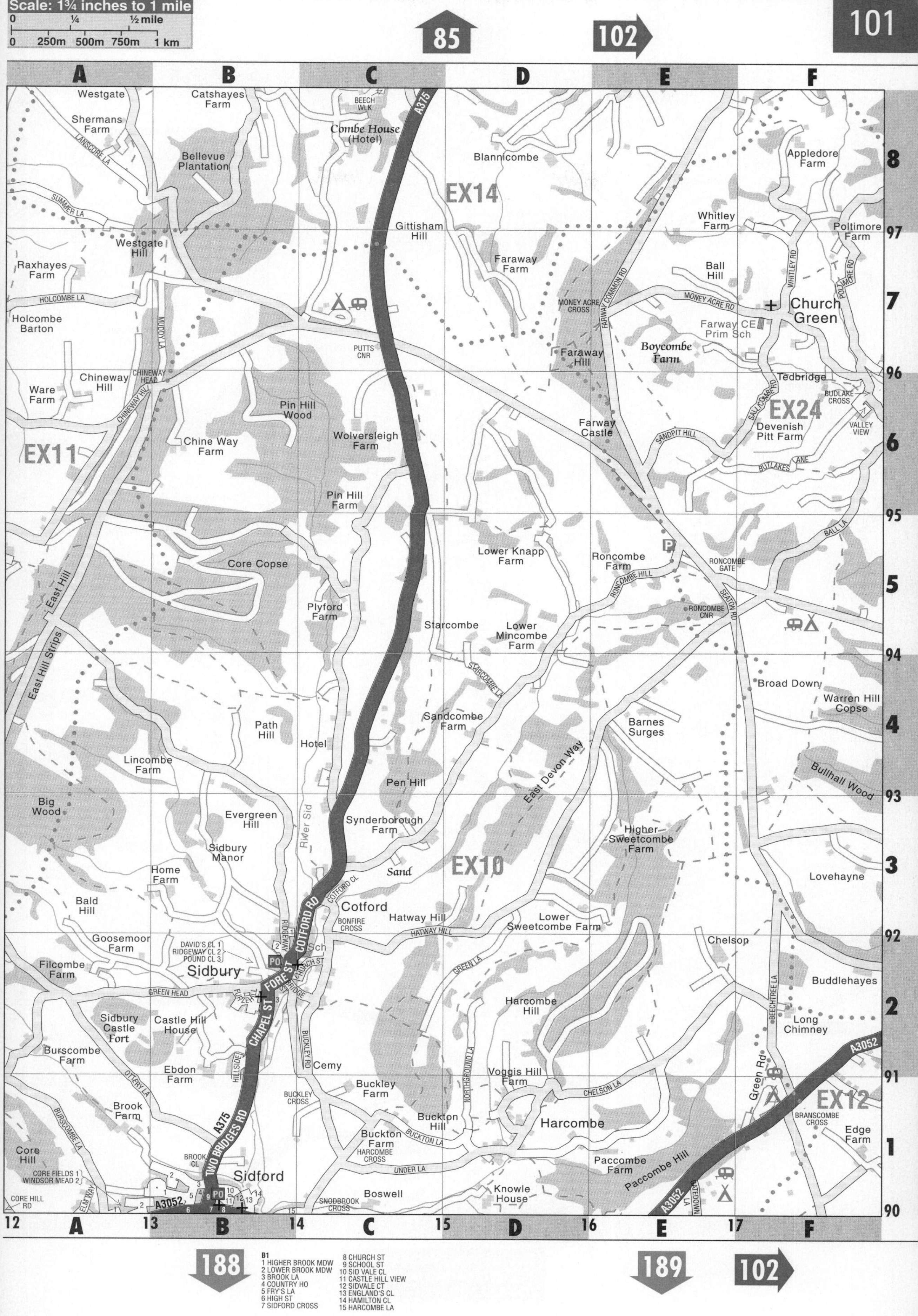

Scale: 1¾ inches to 1 mile
0 ¼ ½ mile
0 250m 500m 750m 1 km
85
102
101
A B C D E F
8 97 7 96 6 95 5 94 4 93 3 92 2 91 1 90
12 13 14 15 16 17
Westgate
Catshayes Farm
Shermans Farm
Bellevue Plantation
Combe House (Hotel)
Blannicombe
Appledore Farm
EX14
Gittisham Hill
Whitley Farm
Poltimore Farm
Westgate Hill
Raxhayes Farm
Faraway Farm
Ball Hill
Holcombe Barton
Money Acre Cross
Church Green
Farway CE Prim Sch
Boycombe Farm
Putts Cnr
Faraway Hill
Chineway Hill
Ware Farm
Chineway Head
Tedbridge
Budlake Cross
Pin Hill Wood
EX24
Farway Castle
Devenish Pitt Farm
Valley View
Chine Way Farm
Wolversleigh Farm
EX11
Pin Hill Farm
Lower Knapp Farm
Roncombe Farm
Roncombe Gate
Core Copse
East Hill
Plyford Farm
Starcombe
Lower Mincombe Farm
Roncombe Cnr
East Hill Strips
Broad Down
Warren Hill Copse
Sandcombe Farm
Path Hill
Hotel
Barnes Surges
Lincombe Farm
East Devon Way
Bullhall Wood
Pen Hill
Big Wood
Evergreen Hill
Synderborough Farm
Higher Sweetcombe Farm
Sidbury Manor
River Sid
Sand
EX10
Home Farm
Lovehayne
Bald Hill
Cotford
Bonfire Cross
Hatway Hill
Lower Sweetcombe Farm
Goosemoor Farm
Chelson
Filcombe Farm
Sidbury
Sch
Buddlehayes
Harcombe Hill
Sidbury Castle Fort
Castle Hill House
Long Chimney
Burscombe Farm
Cemy
Ebdon Farm
Voggis Hill Farm
Buckley Farm
Buckley Cross
Brook Farm
Buckton Hill
Harcombe
EX12
Branscombe Cross
Edge Farm
Core Hill
Buckton Farm
Harcombe Cross
Paccombe Farm
Paccombe Hill
Sidford
Boswell
Knowle House
Snodbrook Cross
Core Hill Rd
Core Fields 1
Windsor Mead 2
A375
A3052
Two Bridges Rd
Chapel St
Fore St
Cotford Rd
Church St
David's Cl 1
Ridgeway Cl 2
Pound Cl 3
Green Head
Ridgeway
Cotford Cl
Green La
Buckley Rd
Hillside
Otterly La
Burscombe La
Elm Way
Brook Cl
Under La
Northground La
Chelson La
Buckton La
Green Rd
Beechtree La
Gatedown La
Starcombe La
Roncombe Hill
Seaton Rd
Ball La
Butlakes Lane
Sandpit Hill
Sallcombe Rd
Money Acre Rd
Whitley Rd
Poltimore Rd
Farway Common Rd
Holcombe La
Summer La
Lanscore La
Muddy La
Chineway Hill
Hatway Hill
Beech Wlk
188
189
102
B1
1 HIGHER BROOK MDW
2 LOWER BROOK MDW
3 BROOK LA
4 COUNTRY HO
5 FRY'S LA
6 HIGH ST
7 SIDFORD CROSS
8 CHURCH ST
9 SCHOOL ST
10 SID VALE CL
11 CASTLE HILL VIEW
12 SIDVALE CT
13 ENGLAND'S CL
14 HAMILTON CL
15 HARCOMBE LA

Scale: 1¾ inches to 1 mile
0 ¼ ½ mile
0 250m 500m 750m 1 km

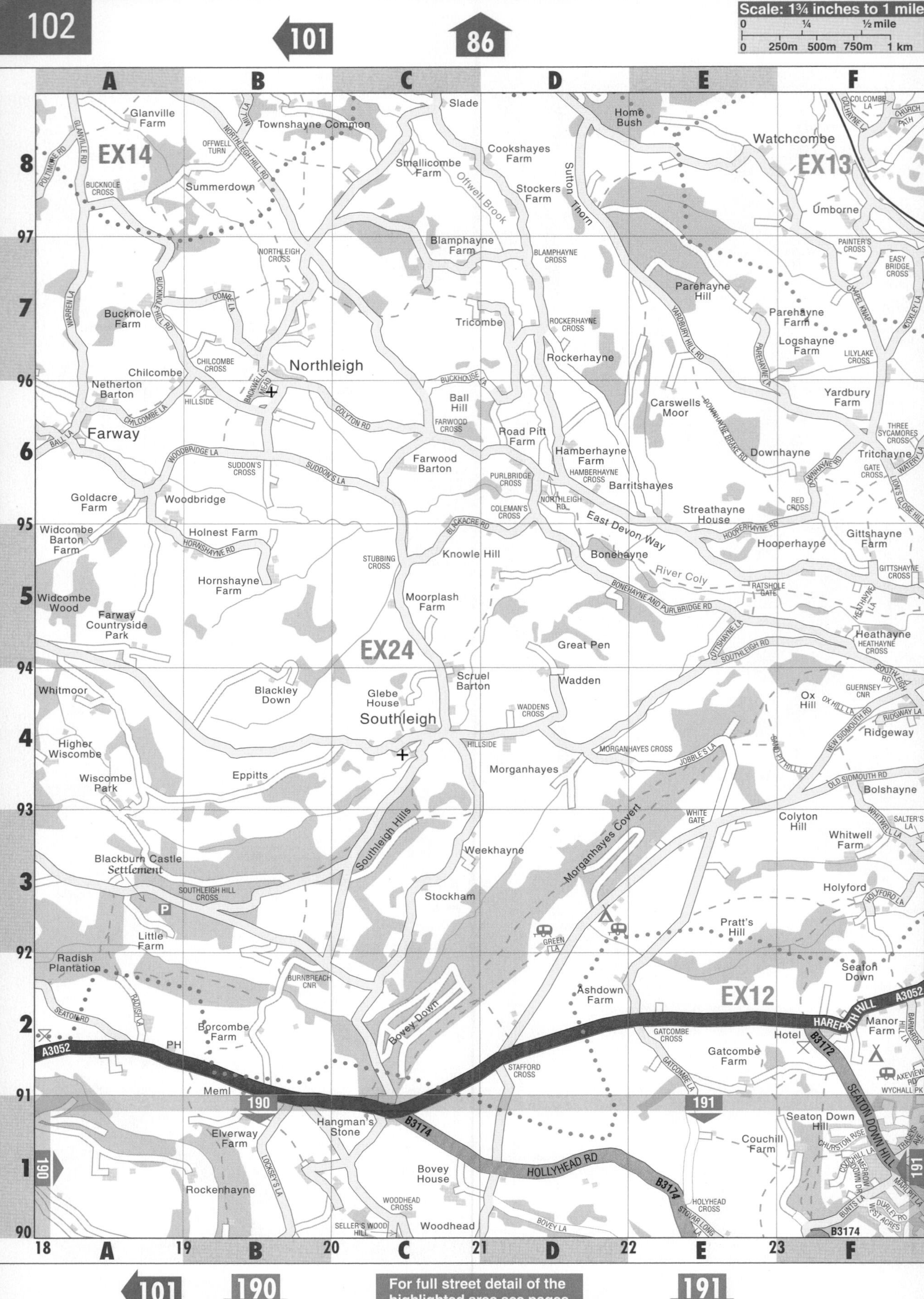

For full street detail of the highlighted area see pages 190 and 191.

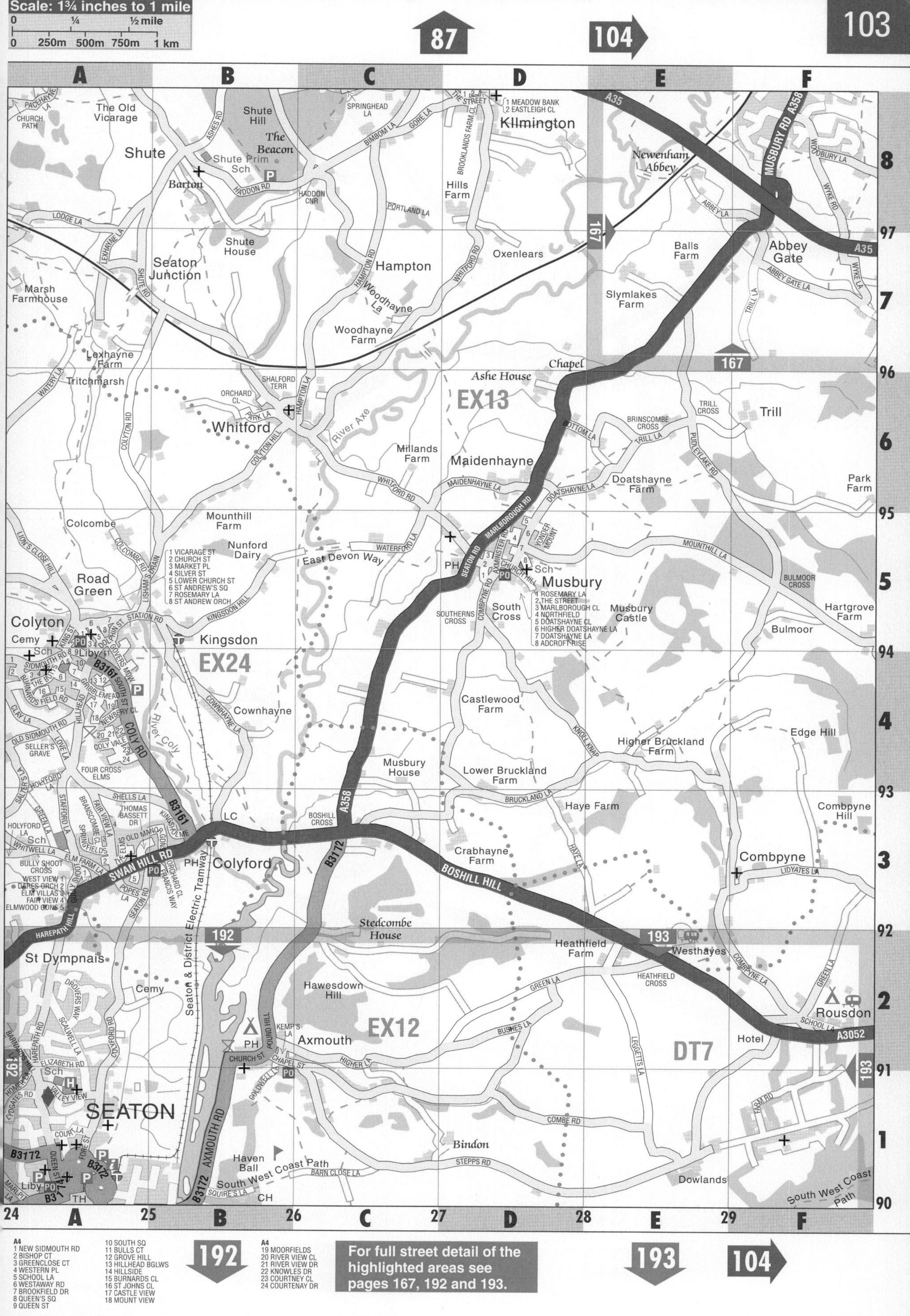

Scale: 1¾ inches to 1 mile
0 ¼ ½ mile
0 250m 500m 750m 1 km
87
104
103
A B C D E F
Shute
The Old Vicarage
Shute Hill
The Beacon
Shute Prim Sch
Barton
Kilmington
1 MEADOW BANK
2 EASTLEIGH CL
Newenham Abbey
Hills Farm
Shute House
Seaton Junction
Hampton
Oxenlears
Balls Farm
Abbey Gate
Marsh Farmhouse
Woodhayne La
Woodhayne Farm
Slymlakes Farm
Lexhayne Farm
Tritchmarsh
Chapel
Ashe House
EX13
Whitford
River Axe
Millands Farm
Maidenhayne
Trill
Doatshayne Farm
Park Farm
Colcombe
Mounthill Farm
Nunford Dairy
East Devon Way
1 VICARAGE ST
2 CHURCH ST
3 MARKET PL
4 SILVER ST
5 LOWER CHURCH ST
6 ST ANDREW'S SQ
7 ROSEMARY LA
8 ST ANDREW ORCH
Road Green
Colyton
Kingsdon
EX24
Musbury
South Cross
1 ROSEMARY LA
2 THE STREET
3 MARLBOROUGH CL
4 NORTHFIELD
5 DOATSHAYNE CL
6 HIGHER DOATSHAYNE LA
7 DOATSHAYNE LA
8 ADCROFT RISE
Musbury Castle
Hartgrove Farm
Bulmoor
Castlewood Farm
Cownhayne
River Coly
Edge Hill
Higher Bruckland Farm
Musbury House
Lower Bruckland Farm
Haye Farm
Combpyne Hill
Colyford
Crabhayne Farm
Combpyne
BOSHILL HILL
Stedcombe House
Seaton & District Electric Tramway
St Dympnais
Heathfield Farm
Westhayes
Hawesdown Hill
EX12
Axmouth
Rousdon
Hotel
DT7
SEATON
Bindon
Haven Ball
South West Coast Path
Dowlands
South West Coast Path
A35
A358
A3052
B3161
B3172
192
193
167
24 25 26 27 28 29
90 91 92 93 94 95 96 97
1 2 3 4 5 6 7 8
A4
1 NEW SIDMOUTH RD
2 BISHOP CT
3 GREENCLOSE CT
4 WESTERN PL
5 SCHOOL LA
6 WESTAWAY RD
7 BROOKFIELD DR
8 QUEEN'S SQ
9 QUEEN ST
10 SOUTH SQ
11 BULLS CT
12 GROVE HILL
13 HILLHEAD BGLWS
14 HILLSIDE
15 BURNARDS CL
16 ST JOHNS CL
17 CASTLE VIEW
18 MOUNT VIEW
A4
19 MOORFIELDS
20 RIVER VIEW CL
21 RIVER VIEW DR
22 KNOWLES DR
23 COURTNEY CL
24 COURTENAY DR
For full street detail of the highlighted areas see pages 167, 192 and 193.
192
193
104

103
88

Scale: 1¾ inches to 1 mile
0 ¼ ½ mile
0 250m 500m 750m 1 km

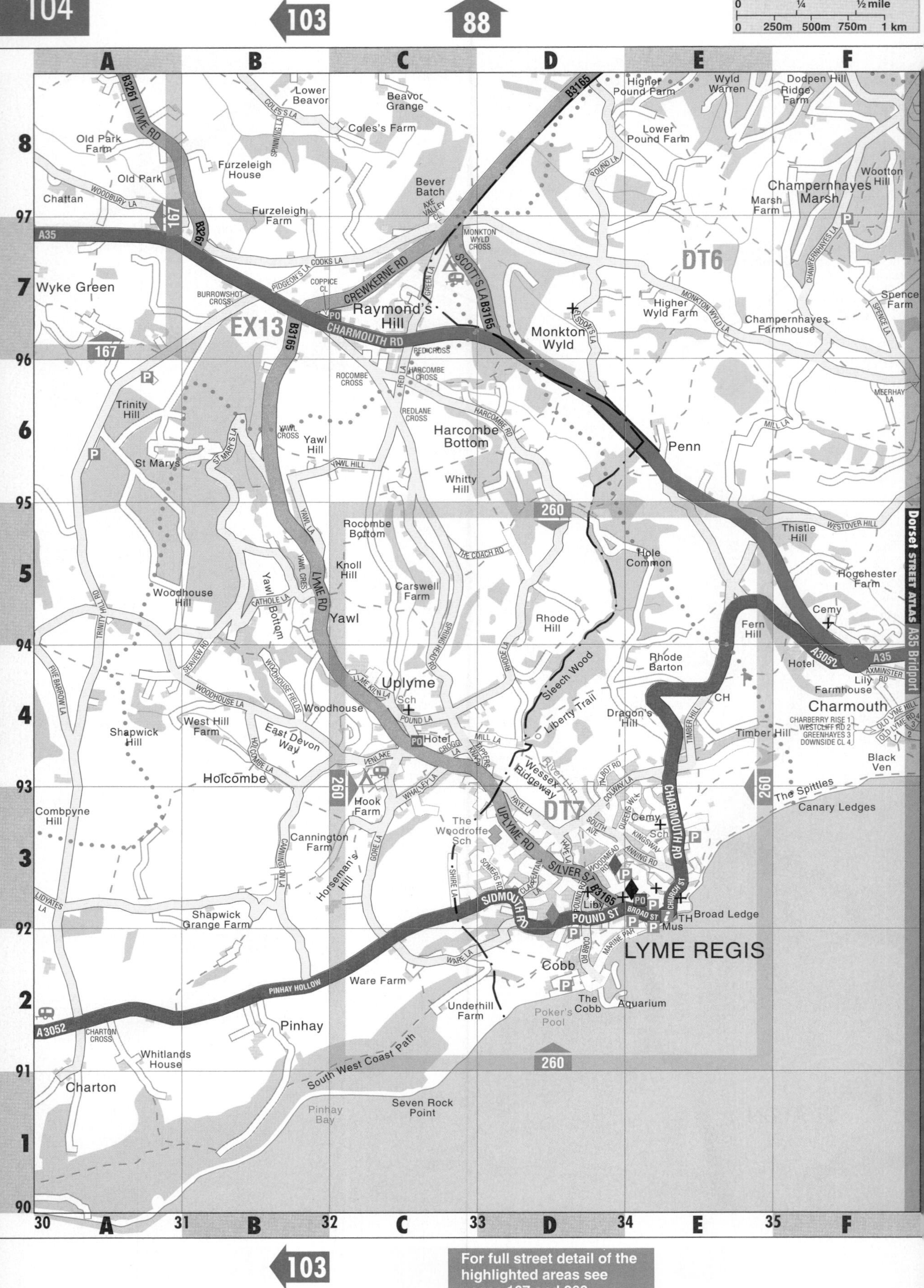

103

For full street detail of the highlighted areas see pages 167 and 260.

Scale: 1¾ inches to 1 mile
0 ¼ ½ mile
0 250m 500m 750m 1 km
90
106
Bridgetown
East Park
PINSLOW CROSS
A388
Hawkadon
Huntsdown
Emsworthy
PL16
Coombe Mill
Downtown Farm
Cobden
Thorne Moor
Druxton
Coombe
THORN MOOR CROSS
CAMP CROSS
CROSS GN
Kellacott
Poole
Peter's Finger
Boldford Bridge
Thorne
KELLACOTT CROSS
Kitcham
WHITEHILL CROSS
Jays
River Carey
Fernhill
A30
TIPPLE CROSS
JAYS CROSS
Ham Mill
Netherbridge
Lower Cookworthy
Carley
Wortham Manor
Higher Cookworthy
COLEMANS CROSS
Nether Bridge
Smallacombe
STONE CROSS
Beara
Stone
Tettaridge Barton
Heale
Two Castles Trail
Yeat
Coombe
Dutson
Liftondown
LIFTONDOWN CROSS
1 WILLAS RD
2 MOORFIELD
3 ARUNDELL GDNS
4 THE CRESCENT
TINHAY CROSS
River Thrushel
Cemy
THE ROWANS
Goodmansleigh
River Tamar
PL15
Welltown Farm
DARKEY LA
NORTH RD
OLD TINHAY
Tinhay
Sch
PO
ARUNDELL CL 5
BROAD ST 6
PARSONAGE CT 7
DUNTZ HILL 8
OAK RIDGE
FORE ST
NEW RD
PH
STATION RD
ASH VALE
PARK WOOD RISE
PARK RD
HANNAFORD RD
HORNAPARK CL
Lifton
Tinhay Mill Ind Est
LEAT RD
Wooladon Farm
Lifton Park
A388
Bamham
Ridgecombe
1 GOLDFINCH CL
2 CHOUGH CL
Bulsworthy Farm
PL16
Moonhouse Plantation
SNOWDROP CRES
FOXGLOVE CL
PRIMROSE WAY
Stourscombe
Newham Manor
Gatherley Wood
ROBIN DR
Lewcoombe
Wishworthy
Harts
Ashleigh
TAVISTOCK RD
3 STOURSCOMBE WOOD
4 GREGORY'S MDW
Treniffle
Turchington
Kellybeare
Newton Farm
LAUNCESTON
Lawhitton Barton
Gatherley
PL19
Yeomans
Winbrook
Hurdon Down
HOLMANS MDW
ST MICHAELS CL
Lawhitton
Hall Farm
Sheers Barton
B3362
Bawcombe
A B C D E F
34 35 36 37 38 39
8 89 7 88 6 87 5 86 4 85 3 84 2 83 1 82
Cornwall STREET ATLAS
A388 Launceston
A30 Launceston, Bodmin
A30 Launceston, Bodmin

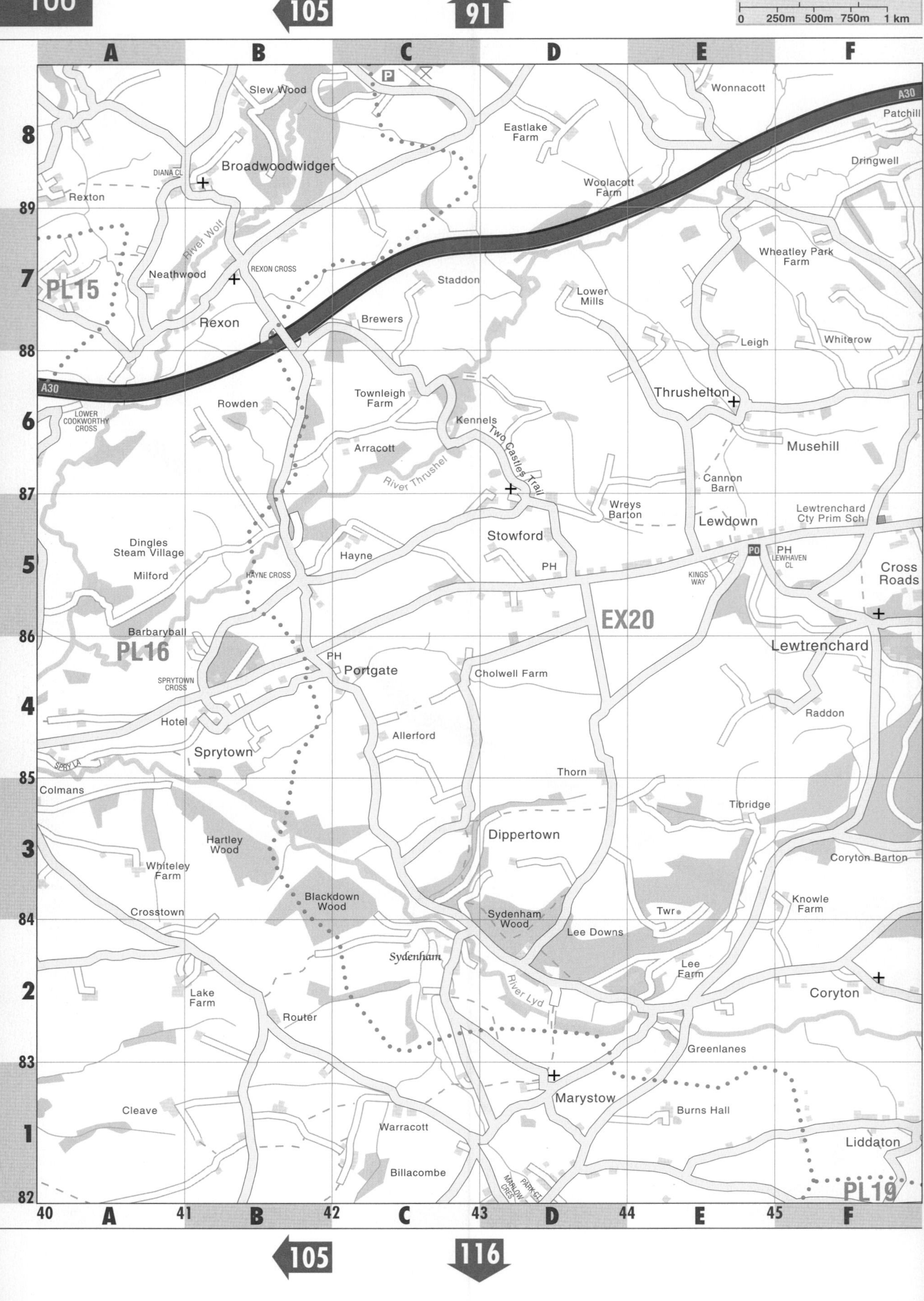
106
105
91
Scale: 1¾ inches to 1 mile
0 ¼ ½ mile
0 250m 500m 750m 1 km
A B C D E F
8 89 7 88 6 87 5 86 4 85 3 84 2 83 1 82
40 41 42 43 44 45
Slew Wood
Wonnacott
A30
Patchill
Eastlake Farm
Dringwell
DIANA CL
Broadwoodwidger
Rexton
Woolacott Farm
River Wolf
Wheatley Park Farm
Neathwood
REXON CROSS
Staddon
PL15
Lower Mills
Rexon
Brewers
Leigh
Whiterow
Rowden
Townleigh Farm
Thrushelton
LOWER COOKWORTHY CROSS
Kennels
Two Castles Trail
Arracott
Musehill
River Thrushel
Cannon Barn
Wreys Barton
Lewtrenchard Cty Prim Sch
Lewdown
Dingles Steam Village
Stowford
Hayne
PO
PH
LEWHAVEN CL
Cross Roads
Milford
HAYNE CROSS
KINGS WAY
EX20
Barbaryball
PL16
Lewtrenchard
Portgate
Cholwell Farm
SPRYTOWN CROSS
Raddon
Hotel
Allerford
Sprytown
SPRY LA
Thorn
Colmans
Tibridge
Dippertown
Hartley Wood
Coryton Barton
Whiteley Farm
Knowle Farm
Blackdown Wood
Crosstown
Sydenham Wood
Twr
Lee Downs
Sydenham
Lee Farm
Lake Farm
River Lyd
Coryton
Router
Greenlanes
Marystow
Cleave
Burns Hall
Warracott
Liddaton
Billacombe
MARLOW CRES
PARK CL
PL19
105
116

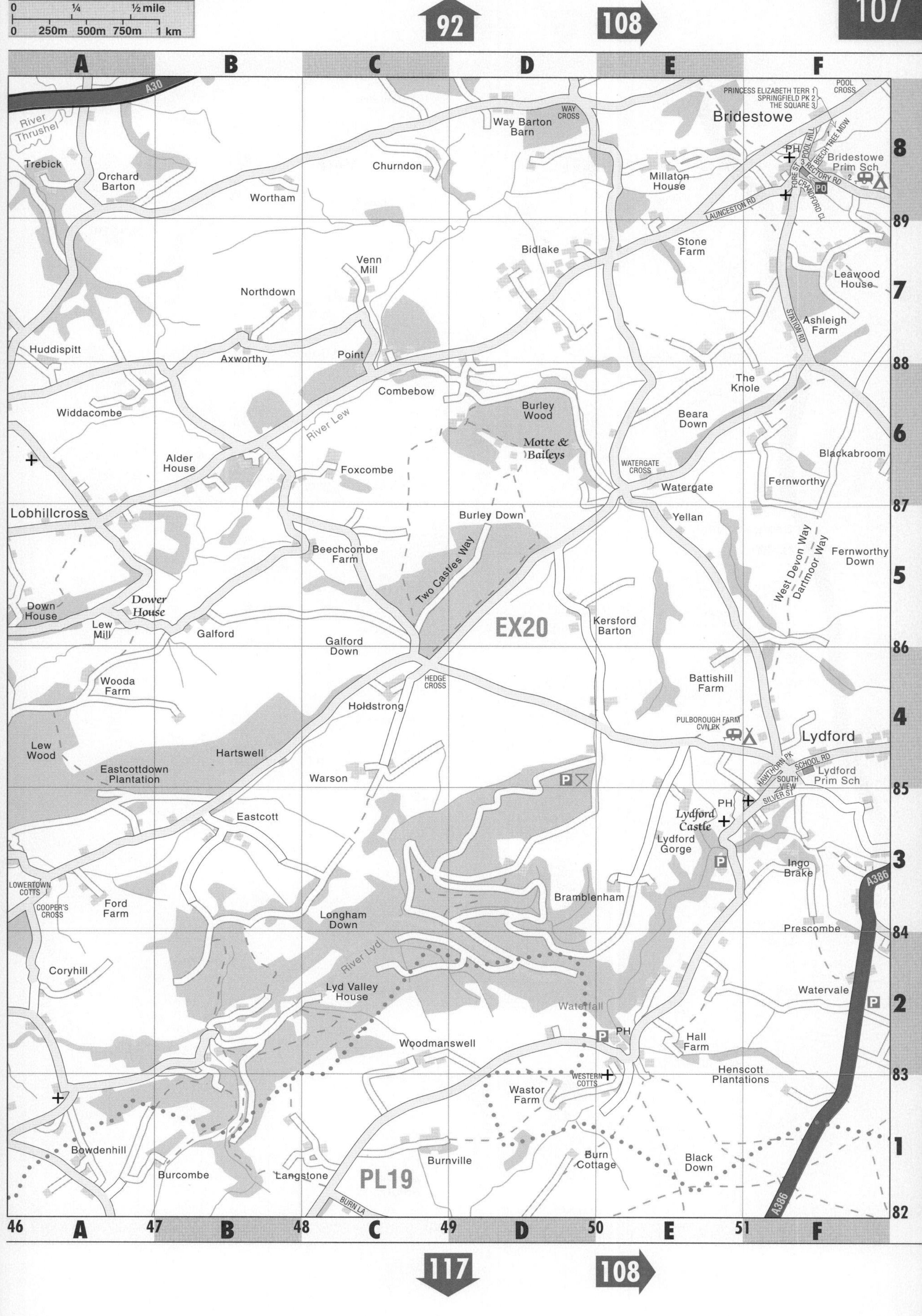
Scale: 1¾ inches to 1 mile
0 ¼ ½ mile
0 250m 500m 750m 1 km
92
108
A B C D E F
A30
River Thrushel
Trebick
Orchard Barton
Wortham
Churndon
Way Barton Barn
WAY CROSS
PRINCESS ELIZABETH TERR 1
SPRINGFIELD PK 2
THE SQUARE 3
POOL CROSS
Bridestowe
PH
POOL HILL
BEECH TREE MDW
FORE ST
RECTORY RD
CRANDFORD CL
Bridestowe Prim Sch
PO
Millaton House
LAUNCESTON RD
Stone Farm
Bidlake
Venn Mill
Northdown
Leawood House
Ashleigh Farm
STATION RD
Huddispitt
Axworthy
Point
Combebow
The Knole
Widdacombe
River Lew
Burley Wood
Beara Down
Motte & Baileys
Alder House
Foxcombe
WATERGATE CROSS
Watergate
Blackabroom
Fernworthy
Lobhillcross
Burley Down
Yellan
Beechcombe Farm
Two Castles Way
West Devon Way
Dartmoor Way
Fernworthy Down
Down House
Dower House
Lew Mill
Galford
EX20
Kersford Barton
Galford Down
Wooda Farm
HEDGE CROSS
Holdstrong
Battishill Farm
PULBOROUGH FARM CVN PK
Lydford
Lew Wood
Hartswell
Eastcottdown Plantation
Warson
HAWTHORN PK
SCHOOL RD
SOUTH VIEW
SILVER ST
Lydford Prim Sch
Eastcott
Lydford Castle
Lydford Gorge
Ingo Brake
LOWERTOWN COTTS
COOPER'S CROSS
Ford Farm
Longham Down
Bramblenham
A386
Prescombe
River Lyd
Coryhill
Lyd Valley House
Waterfall
Watervale
Woodmanswell
Hall Farm
Henscott Plantations
WESTERN COTTS
Wastor Farm
Bowdenhill
Burcombe
Langstone
PL19
Burnville
Burn Cottage
Black Down
BURN LA
8 89 7 88 6 87 5 86 4 85 3 84 2 83 1 82
46 47 48 49 50 51

107
93

Scale: 1¾ inches to 1 mile

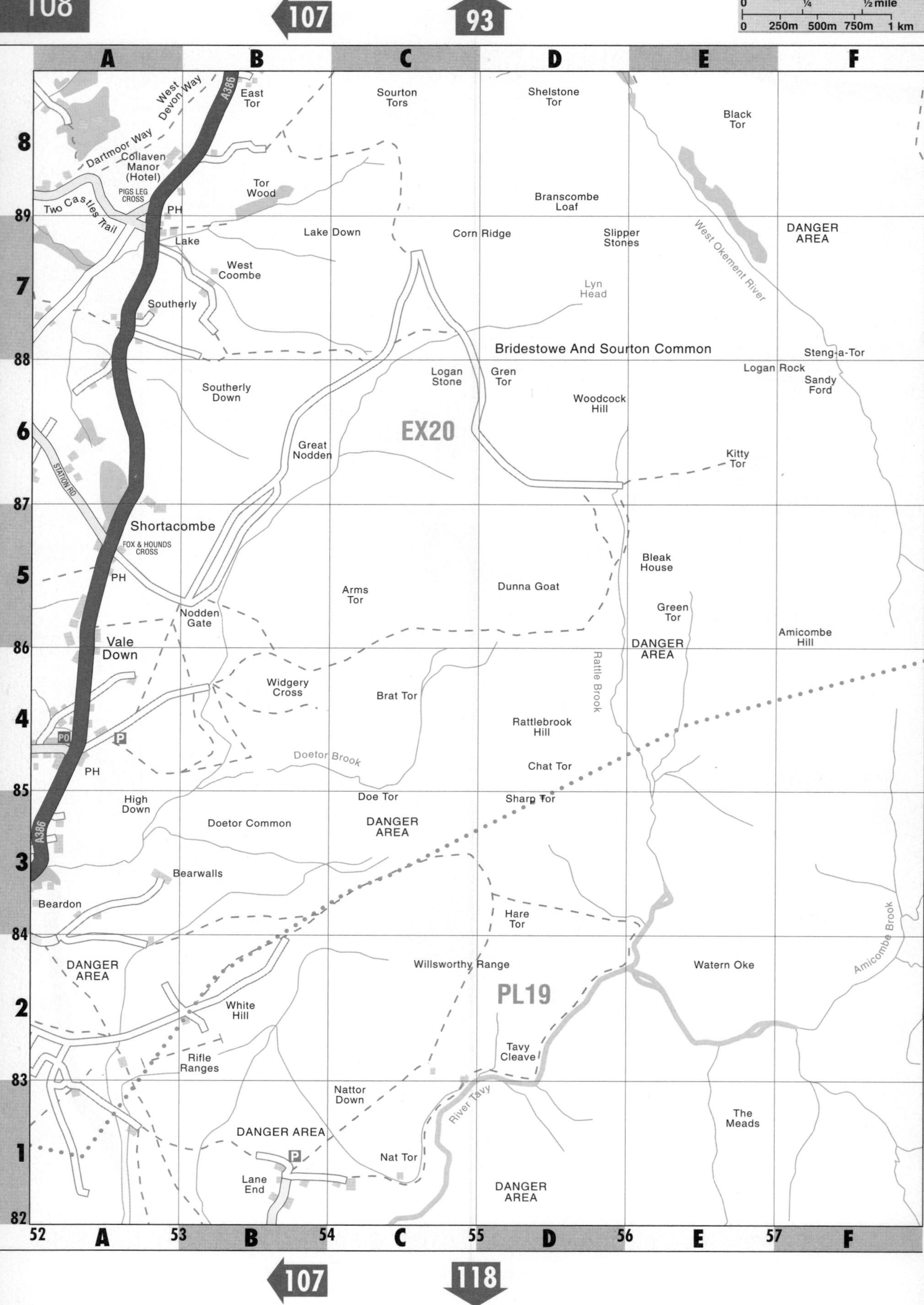

107
118

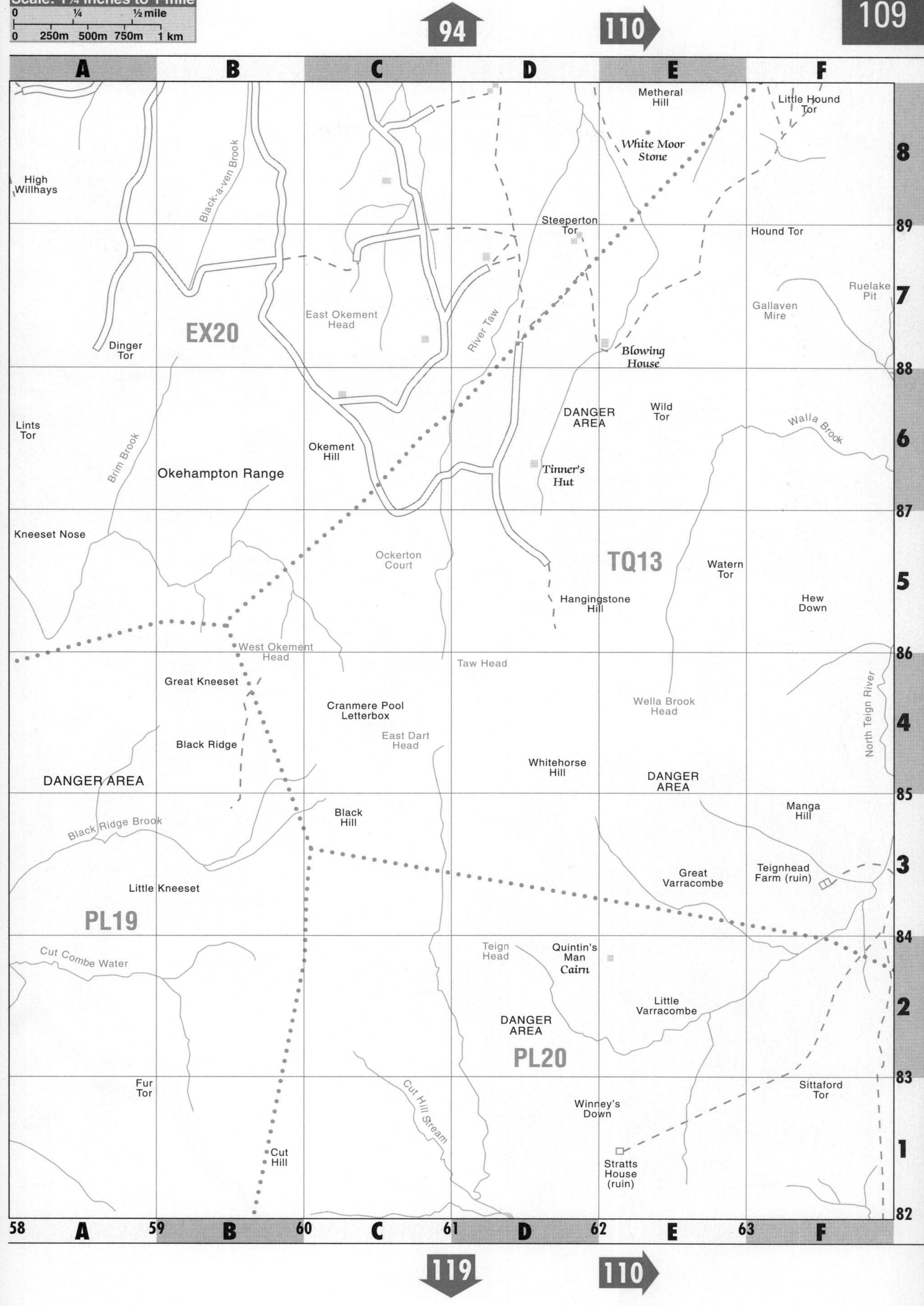
Scale: 1¾ inches to 1 mile
0 ¼ ½ mile
0 250m 500m 750m 1 km
94
110
A
B
C
D
E
F
Metheral Hill
Little Hound Tor
White Moor Stone
8
High Willhays
Black-a-ven Brook
Steeperton Tor
89
Hound Tor
Ruelake Pit
7
Gallaven Mire
East Okement Head
EX20
River Taw
Dinger Tor
Blowing House
88
Wild Tor
DANGER AREA
Walla Brook
Lints Tor
6
Okement Hill
Brim Brook
Okehampton Range
Tinner's Hut
87
Kneeset Nose
Ockerton Court
TQ13
Watern Tor
5
Hew Down
Hangingstone Hill
West Okement Head
86
Taw Head
Great Kneeset
Wella Brook Head
North Teign River
Cranmere Pool Letterbox
4
East Dart Head
Black Ridge
Whitehorse Hill
DANGER AREA
DANGER AREA
85
Manga Hill
Black Hill
Black Ridge Brook
3
Teignhead Farm (ruin)
Great Varracombe
Little Kneeset
PL19
84
Teign Head
Quintin's Man Cairn
Cut Combe Water
Little Varracombe
2
DANGER AREA
PL20
83
Fur Tor
Sittaford Tor
Cut Hill Stream
Winney's Down
1
Cut Hill
Stratts House (ruin)
82
58
59
60
61
62
63
119
110

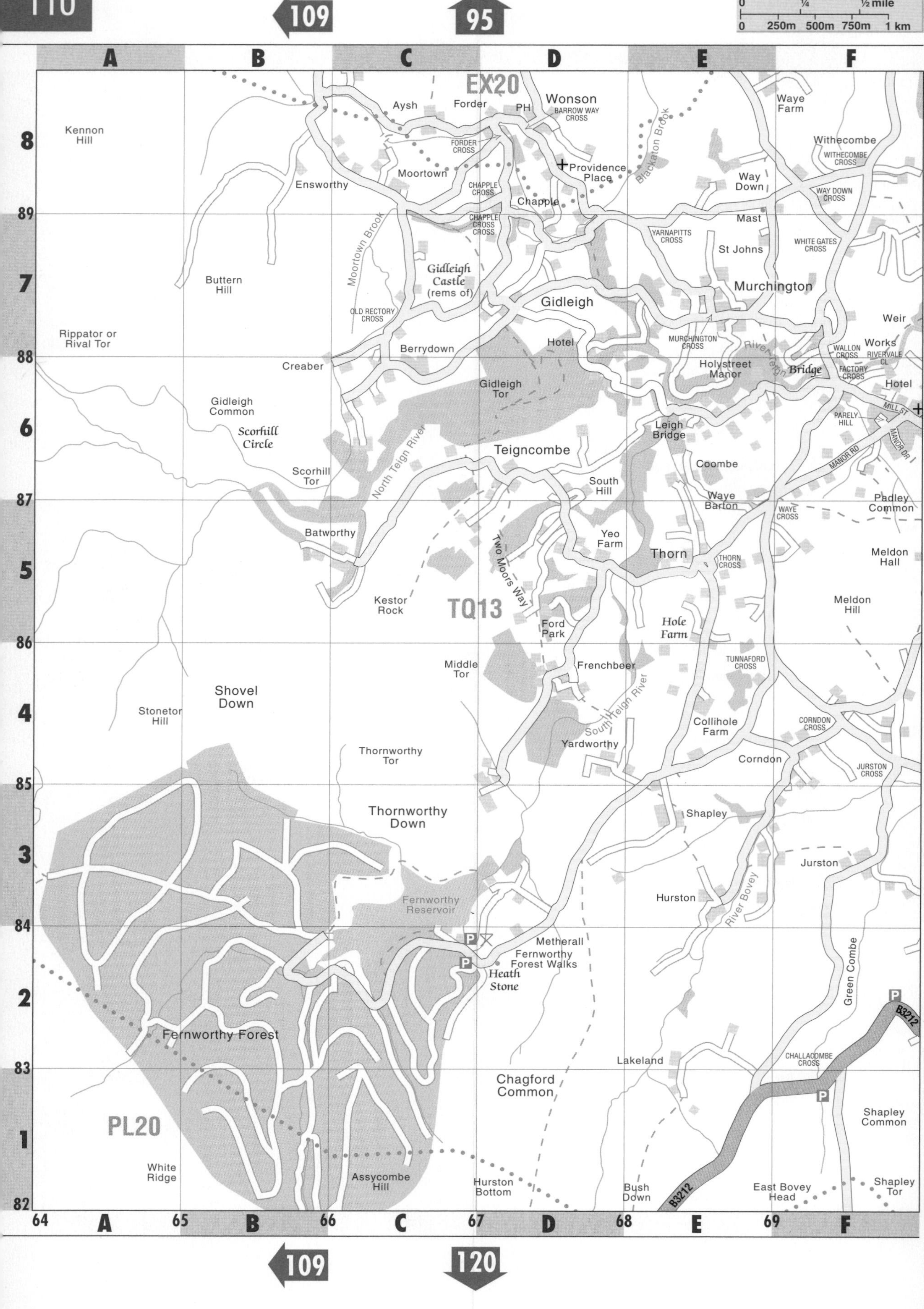
109
95
Scale: 1¾ inches to 1 mile
0 ¼ ½ mile
0 250m 500m 750m 1 km
A B C D E F
8 89 7 88 6 87 5 86 4 85 3 84 2 83 1 82
64 65 66 67 68 69
EX20
TQ13
PL20
Kennon Hill
Aysh
Forder
PH
Wonson
BARROW WAY CROSS
Waye Farm
Withecombe
WITHECOMBE CROSS
FORDER CROSS
Moortown
Providence Place
Blackaton Brook
Ensworthy
CHAPPLE CROSS
Chapple
Way Down
WAY DOWN CROSS
CHAPPLE CROSS CROSS
YARNAPITTS CROSS
Mast
St Johns
WHITE GATES CROSS
Moortown Brook
Buttern Hill
Gidleigh Castle (rems of)
Murchington
Gidleigh
OLD RECTORY CROSS
Weir
Rippator or Rival Tor
Hotel
Works
MURCHINGTON CROSS
River Teign
WALLON CROSS
RIVERVALE CL
Berrydown
Holystreet Manor
Bridge
FACTORY CROSS
Creaber
Hotel
Gidleigh Tor
MILL ST
Gidleigh Common
PARELY HILL
Leigh Bridge
MANOR DR
Scorhill Circle
North Teign River
MANOR RD
Teigncombe
Coombe
Scorhill Tor
South Hill
Padley Common
Waye Barton
WAYE CROSS
Batworthy
Yeo Farm
Thorn
Meldon Hall
THORN CROSS
Two Moors Way
Kestor Rock
Meldon Hill
Ford Park
Hole Farm
Middle Tor
Frenchbeer
TUNNAFORD CROSS
Shovel Down
South Teign River
Stonetor Hill
Collihole Farm
CORNDON CROSS
Yardworthy
Thornworthy Tor
Corndon
JURSTON CROSS
Thornworthy Down
Shapley
Jurston
Fernworthy Reservoir
Hurston
River Bovey
Metherall
Fernworthy Forest Walks
Heath Stone
Green Combe
P
B3212
Fernworthy Forest
Lakeland
CHALLACOMBE CROSS
Chagford Common
Shapley Common
White Ridge
Assycombe Hill
Hurston Bottom
Bush Down
East Bovey Head
Shapley Tor
109
120

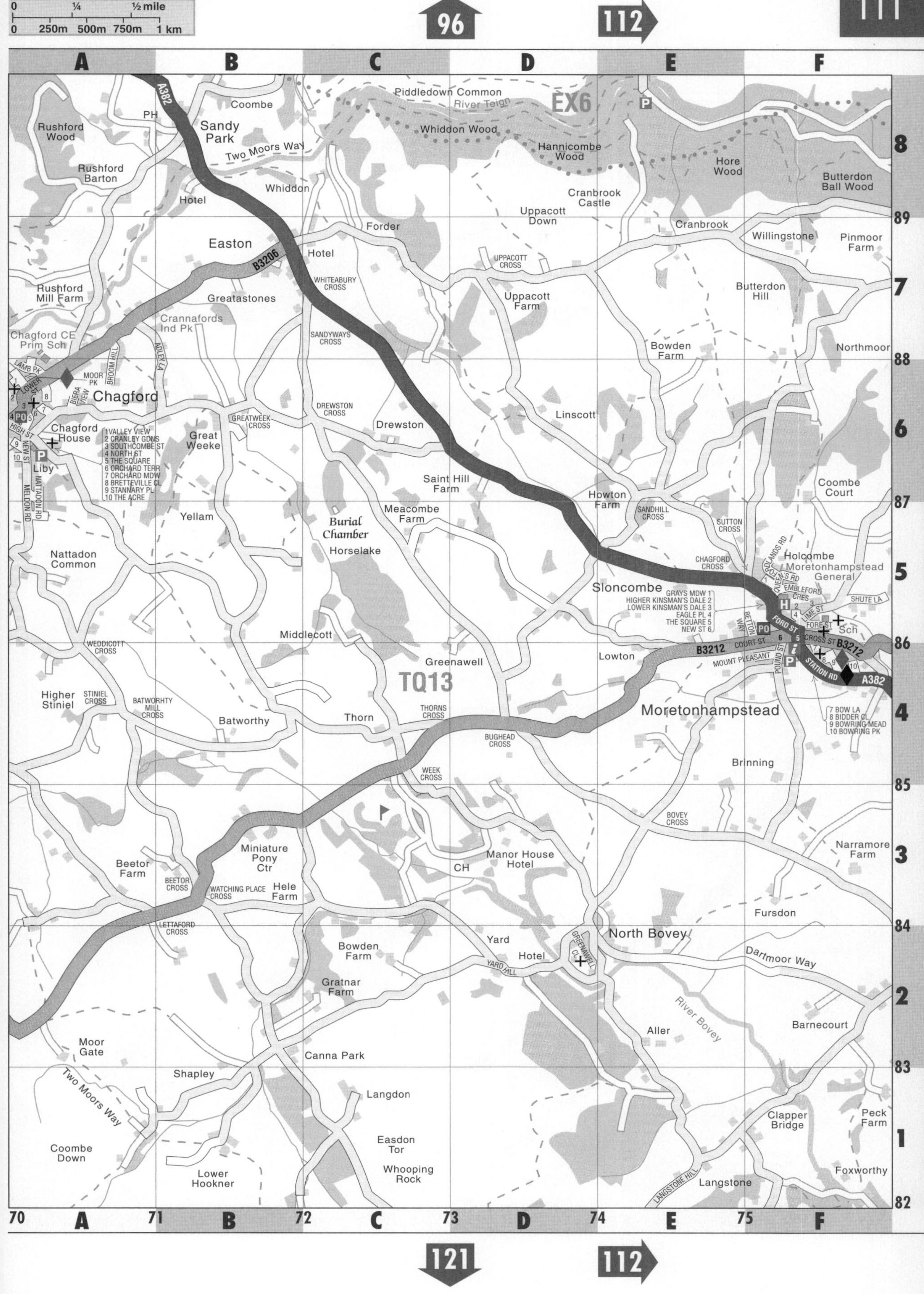
Scale: 1¾ inches to 1 mile
96
112
Chagford
Sandy Park
Easton
Moretonhampstead
North Bovey
Two Moors Way
River Teign
River Bovey
Dartmoor Way
Burial Chamber
TQ13
EX6
121
112

111
97

Scale: 1¾ inches to 1 mile

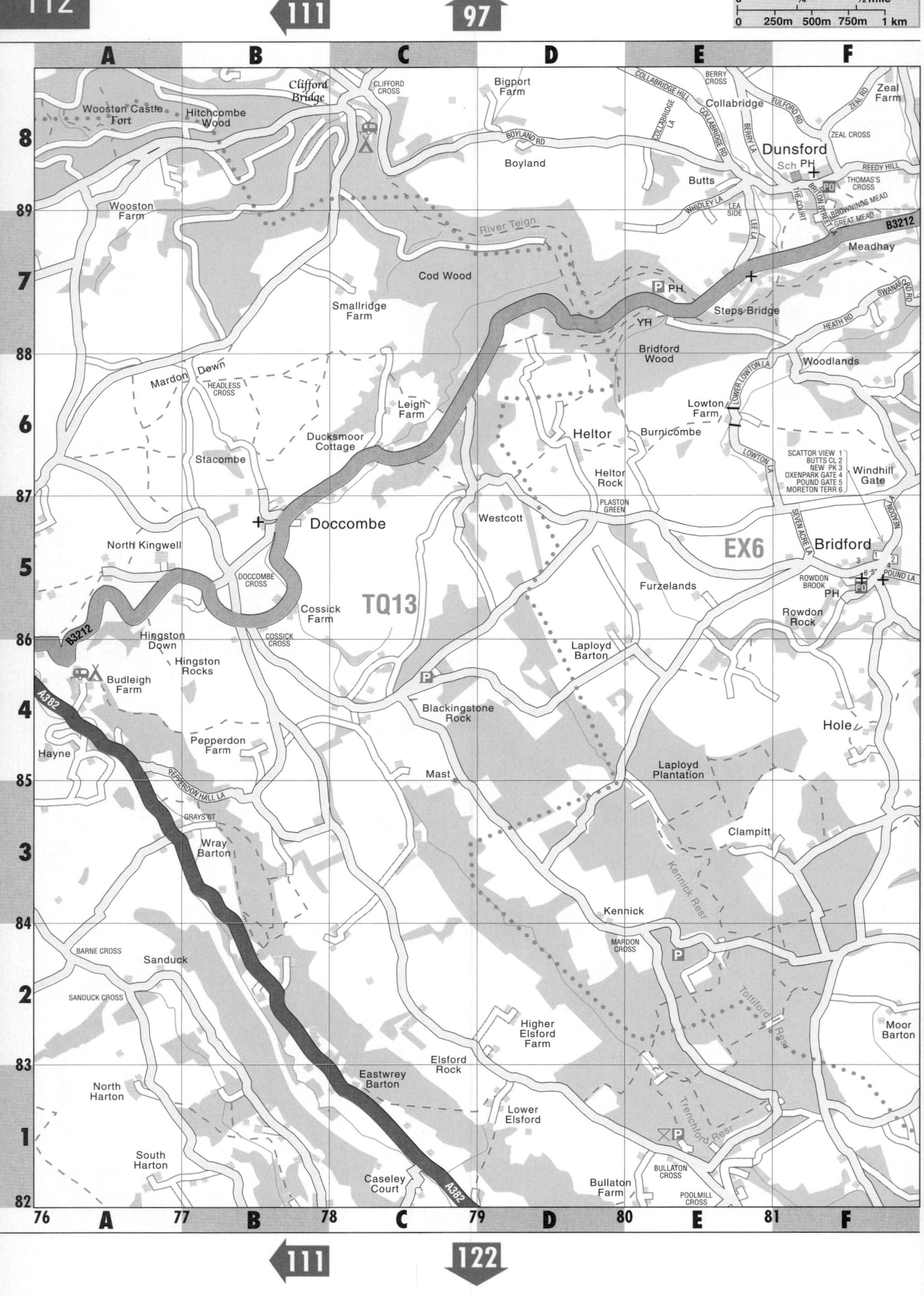

111
122

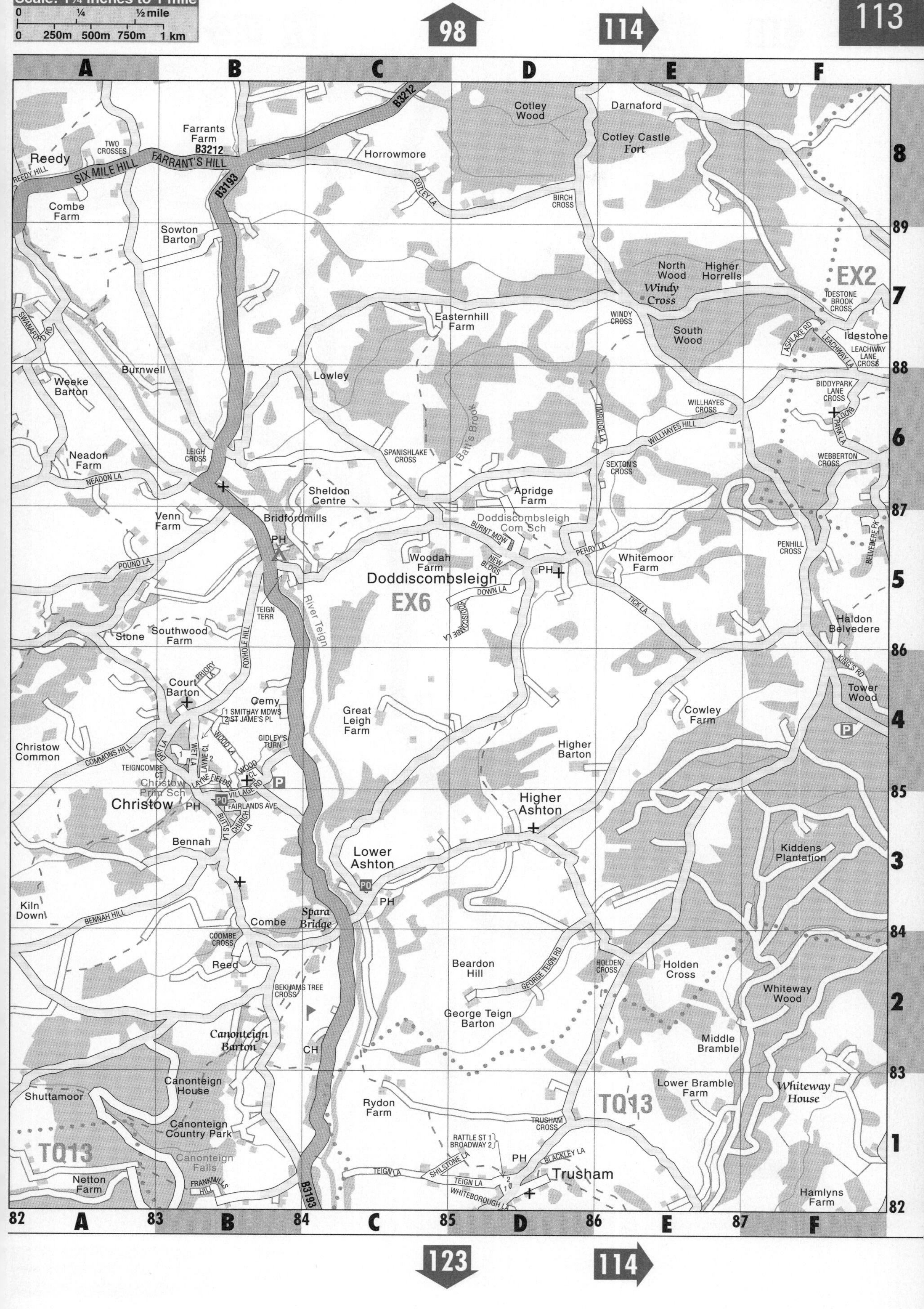
Scale: 1¾ inches to 1 mile
0 ¼ ½ mile
0 250m 500m 750m 1 km
98
114
A B C D E F
8 89 7 88 6 87 5 86 4 85 3 84 2 83 1 82
82 83 84 85 86 87
Reedy
TWO CROSSES
Farrants Farm
B3212
SIX MILE HILL
FARRANT'S HILL
REEDY HILL
B3193
Horrowmore
COTLEY LA
Cotley Wood
Darnaford
Cotley Castle
Fort
BIRCH CROSS
Combe Farm
Sowton Barton
North Wood
Higher Horrells
Windy Cross
EX2
IDESTONE BROOK CROSS
Idestone
WINDY CROSS
South Wood
Easternhill Farm
SWANAFORD RD
ASHLAKE RD
LEACHWAY LA
LEACHWAY LANE CROSS
Burnwell
Weeke Barton
Lowley
BIDDYPARK LANE CROSS
BIDDYPARK LA
WILLHAYES CROSS
WILLHAYES HILL
TIMBRIDGE LA
Batt's Brook
Neadon Farm
LEIGH CROSS
SPANISHLAKE CROSS
SEXTON'S CROSS
WEBBERTON CROSS
NEADON LA
Sheldon Centre
Apridge Farm
Venn Farm
Bridfordmills
Doddiscombsleigh Com Sch
BURNT MDW
PH
PENHILL CROSS
BELVEDERE PK
NEW BLDGS
PERRY LA
Woodah Farm
Whitemoor Farm
POUND LA
Doddiscombsleigh
EX6
DOWN LA
TICK LA
TEIGN TERR
River Teign
Haldon Belvedere
Stone
Southwood Farm
FOXHOLE HILL
KING'S RD
PRIORY
Court Barton
Cemy
Tower Wood
1 SMITHAY MDWS
2 ST JAMES'S PL
Great Leigh Farm
Cowley Farm
Christow Common
COMMONS HILL
DRY LA
WET LA
LAYNE CL
WOOD LA
GIDLEY'S TURN
Higher Barton
TEIGNCOMBE CT
WOOD CL
Christow Prim Sch
LAYNE FIELDS
VILLAGE RD
Christow
PO
FAIRLANDS AVE
Higher Ashton
BUTTS LA
CHURCH LA
Bennah
Kiddens Plantation
Lower Ashton
Kiln Down
BENNAH HILL
Combe
Spara Bridge
COOMBE CROSS
Reed
Beardon Hill
HOLDEN CROSS
Holden Cross
GEORGE TEIGN RD
BEKHAMS TREE CROSS
Whiteway Wood
George Teign Barton
Canonteign Barton
CH
Middle Bramble
Canonteign House
Lower Bramble Farm
Whiteway House
Shuttamoor
Rydon Farm
TQ13
Canonteign Country Park
TRUSHAM CROSS
RATTLE ST 1
BROADWAY 2
Canonteign Falls
SHILSTONE LA
BLACKLEY LA
TEIGN LA
Trusham
Netton Farm
FRANKMILLS HILL
WHITEBOROUGH LA
Hamlyns Farm
123
114

Scale: 1¾ inches to 1 mile
0 ¼ ½ mile
0 250m 500m 750m 1 km

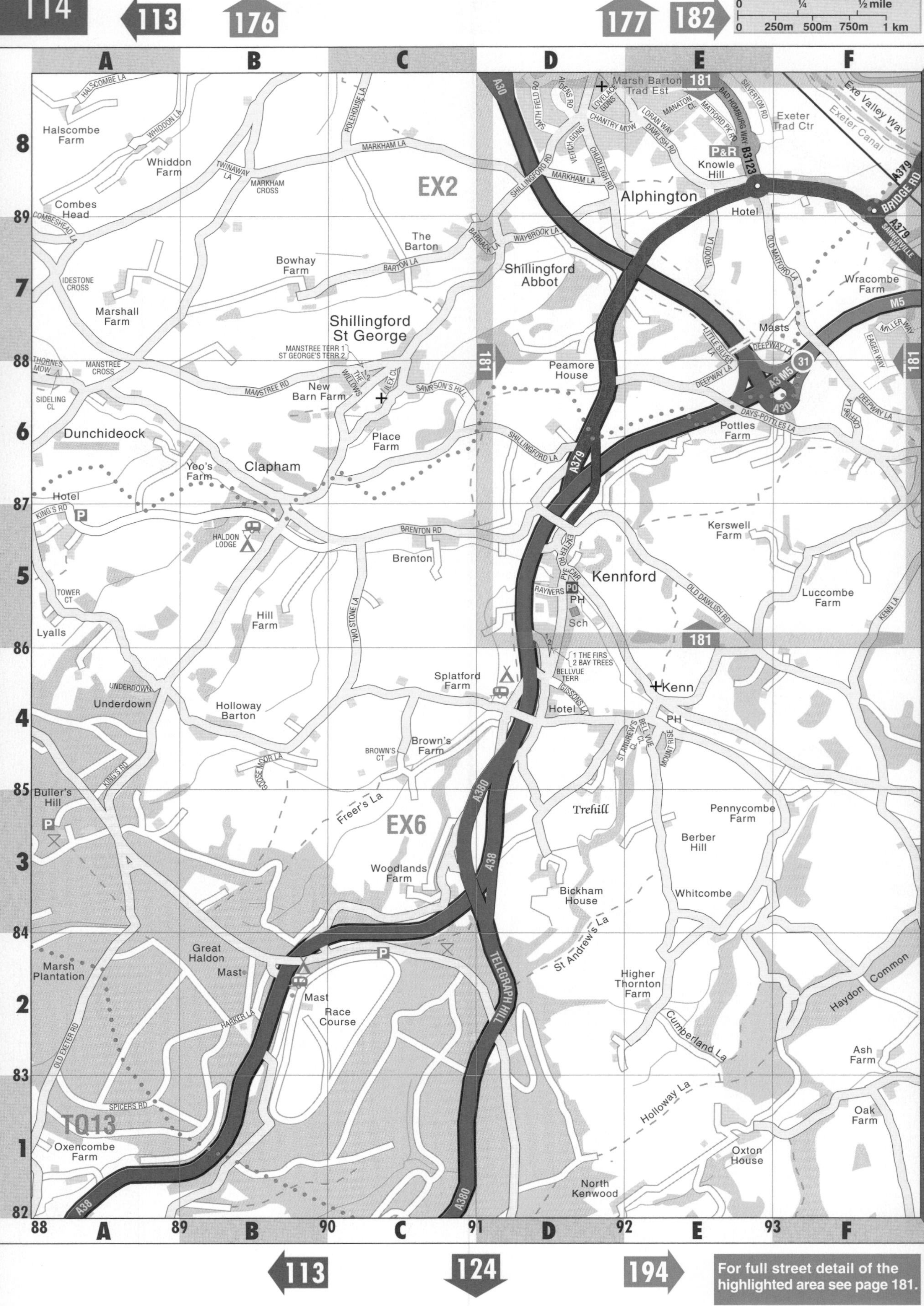

For full street detail of the highlighted area see page 181.

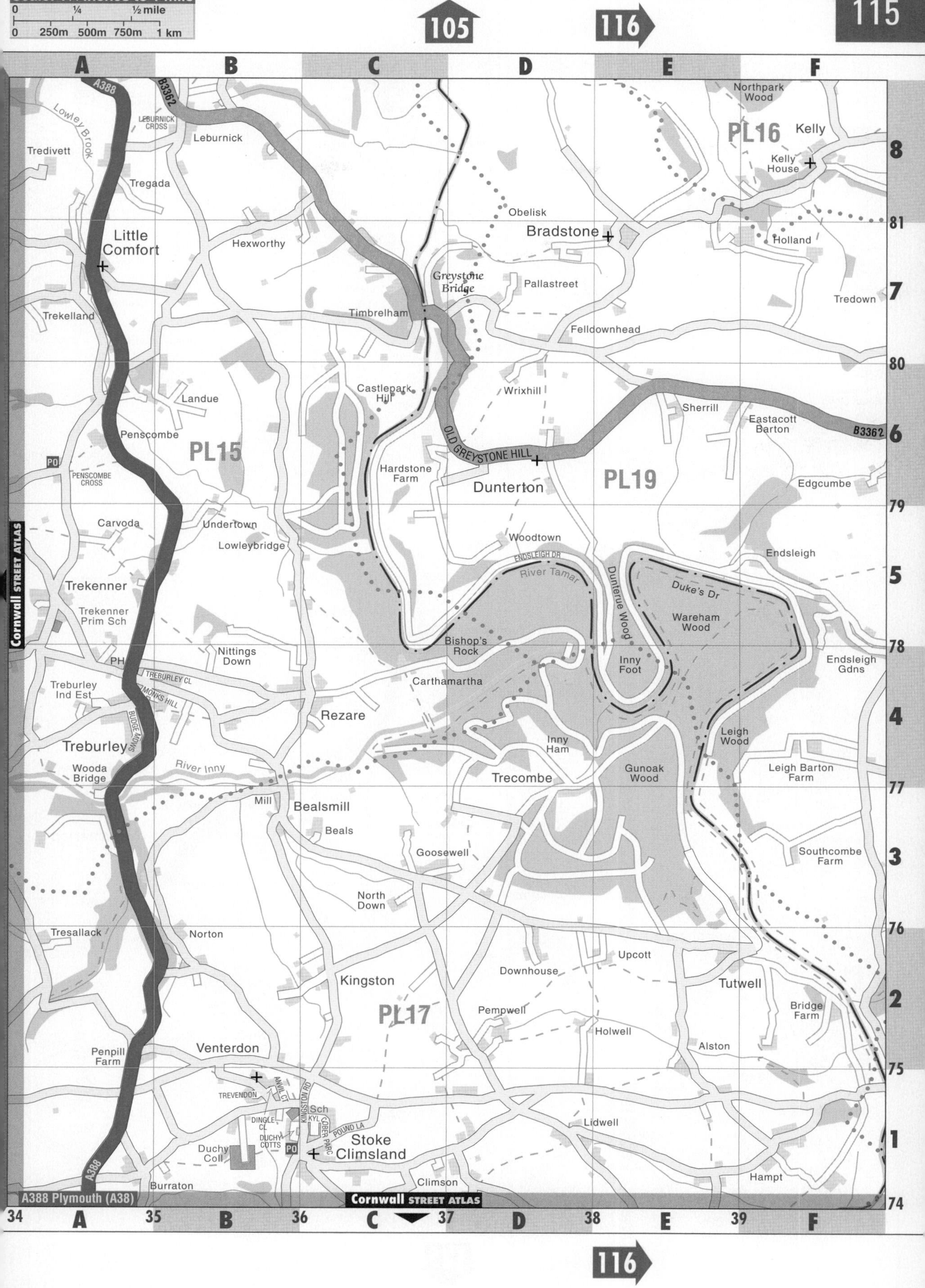
Scale: 1¾ inches to 1 mile
0 ¼ ½ mile
0 250m 500m 750m 1 km
105
116
A B C D E F
Lowley Brook
A388
B3362
LEBURNICK CROSS
Leburnick
Tredivett
Tregada
Little Comfort
Hexworthy
Trekelland
Timbrelham
Greystone Bridge
Obelisk
Bradstone
Pallastreet
Felldownhead
Northpark Wood
PL16
Kelly
Kelly House
Holland
Tredown
Landue
Penscombe
PL15
Castlepark Hill
Wrixhill
Sherrill
Eastacott Barton
OLD GREYSTONE HILL
Hardstone Farm
Dunterton
PL19
Edgcumbe
PO
PENSCOMBE CROSS
Carvoda
Undertown
Lowleybridge
Woodtown
Endsleigh
ENDSLEIGH DR
River Tamar
Dunterue Wood
Duke's Dr
Wareham Wood
Trekenner
Trekenner Prim Sch
Nittings Down
Bishop's Rock
Inny Foot
Endsleigh Gdns
PH
TREBURLEY CL
MONKS HILL
Treburley Ind Est
Carthamartha
BUDGE MDWS
Rezare
Treburley
Wooda Bridge
River Inny
Inny Ham
Leigh Wood
Trecombe
Gunoak Wood
Leigh Barton Farm
Mill
Bealsmill
Beals
Goosewell
Southcombe Farm
North Down
Tresallack
Norton
Upcott
Downhouse
Kingston
Tutwell
PL17
Pempwell
Bridge Farm
Holwell
Alston
Penpill Farm
Venterdon
TREVENDON
ANVIL CT
KINGSTON RD
Sch
KYL
COBER PARC
POUND LA
DINGLE CL
DUCHY COTTS
Lidwell
Duchy Coll
Stoke Climsland
Hampt
Burraton
Climson
A388 Plymouth (A38)
Cornwall STREET ATLAS
8
81
7
80
6
79
5
78
4
77
3
76
2
75
1
74
34 35 36 37 38 39

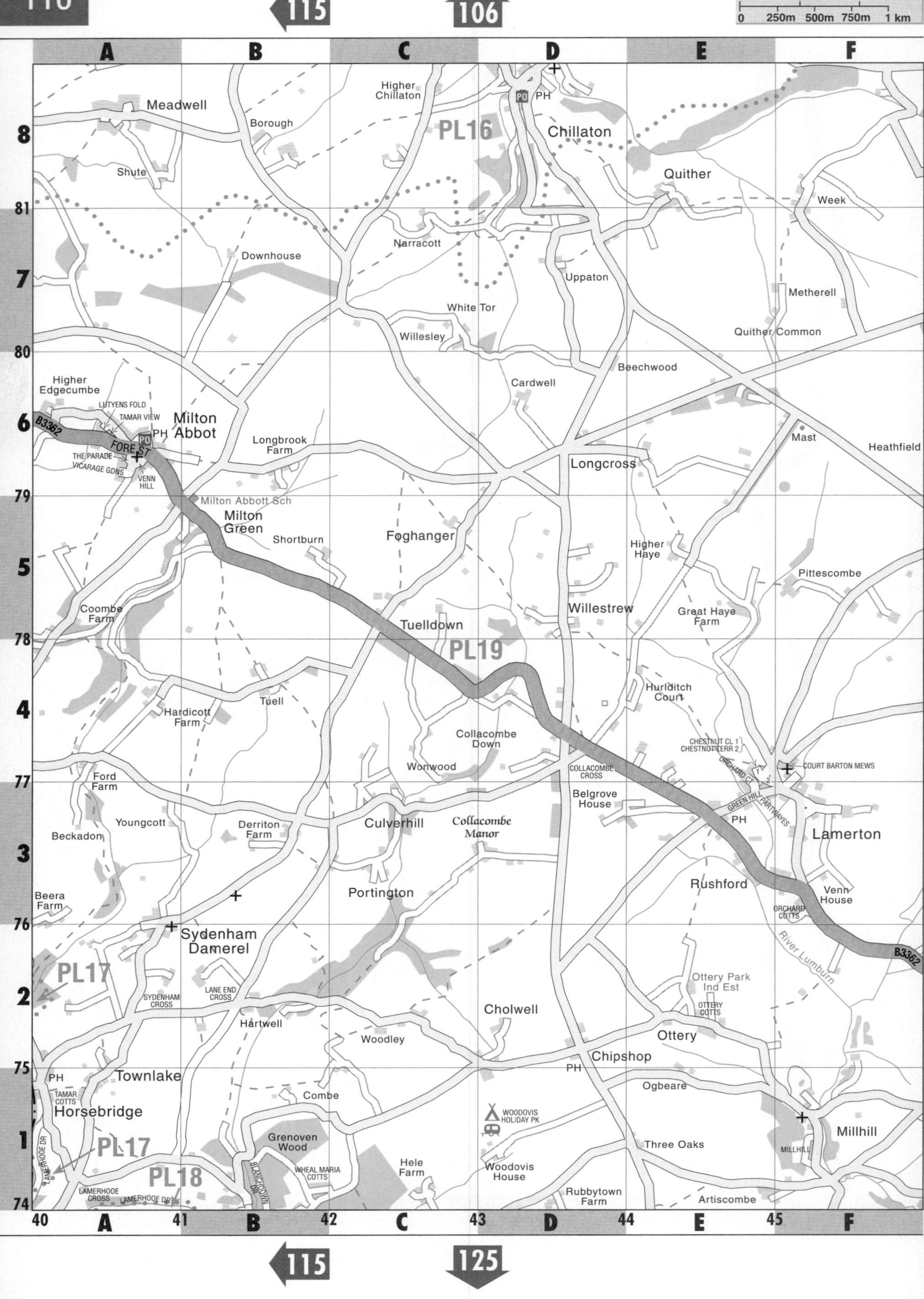
115
106
Scale: 1¾ inches to 1 mile
0 ¼ ½ mile
0 250m 500m 750m 1 km
Meadwell
Borough
Higher Chillaton
PL16
Chillaton
Shute
Quither
Week
Downhouse
Narracott
Uppaton
Metherell
White Tor
Willesley
Quither Common
Beechwood
Cardwell
Higher Edgecumbe
LUTYENS FOLD
TAMAR VIEW
Milton Abbot
B3362
FORE ST
THE PARADE
VICARAGE GDNS
VENN HILL
Longbrook Farm
Longcross
Mast
Heathfield
Milton Abbott Sch
Milton Green
Shortburn
Foghanger
Higher Haye
Pittescombe
Coombe Farm
Willestrew
Great Haye Farm
Tuelldown
PL19
Hurlditch Court
Tuell
Hardicott Farm
Collacombe Down
CHESTNUT CL 1
CHESTNUT TERR 2
COURT BARTON MEWS
ORCHARD CT
Wonwood
COLLACOMBE CROSS
Ford Farm
Belgrove House
GREEN HILL
PARTWAYES
Youngcott
Derriton Farm
Culverhill
Collacombe Manor
Beckadon
Lamerton
Rushford
Portington
Beera Farm
Venn House
ORCHARD COTTS
Sydenham Damerel
River Lumburn
PL17
Ottery Park Ind Est
SYDENHAM CROSS
LANE END CROSS
Cholwell
OTTERY COTTS
Hartwell
Woodley
Ottery
Chipshop
Townlake
TAMAR COTTS
Ogbeare
Horsebridge
Combe
WOODOVIS HOLIDAY PK
Grenoven Wood
Millhill
Three Oaks
LAMERHOOE DR
MILLHILL
Hele Farm
Woodovis House
WHEAL MARIA COTTS
BLANCHDOWN DR
PL18
LAMERHOOE CROSS
Rubbytown Farm
Artiscombe
A B C D E F
8 81 7 80 6 79 5 78 4 77 3 76 2 75 1 74
40 41 42 43 44 45
115
125

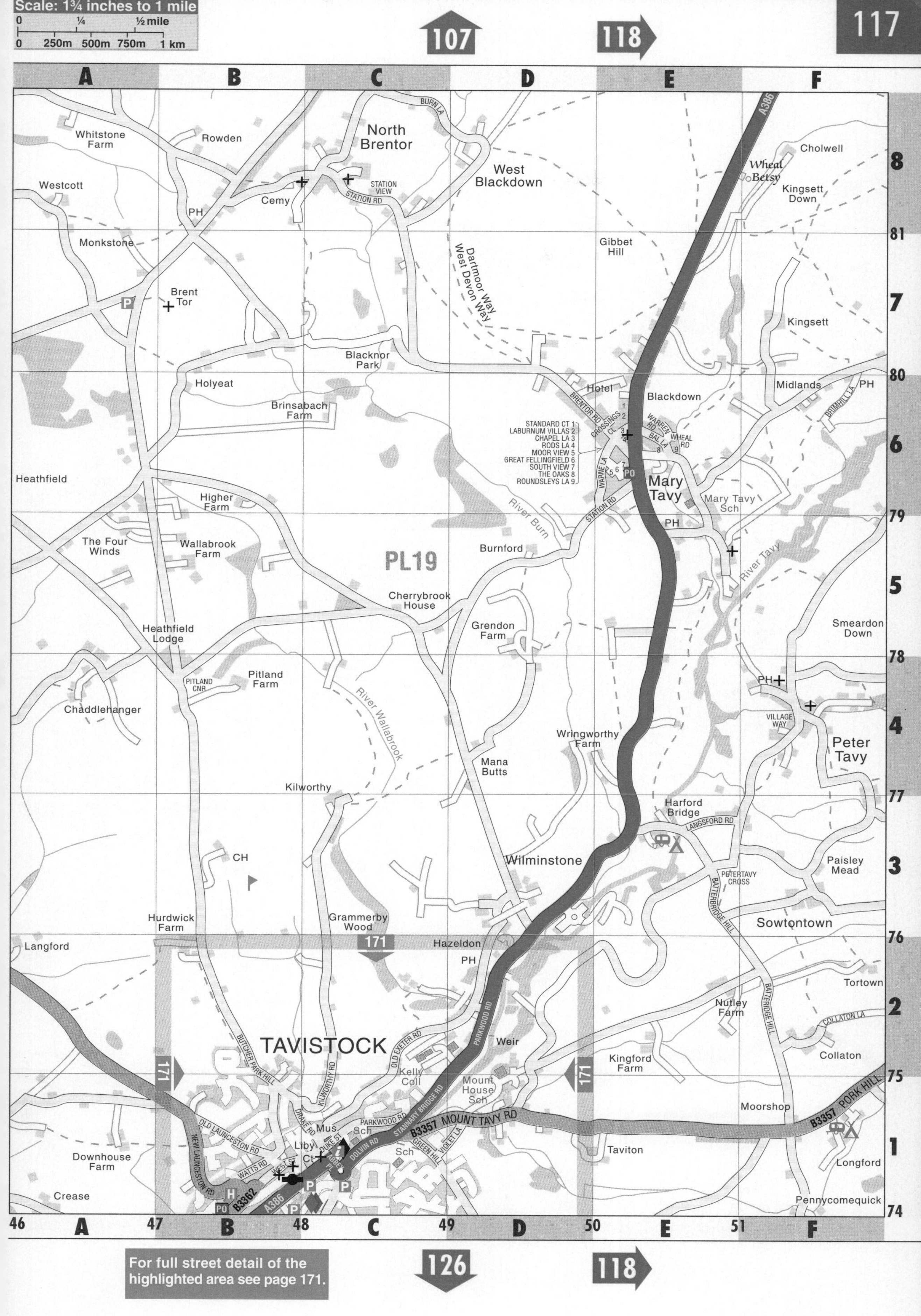

For full street detail of the highlighted area see page 171.

126
118

117
108

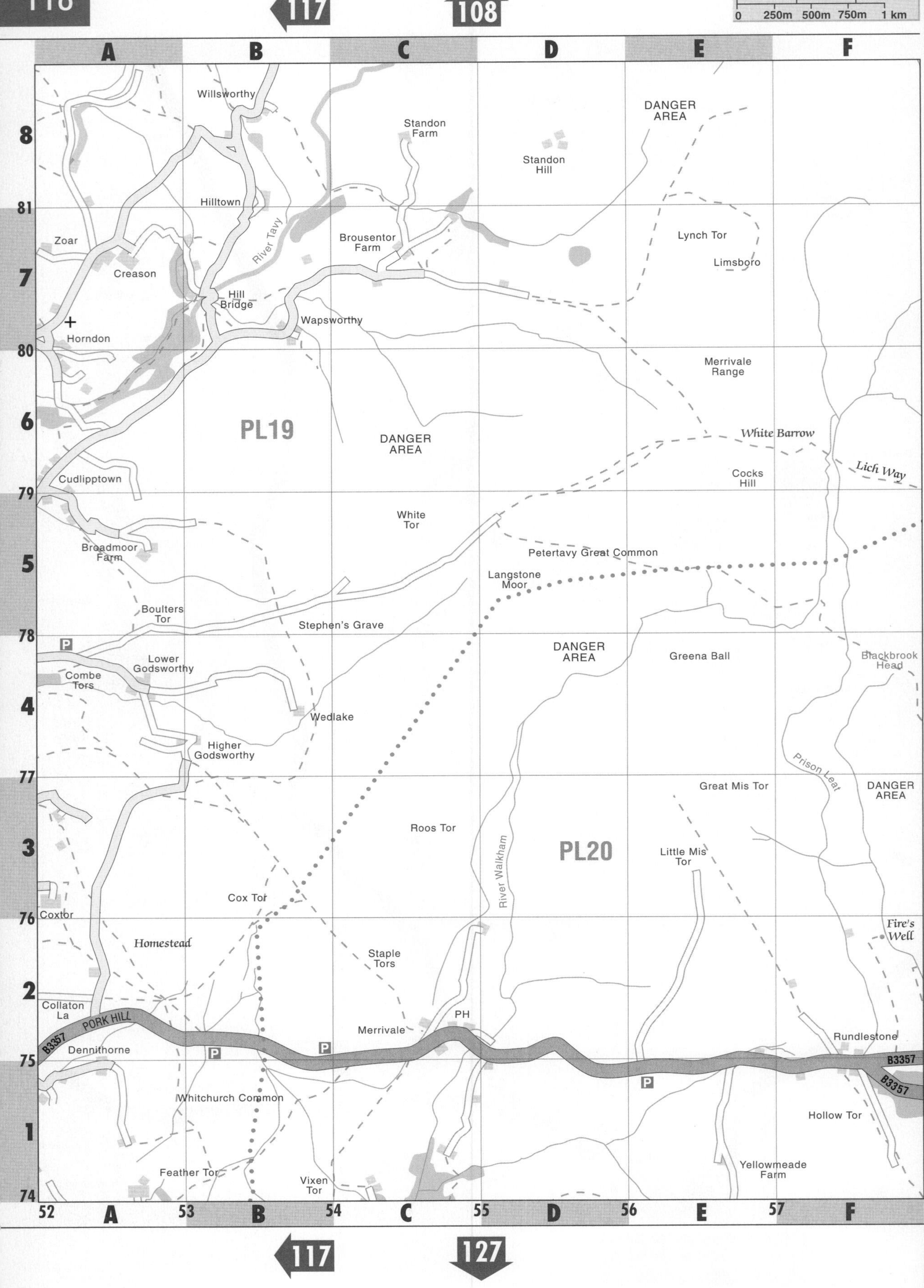

117
127

Scale: 1¾ inches to 1 mile

109
120

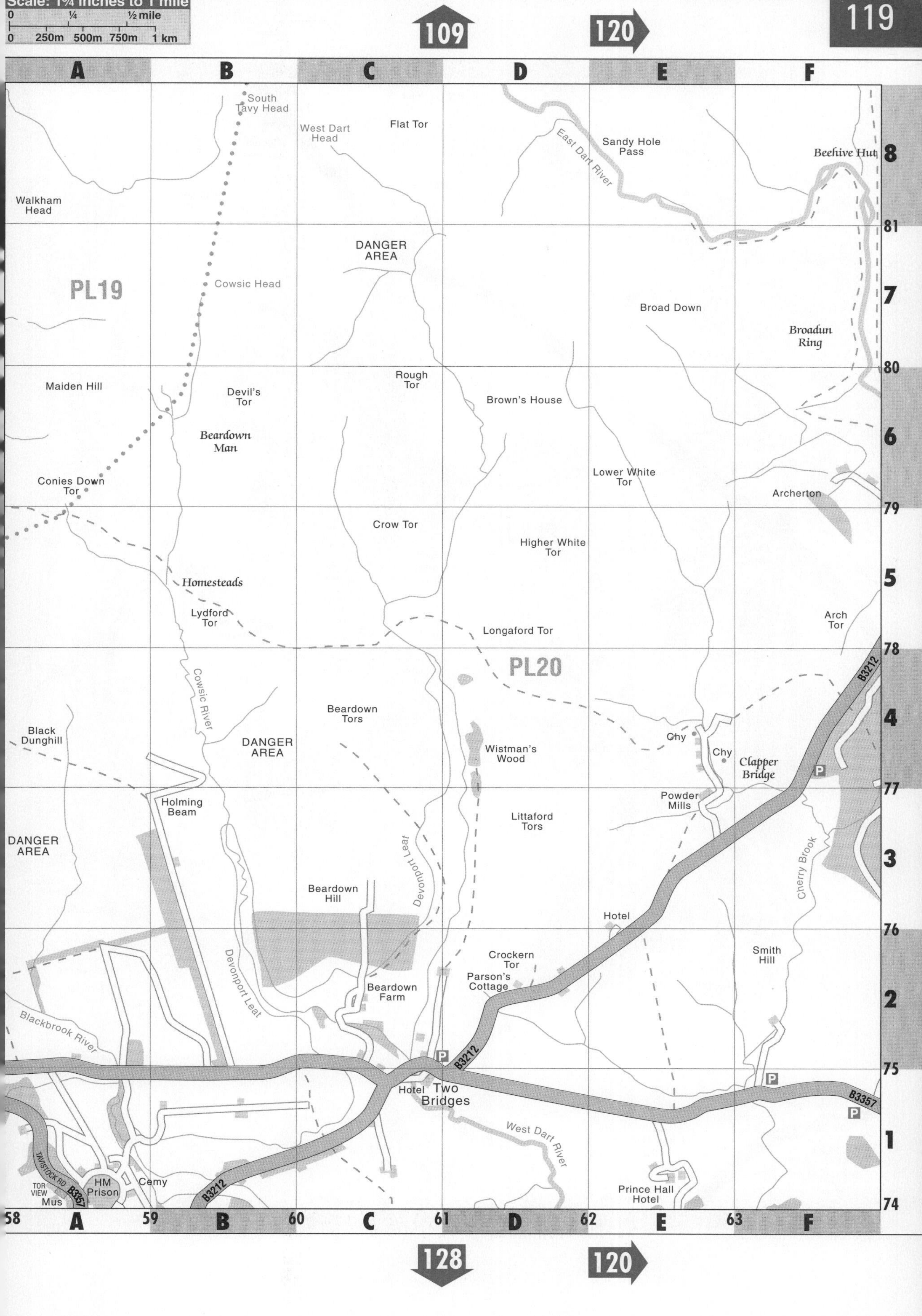

128
120

119
110

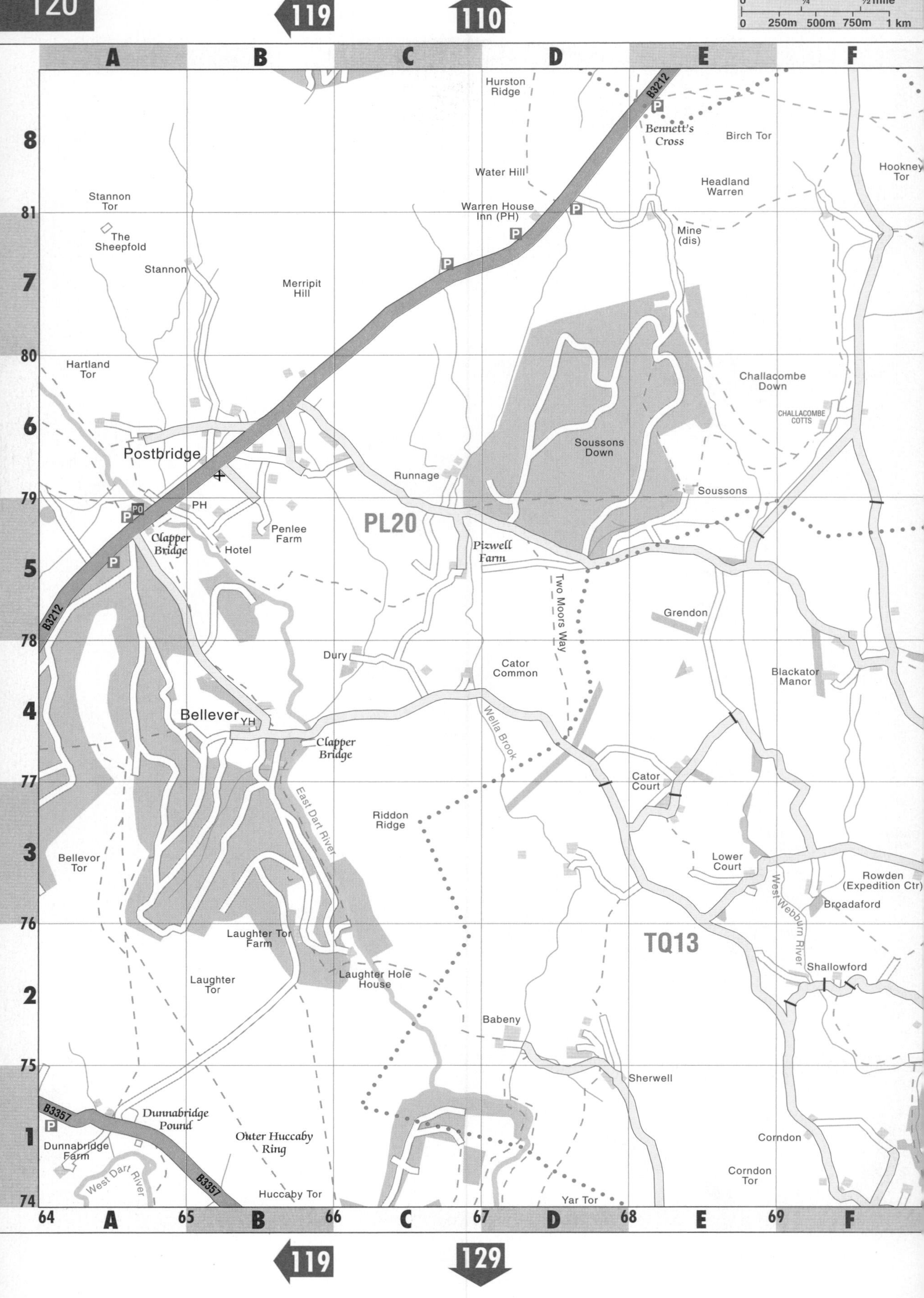

119
129

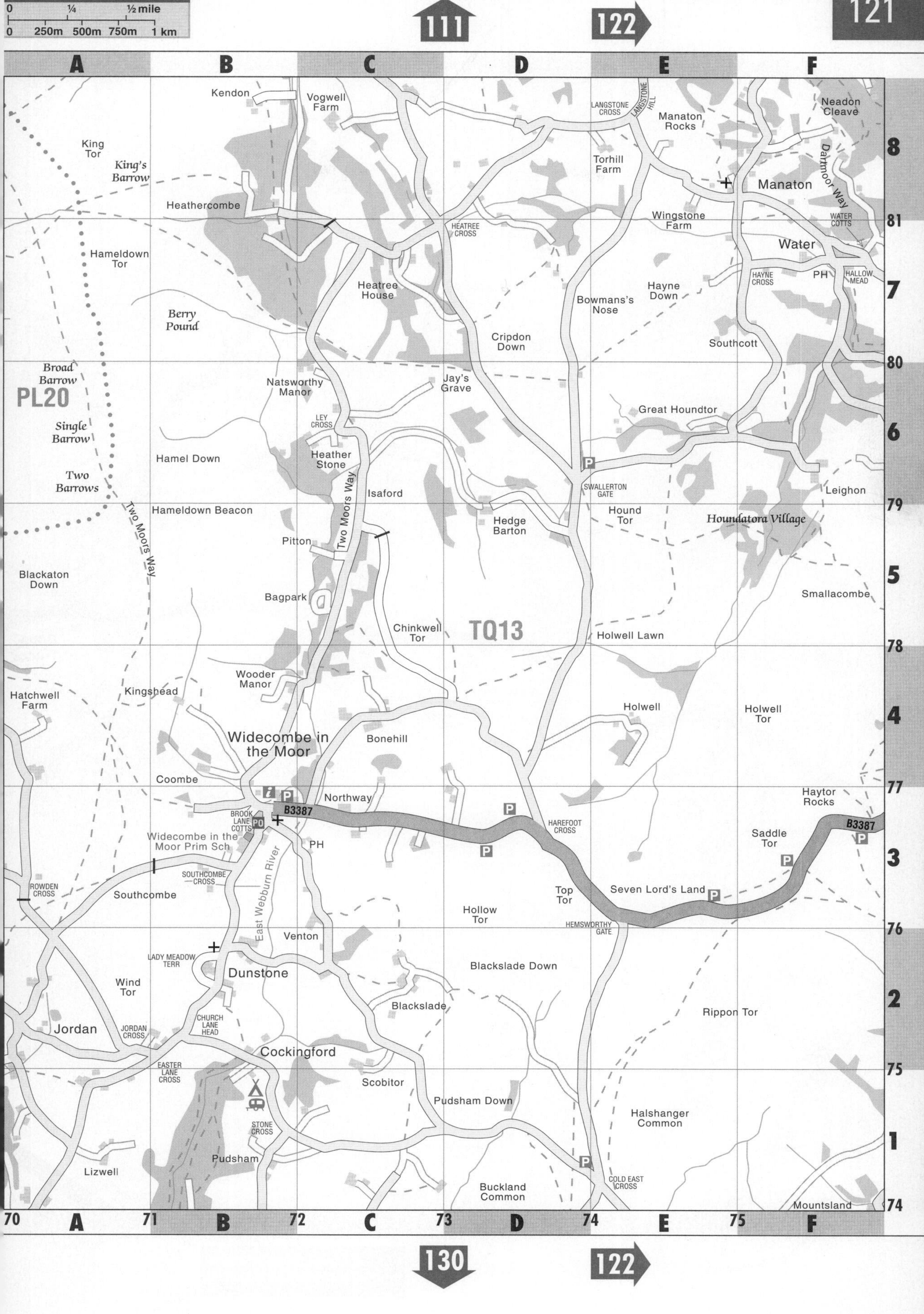
Scale: 1¾ inches to 1 mile
0 ¼ ½ mile
0 250m 500m 750m 1 km
111
122
130
122
Kendon
Vogwell Farm
King Tor
King's Barrow
Heathercombe
Hameldown Tor
Berry Pound
Broad Barrow
PL20
Single Barrow
Two Barrows
Hamel Down
Hameldown Beacon
Two Moors Way
Blackaton Down
Hatchwell Farm
Kingshead
Natsworthy Manor
LEY CROSS
Heather Stone
Isaford
Pitton
Bagpark
Wooder Manor
Widecombe in the Moor
Coombe
BROOK LANE COTTS
PO
Widecombe in the Moor Prim Sch
SOUTHCOMBE CROSS
ROWDEN CROSS
Southcombe
East Webburn River
LADY MEADOW TERR
Dunstone
Wind Tor
Jordan
JORDAN CROSS
CHURCH LANE HEAD
EASTER LANE CROSS
Cockingford
STONE CROSS
Pudsham
Lizwell
Heatree House
HEATREE CROSS
Cripdon Down
Jay's Grave
Chinkwell Tor
TQ13
Hedge Barton
Bonehill
Northway
B3387
PH
Venton
Hollow Tor
Blackslade Down
Blackslade
Scobitor
Pudsham Down
Buckland Common
LANGSTONE CROSS
LANGSTONE HILL
Manaton Rocks
Torhill Farm
Wingstone Farm
Manaton
Neadon Cleave
Dartmoor Way
WATER COTTS
Water
HAYNE CROSS
HALLOW MEAD
Hayne Down
Bowmans's Nose
Southcott
Great Houndtor
SWALLERTON GATE
Hound Tor
Houndatora Village
Leighon
Smallacombe
Holwell Lawn
Holwell
Holwell Tor
HAREFOOT CROSS
Haytor Rocks
Saddle Tor
Top Tor
Seven Lord's Land
HEMSWORTHY GATE
Rippon Tor
Halshanger Common
COLD EAST CROSS
Mountsland
A B C D E F
8 81 7 80 6 79 5 78 4 77 3 76 2 75 1 74
70 71 72 73 74 75

121 112

Scale: 1¾ inches to 1 mile
0 ¼ ½ mile
0 250m 500m 750m 1 km

A B C D E F

Raven's Tor
Lustleigh Cleave
Sharpitor
Nut Crackers
Lustleigh
PETHYBRIDGE
LOWER BROOKFIELD COTTS
KNOWLE RD
Kelly
KELLY CROSS
A382
SLADE CROSS
Wreyland
Cemy
Knowle
Hisley
Houndtor Wood
Becky Falls
Becka Brook
Gradner Rocks
LOWER KNOWLE RD
HATHERLEIGH LA
HAWKMOOR PK
HAWKMOOR COTTS
Shaptor Rock
SHAPTOR CROSS
Beadon Farm
BEADON LA
BOWDEN LA
Stonelands Waste
FURZELEIGH CROSS
LITTLE JOHN'S WLK
LOWER ALLER LA
ALLER LA
HIGHER
FORDER LA
KING'S CROSS
ASHWELL LA
Wolleigh House
River Bovey
Pullabrook Farm
Beckaford Farm
Trendlebere Down
Stone Row
Dartmoor Way
Southbrook
MORETONHAMPSTEAD RD
Whitstone
FURZELEIGH LA
Reddaford Water
Shewte
Black Hill
Yarner Wood
TQ13
GIPSY CNR
SHEWTE CROSS
180
Bovey Tracey
MARY ST
EAST ST
Sch
Parke
Liby
FORE ST
PO
LOWERDOWN
Mine (dis)
Lower Down
LOWERDOWN CROSS
Yarner
B3344
MONKS WAY
STATION RD
Mus
Bovey Tracey
Haytor Down
Challabrook Farm
CHAPPLE RD
Ullacombe Farm
CHALLABROOK LA
Indio
NEWTON RD
Colehayes Park
Whisselwell Farm
STENTIFORD LA
UNDER LA
BRIMLEY RD
ASHBURTON RD
Hotel
BRIMLEY LA
WALLFIELD RD
POTTERY RD
Brimley
Brimley Bsns Pk
GREEN LA
Green Lane
Blue Waters Ind Est
B3387
Haytor Vale
Pinchaford
Slade Mead
Narracombe
Langaller
SMOKEY CROSS
WOODHOUSE CROSS
Wilsworthy
Hotel
Ilsington CE Prim Sch
Ilsington
TIPLEYHILL LA
LEWTHORN CROSS
HONEYWELL LA
TOWN MDW
OLD TOWN HILL
SIMMS HILL
HILLCREST 1
DREWSMEAD 2
Belle Vue
Bag Tor
LENDA LA
Lenda
TIPLEYHILL CROSS
BIRCHANGER CROSS
Great Plantation
Liverton
FOUR CROSS
SIGFORD CROSS
Lounston
WILLIS'S CROSS
KEY CL
Coldeast
Bagtor House
SHAPLEY WAY
BENEDICTS RD
TQ12
FIVE CROSS
Rora Wood
HALFORD CROSS
MOUNTHILL COTTS
BARN PK
Rora House
Halford
BETHELCOMBE CROSS
Higher Sigford
Sch
A38
STAPLEHILL RD
BETHEL CROSS
Horridge
Ramshorn Down
Blackpool

8 81 7 80 6 79 5 78 4 77 3 76 2 75 1 74

76 A 77 B 78 C 79 D 80 E 81 F

121 131

For full street detail of the highlighted area see page 180.

F1
1 LASKEYS HEATH
2 TAYLORS NEWTAKE
3 LEAT MDW
4 ROWELLS MEAD
5 BEAUMONT CL
6 DIVETT DR
7 MUNRO MEAD
8 POMEROY PL
9 FLOWERS MDW
10 KITTERSLEY DR
11 BEANHAY CL
12 BENLEARS ACRE
13 BICKFORDS GN
14 SUMMERLANDS CT
15 SUMMERHILL RD
16 SUMMERHILL CRES
17 SUMMERHILL CL
18 BENEDICTS CL

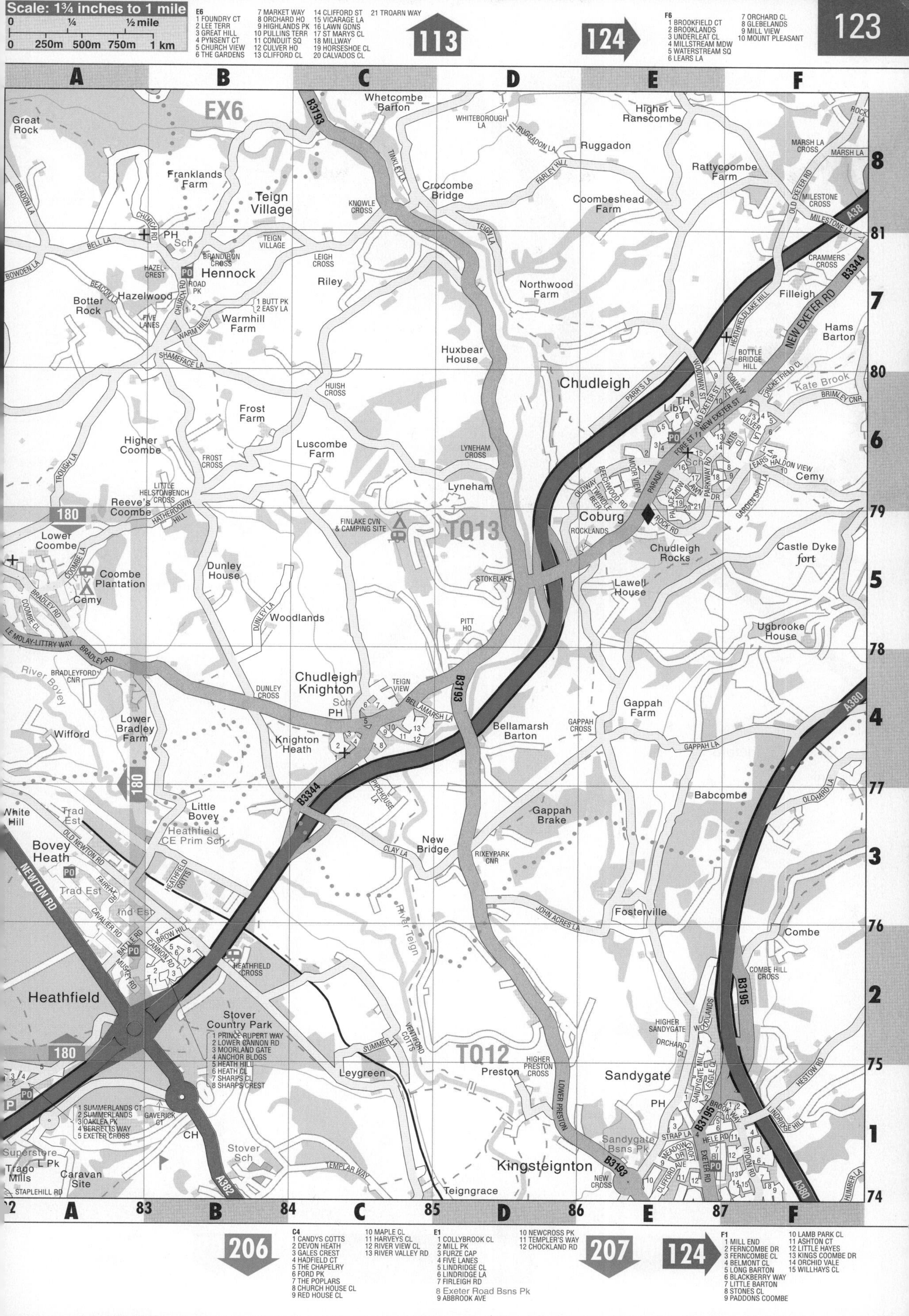
Scale: 1¾ inches to 1 mile
0 ¼ ½ mile
0 250m 500m 750m 1 km
E6
1 FOUNDRY CT
2 LEE TERR
3 GREAT HILL
4 PYNSENT CT
5 CHURCH VIEW
6 THE GARDENS
7 MARKET WAY
8 ORCHARD HO
9 HIGHLANDS PK
10 PULLINS TERR
11 CONDUIT SQ
12 CULVER HO
13 CLIFFORD CL
14 CLIFFORD ST
15 VICARAGE LA
16 LAWN GDNS
17 ST MARYS CL
18 MILLWAY
19 HORSESHOE CL
20 CALVADOS CL
21 TROARN WAY
113
124
F6
1 BROOKFIELD CT
2 BROOKLANDS
3 UNDERLEAT CL
4 MILLSTREAM MDW
5 WATERSTREAM SQ
6 LEARS LA
7 ORCHARD CL
8 GLEBELANDS
9 MILL VIEW
10 MOUNT PLEASANT
A B C D E F
8 81 7 80 6 79 5 78 4 77 3 76 2 75 1 74
EX6
TQ13
TQ12
Great Rock
Franklands Farm
Teign Village
Whetcombe Barton
Whiteborough La
Ruggadon
Higher Ranscombe
Rattycoombe Farm
Crocombe Bridge
Coombeshead Farm
Knowle Cross
Hennock
Brandiron Cross
Teign Village
Leigh Cross
Riley
Hazelwood
Botter Rock
Hazel-crest
Road Pk
1 BUTT PK
2 EASY LA
Warmhill Farm
Five Lanes
Northwood Farm
Huxbear House
Filleigh
Hams Barton
Marsh La Cross
Milestone Cross
Crammers Cross
Bottle Bridge Hill
Chudleigh
Kate Brook
Huish Cross
Frost Farm
Higher Coombe
Luscombe Farm
Lyneham Cross
Frost Cross
Lyneham
Cemy
Little Helstonbench Cross
Reeve's Coombe
180
Lower Coombe
Finlake Cvn & Camping Site
Coburg
Rocklands
Chudleigh Rocks
Castle Dyke fort
Coombe Plantation
Cemy
Dunley House
Stokelake
Lawell House
Woodlands
Pitt Ho
Ugbrooke House
River Bovey
Bradleyford Cnr
Chudleigh Knighton
Teign View
Dunley Cross
Gappah Farm
Wifford
Lower Bradley Farm
Knighton Heath
Bellamarsh Barton
Gappah Cross
Gappah La
Babcombe
White Hill
Trad Est
Little Bovey
Heathfield CE Prim Sch
Gappah Brake
Bovey Heath
New Bridge
Rixeypark Cnr
Trad Est
Ind Est
River Teign
Fosterville
Combe
Heathfield Cross
Combe Hill Cross
Heathfield
Stover Country Park
1 PRINCE RUPERT WAY
2 LOWER CANNON RD
3 MOORLAND GATE
4 ANCHOR BLDGS
5 HEATH HILL
6 HEATH CL
7 SHARPS CL
8 SHARPS CREST
Higher Sandygate
Orchard Cl
Leygreen
Preston
Higher Preston Cross
Sandygate
1 SUMMERLANDS CT
2 SUMMERLANDS
3 OAKLEA PK
4 BERRETTS WAY
5 EXETER CROSS
Gaverick Ct
Superstore
Trago Mills
Caravan Site
Stover Sch
Templar Way
Sandygate Bsns Pk
Kingsteignton
New Cross
Teigngrace
Staplehill Rd
A38
A380
A382
B3193
B3344
B3195
206
207
124
C4
1 CANDYS COTTS
2 DEVON HEATH
3 GALES CREST
4 HADFIELD CT
5 THE CHAPELRY
6 FORD PK
7 THE POPLARS
8 CHURCH HOUSE CL
9 RED HOUSE CL
10 MAPLE CL
11 HARVEYS CL
12 RIVER VIEW CL
13 RIVER VALLEY RD
E1
1 COLLYBROOK CL
2 MILL PK
3 FURZE CAP
4 FIVE LANES
5 LINDRIDGE CL
6 LINDRIDGE LA
7 FIRLEIGH RD
8 Exeter Road Bsns Pk
9 ABBROOK AVE
10 NEWCROSS PK
11 TEMPLER'S WAY
12 CHOCKLAND RD
F1
1 MILL END
2 FERNCOMBE DR
3 FERNCOMBE CL
4 BELMONT CL
5 LONG BARTON
6 BLACKBERRY WAY
7 LITTLE BARTON
8 STONES CL
9 PADDONS COOMBE
10 LAMB PARK CL
11 ASHTON CT
12 LITTLE HAYES
13 KINGS COOMBE DR
14 ORCHID VALE
15 WILLHAYS CL

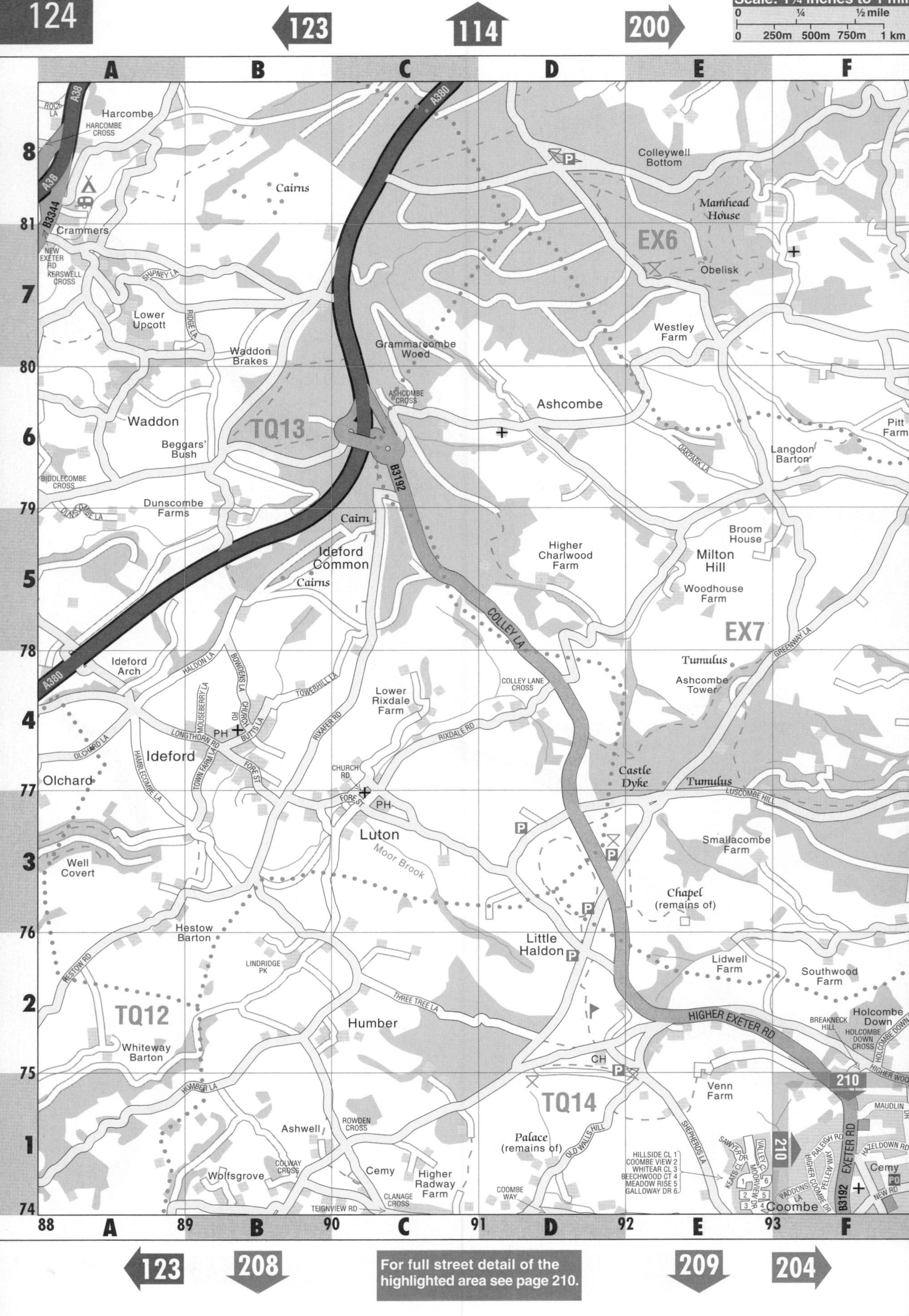

For full street detail of the highlighted area see page 210.

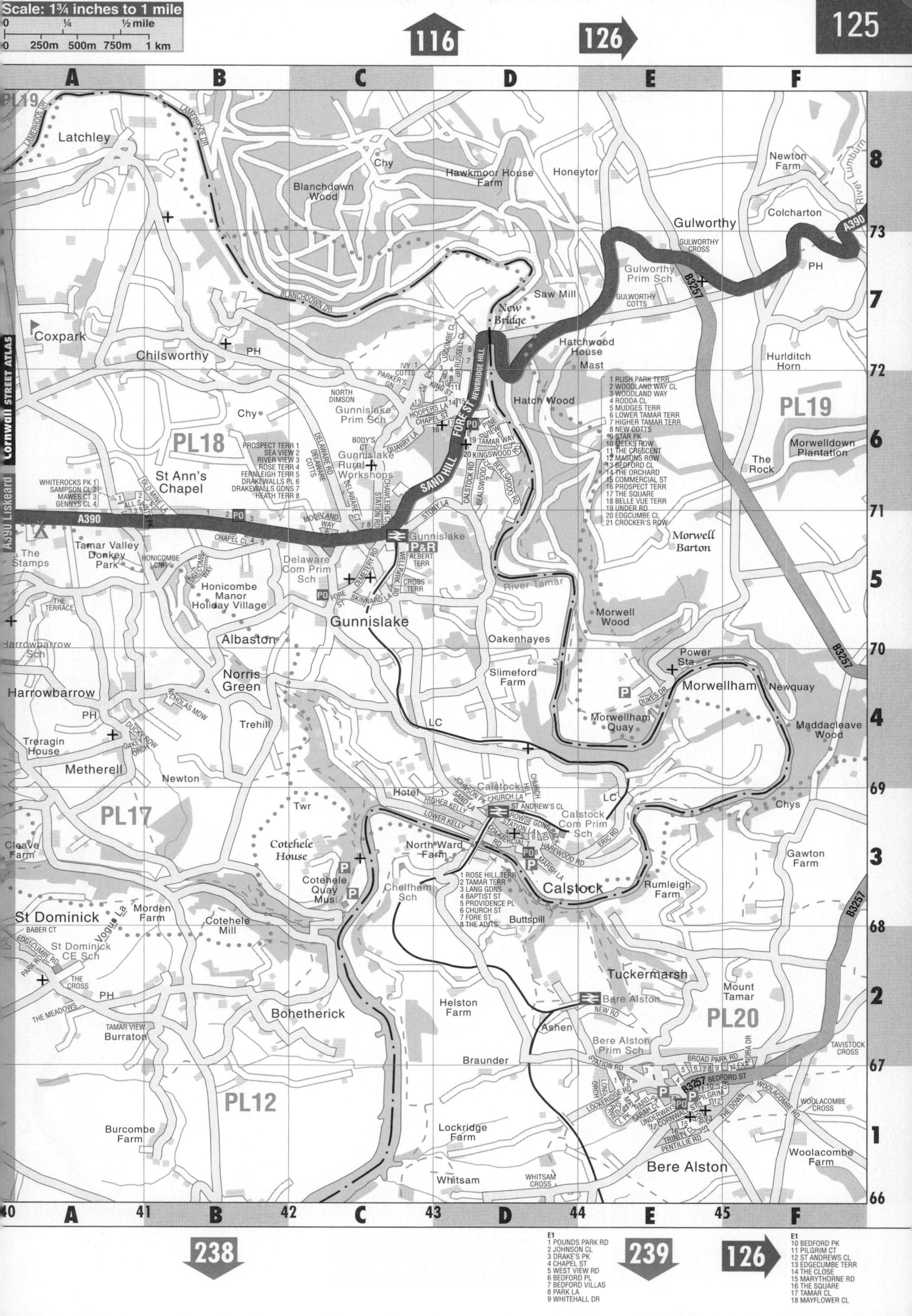

Scale: 1¾ inches to 1 mile
0 ¼ ½ mile
0 250m 500m 750m 1 km
116
126
125
A B C D E F
8
73
7
72
6
71
5
70
4
69
3
68
2
67
1
66
40 41 42 43 44 45
PL19
Latchley
LAMERHOOE DR
Blanchdown Wood
BLANCHDOWN DR
Chy
Hawkmoor House Farm
Honeytor
Newton Farm
River Lumburn
Colcharton
Gulworthy
A390
GULWORTHY CROSS
Gulworthy Prim Sch
B3257
PH
GULWORTHY COTTS
Saw Mill
New Bridge
Coxpark
Chilsworthy
PH
Hatchwood House
Mast
Hurlditch Horn
Hatch Wood
PL19
Chy
PL18
North Dimson
Gunnislake Prim Sch
Gunnislake Rural Workshops
NEWBRIDGE HILL
FORE ST
SAND HILL
1 RUSH PARK TERR
2 WOODLAND WAY CL
3 WOODLAND WAY
4 RODDA CL
5 MUDGES TERR
6 LOWER TAMAR TERR
7 HIGHER TAMAR TERR
8 NEW COTTS
9 STAR PK
10 MEEKS ROW
11 THE CRESCENT
12 MASONS ROW
13 BEDFORD CL
14 THE ORCHARD
15 COMMERCIAL ST
16 PROSPECT TERR
17 THE SQUARE
18 BELLE VUE TERR
19 UNDER RD
20 EDGCUMBE CL
21 CROCKER'S ROW
Morwelldown Plantation
The Rock
PROSPECT TERR 1
SEA VIEW 2
RIVER VIEW 3
ROSE TERR 4
FERNLEIGH TERR 5
DRAKEWALLS PL 6
DRAKEWALLS GDNS 7
HEATH TERR 8
WHITEROCKS PK 1
SAMPSON CL 2
MAWES CT 3
GENNYS CL 4
St Ann's Chapel
Morwell Barton
A390
The Stamps
Tamar Valley Donkey Park
Gunnislake
P&R
Delaware Com Prim Sch
River Tamar
Honicombe Manor Holiday Village
Gunnislake
Morwell Wood
The Terrace
Harrowbarrow Sch
Albaston
Oakenhayes
Power Sta
Norris Green
Slimeford Farm
Morwellham
Newquay
Harrowbarrow
PH
Trehill
Morwellham Quay
Maddacleave Wood
Treragin House
LC
Metherell
Newton
PL17
Twr
Hotel
Calstock
Calstock Com Prim Sch
LC
Chys
Cleave Farm
Cotehele House
North Ward Farm
Gawton Farm
Cotehele Quay Mus
Chelfham Sch
1 ROSE HILL TERR
2 TAMAR TERR
3 LANG GDNS
4 BAPTIST ST
5 PROVIDENCE PL
6 CHURCH ST
7 FORE ST
8 THE ADITS
Calstock
Rumleigh Farm
St Dominick
Morden Farm
Cotehele Mill
Buttspill
B3257
St Dominick CE Sch
Tuckermarsh
Mount Tamar
THE CROSS
PH
Helston Farm
Bere Alston
PL20
Bohetherick
Ashen
Bere Alston Prim Sch
TAVISTOCK CROSS
TAMAR VIEW
Burraton
Braunder
PL12
WOOLACOMBE CROSS
Burcombe Farm
Lockridge Farm
Woolacombe Farm
Whitsam
WHITSAM CROSS
Bere Alston
238
E1
1 POUNDS PARK RD
2 JOHNSON CL
3 DRAKE'S PK
4 CHAPEL ST
5 WEST VIEW RD
6 BEDFORD PL
7 BEDFORD VILLAS
8 PARK LA
9 WHITEHALL DR
239
126
E1
10 BEDFORD PK
11 PILGRIM CT
12 ST ANDREWS CL
13 EDGECUMBE TERR
14 THE CLOSE
15 MARYTHORNE RD
16 THE SQUARE
17 TAMAR CL
18 MAYFLOWER CL
Cornwall STREET ATLAS

125
117
Scale: 1¾ inches to 1 mile
0 ¼ ½ mile
0 250m 500m 750m 1 km
A
B
C
D
E
F
8
73
7
72
6
71
5
70
4
69
3
68
2
67
1
66
46
47
48
49
50
51
TAVISTOCK
BUCTOR PK 1
ABBOTSFIELD CL 2
CREASE LA
UPLANDS
ORCHARD CL
ABBOTSFIELD CRES
CALLINGTON RD
A390
A386
PLYMOUTH RD
PIXON LA
Sch
Coll
Cemy
CH
WHITCHURCH RD
Parswell
171
Crowndale
BROOK LA
Whitchurch
Howell
Caseytown
Warren's Cross
Whitchurch Down
Whitchurch Prim Sch
Brook
CHURCH HILL
Middlemoor
PH
Plaster Down
Anderton
Rixhill
Works
Pennaton
Shillamill
Woodtown
PL19
Tor
West Devon Way
Grenofen
Fullamoor
Birch Wood
Higher Walreddon
Walreddon
BRANSON PK 1
GRENOFEN CL 2
Sortridge
Birchcleave House
F5
1 MADEIRS VILLAS
2 CHAPEL LA
3 GREENWAY CL
4 KNIGHTON TERR
5 WALKHAM TERR
6 THE GREEN
7 SAMPFORD TERR
Grimstone
River Walkham
West Down
Bedford Bridge
Horrabridge
JORDAN LA
Broadwell
Double Waters
WHITCHURCH RD
COPPERFIELDS
CHICHESTER CT
COMMERCIAL RD
BEDFORD RD
Weir
NEW PK
Bucktor
F4
1 RIVERSIDE CL
2 CARADON CT
3 PENCREBER RD
4 CHAPEL LA
5 CHAPEL CL
6 TOWN FARM CL
7 TORBRIDGE RD
8 TOR VIEW
9 PHOENIX CL
10 SOUTH VIEW
11 FILLACE LA
MANOR GDNS
WALKHAMPTON RD
ST JOHN'S RD
YOULDON WAY
WALKHAM MDWS
B3257
PL20
River Tavy
THE OLD STATION
OLD STATION RD
Horrabridge Prim Sch
F3
1 CLONWAY
2 INGRA TOR CL
3 PEW TOR CL
4 LEATHER TOR CL
5 GREAT MIS TOR CL
6 COX TOR CL
7 ASH CL
8 LANGTON RD
9 DEVON TORS RD
Hocklake Farm
Berra Tor
Alston
Uppaton
Uppaton Farm
Hotel
NORTH RD
Coppicetown
St Andrew's CE Prim Sch
NETHERTON EST
Balstone
CROSS PK
Buckland Monachorum
Pound
Roborough Down
VIXEN TOR CL
HARROWBEER LA
GRANGE RD
TAVISTOCK RD
CHAPEL MDW 1
RICHMOND TERR 2
HILLSIDE CL 3
CUXTON MDWS 4
HILL VIEW 5
MODYFORD WLK
THE VILLAGE
OLD QUARRY RD
POUND RD
WOODCHURCH
Hatch Mill
THE CRESCENT
Denham Bridge
Didham Farm
CRAPSTONE TERR 1
GRIMSTONE TERR 2
WOODSIDE 3
THE GLADE 4
MORLEY DR
ABBEY CL
SEATON WAY
WHISTLEY DOWN
BUCKLAND TERR
Yelverton Paperweight Mus
HUNTER'S OAK
Crapstone House
Yelverton Bsns Pk
Crapstone
Axtown
AXTOWN LA
STOKE HILL LA
MOORLAND CT
Leigh
Stokehill
Venton
GREEN LA
Buckland Abbey
CH
Hellingtown
Fishacre Wood
ALLEY HILL
Coombe Farm
Yeoland Farm
YEOLAND LA
Newhouse
Milton Combe
CHURCH HILL
Chubb Tor
125
240
241
For full street detail of the highlighted area see page 171.

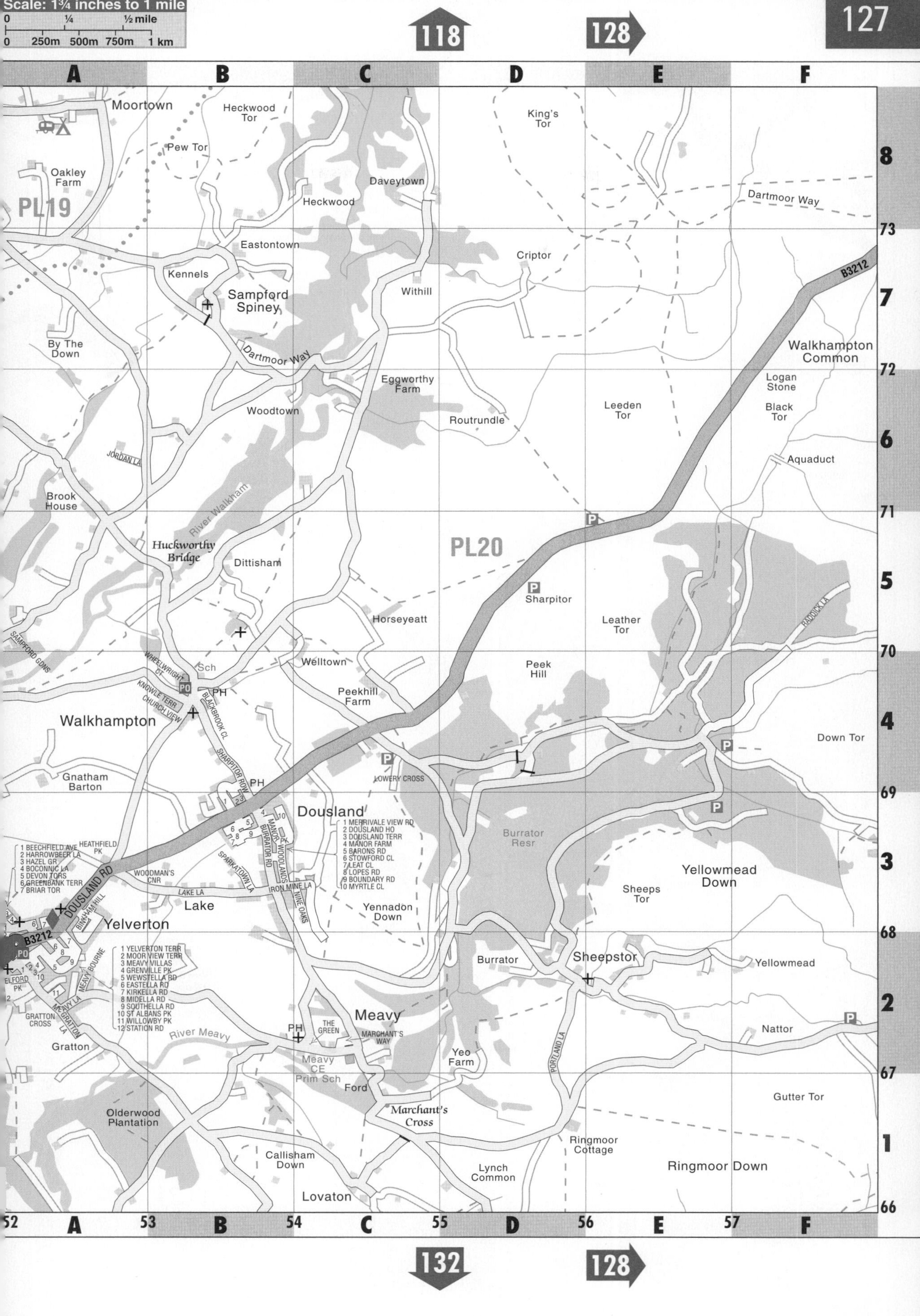
Scale: 1¾ inches to 1 mile
0 ¼ ½ mile
0 250m 500m 750m 1 km
118
128
A B C D E F
Moortown
Heckwood Tor
Pew Tor
King's Tor
Oakley Farm
PL19
Daveytown
Heckwood
Dartmoor Way
Eastontown
Criptor
Kennels
Sampford Spiney
Withill
B3212
By The Down
Dartmoor Way
Walkhampton Common
Eggworthy Farm
Logan Stone
Woodtown
Leeden Tor
Black Tor
Routrundle
JORDAN LA
Aquaduct
River Walkham
Brook House
Huckworthy Bridge
PL20
Dittisham
Sharpitor
Horseyeatt
Leather Tor
RADDICK LA
SAMPFORD GDNS
Sch
Welltown
Peek Hill
WHEELWRIGHT CT
PO
PH
KNOWLE TERR
CHURCH VIEW
BLACKBROOK CL
Peekhill Farm
Walkhampton
Down Tor
SHARPITOR ROW
Gnatham Barton
PH
LOWERY CROSS
Dousland
1 MERRIVALE VIEW RD
2 DOUSLAND HO
3 DOUSLAND TERR
4 MANOR FARM
5 BARONS RD
6 STOWFORD CL
7 LEAT CL
8 LOPES RD
9 BOUNDARY RD
10 MYRTLE CL
Burrator Resr
1 BEECHFIELD AVE
2 HARROWBEER LA
3 HAZEL GR
4 BOCONNIC LA
5 DEVON TORS
6 GREENBANK TERR
7 BRIAR TOR
HEATHFIELD PK
DOUSLAND RD
WOODMAN'S CNR
SPARKATOWN LA
MANOR PK
BURRATOR RD
WOODLANDS
IRON MINE LA
NINE OAKS
LAKE LA
Lake
Yellowmead Down
Sheeps Tor
Yennadon Down
BINKHAM HILL
Yelverton
B3212
PO
Burrator
Sheepstor
Yellowmead
1 YELVERTON TERR
2 MOOR VIEW TERR
3 MEAVY VILLAS
4 GRENVILLE PK
5 WEWSTELLA RD
6 EASTELLA RD
7 KIRKELLA RD
8 MIDELLA RD
9 SOUTHELLA RD
10 ST ALBANS PK
11 WILLOWBY PK
12 STATION RD
MEAVY BOURNE
ELFORD PK
MEAVY LA
GRATTON CROSS
GRATTON LA
Gratton
River Meavy
PH
THE GREEN
Meavy
MARCHANT'S WAY
Nattor
Meavy CE Prim Sch
Yeo Farm
PORTLAND LA
Ford
Marchant's Cross
Gutter Tor
Olderwood Plantation
Ringmoor Cottage
Callisham Down
Lynch Common
Ringmoor Down
Lovaton
8 73 7 72 6 71 5 70 4 69 3 68 2 67 1 66
52 53 54 55 56 57
132
128

127
119

Scale: 1¾ inches to 1 mile

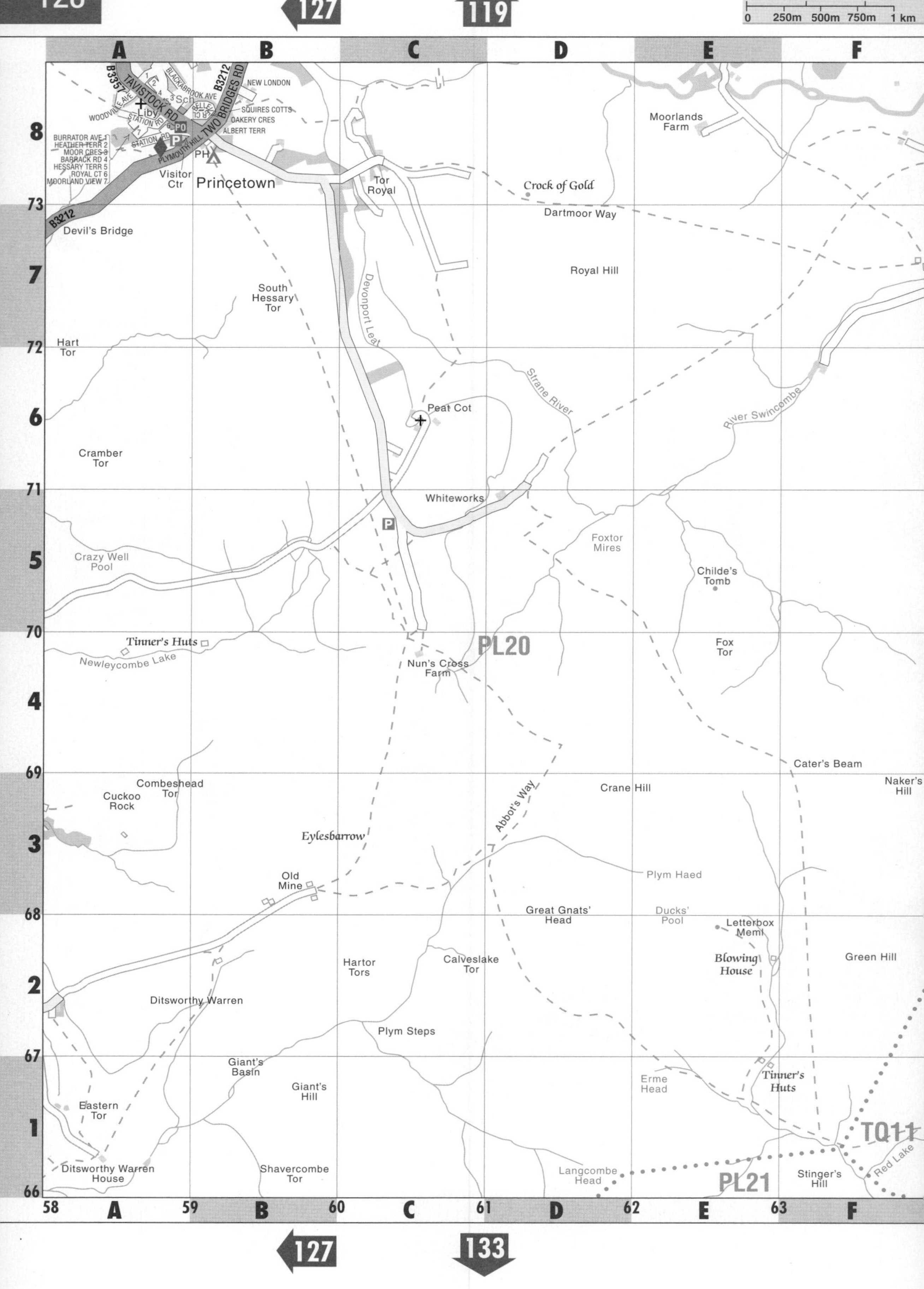
Princetown
Tor Royal
Crock of Gold
Dartmoor Way
Moorlands Farm
Visitor Ctr
Devil's Bridge
Royal Hill
South Hessary Tor
Devonport Leat
Hart Tor
Peat Cot
Strane River
River Swincombe
Cramber Tor
Whiteworks
Foxtor Mires
Crazy Well Pool
Childe's Tomb
Tinner's Huts
Newleycombe Lake
Nun's Cross Farm
PL20
Fox Tor
Cater's Beam
Combeshead Tor
Cuckoo Rock
Abbot's Way
Crane Hill
Naker's Hill
Eylesbarrow
Old Mine
Plym Haed
Great Gnats' Head
Ducks' Pool
Letterbox Meml
Blowing House
Hartor Tors
Calveslake Tor
Green Hill
Ditsworthy Warren
Plym Steps
Giant's Basin
Giant's Hill
Erme Head
Tinner's Huts
Eastern Tor
TQ11
Ditsworthy Warren House
Shavercombe Tor
Langcombe Head
PL21
Stinger's Hill
Red Lake

127
133

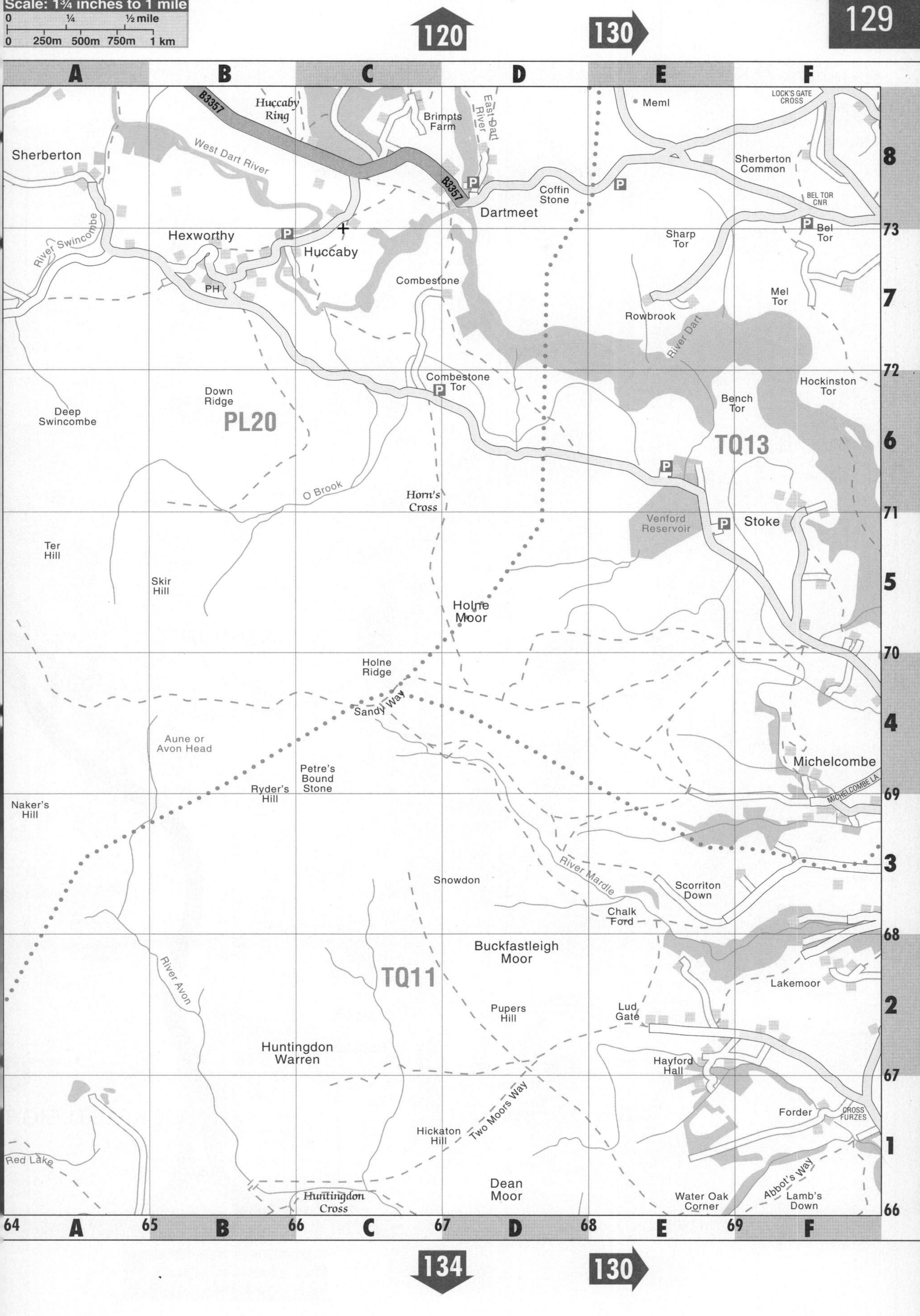
Scale: 1¾ inches to 1 mile
0 ¼ ½ mile
0 250m 500m 750m 1 km
120
130
A B C D E F
Sherberton
Huccaby Ring
B3357
Brimpts Farm
East Dart River
Meml
LOCK'S GATE CROSS
West Dart River
Sherberton Common
Coffin Stone
Dartmeet
BEL TOR CNR
Bel Tor
Hexworthy
Huccaby
Sharp Tor
River Swincombe
PH
Combestone
Mel Tor
Rowbrook
River Dart
Combestone Tor
Hockinston Tor
Down Ridge
Bench Tor
Deep Swincombe
PL20
TQ13
O Brook
Horn's Cross
Venford Reservoir
Stoke
Ter Hill
Skir Hill
Holne Moor
Holne Ridge
Sandy Way
Aune or Avon Head
Michelcombe
Petre's Bound Stone
Ryder's Hill
MICHELCOMBE LA
Naker's Hill
River Mardle
Snowdon
Scorriton Down
Chalk Ford
Buckfastleigh Moor
TQ11
Lakemoor
River Avon
Pupers Hill
Lud Gate
Huntingdon Warren
Hayford Hall
Two Moors Way
Forder
CROSS FURZES
Hickaton Hill
Red Lake
Dean Moor
Abbot's Way
Huntingdon Cross
Water Oak Corner
Lamb's Down
8 73 7 72 6 71 5 70 4 69 3 68 2 67 1 66
64 65 66 67 68 69
134
130

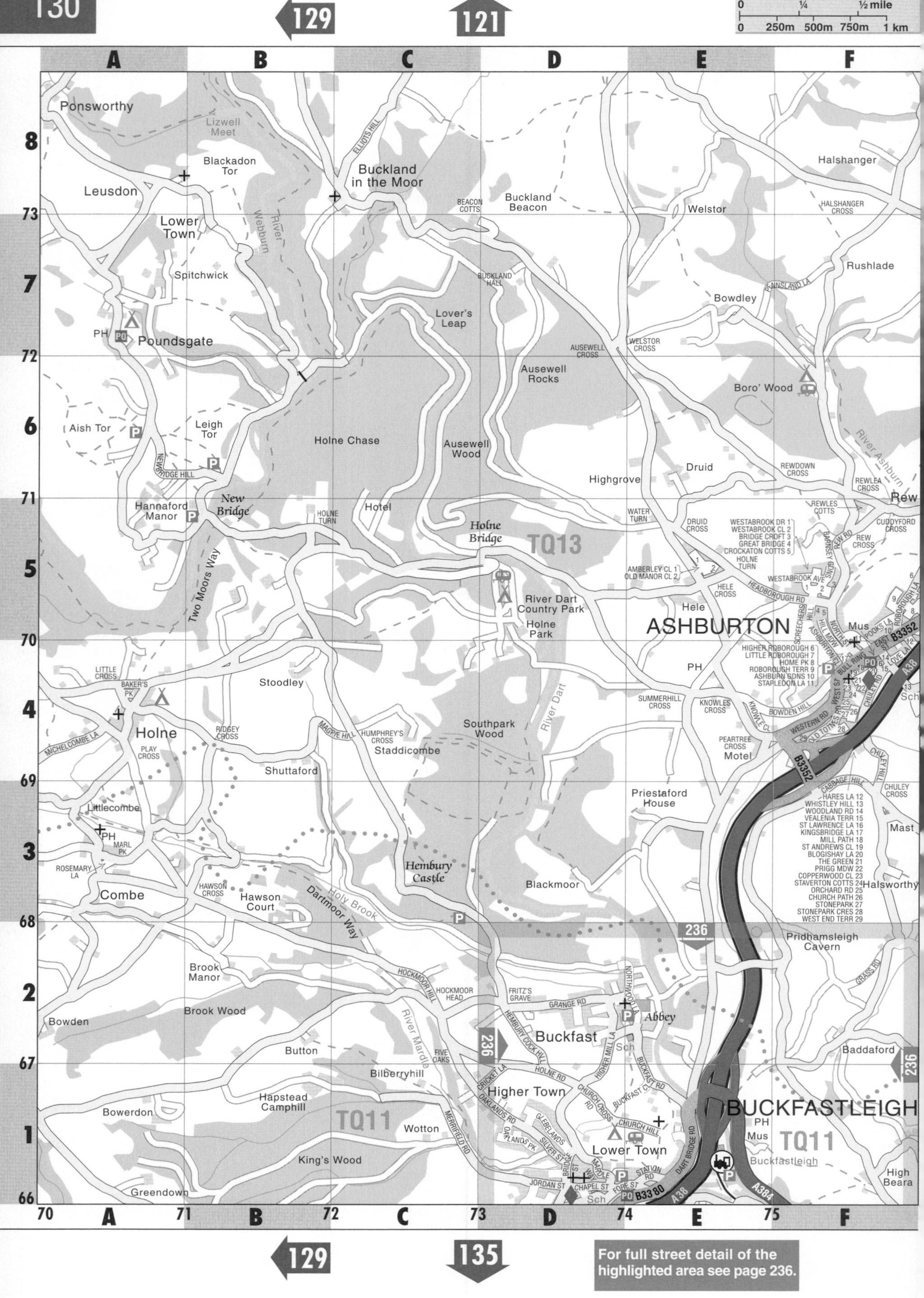

For full street detail of the highlighted area see page 236.

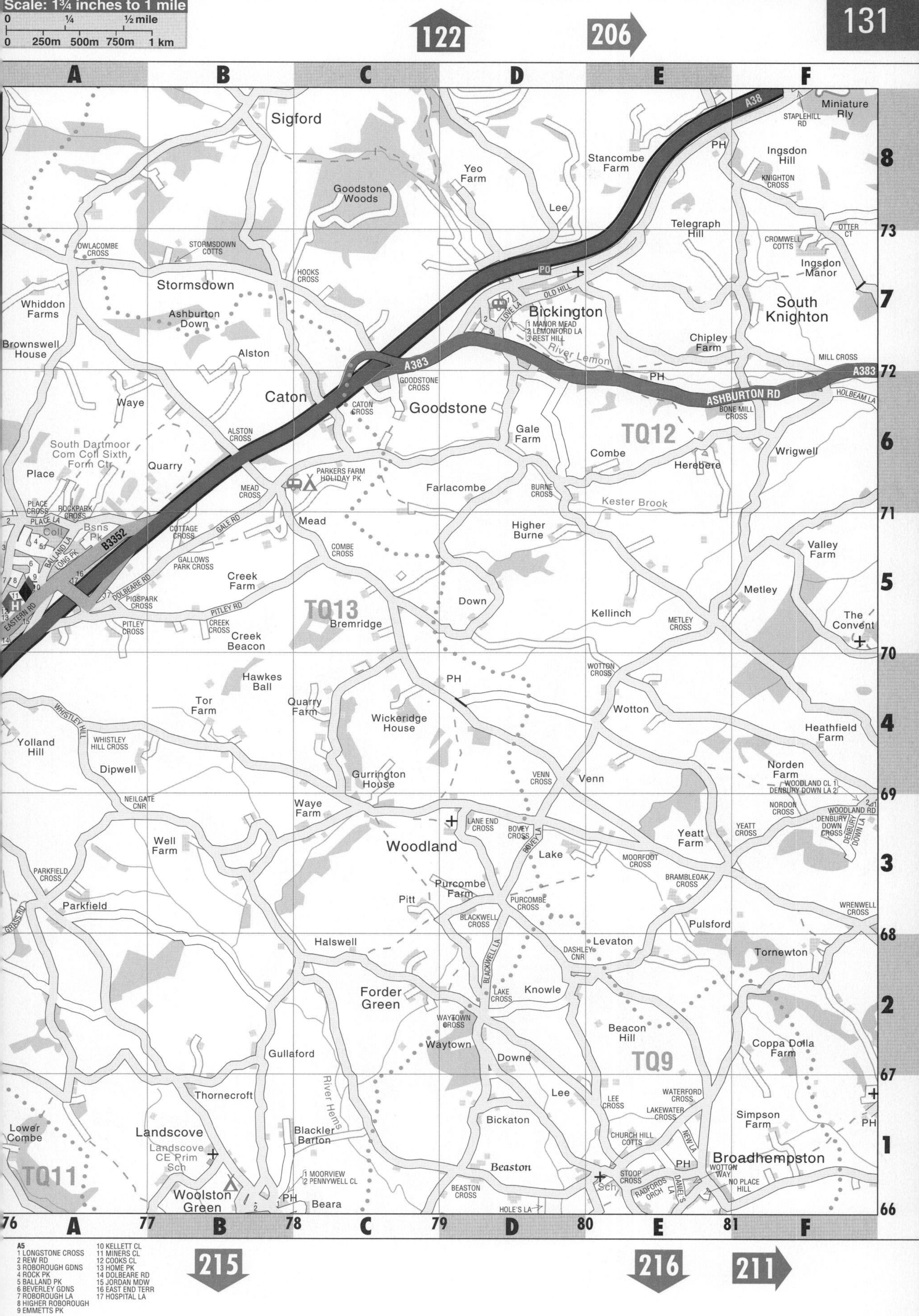
Scale: 1¾ inches to 1 mile
0 ¼ ½ mile
0 250m 500m 750m 1 km
122
206
A B C D E F
Sigford
Goodstone Woods
Yeo Farm
Stancombe Farm
Lee
A38
PH
Miniature Rly
STAPLEHILL RD
Ingsdon Hill
KNIGHTON CROSS
Telegraph Hill
OTTER CT
CROMWELL COTTS
Ingsdon Manor
South Knighton
OWLACOMBE CROSS
STORMSDOWN COTTS
HOOKS CROSS
PO
OLD HILL
Stormsdown
Whiddon Farms
Ashburton Down
Bickington
LOVE LA
1 MANOR MEAD
2 LEMONFORD LA
3 REST HILL
River Lemon
Chipley Farm
Brownswell House
Alston
MILL CROSS
A383
GOODSTONE CROSS
ASHBURTON RD
HOLBEAM LA
Waye
Caton
CATON CROSS
Goodstone
BONE MILL CROSS
ALSTON CROSS
Gale Farm
TQ12
South Dartmoor Com Coll Sixth Form Ctr
Quarry
Combe
Wrigwell
Herebere
Place
PARKERS FARM HOLIDAY PK
MEAD CROSS
Farlacombe
BURNE CROSS
Kester Brook
PLACE CROSS
PLACE LA
ROCKPARK CROSS
Coll
Bsns Pk
B3352
COTTAGE CROSS
GALE RD
Mead
Higher Burne
BALLAND LA
LONG PK
COMBE CROSS
Valley Farm
GALLOWS PARK CROSS
Creek Farm
DOLBEARE RD
PIGSPARK CROSS
Down
Metley
EASTERN RD
TQ13
Bremridge
PITLEY RD
Kellinch
The Convent
PITLEY CROSS
CREEK CROSS
Creek Beacon
METLEY CROSS
WOTTON CROSS
Hawkes Ball
PH
WHISTLEY HILL
Tor Farm
Quarry Farm
Wickeridge House
Wotton
Heathfield Farm
Yolland Hill
WHISTLEY HILL CROSS
Dipwell
Gurrington House
VENN CROSS
Venn
Norden Farm
WOODLAND CL 1
DENBURY DOWN LA 2
NEILGATE CNR
Waye Farm
NORDON CROSS
WOODLAND RD
LANE END CROSS
BOVEY CROSS
BOVEY LA
DENBURY DOWN CROSS
DENBURY DOWN LA
Well Farm
Woodland
Yeatt Farm
YEATT CROSS
Lake
PARKFIELD CROSS
MOORFOOT CROSS
BRAMBLEOAK CROSS
Purcombe Farm
Pitt
Parkfield
PURCOMBE CROSS
WRENWELL CROSS
BLACKWELL CROSS
Pulsford
GRASS RD
Halswell
Levaton
BLACKWELL LA
DASHLEY CNR
Tornewton
Forder Green
LAKE CROSS
Knowle
WAYTOWN CROSS
Beacon Hill
Waytown
Coppa Dolla Farm
Gullaford
Downe
TQ9
Thornecroft
River Hems
Lee
LEE CROSS
WATERFORD CROSS
Lower Combe
Bickaton
LAKEWATER CROSS
Simpson Farm
Landscove
Blackler Barton
CHURCH HILL COTTS
NEW LA
Landscove CE Prim Sch
Beaston
STOOP CROSS
PH
Broadhempston
TQ11
1 MOORVIEW
2 PENNYWELL CL
Sch
WOTTON WAY
NO PLACE HILL
RADFORDS ORCH
DANIELS LA
Woolston Green
PH
Beara
BEASTON CROSS
HOLE'S LA
8
73
7
72
6
71
5
70
4
69
3
68
2
67
1
66
76 77 78 79 80 81
215
216
211
A5
1 LONGSTONE CROSS
2 REW RD
3 ROBOROUGH GDNS
4 ROCK PK
5 BALLAND PK
6 BEVERLEY GDNS
7 ROBOROUGH LA
8 HIGHER ROBOROUGH
9 EMMETTS PK
10 KELLETT CL
11 MINERS CL
12 COOKS CL
13 HOME PK
14 DOLBEARE RD
15 JORDAN MDW
16 EAST END TERR
17 HOSPITAL LA

241
127

Scale: 1¾ inches to 1 mile

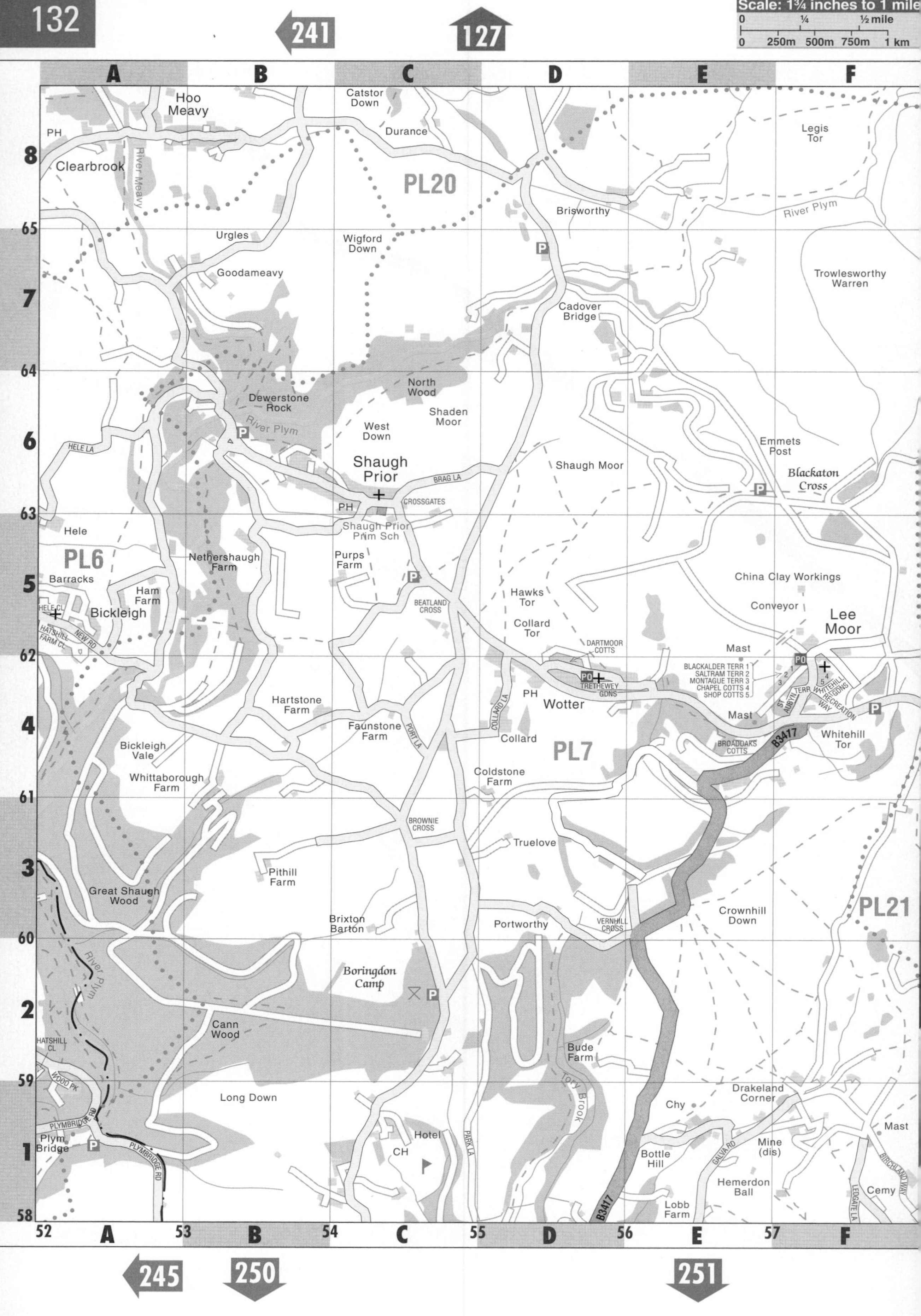

245
250
251

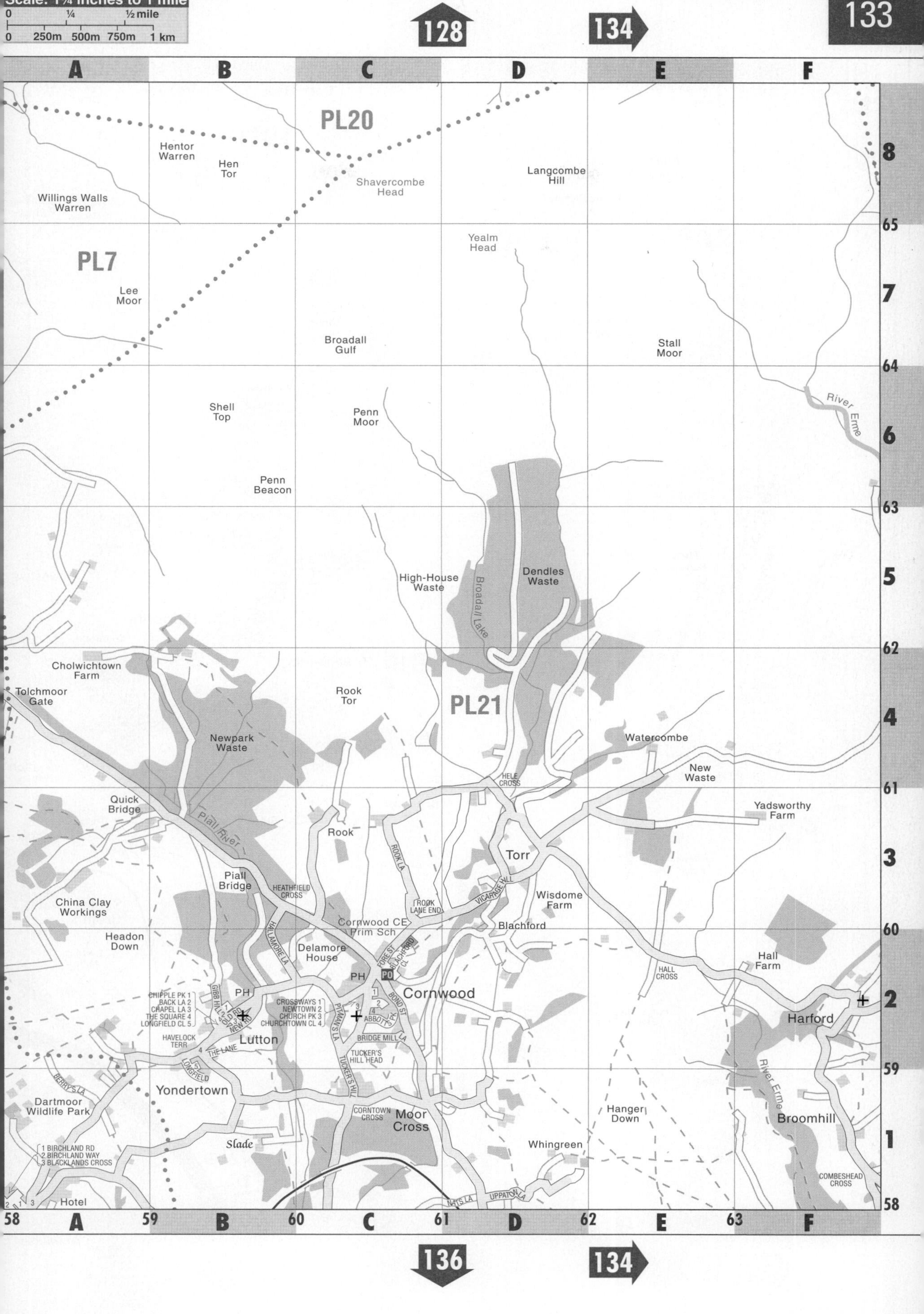

Scale: 1¾ inches to 1 mile
0 ¼ ½ mile
0 250m 500m 750m 1 km
128
134
A B C D E F
PL20
Hentor Warren
Hen Tor
Shavercombe Head
Langcombe Hill
Willings Walls Warren
PL7
Yealm Head
Lee Moor
Broadall Gulf
Stall Moor
Shell Top
Penn Moor
River Erme
Penn Beacon
High-House Waste
Broadall Lake
Dendles Waste
Cholwichtown Farm
Tolchmoor Gate
Rook Tor
PL21
Newpark Waste
Watercombe
New Waste
Hele Cross
Quick Bridge
Piall River
Rook
Yadsworthy Farm
Rook La
Torr
Piall Bridge
Heathfield Cross
Rook Lane End
Vicarage Hill
Wisdome Farm
China Clay Workings
Cornwood CE Prim Sch
Blachford
Headon Down
Hallamore La
Delamore House
Fore St
Blachford Cl
Hall Cross
Hall Farm
PH
Cornwood
Chipple Pk 1
Back La 2
Chapel La 3
The Square 4
Longfield Cl 5
Gibb Hill
Old Rd
New Rd
Crossways 1
Newtown 2
Church Pk 3
Churchtown Cl 4
Pitman's La
Abbots Pk
Bond St
Harford
Havelock Terr
Lutton
The Lane
Bridge Mill La
Tucker's Hill Head
Longfield
Berry's La
Tucker's Hill
River Erme
Yondertown
Dartmoor Wildlife Park
Corntown Cross
Moor Cross
Hanger Down
Broomhill
Slade
Whingreen
1 Birchland Rd
2 Birchland Way
3 Blacklands Cross
Combeshead Cross
Hotel
Nats La
Uppaton La
58 59 60 61 62 63
8 65 7 64 6 63 5 62 4 61 3 60 2 59 1 58
136
134

133
129

Scale: 1¾ inches to 1 mile
0 ¼ ½ mile
0 250m 500m 750m 1 km

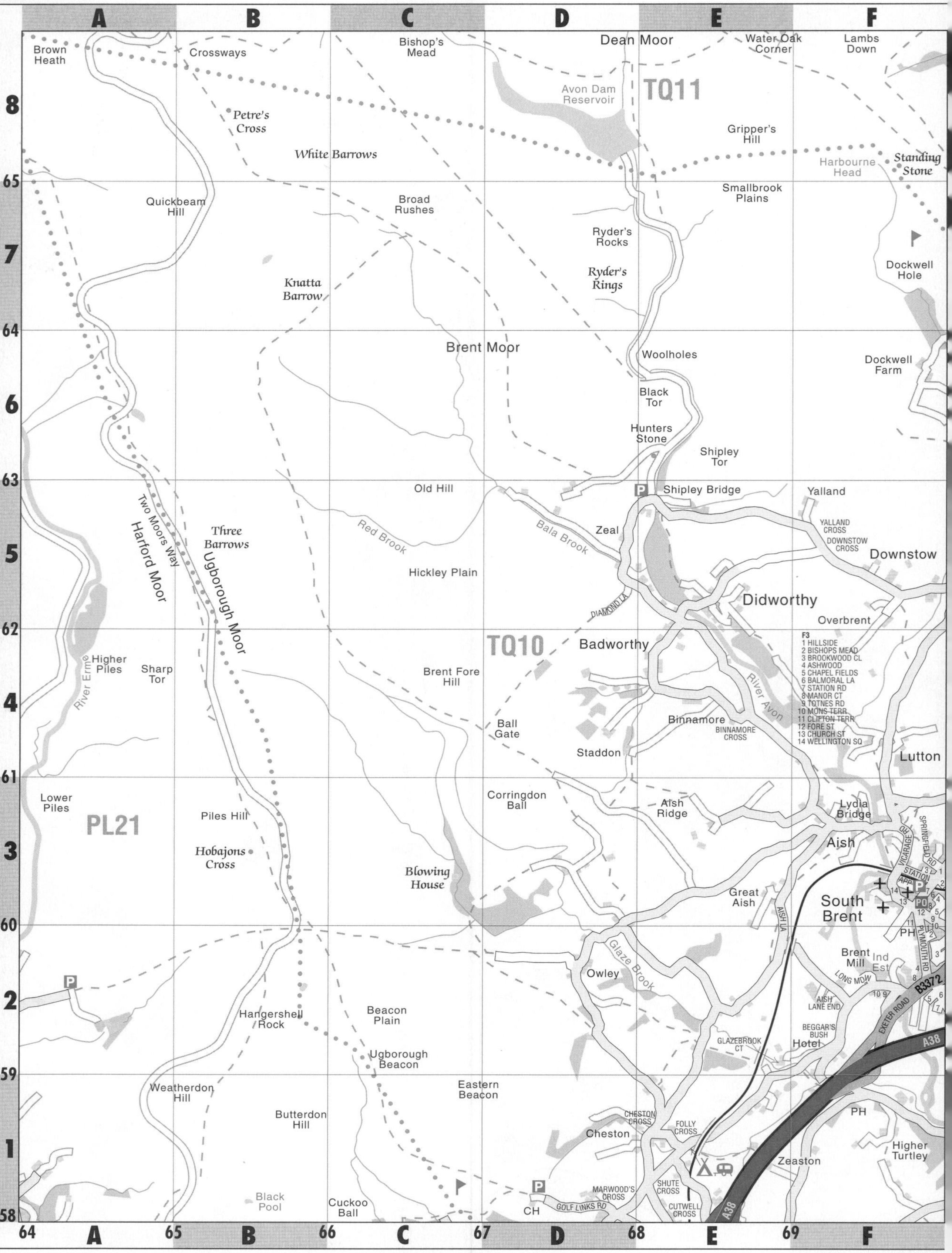

A B C D E F

Brown Heath
Crossways
Bishop's Mead
Dean Moor
Water Oak Corner
Lambs Down
Avon Dam Reservoir
TQ11
8
Petre's Cross
White Barrows
Gripper's Hill
Standing Stone
Harbourne Head
65
Quickbeam Hill
Broad Rushes
Smallbrook Plains
Ryder's Rocks
7
Knatta Barrow
Ryder's Rings
Dockwell Hole
64
Brent Moor
Woolholes
Dockwell Farm
6
Black Tor
Hunters Stone
Shipley Tor
63
Old Hill
Shipley Bridge
Yalland
Yalland Cross
Downstow Cross
Downstow
Two Moors Way
Harford Moor
Three Barrows
Ugborough Moor
Red Brook
Bala Brook
Zeal
5
Hickley Plain
Diamond La
Didworthy
Overbrent
62
TQ10
Badworthy
Higher Piles
Sharp Tor
River Erme
Brent Fore Hill
River Avon

F3
1 HILLSIDE
2 BISHOPS MEAD
3 BROOKWOOD CL
4 ASHWOOD
5 CHAPEL FIELDS
6 BALMORAL LA
7 STATION RD
8 MANOR CT
9 TOTNES RD
10 MONS TERR
11 CLIFTON TERR
12 FORE ST
13 CHURCH ST
14 WELLINGTON SQ

4
Binnamore
Binnamore Cross
Ball Gate
Staddon
Lutton
61
Lower Piles
PL21
Piles Hill
Corringdon Ball
Aish Ridge
Lydia Bridge
3
Hobajons Cross
Aish
Vicarage Hill
Springfield Rd
Station App
Blowing House
Great Aish
Aish La
South Brent
PO
PH
Plymouth Rd
60
Brent Mill
Ind Est
Long Mdw
Glaze Brook
Owley
2
Hangershell Rock
Beacon Plain
Aish Lane End
Exeter Road
B3372
Beggar's Bush
Hotel
Glazebrook Ct
A38
Ugborough Beacon
59
Weatherdon Hill
Eastern Beacon
Butterdon Hill
Chestor Cross
Folly Cross
PH
Cheston
1
Higher Turtley
Zeaston
Black Pool
Cuckoo Ball
Marwood's Cross
Shute Cross
CH
Golf Links Rd
Cutwell Cross
A38
58

64 A 65 B 66 C 67 D 68 E 69 F

133
137

F2
1 WOODHAYE TERR
2 WOODHAYE CL
3 CLOBELLS
4 BEACON TERR
5 ST MICHAELS TERR
6 CORN PARK RD
7 GREENFIELD DR
8 BEACON VIEW
9 AVONDALE HO
10 AVONDALE WLK

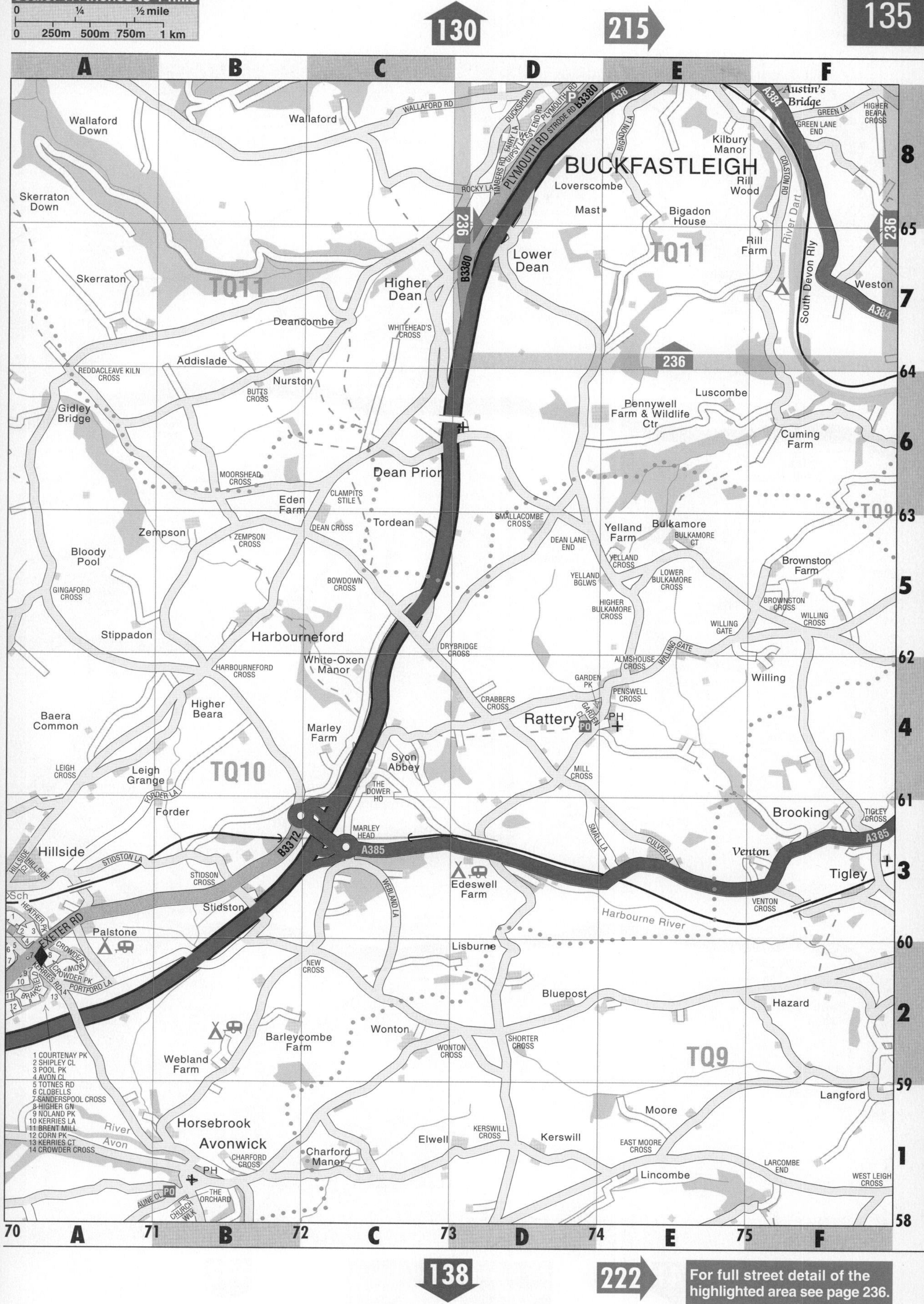

For full street detail of the highlighted area see page 236.

For full street detail of the highlighted area see page 237.

Scale: 1¾ inches to 1 mile

134
138

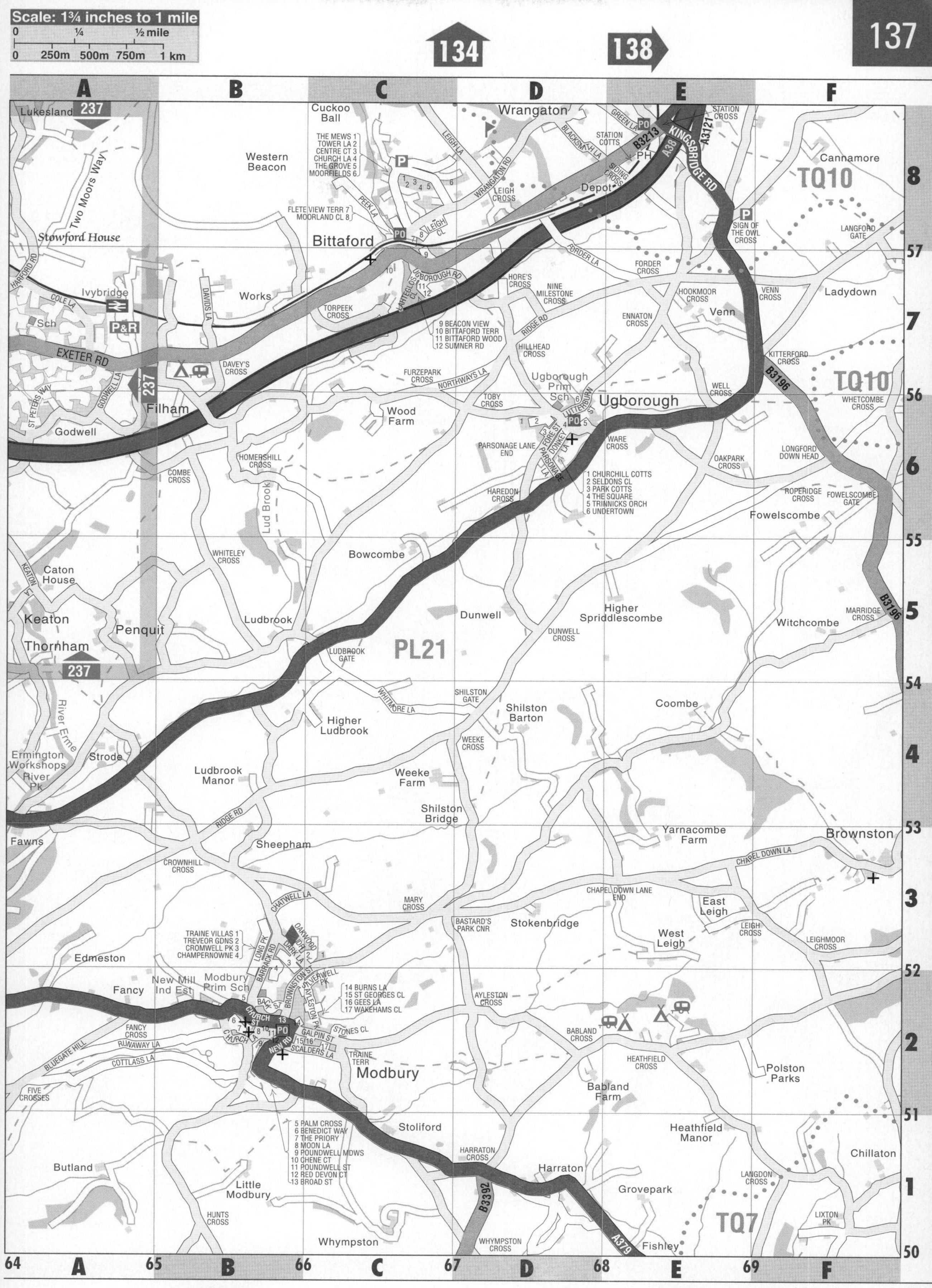

142
143
138

137
135

Scale: 1¾ inches to 1 mile
0 ¼ ½ mile
0 250m 500m 750m 1 km

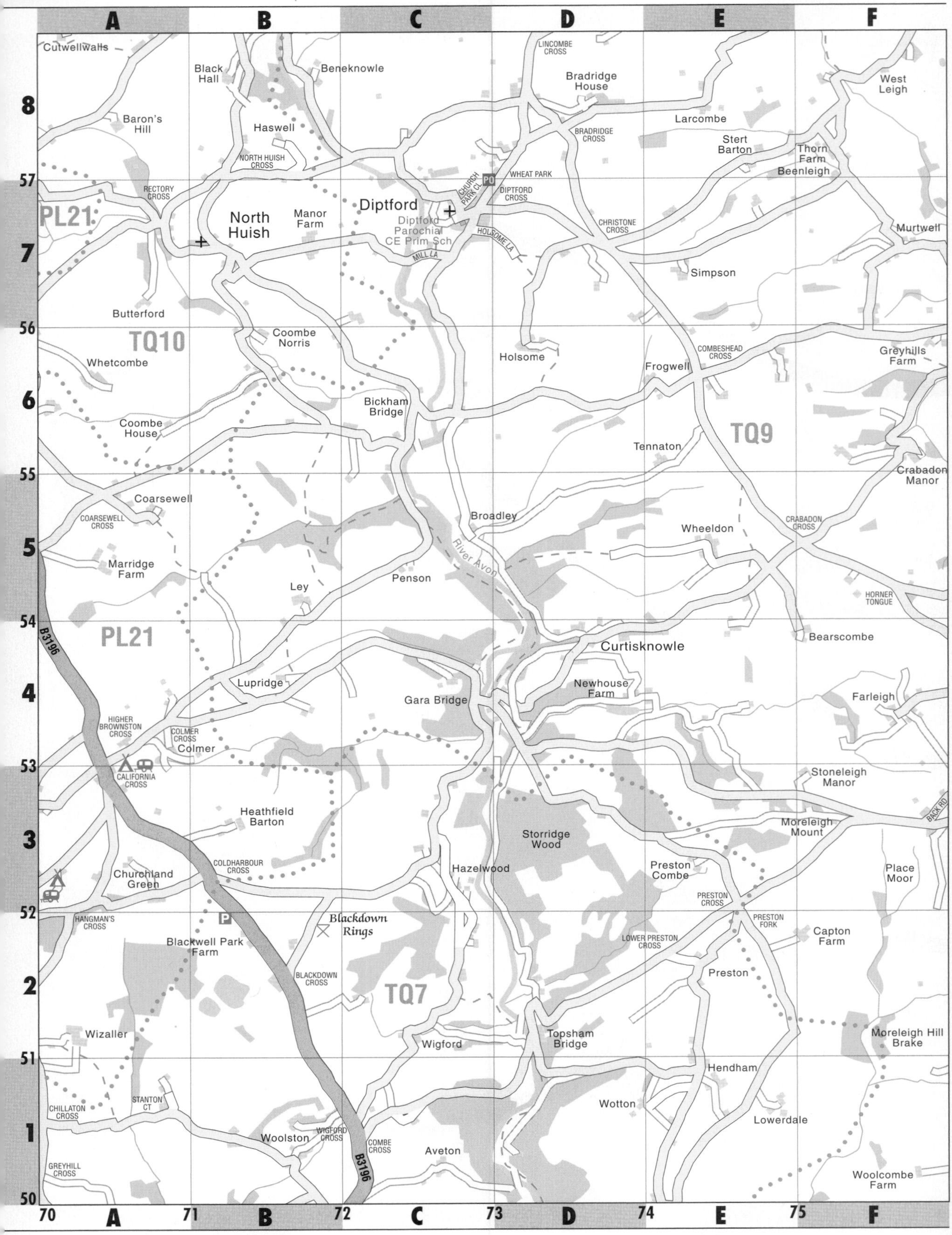

A B C D E F

Cutwellwalls
Black Hall
Beneknowle
Lincombe Cross
Bradridge House
West Leigh
8
Baron's Hill
Haswell
Larcombe
Bradridge Cross
Stert Barton
Thorn Farm
Beenleigh
North Huish Cross
Wheat Park
Church Park Cl
PO
57
Rectory Cross
Diptford Cross
PL21
North Huish
Manor Farm
Diptford
Diptford Parochial CE Prim Sch
Holsome La
Christone Cross
Murtwell
Mill La
7
Simpson
Butterford
56
TQ10
Coombe Norris
Whetcombe
Holsome
Combeshead Cross
Frogwell
Greyhills Farm
6
Bickham Bridge
Coombe House
TQ9
Tennaton
55
Crabadon Manor
Coarsewell
Coarsewell Cross
Broadley
Wheeldon
Crabadon Cross
5
River Avon
Marridge Farm
Penson
Ley
Horner Tongue
54
B3196
PL21
Bearscombe
Curtisknowle
4
Lupridge
Newhouse Farm
Gara Bridge
Farleigh
Higher Brownston Cross
Colmer Cross
Colmer
53
California Cross
Stoneleigh Manor
Heathfield Barton
Back Rd
Storridge Wood
Moreleigh Mount
3
Hazelwood
Preston Combe
Coldharbour Cross
Churchland Green
Place Moor
Preston Cross
52
Hangman's Cross
P
Blackdown Rings
Preston Fork
Capton Farm
Blackwell Park Farm
Lower Preston Cross
Blackdown Cross
2
Preston
TQ7
Wizaller
Topsham Bridge
Moreleigh Hill Brake
Wigford
51
Hendham
Stanton Ct
Chillaton Cross
Wotton
Lowerdale
1
Woolston
Wigford Cross
Combe Cross
Aveton
B3196
Greyhill Cross
Woolcombe Farm
50
70 71 72 73 74 75
A B C D E F

137
143
144

Scale: 1¾ inches to 1 mile

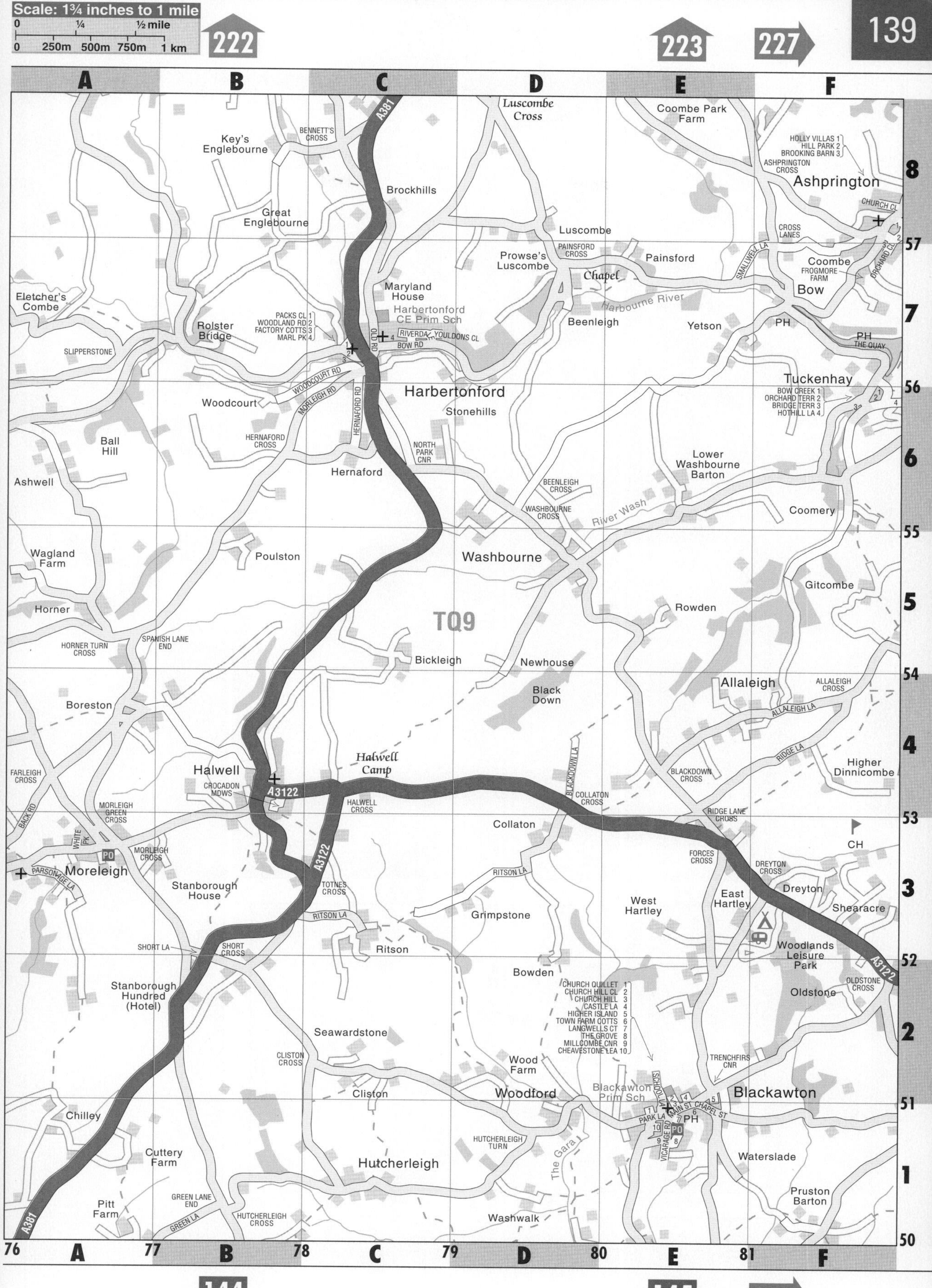

D8
1 WEMBURY MDW
2 HIGHFIELD DR
3 CROSS PARK RD
4 CROSSWAYS
5 COLLIERS CL
6 LABURNUM DR
7 SEA VIEW DR
8 SOUTHLAND PARK CRES
9 HILLCREST CL

Scale: 1¾ inches to 1 mile
0 ¼ ½ mile
0 250m 500m 750m 1 km

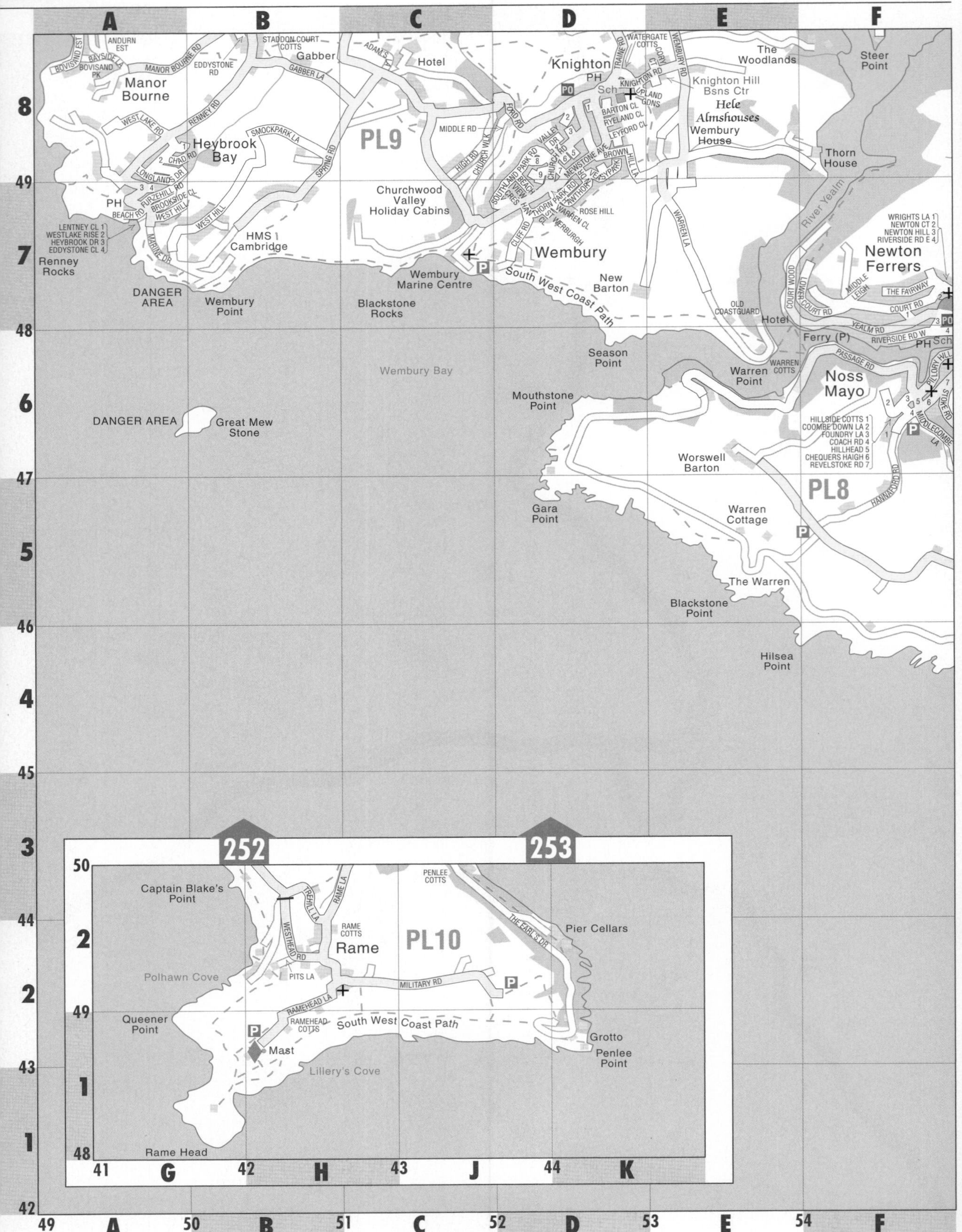

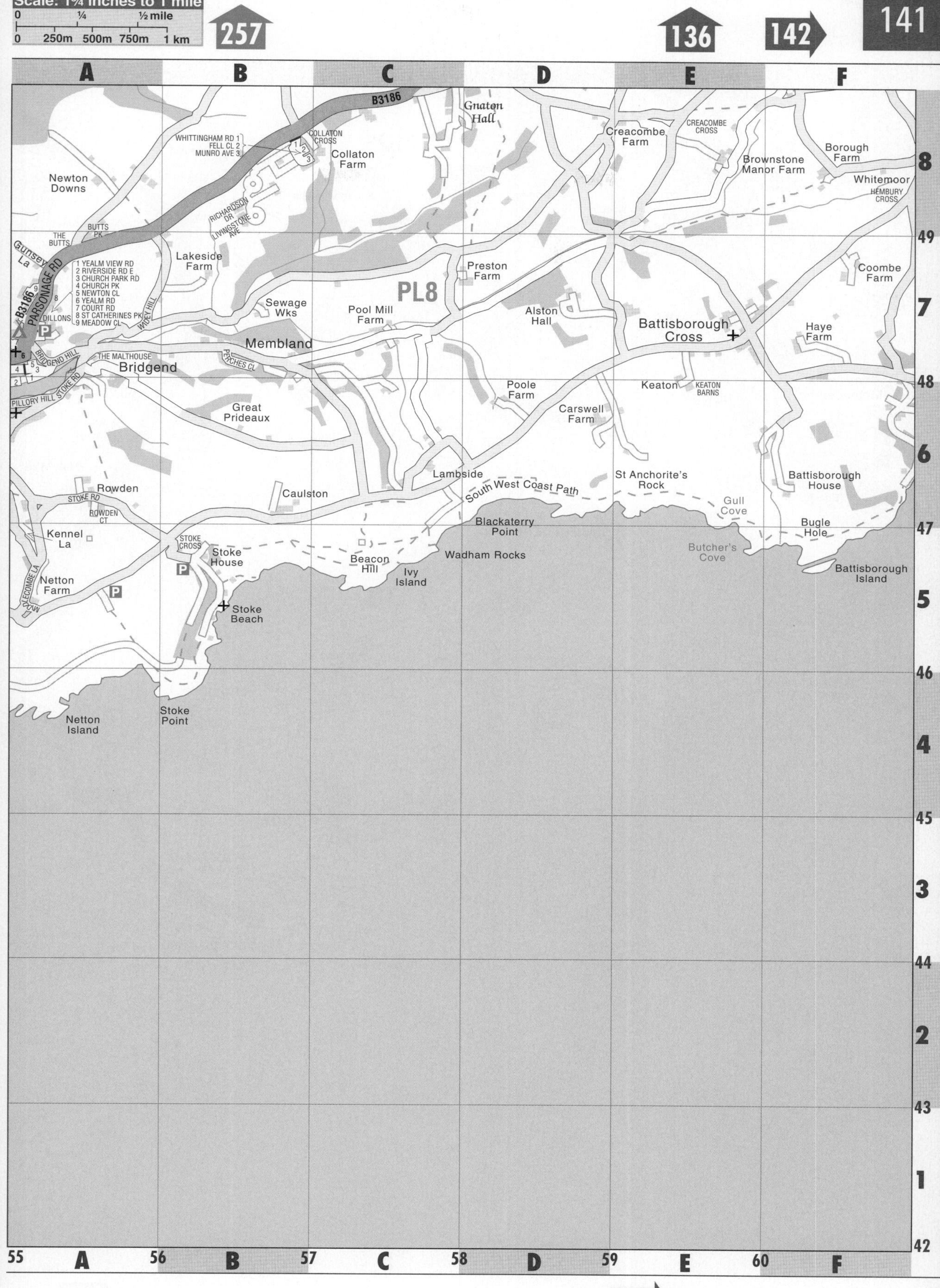
Scale: 1¾ inches to 1 mile
0 ¼ ½ mile
0 250m 500m 750m 1 km
257
136
142
A B C D E F
B3186
Gnaton Hall
Creacombe Farm
CREACOMBE CROSS
Borough Farm
Brownstone Manor Farm
Whitemoor
HEMBURY CROSS
WHITTINGHAM RD 1
FELL CL 2
MUNRO AVE 3
COLLATON CROSS
Collaton Farm
Newton Downs
RICHARDSON DR
LIVINGSTONE AVE
THE BUTTS
BUTTS PK
Gunsey La
PARSONAGE RD
1 YEALM VIEW RD
2 RIVERSIDE RD E
3 CHURCH PARK RD
4 CHURCH PK
5 NEWTON CL
6 YEALM RD
7 COURT RD
8 ST CATHERINES PK
9 MEADOW CL
DILLONS
WIDEY HILL
Lakeside Farm
Sewage Wks
Preston Farm
PL8
Pool Mill Farm
Alston Hall
Coombe Farm
Battisborough Cross
Haye Farm
Membland
THE MALTHOUSE
PERCHES CL
BRIDGEND HILL
Bridgend
PILLORY HILL
STOKE RD
Poole Farm
Keaton
KEATON BARNS
Great Prideaux
Carswell Farm
Lambside
St Anchorite's Rock
Battisborough House
Rowden
Caulston
South West Coast Path
Gull Cove
STOKE RD
ROWDEN CT
Blackaterry Point
Bugle Hole
Kennel La
STOKE CROSS
Stoke House
Wadham Rocks
Butcher's Cove
Beacon Hill
Ivy Island
Battisborough Island
Netton Farm
Stoke Beach
Netton Island
Stoke Point
8
49
7
48
6
47
5
46
4
45
3
44
2
43
1
42
55 A 56 B 57 C 58 D 59 E 60 F

142

141 136 137

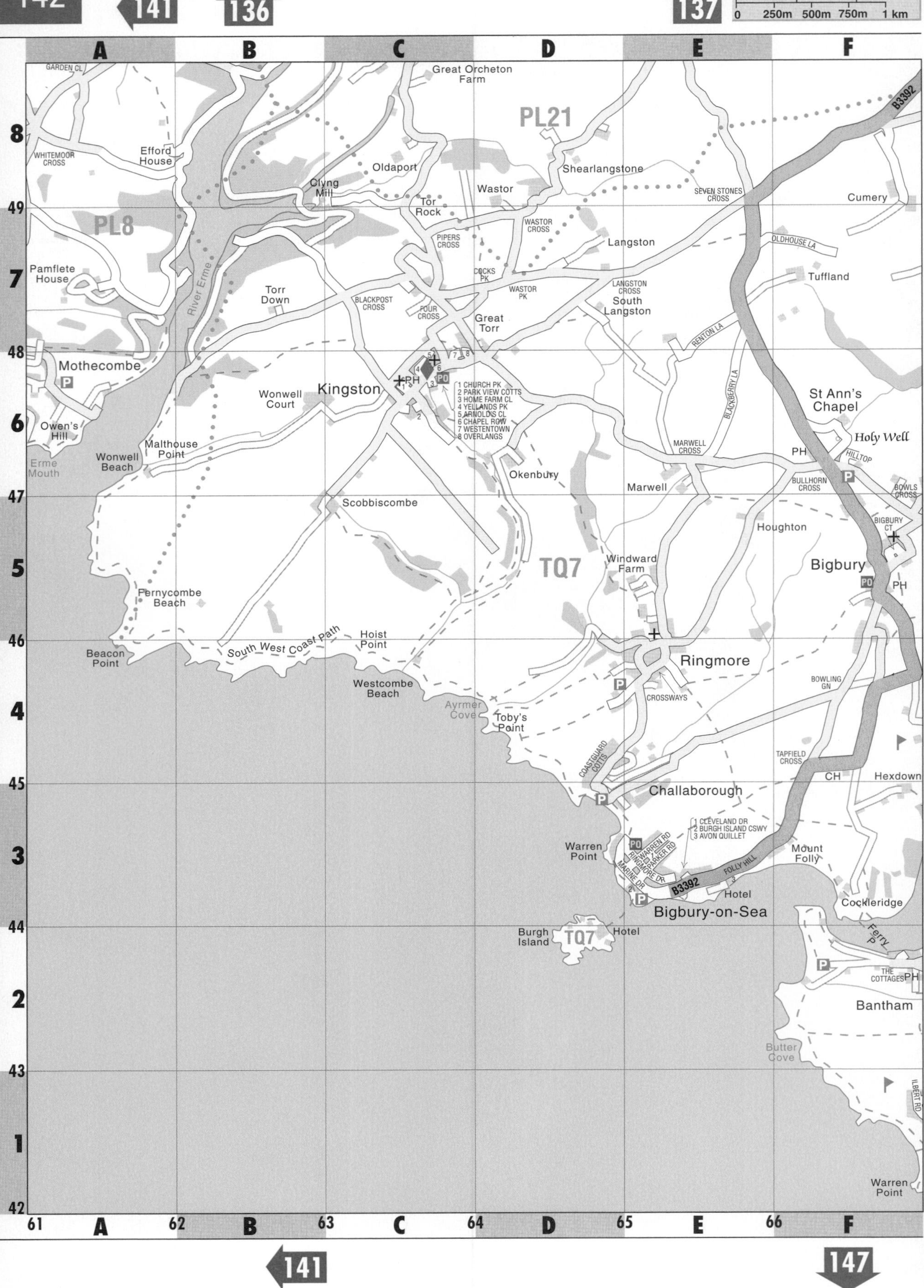

141 147

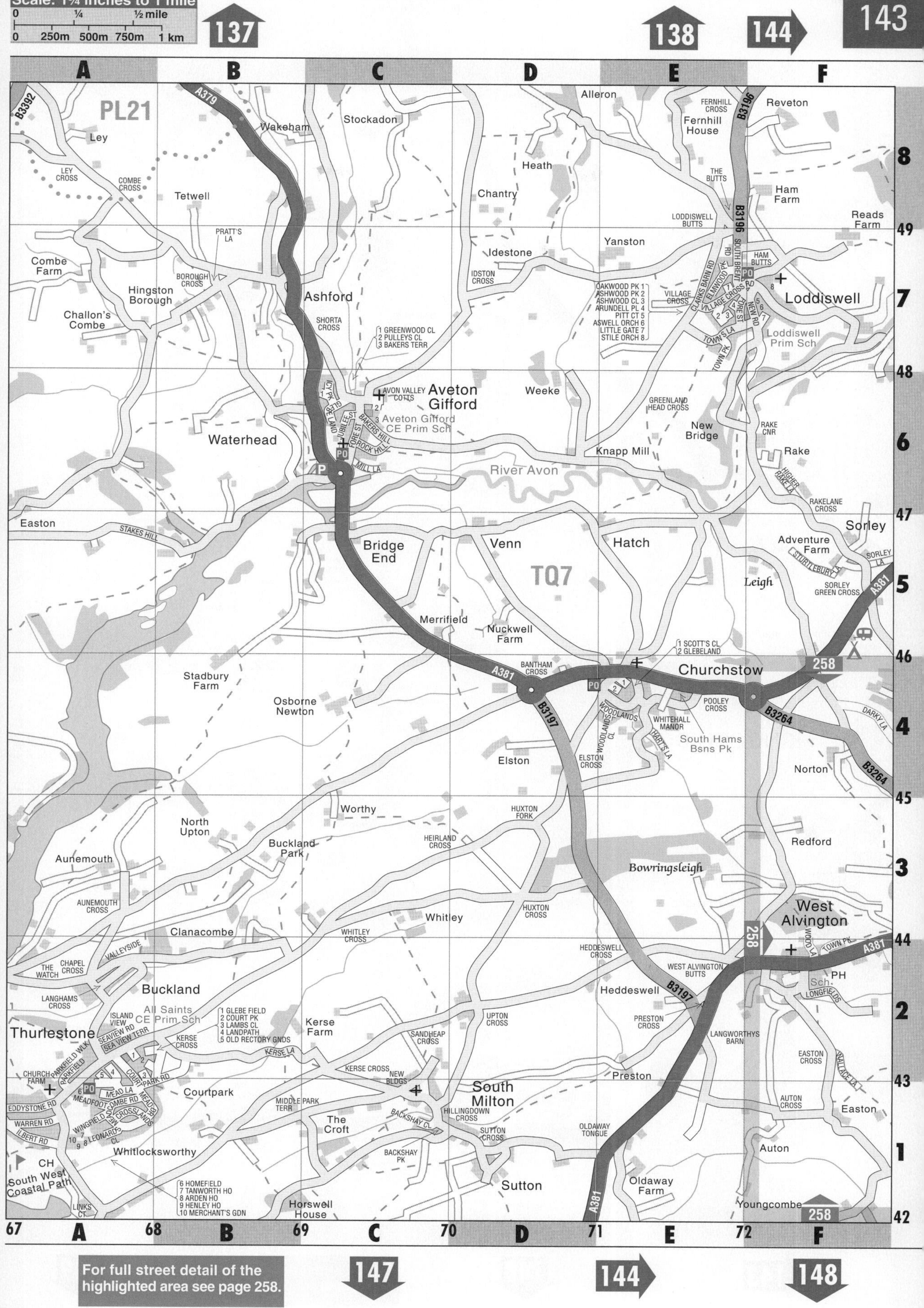

For full street detail of the highlighted area see page 258.

143
138
139

Scale: 1¾ inches to 1 mile
0 ¼ ½ mile
0 250m 500m 750m 1 km

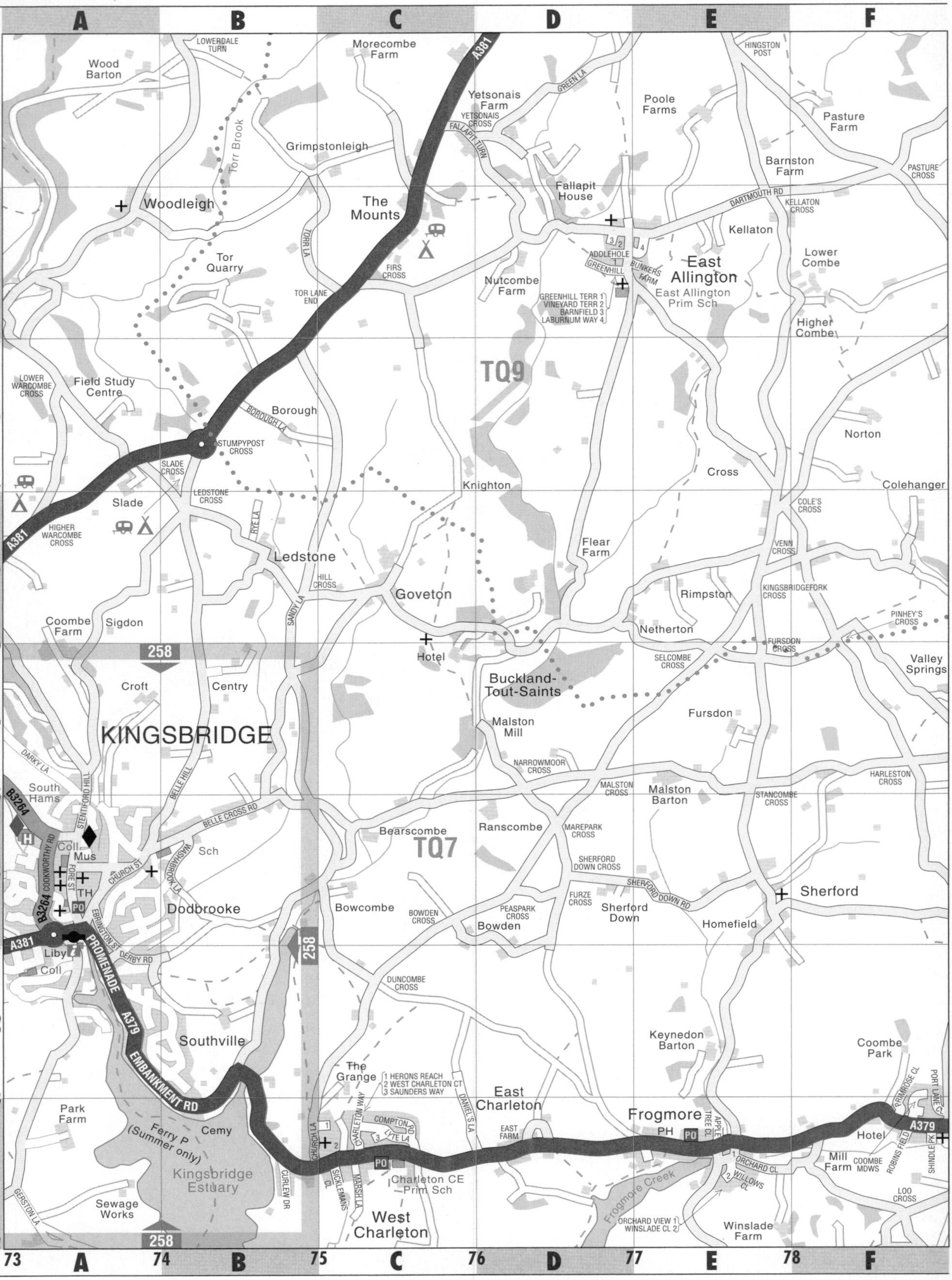
A B C D E F
8 49 7 48 6 47 5 46 4 45 3 44 2 43 1 42
73 74 75 76 77 78
Wood Barton
LOWERDALE TURN
Morecombe Farm
A381
Yetsonais Farm
YETSONAIS CROSS
FALLAPIT TURN
GREEN LA
Poole Farms
HINGSTON POST
Pasture Farm
Torr Brook
Grimpstonleigh
Barnston Farm
PASTURE CROSS
Woodleigh
The Mounts
Fallapit House
DARTMOUTH RD
KELLATON CROSS
Kellaton
Tor Quarry
TORR LA
ADDLEHOLE
GREENHILL
BUNKERS FARM
East Allington
East Allington Prim Sch
Lower Combe
FIRS CROSS
TOR LANE END
Nutcombe Farm
GREENHILL TERR 1
VINEYARD TERR 2
BARNFIELD 3
LABURNUM WAY 4
Higher Combe
LOWER WARCOMBE CROSS
Field Study Centre
TQ9
Borough
BOROUGH LA
STUMPYPOST CROSS
Norton
SLADE CROSS
Knighton
Cross
Slade
LEDSTONE CROSS
RYE LA
Colehanger
COLE'S CROSS
HIGHER WARCOMBE CROSS
Flear Farm
VENN CROSS
Ledstone
HILL CROSS
SANDY LA
Goveton
Rimpston
KINGSBRIDGEFORK CROSS
PINHEY'S CROSS
Coombe Farm
Sigdon
Netherton
Hotel
FURSDON CROSS
SELCOMBE CROSS
Valley Springs
258
Croft
Centry
Buckland-Tout-Saints
Fursdon
Malston Mill
KINGSBRIDGE
DARKY LA
NARROWMOOR CROSS
B3264
South Hams
STENTIFORD HILL
BELLE HILL
MALSTON CROSS
Malston Barton
HARLESTON CROSS
STANCOMBE CROSS
BELLE CROSS RD
Bearscombe
Ranscombe
MAREPARK CROSS
H
Coll
Mus
WASHABROOK LA
Sch
TQ7
COOKWORTHY RD
FORE ST
TH
CHURCH ST
SHERFORD DOWN CROSS
Sherford
Dodbrooke
PO
Bowcombe
BOWDEN CROSS
PEASPARK CROSS
Bowden
FURZE CROSS
Sherford Down
SHERFORD DOWN RD
Homefield
A381
Liby
Coll
ERRINGTON ST
PROMENADE
DERBY RD
DUNCOMBE CROSS
A379
Southville
Keynedon Barton
Coombe Park
PRIMROSE CL
PORT LANE CL
EMBANKMENT RD
The Grange
1 HERONS REACH
2 WEST CHARLETON CT
3 SAUNDERS WAY
DANIEL'S LA
East Charleton
Park Farm
Cemy
CHARLETON WAY
COMPTON RD
LYTE LA
Ferry P (Summer only)
CHURCH LA
EAST FARM
Frogmore
PH
APPLE TREE CL
Hotel
A379
ROBINS FIELD
SHINDLE PK
Kingsbridge Estuary
CURLEW DR
SICKLEMANS CL
MARSH LA
Charleton CE Prim Sch
Frogmore Creek
ORCHARD CL
WILLOWS CL
Mill Farm
COOMBE MDWS
GERSTON LA
Sewage Works
LOO CROSS
West Charleton
ORCHARD VIEW 1
WINSLADE CL 2
Winslade Farm

143
148
149
For full street detail of the highlighted area see page 258.

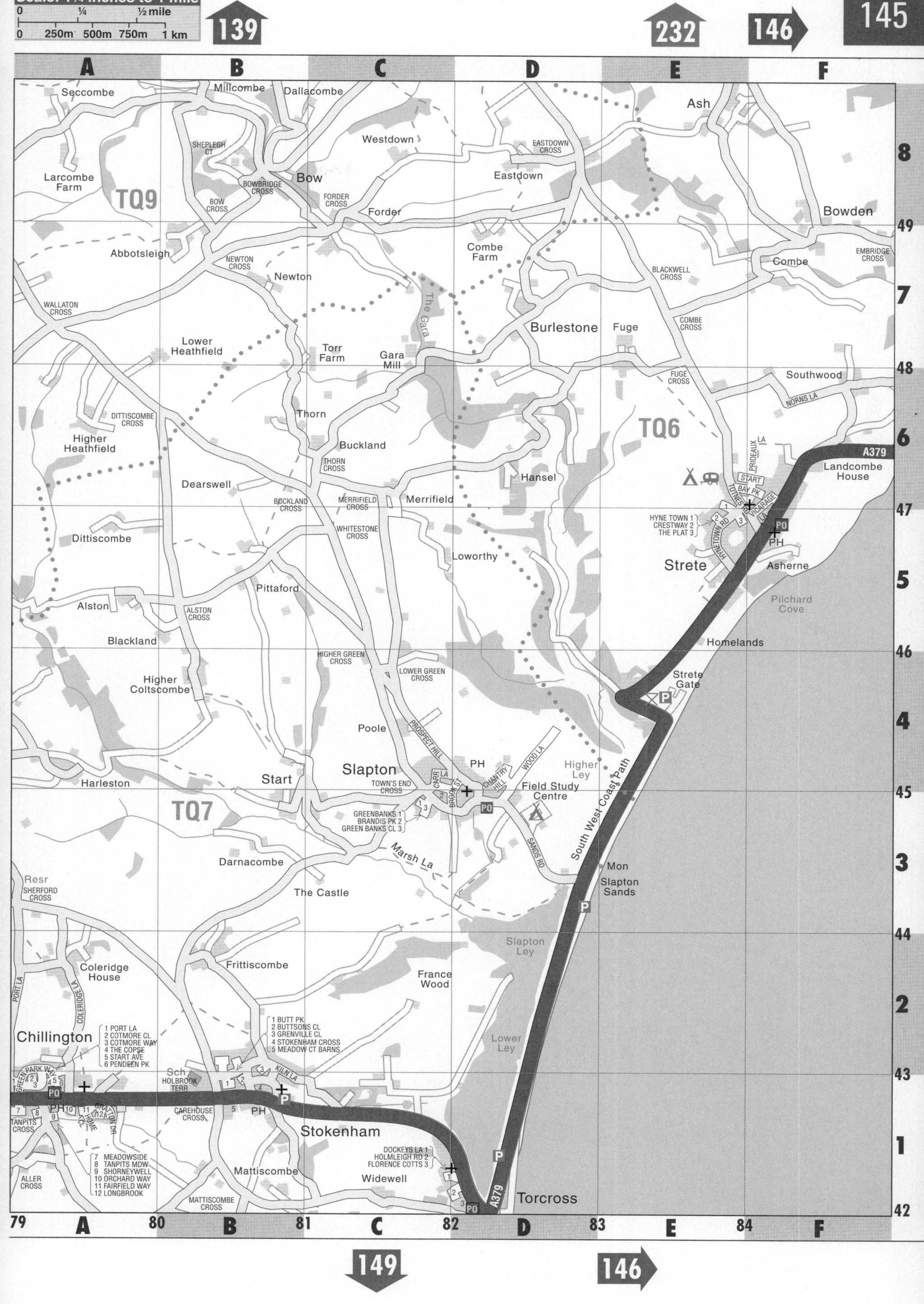
Scale: 1¾ inches to 1 mile
0 ¼ ½ mile
0 250m 500m 750m 1 km
139
232
146
145
A B C D E F
Seccombe
Millcombe
Dallacombe
Ash
Westdown
SHEPLEGH CT
EASTDOWN CROSS
Larcombe Farm
TQ9
BOWBRIDGE CROSS
Bow
Eastdown
BOW CROSS
FORDER CROSS
Forder
Bowden
Abbotsleigh
Combe Farm
EMBRIDGE CROSS
Combe
NEWTON CROSS
BLACKWELL CROSS
Newton
WALLATON CROSS
The Gara
COMBE CROSS
Burlestone
Fuge
Lower Heathfield
Torr Farm
Gara Mill
FUGE CROSS
Southwood
NORNS LA
Thorn
DITTISCOMBE CROSS
TQ6
Higher Heathfield
Buckland
PRIDEAUX LA
A379
Landcombe House
THORN CROSS
START BAY PK
Dearswell
Hansel
TOTNES
VICARAGE LA
BUCKLAND CROSS
MERRIFIELD CROSS
Merrifield
HYNE TOWN 1
CRESTWAY 2
THE PLAT 3
HYNETOWN RD
PO
PH
WHITESTONE CROSS
Dittiscombe
Loworthy
Strete
Asherne
Pittaford
Alston
ALSTON CROSS
Pilchard Cove
Blackland
Homelands
HIGHER GREEN CROSS
LOWER GREEN CROSS
Higher Coltscombe
Strete Gate
P
Poole
PROSPECT HILL
WOOD LA
Higher Ley
PH
Harleston
Start
Slapton
CARR LA
CHANTRY HILL
TOWN'S END CROSS
BROOK ST
Field Study Centre
South West Coast Path
TQ7
GREENBANKS 1
BRANDIS PK 2
GREEN BANKS CL 3
SANDS RD
Marsh La
Darnacombe
Mon
Resr
SHERFORD CROSS
Slapton Sands
The Castle
Slapton Ley
Coleridge House
Frittiscombe
France Wood
PORT LA
COLERIDGE LA
1 PORT LA
2 COTMORE CL
3 COTMORE WAY
4 THE COPSE
5 START AVE
6 PENDEEN PK
1 BUTT PK
2 BUTTSONS CL
3 GRENVILLE CL
4 STOKENHAM CROSS
5 MEADOW CT BARNS
Lower Ley
Chillington
GREEN PARK WAY
Sch
HOLBROOK TERR
KILN LA
PO
PH
GRAFTON DR
HOME CL
TANPITS CROSS
CAREHOUSE CROSS
PH
Stokenham
7 MEADOWSIDE
8 TANPITS MDW
9 SHORNEYWELL
10 ORCHARD WAY
11 FAIRFIELD WAY
12 LONGBROOK
DOCKEYS LA 1
HOLMLEIGH RD 2
FLORENCE COTTS 3
ALLER CROSS
Mattiscombe
Widewell
MATTISCOMBE CROSS
Torcross
79 A 80 B 81 C 82 D 83 E 84 F
8 49 7 48 6 47 5 46 4 45 3 44 2 43 1 42
149
146

145
233
234

145

Scale: 1¾ inches to 1 mile
0 ¼ ½ mile
0 250m 500m 750m 1 km
143
148
A
B
C
D
E
F
Davey Park Farm
A381
Woolston
Southdown
Holwell
Cholwells
Court Barton
Bagton
THURLESTONE ROCK
COURT BARTON HO
BURLEIGH LANE END
MANOR COURT BARNS
Hotel
WATERLEARS CROSS
PITCHINGSTONE CROSS
South Huish
Burleigh Farm
Alston Farm
Great Ledge
Beacon Point
1 WEST PK
2 CHICHESTER CT
3 ANCHOR COTTS
Galmpton
BURLEIGH LA
Woolman Point
GALMPTON CROSS
WEYMOUTH PK
GRAND VIEW RD
HOPE BY-PASS
GREAT LA 1
CHAPEL LA 2
HIGHER TOWN 3
HAY LA 4
LOWER TOWN 5
SHUTE HILL 6
Withymore Farm
EDDYSTONE RISE
BENS CL
SEA VIEW GDNS
Outer Hope
Burton
Yarde Medieval Farmhouse
Shippen
MOORSIDE
LUCKHAMS LA
TOWNSEND CROSS
Yeovil Rock
Hope Cove
CHANNEL VIEW DR
MALBOROUGH GN
SALCOMBE RD
Bolt Tail
Inner Hope
Hope Barton
Sch
7 SHUTE
8 WELL HILL
9 WELL HILL CL
10 PORTLEMORE GDNS
11 PORTLEMORE CL
Fort
WHITE CROSS
TQ7
Redrot Cove
Bolberry
BOLBERRY CROSS
THE QUILLETTS
SHUTE PK
CUMBER CL
COLLATON RD
Collaton
South West Coast Path
1 COASTGUARD COTTS
2 THE SQUARE
Malborough
MALBOROUGH PK
COLLATON CROSS
Whitechurch
Portlemore Barton
12 JUBILEE RD
13 SPARROW PK
PLYMPTON CROSS
Bolberry Down
Hotel
HIGHER COLLATON CROSS
Fernyhole Point
Combe
West Cliff
SOUTH DOWN FARM
Rew
Slippery Point
Hazel Tor
Cathole Cliff
Hotel
DOGWATCH
Lantern Rock
Soar
Soar Mill Cove
The Warren
Steeple Cove
Off Cove
8
41
7
40
6
39
5
38
4
37
3
36
2
35
1
34
66
67
68
69
70
71
148

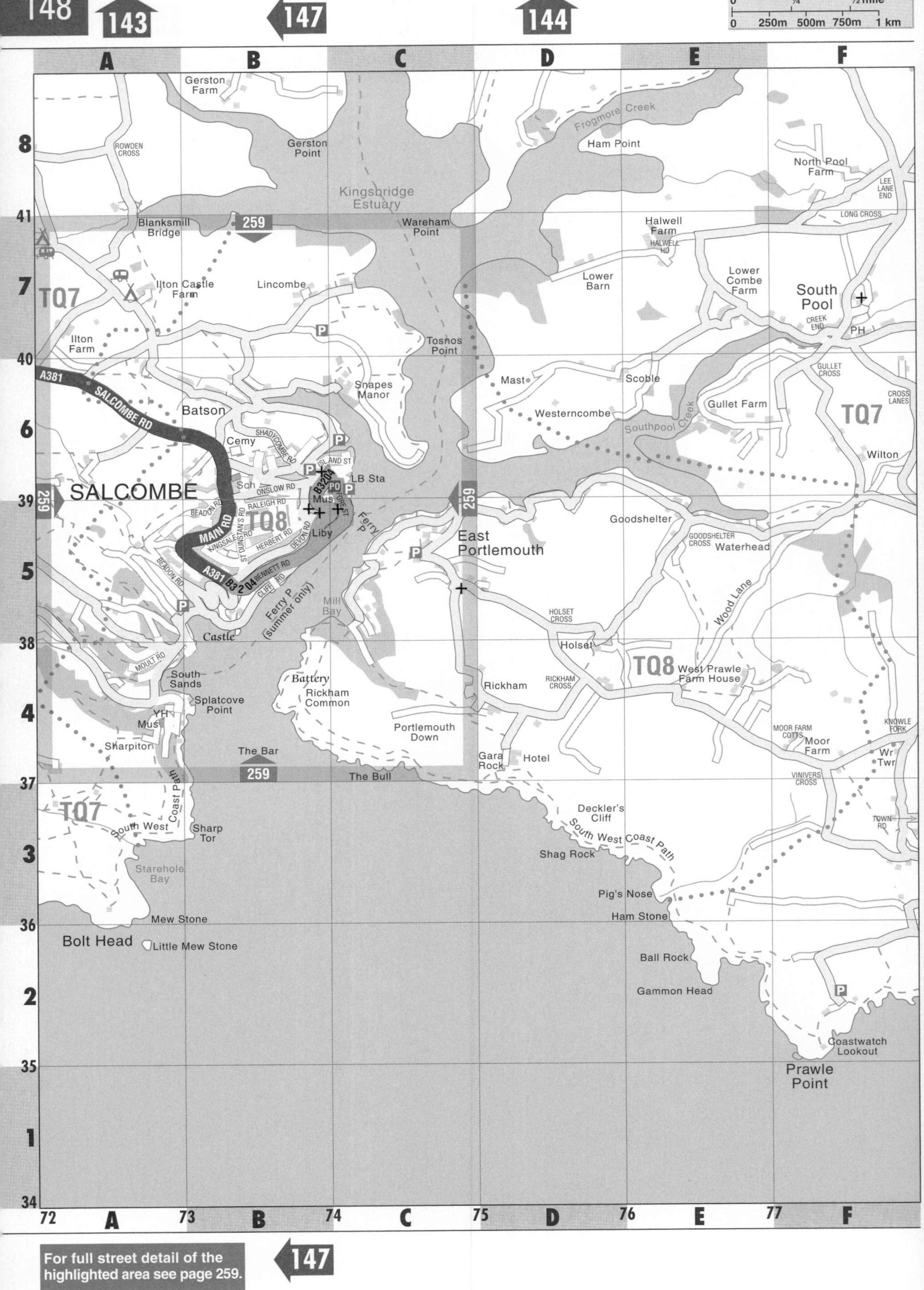

147

For full street detail of the highlighted area see page 259.

Scale: 1¾ inches to 1 mile
0 ¼ ½ mile
0 250m 500m 750m 1 km

145

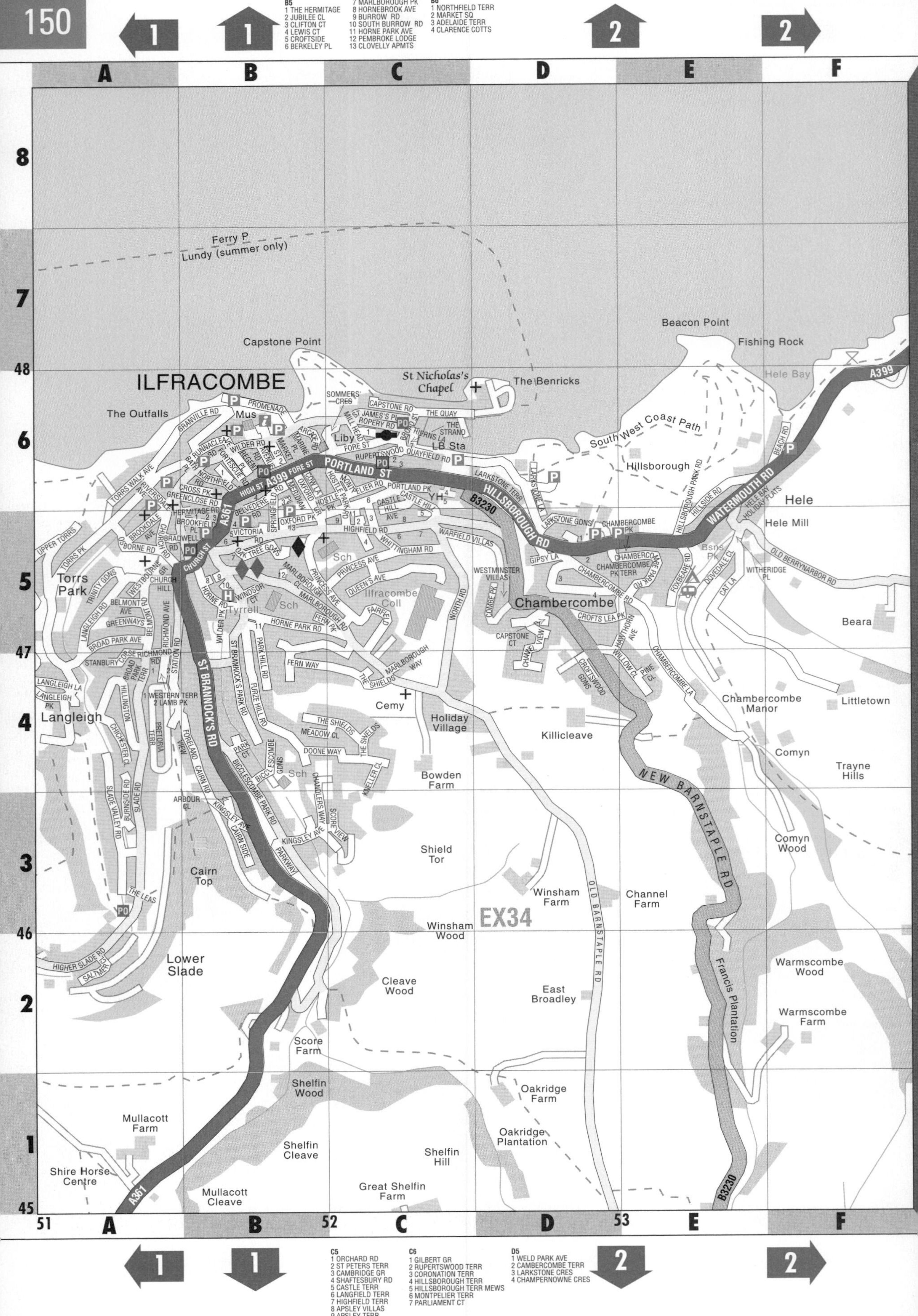
ILFRACOMBE
Ferry P
Lundy (summer only)
Capstone Point
St Nicholas's Chapel
The Benricks
Beacon Point
Fishing Rock
Hele Bay
The Outfalls
South West Coast Path
Hillsborough
Hele
Hele Mill
PORTLAND ST
HILLSBOROUGH RD
WATERMOUTH RD
Torrs Park
Chambercombe
Ilfracombe Coll
Tyrrell
Beara
Langleigh
Cemy
Holiday Village
Killicleave
Chambercombe Manor
Littletown
Comyn
Trayne Hills
Bowden Farm
NEW BARNSTAPLE RD
ST BRANNOCK'S RD
Shield Tor
Cairn Top
Comyn Wood
Winsham Farm
Channel Farm
EX34
Winsham Wood
Lower Slade
OLD BARNSTAPLE RD
Warmscombe Wood
Cleave Wood
East Broadley
Francis Plantation
Warmscombe Farm
Score Farm
Shelfin Wood
Oakridge Farm
Mullacott Farm
Oakridge Plantation
Shelfin Cleave
Shelfin Hill
Shire Horse Centre
Great Shelfin Farm
Mullacott Cleave
A361
A399
B3230

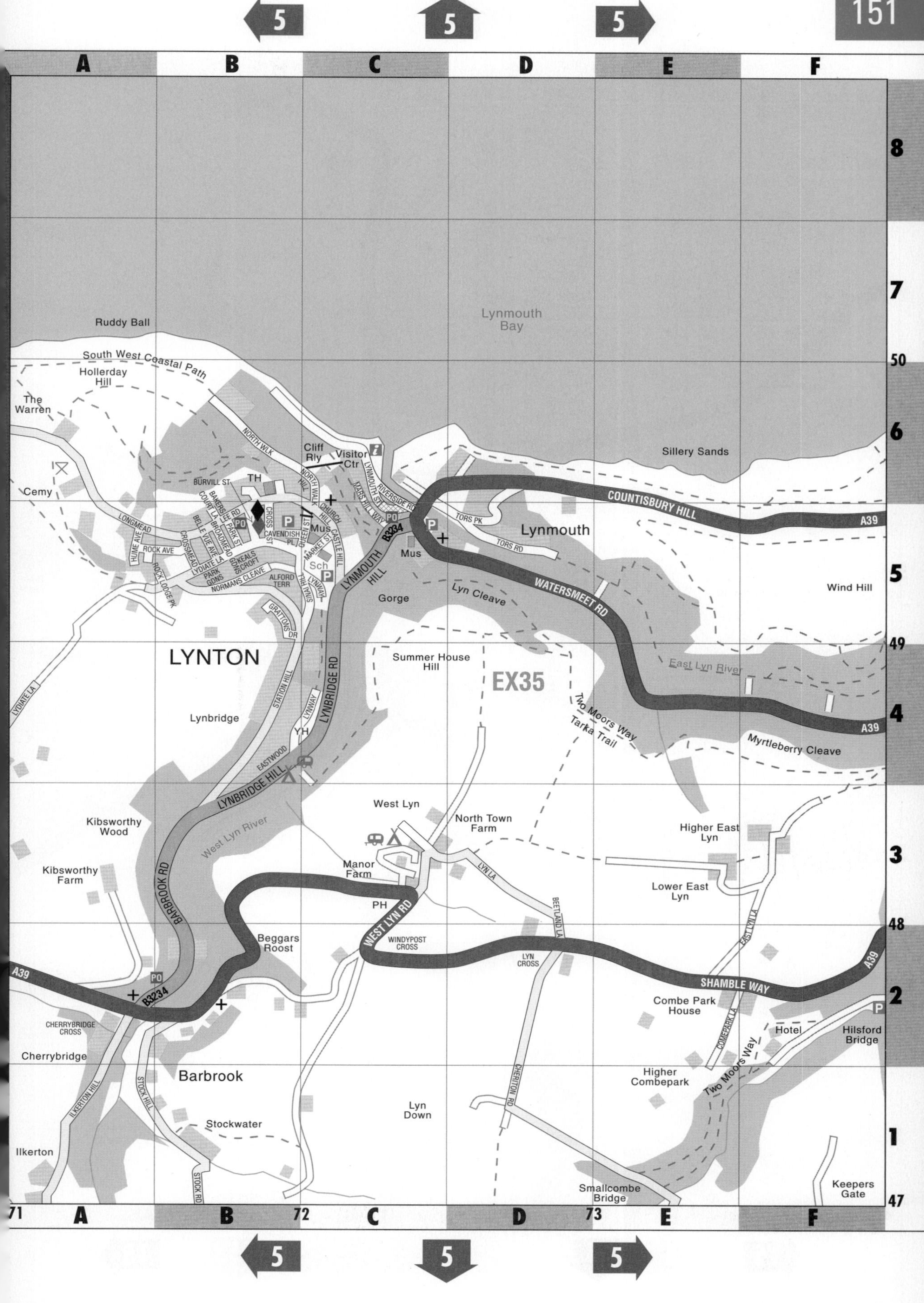
Lynmouth Bay
Ruddy Ball
South West Coastal Path
Hollerday Hill
The Warren
Cemy
Cliff Rly
Visitor Ctr
TH
Sillery Sands
COUNTISBURY HILL
A39
Lynmouth
TORS PK
TORS RD
Mus
Sch
Gorge
Lyn Cleave
WATERSMEET RD
Wind Hill
LYNMOUTH HILL
B3234
LYNTON
Summer House Hill
EX35
East Lyn River
Two Moors Way
Tarka Trail
Myrtleberry Cleave
Lynbridge
LYNBRIDGE RD
STATION HILL
LYNBRIDGE HILL
EASTWOOD
YH
West Lyn
North Town Farm
Higher East Lyn
Kibsworthy Wood
West Lyn River
Kibsworthy Farm
Manor Farm
LYN LA
Lower East Lyn
BARBROOK RD
PH
WEST LYN RD
BEETLAND LA
Beggars Roost
WINDYPOST CROSS
LYN CROSS
EAST LYN LA
SHAMBLE WAY
Combe Park House
COMBEPARK LA
Hotel
Hilsford Bridge
CHERRYBRIDGE CROSS
Cherrybridge
Barbrook
Higher Combepark
ILKERTON HILL
STOCK HILL
CHERITON RD
Lyn Down
Stockwater
Ilkerton
STOCK RD
Smallcombe Bridge
Keepers Gate
LYDIATE LA
LONGMEAD
HUME AVE
ROCK AVE
ROCK LODGE PK
CROSSMEAD
LYDIATE LA
PARK GDNS
NORMANS CLEAVE
ALFORD TERR
GRATTONS DR
SINAI HILL
LYNWAY
BURVILL ST
NORTH WLK
NORTH WALK HILL
CHURCH HILL
LYNMOUTH ST
MARS HILL WAY
RIVERSIDE RD
CROSS ST
CAVENDISH PL
QUEEN ST
MARKET ST
CASTLE HILL
PO
P
A B C D E F
8 7 50 6 5 49 4 3 48 2 1 47
71 72 73

5 5 5 5 5 5

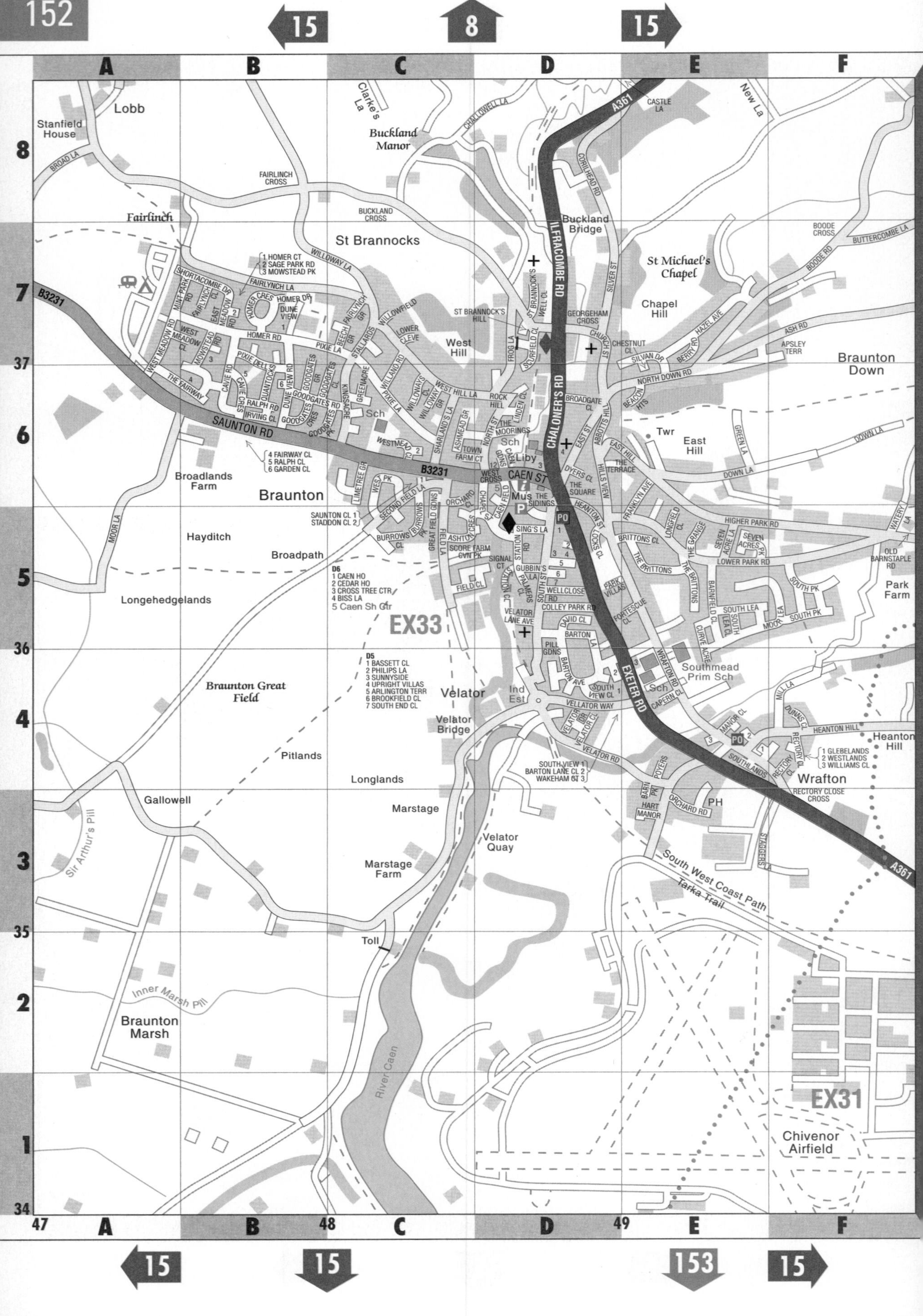
15
8
15
Lobb
Stanfield House
Buckland Manor
Fairlinch
FAIRLINCH CROSS
BUCKLAND CROSS
St Brannocks
Buckland Bridge
St Michael's Chapel
Chapel Hill
West Hill
Braunton Down
East Hill
Braunton
Broadlands Farm
Haydith
Broadpath
Longehedgelands
Park Farm
EX33
Braunton Great Field
Velator
Velator Bridge
Ind Est
Southmead Prim Sch
Heanton Hill
Wrafton
Pitlands
Longlands
Gallowell
Marstage
Velator Quay
Marstage Farm
South West Coast Path
Tarka Trail
Toll
Inner Marsh Pill
Sir Arthur's Pill
Braunton Marsh
River Caen
EX31
Chivenor Airfield
D6
1 CAEN HO
2 CEDAR HO
3 CROSS TREE CTR
4 BISS LA
5 Caen Sh Ctr
D5
1 BASSETT CL
2 PHILIPS LA
3 SUNNYSIDE
4 UPRIGHT VILLAS
5 ARLINGTON TERR
6 BROOKFIELD CL
7 SOUTH END CL
1 HOMER CT
2 SAGE PARK RD
3 MOWSTEAD PK
4 FAIRWAY CL
5 RALPH CL
6 GARDEN CL
SAUNTON CL 1
STADDON CL 2
SOUTH VIEW 1
BARTON LANE CL 2
WAKEHAM CT 3
1 GLEBELANDS
2 WESTLANDS
3 WILLIAMS CL
A361
B3231
SAUNTON RD
ILFRACOMBE RD
CHALONER'S RD
EXETER RD
CAEN ST
A B C D E F
47 48 49
34 35 36 37
1 2 3 4 5 6 7 8
15
15
153
15

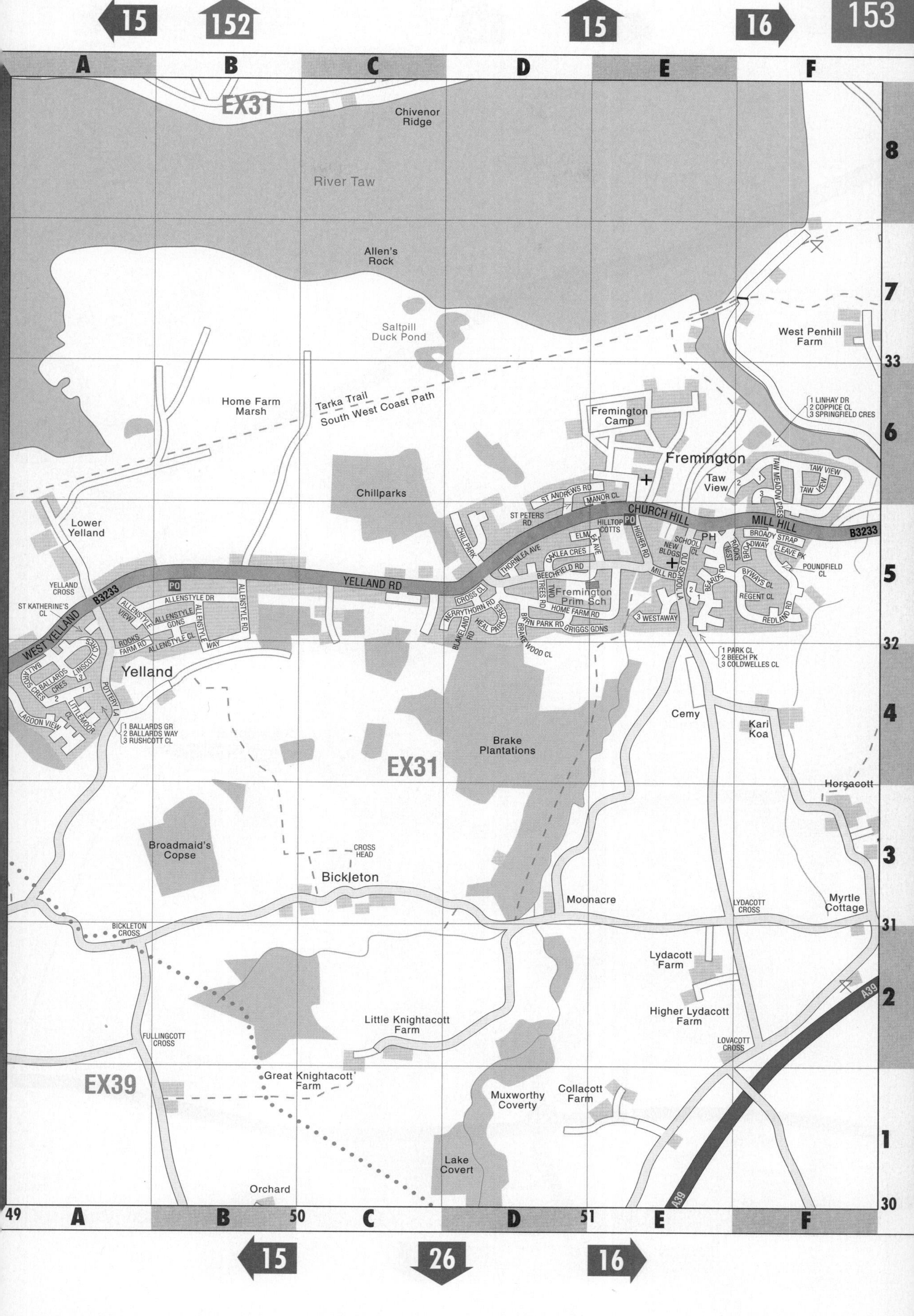

EX31
Chivenor Ridge
River Taw
Allen's Rock
Saltpill Duck Pond
Home Farm Marsh
Tarka Trail
South West Coast Path
Fremington Camp
Fremington
Taw View
Chillparks
Lower Yelland
YELLAND RD
B3233
CHURCH HILL
MILL HILL
Fremington Prim Sch
Yelland
Cemy
Kari Koa
Brake Plantations
Horsacott
Broadmaid's Copse
Bickleton
Moonacre
Myrtle Cottage
Lydacott Farm
Higher Lydacott Farm
Little Knightacott Farm
Great Knightacott Farm
EX39
Muxworthy Coverty
Collacott Farm
Lake Covert
Orchard
West Penhill Farm
1 LINHAY DR
2 COPPICE CL
3 SPRINGFIELD CRES
1 PARK CL
2 BEECH PK
3 COLDWELLES CL
1 BALLARDS GR
2 BALLARDS WAY
3 RUSHCOTT CL
A39

16 16

F5
1 GREEN LA
2 GAMMON WLK
3 LOVERINGS CT
4 HOLLAND WLK
5 MARKET ST
6 CASTLE QUAY CT
7 HOLLAND ST
8 PAIGES LA
9 PATERNOSTER ROW
10 CHURCH LA
11 HORWOOD SQ
12 QUEEN ANNE'S CT
13 THEATRE LA
14 MAIDEN ST
15 BEDFORD ROW
16 SOMERSET PL
17 DIAMOND ST
18 BELLE MEADOW CT

F6
1 ST MARGARETS GDN
2 LOWER ALMSHOUSES
3 REFORM ST
4 YEO VALE HO
5 HALDENE TERR
6 MAPLES CT
7 WARWICK TERR
8 KINGSLEY AVE
9 MARGROVE TERR (MERMAID WLK)
10 BOUTPORT ST
11 GEORGE ST
12 KING EDWARD ST
13 CHARLES ST
14 SEVENTH ST

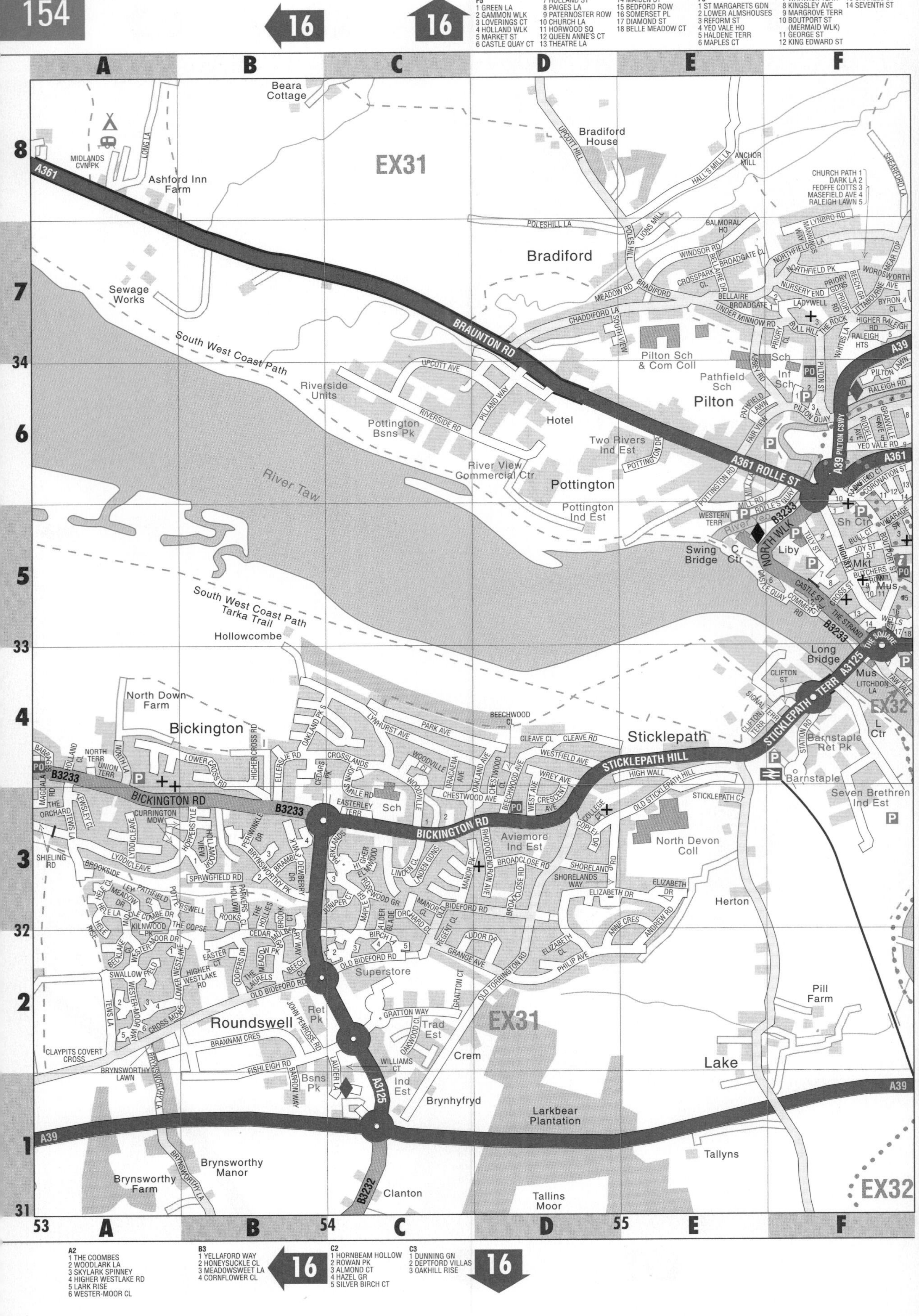

A2
1 THE COOMBES
2 WOODLARK LA
3 SKYLARK SPINNEY
4 HIGHER WESTLAKE RD
5 LARK RISE
6 WESTER-MOOR CL

B3
1 YELLAFORD WAY
2 HONEYSUCKLE CL
3 MEADOWSWEET LA
4 CORNFLOWER CL

C2
1 HORNBEAM HOLLOW
2 ROWAN PK
3 ALMOND CT
4 HAZEL GR
5 SILVER BIRCH CT

C3
1 DUNNING GN
2 DEPTFORD VILLAS
3 OAKHILL RISE

16 16

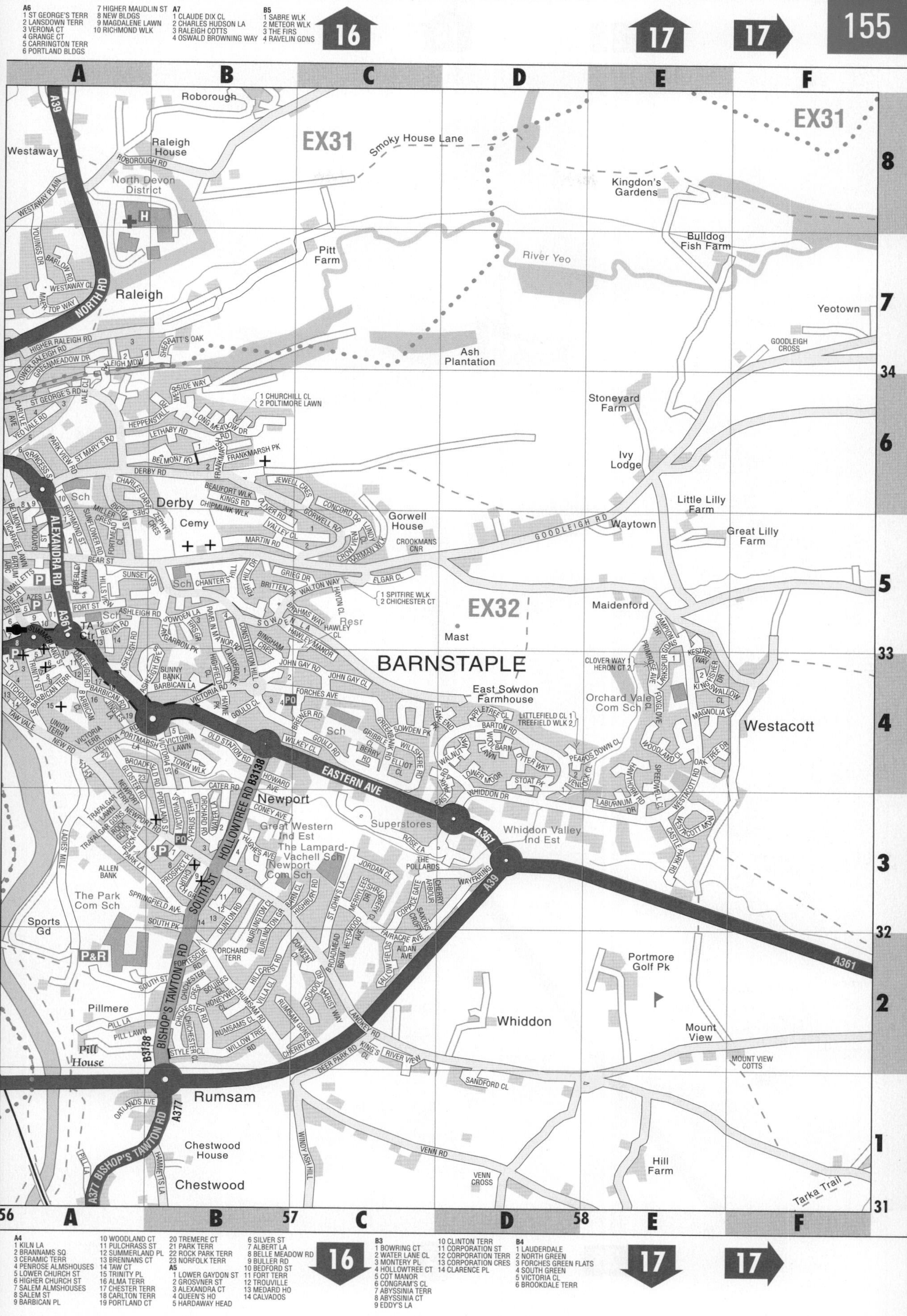
A6
1 ST GEORGE'S TERR
2 LANSDOWN TERR
3 VERONA CT
4 GRANGE CT
5 CARRINGTON TERR
6 PORTLAND BLDGS
7 HIGHER MAUDLIN ST
8 NEW BLDGS
9 MAGDALENE LAWN
10 RICHMOND WLK
A7
1 CLAUDE DIX CL
2 CHARLES HUDSON LA
3 RALEIGH COTTS
4 OSWALD BROWNING WAY
B5
1 SABRE WLK
2 METEOR WLK
3 THE FIRS
4 RAVELIN GDNS
16
17
17
A
B
C
D
E
F
8
7
34
6
5
33
4
3
32
2
1
31
Roborough
Westaway
Raleigh House
ROBOROUGH RD
EX31
Smoky House Lane
EX31
Kingdon's Gardens
North Devon District
WESTAWAY PLAIN
YOUINGS DR
BARLOW RD
WESTAWAY CL
TOP WAY
NORTH RD
A39
Pitt Farm
River Yeo
Bulldog Fish Farm
Raleigh
Yeotown
HIGHER RALEIGH RD
LOWER RALEIGH RD
GREENMEADOW DR
SHERRATT'S OAK
RALEIGH MDW
Ash Plantation
GOODLEIGH CROSS
ST GEORGE'S RD
CARLYLE AVE
YEO VALE RD
VALE CL
WESTSIDE WAY
1 CHURCHILL CL
2 POLTIMORE LAWN
HEPPENSTALL
LONG MEADOW DR
LETHABY RD
Stoneyard Farm
PARK VIEW RD
ST MARY'S RD
BELMONT RD
FRANKMARSH PK
FRANKMARSH RD
Ivy Lodge
PRINCESS ST
DERBY RD
JEWELL CRES
CHARLES DART CRES
BEAUFORT WLK
KINGS RD
CHIPMUNK WLK
OLIVER RD
CONCORD DR
GORWELL RD
Gorwell House
Little Lilly Farm
Sch
Derby
ALEXANDRA RD
MILLER CRES
SUNFLOWER RD
RICHMOND ST
BICTON ST
FORTMEAD CL
ZEPHYR CRES
Cemy
VALLEY CL
MARTIN RD
CROW VIEW
HARTMAN WLK
CROOKMANS CNR
GOODLEIGH RD
Waytown
Great Lilly Farm
BELMONT
VICARAGE LAWN
GAYDON ST
BARUM ARC
BEAR ST
SUNSET HTS
CHANTER'S HILL
FORT HILL DR
GRIEG DR
BRITTEN DR
WALTON WAY
ELGAR CL
1 SPITFIRE WLK
2 CHICHESTER CT
MALLETTS LA
AZES LA
QUEEN ST
FORT ST
ASHLEIGH RD
SOWDEN LA
HAYDN CL
BRAHMS WAY
HAWLEY CL
Resr
EX32
Maidenford
Mast
SUMMERLAND ST
TA Ctr
BEVAN RD
FIRS GR
RAVELIN MANOR RD
CONSTITUTION HILL
BINGHAM CRES
HAWLEY MANOR
GARRON PK
SUNNY BANK
BARBICAN LA
HIGHFIELD RD
LAUDERDALE
JOHN GAY RD
JOHN GAY CL
BARNSTAPLE
CAMPION DR
PRIMROSE AVE
LARKSPUR GDNS
KESTREL WAY
KINGFISHER DR
SWALLOW CL
CLOVER WAY 1
HERON CT 2
TRINITY ST
BARBICAN TERR
BARBICAN RD
OAKLEIGH RD
JINGLES
LITCHDON ST
TAW VALE
UNION TERR
NEW RD
VICTORIA TERR
VICTORIA RD
HAYNE PK
GOULD CL
FORCHES AVE
PO
East Sowdon Farmhouse
Orchard Vale Com Sch
FOXGLOVE
MAGNOLIA CL
Westacott
PORTMARSH LA
VICTORIA ST
VICTORIA LAWN
OLD STATION RD
BREWER RD
Sch
GREENBANK RD
SOWDEN PK
LANE END
APPLETREE CL
BARTON RD
LITTLEFIELD CL 1
TREEFIELD WLK 2
WOODLAND CL
OAK TREE DR
BROADFIELD RD
GLOSTER RD
TOWN WLK
WILKEY CL
GOULD RD
GRIBBLE CL
BERRY RD
ELLIOT CL
WILLSHERE RD
WALNUT WAY
WOODLAND BARN
OTTER WAY
PEARDS DOWN CL
VENLOCK CL
HAWTHORN RD
SPEEDWELL CL
WESTACOTT RD
EASTERN AVE
HOLLOWTREE RD
B3138
HOWARD AVE
CATER RD
NEWPORT RD
PORTLAND ST
ORCHARD RD
WATER LA
LOWER MOOR
STOAT PK
WHIDDON DR
LABURNUM DR
WESTACOTT MDW
CASTLE PARK RD
Newport
CONEY AVE
TRAFALGAR LAWN
ROCK AVE
CYPRUS TERR
Great Western Ind Est
Superstores
A361
Whiddon Valley Ind Est
ROSE LA
THE POLLARDS
The Lampard-Vachell Sch
HUGHES AVE
Newport Com Sch
PARK LA
ALLEN BANK
PROSPECT PL
CHURCH
SOUTH ST
JORDAN CL
ST JOHN'S LA
MERRYLEES DR
SHRUBBERY CL
COPPICE GATE
ARBOUR
CHERRY
WAYFARING
A39
The Park Com Sch
SPRINGFIELD AVE
CLINTON RD
BURLINGTON CL
BURLINGTON GR
BARN CL
HIGHBURY RD
HEYWOOD AVE
SAXONS CROFT
FAIRACRE AVE
AIDAN AVE
A361
Sports Gd
SOUTH PK
P&R
ORCHARD TERR
FORTESCUE RD
CONVENT CL
BROADMEAD
BGLW
FALLOW FIELDS
Portmore Golf Pk
SOUTH ST
CHICHESTER CRES
SQUIRES CL
HONEYWELL
RUMSAM RD
HILLCREST RD
VILLA CL
SCHOOL RD
MARIST WAY
OLD SCHOOL RD
Pillmere
BISHOP'S TAWTON RD
CHICHESTER RD
RUMSAMS CL
WILLOW TREE RD
RUMSAM GDNS
CHERRY GR
Whiddon
Mount View
PILL LA
PILL LAWN
LANDKEY RD
STYLE CL
CHICHESTER CL
KING'S
RIVER VIEW
DEER PARK RD
MOUNT VIEW COTTS
Pill House
B3138
SANDFORD CL
Rumsam
OATLANDS AVE
A377
A377 BISHOP'S TAWTON RD
PILL LA
HAMMETTS LA
Chestwood House
Chestwood
WINDY ASH HILL
VENN RD
VENN CROSS
Hill Farm
Tarka Trail
56
57
58
A
B
C
D
E
F
A4
1 KILN LA
2 BRANNAMS SQ
3 CERAMIC TERR
4 PENROSE ALMSHOUSES
5 LOWER CHURCH ST
6 HIGHER CHURCH ST
7 SALEM ALMSHOUSES
8 SALEM ST
9 BARBICAN PL
10 WOODLAND CT
11 PULCHRASS ST
12 SUMMERLAND PL
13 BRENNANS CT
14 TAW CT
15 TRINITY PL
16 ALMA TERR
17 CHESTER TERR
18 CARLTON TERR
19 PORTLAND CT
20 TREMERE CT
21 PARK TERR
22 ROCK PARK TERR
23 NORFOLK TERR
A5
1 LOWER GAYDON ST
2 GROSVNER ST
3 ALEXANDRA CT
4 QUEEN'S HO
5 HARDAWAY HEAD
6 SILVER ST
7 ALBERT LA
8 BELLE MEADOW RD
9 BULLER RD
10 BEDFORD ST
11 FORT TERR
12 TROUVILLE
13 MEDARD HO
14 CALVADOS
B3
1 BOWRING CT
2 WATER LANE CL
3 MONTERY PL
4 HOLLOWTREE CT
5 COT MANOR
6 CONGRAM'S CL
7 ABYSSINIA TERR
8 ABYSSINIA CT
9 EDDY'S LA
10 CLINTON TERR
11 CORPORATION ST
12 CORPORATION TERR
13 CORPORATION CRES
14 CLARENCE PL
B4
1 LAUDERDALE
2 NORTH GREEN
3 FORCHES GREEN FLATS
4 SOUTH GREEN
5 VICTORIA CL
6 BROOKDALE TERR
16
17
17

25
14

F7
1 COWPARK TERR
2 MORWENNA TERR
3 SPRINGFIELD TERR
4 CHAPEL HO
5 ADMIRALS CT
6 THE SQUARE
7 ST MARGARET'S CT
8 MONDEVILLE WAY
9 ST TERESA'S CT

A
B
3
C
D
44
E
F

25
25

F1
1 WATERLOO TERR
2 CLOVELLY GDNS S
3 WESTCROFT CT
4 TRAFALGAR PL

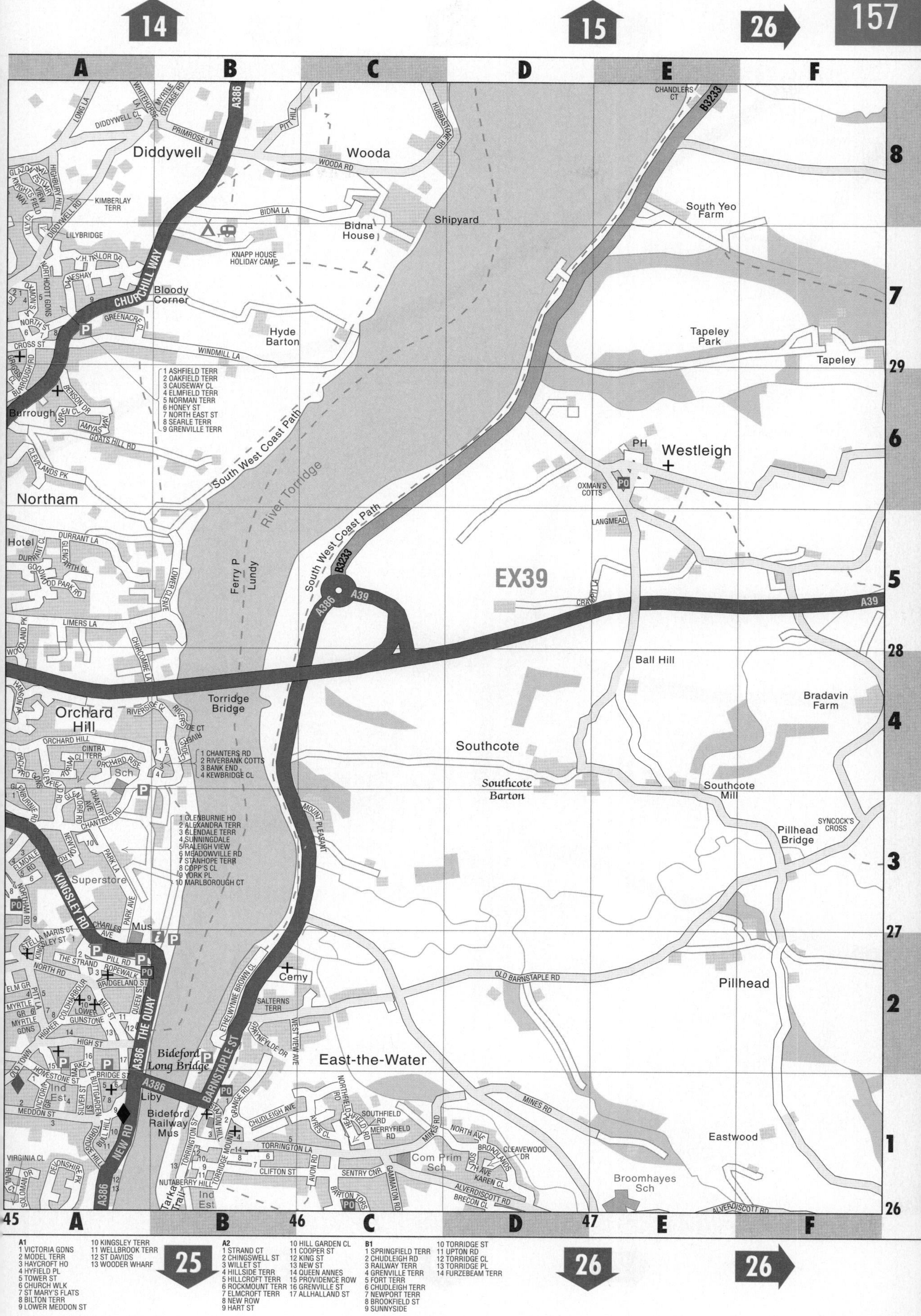
14
15
26
A
B
C
D
E
F
8
7
29
6
5
28
4
3
27
2
1
26
45
46
47
Diddywell
Wooda
Shipyard
Bidna House
KNAPP HOUSE HOLIDAY CAMP
Bloody Corner
Hyde Barton
South Yeo Farm
Tapeley Park
Tapeley
Westleigh
PH
OXMAN'S COTTS
LANGMEAD
Burrough
Northam
Hotel
EX39
Ferry P Lundy
River Torridge
South West Coast Path
Ball Hill
Bradavin Farm
Orchard Hill
Torridge Bridge
Southcote
Southcote Barton
Southcote Mill
SYNCOCK'S CROSS
Pillhead Bridge
Superstore
Mus
Cemy
Pillhead
East-the-Water
Bideford Long Bridge
Liby
Bideford Railway Mus
Com Prim Sch
Broomhayes Sch
Eastwood
Ind Est
Tarka Trail
A386
A39
B3233
CHURCHILL WAY
KINGSLEY RD
THE QUAY
NEW RD
BARNSTAPLE ST
WOODA RD
PRIMROSE LA
WINDMILL LA
GOATS HILL RD
CLEVELANDS PK
DURRANT LA
LIMERS LA
OLD BARNSTAPLE RD
MINES RD
TORRINGTON LA
CLIFTON ST
ALVERDISCOTT RD
1 ASHFIELD TERR
2 OAKFIELD TERR
3 CAUSEWAY CL
4 ELMFIELD TERR
5 NORMAN TERR
6 HONEY ST
7 NORTH EAST ST
8 SEARLE TERR
9 GRENVILLE TERR
1 CHANTERS RD
2 RIVERBANK COTTS
3 BANK END
4 KEWBRIDGE CL
1 GLENBURNIE HO
2 ALEXANDRA TERR
3 GLENDALE TERR
4 SUNNINGDALE
5 RALEIGH VIEW
6 MEADOWVILLE RD
7 STANHOPE TERR
8 COPP'S CL
9 YORK PL
10 MARLBOROUGH CT
A1
1 VICTORIA GDNS
2 MODEL TERR
3 HAYCROFT HO
4 HYFIELD PL
5 TOWER ST
6 CHURCH WLK
7 ST MARY'S FLATS
8 BILTON TERR
9 LOWER MEDDON ST
10 KINGSLEY TERR
11 WELLBROOK TERR
12 ST DAVIDS
13 WOODER WHARF
A2
1 STRAND CT
2 CHINGSWELL ST
3 WILLET ST
4 HILLSIDE TERR
5 HILLCROFT TERR
6 ROCKMOUNT TERR
7 ELMCROFT TERR
8 NEW ROW
9 HART ST
10 HILL GARDEN CL
11 COOPER ST
12 KING ST
13 NEW ST
14 QUEEN ANNES
15 PROVIDENCE ROW
16 GRENVILLE ST
17 ALLHALLAND ST
B1
1 SPRINGFIELD TERR
2 CHUDLEIGH RD
3 RAILWAY TERR
4 GRENVILLE TERR
5 FORT TERR
6 CHUDLEIGH TERR
7 NEWPORT TERR
8 BROOKFIELD ST
9 SUNNYSIDE
10 TORRIDGE ST
11 UPTON RD
12 TORRIDGE CL
13 TORRIDGE PL
14 FURZEBEAM TERR
25
26
26

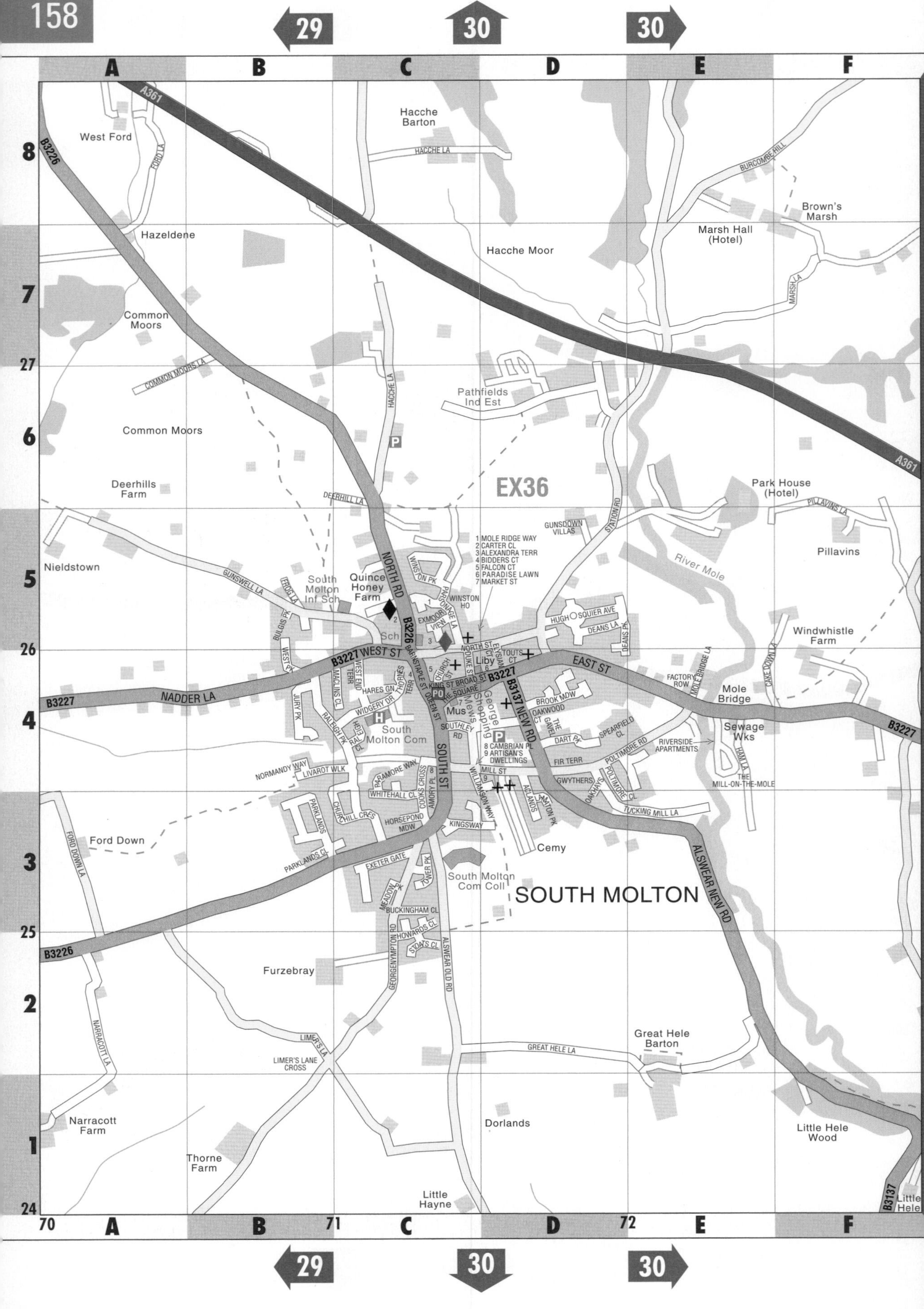
29
30
30
A
B
C
D
E
F
8
7
27
6
5
26
4
3
25
2
1
24
70
71
72
A361
B3226
West Ford
FORD LA
Hacche Barton
HACCHE LA
BURCOMBE HILL
Brown's Marsh
Marsh Hall (Hotel)
Hazeldene
Hacche Moor
MARSH LA
Common Moors
COMMON MOORS LA
Pathfields Ind Est
HACCHE LA
Common Moors
Deerhills Farm
DEERHILL LA
EX36
Park House (Hotel)
PILLAVINS LA
Pillavins
GUNSDOWN VILLAS
STATION RD
1 MOLE RIDGE WAY
2 CARTER CL
3 ALEXANDRA TERR
4 BIDDERS CT
5 FALCON CT
6 PARADISE LAWN
7 MARKET ST
River Mole
Nieldstown
GUNSWELL LA
South Molton Inf Sch
Quince Honey Farm
NORTH RD
WINSTON PK
PARSONAGE LA
WINSTON HO
EXMOOR VIEW
HUGH SQUIER AVE
DEANS LA
DEANS PK
Windwhistle Farm
BULGIS PK
Sch
B3226
NORTH ST
Liby
EAST ST
FACTORY ROW
MOLE BRIDGE LA
CAKE DOWN LA
B3227 WEST ST
BARNSTAPLE ST
KING ST
BROAD ST
B3227
Mole Bridge
WEST PK
MACLINS CL
WEST END TERR
HARES GN
THORNES TERR
CHURCH ST
DUKE ST
THE SQUARE
B3137 NEW RD
BROOK MDW
OAKWOOD CT
B3227
NADDER LA
JURY PK
RALEIGH PK
WIDGERY DR
QUEEN ST
Mus
George Mews Shopping
THE GAVEL
Sewage Wks
B3227
South Molton Com
SOUTHLEY RD
DART PK
SPEARFIELD CL
RIVERSIDE APARTMENTS
HAM LA
8 CAMBRIAN PL
9 ARTISAN'S DWELLINGS
FIR TERR
POLTIMORE RD
NORMANDY WAY
LIVAROT WLK
PARAMORE WAY
SOUTH ST
MILL ST
GWYTHERS
POLTIMORE CL
THE MILL-ON-THE-MOLE
WHITEHALL CL
COOKS CROSS
AMORY PL
WILLIAMSON WAY
ACLANDS
TUCKING MILL LA
PARKLANDS
CHURCHILL CRES
HORSEPOND MDW
KINGSWAY
ALSWEAR NEW RD
FORD DOWN LA
Ford Down
Cemy
PARKLANDS CL
EXETER GATE
TOWER PK
MEADOW
South Molton Com Coll
SOUTH MOLTON
BUCKINGHAM CL
GEORGENYMPTON RD
HOWARDS CL
B3226
STOATS CL
ALSWEAR OLD RD
Furzebray
NARRACOTT LA
LIMER'S LA
LIMER'S LANE CROSS
GREAT HELE LA
Great Hele Barton
Narracott Farm
Dorlands
Little Hele Wood
Thorne Farm
Little Hayne
B3137
Little Hele
70
A
B
71
C
D
72
E
F
29
30
30

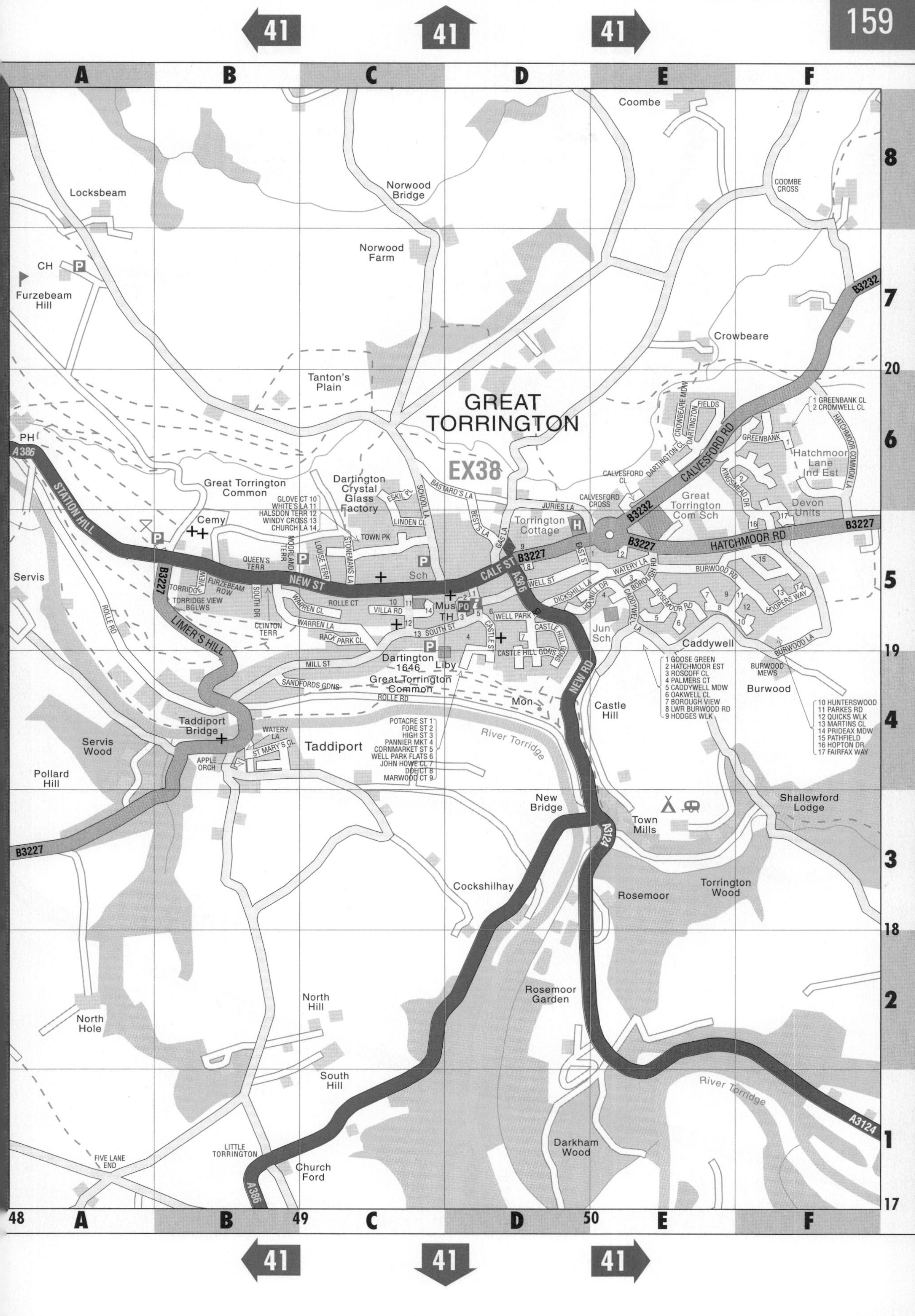
41
41
41
A
B
C
D
E
F
8
7
20
6
5
19
4
3
18
2
1
17
48
49
50
Coombe
Locksbeam
Norwood Bridge
Norwood Farm
COOMBE CROSS
CH
Furzebeam Hill
B3232
Crowbeare
Tanton's Plain
GREAT TORRINGTON
EX38
PH
A386
STATION HILL
Great Torrington Common
Dartington Crystal Glass Factory
GLOVE CT 10
WHITE'S LA 11
HALSDON TERR 12
WINDY CROSS 13
CHURCH LA 14
Cemy
Servis
TOWN PK
LINDEN CL
ESKIL PL
SCHOOL LA
BASTARD'S LA
BEST'S LA
GAS LA
JURIES LA
Torrington Cottage
CALVESFORD CL
CALVESFORD CROSS
CALVESFORD RD
DARTINGTON CL
CROWBEARE MDW
DARTINGTON FIELDS
1 GREENBANK CL
2 CROMWELL CL
GREENBANK
HATCHMOOR COMMON LA
Hatchmoor Lane Ind Est
Great Torrington Com Sch
KINGSMEAD DR
Devon Units
B3227
HATCHMOOR RD
QUEEN'S TERR
MOORLAND TERR
LOUISE TERR
STONEMANS LA
NEW ST
CALF ST
Sch
TORRIDGE VIEW
FURZEBEAM ROW
TORRIDGE VIEW BGLWS
SOUTH DR
ROLLE CT
VILLA RD
WARREN CL
WARREN LA
CLINTON TERR
RACK PARK CL
SOUTH ST
Mus
TH
PO
WELL ST
WELL PARK RD
CASTLE ST
CASTLE HILL GDNS
EAST ST
DICKSHILL LA
HOLWILL DR
WATERY LA
BOROUGH RD
ROSEMOOR RD
CADDYWELL LA
BURWOOD RD
HOOPERS WAY
BURWOOD LA
Jun Sch
Caddywell
ROLLE RD
LIMER'S HILL
B3227
MILL ST
Dartington 1646
Liby
SANDFORDS GDNS
Great Torrington Common
ROLLE RD
Mon
NEW RD
1 GOOSE GREEN
2 HATCHMOOR EST
3 ROSCOFF CL
4 PALMERS CT
5 CADDYWELL MDW
6 OAKWELL CL
7 BOROUGH VIEW
8 LWR BURWOOD RD
9 HODGES WLK
BURWOOD MEWS
Burwood
10 HUNTERSWOOD
11 PARKES RD
12 QUICKS WLK
13 MARTINS CL
14 PRIDEAX MDW
15 PATHFIELD
16 HOPTON DR
17 FAIRFAX WAY
Castle Hill
Taddiport Bridge
Servis Wood
WATERY LA
ST MARY'S CL
APPLE ORCH
Taddiport
POTACRE ST 1
FORE ST 2
HIGH ST 3
PANNIER MKT 4
CORNMARKET ST 5
WELL PARK FLATS 6
JOHN HOWE CL 7
DOE CT 8
MARWOOD CT 9
River Torridge
Pollard Hill
New Bridge
Town Mills
Shallowford Lodge
A3124
B3227
Cockshilhay
Rosemoor
Torrington Wood
Rosemoor Garden
North Hill
North Hole
South Hill
River Torridge
A3124
Darkham Wood
LITTLE TORRINGTON
FIVE LANE END
Church Ford
A386

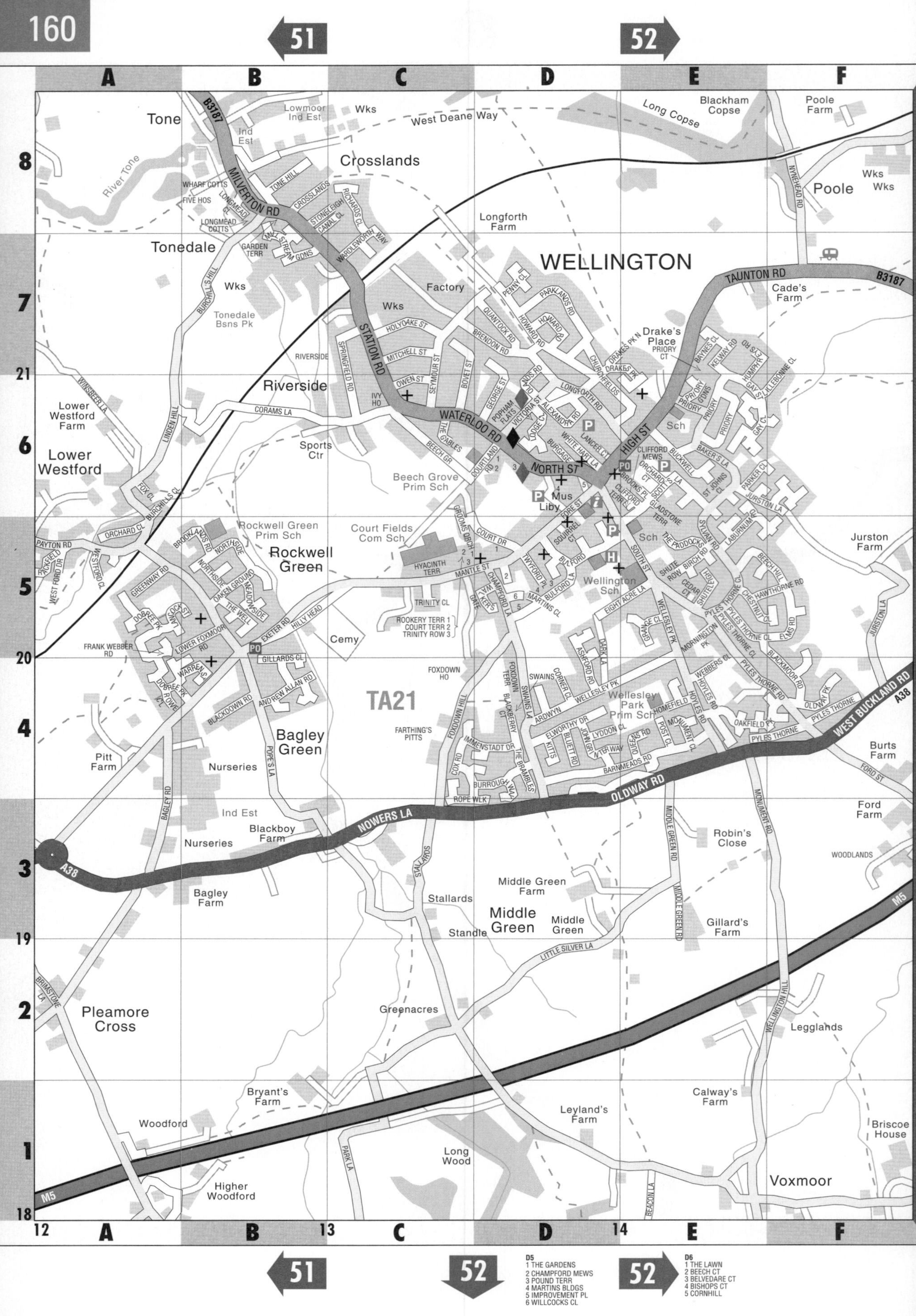
160
51
52
A
B
C
D
E
F
8
7
21
6
5
20
4
3
19
2
1
18
12
13
14
B3187
Tone
Lowmoor Ind Est
Wks
West Deane Way
Long Copse
Blackham Copse
Poole Farm
Ind Est
Crosslands
River Tone
WHARF COTTS
FIVE HOS
LONGMEAD COTTS
MILVERTON RD
TONE HILL
CROSSLANDS
STONELEIGH
CANAL CL
RICHARDS CL
Poole
Wks
Wks
NYNEHEAD RD
Longforth Farm
Tonedale
GARDEN TERR
MILL STREAM GDNS
WARDLEWORTH WAY
WELLINGTON
TAUNTON RD
B3187
Wks
BURCHILLS HILL
Tonedale Bsns Pk
Factory
Wks
Cade's Farm
PENNY CL
PARKLANDS RD
HOWARD RD
QUANTOCK RD
BRENDON RD
HOLYOAKE ST
MITCHELL ST
STATION RD
SPRINGFIELD RD
RIVERSIDE
SEYMOUR ST
BOVET ST
CHURCHFIELDS
DRAKES PK N
Drake's Place
PRIORY CT
DRAKES PK
BAYNES CL
KELWAY RD
WINSBEER LA
Lower Westford Farm
LINDEN HILL
Riverside
CORAMS LA
IVY HO
OWEN ST
GEORGE ST
POPHAM FLATS
VICTORIA ST
ALEXANDRA RD
LONGFORTH RD
WATERLOO RD
PRIORY
PRIORY GDNS
HUMPHREYS RD
GAY ST
Sch
Lower Westford
Sports Ctr
BEECH GR
THE GABLES
COURTLAND RD
NORTH ST
WHITE HART LA
LANCE CL
BURGAGE
HIGH ST
CLIFFORD MEWS
ORCHARD CT
BUCKWELL
BAKER'S LA
PARKER CL
ST JOHNS CL
FOX CL
BURCHILLS CL
Beech Grove Prim Sch
Mus
Liby
CLIFFORD TERR
BROOKS PL
SCOTT'S LA
JURSTON LA
PAYTON RD
ORCHARD CL
Rockwell Green Prim Sch
Court Fields Com Sch
GROOMS ORCH
COURT DR
FORE ST
SQUIRREL CT
GLADSTONE TERR
Sch
THE PADDOCKS
SYLVAN RD
LABURNUM RD
Jurston Farm
Rockwell Green
BROOKLANDS RD
NORTHSIDE
HYACINTH TERR
MANTLE ST
BULFORD
SOUTH ST
SHUTE ROW
BIRCH RD
BEECH HILL
ROCKFIELD
WESTFORD CL
WEST FORD DR
GREENWAY RD
OAKEN GROUND
MEADOWSIDE
THE WELL
CHAMPFORD LA
TWYFORD PL
BULFORD LA
Wellington Sch
CEDAR CT
HAWTHORNE RD
CHESTNUT CL
TRINITY CL
MARTINS CL
EIGHT ACRE LA
WELLESLEY PK
PYLES THORNE CL
ROOKERY TERR 1
COURT TERR 2
TRINITY ROW 3
FRANK WEBBER RD
LOWER FOXMOOR RD
EXETER RD
HILLY HEAD
Cemy
ASHFORD RD
DARK LA
GRANGE CL
MORNINGTON PK
JURSTON LA
PO
GILLARDS CL
FOXDOWN HO
WEBBERS CL
ELMS RD
BLACKMOOR RD
WARRENS
DOBREE PK
BLACKDOWN RD
ANDREW ALLAN RD
TA21
FOXDOWN TERR
SWAINS
CORNER CL
Wellesley Park Prim Sch
HOMEFIELD
HOYLES RD
OLDWAY PK
PYLES THORNE
WEST BUCKLAND RD
A38
FOXDOWN HILL
BLACKBERRY CT
SWAINS LA
ARDWYN
ELWORTHY DR
LYDDON CL
OAKFIELD PK
Bagley Green
FARTHING'S PITTS
IMMENSTADT DR
KITTS
BLUETT RD
JOHN GRAY
QUEENS RD
POST CL
MONUMENT CL
Burts Farm
Pitt Farm
Nurseries
POPE'S LA
COX RD
THE BRAMBLES
BARNMEADS RD
FORD ST
BURROUGH WAY
ROPE WLK
OLDWAY RD
Ford Farm
BAGLEY RD
Ind Est
NOWERS LA
MIDDLE GREEN RD
MONUMENT RD
Robin's Close
Blackboy Farm
Nurseries
WOODLANDS
A38
STALLARDS
Bagley Farm
Middle Green Farm
Stallards
Middle Green
Middle Green
Standle
Gillard's Farm
M5
LITTLE SILVER LA
BRIMSTONE LA
Pleamore Cross
Greenacres
WELLINGTON HILL
Leggllands
Bryant's Farm
Calway's Farm
Leyland's Farm
Woodford
Briscoe House
PARK LA
Long Wood
Voxmoor
Higher Woodford
BEACON LA
M5
51
52
52
D5
1 THE GARDENS
2 CHAMPFORD MEWS
3 POUND TERR
4 MARTINS BLDGS
5 IMPROVEMENT PL
6 WILLCOCKS CL
D6
1 THE LAWN
2 BEECH CT
3 BELVEDARE CT
4 BISHOPS CT
5 CORNHILL

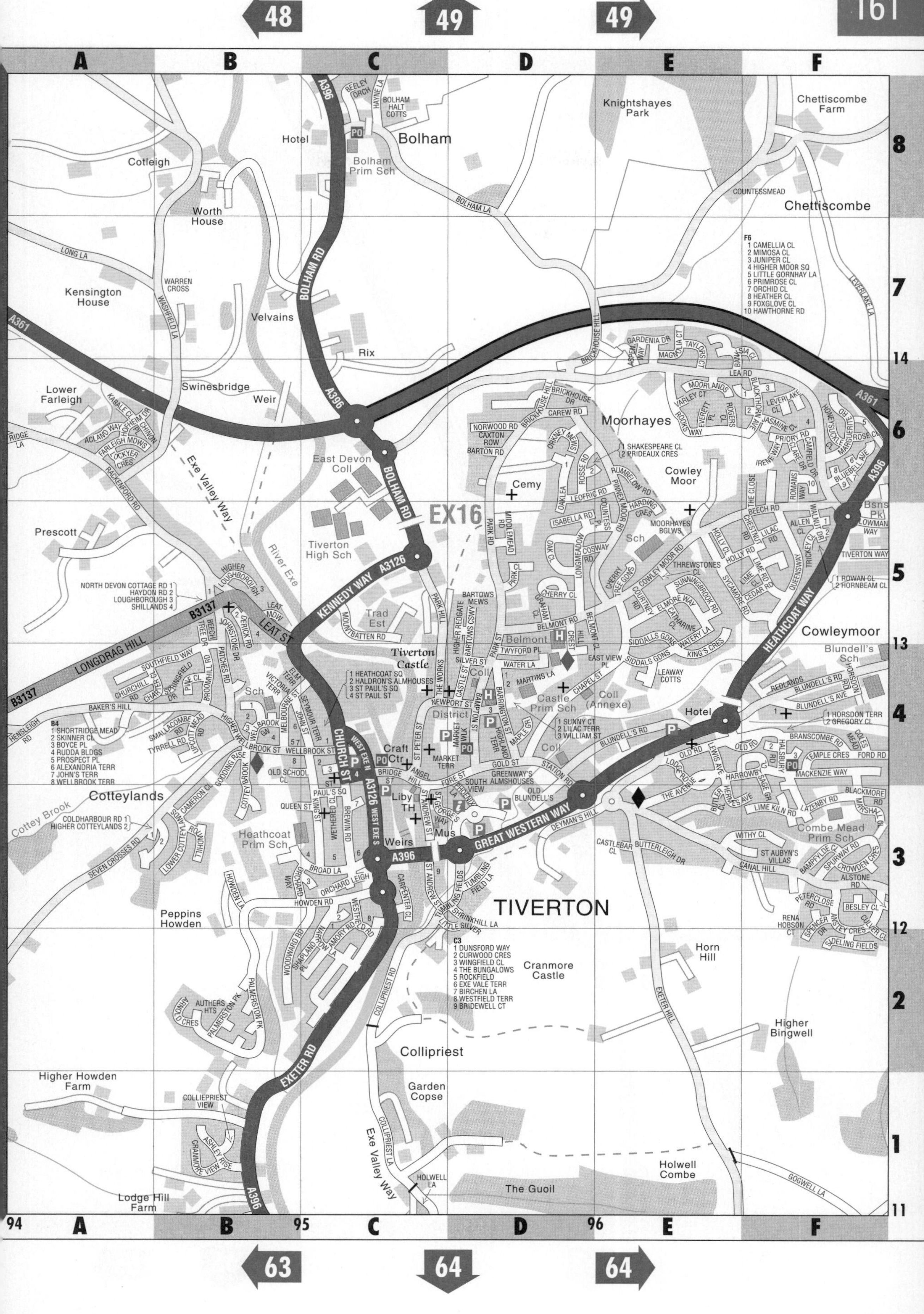
48
49
49
Bolham
Bolham Prim Sch
Hotel
Cotleigh
Worth House
Knightshayes Park
Chettiscombe Farm
Chettiscombe
Kensington House
Velvains
Rix
Lower Farleigh
Swinesbridge
Weir
Moorhayes
Cowley Moor
East Devon Coll
Tiverton High Sch
EX16
Prescott
Trad Est
Tiverton Castle
Cowleymoor
Blundell's Sch
Cotteylands
Heathcoat Prim Sch
Castle Prim Sch
Coll (Annexe)
Combe Mead Prim Sch
Peppins Howden
TIVERTON
Horn Hill
Cranmore Castle
Collipriest
Higher Bingwell
Higher Howden Farm
Garden Copse
Holwell Combe
The Guoil
Lodge Hill Farm
Exe Valley Way
River Exe
F6
1 CAMELLIA CL
2 MIMOSA CL
3 JUNIPER CL
4 HIGHER MOOR SQ
5 LITTLE GORNHAY LA
6 PRIMROSE CL
7 ORCHID CL
8 HEATHER CL
9 FOXGLOVE CL
10 HAWTHORNE RD
NORTH DEVON COTTAGE RD 1
HAYDON RD 2
LOUGHBOROUGH 3
SHILLANDS 4
1 HEATHCOAT SQ
2 HALDRON'S ALMHOUSES
3 ST PAUL'S SQ
4 ST PAUL ST
B4
1 SHORTRIDGE MEAD
2 SKINNER CL
3 BOYCE PL
4 RUDDA BLDGS
5 PROSPECT PL
6 ALEXANDRIA TERR
7 JOHN'S TERR
8 WELLBROOK TERR
COLDHARBOUR RD 1
HIGHER COTTEYLANDS 2
1 SHAKESPEARE CL
2 PRIDEAUX CRES
1 SUNNY CT
2 LILAC TERR
3 WILLIAM ST
1 ROWAN CL
2 HORNBEAM CL
1 HORSDON TERR
2 GREGORY CL
C3
1 DUNSFORD WAY
2 CURWOOD CRES
3 WINGFIELD CL
4 THE BUNGALOWS
5 ROCKFIELD
6 EXE VALE TERR
7 BIRCHEN LA
8 WESTFIELD TERR
9 BRIDEWELL CT
A361
A396
A3126
B3137
BOLHAM RD
KENNEDY WAY
LEAT ST
LONGDRAG HILL
CHURCH ST
WEST EXE S
GREAT WESTERN WAY
HEATHCOAT WAY
EXETER RD
EXETER HILL
BOLHAM LA
LONG LA
WASHFIELD LA
COUNTESSMEAD
LEVERLAKE LA
BRICKHOUSE HILL
PARK HILL
PARK RD
BLUNDELL'S RD
STATION RD
GOLD ST
FORE ST
BAMPTON ST
NEWPORT ST
COLLIPRIEST RD
COLLIPRIEST LA
HOLWELL LA
GOGWELL LA
BUTTERLEIGH DR
CANAL HILL
HOWDEN RD
BROAD LA
WELLBROOK ST
A B C D E F
8 7 6 5 4 3 2 1
14 13 12 11
94 95 96
63
64
64

65
65
65
A
B
C
D
E
F
8
7
12
6
5
11
4
3
10
2
1
09
02
03
04
Catfords Farm
EX16
Swanhams Farm
Yeo Farm
Netherexe
Cott Farm
BROWN'S BRIDGE LA
Muddifords Farm
Slough Farm
WILLAND RD
Fisher's Bridge Farm
Woodcoxhayes Farm
Mountstephen House
B3181
Little Mountstephen
Pitt Farm
Hitchcock's Farm
Braddons Farm
B3440
PH
Culm Vale House
UFFCULME RD
Beggars Bush Cottage
Ind Est
FOUR CROSS WAYS
FOXGLOVE CHASE
Blackdown Pk
SOUTH VIEW EST
STATION RD
GRANVILLE PL
PARK ST
SOUTH VIEW RD
SOUTH VIEW CL
Quick's Farm
Willand Moor
Works
Abattoir
LLOYD MAUNDER RD
BARNES CL
SOMERVILLE RD
SOMERVILLE CL
SOMERVILLE PK
SOMERLEA
FIR CL
SILVER ST
CELANDINE LAWNS
MALLOW CT
WILLAND MOOR MEWS
PEARMAIN CL
BLENHEIM DR
BLENHEIM CL
HAREBELL DR
CORNFLOWER CL
ELDERBERRY WAY
WILLAND MOOR RD
Sch
Burn Rew Farm
Bagster Farm
Spratford Stream
GABLES LEA
GABLES RD
TAMAR'S DR
MAPLE CL
TAMARIND
OAK CRES
CHESTNUT DR
MEADOW PK
BEECH CL
LIME CRES
SYCAMORE CL
VICTORIA CL
PLUM WAY
MULBERRY CL
DAMSON CL
ORCHARD WAY
PEAR DR
APPLE DR
CHERRY CL
BRAMLEY CL
WEBBERS WAY
RECTORY CL
WORCESTER CRES
JAYCROFT
Willand
Weir Mill Farm
Works
Deanhill Farm
DEAN HILL RD
Cemy
PO
ROWES ORCHARD
LANDS
WILLAND OLD VILLAGE
PITFIELD CL
ELMSIDE
HARPITT CL
EX15
River Culm
Woody Park
Gerston Farm
West Lodge
Factory Cottages
163
Skinner's Farm
Kingsley House
Diggerland
163
Five Bridges Farm
STAG CNR
Heron's Bank
Hayne Barton
LONG MOOR
LONG DRAG
Lower Kingsford
M5
B3181
163
163
65
65

65
65
162
162
Moorstone Barton
Kingsley House
Diggerland
Five Bridges Farm
Sutton Barton
Heron's Bank
Spratford Stream
Rull Leat
Hayne Barton
River Culm
Rull Farm
Little Rull
Venn Farm
Ward Cottage
Paulsland Farm
Hembury View
St George's Well
EX15
Mill
River Ken
Kingsmill Ind Est
Service Area
Alexandria Ind Est
Week Farm
Long Bridge
Devon Bsns Pk
Simmonds Pl
Trumps Barn
St Andrew's Hill
Stoneyford
Longbridge Meadow Trad Est
Western Way Ind Est
Cemy
Cullompton
Nursery
HONITON RD
A373
B3181
M5
Bathills
East Culm House
Aller Barton
Sports Ctr
First Bridge
Last Bridge
Upton Farms
CH
Works
Woodmill
Padbrook Hill
Cole Brook
COBURG PL 1
WINDSOR CL 2
DANES MEAD 3
STUART CRES 4
PLANTAGENET DR 5
HANOVER GDNS 6
LANCASTER CL 7
NORMAN DR 8
YORK PL 9
TUDOR GR 10
SPLATFORD DR 11
BEECH CROFT 12
ASH DR 13
1 PEN-Y-DRE
2 GARDEN TERR
3 BELLE VUE TERR
1 MATTHEW'S CT
2 LEYTON CT
3 CHURCH ST
4 QUEEN SQ
5 COCKPIT HILL
6 LWR BULL RING
7 REEDS PL
8 GLOBE CT
9 NEW INN CT
10 DOLPHIN CT
11 FLOOD'S LA
12 APPLEDORE CL
13 WAY'S LA
14 POUND SQ
15 JUBILEE GDNS
HAYMANS GN 1
WOOLCOTT WAY 2
STILE CT 3
ROBIN CL 4
KINGFISHER GDNS 5
TANNERS CL 6
WEAVERS WLK 7
HAWTHORN CL 8
WHEATFIELD CL 9
65
83
65

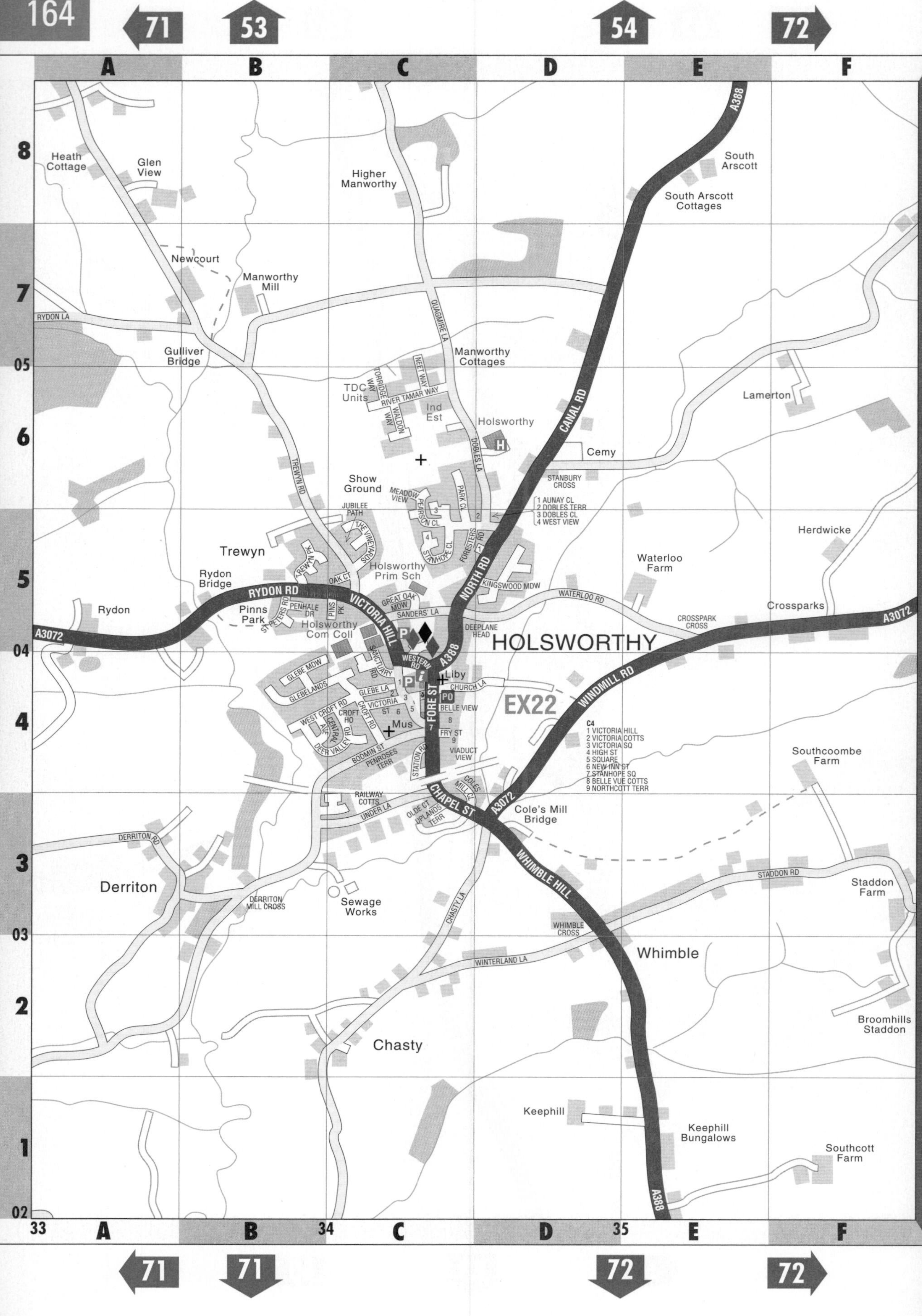
71
53
54
72
Heath Cottage
Glen View
Higher Manworthy
South Arscott
South Arscott Cottages
Newcourt
Manworthy Mill
RYDON LA
QUAGMIRE LA
Gulliver Bridge
Manworthy Cottages
CANAL RD
TDC Units
TORRIDGE WAY
NEET WAY
RIVER TAMAR WAY
WALDON WAY
Ind Est
Holsworthy
Lamerton
DOBLES LA
Cemy
TREWYN RD
Show Ground
STANBURY CROSS
MEADOW VIEW
PEARSON CL
PARK CL
1 AUNAY CL
2 DOBLES TERR
3 DOBLES CL
4 WEST VIEW
JUBILEE PATH
THE VINEYARDS
FORESTERS RD
Herdwicke
Trewyn
STANHOPE CL
Waterloo Farm
Holsworthy Prim Sch
Rydon Bridge
OAK CT
NORTH RD
KINGSWOOD MDW
RYDON RD
VICTORIA HILL
GREAT OAK MDW
WATERLOO RD
Rydon
Pinns Park
PENHALE DR
PINS PK
SANDERS' LA
Crossparks
CROSSPARK CROSS
A3072
ST PETERS RD
Holsworthy Com Coll
DEEPLANE HEAD
HOLSWORTHY
SANCTUARY RD
WESTERN RD
A388
GLEBE MDW
Liby
WINDMILL RD
GLEBELANDS
GLEBE LA
CHURCH LA
PO
VICTORIA ST
FORE ST
BELLE VIEW
EX22
WEST CROFT RD
CROFT HO
CROFT RD
CENTRAL AVE
Mus
FRY ST
C4
1 VICTORIA HILL
2 VICTORIA COTTS
3 VICTORIA SQ
4 HIGH ST
5 SQUARE
6 NEW INN ST
7 STANHOPE SQ
8 BELLE VUE COTTS
9 NORTHCOTT TERR
Southcoombe Farm
DEER VALLEY RD
BODMIN ST
PENROSES TERR
STATION RD
VIADUCT VIEW
COLES MILL CL
RAILWAY COTTS
CHAPEL ST
Cole's Mill Bridge
UNDER LA
OLDE CT
UPLANDS TERR
DERRITON RD
WHIMBLE HILL
STADDON RD
Staddon Farm
Derriton
DERRITON MILL CROSS
Sewage Works
CHASTY LA
WHIMBLE CROSS
Whimble
WINTERLAND LA
Broomhills Staddon
Chasty
Keephill
Keephill Bungalows
Southcott Farm
A B C D E F
8 7 05 6 5 04 4 3 03 2 1 02
33 34 35
71
71
72
72

79 80 80

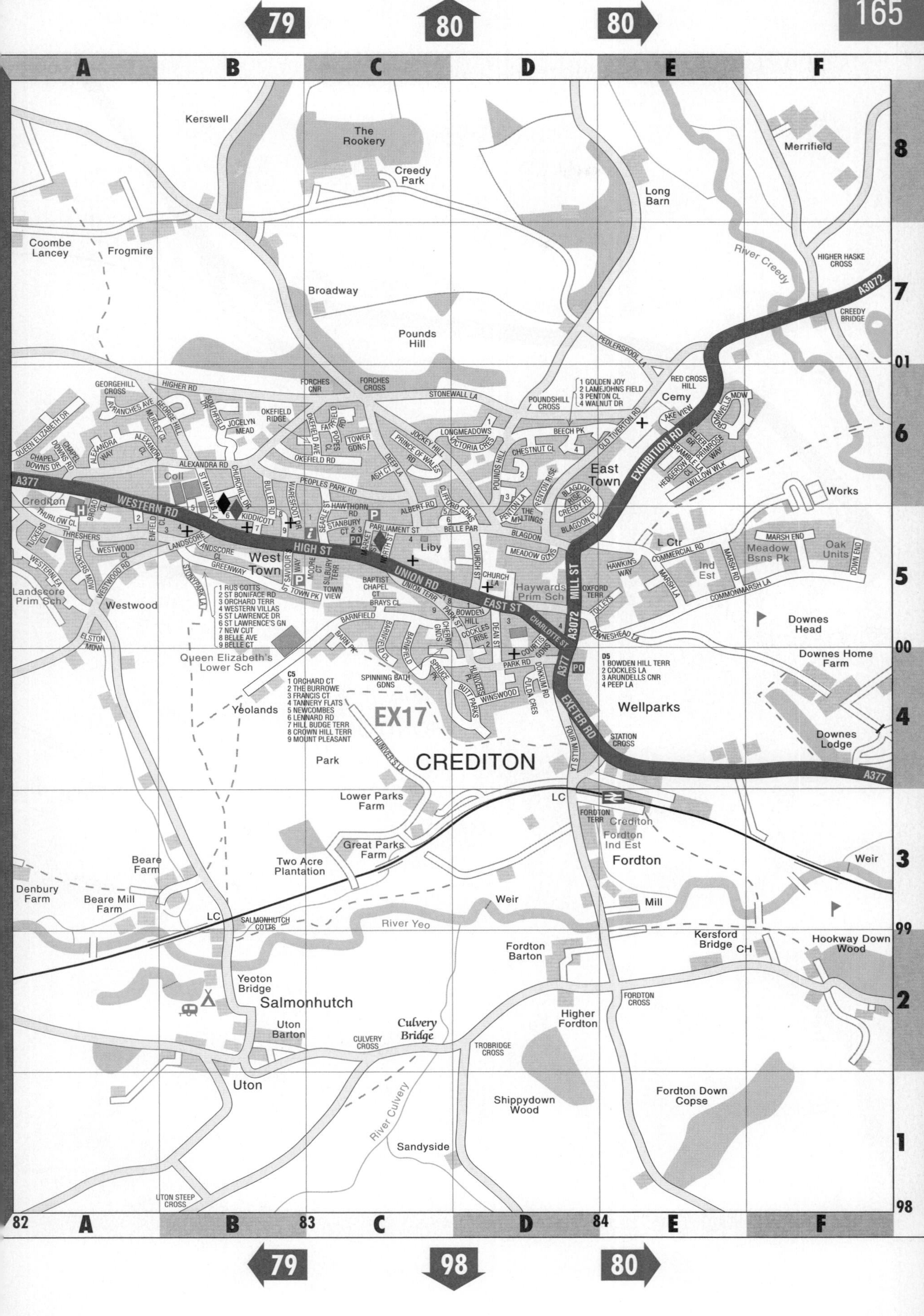

79 98 80

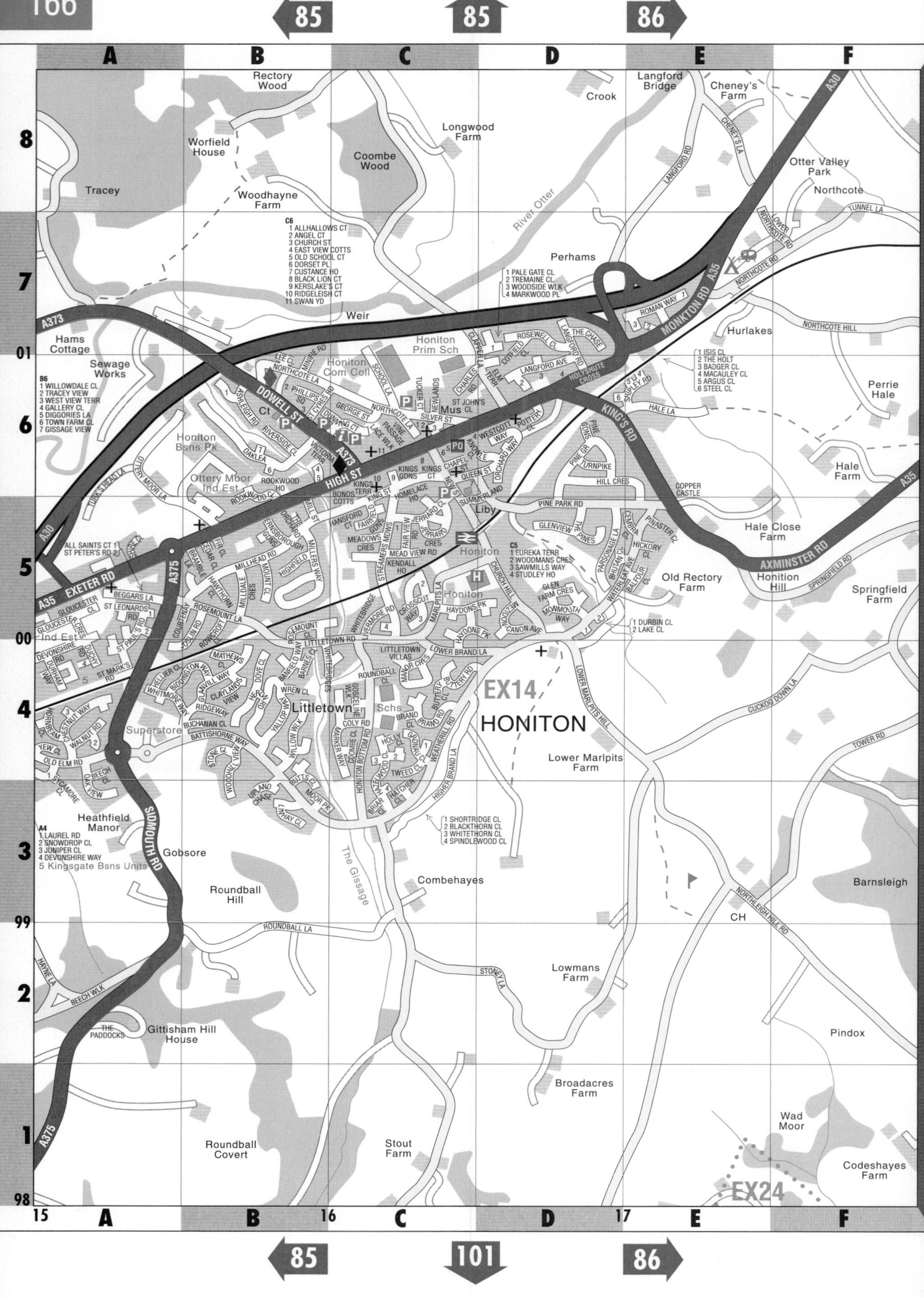
Rectory Wood
Worfield House
Tracey
Woodhayne Farm
Coombe Wood
Longwood Farm
Crook
Langford Bridge
Cheney's Farm
Otter Valley Park
Northcote
River Otter
Perhams
Weir
Hams Cottage
Sewage Works
Honiton Prim Sch
Honiton Com Coll
Hurlakes
Perrie Hale
Honiton Bsns Pk
Ottery Moor Ind Est
Hale Farm
Copper Castle
Hale Close Farm
Liby
Honiton
Old Rectory Farm
Honition Hill
Springfield Farm
Ind Est
Littletown
Schs
EX14
HONITON
Superstore
Lower Marlpits Farm
Heathfield Manor
Gobsore
Roundball Hill
Combehayes
Barnsleigh
CH
Lowmans Farm
Gittisham Hill House
Pindox
Broadacres Farm
Wad Moor
Roundball Covert
Stout Farm
Codeshayes Farm
EX24
C6
1 ALLHALLOWS CT
2 ANGEL CT
3 CHURCH ST
4 EAST VIEW COTTS
5 OLD SCHOOL CT
6 DORSET PL
7 CUSTANCE HO
8 BLACK LION CT
9 KERSLAKE'S CT
10 RIDGELEISH CT
11 SWAN YD
1 PALE GATE CL
2 TREMAINE CL
3 WOODSIDE WLK
4 MARKWOOD PL
1 ISIS CL
2 THE HOLT
3 BADGER CL
4 MACAULEY CL
5 ARGUS CL
6 STEEL CL
B6
1 WILLOWDALE CL
2 TRACEY VIEW
3 WEST VIEW TERR
4 GALLERY CL
5 DIGGORIES LA
6 TOWN FARM CL
7 GISSAGE VIEW
ALL SAINTS CT 1
ST PETER'S RD 2
C5
1 EUREKA TERR
2 WOODMANS CRES
3 SAWMILLS WAY
4 STUDLEY HO
1 DURBIN CL
2 LAKE CL
1 SHORTRIDGE CL
2 BLACKTHORN CL
3 WHITETHORN CL
4 SPINDLEWOOD CL
A4
1 LAUREL RD
2 SNOWDROP CL
3 JUNIPER CL
4 DEVONSHIRE WAY
5 Kingsgate Bsns Units
A30
A35
A373
A375
EXETER RD
HIGH ST
DOWELL ST
KING'S RD
AXMINSTER RD
MONKTON RD
SIDMOUTH RD
NORTHCOTE LA
NORTHCOTE RD
NORTHCOTE HILL
TUNNEL LA
LANGFORD RD
CHENEY'S LA
ROUNDBALL LA
STONEY LA
LOWER MARLPITS HILL
CUCKOO DOWN LA
TOWER RD
NORTHLEIGH HILL RD
HIGHER BRAND LA
LOWER BRAND LA
LITTLETOWN RD
PINE PARK RD
SPRINGFIELD RD
HAYNE LA
BEECH WLK
THE PADDOCKS
The Gissage

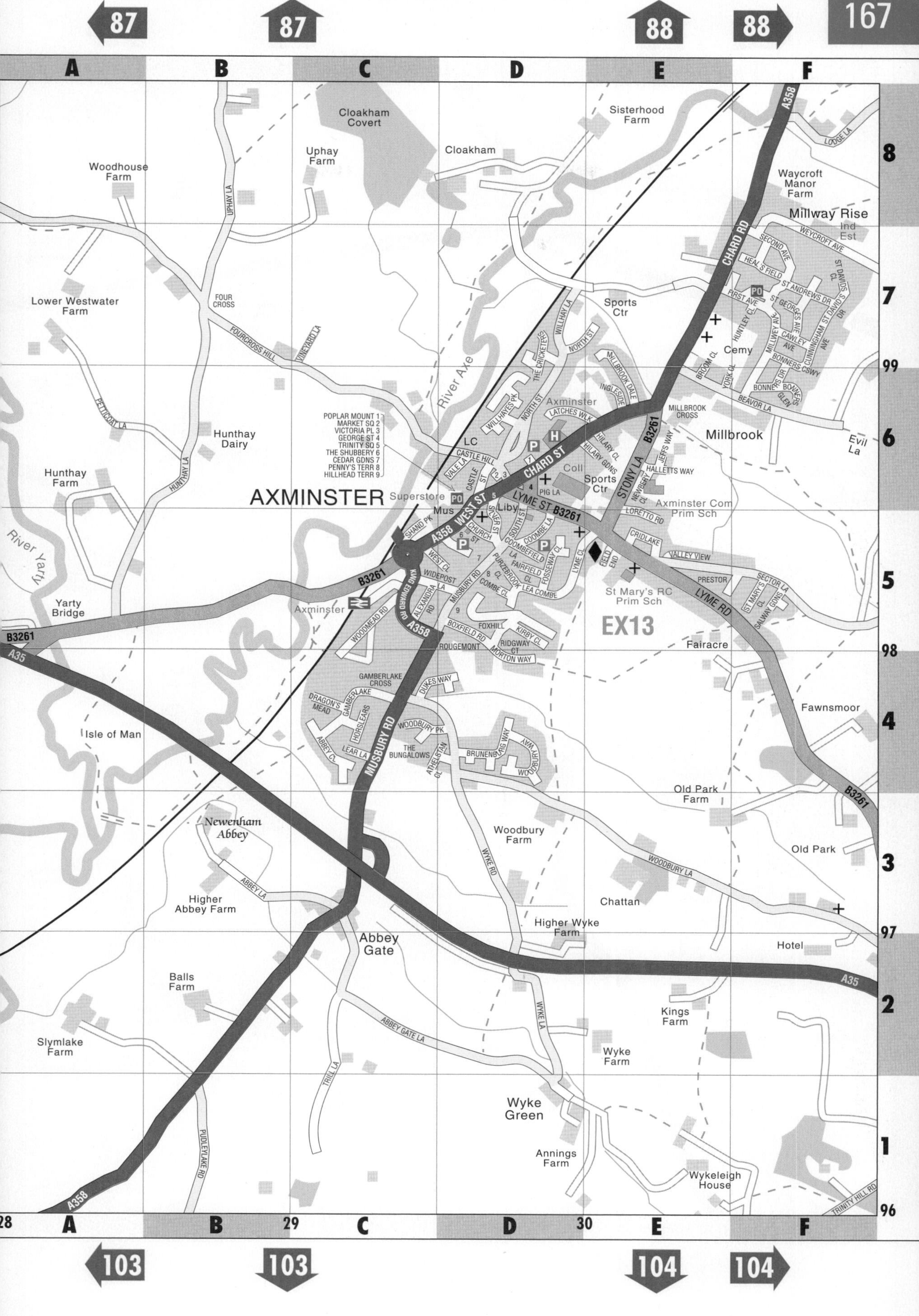

87
87
88
88
A
B
C
D
E
F
8
7
99
6
5
98
4
3
97
2
1
96
28
29
30
103
103
104
104
Cloakham Covert
Sisterhood Farm
Uphay Farm
Cloakham
Woodhouse Farm
Waycroft Manor Farm
Millway Rise
Ind Est
UPHAY LA
CHARD RD
LODGE LA
WEYCROFT AVE
SECOND AVE
HEAL'S FIELD
ST ANDREWS DR
ST DAVIDS CL
ST DAVID'S DR
FIRST AVE
ST GEORGES AVE
HUNTLEY CL
MILLWEY AVE
CAWLEY AVE
CUNNINGHAM AVE
BONNERS CSWY
BONNERS DR
BONNERS GLEN
BROOM CL
YORK CL
BEAVOR LA
Cemy
PO
Lower Westwater Farm
FOUR CROSS
FOURCROSS HILL
VINEYARD LA
Sports Ctr
WILLHAY LA
NORTH ST
THE CRICKETERS
MILLBROOK DALE
INGLESIDE
River Axe
PETTICOAT LA
POPLAR MOUNT 1
MARKET SQ 2
VICTORIA PL 3
GEORGE ST 4
TRINITY SQ 5
THE SHUBBERY 6
CEDAR GDNS 7
PENNY'S TERR 8
HILLHEAD TERR 9
Hunthay Dairy
Axminster
LATCHES WLK
WILLHAYES PK
MILLBROOK CROSS
Millbrook
Evil La
H
P
LC
CASTLE HILL
CHARD ST
HILARY CL
HILARY GDNS
STONY LA
B3261
JEFFS WAY
HALLETTS WAY
Hunthay Farm
HUNTHAY LA
VALE LA
CASTLE ST
Coll
Sports Ctr
NEWBERY CL
AXMINSTER
Superstore
PIG LA
Axminster Com Prim Sch
Mus
WEST ST
A358
Liby
LYME ST B3261
LORETTO RD
SHAND PK
CHURCH ST
SILVER ST
SOUTH ST
COOMBE LA
COOMBEFIELD LA
CRIDLAKE
VALLEY VIEW
River Yarty
WEST CL
FAIRFIELD CL
FOSSEWAY CL
LYME CL
FIELD END
PRESTOR
SECTOR LA
ST MARY'S CL
SALWAY GDNS
LYME RD
B3261
KING EDWARD RD
WIDEPOST LA
PURZEBROOK CL
COMBE CL
LEA COMBE
St Mary's RC Prim Sch
Yarty Bridge
Axminster
ALEXANDRA RD
MUSBURY RD
EX13
WOODMEAD RD
FOXHILL
KIRBY CL
BOXFIELD RD
RIDGWAY CT
Fairacre
B3261
A35
ROUGEMONT
MORTON WAY
GAMBERLAKE CROSS
DUKES WAY
Fawnsmoor
DRAGON'S MEAD
GAMBERLAKE
HORSLEARS
MUSBURY RD
WOODBURY PK
Isle of Man
ABBEY CL
LEAR LA
THE BUNGALOWS
ATHELSTAN CL
BRUNENBURG WAY
WOODBURY WAY
Old Park Farm
B3261
Newenham Abbey
Woodbury Farm
Old Park
WYKE RD
WOODBURY LA
ABBEY LA
Higher Abbey Farm
Chattan
Higher Wyke Farm
Abbey Gate
Hotel
A35
Balls Farm
WYKE LA
Kings Farm
ABBEY GATE LA
Slymlake Farm
Wyke Farm
TRILL LA
Wyke Green
PUDLEYLAKE RD
Annings Farm
Wykeleigh House
TRINITY HILL RD
A358

A
B
C
D
E
F
8
7
95
6
5
94
4
3
93
2
1
92
05
06
07
Cvn Pk
A30
Straightway Head Big Wood
STRETE RALEGH
The Ride
EXETER RD
The Groovy
Cadhay Wood
BIRDCAGE LA
Straitgate Farm
B3174
EXETER RD
Cadhay Bog
B3180
Pitfield Farm
Lowlands Farm
B3174
BRICKYARD RD
TIPTON LA
Tree Tops
TELEGRAPH LA
Mount Houlditch
ALLERCOMBE HILL
Allercombe
Works
Rockbeare Hill
TOADPIT LA
Mill
NEW RD
EX11
P
Upper Linhay
West Hill Court Farm
COURTFIELD CL
Castle Copse
Melton Court
EX5
BENDARROCH RD
ST MARY'S VIEW
ROCKBEARE HILL
WINDMILL LA
MOORLANDS
SCHOOL LA
POTTERS CL
BEECH PK
PERRYS GDNS
OTTER CL
ELSDON LA
CASTLE FARM
LOWER BROAD OAK RD
Westhayes
PO
West Hill
West Hill Prim Sch
EASTFIELD
WEST HILL RD
WARREN PK
ASHLEY BRAKE
Great Copse
HEATHER GRANGE
NEEDLEWOOD CL
EYMORE DR
WARREN CL
Broad Oak Bottom
Cuckoo Down Farm
BROADOAK CL
FORD LA
BIRCH GR
PINEFIELDS CL
Codley Brake
WHITE FARM LA
HAWKINS LA
Little Houndbeare Farm
HIGH BANK
Broad Oak
HYLANDS CL
BRACKEN DOWN
OAK RD
Metcombe Stud
HIGHER BROAD OAK RD
TIPTON CROSS
OAK RD
Aylesbeare Hill
HOUNDBEARE LA
Heathlands
Higher Metcombe
Manor Farm
Hall's Farm
B3180

100
84
100
A B C D E F
8
7
97
6
5
96
4
3
95
2
1
94
08
09
10
168
100
100
A30
EX14
EX11
Escot Park
Higher Gosford Farm
Ye Ash Farm
PATTERSON'S CROSS
Big Wood
LANGLAND LA
TALEFORD CL
TALEFORD VILLAS
Gosford
Fairmile Inn (PH)
Fairmile
GOSFORD LA
Gosford Farm
GOSFORD RD
PITHAM LA
B3177
Woodford Barton
Coombelake
Taleford
River Tale
Little Woodford
REDHILL COTTS
ALFINGTON RD
Four Elms Farm
HOLCOMBE LA
Pitt Farm
River Otter
Woodcote House
Cadhay Barton
Cadhay House
Woodcote Farmhouse
BUTT'S HILL
Cadhay Wood
CADHAY LA
MEADOW CL
BUTTS RD
Cemy
Cadhay Bridge Farm
CORNHILL 1
THE FLEXTON 2
PROSPECT PL 3
BROAD ST 4
WASHBROOK VIEW
HIGHER RIDGEWAY
RIDGEWAY
1 BROOKLAND TERR
2 SHERMAN HO
3 YONDER CNR
4 BROOKLANDS ORCH
5 PLUME OF FEATHERS CL
6 HOLLIS CL
7 BRIDGEFIELD
Thorne Farm
DUNKIRK
Liby
TH
PATERNOSTER ROW
NORTH ST
RALEIGH RD
PATTESON DR
COLERIDGE RD
KINGS AVE
CHINEWAY RD
THE COLLEGE
SILVER ST
GOLD ST
SANDHILL ST
BROOK ST
YONDER ST
BEAUVALE CL
FLUXBROOK
SHUTES MEAD
SLADE CL
TAYLOR CL
FERGUSON CL
GODFREY CL
THORNE FARM WAY
ELIOT CL
HANSFORD WAY
MILL STREAM CT
CANAAN WAY
HIND ST
B3174
PO
JESU ST
Sch
GRANDISSON DR
CHINEWAY GDNS
The Kings Sch
Sports Ctr
THORNE COTTS
Finnimore Ind Est
Ottery St Mary
Cadhay Bog
MILL ST
B3174
EXETER RD
BARRACK RD
ALANS WAY
MOSSOP CL
ST SAVIOURS RD
WINTER'S LA
CHURCH VIEW
LITTLE CL
HIGHLANDS
FRANKLEA CL
TIP HILL
LONGDOGS CL
LONGDOGS LA
ORCHARD CL
HOMEFIELD CL
ST BUDEAUX CL
SPRING GDNS
ST MARYS PK
HIGHER SPRING GDNS
KNIGHTSTONE LA
SLADE RD
Barrack Farm
Island Farm
RIVERSIDE VIEW
HILLCREST
OAK CL
CLAREMONT FIELD
OTTERY ST MARY
Slade Farm
1 VICTORIA TERR
2 MILLCROFT
3 WINDRUSH RISE
4 SPENCER CT
Mill Plantation
Gerway Farm
GERWAY LA
Foxenhole Mill
Foxenholes
SALSTON BARTON
SIDMOUTH RD
Long Copse
SALSTON RIDE
Knightstone Cottage
Salston Manor Hotel
Knightstone
Alder Grove
KNIGHTSTONE RD
Valley View

93
94
94
A
B
C
D
E
F
8
7
96
6
5
95
4
3
94
2
1
93
58
59
60
Mast
Hook
Knowle Farm
Chichacott
Webber Hill Farm
GLENDON CROSS
APPLEDORE HILL
B3215
CHICHACOTT CROSS
B3217
BRIGHTLEY RD
River Okement
Knowle Bridge
Tarka Trail
NORTH RD
CHICHACOTT RD
Barton Farm
Higher Upcott
BEARS FARM COTTS
North Road Ind Est
Oaklands
OKEHAMPTON
LINK RD
CREDITON RD
BARTON RD
Exeter Road Ind Est
RADFORD WAY
CRANMERE RD
HAMELDOWN RD
MERRIVALE RD
BEARDOWN RD
Fatherford Farm
UPCOTT HILL
GLENDALE RD
Okehampton Prim Sch
(Opening 2003)
LODGE HILL
BEANS MDW
VICARAGE RD
CHURCH MDWS
EAST ST
FORE ST
WEST ST
EXETER RD
B3260
Motel
Liby
TH
Mus
DOMEHAYES
CHURCH ST
JUBILEE CL
1 THE CHANTRY
2 SIMMONS CL
Okehampton & Dist
(Closing 2003)
EX20
The Beacon
1 OKETOR CL
2 STEEPERTON CL
3 KESTOR CL
4 ROW TOR CL
5 WHITE TOR CL
6 HARE TOR CL
A30
NORTHAMS MDW 1
BRIGHT VIEW 2
STONEY PARK LA
OLD RD
COURTENAY RD
Okehampton Coll
Ball Hill
Dartmoor Way
Castle
(Closing 2003)
NEW RD
CASTLE LA
LEEZE PARK EST
BRANDIZE PK
PARKLANDS
Okehampton
KLONDYKE RD
PARK VIEW TERR
HIGHLAND VIEW
Castle
West Okement River
West Devon Way
Two Castles Trail
Klondyke
Tarka Trail
West Cleave
East Hill
Well & Cross
CH
CAMP RD
Lower Halstock
East Okement River
Halstock Wood
Moor Brook
Okehampton Camp
MOOR GATE
Okehampton Park
Moorgate Farm
East Bowden
East Bowden Wood
93
94
94

117
117
117

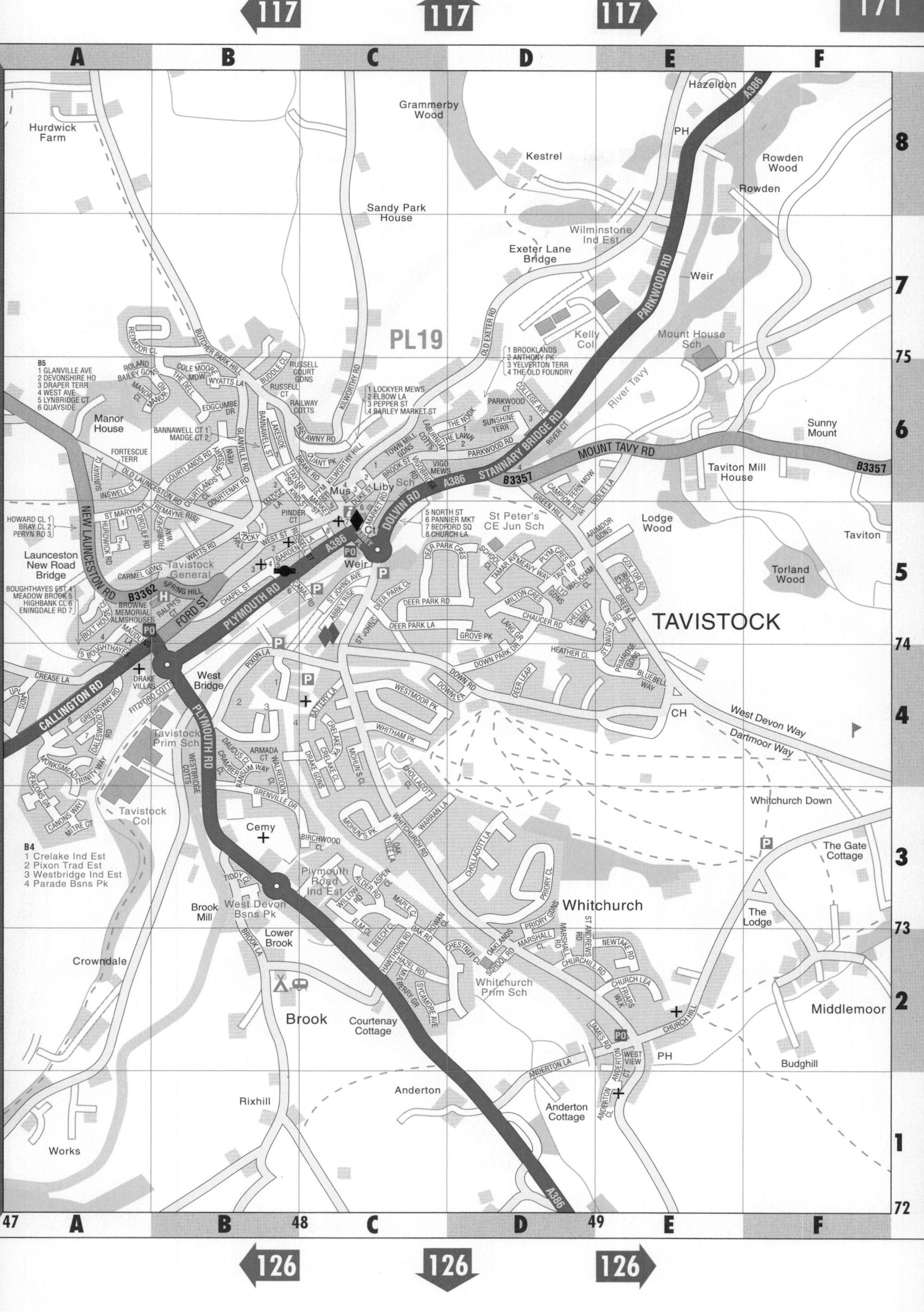

126
126
126

98
81

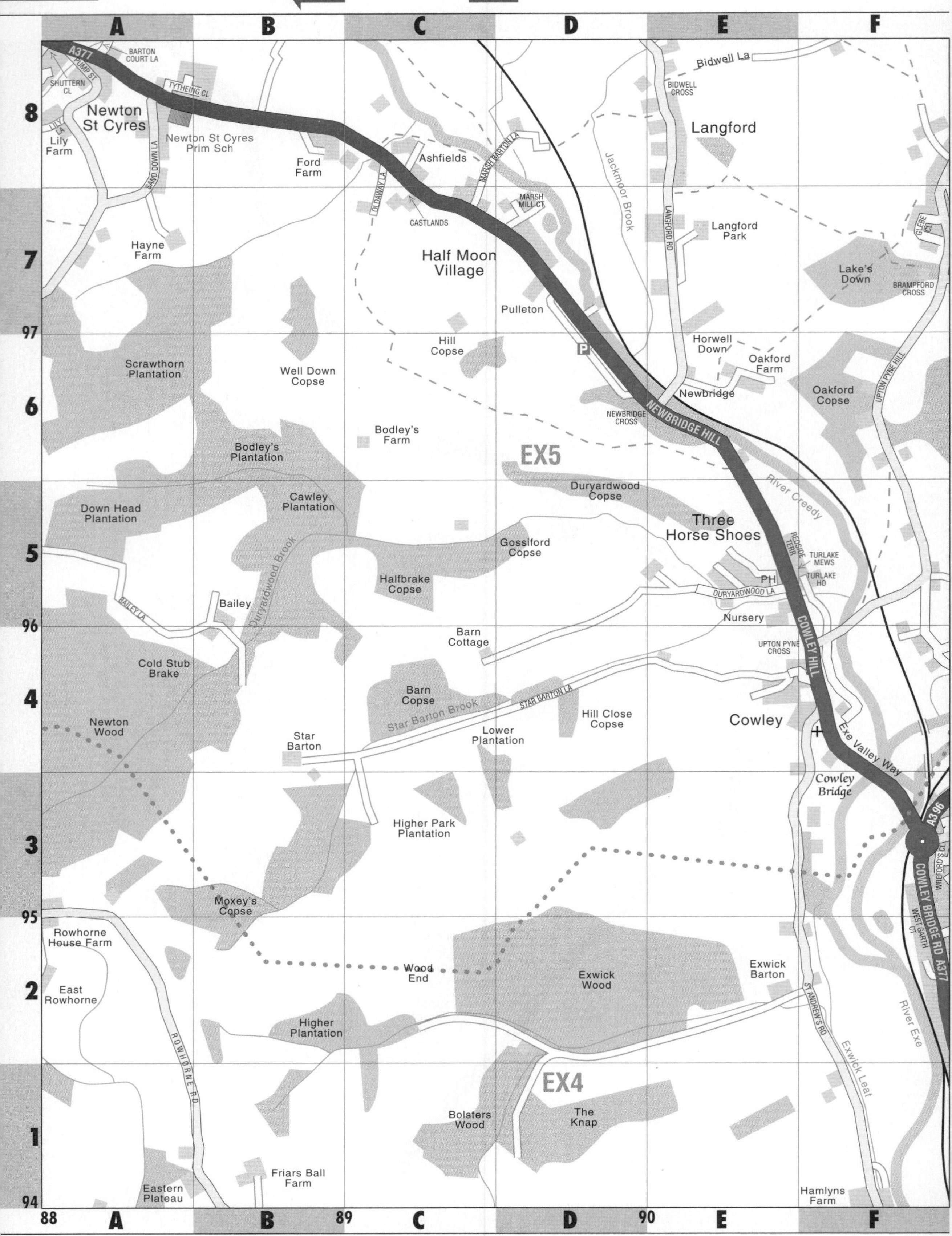
A
B
C
D
E
F
A377
BARTON COURT LA
PUMP ST
SHUTTERN CL
TYTHEING CL
Newton St Cyres
LILY LA
Lily Farm
SAND DOWN LA
Newton St Cyres Prim Sch
Ford Farm
Ashfields
OLDAWAY LA
MARSH BARTON LA
MARSH MILL CT
CASTLANDS
Half Moon Village
Pulleton
Jackmoor Brook
Bidwell La
BIDWELL CROSS
Langford
LANGFORD RD
Langford Park
Lake's Down
GLEBE CL
BRAMPFORD CROSS
Hayne Farm
Hill Copse
Well Down Copse
Scrawthorn Plantation
Horwell Down
Oakford Farm
Newbridge
NEWBRIDGE CROSS
NEWBRIDGE HILL
Oakford Copse
UPTON PYNE HILL
Bodley's Farm
Bodley's Plantation
EX5
Duryardwood Copse
River Creedy
Down Head Plantation
Cawley Plantation
Three Horse Shoes
Gossiford Copse
REDSIDE TERR
TURLAKE MEWS
TURLAKE HO
PH
Halfbrake Copse
Duryardwood Brook
BAILEY LA
Bailey
DURYARDWOOD LA
Nursery
COWLEY HILL
Barn Cottage
UPTON PYNE CROSS
Cold Stub Brake
Barn Copse
STAR BARTON LA
Star Barton Brook
Hill Close Copse
Cowley
Newton Wood
Star Barton
Lower Plantation
Exe Valley Way
Cowley Bridge
A396
Higher Park Plantation
WREFORD'S CL
COWLEY BRIDGE RD A377
Moxey's Copse
WEST GARTH CT
Rowhorne House Farm
Wood End
Exwick Wood
Exwick Barton
East Rowhorne
ST ANDREW'S RD
River Exe
Higher Plantation
ROWHORNE RD
Exwick Leat
EX4
Bolsters Wood
The Knap
Friars Ball Farm
Eastern Plateau
Hamlyns Farm
8
7
97
6
5
96
4
3
95
2
1
94
88
89
90

98
176

81
174

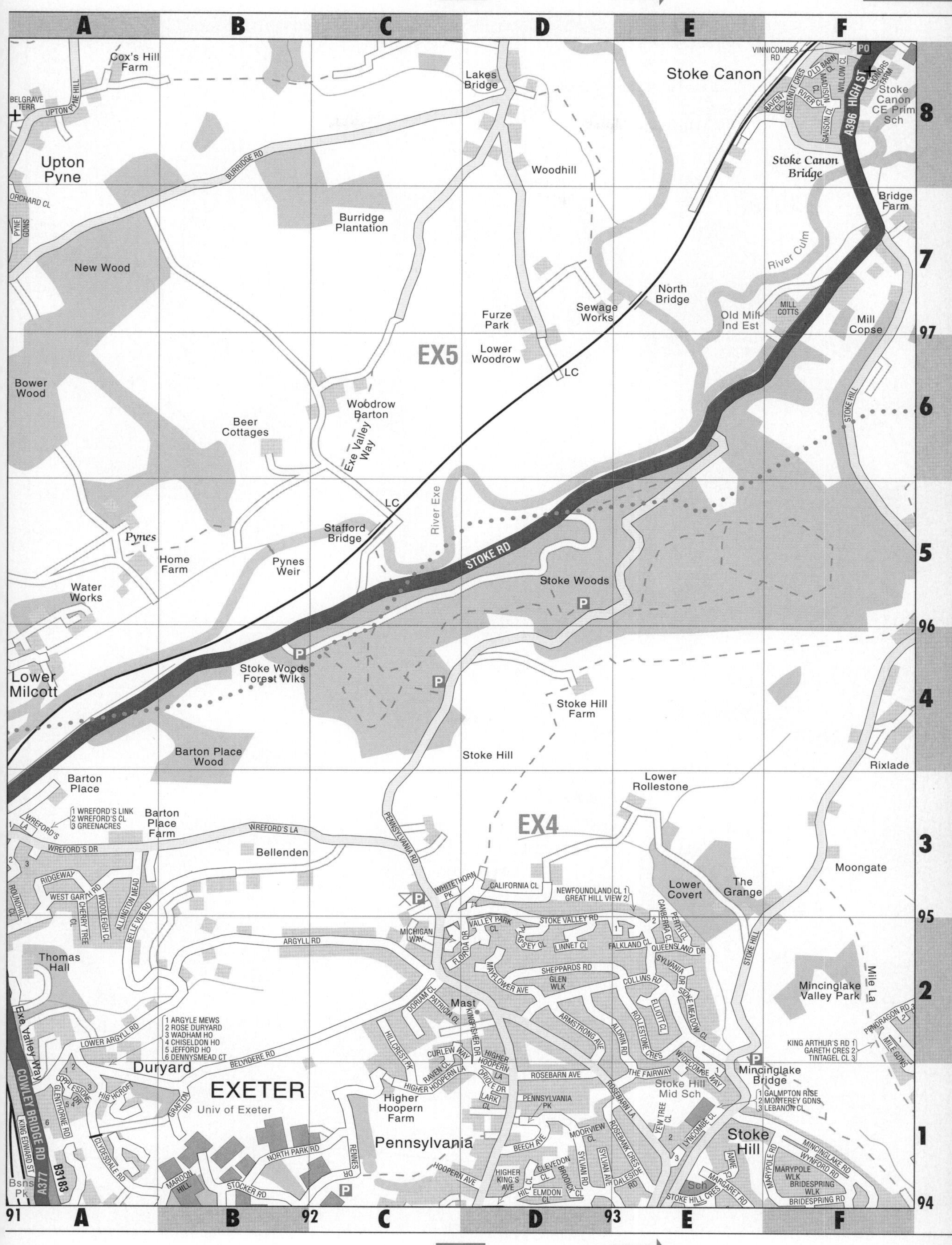

177
174

173
82

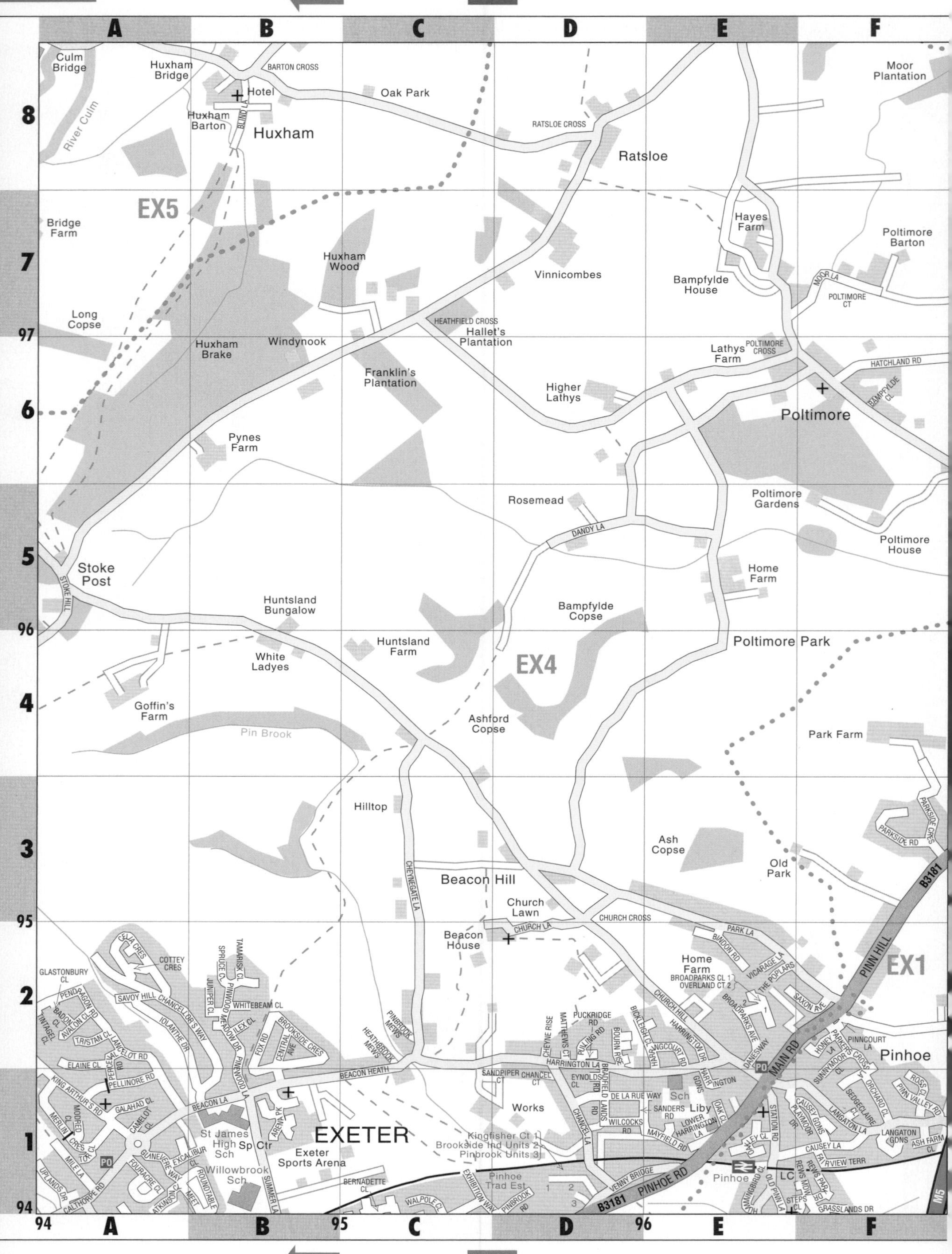

173
178

82
99

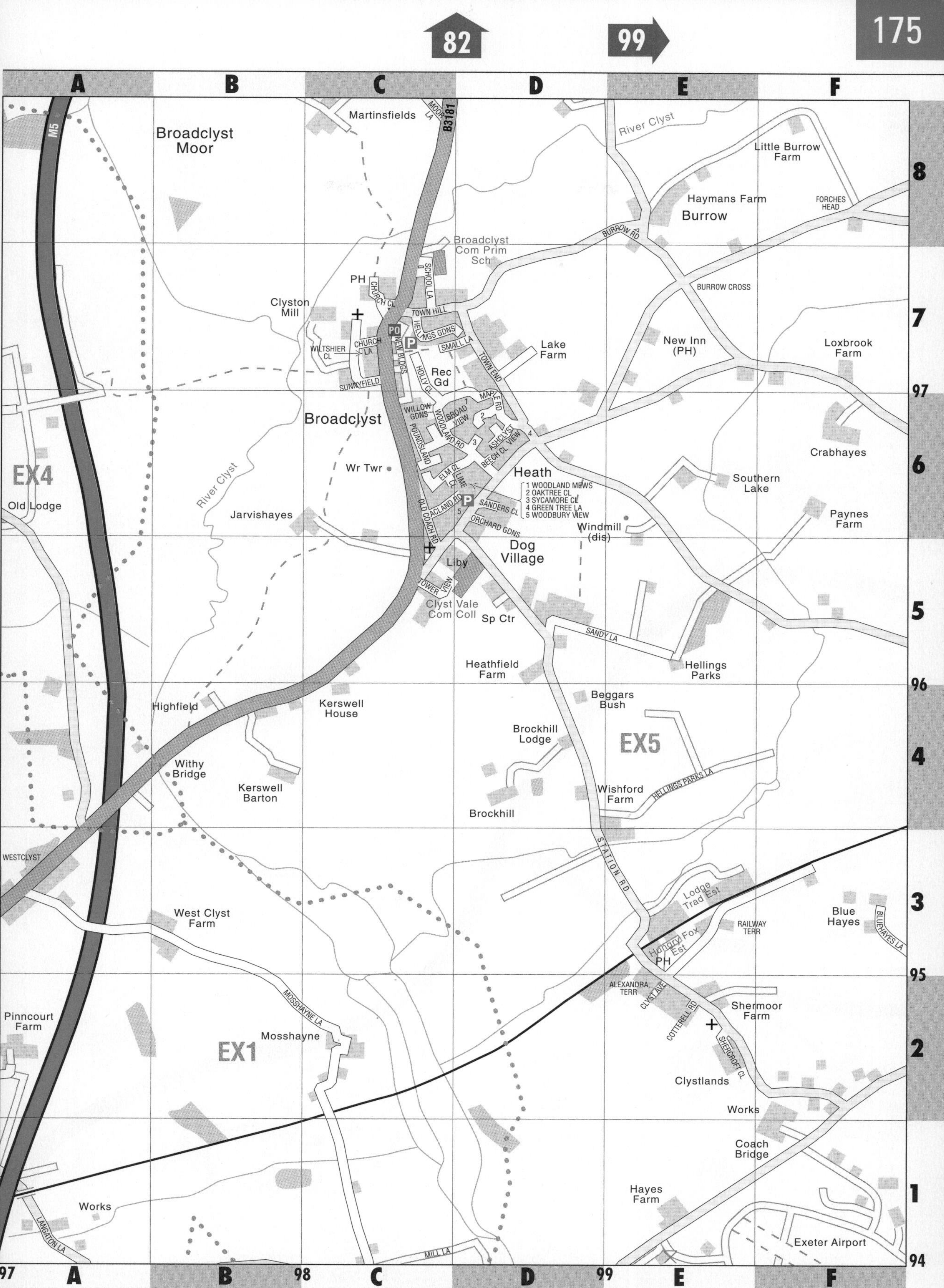
Broadclyst Moor
Martinsfields
B3181
River Clyst
Little Burrow Farm
Haymans Farm
Burrow
FORCHES HEAD
BURROW RD
Broadclyst Com Prim Sch
BURROW CROSS
PH
Clyston Mill
TOWN HILL
SCHOOL LA
CHURCH CL
HELLINGS GDNS
SMALL LA
WILTSHIER CL
CHURCH LA
NEW BLDGS
TOWN END
Lake Farm
New Inn (PH)
Loxbrook Farm
SUNNYFIELD
HOLLY CL
Rec Gd
MAPLE RD
WILLOW GDNS
BROAD VIEW
WOODLAND RD
POUNDSLAND
ASHCLYST VIEW
BEECH CL
Broadclyst
Crabhayes
EX4
Wr Twr
ELM CL
LIME CL
Heath
1 WOODLAND MEWS
2 OAKTREE CL
3 SYCAMORE CL
4 GREEN TREE LA
5 WOODBURY VIEW
Southern Lake
Old Lodge
River Clyst
Jarvishayes
ACLAND RD
SANDERS CL
ORCHARD GDNS
OLD COACH RD
Windmill (dis)
Paynes Farm
Dog Village
Liby
TOWER VIEW
Clyst Vale Com Coll
Sp Ctr
SANDY LA
Heathfield Farm
Hellings Parks
Highfield
Kerswell House
Beggars Bush
Brockhill Lodge
EX5
Withy Bridge
Kerswell Barton
Wishford Farm
HELLINGS PARKS LA
Brockhill
WESTCLYST
STATION RD
Lodge Trad Est
West Clyst Farm
RAILWAY TERR
Blue Hayes
BLUEHAYES LA
Hungry Fox Est
PH
ALEXANDRA TERR
CLYST AVE
COTTERELL RD
Shermoor Farm
Pinncourt Farm
MOSSHAYNE LA
Mosshayne
EX1
SHERCROFT CL
Clystlands
Works
Coach Bridge
Hayes Farm
Works
LANGATON LA
MILL LA
Exeter Airport
M5
A
B
C
D
E
F
8
7
97
6
5
96
4
3
95
2
1
94
97
98
99

179
99

98
172

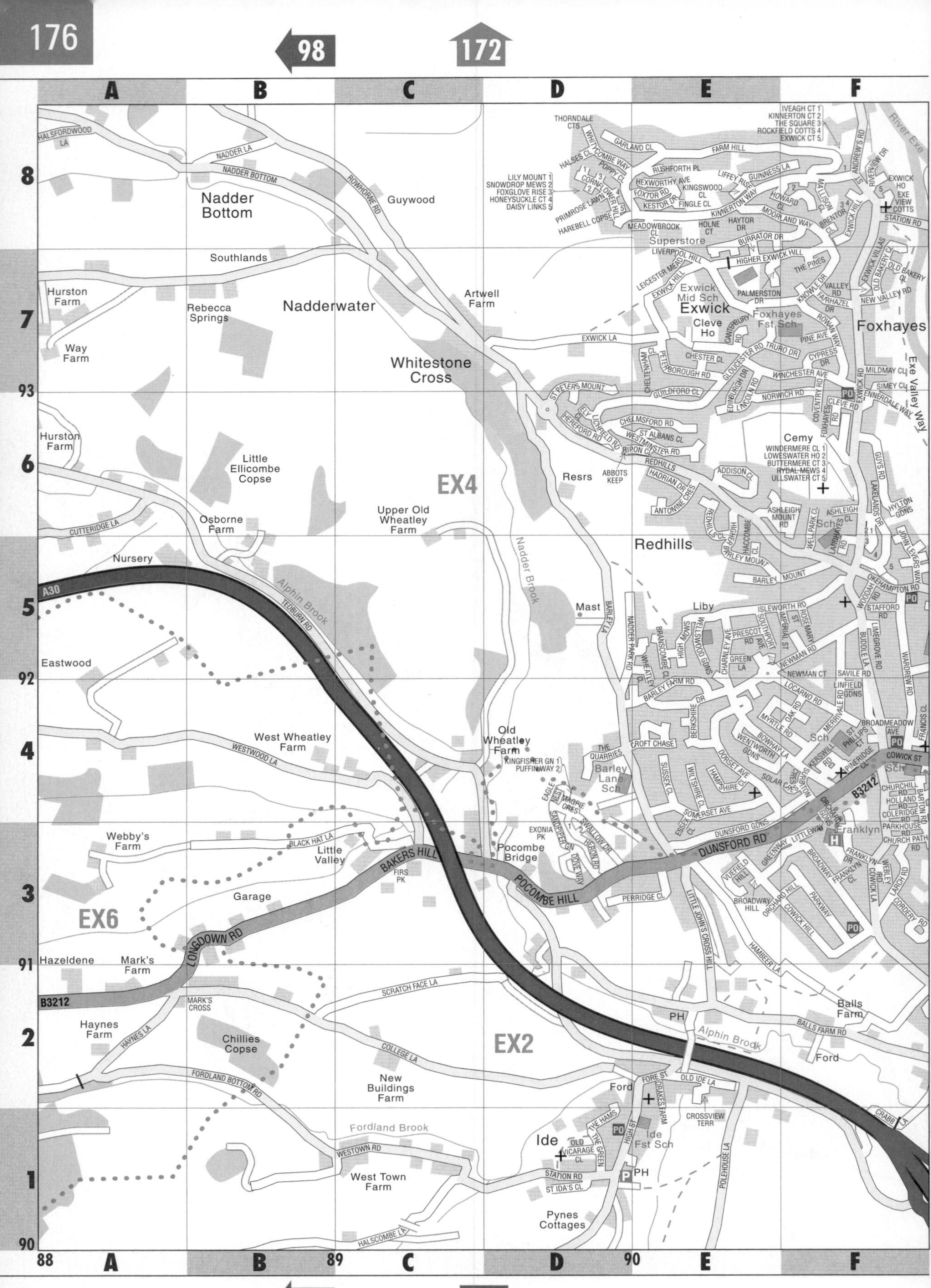
Nadder Bottom
Guywood
Southlands
Hurston Farm
Rebecca Springs
Nadderwater
Artwell Farm
Way Farm
Whitestone Cross
Exwick
Exwick Mid Sch
Foxhayes Fst Sch
Cleve Ho
Foxhayes
Superstore
Hurston Farm
Little Ellicombe Copse
EX4
Resrs
Cemy
Osborne Farm
Upper Old Wheatley Farm
Redhills
Nursery
A30
Mast
Liby
Eastwood
Alphin Brook
Nadder Brook
West Wheatley Farm
Old Wheatley Farm
Barley Lane Sch
Webby's Farm
Little Valley
Pocombe Bridge
Franklyn
Garage
EX6
Hazeldene
Mark's Farm
B3212
Haynes Farm
Chillies Copse
EX2
Balls Farm
Ford
New Buildings Farm
Fordland Brook
Ide
Ide Fst Sch
West Town Farm
Pynes Cottages
NADDER LA
NADDER BOTTOM
ROWHORNE RD
EXWICK LA
CUTTERIDGE LA
TEDBURN RD
WESTWOOD LA
BLACK HAT LA
BAKERS HILL
POCOMBE HILL
DUNSFORD RD
LONGDOWN RD
SCRATCH FACE LA
COLLEGE LA
FORDLAND BOTTOM RD
WESTOWN RD
HALSCOMBE LA
HAYNES LA
BARLEY LA
LITTLE JOHN'S CROSS HILL
POLEHOUSE LA
BALLS FARM RD
COWICK ST
OKEHAMPTON RD
Exe Valley Way
River Exe
LILY MOUNT 1
SNOWDROP MEWS 2
FOXGLOVE RISE 3
HONEYSUCKLE CT 4
DAISY LINKS 5
IVEAGH CT 1
KINNERTON CT 2
THE SQUARE 3
ROCKFIELD COTTS 4
EXWICK CT 5
WINDERMERE CL 1
LOWESWATER HO 2
BUTTERMERE CT 3
RYDAL MEWS 4
ULLSWATER CT 5
KINGFISHER GN 1
PUFFIN WAY 2
88
89
90
93
92
91
90
A
B
C
D
E
F
1
2
3
4
5
6
7
8

98
114

A5
1 EMMANUEL CL
2 EMMANUEL RD
3 LANDSCORE RD
4 CAMBRIDGE ST
5 CORNWALL ST
6 CLARENCE RD
7 CLEVELAND ST
8 OKEHAMPTON PL

173

D8
1 VICTORIA RD
2 WILLOW WLK
3 NEW BLDGS
4 BRIDGE COTTS
5 ROSEWOOD TERR

178

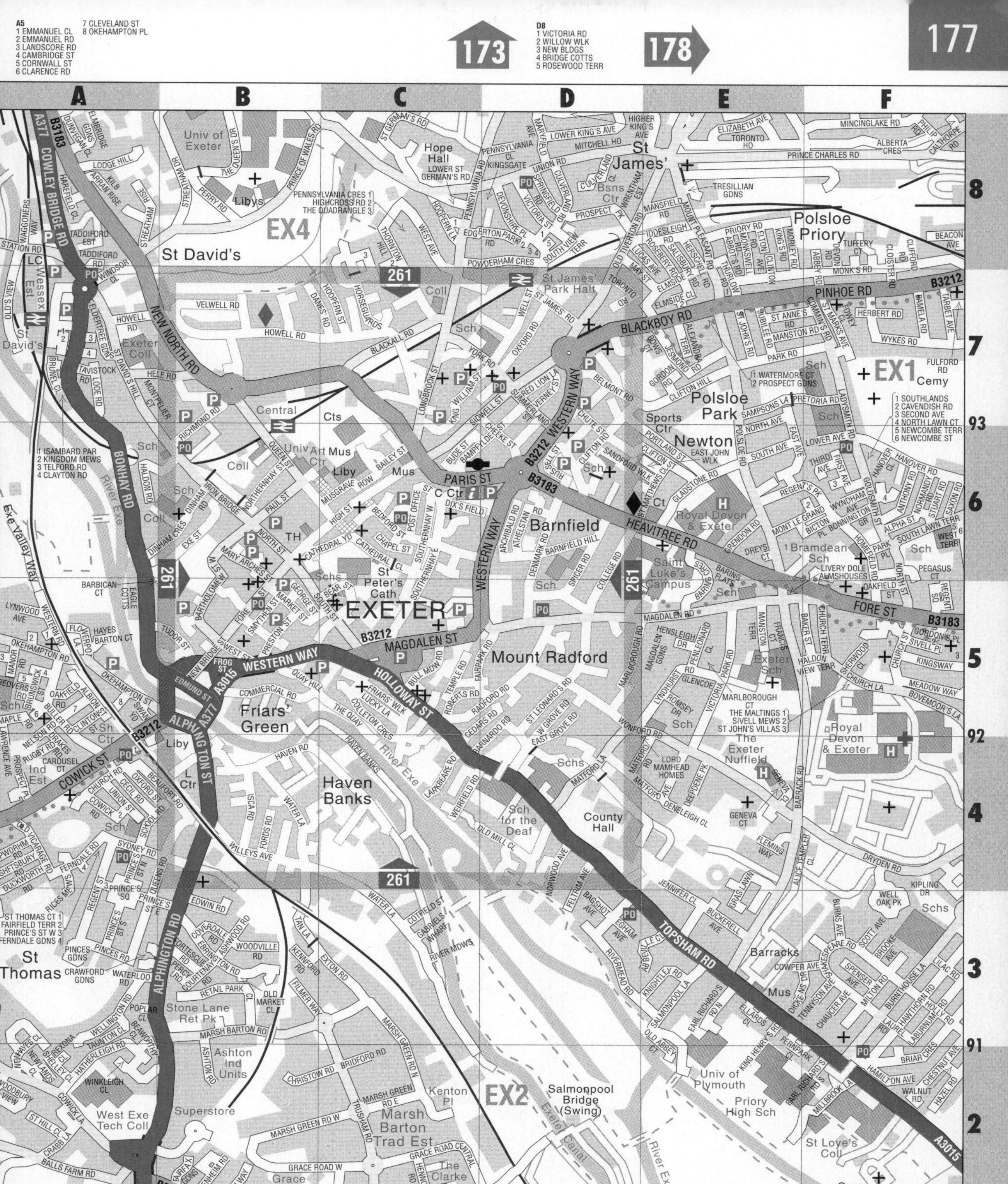

181
178

177
174

C8
1 MARK TWAIN HO
2 FLAYES ALMSHOUSES
3 PEEL ROW
4 ROYSTON CT

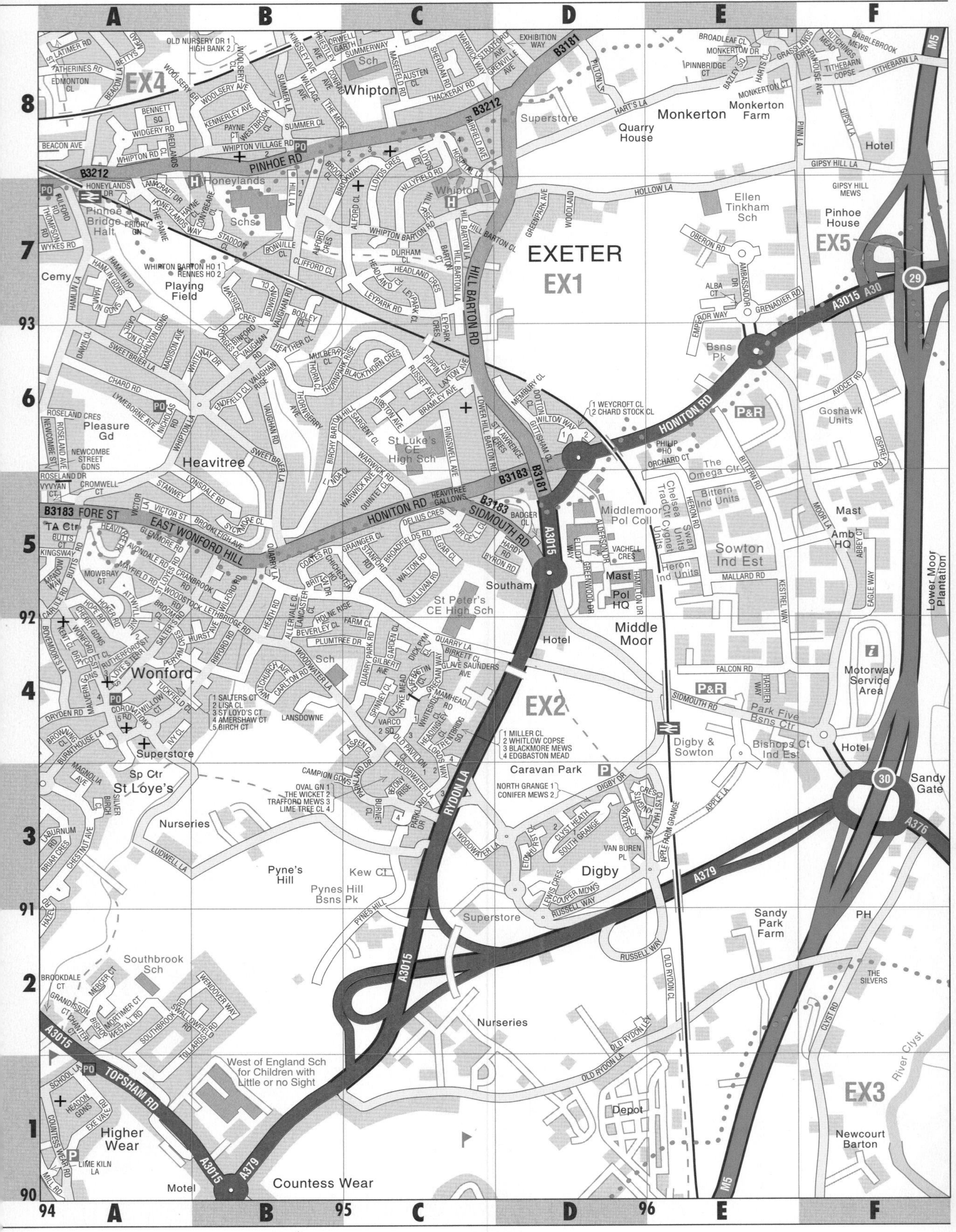

177
182

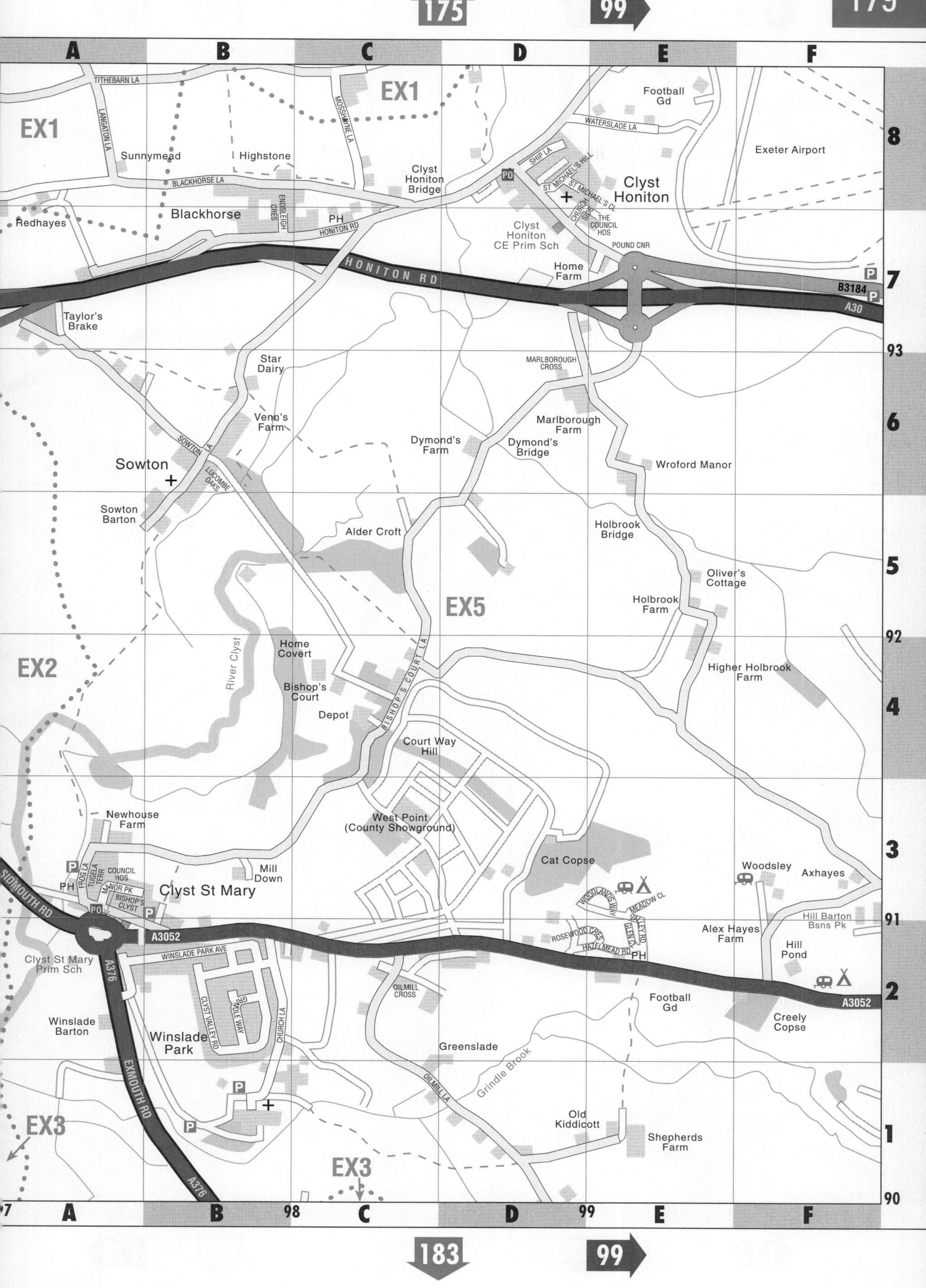
175
99
A
B
C
D
E
F
EX1
EX1
TITHEBARN LA
LANGATON LA
MOSSHAYNE LA
Sunnymead
Highstone
BLACKHORSE LA
Blackhorse
Redhayes
ENDSLEIGH CRES
PH
HONITON RD
Clyst Honiton Bridge
Football Gd
WATERSLADE LA
Exeter Airport
SHIP LA
ST MICHAEL'S HILL
ST MICHAEL'S CL
Clyst Honiton
CHURCH SIDE
THE COUNCIL HOS
Clyst Honiton CE Prim Sch
POUND CNR
Home Farm
HONITON RD
B3184
A30
Taylor's Brake
MARLBOROUGH CROSS
Star Dairy
Venn's Farm
Marlborough Farm
Dymond's Farm
Dymond's Bridge
Wroford Manor
SOWTON LA
LUCOMBE OAKS
Sowton
Sowton Barton
Alder Croft
Holbrook Bridge
Oliver's Cottage
EX5
Holbrook Farm
River Clyst
Home Covert
EX2
BISHOP'S COURT LA
Bishop's Court
Higher Holbrook Farm
Depot
Court Way Hill
Newhouse Farm
West Point (County Showground)
Cat Copse
FROG LA
TUGELA TERR
COUNCIL HOS
Mill Down
PH
MANOR PK
Clyst St Mary
Woodsley
Axhayes
SIDMOUTH RD
BISHOP'S CLYST
PO
WOODLANDS WAY
MEADOW CL
Hill Barton Bsns Pk
A3052
ROSEWOOD CRES
GLEN CL
VALLEY RD
HAZELMEAD RD
PH
Alex Hayes Farm
Hill Pond
Clyst St Mary Prim Sch
WINSLADE PARK AVE
A376
CLYST VALLEY RD
OILMILL CROSS
Football Gd
A3052
Winslade Barton
CHURCH LA
Winslade Park
Creely Copse
Greenslade
Grindle Brook
EXMOUTH RD
OILMILL LA
EX3
Old Kiddicott
Shepherds Farm
EX3
A376
8
7
93
6
5
92
4
3
91
2
1
90
97
98
99
183
99

122
122
C8
1 SOUTHBROOK LA
2 SOUTHBROOK CL
3 ATWAY CL
4 BULLANDS CL
5 MORETONHAMSTEAD RD
D8
1 ORCHARD WAY
2 VICTORIA TERR
3 ORCHARD TERR
4 TOWN HALL PL
5 SOUTHDOWN HO
6 TORVIEW FLATS
7 TRACEY ALMSHOUSES
123
123
A
B
C
D
E
F
8
7
78
6
5
77
4
3
76
2
1
75
80
81
82
Southbrook Farm
SOUTHBROOK LA
A382
WHITSTONE LA
FURZELEIGH LA
Bovey Tracey
Parke Bridge
BONDS MDW
STADDONS VIEW
CROKER'S MDW
MARY ST
TROUGH LA
Lower Coombe
EUREKA TERR
WHITE HEATHER TERR
DEVON HO
Parke
STORRS CL
PRIORY
CROMWELLS WAY
Sch
HIND ST
TH
POUND PL
EAST ST
COLLEGE
ST PETER'S CL
DEVON HOUSE DR
COOMBE LA
Coombe Plantation
ABBEY RD
ABBEY CL
FORE ST
SETT CL
BADGER'S WAY
MOORHAYES
DE TRACEY PK
ST PAUL'S CL
BECKET RD
HIGHER BIBBERY
COOMBE MDW
Cemy
Liby
1 STATION CT
2 ALBERT TERR
3 FAIRFIELD CL
PARKELANDS
FOUNTAIN CT
SOUTH VIEW
BUCKS CL
CHURCHFIELDS DR
MANNINGS MDW
COOMBE CROSS
BRADLEY RD
FIVE WYCHES CROSS
ST JOHN'S LA
DOLPHIN SQ
B3344
Mus
LE MOLAY-LITTRY WAY
HIGH
B3387
Tracey House
Five Wyches Farm
STATION RD
MARLBOROUGH TERR
FORGE PL
BLENHEIM TERR
Bovey Tracey
RENDELLS MDW
DRAKE RD
NEWBURY DR
THE OAKS
DRAKE LA
COOMBE CL
ST THOMAS CL
BRADLEY RD
B3344
HEATHERDENE
INDIO RD
1 HEATHFIELD TERR
2 ST JOHN'S COTTS
BRADLEYFORD CNR
Challabrook Farm
LEALANDS
ST JOHN'S CL
TQ13
River Bovey
CHAPPLE RD
MONKS WAY
Indio
TRACEY VALE
BRIMLEY VALE
NEWTON RD
Indio Pond
Lower Bradley Farm
CHALLABROOK LA
Templer Way
BRIMLEY PK
ASHBURTON RD
BRIMLEY HALT
HEATHFIELD CL
HEATHFIELD MDW
Wifford
Broad Coombe
BRIMLEY GRANGE
BRIMLEY RD
MOOR LA
REDWOODS
KILN RD
KILN CL
UNDER LA
CHAPPLE CROSS
BRIMLEY CT
ASHBURTON
SHAPTOR VIEW
MOOR VIEW
BRIMLEY LA
CHAPPLE CROSS
BRIMLEY CROSS
WALLFIELD RD
POTTERY RD
LANGALLER CL
BROADPARK
THORN CROSS
POTTERY CL
Brimley Bsns Pk
Blue Waters Ind Est
Western Units
Lower Brimley
Caravan Site
Slade Mead
LAKESIDE CL
BIRCHLEA
White Hill
King Charles I Bsns Pk
PARKLANDS WAY
OLD NEWTON RD
Trad Est
1 NORTHWOODS
2 FIVE ACRES
3 MILLWOOD
4 REDWOOD CL
5 OAKBANK
6 WOODLANDS WLK
7 BLUERIDGE
NEW PARK (CVN SITE)
LANGALLER LA
Bovey Heath
Wilsworthy
Langaller
New Park Plantation
Binney Bridge
DRAGOON CL
Samara Bsns Pk
Teignbridge Bsns Ctr
FAIRFAX RD
Crossgrange Trad Est
SABRE CL
HEATHER EST
NEWTON RD
Daneheath Bsns Pk
Heathfield Ind Est
ROUNDHEAD RD
CAVALIER RD
WENTWORTH RD
INTERNATIONAL HO
Belle Vue
BATTLE RD
COLESWORTHY CROSS
TQ12
Templer Way
Great Plantation
Heathfield
Colesworthy
HOLMES RD
DRUM WAY
MUSKET RD
NASEBY DR
FORBES CL
LANGSTONE CL 1
CLIFFORD DR 2
LOWER CANNON RD 3
A382
Old Love Wood
Moor Copse Farm
Old Leys Wood
DRUM BRIDGE
Liverton
Coldeast
LEY CRES
LEY CL
TELEGRAPH VIEW
Woodgate Cotts
CUMMINGS CROSS
CUMMINGS CT
1 SHAPLEY WAY
2 LEAT MDW
A38
LIVERTON CT
POTTERS YD
WOOD COTTS
122
122
123
123

114
177
182
A
B
C
D
E
F
Marsh Barton
Trad Est
Aldens
Bsns Ct
Alphington
River Exe
Country Park
Exe Valley Way
Exeter Canal
Exeter
Trad Ctr
BAD HOMBURG WAY
YEOFORD WAY
P&R
Knowle
Hill
Matford
Bridge
Matford
Barton
Matford Brook
Hotel
MATFORD MEWS
Cotfield
BRIDGE RD
SANNERVILLE WAY
Matford Park
Farm
Wracombe
Farm
MARKHAM LA
SHILLINGFORD RD
CHUDLEIGH RD
DAWLISH RD
Courtneys
Bungalow
WAYBROOK COTTS
WAYBROOK LA
BARTON LA
OAK CL
BARRACK LA
Shillingford
Abbot
EX2
Trood
House
TROOD LA
OLD MATFORD LA
Church Path
Hill Plantation
Barton
Cottage
Peamore
Wood
M5
MILLER WAY
DUNSTER WLK 1
KNIGHTHAYES WLK 2
POWDERHAM WLK 3
DARTINGTON WLK 4
EAGER WAY
REDDAWAY DR
FARM HOUSE RISE
ROUGEMONT CT
Shillingford
Plantation
Little Silver
Plantation
LITTLE SILVER LA
Masts
DEEPWAY LA
Pearce's
Hill
Peamore
Farm
Peamore
House
The
Rock
Peamore
Arch
Silver
Ridge
31
A38
A30
DAYS-POTTLES LA
DEEPWAY GDNS
Dadmouth
Pottles
Farm
Pottles
Wood
SHILLINGFORD LA
Towsington
Cottages
Spurway
Farm
A379
Kenbury
Wood
BRENTON RD
Kerswell
Farm
Resr
EX6
EXETER RD
BEARS COTTS
MILFORD COTTS
PYE CNR
Kenford
OLD DAWLISH RD
Kerswell
Cottages
Luccombe
Farm
BULFORD LA
RAYNERS
PO
PH
Lears
Copse
Brookside
Thatch
SANDFORDS
Kenn CE
Prim Sch
ACACIA MEWS
Horns
Copse
KENN LA
92
93
8
7
89
6
5
88
4
3
87
2
1
86
114
114
182

181
178

181
194

179
184

195
184

183 99

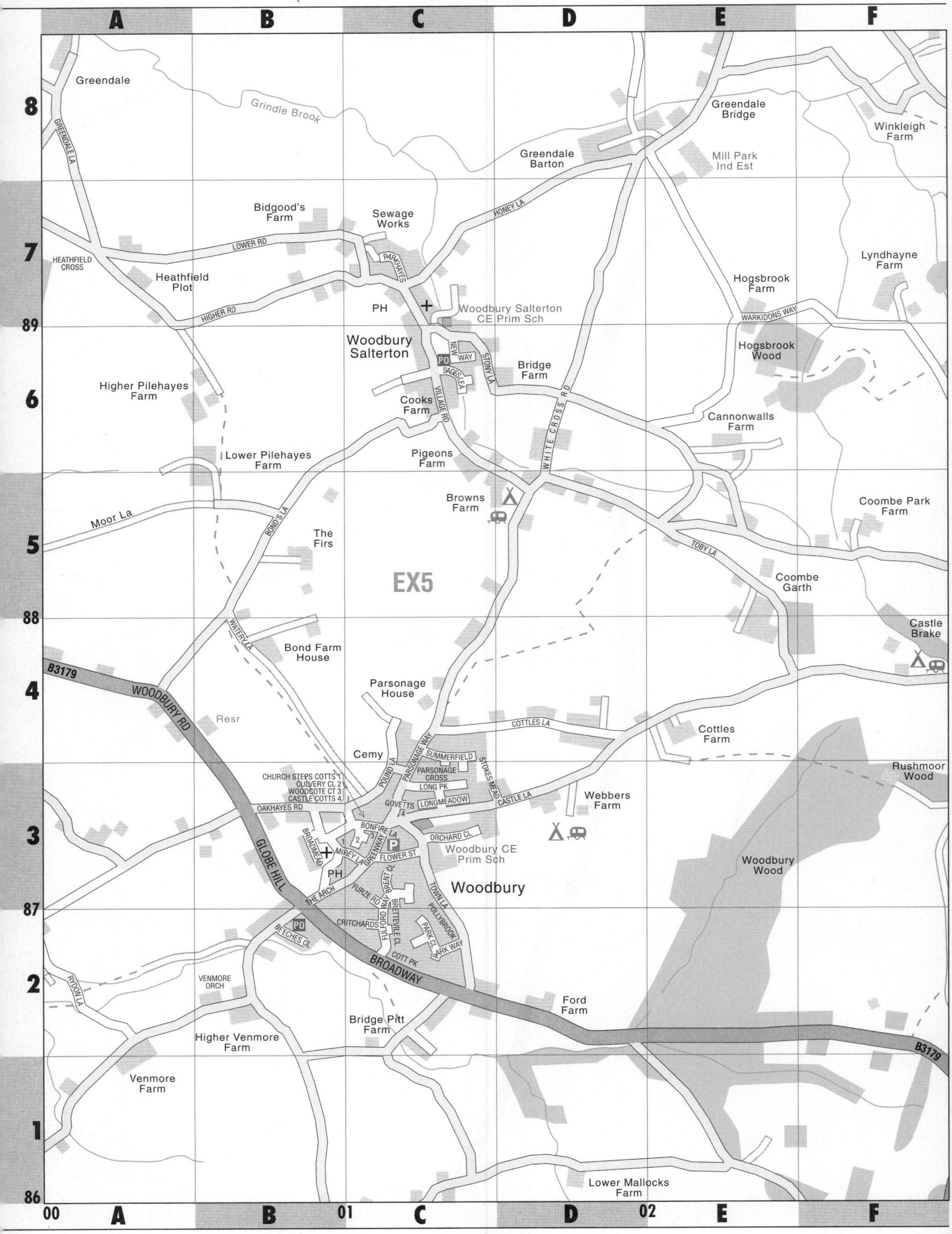

A B C D E F

8 7 89 6 5 88 4 3 87 2 1 86

Greendale
Grindle Brook
GREENDALE LA
Greendale Bridge
Winkleigh Farm
Greendale Barton
Mill Park Ind Est
Bidgood's Farm
Sewage Works
HONEY LA
LOWER RD
PARKHAYES
HEATHFIELD CROSS
Heathfield Plot
Lyndhayne Farm
Hogsbrook Farm
HIGHER RD
PH
Woodbury Salterton CE Prim Sch
WARKIDONS WAY
Woodbury Salterton
NEW WAY
PO
STONY LA
SAGES LEA
Hogsbrook Wood
Bridge Farm
Higher Pilehayes Farm
Cooks Farm
VILLAGE RD
WHITE CROSS RD
Cannonwalls Farm
Pigeons Farm
Lower Pilehayes Farm
Browns Farm
Coombe Park Farm
Moor La
BOND'S LA
The Firs
TOBY LA
EX5
Coombe Garth
Castle Brake
WATERY LA
Bond Farm House
B3179
WOODBURY RD
Parsonage House
Resr
COTTLES LA
Cottles Farm
Cemy
PARSONAGE WAY
SUMMERFIELD
PARSONAGE CROSS
STOKES MEAD
Rushmoor Wood
CHURCH STEPS COTTS 1
CULVERY CL 2
WOODCOTE CT 3
CASTLE COTTS 4
POUND LA
LONG PK
GOVETTS
LONGMEADOW
CASTLE LA
Webbers Farm
OAKHAYES RD
BONFIRE LA
ORCHARD CL
BROADMEAD
MIREY LA
GREENWAY
FLOWER ST
Woodbury CE Prim Sch
GLOBE HILL
PH
Woodbury
Woodbury Wood
THE ARCH
FURZE RD
BRENT CL
TOWN LA
CRITCHARDS
FULFORD WAY
BRETTEVILLE CL
POLLYBROOK
PARK CL
BEECHES CL
PO
PARK WAY
COTT PK
BROADWAY
RYDON LA
VENMORE ORCH
Ford Farm
Bridge Pitt Farm
Higher Venmore Farm
B3179
Venmore Farm
Lower Mallocks Farm

00 A B 01 C D 02 E F

183 196

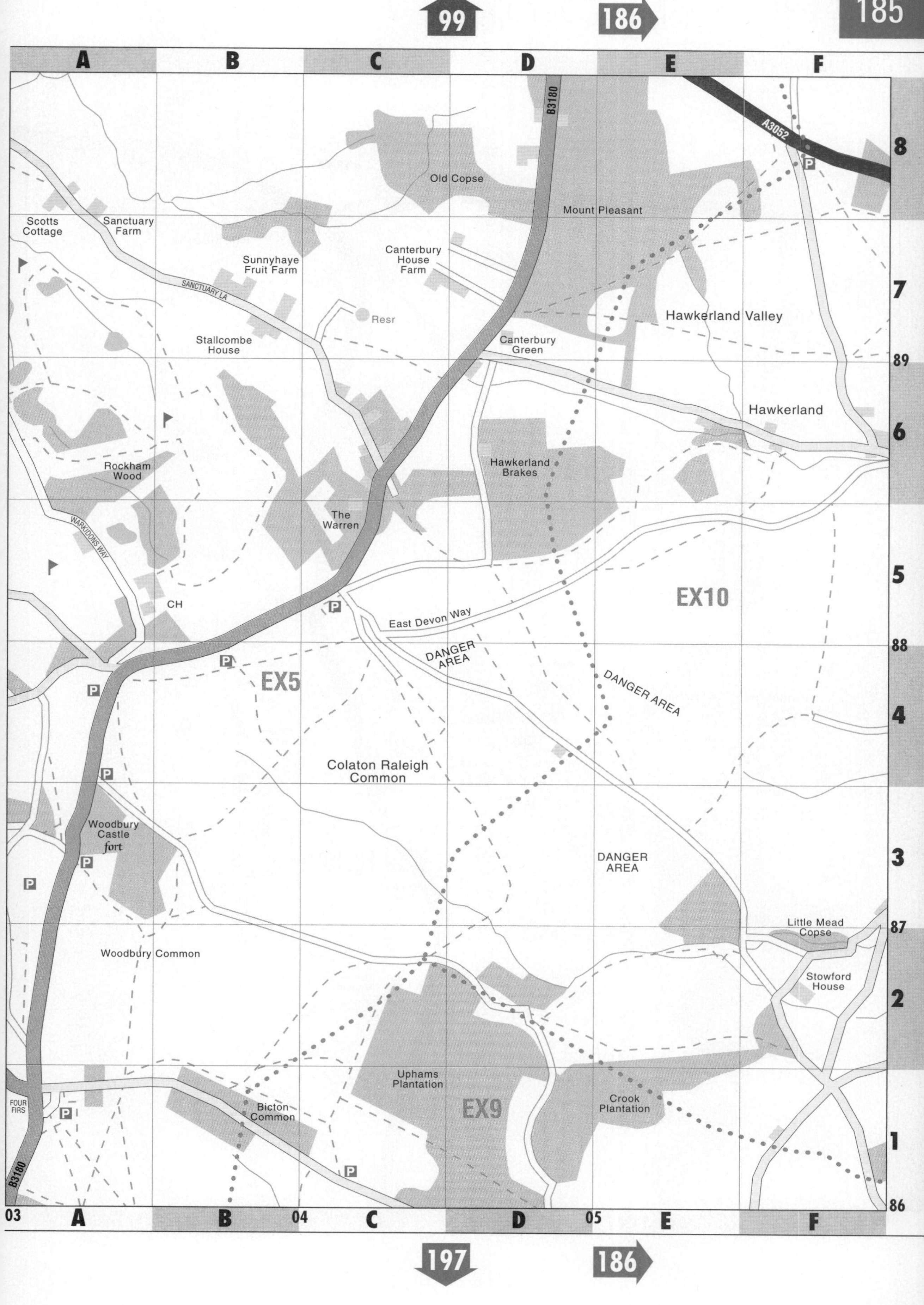
A
B
C
D
E
F
8
7
89
6
5
88
4
3
87
2
1
86
03
04
05
B3180
A3052
Old Copse
Mount Pleasant
Scotts Cottage
Sanctuary Farm
Sunnyhaye Fruit Farm
Canterbury House Farm
SANCTUARY LA
Resr
Hawkerland Valley
Stallcombe House
Canterbury Green
Hawkerland
Rockham Wood
Hawkerland Brakes
The Warren
WARKIDONS WAY
EX10
CH
East Devon Way
DANGER AREA
EX5
DANGER AREA
Colaton Raleigh Common
Woodbury Castle fort
DANGER AREA
Little Mead Copse
Woodbury Common
Stowford House
Uphams Plantation
FOUR FIRS
Bicton Common
EX9
Crook Plantation
P

185
100

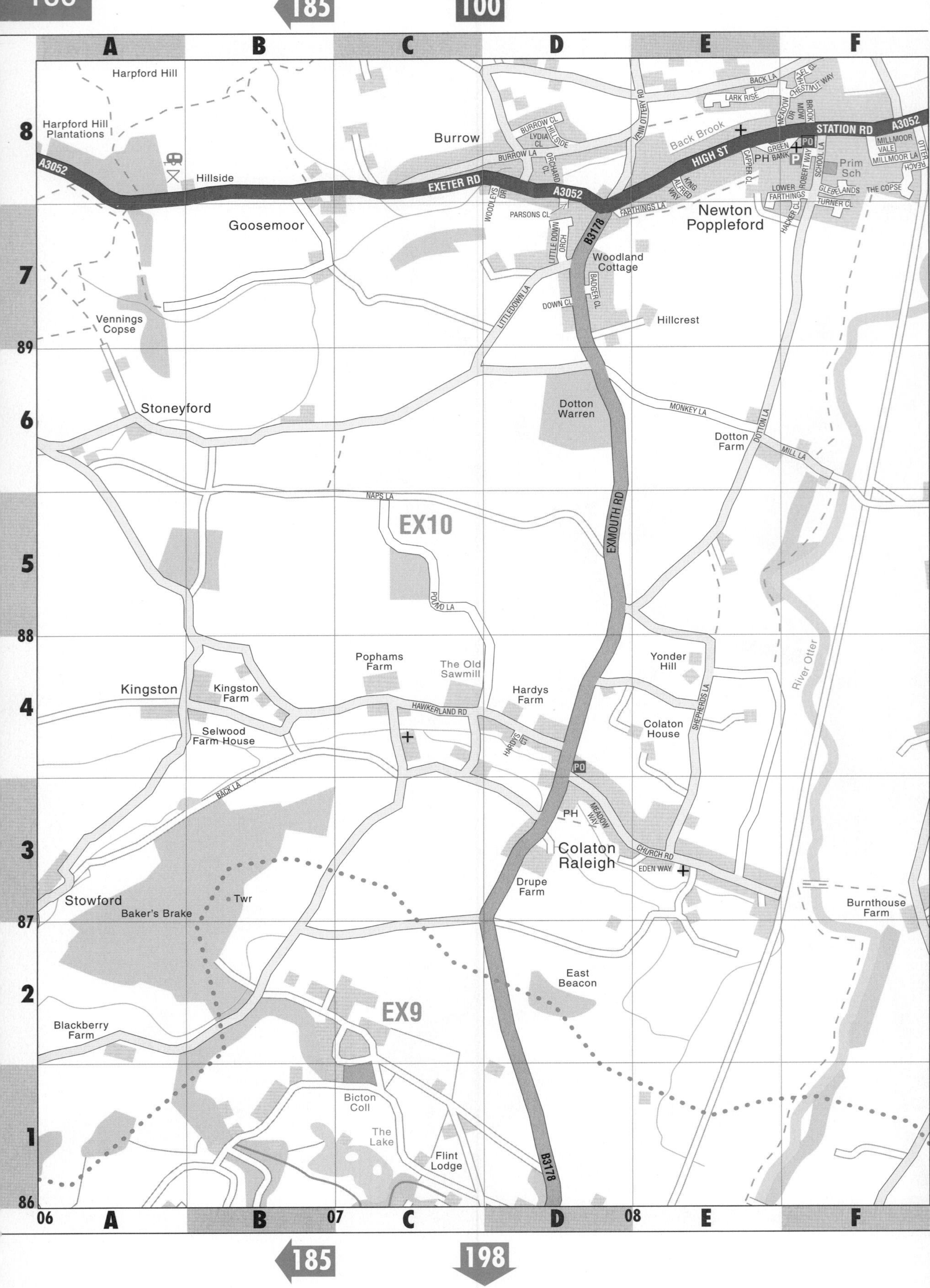

185
198

100
188

199
188

187 101

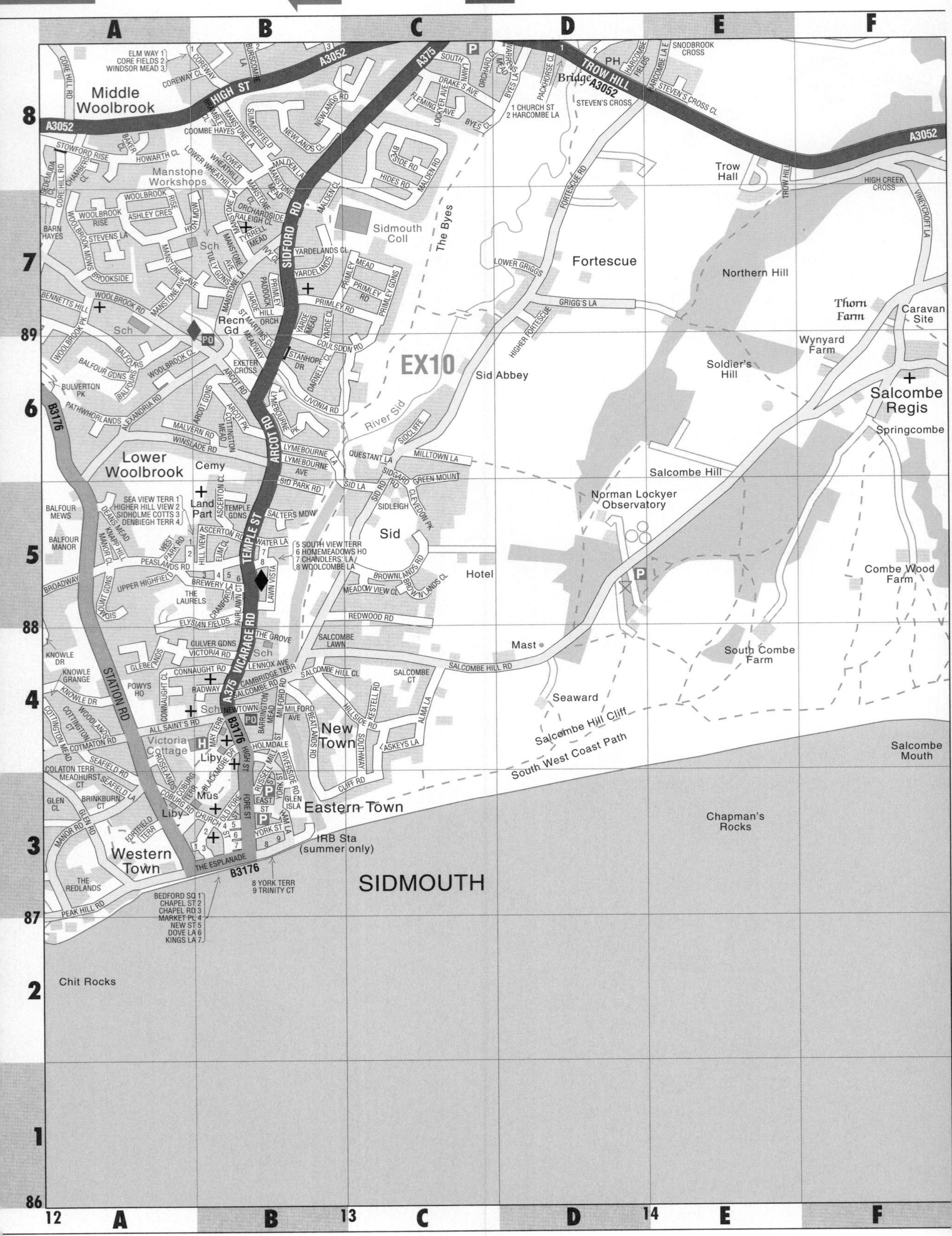
Middle Woolbrook
HIGH ST
A3052
A375
TROW HILL
Trow Hall
Manstone Workshops
Sidmouth Coll
The Byes
SIDFORD RD
Fortescue
Northern Hill
Thorn Farm
Caravan Site
Wynyard Farm
Recn Gd
EX10
Sid Abbey
Soldier's Hill
Salcombe Regis
Springcombe
ARCOT RD
River Sid
Lower Woolbrook
Cemy
Salcombe Hill
Norman Lockyer Observatory
Land Part
TEMPLE ST
Sid
Hotel
Combe Wood Farm
VICARAGE RD
STATION RD
Mast
SALCOMBE HILL RD
South Combe Farm
Seaward
Salcombe Hill Cliff
South West Coast Path
Victoria Cottage
New Town
Salcombe Mouth
Eastern Town
Chapman's Rocks
IRB Sta (summer only)
Western Town
THE ESPLANADE
B3176
SIDMOUTH
Chit Rocks

187

101
190
A
B
C
D
E
F
A3052
Orleigh's Hill
GATEDOWN LA
Bulstone
The Bulstone
Ashton
WESTON CROSS
NORTHERN LA
PACCOMBE POOL LA
Trow Farm
MIRE LA
The Donkey Sanctuary
EX12
Coxe's Farm
Trow
DUNSCOMBE LA
Slade House Farm
SLADE LA
STONELEIGH
Caravan Park
LUGSMOOR LA
GRAMMAR LA
Weston
Higher Weston Farm
Dunscombe Manor Farm
Manor House
(rems of)
Lower Weston Farm
EX10
Dunscombe
Caravan Park
Littlecombe Barn
Daw's Weston
Weston Combe
Dunscombe Coppice
Lincombe
South West Coast Path
Weston Cliff
Coxe's Cliff
Lower Dunscombe Cliff
Weston Mouth
Higher Dunscombe Cliff
Weston Ebb
Hook Ebb
8
7
89
6
5
88
4
3
87
2
1
86
15
16
17
190

101
102

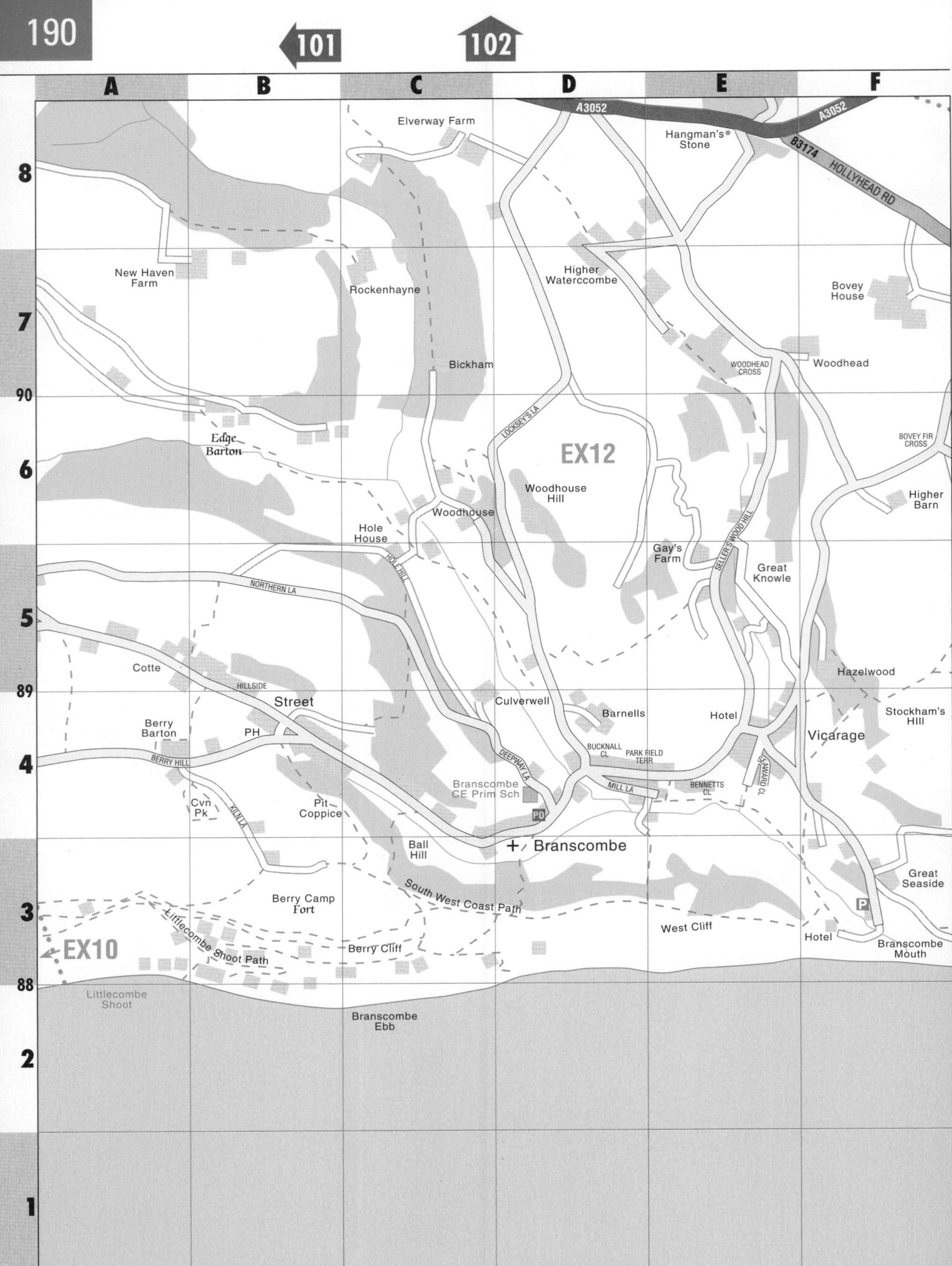
A
B
C
D
E
F
8
7
90
6
5
89
4
3
88
2
1
87
18
19
20
A3052
A3052
B3174
HOLLYHEAD RD
Elverway Farm
Hangman's Stone
New Haven Farm
Rockenhayne
Higher Waterccombe
Bovey House
Bickham
WOODHEAD CROSS
Woodhead
LOCKSEY'S LA
EX12
BOVEY FIR CROSS
Edge Barton
Woodhouse Hill
Higher Barn
Woodhouse
Hole House
HOLE HILL
Gay's Farm
SELLER'S WOOD HILL
Great Knowle
NORTHERN LA
Cotte
Hazelwood
HILLSIDE
Street
Culverwell
Barnells
Hotel
Stockham's Hill
Berry Barton
PH
Vicarage
BERRY HILL
BUCKNALL CL
PARK FIELD TERR
DEEPWAY LA
SEAWARD CL
MILL LA
BENNETTS CL
Branscombe CE Prim Sch
Cvn Pk
KILN LA
Pit Coppice
PO
Ball Hill
Branscombe
Great Seaside
South West Coast Path
Berry Camp Fort
P
West Cliff
Littlecombe Shoot Path
Hotel
EX10
Berry Cliff
Branscombe Mouth
Littlecombe Shoot
Branscombe Ebb

189

102
192

A
B
C
D
E
F
EX24
EX12
HOLLYHEAD RD
GATCOMBE LA
Couchill Farm
HOLLYHEAD CROSS
BOVEY LA
STOVAR LONG LA
PAIZEN LA
B3174
COURT BARTON HILL
PEAZEN FLATS
RATTENBURY COTTS
BERRY LA
NEW RD
TOWNSEND
QUARRY COTTS
QUARRY LA
ASH HILL CT
CAUSEWAY
LONG HILL
Beer CE Prim Sch
Beer Quarry Caves
Pecorama Pleasure Gdns
Beer Heights Light Rly
Cemy
BARLINE
CLAPP'S LA
HIGHER MDWS
THE MEADOWS
LANEHEAD RD
MARE LA
UNDERLEYS
WEST UNDERLEYS
PARK RD
SOUTHDOWN CL
SOUTH DOWN RD
COMMON LA
SEA HILL
SEA VIEW TERR
Beer Roads
Beer
MAIN CUT
FORE ST
CHURCH HILL
CLINTON RISE
Mast
HIGHFIELD TERR 1
MARMORA TERR 2
GORDON TERR 3
ROSE COTTS 4
PIONEER COTTS 5
WEST VIEW 6
THE SQUARE 7
BARNARDS FARM 8
BERRY HILL 9
COMMON HILL
LITTLE LA
BEER HEAD CVN PK
Friar's Park Farm
South Down Farm
Mast
Arratt's Hill
The Hall
South Down Common
South West Coast Path
East Cliff
Hookend Cliff
Under Hookend
Hookend Beach
Sherborne Rocks
Beer Head
B3176
SEATON DOWN HILL
ROMAN WAY
VENBOROUGH CL
CONSTANTINE CL
HONEYDITCHES DR
BOSWELL WAY
UPPER CHURSTON RISE
CHURSTON RISE
SEATON DOWN CL
AUGUSTINE CL
STOWFORD HTS
ALBION CL
TRACEYS AVE
LYDGATES RD
HOMER LA
COUCHILL LA
COUCHILL DR
MERROW DOWN DR
SEATON DOWN RD
MARLPIT LA
GREENWAY
FREMINGTON RD
MARLPIT CL
BUNTS LA
WEST ACRES
DURLEY RD
ALLEYN CT
PADDOCK
SANDS CT
HIGHCLIFFE CRES
WESSITERS
BEER RD
B3174
HIGHCLIFFE CL
HIGHCLYFFE CT
SEAFORTH LODGE
OLD BEER RD
THE GLEN
BEER HILL
Seaton Hole
8
7
90
6
5
89
4
3
88
2
1
87
21
22
23

192

102
103

A
B
C
D
E
F
8
7
91
6
5
90
4
3
89
2
1
88
24
25
26
HAREPATH HILL A3052
A3052
St Dympna's
SEATON RD
COMMON LA
EX24
Axe Marsh
Axmouth Marsh
B3172
Stedcombe Farm
Stedcombe House
Stedcombe Wood
Cemy
Hawkesdown Hill
Seaton & District Electric Tramway
EX12
Axe Farm
POUND HILL
Axmouth
PH
BROOK TERR
CHURCH ST
SOUTHCOOMBE TERR
HIGHER LA
Higher Barn
STEPPS CROSS
GLENWATER CL
COOMBE ORCH
HIGHER AXMOUTH COTTS
Haven Farm
Seaton Prim Sch
Seaton & District
Sewage Works
Seaton Marshes
Parsonage Barn
AXMOUTH RD
Nature Reserve
SEATON
EX12
STEPPS LA
Haven Ball
BARN CLOSE LA
South West Coast Path
STONY CLOSE LA
LYME BAY HOLIDAY VILLAGE
Riverside Workshops
OLD COASTGUARD STA
CH
SQUIRE'S LA
Axmouth Bridge
Haven Higher Barn
Haven Cliff
HARBOUR RD
B3172
B3174
BEER RD
THE SHORELINE
ESPLANADE
Seaton Beach
South West Coast Path
Seaton Bay
Sparrowbush Ledge
QUEEN ST
FORE ST
MANOR RD
THE UNDERFLEET
SEATON DOWN RD
Liby
TH
A4
1 SUNSET HO
2 WEST CLIFF TERR
A5
1 MANOR CL
2 MAJOR TERR
3 THE AVENUE
4 WOODBINE PL
5 BELMONT HO
6 TANYARDS CT
7 THE SQUARE
B4
1 THE BURROW
2 FOSSE WAY CT
3 HOMEBAYE HO
4 HARBOUR CT
5 LYME MEWS
6 BAY CT

191

A
B
C
D
E
F
A3052
BOSHILL HILL
WESTHAYES CVN PK
EX13
Stedcombe Wood
Heathfield Farm
HEATHFIELD CROSS
COMBPYNE LA
Green Lane Farm
GREEN LA
8
GREEN LA
Rousdon
PEEK MEAD
SCHOOL LA
Hotel
A3052
7
Pit Orchard
BUSHES LA
LEGGETTS LA
91
Chadstone
SPRINGHEAD CROSS
DT7
FARM RD
6
Home Farm
COMBE RD
EX12
Bindon
THE GARDENS
Dowlands
5
STEPPS LA
90
4
The Landslip
South West Coast Path
Dowlands Cliffs and Landslips
Culverhole Point
3
89
2
1
88
27
A
B
28
C
D
29
E
F

114
182

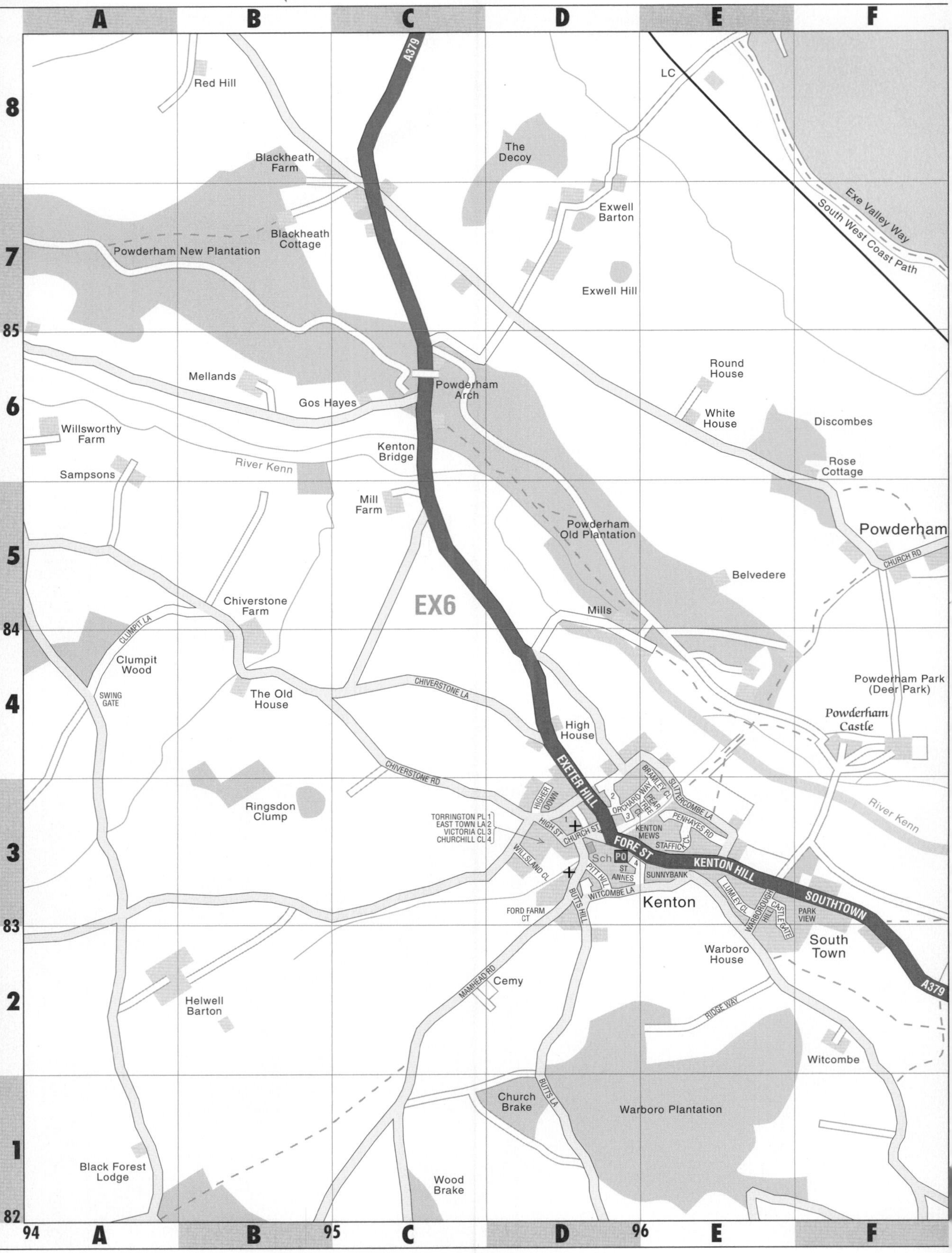

A B C D E F

8 7 85 6 5 84 4 3 83 2 1 82

A379
Red Hill
LC
The Decoy
Blackheath Farm
Exwell Barton
Exe Valley Way
South West Coast Path
Blackheath Cottage
Powderham New Plantation
Exwell Hill
Round House
Mellands
Powderham Arch
Gos Hayes
White House
Discombes
Willsworthy Farm
Kenton Bridge
Rose Cottage
River Kenn
Sampsons
Mill Farm
Powderham Old Plantation
Powderham
CHURCH RD
Belvedere
EX6
Chiverstone Farm
Mills
CLUMPIT LA
Clumpit Wood
SWING GATE
The Old House
CHIVERSTONE LA
Powderham Park (Deer Park)
Powderham Castle
High House
CHIVERSTONE RD
EXETER HILL
HIGHER DOWN
BRAMLEY CL
SLITTERCOMBE LA
ORCHARD WAY
PEAR TREE CL
PENHAYES RD
Ringsdon Clump
River Kenn
TORRINGTON PL 1
EAST TOWN LA 2
VICTORIA CL 3
CHURCHILL CL 4
HIGH ST
CHURCH ST
KENTON MEWS
STAFFICK
FORE ST
Sch
PO
KENTON HILL
WILLSLAND CL
PITT HILL
ST ANNES
SUNNYBANK
WITCOMBE LA
Kenton
SOUTHTOWN
LUMLEY CL
WARBOROUGH HILL
CASTLE GATE
PARK VIEW
FORD FARM CT
BUTTS HILL
Warboro House
South Town
MAMHEAD RD
Cemy
Helwell Barton
RIDGE WAY
Witcombe
Church Brake
BUTTS LA
Warboro Plantation
Black Forest Lodge
Wood Brake

94 95 96

114
200

183
196

201
196

195
184
A
B
C
D
E
F
8
7
85
6
5
84
4
3
83
2
1
82
00
01
02
Woodmanton
Higher Mallocks
EX5
STONY LA
CONIGER CROSS
B3180
Blackhill Quarry
Black Hill
Resr
Blackhill House
HAREFIELD RD
TEDSTONE LA
Tedstone House
Coombe Farm
Lower Coombe Farm
Wotton Brook
Coombe Brake Cottage
Coombe Plantation
East Devon Way
Squabmoor
Lympstone Common
Moorland Cottage
EXE VIEW RD
Exe View House
Horseshoe Cottage
St Peter's Sch
B3179
WRIGHT'S LA
Wotton Farm
Wotton House
Wotton Bridge
WOTTON POUND
WOTTON LA
MARLEY DR
Bystock Wood
Marley Hayes
Big Wood
A376
EXMOUTH RD
Potter's Farm
MARLEY
Goodmores Farm
EX8
HIGHER MARLEY RD
DORCHESTER WAY
Pitt Farm
EXMOUTH
Great Wood
ST JOHN'S RD
Withycombe Barton
SUMMER LA
Manse
POINT IN VIEW COTTS
COURTLANDS LA
COURTLANDS CROSS
A-la Ronde
Bystock Court
BYSTOCK MEWS
THE MEWS
ST JOHNS FARM MEWS
Brixington
WESTMINSTER CL
DINAN WAY
Hulham
PARKSIDE DR
SILVERDALE WAY
Briar Patch
Lower Veiges Plantation
Jun & Inf Sch
BRIXINGTON LA
SEAFIELD AVE
THORNFIELD CL
HULHAM RD
EXETER RD
Withycombe Raleigh
ST JOHN'S RD
Withycombe Brook
Schs
Liverton Bsns Pk
Thorntree Bsns Units
Withycombe Raleigh CE Prim Sch
Pound La Trad Est
Dinan Way Trad Est
SALTERTON RD
B3178
MUDBANK LA
BELLE VUE RD
WITHYCOMBE VILLAGE RD
BRACKENWOOD
BROOKLYN PK
1 MASEY RD
2 NEWLANDS AVE
3 CAROLINE CL
DUKE OF CORNWALL CL 1
PRINCE CHARLES CL 2
SOVEREIGN CL 3
PARTHIA PL 4
SENATE CT 5
HADRIANS WAY
PRINCE OF WALES DR
HOLLAND RD
CHUDLEY CL
BROOKLANDS RD
HALSDON AVE
HIGHBURY PK
CARBERRY AVE
CROSSINGFIELDS DR
PHILLIPPS AVE
GRANGE AVE
SPRINGFIELD RD
BAPTON LA
POUND LA
LANGSTONE DR
HUMPHRIES PK
WILLMOTT CL
CHERISWOOD AVE
NASMITH CL
SOMERVILLE CL
ADMIRALS WLK
BURCH CL
CHESHIRE RD
SOUTHERN WOOD
SYCAMORE CL
ASHFIELD CL
PINE VIEW CL
MEADOWVIEW RD
FIR TREE CL
BROADMEAD
RICHARDS CL
ELLWOOD RD
MARIONS WAY
SPENCER CL
WINSTON RD
MARLBOROUGH CL
EVERGREEN CL
GLOUCESTER RD
SHERWOOD DR
OAKWOOD RISE
VALLEY WAY
LITTLE MDW
IVYDALE
BOOTH WAY
GRENVILLE RD
SCOTT DR
THE MARLES
ELIZABETH RD
FEATHERBED LA
SEYMOUR RD
ROUNDHOUSE LA
RIVERMEAD AVE
LAMPLOUGH RD
WOODLANDS DR
MOUNT PLEASANT AVE
SWISS CL
APRIL CL
WORDSWORTH CL
KEATS CL
SHAKESPEARE WAY
COLERIDGE CL
BRACKENDALE
MARLEY RD
GORSE LA
CHAUCER RISE
SPIDER'S LA
LIME GR
VANSITTART DR
HOLLYMOUNT CL
PINES RD
CEDAR CL
PO

195
202

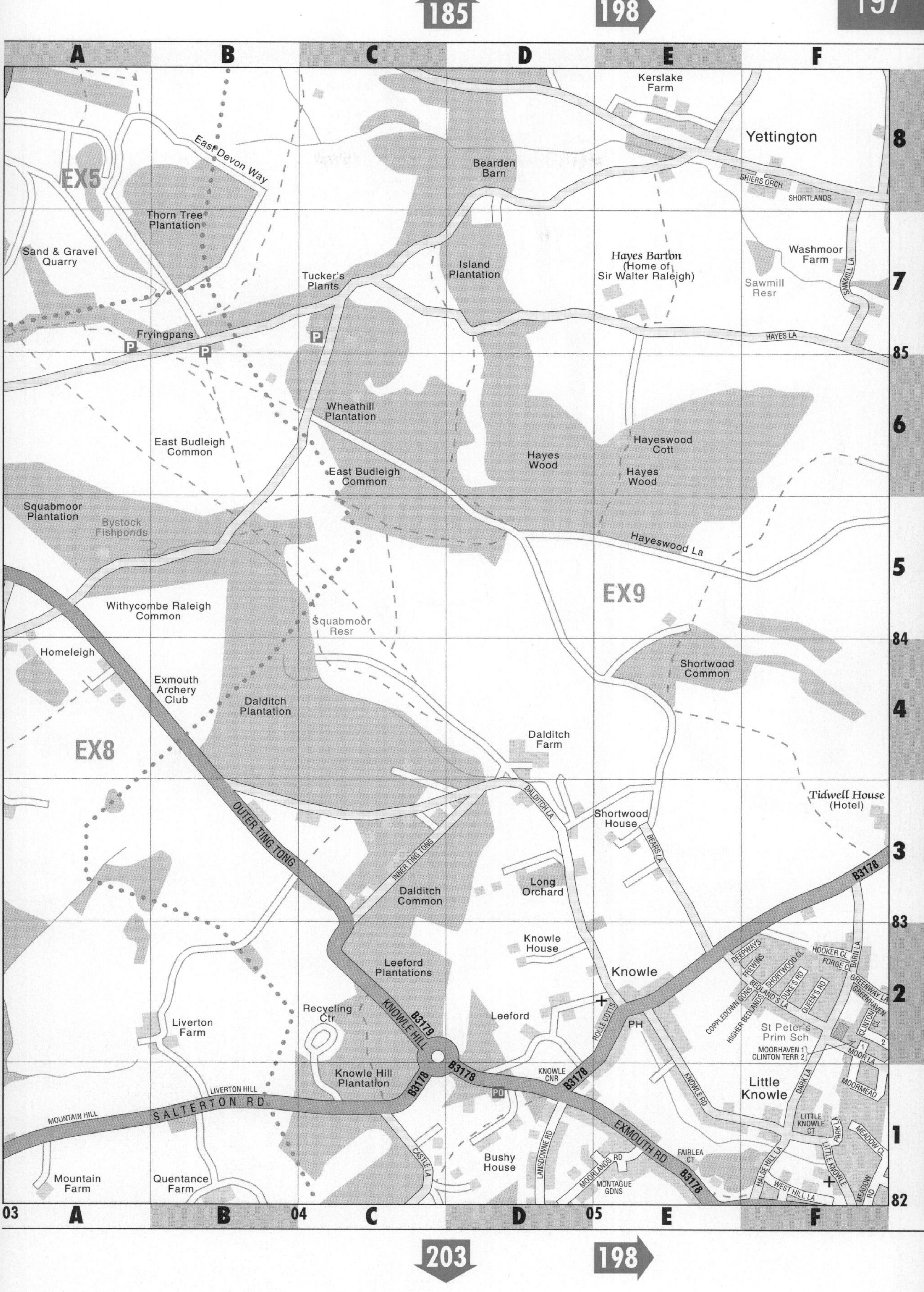
185
198
A
B
C
D
E
F
Kerslake Farm
Yettington
East Devon Way
EX5
Bearden Barn
SHIERS ORCH
SHORTLANDS
Thorn Tree Plantation
Sand & Gravel Quarry
Hayes Barton
(Home of Sir Walter Raleigh)
Washmoor Farm
Island Plantation
Tucker's Plants
Sawmill Resr
SAWMILL LA
Fryingpans
HAYES LA
Wheathill Plantation
East Budleigh Common
Hayeswood Cott
Hayes Wood
East Budleigh Common
Hayes Wood
Squabmoor Plantation
Bystock Fishponds
Hayeswood La
EX9
Withycombe Raleigh Common
Squabmoor Resr
Homeleigh
Shortwood Common
Exmouth Archery Club
Dalditch Plantation
EX8
Dalditch Farm
DALDITCH LA
Tidwell House (Hotel)
Shortwood House
OUTER TING TONG
BEARS LA
INNER TING TONG
Long Orchard
B3178
Dalditch Common
Knowle House
Leeford Plantations
Knowle
DEEPWAYS
FREWINS
HOOKER CL
FORGE CL
BARN LA
GREENWAY LA
GREENHAVEN
COPPLEDOWN GDNS
HIGHER BEDLANDS
BEDLANDS LA
SHORTWOOD CL
DUKE'S RD
QUEEN'S RD
Recycling Ctr
Leeford
ROLLE COTTS
PH
St Peter's Prim Sch
MOORHAVEN 1
CLINTON TERR 2
CLINTON CL
MOOR LA
KNOWLE HILL
B3179
Liverton Farm
Knowle Hill Plantation
B3178
KNOWLE CNR
B3178
KNOWLE RD
Little Knowle
DARK LA
MOORMEAD
LIVERTON HILL
PO
LITTLE KNOWLE CT
PARK LA
MEADOW CL
MOUNTAIN HILL
SALTERTON RD
EXMOUTH RD
FAIRLEA CT
CASTLE LA
LANSDOWNE RD
Bushy House
MOORLANDS RD
HALSE HILL LA
LITTLE KNOWLE
Mountain Farm
Quentance Farm
MONTAGUE GDNS
B3178
WEST HILL LA
MEADOW RD
8
7
85
6
5
84
4
3
83
2
1
82
03
04
05
203
198

197
186

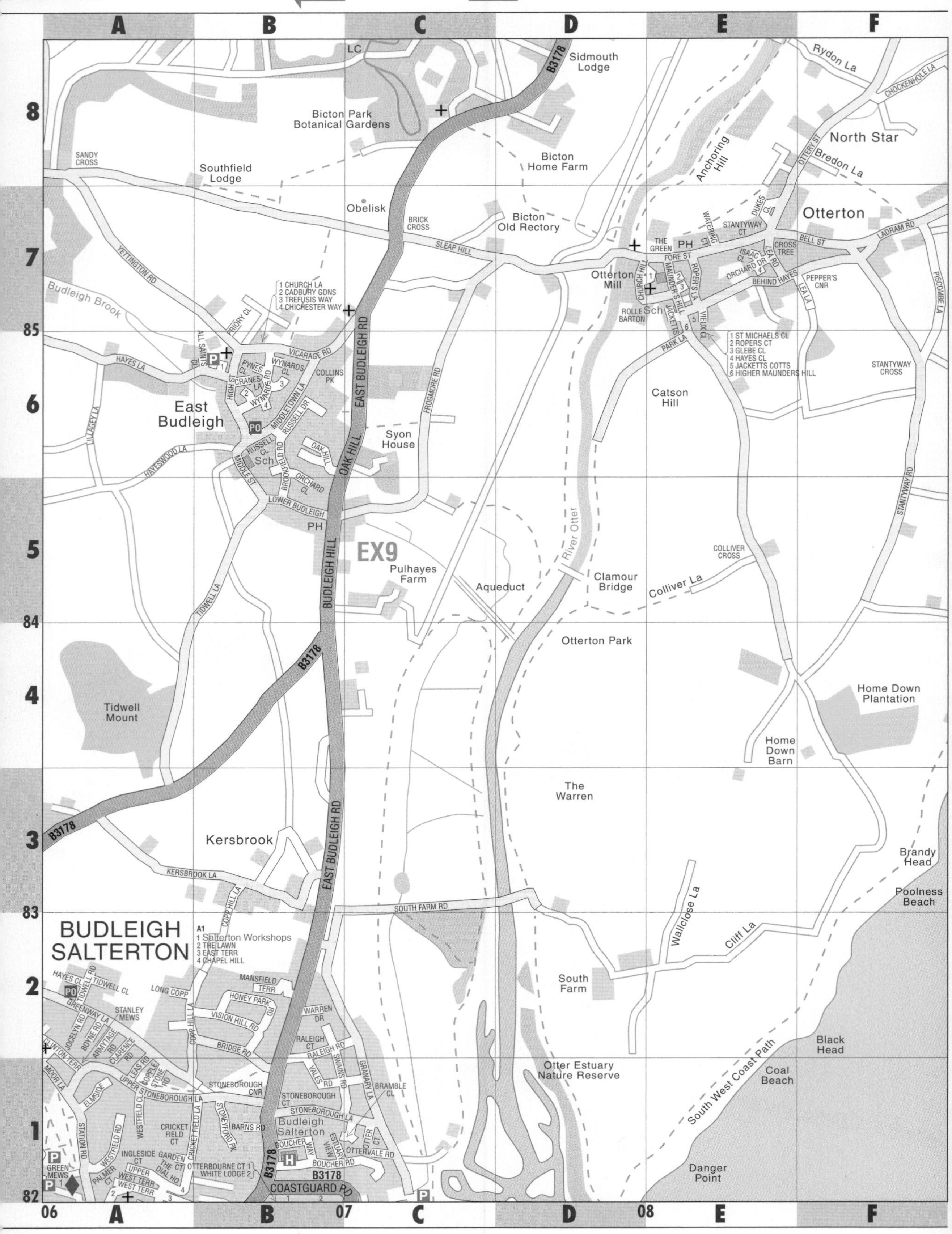
Sidmouth Lodge
Bicton Park Botanical Gardens
Bicton Home Farm
Southfield Lodge
Obelisk
Bicton Old Rectory
North Star
Otterton
Otterton Mill
East Budleigh
Syon House
Catson Hill
EX9
Pulhayes Farm
Aqueduct
Clamour Bridge
Colliver La
Otterton Park
Tidwell Mount
Home Down Plantation
Home Down Barn
The Warren
Kersbrook
Brandy Head
Poolness Beach
BUDLEIGH SALTERTON
South Farm
Black Head
Coal Beach
Otter Estuary Nature Reserve
South West Coast Path
Danger Point
Budleigh Salterton
River Otter
Budleigh Brook

197

187

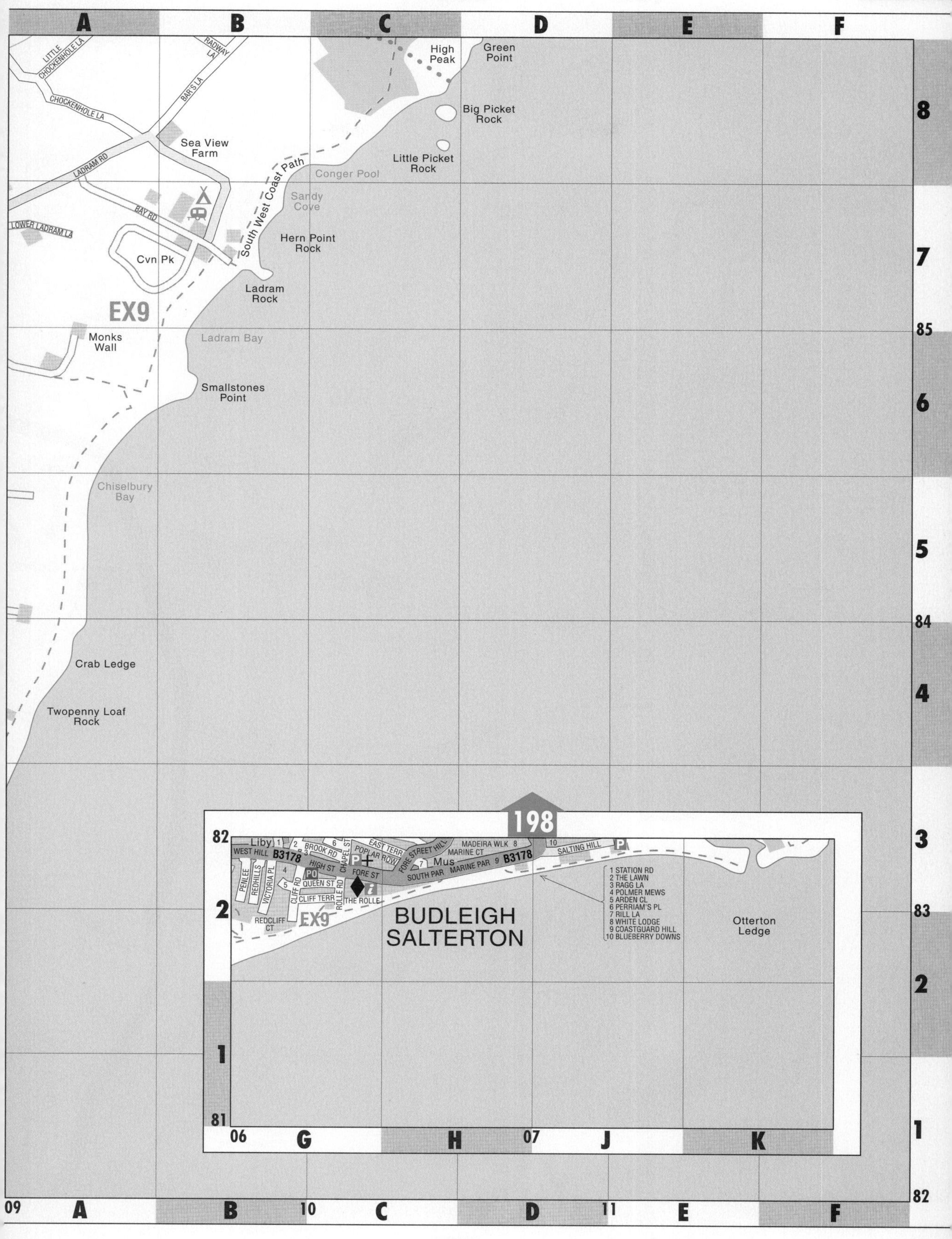

High Peak
Green Point
Big Picket Rock
Little Picket Rock
Sea View Farm
Conger Pool
Sandy Cove
South West Coast Path
Hern Point Rock
Cvn Pk
Ladram Rock
EX9
Monks Wall
Ladram Bay
Smallstones Point
Chiselbury Bay
Crab Ledge
Twopenny Loaf Rock
LITTLE CHOCKENHOLE LA
CHOCKENHOLE LA
RADWAY LA
BAR'S LA
LADRAM RD
BAY RD
LOWER LADRAM LA
198
BUDLEIGH SALTERTON
Otterton Ledge
WEST HILL
B3178
BROOK RD
EAST TERR
POPLAR ROW
FORE STREET HILL
MADEIRA WLK
MARINE CT
SALTING HILL
HIGH ST
CHAPEL ST
FORE ST
SOUTH PAR
MARINE PAR
QUEEN ST
CLIFF TERR
THE ROLLE
PENLEE
REDHILLS
VICTORIA PL
CLIFF RD
ROLLE RD
REDCLIFF CT
Liby
Mus
PO
1 STATION RD
2 THE LAWN
3 RAGG LA
4 POLMER MEWS
5 ARDEN CL
6 PERRIAM'S PL
7 RILL LA
8 WHITE LODGE
9 COASTGUARD HILL
10 BLUEBERRY DOWNS

124
194

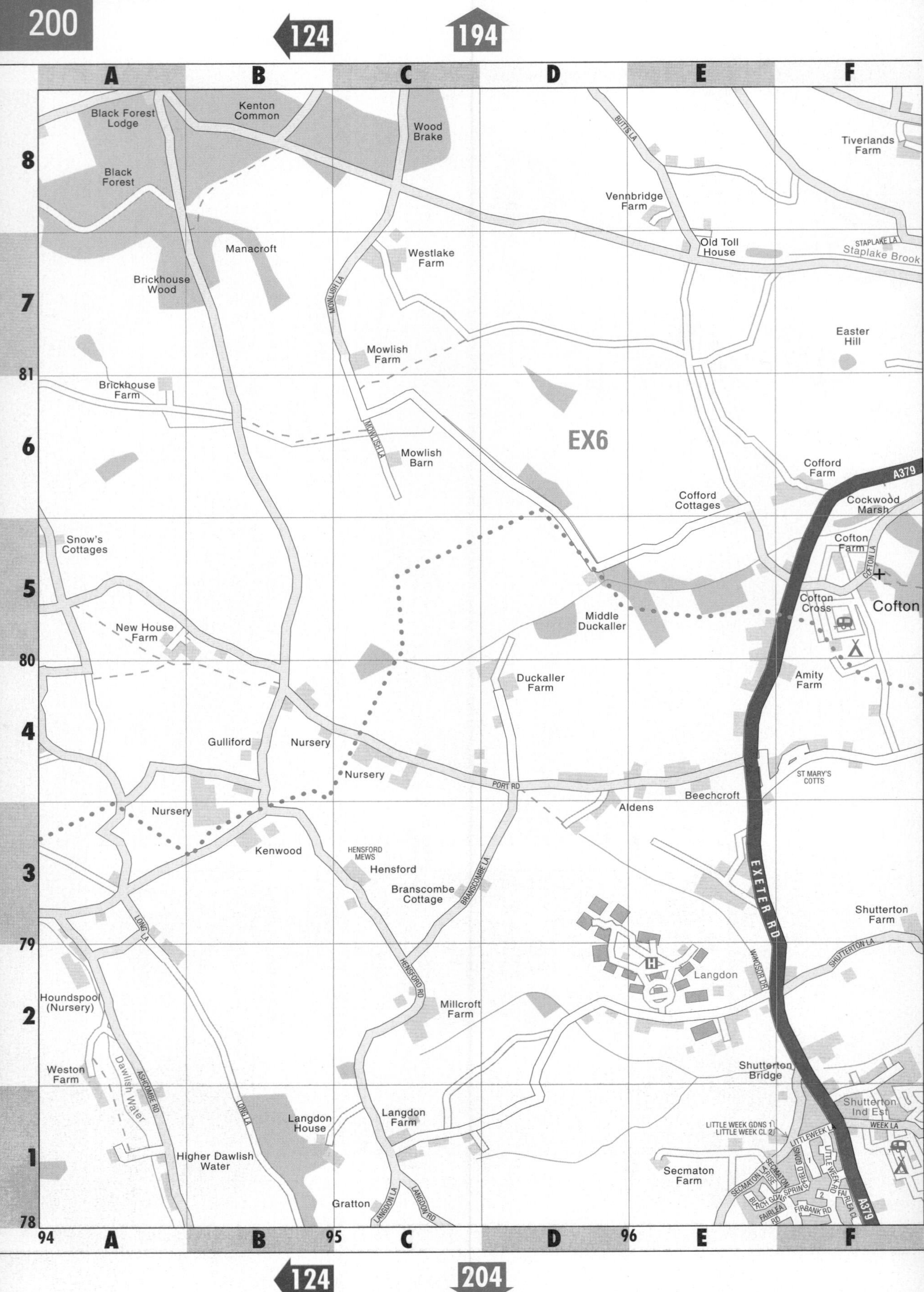

124
204

195
202
A
B
C
D
E
F
Starcross
A379
Jetty
DREW'S CL 1
COOKSON'S RD 2
BRUNEL RD 3
COURTENAY TERR 4
WARBORO TERR 5
CORONATION TERR 6
CHURCH FLATS 7
CHAPPLE CL 8
BISHOPS CL 9
Prim Sch
Staplake
STAPLAKE LA
Old Staplake Farm
GENERALS LA
THE STRAND
River Exe
East Devon Way
Exmouth
Sports Ctr
The Point
EX8
TRINITY RD 1
SCHOONERS CT 2
ROPEWALK HO 3
SAILMAKERS CT 4
CLIPPER WHARF 5
WINDJAMMER CT 6
PENNANT HO 7
MADISON WHARF 8
PIER HEAD 9
SHELLEY CT 10
MAMHEAD VIEW 11
THE MOORINGS 12
Dock
LB Sta
ESPLANADE
ALSTON TERR 1
MORTON CRESCENT MEWS 2
ST ANDREWS HO 3
CLINTON SQ 4
SHARPS CT 5
HARBOUR CT 6
SHELLY REACH 7
ELM GR 8
MANCHESTER ST 9
MANCHESTER RD 10
CLEVELAND PL 11
Southbrook
PH
CHURCH RD
Cockwood Prim Sch
Westwood
Ferry P (summer only)
Cockwood
South West Coast Path
Eastdon
ORCHARD LA
DAWLISH WARREN RD
Eastdon Wood
Eastdon House
Dawlish Warren
Nature Reserve
Dawlish Sands Holiday Park
SHUTTERTON LA
Visitor Ctr
CH
Dawlish Welcome Holiday Park
Dawlish Warren
First Aid Post
Holiday Ctr
Golden Sands Holiday Park
Dawlish Warren
WEEK LA
MOUNT PLEASANT RD
BEACH RD
Langstone Cliff Hotel
8
7
81
6
5
80
4
3
79
2
1
78
97
98
99
205
202

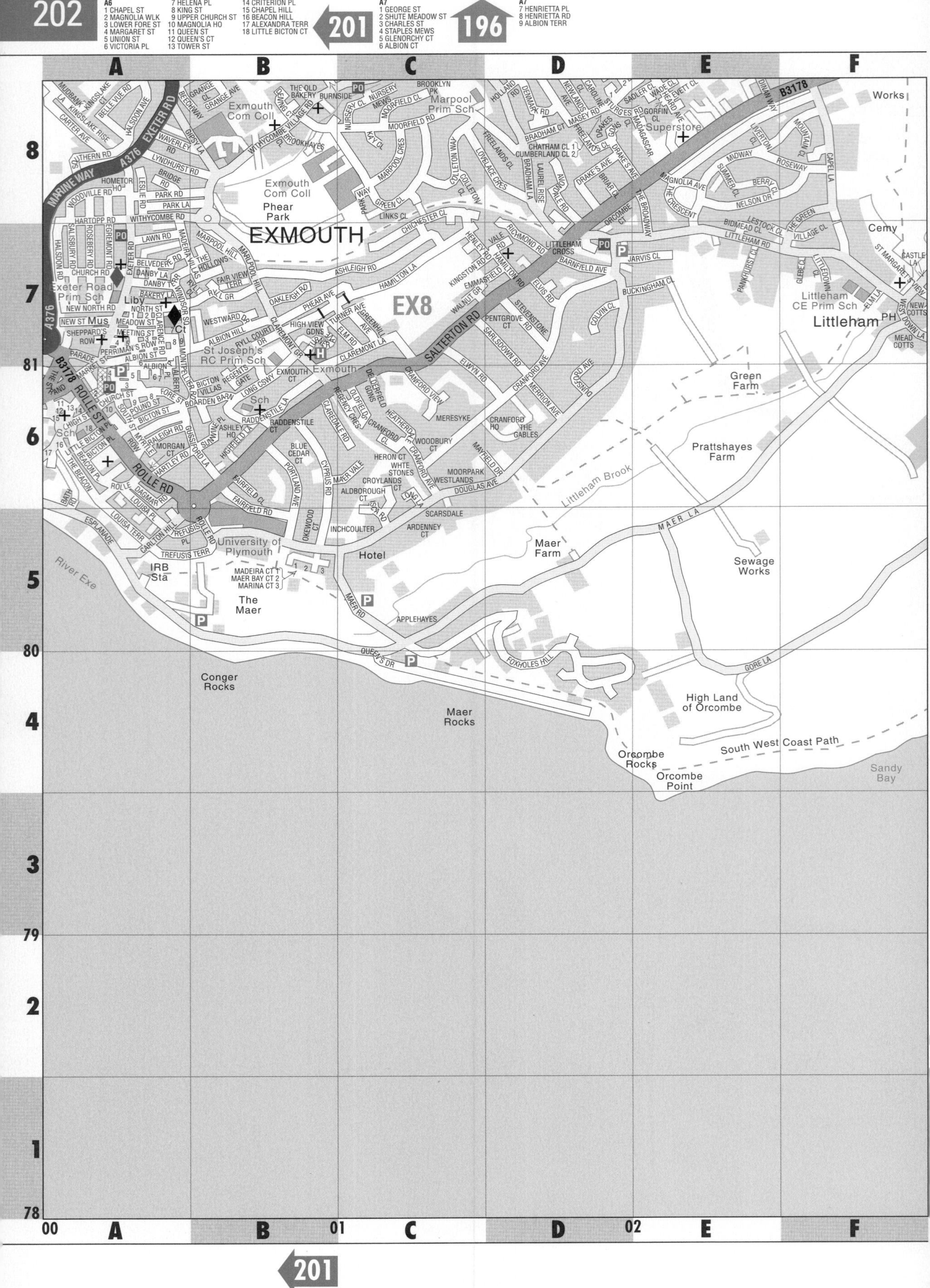
A
B
C
D
E
F
8
7
81
6
5
80
4
3
79
2
1
78
00
01
02
EXMOUTH
EX8
Exmouth Com Coll
Phear Park
Marpool Prim Sch
Superstore
Works
Cemy
Littleham CE Prim Sch
Littleham
Exeter Road Prim Sch
St Joseph's RC Prim Sch
Exmouth
University of Plymouth
Hotel
IRB Sta
The Maer
Maer Farm
Green Farm
Prattshayes Farm
Sewage Works
Littleham Brook
River Exe
Conger Rocks
Maer Rocks
High Land of Orcombe
South West Coast Path
Orcombe Rocks
Orcombe Point
Sandy Bay
MARINE WAY
EXETER RD
A376
B3178
ROLLE ST
ROLLE RD
SALTERTON RD
ESPLANADE
QUEEN'S DR
MAER LA
MAER RD
GORE LA
FOXHOLES HILL
LITTLEHAM RD
DOUGLAS AVE
APPLEHAYES

A
B
C
D
E
F
Quentance Farm
Knowle Hill Plantations
LANSDOWNE RD
West Down
WEST HILL
B3178
WOODLANDS
WEST HILL CT
SHERBROOK HILL
FOUNTAIN HILL
WESTBOURNE TERR
LINKS RD
SHERBROOK CL
NORTHVIEW RD
EX9
CH
Littleham Brook
CASTLE LA
CASTLE COTTS
West Down Beacon
South West Coast Path
Woodlands Farm
ST MARGARET'S VIEW
RODNEY CL
EX8
WEST DOWN LA
World of Country Life
The Floors
Crowden Point
ORCHARD CL
West Down Farm
MEADOW CRES
GORE LA
WEST DOWN VIEW
CEDARS
DEVON CLIFFS HOLIDAY PARK
Littleham Cove
DANGER AREA
Otter Cove
DANGER AREA
Sandy Bay
Straght Point Rifle Range
DANGER AREA
Straight Point
8
7
81
6
5
80
4
3
79
2
1
78
03
04
05

124
200
D6
1 PENFIELD GDNS
2 RED LION PL
3 SIDNEY CT
4 HOOPERN TERR
5 FREDERICK TERR
6 SCHOOL HILL
7 QUEEN LA
8 STOCKTON LA
9 HATCHER ST
10 BLACKSWAN PL
11 LUSCOMBE TERR
12 PRIORY PARK RD
13 HALDON TERR
14 ORCHARD GDNS
15 PRINCES ST
16 KING ST
17 ALBERT ST
18 TOWN TREE HILL
19 GOLDEN TERR
20 OLD MANOR CT
21 BROOKLANDS
22 LAWN TERR
23 ALEXANDER RD
A
B
C
D
E
F
8
7
77
6
5
76
4
3
75
2
1
74
94
95
96
EX7
TQ14
DAWLISH
Rixdale Farm
Radfords
Ford
Fairfield House
The Rise
Luscombe Castle
Luscombe Park
Dawlish Water
Westcote
Gatehouse Farm
Gatehouse Prim Sch
Pathfields Nursery
Dawlish Com Coll
L Ctr
Aller Farm
Oakland Park Sch
Ratcliffe Sch
Cemy
Holcombe Farm
Westbrook
Oakleigh Farm
The Smugglers Inn (PH)
Holcombe
Caravan Pk
East Down
Hole Head
The Parson and Clerk
Higher Holcombe House
Higher Holcombe Farm
Middle Holcombe House
Abbey
Coryton's Cove
Horse Cove
Breakwater
Dawlish
South West Coast Path
TEIGNMOUTH RD
TEIGNMOUTH HILL
EXETER RD
DAWLISH RD
A379
LEYFIELD WLK 1
WESTERN HO 2
SWALLOWS ACRE 3
STANMORE RISE 4
HIGH HOUSE CL 5
KINGSDOWN CL 6
STONELANDS CT 1
STONELANDS TERR 2
STONELANDS MEWS 3
CHURCH VIEW 4
TOWN MILLS 5
E6
1 PRIORY GDNS
2 PRIORY HILL
3 LAWN HILL
4 MALTING CT
5 BELVEDERE CT
6 CARLTON TERR
7 LEIGHAM CT
8 CLEVELAND PL
9 COMMERCIAL RD
10 IDDESLEIGH TERR
11 WHITE CT
12 BEACH ST
13 MARINERS CT
14 RICHMOND CT
15 RICHMOND PL
16 BRUNEL CT
17 STATION RD
18 BROOKDALE TERR
19 CLIFF CT
20 MEWS CT
21 ST MARKS
22 SHAFTESBURY CL
23 SEFTON CT
1 SUNNYLANDS WAY
2 HOLCOMBE CROSS
210
124
210

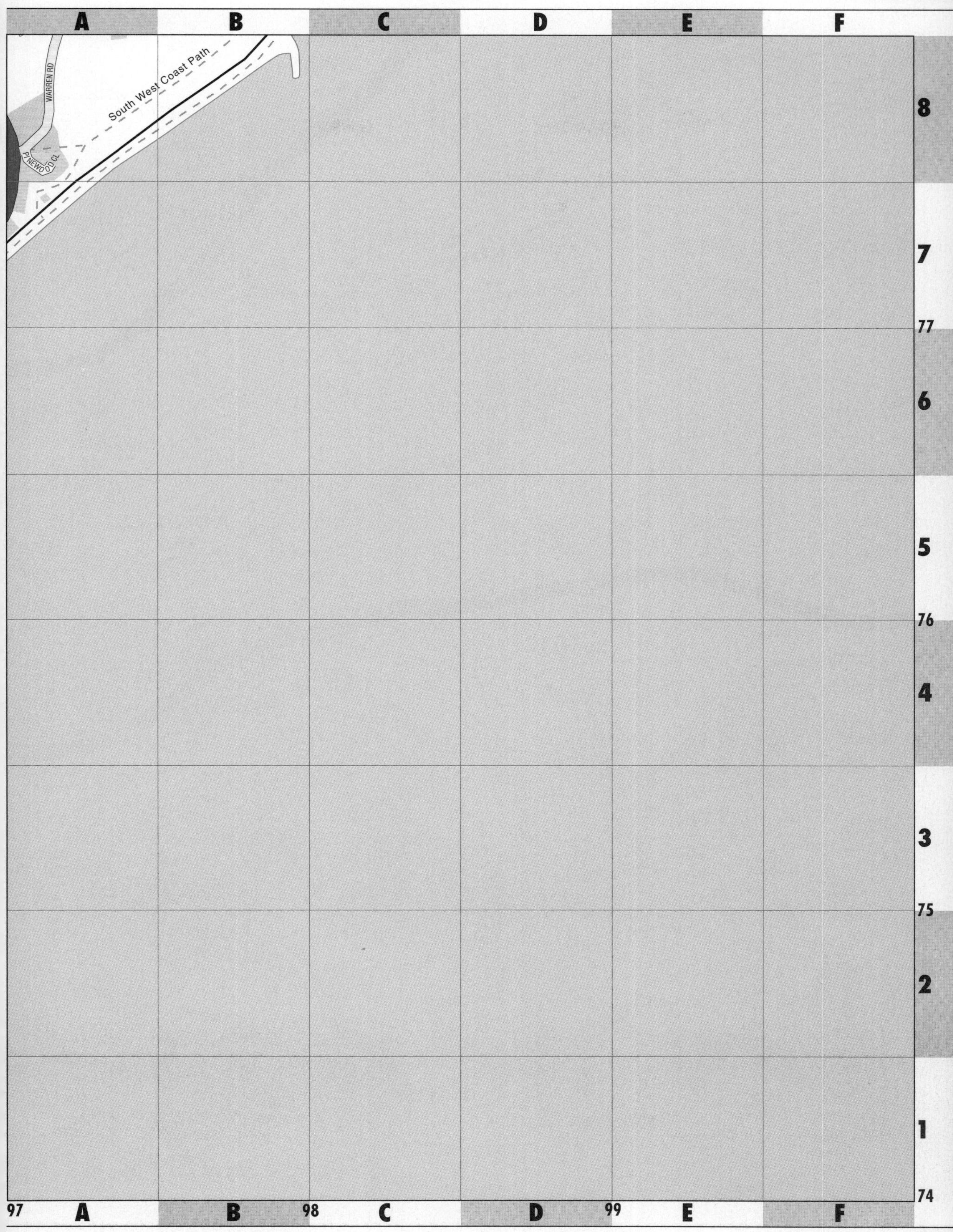
A
B
C
D
E
F
WARREN RD
South West Coast Path
PINEWOOD CL
8
7
77
6
5
76
4
3
75
2
1
74
97
98
99

131
123

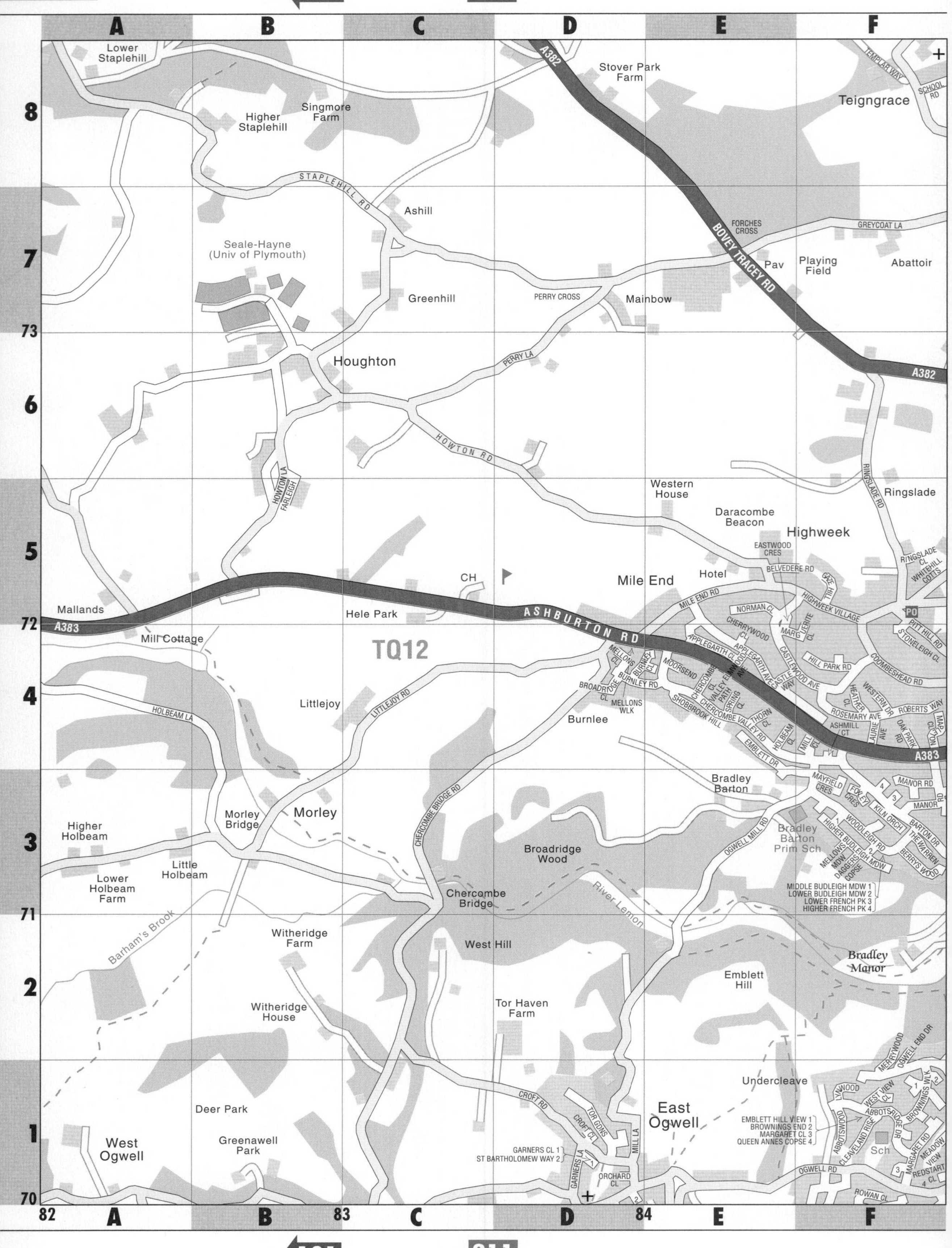

131
211

123
208

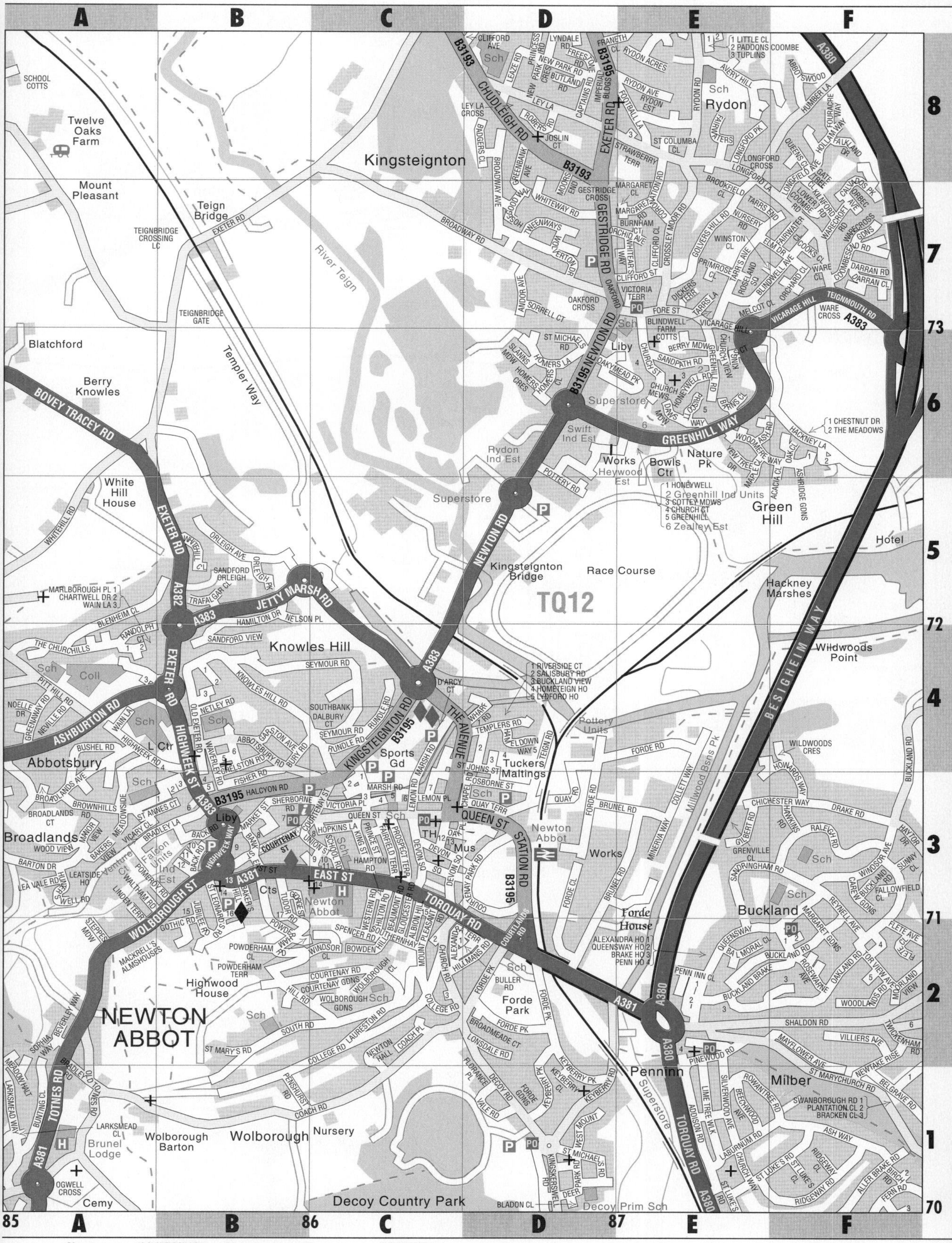
A
B
C
D
E
F
8
7
73
6
5
72
4
3
71
2
1
70
85
86
87
Twelve Oaks Farm
Mount Pleasant
Teign Bridge
Kingsteignton
Rydon
Blatchford
Berry Knowles
White Hill House
River Teign
Templer Way
Knowles Hill
Abbotsbury
Broadlands
NEWTON ABBOT
Highwood House
Wolborough Barton
Wolborough
Nursery
Brunel Lodge
Cemy
OGWELL CROSS
Decoy Country Park
Decoy Prim Sch
Forde Park
Forde House
Newton Abbot
Penninn
Milber
Buckland
Green Hill
Hackney Marshes
Wildwoods Point
Hotel
Race Course
TQ12
Kingsteignton Bridge
Superstore
Rydon Ind Est
Swift Ind Est
Works
Heywood Est
Bowls Ctr
Nature Pk
Tuckers Maltings
Pottery Units
Sports Gd
Millwood Bsns Pk
BESIGHEIM WAY
BOVEY TRACEY RD
ASHBURTON RD
EXETER RD
JETTY MARSH RD
NEWTON RD
GREENHILL WAY
TORQUAY RD
TOTNES RD
WOLBOROUGH ST
EAST ST
QUEEN ST
STATION RD
THE AVENUE
KINGSTEIGNTON RD
HALCYON RD
CHUDLEIGH RD
GESTRIDGE RD
TEIGNMOUTH RD
VICARAGE HILL
A380
A381
A382
A383
B3193
B3195
1 RIVERSIDE CT
2 SALISBURY RD
3 BUCKLAND VIEW
4 HOMETEIGN HO
5 LYDFORD HO
1 HONEYWELL
2 Greenhill Ind Units
3 COTTEY MDWS
4 CHURCH CT
5 GREENHILL
6 Zealley Est
1 LITTLE CL
2 PADDONS COOMBE
3 TUPLINS
1 CHESTNUT DR
2 THE MEADOWS
ALEXANDRA HO 1
QUEENSWAY HO 2
BRAKE HO 3
PENN HO 4
SWANBOROUGH RD 1
PLANTATION CL 2
BRACKEN CL 3
MARLBOROUGH PL 1
CHARTWELL DR 2
WAIN LA 3

B3
1 CORONATION RD
2 POLLYBLANK RD
3 HIGHWEEK RD
4 ST MARY'S CT
5 CHAPEL HILL
6 BRADLEY CT
7 MARKET WLK
8 BEARNE'S LA
9 SUN CT
10 CLARENDON RD
11 GRAFTON RD
12 SALEM PL
13 NEWFOUNDLAND WAY
14 CHURCH CT
15 MANOR COTTS
16 ST LEONARD'S CL
17 HAYTOR TERR

B4
1 PAYNSFORD RD
2 PAYNSFORD MEWS
3 GREENAWAY VILLAS
4 BRUNSWICK HO
5 THURLESTONE RD
6 MILTON RD

C2
1 ALEXANDRA RD
2 CARPENTERS CT
3 MILTON CT

C3
1 CRICKET FIELD RD
2 ELM RD
3 ALBANY ST
4 GLADSTONE PL
5 IMPERIAL MEWS
6 KINGS COTTS
7 ALBERT TERR
8 HOPKINS CT
9 CARLISLE ST
10 SUMMERLAND COTTS
11 SUMMERLAND CT
12 ST PAUL'S RD
13 ST PAUL'S CT
14 CAULFIELD CT
15 NORTHERNHAY

212
208

F2
1 HALDON RISE
2 HALDON CL
3 THE GLEN
4 ELIZABETH SQ
5 WOODLANDS GDNS
6 HACCOMBE PATH

207
124

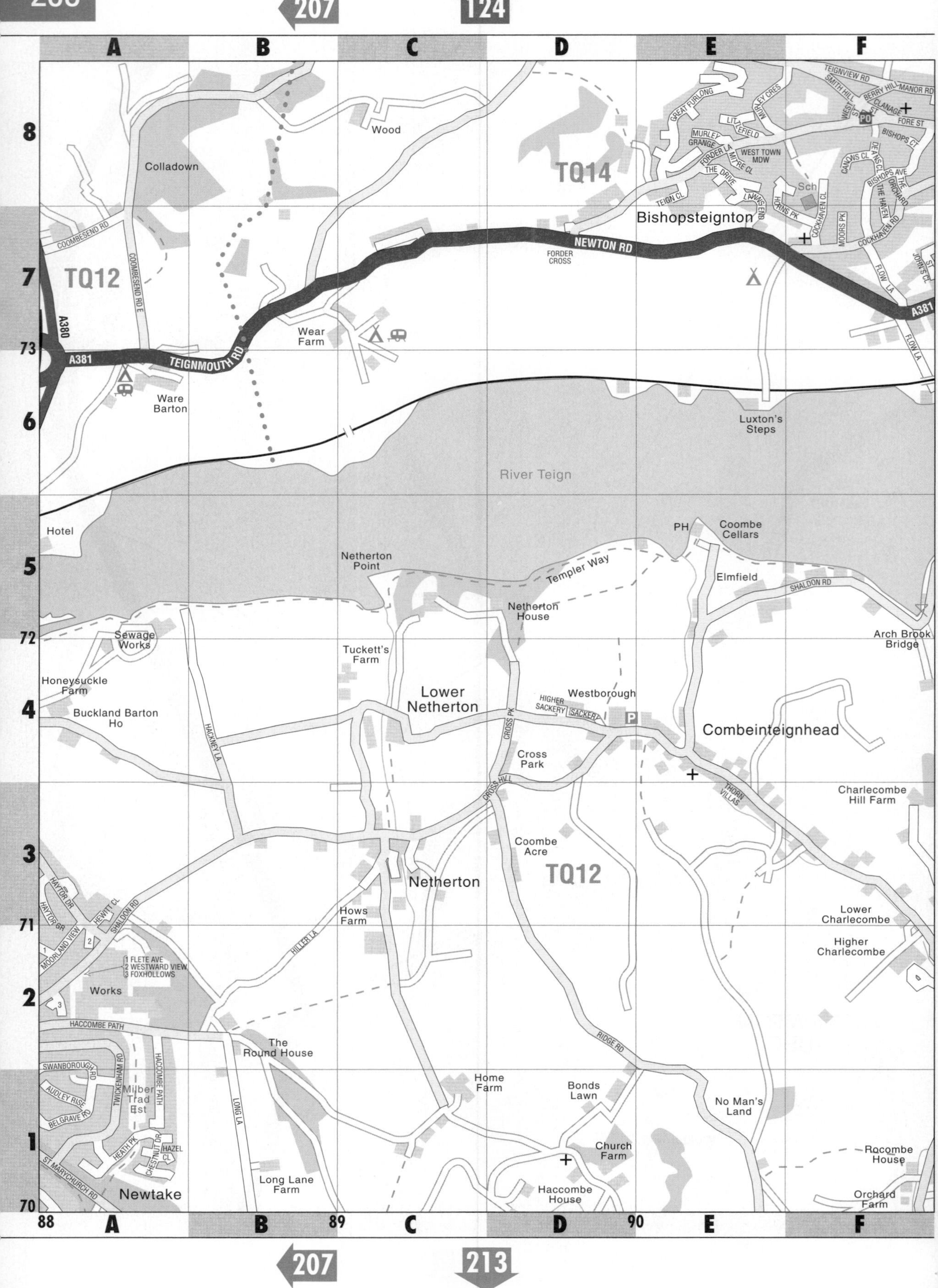

207
213

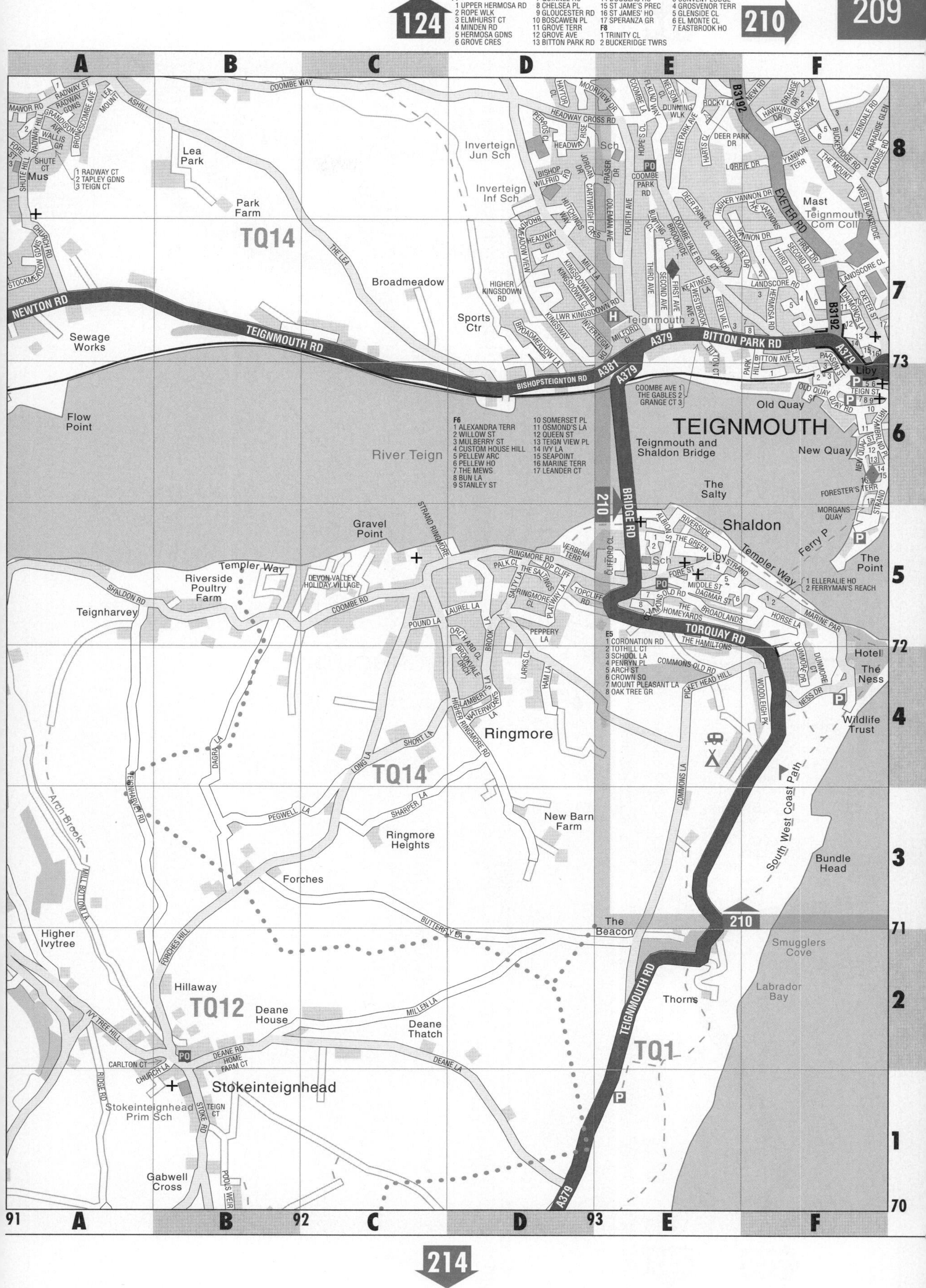
124
210
F7
1 UPPER HERMOSA RD
2 ROPE WLK
3 ELMHURST CT
4 MINDEN RD
5 HERMOSA GDNS
6 GROVE CRES
7 QUINNEL HO
8 CHELSEA PL
9 GLOUCESTER RD
10 BOSCAWEN PL
11 GROVE TERR
12 GROVE AVE
13 BITTON PARK RD
14 DOUGLAS HO
15 ST JAME'S PREC
16 ST JAMES' HO
17 SPERANZA GR
F8
1 TRINITY CL
2 BUCKERIDGE TWRS
3 CONVENT LODGE
4 GROSVENOR TERR
5 GLENSIDE CL
6 EL MONTE CL
7 EASTBROOK HO
A
B
C
D
E
F
TEIGNMOUTH
River Teign
Teignmouth and Shaldon Bridge
Shaldon
Ringmore
Stokeinteignhead
TQ14
TQ12
TQ1
Inverteign Jun Sch
Inverteign Inf Sch
Lea Park
Park Farm
Broadmeadow
Sewage Works
Sports Ctr
Flow Point
Teignmouth Com Coll
Mast
Old Quay
New Quay
The Salty
Gravel Point
Templer Way
Riverside Poultry Farm
Teignharvey
DEVON VALLEY HOLIDAY VILLAGE
The Point
Hotel
The Ness
Wildlife Trust
South West Coast Path
Bundle Head
New Barn Farm
Ringmore Heights
Forches
The Beacon
Smugglers Cove
Labrador Bay
Thorns
Higher Ivytree
Hillaway
Deane House
Deane Thatch
Stokeinteignhead Prim Sch
Gabwell Cross
NEWTON RD
TEIGNMOUTH RD
BISHOPSTEIGNTON RD
A381
A379
B3192
BITTON PARK RD
EXETER RD
BRIDGE RD
TORQUAY RD
COOMBE WAY
SHALDON RD
COOMBE RD
RINGMORE RD
COMMONS OLD RD
COMMONS LA
PICKET HEAD HILL
MARINE PAR
BUTTERFLY LA
MILLEN LA
DEANE RD
DEANE LA
FORCHES HILL
TEIGNHARVEY RD
MILL BOTTOM LA
IVY TREE HILL
STOKE RD
CHURCH LA
CARLTON CT
RIDGE RD
POOLS WEIR
PEGWELL LA
SHARPER LA
LONG LA
SHORT LA
DAGRA LA
HIGHER RINGMORE RD
F6
1 ALEXANDRA TERR
2 WILLOW ST
3 MULBERRY ST
4 CUSTOM HOUSE HILL
5 PELLEW ARC
6 PELLEW HO
7 THE MEWS
8 BUN LA
9 STANLEY ST
10 SOMERSET PL
11 OSMOND'S LA
12 QUEEN ST
13 TEIGN VIEW PL
14 IVY LA
15 SEAPOINT
16 MARINE TERR
17 LEANDER CT
E5
1 CORONATION RD
2 TOTHILL CT
3 SCHOOL LA
4 PENRYN PL
5 ARCH ST
6 CROWN SQ
7 MOUNT PLEASANT LA
8 OAK TREE GR
COOMBE AVE 1
THE GABLES 2
GRANGE CT 3
1 RADWAY CT
2 TAPLEY GDNS
3 TEIGN CT
1 ELLERALIE HO
2 FERRYMAN'S REACH
91
92
93
70
71
72
73
8
7
6
5
4
3
2
1

214

B6
1 TRINITY CL
2 BUCKERIDGE TWRS
3 CONVENT LODGE
4 GROSVENOR TERR
5 GLENSIDE CL
6 EL MONTE CL
7 EASTBROOK HO
TEIGNMOUTH
Holcombe
Shaldon
EX7
TQ14
TQ1
C5
1 BARNSLEY CL
2 LOWER BRIMLEY CL
3 ALWYNS CL
4 HAMBLETON HO
5 ALWYNS CT
6 BELGRAVE TERR
7 ABBEYFIELD HO
8 GLADSTONE TERR
9 SALISBURY TERR
10 SHUTE HILL CRES
11 HEYWOODS CL
12 GLENDARAGH RD
13 LOWER BROOK ST
14 ALBERTA CT
15 MERE LA
16 DAWLISH ST
17 CLIFTON HO
C4
1 ORCHARD HO
2 BICKFORD LA
3 STATION RD
4 HOLLANDS RD
5 POUND LA
6 REGENTS GDNS
7 FRENCH ST
8 FORE ST
9 CLAMPET LA
10 ORCHARD GDNS
11 GEORGE ST
12 BANK ST
13 WELLINGTON ST
14 WATERLOO ST
15 TRIANGLE PL
16 THE TRIANGLE
17 COURTENAY PL
18 REGENT ST
19 BATH TERR
20 CARLTON PL
21 POWDERHAM CT
22 DOLPHIN CT
23 MARINA CT
B4
1 ALEXANDRA TERR
2 WILLOW ST
3 MULBERRY ST
4 CUSTOM HOUSE HILL
5 PELLEW ARC
6 PELLEW HO
7 THE MEWS
8 BUN LA
9 STANLEY ST
10 SOMERSET PL
11 OSMOND'S LA
12 QUEEN ST
13 TEIGN VIEW PL
14 IVY LA
15 SEAPOINT
16 MARINE TERR
17 LEANDER CT
B5
1 UPPER HERMOSA RD
2 ROPE WLK
3 ELMHURST CT
4 MINDEN RD
5 HERMOSA GDNS
6 GROVE CRES
7 QUINNEL HO
8 CHELSEA PL
9 GLOUCESTER RD
10 BOSCAWEN PL
11 GROVE TERR
12 GROVE AVE
13 BITTON PARK RD
14 DOUGLAS HO
15 ST JAMES'S PREC
16 ST JAMES' HO
17 SPERANZA GR
A3
1 CORONATION RD
2 TOTHILL CT
3 SCHOOL LA
4 PENRYN PL
5 ARCH ST
6 CROWN SQ
7 MOUNT PLEASANT LA
8 OAK TREE GR
1 COOMBE AVE
2 INVERTEIGN DR
3 THE GABLES
4 GRANGE CT
1 SOPER WLK
2 SOPER RD
3 DUNNING WLK
4 DUNNING RD
1 DERNCLEUGH GDNS
2 SUNNYLANDS WAY
3 HOLCOMBE CROSS
1 CHILTON AVE
2 BRUNEL CL
3 BARNPARK CL
4 BARNSLEY DR
1 ELLERALIE HO
2 FERRYMAN'S REACH

131
206
212
A
B
C
D
E
F
8
7
69
6
5
68
4
3
67
2
1
66
2
83
84
Sewage Works
Oxenham's Wood
Channing's Wood
Rifel Range
WEST OGWELL CROSS
PH
SUNNY HOLLOW
HM Prison
STUBBINS CROSS
RECTORY RD
Ogwell Grange
Conitor Copse
RYDONBALL CROSS
CONISTON RD
WEBBER CL
REYNELL RD
LUXTON RD
BUTTERCOMBE CL
DAWES CL
DOUGHY LA
PEARTREE CROSS
Peartree Farm
START CROSS
MOORLAND AVE
FAIRVIEW RD
EAST ST
NORTH ST
Prickly Ball Farm (Hedgehog Hospl)
GREENHILL LA
DENBURY RD
Rydon Lodge
RYDON CROSS
HEATHFIELD RD
PO
Sch
WOODLAND RD
WEST ST
DOWN VIEW CL
SOUTH ST
ORCHARD CL
SHUTE LA
Denbury
NEWTON CROSS
1 HEATHFIELD TERR
2 WEST END TERR
New Barn
Denbury Green
IPPLEPEN CROSS
Rydonhill
PH
COPSEY LA
A381
Sharpitor Copse
DORNAFIELD CROSS
TOTNES RD
Ruby Farm
HALWELL CROSS
TQ12
Dornafield
Sunderland Copse
Winnoway Copse
PH
Halwell Farm
TWO MILE OAK CROSS
WHIDDON RD
Blackrock Copse
COURTLAND CROSS
DORNAFIELD LA
Courtlands
Stallage Common
Old Rectory Farm
Clennon's Linhay
Danes
Nursery
Lidmore Copse
Clennor
CH
Olderpark Copse
Clennonpark Wood
DENBURY CROSS
DORNAFIELD CROSS
BEECH TREES LA
TOWNSEND HILL
Park Hill Farm
Lapthorne
Appletrees
TORBRYAN HILL
MOOR RD
DORNAFIELD RD
PARKHILL HO
GRANGE CL
WESLEY TERR 1
THE CAUSEWAY 2
WESLEY VIEW 3
CROFT COTTS 4
ORCHARD DR 5
DORNAFIELD DR W
FULTON CL
DORNAFIELD DR E
ELLIOTT CT
TREMLETT GR
Liby
BROOK RD
DORNAFIELD CL
CAUSWAY CROSS
FOREDOWN RD
Torbryan
Sewage Works
Broadway Farm
COUNTERS CL
BRIDGE ST
EAST ST
THORN ORCH
BARN PARK
NORTH ST
NORTH END CL
BORN CL
LANG WAY
COOKE DR
LEDSGROVE
Butlands Ind Est
PATERNOSTER LA
PO
MOTEHOLE RD
Ipplepen
FORE ST
MAYFAIR RD
CROFT RD
CROFT MDW
CLARENDON RD
PH
CROKERS WAY
ORLEY RD
P
Well Barn Farm
THE GLEBE
DAINTON ELMS CROSS
SILVER ST
NEWHAYES
CLAMPITT RD
BEECH DR
Sch
BLACKSTONE CROSS
Orley Common
CLAMPITT CL
COURT GATE CL
LUSCOMBE CL
BLACKSTONE RD
WRIGWELL CROSS
BILTOR RD
WRIGWELL LA
Orley House
Pool Farm
Barton House
EDGELANDS LA
NEWMAN CROSS
CONNIFORD LA
BELTOR CROSS
Maitlands
POOLE CROSS
Tor Barns
BILTOR RD
A381
Cocklford Bridge
131
217
212

211
207

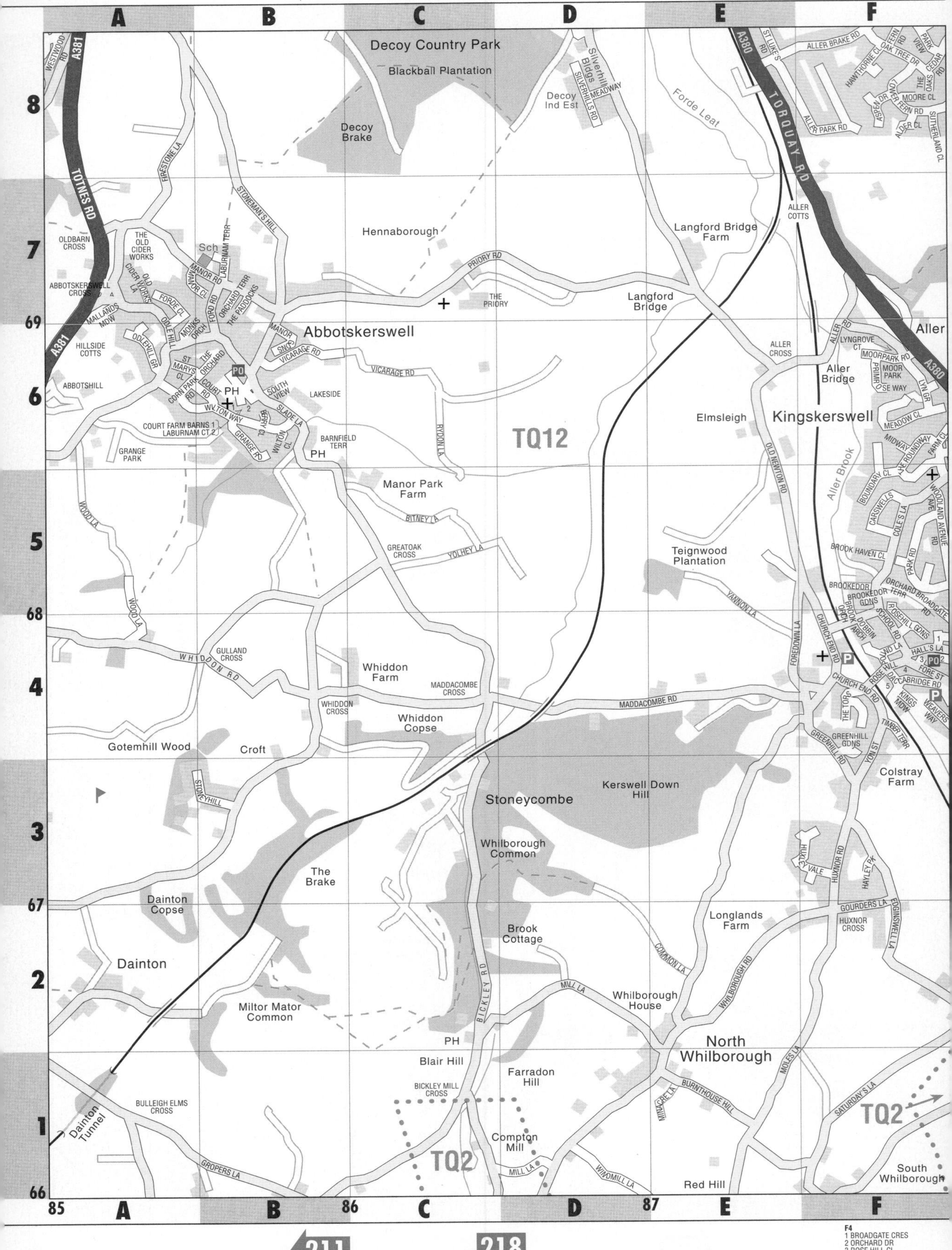

211
218

F4
1 BROADGATE CRES
2 ORCHARD DR
3 ROSE HILL CL
4 GARA LODGE
5 KINGS CT

214

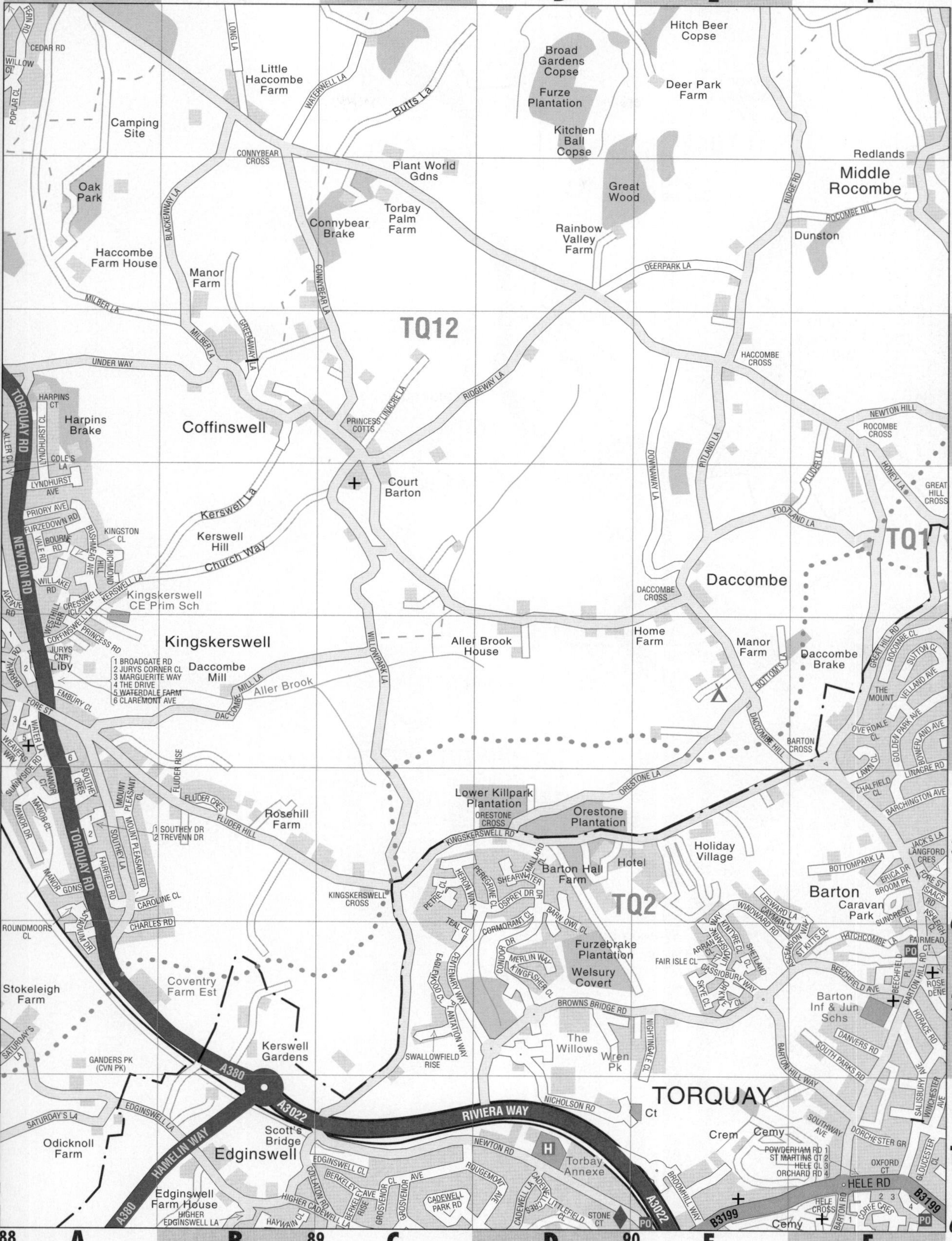

A B C D E F

Little Haccombe Farm
Hitch Beer Copse
Broad Gardens Copse
Deer Park Farm
Furze Plantation
Camping Site
Kitchen Ball Copse
Butts La
Waterwell La
Long La
Cedar Rd
Willow Cl
Fern Rd
Poplar Cl
Connybear Cross
Plant World Gdns
Redlands
Middle Rocombe
Oak Park
Great Wood
Torbay Palm Farm
Connybear Brake
Rocombe Hill
Ridge Rd
Haccombe Farm House
Rainbow Valley Farm
Dunston
Blackenway La
Manor Farm
Deerpark La
Milber La
Connybear La
TQ12
Greenaway La
Under Way
Haccombe Cross
Harpins Ct
Ridgeway La
Linacre La
Harpins Brake
Coffinswell
Princess Cotts
Newton Hill
Rocombe Cross
Lyndhurst Cl
Aller Cl
Cole's La
Court Barton
Downaway La
Pitland La
Fluder La
Honey La
Lyndhurst Ave
Priory Ave
Kerswell La
Great Hill Cross
Furzedown Rd
Kingston Cl
Footland La
Vale Rd
Bourne Rd
Bushmead Ave
Richmond Hill
Kerswell Hill
Church Way
TQ1
Newton Rd
Willake Rd
Kerswell La
Daccombe
Avenue Rd
Westhill Terr
Cresswell Cl
Kingskerswell CE Prim Sch
Daccombe Cross
Coffinswell La
Princess Rd
Home Farm
Great Hill Rd
Rocombe Cl
Sutton Cl
Kingskerswell
Aller Brook House
Manor Farm
Daccombe Brake
Jurys Cnr
Liby
Daccombe Mill
1 Broadgate Rd
2 Jurys Corner Cl
3 Marguerite Way
4 The Drive
5 Waterdale Farm
6 Claremont Ave
Willowpark La
Bottom's La
The Mount
Velland Ave
Barn Rd
Embury Cl
Daccombe Mill La
Aller Brook
Fore St
Overdale Cl
Golden Park Ave
Water La
Weavers Way
Daccombe Hill
Barton Cross
Bowerland Ave
Linacre Rd
Sunnyside Rd
Manor Ct
Southey Cres
Fluder Rise
Lawn Cl
Orestone La
Chalfield Cl
Barchington Ave
Manor Cl
Mount Pleasant Cl
Mount Pleasant Rd
Fluder Cres
Rosehill Farm
Lower Killpark Plantation
Orestone Cross
Orestone Plantation
Manor Dr
Torquay Rd
Southey La
1 Southey Dr
2 Trevenn Dr
Fluder Hill
Kingskerswell Rd
Holiday Village
Jack's La
Langford Cres
Mallard
Barton Hall Farm
Hotel
Bottompark La
Erica Dr
Broom Pk
Fore St
Isaacs Rd
Shearwater Dr
Heron Way
Peregrine Cl
Petrel Cl
Osprey Dr
Manor Gdns
Fairfield Rd
Caroline Cl
Kingskerswell Cross
TQ2
Leeward La
Cayman Cl
Windward Rd
Barton
Caravan Park
Sunrest Cl
Ashleigh Rd
Charles Rd
Teal Cl
Barn Owl Cl
Cormorant Cl
Roundmoors Cl
Stadium Dr
Furzebrake Plantation
Arran Cl
Kintyre Cl
Shetland Cl
Ascension Way
St Kitts Cl
Hatchcombe La
Fairmead Ct
Condor Dr
Merlin Way
Fair Isle Cl
Cassiobury Way
Coventry Farm Est
Eaglewood Cl
Centenary Way
Kingfisher Cl
Welsury Covert
Skye Cl
Beechfield Ave
Beechfield Pl
Barton Hill Rd
Rose Dene
Stokeleigh Farm
Barton Inf & Jun Schs
Browns Bridge Rd
Nightingale Cl
Plantation Way
The Willows
Wren Pk
Danvers Rd
Horace Rd
Saturday's La
Kerswell Gardens
Swallowfield Rise
Barton Hill Way
South Parks Rd
Ganders Pk (Cvn Pk)
A380
Salisbury Ave
Winchester Ave
Torquay
Nicholson Rd
Ct
Saturday's La
A3022
Riviera Way
Southway Ave
Dorchester Gr
Edginswell La
Crem
Cemy
Odicknoll Farm
Hamelin Way
Scott's Bridge
Edginswell
Newton Rd
H
Torbay Annexe
Powderham Rd 1
St Martins Ct 2
Hele Cl 3
Orchard Rd 4
Gloucester Cl
Oxford Ct
Edginswell Cl
Berkeley Ave
Rougemont Ave
Grosvenor Cl
Grosvenor Ave
Collaton Rd
Cadewell Park Rd
Cadewell La
Cadewell Cres
Littlefield Cl
Broomhill Way
Hele Rd
Edginswell Farm House
Higher Edginswell La
Higher Cadewell La
Berkeley Rise
Haywain Cl
Stone Ct
PO
A3022
B3199
Hele Cross
Barton Rd
Corfe Cres
Cemy
B3199
PO

88 A B 89 C D 90 E F
8 7 69 6 5 68 4 3 67 2 1 66

214

213 209

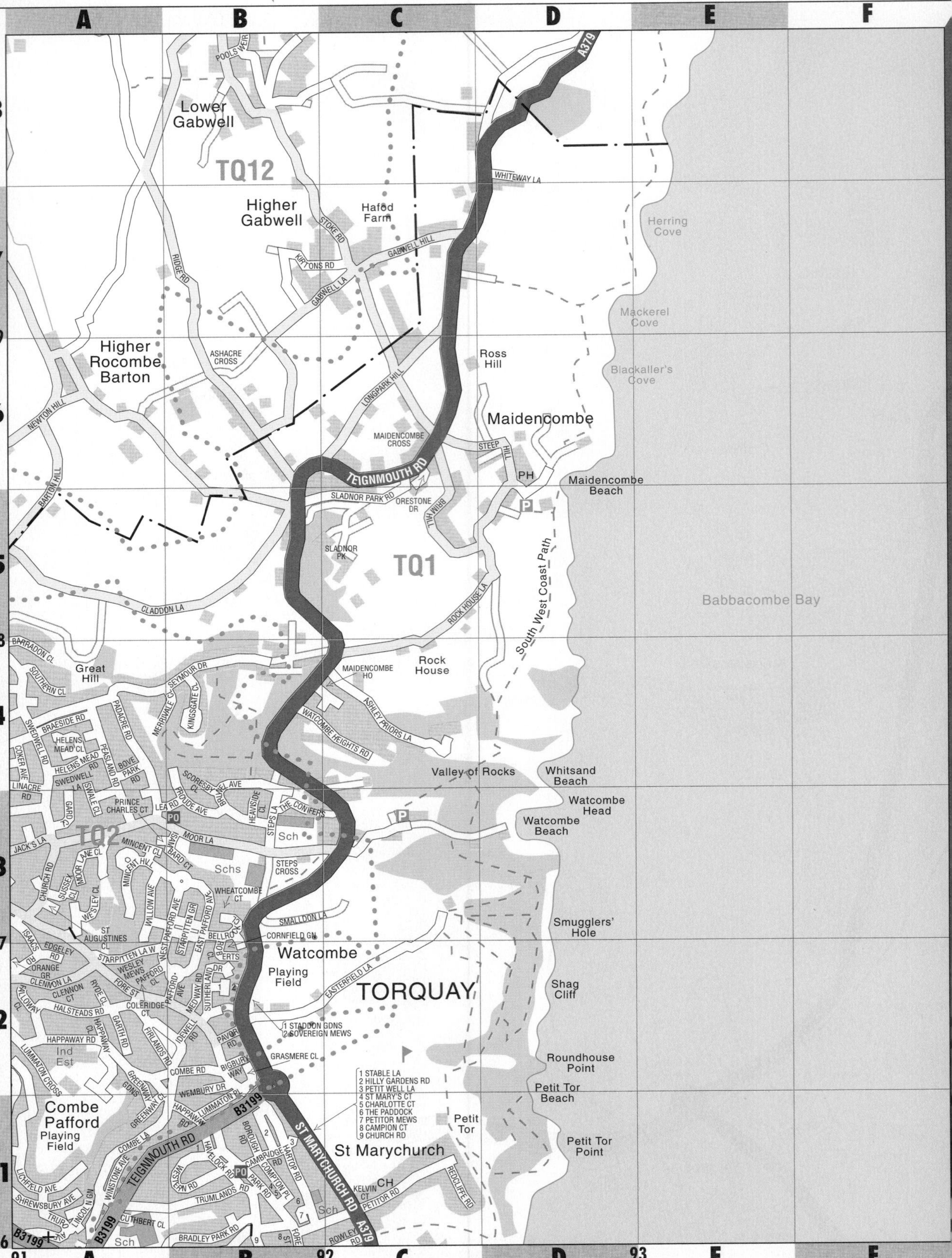

Lower Gabwell
TQ12
Higher Gabwell
Hafod Farm
Herring Cove
Mackerel Cove
Blackaller's Cove
Higher Rocombe Barton
Ross Hill
Maidencombe
ASHACRE CROSS
MAIDENCOMBE CROSS
PH
Maidencombe Beach
TEIGNMOUTH RD
SLADNOR PARK RD
ORESTONE DR
SLADNOR PK
TQ1
South West Coast Path
Babbacombe Bay
CLADDON LA
ROCK HOUSE LA
Great Hill
MAIDENCOMBE HO
Rock House
ASHLEY PRIORS LA
WATCOMBE HEIGHTS RD
Valley of Rocks
Whitsand Beach
Watcombe Head
Watcombe Beach
TQ2
Sch
Schs
STEPS CROSS
Smugglers' Hole
Watcombe
Playing Field
TORQUAY
Shag Cliff
1 STADDON GDNS
2 SOVEREIGN MEWS
GRASMERE CL
Roundhouse Point
Ind Est
1 STABLE LA
2 HILLY GARDENS RD
3 PETIT WELL LA
4 ST MARY'S CT
5 CHARLOTTE CT
6 THE PADDOCK
7 PETITOR MEWS
8 CAMPION CT
9 CHURCH RD
Petit Tor Beach
Combe Pafford
Playing Field
Petit Tor
St Marychurch
Petit Tor Point
ST MARYCHURCH RD
TEIGNMOUTH RD
B3199
A379

213 220

236
131
216

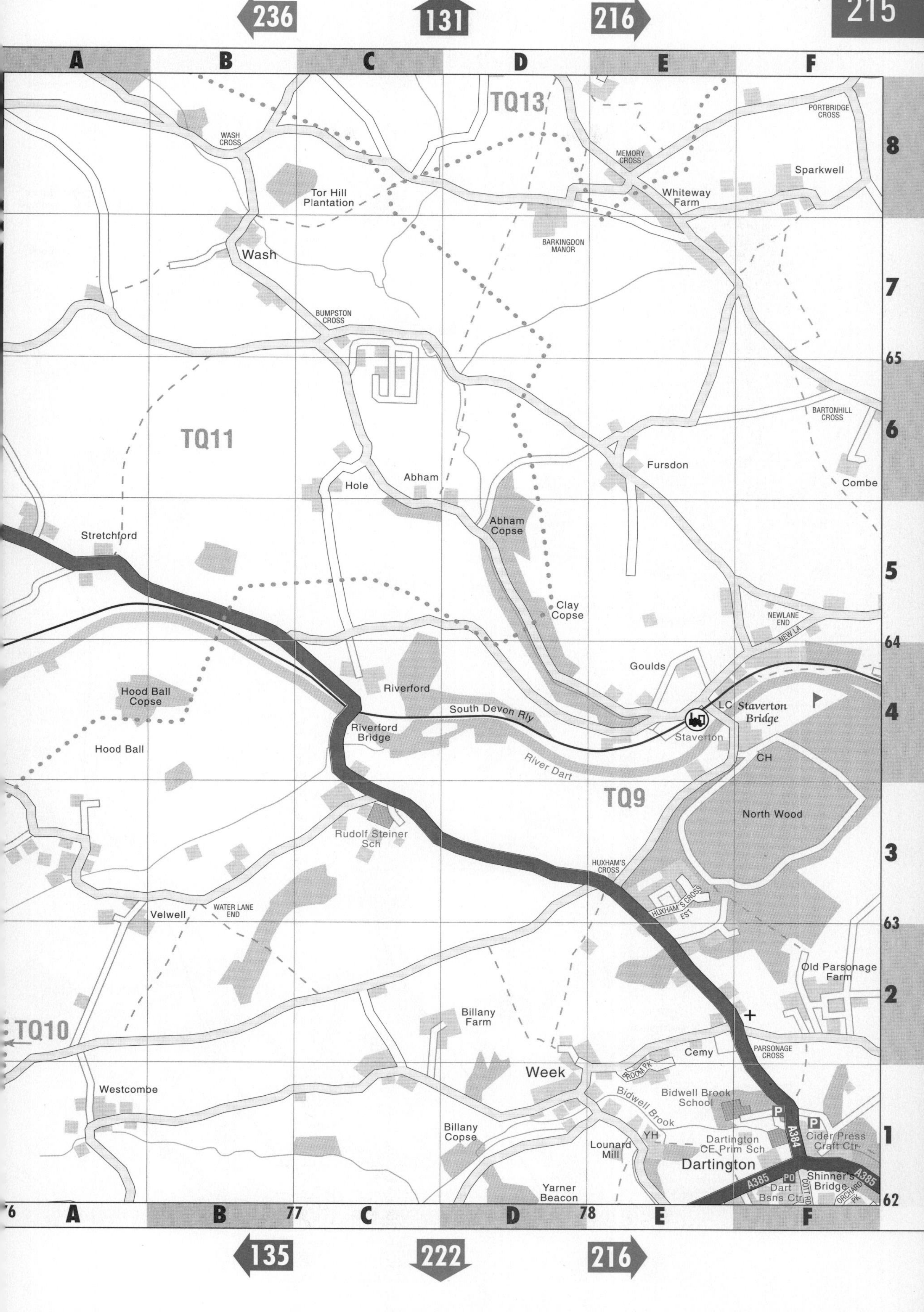

135
222
216

215
131

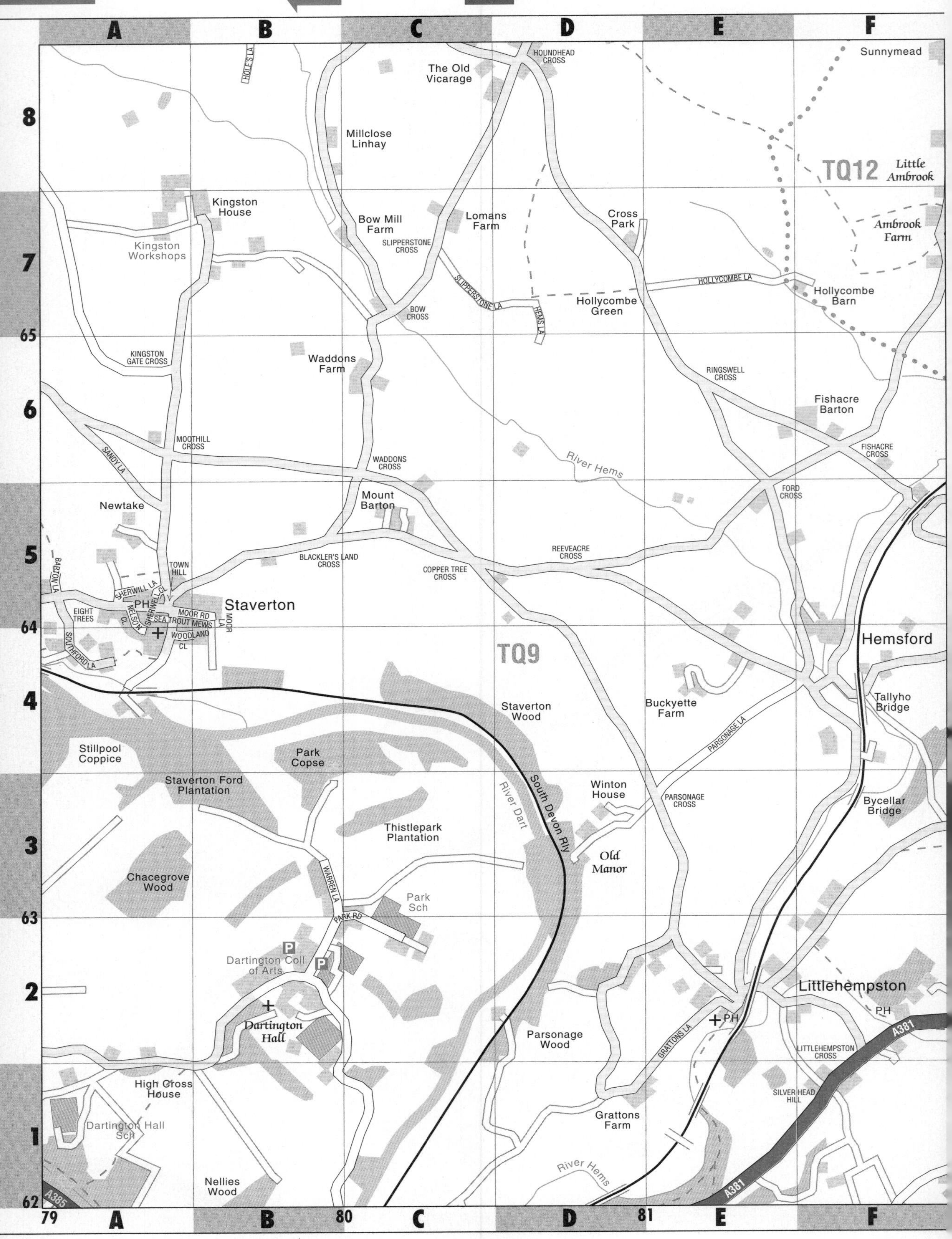

215
223

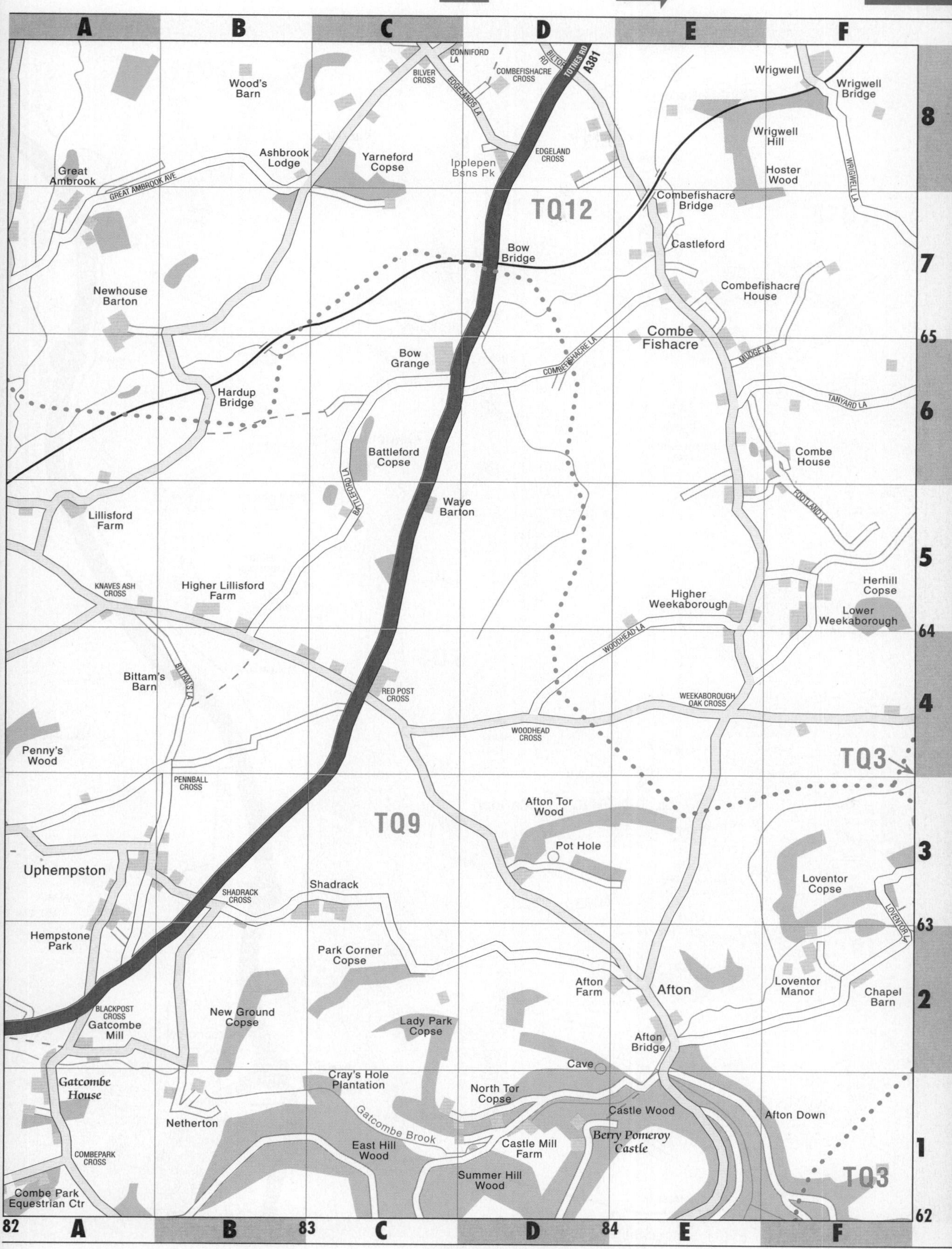
A
B
C
D
E
F
Wood's Barn
CONNIFORD LA
BILVER CROSS
EDGELANDS LA
COMBEFISHACRE CROSS
BILTOR RD
TOTNES RD
A381
Wrigwell
Wrigwell Bridge
Wrigwell Hill
WRIGWELL LA
Hoster Wood
Ashbrook Lodge
Yarneford Copse
Great Ambrook
GREAT AMBROOK AVE
Ipplepen Bsns Pk
EDGELAND CROSS
TQ12
Combefishacre Bridge
Castleford
Bow Bridge
Newhouse Barton
Combefishacre House
Combe Fishacre
Bow Grange
COMBEFISHACRE LA
MUDGE LA
Hardup Bridge
TANYARD LA
Battleford Copse
Combe House
FOOTLAND LA
BATTLEFORD LA
Waye Barton
Lillisford Farm
KNAVES ASH CROSS
Higher Lillisford Farm
Higher Weekaborough
Herhill Copse
Lower Weekaborough
WOODHEAD LA
Bittam's Barn
BITTAM'S LA
RED POST CROSS
WEEKABOROUGH OAK CROSS
WOODHEAD CROSS
Penny's Wood
TQ3
PENNBALL CROSS
Afton Tor Wood
TQ9
Pot Hole
Uphempston
Loventor Copse
SHADRACK CROSS
Shadrack
LOVENTOR
Hempstone Park
Park Corner Copse
Afton Farm
Afton
Loventor Manor
Chapel Barn
BLACKPOST CROSS
Gatcombe Mill
New Ground Copse
Lady Park Copse
Afton Bridge
Cave
Gatcombe House
Cray's Hole Plantation
North Tor Copse
Castle Wood
Afton Down
Netherton
Gatcombe Brook
East Hill Wood
Castle Mill Farm
Berry Pomeroy Castle
COMBEPARK CROSS
Summer Hill Wood
Combe Park Equestrian Ctr
8
7
65
6
5
64
4
3
63
2
1
62
82
83
84

217
212

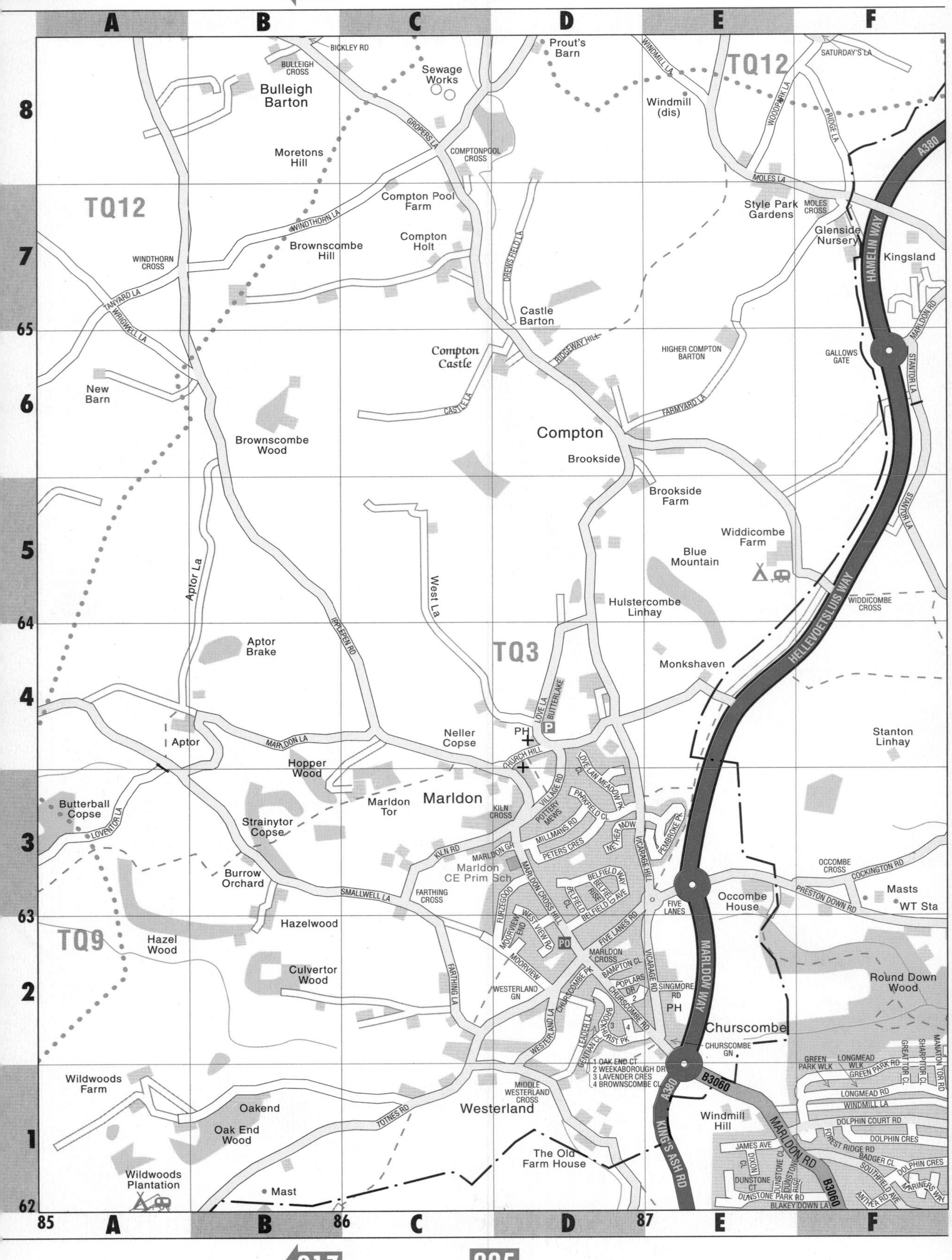

217
225

213
220

F5
1 LANSDOWNE RD
2 LANSDOWNE LA
3 ZION RD
4 PRESTBURY PARK
5 BELGRAVE MEWS
6 BEXLEY LA

F6
1 COLLEGE CT
2 HOMEPALMS HO
3 BRUNSWICK SQ
4 LABURNUM ROW

A6
1 TOR DALE
2 SUNBURY TERR
3 ST IVES CT
4 WILNCOTE LO

A7
1 WILLIS CT
2 EMPIRE CT
3 ORCHARD PL
4 HILL VIEW TERR

B5
1 BETHEL TERR
2 ST MICHAEL'S TERR
3 ALBERT CT
4 MYRTLE ROW

219

B6
1 WELLINGTON PL
2 MOUNT PLEASANT RD
3 WARBERRY VALE
4 ORCHARD RD

B7
1 WARBRO CT
2 PLAINMOOR RD
3 BLYTHSWOOD CRES

214

D5
1 MANORGLADE CT
2 WELLSWOOD MANOR
3 MAXSTOKE CT
4 UNDERHEATH
5 HAZELWOOD

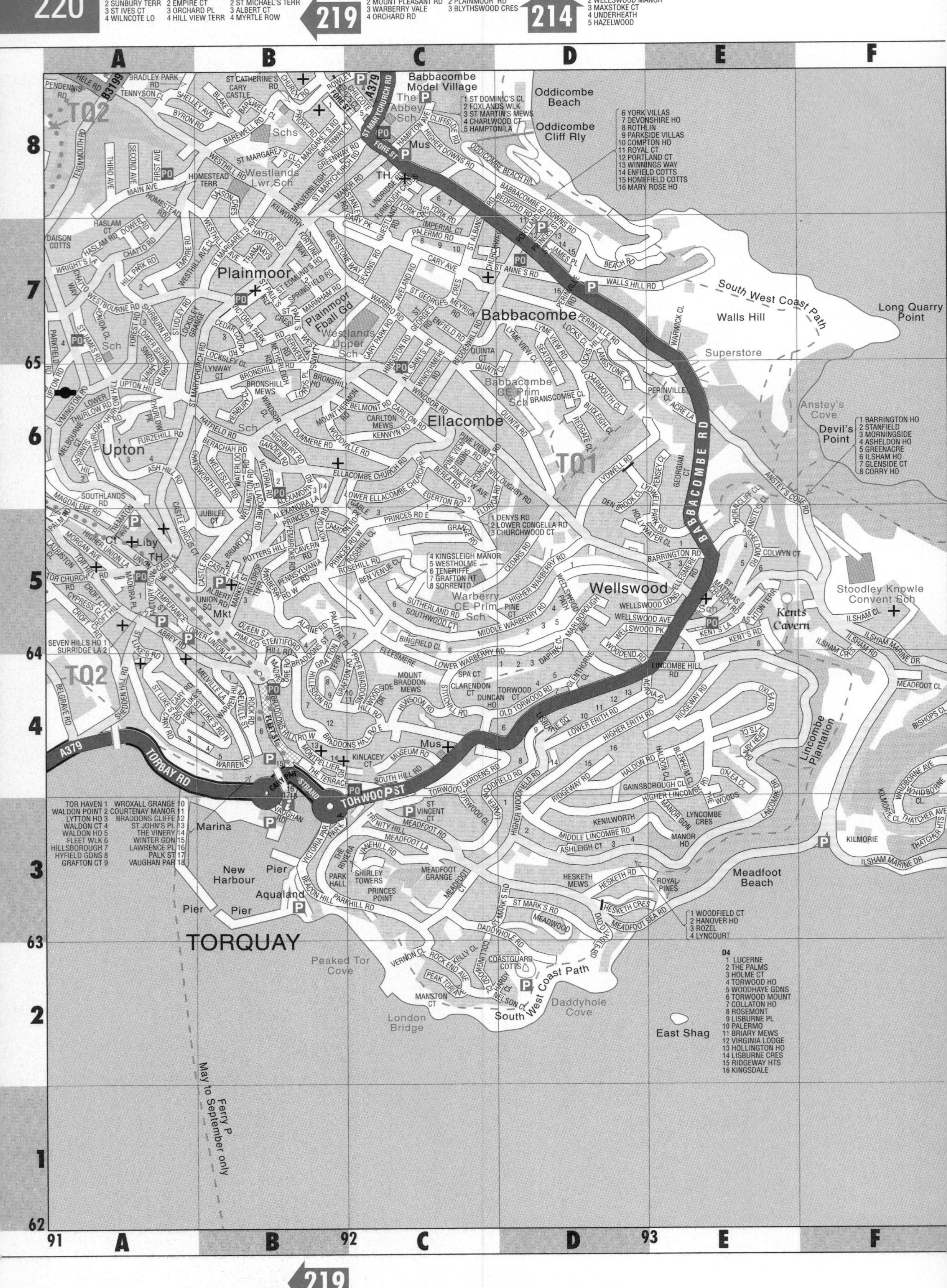

219

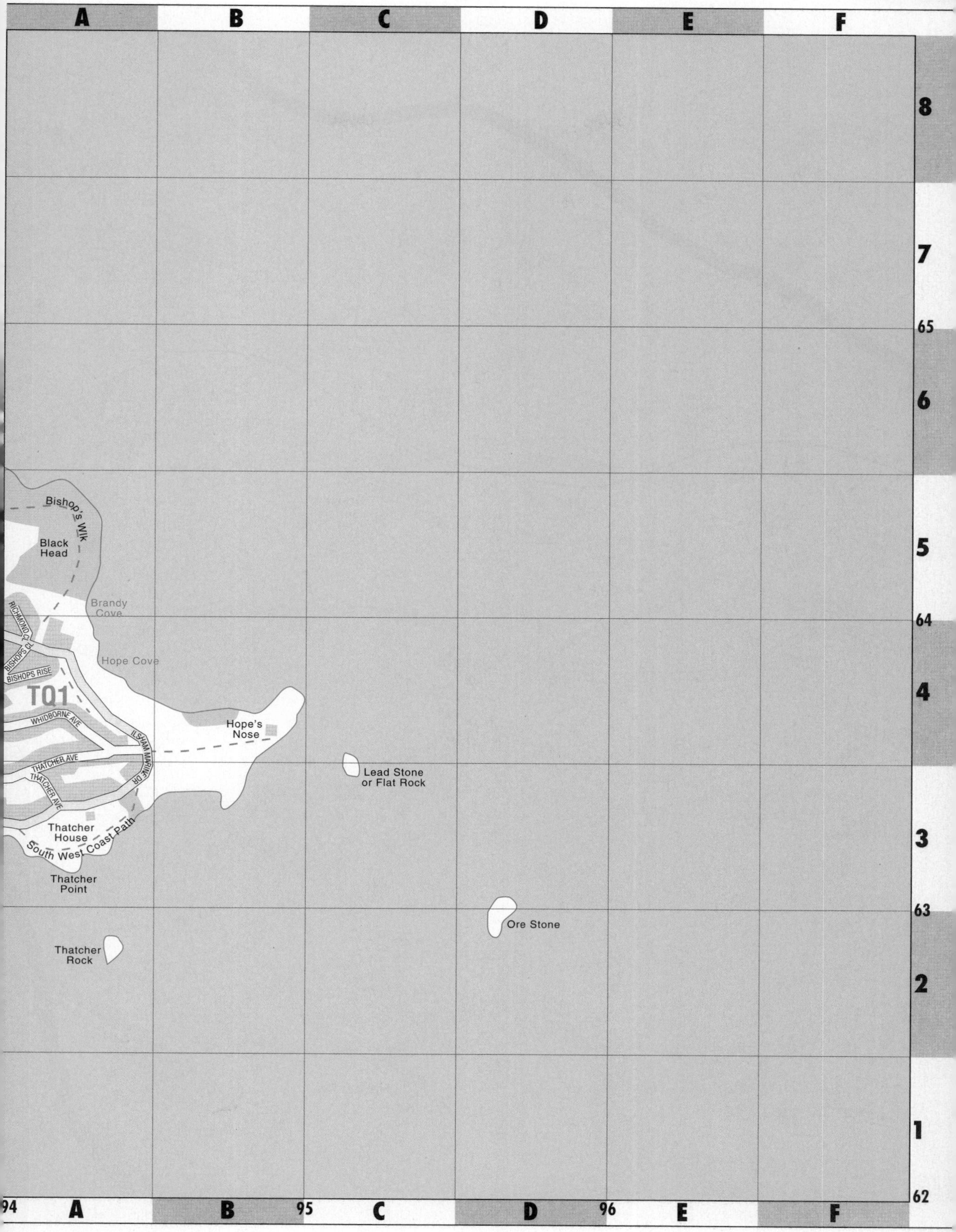

A B C D E F

8
7
65
6
5
64
4
3
63
2
1
62

Bishop's Wlk
Black Head
Brandy Cove
RICHMOND CL
BISHOPS CL
BISHOPS RISE
Hope Cove
TQ1
WHIDBORNE AVE
ILSHAM MARINE DR
Hope's Nose
THATCHER AVE
THATCHER AVE
Lead Stone or Flat Rock
Thatcher House
South West Coast Path
Thatcher Point
Ore Stone
Thatcher Rock

94 A B 95 C D 96 E F

135
215

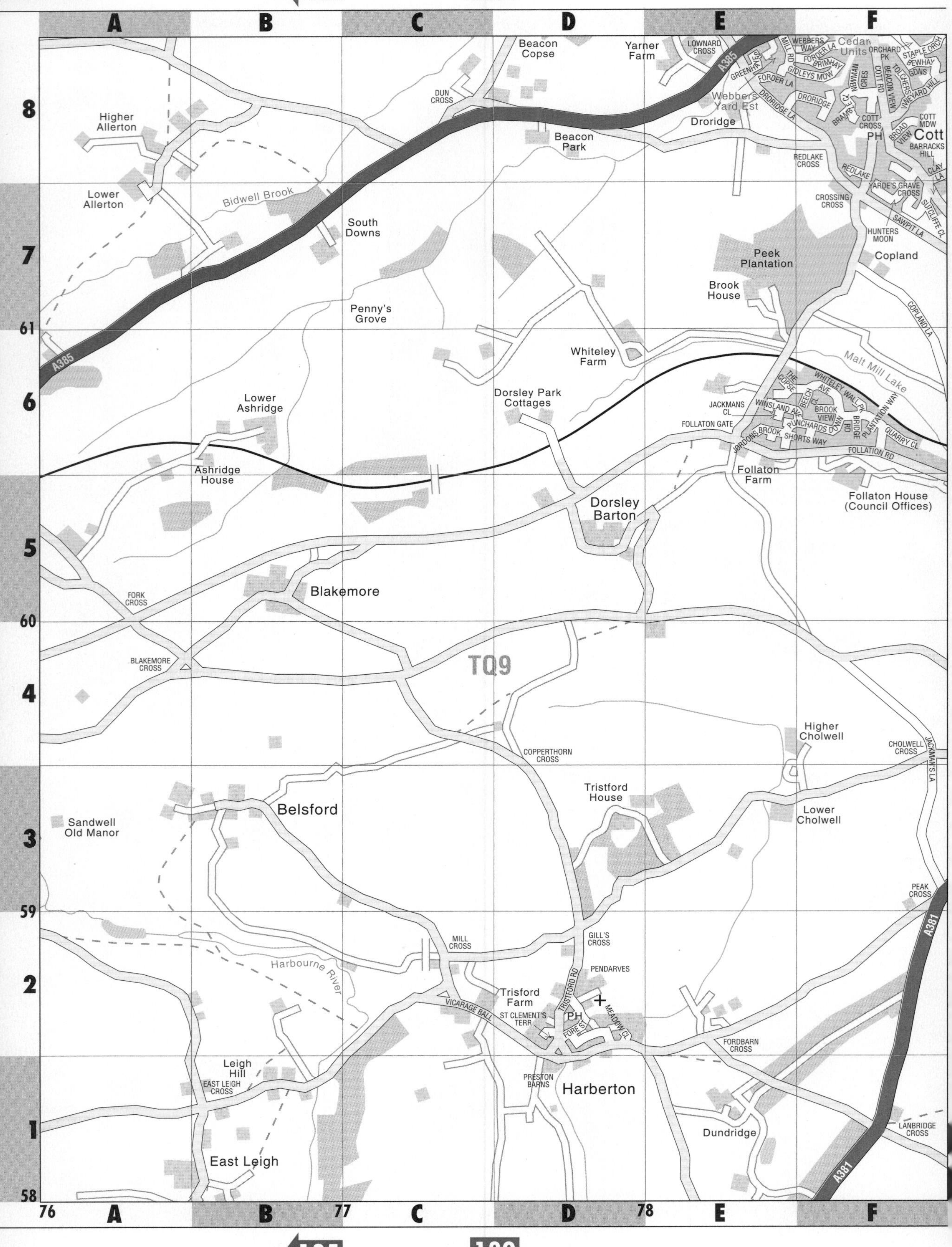

135
139

216

224

E5
1 STAFFORD CT
2 HILLBROOK RISE
3 COLDHARBOUR
4 VARIANT CT

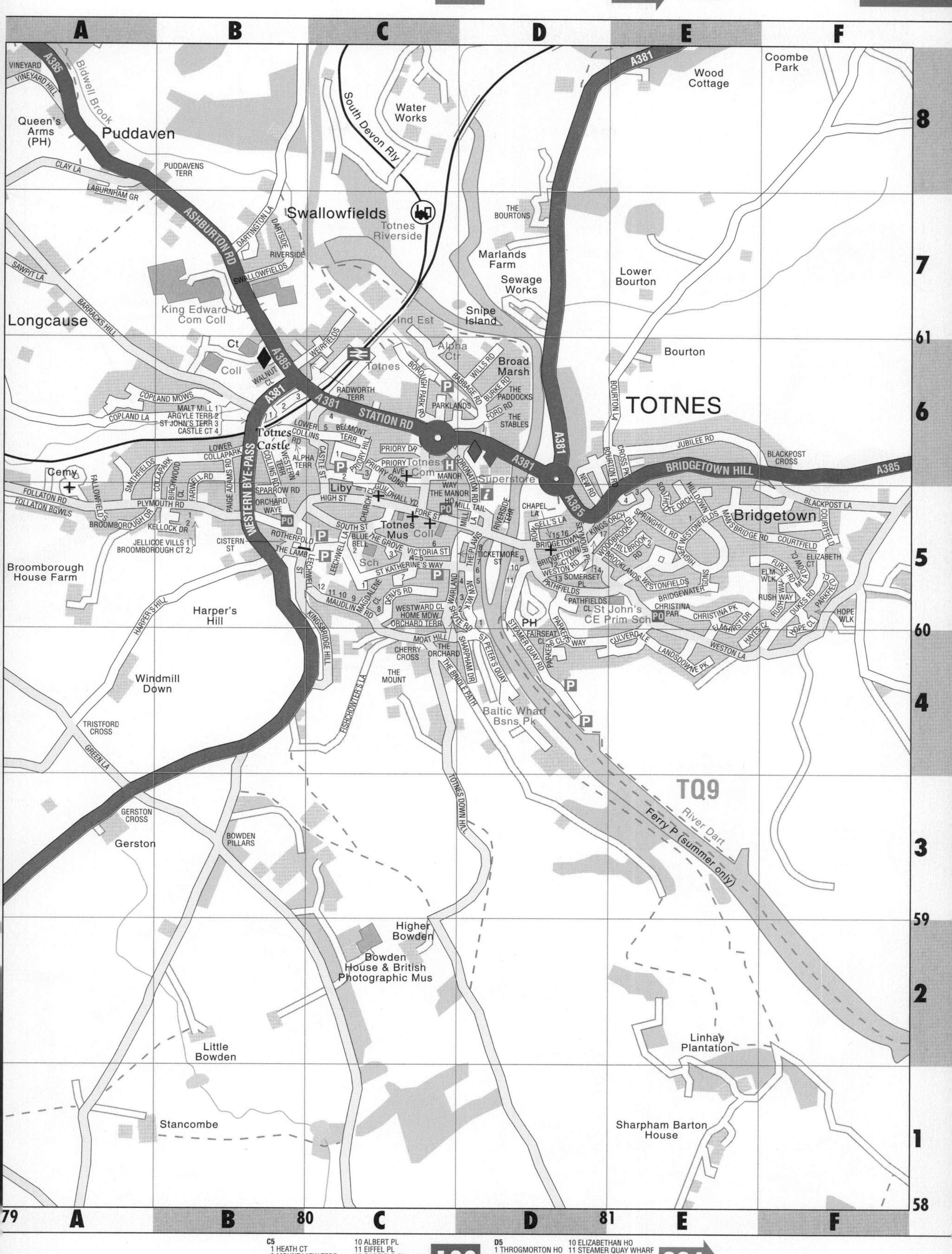

C5
1 HEATH CT
2 MOUNT VIEW TERR
3 GROVE CL
4 VICTORIA CT
5 ST KATHERNE'S MEWS
6 BANK LA
7 THE CARRIONS
8 SUNNYMEAD TERR
9 SHAFTSBURY PL
10 ALBERT PL
11 EIFFEL PL
12 GARFIELD PL

C6
1 ALEXANDRA TERR
2 NORTH ST
3 PRIORY CT
4 QUEEN'S TERR
5 ANTRIM TERR

139

D5
1 THROGMORTON HO
2 TAUNTON CT
3 REEVES CL
4 WINDEATT SQ
5 THE MALTHOUSE
6 APPLE WHARF
7 THE CHAPEL
8 WATERSIDE HO
9 SEYMOUR CT
10 ELIZABETHAN HO
11 STEAMER QUAY WHARF
12 TOLLIT GDN
13 BROAD OAK CRES
14 BARING COTTS
15 DEVON PL
16 DEVON TERR
17 SOMERSET CT

224

223
217

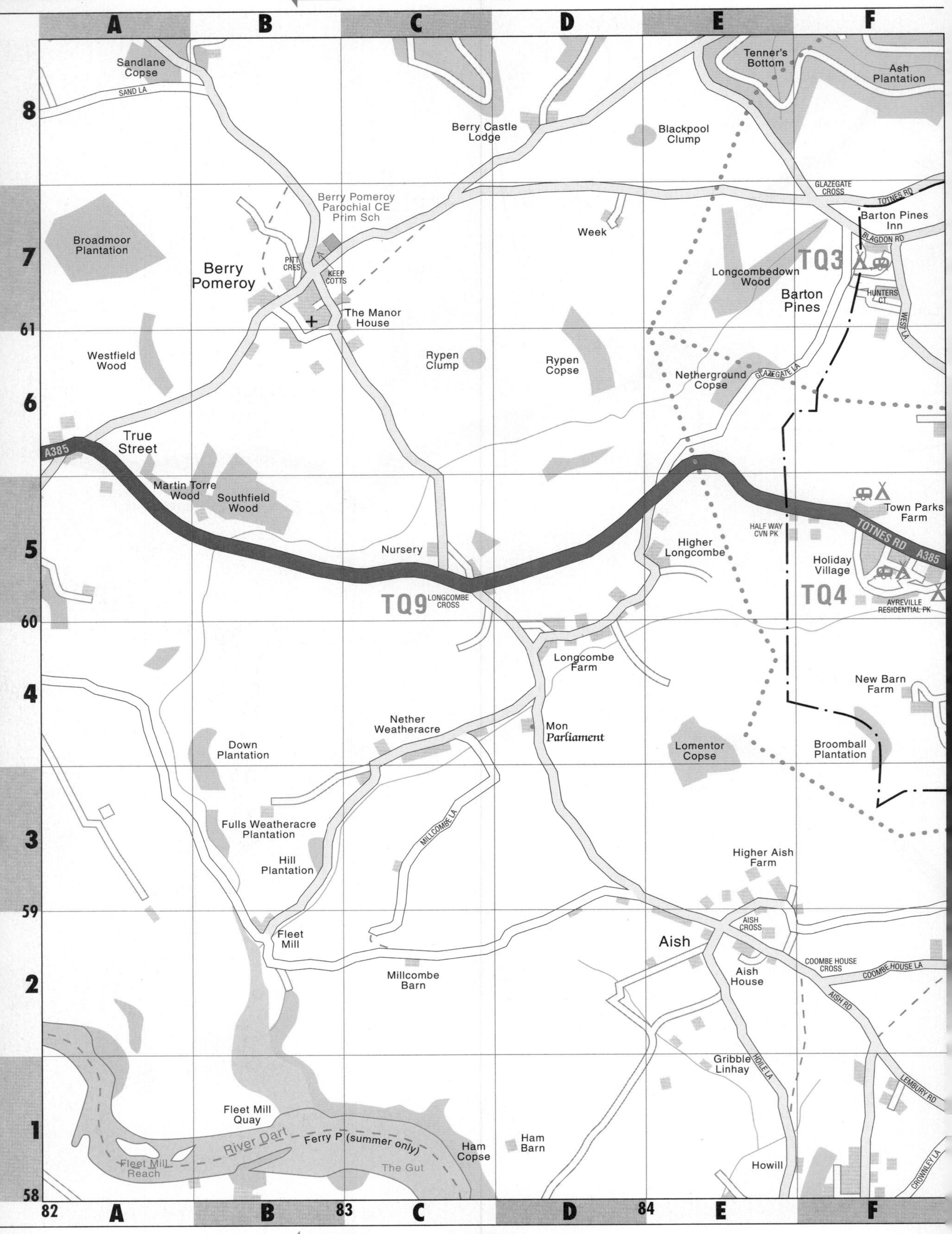

223
227

218
226

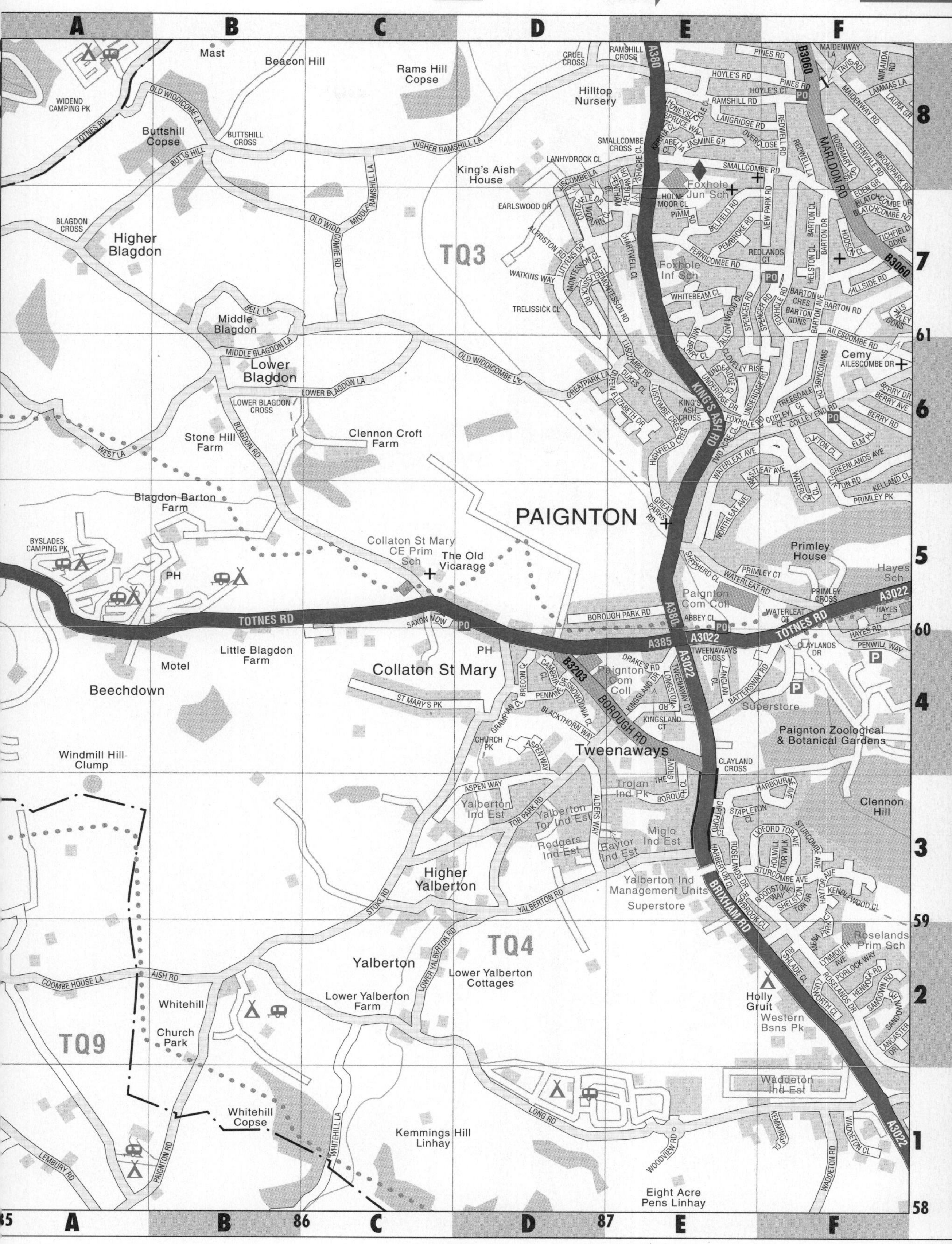

228
226

226
A5
1 HIGHER MANOR TERR
2 CONWAY CRES
3 ELMBANK GDNS
4 MERRITT FLATS
5 FLEMONS CT
A6
1 PLEASANT TERR
2 HILLSIDE TERR
3 CLIFTON BANK
A7
1 KIRKHAM CT
2 LOWER PK
225
219
A B C D E F
8 7 6 5 4 3 2 1
61 60 59 58
88 89 90
Preston
TQ3
Oldway
Oldway Mansion
Oldway Prim Sch
Mayfield Sch
Liby
Paignton & District
Victoria Sh Ctr
Mus
Promenade Pier
PAIGNTON
Paignton (Queen's Park)
Paignton Harbour
Roundham Head
St Michaels
TA Ctr
Seashore Ctr
Paignton Zoo & Botanical Gdns
Goodrington Sands
Torbay L Ctr
Quaywest Waterpark
TQ4
Clennon Hill
Grange Court Holiday Ctr
Goodrington
Sugar Loaf Hill
Saltern Cove
Shell Cove
Tor Bay
South West Coast Path
Paignton & Dartmouth Rly
TORQUAY RD
A3022
B3201
MANOR RD
EUGENE RD
SEAWAY
MARINE DR
ESPLANADE RD
TORBAY RD
HYDE RD
SANDS RD
TOTNES RD
B3060
MARLDON RD
A379
DARTMOUTH RD
1 ROSEMARY CT
2 DOWER CT
3 TAWNY CL
4 THE CLARIDGE
5 SEAWAY GDNS
6 SEAWAY CRES
B7
1 HADDON CT
2 KILLERTON CL
3 MILL LA
4 KIRKHAM ST
B6
1 BRENT RD
2 MILLBROOK RD
3 ST JOHN'S CT
4 CHURCH ST MEWS
5 CROWN AND ANCHOR WAY
6 CHURCH PATH
7 BISHOP'S PL
8 GERSTON PL
9 CROSSWAYS
10 JACK BEARS HO
11 RADFORD HO
12 GREAT WESTERN RD
1 PARKSIDE RD
2 BARRY SQ
1 ADELPHI MANSIONS
2 KINGSWOOD CT
3 CLEVELAND CT
4 MARINA CT
5 HOMEBOURNE HO
6 DENBY HO
7 SUMMERFIELD CT
8 THE MOORINGS
9 THE ANCHORAGE
10 LANCASTER HO
11 ROUNDHAM HO
12 OSMOND LODGE
13 ROSEMOUNT
1 BOSUNS POINT
2 SEABOURNE CT
1 CRYSTAL CL
2 HOOKHILLS RD
BLACKBROOK WLK 1
BIDWELL WLK 2
CHERRY BROOK WLK 3
MONTEREY 4
225
229

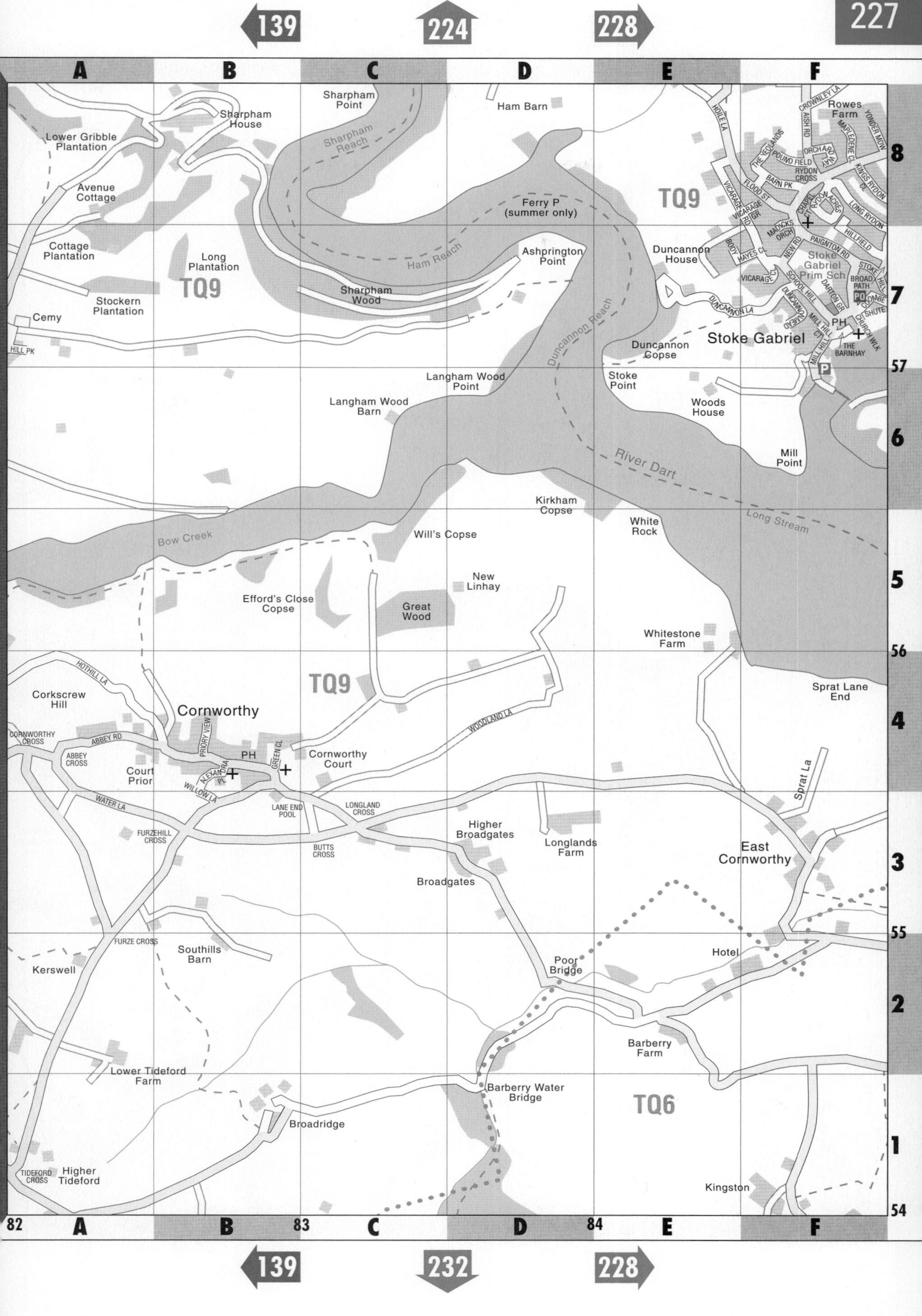
139
224
228
A
B
C
D
E
F
Sharpham Point
Ham Barn
Rowes Farm
Sharpham House
Lower Gribble Plantation
Sharpham Reach
Avenue Cottage
TQ9
Ferry P (summer only)
Cottage Plantation
Long Plantation
Ham Reach
Ashprington Point
Duncannon House
TQ9
Sharpham Wood
Stockern Plantation
Cemy
HILL PK
Duncannon Reach
Duncannon Copse
Stoke Gabriel
Stoke Gabriel Prim Sch
Langham Wood Point
Stoke Point
Langham Wood Barn
Woods House
Mill Point
River Dart
Kirkham Copse
White Rock
Long Stream
Bow Creek
Will's Copse
New Linhay
Efford's Close Copse
Great Wood
Whitestone Farm
Sprat Lane End
Corkscrew Hill
TQ9
Cornworthy
HOTHILL LA
CORNWORTHY CROSS
ABBEY RD
ABBEY CROSS
PRIORY VIEW
PH
GREEN CL
Cornworthy Court
WOODLAND LA
Court Prior
WILLOW LA
WATER LA
LANE END POOL
LONGLAND CROSS
Sprat La
Higher Broadgates
FURZEHILL CROSS
BUTTS CROSS
Longlands Farm
East Cornworthy
Broadgates
FURZE CROSS
Southills Barn
Kerswell
Poor Bridge
Hotel
Barberry Farm
Lower Tideford Farm
Barberry Water Bridge
TQ6
Broadridge
TIDEFORD CROSS
Higher Tideford
Kingston
8
7
57
6
5
56
4
3
55
2
1
54
82
83
84
232

227
225

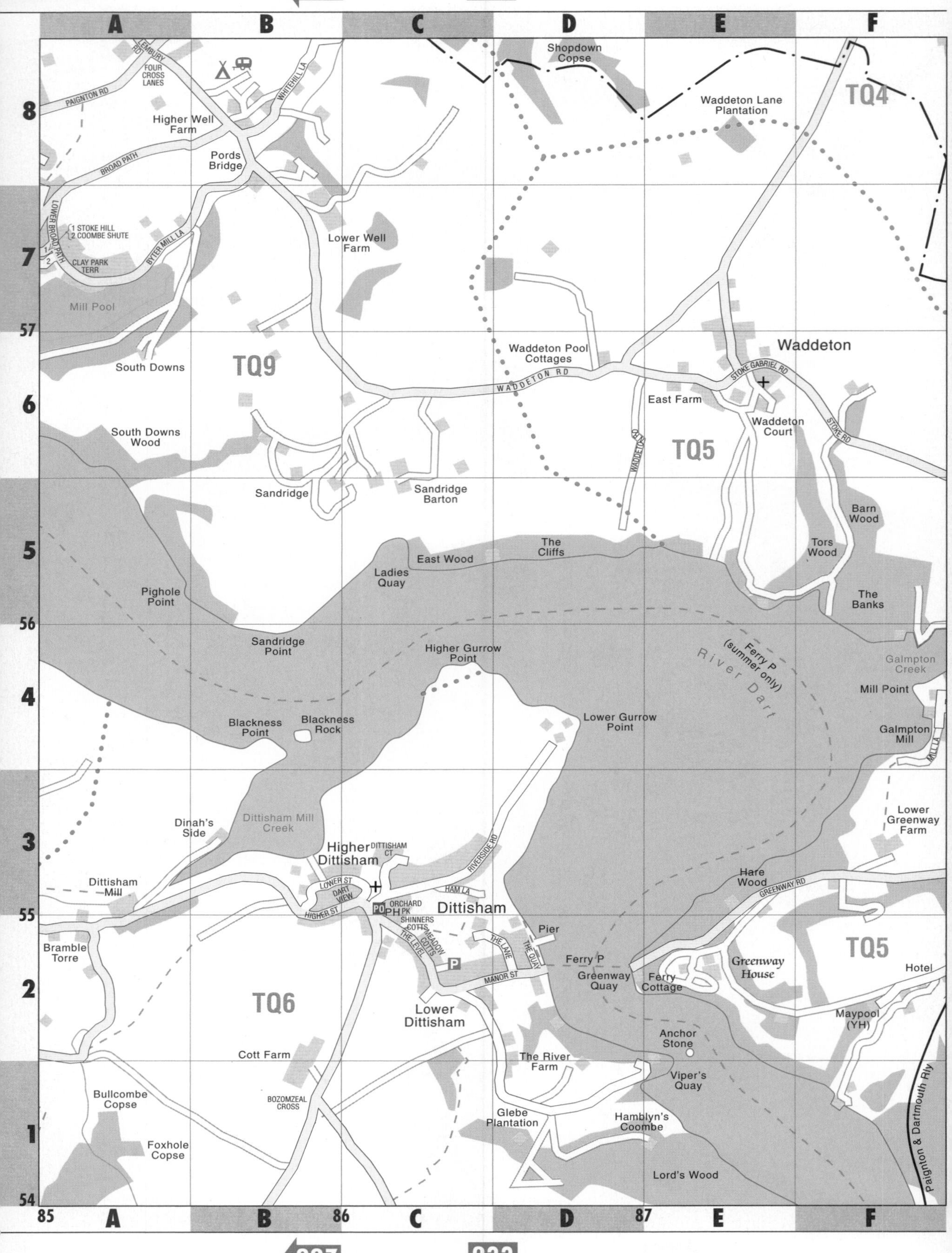

227
233

226
230

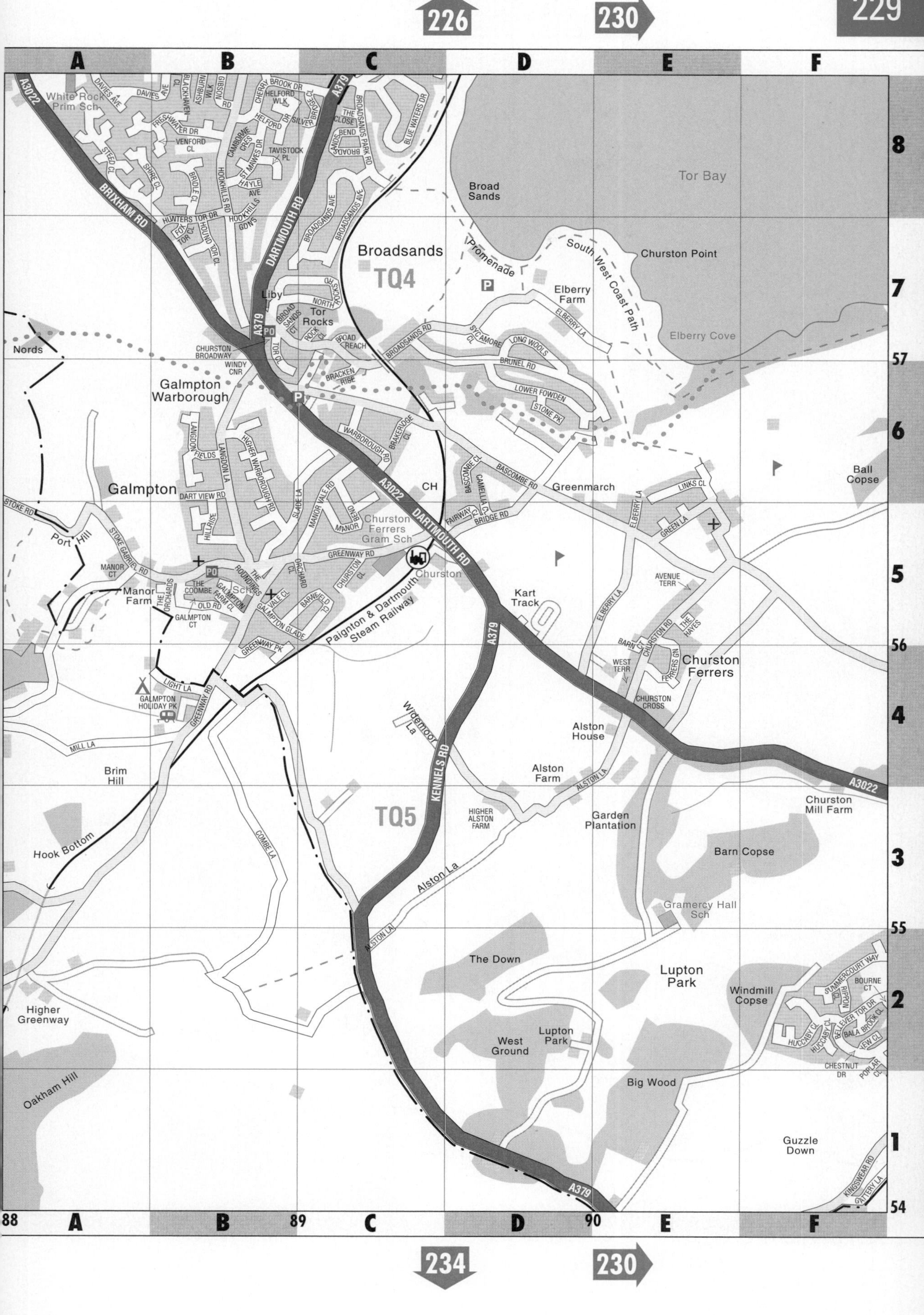

234
230

229

C3
1 GARROW CL
2 EVELEIGH CL
3 DOCTORS RD
4 GREENSWOOD RD
5 CLENNON CT
6 MAYFLOWER DR
7 HANOVER CL
8 ORCHARD CL
C4
1 PRINCE WILLIAM CT
2 SAXON HTS
3 VICTORIA TERR
4 TINKERS WOOD CT
5 WATERMILL CT
6 PARKHAM TWRS
7 CHURCHILL CT
8 BOLTON CT
9 WINDMILL CT
10 WREN CT
C5
1 HARBOUR VIEW CL
2 LINDEN CT
3 PROSPECT RD
4 CHURCH ST
5 CHURCH HILL W
6 CHURCH HILL E
7 APTERS HILL
8 MARKET ST
9 UNION LA
10 SOMERSET CT
D5
1 PARADISE PL
2 FURZE LA
3 THE STRAND
4 PUMP ST
5 ST PETER'S HILL
6 TEMPERANCE PL
7 MARINERS CT
8 HEADLAND CT
9 RANSCOMBE CT

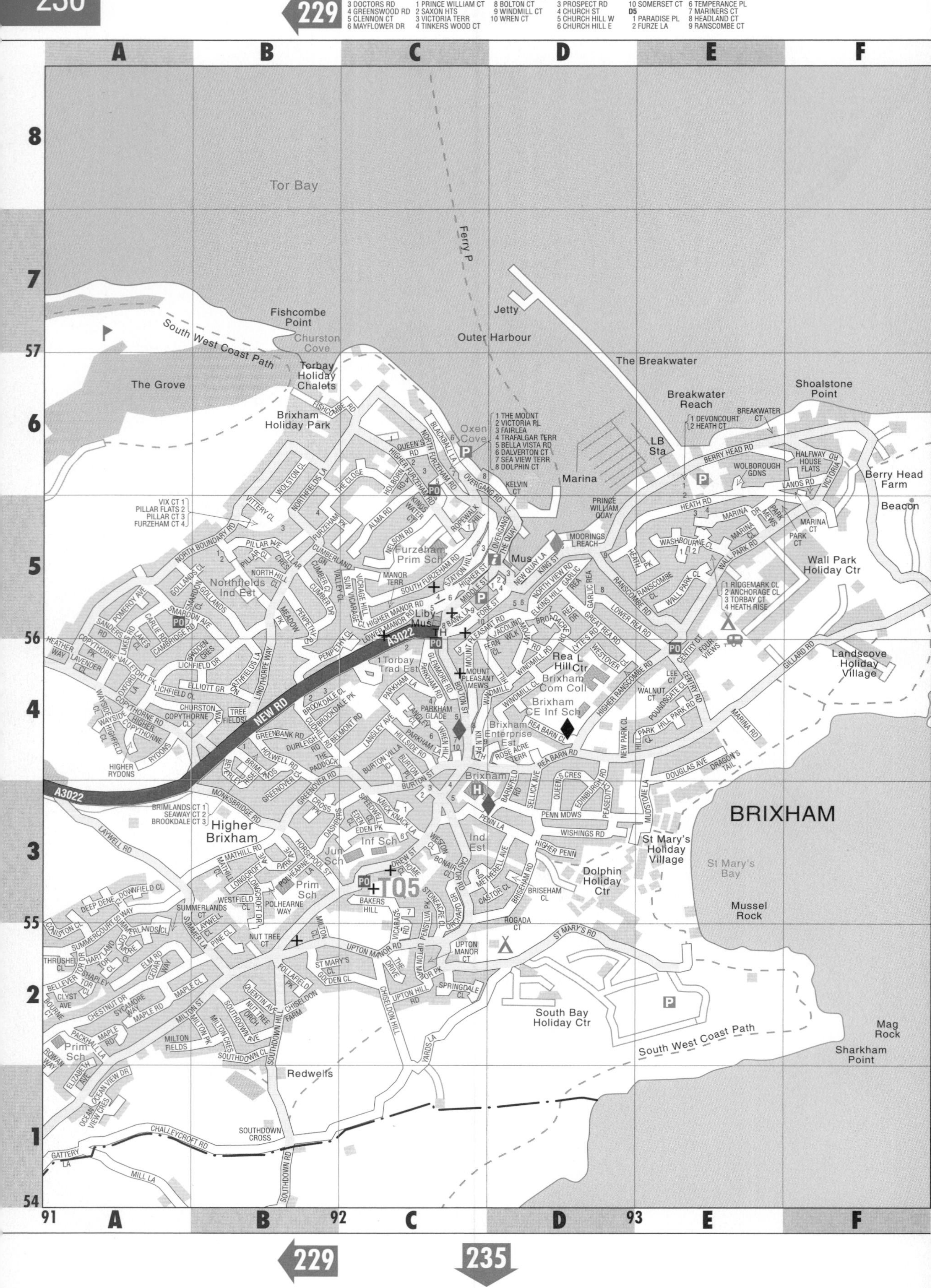

229
235

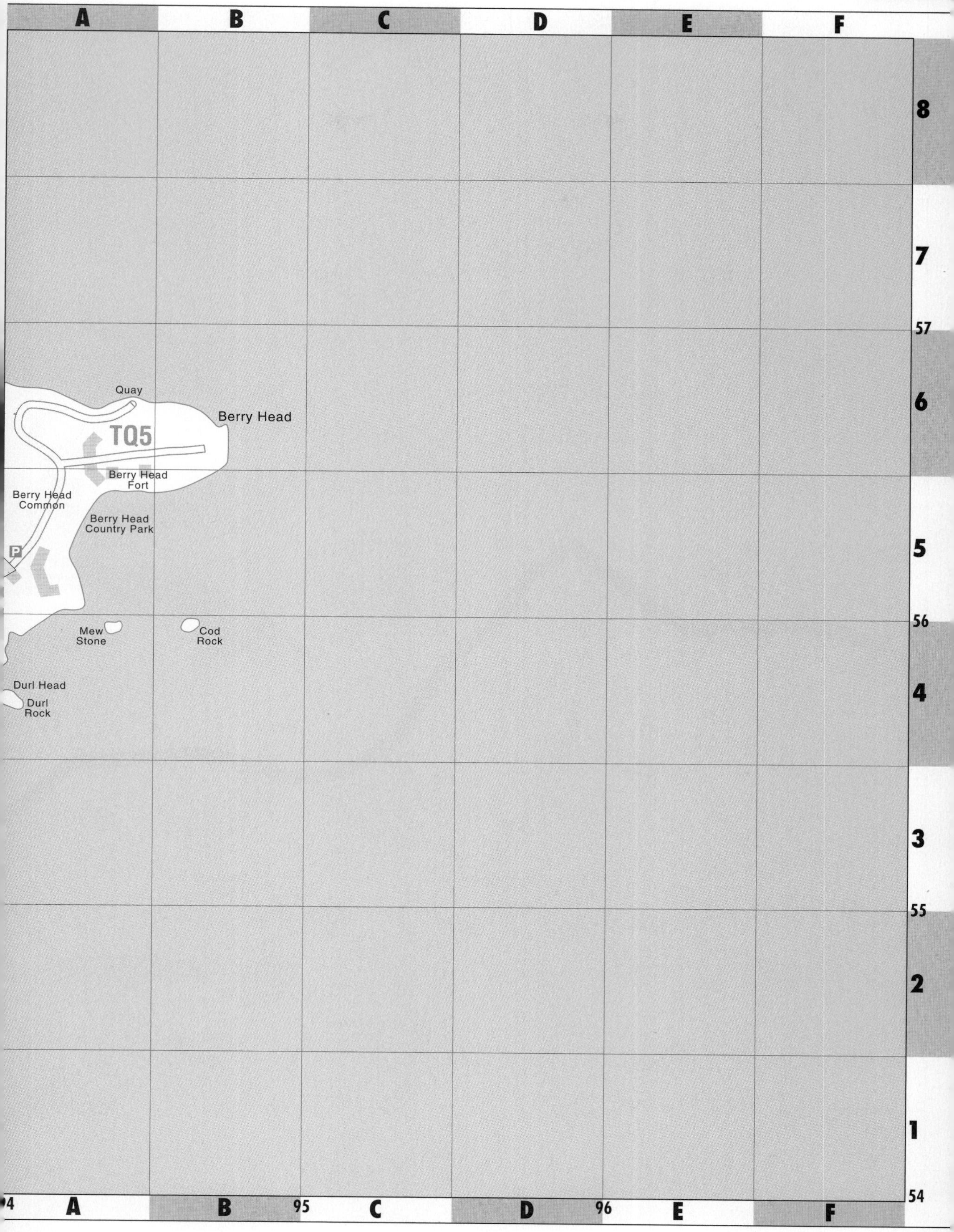

A B C D E F

8
7
57
6
5
56
4
3
55
2
1
54

94 A B 95 C D 96 E F

139
227

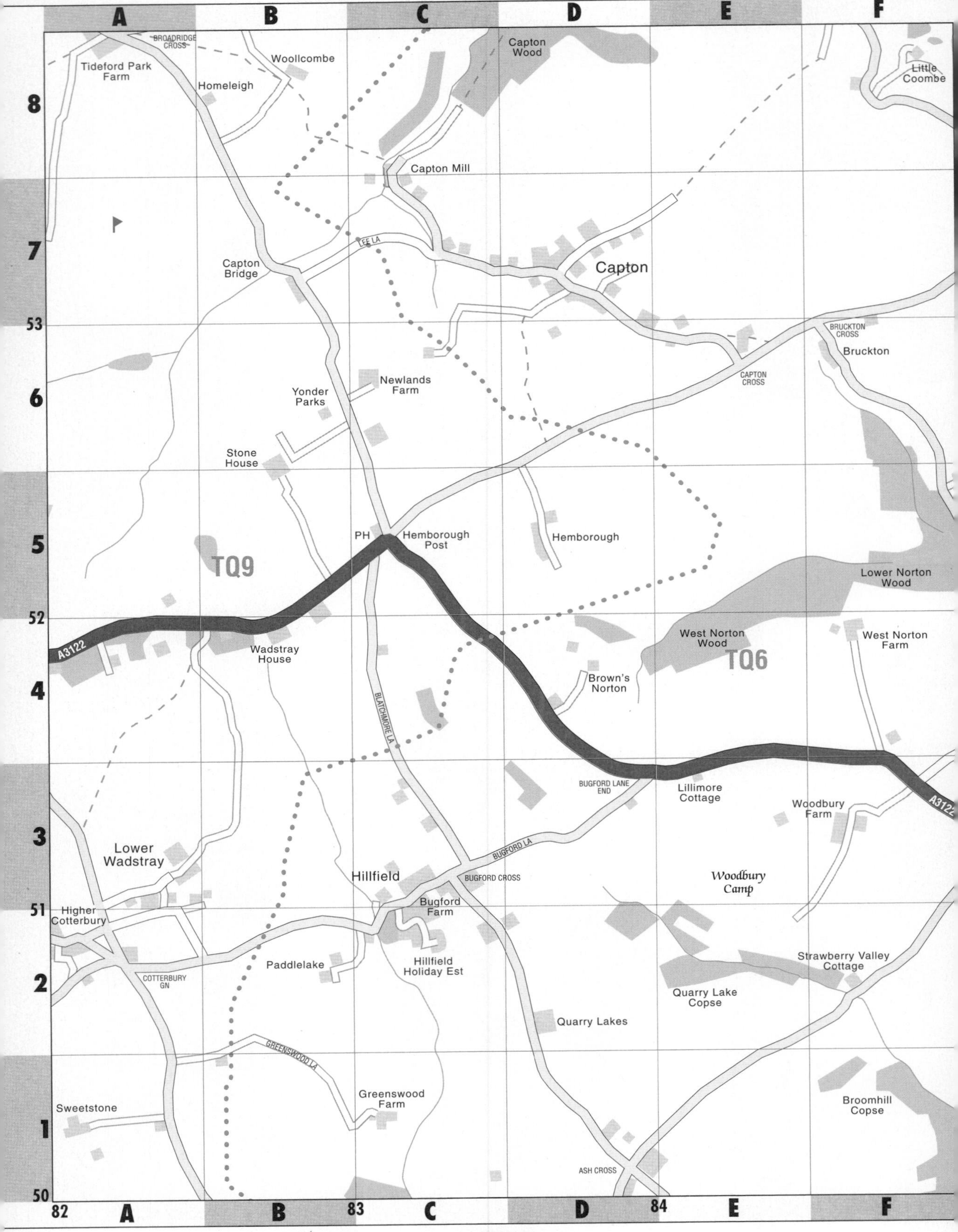

A B C D E F

8 7 53 6 5 52 4 3 51 2 1 50

Tideford Park Farm
BROADRIDGE CROSS
Woollcombe
Homeleigh
Capton Wood
Little Coombe
Capton Mill
LEE LA
Capton Bridge
Capton
BRUCKTON CROSS
Bruckton
CAPTON CROSS
Yonder Parks
Newlands Farm
Stone House
PH
Hemborough Post
Hemborough
TQ9
Lower Norton Wood
A3122
Wadstray House
West Norton Wood
TQ6
West Norton Farm
Brown's Norton
BLATCHMORE LA
BUGFORD LANE END
Lillimore Cottage
Woodbury Farm
A3122
Lower Wadstray
BUGFORD LA
Hillfield
BUGFORD CROSS
Woodbury Camp
Higher Cotterbury
Bugford Farm
Paddlelake
Hillfield Holiday Est
Strawberry Valley Cottage
COTTERBURY GN
Quarry Lake Copse
Quarry Lakes
GREENSWOOD LA
Greenswood Farm
Sweetstone
Broomhill Copse
ASH CROSS

82 A B 83 C D 84 E F

139
145

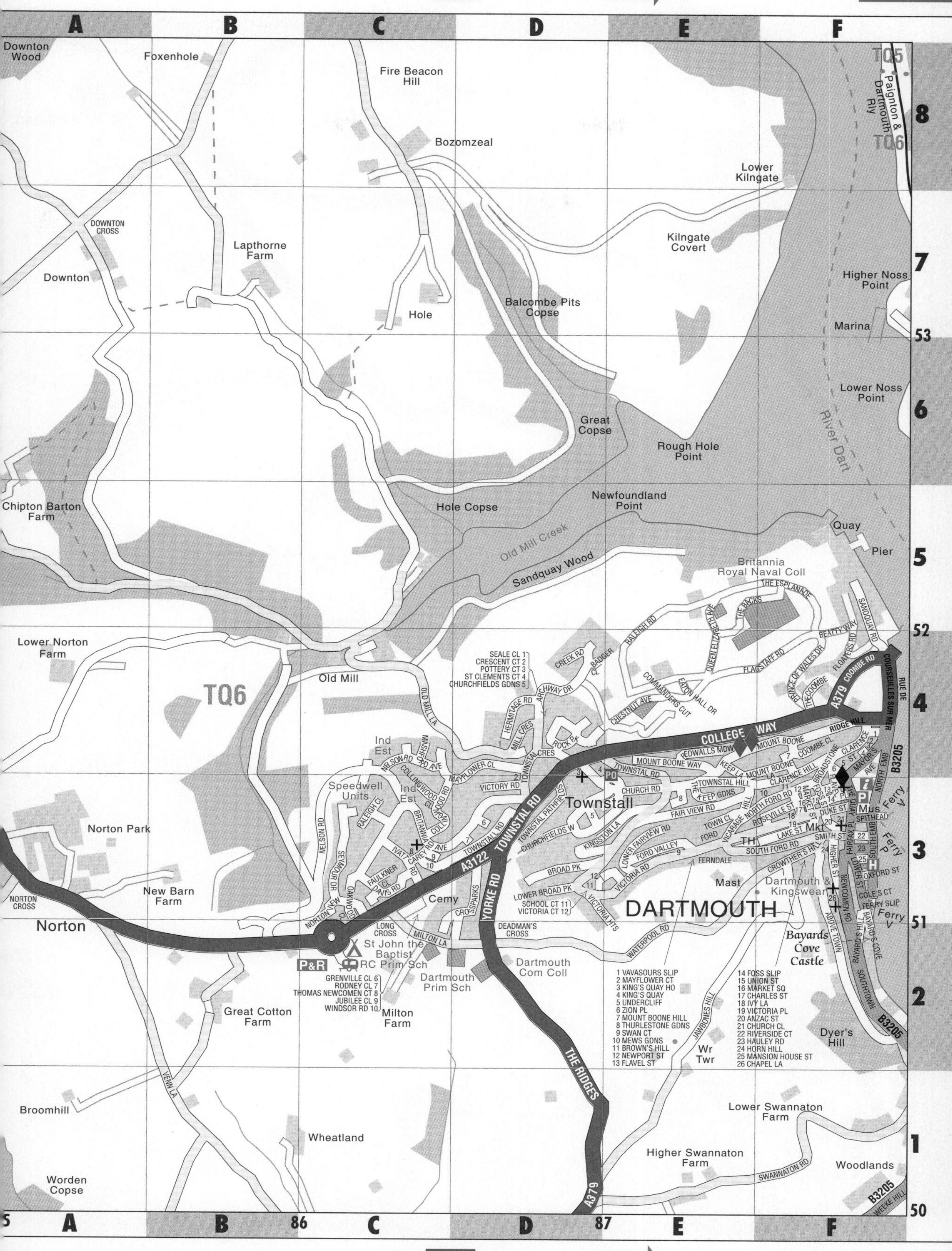
A
B
C
D
E
F
8
7
53
6
5
52
4
3
51
2
1
50
86
87
Downton Wood
Foxenhole
Fire Beacon Hill
Bozomzeal
TQ5
Paignton & Dartmouth Rly
TQ6
Lower Kilngate
DOWNTON CROSS
Lapthorne Farm
Kilngate Covert
Downton
Higher Noss Point
Balcombe Pits Copse
Hole
Marina
Lower Noss Point
Great Copse
Rough Hole Point
River Dart
Chipton Barton Farm
Newfoundland Point
Hole Copse
Old Mill Creek
Quay
Pier
Sandquay Wood
Britannia Royal Naval Coll
THE ESPLANADE
Lower Norton Farm
SEALE CL 1
CRESCENT CT 2
POTTERY CT 3
ST CLEMENTS CT 4
CHURCHFIELDS GDNS 5
Old Mill
TQ6
OLD MILL LA
COLLEGE WAY
RIDGE HILL
COURSEULLES SUR MER
RUE DE
A379
B3205
Ind Est
Speedwell Units
Townstall
Norton Park
Ferry
Mus
Mkt
TH
A3122
TOWNSTAL RD
YORKE RD
New Barn Farm
NORTON CROSS
Norton
Cemy
Mast
DARTMOUTH
Dartmouth & Kingswear
Bayards Cove Castle
LONG CROSS
DEADMAN'S CROSS
St John the Baptist RC Prim Sch
P&R
Dartmouth Com Coll
Dartmouth Prim Sch
GRENVILLE CL 6
RODNEY CL 7
THOMAS NEWCOMEN CT 8
JUBILEE CL 9
WINDSOR RD 10
Great Cotton Farm
Milton Farm
1 VAVASOURS SLIP
2 MAYFLOWER CT
3 KING'S QUAY HO
4 KING'S QUAY
5 UNDERCLIFF
6 ZION PL
7 MOUNT BOONE HILL
8 THURLESTONE GDNS
9 SWAN CT
10 MEWS GDNS
11 BROWN'S HILL
12 NEWPORT ST
13 FLAVEL ST
14 FOSS SLIP
15 UNION ST
16 MARKET SQ
17 CHARLES ST
18 IVY LA
19 VICTORIA PL
20 ANZAC ST
21 CHURCH CL
22 RIVERSIDE CT
23 HAULEY RD
24 HORN HILL
25 MANSION HOUSE ST
26 CHAPEL LA
Dyer's Hill
Wr Twr
THE RIDGES
Broomhill
Lower Swannaton Farm
Wheatland
Higher Swannaton Farm
Woodlands
Worden Copse
SWANNATON RD
WEEKE HILL

233 229

233 146

230

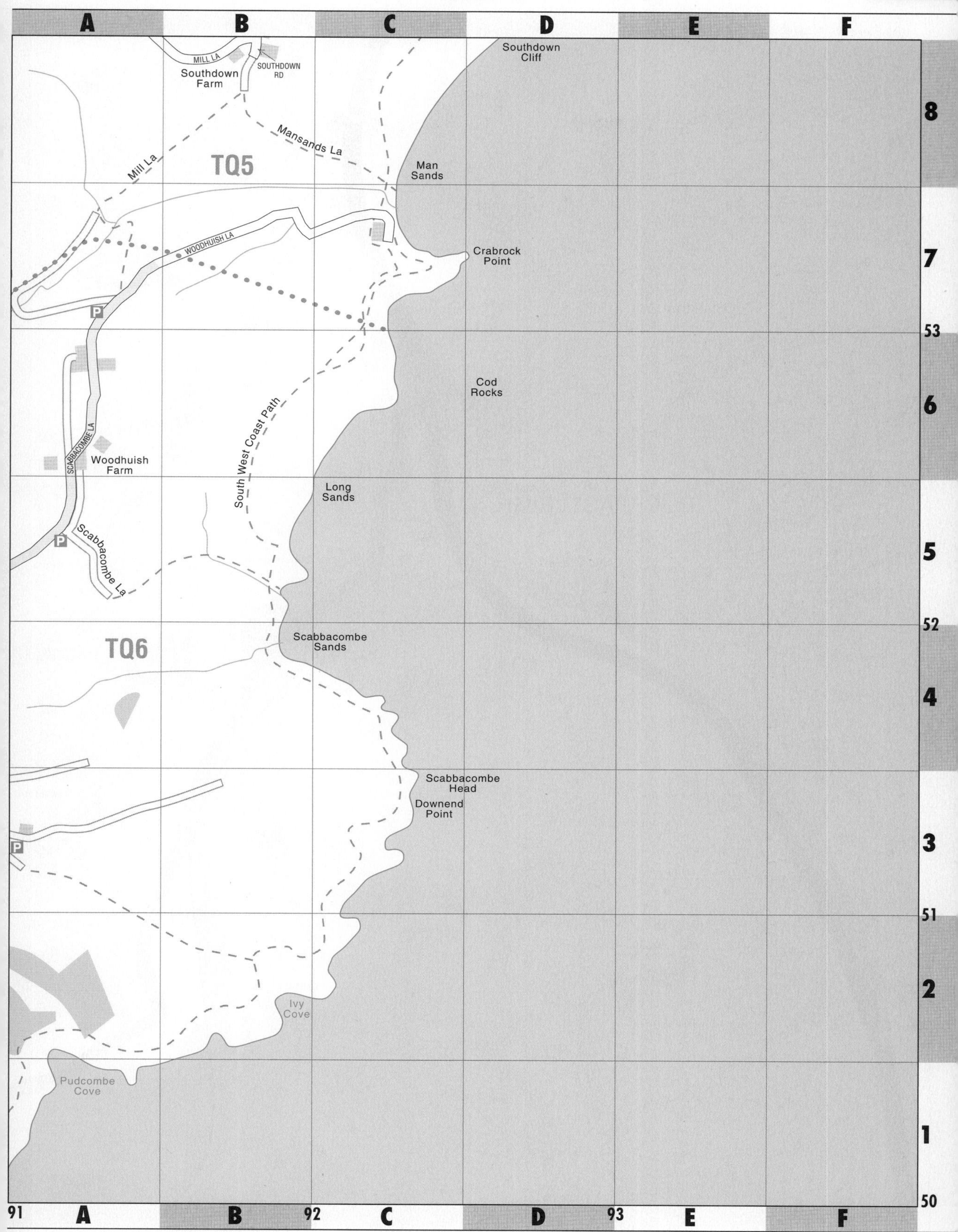
A
B
C
D
E
F
MILL LA
SOUTHDOWN RD
Southdown Farm
Southdown Cliff
8
Mansands La
Mill La
TQ5
Man Sands
WOODHUISH LA
Crabrock Point
7
53
Cod Rocks
6
South West Coast Path
SCABBACOMBE LA
Woodhuish Farm
Long Sands
Scabbacombe La
5
52
TQ6
Scabbacombe Sands
4
Scabbacombe Head
Downend Point
3
51
2
Ivy Cove
Pudcombe Cove
1
50
91
92
93

130 130 131

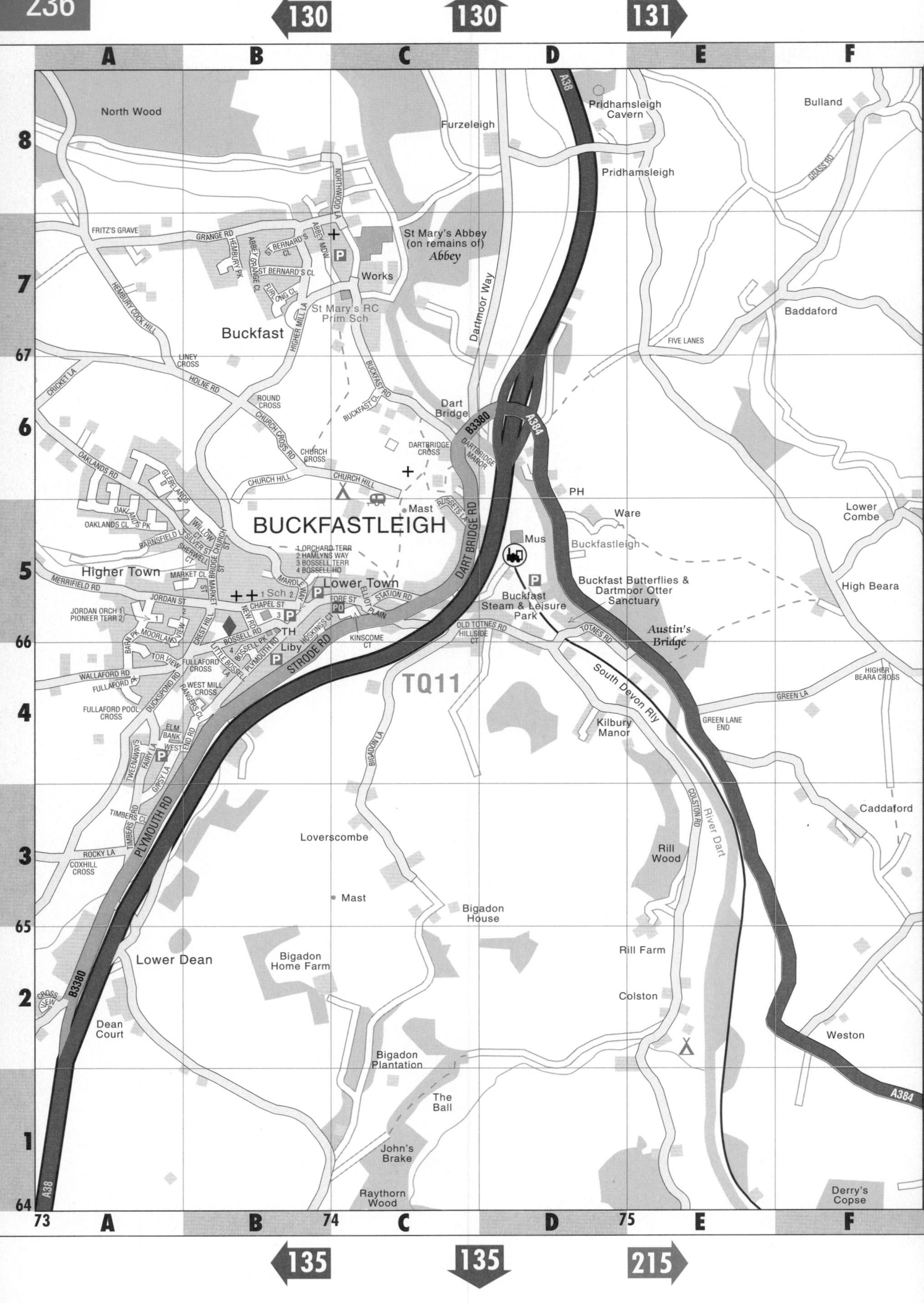

135 135 215

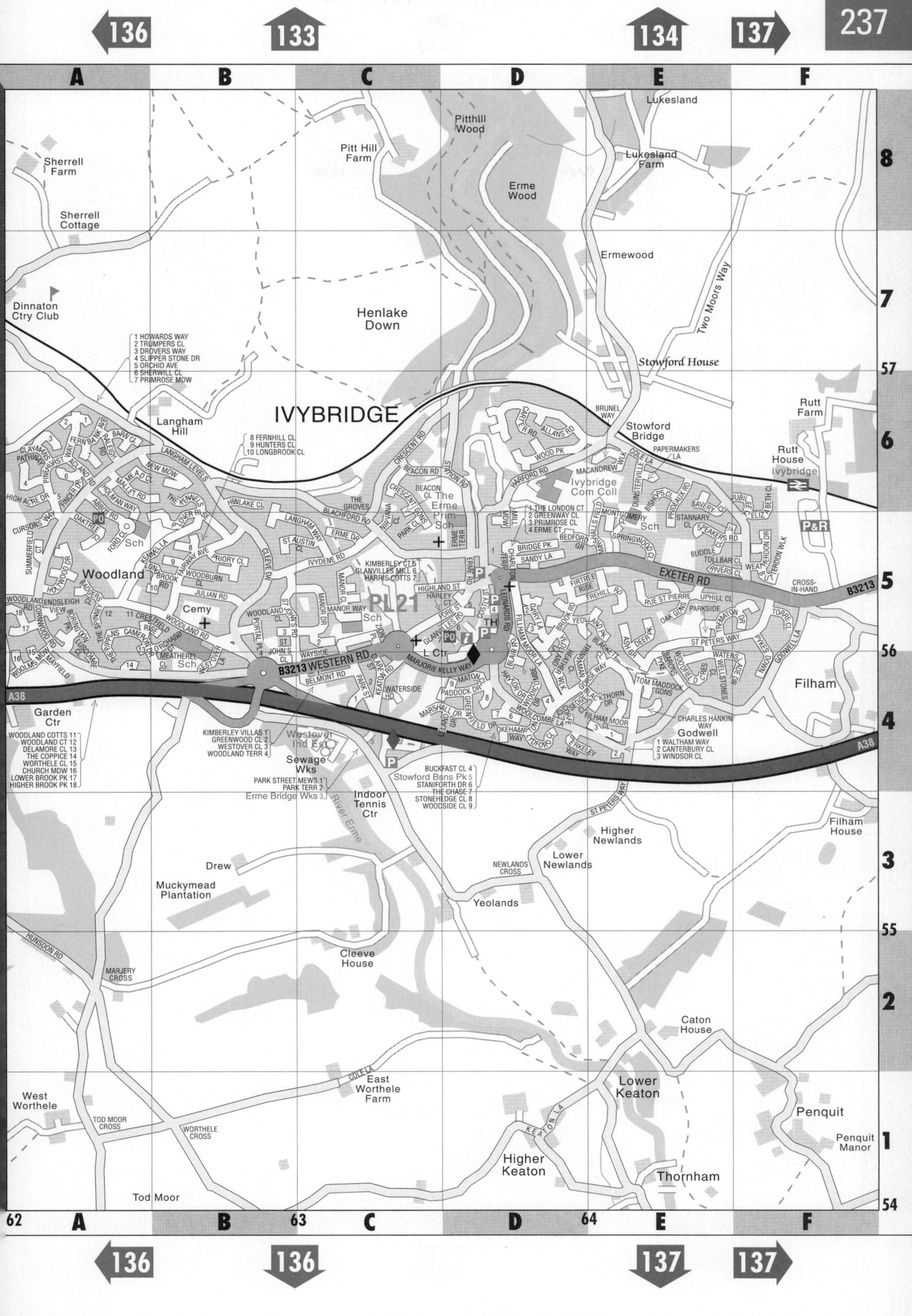
136
133
134
137
A
B
C
D
E
F
8
7
57
6
5
56
4
3
55
2
1
54
Lukesland
Pitthill
Wood
Pitt Hill
Farm
Sherrell
Farm
Lukesland
Farm
Erme
Wood
Sherrell
Cottage
Ermewood
Dinnaton
Ctry Club
Henlake
Down
Two Moors Way
Stowford House
1 HOWARDS WAY
2 TRUMPERS CL
3 DROVERS WAY
4 SLIPPER STONE DR
5 ORCHID AVE
6 SHERWILL CL
7 PRIMROSE MDW
IVYBRIDGE
Langham
Hill
Rutt
Farm
Stowford
Bridge
BRUNEL
WAY
Rutt
House
Ivybridge
8 FERNHILL CL
9 HUNTERS CL
10 LONGBROOK CL
PAPERMAKERS
LA
Ivybridge
Com Coll
Woodland
Cemy
Sch
P&R
EXETER RD
B3213
PL21
CROSS-
IN-HAND
1 THE LONDON CT
2 GREENWAY CL
3 PRIMROSE CL
4 ERME CT
KIMBERLEY CT 5
GLANVILLES MILL 6
HARRIS COTTS 7
B3213 WESTERN RD
MARJORIE KELLY WAY
L Ctr
TH
Filham
A38
Garden
Ctr
WOODLAND COTTS 11
WOODLAND CT 12
DELAMORE CL 13
THE COPPICE 14
WORTHELE CL 15
CHURCH MDW 16
LOWER BROOK PK 17
HIGHER BROOK PK 18
KIMBERLEY VILLAS 1
GREENWOOD CL 2
WESTOVER CL 3
WOODLAND TERR 4
Westover
Ind Est
Sewage
Wks
PARK STREET MEWS 1
PARK TERR 2
Erme Bridge Wks 3
BUCKFAST CL 4
Stowford Bsns Pk 5
STANIFORTH DR 6
THE CHASE 7
STONEHEDGE CL 8
WOODSIDE CL 9
CHARLES HANKIN
WAY
Godwell
1 WALTHAM WAY
2 CANTERBURY CL
3 WINDSOR CL
Indoor
Tennis
Ctr
River Erme
ST PETERS WAY
Higher
Newlands
Filham
House
Lower
Newlands
NEWLANDS
CROSS
Drew
Muckymead
Plantation
Yeolands
Cleeve
House
HUNSDON RD
MARJERY
CROSS
Caton
House
COLE LA
East
Worthele
Farm
Lower
Keaton
West
Worthele
TOD MOOR
CROSS
WORTHELE
CROSS
KEATON LA
Penquit
Penquit
Manor
Higher
Keaton
Thornham
Tod Moor
62
63
64
136
136
137
137

125

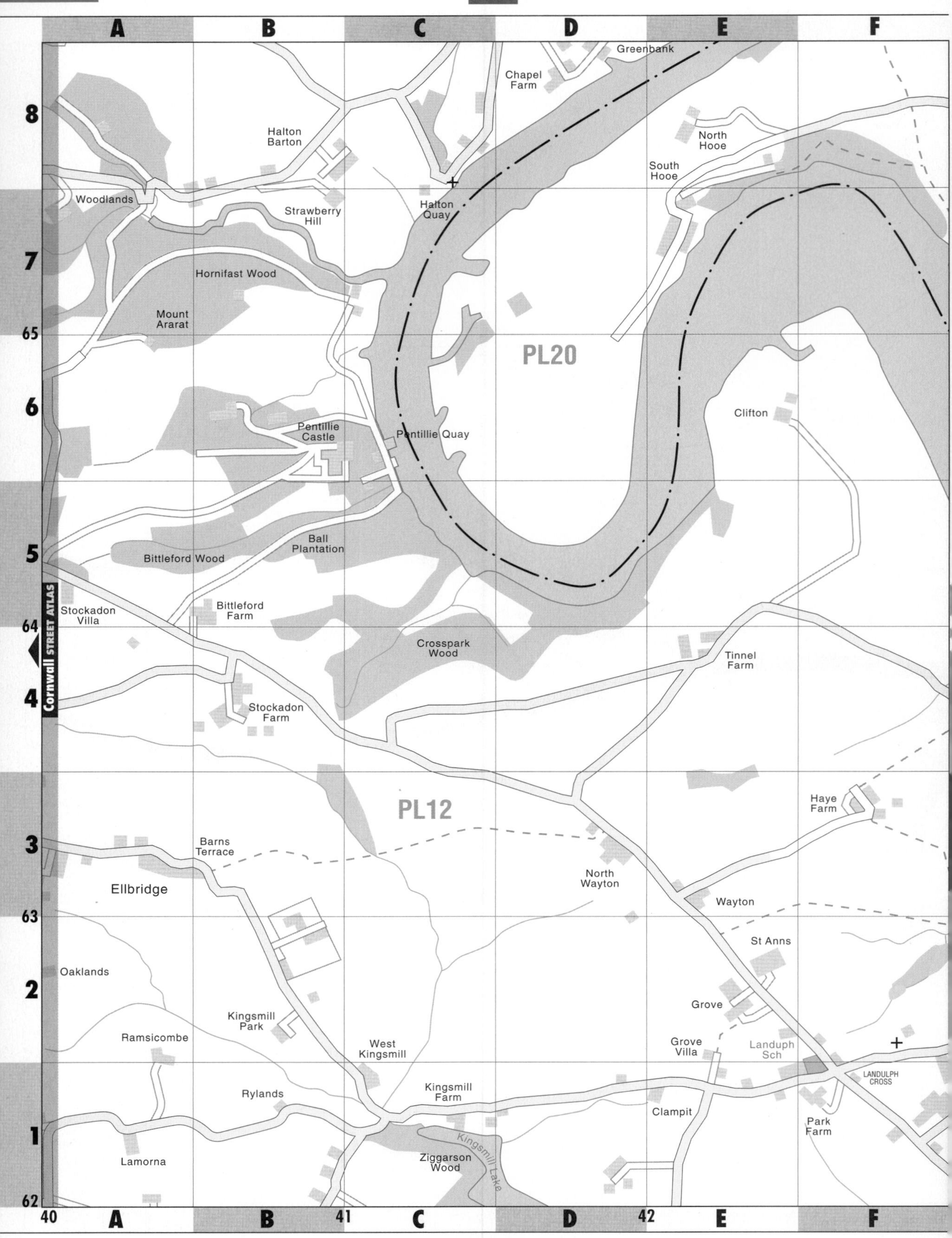
A
B
C
D
E
F
8
7
65
6
5
64
4
3
63
2
1
62
40
41
42
Greenbank
Chapel Farm
Halton Barton
North Hooe
South Hooe
Woodlands
Strawberry Hill
Halton Quay
Hornifast Wood
Mount Ararat
PL20
Clifton
Pentillie Castle
Pentillie Quay
Ball Plantation
Bittleford Wood
Stockadon Villa
Bittleford Farm
Crosspark Wood
Tinnel Farm
Stockadon Farm
Cornwall STREET ATLAS
PL12
Haye Farm
Barns Terrace
Ellbridge
North Wayton
Wayton
St Anns
Oaklands
Grove
Kingsmill Park
Ramsicombe
West Kingsmill
Grove Villa
Landuph Sch
LANDULPH CROSS
Rylands
Kingsmill Farm
Clampit
Park Farm
Kingsmill Lake
Ziggarson Wood
Lamorna

242

125
240
A
B
C
D
E
F
8
7
65
6
5
64
4
3
63
2
1
62
43
44
45
Hewton
Hole's Hole
Cotts
Higher Birch
Wottons Farm
Down Wood
Down Farm
Well Farm
HOLE CROSS
Leeches
Quay
Weir Quay
Cleave Farm
Shangri-La
Hole Farm
River Tamar
Clamoak
Clamoak Poll Wood
Tuckham Bridge
LEY LA
Ley Farm
Clamoak Quay
Ormonde House
Fairway
Shutecombe
Liphil Quay
New Park Farm
Parsonage Farm
PL20
Greystone
HENSBURY LA
TREVETHAN PK
PO
Bere Ferrers
STATION RD
FORE ST
PH
SILVER ST
Bere Ferrers
Bere Barton
Thorn Point
Cargreen
COOMBE LA
COOMBE DR
HOOPERS WAY
PH
Hall
CLOAKE PL
FORE ST
Quays
HILL GDNS
CHURCH LA
Penyoke
PL12
New Barn Farm
Pennard's Point
River Tavy
243
240

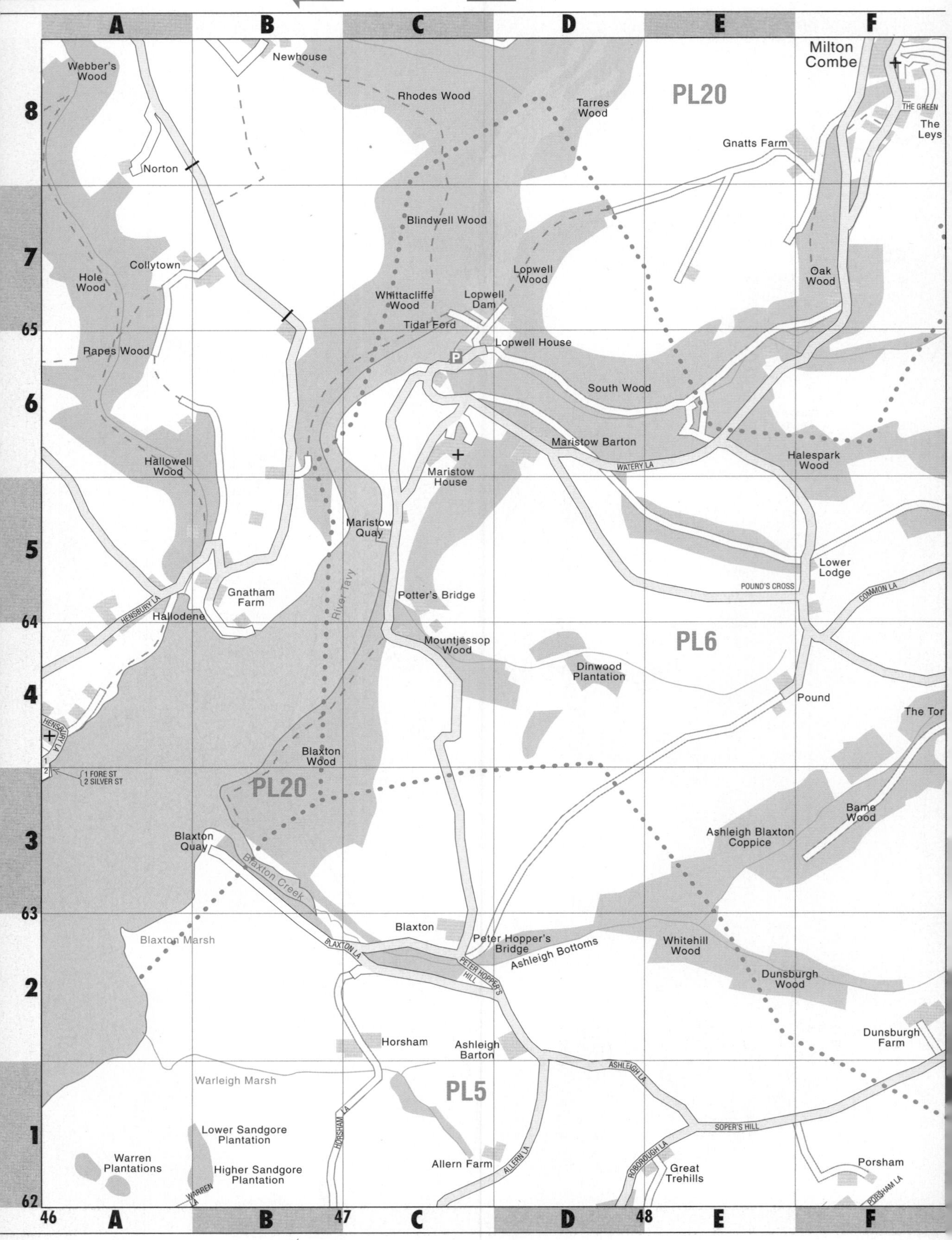

239
126
244
A
B
C
D
E
F
8
7
65
6
5
64
4
3
63
2
1
62
46
47
48
Milton Combe
THE GREEN
The Leys
Webber's Wood
Newhouse
Rhodes Wood
Tarres Wood
PL20
Gnatts Farm
Norton
Blindwell Wood
Collytown
Hole Wood
Lopwell Wood
Oak Wood
Whittacliffe Wood
Lopwell Dam
Tidal Ford
Rapes Wood
Lopwell House
P
South Wood
Maristow Barton
WATERY LA
Halespark Wood
Hallowell Wood
Maristow House
Maristow Quay
River Tavy
Lower Lodge
Gnatham Farm
Potter's Bridge
POUND'S CROSS
COMMON LA
HENSBURY LA
Hallodene
PL6
Mountjessop Wood
Dinwood Plantation
Pound
The Tor
1 FORE ST
2 SILVER ST
Blaxton Wood
PL20
Bame Wood
Ashleigh Blaxton Coppice
Blaxton Quay
Blaxton Creek
Blaxton
Blaxton Marsh
Peter Hopper's Bridge
Ashleigh Bottoms
Whitehill Wood
BLAXTON LA
PETER HOPPER'S HILL
Dunsburgh Wood
Horsham
Ashleigh Barton
Dunsburgh Farm
ASHLEIGH LA
Warleigh Marsh
PL5
HORSHAM LA
SOPER'S HILL
Lower Sandgore Plantation
Warren Plantations
Higher Sandgore Plantation
Allern Farm
ALLERN LA
ROBOROUGH LA
Great Trehills
Porsham
PORSHAM LA
WARREN LA

126
132

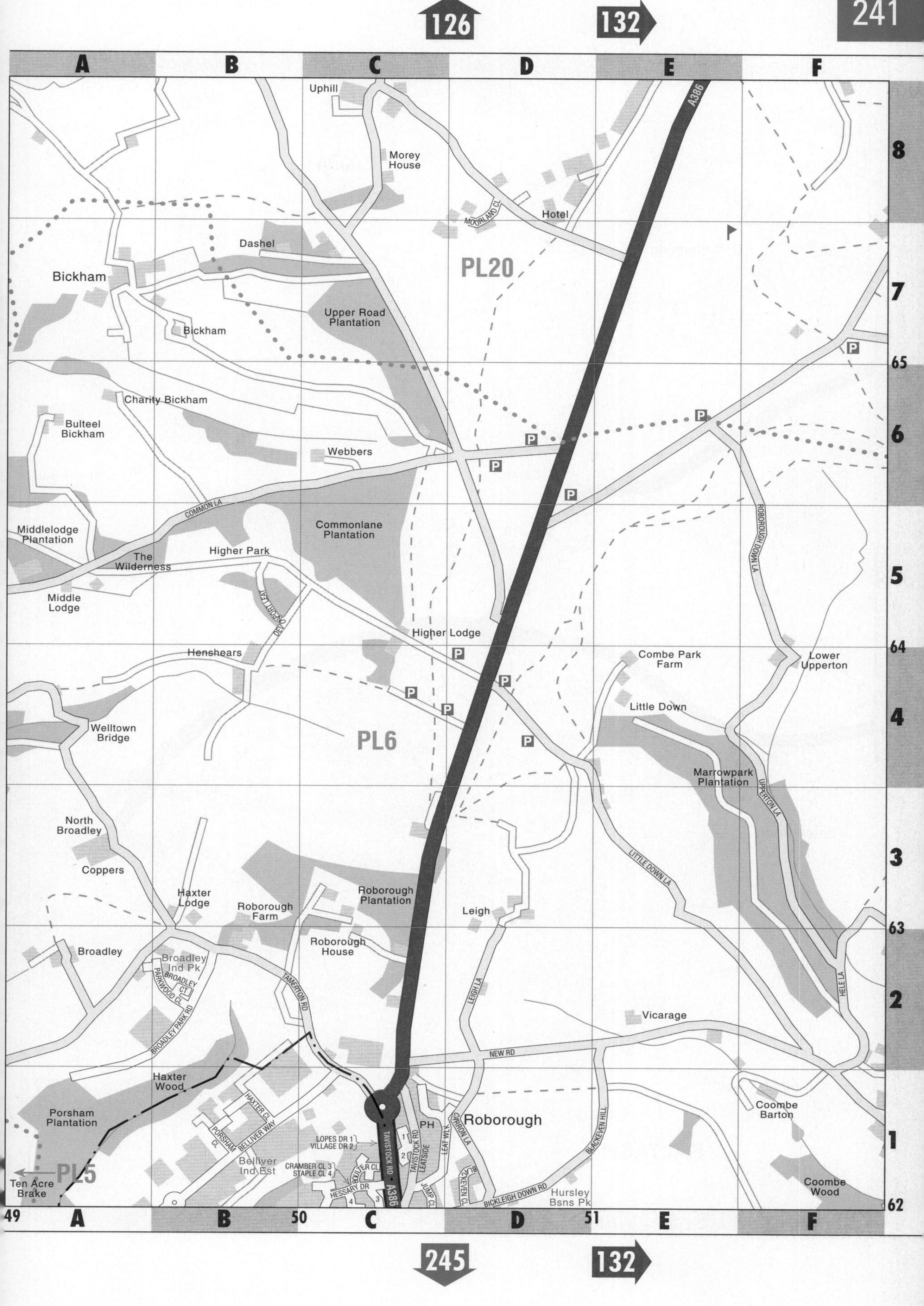

245
132

238

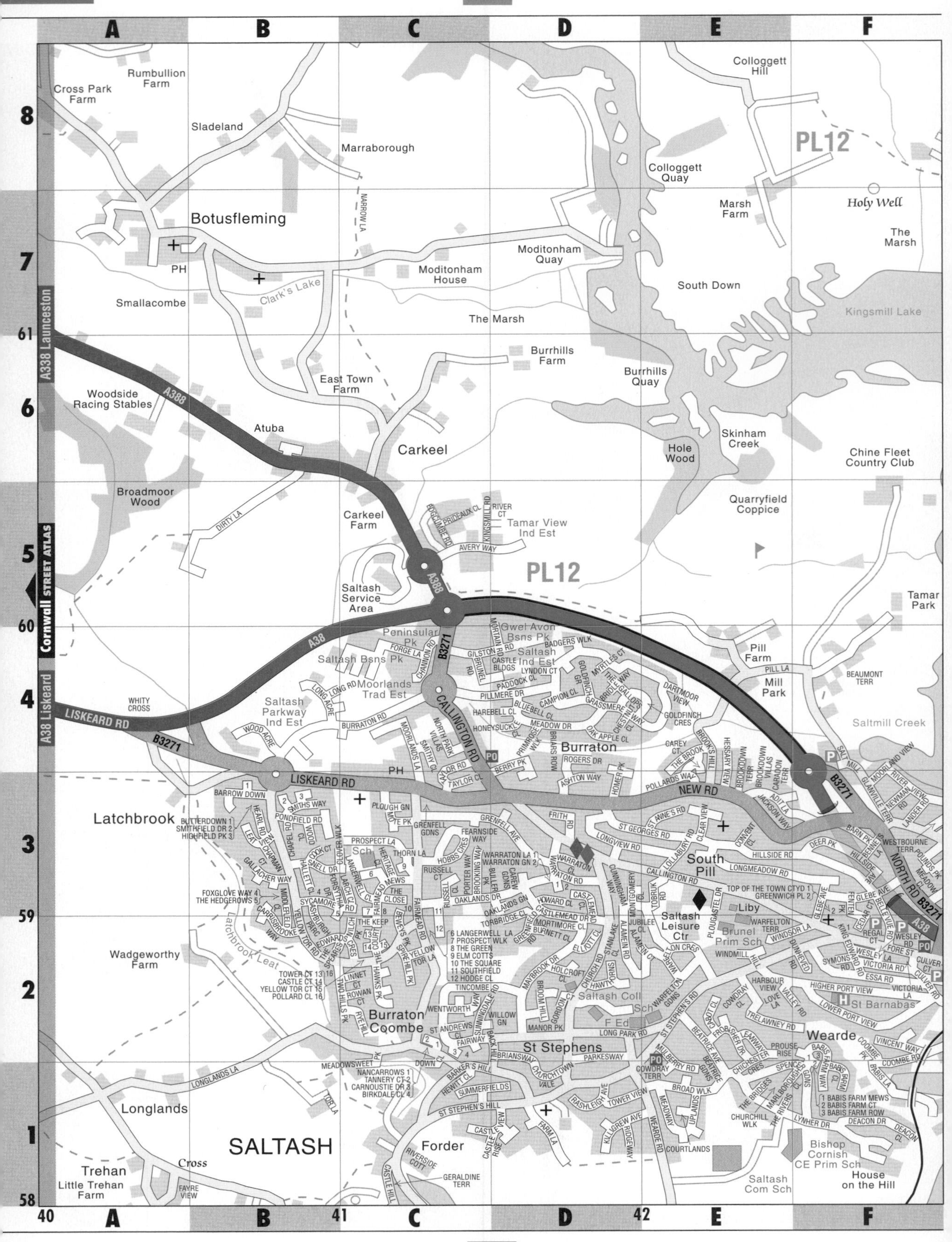
A
B
C
D
E
F
8
7
6
5
4
3
2
1
61
60
59
58
40
41
42
Rumbullion Farm
Cross Park Farm
Sladeland
Marraborough
Colloggett Hill
PL12
Colloggett Quay
Marsh Farm
Holy Well
The Marsh
Botusfleming
PH
Moditonham Quay
Moditonham House
South Down
Smallacombe
Clark's Lake
The Marsh
Kingsmill Lake
A38 Launceston
Burrhills Farm
Burrhills Quay
East Town Farm
Woodside Racing Stables
A388
Atuba
Carkeel
Hole Wood
Skinham Creek
Chine Fleet Country Club
Broadmoor Wood
Quarryfield Coppice
Carkeel Farm
Tamar View Ind Est
Cornwall STREET ATLAS
DIRTY LA
AVERY WAY
PL12
Saltash Service Area
Tamar Park
A38
Peninsular Pk
Gwel Avon Bsns Pk
Saltash Ind Est
Saltash Bsns Pk
Pill Farm
Mill Park
BEAUMONT TERR
A38 Liskeard
WHITY CROSS
LISKEARD RD
Saltash Parkway Ind Est
Moorlands Trad Est
CALLINGTON RD
Saltmill Creek
B3271
Burraton
LISKEARD RD
PH
NEW RD
Latchbrook
South Pill
Saltash Leisure Ctr
Liby
Brunel Prim Sch
St Barnabas
Wadgeworthy Farm
Latchbrook Leat
Burraton Coombe
Saltash Coll
F Ed
Wearde
St Stephens
Longlands
LONGLANDS LA
SALTASH
Forder
Cross
Trehan
Little Trehan Farm
Bishop Cornish CE Prim Sch
Saltash Com Sch
House on the Hill
COURTLANDS

246

A
B
C
D
E
F
8
7
61
6
5
60
4
3
59
2
1
58
44
45
PL12
PL20
PL5
Weir Point
Landulph
Neal Point
Skinham Point
Warleigh House
Warleigh Quay
Warleigh Barton
River Tavy
Tavy Bridge
Park Plantation
Reedwell Plantation
Warleigh Wood
Warleigh Point
River Tamar
Woodlands House
Badgers Park Wood
STATION RD
Warren Point
Tamarton Bridge
Ind Est
LAKESIDE DR
MANSTON CL
TANGMERE AVE
CATTERICK CL
WEST MALLING AVE
DIGBY GR
Liby
DUXFORD CL
HORNCHURCH RD
HORNCHURCH LA
UXBRIDGE DR
NORTHOLT AVE
EXETER CL
MAIDSTONE PL
CROYDON GDNS
MIDDLETON WLK
GRAVESEND WLK
DEBDEN CL
HAWKINGE GDNS
PEMBREY WLK
ST EVAL PL
KENLEY GDNS
BIGGIN HILL
LYMPNE AVE
WESTHAMPNETT PL
ROCHFORD CRES
RUSSET WOOD
COLTISHALL CL
Sports Ctr
Ernesettle Jun & Inf Sch
ERNESETTLE LA
Playing Field
Ernesettle
YELVERTON CL
CULDROSE CL
PERRANPORTH CL
ACKLINGTON PL
BUDSHEAD RD
MARINA RD
QUEENS RD
KINGS RD
KINSALE RD
CROWNHILL RD B3413
DUNCOMBE AVE
SHERFORD CRES
ERNESETTLE CRES
Ernesettle Battery
PL5
THE PARKWAY
B3413
CHATSWORTH GDNS
DALTON GDNS
PRIESTLEY AVE
PLAISTOW CL
St Budeaux Foundation Jun Sch
A38
Ernesettle Farm
TAMAR BRIDGE
Toll
PLYMOUTH
Footpath/Cycleway
Royal Albert Bridge
Saltash
Town Quay
Mary Newman's Cottage
1 ALEXANDRA SQ
2 STATION RD
3 BOSCUNDLE ROW
4 TAMAR TERR
BICKHAM RD
WAVERLEY RD
VICTORIA RD
Mount Tamar Sch
ROW LA
King's Tamerton
NEWTON AVE
NEWTON GDNS
1 ARKWRIGHT GDNS
2 HARGREAVES CL
ADMIRALTY RD
NORMANDY WAY
St Budeaux
LYNHER ST
EVELYN ST
KATHLEAVEN ST
PETER'S PARK LA
TREVITHICK RD
COOMBE WAY
NORMANDY HILL
BLAIRGOWRIE RD
LOUGHBORO RD
VICARAGE GDNS
Riverside
LITTLE ASH GDNS
FLORENCE ST
COLLIN CL
Sch
Tamarside Com Coll
FLAMSTEED CRES
HALLEY GDNS
ADAMS CL
PEMROS RD
WOLSELEY RD
TRELAWNEY PL
PERCY ST
COLEBROOK RD
FERRERS RD
MOOR LA
WESTON MILL RD
WESTON MILL HILL
A3064
MOWHAY RD
FEGAN RD
WARBURTON GDNS
FOULSTON AVE
SCOTT AVE
HAYDON GR
SITHNEY ST
BARNE RD
COLDRENICK ST
FLETEMOOR RD
BRIDWELL RD
YORK RD
TUCKER CL
HAM LA

243
240

243
248

241
132

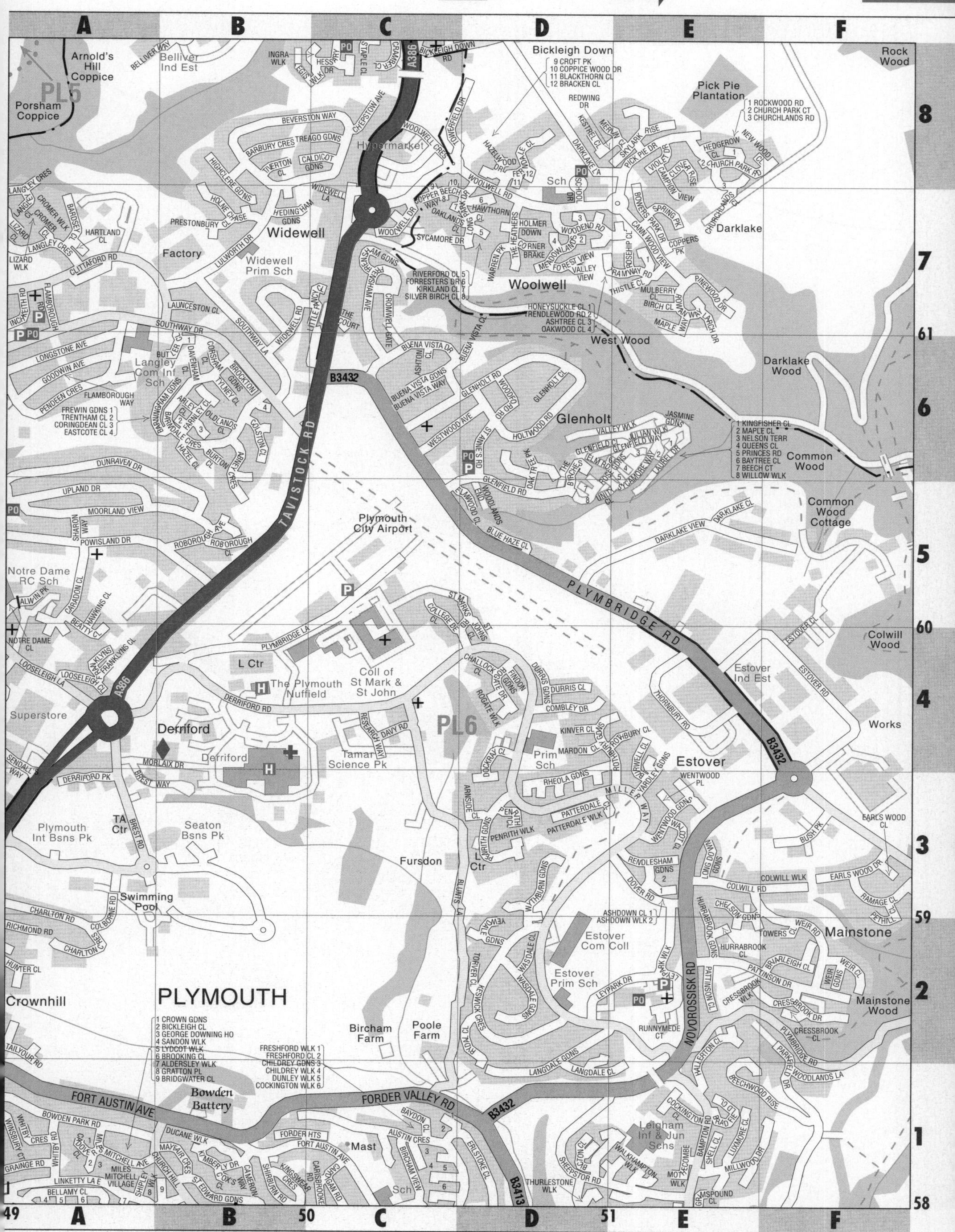

249
132

242

A
B
C
D
E
F
8
7
57
6
5
56
4
3
55
2
1
54
40
41
42
Cornwall STREET ATLAS
A374 Looe (A387)
PL12
PL12
PL11
Trehan
Castle Farm
CASTLE HILL
Trematon Castle
Forder Lake
Marsh Coombe
WEARDE RD
Merryfield View
Henn Point
Wearde Quay
Piers
Shillingham Manor
Antony Passage
Beggar's Island
Quay
St Germans or Lynher River
Jupiter Point
Jetty
Higher Wearlands Plantation
Shillingham Point
Wivelscombe Lake
Jupiter Plantation
Antony Woodland Garden
Tomboy Hill
Great Kithill Plantation
North Wilcove
Wilcove
Ince Point
Ince Castle
Bath House
Wilderness
Antony House
FERRY LA
Antony Park
WILCOVE LA
PENGELLY PK
PENGELLY CL
Maryfield
Coombe Pk
A374
Sports Gd
Borough Farm House
1 FISTRAL CL
2 GWITHIAN CL
Bulland Quay
Horson House
Horson Plantation
Mast
BOROUGH CT
BOROUGH PK
THE MEADOWS
PRIMROSE CL
KYNANCE CL
MULLION CL
TREVITHICK AVE
SENNEN CL
PENLEE PK
LAMORNA PK
TREMATON CL
INCE CL
CARLYON CL
LANGDON DOWN WAY
PENDENNIS CL
WOODLAND WAY
PENTIRE RD
GROVE PK
KERNOW CL
CLEGG AVE
WEST LAKE CL
GOAD AVE
Clift Quay
Bulland
KERNOW CT 3
TRELAWNEY WAY 4
WAY
Trevol Bsns Pk
FISGARD
FROBISHER WAY
WAVISH PK
TRELAWNEY
ADAMS CRES
MURDOCK RD
GURNE CL
DAVY CL
Clift
Longlands Plantation
Cemy
HMS Fisgard
TRELAWNEY RISE
GOAD CL
TRENGROUSE AVE
SYCAMORE DR
Trevol Ho
HAWTHORN AVE
CHESTNUT CL
TREVOL RD
TREVOL PL
Hay
CEDAR CT
CEDAR DR
PENCAIR AVE
TREGONING RD
Trinaway Plantation
A374
TREVORDER RD
TREVORDER CL
PENDILLY AVE
PO
HMS Raleigh
HOLLOWGUTTER LA
ABBOTSCOURT LA
Sports Gd
West Antony
Rifle Range
Eastdowns Lake
Sewage Wks
Efford's Bridge
Deadman's Point
River Tamar Hamoaze
Wolsdon House
St John's Lake

252

F5
1 NEPEAN ST
2 ADELAIDE ST
3 BRUNEL TERR
4 EPWORTH TERR
5 SUSSEX TERR
6 RAILWAY COTTS
7 YORK TERR
8 ST MAWES TERR

253
248

F3
1 CLARENDON HO
2 GARFIELD TERR
3 TRAFALGAR PL
4 THE MEWS
5 NELSON GDNS
6 BEYROUT PL
7 ST MICHAEL'S CT
8 ST MICHAEL'S TERR
9 PORTLAND CT
10 MOLYNEAUX PL
F4
1 ST GEORGES CT
2 HORNBY ST
3 PHILLIMORE ST
4 FREMANTLE GDNS
5 FAIRFAX TERR
6 HARGOOD TERR
7 HARRISON ST
8 KEPPEL TERR
9 HEALY CT
10 BRUNSWICK PL

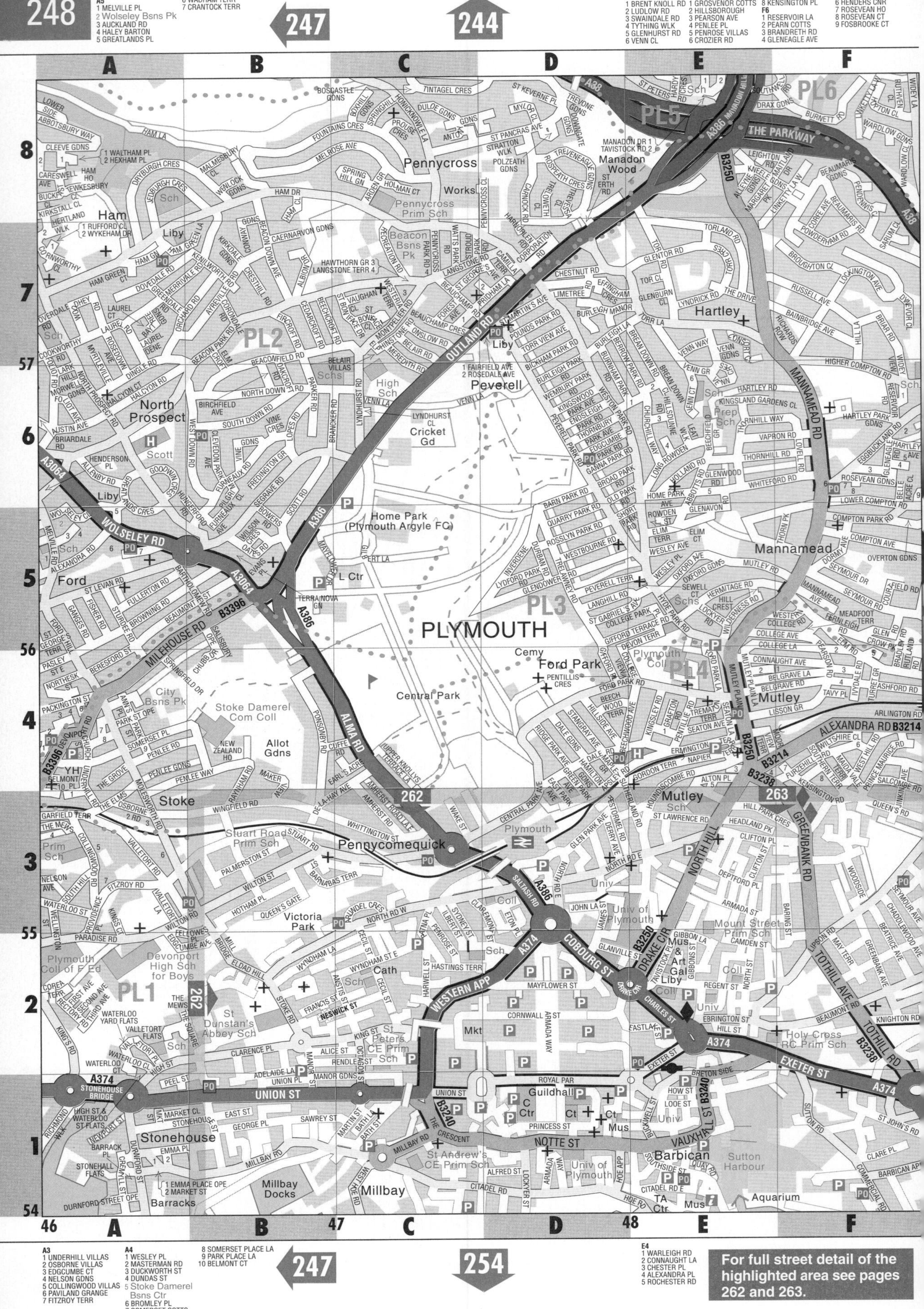
248
A5
1 MELVILLE PL
2 Wolseley Bsns Pk
3 AUCKLAND RD
4 HALEY BARTON
5 GREATLANDS PL
6 WADHAM TERR
7 CRANTOCK TERR
247
244
E6
1 BRENT KNOLL RD
2 LUDLOW RD
3 SWAINDALE RD
4 TYTHING WLK
5 GLENHURST RD
6 VENN CL
F4
1 GROSVENOR COTTS
2 HILLSBOROUGH
3 PEARSON AVE
4 PENLEE PL
5 PENROSE VILLAS
6 CROZIER RD
7 MARINA TERR
8 KENSINGTON PL
F6
1 RESERVOIR LA
2 PEARN COTTS
3 BRANDRETH RD
4 GLENEAGLE AVE
5 GLENEAGLE VILLAS
6 HENDERS CNR
7 ROSEVEAN HO
8 ROSEVEAN CT
9 FOSBROOKE CT
A
B
C
D
E
F
8
7
57
6
5
56
4
3
55
2
1
54
PL1
PL2
PL3
PL4
PL5
PL6
PLYMOUTH
Pennycross
Peverell
Ham
North Prospect
Ford
Stoke
Mutley
Hartley
Mannamead
Ford Park
Pennycomequick
Stonehouse
Millbay
Barbican
Manadon Wood
Home Park (Plymouth Argyle FC)
Central Park
Victoria Park
Millbay Docks
Sutton Harbour
Aquarium
THE PARKWAY
OUTLAND RD
ALMA RD
MILEHOUSE RD
WOLSELEY RD
ALEXANDRA RD
MANNAMEAD RD
NORTH HILL
TOTHILL AVE
EXETER ST
UNION ST
WESTERN APP
COBOURG ST
NOTTE ST
VAUXHALL ST
262
263
46
47
48
A
B
C
D
E
F
A3
1 UNDERHILL VILLAS
2 OSBORNE VILLAS
3 EDGCUMBE CT
4 NELSON GDNS
5 COLLINGWOOD VILLAS
6 PAVILAND GRANGE
7 FITZROY TERR
A4
1 WESLEY PL
2 MASTERMAN RD
3 DUCKWORTH ST
4 DUNDAS ST
5 Stoke Damerel Bsns Ctr
6 BROMLEY PL
7 SOMERSET COTTS
8 SOMERSET PLACE LA
9 PARK PLACE LA
10 BELMONT CT
247
254
E4
1 WARLEIGH RD
2 CONNAUGHT LA
3 CHESTER PL
4 ALEXANDRA PL
5 ROCHESTER RD
For full street detail of the highlighted area see pages 262 and 263.

For full street detail of the highlighted area see page 263.

249
132
E7
1 PERSEVERANCE COTTS
2 BLANCHARD PL
A
B
C
D
E
F
Boringdon Hall
(Hotel)
Triumphal
Arch
China Clay
Works
Hilltops
The
Croft
Brockhole
Wood
Elfordleigh
Wood
Binicliff
Wood
Boringdon
Cottages
Plym Valley Rly
Woodford
Woodford
Jun Sch
Hele's
Sch
Boringdon
Prim Sch
Colebrook
Newnham
Ind Est
Boringdon Mill
Bsns Ctr
Marsh
Mills
B3416
B3417
NEWNHAM RD
STRODE RD
GLEN RD
PLYMOUTH RD
Cot Hill
Trad Est
Ret Pk
Trad Est
Ind & Trad Est
Sewage
Works
Underwood
PL7
Plympton
Plympton
Ridgeway
Sch
Liby
Plympton
St Mary
CE Inf Sch
Old Priory
Jun Sch
Plympton
St Maurice
Longcause
Com Specl
Sch
A38
Amados Hill
Saltram
House
Saltram
Park
Stable
House
Hardwick Wood
Mast
Television
Relay Sta
Telegraph
Cottage
Dorsmouth
Rock
PLYMOUTH
Hardwick
Farm
Heather
Grange
Plympton
St Maurice
Prim Sch
The Belt
Sellar
Acres
Wixenford
Brake
Cemy
New Barne
Farm
Vealeholme
Haye
Farm
Furze
Park
PL9
Wixenford
Farm
Moorcroft
Quarry
Priors Park
Nursery
Haye Road
Nurseries
Higher
Sherford
PL8
COTTAGE MEWS 1
ILBERT COTTS 2
CASTLEHAYES GDNS 3
WOODBINE COTTS 4
DORSMOUTH TERR 5
ST MAURICE MEWS 6
1 TORY BROOK AVE
2 TORY BROOK CT
8
7
57
6
5
56
4
3
55
2
1
54
52
53
54
249
256

B5
1 CALEDONIA CL
2 ELDER CL
3 MAGNOLIA CL
4 TURBILL GDNS
5 PAYNTER WLK
C5
1 EIGHT ACRE CL
2 LAWN CL
3 ORCHARD CL
4 GREAT PARK CL
5 LONG TERRACE CL
6 CYPRESS CL
7 CAMPION CL
8 RODDICK WAY
9 BRANSON CT
132
136
A
B
C
D
E
F
Newnham Park
B3417
Furzeacre Wood
Furzeacre Bridge
Windwhistle
Holly Wood
Lowdamoor
Hemerdon
Old Newnham Farm
Hemerdon Farm
Miners' Arms (PH)
Old Newnham
NEWNHAM RD
WEST PARK HILL
Lodge
Sherwell
Sparkwell Farm
Sparkwell CE Prim Sch
LEDGATE LA
BEECHWOOD CROSS
Hemerdon House
Beechwood
Lodge
Sparkwell Bridge
Moor Bridge
LANGAGE CROSS
Newnham Ind Est
STOGGY LA
Chaddlewood
Langage Science Pk
BEECHWOOD WAY
HOLLAND RD
Higher Langage
Lower Langage
Combe Farm
GLEN RD
Langage Ind Est
Applethorn Slade
SANDY RD
Langage Pk
PL7
Ley Farm
WOLVERWOOD CL
Yealmpstone Farm Prim Sch
B3416
DEEP LA
The Lyneham Inn (PH)
Voss
A38
SPRINGWOOD CL
WOLVERWOOD LA
DEEP LA
Wiverton House
Battisford
Tuxton Farm
Tuxton Wood
Butlas Farm
Wiverton Acre
Blackpool
PL8
East Sherford
8
7
57
6
5
56
4
3
55
2
1
54
55
56
57
257
136

246

Ford
St John's Lake
Vanderbands
Sango Island
St John
PH
Vanderbands Farm
Penhale Lake
Penhale
St John's Down
Mendennick
PL11
Mendennick Hill
B3247
Works
Inswarke
Sewage Wks
Millbrook CE Sch
New Barn
Blindwell
Millbrook Resr
Withnoe Barton
Higher Hounster Farm
Millbrook
Anderton
Withnoe
Tregonhawke Farm
Dadbrook
Cemy
Tregonhawke
Whitsand Bay Holiday Pk
Treninnow Grove
Sollack
Mon
Treninnow
Fourlanesend Com Prim Sch
Treninnow Plantation
The Hats
Whitsand Bay
PL10
Wiggle
South West Coast Path
Wiggle Cliff
Wringford Farm
Wringford Down
Hotel
Knatterbury
Forder
Cornwall STREET ATLAS

247
254

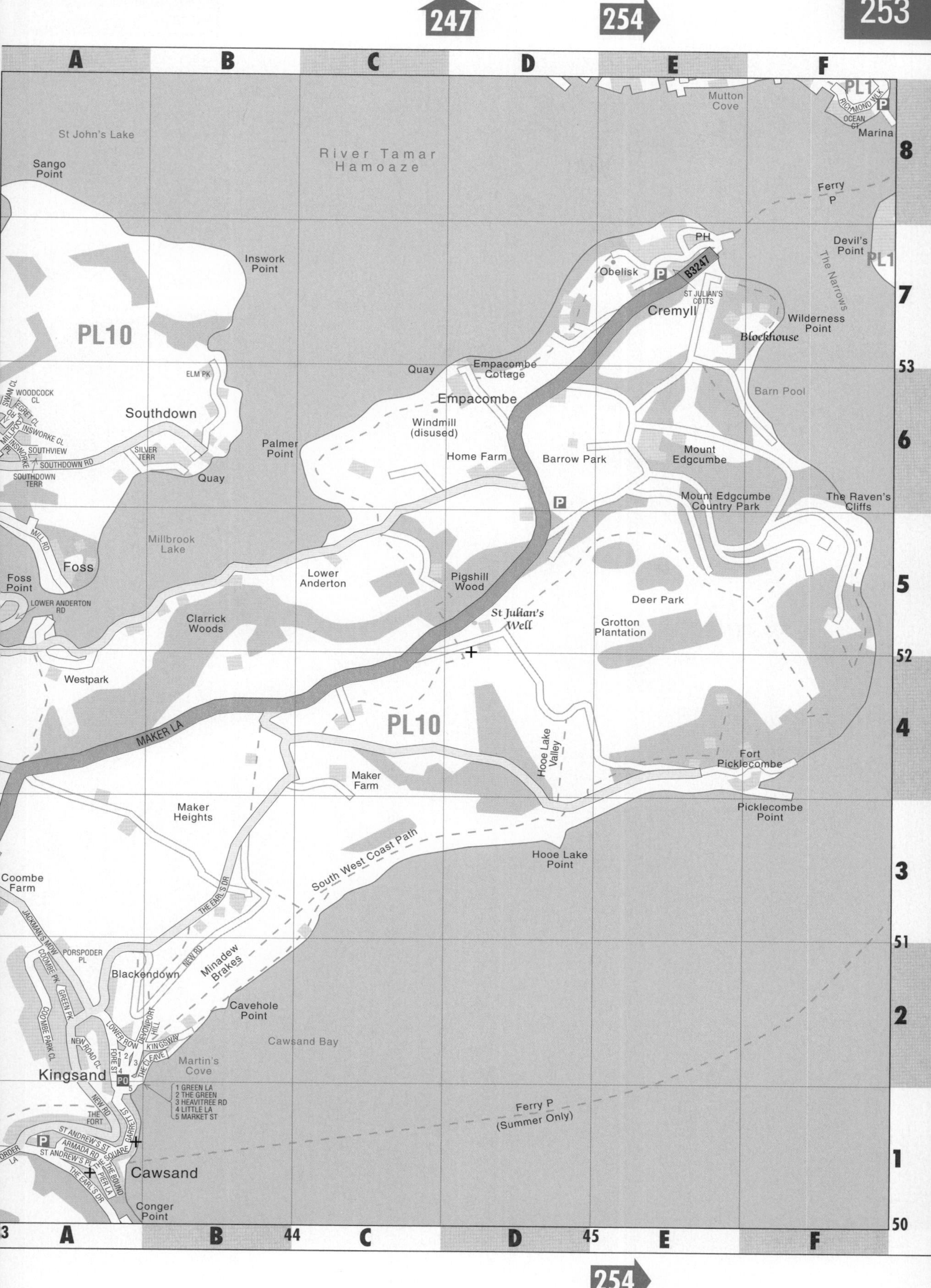
A
B
C
D
E
F
St John's Lake
Sango Point
River Tamar
Hamoaze
Mutton Cove
PL1
Marina
Ferry P
Devil's Point
The Narrows
Inswork Point
PL10
PH
Obelisk
B3247
ST JULIAN'S COTTS
Cremyll
Wilderness Point
Blockhouse
Quay
Empacombe Cottage
Empacombe
ELM PK
Southdown
WOODCOCK CL
EGRET CL
INSWORKE CL
SOUTHVIEW
SOUTHDOWN RD
SOUTHDOWN TERR
SILVER TERR
Quay
Palmer Point
Windmill (disused)
Home Farm
Barrow Park
Mount Edgcumbe
Barn Pool
Mount Edgcumbe Country Park
The Raven's Cliffs
MILL RD
Millbrook Lake
Foss
Foss Point
LOWER ANDERTON RD
Lower Anderton
Pigshill Wood
Deer Park
Clarrick Woods
St Julian's Well
Grotton Plantation
Westpark
PL10
MAKER LA
Hooe Lake Valley
Fort Picklecombe
Maker Farm
Maker Heights
Picklecombe Point
South West Coast Path
Hooe Lake Point
Coombe Farm
THE EARL'S DR
JACKMAN'S MDW
PORSPODER PL
COOMBE PK
Blackendown
NEW RD
Minadew Brakes
GREEN PK
COOMBE PARK CL
DEVONPORT HILL
LOWER ROW
Cavehole Point
Cawsand Bay
KINGSWAY
NEW ROAD CL
FORE ST
THE CLEAVE
Martin's Cove
Kingsand
PO
1 GREEN LA
2 THE GREEN
3 HEAVITREE RD
4 LITTLE LA
5 MARKET ST
NEW RD
THE FORT
GARRETT ST
Ferry P (Summer Only)
ST ANDREW'S ST
ARMADA RD
THE SQUARE
ST ANDREW'S PL
THE BOUND
PIER LA
THE EARL'S DR
Cawsand
Conger Point
8
7
53
6
5
52
4
3
51
2
1
50
44
45

254

253
248
For full street detail of the highlighted area see pages 262 and 263.

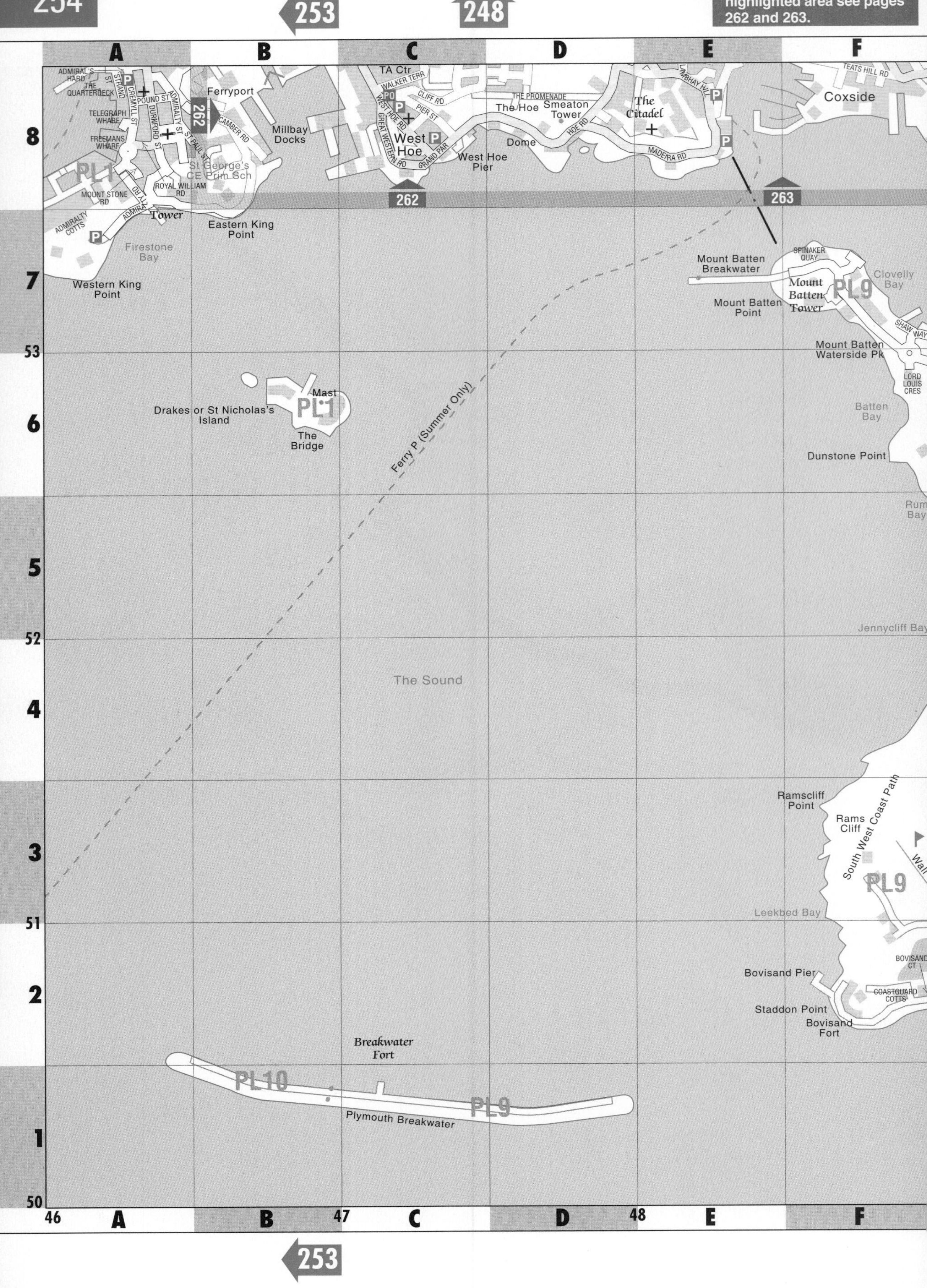

253

For full street detail of the highlighted area see page 263.

249 256

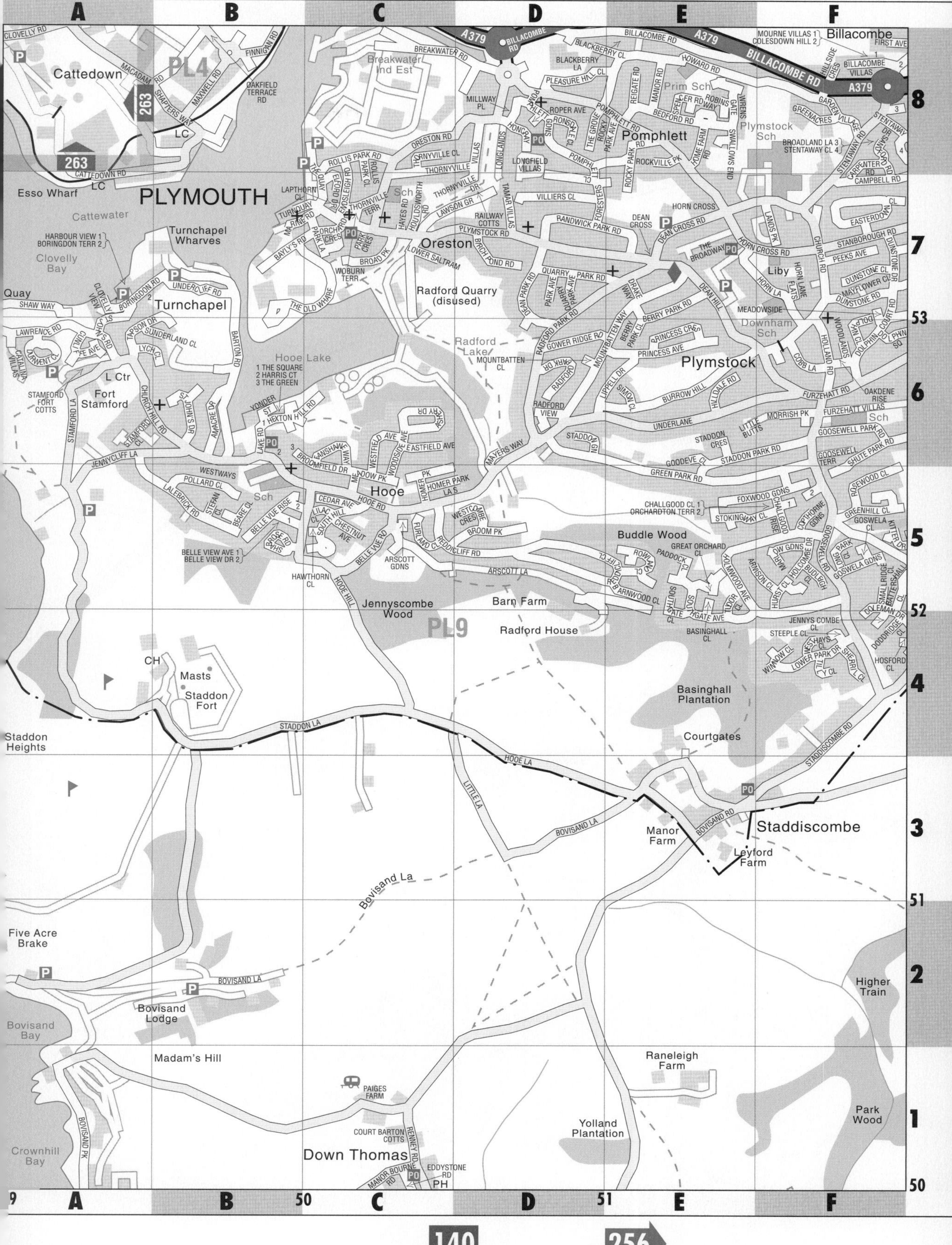

140 256

255
250

255
140

251
136

141
136

143 143 144 144

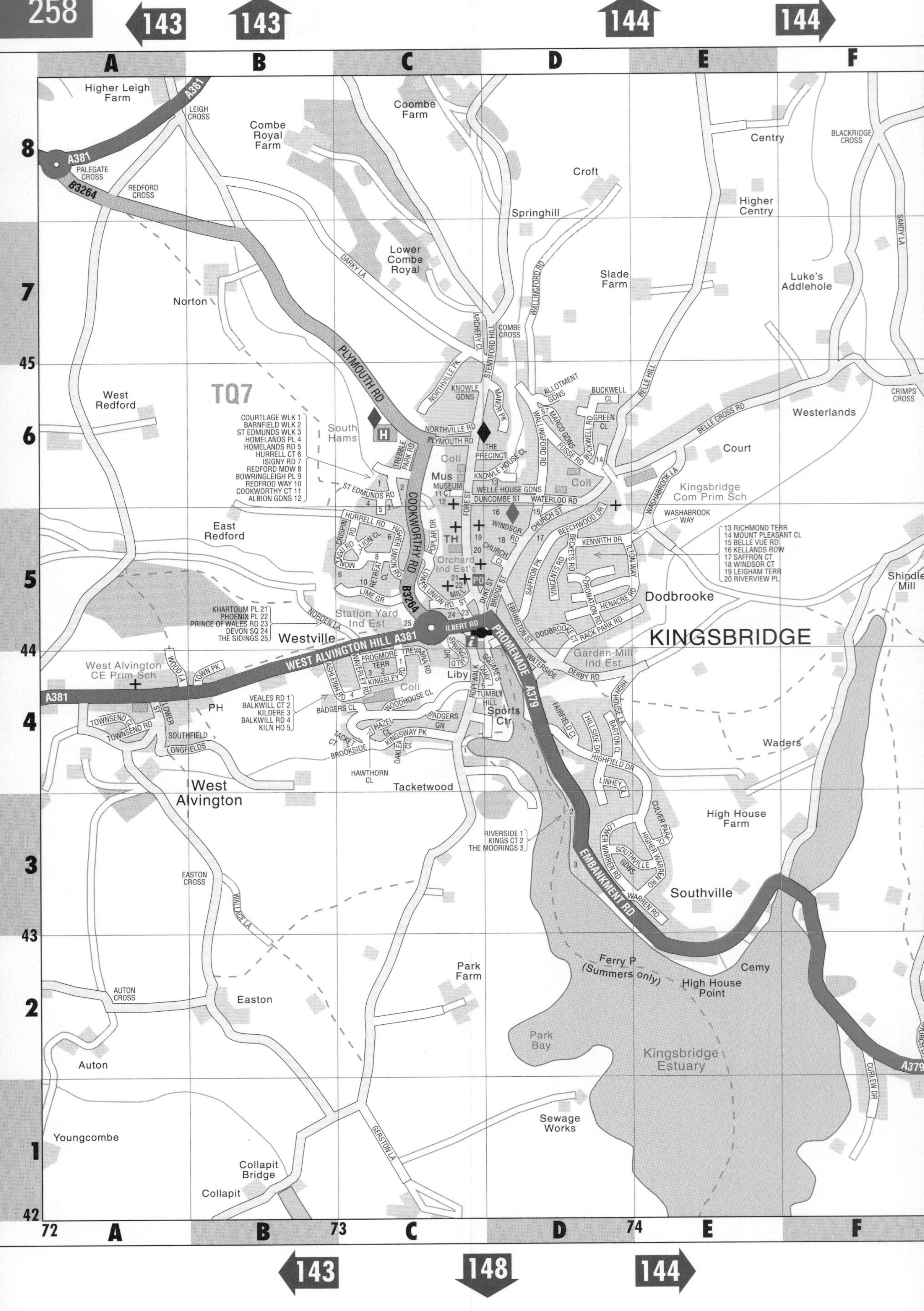

143 148 144

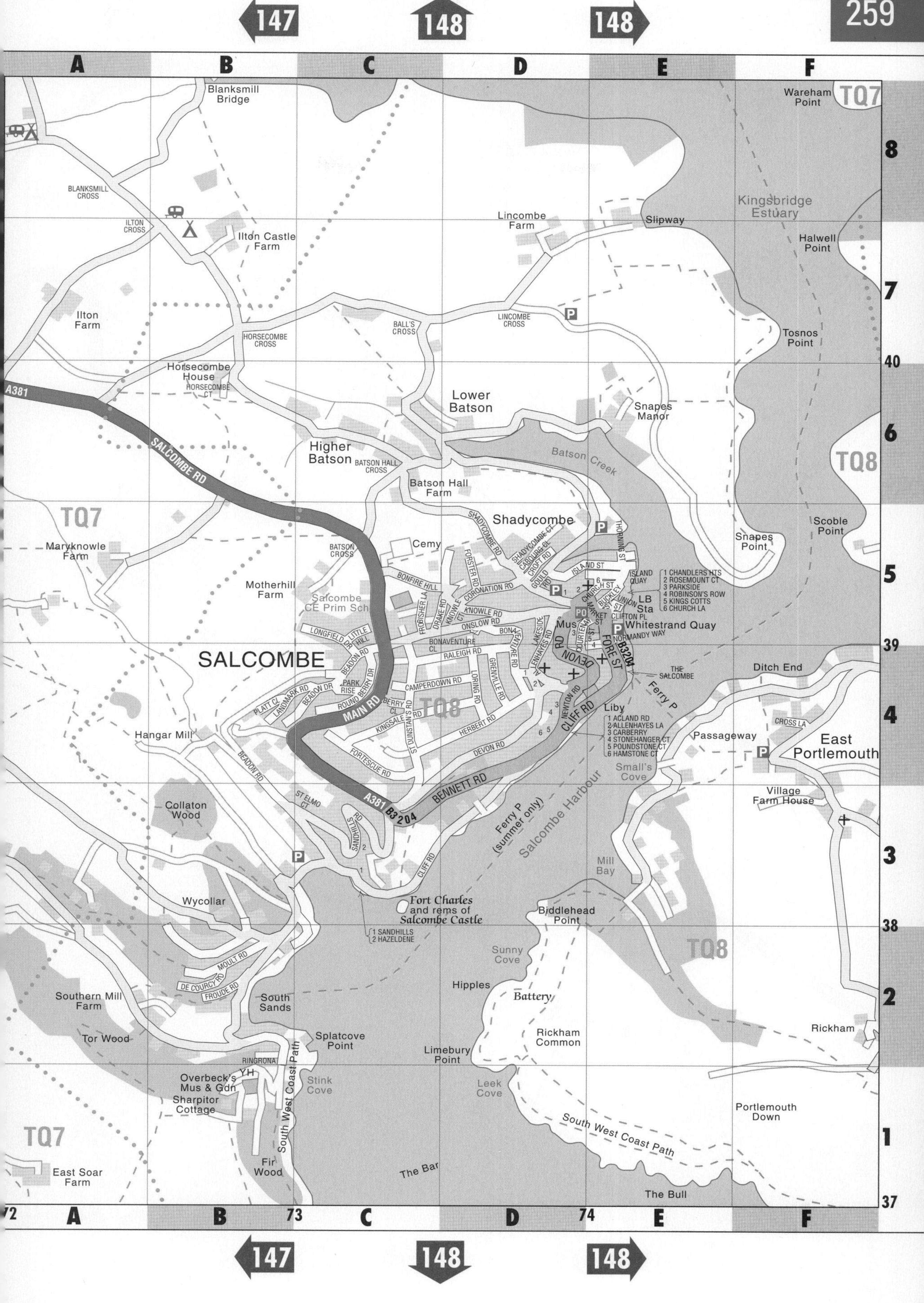

A B C D E F
8 7 40 6 5 39 4 3 38 2 1 37
72 73 74
TQ7
TQ8
Blanksmill Bridge
BLANKSMILL CROSS
ILTON CROSS
Ilton Castle Farm
Ilton Farm
HORSECOMBE CROSS
Horsecombe House
HORSECOMBE CT
A381
SALCOMBE RD
Maryknowle Farm
Motherhill Farm
Higher Batson
BATSON HALL CROSS
Lower Batson
Batson Hall Farm
BALL'S CROSS
LINCOMBE CROSS
Lincombe Farm
Slipway
Kingsbridge Estuary
Wareham Point
Halwell Point
Tosnos Point
Snapes Manor
Batson Creek
Snapes Point
Scoble Point
Shadycombe
Cemy
BATSON CROSS
Salcombe CE Prim Sch
SALCOMBE
MAIN RD
Whitestrand Quay
ISLAND QUAY
LB Sta
Mus
PO
Liby
1 CHANDLERS HTS
2 ROSEMOUNT CT
3 PARKSIDE
4 ROBINSON'S ROW
5 KINGS COTTS
6 CHURCH LA
1 ACLAND RD
2 ALLENHAYES LA
3 CARBERRY
4 STONEHANGER CT
5 POUNDSTONE CT
6 HAMSTONE CT
THE SALCOMBE
Ferry P
Ditch End
Passageway
CROSS LA
East Portlemouth
Small's Cove
Village Farm House
Hangar Mill
Collaton Wood
BENNETT RD
B3204
Ferry P (summer only)
Salcombe Harbour
Mill Bay
Fort Charles and rems of Salcombe Castle
1 SANDHILLS
2 HAZELDENE
Biddlehead Point
Wycollar
Sunny Cove
Hipples
Battery
South Sands
Southern Mill Farm
Tor Wood
Splatcove Point
Limebury Point
Rickham Common
Rickham
RINGRONA
YH
Overbeck's Mus & Gdn
Sharpitor Cottage
Stink Cove
Leek Cove
South West Coast Path
Portlemouth Down
Fir Wood
East Soar Farm
The Bar
The Bull

104 104 104

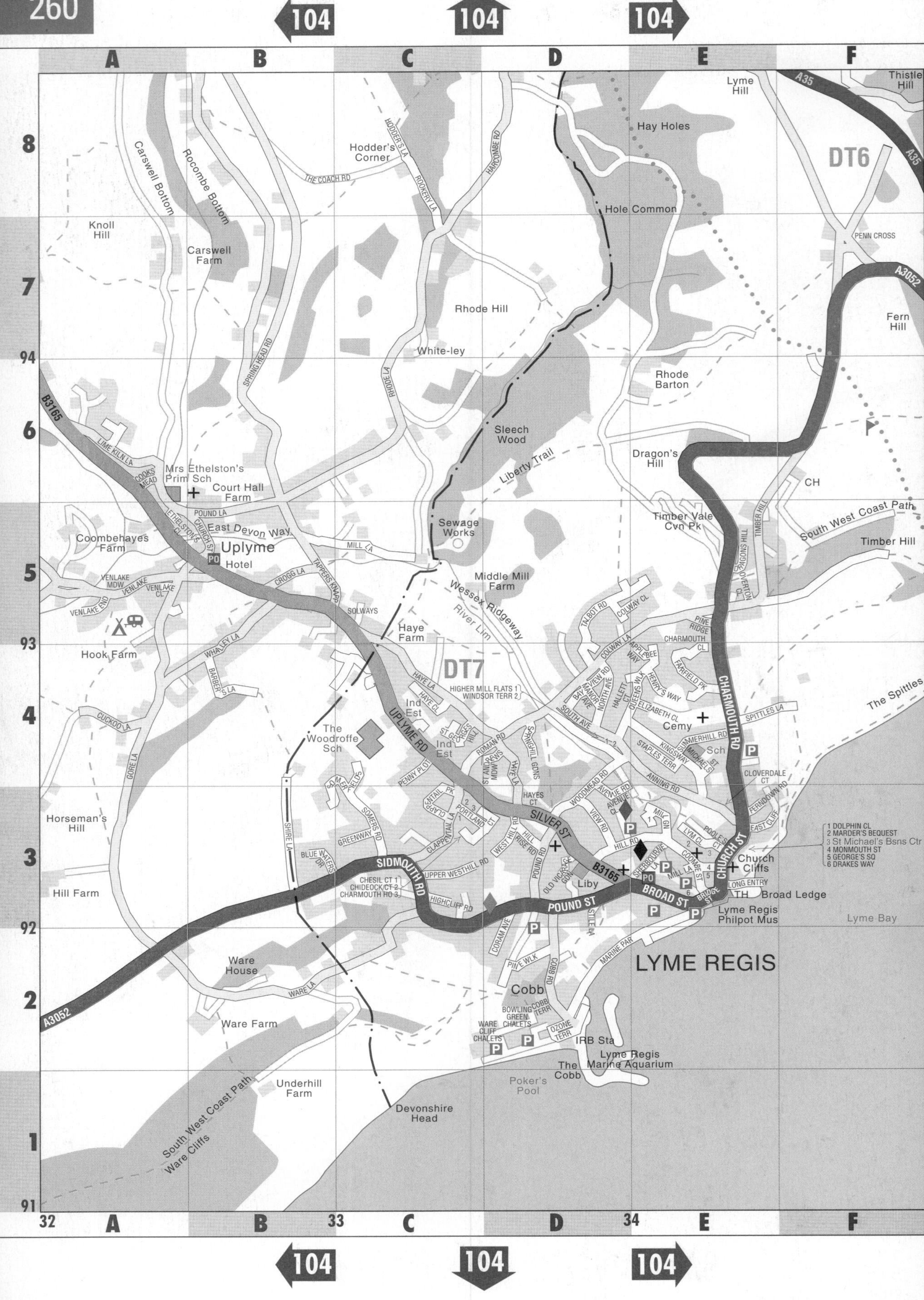

104 104 104

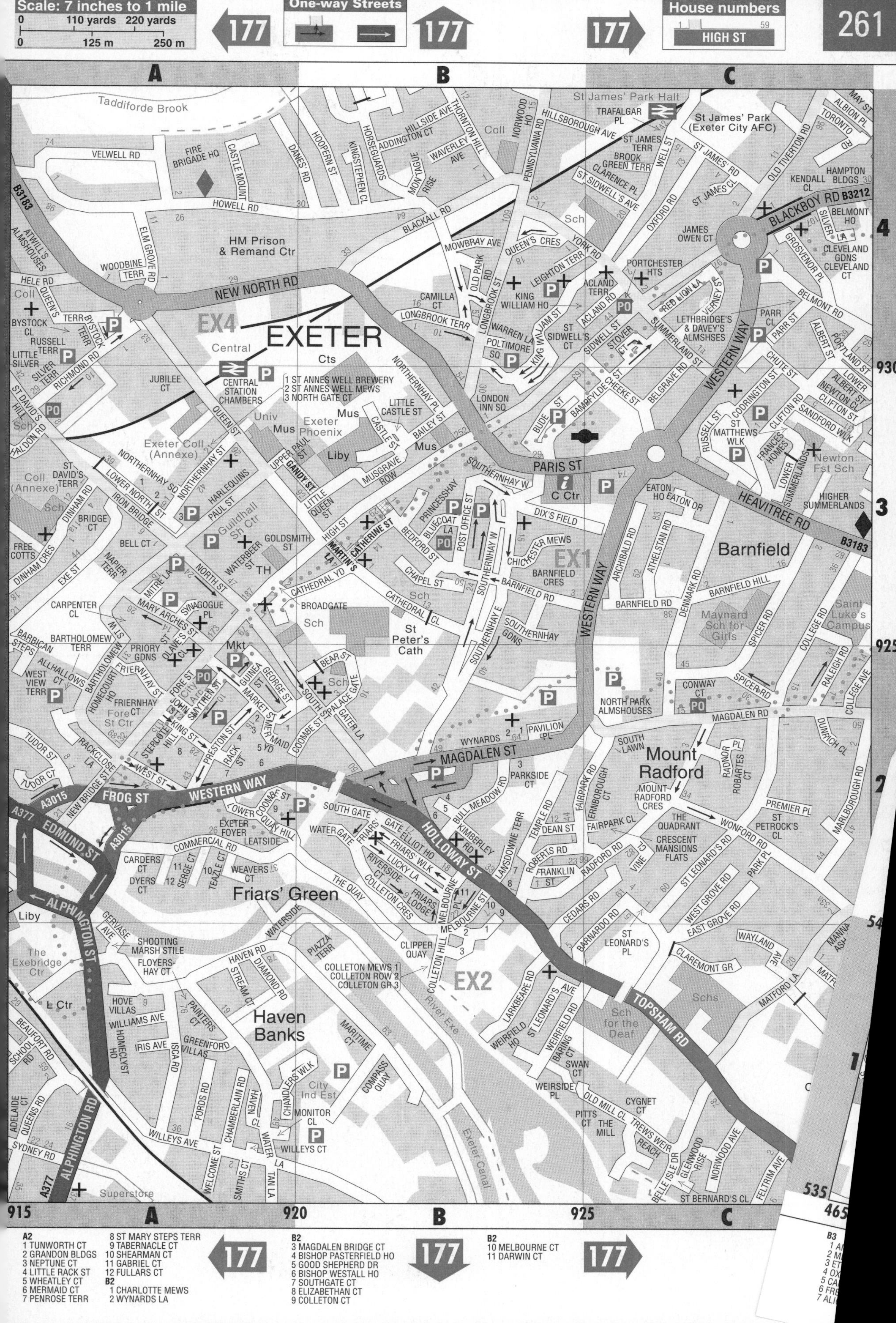

A2
1 TUNWORTH CT
2 GRANDON BLDGS
3 NEPTUNE CT
4 LITTLE RACK ST
5 WHEATLEY CT
6 MERMAID CT
7 PENROSE TERR
8 ST MARY STEPS TERR
9 TABERNACLE CT
10 SHEARMAN CT
11 GABRIEL CT
12 FULLARS CT

B2
1 CHARLOTTE MEWS
2 WYNARDS LA

B2
3 MAGDALEN BRIDGE CT
4 BISHOP PASTERFIELD HO
5 GOOD SHEPHERD DR
6 BISHOP WESTALL HO
7 SOUTHGATE CT
8 ELIZABETHAN CT
9 COLLETON CT

B2
10 MELBOURNE CT
11 DARWIN CT

177 177 177

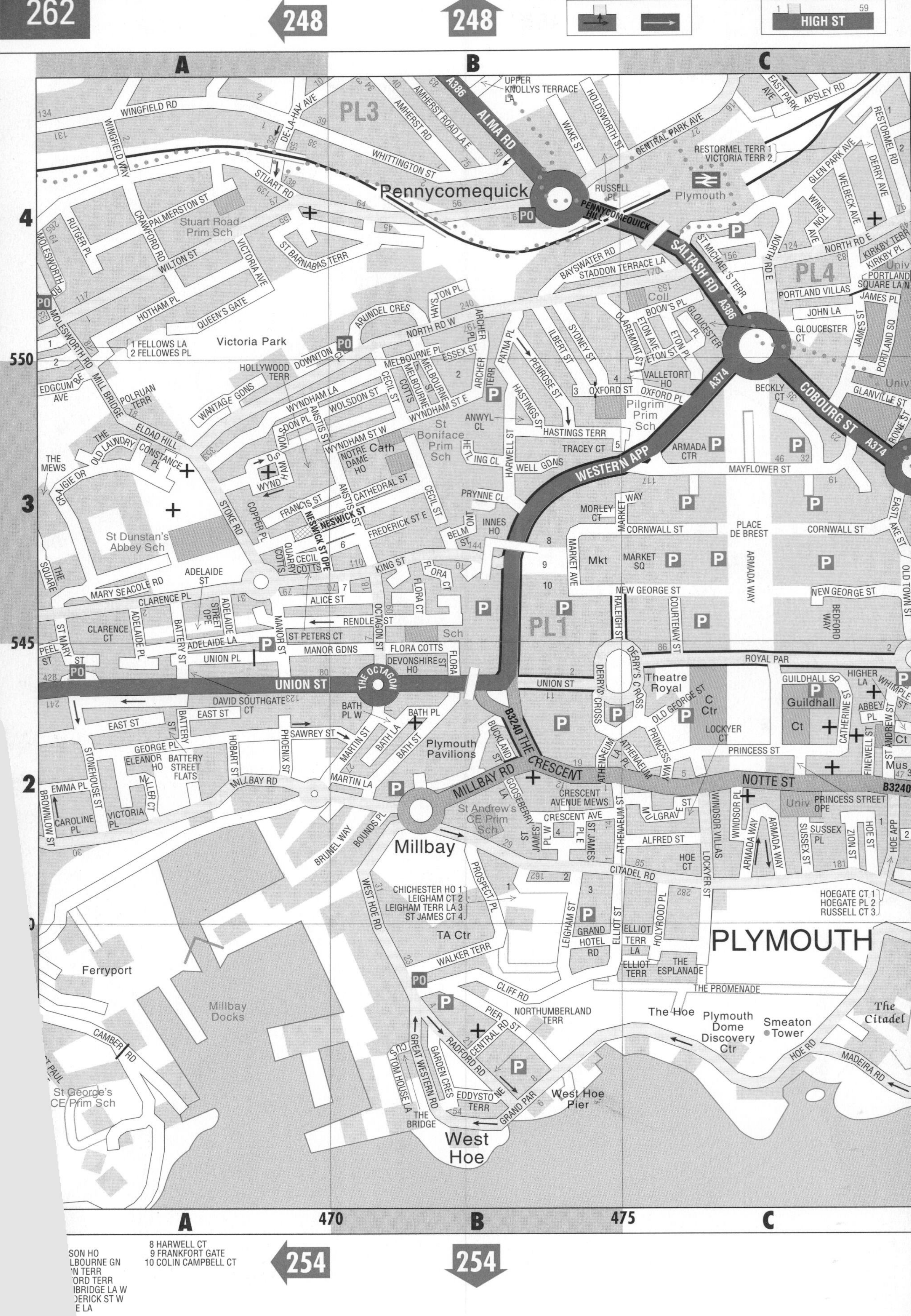

248
248
One-way Streets
House numbers
1
59
HIGH ST
A
B
C
PL3
PL4
PL1
Pennycomequick
Plymouth
PLYMOUTH
Millbay
West Hoe
WINGFIELD RD
WINGFIELD WAY
DE-LA-HAY AVE
AMHERST RD
AMHERST ROAD LA E
A386
ALMA RD
UPPER KNOLLYS TERRACE LA
HOLDSWORTH ST
WAKE ST
CENTRAL PARK AVE
EAST PARK AVE
APSLEY RD
RESTORMEL RD
RESTORMEL TERR 1
VICTORIA TERR 2
WHITTINGTON ST
STUART RD
RUSSELL PL
PENNYCOMEQUICK HILL
GLEN PARK AVE
WELBECK AVE
DERRY AVE
WINSTON AVE
NORTH RD E
KIRKBY TERR
KIRKBY PL
PORTLAND SQUARE LA N
PORTLAND VILLAS
JAMES PL
JOHN LA
JAMES ST
PORTLAND SQ
GLOUCESTER CT
Univ
RUTGER PL
MOLESWORTH RD
PALMERSTON ST
CRAWFORD RD
Stuart Road Prim Sch
WILTON ST
VICTORIA AVE
ST BARNABAS TERR
BAYSWATER RD
STADDON TERRACE LA
SALTASH RD
ST MICHAEL'S TERR
NORTH RD E
Coll
BOON'S PL
CLAREMONT ST
ETON AVE
ETON ST
ETON PL
GLOUCESTER PL
HOTHAM PL
QUEEN'S GATE
HAYSTON PL
ARUNDEL CRES
NORTH RD W
ARCHER PL
PATNA PL
ILBERT ST
SYDNEY ST
1 FELLOWS LA
2 FELLOWES PL
Victoria Park
DOWNTON CL
MELBOURNE PL
ESSEX ST
PENROSE ST
VALLETORT HO
A374
COBOURG ST
BECKLY CT
HOLLYWOOD TERR
CECIL ST
MELBOURNE ST
MELBOURNE COTTS
WYNDHAM ST E
ARCHER TERR
HASTINGS ST
OXFORD ST
OXFORD PL
Pilgrim Prim Sch
GLANVILLE ST
EDGCUMBE AVE
MILL BRIDGE
POLRUAN TERR
WANTAGE GDNS
WYNDHAM LA
WOLSDON ST
ANSTIS ST
DONPL
ANWYL CL
HASTINGS TERR
ROWE ST
ELDAD HILL
THE OLD LAUNDRY
CONSTANCE PL
WYNDHAM ST W
NOTRE DAME HO
Cath
St Boniface Prim Sch
HETLING CL
HARWELL ST
TRACEY CT
WELL GDNS
ARMADA CTR
WESTERN APP
MAYFLOWER ST
THE MEWS
CRAIGIE DR
WYNDHAM SQ
WYND
CATHEDRAL ST
FRANCIS ST
PRYNNE CL
MORLEY CT
MARKET WAY
EASTLAKE ST
St Dunstan's Abbey Sch
STOKE RD
COPPER PL
NESWICK ST
FREDERICK ST E
BELMONT ST
INNES HO
CORNWALL ST
PLACE DE BREST
MARKET AVE
Mkt
MARKET SQ
ARMADA WAY
OLD TOWN ST
THE SQUARE
ADELAIDE ST
MARY SEACOLE RD
QUARRY COTTS
CECIL COTTS
NESWICK ST OPE
KING ST
FLORA CT
CLARENCE PL
ALICE ST
FLORA CT
NEW GEORGE ST
RALEIGH ST
COURTENAY ST
BEDFORD WAY
ST MARY ST
CLARENCE CT
ADELAIDE PL
BATTERY ST
ADELAIDE STREET OPE
MANOR ST
RENDLE ST
ST PETERS CT
OCTAGON ST
Sch
ADELAIDE LA
PEEL ST
UNION PL
MANOR GDNS
FLORA COTTS
DEVONSHIRE HO
FLORA ST
DERRY'S CROSS
ROYAL PAR
UNION ST
THE OCTAGON
Theatre Royal
GUILDHALL SQ
HIGHER LA
WHIMPLE ST
Guildhall
DAVID SOUTHGATE CT
EAST ST
BATH PL W
BATH PL
B3240 THE CRESCENT
C Ctr
OLD GEORGE ST
LOCKYER CT
ABBEY PL
CATHERINE ST
Ct
EAST ST
SAWREY ST
MARTIN ST
BATH LA
BATH ST
BUCKLAND ST
ATHENAEUM ST
ATHENAEUM PL
ATHENAEUM LA
PRINCESS WAY
PRINCESS ST
FINEWELL ST
ST ANDREW ST
GEORGE PL
ELEANOR HO
BATTERY STREET FLATS
STONEHOUSE ST
HOBART ST
PHOENIX ST
Plymouth Pavilions
MILLBAY RD
CRESCENT
NOTTE ST
B3240
Mus
EMMA PL
MILLER CT
MARTIN LA
GOOSEBERRY LA
CRESCENT AVENUE MEWS
WINDSOR PL
PRINCESS STREET OPE
BROWNLOW ST
CAROLINE PL
VICTORIA PL
BRUNEL WAY
BOUNDS PL
St Andrew's CE Prim Sch
CRESCENT AVE
ST JAMES PL W
ST JAMES PL E
MULGRAVE ST
SUSSEX PL
SUSSEX ST
ZION ST
HOE ST
HOE APP
ALFRED ST
HOE CT
WINDSOR VILLAS
LOCKYER ST
PROSPECT PL
CITADEL RD
WEST HOE RD
CHICHESTER HO 1
LEIGHAM CT 2
LEIGHAM TERR LA 3
ST JAMES CT 4
HOEGATE CT 1
HOEGATE PL 2
RUSSELL CT 3
LEIGHAM ST
GRAND HOTEL RD
ELLIOT ST
ELLIOT TERR LA
HOLYROOD PL
TA Ctr
WALKER TERR
ELLIOT TERR
THE ESPLANADE
Ferryport
THE PROMENADE
CLIFF RD
Millbay Docks
NORTHUMBERLAND TERR
PIER ST
The Hoe
Plymouth Dome Discovery Ctr
Smeaton Tower
The Citadel
CAMBER RD
CENTRAL RD
GREAT WESTERN RD
RADFORD RD
GARDEN CRES
CUSTOM HOUSE LA
HOE RD
MADEIRA RD
St George's CE Prim Sch
EDDYSTONE TERR
GRAND PAR
West Hoe Pier
THE BRIDGE
PO
P
4
3
2
550
545
470
475
8 HARWELL CT
9 FRANKFORT GATE
10 COLIN CAMPBELL CT
254
254

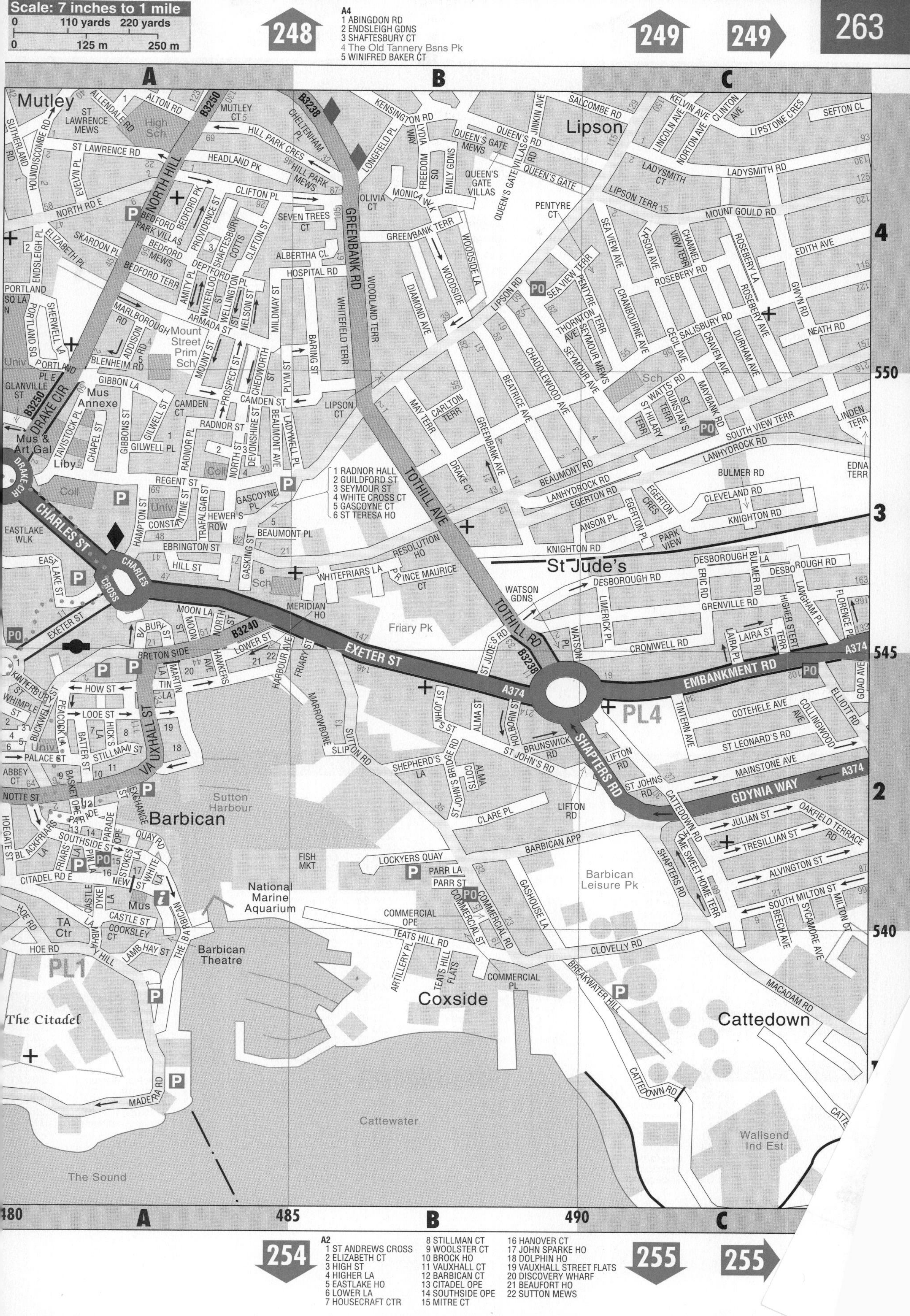
Scale: 7 inches to 1 mile
0 110 yards 220 yards
0 125 m 250 m
248
A4
1 ABINGDON RD
2 ENDSLEIGH GDNS
3 SHAFTESBURY CT
4 The Old Tannery Bsns Pk
5 WINIFRED BAKER CT
249
249
263
A
B
C
Mutley
Lipson
Mount Street Prim Sch
Mus Annexe
Mus & Art Gal
Liby
Coll
Univ
High Sch
4
550
3
545
2
540
1 RADNOR HALL
2 GUILDFORD ST
3 SEYMOUR ST
4 WHITE CROSS CT
5 GASCOYNE CT
6 ST TERESA HO
St Jude's
Friary Pk
PL4
PL1
Barbican
Sutton Harbour
FISH MKT
National Marine Aquarium
Barbican Leisure Pk
Barbican Theatre
TA Ctr
Mus
The Citadel
Coxside
Cattedown
Cattewater
The Sound
Wallsend Ind Est
NORTH HILL
GREENBANK RD
TOTHILL AVE
TOTHILL RD
EXETER ST
EMBANKMENT RD
GDYNIA WAY
SHAPTERS RD
CHARLES ST
CHARLES CROSS
DRAKE CIR
VAUXHALL ST
LIPSON RD
MOUNT GOULD RD
BEAUMONT RD
LANHYDROCK RD
KNIGHTON RD
CATTEDOWN RD
MACADAM RD
CLOVELLY RD
BREAKWATER HILL
COMMERCIAL RD
BARBICAN APP
480
485
490
254
A2
1 ST ANDREWS CROSS
2 ELIZABETH CT
3 HIGH ST
4 HIGHER LA
5 EASTLAKE HO
6 LOWER LA
7 HOUSECRAFT CTR
8 STILLMAN CT
9 WOOLSTER CT
10 BROCK HO
11 VAUXHALL CT
12 BARBICAN CT
13 CITADEL OPE
14 SOUTHSIDE OPE
15 MITRE CT
16 HANOVER CT
17 JOHN SPARKE HO
18 DOLPHIN HO
19 VAUXHALL STREET FLATS
20 DISCOVERY WHARF
21 BEAUFORT HO
22 SUTTON MEWS
255
255

Index

Church Rd **6** Beckenham BR2..........**53** C6

Place name	Location number	Locality, town or village	Postcode district	Page and grid square
May be abbreviated on the map	Present when a number indicates the place's position in a crowded area of mapping	Shown when more than one place has the same name	District for the indexed place	Page number and grid reference for the standard mapping

Public and commercial buildings are highlighted in magenta **Places of interest** are highlighted in blue with a star★

Abbreviations used in the index

Acad	**Academy**	Comm	**Common**	Gd	**Ground**	L	**Leisure**	Prom	**Prom**
App	**Approach**	Cott	**Cottage**	Gdn	**Garden**	La	**Lane**	Rd	**Road**
Arc	**Arcade**	Cres	**Crescent**	Gn	**Green**	Liby	**Library**	Recn	**Recreation**
Ave	**Avenue**	Cswy	**Causeway**	Gr	**Grove**	Mdw	**Meadow**	Ret	**Retail**
Bglw	**Bungalow**	Ct	**Court**	H	**Hall**	Meml	**Memorial**	Sh	**Shopping**
Bldg	**Building**	Ctr	**Centre**	Ho	**House**	Mkt	**Market**	Sq	**Square**
Bsns, Bus	**Business**	Ctry	**Country**	Hospl	**Hospital**	Mus	**Museum**	St	**Street**
Bvd	**Boulevard**	Cty	**County**	HQ	**Headquarters**	Orch	**Orchard**	Sta	**Station**
Cath	**Cathedral**	Dr	**Drive**	Hts	**Heights**	Pal	**Palace**	Terr	**Terrace**
Cir	**Circus**	Dro	**Drove**	Ind	**Industrial**	Par	**Parade**	TH	**Town Hall**
Cl	**Close**	Ed	**Education**	Inst	**Institute**	Pas	**Passage**	Univ	**University**
Cnr	**Corner**	Emb	**Embankment**	Int	**International**	Pk	**Park**	Wk, Wlk	**Walk**
Coll	**College**	Est	**Estate**	Intc	**Interchange**	Pl	**Place**	Wr	**Water**
Com	**Community**	Ex	**Exhibition**	Junc	**Junction**	Prec	**Precinct**	Yd	**Yard**

Index of localities, towns and villages

A

Abbotsham 156 A2
Abbotskerswell 212 B6
Alfington 100 F8
Alswear 30 C1
Appledore 14 F1
Ashbrittle 50 E8
Ashburton 130 E5
Ashcombe 124 D6
Ashford 16 B6
Ashprington 139 F8
Ashreigney 58 F1
Ashwater 90 D6
Atherington 28 A2
Aveton Gifford 143 C6
Avonwick 135 B1
Awliscombe 85 B4
Axminster 167 C6
Axmouth 192 E7
Aylesbeare 99 D2

B

Bampton 34 C1
Barbrook 151 B1
Barnstaple 155 C4
Beacon 85 F8
Beaford 42 D1
Beare 82 E3
Beer 191 E5
Beesands 149 E7
Belstone 94 D4
Bere Alston 125 E1
Bere Ferrers 239 E3
Berry Pomeroy 224 B7
Berrynarbor 2 E3
Bickington (nr Ashburton) 131 D7
Bickington (nr Bideford) 154 B4
Bickleigh (nr Plymouth) 132 A5
Bickleigh (nr Tiverton) 64 A1
Bideford 156 E3
Bigbury 142 F5
Bigbury-on-Sea 142 E3
Bishop's Tawton 16 F1
Bishops Nympton 31 A2
Bishopsteignton 208 E7
Bittaford 137 C8
Black Torrington 74 A8
Blackawton 139 F2
Bolham 161 C8
Bondleigh 77 B7
Bovey Tracey 180 D7
Bow 78 C4
Boyton 89 E2
Bradninch 82 F7
Bradworthy 38 E1
Brampford Speke 81 E1
Brandis Corner 73 B6
Branscombe 190 D3
Bratton Clovelly 92 A2
Bratton Fleming 18 A8
Braunton 152 B6
Brayford 18 F5
Brendon 6 A4
Bridestowe 107 F8
Bridford 112 F5
Bridgerule 70 F6
Brixham 230 E3
Brixton 257 A5
Broadclyst 175 C6
Broadhembury 84 E7
Broadhempston 131 F1
Broadoak 168 D3
Broadwoodkelly 76 D8
Broadwoodwidger 106 B8
Brushford 33 D4
Buck's Mills 24 C2
Buckfast 236 B7
Buckfastleigh 236 B5
Buckland Brewer 40 C7
Buckland in the Moor 130 C8
Buckland Monachorum 126 D3
Buckland St Mary 69 C8
Budlake 82 E3
Budleigh Salterton 198 A2
Burlescombe 51 B3
Burrington 43 F3
Butterleigh 64 C3

C

Cadbury 81 D7
Cadeleigh 63 D3
Calstock 125 D3
Calverleigh 48 E1
Cargreen 239 A2
Cawsand 253 B2
Chagford 111 A6
Challacombe 11 F3
Chapelton 27 F5
Chard Junction 88 E7
Chardstock 88 B7
Charmouth 104 F4
Chawleigh 60 B7
Cheriton Bishop 97 A4
Cheriton Fitzpaine 62 E1
Chevithorne 49 D2
Chillaton 116 D8
Chillington 145 A2
Chilsworthy 53 E1
Chipstable 35 E6
Chittlehamholt 44 B8
Chittlehampton 28 F5
Christow 113 A3
Chudleigh 123 E6
Chudleigh Knighton 123 C4
Chulmleigh 44 F1
Churchinford 68 D7
Churchstow 143 E4
Churston Ferrers 229 E4
Clawton 72 B2
Clayhanger 35 C1
Clovelly 23 E3
Clyst Honiton 179 E8
Clyst Hydon 83 D4
Clyst St George 183 C6
Clyst St Lawrence 83 C3
Clyst St Mary 179 B3
Cobbaton 28 D5
Cockwood 201 B5
Coffinswell 213 B6
Colaton Raleigh 186 D3
Coldridge 59 F2
Colebrooke 79 A3
Colyford 103 B3
Colyton 103 A5
Combe Martin 3 B3
Combe St Nicholas 69 F6
Combeinteignhead 208 E4
Compton 218 D6
Copplestone 79 A6
Cornwood 133 C2
Cornworthy 227 B4
Cove 49 B6
Cowley 172 E4
Crapstone 126 E2
Crediton 165 D4
Crockernwell 96 F3
Croyde 7 E2
Cullompton 163 A3
Culmstock 66 E8

D

Daccombe 213 E5
Dalwood 87 B3
Dartington 215 E1
Dartmouth 233 E3
Dawlish 204 F6
Dawlish Warren 201 A1
Denbury 211 B6
Diptford 138 C7
Dittisham 228 C3
Doddiscombsleigh 113 C5
Dolton 57 F7
Dousland 127 C3
Down St Mary 78 E7
Down Thomas 255 C1
Drewsteignton 96 D2

Dulverton 33 E6
Dunchideock 114 A6
Dunkeswell 67 C2
Dunsford 112 F8
Dunterton 115 D6

E

East Allington 144 E7
East Anstey 32 E5
East Buckland 18 D2
East Budleigh 198 A6
East Ogwell 206 E1
East Portlemouth 259 F4
East Prawle 149 A3
Ebford 183 C4
Edistone 37 C8
Ermington 136 F4
Exbourne 76 C4
Exebridge 33 F3
Exeter 177 C5
Exeter 261 B4
Exminster 182 B4
Exmouth 202 B7
Exton 183 D2

F

Farway 102 A6
Feniton 84 E2
Filleigh 29 C7
Folly Gate 93 F8
Fremington 153 E6
Frithelstock Stone 40 F5
Frogmore 144 E1

G

Galmpton
(nr Paignton) 229 A6
Galmpton
(nr Salcombe) 147 C7
George Nympton 30 A1
Georgeham 8 B2
Germansweek 91 E5
Gittisham 85 B1
Goodleigh 17 C5
Goodrington 226 B2
Great Torrington 159 D6
Greenham 51 B7
Gunnislake 125 C5

H

Halberton 65 B8
Hallsands 149 D5
Halwell 139 B4
Halwill 73 C2
Halwill Junction 73 E2
Harberton 222 D1
Harbertonford 139 C6
Harcombe 101 D1
Harrowbarrow 125 A4
Hartland 22 E3
Hatherleigh 75 C6
Hawkchurch 88 E3
Hawkridge 21 D1
Heasley Mill 19 D3
Heathfield 180 F2
Heddon 29 B7
Hele 82 F5
Hemyock 67 C8
Hennock 123 B7
Hexworthy 129 B7
Heybrook Bay 140 B8
High Bickington 43 B7
Highampton 74 C7
Higher Gabwell 214 B7
Hillhead 234 F8
Hittisleigh 96 D5
Hockworthy 50 D6
Holbeton 136 D1
Holcombe 204 D3
Holcombe Rogus 50 F5
Holemoor 73 B8
Hollocombe 58 F6
Holne 130 A4
Holsworthy 164 D5
Holsworthy Beacon 54 C3
Holywell Lake 51 E7
Honiton 166 D4
Horns Cross 24 E2
Horrabridge 126 F5
Horsebridge 116 A1
Huish Champflower 35 F8
Huntsham 49 F7

I

Iddesleigh 57 F3
Ide 176 D1
Ideford 124 A4
Ilfracombe 150 B6
Ilsington 122 C3
Instow 15 B1
Inwardleigh 75 E2
Ipplepen 211 C2
Ivybridge 237 C6

K

Kennford 181 B2
Kentisbeare 66 A3
Kentisbury 10 E5
Kenton 194 E3
Kilmington 103 D8
King's Nympton 44 E6
Kingsbridge 258 E5
Kingskerswell 213 B4
Kingsteignton 207 C8
Kingston 142 C6
Kingswear 234 B3
Knowle 8 D1
Knowstone 32 A2

L

Lamerton 116 F3
Landkey 17 B2
Langford 172 E8
Langtree 40 F2
Lapford 60 C3
Launceston 105 B2
Lee Mill 136 B6
Lee Moor 132 F5
Lewtrenchard 106 F4
Lifton 105 F4
Littleham 202 F7
Liverton 180 A1
Loddiswell 143 F7
Longdown 98 E1
Lustleigh 122 B7
Luton 124 C3
Lutton 133 B2
Lydford 107 F4
Lyme Regis 260 E2
Lympstone 195 E5
Lynmouth 151 D5
Lynton 151 B4

M

Maidencombe 214 D6
Malborough 147 E6
Marhamchurch 70 A6
Mariansleigh 30 D1
Marldon 218 C3
Marsh 69 B5
Mary Tavy 117 E6
Meavy 127 C2
Meeth 57 C3
Membury 87 D6
Merton 57 A7
Meshaw 45 F6
Metherell 125 A4
Millbrook 252 E5
Millmoor 51 E1
Milton Abbot 116 B6
Milton Combe 126 C1
Milton Damerel 54 D5
Modbury 137 C2
Molland 31 E7
Monkleigh 40 F7
Monkokehampton 76 B8
Monkton 86 A5
Morchard Bishop 61 A2
Morchard Road 78 F7
Morebath 34 B3
Moreleigh 139 A3
Moretonhampstead 111 E4
Morwenstow 36 E2
Musbury 103 D5

N

Nadderwater 176 B7
Newton Abbot 207 A2
Newton Ferrers 140 F7
Newton Poppleford 186 E7
Newton St Cyres 172 A8
Newton St Petrock 55 B7
Newton Tracey 27 A5
North Brentor 117 C8
North Molton 30 D8
North Tamerton 89 C8
North Tawton 77 C4
North Whilborough 212 E2
Northam 157 A6
Northleigh 102 B7
Northlew 74 E1
Noss Mayo 140 F6

O

Oakford 48 C8
Offwell 86 B2
Okehampton 170 A6
Oldways End 32 E3
Otterton 198 F7
Ottery St Mary 169 E3

P

Paignton 226 D6
Parkham 39 E8
Parracombe 4 C2
Pathfinder Village 98 C4
Payhembury 84 D4
Peter Tavy 117 F4
Peters Marland 56 C8
Petrockstow 56 F4
Plymouth 248 C5
Plymouth 262 C1
Plympton 250 E5
Plymstock 255 E6
Plymtree 83 E5
Poltimore 174 F6
Postbridge 120 A6
Princetown 128 B8
Pyworthy 71 D5

R

Rackenford 47 D5
Rame 140 H2
Rattery 135 D4
Rawridge 68 C1
Raymond's Hill 104 C7
Rewe 82 A2
Ringmore 142 E4
Roborough (nr Great
Torrington) 42 F3
Roborough
(nr Plymouth) 241 D1
Rockbeare 99 C6
Rockwell Green 160 B5
Rousdon 193 F7
Runnington 51 F8

S

St Dominick 125 A3
St Giles on the Heath 90 B1
St John 252 C8
Salcombe 259 B4
Salcombe Regis 188 F6
Saltash 242 B1
Sampford Arundel 51 E5
Sampford Chapple 76 E3
Sampford Courtenay 76 F4
Sampford Peverell 50 E1
Sandford 80 A5
Saunton 14 F8
Seaton 192 B5
Shaldon 210 B3
Shaugh Prior 132 C6
Shebbear 55 E4
Sheepwash 56 C1
Shillingford 34 E2
Shillingford Abbot 181 A6
Shillingford St George 114 C7
Shirwell 17 B8
Shobrooke 80 E4
Shop 37 A1
Shute 103 A8
Sidbury 101 B2
Sidford 101 B1
Sidmouth 188 C3
Silverton 82 B5
Simonsbath 13 B2
Skilgate 34 E6
Slapton 145 C4
Sourton 93 B1
South Brent 134 F3
South Molton 158 D3
South Pool 148 F7
South Tawton 95 B5
South Zeal 95 B3
Southleigh 102 C4
Sparkwell 136 A8
Spreyton 95 F7
Staddiscombe 255 F3
Starcross 201 A8
Staverton 216 B5
Stibb Cross 40 C1
Sticklepath 95 A5
Stockland 87 A7
Stockleigh Pomeroy 81 A6
Stoke 22 B3
Stoke Canon 173 E8
Stoke Climsland 115 C1
Stoke Fleming 146 B7
Stoke Gabriel 227 F7
Stokeinteignhead 209 B1
Stokenham 145 C1
Stopgate 68 F4
Strete 145 E5
Sutcombe 54 A6
Swimbridge 17 D1
Sydenham Damerel 116 B2

T

Talaton 84 A2
Taleford 169 C6
Tamerton Foliot 244 B7
Tatworth 88 C8
Tavistock 171 E5
Tedburn St Mary 97 F5
Teigngrace 206 F8
Teignmouth 210 D4
Tetcott 89 F7
Thorverton 81 D5
Throwleigh 95 C1
Thurlestone 143 A2
Tipton St John 100 D2
Tiverton 161 D3
Topsham 182 F5
Torcross 145 D1
Torpoint 247 C3
Torquay 220 B3
Totnes 223 E6
Treburley 115 A4
Trusham 113 D1
Tuckenhay 139 F7
Twitchen 20 D1

U

Uffculme 66 A8
Ugborough 137 E6
Umberleigh 28 D2
Uplowman 50 B2
Uplyme 260 B5
Upottery 68 C2
Upton 34 F8
Upton Pyne 173 A8

V

Venterdon 115 B2
Virginstow 90 D3

W

Walkhampton 127 A4
Wambrook 69 F3
Warkleigh 29 A2
Waterrow 35 F4
Weare Gifford 26 B1
Welcombe 37 A5
Wellington 160 D7
Wembury 140 D7
Wembworthy 59 C4
West Alvington 258 B4
West Anstey 32 C6
West Buckland
(nr Barnstaple) 18 B2
West Buckland
(nr Wellington) 52 F7
West Charleton 144 C1
West Down 8 F5
West Hill 168 E4
West Putford 39 C2
West Worlington 61 A8
Westleigh (Bideford) 157 E6
Westleigh (Wellington) 51 A4
Weston 189 D6
Westward Ho! 156 D8
Westwood 83 C1
Whiddon Down 95 F3
Whimple 99 E7
Whitchurch 171 D3
Whitestone 98 E4
Whitford 103 B6
Whitstone 70 E1
Widecombe in the
Moor 121 B4
Willand 162 E4
Wilmington 86 D3
Winkleigh 58 E2
Witheridge 46 F1
Withypool 21 C6
Wolverstone 85 A7
Woodbury 184 C3
Woodbury Salterton 184 C6
Woolacombe 7 F7
Woolfardisworthy 62 A3
Woolfardisworthy
or Woolsery 38 E7
Wotter 132 D4
Wrafton 152 F4
Wrangaton 137 D8

Y

Yarcombe 69 A3
Yarnscombe 27 E2
Yealmpton 257 E4
Yelland 153 A4
Yelverton 127 A3
Yeoford 79 C1

Z

Zeal Monachorum 78 C7

A

A-la Ronde★ EX8 196 A3
Abbeville Cl EX2 177 E3
Abbey Cl Axminster EX13 167 C4
Bovey Tracey TQ13 180 C7
Crapstone PL20 126 E2
Paignton TQ3 225 E5
Tatworth TA20 88 D8
Teignmouth TQ14 210 C7
Abbey Cross TQ9 227 A4
Abbey Ct Exeter EX2 178 F5
Plymouth PL1 263 A2
Abbey Gate La EX13 167 C2
Abbey Grange Cl TQ11 236 B7
Abbey La EX13 167 B3
Abbey Mdw TQ11 236 B7
Abbey Mews TA20 88 D8
Abbey Pl Plymouth PL1 262 C2
Tavistock PL19 171 C5
Abbey Rd
Barnstaple EX31 154 E6
Bovey Tracey TQ13 180 D7
Cornworthy TQ9 227 A4
Exeter EX4 177 F7
Torquay TQ2 220 A5
Abbey Rise
Okehampton EX20 170 D6
Tavistock PL19 171 C5
Abbey Sch The TQ1 220 C8
Abbeyfield Ho 7 TQ14 210 C5
Abbeyford Ct EX20 170 C5
Abbot Rd PL21 237 A6
Abbot's Cross EX36 31 E6
Abbot's Rd EX4 177 E8
Abbots Cl Lee Mill PL21 136 D6
Woolfardisworthy EX39 38 F8
Abbots Dr EX39 26 A4
Abbots Keep EX4 176 D6
Abbots Mdw EX37 28 F4
Abbotsbury Rd TQ12 207 B4
Abbotsbury Sch TQ12 207 D2
Abbotsbury Way PL2 247 F8
Abbotscourt La PL11 246 A2
Abbotsfield Cl PL19 126 A8
Abbotsfield Cres PL19 126 A8
Abbotsham Cross EX39 25 C4
Abbotsham La EX18 59 C3
Abbotsham Rd EX39 156 E2
Abbotshill TQ12 212 A6
Abbotskerswell Cross
TQ12 212 A7
Abbotskerswell Prim Sch
TQ12 212 B7
Abbotsridge Dr TQ12 206 F1
Abbotswood
East Ogwell TQ12 206 F1
Kingsteignton TQ12 207 F8
Abbotts Hill EX33 152 D6
Abbotts Pk PL21 133 C2
Abbotts Rd PL3 248 E6
Abbrook Ave 9 TQ12 123 E1
Abelia Cl TQ3 225 E8
Aberdeen Ave PL5 244 D2
Abingdon Rd 1 PL4 263 A4
Abney Cres PL6 245 B6
Above Town TQ6 233 F2
Abscott La PL9 255 C5
Abyssinia Ct 8 EX32 155 B3
Abyssinia Terr 7 EX32 155 B3
Acacia Cl Bideford EX39 156 E1
Kingsteignton TQ12 207 F6
Acacia Mews EX6 181 B1
Academic La EX18 44 E1
Acadia Rd TQ1 220 E4
Ackland Pk EX14 84 D2
Acklington Pl PL5 243 E4
Acland Cross EX32 17 B2
Acland Rd
Broadclyst EX5 175 C6
Exeter EX4 261 C4
Ivybridge PL21 237 A6
Landkey EX32 17 B2
Salcombe TQ8 259 D4
Acland Terr EX4 261 C4
Acland Way EX16 161 A6
Aclands EX36 158 D3
Acombe Cross TA3 68 B8
Acre Cl EX39 24 E2
Acre La TQ1 220 E6
Acre Pl PL1 247 F3
Acre Rd EX39 24 E2
Acre The TQ13 111 A6
Ada's Terr EX34 7 F8
Adam's La PL9 140 C8
Adams Cl Plymouth PL5 243 F1
Torpoint PL11 246 F3
Adams Cres PL11 246 E3
Adcroft Rise EX13 103 D5
Adder La EX31 16 B6
Addington Ct EX4 261 B4
Addiscombe La EX6 113 D5
Addison Cl EX4 176 E6
Addison Rd
Newton Abbot TQ12 207 E1
Paignton TQ4 226 A5
Plymouth PL4 263 A4
Addlehole TQ9 144 D7
Adela Rd PL11 247 A3
Adelaide Ct EX2 261 A1
Adelaide La PL1 262 A2
Adelaide Pl PL1 262 A3
Adelaide St
Plymouth PL1 262 A3
2 Plymouth, Ford PL2 247 F5
Adelaide Street Ope
PL1 262 A3
Adelaide Terr 3 EX34 150 B6
Adelphi La TQ4 226 C5
Adelphi Mans TQ4 226 C5
Adelphi Rd TQ4 226 C6
Adit La PL12 242 E3
Adits The PL18 125 D3
Adley La TQ13 111 B7
Admiral's Hard PL1 254 A8
Admirals Ct 5 EX39 156 F7
Admirals Wlk
Exmouth EX8 196 D2
Teignmouth TQ14 210 A8
Admiralty Cotts PL1 254 A7
Admiralty Rd
Plymouth, Millbay PL1 254 A8
Plymouth, St Budeaux PL5 243 C2
Admiralty St
Plymouth, Keyham PL2 247 E6
Plymouth, Millbay PL1 254 A8
Adrian Cl EX39 157 A4
Adworthy La EX17 46 B2
Affeton Castle Cross
EX17 60 F8
Affeton Hill EX17 60 F8
Affeton Moor Cross EX17 46 A2
Agaton Rd PL5 243 E3
Aidan Ave EX32 155 C2
Ailescombe Dr TQ3 225 F6
Ailescombe Rd TQ3 225 F6
Ainslie Terr PL2 247 E7
Aire Gdns PL3 249 B5
Airfield Ind Est EX14 67 B2
Aish Cross TQ9 224 E2
Aish La TQ10 134 E3
Aish Lane End TQ10 134 F2
Aish Pk EX21 55 E4
Aish Rd Paignton TQ4 225 B2
Stoke Gabriel TQ9 224 F2
Alamein Ct PL12 242 E2
Alamein Rd PL12 242 D2
Alandale Cl TQ14 210 C6
Alandale Rd TQ14 210 C6
Alansway EX11 169 C3
Alba Ct EX1 178 E7
Albany Cl EX8 196 E2
Albany Rd TQ3 219 A1
Albany St
3 Newton Abbot TQ12 207 C3
Plymouth PL1 247 E2
Albemarle Villas PL1 247 F3
Albert Ct 3 TQ1 220 B5
Albert La 7 EX32 155 A5
Albert Pl Exmouth EX8 202 A7
10 Totnes TQ9 223 C5
Albert Rd Crediton EX17 165 C5
Plymouth PL2 247 F3
Saltash PL12 243 A2
Torquay TQ1 220 B5
Albert St 17 Dawlish EX7 204 D6
Exeter EX1 261 C4
Albert Terr
Bovey Tracey TQ13 180 C7
Gunnislake PL18 125 C5
7 Newton Abbot TQ12 207 C3
Princetown PL20 128 B8
Alberta Cres EX4 177 F8
Alberta Ct 14 TQ14 210 C5
Albertha Cl PL4 263 B4
Albion Cl EX12 191 F8
Albion Ct
6 Exmouth EX8 202 A7
Torpoint PL11 247 B3
Albion Dr PL2 248 B7
Albion Gdns TQ7 258 C6
Albion Hill Exmouth EX8 202 B7
Newton Abbot TQ12 207 C2
Albion Pl Exeter EX4 261 C4
Exmouth EX8 202 A7
Albion Rd PL11 247 B3
Albion St Exeter EX4 177 A5
Exmouth EX8 202 A7
Teignmouth TQ14 210 A3
Albion Terr 9 EX8 202 A7
Alcester Cl PL2 247 E4
Alcester St PL2 247 F4
Aldborough Ct EX8 202 C6
Alden Wlk PL6 249 B7
Aldens Bsns Ct EX2 181 B8
Aldens Rd EX2 181 B8
Alder Cl
Newton Abbot TQ12 212 F8
Teignmouth TQ14 210 B7
Alder Glade EX31 154 C3
Alder Rd PL19 171 C3
Alderney Rd PL6 244 F7
Alders Way TQ4 225 D3
Aldersley Wlk PL6 245 A1
Alderson Dr EX2 178 D5
Aldridge Mill Hill EX16 48 C6
Aldrin Rd EX4 173 E2
Alexander Rd 23 EX7 204 D6
Alexandra Cl
Crediton EX17 165 A6
Plymouth PL9 256 B8
Alexandra Ct 3 EX32 155 A5
Alexandra Dr PL20 125 F1
Alexandra Ho TQ12 207 E2
Alexandra La TQ1 220 B6
Alexandra Pl
Cornworthy TQ9 227 B4
4 Plymouth PL4 248 E4
Alexandra Rd
Axminster EX13 167 C5
Alexandra Rd *continued*
Barnstaple EX32 155 A5
Crediton EX17 165 B6
1 Newton Abbot TQ12 207 C2
Plymouth, Crownhill PL6 244 F2
Plymouth, Ford PL2 247 F5
Plymouth, Mutley PL4 248 F4
Torquay TQ1 220 B6
Wellington TA21 160 D6
Alexandra Sq PL12 243 A2
Alexandra Terr
Bideford EX39 157 A3
Clyst Honiton EX5 175 E2
Exeter EX4 177 E7
Exmouth EX8 201 F6
Newton Abbot TQ12 207 C2
Plymouth PL2 247 F5
South Molton EX36 158 C5
1 Teignmouth TQ14 210 B4
1 Totnes TQ9 223 C6
Alexandra Way EX17 165 A6
Alexandria Ind Est EX15 163 D4
Alexandria Rd EX10 188 A6
Alexandria Terr 6 EX16 161 B4
Alfington Rd
Alfington EX11 84 F1
Ottery St Mary EX11 169 F6
Alford Cl EX1 178 C7
Alford Cres EX1 178 B7
Alford Terr EX35 151 B5
Alfred Pl PL2 247 F5
Alfred Rd PL2 247 F5
Alfred St PL1 262 C2
Alfriston Rd TQ3 225 D7
Alger Wlk PL6 244 E6
Alice La 7 PL1 262 B3
Alice St PL1 262 A3
Alison Rd TQ3 219 A1
All Hallows Rd TQ3 219 C2
All Saint's Rd EX10 188 A4
All Saints CE Inf Sch
EX10 188 B4
All Saints CE Prim Sch
TQ7 143 A2
All Saints CE Prim Sch
(Marsh) TQ12 207 D3
All Saints Cl EX9 198 B6
All Saints Ct EX14 166 A5
All Saints Pk PL18 125 B5
All Saints Sch EX13 88 A4
All Saints' Rd TQ1 220 C7
Allaleigh Cross TQ9 139 F4
Allaleigh La TQ9 139 F4
Allans Rd PL21 237 D6
Allen Bank EX32 155 A3
Allen Cl EX16 161 F5
Allenby Rd PL2 248 A6
Allendale Rd PL4 263 A4
Allenhayes La TQ8 259 D4
Allenhayes Rd TQ8 259 D4
Allenstyle Cl EX31 153 B5
Allenstyle Dr EX31 153 B5
Allenstyle Gdns EX31 153 B5
Allenstyle Rd EX31 153 B5
Allenstyle View EX31 153 A5
Allenstyle Way EX31 153 B5
Aller Brake Rd TQ12 212 F8
Aller Cl TQ12 213 A6
Aller Cotts TQ12 212 F7
Aller Cross
Chillington TQ7 145 A1
Kentisbeare EX15 65 F1
Kingskerswell TQ12 212 E6
South Molton EX36 29 F7
Aller Gate EX17 78 D5
Aller Grove Cotts EX5 99 F7
Aller Hill
Bishops Nympton EX36 31 A4
Dawlish EX7 204 B5
Aller La EX20 94 F8
Aller Park Rd TQ12 212 F8
Aller Rd Dolton EX19 57 F7
Kingskerswell TQ12 212 F6
Allercombe Cross EX5 99 E5
Allercombe Hill EX5 168 A6
Allercombe La EX5 99 E5
Allerdown Cross EX17 80 A7
Allern La PL5 240 C1
Allerton Wlk PL6 249 B7
Allervale Cl EX2 178 B4
Alley Hill PL20 126 D1
Alleyn Ct EX12 191 F7
Alleyne Gdns PL3 248 E8
Allhalland St 17 EX39 157 A2
Allhallows Ct Exeter EX4 261 A2
1 Honiton EX14 166 C6
Allington Mead EX4 173 A3
Allington Terr EX17 78 F7
Allison La EX17 95 D7
Allotment Dro TA20 69 F5
Allotment Gdns TQ7 258 D6
Allshire La EX16 32 F3
Alma Cotts PL4 263 B2
Alma La EX10 188 C4
Alma Rd Brixham TQ5 230 C5
Plymouth PL3 248 C4
Alma St PL4 263 B2
Alma Terr 16 EX32 155 A4
Almeria Ct PL7 250 D4
Alminstone Cross EX39 39 A7
Almond Ct 3 EX31 154 C2
Almond Dr PL7 251 B6
Almshouse Cross TQ10 135 E4
Alpha Ctr TQ9 223 C6
Alpha Pl 24 EX39 15 A1
Alpha St EX1 177 F6
Alpha Terr TQ9 223 B6
Alphin Brook Rd EX2 177 C1
Alphington Comb Sch
EX2 177 B1
Alphington Rd EX2 177 B3
Alphington St EX2 261 A1
Alpine Rd TQ1 220 B5
Alscott Gdns EX31 27 A4
Alston Cross
Ashburton TQ13 131 B6
Slapton TQ7 145 B5
Alston La TQ5 229 D4
Alston Terr EX8 201 F6
Alstone Rd EX16 161 F3
Alswear New Rd
Alswear EX36 30 C1
South Molton EX36 158 E3
Alswear Old Rd EX36 158 C2
Alta Vista Cl TQ14 210 D7
Alta Vista Rd TQ4 226 C4
Altamira EX3 182 F5
Altamira Cotts EX39 25 D2
Alton Pl PL4 248 E4
Alton Rd PL4 263 A4
Alverdiscott Rd EX39 26 B4
Alvington St PL4 263 C2
Alwin Pk PL6 245 A5
Alwyns Cl 3 TQ14 210 C5
Alwyns Ct 5 TQ14 210 C5
Amacre Dr PL9 255 B6
Amados Cl PL7 250 B4
Amados Dr PL7 250 C4
Amados Rise PL7 250 C4
Ambassador Dr EX1 178 E7
Amberley Cl TQ13 130 E5
American Rd EX33 15 A4
Amershaw Ct EX2 178 A4
Amherst Rd PL3 262 B4
Amherst Road La E PL3 262 B4
Amity Pl PL4 263 A4
Amory Pl EX36 158 C4
Amory Rd Dulverton TA22 33 D6
Tiverton EX16 161 C2
Amyas Way EX39 157 A6
Anchor Bldgs TQ12 123 B2
Anchor Cotts TQ7 147 B7
Anchor Mill EX31 154 E8
Anchorage Cl TQ5 230 E5
Anchorage The TQ4 226 C5
Ander's La TA3 68 E8
Anderton Cl PL19 171 E1
Anderton Ct PL19 171 E2
Anderton La PL19 171 D2
Anderton Rise PL10 252 F4
Andor Ave TQ12 207 D7
Andrew Allan Rd TA21 160 B4
Andrew Cl EX10 187 F8
Andrew Rd EX31 154 E3
Andrew's Hill TA22 33 D6
Andrew's Hill Cross
TA22 33 C6
Andrewshayes La EX13 87 A1
Andurn Cl PL9 256 B6
Andurn Est PL9 140 A8
Angel Ct 2 EX14 166 C6
Angel Hill EX16 161 C4
Angelhill Cross EX36 30 F2
Ann's Pl PL3 248 A4
Anne Cl EX4 173 E1
Anne Cres EX31 154 E3
Annery Kiln Cotts EX39 26 A1
Anning Rd DT7 260 E4
Anson Ho 1 PL1 262 B3
Anson Pl
Plymouth, Devonport PL2 247 F4
Plymouth, St Jude's PL4 263 C3
Anson Rd EX8 196 C2
Anstey Cres EX16 161 F3
Anstey Gate TA22 32 B8
Anstey Way EX39 15 B1
Anstey's Cove Rd TQ1 220 E6
Ansteys Cl TQ1 220 E5
Ansteys Ct EX16 46 E1
Anstis St Plymouth PL1 262 A3
Plymouth PL1 262 B3
Anthea Rd TQ3 218 F1
Anthony Pk PL19 171 D6
Anthony Rd EX1 177 F6
Antonine Cres EX4 176 E6
Antony Gdns PL2 248 C8
Antony Ho★ PL11 246 D5
Antony Rd PL11 247 B3
Antony Woodland Gdn★
PL11 246 D6
Antrim Terr 5 TQ9 223 C6
Anvil Cnr EX22 72 D7
Anvil Ct PL17 115 B1
Anwyl Cl PL1 262 B3
Anzac Ave PL5 244 A4
Anzac St TQ6 233 F3
App's La EX39 25 E2
Apple Cl EX8 196 B3
Apple Dr EX15 162 D4
Apple Farm Grange
EX2 178 E3
Apple La EX2 178 E4
Apple Orch EX38 159 B4
Apple Tree Cl
Frogmore TQ7 144 E1
Witheridge EX16 46 E1
Apple Wharf 6 TQ9 223 D5
Applebee Way DT7 260 E4
Appleby Wlk PL5 244 D4
Appledore Cl EX15 163 B3
Appledore Hill EX20 170 F8
Applegarth Ave TQ12 206 E4
Applegarth Cl TQ12 206 E4
Applehayes EX8 202 C5
Applehayes La EX15 52 F2
Applemede EX5 82 B6
Appletree Cl
Barnstaple EX32 155
Uffculme EX15 66
Appletree Mews 5 EX39 15
Appley Cross TA21 51
April Cl EX8 196
Apsley Rd PL4 248
Apsley Terr
Braunton EX33 152
9 Ilfracombe EX34 150
Apsley Villas 8 EX34 150
Apters Hill 7 TQ5 230
Aqualand★ TQ1 220
Arbour Cl EX34 150
Arbour The PL6 244
Arcade Rd EX34 150
Arcadia PL9 256
Arcadia Rd PL9 256
Arch St 8 TQ14 210
Arch The EX5 184
Archer Pl PL1 262
Archer Terr PL1 262
Archery Cl TQ7 258
Archibald Rd EX1 261
Archipark EX32 17
Archway Ave PL4 249
Archway Dr TQ6 233
Arcot Gdns EX10 188
Arcot Pk EX10 188
Arcot Rd EX10 188
Arden Cl EX9 199
Arden Dr TQ2 219
Arden Gr PL2 248
Arden Ho TQ7 143
Ardenney Ct EX8 202
Ardwyn TA21 160
Arena Pk EX4 174
Argus Cl EX14 166
Argyle Mews EX4 173
Argyle Terr TQ9 223
Argyll Rd EX4 173
Arimoor Gdns PL19 171
Ark Royal Cl PL5 247
Arkwright Gdns PL5 243
Arley Cl PL6 245
Arlington Pl EX34 8 A
Arlington Rd
Plymouth PL4 248
Woolacombe EX34 7
Arlington Terr 4 EX33 152 D
Armada Cl EX12 192 A
Armada Cres TQ2 219 C
Armada Ct PL19 171 B
Armada Ctr PL1 262 C
Armada Dr TQ14 210 A
Armada Rd PL10 253 A
Armada St PL4 263 A
Armada Way
Plymouth PL1 262 C
Plymouth PL1 262 C
Westward Ho! EX39 156 B
Armourwood La EX5 81 D
Armstrong Ave EX4 173 D
Armytage Rd EX9 198 A
Arnison Cl PL9 255 F
Arnold Cres EX16 161 B
Arnold's Cl TQ7 142 C
Arnold's Point PL4 249 C
Arnside Cl PL6 245 D
Arran Cl TQ2 213 E
Arscott Gdns PL9 255 C5
Arscott La PL9 255 D5
Arthington TQ1 219 F7
Arthur Terr PL11 247 B2
Arthurs Cl EX8 196 D2
Artillery Pl PL4 263 B1
Artisan's Dwellings
EX36 158 D4
Arun Cl PL3 249 C5
Arundel Cl EX2 181 B8
Arundel Cres PL1 262 B4
Arundel Terr PL2 247 F4
Arundell Cl PL16 105 E4
Arundell Gdns PL16 105 E4
Arundell Pl TQ7 143 E7
Arundell Rd EX20 77 C4
Arundells Cnr 3 EX17 165 D5
Ascension Way TQ2 213 F2
Ascerton Cl EX10 188 B5
Ascerton Rd EX10 188 B5
Ash Bridge Cross EX20 95 D1
Ash Cl 7 PL20 126 F3
Ash Cross Bradninch EX5 82 F7
Dartmouth TQ6 232 D1
Halberton EX16 65 A6
Oakford EX16 48 D6
Petrockstow EX20 56 F3
Ash Ct Crediton EX17 165 C6
Lee Mill PL21 136 D6
Ash Dr EX15 163 C5
Ash Farm Cl EX1 174 F1
Ash Gr Exmouth EX8 196 B2
Ivybridge PL21 237 E5
Plymouth PL2 247 F7
Seaton EX12 192 A8
Ash Hill Oakford EX16 48 D6
Petrockstow EX20 56 F3
Ash Hill Cross EX16 48 D6
Ash Hill Ct EX12 191 C5
Ash Hill Rd TQ1 220 A6
Ash La Iddesleigh EX19 57 F1
Withypool TA24 21 F6
Woolfardisworthy EX17 62 A2
Ash Mill Hill EX36 31 B2
Ash Plants Cl EX39 156 D2
Ash Rd Braunton EX33 152 F7
Kingsteignton TQ12 207 E6
Ash Vale PL16 105 E4

Ash Way TQ12 207 F1
Ashacre Cross TQ1 214 B7
Ashburgh Parc PL12 242 B3
Ashburn Gdns TQ13 130 F5
Ashburn Wlk TQ4 229 B8
Ashburnham Rd PL5 244 A3
Ashburton & Buckfastleigh Hospl TQ13 131 A5
Ashburton Cl
Ashburton TQ13 130 F4
Bovey Tracey TQ13 180 C5
Ashburton Mus★ TQ13 130 F4
Ashburton Prim Sch TQ13 130 F4
Ashburton Rd
Bickington TQ12 131 F6
Bovey Tracey TQ13 180 C5
Newton Abbot TQ12 206 D4
Totnes TQ9 223 B7
Ashbury Cross EX20 93 B5
Ashby Station Cross EX20 92 C7
Ashclyst View EX5 175 D6
Ashcombe Cl PL7 250 C7
Ashcombe Cross EX7 124 C6
Ashcombe Hill PL8 257 F2
Ashcombe Rd EX7 204 B8
Ashculm Hill EX15 52 C2
Ashdown Cl PL6 245 E3
Ashdown Cross EX22 38 F3
Ashdown Wlk PL6 245 E3
Asheldon Ho TQ1 220 E5
Asheldon Rd TQ1 220 E5
Ashelford Cnr EX31 10 A3
Ashery Dr PL9 255 C6
Ashes Rd Dalwood EX13 87 B1
Shute EX13 103 B8
Ashfield Cl Ashford EX31 16 B6
Exmouth EX8 196 E1
Ashfield La EX31 16 B6
Ashfield Rd TQ2 219 E5
Ashfield Terr EX39 157 A7
Ashford Cl PL3 249 A4
Ashford Cres PL3 249 A4
Ashford Hill PL4 249 A4
Ashford Rd Plymouth PL4 248 F4
Topsham EX3 182 E5
Wellington TA21 160 D4
Ashill TQ14 209 A8
Ashlake Rd EX6 113 F7
Ashleigh EX2 181 A8
Ashleigh Cl Exeter EX4 176 F6
Plymouth PL5 244 C7
Teignmouth TQ14 210 B7
Torquay TQ2 213 F3
Ashleigh Cres EX32 155 B4
Ashleigh Ct TQ1 220 D3
Ashleigh Dr TQ14 210 B7
Ashleigh La PL5 240 D1
Ashleigh Mount TQ14 210 B7
Ashleigh Mount Rd EX4 176 F6
Ashleigh Pk
Bampton EX16 49 C8
Teignmouth TQ14 210 B7
Ashleigh Prim Sch EX32 155 A5
Ashleigh Rd
Barnstaple EX32 155 A5
Exmouth EX8 202 C7
Honiton EX14 166 B6
Kingsbridge TQ7 258 B4
Ashleigh Rise TQ14 210 B7
Ashleigh Way
Plymouth PL7 251 C4
Teignmouth TQ14 210 B7
Ashley Back La EX16 64 A5
Ashley Brake EX11 168 D4
Ashley Cl EX15 66 B8
Ashley Cres EX10 188 A7
Ashley Ho EX8 202 B6
Ashley Priors La TQ1 214 C4
Ashley Rd
Okehampton EX20 170 C5
Uffculme EX15 66 A7
Ashley Rise EX16 161 B1
Ashley Terr EX39 156 F1
Ashley Way EX7 204 F7
Ashmead Gr EX33 152 C6
Ashmill Cross EX21 90 F6
Ashmill Ct TQ12 206 F4
Ashplants Cl EX19 58 F3
Ashprington Cross TQ9 139 F8
Ashridge Gdns
Kingsteignton TQ12 207 F6
Plymouth PL5 244 B2
Ashridge La EX20 77 D6
Ashridge Moor Cross EX20 77 E6
Ashton Cl PL6 245 C6
Ashton Cres EX33 152 C5
Ashton Ct 11 TQ12 123 F1
Ashton Ind Units EX2 177 B2
Ashton Rd EX2 177 B2
Ashton Terr TQ1 220 E5
Ashton Way PL12 242 D3
Ashtown Cross EX16 34 A3
Ashtree Cl PL6 245 D7
Ashtree Gr PL9 256 C8
Ashwater Prim Sch EX21 90 F6
Ashwell La TQ13 122 E6
Ashwood 4 TQ10 134 F3
Ashwood Cl
Loddiswell TQ7 143 E7
Plymouth PL7 251 B5
Ashwood Park Rd PL7 251 C6
Ashwood Pk TQ7 143 E7
Ashwood Rd EX2 177 B3
Aspen Cl Exeter EX2 178 C4
Aspen Cl *continued*
3 Honiton EX14 85 C2
Tavistock PL19 171 C3
Aspen Dr TQ12 212 F8
Aspen Gdns PL7 251 B5
Aspen Way Paignton TQ4 225 D3
Tiverton EX16 161 E7
Astley Ct EX20 170 A5
Astor Dr PL4 249 C3
Aswell Orch TQ7 143 F7
Athelstan Cl EX13 167 D4
Athelstan Rd EX1 261 C3
Athenaeum La PL1 262 B2
Athenaeum Pl PL1 262 C2
Athenaeum St PL1 262 B2
Atherton Pl PL2 247 E4
Atherton Way EX16 64 D7
Atkinson Cl EX4 174 A1
Atlantic Village EX39 25 D4
Atlantic Way EX39 156 D7
Attwyll Ave EX2 178 A5
Atway Cl 3 TQ13 180 C8
Atwill's Almshouses EX4 261 A4
Atworthy Cross EX22 38 D3
Auckland Rd 3 PL2 248 A5
Auction Way EX39 38 F8
Audley Ave TQ2 219 F8
Audley Rise TQ12 208 A1
Augustine Cl EX12 191 F8
Aunay Cl EX22 164 D5
Aune Cl TQ10 135 B1
Aunemouth Cross TQ7 143 A3
Ausewell Cross TQ13 130 D7
Austen Cl EX4 178 C8
Austin Ave PL2 248 A6
Austin Cres PL6 245 C1
Austin Farm Prim Sch PL6 249 C7
Authers Hts EX16 161 B2
Auton Cross TQ7 258 A2
Avalon Cl EX4 174 A2
Aveland Rd TQ1 220 C7
Avent Wlk PL7 250 F7
Avenue Cl DT7 260 D3
Avenue Rd
Bovey Tracey TQ13 180 C6
Ilfracombe EX34 150 B6
Kingskerswell TQ12 213 A5
Lyme Regis DT7 260 D3
Torquay TQ2 219 F5
Avenue Terr TQ5 229 E5
Avenue The Exton EX3 183 C1
Newton Abbot TQ12 207 D4
3 Seaton EX12 192 A5
Tiverton EX16 161 E3
Avery Hill TQ12 207 E8
Avery Way PL12 242 C5
Aveton Gifford CE Prim Sch TQ7 143 C6
Aviemore Ind Est EX31 154 D3
Avoca Ave TQ1 219 F6
Avocet Dr EX3 183 C2
Avocet Rd EX2 178 F6
Avon Cl Plymouth PL3 249 D6
South Brent TQ10 135 A2
Avon La EX39 156 D7
Avon Quillet TQ7 142 E3
Avon Rd Bideford EX39 157 C1
Torquay TQ2 219 B7
Avon Valley Cotts TQ7 143 C6
Avondale Ho 9 TQ10 134 F2
Avondale Rd Exeter EX2 178 A5
Exmouth EX8 202 D8
Avondale Wlk 10 TQ10 134 F2
Avranches Ave EX17 165 A6
Awliscombe Prim Sch EX14 85 B4
Axe Cl PL3 249 D6
Axe Vale Cvn Pk EX12 192 B6
Axe Valley Cl EX13 104 C7
Axe Valley Com Coll The EX13 167 D6
Axeford TA20 88 E8
Axeford Mdws TA20 88 E8
Axeview Rd EX12 192 A7
Axminster Com Prim Sch EX13 167 E6
Axminster Hospl EX13 167 D6
Axminster Mus★ EX13 167 D5
Axminster Rd
Charmouth DT6 104 F4
Honiton EX14 166 F5
Musbury EX13 103 D5
Offwell EX14 86 A3
Tatworth TA20 88 C8
Axminster Sta EX13 167 C5
Axmouth Rd EX12 192 C5
Axtown La PL20 126 F2
Aycliffe Gdns PL7 251 A3
Aylesbury Cres PL5 244 B5
Aylescott Cross EX37 43 E3
Aylescott Hill EX34 9 A4
Aylescott La EX34 9 A4
Ayleston Cross PL21 137 D2
Ayleston Pk PL21 137 C2
Aylwin Cl PL7 250 E6
Ayres Cl EX39 157 C1
Ayreville Rd PL2 248 B7
Ayreville Residential Pk TQ4 224 F5
Aysha Gdns EX39 156 D8
Ayshford EX15 66 A7
Azalea Cl EX14 67 C1
Azes La EX32 155 A5

B

Babbacombe CE Prim Sch TQ1 220 D6
Babbacombe Cl PL6 249 E8
Babbacombe Downs Rd TQ1 220 D8
Babbacombe Model Village★ TQ1 220 C8
Babbacombe Rd TQ1 220 E6
Babbage Rd TQ9 223 D6
Babbages EX31 154 A4
Babblebrook Mews EX1 178 F8
Babeleigh Cl EX39 40 B7
Babeleigh Water EX39 39 E7
Baber Ct PL12 125 A2
Babis Farm Cl PL12 242 F1
Babis Farm Ct PL12 242 F1
Babis Farm Mews PL12 242 F2
Babis Farm Row PL12 242 F1
Babis Farm Way PL12 242 F2
Babis La PL12 242 F1
Babland Cross PL21 137 D2
Bableigh Cross EX32 28 B8
Bableigh Rd EX32 17 B1
Babylon La EX5 82 B5
Back Hill PL12 242 D2
Back Hill Ind Est EX18 44 E1
Back La Abbotsham EX39 156 A1
Bickleigh EX16 63 D2
Black Torrington EX21 74 A8
Bradninch EX5 82 E6
Chittlehampton EX37 28 F4
Chulmleigh EX18 44 E1
Colaton Raleigh EX10 186 B3
Copplestone EX17 79 A4
Ermington PL21 136 F3
Frithelstockstone EX38 40 F5
Lutton PL21 133 B2
Merton EX20 57 A7
Newton Poppleford EX10 186 E8
North Molton EX36 30 D8
Plymouth PL7 250 E4
Sandford EX17 80 A5
Sidmouth EX10 187 C7
Sticklepath EX20 95 A5
Stockland EX14 87 A5
Back Rd Calstock PL18 125 D3
Moreleigh TQ9 139 A3
Newton Abbot TQ12 207 B3
Back St Bampton EX16 34 B1
Modbury PL21 137 B2
Woolfardisworthy EX39 38 F8
Back's Hill Crediton EX17 79 F7
Sandford EX17 80 A7
Backfield 7 EX39 15 A1
Backs The TQ6 233 E5
Backshay Cl TQ7 143 C1
Backshay Pk TQ7 143 C1
Backstone La EX16 47 B6
Backswood La EX16 64 B4
Backways La TA21 51 F6
Backwells Mead EX24 102 B6
Bad Homburg Way EX2 181 D8
Badgaver La EX34 3 B3
Badger Cl
Dartmouth TQ6 233 D4
Exeter EX2 178 D5
Honiton EX14 166 E7
Newton Poppleford EX10 186 D7
Paignton TQ3 218 F1
Badger's Way TQ13 180 D7
Badgers Cl
Ivybridge PL21 237 A5
Kingsbridge TQ7 258 C4
Kingsteignton TQ12 207 D8
Badgers Gn TQ7 258 C4
Badgers Wlk PL12 242 D4
Badlake Cl EX7 204 C7
Badlake Hill EX7 204 C7
Badlake La EX36 32 D6
Badlake Moor Cross TA22 32 D7
Badon Cl EX4 174 A2
Bagley Rd TA21 160 A3
Bagmore Hill EX5 82 F8
Bagshot Ave EX2 177 D3
Bailey La EX5 98 F7
Bailey St EX4 261 B3
Bailey Terr EX22 70 F5
Bailey's Knapp EX16 50 B4
Baileys Mdw TQ6 146 B7
Bainbridge Ave PL3 248 F7
Bainbridge Ct PL7 250 E7
Baker Cl EX10 188 A8
Baker St EX2 177 F5
Baker's Cross TA3 68 A7
Baker's Hill
Newton Abbot TQ12 207 B3
Tiverton EX16 161 A4
Baker's La
Churchinford TA3 68 A7
Wellington TA21 160 E6
Baker's Pk TQ13 130 A4
Bakers Cl PL7 251 C5
Bakers Cotts EX8 195 F5
Bakers Court La EX35 151 B5
Bakers Hill
Aveton Gifford TQ7 143 C6
Brixham TQ5 230 C3
Exeter EX2 176 C3
Bakers Mead EX13 87 A1
Bakers Pl PL1 247 F1
Bakers Terr TQ7 143 C6
Bakers View TQ12 207 A3
Bakery La EX8 202 A7
Bakery Mdw EX16 62 B5
Bakery Way EX32 17 B2
Bal La PL19 117 E6
Bala Brook Cl TQ5 229 F2
Baldwin Dr EX20 170 D6
Balfour Cl EX14 166 E5
Balfour Gdns EX10 188 A6
Balfour Manor EX10 188 A5
Balfour Manor Ct EX10 187 F5
Balfour Mews EX10 188 A5
Balfour Terr
Kilmington EX13 87 C1
Plymouth PL2 247 E4
Balfours EX10 188 A6
Balkwill Ct TQ7 258 C4
Balkwill Rd TQ7 258 C4
Balkwills Cotts EX21 55 E4
Ball Hill EX17 63 A2
Ball Hill La EX20 170 D5
Ball La EX24 101 F5
Ball's Cross TQ8 259 C7
Balland La TQ13 131 A5
Balland Pk 5 TQ13 131 A5
Ballards Cres EX31 153 A4
Ballards Gr EX31 153 A4
Ballards Way EX31 153 A4
Balleroy Cl EX21 55 E4
Ballhill La EX16 49 B8
Balls Cnr Burrington EX37 44 A3
Merton EX20 57 C8
Balls Corner Cross EX20 57 C8
Balls Cross EX36 20 B2
Balls Farm Rd EX2 176 F2
Balls Hill EX37 44 A2
Balmoral Ave PL2 247 F5
Balmoral Cl TQ12 207 E2
Balmoral Cres EX20 170 D5
Balmoral Gdns EX3 182 F5
Balmoral Ho EX31 154 E7
Balmoral La 6 TQ10 134 F3
Baltic Wharf Bsns Pk TQ9 223 D4
Bampfylde Way PL6 244 D6
Bampfylde Cl
Poltimore EX4 174 F6
Tiverton EX16 161 F3
Bampfylde Cross EX36 19 D2
Bampfylde Rd TQ2 219 F5
Bampfylde St EX1,EX4 261 C3
Bampfylde Way PL6 244 E6
Bampton Cl TQ3 218 D2
Bampton Down Rd EX16 49 F7
Bampton Prim Sch EX16 34 B1
Bampton Rd PL6 245 E1
Bampton St EX16 161 D4
Bamson La EX16 62 B6
Banbury Pk TQ2 219 C8
Banfield Way EX14 166 B4
Bank End EX39 157 B4
Bank La Brixham TQ5 230 C5
6 Totnes TQ9 223 C5
Bank Sq TA22 33 D6
Bank St
Newton Abbot TQ12 207 B3
12 Teignmouth TQ14 210 C4
Bankland La EX20 77 D8
Banksia Cl EX16 161 E7
Bankside EX8 196 C3
Bannawell St PL19 171 B6
Bantham Cross TQ7 143 D4
Baptist Chapel Ct EX17 165 C5
Baptist St PL17 125 D3
Bapton Cl EX8 196 B2
Bapton La EX8 196 B1
Bar's La EX9,EX10 199 B8
Barber's La Uplyme DT7 260 B4
West Buckland TA21 52 F7
Barbican App PL4 263 B2
Barbican Cl EX32 155 A4
Barbican Ct Exeter EX4 177 A5
12 Plymouth PL4 263 A2
Barbican La EX32 155 B4
Barbican Leisure Pk PL4 263 C2
Barbican Pl 9 EX32 155 A4
Barbican Rd
Barnstaple EX32 155 A4
Plymouth PL7 250 E4
Barbican Stps
Exeter EX4 177 A6
Exeter EX4 261 A2
Barbican Terr EX32 155 A4
Barbican The PL1 263 A2
Barbican Theatre PL1 263 A1
Barbrook Rd EX35 151 B3
Barbury Cres PL6 245 B8
Barchington Ave TQ2 213 F3
Barcombe Hts TQ3 226 B8
Barcombe La TQ3 226 B8
Barcombe Mews TQ3 226 B8
Barcombe Rd TQ3 226 A8
Barcote Wlk PL6 249 C8
Bardsey Cl PL6 245 A7
Barewell Cl TQ1 220 B8
Barewell Rd TQ1 220 B8
Barfield Cl EX19 57 F7
Barfield Rd EX19 57 F7
Baring Cotts 14 TQ9 223 D5
Baring Cres EX1 177 E6
Baring Ct EX2 261 B1
Baring Flats EX1 177 E6
Baring St PL4 263 B4
Barker's Hill PL12 242 C1
Barkers Way EX20 77 C4
Barkingdon Manor TQ9 215 D7
Barlands Way EX19 57 F7
Barley Cl EX15 163 B2
Barley Farm Rd EX4 176 E4
Barley La EX4 176 D5
Barley Lane Sch EX4 176 D4
Barley Market St PL19 171 C6
Barley Mount EX4 176 F5
Barley Wlk EX6 201 A8
Barleycorn Field 6 EX32 17 B2
Barline EX12 191 D5
Barlow Rd EX31 155 A7
Barn Cl Barnstaple EX32 155 C3
Ivybridge PL21 237 A6
Plymouth PL7 251 D4
Shebbear EX21 55 E4
Whiddon Down EX20 95 F3
Barn Close La EX12 192 E5
Barn Cross EX14 85 F8
Barn Ct TQ5 229 E4
Barn Hayes EX10 187 F7
Barn Hill EX17 78 F7
Barn La EX9 197 F2
Barn Meads Rd TA21 160 E4
Barn Owl Cl TQ2 213 D3
Barn Park Cl TQ12 211 E2
Barn Park Rd
Fremington EX31 153 D5
Plymouth PL3 248 D6
Barn Pk Ashwater EX21 90 E6
Buckfastleigh TQ11 236 A5
Crediton EX17 165 C5
Liverton TQ12 122 F1
Saltash PL12 242 F3
Stoke Gabriel TQ9 227 F8
Wrafton EX33 152 E3
Barn Rd TQ4 226 C2
Barnacott Cross EX39 26 D8
Barnardo Rd EX2 261 C1
Barnards Farm EX12 191 D5
Barnards Hill La EX12 192 A7
Barncroft EX22 39 C1
Barndale Cres PL6 245 B6
Barne Barton Prim Sch PL5 247 D8
Barne Cl PL5 247 C8
Barne Cross TQ13 112 A2
Barne La PL5 243 D1
Barne Rd PL5 247 C8
Barnes Cl Honiton EX14 166 B4
Willand EX15 162 C5
Barnes Close Mead TA22 33 D6
Barnfield Crediton EX17 165 C5
East Allington TQ9 144 D7
Barnfield Ave EX8 202 D7
Barnfield Cl
Braunton EX33 152 E5
Crediton EX17 165 C5
Galmpton TQ5 229 C5
Barnfield Cres EX1 261 B3
Barnfield Dr PL7 251 C5
Barnfield Hill EX1 261 C3
Barnfield Rd
Brixham TQ5 230 D3
Exeter EX1 261 B3
Exeter EX1 261 C3
Paignton TQ3 226 A7
Torquay TQ2 219 D2
Barnfield Terr TQ12 212 B6
Barnfield Wlk TQ7 258 C6
Barnhay 6 EX16 34 B1
Barnhay The TQ9 227 F7
Barnhill Rd TQ12 213 A4
Barningham Gdns PL6 245 A6
Barnmeads Rd TA21 160 E4
Barnpark Cl TQ14 210 C6
Barnpark Rd TQ14 210 C5
Barnpark Terr TQ14 210 C6
Barns Cl Bradninch EX5 82 F6
Kingsteignton TQ12 207 E6
Barns Close Ind Est TA22 33 D6
Barns Rd EX9 198 B1
Barnsclose TA22 33 D6
Barnsclose N TA22 33 D6
Barnsclose W TA22 33 D6
Barnsey Gdns TQ13 130 F5
Barnsfield La TQ11 236 A5
Barnshill Cl EX17 62 F1
Barnsley Cl 1 TQ14 210 C5
Barnsley Dr TQ14 210 C6
Barnstaple C Ctr EX31 154 E5
Barnstaple Cl
Chittlehampton EX37 28 F4
Plymouth PL6 249 E7
Barnstaple Cross
Burrington EX37 43 C3
Crediton EX17 79 E4
Barnstaple Ret Pk EX31 154 F4
Barnstaple St
Bideford EX39 157 B2
South Molton EX36 158 C4
Winkleigh EX19 58 F3
Barnstaple Sta EX31 154 F4
Barnstone Ct EX2 181 A8
Barntown Gate EX19 58 E1
Barntown La EX19 58 D1
Barnwood Cl PL9 255 E5
Barons Pyke PL21 237 E4
Barons Rd PL20 127 B3
Barossa Rd PL11 247 B3
Barpark Cnr EX15 52 E3
Barrack La EX2 114 C7
Barrack Pl PL1 248 A1
Barrack Rd Exeter EX2 177 E4
Modbury PL21 137 B3
Ottery St Mary EX11 169 C3
Barrack St PL1 247 E2
Barracks Hill TQ9 223 A7
Barradon Cl TQ2 214 A4
Barrington Ho TQ1 220 E5

Barrington Mead EX10 188 B4
Barrington Rd TQ1 220 E5
Barrington St EX16 161 D4
Barris EX17 60 C3
Barron Way EX31 154 B1
Barrow Down PL12 242 B3
Barrow Rd EX14 84 C4
Barrow Way Cross
EX20 110 D8
Barrowdale Cl EX8 196 C3
Barry Sq TQ4 226 C6
Bartholomew Rd PL2 248 B5
Bartholomew St W EX4 261 A2
Bartholomew Terr EX4 261 A2
Barton Ave
Braunton EX33 152 D4
Paignton TQ3 225 F7
Plymouth PL2 247 E5
Barton Cl
Cheriton Fitzpaine EX17 62 E1
Exton EX3 183 C1
Kingsbridge TQ7 258 D4
Paignton TQ3 225 F7
Parkham EX39 39 E8
Plymouth PL7 251 C5
Stoke Canon EX5 81 F1
Wembury PL9 140 D8
Barton Close La EX33 8 B4
Barton Cnr EX17 61 B2
Barton Cotts EX20 95 C1
Barton Court La EX5 172 A8
Barton Cres Dawlish EX7 204 C6
Paignton TQ3 225 F7
Barton Cross
East Anstey EX16 32 E5
Filleigh EX32 29 A6
Heasley Mill EX36 19 C2
Instow EX39 15 B2
Morchard Bishop EX17 61 C2
Poltimore EX5 174 B8
Sandford EX17 80 C6
Torquay TQ2 213 F4
Barton Ct Ashwater EX21 90 E6
Exeter EX1 178 C7
Parkham EX39 39 E8
Barton Dr
Newton Abbot TQ12 206 F3
Paignton TQ3 225 F7
Barton Gate La 3 EX34 3 A3
Barton Gdns TQ3 225 F7
Barton Head Cross EX20 76 C4
Barton Hill
Berrynarbor EX34 2 E4
Daccombe TQ1,TQ12 214 A6
Dawlish EX7 204 D6
North Tawton EX20 77 C4
Barton Hill Rd TQ2 213 F2
Barton Hill Way TQ2 213 F2
Barton Ho EX39 26 A4
Barton Inf Sch TQ2 213 F2
Barton Jun Sch TQ2 213 F2
Barton La Berrynarbor EX34 2 E4
Bratton Fleming EX31 11 D3
Braunton EX33 152 D5
Brayford EX32 18 F4
Dawlish EX7 204 D6
Lapford EX17 60 A2
Shillingford Abbot EX2 114 C7
Staverton TQ9 216 A5
Witheridge EX16 46 E1
Barton Lane Cl EX33 152 D4
Barton Meadow Rd EX37 43 B7
Barton Mews Exton EX3 183 C1
Millbrook PL10 252 F6
Parkham EX39 39 E8
Tipton St John EX11 100 B2
Barton Orch EX10 100 D2
Barton Paddocks EX10 100 D2
Barton Rd
Barnstaple EX32 155 D4
Buckland Brewer EX39 40 B7
Exeter EX2 176 F4
Ilfracombe EX34 8 F5
Okehampton EX20 170 C5
Paignton TQ3 225 F7
Parkham EX39 39 E8
Plymouth PL9 255 B6
Tiverton EX16 161 D6
Torquay TQ2 219 E7
Woolacombe EX34 7 F6
Barton Rd Ind Units
TQ2 219 E8
Barton Rise EX14 84 E2
Barton St EX20 77 C4
Barton Steep EX35 5 E4
Barton Terr EX7 204 D6
Barton The TA4 35 E8
Barton Tors EX39 157 C1
Barton Villas EX7 204 C6
Bartonbury Cross EX17 78 E6
Bartonhill Cross TQ9 215 F6
Bartows Cswy EX16 161 D5
Bartows Mews EX16 161 D5
Bartridge Hill EX31 27 A5
Barum Arc EX32 155 A5
Barum Cl TQ3 226 C7
Barwick Cross EX19 58 B2
Bary Cl EX17 62 F1
Bary Hill Cross EX17 62 F1
Bary La EX17 62 F1
Bascombe Cl TQ5 229 D6
Bascombe Rd TQ5 229 D6
Basinghall Cl PL9 255 E5
Basket Ope PL4 263 A2
Bason Cross EX22 55 B2
Bassett Cl EX39 156 F8
Bassetts Farm Prim Sch
EX8 196 E1
Bassetts Gdns EX8 196 D2
Bastard's La EX38 159 D6
Bastard's Park Cnr
PL21 137 D3
Batcombe La EX5 81 F6
Bate Cl EX2 177 A1
Bath Cl EX14 84 D2
Bath Ct EX39 156 C7
Bath Hotel Rd EX39 156 C7
Bath La Plymouth PL1 262 B2
Torquay TQ2 219 F5
Bath Meadow Dr TA22 33 E6
Bath Pl Ilfracombe EX34 150 B6
Plymouth PL1 262 B2
Bath Pl W PL1 262 B2
Bath Rd EX8 202 A6
Bath St PL1 262 B2
Bath Terr 6 Instow EX39 15 B1
19 Teignmouth TQ14 210 C4
Batson Cross TQ8 259 C5
Batson Gdns TQ4 226 B4
Batson Hall Cross TQ8 259 C6
Batsworthy Cross EX16 46 F7
Batsworthy Hill EX16 47 A7
Batt's La EX11 169 D3
Battens EX14 87 A7
Battens Cross EX16 65 C8
Batter St PL4 263 A2
Batterbridge Hill PL19 117 E3
Batteridge Hill PL19 117 F2
Battershall Cl PL9 255 F5
Battersway Rd TQ4 225 E4
Battery La PL19 171 C4
Battery St PL1 262 A2
Battery Street Flats
PL1 262 A2
Battishorne Way EX14 166 B4
Battle Rd TQ12 180 F2
Battle St EX15 52 E1
Battledown Cross EX21 55 F4
Battleford La TQ9 217 C5
Battleton TA22 33 D6
Batts Pk EX15 66 C6
Batworthy Mill Cross
TQ13 111 A4
Bavent Cl EX5 173 F8
Baxter Cl EX2 178 D3
Baxworthy Cross EX39 23 A1
Bay Ct EX12 192 B4
Bay Rd EX9 199 A7
Bay Trees EX6 114 D4
Bay View TQ3 219 D1
Bay View Cl TQ6 146 B7
Bay View Ct EX39 156 F6
Bay View Dr TQ14 210 C6
Bay View Est TQ6 146 B7
Bay View Rd
Northam EX39 156 E6
Woolacombe EX34 7 F6
Bayard's Cove TQ6 233 F3
Bayard's Hill TQ6 233 F3
Bayclose La EX31 10 D6
Baydon Cl PL6 245 C1
Bayly's Rd PL9 255 B7
Baymount Rd TQ3 226 A7
Baynes Cl TA21 160 E7
Bayside La PL9 140 A8
Bayswater Rd PL1 262 B4
Baythorpe Lodge TQ2 219 E2
Baytor Ind Est TQ4 225 D3
Baytree Cl PL6 245 D6
Baytree Gdns PL2 248 A7
Bayview Rd DT7 260 D4
Baze La EX35 6 B4
Bazley Sq EX1 178 E8
Beach Rd Croyde EX33 7 D2
Dawlish Warren EX7 201 B2
Heybrook Bay PL9 140 A7
Ilfracombe EX34 150 F6
Paignton TQ4 226 C6
Seaton EX12 192 B4
Torquay TQ1 220 D7
Westward Ho! EX39 156 D7
Woolacombe EX34 8 A6
Beach St 11 EX7 204 E6
Beach View Cres PL9 140 D7
Beacon Ave EX4 178 A8
Beacon Bsns Pk PL2 248 C7
Beacon Cl PL21 237 C6
Beacon Cotts TQ13 130 C7
Beacon Cross
Bradninch EX5 82 F7
Copplestone EX17 79 D6
North Tawton EX20 77 A2
South Molton EX36 45 C5
Talaton EX5 84 B1
Beacon Down Ave PL2 248 B7
Beacon Down Cnr EX6 98 D2
Beacon Down Cross
EX20 93 E5
Beacon Down Hill EX20 93 F5
Beacon Heath EX4 174 C1
Beacon Hill Bradninch EX5 82 F7
16 Exmouth EX8 202 A6
Torquay TQ1 220 B3
Beacon Hill La EX14 87 A5
Beacon Ho PL3 249 D4
Beacon Hts EX33 152 E6
Beacon La
Bovey Tracey TQ13 123 A7
Cullompton EX15 65 A3
Exeter EX4 178 A8
Kingswear TQ6 234 A2
Wellington TA21 52 C4
Beacon Park Rd PL2 248 B7
Beacon Pk PL15 89 D2
Beacon Pl EX8 202 A6
Beacon Rd Bradninch EX5 82 F7
Ivybridge PL21 237 C6
Kingswear TQ6 234 A2
Beacon Rise EX18 44 E1
Beacon Terr 4 TQ10 134 F2
Beacon The EX8 202 A6
Beacon View
Bittaford PL21 137 C7
Dartington TQ9 222 F8
8 South Brent TQ10 134 F2
Beacondown Cross EX16 63 E8
Beaconfield Rd PL2 248 B7
Beaconpark La EX20 95 D3
Beaconsfield Cross EX22 72 E6
Beadon Dr TQ8 259 C4
Beadon La TQ13 123 A8
Beadon Rd
Salcombe TQ8 259 B4
Salcombe TQ8 259 C4
Beaford Com Prim Sch
EX19 42 D1
Bealey Court Cross EX18 45 E2
Bealswood Cl PL18 125 D6
Bealswood Rd PL18 125 D6
Beanhay Cl 11 TQ12 122 F1
Beans Mdw EX20 170 A5
Beaple's Moor Cross
EX36 47 A8
Bear St Barnstaple EX32 155 A5
Exeter EX1 261 B2
Beara Cross
Bratton Fleming EX31 18 A8
Highampton EX21 74 A6
King's Nympton EX37 44 F6
Roborough EX38 42 E6
Beara Down Cross EX31 8 F1
Beara Head EX38 42 E6
Beara Hill EX32 19 A5
Beara Hill Head EX36 19 B6
Beara La
Bratton Fleming EX31 18 A8
Combe Martin EX34 3 C3
Beardown Rd EX20 170 E5
Beards Rd EX31 153 E5
Beare Bridge Rd EX20 170 C6
Beare Cl PL9 255 B5
Beare Copse La EX19 58 F2
Beare La Beare EX5 82 E3
Bondleigh EX20 77 B7
Beare Lane Cross EX20 77 B7
Beare Sq EX5 82 E4
Bearne's La 8 TQ12 207 B3
Bearne's Prim Sch
TQ12 207 C3
Bears Cotts EX6 181 B2
Bears Farm Cotts EX20 170 B7
Bears La EX9 197 E3
Bearsdown Cl PL6 249 C8
Bearsdown Rd PL6 249 C8
Beaston Cross TQ9 131 D1
Beatland Cross PL7 132 C5
Beatlands Rd EX10 188 B4
Beatrice Ave
Plymouth Keyham PL2 247 E5
Plymouth St Jude's PL4 263 B3
Saltash PL12 242 E2
Beatrice Gdns PL12 242 E1
Beattie Rd PL5 247 B8
Beatty Cl PL6 245 A4
Beatty Way TQ6 233 F4
Beauchamp Cres PL2 248 C7
Beauchamp Rd PL2 248 C7
Beaudyn Wlk 5 PL6 249 C7
Beaufort Cl EX16 50 D1
Beaufort Ho 21 PL4 263 A2
Beaufort Rd EX2 261 A1
Beaufort Wlk EX32 155 B6
Beauly Cl PL7 251 A5
Beaumaris Gdns PL3 248 F8
Beaumaris Rd PL3 248 F7
Beaumont Ave PL4 263 A3
Beaumont Cl
5 Liverton TQ12 122 F1
Torquay TQ2 219 D6
Beaumont Pl PL4 263 A3
Beaumont Rd
Newton Abbot TQ12 207 C3
Plymouth PL4 263 B3
Beaumont St PL2 248 A5
Beaumont Terr PL12 242 F4
Beauvale Cl EX11 169 E4
Beavers Brook Cl TQ3 219 B2
Beavor La EX13 167 F6
Beaworthy Cl EX2 177 A3
Beccott Cross EX31 10 D4
Becket Rd TQ13 180 E7
Beckets Rd TQ7 258 D5
Beckford Cl PL7 251 A5
Beckford Cross EX13 87 C4
Beckham Pl PL3 249 A6
Becklake Cl EX31 154 A2
Beckland Cross EX39 22 F4
Beckly Ct PL1 262 C3
Becky Falls★ TQ13 122 A7
Bede Gdns PL5 244 C1
Bedford Cl PL18 125 C6
Bedford Gr PL21 237 D5
Bedford Mews PL4 263 A4
Bedford Park Villas PL4 263 A4
Bedford Pk
10 Bere Alston PL20 125 E1
Plymouth PL4 263 A4
Bedford Pl 6 PL20 125 E1
Bedford Rd
Horrabridge PL20 126 F4
Plymouth PL9 255 E8
Bedford Rd continued
Torquay TQ1 220 D8
Bedford Row 15 EX31 154 F5
Bedford Sq
Sidmouth EX10 188 B3
Tavistock PL19 171 C5
Bedford St
10 Barnstaple EX32 155 A5
Bere Alston PL20 125 E1
Exeter EX1 261 B3
Plymouth PL2 247 F5
Bedford Terr PL4 263 A4
Bedford Villas 7 PL20 125 E1
Bedford Way PL1 262 C3
Bedlam La EX13 87 C6
Bedland's La EX9 197 F2
Beech Ave Exeter EX4 173 D1
Plymouth PL4 263 C2
Beech Bank EX39 25 D4
Beech Cl Barnstaple EX31 154 B2
Broadclyst EX5 175 D6
Honiton EX14 166 A4
Tavistock PL19 171 C2
Torpoint PL11 247 A3
Totnes TQ9 222 F6
Willand EX15 162 D4
Beech Croft EX15 163 C5
Beech Ct Plymouth PL6 245 D5
2 Wellington TA21 160 D6
Beech Dr
Down St Mary EX17 78 E7
Ipplepen TQ12 211 E2
Beech Gr
Barnstaple EX31 154 F7
Braunton EX33 152 C7
Wellington TA21 160 C6
Beech Grove Prim Sch
TA21 160 C6
Beech Hill TA21 160 F5
Beech Hill Cross EX17 61 B3
Beech La EX13 88 E1
Beech Lea EX18 58 F8
Beech Pk Crediton EX17 165 D6
Fremington EX31 153 E5
Holsworthy Beacon EX22 54 C3
West Hill EX11 168 D4
Beech Rd Lee Mill PL21 136 C7
Stibb Cross EX38 40 D1
Beech Tree Cross TA22 33 C7
Beech Tree Dr EX16 161 B5
Beech Tree Mdw EX20 107 F8
Beech Trees La TQ12 211 C3
Beech Wlk EX14 85 C1
Beechcroft Rd
Plymouth Lower Compton
PL3 249 A6
Plymouth, Beacon Park
PL2 248 B7
Beeches Cl EX5 184 B2
Beeches The
Okehampton EX20 76 E1
Woolfardisworthy EX39 38 F8
Beechfield Ave
Torquay TQ2 213 F2
Yelverton PL20 127 A3
Beechfield Gr PL3 248 E6
Beechfield Pl TQ2 213 F2
Beechfield Rd EX31 153 D5
Beeching Cl EX21 73 E3
Beechtree La EX10,E12 101 F2
Beechway EX8 202 A8
Beechwood Ave
Barnstaple EX31 154 D4
Newton Abbot TQ12 207 E1
Plymouth PL4 248 D4
Beechwood Cl EX31 154 D4
Beechwood Cres EX7 201 A2
Beechwood Cross PL7 251 F7
Beechwood Ct TQ14 124 E1
Beechwood Dr TQ7 258 D5
Beechwood Rd TQ13 123 E6
Beechwood Rise PL6 245 E1
Beechwood Terr PL4 248 D4
Beechwood Way PL7 251 D5
Beeley Orch EX16 161 C8
Beenleigh Cross TQ9 139 D6
Beer CE Prim Sch EX12 191 C5
Beer Cross EX20 94 E6
Beer Head Cvn Pk EX12 191 D4
Beer Heights Light Rly★
EX12 191 C5
Beer Hill Clawton EX21 72 B1
Seaton EX12 191 E6
Beer La Burlescombe EX16 51 B2
Dulverton TA22 33 B5
Witheridge EX16 62 C6
Zeal Monachorum EX17 78 C7
Beer Quarry Caves★
EX12 191 A5
Beer Rd EX12 191 E6
Beerash Cross EX16 63 B4
Beere Cross EX36 32 A5
Beerhill La EX20 76 F5
Beers Hill EX17 79 A5
Beesands TQ7 149 E7
Beeson Cross TQ7 149 D7
Beeson Pool TQ7 149 C8
Beeston Wlk 6 PL6 249 C7
Beetham La TA20 69 E6
Beetland La EX35 151 D2
Beetor Cross TQ13 111 B3
Beggar's Bush TQ10 134 F2
Beggars La EX14 166 A5
Behind Hayes EX9 198 E7
Bekhams Tree Cross
EX6 113 B2
Bel Tor Cnr TQ13 129 F8
Belair Rd PL2 248 C7
Belair Villas PL2 248 C7
Belcombe Dro TA20 69 E7
Belfield Ave TQ3 218 D3
Belfield Cl TQ3 218 D3
Belfield Rd TQ3 225 E7
Belfield Rise TQ3 218 D3
Belfield Way TQ3 218 D3
Belgrave La PL4 248 F4
Belgrave Mews 5 TQ2 219 F5
Belgrave Rd Exeter EX1 261 C3
Newton Abbot TQ12 207 F1
Plymouth PL4 248 F4
Torquay TQ2 219 F5
Belgrave Terr
6 Teignmouth TQ14 210 C5
Upton Pyne EX5 173 A8
Bell Cl PL7 250 F6
Bell Ct EX4 261 A3
Bell La
Bovey Tracey TQ13 123 A7
Paignton TQ3 225 B7
Bell Mdw EX16 64 A2
Bell St EX9 198 F7
Bella Vista Rd TQ5 230 C6
Belladown Hill EX31 27 A6
Bellaire EX31 154 E7
Bellaire Dr EX31 154 E7
Bellamarsh La TQ13 123 C4
Bellamy Cl PL6 245 A1
Belle Acre Cl PL3 248 F6
Belle Ave EX17 165 B5
Belle Cross Rd TQ7 258 E6
Belle Ct EX17 165 B5
Belle Hill TQ7 258 E6
Belle Isle Dr EX2 261 C1
Belle Meadow Ct 18
EX32 154 F5
Belle Meadow Rd 8
EX32 155 A5
Belle Par EX17 165 D5
Belle View EX22 164 C4
Belle View Terr TA20 88 C8
Belle Vue EX18 60 A7
Belle Vue Ave
Lynton EX35 151 B5
Plymouth PL9 255 B5
Belle Vue Cl EX6 114 E4
Belle Vue Cotts 8 EX22 164 C4
Belle Vue Cross EX38 42 A8
Belle Vue Dr PL9 255 B5
Belle Vue Rd Exeter EX4 173 A2
Exmouth EX8 202 A8
Kingsbridge TQ7 258 D5
Paignton TQ4 226 C5
Plymouth PL9 255 C5
Saltash PL12 242 F2
Belle Vue Rise PL9 255 B5
Belle Vue Terr
Bideford EX39 156 F2
Cullompton EX15 163 C4
Gunnislake PL18 125 D6
Bellever Cl PL20 128 B8
Bellever Tor Dr TQ5 229 F2
Bellevue Sq PL11 247 B2
Bellingate EX17 79 A2
Bellingham Cres PL7 251 C4
Belliver Ind Est PL6 241 B1
Belliver Way PL6 241 B1
Bellows Pk PL8 257 B5
Bellrock Cl TQ2 214 B3
Bells Cl EX18 60 A7
Bellvue Terr EX6 114 D4
Belmont EX32 155 A5
Belmont Ave
Combe Martin EX34 2 F4
Ilfracombe EX34 150 A5
Belmont Cl
4 Kingsteignton TQ12 123 F1
Tiverton EX16 161 D5
Belmont Ct 10 PL3 248 A4
Belmont Ho Exeter EX4 261 C4
5 Seaton EX12 192 A5
Belmont Hospl EX16 161 D5
Belmont Pl PL3 248 A4
Belmont Rd
Barnstaple EX32 155 B6
Brixham TQ5 230 C4
Exeter EX1 261 C4
Ilfracombe EX34 150 A5
Ivybridge PL21 237 C4
Tiverton EX16 161 D5
Torquay TQ1 220 C6
Belmont St PL1 262 B3
Belmont Terr
Exmouth EX8 196 C1
Totnes TQ9 223 C6
Belstone Cl PL5 244 A3
Belstone Cnr Cross EX20 76 E1
Belstone Cross EX20 94 E4
Beltor Cross TQ12 211 D1
Belvedare Ct 3 TA21 160 D6
Belvedere Cl EX3 182 E6
Belvedere Ct 5 EX7 204 E6
Belvedere Pk EX2 113 F5
Belvedere Rd
Exmouth EX8 202 A7
Ilfracombe EX34 150 B6
Newton Abbot TQ12 206 E5
Plymouth PL4 249 B2
Belvidere Rd EX4 173 B2
Belvoir Rd EX39 156 F2
Ben Jonson Cl TQ2 219 D6
Ben Venue Cl TQ1 220 C5
Benbow St PL2 247 F4
Bench Tor Cl TQ2 219 B7
Bendarroch Rd EX11 168 D5
Bendarroch Sch EX5 99 E2
Bendibus Cross EX22 72 E2

Bendibus Hill EX21 72 E3
Bendle La EX36 30 E8
Bendle Lane Cross EX36 30 E8
Bendley Hill EX16 46 E1
Benedict Cl TQ14 210 C7
Benedict Way PL21 137 B2
Benedicts Cl 18 TQ12 122 F1
Benedicts Rd TQ12 122 F1
Benlears Acre 12 TQ12 122 F1
Benley Cross EX18 45 D2
Bennah Hill EX6 113 A3
Bennets La PL12 242 F3
Bennett Cl EX2 181 B8
Bennett Rd TQ8 259 D3
Bennett Sq EX4 178 A8
Bennett St PL1 247 E1
Bennett's Cross TQ9 139 C8
Bennetts Cl EX12 190 E4
Bennetts Hill EX10 187 F7
Bens Cl TQ7 147 D7
Benson Cl EX16 46 E1
Benson Dr EX39 157 A6
Benton Cross EX32 18 B7
Benton La EX31 18 B7
Benton Rd EX32 18 B8
Berachah Rd TQ1 220 B6
Bere Alston Prim Sch PL20 125 E1
Bere Alston Sta PL20 125 E2
Bere Ferrers Sta PL20 239 E3
Bere Hill EX7 204 B6
Berea Rd TQ1 220 C6
Beresford St PL2 248 A4
Berkeley Ave TQ2 213 C1
Berkeley Pl 6 EX34 150 B5
Berkeley Rise TQ2 213 C1
Berkeley Way PL21 237 D4
Berkshire Dr Exeter EX4 176 E4
Plymouth PL2 247 F5
Bernadette Cl EX4 174 C1
Berner's Cross EX19 58 F4
Bernice Cl PL4 249 B4
Bernice Terr PL4 249 B4
Berretts Way TQ12 123 A1
Berrow Park Rd PL3 248 E6
Berry Ave TQ3 225 F6
Berry Cl
Abbotskerswell TQ12 212 B6
Exmouth EX8 202 E8
Salcombe TQ8 259 C4
Berry Cross
Dunsford EX6 112 E8
Shebbear EX21 55 D5
Berry Down Cross EX34 9 F6
Berry Dr TQ3 226 A6
Berry Head Country Pk* TQ5 231 A5
Berry Head Gdns PL6 244 E1
Berry Head Rd TQ5 230 E6
Berry Hill Beer EX12 191 D5
Bishopsteignton TQ14 208 F8
Branscombe EX12 190 B4
North Tawton EX20 59 C1
Berry La Axminster EX13 88 F3
Beer EX12 191 D6
Combe Martin EX34 2 F4
Dunsford EX6 112 E8
Berry Mdw TQ12 207 E6
Berry Park Cl PL9 255 E6
Berry Park Rd PL9 255 E7
Berry Pk PL12 242 D4
Berry Pomeroy Castle* TQ9 217 D1
Berry Pomeroy Parochial CE Prim Sch TQ9 224 B7
Berry Rd Barnstaple EX32 155 C4
Braunton EX33 152 E7
Paignton TQ3 225 F6
Berry's Ground La EX31 4 C5
Berry's La PL7 133 A1
Berryball Fields EX20 170 C6
Berrybrook Mdw EX6 182 B3
Berrydown Cross EX34 2 F1
Berrynarbor Prim Sch EX34 2 E3
Berrys Wood TQ12 206 F3
Berthon Rd PL5 247 C8
Berwick Ave PL5 244 E3
Besigheim Way TQ12 207 F4
Besley Cl EX16 161 F3
Best's La EX38 159 D5
Betham Hill EX16 46 F2
Betham La EX18 59 B6
Bethel Cross TQ12 122 C1
Bethel Terr 1 TQ1 220 B5
Bethelcombe Cross TQ12 122 C1
Betjeman Wlk PL5 244 C3
Betjemen Dr EX8 196 C3
Betony Rise EX2 178 C3
Betton Way TQ13 111 F5
Bettys Mead EX4 178 A8
Beuvron Cl EX39 38 F8
Bevan Rd EX32 155 A5
Beverley Cl EX2 178 B4
Beverley Gdns 6 TQ13 131 A5
Beverley Rd PL3 249 C4
Beverley Rise TQ5 230 B4
Beverley Way TQ12 207 A2
Beverston Way PL6 245 B8
Bevil Cl EX39 157 A1
Beweys Pk PL12 242 C2
Bewhay Gdns TQ9 222 F8
Bewsley Hill EX17 79 B5
Bexley La 6 TQ2 219 F5
Beyrout Pl 6 PL1 247 F3
Bhutan Cl EX14 166 D5
Bibors Hill TA4 35 E4
Bicclescombe Gdns EX34 150 B4
Bicclescombe Park Rd EX34 150 B4
Bickell Cross EX32 28 C6
Bickern Rd PL11 247 B3
Bickerton Top TQ7 149 C5
Bickfont Hill EX31 11 F4
Bickford La 2 TQ14 210 C4
Bickfords Gn 18 TQ12 122 F1
Bickham La EX16 47 E7
Bickham Park Rd PL3 248 D7
Bickham Rd PL5 243 D2
Bickingcott Cross EX36 31 C7
Bickingcott Hill EX36 31 C8
Bickington Lodge EX31 16 A3
Bickington Rd EX31 154 C3
Bickleigh Castle* EX16 63 F1
Bickleigh Cl Exeter EX4 174 D2
Plymouth PL6 245 A1
Bickleigh Down CE Prim Sch PL6 245 D7
Bickleigh Down Rd PL6 241 D1
Bickleigh-on-Exe CE Prim Sch EX16 64 A2
Bickleton Cross EX31 153 A2
Bickley Mill Cross TQ12 212 C1
Bickley Rd TQ12 212 C2
Bickwell House La EX10 187 E5
Bickwell La EX10 187 F5
Bickwell Valley EX10 187 F4
Bickwill Cross EX36 46 D8
Bicton Cl PL6 245 D1
Bicton Coll EX9 186 C1
Bicton Park Botanical Gdns* EX9 198 C8
Bicton Pl Exeter EX1 177 F6
Exmouth EX8 202 A6
Bicton St
Barnstaple EX32 155 A5
Exmouth EX8 202 A6
Bicton Villas EX8 202 B6
Bidbrooke La EX36 32 A6
Biddacott Cross EX37 28 E4
Biddamoor La EX19 42 C2
Bidder Cl TQ13 111 F4
Bidders Cl TQ6 146 B7
Bidders Ct EX36 158 C4
Biddick Dr PL2 247 F6
Biddington Way EX14 166 A4
Biddlecombe Cross TQ13 124 A6
Biddypark La EX2 113 F6
Biddypark Lane Cross EX2 113 F6
Bideford & Torridgeside Hospl EX39 156 F2
Bideford Coll EX39 156 E1
Bideford Railway Mus* EX39 157 B1
Bideford Wlk PL6 249 E8
Bidmead Cl EX8 202 E7
Bidna La EX39 157 B8
Bidwell Brook Dr TQ4 226 C1
Bidwell Brook Sch TQ9 215 F1
Bidwell Cross
Langford EX5 172 E8
Thorverton EX5 81 E6
Bidwell La
Brampford Speke EX5 81 C1
Thorverton EX5 81 F6
Bidwell Wlk TQ4 226 B1
Biera View TQ13 111 A6
Big Sheep (Farm Pk) The* EX39 156 B1
Bigadon La TQ11 236 C4
Bigbury Ct TQ7 142 F5
Bigbury Way TQ2 214 B2
Bigbury Wlk PL6 249 E8
Biggin Hill PL5 243 F4
Bilbie Cl EX15 163 B3
Bilbury St PL4 263 A3
Billacombe Rd PL9 249 E1
Billacombe Villas PL9 255 F8
Billhole La EX17 61 C6
Billing Cl PL6 244 D6
Billington Cl PL6 249 B7
Bilton Terr 8 EX39 157 A1
Biltor Rd TQ12 211 D1
Bilver Cross TQ12 217 C8
Bimbom La EX13 103 C8
Bindon Rd EX4 174 E2
Binford Cl EX1 178 B6
Bingfield Cl TQ1 220 C5
Bingham Cres EX32 155 B4
Binhamy Rd EX23 70 A8
Binkham Hill PL20 127 A3
Binnamore Cross TQ10 134 E4
Binneford Cross EX17 96 F8
Binneford Hill EX17 62 B2
Birch Cl PL6 245 E7
Birch Cross
Doddiscombsleigh EX6 113 D8
Zeal Monachorum EX17 78 B8
Birch Ct EX2 178 A4
Birch End EX5 99 C5
Birch Gr EX11 168 D3
Birch La Barnstaple EX31 154 C2
Landkey EX32 17 D3
Morchard Bishop EX17 61 A2
Zeal Monachorum EX17 78 A8
Birch Pond Rd PL9 255 D7
Birch Rd Landkey EX32 17 B2
Landkey EX32 17 D2
Lympstone EX8 195 F5
Newton Abbot TQ12 207 F1
Wellington TA21 160 E5
Birch Wlk TQ2 219 C8
Bircham View PL6 245 C1
Birchanger Cross TQ13 122 B2
Birchen La
Highampton EX20,EX21 74 E5
7 Tiverton EX16 161 C3
Birchen Tree Cross EX15 66 C4
Birchenbeer Cnr EX17 61 C1
Birches The PL6 245 D6
Birchfield Ave PL2 248 B6
Birchill Cross EX13 88 A6
Birchland Rd PL7 133 A1
Birchland Way PL7 136 A8
Birchlea TQ13 180 C4
Birchman's Cross EX17 78 E1
Birchpark La EX20 77 B4
Birchwood Cl
Tavistock PL19 171 C3
Totnes TQ9 223 B5
Birchwood Gdns PL7 251 A7
Birchwood Rd EX8 196 D2
Birchy Barton Hill EX1 178 B6
Birdcage La EX11 168 E8
Birdshaven TQ2 219 E5
Birdswell La EX34 2 E3
Birkbeck Cl PL7 250 E7
Birkdale Cl PL12 242 C2
Birkett Cl EX2 178 C4
Biscombe Cross TA3 67 E8
Biscombe Gdns PL12 243 A2
Bishmill Gate EX36 30 E4
Bishop Cornish CE Prim Sch PL12 242 F1
Bishop Ct 2 EX24 103 A4
Bishop Pasterfield Ho 4 EX2 261 B2
Bishop Westall Ho 6 EX2 261 B2
Bishop Westall Rd EX2 178 A2
Bishop Wilfrid Rd TQ14 209 D8
Bishop's Clyst EX5 179 A3
Bishop's Court La EX5 179 C4
Bishop's Hill TA21 51 B7
Bishop's Nympton Cross EX36 30 F1
Bishop's Pl 7 TQ3 226 B6
Bishop's Tawton Prim Sch EX32 16 E1
Bishop's Tawton Rd
Barnstaple EX32 155 B2
Bishop's Tawton EX32 16 E1
Bishops Ave TQ14 208 F8
Bishops Cl
Ivybridge PL21 237 E6
Starcross EX6 201 B8
Torquay TQ1 221 A4
Bishops Court Ind Est EX2 178 E4
Bishops Ct
Bishopsteignton TQ14 208 F8
4 Wellington TA21 160 D6
Bishops Mead 2 TQ10 134 F3
Bishops Nympton EX36 31 C1
Bishops Rise
Kentisbeare EX15 66 A3
Torquay TQ1 221 A4
Bishopsteignton Rd TQ14 209 D6
Bishopsteignton Sch TQ14 208 F8
Biss La 4 EX33 152 D6
Bitney La TQ12 212 C5
Bittadon La EX31 9 C4
Bittaford Terr PL21 137 C7
Bittaford Wood PL21 137 C7
Bittam's La TQ9 217 B4
Bittern Ind Units EX2 178 E5
Bittern Rd EX1 178 E6
Bittery Cross EX5 84 B2
Bitton Ave TQ14 210 B5
Bitton Ct TQ14 210 A5
Bitton Park Rd 18 TQ14 210 B5
Blachford Cl PL21 133 C2
Blachford Rd PL21 237 C5
Black Dog Cross EX17 61 E4
Black Gate EX22 73 B8
Black Hat La EX6 176 B3
Black Horse Cnr EX18 59 C4
Black La Hemyock EX15 52 D2
Holcombe Rogus TA21 50 E6
Black Lion Ct 8 EX14 166 C6
Black Torrington CE Prim Sch EX21 74 A8
Blackabrook Ave PL20 128 A8
Blackacre Rd EX24 102 C6
Blackalder Terr PL7 132 F4
Blackall Gdns PL6 244 D6
Blackall Rd EX4 261 B4
Blackaller La EX16 33 C1
Blackawton Prim Sch TQ9 139 E2
Blackball La TQ5 230 C6
Blackberry Cl PL9 255 E8
Blackberry Ct TA21 160 D4
Blackberry La
Bigbury TQ7 142 E6
Plymouth PL9 255 E8
Blackberry Way 6 TQ12 123 F1
Blackboy Rd EX1 177 E7
Blackbrook Ave TQ4 226 B1
Blackbrook Cl PL20 127 B4
Blackbrook Wlk TQ4 226 B1
Blackditch Cross EX17 60 B1
Blackditch La EX17 78 B8
Blackdown Cross
Cornworthy TQ9 139 E4
Loddiswell TQ7 138 B2
Tedburn St Mary EX17 97 E8
Blackdown La
Halwell TQ9 139 D4
Tedburn St Mary EX4 98 C5
Blackdown Pk EX15 162 C5
Blackdown Rd TA21 160 B4
Blackdown View
2 Hemyock EX15 67 B8
Sampford Peverell EX16 50 C1
Blackdown Visitors Ctr* EX15 52 D3
Blackenway La TQ12 213 B7
Blackerton Cross EX16 32 E3
Blackett Cl PL21 237 E4
Blackeven Cl PL6 241 D1
Blackeven Hill PL6 241 E1
Blackfriars La PL1 263 A2
Blackgate Cross EX39 26 C7
Blackhaven Cl TQ4 229 B8
Blackhayes La EX14 68 F1
Blackhorse La EX5 179 B8
Blackler's Land Cross TQ9 216 B5
Blackley La TQ13 113 D1
Blackmoor Rd TA21 160 F4
Blackmore Cres PL6 244 D6
Blackmore Ct EX8 196 E1
Blackmore Dr EX10 188 B4
Blackmore Mews EX2 178 C4
Blackmore Rd EX16 161 F3
Blackpool CE Prim Sch TQ12 122 F1
Blackpool Cross EX17 78 D4
Blackpool Hill TQ6 146 A6
Blackpool Rd EX17 78 D4
Blackpool Valley Rd TQ6 146 A7
Blackpost Cross
Kingston TQ7 142 C7
Totnes TQ9 223 F6
Totnes, Littlehempston TQ9 217 A2
Blackpost La TQ9 223 F5
Blackridge Cross TQ7 258 F8
Blacksmith La TQ10 137 D8
Blacksmiths Cnr EX17 81 A6
Blackstone Cl PL9 256 B6
Blackstone Cross TQ12 211 D1
Blackstone Rd TQ12 211 D1
Blackswan Pl 10 EX7 204 D6
Blackthorn Ave EX16 161 F6
Blackthorn Cl
Honiton EX14 166 C4
Plymouth, Honicknowle PL5 244 B3
Plymouth, Woolwell PL6 245 D8
Sidmouth EX10 187 F8
Blackthorn Cres EX1 178 C5
Blackthorn Dr PL21 237 E4
Blackthorn Way TQ4 225 D4
Blackwalls La EX18 60 B7
Blackwater La EX13 88 F3
Blackwater Rd EX15 66 E8
Blackwell Cross
Broadhempston TQ13 131 D3
Strete TQ6 145 E7
Blackwell La TQ13 131 D2
Bladder La PL5 244 E2
Bladon Cl TQ12 207 D1
Blagaton Gate EX21 73 B1
Blagdon EX17 165 D5
Blagdon Cl EX17 165 D5
Blagdon Cross
Ashwater EX21 90 C7
Paignton TQ3 225 A7
Blagdon Lodge Cross EX21 90 C8
Blagdon Rd TQ3 225 B6
Blagdon Rise EX17 165 D6
Blagrove Hill EX17 46 C3
Blair Rd PL21 237 D5
Blairgowrie Rd PL5 243 C2
Blake Cl TQ1 220 B8
Blake Gdns PL5 244 C3
Blakeland Rd EX31 153 D5
Blakemore Cross TQ9 222 A4
Blakes Hill Rd EX32 17 B2
Blakewell Cross
Chittlehampton EX37 28 E3
Umberleigh EX37 28 D3
Blakewell Hill EX32 18 E2
Blakey Down La TQ3 218 F1
Blamphayne Cross EX24 102 D7
Blanchard Pl 2 PL7 250 E7
Blanchdown Dr PL18 125 C7
Blandford Rd PL3 249 C6
Blanksmill Cross TQ7 259 A8
Blatchborough Cross EX22 38 B1
Blatchcombe Dr TQ3 225 F7
Blatchcombe Rd TQ3 226 A7
Blatchfords Ct EX20 170 B5
Blatchmore La TQ6 232 C4
Blaxton La PL5 240 C2
Blenheim Cl
Newton Abbot TQ12 207 A5
Torquay TQ1 220 E4
Willand EX15 162 D5
Blenheim Ct EX2 177 C1
Blenheim Dr EX15 162 D4
Blenheim La EX20 76 C4
Blenheim Rd Exeter EX2 177 B2
Plymouth PL4 263 A4
Blenheim Terr TQ13 180 C7
Bligh Cl TQ14 210 A8
Blights Hill EX16,TA22 33 F3
Blind Acres La EX33 15 A8
Blind La Aylesbeare EX5 99 E2
Blind La *continued*
Buckland St Mary TA20 69 A8
Poltimore EX5 174 B8
Blindwell Ave TQ12 207 F7
Blindwell Farm Cotts TQ12 207 E7
Blindwell Hill PL10 252 E5
Blindwell La TA4 34 E6
Blindwylle Rd TQ2 219 E5
Blogishay La TQ13 130 F4
Bloomball Cl PL3 249 B6
Blossom Cl EX14 67 C1
Blue Anchor Cross EX14 84 B4
Blue Bell TQ9 223 C5
Blue Cedar Ct EX8 202 B6
Blue Gate TA24 19 F8
Blue Haze Cl PL6 245 D5
Blue La EX17 96 A3
Blue Waters Dr
Lyme Regis DT7 260 B3
Paignton TQ4 229 C8
Blue Waters Ind Est TQ13 180 C5
Bluebell Ave EX16 161 F6
Bluebell Cl Saltash PL12 242 D4
Seaton EX12 192 B7
Bluebell Rd EX14 67 C1
Bluebell Way PL19 171 E4
Blueberry Downs EX9 199 J2
Bluecoat La EX1 261 B3
Bluecoat Sch The EX31 154 F6
Bluegate Hill PL21 137 A2
Bluehayes La
Clyst Honiton EX5 175 F3
Rockbeare EX5 99 A5
Blueridge TQ13 180 C4
Bluett Rd TA21 160 D4
Blundell's Ave EX16 161 F4
Blundell's Rd
Tiverton EX15 64 D8
Tiverton EX16 161 E4
Blundell's Sch EX16 161 F4
Blunts La PL6 245 C3
Blyth Ct EX39 156 B6
Blythswood Cres 3 TQ1 220 B7
Boarden Barn EX8 202 B6
Boasley Cross EX20 92 E4
Boasley Cross Prim Sch EX20 92 E4
Bockland Cl EX15 163 A3
Boconnic La PL20 127 A3
Bodley Cl EX1 178 B7
Bodley Cross EX31 4 D1
Bodley La EX31 4 C2
Bodmin Rd PL5 244 D3
Bodmin St EX22 164 C4
Body Hayes Cl TQ9 227 F7
Body's Ct PL18 125 C6
Bogtown Cross EX20 92 D8
Bolberry Cross TQ7 147 E6
Boldventure PL8 257 F3
Boldventure Cross EX21 91 E6
Bolham Halt Cotts EX16 161 C8
Bolham La EX16 161 D8
Bolham Prim Sch EX16 161 C8
Bolham Rd EX16 161 C7
Bolt House Cl PL19 171 A5
Bolton Ct 8 TQ5 230 C4
Bolton St TQ5 230 C4
Bommertown Cross EX36 32 A4
Bonair Cl TQ5 230 C3
Bonaventure Cl TQ8 259 D5
Bonaventure Rd TQ8 259 D5
Bond La EX16 62 F5
Bond St Beaford EX19 42 D2
Cornwood PL21 133 C2
Plymouth PL6 244 E6
Bond's La EX5 184 B5
Bondhouse La EX6 98 E3
Bondleigh Bridge Cross EX20 77 B7
Bondleigh Cross EX20 77 B7
Bondleigh Moor Cross EX20 76 F6
Bondleigh Wood Cross EX20 77 B7
Bonds Cotts EX14 166 C6
Bonds Cross
Chulmleigh EX18 44 E1
Petrockstow EX20 56 C5
Bonds Mdw TQ13 180 C8
Bone Mill Cross TQ12 131 F6
Bonehayne & Purlbridge Rd EX24 102 E5
Bonfire Cross EX10 101 C3
Bonfire Hill
Black Torrington EX21 74 A8
Salcombe TQ8 259 C5
Bonfire La EX5 184 C3
Bonhay Cl EX6 201 B8
Bonhay Rd Exeter EX4 177 A6
Starcross EX6 201 B8
Boniford Cross EX14 87 A4
Bonners Cswy EX13 167 F7
Bonners Dr EX13 167 F6
Bonners Glen EX13 167 F6
Bonnicott La EX33 7 D1
Bonnington Gr EX1 177 F6
Bonny Cross
Bampton EX16 34 B3
Clayhanger EX16 35 B1
Bonville Cl EX1 178 B7
Bonville Cres EX16 64 D7

- Bonville Rd PL6 244 E6
- Boobery EX16 50 D1
- Boode Cross EX33 152 F7
- Boode Rd EX33 152 F7
- Booklands EX32 18 B2
- Boon's Pl PL1 262 C4
- Booth Way EX8 196 B2
- Borden Gate EX16 50 B8
- Border Rd 13 EX14 85 C2
- Boringdon Ave PL5 247 D8
- Boringdon Cl PL7 250 D7
- Boringdon Hill PL7 250 E7
- Boringdon Mill Bsns Ctr PL7 250 F6
- Boringdon Pk PL21 237 A5
- Boringdon Prim Sch PL7 250 D7
- Boringdon Rd
  - Plymouth, Plympton PL7 250 D6
  - Plymouth, Turnchapel PL9 255 A7
- Boringdon Terr
  - Plymouth, Plympton PL7 250 D6
  - Plymouth, Turnchapel PL9 255 A7
- Boringdon Villas PL7 250 D6
- Borne Cross EX37 44 B2
- Borough Cl TQ4 225 E3
- Borough Cross
  - Aveton Gifford TQ7 143 B7
  - Bridgerule EX22 70 E5
  - Chilsworthy EX22 53 E2
  - Newton Tracey EX31 27 A3
  - Woolacombe EX34 1 B1
- Borough Ct PL11 246 E4
- Borough La TQ9 144 B6
- Borough Park Rd
  - Paignton TQ3 225 E5
  - Totnes TQ9 223 C6
- Borough Pk PL11 246 E4
- Borough Rd
  - Combe Martin EX34 2 F4
  - Great Torrington EX38 159 E5
  - Paignton TQ4 225 E4
  - Torquay TQ1 214 B1
- Borough The PL8 257 F4
- Borough View EX38 159 E5
- Borrowdale Cl PL6 244 D5
- Boscastle Gdns PL2 248 C8
- Boscawen Pl
  - Plymouth PL2 247 E4
  - 10 Teignmouth TQ14 210 B5
- Boscundle Row PL12 243 A2
- Boshill Hill Axmouth DT7 193 C8
  - Colyford DT7,EX12 103 D3
- Bossell Ho TQ11 236 B4
- Bossell Pk TQ11 236 B4
- Bossell Rd TQ11 236 B5
- Bossell Terr TQ11 236 B5
- Bosuns Point TQ4 226 C4
- Boswell Cl PL5 244 B2
- Boswell Way EX12 191 F8
- Boswell's La EX20 77 D4
- Boswell's Lane End EX20 77 D4
- Bottle Bridge Hill TQ13 123 F7
- Bottle Pk PL21 136 B6
- Bottom La EX13 103 D6
- Bottom's La TQ12 213 E4
- Bottompark La TQ2 213 F3
- Bottoms La EX33 8 B2
- Bottreaux Mill Cross EX36 32 A5
- Boucher Rd EX9 198 B1
- Boucher Way EX9 198 B1
- Boucher's La TA4 35 E4
- Bouchiers Cl EX20 77 C5
- Boughmore La EX10 187 F3
- Boughmore Rd EX10 187 F4
- Boughthayes Est PL19 171 A5
- Boulden Cl PL7 251 C5
- Boulter Cl PL6 241 C1
- Bound The PL10 253 A1
- Boundary Cl TQ12 212 F5
- Boundary Pk
  - Bideford EX39 26 F4
  - Seaton EX12 192 A8
- Boundary Rd
  - Dousland PL20 127 B3
  - Torquay TQ2 219 D5
- Bounds Cross EX22 71 A4
- Bounds Pl PL1 262 B2
- Boundy's Cross EX17 61 B8
- Bounsells La EX20 57 A7
- Bountice La EX34 2 D2
- Bourchier Cl 13 EX16 34 B1
- Bourchier Dr 12 EX16 34 B1
- Bourn Rise EX4 174 D2
- Bourne Bridge Cross EX36 46 A5
- Bourne Cl PL3 249 D6
- Bourne Ct TQ5 229 F2
- Bourne Rd TQ12 213 A5
- Bourton La TQ9 223 E6
- Bourton Rd TQ9 223 E6
- Bourtons The TQ9 223 D7
- Boutport St EX31 154 F5
- Boutport St (Mermaid Wlk) EX31 154 F6
- Boutport Street (Mermaid Wlk) 10 EX31 154 F6
- Bovacott La EX22 73 C7
- Bove Park Rd TQ2 214 A4
- Bovemoor's La EX2 178 A4
- Bovet St TA21 160 C6
- Bovey Cross
  - Broadhempston TQ13 131 D3
  - Moretonhampstead TQ13 111 E3
- Bovey Fir Cross EX12 190 F6
- Bovey La EX12 191 B7
- Bovey Tracey Hospl TQ13 180 D8
- Bovey Tracey Prim Sch TQ13 180 C8
- Bovey Tracey Rd TQ12 206 F6
- Boville La PL9 256 C7
- Bovisand Ct PL9 254 F2
- Bovisand Est PL9 140 A8
- Bovisand La
  - Down Thomas PL9 255 B2
  - Staddiscombe PL9 255 D3
- Bovisand Pk
  - Down Thomas PL9 255 A1
  - Heybrook Bay PL9 140 A8
- Bovisand Rd PL9 255 E3
- Bow Beer Cross EX17 78 A1
- Bow Com Prim Sch EX17 78 C4
- Bow Creek TQ9 139 F6
- Bow Cross
  - Blackawton TQ9 145 B8
  - Staverton TQ9 216 C7
- Bow La TQ13 111 F4
- Bow Mill La EX17 78 B4
- Bow Rd TQ9 139 C7
- Bow Station Cross EX17 78 C2
- Bowbeer La EX17 78 B1
- Bowbridge Cross TQ9 145 B8
- Bowd Ct EX10 100 E1
- Bowden Cnr EX31 9 F3
- Bowden Cross
  - Buckland Brewer EX39 40 B8
  - Drewsteignton EX6 96 E3
  - Kingsbridge TQ7 144 C3
- Bowden Farmhouse PL8 257 F4
- Bowden Gn EX39 25 E4
- Bowden Hill
  - Ashburton TQ13 130 F4
  - Crediton EX17 165 D5
  - Newton Abbot TQ12 207 C2
  - Yealmpton PL8 257 F4
- Bowden Hill Terr 1 EX17 165 D5
- Bowden House & British Photographic Mus* TQ9 223 C2
- Bowden La TQ13 123 A7
- Bowden Park Rd PL6 245 A1
- Bowden Pillars TQ9 223 B3
- Bowden Rd TQ12 211 E2
- Bowdens La
  - Ideford TQ13 124 B4
  - Shillingford EX16 34 E3
- Bowdown Cross TQ10 135 C5
- Bowerhayes Cross EX14 67 C3
- Bowerhayes La EX14 67 C3
- Bowering Ct 1 EX32 155 B3
- Bowerland Ave TQ2 213 F4
- Bowerland Cross EX20 93 D3
- Bowerland Rd EX20 93 D4
- Bowers Park Dr PL6 245 E7
- Bowers Rd PL2 248 B5
- Bowerthy La EX17 60 D4
- Bowhay Cl EX21 74 A8
- Bowhay La
  - Combe Martin EX34 3 A3
  - Exeter EX4 176 E4
- Bowhays Wlk 2 PL6 249 C7
- Bowhill EX5 83 A7
- Bowland Cl TQ4 226 A2
- Bowley Mdw EX5 82 F6
- Bowling Gn TQ7 142 F4
- Bowling Green Chalets DT7 260 D2
- Bowling Green La
  - Combe Martin EX34 3 A3
  - Hatherleigh EX20 75 B7
- Bowls Cross Bigbury TQ7 142 F5
  - Stoke Canon EX4 82 C1
- Bowls Ctr TQ12 207 E6
- Bowman's Terr EX20 77 B4
- Bowpound Cross EX17 78 C3
- Bowring Cl EX1 178 B7
- Bowring Mead TQ13 111 F4
- Bowring Pk TQ13 111 F4
- Bowringleigh Pl TQ7 258 C5
- Bows Ct EX1 177 E7
- Box's Cnr EX18 60 B6
- Boxfield Rd EX13 167 D5
- Boxhill Cl PL5 244 B3
- Boxhill Gdns PL2 248 C8
- Boyce Pl 3 EX16 161 B4
- Boyds Dr TQ14 210 C5
- Boyes Cl EX16 65 A7
- Boyland Rd EX6 112 D8
- Boyne Rd EX9 198 A2
- Boyton Com Prim Sch PL15 89 D3
- Bozomzeal Cross TQ6 228 B1
- Bracken Cl
  - 10 Honiton EX14 85 C2
  - Newton Abbot TQ12 212 F8
  - Plymouth PL6 245 D8
- Bracken Down EX11 168 D2
- Bracken Rise TQ4 229 C6
- Bracken Way EX7 201 A2
- Brackendale EX8 196 C4
- Brackenwood EX8 196 C1
- Bradaford Cross EX21 90 F6
- Bradbury La EX32 29 D6
- Bradden Cres TQ5 230 B4
- Braddon Cnr EX16 81 D8
- Braddons Cliffe TQ1 220 B4
- Braddons Hill PL7 250 B7
- Braddons Hill Rd E TQ1 220 C4
- Braddons Hill Rd W TQ1 220 B4
- Braddons St TQ1 220 B4
- Bradfield Cl PL6 245 E1
- Bradfield House Sch EX15 65 F4
- Bradfield Rd EX4 174 D1
- Bradford Cl Exmouth EX8 196 C3
  - Plymouth PL6 249 B7
- Bradford Cross EX16 47 A3
- Bradford Moor Hill EX16 47 A3
- Bradford Prim Sch EX22 73 B8
- Bradham Ct EX8 202 D8
- Bradham La EX8 202 D8
- Bradiford EX31 154 E7
- Bradley Barton Prim Sch TQ12 206 E3
- Bradley Ct 6 TQ12 207 B3
- Bradley La TQ12 207 A3
- Bradley Manor* TQ12 206 F2
- Bradley Park Rd TQ1 214 B1
- Bradley Rd
  - Bovey Tracey TQ13 180 E7
  - Newton Abbot TQ12 207 A1
  - Plymouth PL4 248 F4
- Bradley Rowe Fst Sch EX2 177 F3
- Bradley Rowe Mid Sch EX2 177 F3
- Bradleyford Cnr TQ13 180 F6
- Bradman Way EX2 177 C2
- Bradninch Cross EX32 17 D4
- Bradninch Prim Sch EX5 83 A6
- Bradridge Cross TQ9 138 D8
- Bradwell EX34 150 A5
- Bradwell Rd EX34 8 D5
- Bradworthy Com Prim Sch EX22 38 E1
- Bradworthy Cross EX22 53 D7
- Brady Cl EX17 80 B5
- Braemar Cl PL7 251 C4
- Braeside Rd
  - Paignton TQ4 226 C4
  - Torquay TQ2 214 A4
- Brag La PL7 132 C6
- Braggs Hill PL15 89 E3
- Braggs' Hill EX37 43 B7
- Brahms Way EX32 155 C5
- Brake Ho TQ12 207 E2
- Brake La PL10 252 B5
- Brake Rd PL5 244 E2
- Brake Wood Cl EX31 153 D5
- Brakefield TQ10 135 A2
- Brakeridge Cl TQ5 229 C6
- Bramble Cl
  - Budleigh Salterton EX9 198 C1
  - Dartington TQ9 222 F8
  - Plymouth PL3 249 B7
  - Sidmouth EX10 188 B8
  - Torquay TQ2 219 D5
- Bramble La
  - Brampford Speke EX5 81 C1
  - Crediton EX17 165 E6
  - Honiton EX14 166 B5
- Bramble Mead EX5 99 D2
- Bramble Path 7 EX32 17 B2
- Bramble Wlk
  - Barnstaple EX31 154 B3
  - 1 Plymouth PL6 249 C7
- Brambleoak Cross TQ12 131 E3
- Brambles The TA21 160 D4
- Bramdean Sch EX1 177 F6
- Bramfield Pl PL6 249 D7
- Bramley Ave EX1 178 C6
- Bramley Cl Kenton EX6 194 E3
  - Willand EX15 162 D4
- Bramley Gdns EX5 99 E7
- Bramley Mdw EX32 17 C2
- Bramley Rd PL3 249 C4
- Bramley Way EX15 66 C6
- Brampford Cross EX5 172 F7
- Brampford Speke CE Prim Sch EX5 81 E1
- Brampton Down Cross EX16 49 F8
- Branches Cross EX22 54 E3
- Brancker Rd PL2 248 C6
- Brand Cl EX14 166 C4
- Brand Rd EX14 166 C4
- Brandiron Cross EX6 123 B7
- Brandirons Cnr EX17 79 C5
- Brandis Cnr
  - Great Torrington EX20 41 F1
  - North Tawton EX17 77 F1
  - Petrockstow EX20 56 C6
  - Rackenford EX16 47 F1
- Brandis Cross EX20 95 E4
- Brandis La EX20 95 E4
- Brandis Pk TQ7 145 C3
- Brandise Cross EX17 79 C2
- Brandise Hill EX20 56 F3
- Brandize Pk EX20 170 B3
- Brandon Rd PL3 249 C4
- Brandreth Rd 3 PL3 248 F6
- Brandy Wells EX37 44 E6
- Branksome Cl TQ3 219 C2
- Brannam Cres EX31 154 B2
- Brannams Sq 2 EX32 155 A4
- Branscombe CE Prim Sch EX12 190 D4
- Branscombe Cl
  - Colyford EX24 103 A3
  - Exeter EX4 176 E5
  - Torquay TQ1 220 D6
- Branscombe Cross EX10 101 F1
- Branscombe Gdns PL5 244 A3
- Branscombe La EX7 200 C3
- Branscombe Rd EX16 161 F4
- Bransgrove Hill EX18 59 B5
- Bransgrove La EX18 59 B5
- Branson Ct 9 PL7 251 C5
- Branson Pk PL19 126 D6
- Brantwood Cl TQ4 226 A4
- Brantwood Cres TQ4 226 A3
- Brantwood Dr TQ4 226 A3
- Bratton Cross EX31 17 E7
- Bratton Fleming Prim Sch EX31 18 A8
- Braundsworthy Cross EX21 73 E8
- Braunton Caen Prim Sch EX33 152 D6
- Braunton Mus* EX33 152 D6
- Braunton Rd EX31 154 D7
- Braunton Sch & Com Coll EX33 152 E4
- Braunton Wlk PL6 249 E8
- Bray Cl Burlescombe EX16 51 B3
  - Tavistock PL19 171 A5
- Bray Hill EX32 18 F3
- Bray Mill Cross EX37 29 D4
- Brayford Cl PL5 244 B3
- Brayford Prim Sch EX32 18 F5
- Brayhams Terr EX20 170 C6
- Brayley Hill EX32 18 E1
- Brays Cl EX17 165 C5
- Braytown Cotts EX32 18 F5
- Breach Cotts TA21 51 F5
- Breach Hill TA21 51 F5
- Breaka La EX19 57 E5
- Breakneck Cross EX37 28 F5
- Breakneck Hill
  - Chittlehampton EX37 28 F5
  - Teignmouth TQ14 210 B8
- Breakwater Ct TQ5 230 E6
- Breakwater Hill PL4 263 C1
- Breakwater Ind Est PL9 255 C8
- Breakwater Rd PL9 255 C8
- Brean Down Cl PL3 248 E6
- Brean Down Rd PL3 248 E7
- Brecon Cl Bideford EX39 157 D1
  - Paignton TQ4 225 D4
  - Plymouth PL3 249 A7
- Bremley Cross EX36 31 F7
- Brendon Cross EX39 39 F6
- Brendon Hill EX17 79 C6
- Brendon Rd TA21 160 D7
- Brendon Two Gates TA24 13 A6
- Brendons Ave TQ2 219 C3
- Brendons The EX16 50 D1
- Brennacott Rd EX39 25 D4
- Brennans Ct 13 EX32 155 A4
- Brent Cl EX5 184 C3
- Brent Hill PL8 136 D1
- Brent Knoll Rd 1 PL3 248 E6
- Brent Mill TQ10 135 A2
- Brent Mill Ind Est TQ10 134 F2
- Brent Rd 1 TQ3 226 B6
- Brent Tor* PL19 117 B7
- Brentford Ave PL5 244 B5
- Brenton Rd EX6 114 C5
- Brentor Cl EX4 176 F8
- Brentor Rd
  - Mary Tavy PL19 117 D6
  - Plymouth PL4 249 B2
- Brest Rd PL6 245 A3
- Brest Way PL6 245 A3
- Breton Side PL4 263 A2
- Breton Way EX8 196 E1
- Brett Wlk PL7 250 F7
- Bretteville Cl EX5 184 C3
- Bretteville Cl TQ13 111 A6
- Brewer Rd EX32 155 C4
- Brewers Hill EX39 39 F8
- Brewers La EX39 39 F8
- Brewery La EX10 188 B5
- Brewin Rd EX16 161 C3
- Briansway PL12 242 D2
- Briar Cl Exmouth EX8 202 D8
  - Honiton EX14 166 C3
- Briar Cres EX2 177 F2
- Briar Rd PL3 248 F7
- Briar Tor PL20 127 A3
- Briardale Rd PL2 247 F6
- Briarleigh Cl PL6 245 F2
- Briars Row PL12 242 D4
- Briary La TQ1 220 B5
- Briary Mews 11 TQ1 220 D4
- Brick Cross EX9 198 C7
- Brickhouse Dr EX16 161 D6
- Brickhouse Hill EX16 161 D6
- Brickyard La EX6 201 A8
- Brickyard Rd EX5 168 A7
- Bridespring Rd EX4 173 F1
- Bridespring Wlk EX4 173 F1
- Bridewell Ct 9 EX16 161 C3
- Bridford Rd EX2 177 C2
- Bridge Cl EX5 82 D3
- Bridge Cotts
  - Chard Junction TA20 88 D8
  - 4 Exeter EX4 177 D8
  - Lympstone EX8 195 D5
- Bridge Croft TQ13 130 F5
- Bridge Cross
  - Bishops Nympton EX36 30 F4
  - Burrington EX37 44 B4
- Bridge Ct EX4 261 A3
- Bridge End EX36 31 C5
- Bridge Hill EX3 182 F5
- Bridge La Budlake EX5 82 D3
  - 7 Instow EX39 15 B1
- Bridge Mill La PL21 133 C2
- Bridge Pk Ashwater EX21 90 F6
  - Bridgerule EX22 70 F5
- Bridge Pk *continued*
  - Ivybridge PL21 237 D5
- Bridge Plats Way EX39 156 E2
- Bridge Rd
  - Budleigh Salterton EX9 198 B2
  - Churston Ferrers TQ5 229 D5
  - Exeter EX2,EX6 182 A8
  - Exmouth EX8 202 A8
  - Kingswear TQ5,TQ6 234 B7
  - Teignmouth TQ14 210 A3
  - Torquay TQ2 219 F5
  - Totnes TQ9 222 F6
- Bridge Reeve Cross EX18 59 C8
- Bridge Ret Pk TQ2 219 E8
- Bridge St Bideford EX39 157 A1
  - Buckfastleigh TQ11 236 B5
  - Dulverton TA22 33 D6
  - Hatherleigh EX20 75 C7
  - Ipplepen TQ12 211 D2
  - Kingsbridge TQ7 258 D5
  - Lyme Regis DT7 260 E3
  - Sidbury EX10 101 B2
  - Tiverton EX16 161 C4
  - Uffculme EX15 66 A7
- Bridge Terr
  - Ashprington TQ9 139 F6
  - Bampton EX16 34 B1
- Bridge The PL1 262 B1
- Bridge View EX5 99 C6
- Bridgefield EX11 169 E4
- Bridgehill Garth EX3 182 F5
- Bridgehouse Cross EX15 52 D1
- Bridgeland St EX39 157 A2
- Bridgemoor Cross EX22 71 B6
- Bridgend Hill PL8 141 A7
- Bridgerule CE Prim Sch EX22 70 F5
- Bridgerule Ind Est EX22 70 E4
- Bridges The PL12 242 E1
- Bridgetown TQ9 223 D5
- Bridgetown Ct TQ9 223 D5
- Bridgetown Hill TQ9 223 E6
- Bridgewater Gdns TQ9 223 E5
- Bridgwater Cl PL6 245 B1
- Bridle Cl Paignton TQ4 229 B8
  - Plymouth PL7 251 B7
- Bridle Path The TQ9 223 C4
- Bridle Way PL12 242 D4
- Bridwell Ave EX15 65 F7
- Bridwell Cl PL5 247 E8
- Bridwell La N PL5 247 E8
- Bridwell Rd PL5 247 E8
- Bright View EX20 170 A4
- Brightley Cross EX20 94 B8
- Brightley Rd EX20 170 C8
- Brim Brook Ct TQ2 219 B8
- Brim Hill TQ1 214 C5
- Brimacombe Rd EX39 22 E3
- Brimford Cross EX39 38 A4
- Brimhay TQ9 222 F8
- Brimhill Cl PL7 251 B3
- Brimhill La PL19 117 F6
- Brimlands TQ5 230 B4
- Brimlands Ct TQ5 230 B4
- Brimley Bsns Pk TQ13 180 C5
- Brimley Cnr TQ13 123 F6
- Brimley Cross
  - Bovey Tracey TQ13 180 B5
  - Hemyock TA3 52 F1
- Brimley Ct TQ13 180 B5
- Brimley Dr TQ14 210 C5
- Brimley Grange TQ13 180 B5
- Brimley Halt TQ13 180 C5
- Brimley Hill EX13 88 D2
- Brimley La TQ13 180 A5
- Brimley Pk TQ13 180 C5
- Brimley Rd
  - Axminster EX13 88 D3
  - Bovey Tracey TQ13 180 B5
- Brimley Vale TQ13 180 C6
- Brimpenny Rd EX8 196 C1
- Brimstone La
  - Rockwell Green TA21 160 A2
  - Sampford Arundel TA21 51 F6
  - Sampford Peverell EX16 50 E2
- Brindifield La EX17 62 A5
- Brindiwell Cross EX17 63 B3
- Brindiwell Hill EX17 63 B2
- Brinkburn Ct EX10 188 A3
- Brinscombe Cross EX13 103 E6
- Brinscombe La
  - Bratton Fleming EX31 10 F3
  - Membury EX13 87 E6
- Brinsworthy Cross EX36 19 F1
- Briseham Cl TQ5 230 D3
- Briseham Rd TQ5 230 D3
- Brismar Wlk 3 PL6 249 C7
- Britannia Ave TQ6 233 C3
- Britannia Pl PL4 249 B2
- Britannia Royal Naval Coll TQ6 233 F5
- Britannia Way EX39 156 E7
- Briton St 2 EX16 34 C1
- Briton Streetlane EX6 112 F7
- Brittany Rd EX8 196 C4
- Britten Dr
  - Barnstaple EX32 155 B5
  - Exeter EX2 178 B5
- Britton Cl EX16 65 A7
- Brittons Cl EX33 152 E5
- Brittons The EX33 152 E5
- Briwere Rd TQ1 219 E7
- Brixham CE Inf Sch TQ5 230 D4
- Brixham Com Coll TQ5 230 D4
- Brixham Cross TQ5 234 E8
- Brixham Enterprise Est TQ5 230 D4

Brixham Hospl TQ5 230 C3
Brixham Rd
Kingswear TQ6 234 B3
Paignton TQ4 225 E3
Brixham Wlk PL6 249 E8
Brixington Dr EX8 196 D1
Brixington Inf Sch EX8 196 C2
Brixington Jun Sch EX8 196 C3
Brixington La EX8 196 C2
Brixton Lodge Gdns PL8 256 F5
Broad Cl Crediton EX17 165 A6
North Molton EX36 30 E8
Broad Croft EX13 87 E8
Broad La Appledore EX39 14 F1
Braunton EX33 152 A8
Hawkridge TA22 21 D1
Tiverton EX16 161 C3
Broad Lane Head TA22 21 D1
Broad Oak Cres [13] TQ9 223 D5
Broad Park Ave EX34 150 A5
Broad Park Cl EX33 7 E2
Broad Park Rd
Bere Alston PL20 125 E2
Exmouth EX8 196 C1
Plymouth PL3 248 D6
Broad Park Terr EX34 150 A4
Broad Path
Stoke Gabriel TQ9 228 A8
Uffculme EX15 66 A8
Broad Pk Dartmouth TQ6 233 D3
Plymouth PL9 255 C7
Broad Rd
Kentisbeare EX15 66 C1
Kingswear TQ6 234 D5
Broad Reach TQ4 229 C7
Broad St
Black Torrington EX21 74 A8
Churchinford TA3 68 A7
Ilfracombe EX34 150 C6
Lifton PL16 105 E4
Lyme Regis DT7 260 E3
Modbury PL21 137 B2
Ottery St Mary EX11 169 D3
South Molton EX36 158 C4
Broad View
Broadclyst EX5 175 C6
Dartington TQ9 222 F8
Broad Wlk PL12 242 E1
Broadacre Dr TQ5 230 D5
Broadclose Hill EX16 46 F6
Broadclose Rd EX31 154 D3
Broadclyst Com Prim Sch EX5 175 C7
Broaddown Cross EX14 86 A1
Broadfield Rd EX32 155 B4
Broadfields Rd EX2 178 C5
Broadgate
Barnstaple EX31 154 E7
Exeter EX1 261 A3
Broadgate Cl
Barnstaple EX31 154 E7
Braunton EX33 152 D6
Broadgate Cres [1] TQ12 212 F4
Broadgate La EX17 61 B2
Broadgate Rd TQ12 213 A4
Broadhayes Cross EX14 86 E5
Broadhembury Cross EX14 84 E7
Broadhempston Prim Sch TQ9 131 E1
Broadland Gdns PL9 256 A8
Broadland La PL9 255 F8
Broadlands
Bideford EX39 157 D1
Northam EX39 156 F8
Teignmouth TQ14 210 A3
Thorverton EX5 81 E4
Broadlands Ave TQ12 207 A3
Broadlands Cl PL7 251 A3
Broadlands Ct TQ12 207 A3
Broadlands Rd TQ4 226 A4
Broadleaf Cl EX1 178 E8
Broadley Ct PL6 241 B2
Broadley Dr TQ2 219 C3
Broadley Ind Pk PL6 241 B2
Broadley Park Rd PL6 241 B2
Broadmead Exmouth EX8 196 D2
Woodbury EX5 184 B3
Broadmead Bglws EX32 155 C2
Broadmead Cross EX16 48 A5
Broadmead Gdns EX35 151 B5
Broadmeade Ct TQ12 207 D2
Broadmeadow Ave EX4 176 F4
Broadmeadow La TQ14 209 D7
Broadmeadow View TQ14 209 D7
Broadmoor Cross EX37 29 A2
Broadmoor La EX20 170 A5
Broadoak Cl EX11 168 D3
Broadoak Hill EX31 4 C3
Broadoaks Cotts PL7 132 E4
Broadpark
Bovey Tracey TQ13 180 B5
Brampford Speke EX5 81 E1
Broadpark La EX20 95 D4
Broadpark Rd
Paignton TQ3 226 A7
Torquay TQ2 219 D2
Broadparks Ave EX4 174 E2
Broadparks Cl EX4 174 E2
Broadridge Cl TQ12 206 D4
Broadridge Cross TQ9 232 A8
Broadridge La EX17 61 A4
Broadsands Ave TQ4 229 C7
Broadsands Bend TQ4 229 C8
Broadsands Ct TQ4 229 B7
Broadsands Park Rd TQ4 229 C8
Broadsands Rd TQ4 229 C7
Broadshell Cross EX22 71 D5
Broadstone TQ6 233 F4
Broadstone Park Rd TQ2 219 D3
Broadway Exeter EX2 176 F3
Fremington EX31 153 F5
Sidmouth EX10 187 F5
Trusham TQ13 113 D1
Woodbury EX5 184 C2
Broadway Ave TQ12 207 D7
Broadway Hill EX2 176 E3
Broadway La EX33 7 D3
Broadway Rd TQ12 207 C7
Broadway The
Exmouth EX8 202 E8
Plymouth PL9 255 E7
Broadways Head EX14, TA20 68 F6
Broadwoodwidger Prim Sch PL16 91 A4
Broady Strap EX31 153 F5
Brock Ho [10] PL4 263 A2
Brockhole La EX13,TA20 88 B7
Brockhurst Pk TQ3 218 D2
Brockington's Rd EX5 99 C8
Brockley Rd PL3 249 C4
Brocks Cross EX17 79 A2
Brockscombe Cross EX21 91 F5
Brockton Gdns PL6 245 B6
Brodick Cl EX4 173 D1
Bromhead Ct PL6 249 A8
Bromley Pl [6] PL2 248 A4
Bronescombe Ave TQ14 209 A8
Bronshill Ho TQ1 220 B6
Bronshill Mews TQ1 220 B6
Bronshill Rd TQ1 220 B6
Bronte Pl PL5 244 D1
Brook Cl Exeter EX1 178 B8
Holcombe EX7 210 E8
Plymouth PL7 251 A3
Sidford EX10 101 B1
Brook Ct EX31 154 B3
Brook Green Terr EX4 261 C4
Brook Haven Cl TQ12 212 F5
Brook La Calverleigh EX16 48 F2
Shaldon TQ14 209 D5
[3] Sidford EX10 101 B1
Tavistock PL19 171 B2
Brook Lane Cotts TQ13 121 B3
Brook Mdw Exmouth EX8 196 C1
Newton Poppleford EX10 186 F8
South Molton EX36 158 D4
Brook Orch TQ12 212 F4
Brook Rd
Budleigh Salterton EX9 199 G2
Cullompton EX15 163 B2
Dolton EX19 57 F7
Ipplepen TQ12 211 D2
Ivybridge PL21 237 D5
Brook St Bampton EX16 34 B1
Dawlish EX7 204 D6
Ottery St Mary EX11 169 E3
Slapton TQ7 145 C3
Tavistock PL19 171 C6
Brook Terr EX12 192 D7
Brook The PL12 242 E4
Brook View TQ9 222 F6
Brook Way TQ12 123 F1
Brookdale EX11 169 E4
Brookdale Ave EX34 150 A5
Brookdale Cl TQ5 230 B4
Brookdale Ct
Brixham TQ5 230 B4
Exeter EX2 178 A2
Brookdale Pk TQ5 230 B4
Brookdale Terr
[6] Barnstaple EX32 155 B4
[18] Dawlish EX7 204 E6
Brookdown Terr PL12 242 E3
Brookdown Villas PL12 242 E3
Brooke Ave EX2 177 F3
Brooke Cl Saltash PL12 243 A2
Sampford Courtenay EX20 76 F3
Brooke Rd EX16 46 E1
Brookedor TQ12 212 F5
Brookedor Gdns TQ12 212 F5
Brookfield EX39 25 E4
Brookfield Cl
[5] Braunton EX33 152 D5
Kingsteignton TQ12 207 E7
Paignton TQ3 226 C8
Plymouth PL7 251 B5
Brookfield Ct [1] TQ13 123 F6
Brookfield Dr
[7] Colyton EX24 103 A4
Teignmouth TQ14 210 C7
Brookfield Gdns EX2 177 B1
Brookfield Pl EX34 150 B5
Brookfield Rd EX9 198 B6
Brookfield St [8] EX39 157 B1
Brookhayes Cl EX8 202 B8
Brookhill TQ6 234 B2
Brooking Barn TQ9 139 F8
Brooking Way PL12 242 C3
Brookingfield Cl PL7 250 C5
Brookland Terr EX11 169 E3
Brooklands
[2] Chudleigh TQ13 123 F6
[21] Dawlish EX7 204 D6
Tavistock PL19 171 D6
Totnes TQ9 223 D5
Brooklands Cross EX10 100 C1
Brooklands Ct PL6 244 E3
Brooklands Farm Cl EX13 103 D8
Brooklands La TQ2 219 E4
Brooklands Orch EX11 169 E4
Brooklands Rd
Exmouth EX8 196 D1
Rockwell Green TA21 160 B5
Brookleigh Ave EX1 178 B5
Brooklyn Pk EX8 196 C1
Brooks Hill EX15 66 C8
Brooks La PL10 252 F5
Brooks Pl TA21 160 E6
Brookside
Barnstaple EX31 154 A3
Kingsbridge TQ7 258 C4
Pathfinder Village EX6 98 C4
Sidmouth EX10 188 A7
Brookside Cl
Heybrook Bay PL9 140 A7
Teignmouth TQ14 210 A5
Brookside Cres EX4 174 B2
Brookside Ind Units EX4 174 D1
Brookside Villas [20] EX34 3 A3
Brookvale Orch TQ14 209 D4
Brookway EX1 178 C7
Brookwood Cl [3] TQ10 134 F3
Brookwood Rd PL9 256 D7
Broom Cl Axminster EX13 167 E6
Dawlish EX7 204 F8
Exeter EX2 178 A5
Broom Hill
Chagford TQ13 111 A6
Saltash PL12 242 D2
Broom La EX13 88 C5
Broom Pk Dartington TQ9 215 E1
Plymouth PL9 255 D5
Torquay TQ2 213 F3
Broom's La TA3 68 C7
Broomball Cross TA22 32 F5
Broomball La EX16 32 E5
Broomborough Ct TQ9 223 B5
Broomborough Dr TQ9 223 A5
Broomfield Dr PL9 255 C5
Broomham Cross EX37 45 A7
Broomhayes Sch EX39 157 E1
Broomhill Cross
Chilsworthy EX22 53 B3
Copplestone EX17 79 A4
Broomhill Rd EX16 161 B4
Broomhill Villas EX32 18 E5
Broomhill Way TQ2 213 E1
Broomhouse La EX36 30 A2
Broomhouse Pk EX16 46 E1
Broughton Cl PL3 248 F7
Brow Hill TQ12 123 B2
Brown Down La TA20 68 F7
Brown's Bridge La EX15 65 B7
Brown's Ct EX6 114 C4
Brown's Hill TQ6 233 F3
Brown's Hill Head EX37 27 F2
Browne Meml Almshouses PL19 171 A5
Brownhill La PL9 140 D8
Brownhills Rd TQ12 207 A3
Brownie Cross PL7 132 C3
Browning Cl EX2 178 A4
Browning Rd PL2 248 A5
Brownings End TQ12 206 F1
Brownings Mead EX6 112 F7
Brownings Wlk TQ12 206 F1
Brownlands Cl EX10 188 C5
Brownlands Rd EX10 188 C5
Brownlees EX6 182 A4
Brownlow St PL1 262 A2
Browns Bridge Rd TQ2 213 D2
Brownscombe Cl TQ3 218 D2
Brownsey La TA20 69 C5
Brownston Cross TQ10 135 F5
Brownston St PL21 137 B2
Brownstone Cross EX17 61 C3
Brownstone Moor Cross EX17 61 D4
Broxfords Hill EX17 80 C7
Broxton Dr PL9 249 E1
Bruckland La EX12,EX13 103 D3
Bruckton Cross TQ6 232 F6
Brunel Ave Plymouth PL2 247 F5
Torquay TQ2 214 B4
Brunel Cl Exeter EX4 177 A7
Teignmouth TQ14 210 C6
Brunel Ct [16] EX7 204 E6
Brunel Lodge Hospl TQ12 207 A1
Brunel Mews TQ2 219 F4
Brunel Prim Sch PL12 242 E2
Brunel Rd
Newton Abbot TQ12 207 D3
Paignton TQ4 229 D6
Saltash PL12 242 C4
Starcross EX6 201 A8
Brunel Terr [3] PL2 247 F5
Brunel Way
Ivybridge PL21 237 E6
Plymouth PL1 262 A2
Brunenburg Way EX13 167 D4
Brunswick Ho [4] TQ12 207 B4
Brunswick Pl
Dawlish EX7 204 E6
[10] Plymouth PL2 247 F4
Brunswick Rd PL4 263 B2
Brunswick Sq [3] TQ1 219 F6
Brunswick St Exeter EX4 177 A5
Teignmouth TQ14 210 C4
Brunswick Terr TQ1 219 F6
Brushford Cross TA22 33 E4
Brushford La
Chevithorne EX16 49 F3
Brushford La *continued*
Chulmleigh EX18 59 D2
Brushford New Rd TA22 33 E4
Brynmoor Cl PL3 249 A7
Brynmoor Pk PL3 249 A6
Brynmoor Wlk PL3 249 A6
Brynsworthy La EX31 154 A1
Brynsworthy Lawn EX31 154 A2
Brynsworthy Pk EX31 154 B3
Bubrook La EX6 96 F2
Buchanan Cl EX14 166 B4
Buckerell Cross EX14 84 F2
Buckerell Ave EX2 177 E3
Buckeridge Ave TQ14 210 B6
Buckeridge Rd TQ14 210 B6
Buckeridge Twrs [2] TQ14 210 B6
Buckfast Abbey★ TQ11 236 C7
Buckfast Butterflies & Dartmoor Otter Sanctuary★ TQ11 236 D5
Buckfast Cl
Buckfast TQ11 236 C6
Ivybridge PL21 237 D4
Plymouth PL2 248 A8
Buckfast Rd TQ11 236 C6
Buckfast Steam & Leisure Pk★ TQ11 236 D5
Buckfastleigh Prim Sch TQ11 236 B5
Buckfastleigh Sta TQ11 236 D5
Buckgrove Cotts EX38 42 B6
Buckham Cross EX36 45 D7
Buckham Hill EX36 45 D7
Buckhouse La EX24 102 C7
Buckingham Cl
Exmouth EX8 202 E7
South Molton EX36 158 C3
Buckingham Pl PL5 243 E2
Buckland Abbey★ PL20 126 C1
Buckland Brake TQ12 207 E2
Buckland Brewer Prim Sch EX39 40 C7
Buckland Cl PL7 250 D7
Buckland Cross
Braunton EX33 152 C8
Slapton TQ7 145 C6
Buckland Hall TQ13 130 D7
Buckland Rd
Georgeham EX33 8 B3
Newton Abbot TQ12 207 F4
Buckland St PL1 262 B2
Buckland St Mary CE Prim Sch TA20 69 D8
Buckland Terr PL20 126 F2
Buckland View
Buckland Brewer EX39 40 B7
Newton Abbot TQ12 207 D4
Buckleigh Cross EX39 156 C6
Buckleigh Rd EX39 156 C5
Buckley Cross EX10 101 C1
Buckley Rd EX10 101 C2
Buckley St TQ8 259 E5
Bucknall Cl EX12 190 D4
Bucknill Cl EX6 182 A4
Bucknole Cross EX14 102 A8
Bucknole Hill Rd EX24 102 A7
Bucks Cl TQ13 180 D7
Buckshots Cross EX14 69 A4
Buckton La EX10 101 C1
Buckwell TA21 160 E6
Buckwell Cl TQ7 258 D6
Buckwell Rd TQ7 258 D6
Buckwell St PL1,PL4 263 A2
Buctor Pk PL19 126 A8
Buddle Cl Ivybridge PL21 237 E5
Plymouth PL9 256 A5
Tavistock PL19 171 B6
Buddle La Exeter EX4 176 F5
Hatherleigh EX20 75 C7
Bude Hill EX19 59 A3
Bude Moor Cross EX19 76 D7
Bude St Appledore EX39 15 A1
Exeter EX4 261 B3
Budge Mdws PL15 115 A4
Budgett's Cross TA21 52 F6
Budgetts TA21 52 F6
Budlake Cross EX24 101 F6
Budlake Rd EX2 177 C1
Budlake Units EX2 177 C1
Budleigh Cl
Plymouth PL9 255 F5
Torquay TQ1 220 D6
Budleigh Hill EX9 198 B5
Budleigh Salterton Hospl EX9 198 B1
Budshead Gn PL5 244 C4
Budshead Rd PL5 244 C4
Budshead Way PL5 244 E2
Buena Vista Cl PL6 245 D6
Buena Vista Dr PL6 245 C6
Buena Vista Gdns PL6 245 C6
Buena Vista Way PL6 245 C6
Bugford Cross TQ6 232 C3
Bugford La TQ6 232 D3
Bugford Lane End TQ6 232 D3
Bughead Cross TQ13 111 D4
Bughole La TA21 51 E8
Building's Cross EX17 63 A4
Bulford TA21 160 D5
Bulford La Kennford EX6 181 B1
Wellington TA21 160 D5
Bulgis Pk EX36 158 B5
Bulkamore Ct TQ10 135 E5
Bull Ct EX31 154 F5
Bull Hill Barnstaple EX31 154 F7
Bideford EX39 157 A1
Bull Meadow Rd EX2 261 B2
Bull Point Prim Sch PL5 247 B8
Bull Ring TQ13 130 F4
Bull's La TA20 88 C8
Bullaford Gate EX36 31 E4
Bulland Cross EX20 76 E4
Bulland La
Cheriton Fitzpaine EX17 62 D3
Sampford Courtenay EX20 76 F4
Bullands Cl [4] TQ13 180 C8
Bullaton Cross TQ13 112 E1
Bulleid Cl PL2 247 F7
Bulleigh Cross TQ12 218 B8
Bulleigh Elms Cross TQ12 212 A1
Bullen St EX5 81 E5
Bullens Cl EX5 81 E4
Buller Cl Plymouth PL7 250 F4
Torpoint PL11 247 A3
Buller Pk PL12 242 D3
Buller Rd
[9] Barnstaple EX32 155 A5
Crediton EX17 165 B6
Exeter EX4 177 A5
Newton Abbot TQ12 207 D2
Torpoint PL11 247 B3
Bullfinch Cl EX15 163 A2
Bullhead Cross EX19 58 B2
Bullhorn Cross TQ7 142 F6
Bullow View EX19 58 F2
Bulls Ct [11] EX24 103 A4
Bully Shoot Cross EX24 103 A3
Bulmer Rd PL4 263 C3
Bulmoor Cross EX13 103 F5
Bulteel Gdns PL6 244 E7
Bulverton Pk EX10 187 F6
Bulworthy Cross EX16 47 E5
Bulworthy Knap EX16 47 E5
Bumpston Cross TQ11 215 C7
Bun La [8] TQ14 210 B4
Bungalows The
Axminster EX13 167 C4
[4] Tiverton EX16 161 C3
Bunkers Farm TQ9 144 E7
Bunn Rd EX8 196 D4
Bunneford Cross EX15 64 E1
Bunson Gate EX18 45 A4
Bunting Cl
Newton Abbot TQ12 207 A1
Teignmouth TQ14 210 A5
Bunts La EX12 191 F7
Bunyan Cl PL5 244 C2
Burch Cl EX8 196 E2
Burch Gdns EX7 200 E1
Burches Cross EX16 48 A1
Burchill's Hill TA21 160 B7
Burchills Cl TA21 160 A6
Burcombe Hill EX36 158 E8
Burdon La EX21 74 C7
Burgage TA21 160 D6
Burgh Island Cswy TQ7 142 E3
Burgmanns Hill EX8 195 D5
Burke Rd TQ9 223 D6
Burland Cross EX31 9 B4
Burland La EX33 8 F1
Burlands The EX14 84 D2
Burleigh La
Malborough TQ7 147 E7
Plymouth PL3 248 D7
Burleigh Lane End TQ7 147 E8
Burleigh Manor PL3 248 D7
Burleigh Park Rd PL3 248 D6
Burleigh Rd TQ2 219 C7
Burlescombe CE Prim Sch EX16 51 B3
Burlington Cl EX32 155 B3
Burlington Gr EX32 155 B2
Burn La Lydford PL19 107 C1
North Brentor PL19 117 C8
Burn River Rise TQ2 219 B8
Burnard Cl PL6 244 E7
Burnards Cl [15] EX24 103 A4
Burnards Field Rd EX24 103 A4
Burnbreach Cnr EX24 102 B2
Burnbridge Hill EX16 63 D2
Burne Cross TQ12 131 D6
Burnet Cl EX2 178 C3
Burnett Cl PL12 242 D2
Burnett Rd PL6 248 F8
Burnham Cl EX12 192 A8
Burnham Ct TQ12 207 E7
Burnham Park Rd PL3 248 D6
Burnistone Cl PL7 251 A3
Burnley Cl TQ12 206 D4
Burnley Rd TQ12 206 D4
Burns Ave Exeter EX2 177 F3
Plymouth PL5 244 C2
Burns Ct EX7 204 E5
Burns La PL21 137 B2
Burnside EX8 196 B1
Burnside Rd EX34 150 A3
Burnsome La EX14,EX15 67 B5
Burnt Mdw EX6 113 D5
Burnthouse Cross EX14 67 B5
Burnthouse Hill TQ12 212 E1
Burnthouse La EX2 177 F3
Burraton Com Prim Sch PL12 242 C3
Burraton Cross PL21 136 D4
Burraton Rd PL12 242 C4
Burrator Ave PL20 128 A8
Burrator Dr EX4 176 E8
Burrator Rd PL20 127 B3
Burridge Ave TQ2 219 D5

Burridge Cross EX18 58 F8
Burridge Moor Cross
EX18 60 E6
Burridge Rd
Torquay TQ2 219 D5
Upton Pyne EX5 173 B8
Burrington Dr EX17 80 E4
Burrington Ind Est PL5 244 A1
Burrington Moor Cross
EX37 43 C3
Burrington Primary Sch
EX37 43 F3
Burrington Rd PL5 244 A1
Burrington Way PL5 244 B1
Burrough Rd EX39 157 A6
Burrough Way TA21 160 D4
Burrow Cl EX10 186 D8
Burrow Cnr
Butterleigh EX16 64 C4
Dalwood EX13 86 F2
Burrow Cross
Broadclyst EX5 175 F8
Budlake EX5 82 E1
Monkokehampton EX19 76 A8
Witheridge EX17 46 A4
Burrow Ctyd EX16 64 C4
Burrow Farm Gdns★
EX13 87 A2
Burrow Hill PL9 255 E6
Burrow Knap EX13 87 A2
Burrow Knap Way EX13 86 F2
Burrow La Ashbrittle TA21 50 D8
Bow EX17 78 A5
Newton Poppleford EX10 186 D8
Burrow Rd
Broadclyst EX5 175 E8
9 Ilfracombe EX34 150 B5
Seaton EX12 192 B4
Burrow The 1 EX12 192 B4
Burrowe The 2 EX17 165 C5
Burrowplot Cross EX17 59 F2
Burrows Cl EX33 152 C5
Burrows Close La EX33 15 A7
Burrows La EX39 14 F1
Burrows Pk EX33 152 C5
Burrows Way EX39 156 F8
Burrowshot Cross EX13 104 B7
Burscombe La EX10 101 A1
Bursdon Moor Cross
EX39 37 E7
Bursledon Ct EX7 204 F6
Burston Cross EX17 78 B4
Burston La EX16 34 A4
Burton Cl PL6 245 B6
Burton Mus & Art Gallery★
EX39 157 A2
Burton Pl TQ5 230 C4
Burton Rd EX39 156 E1
Burton St TQ5 230 C3
Burton Villa Cl TQ5 230 C4
Burvill St EX35 151 B5
Burwell Cl PL6 245 E4
Burwell La EX36 30 F7
Burwood La EX38 159 F5
Burwood Mews EX38 159 F4
Burwood Rd EX38 159 E5
Bury Cross Lapford EX17 60 D2
Petrockstow EX20 56 F5
Bury Rd TQ12 207 B4
Bury The EX5 81 E5
Buscombe La EX31 11 E2
Bush Cnr EX18 58 F8
Bush Cross EX18 58 F8
Bush Pk PL6 245 F3
Bushayes Cnr EX3 183 C6
Bushel Rd TQ12 207 A4
Bushes La EX12,DT7 193 B7
Bushmead Ave TQ12 213 A5
Bussell's Moor Cross
EX36 32 C4
Butcher Park Hill PL19 171 B7
Butcher's Moor La EX19 58 E4
Butchers Row EX31 154 F5
Butcombe La EX17 61 D1
Bute Rd PL4 249 A4
Butlakes La EX24 101 F6
Butland Ave TQ3 219 C1
Butland Rd TQ12 207 D8
Butlands Ind Est TQ12 211 F2
Butler Cl Plymouth PL6 245 B6
Tiverton EX16 161 E3
Butler Way EX14 86 A6
Butsford La EX17 79 A3
Butt Park Rd PL5 244 B3
Butt Parks EX17 165 D4
Butt Pk
Bovey Tracey TQ13 123 B7
Stokenham TQ7 145 B1
Butt's Hill EX11 169 E4
Buttercombe Cl TQ12 211 F8
Buttercombe La
Braunton EX33 15 E8
Ilfracombe EX34 8 E5
Knowle EX31,EX34 8 F1
Buttercup Cl EX12 192 B8
Butterdon Wlk PL21 237 F5
Butterdown PL12 242 B3
Butterfly La TQ12 209 C2
Butterlake TQ3 218 D3
Butterleigh Dr EX16 161 E3
Buttermere Ct EX4 176 F5
Buttermoor Cross EX16 48 D3
Buttery Cl EX14 166 C4
Buttery Rd EX14 166 C4
Buttgarden St EX39 157 A1
Buttle's Cross TA3 68 C7
Buttle's La TA3 68 B6
Button La EX31 11 A1
Buttonhill Cross EX31 18 A8
Butts Cl Bridford EX6 112 F5
Chawleigh EX18 60 B7
Honiton EX14 166 B4
Witheridge EX16 46 E1
Butts Cross
Buckfastleigh TQ11 135 B6
Cornworthy TQ9 227 C3
Butts Ct EX2 178 A5
Butts Hill Kenton EX6 194 D3
Paignton TQ3 225 B8
Butts La Christow EX6 113 B3
Ideford TQ13 124 B4
Kenton EX6 194 D1
Starcross EX6 200 D8
Butts Pk PL8 141 A7
Butts Rd Exeter EX2 178 A5
Ottery St Mary EX11 169 E4
Butts The Colyton EX24 103 A4
Loddiswell TQ7 143 E8
Newton Ferrers PL8 141 A7
Butts Way EX20 77 C4
Buttsbear Cross EX22 70 E7
Buttsford Terr PL21 136 B6
Buttshill Cross TQ3 225 B8
Buttsons Cl TQ7 145 B1
Buzzacott Cl EX34 3 B2
Buzzacott La EX34 3 B2
Byard Cl PL5 243 E1
Bycott La EX18 45 B4
Bydown Cross EX32 28 D8
Bye Cross EX33 8 B3
Byes Cl EX10 188 C8
Byes La EX10 188 D8
Byeside Rd EX10 188 C8
Bygones Mus★ TQ1 220 C8
Byland Rd PL3 249 A6
Byron Ave PL5 244 C2
Byron Cl EX31 154 F7
Byron Rd Exeter EX2 178 C5
Torquay TQ1 220 A8
Byron Way EX8 196 C3
Byslades Camping Pk
TQ4 225 A5
Bystock Cl EX4 261 A4
Bystock Mews EX8 196 E3
Bystock Rd EX8 196 D4
Bystock Terr EX4 261 A4
Byter Mill La TQ9 228 A7
Byways Cl EX31 153 F5

C

Cabbage Hill TQ13 130 F4
Cabbage La EX14 85 A3
Cabot Cl PL12 242 E2
Cabourg Cl TQ8 259 D5
Cadbury Cross EX17 81 C8
Cadbury Gdns EX9 198 B6
Caddiford Cross EX17 97 B6
Cadditon Cross EX20 76 F7
Caddsdown Ind Pk EX39 25 D4
Caddywell La EX38 159 E5
Caddywell Mdw EX38 159 E5
Cadewell Cres TQ2 213 D1
Cadewell La TQ2 219 C8
Cadewell Park Rd TQ2 213 C1
Cadford La EX19 59 B3
Cadhay Ho★ EX11 169 B5
Cadhay La EX11 169 B4
Cadlake La EX20 77 A3
Cadleigh Cl PL21 136 D6
Cadleigh Court La EX16 63 D2
Cadleigh Cross PL21 136 D7
Cadleigh La PL21 136 D6
Cadover Cl PL6 245 A1
Cadwell Rd TQ3 226 B7
Caen Field EX33 152 D6
Caen Gdns EX33 152 D6
Caen Ho 1 EX33 152 D6
Caen Sh Ctr 5 EX33 152 D6
Caen St EX33 152 D6
Caernarvon Gdns PL2 248 B7
Caffyns Cross EX35 5 A4
Cairn Rd EX34 150 B4
Cairn Side EX34 150 B3
Cake Down La EX36 158 E4
Calder Cl PL3 249 B6
Caldicot Gdns PL6 245 C8
Caledonia Cl 1 PL7 251 B5
Calf St EX38 159 D5
California Cl EX4 173 D3
California Cross PL21 138 A3
California Gdns PL3 249 D6
Caller's La EX15 52 D1
Callington Rd
Saltash PL12 242 E3
Tavistock PL19 171 A4
Calstock Com Prim Sch
PL18 125 D3
Calstock Rd PL18 125 D6
Calstock Sta PL17 125 D3
Calthorpe Rd EX4 177 F8
Calvados 14 EX32 155 A5
Calvados Cl 20 TQ13 123 E6
Calvados Pk TQ12 207 F7
Calverleigh Cross EX16 48 C1
Calvesford Cl EX38 159 E6
Calvesford Cross EX38 159 E5
Calvesford Rd EX38 159 E6
Calvez Cl PL10 252 F6
Camber Rd PL1 262 A1
Cambercombe Terr 2
EX34 150 D5
Camborne Cl PL5 244 A5
Camborne Cres TQ4 229 B8
Cambrian Cl TQ4 225 D4
Cambridge Gr 3 EX34 150 C5
Cambridge La W 5 PL1 262 B3
Cambridge Rd
Brixham TQ5 230 A4
Plymouth PL2 247 F5
Torquay TQ1 214 B1
Cambridge St 4 EX4 177 A5
Cambridge Terr EX10 188 B4
Camden Ct PL4 263 A3
Camden Rd TQ1 220 B5
Camden St PL4 263 A3
Came Cross EX14 84 C7
Camellia Cl
Churston Ferrers TQ5 229 D5
1 Tiverton EX16 161 F6
Camelot Cl EX4 174 A1
Cameron Cl EX16 161 B3
Cameron Dr PL21 237 A5
Cameron Way PL6 245 B1
Camfield Dr EX16 161 F6
Camilla Ct EX4 261 B4
Camilla Terr PL2 248 D7
Camp Cross PL15 105 E7
Camp Rd EX20 170 C2
Campbell Rd PL9 255 F7
Campbellhayes Hill EX16 47 A1
Camperdown Rd TQ8 259 C4
Camperdown St PL2 247 F4
Camperdown Terr EX8 201 F6
Camperknowle Cl PL10 252 F6
Campian Way 11 EX14 85 C2
Campion Cl
7 Plymouth PL7 251 C5
Saltash PL12 242 D4
Campion Ct TQ1 214 B1
Campion Dr EX32 155 E5
Campion Gdns EX2 178 C3
Campion Rise PL19 171 D6
Campion View PL6 245 E8
Camps Cross EX17 80 E2
Canaan Way EX11 169 D3
Canada Hill Com Prim Sch
TQ12 206 F1
Canal Cl TA21 160 B8
Canal Hill EX16 161 F3
Canal Rd
Holsworthy EX22 164 D6
Tavistock PL19 171 B5
Canberra Cl EX4 173 E2
Candish Dr PL9 256 D7
Candys Cotts 1 TQ13 123 C4
Cane's Cotts PL8 257 A5
Canefields Ave PL7 251 B3
Canhaye Cl PL7 251 A3
Cann Gdns PL6 244 D6
Cann Wood View PL6 245 E7
Cannington La
Lyme Regis DT7 104 B3
Uplyme DT7 260 A5
Cannon Rd
Bovey Tracey TQ12 123 B2
Heathfield TQ12 180 F2
Cannon St PL1 247 D2
Canns Water EX39 39 C6
Canon Way EX2 181 B8
Canons Cl TQ14 208 F8
Canons Way PL19 171 A3
Canonteign Ctry Pk★
EX6 113 B1
Canonteign Falls★ EX6 113 B1
Canterbury Cl
Feniton EX14 84 D2
Ivybridge PL21 237 E4
Canterbury Dr PL5 244 B4
Canterbury Rd EX4 176 E7
Canterbury Way EX8 196 E4
Capel La EX8 202 F8
Capern Cl EX33 152 E4
Capern Rd EX39 156 F1
Capper Cl EX10 186 E8
Capstone Ct EX34 150 D5
Capstone Par EX34 150 C7
Capstone Rd EX34 150 C6
Captain Brooks Cross
EX39 39 B8
Captain's Cross EX16 63 C3
Captains Gdns PL5 244 E1
Captains Rd TQ12 207 D8
Capton Cross TQ6 232 E6
Caradon Cl PL6 245 A5
Caradon Ct 2 PL20 126 F4
Caradon Terr PL12 242 E3
Carbeile Rd PL11 247 A2
Carbeile Sch PL11 247 A3
Carberry TQ8 259 D4
Carberry Ave EX8 196 A1
Carders Ct EX2 261 A2
Cardiff Cl PL7 251 B4
Cardigan Rd PL6 245 C1
Cardinal Ave PL5 247 D8
Carehouse Cross TQ7 145 B1
Careswell Ave PL2 247 F8
Carew Ave PL5 244 B3
Carew Gdns
Newton Abbot TQ12 207 F3
Plymouth PL5 244 B3
Saltash PL12 242 D3
Carew Gr PL5 244 B3
Carew Rd EX16 161 D6
Carew Terr PL11 247 B2
Carew Wharf PL11 247 C2
Carey Ct PL12 242 E3
Carey Rd TQ6 233 C3
Carhaix Way EX7 204 F8
Carisbrooke Rd PL6 245 C1
Carlie Rd TQ5 230 A5
Carlile Rd EX2 178 A5
Carlisle Rd PL5 244 D3
Carlisle St 9 TQ12 207 C3
Carlton Cl Paignton TQ3 219 C2
Plymouth PL3 249 B5
Carlton Ct TQ12 209 B2
Carlton Dr TQ3 219 C2
Carlton Hill EX8 202 A5
Carlton Mews TQ1 220 C6
Carlton Pl 20 TQ14 210 C4
Carlton Rd Exeter EX2 178 B4
Torquay TQ1 220 C6
Carlton Terr
18 Barnstaple EX32 155 A4
6 Dawlish EX7 204 E6
Plymouth, Lipson PL4 263 B3
Plymouth, Weston Mill PL5 247 E8
Carlyle Ave EX32 155 A6
Carlyon Cl Exeter EX1 178 A6
Torpoint PL11 246 F4
Carlyon Gdns EX1 178 A6
Carmarthen Rd PL4 249 B2
Carmel Gdns PL19 171 A5
Carnegie N EX39 156 F6
Carnegie S EX39 156 F6
Carnock Rd PL2 248 D8
Carnoustie Dr PL12 242 C2
Carolina Gdns PL2 247 F7
Caroline Cl Exmouth EX8 196 D1
Kingskerswell TQ12 213 A3
Caroline Pl PL1 262 A2
Carousel Ct EX4 177 A4
Carpenter Cl Exeter EX4 261 A3
Tiverton EX16 161 C3
Carpenter Rd PL9 255 F8
Carpenter's Cross EX18 60 A5
Carpenters Ct 2 TQ12 207 C2
Carr La TQ7 145 C4
Carradale Rd PL6 249 C7
Carrington Terr 5
EX32 155 A6
Carrionpit La EX19 58 F3
Carrions The 7 TQ9 223 C5
Carrisbrooke Way PL12 242 B2
Carroll Rd PL5 244 C2
Carron La PL6 241 D1
Carswells TQ12 212 F5
Carter Ave EX8 202 A8
Carter Cl EX36 158 C5
Carter Rd PL21 237 D6
Carters Cross EX13 87 A3
Cartwright Cres TQ14 209 D8
Cary Ave TQ1 220 C7
Cary Castle TQ1 220 B8
Cary Par TQ2 220 B4
Cary Park Rd TQ1 220 C7
Cary Pk TQ1 220 C7
Cary Rd Paignton TQ3 219 A1
Torquay TQ2 220 A4
Case Gdns EX12 192 B6
Caseberry La EX5 82 E6
Cassiobury Way TQ2 213 E2
Castlands EX5 172 C7
Castle Acre Gdns PL3 249 B5
Castle Bank Gdns PL3 249 B5
Castle Barbican PL7 250 E4
Castle Bldgs PL12 242 D4
Castle Carey Gdns PL3 249 B5
Castle Cir TQ1 220 A5
Castle Circus Ct TQ1 220 A5
Castle Cotts
Exmouth EX8 203 A7
Wellington TA21 52 D8
Woodbury EX5 184 C3
Castle Cross
Axminster EX13 88 D4
Bratton Clovelly EX20 92 C6
Membury EX13 87 E4
Castle Ct Saltash PL12 242 C2
Totnes TQ9 223 B6
Castle Drogo★ EX6 96 C1
Castle Dyke La PL1 263 A2
Castle Farm EX11 168 E4
Castle Gate EX6 194 E3
Castle Hill
Axminster EX13 167 D6
Berrynarbor EX34 2 E3
Ilfracombe EX34 150 C6
Lynton EX35 151 C5
Saltash PL12 242 C1
Seaton EX12 192 A4
Castle Hill Ave EX34 150 C6
Castle Hill Gdns EX38 159 D5
Castle Hill View 11
EX10 101 B1
Castle Hospl EX20 170 B4
Castle La Blackawton TQ9 139 E2
Budleigh Salterton EX9 197 C1
Exmouth EX8,EX9 203 B8
Okehampton EX20 170 A3
Paignton TQ3 218 C6
Plymouth PL7 250 E4
Torquay TQ1 220 B5
Woodbury EX5 184 D3
Castle Mdw EX39 40 B8
Castle Mount EX4 261 A4
Castle Park Rd EX32 155 E3
Castle Pk EX15 67 B8
Castle Prim Sch EX16 161 D4
Castle Quay EX31 154 F5
Castle Quay Ct 6 EX31 154 F5
Castle Rd Dartmouth TQ6 234 B1
Kingswear TQ6 234 A2
Okehampton EX20 170 B4
Torquay TQ1 220 B5
Wellington TA21 52 D8
Castle Rise Plymouth PL3 249 B4
Castle Rise *continued*
Saltash PL12 242 D1
Castle St Axminster EX13 167 D6
Bampton EX16 34 B1
Barnstaple EX31 154 F5
Combe Martin EX34 3 A3
Exeter EX4 261 B3
Great Torrington EX38 159 D5
Northam EX39 156 F6
Plymouth PL1 263 A2
Tiverton EX16 161 D4
Totnes TQ9 223 C6
Winkleigh EX19 58 F3
Castle Terr 5 EX34 150 C5
Castle View
17 Colyton EX24 103 A4
Saltash PL12 242 D1
Castle Way TQ12 206 E4
Castle Wood La TA20 69 F1
Castlebar Cl EX16 161 E3
Castlehayes Gdns PL7 250 E4
Castlemead Cl PL12 242 D3
Castlemead Dr PL12 242 D3
Castleton Cl PL3 249 A4
Castleton Tor TQ1 219 F7
Castlewood Ave TQ12 206 F4
Castor Cl TQ5 230 D3
Castor La TQ4 226 B1
Castor Rd TQ5 230 C3
Cat La EX34 150 E5
Catalina Cl EX14 67 C1
Catalina Villas PL9 255 A6
Cater Rd EX32 155 B4
Cath of St Mary & St
Boniface PL1 262 B3
Catharine Cl EX16 161 E5
Cathcart Ave PL4 249 B2
Cathedral Cl EX1 261 B3
Cathedral Sch The
Exeter EX1 261 B3
Exeter EX2 261 B2
Exeter EX4 261 A3
Cathedral St PL1 262 B3
Cathedral Yd EX1 261 B3
Catherine St Exeter EX1 261 B3
Plymouth PL1 262 C2
Cathole La DT7 104 B5
Catkill Cross EX36 46 C7
Catmoor Cross EX13 88 A5
Caton Cross TQ12 131 C6
Catriage Hill EX32 18 C2
Catsborough Cross EX39 40 E6
Catshole La EX39 156 F1
Catsmoor Cross EX20 92 F1
Catson Gn PL8 257 A5
Catt's La TA21 52 E6
Cattedown Rd PL4 263 C1
Catterick Cl PL5 243 E5
Cattewater Rd PL4 249 B1
Cauleston Cl EX8 196 A2
Caulfield Ct 14 TQ12 207 C3
Caumont Cl EX15 65 F7
Caunters Cl TQ12 211 D2
Causeway EX12 191 D5
Causeway Cl EX39 157 A7
Causeway End EX14 84 D7
Causeway The TQ12 211 D2
Causey Gdns EX1 174 F1
Causey La EX1 174 F1
Causway Cross TQ12 211 E2
Cavalier Rd TQ12 180 F3
Cavendish Cl EX7 204 C7
Cavendish Pl EX35 151 B5
Cavendish Rd Exeter EX1 177 F6
Plymouth PL4 249 B1
Cavern Rd TQ1 220 B5
Cavie Cres EX33 152 B6
Cavie Rd EX33 152 B6
Cawley Ave EX13 167 F7
Cawley's La EX14 86 F6
Caxton Gdns PL5 244 C1
Caxton Row EX16 161 D6
Cayley Way PL5 243 F2
Cayman Cl TQ2 213 E3
Cecil Ave Paignton TQ3 226 B8
Plymouth PL4 263 C4
Cecil Cotts PL1 262 A3
Cecil Mews TQ3 226 B7
Cecil Rd Exeter EX2 177 A4
Paignton TQ3 226 B7
Cecil St PL1 262 B3
Cecilia Rd TQ3 219 B1
Cedar Ave PL9 255 C5
Cedar Cl Exmouth EX8 196 D3
Honiton EX14 166 B5
Seaton EX12 192 A7
Teignmouth TQ14 210 D7
Torpoint PL11 246 F2
Cedar Court Rd TQ1 220 B7
Cedar Ct Saltash PL12 242 F2
Wellington TA21 160 E5
Cedar Dr PL11 246 F2
Cedar Gdns EX13 167 D5
Cedar Gr EX31 154 B2
Cedar Ho 2 EX33 152 D6
Cedar Rd
Newton Abbot TQ12 212 F8
Paignton TQ3 219 C1
Tiverton EX16 161 F5
Cedar Units TQ9 222 F8
Cedar Way Bideford EX39 25 D4
Brixham TQ5 230 A2
Cedarcroft Rd PL2 248 B7
Cedars EX8 203 B6
Cedars Pk EX31 154 B4
Cedars Rd Exeter EX2 261 B2
Torquay TQ1 220 D5
Celandine Cl EX12 192 B7

Celandine Gdns PL7 251 C5
Celandine Lawns EX15 162 D5
Celia Cres EX4 174 A2
Cembra Cl EX14 166 E5
Cemetery La EX5 82 F6
Cemetery Rd PL18 125 C5
Centenary Way TQ2 213 C2
Centery La Barnstaple EX31 9 C5
Parracombe EX31 4 D2
Central Ave
Exeter, Countess Wear EX2 182 D7
Exeter, Whipton EX4 174 B2
Holsworthy EX22 164 B4
Lee Mill PL21 136 C6
Paignton TQ3 226 B7
Central CE Mid Sch EX2 261 C1
Central Fst Sch EX2 261 C1
Central Park Ave PL4 262 C4
Central Rd PL1 262 B1
Central Sta EX4 261 A4
Central Station Chambers EX4 261 A3
Centre Ct PL21 137 C8
Centry Ct TQ5 230 E4
Centry Rd TQ5 230 E4
Century Dr EX39 156 E6
Ceramic Terr 3 EX32 155 A4
Chackrell La EX16 50 F2
Chad Rd PL9 140 A8
Chaddiford La EX31 154 D7
Chaddlewood Ave PL4 263 B3
Chaddlewood Cl PL7 251 A4
Chaddlewood Ho PL7 251 B5
Chaddlewood Inf Sch PL7 251 A5
Chaddlewood Prim Sch PL7 251 A5
Chaffcombe Cross EX17 78 F5
Chaffcombe La EX17 79 A6
Chaffinch Dr EX15 163 B2
Chagford CE Prim Sch TQ13 111 A7
Chagford Cross TQ13 111 E5
Chagford Wlk PL6 249 E8
Chains Rd EX16 50 C1
Chalcombe Rocks La TA4 34 E5
Chalfield Cl TQ2 213 F3
Challabrook La TQ13 180 B6
Challacombe Cotts PL20 120 F6
Challacombe Cross
Bratton Fleming EX31 11 F3
Chagford TQ13 110 F2
Chulmleigh EX18 45 A2
Challacombe Hill EX34 8 A5
Challacombe Hill Rd EX34 7 F6
Challenger Cross EX13 87 E7
Challeycroft Rd TQ5 230 A1
Challgood Cl PL9 255 F5
Challgood Rise PL9 255 F5
Challick La TA4 35 F6
Challock Cl PL6 245 D4
Challowell La EX33 152 D8
Chaloner's Rd EX33 152 D6
Chambercombe La EX34 150 E4
Chambercombe Manor* EX34 150 E4
Chambercombe Park Rd EX34 150 E5
Chambercombe Pk EX34 150 E5
Chambercombe Pk Terr EX34 150 E5
Chambercombe Rd EX34 150 D5
Chamberlain Rd EX2 261 A1
Chamberlayne Dr PL7 250 E6
Chambers Cl EX10 188 A8
Champernhayes La DT6 104 F7
Champernowne PL21 137 B3
Champernowne Cres 4 EX34 150 D5
Champford La TA21 160 D5
Champford Mews 2 TA21 160 D5
Champion Cross TA4 35 E3
Chancel Ct EX4 174 D1
Chancel La EX4 174 D1
Chancellor's Way EX4 174 A2
Chandlers Ct 9 EX39 15 B1
Chandlers Hts TQ8 259 D5
Chandlers Way EX34 150 B3
Chandlers Wlk EX2 261 A1
Chandlers' La EX10 188 B5
Change La TA4 34 D6
Channel Park Ave PL3 249 B5
Channel Sch (Language) EX34 150 B4
Channel View
Ilfracombe EX34 150 D5
Woolacombe EX34 1 A2
Channel View Dr TQ7 147 B6
Channel View Terr PL4 263 C4
Channon Rd PL12 242 C4
Chanter Ct EX2 178 A2
Chanter's Hill EX32 155 B5
Chanters Rd EX39 157 A3
Chantry Ave EX39 157 A3
Chantry Cl TQ14 210 D7
Chantry Ct PL7 250 B5
Chantry Hill TQ7 145 D4
Chantry Mdw EX2 181 B8
Chantry The EX20 170 C5
Chapel Cl
Gunnislake PL18 125 B5
Halberton EX16 65 A8
5 Horrabridge PL20 126 F4
Petrockstow EX20 56 F4
Chapel Cnr EX22 70 F5
Chapel Cotts PL7 132 F4
Chapel Cross
Dunkeswell EX14 67 C2
Iddesleigh EX19 57 E3
Petrockstow EX20 56 F8
Thorverton EX5 81 D5
Thurlestone TQ7 143 A2
Witheridge EX16 62 B5
Chapel Ct
Stoke Gabriel TQ9 227 F8
Swimbridge EX32 28 E8
Torquay TQ1 219 F7
Chapel Down La PL21 137 F3
Chapel Down Lane End PL21 137 E3
Chapel Downs Dr EX17 165 A6
Chapel Downs Rd EX17 165 A6
Chapel Fields 5 TQ10 134 F3
Chapel Hill
4 Budleigh Salterton EX9 198 A1
Cheriton Fitzpaine EX17 62 F1
Clyst St George EX3 183 C6
15 Exmouth EX8 202 A6
Longdown EX6 98 E2
5 Newton Abbot TQ12 207 B3
Uffculme EX15 66 A7
Chapel Hill Cross EX17 62 F1
Chapel Ho 4 EX39 156 F7
Chapel Knap EX13,EX24 102 F7
Chapel La
Combe Martin EX34 3 A3
Dartmouth TQ6 233 F3
Folly Gate EX20 93 F8
4 Horrabridge PL20 126 F4
Lutton PL21 133 B2
Malborough TQ7 147 E6
Mary Tavy PL19 117 E6
Ottery St Mary EX11 169 E4
Stoke Fleming TQ6 146 B7
Totnes TQ9 223 D5
Yealmpton PL8 257 F4
Chapel Mdw PL20 126 C3
Chapel Rd
Brampford Speke EX5 81 E1
Bratton Clovelly EX20 92 A2
Exeter EX2 177 B1
Lympstone EX8 195 D5
Newton Abbot TQ12 207 D3
Parkham EX39 39 E8
Saltash PL12 242 B3
Sidmouth EX10 188 B3
Yealmpton PL8 136 A2
Chapel Row TQ7 142 C6
Chapel St Axmouth EX12 192 D7
4 Bere Alston PL20 125 E1
Blackawton TQ9 139 E1
Braunton EX33 152 D5
Buckfastleigh TQ11 236 B5
Budleigh Salterton EX9 199 G2
Dolton EX19 57 F7
Dulverton TA22 33 D6
Ermington PL21 136 F4
Exeter EX1 261 B3
1 Exmouth EX8 202 A6
Georgeham EX33 8 A2
Gunnislake PL18 125 D6
Holsworthy EX22 164 C3
Honiton EX14 166 C6
Morchard Bishop EX17 61 A2
Plymouth PL4 263 A3
Plymouth, Mount Wise PL1 247 E2
Sidbury EX10 101 B2
Sidmouth EX10 188 B3
Tavistock PL19 171 B5
Tiverton EX16 161 D4
Woolfardisworthy EX39 38 F7
Chapel The 7 TQ9 223 D5
Chapel Way PL3 249 A6
Chapeldown Rd PL11 247 A2
Chapelry The 5 TQ13 123 C4
Chapelton Sta EX37 28 A4
Chapeltown Cross EX5 63 C1
Chapman Ct PL12 242 B3
Chapmans Gn EX22 54 C4
Chapmans Ope PL1 247 D2
Chapple Cl EX6 201 B8
Chapple Cross
Bovey Tracey TQ13 180 B5
Chagford TQ13 110 D8
Dolton EX19 57 E6
Chapple Cross Cross TQ13 110 D8
Chapple La EX20 76 E4
Chapple Rd
Bovey Tracey TQ13 180 A6
Witheridge EX16 46 E1
Chapplecroft Rd EX13 87 E5
Charberry Rise DT6 104 F4
Chard Ave 4 EX5 99 E8
Chard Barton PL5 244 B3
Chard Rd Axminster EX13 88 B4
Exeter EX1 178 A6
Plymouth PL5 243 D2
Chard St Axminster EX13 167 D6
Chardstock EX13 88 B7
Chard Stock Cl EX1 178 D6
Charfield Dr PL6 249 A8
Charford Cross TQ10 135 B1
Charlacott Cross
Newton Tracey EX31 27 B6
Newton Tracey EX31 27 B7
Charlemont Rd TQ14 210 B8
Charles Ave EX39 157 A2
Charles Cross
East Buckland EX32 18 E3
Plymouth PL4 263 A3
Charles Dart Cres EX32 155 A6
Charles Hankin Way PL21 237 E4
Charles Hudson La 2 EX31 155 A7
Charles Rd Honiton EX14 166 C6
Kingskerswell TQ12 213 A2
Charles St
13 Barnstaple EX32 154 F6
Dartmouth TQ6 233 F3
3 Exmouth EX8 202 A7
Plymouth PL1 263 A3
Charles Terr PL3 249 A6
Charleton CE Prim Sch TQ7 144 C1
Charleton Way TQ7 144 C1
Charlotte Cl TQ2 219 F8
Charlotte Ct TQ1 214 B1
Charlotte Mews 1 EX2 261 B2
Charlotte St
Crediton EX17 165 D5
Plymouth PL2 247 E4
Charlton Cres PL6 245 A2
Charlton Ho EX7 204 F6
Charlton Rd PL6 245 A3
Charlton Terr PL21 237 D5
Charlwood Ct TQ1 220 C8
Charmoor Dro TA20 69 F8
Charmouth Cl
Lyme Regis DT7 260 E4
Torquay TQ1 220 D6
Charmouth Ho DT7 260 C3
Charmouth Rd
Lyme Regis DT7 260 E4
Raymond's Hill EX13 104 C7
Charneymore Cross EX18 44 E1
Charnhill Cl PL9 256 A6
Charnhill Way PL9 256 A6
Charnley Ave EX4 176 E5
Charter Cl EX16 161 B4
Charton Cross DT7 104 A2
Chartwell Cl TQ3 225 E7
Chartwell Dr TQ12 207 A4
Charwell Mdw EX5 82 F6
Chase The Honiton EX14 166 D7
Ivybridge PL21 237 D4
Chasty La EX22 164 C3
Chatham Cl EX8 202 D8
Chatsworth Gdns PL5 243 F3
Chatsworth Rd TQ1 220 B6
Chatto Rd TQ1 220 A7
Chatto Way TQ1 220 A7
Chatwell La PL21 137 B3
Chaucer Ave EX2 177 F3
Chaucer Prim Sch PL5 244 C2
Chaucer Rd PL19 171 D5
Chaucer Rise EX8 196 C3
Chaucer Way PL5 244 C1
Chawleigh Cl PL18 125 C5
Chawleigh Hill EX18 59 F8
Chawleigh Prim Sch EX18 60 B7
Chawleigh Week Cross EX18 59 E8
Chawleigh Week La EX18 59 D8
Chawleigh Week Mill Cross EX18 59 D8
Cheavestone Lea TQ9 139 E1
Checkridge La EX13 88 D2
Chedworth St PL4 263 A3
Cheeke St EX1 261 C3
Cheese La EX10 187 F4
Cheglinch Cnr EX34 8 F5
Cheglinch La EX34 8 F6
Cheldon Cross
Chawleigh EX18 60 D8
Chulmleigh EX18 45 D2
Chelfham Mill Sch EX32 17 C6
Chelfham Sch PL20 125 C3
Chelmer Cl PL7 251 A5
Chelmsford Pl PL5 244 C4
Chelmsford Rd EX4 176 E6
Chelsea Pl 8 TQ14 210 B5
Chelson Gdns PL6 245 E3
Chelson La EX10 101 E1
Chelston Rd
Newton Abbot TQ12 207 B4
Torquay TQ2 219 E3
Chelston Terr TA21 52 D8
Cheltenham Cl EX4 176 E7
Cheltenham Pl PL4 263 B4
Chene Ct PL21 137 B2
Cheney's La EX14 166 E8
Chepstow Ave PL6 245 C8
Chepstow Cl EX2 182 B8
Chequers Haigh PL8 140 F6
Chercombe Bridge Rd TQ12 206 C3
Chercombe Cl TQ12 206 E4
Chercombe Valley Rd TQ12 206 E4
Cheriswood Ave EX8 196 D1
Cheriswood Cl EX8 196 D1
Cheriton Bishop Com Prim Sch EX6 97 B4
Cheriton Cl PL5 244 A3
Cheriton Cross
Cadbury EX5 81 C8
Cheriton Fitzpaine EX17 80 D7
Cheriton Fitzpaine Prim Sch EX17 62 E1
Cheriton Hill EX35 5 D3
Cheriton Mill Cross EX17 62 E2
Cheriton Rd EX35 151 D1
Cherry Arbour EX32 155 C3
Cherry Brook Dr TQ4 229 B8
Cherry Brook Wlk TQ4 226 B1
Cherry Cl
Cheriton Fitzpaine EX17 62 F1
Exmouth EX8 196 C3
5 Honiton EX14 85 C2
Tiverton EX16 161 D5
Willand EX15 162 D4
Cherry Cross TQ9 223 C4
Cherry Dr EX12 192 A5
Cherry Gdns
Crediton EX17 165 C5
Exeter EX2 178 A4
Paignton TQ3 226 A7
Cherry Gr EX32 155 C2
Cherry Mdw EX17 62 F1
Cherry Park Cl TQ2 219 D2
Cherry Pk Appledore EX39 14 F1
Plymouth PL7 251 A3
Cherry Tree Cl
Exeter EX4 173 A2
Rockbeare EX5 99 B6
Cherry Tree Dr
Brixton PL8 257 A5
3 Landkey EX32 17 B2
Cherry Tree Gdns EX16 161 E5
Cherry Tree La PL7 251 A4
Cherrybridge Cross EX35 151 A2
Cherryford La EX31 4 C4
Cherrywood Cl TQ12 206 E4
Cheshire Dr PL6 244 D6
Cheshire Rd EX8 196 E2
Chesil Ct DT7 260 C3
Chester Cl EX4 176 E7
Chester Ct EX8 201 F7
Chester Pl 3 PL4 248 E4
Chester Terr 17 EX32 155 A4
Chesterfield Rd PL3 249 B4
Chestermoor Cross EX20 92 D5
Chesterton Cl PL5 244 C3
Chestnut Ave
Cullompton EX15 163 C2
Dartmouth TQ6 233 E4
Exeter EX2 178 A3
Plymouth PL9 255 C5
Torquay TQ2 219 F4
Chestnut Cl
Braunton EX33 152 E6
Cheriton Bishop EX6 97 B4
Crediton EX17 165 D6
Exmouth EX8 196 C3
Lamerton PL19 116 E4
Saltash PL12 242 D4
Seaton EX12 192 A7
Tavistock PL19 171 D2
Torpoint PL11 246 F3
Wellington TA21 160 E5
Chestnut Cres EX5 173 F8
Chestnut Ct EX2 181 B8
Chestnut Dr
Bideford EX39 25 D4
Brixham TQ5 230 A2
Kingsteignton TQ12 207 F6
Newton Abbot TQ12 208 A1
Willand EX15 162 C4
Chestnut Pk TQ7 149 D7
Chestnut Rd
Plymouth PL3 248 D7
Tiverton EX16 161 F5
Chestnut Terr PL19 116 E3
Chestnut View EX13 87 D6
Chestnut Way
Honiton EX14 166 A4
Newton Poppleford EX10 186 F8
Chestnut Wlk EX7 204 C5
Chestnuts The EX5 99 D2
Cheston Cross TQ10 134 E1
Chestwood Ave EX31 154 C3
Chestwood Cl EX31 154 D4
Cheyne Rise EX4 174 D2
Cheynegate La EX4 174 C3
Cheyney Cross EX36 30 B2
Cheyney La EX36 30 B2
Chibbet Hill TA24 21 B8
Chibbet Post TA24 21 C8
Chichacott Cross EX20 170 F7
Chichacott Rd EX20 170 D7
Chichester Cl
Barnstaple EX32 155 B2
Exmouth EX8 202 C8
Ilfracombe EX34 150 A4
11 Instow EX39 15 B1
Chichester Cres
Barnstaple EX32 155 B2
Saltash PL12 242 E1
Chichester Ct
Barnstaple EX32 155 C5
Galmpton TQ7 147 B7
Horrabridge PL20 126 F4
Chichester Ho
Exeter EX2 178 B5
Plymouth PL1 262 B2
Chichester Mews EX1 261 B3
Chichester Pk EX34 8 A6
Chichester Pl 7 EX16 64 D7
Chichester Rd EX32 155 B2
Chichester Way
East Budleigh EX9 198 B6
Newton Abbot TQ12 207 F3
Westward Ho! EX39 156 C6
Chideock Ct DT7 260 C3
Chilbridge La EX31 17 B8
Chilcombe Cross EX24 102 B7
Chilcombe La EX24 102 A6
Chilcote Cl TQ1 220 C8
Chilcott Cl 5 EX16 64 D7
Chilcott Cross TA22 33 A7
Chilcott La TA22 33 A7
Childrey Gdns PL6 245 C1
Childrey Wlk PL6 245 C1
Chill Pits La EX13 88 B8
Chilla Chapel EX21 73 E4
Chilla Rd EX21 73 E3
Chillaton Cross TQ7 138 A1
Chillpark EX31 153 D5
Chiltern Cl TQ2 219 D3
Chiltern Cross EX16 34 B2
Chilton Ave TQ14 210 C6
Chilton Cl PL6 249 B7
Chilton Gate EX16 81 D8
Chilton La EX17 80 E7
Chilverton Cross EX17 59 F1
Chilverton Hill Gate EX17 59 F1
Chilverton La EX17 59 F1
Chineway Gdns EX11 169 F3
Chineway Head EX11 101 B6
Chineway Hill EX11 101 A6
Chineway Rd EX11 100 F6
Chingswell St 2 EX39 157 A2
Chinkwell Rise TQ2 219 B8
Chinon Pl EX16 161 A6
Chinston Cl EX14 85 B4
Chipmunk Wlk EX32 155 B6
Chipple Pk PL21 133 B2
Chircombe La EX39 157 A4
Chiseldon Farm TQ5 230 B2
Chiseldon Hill TQ5 230 C2
Chiseldon Ho EX4 173 A1
Chittleburn Cross PL8 256 E5
Chittleburn Hill PL8 256 E5
Chittlehampton CE Prim Sch EX37 28 F4
Chivelstone Cross TQ7 149 A5
Chivenor Ave PL5 243 D4
Chivenor Cross EX31 15 E5
Chiverstone La EX6 194 C4
Chiverstone Rd EX6 194 C4
Chockenhole La EX9 199 A8
Chockland Rd 12 TQ12 123 E1
Cholhouse La EX20 77 C7
Chollacott Cl PL19 171 C4
Chollacott La PL19 171 D3
Chollaton Cross EX22 39 E1
Cholloway's Cross EX37 44 A7
Cholwell Cross TQ9 222 F4
Chope Rd EX39 156 F6
Chopes Cl EX39 26 A4
Chough Cl PL15 105 A2
Christ Cross EX5 82 C8
Christcross La EX5 82 D7
Christian Mill Bsns Pk PL6 244 E4
Christina Par TQ9 223 F5
Christina Pk TQ9 223 E5
Christone Cross TQ9 138 D7
Christow Prim Sch EX6 113 B4
Christow Rd EX2 177 B2
Chrystel Cl EX10 100 D2
Chubb Dr PL3 248 B4
Chubb Rd EX39 26 A4
Chubs Cross EX20 77 F5
Chubworthy Cross TA4 35 D5
Chudleigh Ave EX39 157 B1
Chudleigh CE Com Prim Sch TQ13 123 E6
Chudleigh Knighton CE Prim Sch TQ13 123 C4
Chudleigh Rd
2 Bideford EX39 157 B1
Exeter EX2 181 B7
Kingsteignton TQ12 207 D8
Plymouth PL4 249 A4
Chudleigh Terr 6 EX39 157 B1
Chudley Cl EX8 196 D1
Chuggaton Cross EX37 28 C5
Chuley Cross TQ13 130 F3
Chuley Hill TQ13 130 F4
Chuley Rd TQ13 130 F4
Chulmleigh Hill EX18 44 E1
Chulmleigh Prim Sch EX18 44 E1
Chulmleigh Rd
Morchard Bishop EX17 61 A2
Winkleigh EX19 58 F3
Church Ave EX20 170 A5
Church Cl
Ashprington TQ9 139 F8
Aylesbeare EX5 99 D2
Bratton Fleming EX31 18 A8
Broadclyst EX5 175 C7
Chulmleigh EX18 44 E1
Dartmouth TQ6 233 F3
Dolton EX19 57 F6
Goodleigh EX32 17 B5
Kingsbridge TQ7 258 D5
Lapford EX17 60 D3
Plymouth PL7 250 B7
Totnes TQ9 223 C5
Witheridge EX16 62 B5
Yealmpton PL8 257 F4
Church Cross
Buckfastleigh TQ11 236 B6
Cheriton Fitzpaine EX17 62 E1
Exeter EX4 174 D3
Filleigh EX32 29 C6
Sandford EX17 80 A5
Church Cross Rd TQ11 236 B6
Church Ct
Kingsteignton TQ12 207 E6
14 Newton Abbot TQ12 207 B3

Church Dr TA21 52 F7
Church End Rd TQ12 212 F4
Church Farm TQ7 143 A1
Church Fields TA21 160 E6
Church Flats EX6 201 B8
Church Gr EX32 155 B3
Church Hill
Awliscombe EX14 85 B4
Beer EX12 191 D5
Blackawton TQ9 139 E1
Brendon EX35 5 F4
Buckfastleigh TQ11 236 C6
Calstock PL18 125 D3
Exeter EX4 174 E2
Fremington EX31 153 E5
Holbeton PL8 136 D1
Honiton EX14 166 D5
Ilfracombe EX34 150 A5
Kingswear TQ6 234 A2
Lynton EX35 151 C5
Marldon TQ3 218 D4
Milton Combe PL20 126 C1
Musbury EX13 103 D5
Otterton EX9 198 D7
Plymouth PL6 245 B1
Tavistock PL19 171 E2
Tedburn St Mary EX6 97 F5
Winkleigh EX19 58 F3
Church Hill Cl TQ9 139 E2
Church Hill Cotts TQ9 131 E1
Church Hill Cross EX20 94 E7
Church Hill E 6 TQ5 230 C5
Church Hill La EX33 8 D1
Church Hill Rd PL9 255 A6
Church Hill W 5 TQ5 230 C5
Church House Cl 8 TQ13 123 C4
Church La Alfington EX11 84 F1
10 Barnstaple EX31 154 F5
Bideford EX39 25 E2
Bittaford PL21 137 C8
Bridford EX6 112 F5
Broadclyst EX5 175 C7
Calstock PL18 125 D3
Cargreen PL12 239 A1
Christow EX6 113 B3
Clyst St Mary EX5 179 B2
Crediton EX17 165 D5
Dulverton TA22 33 D6
East Budleigh EX9 198 B6
Exeter, Heavitree EX2 177 F5
Exeter, Pinhoe EX4 174 D2
Feniton EX14 84 E2
Frithelstockstone EX38 40 F5
Great Torrington EX38 159 C5
Hatherleigh EX20 75 C7
Holsworthy EX22 164 C4
Kentisbeare EX14 66 F3
Kingsbridge TQ7 258 F2
Langtree EX38 40 F2
Membury EX13 87 D5
Modbury PL21 137 B2
Parracombe EX31 4 D1
Salcombe TQ8 259 E5
Shobrooke EX17 80 E4
St John PL11 252 B8
Stokeinteignhead TQ12 209 B2
Swimbridge EX32 28 E8
Tavistock PL19 171 C5
Torquay TQ2 219 F5
Whitestone EX4 98 E4
Winkleigh EX19 58 F3
Yealmpton PL8 257 F4
Church Lake 8 EX32 17 B2
Church Lane Head TQ13 121 B2
Church Lea PL19 171 E2
Church Mdw
High Bickington EX37 43 B7
Ivybridge PL21 237 A4
Landkey EX32 17 B2
Church Mdws
Bratton Clovelly EX20 92 A2
Okehampton EX20 170 A5
Church Mead EX14 85 B1
Church Mews TQ12 207 E6
Church Park Cl TQ9 138 C7
Church Park Ct PL6 245 E8
Church Park Rd
Newton Ferrers PL8 141 A7
Plymouth PL6 245 E8
Yealmpton PL8 136 A2
Church Parks EX17 80 A5
Church Path
Ashburton TQ13 130 F4
Barnstaple EX31 154 F7
Halberton EX16 65 A7
Okehampton EX20 170 A5
6 Paignton TQ3 226 B6
Shute EX13 102 F8
Church Path Rd EX2 176 F3
Church Pk Bideford EX39 25 A3
Cornwood PL21 133 C2
Horrabridge PL20 126 F4
Kingston TQ7 142 C6
Newton Ferrers PL8 141 A7
Paignton TQ4 225 D4
Church Pool EX34 8 F5
Church Quillet TQ9 139 E1
Church Rd
Bishopsteignton TQ14 209 A7
Bovey Tracey TQ13 123 B7
Churchinford TA3 68 C8
Cockwood EX6 201 A6
Colaton Raleigh EX10 186 E3
Church Rd *continued*
Dartmouth TQ6 233 E3
Exeter, Alphington EX2 177 B1
Exeter, St Thomas EX2 177 A4
Exmouth EX8 202 A7
Georgeham EX33 8 A2
Highampton EX21 74 C7
Ideford TQ13 124 B4
Ilfracombe EX34 150 A5
Kenton EX6 194 F5
Luton TQ13 124 C4
Lympstone EX8 195 E5
Newton Abbot TQ12 207 C2
Plymouth, Plympton PL7 250 F4
Plymouth, Plymstock PL9 255 F7
Saltash PL12 242 D2
Silverton EX5 82 B5
Stoke Fleming TQ6 146 B7
Torquay, Barton TQ2 214 A3
Torquay, St Marychurch TQ1 220 B8
Wembury PL9 140 D8
Whimple EX5 99 E7
Church Row La PL5 244 C6
Church Side EX5 179 D7
Church St
Axminster EX13 167 D5
Axmouth EX12 192 D7
Bradninch EX5 83 A7
Braunton EX33 152 D7
4 Brixham TQ5 230 C5
Buckfastleigh TQ11 236 B5
Calstock PL18 125 D3
Colyton EX24 103 A5
Combe Martin EX34 3 A3
Crediton EX17 165 D5
Cullompton EX15 163 C3
Dawlish EX7 204 C6
Dolton EX19 57 F7
Ermington PL21 136 F4
Exeter EX2 177 F5
Exmouth EX8 202 A6
3 Honiton EX14 166 C6
Ilfracombe EX34 150 B5
Kenton EX6 194 D3
Kingsbridge TQ7 258 D5
Kingsteignton TQ12 207 E6
Lyme Regis DT7 260 E3
Modbury PL21 137 B2
Morchard Bishop EX17 61 B2
Okehampton EX20 170 B5
Paignton TQ3 226 B6
Plymouth PL3 248 A4
Salcombe TQ8 259 E5
Sandford EX17 80 A5
Sidbury EX10 101 C2
8 Sidford EX10 101 B1
Sidmouth EX10 188 B3
13 South Brent TQ10 134 F3
South Molton EX36 158 C4
Starcross EX6 201 B8
Tiverton EX16 161 C4
Torquay TQ2 219 F5
Uplyme DT7 260 B5
Witheridge EX16 46 E1
Church St Mews 4 TQ3 226 B6
Church Steps Cotts EX5 184 B3
Church Stile EX6 182 B4
Church Terr
7 Bampton EX16 34 B1
Exeter EX2 177 F5
Church View
Bideford EX39 26 A1
5 Chudleigh TQ13 123 E6
Dawlish EX7 204 C6
Kingsteignton TQ12 207 E6
Ottery St Mary EX11 169 D3
Sutcombe EX22 54 A6
Walkhampton PL20 127 B4
Church Way
Newton Abbot TQ12 207 E1
Plymouth PL5 247 E8
Yealmpton PL8 257 F4
Church Ways EX20 95 B5
Church Wlk
Avonwick TQ10 135 B1
6 Bideford EX39 157 A1
Stoke Gabriel TQ9 227 F7
Wembury PL9 140 C8
Churchfield Rd 26 EX39 15 A1
Churchfields TA21 160 D7
Churchfields Dr TQ13 180 D7
Churchfields Gdns TQ6 233 D3
Churchfields W TQ6 233 D3
Churchford Rd EX33 8 D1
Churchgate EX36 30 E1
Churchill EX34 8 F4
Churchill Ave EX7 204 D5
Churchill Cl
Barnstaple EX32 155 B6
Kenton EX6 194 D3
Churchill Cotts PL21 137 D6
Churchill Cres EX36 158 C3
Churchill Ct
7 Brixham TQ5 230 C4
Lympstone EX8 195 E6
Churchill Dr
Crediton EX17 165 B6
Teignmouth TQ14 210 C6
Churchill Gdns EX17 78 C7
Churchill Hill EX31 10 C4
Churchill La
Axminster EX13 88 A5
Calverleigh EX16 48 C3
Chipstable TA4 35 C5
Churchill Rd
Bideford EX39 26 A4
Exeter EX2 176 F4
Churchill Rd *continued*
Exmouth EX8 196 D2
Tavistock PL19 171 D2
Tiverton EX16 161 A4
Churchill Way
Appledore EX39 14 F1
Northam EX39 157 A7
Plymouth PL3 248 E6
Churchill Wlk PL12 242 E1
Churchills 11 EX15 67 B8
Churchills The TQ12 207 A4
Churchlands EX17 78 C4
Churchlands Cl PL6 245 E7
Churchlands Rd PL6 245 E8
Churchstanton Prim Sch TA3 68 B8
Churchstow Wlk PL6 249 E8
Churchtown Cl PL21 133 C2
Churchtown Vale PL12 242 D1
Churchward Rd TQ3 226 B7
Churchwater La EX18 58 D8
Churchway TQ1 220 C7
Churchwood Ct TQ1 220 C5
Churchyard La EX17 61 C7
Churscombe Gn TQ3 218 E2
Churscombe Pk TQ3 218 D2
Churscombe Rd TQ3 218 D2
Churston Broadway TQ4 229 B7
Churston Cl TQ5 229 C5
Churston Cross
Churston Ferrers TQ5 229 E4
West Putford EX22 39 B2
Churston Ferrers Gram Sch TQ5 229 C5
Churston Rd TQ5 229 E5
Churston Rise EX12 191 F8
Churston Sta TQ5 229 C5
Churston Way TQ5 230 B4
Chute St EX1 261 C4
Cider Press Craft Ctr* TQ9 215 F1
Cinders La TQ6 146 B7
Cintra Terr EX39 157 A4
Cistern St TQ9 223 B5
Citadel Ope 13 PL1 263 A2
Citadel Rd PL1 262 C2
Citadel Rd E PL1 263 A2
Citadel The* PL1 263 A1
City Arc EX4 261 A2
City Bsns Pk PL3 248 A4
City Ind Est EX2 261 B1
City Mus & Art Gal* PL4 263 A3
City Mus & Art Gal Annexe* PL4 263 A3
Claddon La TQ1,TQ2 214 A5
Clampet La 9 TQ14 210 C4
Clampits Stile TQ11 135 C6
Clampitt Cl TQ12 211 D1
Clampitt Rd TQ12 211 D2
Clampitts EX15 163 B2
Clanage Cross TQ14 124 C1
Clanage St TQ14 208 F8
Clannaborough Cross EX17 78 E5
Claponmill Cross EX5 83 B2
Clapp's La Beer EX12 191 D5
Seaton EX12 192 B5
Clappentail La DT7 260 C3
Clappentail Pk DT7 260 C3
Clapper Cross
Bondleigh EX20 77 B8
Zeal Monachorum EX17 78 B5
Clapper La EX14 166 C7
Clapperbrook La EX2 177 B1
Clapworthy Cider Mill* EX36 29 D2
Clapworthy Cross EX36 29 D2
Clara Pl EX3 182 E5
Clare Dr EX16 161 F6
Clare Pl PL4 263 B2
Clare St PL21 237 C4
Claredale Rd EX8 202 B6
Claremont Ave TQ12 213 A4
Claremont Field EX11 169 D3
Claremont Gr Exeter EX2 261 C1
Exmouth EX8 202 B7
Claremont La EX8 202 C7
Claremont Pl EX20 75 C7
Claremont St PL1 262 C4
Clarence Cotts 4 EX34 150 B6
Clarence Ct PL1 262 A3
Clarence Hill TQ6 233 F4
Clarence Ho TQ2 219 E6
Clarence Pl
14 Barnstaple EX32 155 B3
Exeter EX4 261 C4
Plymouth, Morice Town PL2 247 E4
Plymouth, Stonehouse PL1 262 A3
Clarence Rd
Budleigh Salterton EX9 198 A2
6 Exeter EX4 177 A5
Exmouth EX8 202 A7
Torpoint PL11 247 B3
Clarence St TQ6 233 F4
Clarendon Cl TQ1 219 F6
Clarendon Ct TQ1 220 C4
Clarendon Ho 1 PL1 247 F3
Clarendon Rd
Ipplepen TQ12 211 D2
10 Newton Abbot TQ12 207 B3
Claridge The TQ3 226 C8
Clarke Cl EX15 65 F7
Clarke Ctr The EX2 177 C2
Clarke Mead EX2 178 C4
Clarks Barn Rd TQ7 143 E7
Clarks La EX20 57 A6
Clatworthy La EX32 29 E6
Claude Dix Cl 1 EX31 155 A7
Claw Cross EX39 38 F5
Claw Hill EX16 62 F4
Claw Pk EX22 72 B2
Clawford Cross EX22 72 D3
Clawton Prim Sch EX21 72 B1
Clay La
Chudleigh Knighton TQ13 123 C3
Colyton EX24 103 A4
Copplestone EX17 79 A6
Dartington TQ9 223 A8
Lympstone EX8 195 E4
Teignmouth TQ14 210 B5
Uffculme EX15 66 A8
Clay Park Terr TQ9 228 A7
Clayford La TA22 33 C5
Clayford Rd TA22 33 C5
Clayhidon Crossway EX15 52 E2
Clayland Cross TQ4 225 E4
Claylands Dr TQ4 225 F4
Claylands View EX14 166 B4
Claymans Pathway PL21 237 A6
Claypark Hill EX16 47 D5
Claypits Covert Cross EX31 154 A2
Clayton Pl PL4 249 B2
Clayton Rd Exeter EX4 177 A7
Plymouth PL4 249 B2
Clear View PL12 242 E3
Clearbrook Ave PL5 243 E1
Cleave Cl
Barnstaple EX31 154 D4
Tedburn St Mary EX6 97 F4
Cleave Cross EX14 86 C3
Cleave Hill Dolton EX19 57 E6
South Molton EX36 46 A6
Cleave La
Bishop's Tawton EX32 27 F7
Burrington EX37 44 A2
Chapelton EX32 28 A7
Wilmington EX14 86 C3
Cleave Lane End EX32 27 F7
Cleave Pk EX31 153 F5
Cleave Rd EX31 154 D4
Cleave The PL10 253 B2
Cleaveanger La EX17 60 B1
Cleaveland Rise TQ12 206 F1
Cleaves Cl EX5 81 E5
Cleavewood Dr EX39 157 D1
Cleeve Dr PL21 237 B5
Cleeve Gdns PL2 248 A8
Cleeve The EX15 66 E8
Clegg Ave PL11 246 E3
Clement Rd PL7 251 B5
Clement's La EX32 28 B8
Clennon Ave TQ4 226 B4
Clennon Ct
5 Brixham TQ5 230 C3
Torquay TQ2 214 A2
Clennon Dr TQ4 226 B4
Clennon Gdns TQ4 226 B4
Clennon Hts TQ4 226 B4
Clennon La TQ2 214 A2
Clennon Pk TQ4 226 B4
Clennon Rise TQ4 226 B4
Clennon Summit TQ4 226 B4
Clerk Cl EX8 196 C2
Cleve Rd EX4 176 F6
Clevedon Cl EX4 173 D1
Clevedon Park Ave PL2 248 B6
Clevedon Pk EX10 188 C5
Cleveland Ct Exeter EX1 261 C4
Paignton TQ4 226 C5
Cleveland Dr TQ7 142 E3
Cleveland Gdns EX1 261 C4
Cleveland Pl
8 Dawlish EX7 204 E6
Exmouth EX8 201 F6
Cleveland Rd
Paignton TQ4 226 C5
Plymouth PL4 263 C3
Torquay TQ2 219 F6
Cleveland St 7 EX4 177 A5
Cleveland Terr EX39 156 C7
Clevelands Pk EX39 157 A6
Cleverdon Cross EX22 53 F8
Cleverhayes La EX14 86 B4
Cliff Bastin Cl EX2 178 C4
Cliff Ct 19 EX7 204 E6
Cliff Ho TQ4 226 D5
Cliff La PL10 252 A4
Cliff Park Ave TQ4 226 C3
Cliff Park Ct TQ4 226 C3
Cliff Park Rd TQ4 226 C2
Cliff Rd
Budleigh Salterton EX9 199 G2
Paignton TQ4 226 D5
Plymouth PL1 262 B1
Salcombe TQ8 259 C3
Sidmouth EX10 188 C3
Teignmouth TQ14 210 D7
Torquay TQ2 219 E2
Wembury PL9 140 D7
Cliff Terr EX9 199 G2
Cliffden Cl TQ14 210 C5
Clifford Ave TQ12 123 E1
Clifford Cl
13 Chudleigh TQ13 123 E6
Exeter EX1 178 B7
Kingsteignton TQ12 207 E7
Plymouth PL5 243 E2
Teignmouth TQ14 210 A3
Clifford Cross EX6 112 C8
Clifford Dr TQ12 180 F2
Clifford Gdns EX17 165 D5
Clifford Mews TA21 160 E6
Clifford Rd EX4 177 F8
Clifford St
14 Chudleigh TQ13 123 E6
Kingsteignton TQ12 207 E7
Clifford Terr TA21 160 E6
Cliffside Rd TQ1 220 C8
Clifton Ave PL7 250 E7
Clifton Bank 3 TQ3 226 A6
Clifton Cl Paignton TQ3 225 F6
Plymouth PL7 250 E7
Clifton Cres TQ3 226 A6
Clifton Ct 3 EX34 150 B5
Clifton Gdns TQ3 226 A6
Clifton Gr TQ3 226 A6
Clifton Hill EX1 177 E7
Clifton Ho 17 TQ14 210 C5
Clifton La EX31 10 B4
Clifton Pl Dawlish EX7 204 C6
Plymouth PL4 263 A4
Salcombe TQ8 259 E5
Clifton Rd Exeter EX1 261 C3
Paignton TQ3 226 A6
Clifton Rise TQ3 226 A6
Clifton St
Barnstaple EX31 154 F4
Bideford EX39 157 B1
Exeter EX1 177 E6
Plymouth PL4 263 A4
Clifton Terr
Barnstaple EX31 154 E4
11 South Brent TQ10 134 F3
Climsland Rd TQ4 226 A5
Clinton Ave Exeter EX4 177 E8
Plymouth PL4 249 A4
Clinton CE Prim Sch The EX20 57 A6
Clinton Cl EX9 197 F2
Clinton Gdns EX20 57 A7
Clinton Rd EX32 155 B3
Clinton Rise EX12 191 E6
Clinton Sq EX8 201 F6
Clinton St EX4 177 A5
Clinton Terr
10 Barnstaple EX32 155 B3
Budleigh Salterton EX9 198 A2
Great Torrington EX38 159 B5
Merton EX20 57 A7
Millbrook PL10 252 F6
Clipper Quay EX2 261 B1
Clipper Wharf EX8 201 E6
Cliston Ave EX8 196 E2
Cliston Cross TQ9 139 C2
Cliston La EX20 76 E4
Clittaford Rd PL6 244 F7
Clittaford View PL6 244 E7
Cliveden Rd EX39 26 A4
Cloake Pl PL12 239 A2
Clobells 3 TQ10 134 F2
Cloggshill Cross EX31 27 B1
Cloister Rd EX4 177 F7
Clonway 1 PL20 126 F3
Close The
14 Bere Alston PL20 125 E1
Brixham TQ5 230 C6
Holcombe EX7 210 F8
Paignton TQ4 229 C8
Rewe EX5 82 A2
Saltash PL12 242 C3
Seaton EX12 192 A5
Tiverton EX16 161 F6
Cloutman's La EX33 7 E2
Clovelly Apmts 13 EX34 150 B5
Clovelly Cl EX39 156 E1
Clovelly Cross EX39 23 D2
Clovelly Gdns N EX39 156 E1
Clovelly Gdns S 2 EX39 156 F1
Clovelly Prim Sch EX39 23 D3
Clovelly Rd Bideford EX39 25 D4
Plymouth PL4 263 C1
Clovelly Rise
Dawlish EX7 204 D5
Paignton TQ3 225 E6
Clovelly View PL9 255 A7
Clover Dr EX15 163 B2
Clover Rise PL6 245 E8
Clover Way EX32 155 E4
Clover Wlk PL12 242 C3
Cloverdale Ct DT7 260 E3
Clowance Cl PL1 247 F1
Clowance La PL1 247 E1
Clowance St PL1 247 F1
Cluden Cl EX2 181 B8
Cluden Rd EX39 156 F6
Clumpit La EX6 194 A4
Clyde St PL2 247 F5
Clydesdale Rd EX4 173 A1
Clyst Ave Brixham TQ5 230 A2
Clyst Honiton EX5 175 E2
Clyst Halt Ave EX2 178 E3
Clyst Heath EX2 178 D3
Clyst Honiton CE Prim Sch EX5 179 D7
Clyst Rd Exeter EX3 178 F2
Topsham EX3 182 F7
Clyst St Mary Prim Sch EX5 179 A2
Clyst Units EX2 177 D1
Clyst Vale Com Coll EX5 175 D5
Clyst Valley Rd EX5 179 B2
Clyst William Cross EX15 84 B5
Clyston Hydon Prim Sch EX15 83 D4
Coach Dr EX39 25 F4
Coach Ho The TQ3 226 C7
Coach House Mews PL9 256 B6

Coach Pl TQ12 ....207 C2
Coach Rd
Newton Abbot TQ12 .....207 B1
Noss Mayo PL8 ....140 F6
Silverton EX5 ....82 B6
Coach Rd The DT7 .....260 B8
Coarsewell Cross PL21 .138 A5
Coastguard Cotts
Bigbury-on-Sea TQ7 .....142 D4
Dawlish EX7 ....204 F6
Down Thomas PL9 ....254 F2
Galmpton TQ7 ....147 B6
Stoke EX39 ....22 B3
Torquay TQ1 ....220 D2
Coastguard Hill EX9 ...199 H2
Coastguard Rd EX9 ....198 B1
Coates Rd EX2 ....178 B5
Cob Castle TA21 ....52 D8
Cob Mdw EX20 ....75 C7
Cobb La PL9 ....255 F6
Cobb Rd DT7 ....260 D2
Cobb Terr DT7 ....260 D2
Cobb The★ DT7 ....260 D2
Cobbacombe Cross EX16 49 D6
Cobbaton Combat Collection Mus★ EX37 ....28 D5
Cobbaton Cross EX37 ...28 D6
Cobbett Rd PL5 ....244 B2
Coblands Cross EX5 .....82 A7
Cobley La Bideford EX39 ..26 C6
Lapford EX17 ....60 E4
West Worlington EX17 .....60 F6
Cobourg St PL1 ....262 C3
Coburg Cl TA21 ....52 F7
Coburg Pl EX15 ....163 C6
Coburg Rd EX10 ....188 A3
Coburg Terr EX10 ......188 A3
Cockeram's Rd EX5 .....99 C8
Cockhaven Cl TQ14 .....208 F7
Cockhaven Rd TQ14 ....208 F7
Cockington Cl PL6 .....245 E1
Cockington Country Pk★ TQ2 ....219 B4
Cockington La
Paignton TQ3 ....219 C1
Torquay TQ2 ....219 D4
Cockington Prim Sch TQ2 ....219 F5
Cockington Rd TQ3 ....219 A3
Cockington Wlk PL6 ...245 C1
Cockland Hill TA21 ......51 C8
Cockland La EX16 ....48 F3
Cockles La [2] EX17 ....165 D5
Cockles Rise EX17 .....165 D5
Cockpit Hill EX15 ......163 C3
Cockram's La EX37 ......43 F7
Cockrams Butt Cross EX37 ....29 B1
Cocks Pk PL21 ....142 D7
Cockspark La EX14 ......84 F8
Cocktree Throat EX20 ...95 C8
Cockwood Prim Sch EX6 ....201 B6
Codden Cross EX32 .....28 A8
Codden Hill Cross EX32 .27 E8
Coddiford Cross EX17 ...62 E2
Coddiford Hill EX17 .....62 E1
Coddiford La EX17 ......62 F2
Codrington St EX1 .....261 C3
Coffins La EX6 ....181 F4
Coffinswell La TQ12 ...213 A4
Coffintree Cross EX17 ...80 F6
Coffintree Hill EX17 .....80 F7
Cofton Hill EX6 ....201 A5
Cofton La EX6 ....200 F5
Cofton Rd EX2 ....177 D1
Coil Cross EX31 ....10 B6
Coker Ave TQ2 ....214 A4
Cokers Elm EX14 ....87 A7
Cokers Elm Cross EX14 ..87 A7
Colands Ct EX2 ....181 A8
Colaton La EX5 ....81 E5
Colaton Terr EX10 ......188 A4
Colborne Rd PL6 ....245 A2
Colcombe La
Dalwood EX13 ....86 F1
Shute EX13 ....102 F8
Colcombe Rd EX24 .....103 A5
Cold East Cross TQ13 ...121 E1
Coldharbour
Bideford EX39 ....157 A2
[3] Totnes TQ9 ....223 E5
Uffculme EX15 ....66 A7
Coldharbour Cross
Chilsworthy EX22 ....53 E1
Loddiswell PL21 ....138 B3
Coldharbour Rd EX16 ..161 A3
Coldrenick St PL5 ......243 D1
Coldwell La EX12 ......192 D6
Coldwelles Cl EX31 .....153 E5
Cole La Ivybridge PL21 ..237 E6
Ivybridge, Higher Keaton PL21 ....237 C1
Cole Moore Mdw PL19 .171 B6
Cole's Cnr EX18 ....59 C8
Cole's Cotts PL7 ....250 E6
Cole's Cross TQ9 ......144 F5
Cole's Ct TQ6 ....233 F3
Cole's La TQ12 ....212 F5
Colebrook La PL7 ......250 E7
Colebrook Rd
Plymouth, Plympton PL7 ..250 E6
Plymouth, St Budeaux PL5 243 D1
Colebrooke La EX15 .....65 A1
Coleford Hill EX16 ......48 B6
Coleman Ave TQ14 .....210 A5
Coleman Dr PL9 ....255 F4
Coleman's Cross EX24 .102 D6
Colemans Cross PL15 ..105 B5
Coleridge Ave PL6 .....244 F2
Coleridge Cl EX8 ......196 C4
Coleridge Ct TQ2 ......214 A2
Coleridge La TQ7 ......145 A2
Coleridge Rd Exeter EX2 176 F4
Ottery St Mary EX11 .....169 F4
Plymouth PL4 ....249 A4
[8] Tiverton EX16 ....64 D7
Coles Mead EX16 ......161 F4
Coles Mill Cl EX22 .....164 C4
Coles's La EX13 ....104 B8
Colesdown Hill PL9 ....250 B1
Colesworthy Cross TQ12 ....180 B2
Colhayne La
Dalwood EX13 ....86 F1
Shute EX13 ....102 F8
Colin Campbell Ct [10] PL1 ....262 B3
Colin Rd TQ3 ....226 C7
Coll Ct EX15 ....66 A7
Coll of St Mark & St John PL6 ....245 C4
Collabear Cnr EX31 .....27 D8
Collabridge Hill EX6 ...112 E8
Collabridge La EX6 ....112 E8
Collabridge Rd EX6 ....112 E8
Collacombe Cross PL19 116 D4
Collacott Cross EX38 ....40 F2
Collacotts La EX19 ......59 B2
Collaford Cl PL7 ....251 A4
Collapark TQ9 ....223 B6
Collard La PL7 ....132 D4
Collaton Cross
Halwell TQ9 ....139 D4
Malborough TQ7 ....147 F6
Yealmpton PL8 ....141 B8
Collaton Ct TQ2 ....219 C8
Collaton Ho [7] TQ1 .....220 D4
Collaton La PL19 ....117 F2
Collaton Rd
Malborough TQ7 ....147 F6
Torquay TQ2 ....219 C8
Collaton St Mary CE Prim Sch TQ3 ....225 C5
Collatons Wlk EX17 .....78 C4
College TQ13 ....180 E8
College Ave Exeter EX2 .261 C2
Plymouth PL3 ....248 E5
Tavistock PL19 ....171 D6
College Cl EX39 ....156 C6
College Ct
Barnstaple EX31 ....154 D3
[1] Torquay TQ1 ....219 F6
College Dean Cl PL6 ...245 C5
College Gn Bideford EX39 156 F2
Uffculme EX15 ....66 A7
College La
Clyst Hydon EX5,EX15 .....83 B5
Ide EX2 ....176 C2
Plymouth PL4 ....248 F4
College Park Pl PL3 ...248 E5
College Rd
Cullompton EX15 ....163 C4
Exeter EX1 ....261 C3
Newton Abbot TQ12 .....207 C2
Plymouth PL2 ....247 E5
Shebbear EX21 ....55 F4
College Road Prim Sch PL2 ....247 E5
College The EX11 ......169 D4
College View PL3 ......248 E4
College Way TQ6 ......233 E4
Collerton Ct [9] EX2 ....261 B2
Colleton Cl EX8 ....202 C8
Colleton Cres EX2 .....261 B2
Colleton Gate EX18 .....44 C1
Colleton Gr EX2 ....261 B1
Colleton Hill EX2 ......261 B1
Colleton Mews EX2 ....261 B1
Colleton Row EX2 .....261 B1
Colleton Way EX8 .....202 C8
Collett Way TQ12 ......207 E3
Colley Cres TQ3 ....226 A6
Colley End Pk TQ3 .....226 A6
Colley End Rd TQ3 .....226 A6
Colley La EX7,TQ13 ....124 D5
Colley Lane Cross TQ13 124 D4
Colley Park Rd EX33 ...152 D5
Colleybrook Cl [1] TQ12 .123 E1
Colliepriest View EX16 .161 B1
Colliers Cl [5] PL9 ....140 D8
Collin Cl PL5 ....243 D1
Collingsdown Cross EX39 39 F4
Collingwood Ave PL4 ..263 C2
Collingwood Cl
Dartmouth TQ6 ....233 C3
Torquay TQ1 ....220 C2
Collingwood Rd
Dartmouth TQ6 ....233 C3
Paignton TQ4 ....226 A5
Plymouth PL1 ....248 A3
Collingwood Villas [5] PL1 ....248 A3
Collins Pk EX9 ....198 B6
Collins Rd Exeter EX4 ..173 E2
Totnes TQ9 ....223 B6
Collipriest La EX16 .....161 C1
Collipriest Rd EX16 ....161 C2
Colliton Cross EX14 ....84 C6
Colliver Cross EX9 .....198 E5
Collyland La EX17 ......62 C3
Colmer Cross PL21 ....138 A4
Colne Gdns PL3 ....249 B5
Colscott Cross EX22 ....39 C1
Colston Cl PL6 ....245 B6
Colston Cross EX13 .....88 B4
Colston La EX16 ....47 E1
Colston Rd TQ11 ....236 E3
Coltishall Cl PL5 ....243 F4
Coltness Rd PL9 ....256 B5
Coltsfield Cl PL6 ....249 B8
Columbjohn Cross EX5 ..82 B2
Colvin Cl EX8 ....202 D7
Colway Cl DT7 ....260 D5
Colway Cross TQ14 ....124 B1
Colway La
Chudleigh TQ13 ....123 F6
Lyme Regis DT7 ....260 D4
Colwill Rd PL6 ....245 E3
Colwill Wlk PL6 ....245 F3
Colwyn Ct TQ1 ....220 E5
Colwyn Rd PL11 ....247 A3
Coly Rd Colyton EX24 ...103 B4
Honiton EX14 ....166 C4
Coly Vale EX24 ....103 A4
Colyford Rd EX12 ......192 B7
Colyton Cross EX14 .....86 C2
Colyton Gram Sch EX24 103 A3
Colyton Hill EX13,EX24 ..103 B6
Colyton Prim Sch EX24 .103 A4
Colyton Rd
Northleigh EX24 ....102 C6
Whitford EX13,EX24 ....103 A6
Combas La EX33 ....7 E2
Combe Beacon La TA20 ..69 F7
Combe Cl EX13 ....167 D5
Combe Cross
Ashburton TQ13 ....131 C5
Aveton Gifford PL21 .....143 A8
Ivybridge PL21 ....137 B6
Kingsbridge TQ7 ....258 D7
Loddiswell TQ7 ....138 C1
Shillingford EX16 ....34 D4
Strete TQ6 ....145 E7
Combe Hill EX15 ....52 C2
Combe Hill Cross TQ12 .123 F2
Combe Hill Dro TA20 ....69 F5
Combe La
Combe St Nicholas TA20 ...69 E5
Dulverton TA22 ....33 D6
East Anstey TA22 ....32 F6
Galmpton TQ5 ....229 B3
North Tawton EX17 ......77 F1
Northleigh EX24 ....102 B7
Spreyton EX17 ....95 F8
Torquay TQ2 ....214 A1
Combe Martin Cty Prim Sch EX34 ....2 F4
Combe Martin Wildlife & Dinosaur Pk★ EX34 .....3 C2
Combe Martin Wildlife Park Rly★ EX34 ....3 C2
Combe Mead Prim Sch EX16 ....161 F3
Combe Moor La EX17 ...77 F1
Combe Pafford Sch TQ2 ....214 B3
Combe Pk EX34 ....150 D5
Combe Rd
Axmouth EX12,DT7 ......193 B6
Torquay TQ2 ....214 B2
Combefishacre Cross TQ12 ....217 D8
Combefishacre La TQ9, TQ12 ....217 D6
Combehead Droveway EX13 ....86 E3
Combehead La EX13 ....86 F3
Combeland La TA22 ....34 A5
Combepark Cross TQ9 .217 A1
Comber's Cross EX31 ...27 E6
Combesdown Cross EX22 ....72 C6
Combeshead Cross
Cornwood PL21 ....133 F1
Diptford TQ9 ....138 E6
Heasley Mill EX36 ....19 C2
Combeshead La
Dunchideock EX2 ....114 A7
West Anstey EX36 ....32 A7
Combley Dr PL6 ....245 D4
Combpyne La DT7,EX13 .193 E8
Combpyne Rd EX13 ....103 D5
Combrew La EX31 ....16 A3
Combsland Cross EX36 ..31 B4
Combsland New Cross EX36 ....31 B4
Comburg Cl EX8 ....196 E3
Comepark La EX35 .....151 E2
Comer's Cross TA24 .....21 E6
Comer's Gate TA24 .....21 E6
Comers La EX34 ....3 B3
Comilla Cl EX8 ....196 C3
Commanders Cut TQ6 ..233 E4
Commercial Ope PL4 ..263 B2
Commercial Pl PL4 ....263 B1
Commercial Rd
Barnstaple EX31 ....154 F5
Calstock PL18 ....125 D3
Crediton EX17 ....165 E5
[9] Dawlish EX7 ....204 E6
Exeter EX2 ....261 A2
Horrabridge PL20 ....126 F4
Paignton TQ4 ....226 B6
Plymouth PL4 ....263 B2
Uffculme EX15 ....66 A7
Commercial St
Gunnislake PL18 ....125 D6
Plymouth PL4 ....263 B2
Commin's Rd EX1 ......177 F7
Commodore Cl EX39 ...156 E7
Common Head EX37 ....43 C3
Common Hill EX12 .....191 D4
Common La Beer EX12 ..191 D5
Common La *continued*
Huish Champflower TA4 ...35 D7
Kingskerswell TQ12 ......212 E2
Milton Combe PL6 ....241 B5
Seaton EX24 ....192 B8
Common Mews EX39 ...156 E7
Common Moors La EX36 ....158 A6
Commonmarsh La EX17 165 E5
Commons Gate EX22 ....89 E8
Commons Hill EX6 .....113 A4
Commons La TQ14 .....210 A2
Commons Old Rd
Shaldon TQ14 ....210 A2
Shaldon TQ14 ....210 A3
Community College The EX18 ....44 E1
Compass Dr PL7 ....251 A7
Compass Quay EX2 ....261 B1
Compton Ave PL3 ......249 A5
Compton Castle★ TQ3 .218 C6
Compton CE Prim Sch PL3 ....249 A6
Compton Ho TQ1 ......220 C7
Compton Knoll Cl PL3 ..249 A6
Compton Leigh PL3 ....249 A6
Compton Park Rd PL3 ..248 F5
Compton Pl TQ1 ....214 B1
Compton Rd TQ7 ......144 C1
Compton Vale PL3 .....249 A5
Comptonpool Cross TQ3 ....218 C8
Concord Dr EX32 ......155 C5
Concorde Rd EX8 ......196 F1
Condor Dr TQ2 ....213 D2
Conduit Sq [11] TQ13 ....123 E6
Coney Ave EX32 ....155 B3
Coneypark La EX34 ......3 A3
Congella Rd TQ1 ......220 C6
Congram's Cl [6] EX32 ..155 B3
Congreve Gdns PL5 ....244 C1
Conifer Cl EX15 ....163 C5
Conifer Mews EX2 .....178 D3
Conifers The TQ2 ......214 B3
Conigar Cl EX15 ....67 B8
Conigar La EX15 ....67 A7
Coniger Cross EX8 .....196 B7
Coniston Cl TQ5 ....230 A2
Coniston Gdns PL6 ....244 F4
Coniston Rd TQ12 .....211 F8
Connaught Ave PL4 ....248 F4
Connaught Cl EX10 ....188 A4
Connaught La [2] PL4 ...248 E4
Connaught Rd EX10 ....188 A4
Conniford La TQ12 .....211 D1
Connybear Cross TQ12 .213 B8
Connybear La TQ12 ....213 C7
Conqueror Dr PL5 .....244 E1
Conrad Ave EX4 ....178 B8
Conrad Rd PL5 ....244 D1
Consort Cl PL3 ....248 E7
Constable Cl PL5 ......244 D3
Constance Pl PL1 ......262 A3
Constantine Cl EX12 ...191 F8
Constantine St PL4 ....263 A3
Constitution Hill EX32 ..155 B4
Contour Hts TQ6 ......234 A3
Convent Cl
Barnstaple EX32 ....155 C2
Saltash PL12 ....242 E3
Convent Fields EX10 ...187 F4
Convent Lodge [3] TQ14 210 B6
Convent Rd EX10 ......187 F4
Conway Cres [2] TQ4 ....226 A5
Conway Ct EX1 ....261 C2
Conway Gdns PL2 .....248 B7
Conway Rd TQ4 ....226 B5
Conybeare Cl EX4 .....178 B7
Conybeare Dr EX39 ....156 E6
Conyngham Ct PL6 ....249 A8
Cooban Ct PL6 ....249 A8
Cook Ct PL12 ....242 B3
Cooke Dr TQ12 ....211 E2
Cooks Cl
[12] Ashburton TQ13 ......131 A5
Kingsteignton TQ12 .....207 F7
Cooks Cross EX36 .....158 C3
Cooks La EX13 ....104 B7
Cooks Mead DT7 ......260 A6
Cooksley Ct PL1 ....263 A1
Cookson's Rd EX6 .....201 A8
Cookworthy Ct TQ7 ...258 C6
Cookworthy Moor Forest Wlk★ EX21 ....73 B4
Cookworthy Mus★ TQ7 258 C6
Cookworthy Rd
Kingsbridge TQ7 ....258 C5
Plymouth PL2 ....247 F6
Coombe Ave TQ14 .....210 A5
Coombe Ball Hill
West Worlington EX17 ....61 C8
Witheridge EX16 ....46 D1
Coombe Cl
Bovey Tracey TQ13 ......180 E7
Dartmouth TQ6 ....233 F4
Goodleigh EX32 ....17 B5
Honiton EX14 ....166 C4
Coombe Cross
Barnstaple EX32 ....17 B4
Bovey Tracey TQ13 ......180 E7
Christow EX6 ....113 B2
Great Torrington EX38 ....159 F8
Coombe Dean Sch PL9 .256 A6
Coombe Down La PL8 ..140 F6
Coombe Dr PL12 ......239 A2
Coombe Hayes EX10 ...188 B8
Coombe Hill EX16 ....47 F1
Coombe House Cross TQ9 ....224 F2
Coombe House La TQ9 .225 A2
Coombe La
Axminster EX13 ....167 D5
Bickleigh EX16 ....63 C3
Bovey Tracey TQ13 ......180 F8
Cadbury EX5 ....81 C7
Cargreen PL12 ....239 A2
Chulmleigh EX18 ....44 E4
Plymouth PL5 ....244 D7
Silverton EX5 ....82 B7
Teignmouth TQ14 ....210 A7
Tiverton EX16,EX17 ....63 B3
Witheridge EX16 ....62 B6
Coombe Mdw TQ13 ....180 E7
Coombe Mdws TQ7 ....144 F1
Coombe Orch EX12 ....192 E6
Coombe Park Cl PL10 ..253 A2
Coombe Park La PL5 ..244 A3
Coombe Park Rd TQ14 .210 A6
Coombe Pk
Cawsand PL10 ....253 A2
Saltash PL12 ....242 F2
Coombe Rd
Dartmouth TQ6 ....233 F4
Paignton TQ3 ....219 C1
Saltash PL12 ....243 A2
Shaldon TQ14 ....209 C5
Coombe Shute TQ9 ....227 F7
Coombe St Exeter EX1 ..261 B2
Lyme Regis DT7 ....260 E3
Coombe The
Dartmouth TQ6 ....233 F4
Galmpton TQ5 ....229 B5
Coombe Vale EX10 .....100 D2
Coombe Vale Rd TQ14 .210 A5
Coombe View
Plymouth PL2 ....247 F7
Teignmouth TQ14 ....124 E1
Coombe Way
Bishopsteignton TQ14 ....209 B8
Plymouth PL5 ....243 F1
Coombefield La EX13 ..167 D5
Coombes The [1] EX31 ..154 A2
Coombesend Rd
Kingsteignton TQ12 ......207 F7
Kingsteignton TQ12 ......208 A7
Coombesend Rd E TQ12 ....208 A7
Coombeshead Coll TQ12 ....207 A4
Coombeshead Rd TQ12 .206 F4
Cooper St [11] EX39 .....157 A2
Cooper's Cross EX18 ....60 C6
Cooper's Cross EX20 ...107 A3
Coopers Cross EX37 .....44 E6
Coopers Dr EX31 ......154 B2
Coopers Hill EX19 ....58 F3
Coot Hide EX16 ....50 D1
Copland La TQ9 ....223 A6
Copland Mdws TQ9 ....223 B6
Copleston Rd PL6 .....244 E5
Copley Cl TQ3 ....225 F6
Copley Dr EX31 ....154 D3
Copp Hill La EX9 ......198 A2
Copp Path EX7 ....204 C5
Copp's Cl EX39 ....157 A3
Coppard Mdws PL7 ....250 B6
Copper Beech Way PL6 245 C7
Copper Castle EX14 ....166 E6
Copper Cl EX39 ....38 F8
Copper Pl PL1 ....262 A3
Copper Tree Cross TQ9 .216 C5
Copperfield Cl EX8 ....196 E1
Copperfields PL20 .....126 E5
Coppers Pk PL6 ....245 E7
Copperthorn Cross TQ9 222 D4
Copperwood Cl TQ13 ..130 F4
Coppice Cl
Fremington EX31 ....153 F6
Raymond's Hill EX13 .....104 B7
Coppice Gate EX32 ....155 C3
Coppice Gdns PL5 .....244 E2
Coppice La EX17 ....80 A7
Coppice The
Dawlish EX7 ....204 D4
Ivybridge PL21 ....237 A4
Coppice Wood Dr PL6 ..245 C7
Coppledown Gdns EX9 .197 F2
Copplestone Dr EX4 ...173 A1
Copplestone Prim Sch EX17 ....79 B5
Copplestone Rd EX9 ...198 A1
Copplestone Sta EX17 ...79 A6
Copse EX8 ....196 E2
Copse Cl PL7 ....250 D4
Copse Hill La EX20 ......77 B7
Copse Rd PL7 ....250 D4
Copse The
Barnstaple EX31 ....154 B3
Chillington TQ7 ....145 A1
Exeter EX2 ....182 C7
Newton Poppleford EX10 .186 F8
Okehampton EX20 ....170 D6
Totnes TQ9 ....222 E6
Copsey La TQ12 ....211 B6
Copstone EX39 ....39 E7
Copstone Hill EX17 .....61 D5
Copthorne Gdns PL9 ...255 F5
Copydown La EX5 ......82 D6
Copythorne Cl TQ5 ....230 A4
Copythorne Pk TQ5 ....230 A4
Copythorne Rd TQ5 ....230 A4
Coral Ave EX39 ....156 D7

Coram Ave DT7 260 D2
Corams La TA21 160 B6
Corbyn Ct TQ2 219 E3
Cordery Rd EX2 176 F3
Core Fields EX10 188 B8
Core Hill Rd EX10 100 F1
Corea Terr PL1 248 A2
Coreway EX10 188 B8
Coreway Cl EX10 188 B8
Corfe Ave PL3 248 F8
Corfe Cl PL21 237 D4
Corfe Cres TQ2 213 F1
Corilhead Rd EX33 152 D8
Coringdean Cl PL6 245 B6
Cormorant Cl TQ2 213 D3
Corn Mill Cres EX2 177 A1
Corn Park Rd
Abbotskerswell TQ12 212 A6
6 South Brent TQ10 134 F2
Corn Pk TQ10 135 A2
Cornacre Cl TQ2 219 C7
Cornacre Rd TQ2 219 C7
Cornborough Rd EX39 156 B6
Corndon Cross TQ13 110 F4
Corner Brake PL6 245 D7
Corner Cl TA21 160 D4
Corner Cotts EX16 65 A7
Corner La
Combe Martin EX34 3 B3
Halberton EX16 65 A7
Cornermoor Cross EX16 47 C1
Cornfield Gdns PL7 251 B7
Cornfield Gn TQ2 214 B2
Cornflower Cl
4 Barnstaple EX31 154 B3
Willand EX15 162 E5
Cornflower Hill EX4 176 D8
Cornhill Hemyock EX15 67 B8
Ottery St Mary EX11 169 D4
5 Wellington TA21 160 D6
Cornlands EX16 50 D1
Cornmarket St EX38 159 D5
Cornridge View EX20 93 C2
Corntown Cross PL21 133 C1
Cornwall Beach PL1 247 D2
Cornwall St
Bere Alston PL20 125 E1
5 Exeter EX4 177 A5
Plymouth PL1 262 C3
Plymouth, Morice Town PL1 247 D2
Cornwood CE Prim Sch PL21 133 C2
Cornwood Rd
Ivybridge PL21 237 A5
Plymouth PL7 251 B4
Cornworthy Cl PL2 248 A7
Cornworthy Cross TQ9 227 A4
Coronation Ave EX7 204 D5
Coronation Cres EX15 66 A7
Coronation Pl
Plymouth PL5 247 E8
Shebbear EX21 55 E4
Coronation Rd
Bideford EX39 156 F1
Exeter EX2 178 A4
Kingsbridge TQ7 258 D5
Kingsteignton TQ12 207 E7
1 Newton Abbot TQ12 207 B3
Salcombe TQ8 259 D5
1 Teignmouth TQ14 210 A3
Totnes TQ9 223 D6
Coronation St EX32 154 F6
Coronation Terr
Abbotsham EX39 156 A2
3 Ilfracombe EX34 150 C6
Starcross EX6 201 B8
Coronation Villas EX18 59 C4
Corondale Rd PL2 248 B7
Corporation Cres 13 EX32 155 B3
Corporation Rd PL2 248 D7
Corporation St 11 EX32 155 B3
Corporation Terr 12 EX32 155 B3
Corry Ho TQ1 220 E5
Corscombe La EX20 94 E6
Corsham Cl PL6 245 B6
Corsham Rd TQ4 226 A5
Corstone Cross EX19 76 D7
Cory Ct PL9 140 E8
Coryton Cl EX7 204 E6
Coryton La EX13 87 C1
Cosdon Pl PL6 244 F1
Cosgates Feet or County Gate EX35 6 D5
Cossick Cross TQ13 112 B5
Costly St PL21 237 D5
Cosway Rd EX16 161 D5
Cot Green Cross EX14 85 B5
Cot Hill PL7 250 B5
Cot Hill Trad Est PL7 250 B6
Cot La EX5 82 D5
Cot Manor 5 EX32 155 B3
Cotehele Ave
Plymouth, Keyham PL2 247 F5
Plymouth, Prince Rock PL4 263 C2
Cotehele Dr TQ3 225 D7
Cotehele Ho* PL12 125 C3
Cotehele Quay Mus* PL12 125 C3
Coteland La EX32 18 F1
Coteland Lane End EX32 18 F1
Cotfield Cl EX14 166 D7
Cotfield St EX2 177 C3
Cotford Cl EX10 101 C3
Cotford Rd EX10 101 C3
Cotlands EX10 187 F3
Cotleigh Cross EX14 86 C5
Cotleigh Crossing EX14 68 C1
Cotley La EX6 113 C8
Cotmaton Rd EX10 187 F3
Cotmore Cl Brixham TQ5 230 A2
Chillington TQ7 145 A1
Cotmore Way TQ7 145 A1
Cotswold Cl TQ2 219 D3
Cott Cross
Bishops Nympton EX36 31 C2
Chawleigh EX18 59 E6
Dartington TQ9 222 F8
Membury EX13 87 C7
Cott Hill EX31 10 D1
Cott La Croyde EX33 7 E1
Petrockstow EX20 56 F4
Cott Mdw TQ9 222 F8
Cott Pk EX5 184 C2
Cott Rd TQ9 222 F8
Cottage Cl EX33 8 D1
Cottage Cross
Ashburton TQ13 131 B5
Cheriton Bishop EX6 97 B4
Cottage La TA22 33 D6
Cottage Mews PL7 250 E4
Cottages The TQ7 142 F2
Cotterbury Gn TQ9 232 A2
Cotterell Rd EX5 175 E2
Cotters Cl EX15 66 A3
Cottey Brook EX16 161 B4
Cottey Cres EX4 174 A2
Cottey Mdws TQ12 207 E6
Cottingham Cres EX39 156 F3
Cottington Ct EX10 188 A4
Cottington Mead
Sidmouth, Lower Woolbrook EX10 188 B6
Sidmouth, Weston Town EX10 188 A4
Cottlass La PL21 137 A2
Cottles La EX5 184 D4
Cotton Cl PL7 250 F4
Cotton La
Cheriton Fitzpaine EX17 63 A3
Tiverton EX16 63 B5
Cottshayne La EX24 102 E5
Couchill Dr EX12 191 F8
Couchill La EX12 191 F8
Coulsdon Rd EX10 188 B6
Coulson Cross EX20 76 F8
Coulsworthy Crook EX34 3 D2
Coulsworthy La EX34 3 E2
Council Hos Brixton PL8 257 B5
Clyst St Mary EX5 179 A3
Council Hos The EX5 179 E7
Council Houses The TQ7 149 D7
Countess Pl EX16 161 E5
Countess Wear Comb Sch EX2 182 B8
Countess Wear Rd EX2 182 A8
Countessmead EX16 161 F8
Counties Cres EX6 201 B7
Countisbury Hill EX35 151 E5
Country Ho 4 EX10 101 B1
County Cl PL7 251 A5
Couper Mdws EX2 178 D3
Coursebeer La EX20 95 E5
Court Baron Cross EX14 84 E3
Court Barton Cotts PL9 255 C1
Court Barton Hill EX12 191 D6
Court Barton Ho TQ7 147 D8
Court Barton Mews PL19 116 F4
Court Dr
Cullompton EX15 163 C5
Wellington TA21 160 D5
Court Farm Barns TQ12 212 B6
Court Field La TA20 69 E5
Court Fields Com Sch TA21 160 C5
Court Gate Cl TQ12 211 C1
Court Gdns EX16 48 D5
Court La Bampton EX16 34 D4
Seaton EX12 192 A6
Court Moors La TA21 51 E5
Court Orch EX5 81 A1
Court Park Rd TQ7 143 A1
Court Pk TQ7 143 A2
Court Rd
Abbotskerswell TQ12 212 B6
Newton Ferrers PL8 140 F7
Torquay TQ2 219 C5
Court St TQ13 111 F4
Court Terr TA21 160 C5
Court The Dunsford EX6 112 F8
Plymouth PL6 245 C7
Saltash PL12 242 C2
Court View PL8 256 F4
Court Way EX16 50 D1
Court Wlk EX19 58 F3
Court Wood PL8 140 E7
Courtenay EX14 166 A5
Courtenay Cl EX6 195 A1
Courtenay Cotts EX16 48 F2
Courtenay Dr 24 EX24 103 A4
Courtenay Gdns
Exeter EX2 181 A8
Newton Abbot TQ12 207 C2
Courtenay Manor TQ1 220 C4
Courtenay Park Rd TQ12 207 D3
Courtenay Pk TQ10 135 A3
Courtenay Pl 17 TQ14 210 C4
Courtenay Rd Exeter EX2 177 B3
Courtenay Rd *continued*
Newton Abbot TQ12 207 C2
Okehampton EX20 170 C4
Paignton TQ4 226 C2
Tavistock PL19 171 B6
Courtenay St
Newton Abbot TQ12 207 B3
Plymouth PL1 262 C3
Salcombe TQ8 259 D5
Courtenay Terr EX6 201 B8
Courtfield TQ9 223 F5
Courtfield Cl EX11 168 D5
Courtfield Rd PL3 248 F5
Courthayes Cross EX5 81 E5
Courthayes La EX5 81 F5
Courtis Gdns EX17 165 D5
Courtlage Wlk TQ7 258 C6
Courtland Cres PL7 250 D7
Courtland Cross TQ12 211 A4
Courtland Rd
Paignton TQ3 226 B7
Torquay TQ2 219 B7
Wellington TA21 160 D6
Courtlands PL12 242 E1
Courtlands Cl PL19 171 B6
Courtlands Cross EX8 196 A3
Courtlands La EX8 195 F3
Courtlands Rd
Newton Abbot TQ12 207 D2
Tavistock PL19 171 B6
Courtlands Sch PL6 244 F1
Courtney Cl 23 EX24 103 A4
Courtney Rd EX16 161 E5
Cousens Cl EX7 204 F8
Cousin's Cross TQ7 149 A6
Cove Hill EX16 49 C6
Cove Mdw PL11 247 A6
Coventry Cl EX14 84 D2
Coventry Farm Est TQ12 213 B2
Coventry Rd EX4 176 F6
Coverdale Pl PL5 244 C1
Coverdale Rd Exeter EX2 177 B3
Paignton TQ3 226 B6
Cow Down Rd TA20 88 F8
Cow La EX34 150 B6
Cowdray Cl PL12 242 E2
Cowdray Terr PL12 242 E1
Cowflop Cross EX18 43 A1
Cowick Fst Sch EX2 176 F4
Cowick Hill EX2 176 F3
Cowick La EX2 176 F3
Cowick Rd EX2 177 A4
Cowick St EX4 177 A4
Cowley Bridge Rd EX4 173 A1
Cowley Bridge Rd Bsns Pk EX4 173 A1
Cowley Hill EX5 172 F4
Cowley Moor Rd EX16 161 E5
Cowley Rd PL5 244 D3
Cowley Wood Head EX31 4 A2
Cowley Wood Hill EX31 4 A2
Cownhayne La EX24 103 B4
Cowpark Terr 1 EX39 156 F7
Cowper Ave EX2 177 F3
Cox Rd TA21 160 C4
Cox Tor Cl 6 PL20 126 F3
Cox Tor Rd PL19 171 E5
Cox's Cl PL6 245 B1
Coxhill Cross TQ11 236 A3
Coxley La EX13 102 F7
Coxmoor Cross EX17 78 A1
Coxmoor La EX17 78 A2
Coxs Mdw EX22 89 F7
Coypool Rd PL7 250 A6
Crabadon Cross TQ9 138 F5
Crabb La EX2 177 A2
Crabbers Cross TQ10 135 D4
Crabbs Cl PL15 90 C1
Crabtree Cl PL3 249 F5
Crabtree Villas PL3 249 E5
Crackaway La EX34 9 A4
Crackston Cl PL6 249 B7
Craigie Dr PL1 262 A3
Craigmore Ave PL2 247 F5
Cramber Cl
Roborough PL6 245 C8
Tavistock PL19 171 B4
Crammer Ash Cross EX15 84 C8
Crammers Cross TQ13 123 F7
Cramp La EX36 31 E6
Crampit La EX39 157 E5
Cranapool Cross EX22 54 E3
Cranbourne Ave PL4 263 C4
Cranbrook Rd EX2 178 A5
Crandford Cl EX20 107 F8
Crandons Cross EX14 87 B6
Cranes La EX9 198 B6
Cranfield PL7 250 C7
Cranford EX10 188 B5
Cranford Ave EX8 202 D6
Cranford Cl EX8 202 C6
Cranford Cross
Great Torrington EX38 42 C8
Woolfardisworthy EX39 39 A8
Cranford Ho EX8 202 D6
Cranford Rd TQ3 219 A1
Cranford View EX8 202 C6
Cranishaies La EX5 83 B7
Cranley Gdns TQ13 111 A6
Cranmere Ct EX2 181 C8
Cranmere Rd
Okehampton EX20 170 E6
Plymouth PL3 249 A6
Cranmore View EX16 161 B1
Crannafords Ind Pk TQ13 111 B7
Crantock Terr 7 PL2 248 A5
Craon Gdns EX20 170 D6
Crapstone Terr PL20 126 E2
Crashaw Cl PL5 244 D3
Craven Ave PL4 263 C4
Crawford Gdns EX2 177 A3
Crawford Rd PL1 262 A4
CRC Units EX2 177 D1
Creacombe Barton Cross EX16 46 F6
Creacombe Cross PL8 141 E8
Creacombe Parsonage Cross EX16 47 A5
Creacombemoor Cross EX16 47 A6
Crealy Pk* EX5 99 A1
Creamery Cl PL8 136 A2
Crease La PL19 171 A4
Crediton Cross EX17 62 D3
Crediton Hospl EX17 165 A6
Crediton La EX6 97 C5
Crediton Lane End EX6 97 C4
Crediton Rd
Okehampton EX20 170 C5
Okehampton EX20 170 D6
Crediton Sta EX17 165 E3
Crediton Wlk PL6 249 E8
Creedy Bridge EX17 165 F7
Creedy Cross EX17 62 A2
Creedy Rd Crediton EX17 165 D5
Plymouth PL3 249 C5
Creedy View EX5 80 F2
Creek Cross TQ13 131 B5
Creek End TQ7 148 F7
Creek Rd TQ6 233 D4
Creel Cl EX2 181 C8
Crelake Cl PL19 171 C4
Crelake Ind Est 1 PL19 171 B4
Crelake Pk PL19 171 C4
Cremyll Rd PL11 247 B2
Cremyll St PL1 254 A8
Crescent Ave
Barnstaple EX31 154 D3
Plymouth PL1 262 B2
Crescent Avenue Mews PL1 262 B2
Crescent Ct TQ6 233 D4
Crescent Gdns PL21 237 C6
Crescent Mansions Flats EX2 261 C2
Crescent Rd PL21 237 C6
Crescent The
Brixton PL8 257 A5
Crapstone PL20 126 E3
Exmouth EX8 202 E8
Gunnislake PL18 125 D6
Kilmington EX13 87 C1
Lifton PL16 105 E4
Pathfinder Village EX6 98 B4
Plymouth PL1 262 B2
Cresents Gdns PL21 237 C6
Cressbrook Cl PL6 245 F2
Cressbrook Dr PL6 245 F2
Cressbrook Wlk PL6 245 E2
Cresswell Cl TQ12 213 A5
Crest Hill TQ11 236 B5
Crestfield Rise PL21 237 A5
Cresthill Rd PL2 248 B7
Crestway TQ6 145 E5
Crewkerne Rd EX13 104 C7
Crewkerne Turning EX13 88 C6
Cricket Cl EX18 44 F1
Cricket Field Ct EX9 198 A1
Cricket Field La EX9 198 A1
Cricket Field Rd 1 TQ12 207 C3
Cricket La TQ11 236 A6
Cricket Pk EX23 70 A6
Cricketers The EX13 167 D7
Cricketfield Cl TQ13 123 F6
Cricketfield Rd TQ2 219 F7
Cridlake EX13 167 E5
Crimps Cross TQ7 258 F6
Crispin Rd TQ7 258 C5
Critchards EX5 184 C2
Criterion Pl 14 EX8 202 A6
Crocadon Mdws TQ9 139 B4
Crockaton Cotts TQ13 130 F5
Crocken Tor Rd EX20 170 D5
Crocker's Row PL18 125 D6
Crockernwell Ct EX6 96 F3
Crockers Way PL15 90 C1
Crockwells Cl EX6 182 B3
Crockwells Rd EX6 182 B4
Croft Chase EX4 176 E4
Croft Cl TQ12 206 D1
Croft Cotts TQ12 211 D2
Croft Ct TQ2 220 A5
Croft Hill TQ2 220 A5
Croft Ho EX22 164 C4
Croft La Brushford TA22 33 C4
Skilgate TA4 34 E6
Spreyton EX17 96 A6
Croft Mdw TQ12 211 D2
Croft Orch TQ12 211 D2
Croft Pk PL6 245 C7
Croft Rd
East Ogwell TQ12 206 D1
Holsworthy EX22 164 C4
Ipplepen TQ12 211 D2
Salcombe TQ8 259 D5
Torquay TQ1 220 A5
Croft The EX20 95 A4
Croft's Est EX17 80 A5
Crofts Lea EX34 2 E3
Crofts Lea Pk EX34 150 D5
Croftside 5 EX34 150 B5
Croftswood Gdns EX34 150 D4
Crogg La DT7 260 B5
Croker's Mdw TQ13 180 C8
Crokers Way TQ12 211 D2
Cromartie Point Flats TQ2 219 E2
Cromartie Rd PL4 249 B1
Cromer Cl PL6 245 A7
Cromer Wlk PL6 245 A7
Cromwell Cl EX38 159 F6
Cromwell Cotts TQ12 131 F7
Cromwell Ct EX1 178 A5
Cromwell Gate PL6 245 C7
Cromwell Pk
Modbury PL21 137 B3
Tiverton EX16 64 D6
Cromwell Rd PL4 263 C3
Cromwells Mdw EX17 165 E6
Cromwells Way TQ13 180 C8
Crooke La EX20 77 E3
Crooked Oaks EX36 30 C1
Crookeder Cl PL9 256 A5
Crooklake Hill EX5 98 E8
Crookmans Cnr EX32 155 C5
Croscombe La EX35 4 E4
Cross Cl EX31 153 D5
Cross Farm Ct 5 EX32 16 E1
Cross Furzes TQ11 129 F1
Cross Gate EX32 18 F6
Cross Gn PL15 105 E7
Cross Head EX31 153 C3
Cross Hill
Cheriton Fitzpaine EX17 80 C8
Combeinteignhead TQ12 208 D3
Crediton EX17 79 E5
Plymouth PL2 247 E4
Cross Hill Cross EX17 80 C8
Cross La Berrynarbor EX34 2 E3
Brendon EX35 6 A4
East Portlemouth TQ8 259 F4
Cross Lane Cross EX36 19 D1
Cross Lanes
Ashprington TQ9 139 F8
Ashwater EX21 90 F6
South Pool TQ7 148 F6
Cross Mdw EX17 96 A7
Cross Mdws EX31 154 A2
Cross Moor La EX36 31 E2
Cross Park Ave PL6 244 F1
Cross Park Rd
Plymouth PL6 244 F1
3 Wembury PL9 140 D8
Cross Park Way PL6 244 F1
Cross Parks
Cullompton EX15 163 A2
High Bickington EX37 43 C7
Cross Pk Brixham TQ5 230 B3
Brixton PL8 257 B5
Buckland Monachorum PL20 126 D3
Combeinteignhead TQ12 208 D4
Ilfracombe EX34 150 B6
South Zeal EX20 95 A4
Totnes TQ9 223 E6
Cross Side Hill EX36 31 F2
Cross St Barnstaple EX31 154 F5
Combe Martin EX34 2 F4
Lynton EX35 151 B5
Moretonhampstead TQ13 111 F5
Northam EX39 157 A7
Seaton EX12 192 A5
Cross Terr PL18 125 C5
Cross The Kilmington EX13 87 D1
St Dominick PL12 125 A2
Cross Tree EX9 198 E7
Cross Tree Ctr 3 EX33 152 D6
Cross View
Buckfastleigh TQ11 236 A2
Exeter EX2 177 B1
Cross-in-Hand PL21 237 F5
Crosscut Way EX14 166 C5
Crossgate EX18 59 C7
Crossgates PL7 132 C6
Crossgrange Trad Est TQ12 180 F3
Crosshill La EX6 97 A5
Crossing Cross TQ9 222 F7
Crossingfields Dr EX8 196 A1
Crossings Cl PL19 117 E6
Crossland La EX14 68 C2
Crosslands
Barnstaple EX31 154 C4
Thurlestone TQ7 143 A1
Wellington TA21 160 B8
Crossley Moor Rd TQ12 207 E7
Crossmead EX35 151 B5
Crossmoor Cross EX16 47 E1
Crosspark Ave TQ2 219 C8
Crosspark Cl EX31 154 E7
Crosspark Cres EX31 17 A7
Crosspark Cross
Bradworthy EX22 38 E1
Holsworthy EX22 164 E5
Crosspark Hill EX16 48 C8
Crossparks
Dartmouth TQ6 233 D3
Tiverton EX16 64 F6
Crossview Terr EX2 176 E2
Crosswater EX23 36 F1
Crossway Paignton TQ4 226 C2
Plymouth PL7 250 D7
Crossway Ave PL4 249 B3
Crossway Cross EX20 94 E6
Crossway Hill EX17 61 F2
Crossways
Cornwood PL21 133 C2
Milton Damerel EX22 54 E5
9 Paignton TQ4 226 B6
Ringmore TQ7 142 E4

Crossways continued
Tatworth TA20 .88 D8
4 Wembury PL9 .140 D8
Whitestone EX4 .98 E4
Crow Bridge EX15 .163 B3
Crow Gn EX15 .163 B3
Crow La EX16 .47 C3
Crow Pk PL3 .248 F5
Crow View EX32 .155 C5
Crowbeare Mdw EX38 .159 E6
Crowborough Rd EX33 .8 A2
Crowbridge Pk EX15 .163 B2
Crowden Cres EX16 .161 F3
Crowden Cross EX20 .74 D2
Crowden Rd EX20 .74 E2
Crowder Cross TQ10 .135 A2
Crowder Mdw TQ10 .135 A2
Crowder Pk TQ10 .135 A2
Crowder's Cross EX14 .84 C3
Crowdhole Cross EX16 .46 F4
Crowdhole Hill EX16 .46 F4
Crown & Anchor Way 5 TQ3 .226 B6
Crown Gdns PL6 .245 A1
Crown Hill Halberton EX16 64 F7
West Buckland TA21 .52 F7
Crown Hill Terr 8 EX17 165 C5
Crown Mews TA21 .52 F7
Crown Sq 6 TQ14 .210 A3
Crowndale Ave PL3 .249 A6
Crownhill Cross PL21 .137 B3
Crownhill Ct
Plymouth PL6 .244 F2
Torquay TQ2 .219 E6
Crownhill Fort★ PL6 .244 F3
Crownhill Fort Rd PL6 .244 F3
Crownhill La EX5 .81 C5
Crownhill Pk TQ2 .219 E6
Crownhill Rd PL5 .244 C3
Crownhill Rise TQ2 .219 E6
Crownley La TQ9 .227 F8
Crowther's Hill TQ6 .233 F3
Croyde Rd EX33 .7 D1
Croyden Cross EX22 .55 A4
Croydon Gdns PL5 .243 E4
Croylands Ct EX8 .202 C6
Croyle Cross EX15 .66 A4
Crozier Rd 6 PL4 .248 F4
Cruel Cross TQ3 .225 D8
Cruffen Cross EX33 .8 B1
Cruffen La EX33 .8 B1
Cruwy's Morchard Mill La EX16 .63 A7
Cruwys Morchard Hill EX16 .63 A7
Crystal Cl TQ4 .226 C2
Cuckoo Down La EX14 .166 E4
Cuckoo Hill EX17 .61 C3
Cuckoo La DT7 .260 A4
Cuckoo's La EX32 .28 B5
Cuddeford Cnr EX4 .98 C6
Cuddenhay La EX17 .46 A2
Cuddyford Cross TQ13 .130 F5
Cudemoor Cross EX38 .41 A1
Cudhill Rd TQ5 .230 B4
Cudmore Pk EX16 .64 D6
Cuffe Rd PL3 .248 C4
Culdrose Cl PL5 .243 E4
Cullaford Cross EX17 .95 E8
Cullompton Com Coll EX15 .163 C2
Cullompton Hill EX5 .83 A7
Culm Cl TQ2 .219 B8
Culm Cross EX20 .77 A4
Culm Haven EX15 .66 A7
Culm Lea EX15 .163 E3
Culm Valley Way EX15 .65 F7
Culmbridge La EX15 .67 B7
Culme Cl EX14 .67 C1
Culme Rd PL3 .249 A5
Culme Way EX14 .67 C1
Culmstock Prim Sch EX15 .51 E1
Culmstock Rd EX15 .67 B8
Culver Cl Bradninch EX5 .83 A6
Plymouth PL6 .249 A8
Tiverton EX16 .161 F3
Culver Ct PL12 .242 F2
Culver Gdns EX10 .188 B4
Culver Ho 12 TQ13 .123 E6
Culver La Chudleigh TQ13 123 F6
Rattery TQ10 .135 E3
Culver Park Cl TQ7 .258 E3
Culver Rd PL12 .242 F2
Culver Way PL6 .249 A7
Culverdale TQ9 .223 E4
Culverlake La EX13 .88 G3
Culverland Cl EX4 .177 D8
Culverland Rd EX4 .177 D8
Culvert Rd EX5 .81 F1
Culverwood Cl PL7 .251 C6
Culvery Cl EX5 .184 C3
Culvery Cross EX17 .165 C2
Culvery Gn TQ2 .219 B8
Cumber Cl Brixham TQ5 .230 B5
Malborough TQ7 .147 F6
Cumber Dr TQ5 .230 B5
Cumberland Cl EX8 .202 D8
Cumberland Gn TQ5 .230 B5
Cumberland Rd PL1 .247 F1
Cumberland St PL1 .247 E2
Cummings Cross TQ12 .180 C1
Cummings Ct TQ12 .180 C1
Cummins Cnr EX6 .97 E5
Cummins La EX14 .87 B6
Cundy Cl PL7 .250 A7
Cunliffe Ave PL9 .255 A6
Cunningham Ave EX13 .167 F7
Cunningham Rd
Exmouth EX8 .196 D2
Plymouth PL5 .244 C8
Cunningham Way PL12 .242 D3
Cunningham's La EX10 .187 F3
Cuppiers Piece Cross EX19 .43 A1
Curledge St TQ4 .226 B5
Curledge Street Prim Sch TQ4 .226 B5
Curlew Cl EX20 .170 A6
Curlew Dr TQ7 .258 F1
Curlew Mews PL3 .249 C4
Curlew Way EX4 .173 D2
Currington Mdw EX31 .154 A3
Curriton Hill EX17 .61 C5
Curriton La EX17 .61 B6
Curscombe Cross EX14 .84 F4
Curscombe La EX14 .84 F4
Cursons Way PL21 .237 A5
Curtis Cross EX22 .54 B3
Curtis St PL1 .247 E1
Curve Acre EX33 .152 E5
Curwood Cres 2 EX16 .161 C3
Cussacombe EX36 .20 D1
Cussacombe Gate EX36 .20 E1
Custance Ho 7 EX14 .166 C6
Custom House Hill 4 TQ14 .210 B4
Custom House La PL1 .262 B1
Custom La EX16 .64 B4
Cut Tongue La TA20 .69 F7
Cuthays La EX13 .88 B1
Cuthbert Cl TQ1 .214 A1
Cuthbert Mayne Joint RC & CE Sch TQ1 .214 A1
Cutland Cross EX18 .44 D4
Cutliffe La EX39 .22 D3
Cutteridge La EX4 .176 A6
Cutwell Cross TQ10 .134 E1
Cuxton Mdws PL20 .126 C3
Cygnet Ct EX2 .261 C1
Cygnet Units EX2 .178 E5
Cypress Cl
12 Honiton EX14 .85 C2
6 Plymouth PL7 .251 C5
Torquay TQ2 .220 A5
Cypress Dr EX4 .176 F7
Cyprus Rd EX8 .202 B6
Cyprus Terr EX32 .155 B3

D

D'arcy Ct TQ12 .207 C4
Dabby La EX6 .97 B4
Daccabridge Rd TQ12 .212 F4
Daccombe Cross TQ12 .213 E5
Daccombe Hill TQ2, TQ12 .213 E4
Daccombe Mill La TQ12 213 B4
Daddon Hill EX39 .156 E6
Daddyhole Rd TQ1 .220 D3
Daggeridge Plain EX16 .63 B4
Daggers Copse TQ12 .206 F3
Dagmar Rd EX8 .202 A6
Dagmar St TQ14 .210 A3
Dagra La TQ12,TQ14 .209 B4
Daimonds La TQ14 .210 B5
Dainton Elms Cross TQ12 .211 F2
Dainton Mews TQ4 .226 B5
Dairs Orch TA20 .88 C8
Dairy Cl EX6 .182 B3
Dairy Hill TQ2 .219 C7
Dairy La PL21 .237 D5
Daison Cotts TQ1 .220 A7
Daison Cres TQ1 .220 B8
Daisy Links EX4 .176 D8
Dalbury Ct TQ12 .207 C4
Dalditch La EX9 .197 D3
Dale Ave PL6 .249 C7
Dale Gdns PL4 .248 D4
Dale Rd PL4 .248 D4
Daleside Rd EX4 .173 E1
Daleswood Rd PL19 .171 A4
Dalton Gdns PL5 .243 E3
Dalverton Ct TQ5 .230 C6
Dalwood La EX13 .87 B3
Dalwood Prim Sch EX13 .87 A3
Dame Hannah Rogers' Sch PL21 .237 B5
Damerel Cl PL1 .247 F2
Damson Cl EX15 .162 D4
Danby Heights Cl TQ1 .220 E4
Danby La EX8 .202 A7
Danby Terr EX8 .202 A7
Dandy La EX4 .174 D5
Daneheath Bsns Pk TQ12 .180 F3
Danes Cl EX14 .68 C2
Danes Cross EX5 .82 C2
Danes Hill EX4,EX5 .82 C2
Danes Mead EX15 .163 C6
Danes' Rd EX4 .261 B4
Daneshay EX39 .157 A7
Daneshill Cross EX13 .87 B3
Danesway EX4 .174 E2
Daniel's Grave EX16 .62 D4
Daniel's La
Broadhempston TQ9 .131 E1
West Charleton TQ7 .144 C1
Danum Dr PL7 .251 B3
Danvers Rd TQ2 .213 F2
Daphne Cl TQ1 .220 D5
Dares Orch EX24 .103 A3
Dark La Barnstaple EX31 .154 F7
Budleigh Salterton EX9 .197 F1
Dark La continued
Hockworthy EX16 .50 B8
Modbury PL21 .137 B3
Northlew EX20 .74 D2
Sidmouth EX10 .187 F6
Thorverton EX5 .81 E5
Wellington TA21 .160 D5
Dark Street La PL7 .250 E4
Darkey La Lifton PL16 .105 E4
Okehampton EX20 .170 A5
Darklake Cl PL6 .245 E5
Darklake La PL6 .245 D8
Darklake View PL6 .245 E5
Darky La Chulmleigh EX18 .59 E8
Kingsbridge TQ7 .258 C7
Darlick Cnr EX36 .20 C4
Darnell Cl EX10 .188 B6
Darracott Cross EX38 .41 E8
Darracott Hill EX39 .37 B4
Darran Cl TQ12 .207 F7
Darran Rd TQ12 .207 F7
Dart Ave TQ2 .219 C7
Dart Bridge Rd TQ11 .236 C5
Dart Bsns Ctr TQ9 .215 F1
Dart Cl Braunton EX31 .15 E5
Plymouth PL3 .249 D7
St Giles on the Heath PL15 .90 C1
Dart Hill EX16 .46 D2
Dart Pk EX36 .158 D4
Dart View TQ6 .228 C3
Dart View Rd TQ5 .229 B6
Dartbridge Cross TQ11 .236 C6
Dartbridge Manor TQ11 236 C6
Dartington CE Prim Sch TQ9 .215 F1
Dartington Cl EX38 .159 E6
Dartington Coll of Arts TQ9 .216 B2
Dartington Crystal Glass Factory★ EX38 .159 C6
Dartington Fields EX38 .159 E6
Dartington Hall TQ9 .216 B2
Dartington Hall Sch TQ9 .216 A1
Dartington La TQ9 .223 B7
Dartington Wlk
Exminster EX6 .181 F5
Plymouth PL6 .249 E8
Dartmeet★ PL20 .129 D8
Dartmeet Ave PL3 .249 B6
Dartmoor Cotts PL7 .132 D4
Dartmoor Prison Mus★ PL20 .119 A1
Dartmoor View
Chulmleigh EX18 .44 E1
Plymouth PL4 .249 C3
Saltash PL12 .242 E4
Woolfardisworthy EX17 .61 E4
Dartmoor Wildlife Pk★ PL7 .133 A1
Dartmouth & Kingswear Hospl TQ6 .233 F3
Dartmouth Castle★ TQ6 .234 B1
Dartmouth Com Coll TQ6 .233 D2
Dartmouth Hill TQ6 .146 B7
Dartmouth Mus★ TQ6 .233 F3
Dartmouth Prim Sch TQ6 .233 D2
Dartmouth Rd
East Allington TQ9 .144 E7
Paignton TQ4,TQ5 .226 C3
Stoke Fleming TQ6 .146 B8
Dartmouth Wlk PL6 .249 E8
Darton Gr TQ9 .227 F7
Dartridge La EX18 .44 D1
Dartside TQ9 .223 B7
Darwin Cres PL3 .249 D5
Darwin Ct 11 EX2 .261 B2
Dashley Cnr TQ9 .131 D2
Dashpers TQ5 .230 B3
Daucus Cl PL19 .171 B4
Davenham Cl PL6 .245 B6
Davey's Cross PL21 .137 B7
Daveycourt La EX20 .95 F3
David Cl Braunton EX33 .152 D5
Plymouth PL7 .250 F6
David Rd TQ3 .226 A7
David Southgate Ct PL1 262 A2
David's Cl EX10 .101 B2
David's Hill EX33 .8 A2
Davids La PL21 .137 B7
Davies Ave TQ4 .229 A8
Davies Cl EX5 .82 B6
Davis Ave TQ2 .219 D6
Davis Rd TQ6 .233 C3
Davy Cl PL11 .246 F3
Davy Rd PL6 .245 C4
Dawes Cl TQ12 .211 F8
Dawes Ct TQ4 .226 B5
Dawes La Millbrook PL10 .252 E5
Plymouth PL9 .256 D7
Dawlish Com Coll EX7 .204 F7
Dawlish Mus★ EX7 .204 D6
Dawlish Rd Exeter EX2 .181 C8
Teignmouth TQ14 .210 C6
Dawlish St 16 TQ14 .210 C5
Dawlish Sta EX7 .204 E6
Dawlish Warren Rd EX6 201 B4
Dawlish Warren Sta EX7 .201 B2
Dawlish Wlk PL6 .249 E8
Dawn Cl EX1 .178 A6
Daws Ct PL12 .243 A2
Daws Mdw TQ12 .207 E6
Dawson Cl PL5 .243 E1
Daymond Rd PL5 .243 D2
Days-Pottles La EX6, EX2 .181 D4
Dayton Cl PL6 .244 E3
De Bathe Cross EX20 .77 C3
De Courcy Rd TQ8 .259 B2
De La Rue Way EX4 .174 D1
De Tracey Pk TQ13 .180 D7
De-La-Hay Ave PL3 .262 A4
Deacon Cl EX2 .181 B8
Deacon Dr PL12 .242 F1
Deacons Gn PL19 .171 A3
Dead La EX15 .65 F2
Dead Road Cross EX15 .65 F2
Deadman's Cross TQ6 .233 D2
Dean Cross
Goodleigh EX32 .17 E4
Ilfracombe EX34 .8 E5
Lynton EX35 .5 A5
Plymouth PL9 .255 E7
South Brent TQ10 .135 C5
Dean Cross Rd PL9 .255 E7
Dean Hill PL9 .255 E7
Dean Hill Rd EX15 .162 B3
Dean La Combe Martin EX31 .3 E1
Ilfracombe EX34 .8 F5
Lynton EX35 .5 A5
Dean Lane End TQ10 .135 D5
Dean Park Rd PL9 .255 D7
Dean Rd PL7 .250 D6
Dean St Crediton EX17 .165 D5
Exeter EX2 .261 B2
Dean Steep EX35 .5 A4
Deane Cl EX33 .8 D1
Deane La TQ12 .209 D2
Deane Rd TQ12 .209 B2
Deane Way TA20 .88 D8
Deans Cl
Bishopsteignton TQ14 .208 F8
Northam EX39 .156 F7
Deans La EX36 .158 D5
Deans Mead EX10 .188 A5
Deans Pk EX36 .158 D5
Debden Cl PL5 .243 D4
Deckport Cross EX20 .75 D7
Decoy Country Pk★ TQ12 .207 C1
Decoy Ind Est TQ12 .212 D8
Decoy Prim Sch TQ12 .207 D1
Decoy Rd TQ12 .207 D1
Deeble Cl PL7 .250 E7
Deep Cut Cross EX14 .67 C2
Deep Dene Cl TQ5 .230 A3
Deep La Crediton EX17 .165 C6
High Bickington EX37 .43 D7
Plymouth PL7 .251 C3
Deepdene Pk EX2 .177 E4
Deeplane Head EX22 .164 C5
Deepway Gdns EX6 .181 F4
Deepway La
Branscombe EX12 .190 D4
Exeter EX2 .181 D4
Exminster EX6 .182 A4
Deepways EX9 .197 F2
Deer Leap PL19 .171 D4
Deer Park Ave TQ14 .210 A6
Deer Park Cl
Tavistock PL19 .171 C5
Teignmouth TQ14 .210 A6
Deer Park Cres PL19 .171 C5
Deer Park Dr
Plymouth PL3 .249 D7
Teignmouth TQ14 .210 A6
Deer Park La PL19 .171 C5
Deer Park Rd
Barnstaple EX32 .155 C2
Newton Abbot TQ12 .207 D1
Stoke Fleming TQ6 .146 B8
Tavistock PL19 .171 C5
Deer Pk Ivybridge PL21 .237 E5
Saltash PL12 .242 F3
Deer Valley Rd EX22 .164 C4
Deerhill La EX36 .158 C6
Deerpark La TQ12 .213 E7
Deers Leap Cl TQ3 .219 B2
Defoe Cl PL5 .244 C1
Delacombe Cl PL7 .250 F7
Delamere Rd PL6 .249 D7
Delamore Cl PL21 .237 A5
Delaware Com Prim Sch PL18 .125 C5
Delaware Cotts PL18 .125 C6
Delaware Ct PL18 .125 C5
Delaware Gdns PL2 .247 F7
Delaware Rd PL18 .125 C6
Delderfield Gdns EX8 .202 C6
Delia Gdns EX5 .99 C5
Delius Cres EX2 .178 C5
Dell The Plymouth PL7 .250 B6
Tavistock PL19 .171 B6
Delve's Grave Cross EX38 .41 F8
Den Brook Cl TQ1 .220 D6
Den Cres TQ14 .210 C4
Den Prom TQ14 .210 C4
Den Rd TQ14 .210 C4
Den The TQ14 .210 C4
Denbiegh Terr EX10 .188 B5
Denbow Cross EX5 .99 A2
Denbury Cross TQ12 .211 D3
Denbury Down Cross TQ12 .131 F3
Denbury Down La TQ12 131 F3
Denbury Prim Sch TQ12 .211 A6
Denbury Rd TQ12 .211 E6
Denby Ho TQ4 .226 C5
Dencroft La EX14 .87 A5
Dendy Rd TQ4 .226 B6
Dene Cl EX8 .196 D1
Dene's Cl 2 EX32 .17 B2
Deneleigh Cl EX2 .177 E4
Deneridge Cross EX17 .60 F6
Deneridge Hill EX17 .61 A5
Denes Rd EX32 .17 B2
Dengie Cl PL7 .251 B5
Denham Cl PL5 .244 C2
Dening Ct EX8 .202 B8
Denise Cl EX2 .181 B8
Denmark Rd
Exeter EX1,EX2 .261 C3
Exmouth EX8 .202 D8
Denners Way EX15 .66 A7
Dennington Cross EX32 .28 D8
Dennington Hill EX32 .28 D8
Dennington La
Churchinford EX14 .68 F6
Dulverton TA22 .33 B4
Dennis Cl PL5 .247 C7
Dennis Cross EX19 .57 F7
Dennis's Down Cross EX6 .96 C5
Dennysmead Ct EX4 .173 A1
Densdon Gate EX16 .46 E6
Densdon Rd EX36 .46 E6
Densham La EX17 .61 F4
Denver Cl EX3 .182 E6
Denver Rd EX3 .182 E6
Denys Rd Torquay TQ1 .220 C5
Totnes TQ9 .223 C5
Deptford Pl PL4 .263 A4
Deptford Villas 2 EX31 .154 C3
Derby Rd
Barnstaple EX32 .155 B6
Kingsbridge TQ7 .258 D4
Plymouth PL5 .244 C4
Derick Rd EX16 .161 B5
Derncleugh Gdns EX7 .210 F8
Derrell Rd TQ4 .226 A4
Derriford Hospl PL6 .245 B4
Derriford Pk PL6 .245 A3
Derriford Rd PL6 .245 B4
Derriton Mill Cross EX22 .164 B3
Derriton Rd EX22 .71 E6
Derry Ave PL4 .262 C4
Derry's Cross PL1 .262 B2
Derwent Ave PL3 .249 C5
Derwent Rd TQ1 .220 B7
Derworthy Cross EX22 .54 D6
Derworthy La EX22 .54 D6
Desborough La PL4 .263 C3
Desborough Rd PL4 .263 C3
Deveron Cl PL7 .251 A5
Devon & Cornwall Pol HQ (Middlemoor) EX2 .178 D5
Devon Bsns Pk EX15 .163 D4
Devon Cliffs Holiday Pk EX8 .203 B5
Devon Heath 2 TQ13 .123 C4
Devon Ho TQ13 .180 E8
Devon House Dr TQ13 .180 E8
Devon Pl 15 TQ9 .223 D5
Devon Rd Exeter EX4 .177 F8
Salcombe TQ8 .259 D4
Devon Sq
Kingsbridge TQ7 .258 C5
Newton Abbot TQ12 .207 C3
Devon Terr Plymouth PL3 248 E5
16 Totnes TQ9 .223 D5
Devon Tors PL20 .127 A3
Devon Tors Rd 9 PL20 .126 F3
Devon Units Exeter EX2 .177 C1
Great Torrington EX38 .159 F6
Devon Valley Holiday Village TQ14 .209 C5
Devon View EX7 .201 B2
Devoncourt TQ5 .230 E6
Devondale Ct EX7 .201 B2
Devonia Cl PL7 .250 E7
Devonport High Sch for Boys PL1 .248 A2
Devonport High Sch for Girls PL2 .248 C6
Devonport Hill
Cawsand PL10 .253 A2
Plymouth PL1 .247 F1
Devonport Leat PL6 .241 B5
Devonport Rd PL3 .247 F3
Devonport Sta PL1 .247 F3
Devons' Rd TQ1 .220 C7
Devonshire Ct 16 EX14 .85 C2
Devonshire Gdns EX20 .77 C4
Devonshire Ho
Plymouth PL1 .262 B2
2 Tavistock PL19 .171 B5
Torquay TQ1 .220 C8
Devonshire Pk EX39 .157 A1
Devonshire Pl EX4 .177 D8
Devonshire Rd EX14 .85 C2
Devonshire St PL4 .263 A3
Dewberry Dr EX31 .154 B3
Deyman's Hill EX16 .161 D3
Dial Ho The EX9 .198 A1
Dial St EX19 .58 F3
Diamond Ave PL4 .263 B4
Diamond La TQ10 .134 D5
Diamond Rd EX2 .261 A1
Diamond St 17 EX32 .154 F5
Diana Cl PL16 .106 A8
Diane Cl EX8 .196 D4
Dibbon's La EX34 .1 D2
Dick Pym Cl EX2 .178 C4
Dick's Hill EX36 .46 E8

Dickens Dr EX2 177 F3
Dickens Rd PL5 244 B1
Dickers Terr TQ12 207 E7
Dickiemoor La PL5 244 C2
Dickna St PL15 90 C1
Dickshill La EX38 159 D5
Diddywell Cl EX39 157 A8
Diddywell Rd EX39 157 A8
Dieppe Cl PL1 247 F2
Digby Dr EX2 178 D3
Digby Gr PL5 243 F5
Digby Sowton Sta EX2 178 E4
Diggerland★ EX15 163 E8
Diggories La 5 EX14 166 B6
Dillons PL8 141 A7
Dillybridge Hill EX6 97 D4
Dinan Way EX8 196 E3
Dinan Way Trad Est EX8 196 F1
Dince Hill Cl EX5 99 E7
Dingle Cl PL17 115 B1
Dingle Rd
Plymouth, North Prospect PL2 248 A6
Plymouth, Plympton PL7 250 C6
Dingles Steam Village★ PL16 106 A5
Dingwall Ave PL5 244 E3
Dinham Cres EX4 261 A3
Dinham Rd EX4 261 A3
Dinne Ford St EX5 81 E5
Dinnis Cl EX6 97 F4
Dipford Gate EX16 48 C3
Dipford La EX16 48 C4
Diptford Cl TQ4 225 E3
Diptford Cross TQ9 138 C7
Diptford Parochial CE Prim Sch TQ9 138 C7
Dirty La PL12 242 B5
Discovery Wharf 20 PL4 263 A2
Distine Cl PL3 249 B7
District Hospl EX16 161 D4
Ditch End Cross EX32 18 C7
Ditchett Cross EX16 46 E6
Dittiscombe Cross TQ9 145 A6
Dittisham Ct TQ6 228 C3
Dittisham Wlk PL6 249 E8
Ditton Ct PL6 249 A8
Divett Dr 6 TQ12 122 F1
Dix's Field EX1 261 B3
Dixon Cl TQ3 218 E1
Dixon Pl PL2 247 F4
Dixon Terr PL8 257 F3
Doatshayne Cl EX13 103 D5
Doatshayne La
Musbury EX13 103 D5
Musbury EX13 103 D6
Dobbin Arch TQ12 212 F4
Dobbsmoor Cross EX18 44 F3
Dobles Cl EX22 164 C5
Dobles La EX22 164 C6
Dobles Terr EX22 164 D5
Dobree Pk TA21 160 A4
Doccombe Cross TQ13 112 B5
Dock Rd EX8 201 E6
Dockeys La TQ7 145 D1
Dockray Cl PL6 245 D4
Dockworthy Cross EX18 60 C8
Dockyard Halt PL2 247 E4
Docton Mill & Gdns★ EX39 22 B1
Doctors Cnr EX16 61 D7
Doctors Rd 3 TQ5 230 C3
Dodbrooke Ct TQ7 258 D5
Doddiscombsleigh Com Sch EX6 113 D5
Doddridge Cl PL9 255 F4
Dodscott Cross EX38 42 B7
Doe Ct EX38 159 D5
Dog Down Cross EX16 50 A8
Doggie La EX34 1 E2
Dogwatch TQ7 147 E4
Doidges Farm Cl PL6 249 B8
Dokkum Rd EX17 165 D4
Dolbeare Rd
14 Ashburton TQ13 131 A5
Ashburton TQ13 131 A5
Dole Park Cross E EX37 43 D5
Dole Park Cross W EX37 43 C5
Dolepark La EX37 43 D5
Dolphin Cl
Lyme Regis DT7 260 E3
Plymouth PL9 255 F6
Dolphin Court Rd
Paignton TQ3 218 F1
Plymouth PL9 255 F6
Dolphin Cres TQ3 218 F1
Dolphin Ct Brixham TQ5 230 C6
Cullompton EX15 163 C3
Northam EX39 156 E7
22 Teignmouth TQ14 210 C4
Dolphin Ho 18 PL4 263 A2
Dolphin Sch The EX8 202 B6
Dolphin Sq
Bovey Tracey TQ13 180 C7
Plymouth PL9 255 F6
Dolphin St EX24 103 A5
Dolton CE Prim Sch EX19 57 E7
Dolvin Rd PL19 171 C5
Domehayes EX20 170 B5
Donkey La
Millbrook PL10 252 C4
Ugborough PL21 137 D6
Donkey Sanctuary The★ EX10 189 B7
Donnington Dr PL3 249 C7
Doomsford La EX37 44 B5
Doone Way EX34 150 C4
Dorchester Ave PL5 244 D4
Dorchester Gr TQ2 213 F1
Dorchester Way EX8 196 D4
Doreena Rd PL9 256 C7
Doriam Cl EX4 173 C2
Dormy Ave PL3 248 F5
Dornafield Cl TQ12 211 D2
Dornafield Cross
Abbotskerswell TQ12 211 E5
Ipplepen TQ12 211 D3
Dornafield Dr E TQ12 211 E2
Dornafield Dr W TQ12 211 D2
Dornafield La TQ12 211 E4
Dornafield Rd TQ12 211 D3
Dornaford Cross EX20 76 C2
Dorridge Gate EX37 28 D3
Dorset Ave EX4 176 E4
Dorset Pk PL15 89 D2
Dorset Pl 6 EX14 166 C6
Dorsmouth Terr PL7 250 E4
Dosson Gr TQ1 219 E7
Dotheridge La EX39 25 A1
Dotton Cl EX1 178 D6
Dotton La EX10 186 E6
Doughy La TQ12 211 A7
Douglas Ave
Brixham TQ5 230 E4
Exmouth EX8 202 C6
Douglas Dr PL9 256 A6
Douglas Ho 14 TQ14 210 B5
Douglass Rd PL3 249 C6
Dousland Ho PL20 127 B3
Dousland Rd PL20 127 A3
Dousland Terr PL20 127 B3
Dove Cl Cullompton EX15 163 A2
Honiton EX14 166 B4
Dove Gdns PL3 249 D7
Dove La EX10 188 B3
Dove Way EX2 176 D3
Dovedale Cl EX34 150 E5
Dovedale Rd PL2 248 A7
Dover Rd PL6 245 E3
Dover's Hill EX17 80 E8
Dowell St EX14 166 B6
Dower Ct TQ3 226 C8
Dower Ho The TQ10 135 C4
Dower Rd TQ1 220 A7
Down Cl
Newton Poppleford EX10 186 D7
Saltash PL12 242 C2
Down Cross EX16 47 A2
Down End EX17 165 F5
Down Hill
Morchard Bishop EX17 78 F8
Rackenford EX16 47 A3
Down La Braunton EX33 152 E6
Combe Martin EX31 10 F6
Doddiscombsleigh EX6 113 D5
Georgeham EX33 8 A4
Georgeham, North Buckland EX33 8 B3
Knowle EX33 8 F2
Molland EX36 31 E7
Rackenford EX16 47 A3
Winkleigh EX19 58 D4
Down Park Dr PL19 171 D4
Down Rd Instow EX39 15 B1
Plymouth PL7 251 C5
Tavistock PL19 171 D4
Down St Mary Vineyard★ EX17 78 D7
Down The PL20 125 F1
Down View Rd TQ12 211 A6
Downash La EX13 88 E3
Downaway La TQ12 213 E5
Downeshead La EX17 165 E5
Downfield Cl TQ5 230 A3
Downfield Dr PL7 250 F5
Downfield Way PL7 250 F5
Downfield Wlk PL7 250 F5
Downgate Gdns PL2 248 D8
Downham Gdns PL5 244 C7
Downham Sch PL9 255 F7
Downhayne Hill EX17 62 B1
Downhayne Rd EX24 102 F6
Downland Cross EX39 23 E2
Downlands Cross EX15 66 E2
Downlands La TA3 52 F1
Downlea PL19 171 D4
Downmoor Cross EX38 55 B8
Downs Rd EX39 15 C1
Downs View EX22 54 D6
Downside Ave PL6 249 C7
Downside Cl DT6 104 F4
Downstow Cross TQ10 134 F5
Downton Cl PL1 262 A4
Downton Cross TQ6 233 A7
Dowrich Cross EX17 80 A7
Dracaena Ave EX31 154 C4
Dragdown Hill EX17 95 F7
Dragon Hill EX38 40 F2
Dragon's Mead EX13 167 C4
Dragon's Tail TQ5 230 E4
Dragons Hill DT7 260 E5
Dragoon Cl TQ12 180 E3
Drake Ave
Teignmouth TQ14 210 A8
Torquay TQ2 219 C6
Drake CE Prim Sch EX9 198 B6
Drake Cir PL1,PL4 263 A3
Drake Cl EX39 156 B6
Drake Ct PL4 263 B3
Drake Dr TQ4 226 B2
Drake Gdns PL19 171 C4
Drake La TQ13 180 E7
Drake Prim Sch PL2 247 E6
Drake Rd
Bovey Tracey TQ13 180 E7
Newton Abbot TQ12 207 F3
Salcombe TQ8 259 C5
Tavistock PL19 171 C6
Drake Villas PL19 171 A4
Drake Way PL9 255 E7
Drake's Ave Exmouth EX8 202 D8
Sidmouth EX10 188 C8
Drake's Cross EX37 44 A7
Drake's Pk 3 PL20 125 E1
Drake's Rd TQ4 225 E4
Drakefield Dr PL12 243 A3
Drakes Cl PL6 244 F4
Drakes Cres TA20 88 D8
Drakes Farm EX2 176 E2
Drakes Gdns EX8 202 D8
Drakes Mdw
Cheriton Fitzpaine EX17 62 F1
Yarcombe EX14 69 A3
Drakes Pk TA21 160 D7
Drakes Pk N TA21 160 D7
Drakes Rd EX4 177 A4
Drakes Way DT7 260 E3
Drakewalls Gdns PL18 125 C5
Drakewalls Pl PL18 125 C5
Draper Terr 3 PL19 171 B5
Drapers Cl EX34 3 B3
Drax Gdns PL6 248 E8
Draycott Cl EX2 178 A4
Drayford Rd EX16 46 E1
Drayton Rd PL5 244 C1
Drayway Cross EX16 63 D1
Drayway La EX16 63 E1
Drew St TQ5 230 C3
Drew's Cl EX6 201 A8
Drews Field La TQ3 218 D7
Drewsmead TQ13 122 C3
Drewston Cross TQ13 111 C6
Drewstone Cross EX36 30 E6
Dreys Ct EX1 177 E6
Dreyton Cross TQ9 139 F3
Drift La EX14 66 F3
Drift Lane Cross EX14 66 F3
Drift The TA20 88 E8
Drive The
Bishopsteignton TQ14 208 E8
Brixham TQ5 230 C2
Dawlish EX7 204 E6
Exeter EX5 99 B3
Holbeton PL8 136 D1
Kingskerswell TQ12 213 A4
Plymouth PL3 248 E7
Droridge TQ9 222 F8
Droridge La TQ9 222 E8
Drove Way TA3 68 C8
Drovers Way
Ivybridge PL21 237 A6
Seaton EX12 192 B8
Druid Cross TQ13 130 E5
Drum Bridge TQ12 180 F1
Drum Way TQ12 180 F2
Drummond Cl PL2 247 F7
Drummond Pl PL1 247 F3
Drunken Bridge Hill PL7 250 D4
Dry La Christow EX6 113 B4
Okehampton EX20 93 D5
Drybridge Cross TQ10 135 C5
Dryburgh Cres PL2 248 A8
Dryden Ave PL5 244 C1
Dryden Cotts EX5 99 D2
Dryden Rd EX2 177 F4
Dryfield EX6 182 B4
Drymump Hill EX36 45 F7
Dualstone Cross EX22 71 C3
Dubbs Cross EX21 90 E3
Ducane Wlk PL6 245 B1
Duchy Ave TQ3 219 B2
Duchy Coll PL17 115 B1
Duchy Cotts PL17 115 B1
Duchy Dr TQ3 219 B2
Duchy Gdns TQ3 219 A3
Duchy Pk TQ3 219 A2
Duchy Rd EX14 166 A4
Duchy Sch The EX5 82 F6
Duck La EX20 76 C5
Ducks Orch EX6 182 B3
Ducksmoor Cross EX16 63 E8
Duckspond Rd TQ11 236 A4
Duckworth Rd EX2 177 A4
Duckworth St 3 PL2 248 A4
Ducky Row PL17 125 A4
Dudley Gdns PL6 249 B8
Dudley Rd PL7 250 B5
Dudley Way EX39 156 B6
Dudmoor La EX31 10 B4
Duerdon Cross EX39 38 E6
Duke Of Cornwall Cl EX8 196 E1
Duke St Cullompton EX15 163 C2
Dartmouth TQ6 233 F3
Kingsbridge TQ7 258 D5
Plymouth PL1 247 E2
South Molton EX36 158 C4
Tavistock PL19 171 C6
Duke's Rd EX9 197 F2
Dukes Cl Otterton EX9 198 E7
Paignton TQ3 225 E6
Dukes Cres EX8 196 E1
Dukes Dr PL19 125 E4
Dukes Mdw EX15 163 C2
Dukes Orch EX5 82 F6
Dukes Rd TQ9 223 F5
Dukes Way EX13 167 C4
Dulcis Cross EX13 87 C2
Dulford Bsns Pk EX15 66 B1
Dulford Cross EX15 66 B1
Duloe Gdns PL2 248 C8
Dulverton Com Sch TA22 33 D6
Dulverton La TA4 35 D7
Dumfries Ave PL5 244 D3
Dumpdon La EX14 85 F6
Dumpdon View EX14 86 A6
Dun Cross TQ9 222 C8
Duncan Ho TQ1 220 C4
Duncan St PL1 247 E1
Duncannon La TQ9 227 E7
Duncannon Mead TQ9 227 F7
Dunclair Pk PL3 249 D5
Duncombe Ave PL5 244 A2
Duncombe Cross TQ7 144 C2
Duncombe St TQ7 258 D6
Dundas St 4 PL2 248 A4
Dundonald St PL2 247 F4
Dune View
Braunton EX33 152 B7
Westward Ho! EX39 156 D7
Dune View Rd EX33 152 B6
Dunheved Rd PL12 242 F2
Dunkeswell Airfield EX14 67 B2
Dunkeswell Bsns Pk EX14 67 B2
Dunkeswell Cl PL2 247 F8
Dunkirk EX11 169 C4
Dunley Cross TQ13 123 B4
Dunley La TQ13 123 B5
Dunley Wlk PL6 245 C1
Dunmere Rd TQ1 220 B6
Dunmore Ct TQ14 210 B2
Dunmore Dr TQ14 210 B2
Dunn La EX39 25 E2
Dunn's Hill TA21 51 A6
Dunnet Rd PL6 244 D7
Dunning Ct EX14 166 B6
Dunning Gn 1 EX31 154 C3
Dunning Rd TQ14 210 A7
Dunning Wlk
Teignmouth TQ14 210 A6
Teignmouth TQ14 210 A7
Dunns Cl EX33 152 F4
Dunraven Dr PL6 245 A5
Dunrich Cl EX2 261 C2
Dunscombe La
Chudleigh TQ13 124 A5
Sidmouth EX10 189 B7
Dunsdon Cross EX22 53 C3
Dunsford Cl EX8 202 D6
Dunsford Gdns EX4 176 E3
Dunsford Hill EX5 81 E3
Dunsford Prim Sch EX6 112 F8
Dunsford Rd EX2 176 E3
Dunsford Way 1 EX16 161 C3
Dunsgreen La EX15 67 D8
Dunsland Cross EX22 73 A6
Dunsley Hill EX16,EX36 32 D5
Dunster Cl PL7 251 C4
Dunster Wlk EX6 181 F5
Dunsterville Rd PL21 237 E6
Dunstone Ave PL9 256 A7
Dunstone Cl
Paignton TQ3 218 E1
Plymouth PL9 255 F7
Dunstone Cross TQ7 149 C7
Dunstone Ct TQ3 218 E1
Dunstone Dr PL9 255 F7
Dunstone La PL9 256 B7
Dunstone Park Rd TQ3 218 E1
Dunstone Prim Sch PL9 256 A8
Dunstone Rd
Plymouth, Plymstock PL9 255 F7
Plymouth, St Budeaux PL5 243 F3
Dunstone Rise TQ3 218 E1
Dunstone View PL9 256 A7
Duntz Hill PL16 105 E4
Dunvegan Cl EX4 177 A8
Dunwell Cross PL21 137 D5
Dural Cross EX22 38 B3
Durant Ho EX20 77 C4
Durban Rd PL3 248 D5
Durbin Cl EX14 166 D5
Durdon Cross EX20 75 A1
Dure La EX36 30 E8
Durham Ave PL4 263 C4
Durham Cl Exeter EX1 178 C7
Exmouth EX8 196 D4
Paignton TQ3 219 B1
Durham Way EX14 166 A4
Durleigh Rd TQ5 230 B4
Durlestone Cross TQ7 149 B8
Durley Rd EX12 191 F7
Durleymoor Cross EX16 50 F4
Durnford St PL1 248 A1
Durnford Street Ope PL1 248 A1
Durrant Cl Northam EX39 157 A5
Plymouth PL1 247 E3
Durrant La EX39 157 A5
Durris Cl PL6 245 D4
Durris Gdns PL6 245 D4
Dursley Way EX39 156 E2
Durwent Cl PL9 255 A6
Duryardwood La EX5 172 E5
Dux Cross EX22 71 B6
Duxford Cl PL5 243 E5
Dyehouse Cnr TA22 34 A6
Dyehouse Cross TA22 33 F5
Dyehouse La TA22 34 A5
Dyers Cl Braunton EX33 152 D6
West Buckland TA21 52 F7
Dyers Ct EX2 261 A2
Dyke Hill Terr TA20 88 D8
Dymond Rd EX39 156 F1
Dynevor Cl PL3 248 F7

E

Eager Way EX6 181 F5
Eagle Cl TQ12 123 E1
Eagle Cotts EX4 177 A5
Eagle Ct TQ2 219 E8
Eagle Nest EX2 176 D3
Eagle Pl TQ13 111 F5
Eagle Rd PL7 251 C4
Eagle Way EX2 178 F5
Eaglewood Cl TQ2 213 C2
Earl Richard's Rd N EX2 177 E3
Earl Richard's Rd S EX2 177 F2
Earl's Acre PL3 248 C4
Earl's Dr The
Cawsand PL10 253 A1
Cawsand, Kingsand PL10 253 B3
Earl's Dr The PL10 140 J2
Earls Ct TQ1 219 F6
Earls Mill Rd PL7 250 E6
Earls Wood Cl PL6 245 F3
Earls Wood Dr PL6 245 F3
Earlswood Dr TQ3 225 D7
East Allington Prim Sch TQ9 144 D7
East Anstey Prim Sch EX16 32 E5
East Ash Cross
Bradworthy EX22 38 F3
Whiddon Down EX20 95 D2
Whiddon Down EX20 95 E1
East Ave EX1 177 E6
East Ball Hill EX39 22 E3
East Buckland Cross EX32 18 D2
East Budleigh Rd
Budleigh Salterton EX9 198 B3
East Budleigh EX9 198 C6
East Butterleigh Cross EX15 64 E3
East Challacombe La EX34 3 B4
East Cl EX16 46 E1
East Cliff DT7 260 E3
East Cliff Cl EX7 204 E7
East Cliff Gdns EX7 204 E7
East Cliff Rd EX7 204 E7
East Cliff Wlk TQ14 210 D7
East Coombe Cross EX17 81 A6
East Coombe La TA4 35 D8
East Devon Bsns Pk EX14 86 C3
East Devon Coll EX16 161 C6
East Devon Coll (Annexe) EX16 161 D4
East Down Cross
Barnstaple EX34 9 F6
Okehampton EX20 93 D8
East Dr EX8 196 A1
East End EX17 62 D3
East End Terr 16 TQ13 131 A5
East Farm TQ7 144 D1
East Grove Rd EX2 261 C2
East Hill EX33 152 E6
East John Wlk EX1 177 E6
East Leigh Cross
Harberton TQ9 222 B1
Zeal Monachorum EX17 77 F8
East Lyn La EX35 151 F2
East Mead EX15 67 B8
East Meadow Rd EX33 152 B7
East Mere Cross EX16 50 B2
East Moore Cross TQ9 135 E1
East Nymph La EX17 95 E6
East Pafford Ave TQ2 214 B3
East Park Ave PL4 262 C4
East Park Cl EX19 58 F3
East Park Rd EX32 155 D4
East Pk EX39 38 F8
East Pugsley Cross EX37 29 B2
East Rowley La EX36 45 D5
East Sherford Cross PL8 257 A8
East St Ashburton TQ13 130 F5
Bishop's Tawton EX32 16 E1
Black Torrington EX21 74 A8
Bovey Tracey TQ13 180 D8
Braunton EX33 152 D6
Chittlehampton EX37 28 F4
Chulmleigh EX18 44 E1
Crediton EX17 165 D5
Denbury TQ12 211 A7
Great Torrington EX38 159 D5
Ipplepen TQ12 211 E2
Newton Abbot TQ12 207 C3
Okehampton EX20 170 C5
Plymouth PL1 262 A2
Sheepwash EX21 56 C1
Sidmouth EX10 188 B3
South Molton EX36 158 D4
Torquay TQ2 219 F6
Uffculme EX15 66 A7
East Tapps La EX16 33 B2
East Terr EX9 199 H2
East Town La EX6 194 D3
East View Cotts 4 EX14 166 C6
East View Pl EX16 161 E4
East Village Cross EX17 80 C8
East Way PL21 136 D6
East Wonford Hill EX2 178 B5
East Worlington Cross EX17 61 B8
East Worlington Sch EX17 61 B8

East Youlstone Cross
EX23 .....37 F2
East-the-Water Com Prim Sch EX39 .....157 C1
Eastacombe Cross
Barnstaple EX31 .....16 B1
Northlew EX20 .....74 E2
Eastacombe La EX31 .....15 E6
Eastacombe Rise EX31 .....15 E6
Eastacott Cross EX37 .....28 E2
Eastacott La EX34 .....8 B6
Eastbourne Terr EX39 .....156 D7
Eastbrook Ho 7 TQ14 .....210 B6
Eastbury Ave PL5 .....244 A2
Eastchurch La EX6 .....96 D6
Eastcoombe La EX17 .....81 A6
Eastcote Cl PL6 .....245 B6
Eastcott Cross EX23 .....37 D2
Eastdown EX39 .....22 F3
Eastdown Cross TQ9 .....145 D8
Eastella Rd PL20 .....127 A2
Easter Close Cross EX31 .....3 D1
Easter Ct EX31 .....154 B2
Easter Ground La EX34 .....8 F5
Easter Hill EX37 .....28 B2
Easter La Berrynarbor EX34 .....2 E3
Brendon EX35 .....6 B4
Easter Lane Cross TQ13 121 B2
Easter St EX32 .....16 E1
Easterbrook La EX6 .....96 D8
Easterdown Cl PL9 .....255 F7
Easterfield La TQ1 .....214 C2
Easterley Terr EX31 .....154 C3
Eastern Ave
Barnstaple EX32 .....155 C4
Exeter EX2 .....182 C7
Eastern Espl TQ4 .....226 C6
Eastern Rd
Ashburton TQ13 .....131 A5
Zeal Monachorum EX17 .....78 C7
Eastern Wood Rd PL7 .....251 D4
Easterntown PL8 .....136 D1
Eastfield EX11 .....168 D4
Eastfield Ave PL9 .....255 C6
Eastfield Cres PL3 .....249 A6
Eastfield Orch EX15 .....66 A8
Easthay La TA20 .....88 F4
Eastington Cross EX17 .....60 E4
Eastington Hill EX17 .....60 E3
Eastlake Ho 5 PL1 .....263 A2
Eastlake St PL1 .....263 A3
Eastlake Wlk PL1 .....263 A3
Eastlands EX15 .....67 B8
Eastleigh Cl EX13 .....103 D8
Eastmoor La TA4 .....34 E8
Easton Cross
Hittisleigh EX6 .....96 C5
Kingsbridge TQ7 .....258 B3
Easton La EX16 .....50 D1
Easton Moor Cross EX31 27 C1
Eastwood EX35 .....151 B4
Eastwood Cres TQ12 .....206 E4
Eastwood La EX6 .....96 C7
Easy Bridge Cross EX13 102 F7
Easy La TQ13 .....123 B7
Eaton Ct TQ14 .....210 B7
Eaton Dr EX1 .....261 C3
Eaton Hall Dr TQ6 .....233 E4
Eaton Ho EX1 .....261 C3
Eaton Pl TQ4 .....226 B5
Ebberley Lawn EX32 .....155 A5
Ebberly Arms EX38 .....42 F6
Ebberly Cross EX19 .....42 E5
Ebenezer Rd TQ3 .....226 A5
Ebford La EX3 .....183 D4
Ebrington Rd EX2 .....177 B3
Ebrington St
Kingsbridge TQ7 .....258 D5
Plymouth PL4 .....263 A3
Eddy's La 9 EX32 .....155 B3
Eddystone Cl
Heybrook Bay PL9 .....140 A7
Plymouth PL3 .....249 C6
Eddystone Rd
Down Thomas PL9 .....255 C1
Thurlestone TQ7 .....143 A1
Eddystone Rise TQ7 .....147 D7
Eddystone Terr PL1 .....262 B1
Eden Cl TQ5 .....230 C3
Eden Gr TQ3 .....225 F7
Eden Park Cty Jun & Inf Schs TQ5 .....230 C3
Eden Pk TQ5 .....230 C3
Eden Way EX10 .....186 E3
Edenvale Rd TQ3 .....225 F8
Edgar Terr PL4 .....249 A4
Edgbaston Mead EX2 .....178 C4
Edgcumbe Ave PL1 .....262 A3
Edgcumbe Cl PL18 .....125 D6
Edgcumbe Cres PL10 .....252 F6
Edgcumbe Ct 3 PL3 .....248 A3
Edgcumbe Dr PL19 .....171 B6
Edgcumbe Park Rd PL3 248 D6
Edgcumbe Rd PL12 .....242 C5
Edgecombe Way PL18 .....125 B5
Edgecumbe Rd PL12 .....125 A2
Edgecumbe Terr 13 PL20 .....125 E1
Edgehill Coll EX39 .....156 F2
Edgeland Cross TQ12 .....217 D8
Edgelands La TQ12 .....211 C1
Edgeley Rd TQ2 .....214 A2
Edgerley Cross EX17 .....60 C1
Edgerton Park Rd EX4 .....177 D8
Edgeworthy Hill EX16 .....62 C8
Edgiford Cross EX18 .....45 B1
Edginswell Cl TQ2 .....213 C1
Edginswell La TQ2,TQ12 213 A1
Edinburgh Cres EX8 .....195 E6
Edinburgh Dr EX4 .....176 E6
Edinburgh Rd TQ5 .....230 D3
Edinburgh St PL1 .....247 E1
Edith Ave PL4 .....263 C4
Edith St PL5 .....243 D1
Edmonton Cl EX4 .....178 A8
Edmund St EX2,EX4 .....261 A2
Edna Terr PL4 .....263 C3
Edwards Cl PL7 .....251 B4
Edwards Cres PL12 .....242 C2
Edwards Dr
Plymouth PL7 .....251 B5
Westward Ho! EX39 .....156 E7
Edwards Rd PL15 .....90 C1
Edwin Rd EX2 .....177 B3
Effingham Cres PL3 .....248 D7
Efford Barns EX17 .....81 B4
Efford Cres PL3 .....249 B6
Efford La PL3 .....249 B5
Efford Pathway
Plymouth PL3 .....249 C6
Plymouth PL3 .....249 D5
Efford Rd PL3 .....249 B6
Efford Wlk PL3 .....249 B6
Egerton Cres PL4 .....263 C3
Egerton Pl PL4 .....263 C3
Egerton Rd Plymouth PL4 263 C3
Torquay TQ1 .....220 C6
Egg Moor La EX13 .....88 A7
Eggbuckland Com Coll PL6 .....249 A8
Eggbuckland Rd PL3 .....249 C7
Eggbuckland Vale Prim Sch PL6 .....249 A8
Eggesford Country Ctr★ EX18 .....59 E6
Eggesford Cross EX17 .....60 A3
Eggesford Fourways EX18 .....59 E5
Eggesford Rd EX19 .....58 F3
Eggesford Sta EX18 .....59 E6
Egham Ave EX2 .....177 D3
Egremont Cross EX14 .....84 C6
Egremont Rd EX8 .....202 A7
Egret Cl PL10 .....253 A6
Egypt La EX18 .....44 E1
Eiffel Pl 11 TQ9 .....223 C5
Eight Acre Cl 1 PL7 .....251 C5
Eight Acre La TA21 .....160 E5
Eight Trees TQ9 .....216 A5
El Monte Cl 6 TQ14 .....210 B6
Elaine Cl Exeter EX4 .....174 A2
Plymouth PL7 .....250 B5
Elba Cl TQ4 .....226 C1
Elberry La
Churston Ferrers TQ5 .....229 E5
Paignton TQ4 .....229 D7
Elbow La PL19 .....171 C6
Elburton Prim Sch PL9 .....256 C7
Elburton Rd PL9 .....256 B8
Eldad Hill PL1 .....262 A3
Elder Cl 2 PL7 .....251 B5
Elder Gr EX17 .....165 E6
Elderberry Way EX15 .....162 E5
Eldertree Gdns EX4 .....177 A7
Eleanor Ho PL1 .....262 A2
Elford Cres PL7 .....250 E7
Elford Dr PL9 .....255 C7
Elford Pk PL20 .....127 A2
Elgar Cl Barnstaple EX32 .....155 C5
Exeter EX2 .....178 C5
Elgin Cres PL5 .....244 E3
Elim Cl EX10 .....188 B5
Elim Ct PL3 .....248 E5
Elim Terr PL3 .....248 E5
Eliot Cl EX11 .....169 C3
Eliot St PL5 .....247 E8
Elizabeth Ave
Brixham TQ5 .....230 A1
Exeter EX4 .....177 E8
Elizabeth Cl
Barnstaple EX31 .....154 D2
Ivybridge PL21 .....237 F5
Lyme Regis DT7 .....260 E4
2 Whimple EX5 .....99 E8
Elizabeth Ct
2 Plymouth PL1 .....263 A2
Torquay TQ2 .....219 F5
Totnes TQ9 .....223 F5
Elizabeth Dr EX31 .....154 D3
Elizabeth Lea Cl EX22 .....38 E1
Elizabeth Pl PL4 .....263 A4
Elizabeth Rd
Exmouth EX8 .....196 C2
Seaton EX12 .....192 A7
Elizabeth Sq 4 TQ12 .....207 F2
Elizabethan Ct 8 EX2 .....261 B2
Elizabethan Ho 10 TQ9 .....223 D5
Elizabethan House (Mus) The★ PL1 .....263 A2
Elkins Hill TQ5 .....230 D5
Ellacombe Church Rd TQ1 .....220 C6
Ellacombe Cty Prim Sch TQ1 .....220 B6
Ellacombe Rd TQ1 .....220 B6
Ellards Cl EX2 .....177 E3
Ellen Tinkham Sch EX1 .....178 E7
Elleralie Ho TQ14 .....210 B3
Ellerhayes EX5 .....82 D4
Ellersdown La TA22 .....33 E4
Ellerslie Rd EX31 .....154 B4
Ellesmere TQ1 .....220 C4
Ellesmere Rd TQ1 .....220 E5
Elley Cross EX17 .....79 B2
Elliot Cl EX32 .....155 C4
Elliot Ho EX2 .....261 B2
Elliot Plain TQ11 .....236 C5
Elliot Sq PL11 .....247 B3
Elliot St PL1 .....262 B1
Elliot Terr PL1 .....262 C1
Elliot Terrace La PL1 .....262 C1
Elliots Hill TQ13 .....130 C8
Elliott Cl Exeter EX4 .....173 E2
Saltash PL12 .....242 D2
Elliott Ct TQ12 .....211 C2
Elliott Gr TQ5 .....230 B4
Elliott Rd PL4 .....249 B1
Elliott Way EX2 .....178 D5
Elliott's Hill EX17 .....61 C3
Elliotts Hill PL8 .....257 A4
Ellmead Cross EX20 .....93 F7
Ellwood Rd EX8 .....196 D2
Elm Bank TQ11 .....236 A4
Elm Cl Broadclyst EX5 .....175 C6
Stibb Cross EX38 .....40 D1
Tavistock PL19 .....171 C3
Elm Cotts Barnstaple EX31 16 A3
Saltash PL12 .....242 C3
Elm Cres PL3,PL4 .....249 A4
Elm Ct EX6 .....201 B8
Elm Dr TQ12 .....207 F7
Elm Farm La EX24 .....103 A3
Elm Gr Bideford EX39 .....156 F2
Exmouth EX8 .....201 F6
Plymouth PL7 .....250 E5
Teignmouth TQ14 .....210 B8
Elm Grove Ave EX3 .....182 F5
Elm Grove Cl EX7 .....204 E7
Elm Grove Dr EX7 .....204 E7
Elm Grove Gdns EX3 .....182 F5
Elm Grove Rd
Dawlish EX7 .....204 E7
Exeter EX4 .....261 A4
Topsham EX3 .....182 F5
Elm La EX8 .....202 F7
Elm Orch EX12 .....192 D7
Elm Pk Millbrook PL10 .....253 B6
Paignton TQ3 .....225 F6
Elm Rd Brixham TQ5 .....230 A2
Exmouth EX8 .....202 C7
2 Newton Abbot TQ12 .....207 C3
Plymouth, Glenholt PL6 .....245 D6
Plymouth, Mannamead PL4 .....248 D6
Elm Terr Honiton EX14 .....166 D6
Tiverton EX16 .....161 B4
Elm Tree Cl PL8 .....257 F4
Elm Tree Pk PL8 .....136 A2
Elm Units EX2 .....177 D1
Elm Villas EX24 .....103 A3
Elm Way EX10 .....101 A1
Elm Wlk TQ9 .....223 F5
Elmbank Gdns 3 TQ4 .....226 A5
Elmbank Rd TQ4 .....226 A5
Elmbridge Gdns EX4 .....177 A8
ElmCroft PL2 .....248 B7
Elmcroft Terr 7 EX39 .....157 A2
Elmdale Rd EX39 .....157 A3
Elmdon Cl EX4 .....173 D1
Elmfield Cres EX8 .....196 B2
Elmfield Mdw EX20 .....74 E1
Elmfield Rd
Barnstaple EX31 .....16 A3
Seaton EX12 .....192 A7
Elmfield Terr EX39 .....157 A7
Elmhirst Dr TQ9 .....223 E5
Elmhurst Ct 3 TQ14 .....210 B5
Elmlea Ave EX31 .....153 E5
Elmore Way EX16 .....161 E5
Elms Rd TA21 .....160 F5
Elms The Colyford EX24 .....103 A3
Plymouth PL3 .....248 A3
Elmside
Budleigh Salterton EX9 .....198 A1
Exeter EX4 .....177 E7
Willand EX15 .....162 D3
Elmside Cl EX4 .....177 E7
Elmsleigh EX32 .....27 E8
Elmsleigh Pk TQ4 .....226 B5
Elmsleigh Rd TQ4 .....226 B5
Elmwood Ave TQ12 .....206 E4
Elmwood Cl PL6 .....245 D5
Elmwood Cres EX7 .....204 E7
Elmwood Gdns EX24 .....103 A3
Elmwood Pk TQ7 .....143 E7
Elphinstone Rd PL2 .....248 C7
Elsdale Rd TQ4 .....226 A4
Elsdon La EX11 .....168 E4
Elsdon's La DT6 .....104 D7
Elston Cross
Chulmleigh EX18 .....44 C3
Churchstow TQ7 .....143 D4
Copplestone EX17 .....79 C6
Elston La EX17 .....79 B5
Elston Mdw EX17 .....165 A5
Elstone Cross EX18 .....44 C3
Elton Rd EX4 .....177 E8
Elvis Rd EX8 .....202 D7
Elwell Cross EX32 .....18 B2
Elwell Rd PL12 .....243 A2
Elwick Gdns PL3 .....249 B5
Elworthy Cross EX16 .....47 C2
Elworthy Dr TA21 .....160 D4
Elworthy Hill EX16 .....47 D2
Elwyn Rd EX8 .....202 C6
Ely Cl Exeter EX4 .....176 D6
Feniton EX14 .....84 D2
Elysian Ct EX36 .....158 D5
Elysian Fields EX10 .....188 B5
Embankment La PL4 .....249 B2
Embankment Rd
Kingsbridge TQ7 .....258 D3
Plymouth PL4 .....249 B2
Embankment Road La N PL4 .....249 B2
Embercombe Cross EX32 18 F1
Embleford Cross TQ13 .....111 F5
Emblett Dr TQ12 .....206 E4
Emblett Hill View TQ12 .....206 F1
Embridge Cross TQ6 .....145 F7
Embridge Hill TQ6 .....146 A7
Embury Cl TQ12 .....213 A4
Emily Gdns PL4 .....263 B4
Emma Pl PL1 .....248 A1
Emma Place Ope PL1 .....248 A1
Emmanuel Cl 1 EX4 .....177 A5
Emmanuel Rd 2 EX4 .....177 A5
Emmasfield EX8 .....202 D7
Emmetts Pk 9 TQ13 .....131 A5
Emperor Way EX1 .....178 E7
Empire Ct 2 TQ1 .....220 A7
Empire Rd TQ1 .....220 A7
Empsons Cl EX7 .....204 C6
Empsons Hill EX7 .....204 C6
Endfield Cl EX1 .....178 B6
Endsleigh Cres EX5 .....179 B7
Endsleigh Dr PL15,PL19, PL17 .....115 D5
Endsleigh Gdns 2 PL4 .....263 A4
Endsleigh Park Rd PL3 .....248 D6
Endsleigh Pk EX23 .....70 A6
Endsleigh Pl PL4 .....263 A4
Endsleigh Rd PL9 .....255 C7
Endsleigh View PL21 .....237 A5
Enfield Cl EX17 .....165 A5
Enfield Cotts TQ1 .....220 D7
Enfield Rd TQ1 .....220 C7
England's Cl 13 EX10 .....101 B1
Eningdale Rd PL19 .....171 A4
Ennaton Cross PL21 .....137 E7
Ennerdale Gdns PL6 .....244 E5
Ennerdale Way EX4 .....176 F6
Ennisfarne Rd EX39 .....156 B7
Ensign Ct EX39 .....156 E7
Ensis Cross EX31 .....27 D5
Entrance Cross EX37 .....44 B7
Epping Cres PL6 .....249 D7
Epworth Terr 4 PL2 .....247 F5
Eric Rd Calstock PL18 .....125 E3
Plymouth PL4 .....263 C3
Erica Dr TQ2 .....213 F3
Erith Ave PL2 .....247 E7
Erle Gdns PL7 .....250 F3
Erlstoke Cl PL6 .....245 D1
Erme Bridge Wks PL21 .....237 C4
Erme Ct PL21 .....237 D5
Erme Dr PL21 .....237 C5
Erme Gdns PL3 .....249 C5
Erme Pk PL21 .....136 F3
Erme Prim Sch The PL21 .....237 D5
Erme Rd PL21 .....237 D5
Erme Terr PL21 .....237 D5
Ermeside Cotts PL21 .....136 F4
Ermington Prim Sch PL21 .....136 F4
Ermington Terr PL4 .....248 E4
Ermington Workshops PL21 .....137 A4
Ernborough Ct EX2 .....261 C2
Ernesettle Cres PL5 .....243 E3
Ernesettle Gn PL5 .....243 E4
Ernesettle Jun & Inf Sch PL5 .....243 F4
Ernesettle La PL5 .....243 D4
Ernesettle Rd PL5 .....243 E3
Ernsborough Gdns EX14 .....166 B5
Escot Park Animal Ctr & Gdns★ EX11 .....84 C1
Eskil Pl EX38 .....159 C6
Esmonde Gdns PL5 .....247 B8
Esplanade Exmouth EX8 .....202 A5
Seaton EX12 .....192 B4
Teignmouth TQ14 .....210 C4
Esplanade Rd TQ4 .....226 C6
Esplanade The
Dartmouth TQ6 .....233 F5
Plymouth PL1 .....262 C1
Sidmouth EX10 .....188 B3
Woolacombe EX34 .....7 F7
Essa Rd PL12 .....242 F2
Essex Cl EX4 .....176 E4
Essex St PL1 .....262 B4
Essington Cl EX8 .....196 B3
Essington La EX20 .....77 D4
Essington Rd EX20 .....77 C4
Essinton Ct EX8 .....196 B3
Estover Cl PL6 .....245 F5
Estover Com Coll PL6 .....245 D2
Estover Ind Est PL6 .....245 E4
Estover Prim Sch PL6 .....245 D2
Estover Rd PL6 .....245 F4
Estuary Bsns Pk EX31 .....15 C3
Estuary CT EX8 .....201 E6
Estuary View
Budleigh Salterton EX9 .....198 B1
Northam EX39 .....157 A8
Yelland EX31 .....15 C2
Esworthy Cross EX16 .....32 F1
Ethelston's Cl DT7 .....260 A5
Ethelwynne Brown Cl EX39 .....157 B2
Eton Ave PL1 .....262 C4
Eton Cl EX39 .....156 F3
Eton Pl PL1 .....262 C4
Eton St PL1 .....262 C4
Eton Terr 3 PL1 .....262 B3
Etonhurst Cl EX2 .....178 D3
Eugene Rd TQ3 .....226 C8
Eureka Terr
Bovey Tracey TQ13 .....180 D8
1 Honiton EX14 .....166 C5
Europa Pk EX34 .....8 B6
Evans Pl PL2 .....248 B5
Eveleigh Cl 2 TQ5 .....230 C3
Evelyn Pl PL4 .....263 A4
Evelyn St PL5 .....243 D1
Evenden Ct PL11 .....247 A3
Everest Dr EX12 .....192 A7
Everett Pl EX16 .....161 E6
Evergreen Cl EX8 .....196 D3
Evett Cl EX8 .....202 E8
Ewin's Ash EX14 .....85 C8
Eworthy Cross EX21 .....91 E6
Exbourne Cross EX20 .....76 C4
Exbourne Prim Sch EX20 76 C4
Excalibur Cl EX4 .....174 A1
Exchange St PL1 .....263 A2
Exe Cl EX31 .....15 E5
Exe Gdns PL3 .....249 C7
Exe Hill TQ2 .....219 B8
Exe St Exeter EX4 .....261 A3
Topsham EX3 .....182 F5
Exe Units EX2 .....177 D1
Exe Vale Rd EX2 .....178 A1
Exe Vale Terr 6 EX16 .....161 C3
Exe View Cotts EX4 .....176 F8
Exe View Rd EX8 .....196 C6
Exebridge Ctr The EX4 .....261 A1
Exebridge Ind Est TA22 .....33 F3
Exeter Airport EX5 .....99 A4
Exeter Airport Bsns Pk EX5 .....99 A4
Exeter Cl Feniton EX14 .....84 D2
Plymouth PL5 .....243 D4
Exeter Coll EX4 .....177 A7
Exeter Coll (Annexe) EX4 .....261 A3
Exeter Coll Bishop Blackall Annex EX4 .....261 B4
Exeter Cross
Bovey Tracey TQ12 .....123 A1
Sidmouth EX10 .....188 B6
Exeter Foyer EX2 .....261 A2
Exeter Gate EX36 .....158 C3
Exeter Hill
Cullompton EX15 .....163 B2
Kenton EX6 .....194 D3
Shobrooke EX17 .....80 F5
Tiverton EX16 .....161 E2
Exeter Hill Cross EX17 .....80 F4
Exeter Nuffield Hospl The EX2 .....177 E4
Exeter Phoenix EX1 .....261 B3
Exeter Rd Braunton EX33 152 E4
Crediton EX17 .....165 D4
Cullompton EX15 .....163 B2
Dawlish EX7 .....200 E3
Exmouth EX8 .....196 A2
Exmouth EX8 .....202 A7
Honiton EX14 .....166 A5
Ivybridge PL21 .....237 E5
Kennford EX6 .....181 A2
Kingsteignton TQ12 .....207 D8
Newton Abbot TQ12 .....207 B5
Newton Poppleford EX10 .....186 C8
Okehampton EX20 .....170 D5
Ottery St Mary EX11 .....169 A3
Rockwell Green TA21 .....160 B5
Silverton EX5 .....82 B5
South Brent TQ10 .....135 A3
Teignmouth TQ14 .....210 B6
Tiverton EX16 .....64 B4
Topsham EX2,EX3 .....182 D6
West Hill EX11 .....168 E7
Whiddon Down EX20 .....95 F3
Whimple EX5 .....168 B8
Winkleigh EX19 .....58 F2
Exeter Road Bsns Pk 8 TQ12 .....123 E1
Exeter Road Ind Est EX20 .....170 E6
Exeter Road Prim Sch EX8 .....202 A7
Exeter Sch EX2 .....177 E5
Exeter St
North Tawton EX20 .....77 C4
Plymouth PL4 .....263 A3
Plymouth PL4 .....263 B2
Teignmouth TQ14 .....210 B5
Exeter Trad Ctr EX2 .....181 E8
Exeter YH★ EX2 .....182 A8
Exhibition Rd EX17 .....165 E6
Exhibition Way EX4 .....178 D8
Exminster Com Prim Sch EX6 .....182 A4
Exminster Hill EX6 .....182 B2
Exminster Marshes (Nature Reserve)★ EX6 .....182 D3
Exmoor Gdns TA22 .....33 D6
Exmoor National Park Visitor Ctr★ EX35 .....151 C6
Exmoor Steam Rly★ EX32 .....11 C1
Exmoor View EX36 .....158 C5
Exmoor Zoo★ EX31 .....11 B3
Exmouth CE Prim Sch EX8 .....202 A6
Exmouth Com Coll EX8 .....202 B8
Exmouth Ct EX8 .....202 B6
Exmouth Hospl EX8 .....202 B7
Exmouth Mus★ EX8 .....202 A7
Exmouth Rd
Budleigh Salterton EX9 .....197 E1

Exmouth Rd *continued*
Clyst St Mary EX5 ....179 A1
Exton EX3 ....183 C3
Lympstone EX8 ....195 F7
Newton Poppleford EX10 .186 D5
Plymouth PL1 ....247 F3
Exmouth Sta EX8 ......201 F7
Exonia Pk EX2 ....176 D3
Exton La EX3 ....183 C2
Exton Rd EX2 ....177 C3
Exton Sta EX3 ....183 C1
Exwick Ct EX4 ....176 F8
Exwick Hill EX4 ....176 E7
Exwick Ho EX4 ....176 F8
Exwick La EX4 ....176 D7
Exwick Mid Sch EX4 ...176 E7
Exwick Rd EX4 ....176 F7
Eyewell Gn EX12 ....192 A6
Eymore Dr EX11 ....168 C3
Eyrecourt Rd EX12 .....192 A4

F

Factory Cotts TQ9 .....139 C7
Factory Cross TQ13 ....110 F6
Factory La TA20 ....88 D8
Factory Ope 1 EX39 ....15 A1
Factory Row
South Molton EX36 ......158 E4
Torquay TQ2 ....220 A5
Fair Isle Cl TQ2 ....213 E2
Fair Oak Cl EX5 ....99 A4
Fair View
Barnstaple EX31 ....154 E6
Colyford EX24 ....103 A3
Fair View La EX24 ......103 A3
Fair View Rd
Dartmouth TQ6 ....233 E3
Honiton EX14 ....166 C5
Fair View Terr EX8 .....202 B7
Fairacre Ave EX32 ......155 C2
Fairfax Gdns EX2 ....177 B2
Fairfax Pl TQ6 ....233 F3
Fairfax Rd TQ12 ....180 F3
Fairfax Terr 5 PL2 .....247 F4
Fairfax Way EX38 ....159 F5
Fairfield
Bratton Fleming EX31 .....18 A8
Ilfracombe EX34 ....150 C5
Plymouth PL7 ....250 E7
Sampford Peverell EX16 ...50 D1
Fairfield Ave Exeter EX4 .178 C8
Plymouth PL2 ....248 C7
Fairfield Cl
Axminster EX13 ....167 D5
Bovey Tracey TQ13 ......180 C7
Exmouth EX8 ....202 B6
Kingsbridge TQ7 ....258 D4
Fairfield Gdns EX14 ....166 C5
Fairfield Gn TA3 ....68 D7
Fairfield Pk DT7 ....260 E4
Fairfield Rd
Crediton EX17 ....165 C6
Exeter EX2 ....181 B8
Exmouth EX8 ....202 B5
Kingskerswell TQ12 .....213 A3
Torquay TQ2 ....219 F8
Fairfield Terr Exeter EX2 177 A4
Newton Abbot TQ12 .....207 C3
Fairfield Way TQ7 ......145 A1
Fairhazel Dr EX4 ....176 F7
Fairholme Rd EX34 ....7 F6
Fairlands Ave EX6 ......113 B3
Fairlawn Ct EX10 ....188 B5
Fairlawns Pk TQ4 ....226 B2
Fairlea TQ5 ....230 C6
Fairlea Cl EX7 ....200 F1
Fairlea Cres EX39 ......156 F6
Fairlea Ct EX9 ....197 E1
Fairlea Rd EX7 ....200 F1
Fairlinch Cross EX33 ...152 B8
Fairlynch Cl EX33 ......152 B7
Fairlynch Gr EX33 ......152 C7
Fairlynch La EX33 ......152 B7
Fairlynch Mus EX9 .....199 H2
Fairmead EX10 ....187 F8
Fairmead Ct TQ2 ....213 F2
Fairmead Mews PL12 ...242 C3
Fairmead Rd PL12 ......242 C2
Fairpark Cl EX2 ....261 C2
Fairpark Rd EX2 ....261 B2
Fairplace Terr EX20 ....170 B5
Fairseat Cl TQ9 ....223 D4
Fairview Ave PL3 ....249 D5
Fairview Rd TQ12 ....211 A7
Fairview Terr EX1 ......174 F1
Fairview Way PL3 ......249 E5
Fairwater Cl TQ12 .....207 F7
Fairwaters TQ12 ....207 E8
Fairway Appledore EX39 ...14 F1
Saltash PL12 ....242 C2
Tiverton EX16 ....64 E8
Fairway Ave PL21 ......237 B5
Fairway Cl
Braunton EX33 ....152 B6
Churston Ferrers TQ5 ...229 D5
Fairway The
Braunton EX33 ....152 B6
Exeter EX4 ....173 E1
Newton Ferrers PL8 .....140 F7
Fairways Cl EX37 ....43 B6
Fairways Dr EX37 ....43 B6
Fairways The EX39 .....156 D7
Fairways View EX37 ......43 C6
Fairy La TQ11 ....236 A4
Falcon Ct EX36 ....158 C4
Falcon Rd EX2 ....178 E4
Falcon Units TQ12 .....207 A3
Falkedon Cross EX17 .....96 A6
Falkland Cl EX4 ....173 E2
Falkland Dr TQ12 ....207 F8
Falkland Rd TQ2 ....219 F5
Falkland Way TQ14 .....210 A6
Fallapit Turn TQ9 ......144 C8
Fallow Fields EX32 .....155 C2
Falloway Cl TQ2 ....214 A2
Fallowfield Cl TQ12 ....207 F3
Fallowfields TQ9 ....223 A5
Falmouth Cl TQ2 ....219 B8
Fancy Cross PL21 ....137 A2
Fanny's Cross EX36 ......46 E7
Fanny's La EX17 ....80 B5
Fannys Lane Cross EX17 .80 B5
Fanshawe Way PL9 .....255 C6
Far View Rd EX20 ......170 C5
Faraday Mill Bsns Pk
PL4 ....249 B1
Faraday Rd PL4 ....249 B1
Farleigh TQ12 ....206 B5
Farleigh Back Rd EX16 ..63 C2
Farleigh Cross TQ9 ....139 A4
Farleigh Front Rd EX16 ..63 C2
Farleigh Mdws EX16 ...161 A6
Farley Hill TQ13 ....123 D8
Farley La EX35 ....5 E3
Farley's Grave EX20 .....77 E7
Farm Cl Exeter EX2 .....178 C4
Kingskerswell TQ12 .....212 F6
Plymouth PL7 ....250 C7
Farm Hill EX4 ....176 E8
Farm House Rise EX6 ..181 F4
Farm La Plymouth PL5 ..244 B2
Saltash PL12 ....242 D1
Farm Rd DT7 ....193 E6
Farm Way EX14 ....84 D2
Farmer Frank's La EX19 ..58 F2
Farmhouse Ave EX1 ....178 F8
Farmyard La TQ3 ......218 E6
Farnham Terr TQ3 .....226 C7
Farnley Cl PL6 ....245 B6
Farpark Hill La EX31 ......9 A1
Farrant's Hill EX6 .....113 B8
Farriel La EX34 ....8 F5
Farringdon Cross
Cheriton Fitzpaine EX17 ...80 E7
Exeter EX5 ....99 A1
Farringdon Ct EX5 ....99 B2
Farringdon Hill EX17 .....80 E7
Farringdon Rd PL4 .....249 B3
Farthing Cross TQ3 ....218 C3
Farthing Down TA21 ......51 E7
Farthing La TQ3 ....218 C2
Farthing Lake Cross
EX32 ....29 A7
Farthing's Pitts TA21 ..160 C4
Farthingland Cross EX20 .76 B5
Farthings La EX10 .....186 E7
Farthings Lodge Bsns Ctr
EX15 ....83 F6
Farway CE Prim Sch
EX24 ....101 F7
Farway Common Rd
EX14,EX24 ....101 E7
Farway Countryside Pk★
EX24 ....102 A5
Farwell Rd TQ9 ....223 B6
Farwood Cross EX24 ...102 C6
Fatacott Cross EX39 .....22 F5
Fatherford Rd EX20 ....170 D5
Faulkner Cl TQ6 ....233 C3
Fawns Cl PL21 ....136 F4
Fay Rd EX7 ....204 E6
Fayre View PL12 ....242 B1
Fearnside Way PL12 ...242 C3
Featherbed La
Clayhanger EX16 ....35 C1
Exmouth EX8 ....196 B2
Monkton EX14 ....86 D6
Offwell EX14 ....86 B2
Featherstone Rd EX8 ..196 A2
Federation Rd PL3 .....249 C4
Fegan Rd PL5 ....243 B1
Fell Cl PL8 ....141 B8
Fellowes Pl PL1 ....248 A2
Fellows La PL1 ....262 A4
Feltrim Ave EX2 ....261 C1
Feniton CE Prim Sch
EX14 ....84 E2
Feniton Gdns EX14 ....84 D2
Feniton Sta EX14 ....84 D2
Fenten Pk PL12 ....242 F3
Feoffe Cotts EX31 ......154 F7
Ferguson Cl EX11 ......169 B3
Fern Cl Brixham TQ5 ...230 D4
Okehampton EX20 ....170 C6
Plymouth PL7 ....251 C5
Fern Mdw
Okehampton EX20 ....170 C6
Tavistock PL19 ....171 D6
Fern Pk EX34 ....150 B5
Fern Rd TQ12 ....207 F1
Fern Way EX34 ....150 B4
Fernbank Ave PL21 ....237 A6
Ferncombe Cl 3 TQ12 ..123 F1
Ferncombe Dr 2 TQ12 ..123 F1
Ferndale TQ6 ....233 E3
Ferndale Ave PL2 ......247 E7
Ferndale Cl
8 Honiton EX14 ....85 C2
Plymouth PL6 ....245 D8
Ferndale Gdns EX2 ....177 A4
Ferndale Mews TQ2 ...219 B7
Ferndale Rd Exeter EX2 .177 A4
Plymouth PL2 ....247 F7
Teignmouth TQ14 ....210 B6
Torquay TQ2 ....219 B7
Ferndown Cl EX39 .....156 E2
Ferndown Rd DT7 ......260 E3
Ferne Animal Sanctuary★
TA20 ....69 D2
Fernhill Cl PL21 ....237 B5
Fernhill Cross TQ7 .....143 E8
Fernicombe Rd TQ3 ...225 E7
Fernleigh Cl EX20 ....77 C4
Fernleigh Rd PL3 ......248 F5
Fernleigh Terr PL18 ...125 B5
Fernpark Cl EX2 ....177 F3
Fernworthy Cl
Copplestone EX17 ....79 B5
Torquay TQ2 ....219 A7
Fernworthy Forest Walks★
TQ13 ....110 D2
Fernworthy Gdns EX17 ...79 B5
Fernworthy Pk EX17 .....79 B5
Ferrers Gn TQ5 ....229 E4
Ferrers Rd PL5 ....243 E1
Ferry La PL11 ....246 D5
Ferry Rd Plymouth PL1 ..247 E3
Topsham EX3 ....182 E5
Ferry Slip TQ6 ....233 F3
Ferry St PL11 ....247 C3
Ferryman's Reach
TQ14 ....210 B3
Feversham Pl PL7 .....251 B6
Fiddlecott La EX18 ....60 B6
Field Cl Braunton EX33 ..152 C5
Paignton TQ3 ....219 B2
Field End EX13 ....167 E5
Field La Ashford EX31 ....16 B6
Braunton EX33 ....152 C5
Filham Moor Cl PL21 ...237 E4
Fillace La 11 PL20 ......126 F4
Filleigh Com Prim Sch
EX32 ....29 C6
Filleigh Mill New Rd
EX32 ....29 D7
Filleigh Moor Cross
EX17 ....60 D5
Filleighmoor Gate EX21 .56 C3
Fillham Moor La PL21 ..237 D5
Filmer Way EX2 ....177 B3
Fincer Dr PL21 ....237 A6
Finch Cl PL3 ....249 D4
Finch Foundary Mus of Rural
Industry★ EX20 ....95 A5
Finches Cl PL9 ....256 C7
Findon Gdns PL6 ......245 D4
Finewell St PL1 ....262 C2
Fingle Cl EX4 ....176 E8
Fingle Glen EX6 ....98 B4
Finlake Cvn & Camping Site
TQ13 ....123 C5
Finnigan Rd PL4 ....249 B1
Finnimore Ind Est EX11 169 C3
Fir Cl Honiton EX14 ....166 B5
Willand EX15 ....162 D5
Fir Terr EX36 ....158 D4
Fir Tree Cl EX8 ....196 E2
Firbank Rd EX7 ....200 F1
Fircroft Rd PL2 ....248 B7
Fire Beacon Cross
Bishop's Tawton EX31 .....27 D7
Chittlehampton EX37 ......29 B2
Fire Beacon La EX10 ...100 E1
Fire Brigade HQ EX4 ...261 A4
Fire Stone Cross EX20 ....95 C4
Firebeacon Cross EX39 ...37 C7
Firebeacon La
Bolham EX16 ....49 C3
Chittlehampton EX37 ......29 B2
Firestone Cross EX20 .....95 C3
Firestone La TQ12 .....212 A8
Firlands TQ14 ....210 B7
Firlands Rd TQ2 ....214 A2
Firleigh Rd 7 TQ12 ....123 E1
Firs Cross TQ9 ....144 C7
Firs Gr EX32 ....155 B5
Firs Pk EX2 ....176 C3
Firs The
3 Barnstaple EX32 ......155 B5
Kennford EX6 ....114 D4
Wilmington EX14 ....86 D2
First Ave Axminster EX13 .167 F7
Dawlish EX7 ....204 D5
Exeter, Countess Wear
EX2 ....182 D7
Exeter, Heavitree EX1 ...177 F6
Plymouth, Billacombe PL9 .255 F8
Plymouth, Stoke PL1 ....248 A2
Teignmouth TQ14 ....210 A5
Torquay TQ1 ....220 A8
First Dr Teignmouth TQ14 .210 B5
Teignmouth TQ14 ....210 D6
First Raleigh EX39 .....156 E3
Firtree Rise PL21 ......237 D5
Firway Cross EX16 ....34 C3
Fisgard Way PL11 ......246 D3
Fish Mkt PL4 ....263 B2
Fishacre Cl TQ3 ....225 E8
Fishacre Cross TQ9 ....216 F6
Fishchowter's La TQ9 ..223 C4
Fishcombe Rd TQ5 .....230 B6
Fisher Rd
Newton Abbot TQ12 .....207 B3
Plymouth PL2 ....248 A5
Fisher St TQ4 ....226 B5
Fisher's Hill TA21 ....51 D7
Fishers Mead TA22 ......33 D6
Fisherton Cross EX37 ....28 C2
Fishingclose Cross EX20 .76 F6
Fishleigh Cross EX20 ....75 C8
Fishleigh Rd EX31 .....154 B2
Fistral Cl PL11 ....246 F4
Fitzford Cotts PL19 ....171 B4
Fitzroy Rd PL1 ....248 A3
Fitzroy Terr 7 PL1 .....248 A3
Five Acres TQ13 ....180 C4
Five Barrow La EX13 ...104 A4
Five Barrows Cross EX36 19 D7
Five Bridges Cross EX15 .67 C7
Five Cross TQ12 ....122 C1
Five Cross Way
Brayford EX31 ....18 F8
Plymtree EX15 ....83 E8
West Buckland TA21 ......52 F6
Five Cross Ways TA22 ....32 F7
Five Crosses
Modbury PL21 ....137 A2
Rackenford EX16 ....47 C1
Five Crossway EX36 ......46 D8
Five Elms Cross EX5 .....80 E1
Five Elms La EX5 ....80 E1
Five Hos TA21 ....160 B8
Five Lane End EX38 ....159 A1
Five Lanes
Bovey Tracey TQ13 .....123 B7
Buckfastleigh TQ11 .....236 E7
4 Kingsteignton TQ12 ...123 E1
Marldon TQ3 ....218 E3
Five Lanes Cross EX22 ...54 D8
Five Lanes Rd TQ3 ....218 D2
Five Mile Hill EX6 ....98 C4
Five Mile Hill Cross EX6 .98 C4
Five Oaks TQ11 ....130 C2
Five Oaks Cross
Brampford Speke EX5 .....81 C1
Burrington EX37 ....43 D4
Five Turnings EX34 ....3 A4
Five Wyches Cross
TQ13 ....180 B7
Flagstaff Rd TQ6 ....233 F4
Flamborough Rd PL6 ...245 A7
Flamborough Way PL6 .245 A6
Flamsteed Cres PL5 ....243 E1
Flavel Pl TQ6 ....233 F3
Flavel St TQ6 ....233 F3
Flayes Almshouses 2
EX4 ....178 C8
Fleet St Plymouth PL2 ...247 E6
Torquay TQ1 ....220 B4
Fleet Wlk TQ2 ....220 B4
Fleming Ave EX10 ......188 C8
Fleming Way EX2 ......177 E4
Flemons Ct 5 TQ4 .....226 A5
Fletcher Cl TQ2 ....219 E7
Fletcher Cres PL9 ......256 B6
Fletcher Way PL9 ......256 A6
Flete★ PL21 ....136 E2
Flete Ave TQ12 ....207 F2
Flete Cl TQ12 ....207 F2
Flete View Terr PL21 ...137 C8
Fletemoor Rd PL5 ......243 E1
Flexapark EX34 ....3 A3
Flexi Units EX2 ....177 C1
Flexton The EX11 ......169 D4
Flightway EX14 ....67 B3
Floaters Rd TQ6 ......233 F4
Flood St TQ9 ....227 F8
Flood's La EX15 ....163 B3
Flora Cotts PL1 ....262 B2
Flora Ct PL1 ....262 B3
Flora St PL1 ....262 B2
Florance Pl TQ12 ......207 D1
Florence Cotts TQ7 ....145 D1
Florence Pl PL4 ....263 C3
Florence St PL5 ....243 D1
Florida Dr EX4 ....173 D2
Florida Gdns PL3 ......249 C6
Florida Rd TQ1 ....220 C6
Flow La TQ14 ....208 F7
Flower St EX5 ....184 C3
Flowerpot La EX4 .....177 A5
Flowers Mdw 9 TQ12 ...122 F1
Floyd Cl PL2 ....247 F7
Floyers-Hay Ct EX2 ....261 A1
Floyte La EX6 ....98 B5
Fluder Cres TQ12 ......213 B3
Fluder Hill TQ12 ....213 B3
Fluder La TQ12 ....213 F5
Fluder Rise TQ12 ......213 B3
Foldhay Cross EX17 .....78 A6
Foliot Ave PL2 ....248 A6
Foliot Rd PL2 ....248 A6
Follafield Pk TQ5 ......230 B4
Follaton Bglws TQ9 ....223 A5
Follaton Gate TQ9 .....222 E6
Follaton Rd TQ9 ....222 F6
Follett Rd Tiverton EX16 ..64 D7
Topsham EX3 ....182 E5
Folley La EX4 ....98 D4
Folly Cross TQ10 ......134 E1
Folly Gate Cross EX20 ...93 F8
Folly Goyle Cross EX19 ...43 B3
Folly Hill TQ7 ....142 E3
Folly La
Buckland St Mary TA20 ....69 D8
South Molton EX36 ....30 D4
Football La TQ12 ....207 E8
Footland La
Daccombe TQ12 ....213 F5
Ipplepen TQ12 ....217 F5
Footland Rd TQ4 ......226 A4
Footpark La EX6 ....96 D2
Forbes Cl TQ12 ....180 F2
Forcefield Rd EX15 ....163 B2
Forces Cross TQ9 .....139 E3
Forches Ave EX32 .....155 C4
Forches Cnr EX17 .....165 C6
Forches Cross
Burrington EX37 ....43 F4
Crediton EX17 ....165 C6
Langtree EX38 ....40 F1
Newton Abbot TQ12 .....206 E7
Forches Cross Prim Sch
EX32 ....155 C4
Forches Green Flats 3
EX32 ....155 B4
Forches Head EX5 .....175 F8
Forches Hill TQ12 ......209 B2
Ford TQ6 ....233 E3
Ford Cl PL21 ....237 A5
Ford Cres EX22 ....53 E8
Ford Cross
Bishops Nympton EX36 ....31 D1
Chawleigh EX18 ....59 E7
Chillington TQ7 ....149 A7
Chulmleigh EX18 ....44 D2
Combe Martin EX31 ....10 D5
Hittisleigh EX6 ....96 D4
Molland EX36 ....31 F7
Monkton EX14 ....86 A5
Oakford EX16 ....48 D5
South Zeal EX20 ....95 A4
Staverton TQ9 ....216 E5
Tedburn St Mary EX17 ....97 D8
Ford Down La EX36 ...158 A3
Ford Farm Ct EX6 .....194 D3
Ford Hill Bow EX17 ......78 F4
Cheriton Bishop EX6,EX17 ..97 C6
Combe Martin EX31 ....10 D5
Hartland EX39 ....22 E3
Plymouth PL2 ....248 A5
Thorverton EX5 ....81 E6
Ford La Combe Martin EX31 10 B5
South Molton EX36 .....158 A8
Tiverton EX16 ....63 B6
West Hill EX11 ....168 E3
Whitestone EX4 ....98 E4
Ford Lane Cross EX6 ....96 D4
Ford Moor Cross EX18 ...59 E7
Ford Orch EX16 ....50 D1
Ford Park La PL4 ......248 E4
Ford Park Rd PL4 ......248 D4
Ford Pk 6 TQ13 ....123 C4
Ford Plain EX5 ....81 E5
Ford Prim Sch PL2 .....248 A5
Ford Rd
Abbotskerswell TQ12 ....212 B7
Bampton EX16 ....34 C1
Tiverton EX16 ....64 D7
Totnes TQ9 ....223 D6
Wembury PL9 ....140 D8
Yealmpton PL8 ....136 A2
Ford Rise EX39 ....25 F4
Ford St
Moretonhampstead TQ13 .111 F5
Tavistock PL19 ....171 B5
Wellington TA21 ....160 F4
Ford Valley TQ6 ....233 E3
Fordbarn Cross TQ9 ...222 E2
Forde Abbey★ TA20 .....88 F8
Forde Cl
Abbotskerswell TQ12 ....212 A7
Newton Abbot TQ12 .....207 D3
Forde Cross EX17 ....80 F8
Forde Gdns TQ12 ......207 D1
Forde Ho TQ12 ....207 E2
Forde La EX38 ....26 E2
Forde Pk TQ12 ....207 D2
Forde Rd TQ12 ....207 D3
Fordens La EX7 ....204 C3
Forder Cross
Bishopsteignton TQ14 ...208 D7
Blackawton TQ9 ....145 C8
Chagford EX20 ....110 D8
Ugborough PL21 ....137 E7
Forder Hill PL10 ....252 F1
Forder Hts PL6 ....245 B1
Forder La
Bishopsteignton TQ14 ...208 E8
Bovey Tracey TQ13 .....122 E7
Cawsand PL10 ....252 F1
Dartington TQ9 ....222 E8
Dartington TQ9 ....222 F8
South Brent TQ10 ......135 B4
Ugborough PL21 ....137 D7
Forder Valley Rd PL6 ...249 D8
Fordishaies La EX5,EX15 .82 F8
Fordland Bottom Rd
EX2,EX6 ....176 B2
Fordlands Cres EX39 ...156 F4
Fordlands Rd TQ13 .....111 F5
Fordmill Cross EX16 .....34 D1
Fordmoor Cross EX16 ...48 C8
Fords Rd EX2 ....261 A1
Fordton Cross EX17 ...165 E2
Fordton Ind Est EX17 ..165 E3
Fordton Terr EX17 .....165 D3
Fordworth Cotts TQ7 ...149 D5
Fore St
Aveton Gifford TQ7 .....143 C6
9 Bampton EX16 ....34 B1
Beer EX12 ....191 D5
Bere Alston PL20 ....125 E1
Bere Ferrers PL20 ....239 F3
Bishopsteignton TQ14 ...208 F8
Bovey Tracey TQ13 .....180 D7
Bradninch EX5 ....82 F6
Bridestowe EX20 ....107 F8
Brixham TQ5 ....230 C5
Buckfastleigh TQ11 .....236 C5
Budleigh Salterton EX9 ..199 G2
Calstock PL18 ....125 D3
Cargreen PL12 ....239 A2
Cawsand PL10 ....253 A2
Chudleigh TQ13 ....123 E6

Fore St *continued*
Chulmleigh EX18 ....44 E1
Cornwood PL21 ....133 C2
Cullompton EX15 ....163 C3
Culmstock EX15 ....66 E8
Dartmouth TQ6 ....234 A3
Dolton EX19 ....57 F7
Dulverton TA22 ....33 D6
Exbourne EX20 ....76 C5
Exeter EX4 ....261 A2
Exeter, Heavitree EX1 ....177 F5
Exmouth EX8 ....202 A6
Great Torrington EX38 ....159 D5
Gunnislake PL18 ....125 C5
Gunnislake PL18 ....125 D6
Harberton TQ9 ....222 D2
Hartland EX39 ....22 E3
7 Hemyock EX15 ....67 B8
Holbeton PL8 ....136 D1
Holcombe Rogus TA21 ....50 F5
Holemoor EX22 ....73 C8
Holsworthy EX22 ....164 C4
Ide EX2 ....176 E2
Ideford TQ13 ....124 B4
Ilfracombe EX34 ....150 C6
Ipplepen TQ12 ....211 D2
Ivybridge PL21 ....237 D5
Kentisbeare EX15 ....66 A3
Kenton EX6 ....194 D3
Kingsbridge TQ7 ....258 C6
Kingskerswell TQ12 ....213 A4
Kingsteignton TQ12 ....207 E7
Langtree EX38 ....40 E2
Lifton PL16 ....105 E4
Loddiswell TQ7 ....143 E7
Luton TQ13 ....124 C3
Millbrook PL10 ....252 E5
Milton Abbot PL19 ....116 A6
Morchard Bishop EX17 ....61 A2
Moretonhampstead TQ13 ....111 F5
North Molton EX36 ....30 D8
North Tawton EX20 ....77 B4
Northam EX39 ....156 F6
Okehampton EX20 ....170 B5
Otterton EX9 ....198 E7
Plymouth, Devonport PL1 ....247 F2
Plymouth, Plympton PL7 ....250 E4
Plymouth, Tamerton Foliot PL5 ....244 B6
Salcombe TQ8 ....259 E4
Saltash PL12 ....242 F2
Seaton EX12 ....192 B5
Shaldon TQ14 ....210 A3
Shebbear EX22 ....55 D1
Sidbury EX10 ....101 B2
Sidmouth EX10 ....188 B3
Silverton EX5 ....82 B5
12 South Brent TQ10 ....134 F3
South Tawton EX20 ....95 B5
Tatworth TA20 ....88 D8
8 Teignmouth TQ14 ....210 C4
Tiverton EX16 ....161 D4
Topsham EX3 ....182 F5
Torpoint PL11 ....247 B3
Torquay, Barton TQ2 ....214 A2
Torquay, St Marychurch TQ1 ....220 B8
Totnes TQ9 ....223 C5
Uffculme EX15 ....66 A7
Ugborough PL21 ....137 D6
Wellington TA21 ....160 D6
Winkleigh EX19 ....58 F3
Witheridge EX16 ....46 E1
Yealmpton PL8 ....257 F4
Fore Street Ctr EX4 ....261 A2
Fore Street Hill EX9 ....199 H2
Foredown La TQ12 ....212 E4
Foredown Rd TQ12 ....211 E2
Foreland View EX34 ....150 B4
Forest Ave PL2 ....248 C7
Forest Hill EX39 ....25 F4
Forest Houses EX21 ....73 B4
Forest Rd TQ1 ....220 A7
Forest Ridge Rd TQ3 ....218 F1
Forest View PL6 ....245 D7
Forester's Terr TQ14 ....210 B4
Foresters Rd
Holsworthy EX22 ....164 C5
Plymouth PL9 ....255 D7
Foretown EX15 ....83 D3
Forge Cl EX9 ....197 F2
Forge End EX19 ....58 F2
Forge La Butterleigh EX15 ....64 D3
Saltash PL12 ....242 C4
Forge Pl TQ13 ....180 C7
Forge Way EX15 ....163 C3
Forges Hill EX15 ....64 F3
Forgeway Cl TQ2 ....219 D4
Fork Cross TQ9 ....222 A5
Forrest Units EX2 ....177 D1
Forresters Dr PL6 ....245 D7
Forster Rd TQ8 ....259 D5
Forsythia Dr PL12 ....242 C3
Fort Austin Ave PL6 ....245 C1
Fort Hill Dr EX32 ....155 B5
Fort St EX32 ....155 A5
Fort Terr
11 Barnstaple EX32 ....155 A5
5 Bideford EX39 ....157 B1
Plymouth PL6 ....244 F3
Fort The PL10 ....253 A1
Fortescue Cl EX33 ....152 E5
Fortescue Cross EX5 ....81 E2
Fortescue Pl PL3 ....249 A6
Fortescue Rd
Barnstaple EX32 ....155 B2
Exeter EX2 ....177 B3
Ilfracombe EX34 ....150 B6

Fortescue Rd *continued*
Paignton TQ3 ....219 C1
Salcombe TQ8 ....259 C4
Sidmouth EX10 ....188 D7
Fortescue Terr PL19 ....171 A6
Fortfield EX12 ....192 B5
Fortfield Terr EX10 ....188 A3
Forth Gdns PL3 ....249 D6
Fortmead Cl EX32 ....155 A5
Forton Rd EX8 ....196 C1
Fortune Way TQ1 ....220 B7
Forward Gn EX5 ....82 E7
Fosbrooke Ct 9 PL3 ....248 F6
Fosketh Hill EX39 ....156 C6
Fosketh Terr EX39 ....156 C6
Foss Slip TQ6 ....233 F3
Foss St TQ6 ....233 F3
Fosse Rd TQ7 ....258 D6
Fosse Way Ct 2 EX12 ....192 B4
Fosseway Cl EX13 ....167 D5
Fosterlea EX15 ....163 B3
Foulston Ave PL5 ....247 B8
Foundry Ct 1 TQ13 ....123 E6
Foundry La PL8 ....140 F6
Fountain Ct TQ13 ....180 D7
Fountain Hill EX9 ....203 F8
Fountains Cres PL2 ....248 C8
Four Acres EX39 ....156 D2
Four Acres Cl EX14 ....86 B2
Four Cross
Axminster EX13 ....167 B7
Ilsington TQ12 ....122 C2
Kingston TQ7 ....142 C7
Wilmington EX14 ....86 C4
Four Cross Elms EX24 ....103 A4
Four Cross Lanes TQ9 ....228 A8
Four Cross Way EX32 ....11 C1
Four Cross Ways
Cheriton Bishop EX6 ....97 A4
North Tawton EX20 ....77 D4
Willand EX15 ....162 D5
Winkleigh EX19 ....58 D2
Four Crossways EX18 ....44 E1
Four Elms
Holcombe Rogus TA21 ....51 A6
Sidmouth EX10 ....187 C8
Four Elms Hill EX10 ....187 B8
Four Firs EX5 ....185 A1
Four Lanes EX15 ....84 B8
Four Mills La EX17 ....165 D4
Four Oaks EX32 ....17 B2
Four Oaks Cl 1 EX32 ....17 B2
Four Oaks Cross EX32 ....17 B2
Four Oaks Rd EX6 ....97 F4
Four Views TQ5 ....230 E4
Four Ways Cotts EX18 ....59 E4
Four Ways Dr EX18 ....44 E1
Four White Gates Cross EX37 ....29 B4
Fouracre Cl EX4 ....174 A1
Fouracre Way TQ12 ....207 F8
Fourcross Hill EX13 ....167 B7
Fourlanesend Com Prim Sch PL10 ....252 F3
Fourth Ave TQ14 ....210 A6
Fourways Cross EX15 ....67 C8
Fowelscombe Gate PL21 ....137 F6
Fowey Ave TQ2 ....219 B8
Fowey Cl EX1 ....177 F7
Fowey Gdns PL3 ....249 D6
Fowey Rd EX31 ....15 E5
Fowler Cl EX6 ....182 A4
Fowley Cross EX20 ....93 D5
Fox & Hounds Cross EX20 ....108 A5
Fox Cl Okehampton EX20 ....170 D6
Rockwell Green TA21 ....160 A6
Fox Field Cl PL3 ....249 C5
Fox Hill EX39 ....156 F6
Fox Rd EX4 ....174 B2
Fox Tor Cl TQ4 ....229 B7
Fox's Cnr EX10 ....187 F2
Fox's Cross EX17 ....63 B1
Foxbeare Rd EX34 ....150 E5
Foxdown Hill TA21 ....160 C4
Foxdown Ho TA21 ....160 C4
Foxdown Terr TA21 ....160 D4
Foxes Lair EX20 ....170 A6
Foxes' Cross EX38 ....26 E1
Foxglove Chase EX15 ....162 D5
Foxglove Cl
Barnstaple EX32 ....155 E4
Dunkeswell EX14 ....67 C1
Launceston PL15 ....105 A2
9 Tiverton EX16 ....161 F6
Foxglove Rd EX12 ....192 B7
Foxglove Rise EX4 ....176 D8
Foxglove Way PL12 ....242 B3
Foxhayes Fst Sch EX4 ....176 F7
Foxhayes Rd EX4 ....176 F6
Foxhill EX13 ....167 D5
Foxhole Hill EX6 ....113 B4
Foxhole Inf Sch TQ3 ....225 E7
Foxhole Jun Sch TQ3 ....225 E8
Foxhole La EX39 ....156 F6
Foxhole Rd Paignton TQ3 ....225 F7
Torquay TQ2 ....219 D5
Foxholes Hill EX8 ....202 D4
Foxhollows TQ12 ....208 A2
Foxlands Wlk TQ1 ....220 C8
Foxley Cres TQ12 ....206 F3
Foxtor Cl PL5 ....244 B3
Foxtor Rd EX4 ....176 E8
Foxwood Gdns
Plymouth, Plymstock PL9 ....255 F5
Plymouth, Southway PL6 ....244 E5
Foyle Cl PL7 ....251 A5

Frances Homes EX1 ....261 C3
Francis Cl EX4 ....176 F4
Francis Court Cotts EX5 ....82 D2
Francis Cres 4 EX16 ....64 D7
Francis Ct
3 Crediton EX17 ....165 C5
Exeter EX2 ....177 E5
Francis Dr EX39 ....156 C6
Francis St PL1 ....262 A3
Francis Way EX24 ....103 B3
Franeth Cl TQ12 ....207 E8
Frank Webber Rd TA21 ....160 A5
Frankford La EX6 ....97 F5
Frankfort Gate 9 PL1 ....262 B3
Franklea Cl EX11 ....169 D3
Franklin St EX2 ....261 B2
Franklyn Ave EX33 ....152 E6
Franklyn Cl EX2 ....176 F3
Franklyn Dr EX2 ....176 F3
Franklyn Hospl EX2 ....176 F3
Franklyns Cl PL6 ....245 A4
Franklyns' PL6 ....245 A4
Frankmarsh Pk EX32 ....155 B6
Frankmarsh Rd EX32 ....155 B6
Frankmills Hill EX6 ....113 B1
Fraser Dr TQ14 ....210 A6
Fraser Pl PL5 ....244 C7
Fraser Rd Exmouth EX8 ....196 D2
Plymouth PL5 ....244 C7
Fraser Sq PL5 ....244 C7
Frederick St E PL1 ....262 B3
Frederick St W 6 PL1 ....262 B3
Frederick Terr 5 EX7 ....204 D6
Fredington Gr PL2 ....248 B6
Free Cotts EX4 ....261 A3
Freedom Sq PL4 ....263 B4
Freelands Cl EX8 ....202 D8
Freemans Wharf PL1 ....254 A8
Freestone Rd TQ12 ....207 D8
Fremantle Gdns 4 PL2 ....247 F4
Fremantle Pl PL2 ....247 F4
Fremington Prim Sch EX31 ....153 D5
Fremington Rd EX12 ....191 F7
French Cl EX5 ....82 B6
French St 7 TQ14 ....210 C4
Frenchstone Cross EX36 ....30 B2
Frensham Ave PL6 ....245 C7
Frensham Gdns PL6 ....245 C7
Freshford Cl PL6 ....245 C1
Freshford Wlk PL6 ....245 C1
Freshwater Dr TQ4 ....229 B8
Frewin Gdns PL6 ....245 B6
Frewins EX9 ....197 F2
Friar's Hele Cross EX20 ....57 B2
Friars Lodge EX2 ....261 B2
Friars Wlk PL19 ....171 E2
Friars' Gate EX2 ....261 B2
Friars' La PL1 ....263 A2
Friars' Wlk EX2 ....261 B2
Friary Pk PL4 ....263 B3
Friary St PL4 ....263 B3
Friernhay Ct EX4 ....261 A2
Friernhay St EX4 ....261 A2
Frith Rd PL12 ....242 D3
Fritz's Grave TQ11 ....236 A7
Frobisher App PL5 ....244 E2
Frobisher Cl TQ14 ....210 A8
Frobisher Dr PL12 ....242 E2
Frobisher Gn TQ2 ....219 C6
Frobisher La TQ8 ....259 C5
Frobisher Rd EX8 ....196 C2
Frobisher Way
Paignton TQ4 ....226 B2
Tavistock PL19 ....171 B5
Torpoint PL11 ....246 D3
Frog La Braunton EX33 ....152 D7
Clyst St Mary EX5 ....179 A3
Holcombe Rogus TA21 ....50 F5
South Molton EX36 ....158 B5
Frog St Bampton EX16 ....34 B1
Exeter EX1,EX2 ....261 A2
Woolacombe EX34 ....7 F6
Frogbury Cross EX17 ....59 F1
Froggy Mill Cross EX6 ....97 C5
Frogmore Ave
Plymouth PL6 ....249 B7
Plymouth PL6 ....249 C7
Frogmore Cross EX5 ....82 F3
Frogmore Ct PL6 ....249 B7
Frogmore Farm TQ9 ....139 F7
Frogmore Rd EX9 ....198 C6
Frogmore Terr TQ7 ....258 C4
Frogstreet Hill EX33 ....8 A2
Frogwell Cross TA4 ....34 D6
Frome Cl PL7 ....251 A4
Frontfield Cres PL6 ....244 E5
Frost Cross
Bovey Tracey TQ13 ....123 B6
Morchard Bishop EX17 ....61 B1
Frost's Cnr EX19 ....42 D1
Froude Ave TQ2 ....214 B3
Froude Rd TQ8 ....259 B2
Fry St EX22 ....164 C4
Fry's La 5 EX10 ....101 B1
Fuge Cross TQ6 ....145 E6
Fuidge Cross EX17 ....96 A5
Fuidge La EX17 ....96 A5
Fulda Cres EX17 ....165 D4
Fulford Cl EX6 ....97 F4
Fulford Dr EX15 ....163 B2
Fulford Rd
Cheriton Bishop EX6 ....97 D1
Dunsford EX6 ....112 F8
Exeter EX1 ....177 F7
Fulford Way EX5 ....184 C2
Fullaford Cross TQ11 ....236 B4
Fullaford Hill EX31 ....18 E8

Fullaford Pk TQ11 ....236 A4
Fullaford Pool Cross TQ11 ....236 A4
Fullars Ct 12 EX2 ....261 A2
Fullerton Rd PL2 ....248 A5
Fullingcott Cross EX39 ....153 A2
Fulton Cl TQ12 ....211 D2
Furland Cl PL9 ....255 C5
Furley Cross EX13 ....87 D6
Furlong Cl TQ11 ....236 B7
Furlong Cotts EX16 ....51 A4
Furneaux Ave PL2 ....248 B5
Furneaux Rd PL2 ....248 B6
Furness Cl TQ4 ....226 A2
Furrough Cross TQ1 ....220 C8
Fursdon Cl PL9 ....256 C6
Fursdon Cross
East Allington TQ7 ....144 E4
Hittisleigh EX6 ....96 C5
Fursdon Ho★ EX5 ....81 E7
Fursdon La EX6 ....96 B5
Furse Pk PL5 ....247 C7
Fursham Cross EX6 ....96 B4
Furze Cap 3 TQ12 ....123 E1
Furze Cross
Bridgerule EX22 ....71 A5
Chittlehampton EX37 ....29 A5
Cornworthy TQ9 ....227 A2
Kingsbridge TQ7 ....144 D3
Furze Gdns EX23 ....37 A1
Furze Hill Rd EX34 ....150 B4
Furze La 2 TQ5 ....230 D5
Furze Park La EX31 ....9 B2
Furze Park Rd EX31 ....18 A8
Furze Rd Totnes TQ9 ....223 F5
Woodbury EX5 ....184 C3
Furzeacre Cl PL7 ....251 A7
Furzebeam Row EX38 ....159 B5
Furzebeam Terr 14 EX39 ....157 B1
Furzebrook EX11 ....169 E4
Furzedown Cross
Copplestone EX17 ....79 A5
South Zeal EX20 ....95 A6
Furzedown Rd TQ12 ....213 A5
Furzegood TQ3 ....218 D3
Furzeham Ct TQ5 ....230 B5
Furzeham Pk TQ5 ....230 B5
Furzeham Prim Sch TQ5 ....230 C5
Furzehatt Ave PL9 ....256 A6
Furzehatt Park Rd PL9 ....256 A6
Furzehatt Rd PL9 ....255 F6
Furzehatt Rise PL9 ....256 A6
Furzehatt Villas PL9 ....255 F6
Furzehatt Way PL9 ....256 A6
Furzehill EX10 ....101 B2
Furzehill Cross TQ9 ....227 B3
Furzehill Rd
Heybrook Bay PL9 ....140 A7
Plymouth PL4 ....248 F4
Torquay TQ1 ....220 A6
Furzeland Hill EX17 ....79 C6
Furzeleigh Cross TQ13 ....122 F6
Furzeleigh La TQ13 ....180 D8
Furzepark Cross
Bittaford PL21 ....137 C7
Dolton EX19 ....58 A5
Furzepark La
Combe Martin EX31 ....10 E6
Hartland EX39 ....22 E3
Fyldon Hill EX36 ....19 D5

G

Gabber La PL9 ....140 B8
Gable Pk TQ1 ....220 C6
Gables Lea EX15 ....162 C4
Gables Rd EX15 ....162 C4
Gables The
Combe Martin EX34 ....2 F4
Exmouth EX8 ....202 D6
Teignmouth TQ14 ....210 A5
Wellington TA21 ....160 C6
Gabriel Ct 11 EX2 ....261 A2
Gabriels Wharf EX2 ....177 C3
Gabwell Hill TQ1,TQ12 ....214 C7
Gabwell La TQ12 ....214 C7
Gaddacombe Cross EX20 ....91 D1
Gains Cross EX22 ....53 C3
Gainsborough Cl TQ1 ....220 E4
Gainsborough Dr EX39 ....156 B6
Gala Cross PL8 ....257 F1
Galahad Cl EX4 ....174 A1
Gale Rd TQ13 ....131 B5
Gales Crest 3 TQ13 ....123 C4
Galileo Cl PL7 ....250 E6
Gallacher Way PL12 ....242 B3
Galleon Way EX39 ....156 E7
Gallery Cl 4 EX14 ....166 B6
Galloping La EX39 ....39 B8
Gallops The PL12 ....242 D4
Galloway Dr TQ14 ....124 E1
Gallows Gate TQ3 ....218 F6
Gallows Park Cross TQ13 ....131 B5
Galmpton CE Prim Sch TQ5 ....229 B5
Galmpton Cross TQ7 ....147 D7
Galmpton Ct TQ5 ....229 B5
Galmpton Farm Cl TQ5 ....229 B5
Galmpton Glade TQ5 ....229 B5
Galmpton Holiday Pk TQ5 ....229 B4
Galmpton Rise EX4 ....173 E1
Galpin St PL21 ....137 C2
Galsworthy Cl PL5 ....244 C2

Galsworthy Sq EX4 ....178 C8
Galva Rd Plymouth PL7 ....251 C8
Sparkwell PL7 ....132 E1
Gamberlake EX13 ....167 C4
Gamberlake Cross EX13 ....167 C4
Gamblyn Cross TA4 ....34 F5
Gammaton Moor Cross EX39 ....26 D3
Gammaton Rd EX39 ....26 B4
Gammon Wlk 2 EX31 ....154 F5
Gammons Hill EX13 ....87 D1
Ganders Pk (Cvn Pk) TQ2 ....213 A2
Gandy St EX4 ....261 A3
Ganges Rd PL2 ....248 A5
Ganna Park Rd PL3 ....248 D6
Gapemouth Cnr EX13 ....87 C1
Gappah Cross TQ13 ....123 E4
Gappah La TQ13 ....123 E4
Gara Cl PL9 ....256 B6
Gara Lodge 4 TQ12 ....212 F4
Gard Cl TQ2 ....214 A3
Garden Cl Braunton EX33 ....152 B6
Exeter EX2 ....178 C4
Holbeton PL8 ....142 A8
Plymouth PL7 ....251 D5
Rattery TQ10 ....135 D4
Garden Cres PL1 ....262 B1
Garden Ct EX9 ....198 A1
Garden La PL19 ....171 B5
Garden Mill Ind Est TQ7 ....258 D4
Garden Park Cl PL9 ....256 C7
Garden Pk TQ10 ....135 D4
Garden Rd TQ1 ....220 B6
Garden Spot La TQ13 ....123 F6
Garden St PL2 ....247 E4
Garden Terr
Cullompton EX15 ....163 C4
Wellington TA21 ....160 B7
Garden Village PL9 ....255 F8
Gardenia Dr EX16 ....161 E7
Gardens The
6 Chudleigh TQ13 ....123 E6
Dulverton TA22 ....33 D7
Rousdon DT7 ....193 E5
1 Wellington TA21 ....160 D5
Gardiner Cl EX5 ....82 A1
Gards La PL5 ....243 E2
Gareth Cres EX4 ....173 F2
Garfield Pl 12 TQ9 ....223 C5
Garfield Rd TQ4 ....226 C6
Garfield Terr PL1,PL3 ....248 A3
Garland Cl EX4 ....176 E8
Garland Cross EX37 ....45 B5
Garland's La EX16 ....64 A5
Garlandhayes La EX15 ....52 E2
Garlic Rea TQ5 ....230 D5
Garliford La EX36 ....30 F4
Garners Cl TQ12 ....206 D1
Garners La TQ12 ....206 D1
Garratt Cl EX8 ....196 C3
Garrett St PL10 ....253 A1
Garrick Cl PL5 ....244 C2
Garrison Cl PL1 ....247 E1
Garrow Cl 1 TQ5 ....230 C3
Garston Ave TQ12 ....207 B4
Garston Cl PL9 ....256 A8
Garth Rd TQ2 ....214 A2
Gas La EX38 ....159 D5
Gascoyne Ct PL4 ....263 A3
Gascoyne Pl PL4 ....263 A3
Gashay La EX13 ....88 H3
Gashouse La PL4 ....263 B2
Gasking St PL4 ....263 A3
Gatcombe Cross EX12 ....102 E2
Gatcombe La Beer EX12 ....191 C8
Seaton EX12 ....102 E2
Gate Cl EX13 ....88 E3
Gate Cross EX24 ....102 F6
Gate Field Rd EX39 ....156 E2
Gate Tree Cl TQ12 ....207 F7
Gatedown La
Salcombe Regis EX10 ....101 E1
Sidmouth EX10 ....189 D8
Gatehouse Cl
Cullompton EX15 ....163 B3
Dawlish EX7 ....204 E7
Gatehouse Hill EX7 ....204 E7
Gatehouse Prim Sch EX7 ....204 E8
Gatehouse Rise EX7 ....204 E7
Gater La EX1 ....261 B2
Gattery La TQ5 ....229 F1
Gavel The EX36 ....158 D4
Gaverick Ct TQ12 ....123 B1
Gay Cl TA21 ....160 E6
Gay St TA21 ....160 E6
Gaydon St EX32 ....155 A5
Gays Cross EX17 ....79 C7
Gays La EX17 ....79 C7
Gaze Hill TQ12 ....206 F5
Gdynia Way PL4 ....263 C2
Geasons La PL7 ....250 E5
Gees La PL21 ....137 C2
Generals Cl EX6 ....201 A7
Generals La EX6 ....201 B7
Genesis La 2 EX34 ....3 A3
Geneva Cl EX2 ....177 E4
Geneva Ct Bideford EX39 ....156 F1
Exeter EX2 ....177 E4
Geneva Pl EX39 ....156 F1
Gennys Cl PL18 ....125 B6
Gentian Cl TQ3 ....218 D2
George Ave PL7 ....250 F6

George Cross PL7 250 F5
George Downing Ho PL6 245 A1
George Hill EX17 165 B6
George La Kilmington EX13 87 C1
Plymouth PL7 250 F5
George Nympton Cross EX36 30 A2
George Pl PL1 262 A2
George Rd TQ3 219 B1
George Shopping Mews EX36 158 C4
George Sq PL1 247 F1
George St
Axminster EX13 167 D6
11 Barnstaple EX32 154 F6
Exeter EX1 261 A2
1 Exmouth EX8 202 A4
Honiton EX14 166 C6
Newton Abbot TQ12 207 B3
Okehampton EX20 170 B5
Plymouth PL1 247 F1
11 Teignmouth TQ14 210 C4
Wellington TA21 160 D6
George Teign Rd EX6 113 D2
George's Sq DT7 260 E3
Georgeham Cross EX33 152 D7
Georgeham Prim Sch EX33 8 A2
Georgeham Rd
Croyde EX33 7 F2
Woolacombe EX34 8 B5
Georgehill Cross EX17 165 A6
Georgenympton Rd EX36 158 C2
Georges Cl EX1 178 B6
Georgia Cres PL3 249 C6
Georgian Ct TQ1 220 E6
Gerald Dinnis Units EX2 177 D1
Geraldine Terr PL12 242 C1
Gerbestone La TA21 52 E6
Gerrydown Rd EX19 58 D3
Gerston Cross TQ9 223 A3
Gerston La TQ7 258 C1
Gerston Pl 8 TQ3 226 B6
Gerston Rd TQ4 226 B6
Gervase Ave EX2 261 A1
Gerway La EX11 169 E2
Gestridge Cross TQ12 207 D7
Gestridge Rd TQ12 207 D7
Giant's Grave TA20 69 D7
Giant's Grave Rd TA20 69 D7
Gibb Hill PL21 133 B2
Gibbon La PL4 263 A3
Gibbons St PL4 263 A3
Giblands Cross EX20 170 D5
Giblands Pk EX20 170 D5
Gibraltar Rd EX8 195 E6
Gibson Cl EX8 196 E1
Gibson Dr TQ4 226 A1
Gibson Gdns TQ4 226 A1
Gibson Rd TQ4 226 A1
Gidcott Cross EX22 55 A4
Gidley Arms Cross EX36 46 A5
Gidley Cross EX36 46 B4
Gidley's Turn EX6 113 B4
Gidleys Mdw TQ9 222 F8
Gifford Pl PL3 248 D4
Gifford Terrace Rd PL3 248 E5
Gilbert Ave Exeter EX2 178 C4
Teignmouth TQ14 210 A7
Gilbert Cl TQ2 219 D6
Gilbert Ct PL7 251 B6
Gilbert Gr 1 EX34 150 C6
Gilbert La PL2 248 C5
Gilbert Rd TQ12 207 E3
Gilbert Way TQ4 226 A3
Gill Pk PL3 249 B5
Gill's Cross TQ9 222 D2
Gillard Rd TQ5 230 F4
Gillard Way PL21 136 D6
Gillards Cl TA21 160 B4
Gillards Mead TA3 68 D7
Gillscott Cross EX17 60 B1
Gilpin Cl EX7 204 F8
Gilston Rd PL12 242 D4
Gilwell Ave PL9 256 B7
Gilwell Pl PL4 263 A3
Gilwell St PL4 263 A3
Gingaford Cross TQ10 135 A5
Gipsies Cnr EX17 79 F6
Gipsies La EX17 79 F6
Gipsy Cnr Barnstaple EX31 9 C1
Bovey Tracey TQ13 122 D5
Budlake EX5 82 E1
Gipsy Cross EX15 67 A5
Gipsy Dro TA20 69 F6
Gipsy Hill La EX1 178 F8
Gipsy Hill Mews EX1 178 F7
Gipsy La Barnstaple EX31 9 F3
Bideford EX39 25 B4
Buckfastleigh TQ11 236 A4
Exeter EX1 178 F8
Exmouth EX8 202 B8
Ilfracombe EX34 150 D5
Ivybridge PL21 136 D7
Sampford Arundel TA21 51 D5
Girt La EX34 3 B4
Gissage Hill EX17 78 B7
Gissage View 7 EX14 166 B6
Gissons EX6 182 B4
Gissons La EX6 114 D4
Gittisham Cl EX1 178 D6
Gittisham Farm Cross EX14 85 A1
Gittshayne Cross EX24 102 F5
Glade The PL20 126 E2
Gladstone Pl 4 TQ12 207 C3
Gladstone Rd EX1 177 E6
Gladstone Terr
8 Teignmouth TQ14 210 C5
Wellington TA21 160 E6
Glanvill Way EX14 166 B4
Glanville Ave 1 PL19 171 B5
Glanville Rd
Offwell EX14 102 A8
Tavistock PL19 171 B6
Glanville St PL1,PL4 262 C3
Glanville Terr PL12 242 F3
Glanvilles Mill PL21 237 D5
Glanvilles Rd PL21 237 D5
Glascott Cl EX20 75 B6
Glasshouse La EX2 182 B7
Glastonbury Cl EX4 174 A2
Glave Saunders Ave EX2 178 C4
Glazebrook Ct TQ10 134 E2
Glazegate Cross TQ3 224 F7
Glazegate La TQ3,TQ4, TQ9 224 E6
Glazon Way EX39 157 A8
Glebe Ave PL12 242 F3
Glebe Cl Exmouth EX8 202 F7
Lympstone EX8 195 E6
Otterton EX9 198 E7
Upton Pyne EX5 172 F7
Glebe Cotts EX5 99 B1
Glebe Ct EX39 156 F6
Glebe Field TQ7 143 A2
Glebe Hos EX39 156 A1
Glebe La EX22 164 C4
Glebe Land TQ7 143 C6
Glebe Mdw EX22 164 B4
Glebe The
Cheriton Fitzpaine EX17 62 D3
Ipplepen TQ12 211 C2
Thorverton EX5 81 E4
Glebefields EX39 156 F6
Glebeland
Churchstow TQ7 143 E4
Down St Mary EX17 78 E7
Glebeland Villas EX36 31 A2
Glebeland Way TQ2 219 B8
Glebelands
Buckfastleigh TQ11 236 A6
Cheriton Bishop EX6 97 B4
8 Chudleigh TQ13 123 F6
Exminster EX6 182 A4
Holsworthy EX22 164 B4
Lympstone EX8 195 E6
Newton Poppleford EX10 186 F8
Sidmouth EX10 188 A4
Witheridge EX16 62 B5
Wrafton EX33 152 E4
Glebelands Rd EX16 64 D7
Glen Cl Clyst St Mary EX5 179 E2
Sidmouth EX10 188 A3
Glen Farm Cres EX14 166 D5
Glen Gdns EX39 156 F4
Glen Isla EX10 188 B3
Glen Lyn Gorge★ EX35 151 C5
Glen Park Ave PL4 262 C4
Glen Park Prim Sch PL7 251 B5
Glen Rd Paignton TQ3 226 B7
Plymouth, Mannamead PL3 248 F5
Plymouth, Plympton PL7 250 F6
Sidmouth EX10 188 A3
Glen The Beer EX12 191 E6
3 Newton Abbot TQ12 207 F2
Okehampton EX20 170 B4
Glen Wlk EX4 173 D2
Glenavon Rd PL3 248 E5
Glenburn Cl PL3 248 E7
Glenburnie Ho EX39 157 A3
Glenburnie Rd EX39 157 A3
Glencarnock Cl TQ1 219 E7
Glencoe EX2 177 E5
Glendale Rd EX20 170 A6
Glendale Terr EX39 157 A3
Glendaragh Rd 12 TQ14 210 C5
Glendon Cross EX20 170 F8
Glendower Rd PL3 248 D5
Gleneagle Ave 4 PL3 248 F6
Gleneagle Rd PL3 248 F6
Gleneagle Villas 5 PL3 248 F6
Glenfield Cl PL6 245 D6
Glenfield Rd
Bideford EX39 157 A4
Plymouth PL6 245 D5
Glenfield Way PL6 245 E6
Glengarth Cl EX39 157 A5
Glenholt Cl PL6 245 D6
Glenholt Rd PL6 245 D6
Glenhurst Rd 5 PL3 248 E6
Glenmore Ave PL2 247 F5
Glenmore Rd
Brixham TQ5 230 C4
Exeter EX2 178 A5
Glennaven Cl PL7 251 C6
Glenorchy Ct 5 EX8 202 A7
Glenside Cl 5 TQ14 210 B6
Glenside Ct TQ1 220 E5
Glenside Rise PL7 250 E6
Glenthorne Cl TQ1 220 D4
Glenthorne Rd EX4 173 A1
Glentor Rd PL3 248 E7
Glentorr Rd EX39 157 A3
Glenview EX14 166 D5
Glenwater Cl EX12 192 D6
Glenwood Rd PL3 248 E6
Glenwood Rise EX2 261 C1
Globe Ct EX15 163 C3
Globe Hill EX5 184 B3
Globe La EX3 182 F4
Globefield EX3 182 F5
Gloster Rd EX32 155 A4
Gloucester Cl
Honiton EX14 166 A5
Torquay TQ2 213 F1
Gloucester Cres EX14 166 A5
Gloucester Ct PL1 262 C4
Gloucester Pl PL1 262 C4
Gloucester Rd
Exeter EX4 176 E7
Exmouth EX8 196 E3
Newton Abbot TQ12 207 C3
9 Teignmouth TQ14 210 B5
Glove Ct EX38 159 C5
Gloyn Pk EX22 53 E1
Glynsmead TA20 88 C8
Gnome Reserve★ EX22 39 B2
Goad Ave Plymouth PL4 263 C2
Torpoint PL11 246 E3
Goad Cl PL11 246 F3
Goaman Pk EX39 22 E3
Goaman Rd EX39 26 A4
Goats Hill Rd EX39 157 A6
Goblin Hill EX17 79 C4
Goblin La EX15 163 C4
Godborough View EX39 156 D2
Godding Gdns PL6 244 E6
Godford Cross EX14 85 B5
Godfrey Ave TQ3 219 B2
Godfrey Cl EX11 169 C3
Godfreys Gdns EX17 78 C4
Godhams La TA4 35 A7
Godolphin Cl EX5 81 A1
Godwell La PL21 237 F5
Gogwell La Cove EX16 49 B5
Tiverton EX16 161 F1
Gold Coast Holiday Village EX34 8 C6
Gold St
Ottery St Mary EX11 169 D4
Tiverton EX16 161 D4
Goldburn Cross EX20 76 B1
Golden Cl TQ5 230 B2
Golden Hinde Mus★ TQ5 230 D5
Golden Inn Cross EX21 74 C7
Golden Joy EX17 165 D6
Golden La EX14 66 F2
Golden Lane Cross EX14 66 E2
Golden Park Ave TQ2 213 F4
Golden Sq EX14 86 E6
Golden Terr 19 EX7 204 D6
Goldfinch Cl PL15 105 A2
Goldfinch Cres PL12 242 E4
Goldfinch Gr
Cullompton EX15 163 A2
Saltash PL12 242 D4
Golds Cross EX6 97 E4
Golds La EX6 97 E5
Goldscross Hill EX6 97 D4
Goldsmith Gdns PL5 244 D3
Goldsmith St Exeter EX4 261 A3
Exeter, Heavitree EX1 177 F6
Goldsmiths La EX13 88 A4
Goldsmoor Gate EX16 50 E3
Golf Links Rd
South Brent TQ10 134 D1
Westward Ho! EX39 156 D7
Golland La EX37 44 B2
Gollands TQ5 230 B5
Gollands Cl TQ5 230 A5
Gollands La
Copplestone EX17 79 B8
Morchard Bishop EX17 61 B1
Golvers Hill Rd TQ12 207 E7
Good Shepherd Dr 5 EX2 261 B2
Goodacre Cross PL16 91 B1
Goodeve Cl PL9 255 E6
Goodgates Cl EX33 152 C6
Goodgates Cres EX33 152 B6
Goodgates Gr EX33 152 B6
Goodgates Pk EX33 152 C6
Goodgates Rd EX33 152 B6
Goodiford Cross EX15 65 F3
Gooding Rise EX16 161 B4
Goodleigh Cross EX32 155 F7
Goodleigh La EX19 58 E3
Goodleigh Prim Sch EX32 17 B5
Goodleigh Rd EX32 155 D5
Goodridge Cl EX7 204 E8
Goodrington Rd TQ4 226 B1
Goodrington Sands Sta TQ4 226 C4
Goodshelter Cross TQ8 148 E5
Goodstone Cross TQ12 131 C6
Goodstone Way TQ4 225 F3
Goodwells Head EX32 18 C3
Goodwin Ave PL6 245 A6
Goodwin Cres PL2 248 A6
Goodwood Park Rd EX39 157 A5
Goose Moor La EX6 114 B4
Gooseberry La PL1 262 B2
Gooseford Cross EX20 95 D2
Gooseford La PL11 252 C8
Goosewell Hill PL6 249 C8
Goosewell Park Rd PL9 255 F6
Goosewell Prim Sch PL9 255 F6
Goosewell Rd PL9 255 F5
Goosewell Terr PL9 255 F6
Gora La EX34 8 A6
Gordon Ct PL12 242 D2
Gordon Rd Exeter EX1 177 E7
Topsham EX3 182 E6
Gordon Terr Beer EX12 191 D5
Plymouth PL4 248 E4
Gordon's Pl EX1 177 F5
Gore La Exmouth EX8 202 E4
Kilmington EX13 103 C8
Uplyme DT7 260 A4
Gorhuish Cross EX20 75 C1
Gorlegg TA21 51 E5
Gornhay Cross EX16 64 D8
Gorrans Down EX39 22 F1
Gorse La EX8 196 D4
Gorse Way
Ivybridge PL21 237 E4
Sidmouth EX10 187 F4
Gorsey Cl PL5 244 E2
Gorvin Cross EX39 38 B6
Gorway TQ14 210 C6
Gorwell Rd EX32 155 C5
Gorwood Rd EX39 40 B7
Gorwyn La EX6 97 C4
Gosceline Wlk EX14 166 C4
Gosford La EX11 169 C7
Gosford Rd EX11 169 D7
Goshawk Units EX2 178 F6
Goshen Rd TQ2 219 E4
Goss Mdw EX17 78 C4
Gostwick Cl EX20 77 C4
Goswela Cl PL9 255 F5
Goswela Gdns PL9 255 F5
Gothic Rd TQ12 207 B2
Gould Cl EX32 155 B4
Gould Rd
Barnstaple EX32 155 C4
Salcombe TQ8 259 D5
Gourders La TQ12 212 F2
Goutsford Gate PL21 136 F2
Govers Mdw EX24 103 A4
Govetts EX5 184 C3
Gower Ridge Rd PL9 255 D6
Goyle Acre La EX13 87 D4
Grace Par EX2 177 B2
Grace Rd Central EX2 177 C2
Grace Rd W EX2 177 B2
Graddon Cross
Black Torrington EX21 73 F6
Okehampton EX20 93 E4
Grafton Ct TQ1 220 B4
Grafton Hts TQ1 220 C5
Grafton Rd Exeter EX4 173 B1
11 Newton Abbot TQ12 207 B3
Plymouth PL4 248 E4
Torquay TQ1 220 B4
Grafton Terr TQ1 220 B4
Graham Cl EX16 161 D5
Graham Rd TQ3 219 A1
Grainge Rd PL6 245 A1
Grainger Cl EX2 178 C5
Gramercy Hall Sch TQ5 229 E3
Grammar La EX10 189 D7
Grampian Cl TQ4 225 D4
Granary La EX9 198 C1
Granby Ct PL1 247 E2
Granby Gn PL1 247 E2
Granby Pl PL1 247 E2
Granby St PL1 247 E2
Granby Way PL1 247 E2
Grand Hotel Rd PL1 262 B1
Grand Par PL1 262 B1
Grand View Rd TQ7 147 B7
Grand Western Canal (Country Pk)★ EX16 50 F2
Grandison Ave TQ14 209 A8
Grandisson Ct EX2 178 A2
Grandisson Dr EX11 169 F3
Grandon Bldgs 2 EX1 261 A2
Grange Ave
Barnstaple EX31 154 C2
Exmouth EX8 202 B8
Paignton TQ4 226 B2
Grange Cl
Bratton Fleming EX32 18 A8
Exmouth EX8 202 B8
Ipplepen TQ12 211 C3
Lympstone EX8 195 F5
Wellington TA21 160 E5
Grange Cotts
Plymouth PL7 250 F4
Rockbeare EX5 99 C6
Grange Cross EX14 84 D7
Grange Ct
4 Barnstaple EX32 155 A6
Teignmouth TQ14 210 A5
Grange Dr TQ14 210 B6
Grange Heights Cl TQ4 226 A1
Grange Hill EX32 18 B8
Grange Hts TQ4 226 A2
Grange La EX20 57 A7
Grange Pk TQ12 212 A6
Grange Rd
Abbotskerswell TQ12 212 B6
Bideford EX39 157 B1
Buckfast TQ11 236 B7
Paignton TQ4 226 B2
Plymouth PL7 251 A4
Torquay TQ1 220 C5
Yelverton PL20 126 F3
Grange The EX33 152 E5
Grange View TQ4 226 A2
Grant's Hill EX16,TA22 33 F2
Grantham Cl PL7 250 B4
Grantland Hill EX16,EX17 63 A4
Grantlands EX15 66 A7
Grantley Gdns PL3 249 A5
Granville Ave EX32 154 F6
Granville Pl EX15 162 C5
Granville Rd EX34 150 B6
Gras Lawn EX2 177 E4
Grasmere Cl
Plymouth PL6 244 E5
Torquay TQ2 214 B2
Grass Rd Ashburton TQ13 131 A3
Buckfastleigh TQ11 236 F8
Grassendale Ave PL2 247 F7
Grasslands Dr EX1 178 F8
Grassmere Way PL12 242 D4
Grasspark Hill EX32 18 E3
Grassy La PL8 136 C4
Grattan La EX31 16 B6
Grattans Way EX17 78 C4
Gratton Cl TQ6 146 B8
Gratton Cross
Shebbear EX22 55 A5
Yelverton PL20 127 A2
Gratton Ct EX31 154 C2
Gratton Dr TQ7 145 A1
Gratton La Barnstaple EX31 9 C5
Brendon EX35 6 A4
Chulmleigh EX18 59 D3
Combe Martin EX31 3 F2
Yelverton PL20 127 A2
Gratton Way EX31 154 C2
Grattons Dr EX35 151 B5
Grattons La TQ9 216 E2
Gravel La EX12 192 B7
Gravel Pit Cross EX36 20 A6
Gravel Wlk EX15 163 C3
Gravesend Gdns PL11 247 B3
Gravesend Wlk PL5 243 D4
Gray Cres PL5 247 C8
Gray's Hill EX15 52 D1
Gray's La EX15 52 D1
Graybridge Rd PL20 126 F4
Graynfylde Dr EX39 157 B2
Grays Ct TQ13 112 B3
Grays Mdw TQ13 111 F5
Great Ambrook Ave TQ12 217 A7
Great Berry Rd PL6 244 F1
Great Bridge TQ13 130 F5
Great Burrow Rise EX39 156 F8
Great Churchway PL9 256 A7
Great Cl EX15 51 E1
Great Fellingfield PL19 117 E6
Great Field Gdns EX33 152 C5
Great Furlong TQ14 208 E8
Great Headland Cres TQ3 219 D1
Great Headland Rd TQ3 219 C1
Great Hele La EX36 158 D2
Great Hill 3 TQ13 123 E6
Great Hill Cross TQ1 213 F5
Great Hill Rd TQ2 213 F4
Great Hill View EX4 173 E2
Great La TQ7 147 E6
Great Lightleigh La EX18 44 F5
Great Links Tor Rd EX20 170 E5
Great Mdw TA22 33 D6
Great Mead EX6 112 F7
Great Mis Tor Cl 5 PL20 126 F3
Great Oak Cross EX5 81 D2
Great Oak Mdw EX22 164 C5
Great Orchard Cl PL9 255 E5
Great Park Cl 4 PL7 251 C5
Great Parks Rd TQ3 225 E5
Great Pitford La EX18 58 D6
Great Rea Rd TQ5 230 D5
Great Ringaton La EX36 32 B6
Great Tor Cl TQ3 218 F1
Great Torrington Bluecoat CE Inf Sch EX38 159 C5
Great Torrington Com Sch EX38 159 E5
Great Torrington Jun Sch EX38 159 E5
Great Western Cl TQ4 226 C4
Great Western Ind Est EX32 155 B3
Great Western Rd
12 Paignton TQ4 226 B6
Plymouth PL1 262 B1
Great Western Way EX16 161 D3
Great Woodford Dr PL7 250 B6
Greatfield Rd PL3 249 B7
Greatlands Cres PL2 248 A6
Greatlands Pl 5 PL2 248 A5
Greatoak Cross TQ12 212 C5
Greatpark La TQ3 225 D6
Greatweek Cross TQ13 111 B6
Greatwood Terr EX3 182 F5
Grebe Cl PL7 250 F5
Grecian Way EX2 178 C4
Greebys The TQ3 226 A6
Green Bank EX10 186 E8
Green Banks Cl TQ7 145 C3
Green Cl Cornworthy TQ9 227 B4
Exmouth EX8 202 C8
Kingsbridge TQ7 258 D6
Green Close La EX31 10 B5
Green End La EX15 83 F5
Green Gate EX16 50 C2
Green Gdns EX39 156 E6
Green Head EX10 101 B2
Green Hill
Cheriton Fitzpaine EX16, EX17 62 D3
Lamerton PL19 116 E3
Sampford Courtenay EX20 76 F3
Tavistock PL19 171 D5
Green Knap La TA20 69 F2

Green La
23 Appledore EX39 15 A1
Axmouth EX12,DT7 193 B8
1 Barnstaple EX31 154 F5
Beaford EX19 42 D1
Bittaford TQ10 137 E8
Blackawton TQ9 139 B1
Braunton EX33 152 E6
Buckfastleigh TQ11 236 F4
Cawsand PL10 253 A2
Chard Junction TA20 88 D7
Chardstock EX13 88 B7
Cheriton Bishop EX6 97 C2
Churston Ferrers TQ5 229 E5
Colyford EX24 103 A3
East Allington TQ9 144 D8
Exeter EX4 176 E5
Exton EX3 183 B2
Hatherleigh EX20 75 D7
Ilsington TQ13 122 C4
Merton EX20 57 A7
Rackenford EX16 47 C5
Raymond's Hill EX13 104 C7
Rewe EX5 82 A2
Rousdon DT7 193 F8
Sampford Arundel TA21 51 F4
Sidbury EX10 101 D2
Southleigh EX24 102 D3
Spreyton EX17 96 A7
Swimbridge EX32 28 B8
Tavistock PL19 171 E5
Totnes TQ9 223 A4
Yelverton PL20 126 F1
Green Lane End
Blackawton TQ9 139 B1
Buckfastleigh TQ11 236 E4
Green Lanes Sh Ctr
EX31 154 F5
Green Mews EX9 198 A1
Green Mount EX10 188 C6
Green Park Ave PL4 248 D4
Green Park Rd
Paignton TQ3 218 F1
Plymouth PL9 255 E5
Green Park Way TQ7 145 A1
Green Park Wlk TQ3 218 F1
Green Pk PL10 253 A2
Green The
Ashburton TQ13 130 F4
Bridgerule EX22 70 F5
Brushford TA22 33 E4
Cawsand PL10 253 A2
Down St Mary EX17 78 E7
Exmouth EX8 202 F8
6 Horrabridge PL20 126 F5
Ide EX2 176 D1
Meavy PL20 127 C2
Milton Combe PL20 240 F8
Otterton EX9 198 E7
Plymouth PL9 255 B6
Saltash PL12 242 C3
Teignmouth TQ14 210 A3
Whimple EX5 99 E8
Green Tree La EX5 175 D6
Greenacre
Braunton EX33 152 C6
Torquay TQ1 220 E5
Greenacre Cl
Bradworthy EX22 53 E8
North Tawton EX20 77 C4
Northam EX39 157 A7
Greenacres Exeter EX4 173 A3
Plymouth PL9 255 F8
Greenacres Cl EX14 84 D1
Greenaway EX17 61 A2
Greenaway La TQ12 213 B6
Greenaway Rd TQ12 207 A4
Greenaway Villas 3
TQ12 207 B4
Greenawell Cl TQ13 111 D2
Greenbank EX38 159 F6
Greenbank Ave
Kingsteignton TQ12 207 D8
Plymouth PL4 263 B3
Greenbank Cl EX38 159 F6
Greenbank Rd
Barnstaple EX32 155 C4
Brixham TQ5 230 B4
Plymouth PL4 263 B4
Greenbank Terr
Plymouth PL4 263 B4
Yelverton PL20 127 A3
Greenbanks TQ7 145 C3
Greenclose Ct 3 EX24 103 A4
Greenclose Rd EX34 150 B6
Greendale Cross EX5 183 F7
Greendale La Exeter EX5 99 A1
Woodbury Salterton EX5 184 A8
Greendale Rd PL2 248 A7
Greendown Cross EX20 74 C2
Greenfield Dr
Ivybridge PL21 237 D4
7 South Brent TQ10 134 F2
Greenfield Rd
Paignton TQ3 219 A1
Saltash PL12 242 D2
Greenfield Terr TA20 88 D8
Greenfield Villas EX2 261 A1
Greenhaven EX9 197 F2
Greenhayes
Charmouth DT6 104 F4
Dartington TQ9 222 E8
Greenhays Foot EX13 88 B6
Greenhill
East Allington TQ9 144 D7
Kingsteignton TQ12 207 E6
Greenhill Ave
Exmouth EX8 202 C7
Greenhill Ave *continued*
Lympstone EX8 195 E5
Greenhill Cl PL9 255 F5
Greenhill Cross
Knowle EX33 8 E1
Knowstone EX36 32 B2
Sampford Chapple EX20 77 A3
Witheridge EX16 62 D3
Greenhill Gdns TQ12 212 F3
Greenhill Ind Units
TQ12 207 E6
Greenhill La TQ12 211 B6
Greenhill Rd
Kingskerswell TQ12 212 F4
Kingsteignton TQ12 207 E6
Greenhill Terr TQ9 144 D7
Greenhill Way TQ12 207 E6
Greenings Rd EX39 40 C7
Greenlake Cross EX39 22 D1
Greenland PL10 252 F5
Greenland Head Cross
Churchstow TQ7 143 E6
Witheridge EX16 62 E6
Greenlands Ave TQ3 225 F6
Greenlane Cross EX36 31 C8
Greenlees Dr PL7 251 B3
Greenmeadow Dr EX31 155 A7
Greenover Cl TQ5 230 B3
Greenover Rd TQ5 230 B3
Greenpark Ave EX1 178 D7
Greenpark Rd EX8 196 D2
Greenslade Cross EX20 77 A3
Greenslade Rd EX16 46 E1
Greenslinch La EX5 82 D6
Greensway Rd PL19 171 A4
Greenswood La TQ6 232 B1
Greenswood Rd 4 TQ5 230 C3
Greenway Crediton EX17 165 B5
Exeter EX2 176 F3
Halberton EX16 65 A8
Lyme Regis DT7 260 C3
Seaton EX12 191 F7
Woodbury EX5 184 C3
Greenway Ave PL7 250 B6
Greenway Cl
3 Horrabridge PL20 126 F5
Ivybridge PL21 237 D5
Torquay TQ2 214 A1
Greenway Gate EX16 34 E1
Greenway Gdns TQ2 214 A2
Greenway La
Ashcombe EX7 124 F5
Awliscombe EX14 85 B5
Beacon EX14 85 D8
Budleigh Salterton EX9 198 A2
Sidmouth EX10 187 E8
Torquay TQ1 220 B8
Greenway Pk TQ5 229 B4
Greenway Rd
Galmpton TQ5 229 B4
Paignton TQ5 228 E3
Rockwell Green TA21 160 A5
Torquay, Chelston TQ2 219 E4
Torquay, St Marychurch
TQ1 220 B8
Greenway's Almshouses
EX16 161 D4
Greenways EX34 150 A5
Greenwich Pl PL12 242 F3
Greenwood Cl
Aveton Gifford TQ7 143 C6
Ivybridge PL21 237 C5
Greenwood Dr EX2 178 D5
Greenwood Park Cl PL7 251 B6
Greenwood Park Rd
PL7 251 B6
Greenwoods The EX39 22 E3
Gregory Cl Bow EX17 78 C4
Tiverton EX16 161 F4
Gregory Terr EX39 22 E3
Gregory's Mdw PL15 105 A2
Grenadier Rd EX1 178 E7
Grendon Ct TQ14 210 A5
Grendon La EX16 46 E4
Grendon Rd EX1 177 E6
Grenfell Ave PL12 242 D3
Grenfell Gdns PL12 242 C3
Grenofen Cl PL19 126 D6
Grenville Ave Exeter EX4 178 D8
Teignmouth TQ14 210 A7
Torquay TQ2 219 D6
Grenville Cl
Dartmouth TQ6 233 D3
Newton Abbot TQ12 207 E3
Stokenham TQ7 145 B2
Grenville Coll EX39 156 F2
Grenville Coll (Moreton
House) EX39 156 D1
Grenville Ct PL7 251 C6
Grenville Dr PL19 171 B3
Grenville Est The EX39 25 E4
Grenville Estate Cres
EX39 25 E4
Grenville Pk PL20 127 A2
Grenville Rd
Exmouth EX8 196 C2
Plymouth PL4 263 C3
Salcombe TQ8 259 D4
Grenville Road La S
PL4 249 B2
Grenville St 16 EX39 157 A2
Grenville Terr
4 Bideford EX39 157 B1
Northam EX39 157 A7
Grenville Way TQ4 226 B3
Gresham Cl PL5 244 C7
Greycoat La TQ12 206 F7
Greyhill Cross TQ7 138 A1
Greysand Cres 31 EX39 15 A1
Greysholt Cross EX32 28 B8
Greystoke Ave PL6 249 D7
Greystone Cross EX6 96 E2
Greystone Way TQ1 220 C7
Gribble Cl EX32 155 C4
Gribble La EX5 99 D6
Gribbleford Cross EX20 75 A4
Gribblemead EX24 103 A4
Grieg Dr EX32 155 C5
Griffin Way PL9 256 C6
Grigg's La EX10 188 D7
Griggs Cl Northam EX39 157 A6
Plymouth PL7 251 B4
Griggs Gdns EX31 153 D5
Grimspound Cl PL6 249 E8
Grimstone Terr PL20 126 E2
Grinacombe Cross PL16 91 B2
Grinacombe Moor cross
PL16 91 B2
Grindhill Cross EX20 92 D5
Grindle Way EX5 179 B2
Grizedale Rd PL6 249 D7
Gronau Cl EX14 166 C4
Grooms Orch TA21 160 C5
Gropers La
Ipplepen TQ3,TQ12 218 C8
North Whilborough TQ12 212 B1
Gropy La
Bishops Nympton EX36 31 D1
South Molton EX36 46 D8
Grosvenor Ave TQ2 213 C1
Grosvenor Cl TQ2 213 C1
Grosvenor Cotts 1 PL4 248 F4
Grosvenor Pl EX1 261 C4
Grosvenor Rd
Paignton TQ4 226 B5
Plymouth PL6 244 F2
Grosvenor St 2 EX32 155 A5
Grosvenor Terr
Paignton TQ4 226 B5
4 Teignmouth TQ14 210 B6
Groundhead Rd EX14 86 F6
Grove Ave 12 TQ14 210 B5
Grove Cl 3 TQ9 223 C5
Grove Cres 6 TQ14 210 B5
Grove Cross EX22 39 D3
Grove Ct Dawlish EX7 204 F6
Teignmouth TQ14 210 C6
Grove Hill
12 Colyton EX24 103 A4
Topsham EX3 182 F5
Grove Ho EX3 182 F5
Grove La EX36 32 D6
Grove Mdw EX20 94 F5
Grove Pk Tavistock PL19 171 D5
Torpoint PL11 246 E3
Grove Prim Sch The
TQ9 223 C5
Grove Rd EX5 99 F7
Grove Terr 11 TQ14 210 B5
Grove The Bittaford PL21 137 C8
Blackawton TQ9 139 E1
Paignton TQ4 225 E4
Plymouth, Plymstock PL9 255 D8
Plymouth, Stoke PL3 248 A4
Sidmouth EX10 188 B4
Totnes TQ9 223 C5
Woolacombe EX34 7 F6
Groves The PL21 237 C6
Gubbin's La EX33 152 D5
Guernsey Cnr EX24 102 F4
Guestland Rd TQ1 220 C7
Guildford Cl Exeter EX4 176 E6
Plymouth PL5 244 E3
Guildford St PL4 263 A3
Guildhall Sh Ctr EX4 261 A3
Guildhall Sq PL1 262 C2
Guildhall Yd TQ9 223 C5
Guinea St EX1 261 A2
Guinevere Way EX4 174 A1
Guinness La EX4 176 E8
Gulland Cross TQ12 212 B4
Gullet Cross TQ7 148 F6
Gulliver La EX20 77 D7
Gully La EX14 86 C5
Gully Shoot EX24 103 A3
Gullyhole Hill EX36 31 F7
Gulway Mead TA20 88 D8
Gulworthy Cotts PL19 125 E7
Gulworthy Cross PL19 125 E7
Gulworthy Prim Sch
PL19 125 E7
Gun Cross EX32 17 F3
Gun La EX36 19 D4
Gunnislake Prim Sch
PL18 125 C6
Gunnislake Rural Workshops
PL18 125 C6
Gunnislake Sta PL18 125 C5
Gunsdown Villas EX36 158 D5
Gunstone Cross EX17 79 E2
Gunstone Mill Cross
EX17 79 E1
Gunswell La EX36 158 B5
Gurnard Wlk PL3 249 C6
Gurney Cl PL11 246 F3
Gurneys The TQ3 226 A5
Guscott La EX38 26 E2
Gussiford La EX8 202 B6
Guy Miles Way PL5 244 B3
Guys Rd EX4 176 F6
Gwel Avon Bsns Pk
PL12 242 D4
Gwithian Cl PL11 246 F4
Gwyn Rd PL4 263 C4
Gwythers EX36 158 D4

H

Hacche La EX36 158 C6
Haccombe Cl EX4 176 E5
Haccombe Cross TQ12 213 E6
Haccombe Path TQ12 208 A2
Hacker Cl EX10 186 F7
Hackney La
Kingsteignton TQ12 207 F6
Newton Abbot TQ12 208 B4
Hackney Marsh (Nature Pk)
TQ12 207 E6
Hackpen Cross Way
EX15 66 E6
Hackworthy Cnr EX4 98 F5
Hackworthy Cross EX6 97 E5
Hackworthy Cross La
EX6 97 E5
Hackworthy La
Nadderwater EX4 98 F5
Tedburn St Mary EX6 97 E4
Haddacott Cross EX38 26 F3
Haddington Rd PL2 247 F4
Haddon Cnr EX13 103 C8
Haddon Ct 1 TQ3 226 B7
Haddon La TA4 34 C7
Haddon Rd EX13 103 B8
Hadfield Ct 4 TQ13 123 C4
Hadrian Dr EX4 176 E6
Hadrians Way EX8 196 D1
Halberton Prim Sch
EX16 65 A7
Halcyon Ct PL2 248 A6
Halcyon Rd
Newton Abbot TQ12 207 B3
Plymouth PL2 248 A6
Haldene Terr 5 EX32 154 F6
Haldon Ave TQ14 210 C6
Haldon Belvedere★
EX6 113 F5
Haldon Cl
2 Newton Abbot TQ12 207 F2
Topsham EX3 182 E6
Torquay TQ1 220 E4
Haldon Ct EX8 196 B2
Haldon La TQ13 124 B4
Haldon Lodge EX6 114 B5
Haldon Pl PL5 244 A3
Haldon Rd Exeter EX4 177 A6
Torquay TQ1 220 D4
Haldon Rise 1 TQ12 207 F2
Haldon Terr 13 EX7 204 D6
Haldon View TQ13 123 F6
Haldon View Terr EX2 177 F5
Haldron's Almshouses
EX16 161 C4
Hale La EX14 166 E6
Haley Barton 4 PL2 248 A5
Haley Cl EX8 196 C2
Half Moon The EX13 87 E8
Half Way Cvn Pk TQ4 224 E5
Halford Cross TQ12 122 E1
Halfpenny Cross EX16 49 B7
Halfsbury Cross EX37 43 E4
Halfway House Flats
TQ5 230 F6
Hall Cross PL21 133 E2
Hall Hill EX35 6 B5
Hall La EX7 210 E8
Hall Mus★ TQ8 259 E5
Hall's La TQ12 212 F4
Hall's Mill La EX31 154 E8
Hallamore La PL21 133 B2
Hallerton Cl PL6 245 E2
Hallett Cl PL12 242 B3
Hallett Ct DT7 260 D4
Halletts Way EX13 167 E6
Halley Gdns PL5 243 E1
Hallow Mead TQ13 121 F7
Halls Cross EX31 10 E4
Halmpstone Cross EX32 28 C7
Halsbury Rd EX16 161 F4
Halscombe La EX2 176 C1
Halsdon Ave EX8 196 A1
Halsdon Cross EX22 54 C1
Halsdon La EX8 196 A2
Halsdon Rd EX8 202 A7
Halsdon Terr EX38 159 C5
Halse Hill La EX9 197 F1
Halse La
North Tawton EX20 77 D4
West Worlington EX17 61 B6
Halsegate Cross EX20 77 D3
Halses Cl EX4 176 D8
Halsewood Gate EX15 64 E2
Halsey Lake Cross EX31 10 D1
Halsfordwood La EX4 98 F4
Halshanger Cross TQ13 130 F8
Halsteads Rd TQ2 214 A2
Halswell Cross EX36 29 D2
Halwell Cross
Denbury TQ12 211 A5
Halwell TQ9 139 C4
Halwell Ho TQ7 148 E7
Halwill Prim Sch EX21 73 C2
Halyards EX3 182 E5
Ham Butts TQ7 143 F7
Ham Cl PL2 248 B8
Ham Cross EX13 86 F4
Ham Dr PL2 248 B7
Ham Gn PL2 248 A7
Ham Green Ct PL2 248 A7
Ham Green La PL2 248 A7
Ham Hill Ashreigney EX18 58 E8
Combe St Nicholas TA20 69 F8
Ham Ho PL2 248 A8
Ham La Colyton EX24 103 A4
Ham La *continued*
Dittisham TQ6 228 C3
Plymouth PL2 248 A8
Shaldon TQ14 209 D4
Sidmouth EX10 188 B3
South Molton EX36 158 E4
Ham Rd Dalwood EX13 87 A3
Wellington TA21 52 D8
Hambeer La EX2 176 E3
Hamberhayne Cross
EX24 102 D6
Hamble Cl PL3 249 D7
Hamblecombe La TQ13 124 A4
Hambleton Ho 4 TQ14 210 C5
Hameldown Cl TQ2 219 B7
Hameldown Rd EX20 170 E5
Hameldown Way TQ12 207 D4
Hamelin Way TQ2,TQ3 219 A8
Hamilton Ave EX2 177 F2
Hamilton Cl Bideford EX39 25 E4
14 Sidford EX10 101 B1
Hamilton Dr Exeter EX2 178 D5
Newton Abbot TQ12 207 B5
Hamilton Gdns PL4 248 D4
Hamilton Gr EX6 201 B7
Hamilton La EX8 202 C7
Hamilton Rd
Exmouth EX8 202 D7
Topsham EX3 182 E6
Hamiltons The TQ14 210 A3
Hamley La TA20 69 E8
Hamlin Gdns EX1 178 A7
Hamlin Ho EX1 178 A7
Hamlin La EX1 178 A7
Hamlintoo La EX17 95 E7
Hamlyns Way TQ11 236 B5
Hammett Rd EX15 163 B3
Hammetts La
Barnstaple EX32 155 B1
Bishop's Tawton EX32 16 E1
Hammond Croft Way
EX2 181 B8
Hamoaze Ave PL5 247 D8
Hamoaze Pl PL1 247 D2
Hamoaze Rd PL11 247 B2
Hampshire Cl EX4 176 E4
Hampson Cross EX17 78 A4
Hampson La EX17 78 A4
Hampton Ave TQ1 220 C8
Hampton Bldgs EX4 261 C4
Hampton La
Torquay TQ1 220 C8
Whitford EX13 103 C6
Hampton Rd
Newton Abbot TQ12 207 C3
Whitford EX13 103 C7
Hampton St PL4 263 A3
Hams The EX2 176 D1
Hamslade Cross EX16 48 D8
Hamslade Hill EX16 48 D8
Hamstone Ct TQ8 259 D4
Hamway La TA20 69 F8
Hancock Cl PL6 244 D6
Hand & Pen Cotts EX5 99 E6
Hanger La EX14 84 F8
Hanging La EX35 5 A3
Hangman Path EX34 2 F4
Hangman's Cross PL21 138 A2
Hangman's Hill EX16 48 D7
Hangman's Hill Cross
EX16 48 E7
Hangmans Cnr EX17 165 E1
Hankford Cross EX22 39 E2
Hannaburrow La EX33 14 F8
Hannaford Cross EX32 28 C8
Hannaford La EX32 28 D8
Hannaford Rd
Lifton PL16 105 E3
Noss Mayo PL8 140 F5
Hannaton Cross EX32 28 D8
Hannock Ct EX2 181 D8
Hanover Cl
7 Brixham TQ5 230 C3
Exeter EX1 177 F6
Plymouth PL3 249 B5
Hanover Ct Exeter EX2 181 C8
16 Plymouth PL1 263 A2
Hanover Gdns EX15 163 C5
Hanover Ho TQ1 220 D3
Hanover Rd Exeter EX1 177 F6
Plymouth PL3 249 C4
Hansetown Rd TA4 34 F8
Hansford Cross
Ashreigney EX18 44 A1
Burrington EX37 44 B2
Hansford Ct EX14 166 C5
Hansford Way EX11 169 C3
Hanson Pk EX39 157 A4
Happaway Cl TQ2 214 A2
Happaway Rd TQ2 214 A2
Harberton Cl TQ4 225 E3
Harbertonford CE Prim Sch
TQ9 139 C7
Harbour Ave
Plymouth PL4 263 A2
Plymouth, Camels Head
PL5 247 E8
Harbour Ct Exmouth EX8 201 F6
4 Seaton EX12 192 B4
Harbour Rd EX12 192 B4
Harbour St PL11 247 B3
Harbour View
Plymouth PL9 255 A7
Saltash PL12 242 E2

Harbour View Cl 1 TQ5 230 C5
Harbourne Ave TQ4 225 F3
Harbourneford Cross TQ10 135 B4
Harcombe Cross
Chudleigh TQ13 124 A8
Raymond's Hill EX13 104 C6
Sidbury EX10 101 C1
Harcombe Fields EX10 188 D8
Harcombe La EX10 188 D8
Harcombe La E EX10 188 E8
Harcombe Rd
Raymond's Hill DT7 104 D6
Uplyme DT7 260 D8
Hardaway Head 5 EX32 155 A5
Harding Cres EX16 161 E5
Hardisworthy Cross EX39 37 B7
Hardy Cl TQ1 220 C2
Hardy Cres PL5 244 E1
Hardy Rd EX2 178 D5
Hardys Ct EX10 186 D4
Hare La EX4 98 D4
Hare Tor Cl EX20 170 E5
Harebell Cl PL12 242 D4
Harebell Copse EX4 176 D8
Harebell Dr EX15 162 E5
Haredon Cross PL21 137 D6
Harefield Cl EX4 177 A8
Harefield Cotts EX8 195 D5
Harefield Dr
Lympstone EX8 195 F5
Stoke Fleming TQ6 146 B7
Harefield Rd EX8 195 F6
Harefoot Cross TQ13 121 D3
Harepath Hill EX12 192 A8
Harepath Rd EX12 192 A7
Harepathstead Rd EX5 83 B1
Harepie Cross EX31 27 D6
Hares Gn EX36 158 C4
Hares La TQ13 130 F4
Haresdown Cross EX36 47 C7
Hareston Cl PL7 251 B3
Hareston Cross PL8 257 D8
Harestone Cross EX13 88 B7
Harewood Cl PL7 250 E5
Harewood Cres PL5 244 B2
Harewood Rd PL18 125 D3
Harford Cross EX32 17 C2
Harford La EX6,EX17 97 F7
Harford Rd
Ivybridge PL21 237 D6
Landkey EX32 17 B2
Hargood Terr 6 PL2 247 F4
Hargreaves Cl PL5 243 F2
Harker La EX6 114 B2
Harlech Cl PL3 249 A7
Harlequins EX4 261 A3
Harleston Cross TQ7 144 F4
Harley Ct PL21 237 D5
Harman Wlk EX32 155 C5
Harnorlen Rd PL2 248 D7
Haroldsleigh Ave PL5 244 E2
Harp La EX5 99 E2
Harp's Corner Cross EX36 46 C6
Harper's Hill
Northlew EX20 74 E2
Totnes TQ9 223 A5
Harpins Ct TQ12 213 A6
Harpitt Cl EX15 162 C3
Harpson Hill EX36 31 F1
Harpson La
Bishops Nympton EX36 31 F1
South Molton EX36 46 F8
Harracott Cross EX31 27 E6
Harraton Cross PL21 137 D1
Harrier Way EX2 178 E4
Harriers Cl EX12 192 A6
Harriet Gdns PL7 250 B6
Harringcourt Rd EX4 174 E2
Harrington Dr EX4 174 E2
Harrington Gdns EX4 174 E1
Harrington La EX4 174 D2
Harris Cl EX16 51 A4
Harris Cotts PL21 237 C5
Harris Cross EX39 38 D8
Harris Ct PL9 255 B6
Harris Way PL21 136 B6
Harrison St 7 PL2 247 F4
Harrowbarrow Sch PL17 125 A4
Harrowbeer La PL20 126 F3
Harrowby Cl EX16 161 F4
Hart Manor EX33 152 E3
Hart St 9 EX39 157 A2
Hart's La Churchstow TQ7 143 E4
Exeter EX1 178 D8
Huish Champflower TA4 35 D7
Hartland Abbey* EX39 22 C3
Hartland Cl PL6 245 A7
Hartland Cross EX17 79 C4
Hartland Prim Sch EX39 22 E3
Hartland Quay Mus* EX39 22 A3
Hartland Tor Cl TQ5 230 A2
Hartland View Rd EX34 8 C6
Hartley Ave PL3 249 A6
Hartley Ct PL3 249 A6
Hartley Park Gdns PL3 248 F6
Hartley Rd Exmouth EX8 202 A6
Paignton TQ4 226 A5
Plymouth PL3 248 E6
Hartnoll Cross EX16 64 E8
Harton Cross EX39 22 E3
Harton Way EX39 22 E3
Hartop Rd TQ1 214 B1
Hartopp Rd EX8 202 A8
Harts Cl Exeter EX1 178 E8
Teignmouth TQ14 210 A6
Hartwell Ave PL9 256 D7
Harvest La EX39 156 D2
Harvey Ave PL4 249 B1
Harvey St PL11 247 B3
Harveys Cl
11 Chudleigh Knighton TQ13 123 C4
Sampford Courtenay EX20 76 F4
Harwell Ct 8 PL1 262 B3
Harwell St PL1 262 B3
Harwood Ave PL5 244 C7
Harwood Cl EX8 196 D1
Hask La EX6 96 D3
Haskins Cross EX14 84 C5
Haslam Ct TQ1 220 A7
Haslam Rd TQ1 220 A7
Hastings St PL1 262 B3
Hastings Terr PL1 262 B3
Haswell Cl PL6 249 A8
Hat La PL10 252 F2
Hatchcombe La TQ2 213 F2
Hatcher Cl EX14 166 C3
Hatcher St 9 EX7 204 D6
Hatchland Rd EX4 174 F6
Hatchmoor Common La EX38 159 F6
Hatchmoor Ind Est EX20 75 B6
Hatchmoor Lane Ind Est EX38 159 F6
Hatchmoor Rd EX38 159 F5
Hatfield Rd TQ1 220 B6
Hatherdown Hill TQ13 123 B6
Hatherleigh La TQ13 122 D7
Hatherleigh Prim Sch EX20 75 C7
Hatherleigh Rd
Exeter EX2 177 A2
Okehampton EX20 93 F7
Winkleigh EX19 58 E2
Hatherton La EX20 76 E2
Hatshill Cl PL6 132 A2
Hatshill Farm Cl PL6 132 A5
Hatway Hill EX10 101 C3
Hauley Rd TQ6 233 F3
Have's Hill EX17 61 C8
Havelock Rd TQ1 214 B1
Havelock Terr
Lutton PL21 133 B2
Plymouth PL2 247 F3
Haven Cl EX2 261 A1
Haven Rd EX2 261 A1
Haven The TQ14 208 F7
Havenview Rd EX12 192 A5
Hawarden Cotts PL4 249 B1
Hawcombe La EX33 8 E1
Haweswater Cl PL6 244 E4
Hawkchurch Cross EX13 88 E2
Hawkchurch Prim Sch EX13 88 E3
Hawkchurch Rd EX13 88 E3
Hawkerland Rd EX10 186 C4
Hawkers Ave PL4 263 A2
Hawkesdown Cl EX12 192 D7
Hawkin's La TA4 35 E7
Hawkinge Gdns PL5 243 E4
Hawkins Ave TQ2 219 C7
Hawkins Cl PL6 245 A5
Hawkins Dr TQ14 210 B6
Hawkins La EX11 168 E3
Hawkins Rd TQ12 207 F3
Hawkins Way EX17 165 E5
Hawkmoor Cotts TQ13 122 E7
Hawkmoor Hill EX13,DT6 88 H2
Hawkmoor Pk TQ13 122 E7
Hawkridge Cross
Hawkridge TA22 21 D1
Umberleigh EX37 28 C4
Hawkridge Rd EX31 15 E5
Hawks Pk PL12 242 C2
Hawksdown View EX12 192 A7
Hawkwell Cross EX16 32 F4
Hawley Cl EX32 155 C5
Hawley Cross EX13 86 F3
Hawley Manor EX32 155 C5
Hawson Cross TQ11 130 B3
Hawthorn Ave
Ilfracombe EX34 150 D5
Torpoint PL11 246 F3
Hawthorn Cl
Cullompton EX15 163 B2
Honiton EX14 166 B5
Kingsbridge TQ7 258 C4
Plymouth, Hooe PL9 255 C5
Plymouth, Woolwell PL6 245 D7
Hawthorn Dr
Sidmouth EX10 187 F8
Wembury PL9 140 D7
Hawthorn Gr
Exmouth EX8 196 E1
Plymouth PL2 248 C7
Hawthorn Park Cl TQ2 219 D3
Hawthorn Park Rd PL9 140 D7
Hawthorn Pk
Bideford EX39 156 E1
Lydford EX20 107 F4
Hawthorn Rd
Barnstaple EX32 155 E4
Crediton EX17 165 C5
Exeter EX2 177 F3
Tavistock PL19 171 C2
Hawthorn Way
Exeter EX2 181 A8
Hawthorn Way *continued*
Plymouth PL3 249 B7
Hawthorne Cl TQ12 212 F8
Hawthorne Rd
10 Tiverton EX16 161 F6
Wellington TA21 160 F5
Hawthorns PL12 242 D2
Haxter Cl PL6 241 B1
Haxton Down La EX31 18 B8
Haxton La EX31 18 A8
Hay La TQ7 147 E6
Haycroft Ho 8 EX39 157 A1
Haycross Hill EX21 55 D4
Haydn Cl EX32 155 C5
Haydon Cross EX16 48 C4
Haydon Gr PL5 243 C1
Haydon Rd EX16 161 B5
Haydons Pk EX14 166 C5
Haye Cl DT7 260 C4
Haye La
Colyford DT7,EX13 103 D3
Lyme Regis DT7 260 D4
Haye Rd PL7,PL9 250 C1
Haye Rd S PL9 256 C7
Hayes Barton* EX9 197 E7
Hayes Barton Ct EX4 177 A5
Hayes Cl
Budleigh Salterton EX9 198 A2
Otterton EX9 198 E7
Totnes TQ9 223 E4
Hayes Copse EX32 17 B2
Hayes Cross EX21 55 E3
Hayes Ct Lyme Regis DT7 260 D3
Paignton TQ4 225 F5
Hayes Gdns TQ4 226 A4
Hayes La Ashreigney EX18 58 D8
East Budleigh EX9 198 A6
Hayes Rd Paignton TQ4 226 A5
Plymouth PL9 255 C7
Hayes Sch TQ4 225 F5
Hayes The TQ5 229 E5
Hayeswood La EX9 198 A6
Hayfield Rd EX20 76 C5
Hayle Ave TQ4 229 B8
Hayley Pk TQ12 212 F3
Haymans Cl EX15 163 B2
Haymans Gn EX15 163 B2
Hayne Cl Exeter EX4 178 A7
Tipton St John EX10 100 D2
Hayne Cross
Bampton EX16 34 B4
Bishops Nympton EX36 31 A4
Cheriton Fitzpaine EX17 63 A2
Kentisbeare EX15 66 F5
Lewtrenchard EX20 106 B5
Lustleigh TQ13 121 F7
Plymtree EX15 83 F6
Zeal Monachorum EX17 78 B6
Hayne Hill EX10 100 D2
Hayne Ho EX16 49 B2
Hayne La Bolham EX16 49 B2
Butterleigh EX15 64 C2
Honiton EX14 85 C2
Silverton EX5 82 C4
Wilmington EX14 86 D3
Hayne Pk
Barnstaple EX32 155 B4
Tipton St John EX10 100 D2
Hayne Town Cross EX37 44 B8
Haynes La EX6 176 A2
Hayrish Cross EX20 95 B7
Hayston Pl PL1 262 B4
Haytor Ave TQ4 225 F3
Haytor Cl Plymouth PL5 244 B3
Teignmouth TQ14 209 D8
Haytor Dr Exeter EX4 176 E7
Ivybridge PL21 237 D4
Newton Abbot TQ12 208 A3
Haytor Gr TQ12 208 A3
Haytor Rd TQ1 220 B7
Haytor Terr 17 TQ12 207 B3
Haytown Pottery* EX22 39 E1
Haywain Cl TQ2 213 B1
Haywards Prim Sch EX17 165 D5
Hazel Ave EX33 152 E7
Hazel Cl Kingsbridge TQ7 258 C4
Newton Abbot TQ12 208 A1
Newton Poppleford EX10 186 F8
Plymouth PL6 245 B6
Seaton EX12 192 A7
Teignmouth TQ14 210 C8
Hazel Dr PL9 256 C7
Hazel Gr
4 Barnstaple EX31 154 C2
Plymouth PL9 256 C7
Rockbeare EX5 99 C5
Yelverton PL20 127 A3
Hazel Rd Exeter EX2 177 F2
Tavistock PL19 171 C2
Hazel-Crest TQ13 123 B7
Hazeldene TQ8 259 C3
Hazeldene Cl PL21 136 B6
Hazeldene Gdns EX8 196 A1
Hazeldown Prim Sch TQ14 210 B8
Hazeldown Rd TQ14 210 B7
Hazelmead Rd EX5 179 E2
Hazelstone EX5 82 E2
Hazelwood 5 TQ1 220 D5
Hazelwood Cl EX14 166 C4
Hazelwood Cres PL9 256 D7
Hazelwood Dr
Dawlish Warren EX7 201 A2
Plymouth PL6 245 D8
Head Hill EX18,EX37 44 C5
Head Weir Rd EX15 163 C5
Headborough Rd TQ13 130 F5
Headgate EX36 20 B1
Headingley Cl EX2 178 C4
Headland Cl EX1 178 C7
Headland Cres EX1 178 C7
Headland Cross EX17 96 A6
Headland Ct
8 Brixham TQ5 230 D5
Woolacombe EX34 7 F8
Headland Gr TQ3 219 C1
Headland La EX17 96 A5
Headland Park Rd TQ3 219 C1
Headland Pk PL4 263 A4
Headland Rd TQ2 219 E2
Headlands The TQ2 219 E2
Headlands View Ave EX34 1 B1
Headless Cross TQ13 112 B6
Headon Cross EX22 72 C5
Headon Gdns EX2 178 A1
Headson Cross EX20 91 D1
Headstock Rd TA20 88 E7
Headway Cl TQ14 209 D7
Headway Cross Rd TQ14 209 D8
Headway Rise TQ14 209 D8
Heal Park Cres EX31 153 D5
Heal's Field EX13 167 F7
Heale Down La EX31 4 A3
Healy Ct 9 PL2 247 F4
Healy Pl PL2 247 F4
Heanton Hill EX33 152 F4
Heanton Hill La EX31 15 E6
Heanton St EX33 152 D5
Heanton Terr PL10 252 E6
Heard Ave EX8 202 E8
Heard Cl EX39 22 E3
Hearl Rd PL12 242 B3
Hearson Cross EX32 28 B8
Heasley Cross EX36 19 C3
Heasley La EX36 19 D3
Heasley Mill Cross EX36 19 D3
Heath Cl
Bovey Tracey TQ12 123 B2
17 Honiton EX14 85 C2
Heath Comm EX13 87 E6
Heath Cross
Spreyton EX17 96 A8
Tedburn St Mary EX4 98 C5
Tiverton EX16 63 A5
Heath Ct Brixham TQ5 230 E6
1 Totnes TQ9 223 C5
Heath Hill TQ12 123 B2
Heath La Hollocombe EX19 58 F5
Tedburn St Mary EX6 98 C4
Tiverton EX16 63 A6
Heath Pk Brixham TQ5 230 E5
Newton Abbot TQ12 208 A1
Heath Rd Brixham TQ5 230 E5
Dunsford EX6 112 F7
Exeter EX2 178 B5
Spreyton EX17 95 F8
Heath Rise TQ5 230 E5
Heath Terr PL18 125 C5
Heathayne Cross EX24 102 F5
Heathayne La EX24 102 F5
Heathbrook Mews EX4 174 C2
Heathcoat Fst Sch EX16 161 B3
Heathcoat Prim Sch EX16 161 B3
Heathcoat Sq EX16 161 C4
Heathcoat Way EX16 161 F5
Heather Cl Exeter EX1 178 B6
9 Honiton EX14 85 C2
Newton Abbot TQ12 206 F4
Okehampton EX20 170 B5
Seaton EX12 192 B7
Tavistock PL19 171 D4
Teignmouth TQ14 210 B7
8 Tiverton EX16 161 F6
Heather Est TQ12 180 F3
Heather Grange EX11 168 D4
Heather Pk TQ10 135 A3
Heather Terr PL20 128 A8
Heather Way TQ5 230 A4
Heather Wlk PL21 237 D4
Heatherdale EX8 202 C6
Heatherdene TQ13 180 C7
Heatherfield EX6 98 C4
Heathers The
Okehampton EX20 170 D6
Plymouth PL6 245 D7
Heathfield CE Prim Sch TQ12 123 B3
Heathfield Cl TQ13 180 C5
Heathfield Cotts TQ12 123 B3
Heathfield Cross
Axmouth DT7 193 D8
Bovey Tracey TQ12 123 B2
Cornwood PL21 133 C3
Exeter EX5 184 A7
Modbury PL21 137 E2
Poltimore EX4 174 C7
Heathfield Ind Est TQ12 180 F3
Heathfield Mdw TQ13 180 D5
Heathfield Pk PL20 127 A3
Heathfield Rd
Bideford EX39 157 C1
Denbury TQ12 211 A6
Plymouth PL4 249 B3
Heathfield Terr
Bovey Tracey TQ13 180 C6
Denbury TQ12 211 A6
Heathfieldlake Hill TQ13 123 F7
Heathland View EX38 40 D1
Heathlands Ct TQ14 210 A8
Heathlands Rise TQ14 210 A8
Heathpark Ind Est EX14 166 A5
Heathpark Way 15 EX14 85 C2
Heaton Lea EX31 15 E6
Heatree Cl TQ14 210 B8
Heatree Cross TQ13 121 D7
Heaviside Cl TQ2 214 B3
Heavitree Gallows EX1 178 C5
Heavitree Pk EX1 178 A5
Heavitree Rd
Cawsand PL10 253 A2
Exeter EX1 177 E6
Heddeswell Cross TQ7 143 E2
Heddon Cross
Heddon EX32 29 A7
Milton Damerel EX22 54 C5
Hederman Cl EX5 82 B5
Hedge Cross EX20 107 C4
Hedgehog Hospl (Prickly Ball Farm)* TQ12 211 F7
Hedgend Rd EX14 86 B5
Hedgerow Cl
Crediton EX17 165 E6
Plymouth PL6 245 E8
Hedgerows The PL12 242 B3
Hedingham Cl PL7 251 C4
Hedingham Gdns PL6 245 B7
Heggadon Cl EX5 83 A7
Heiffers La EX16 47 A5
Heirland Cross TQ7 143 D3
Hele Almshouses PL9 140 E8
Hele Barton Cross EX17 61 D6
Hele Bay Holiday Flats EX34 150 E5
Hele Cl Barnstaple EX31 154 A3
Bickleigh PL6 132 A5
Torquay TQ2 213 F1
Hele Cross
Ashburton TQ13 130 E5
Bradworthy EX22 38 E4
Cornwood PL21 133 D4
King's Nympton EX37 44 D7
St Giles on the Heath PL15 90 B3
Torquay TQ2 213 F1
Hele Gdns PL7 251 A4
Hele Hill EX17 61 C5
Hele La Barnstaple EX31 154 A3
Frithelstockstone EX38 40 F5
Roborough PL6 241 F2
Shaugh Prior PL6,PL7 132 A6
Hele Lane Hill EX17 61 D6
Hele Rd Bradninch EX5 82 F6
Exeter EX4 261 A4
Kingsteignton TQ12 123 E1
Torquay TQ2 213 F1
Hele Rise EX31 154 A3
Hele's Sch PL7 250 C6
Hele's Terr PL4 249 B2
Helebridge Rd EX23 70 A6
Helena Pl 7 EX8 202 A6
Helens Mead Cl TQ2 214 A4
Helens Mead Rd TQ2 214 A4
Helford Dr TQ4 229 B8
Helford Wlk TQ4 229 B8
Heligan Dr TQ3 225 E8
Hellevoetsluis Way TQ3 218 F4
Hellier Cl EX14 166 A4
Hellinghayes La EX16 46 C3
Hellings Gdns EX5 175 C7
Hellings Parks La EX5 175 E4
Helmdon Rise TQ2 219 B8
Helston Cl TQ3 225 F7
Hembury Cock Hill TQ11 236 A7
Hembury Cross
Holbeton PL8 141 F8
Stibb Cross EX38 40 C4
Hembury Fort Cross EX14 84 E5
Hembury Pk TQ11 236 B7
Hemerdon Hts PL7 251 A6
Hemerdon La PL7 251 C8
Hemerdon Way PL7 250 D6
Hems Brook Ct TQ2 219 B8
Hems La TQ9 216 D7
Hemsworthy Gate TQ13 121 E3
Hemyock Castle* EX15 67 B8
Hemyock Prim Sch EX15 67 B8
Hemyock Rd EX15 66 E8
Hen St EX5 83 A7
Henacre Rd TQ7 258 D5
Henacroft Cross EX19 58 B3
Henbury Cl TQ1 220 B6
Henceford Cross EX17 62 A6
Henderbarrow Cross EX21 73 E1
Henders Cnr 6 PL3 248 F6
Henderson Pl PL2 247 F6
Hendon Cross EX16 50 B8
Hendwell Cl PL6 244 E6
Heneaton Sq EX2 182 B8
Henlake Cl PL21 237 B6
Henley Cl EX13 88 B7
Henley Dr PL5 244 C7
Henley Ho TQ7 143 A1
Henley Rd EX8 202 C7
Hennapyn Rd TQ2 219 E3
Hennock Rd Exeter EX2 177 D1
Paignton TQ4 225 F2
Hennock Rd Central EX2 177 C1
Hennock Rd N EX2 177 C2
Hennock Sch TQ13 123 B7
Henrietta Pl 7 EX8 202 A7
Henrietta Rd 8 EX8 202 A7
Henry Cl PL21 136 B6
Henry Lewis Cl 7 EX5 99 E8
Henry's Way DT7 260 E4
Hensbury La PL20 239 F4
Hensford Mews EX7 200 C3
Hensford Rd EX7 200 C2

Hensleigh Dr EX2 177 E5
Hensleigh Rd EX16 63 F7
Hensons Dr EX16 51 A3
Henstill La EX17 79 F7
Henty Ave EX7 204 F7
Henty Cl EX7 204 F8
Heppenstall Rd EX32 155 B6
Herbert Ho TA22 33 D6
Herbert Pl PL2 247 E4
Herbert Rd Exeter EX1 177 F7
Salcombe TQ8 259 D4
Torquay TQ2 219 D4
Herbert St PL2 247 E4
Herdicott Cross EX22 71 F2
Hereford Cl EX8 196 D4
Hereford Rd Exeter EX4 176 D6
Plymouth PL5 244 B5
Heritage Cl PL12 242 C3
Hermes Ave EX16 161 E3
Hermitage Rd
Dartmouth TQ6 233 D4
Ilfracombe EX34 150 B6
Plymouth PL3 248 E5
Hermitage The 1 EX34 150 B5
Hermosa Gdns 5 TQ14 210 B5
Hermosa Rd TQ14 210 B5
Hern La PL8 257 F4
Hernaford Cross TQ9 139 B6
Hernaford Rd TQ9 139 C6
Heron Cl PL10 252 F6
Heron Ct Barnstaple EX32 155 E4
Exmouth EX8 202 C6
Heron Ind Units EX2 178 E5
Heron Rd
Exeter, Redhills EX2 176 D3
Exeter, Sowton EX2 178 E5
Honiton EX14 166 B4
Heron Way
Cullompton EX15 163 B2
Torquay TQ2 213 C3
Herons Brook EX20 170 A6
Herons Reach TQ7 144 C1
Herschel Gdns PL5 243 E1
Herschell Rd EX4 177 E8
Hertland Wlk PL2 248 A7
Hescane Pk EX6 97 B4
Hesketh Cres TQ1 220 D3
Hesketh Mews TQ1 220 D3
Hesketh Rd TQ1 220 D3
Hessary Dr PL6 241 C1
Hessary Terr PL20 128 A8
Hessary View
Saltash PL12 242 E4
Tavistock PL19 171 B6
Hestow Rd TQ12 123 F1
Hetling Cl PL1 262 B3
Hewer's Row PL4 263 A3
Hewitt Cl
Newton Abbot TQ12 208 A3
Saltash PL12 242 C1
Hexham Pl PL2 248 A8
Hexton Hill Rd PL9 255 B6
Hexworthy Ave EX4 176 E8
Heybrook Ave PL5 243 D1
Heybrook Dr PL9 140 A7
Heydon's La EX10 188 A4
Heyswood Ave EX32 155 C2
Heywood Cl Hartland EX39 22 E3
Torquay TQ2 219 E7
Heywood Cross EX18 59 D5
Heywood Dr EX6 201 A8
Heywood Est TQ12 207 D6
Heywood Rd EX39 156 F5
Heywoods Cl 11 TQ14 210 C5
Heywoods Rd TQ14 210 C5
Hibernia Terr PL5 247 E8
Hick's La PL4 263 A2
Hickory Cl EX14 166 E5
Hickory Dr PL7 251 B5
Hidden Valley Cvn Pk
EX34 8 D4
Hides Rd EX10 188 C8
Hidewood La EX15 52 F1
Hierns La EX34 150 C6
High Acre Dr PL21 237 A6
High Bank Exeter EX4 178 B8
West Hill EX11 168 D3
High Bullen EX5 82 B6
High Bullen Cross EX36 19 E1
High Bullen La EX35 5 B3
High Cl TQ13 180 E7
High Cott EX36 19 C2
High Creek Cross EX10 188 F8
High Cross Bampton EX16 34 A1
12 Combe Martin EX34 3 A3
High Cross Ho* TQ9 216 A1
High Gate EX16 62 F6
High House Cl EX7 204 E7
High House La TQ7 258 D4
High Mdw EX10 188 B7
High Mdws EX4 176 E5
High Park Cl EX39 25 D4
High Rd PL9 140 C8
High St Bampton EX16 34 B1
Barnstaple EX31 154 F5
Bideford EX39 157 A2
Budleigh Salterton EX9 199 G2
Chagford TQ13 111 A6
Clovelly EX39 23 D3
Combe Martin EX34 3 A3
Crediton EX17 165 C5
Cullompton EX15 163 C3
Dawlish EX7 204 E6
Dulverton TA22 33 D6
East Budleigh EX9 198 B6
Exbourne EX20 76 C4
Exeter EX4 261 B3
Exmouth EX8 202 A6
High St *continued*
Great Torrington EX38 159 D5
Halberton EX16 65 A7
Hatherleigh EX20 75 C7
Hemyock EX15 67 B8
High Bickington EX37 43 B7
4 Holsworthy EX22 164 C4
Ide EX2 176 D1
Ilfracombe EX34 150 B6
Kentisbeare EX15 66 A3
Kenton EX6 194 D3
Newton Poppleford EX10 186 E8
North Tawton EX20 77 C4
Okehampton EX20 170 B5
3 Plymouth PL1 263 A2
Plymouth, Stonehouse PL1 248 A2
Sidford EX10 188 B8
Sidmouth EX10 188 B4
Silverton EX5 82 B6
Stoke Canon EX5 173 F8
Swimbridge EX32 28 E8
Topsham EX3 182 E6
Totnes TQ9 223 C5
Uffculme EX15 66 A7
Wellington TA21 160 E6
Winkleigh EX19 58 F3
High Street & Waterloo
Street Flats PL1 248 A1
High View Bideford EX39 156 E1
Feniton EX14 84 E2
Sheepwash EX21 56 C1
High View Gdns EX8 202 B7
High View Terr EX39 156 C6
High Wall EX31 154 E4
High Way EX16 48 D8
Highampton Com Prim Sch
EX21 74 C7
Highampton Cross EX21 74 C7
Highaton Head Cross
EX36 32 C4
Highbank Cl PL19 171 A4
Highbarrow Cross EX22 54 A4
Highbury Cres PL7 250 D7
Highbury Hill EX39 157 A8
Highbury Pk EX8 196 A1
Highbury Rd
Barnstaple EX32 155 C3
Torquay TQ1 220 B6
Highclere Gdns PL6 245 B8
Highcliff Ct EX7 204 E6
Highcliff Rd DT7 260 C3
Highcliffe Cl
Lympstone EX8 195 D4
Seaton EX12 191 F6
Highcliffe Cres EX12 191 F6
Highcliffe Mews TQ4 226 C4
Highclyffe Ct EX12 191 F6
Highcroft EX4 173 A1
Highcross Rd EX4 177 C8
Highdown Cross EX39 23 A4
Higher Aboveway EX6 182 B3
Higher Aller La TQ13 122 E6
Higher Alston Farm
TQ5 229 D3
Higher Anderton Rd
PL10 252 F5
Higher Audley Ave TQ2 219 F8
Higher Axmouth Cotts
EX12 192 F6
Higher Barley Mount
EX4 176 E5
Higher Beara Cross
TQ11 236 F4
Higher Bedlands EX9 197 F2
Higher Bibbery TQ13 180 E7
Higher Brand La EX14 166 C4
Higher Brimley Rd
TQ14 210 C5
Higher Brixham Prim Sch
TQ5 230 A2
Higher Broad Oak Rd
EX11 168 D2
Higher Brook Mdw 1
EX10 101 B1
Higher Brook Pk PL21 237 A5
Higher Brownston Cross
PL21 138 A4
Higher Buckeridge Rd
TQ14 210 B7
Higher Budleigh Mdw
TQ12 206 F3
Higher Bulkamore Cross
TQ10 135 E5
Higher Bull Ring EX15 163 C3
Higher Bulworthy Cross
EX16 47 E4
Higher Bulworthy La
EX16 47 E4
Higher Buzzacott La EX34 3 C3
Higher Cadewell La
TQ2 219 C8
Higher Cheglinch La EX34 8 F6
Higher Church St 6
EX32 155 A4
Higher Churchway PL9 256 A7
Higher Clevelands EX39 156 F6
Higher Collaton Cross
TQ7 147 F6
Higher Compton Barton
TQ3 218 E6
Higher Compton Rd
PL3 248 F6
Higher Contour Rd TQ6 234 B3
Higher Coombe Dr
TQ14 210 A7
Higher Coombses TA20 88 D8
Higher Copythorne TQ5 230 A4
Higher Cotteylands
EX16 161 B3
Higher Cross EX15 51 C1
Higher Cross Rd EX31 154 B4
Higher Davis Cl EX32 17 F6
Higher Dean TQ11 135 C7
Higher Dean La EX34 3 B3
Higher Doats Hayne La
EX13 103 D5
Higher Down EX6 194 D3
Higher Downs Rd TQ1 220 C8
Higher Dr EX7 204 F8
Higher East St EX36 30 D8
Higher Edginswell La
TQ2 219 B8
Higher Efford Rd PL3 249 B5
Higher Elmwood EX31 154 C3
Higher Elstone Cross
EX18 44 D3
Higher Erith Rd TQ1 220 D4
Higher Exeter Rd TQ14 124 E2
Higher Exwick Hill EX4 176 F8
Higher Forches Cross
EX17 60 D4
Higher Fortescue EX10 188 D7
Higher French Pk TQ12 206 F3
Higher Furzeham Rd
TQ5 230 C6
Higher Gn TQ10 135 A2
Higher Green Cross
TQ7 145 C4
Higher Greenway La
EX10 187 E7
Higher Gunstone EX39 157 A2
Higher Haske Cross
EX17 165 F7
Higher Hewish La EX31 9 D4
Higher Hill View EX10 188 A5
Higher Ho EX38 42 B5
Higher Holcombe Cl
TQ14 210 C7
Higher Holcombe Dr
TQ14 210 C8
Higher Holcombe Rd
TQ14 210 C8
Higher Hoopern La EX4 173 C1
Higher Island TQ9 139 E2
Higher Kelly PL18 125 D3
Higher King's Ave EX4 177 D8
Higher Kingsdown Rd
TQ14 209 D7
Higher Kinsman's Dale
TQ13 111 F5
Higher La Axmouth EX12 192 E7
Plymouth PL1 262 C2
Higher Ley EX17 60 B3
Higher Lincombe Rd
TQ1 220 E3
Higher Loughborough
EX16 161 B5
Higher Manor Rd TQ5 230 C5
Higher Manor Terr 1
TQ3 226 A5
Higher Marley Rd EX8 196 D4
Higher Maudlin St 7
EX32 155 A6
Higher Maunders Hill
EX9 198 E7
Higher Mdws Beer EX12 191 D5
High Bickington EX37 43 B7
Higher Mead EX15 67 B8
Higher Mill Flats DT7 260 D4
Higher Mill La
Buckfast TQ11 236 B7
Cullompton EX15 163 C3
Higher Millhayes EX15 52 B1
Higher Mogworthy Cross
EX16 47 D4
Higher Moor Sq 4
EX16 161 F6
Higher Mowles PL3 249 B6
Higher Newclose La
EX31 16 B6
Higher Park Cl PL7 251 B3
Higher Park Rd EX33 152 E5
Higher Penn TQ5 230 D3
Higher Pk TQ7 149 A3
Higher Polsham Rd
TQ3 226 B7
Higher Port View PL12 242 F2
Higher Preston Cross
TQ12 123 D1
Higher Rake La TQ7 143 F6
Higher Raleigh Rd EX31 155 A7
Higher Ramshill La TQ3 225 C8
Higher Ranscombe Rd
TQ5 230 D4
Higher Rd Crediton EX17 165 B6
Fremington EX31 153 E5
Woodbury Salterton EX5 184 B7
Higher Redgate EX16 161 D5
Higher Ridgeway EX11 169 E4
Higher Ringmore Rd
TQ14 209 D4
Higher Roborough 8
TQ13 131 A5
Higher Rydons TQ5 230 A4
Higher Sackery TQ12 208 D4
Higher Sandygate TQ12 123 E2
Higher Shapter Cl EX3 182 F4
Higher Shapter St EX3 182 F4
Higher Slade Rd EX34 150 A2
Higher Spring Gdns
EX11 169 E3
Higher St Brixham TQ5 230 C5
Cullompton EX15 163 C4
Dartmouth TQ6 233 F3
Dittisham TQ6 228 B2
Higher St *continued*
Hatherleigh EX20 75 C7
Kingswear TQ6 234 A3
Higher Stert Terr PL4 263 C3
Higher Summerlands
EX1 261 C3
Higher Tamar Terr
PL18 125 D7
Higher Town
Malborough TQ7 147 E6
Sampford Peverell EX16 50 C1
Higher Tuckers Pk EX22 38 E1
Higher Union La TQ2 220 A5
Higher Union Rd TQ7 258 C5
Higher Venn Cross EX32 17 A1
Higher Warberry Rd
TQ1 220 D5
Higher Warborough Rd
TQ5 229 B6
Higher Warcombe Cross
TQ7 144 A5
Higher Warren Rd TQ7 258 C3
Higher Way EX10 187 A8
Higher Wear Rd EX2 182 C7
Higher Weaver Cross
EX15 83 E7
Higher Wellbrook St
EX16 161 B4
Higher Westlake Rd
4 Barnstaple EX31 154 A2
Barnstaple EX31 154 B2
Higher Westonfields
TQ9 223 E5
Higher Woodfield Rd
TQ1 220 D3
Higher Woodford La
PL7 250 C7
Higher Woodway Cl
TQ14 210 C7
Higher Woodway Rd
TQ14 210 B8
Higher Woolbrook Pk
EX10 187 F7
Higher Yannon Dr TQ14 210 A6
Highermoor Cross EX22 53 B1
Highfield Honiton EX14 166 B5
Lapford EX17 60 D3
Northam EX39 156 F6
Topsham EX3 182 F7
Highfield Cl
Barnstaple EX32 155 B4
Brixham TQ5 230 A4
High Bickington EX37 43 B7
Plymouth PL3 249 C5
Highfield Cres TQ3 225 E6
Highfield Dr
Kingsbridge TQ7 258 D4
2 Wembury PL9 140 D8
Highfield Gdns EX34 3 A3
Highfield La EX8 202 B6
Highfield Pk PL12 242 B3
Highfield Prim Sch PL3 249 C5
Highfield Rd
Dunkeswell EX14 67 C1
Ilfracombe EX34 150 C5
Highfield Terr
Beer EX12 191 D5
7 Ilfracombe EX34 150 C5
2 Bishop's Tawton EX32 16 E1
Highglen Dr PL7 251 B7
Highgrove Pk TQ14 210 C7
Highland Cl TQ2 219 C6
Highland Rd TQ2 219 C5
Highland St PL21 237 D5
Highland Terr
Tiverton EX16 161 D4
Uffculme EX15 66 A7
Highland View EX20 170 C3
Highlands EX11 169 D3
Highlands Pk 9 TQ13 123 E6
Highridge Cross EX37 45 B7
Highstead Cross EX22 73 C8
Highweek Com Prim Sch
TQ12 207 A3
Highweek Cross EX21 73 E8
Highweek Rd
Newton Abbot TQ12 207 A4
3 Newton Abbot TQ12 207 B3
Highweek St TQ12 207 B3
Highweek Village TQ12 206 F5
Highweek Way TQ12 207 B3
Highwell Rd EX12 192 A5
Highworthy Cross EX21 55 E3
Hilary Cl EX13 167 E6
Hilary Gdns EX13 167 E6
Hill Barton Bsns Pk
Clyst St Mary EX5 179 F2
Exeter EX5 99 A1
Hill Barton Cl EX1 178 C7
Hill Barton La EX1 178 C7
Hill Barton Rd EX2 178 C7
Hill Budge Terr 7 EX17 165 C5
Hill Cl Exeter EX4 173 D1
Plymouth PL7 250 D4
Hill Cres EX14 166 D6
Hill Crest Exminster EX6 182 A4
Kilmington EX13 87 C1
Plymouth PL3 248 E5
South Tawton EX20 95 B5
Tiverton EX16 161 D5
Hill Crest Sch EX8 196 E1
Hill Cross Cobbaton EX32 28 B5
Kingsbridge TQ7 144 B5
Hill Dr EX8 196 B3
Hill Garden Cl 10 EX39 157 A2
Hill Gdns PL12 239 A2
Hill Head EX37 28 F4
Hill Head Cross
Chittlehampton EX37 28 F4
King's Nympton EX37 44 C5
Hill La Chipstable TA4 35 C6
Exeter EX1 178 B7
Plymouth PL3 248 F7
Waterrow TA4 35 E5
Whitestone EX4 98 E4
Hill Mdw TQ13 130 F5
Hill Park Cl TQ5 230 E4
Hill Park Cres PL4 263 A4
Hill Park Mews PL4 263 B4
Hill Park Rd Brixham TQ5 230 E4
Newton Abbot TQ12 206 F4
Torquay TQ1 220 A7
Hill Park Terr TQ4 226 C5
Hill Path PL5 243 F5
Hill Pk Ashprington TQ9 139 F8
Beesands TQ7 149 C6
Hill Rd Bondleigh EX20 77 C7
Lyme Regis DT7 260 D3
Newton Abbot TQ12 207 B2
Hill Rise EX1 178 C7
Hill Rise Rd DT7 260 D3
Hill Side Cross EX36 45 F5
Hill St PL4 263 A3
Hill The EX13 87 C1
Hill Top Crest PL5 243 E2
Hill View
Buckland Monachorum
PL20 126 C3
Sidmouth EX10 188 B5
Hill View Terr 4 TQ1 220 A7
Hill's La EX14 86 C5
Hillbrook Rd TQ9 223 E5
Hillbrook Rise 2 TQ9 223 E5
Hillcliffe Terr 30 EX39 15 A1
Hillcrest Ilsington TQ13 122 C3
Oakford EX16 48 D5
Ottery St Mary EX11 169 D3
Hillcrest Cl Plymouth PL7 251 A5
9 Wembury PL9 140 D8
Hillcrest Dr PL7 251 A4
Hillcrest Pk EX4 173 C2
Hillcrest Rd
Barnstaple EX32 155 B2
Bideford EX39 26 A4
Silverton EX5 82 C6
Hillcroft Terr 5 EX39 157 A2
Hilldale Rd PL9 255 E6
Hilldean Cl PL5 244 C7
Hilldown TQ9 223 E5
Hilldown Cross EX17 78 D2
Hilldown La EX17 78 D2
Hilldown Rd EX17 78 C3
Hilldrop Terr TQ1 220 B5
Hiller La TQ12 208 B2
Hillerton Cross EX17 78 B1
Hillesdon Rd TQ1 220 B4
Hillfield South Zeal EX20 95 A4
Stoke Gabriel TQ9 227 F7
Hillhead Colyton EX24 103 A4
Halberton EX16 65 A7
Noss Mayo PL8 140 F6
Hillhead Bglws 13 EX24 103 A4
Hillhead Cross PL21 137 D7
Hillhead Pk TQ5 234 E8
Hillhead Terr EX13 167 D5
Hillhouse EX14 69 A3
Hilliers EX19 57 F7
Hillingdown Cross TQ7 143 D1
Hillington EX34 150 A4
Hillmans Rd TQ12 207 D2
Hillmoor Cross EX21 73 F7
Hillrise TQ5 229 B5
Hills View
Barnstaple EX32 155 A5
Braunton EX33 152 D6
Hillsborough
2 Plymouth PL4 248 F4
Torquay TQ1 220 B4
Hillsborough Ave EX4 261 B4
Hillsborough Cross EX22 71 C7
Hillsborough Park Rd
EX34 150 E5
Hillsborough Rd EX34 150 D5
Hillsborough Terr 4
EX34 150 C6
Hillsborough Terr Mews 5
EX34 150 C6
Hillsdunne Rd PL3 248 E6
Hillside Branscombe EX12 190 B5
14 Colyton EX24 103 A4
Honiton EX14 85 E5
Newton Poppleford EX10 186 D8
Northleigh EX24 102 B6
Payhembury EX14 84 C4
Sidbury EX10 101 B2
South Brent TQ10 135 A3
Southleigh EX24 102 C4
Talaton EX5 84 B1
Hillside Ave Exeter EX4 261 B4
Plymouth PL4 248 D4
Saltash PL12 242 F3
Hillside Cl
Buckland Monachorum
PL20 126 C3
South Brent TQ10 135 A3
Teignmouth TQ14 124 E1
Hillside Cotts
Abbotskerswell TQ12 212 A6
Noss Mayo PL8 140 F6
Hillside Cres PL9 255 F8
Hillside Cross EX22 72 F4
Hillside Ct TQ11 236 C5

Hillside Dr
Kingsbridge TQ7 ....258 D4
Yealmpton PL8 ....257 F3
Hillside Rd Brixham TQ5 .230 C4
Ilfracombe EX34 ....150 E5
Paignton TQ3 ....225 F7
Saltash PL12 ....242 E3
Sidmouth EX10 ....188 C4
Hillside Sch PL5 ....244 B4
Hillside Terr
4 Bideford EX39 ....157 A2
Kingswear TQ6 ....234 A3
2 Paignton TQ3 ....226 A6
Hillside Way PL8 ....136 A2
Hilltop TQ7 ....142 F6
Hilltop Cotts EX31 .....153 E5
Hilltop Rd EX39 ....156 E4
Hilltown Cross
Chittlehampton EX37 .....29 B2
Okehampton EX20 ....93 E5
Rackenford EX16 ....47 D2
Hilltown Hill EX36 ....31 C5
Hilltown La EX18 ....59 F5
Hillway La EX10 .....187 A7
Hilly Gardens Rd TQ1 ..214 B1
Hilly Head TA21 ....160 B5
Hillyfield Rd EX1 ....178 C7
Hillymead EX12 ....192 B6
Hilton Ave PL5 ....244 D1
Hilton Cres TQ3 ....219 C1
Hilton Dr TQ3 ....219 C1
Hilton Rd
Marhamchurch EX23 .....70 A6
Monkleigh EX39 ....40 F7
Newton Abbot TQ12 .....207 C3
Hinam Cross TA22 ....33 B7
Hind St
Bovey Tracey TQ13 .....180 D8
Ottery St Mary EX11 .....169 D3
Hindharton La EX39 .....22 E3
Hingston Ct PL6 ....249 A8
Hingston Post TQ9 .....144 E8
Hingston Rd TQ1 ....220 C7
Hirmandale Rd PL5 .....243 F3
Hittisleigh Cross EX6 .....96 D6
Hittisleigh Mill La EX6 ..96 D5
Hittsford La EX36 ....32 A1
Hobart St PL1 ....262 A2
Hobb's Hill EX33 ....7 E2
Hobbacott La EX23 .....70 A6
Hobbs Cres PL12 ....242 C3
Hobbs La EX32 ....18 E2
Hobbs Way EX17 ....78 B4
Hobby Dr The EX39 .....23 E3
Hobby House La EX36 ...30 C1
Hobbymoor Cross EX17 ..60 A1
Hockmoor Head TQ11 ..130 C2
Hockmoor Hill TQ11 ...130 C2
Hodder's La DT7 ....260 C8
Hodders Way PL12 .....239 A2
Hodge Cl PL12 ....242 C2
Hodges Wlk EX38 ....159 E5
Hodson Cl TQ3 ....225 F7
Hoe App PL1 ....262 C2
Hoe Ct PL1 ....262 C2
Hoe Rd PL1 ....262 C1
Hoe St PL1 ....262 C2
Hoe The PL1 ....262 C1
Hoegate Ct PL1 ....262 C2
Hoegate Pl PL1 ....262 C2
Hoegate St PL1 ....263 A2
Hofheim Dr EX16 ....161 A6
Hogarth Cl PL9 ....256 B6
Hogarth Wlk PL9 ....256 B6
Hoile La TQ9 ....224 E1
Hoker Rd EX2 ....178 A5
Holbeam Cl TQ12 ....206 E4
Holbeam La
Bickington TQ12 ....131 F6
Newton Abbot TQ12 .....206 A4
Holbeton Sch PL8 ....136 D1
Holborn Pl PL7 ....250 E6
Holborn Rd TQ5 ....230 C6
Holborn St PL4 ....263 B2
Holbrook Terr TQ7 .....145 B1
Holcombe Barton Cnr
EX6 ....98 D2
Holcombe Cross EX7 ...210 F8
Holcombe Down Cross
TQ14 ....124 F2
Holcombe Down Rd
EX7,TQ14 ....204 A4
Holcombe Dr
Holcombe EX7 ....210 F8
Plymouth PL9 ....255 F5
Holcombe La
Ottery St Mary EX11 .....100 F7
Uplyme DT7 ....104 B4
Holcombe Rd TQ14 .....210 E8
Holcroft Cl PL12 ....242 D2
Holden Cross EX6 ....113 E2
Holdridge La EX36 .....30 D8
Holdstone Way EX34 .....3 B2
Holdsworth St PL4 .....262 B4
Hole Ball Cross EX21 ...92 A8
Hole Cleave Rd EX33 .....8 A1
Hole Cross Halwill EX21 ...73 F1
Hittisleigh EX6 ....96 E4
Yelverton PL20 ....239 E7
Hole Ct EX20 ....75 C7
Hole Hill
Branscombe EX12 ....190 C5
Exbourne EX20 ....76 C4
Witheridge EX16 ....46 F2
Hole La Chulmleigh EX18 ..45 B3
Hole La *continued*
Combe Martin EX31 ....10 B6
Croyde EX33 ....7 F1
North Tawton EX20 ....77 E6
Hole's La
Broadhempston TQ9 .....131 D1
Staverton TQ9 ....216 B8
Holebay Cl PL9 ....256 A5
Holebrook Cross EX20 ...76 C4
Holebrook La EX20 ....76 C5
Holemoor Cross EX22 ...73 C8
Holemore Cross EX14 ...68 C5
Holestone La EX10 .....187 A1
Holewater Cross EX32 ...19 A6
Holewater Hill EX32 .....19 A6
Holewell La EX6 ....96 E4
Hollacombe Brake PL9 .256 C1
Hollacombe Cross
Holsworthy EX22 ....72 D6
Yeoford EX17 ....79 D3
Hollacombe La TQ3 .....219 D1
Hollam Cross TA22 ....33 E7
Hollam Dr TA22 ....33 D6
Hollam La TA22 ....33 D7
Hollam Way TQ12 ....207 F8
Hollamoor View EX31 ..154 B3
Holland Cl EX31 ....154 A4
Holland Copse EX6 ....98 C4
Holland Rd Exeter EX2 ..176 F4
Exmouth EX8 ....196 D1
Plymouth, Chaddlewood
PL7 ....251 D5
Plymouth, Peverell PL3 ...248 E6
Plymouth, Plymstock PL9 .255 F6
Holland St 7 EX31 .....154 F5
Holland Wlk 4 EX31 ...154 F5
Holland's La TA4 ....35 E8
Holland's Wash Dro TA20 69 F5
Hollands Park Ave EX34 ..3 A3
Hollands Rd 4 TQ14 ...210 C4
Holley Cl EX6 ....182 A4
Holley Pk EX20 ....170 D6
Holleys Cl TA20 ....88 D8
Hollies The EX31 ....154 B3
Hollingarth Way EX15 ...67 B8
Hollington Ho 13 TQ1 ..220 D4
Hollis Cl EX11 ....169 E4
Hollocombe Cnr EX18 ...58 D6
Hollocombe Moor Gate
EX18 ....58 D7
Hollocombe Moor Head
EX18 ....58 D7
Hollow Head Cross
EX10 ....100 F2
Hollow La EX1 ....178 E7
Hollow Pits Ct EX2 .....181 B8
Hollow Tree Cross EX18 .60 A7
Holloway Gdns PL9 ....256 A5
Holloway St EX2 ....261 B2
Holloway The TA21 ....51 E7
Hollowcombe Cross
PL21 ....136 E3
Hollowcombe Head
TQ7 ....149 C5
Hollowgutter La PL11 ..246 C2
Hollows The
Exmouth EX8 ....202 B7
Plymouth PL9 ....256 B8
Hollowtree Ct 4 EX32 ..155 B3
Hollowtree Rd EX32 .....155 B3
Holly Cl Broadclyst EX5 ..175 C7
Honiton EX14 ....166 C4
Tiverton EX16 ....161 E5
Holly Ct PL6 ....249 E7
Holly Park Cl PL5 ....244 A5
Holly Park Dr PL5 ....244 A5
Holly Rd Exeter EX2 .....177 F3
Tiverton EX16 ....161 E5
Holly Villas TQ9 ....139 F8
Holly Water Rd EX17 ...62 E1
Holly Way EX15 ....163 C5
Holly Wlk EX8 ....196 D3
Hollycombe Cross EX20 .95 E4
Hollycombe La TQ9 .....216 E7
Hollycroft Rd PL3 ....249 A7
Hollyford La EX17 ....62 C2
Hollyhead Cross EX12 ..191 C7
Hollyhead Rd EX12 .....191 B8
Hollymount Cl EX8 .....196 C3
Hollywater Cl TQ1 .....220 D5
Hollywood Terr PL1 .....262 A3
Holm Cross EX17 ....59 F2
Holm Hill EX17 ....59 E2
Holmacott Cross EX39 ..26 E7
Holman Cl EX7 ....204 F8
Holman Ct PL2 ....248 C8
Holman Way
Ivybridge PL21 ....237 A6
Topsham EX3 ....182 F5
Holmans Bldgs PL1 .....247 D2
Holmans Mdw PL15 .....105 B1
Holmbush Way PL8 .....257 A4
Holmdale EX10 ....188 B4
Holme Ct 3 TQ1 ....220 D4
Holmead Cross EX16 .....48 B3
Holmer Down PL6 ....245 D7
Holmes Ave PL3 ....249 B5
Holmes Rd TQ12 ....180 F2
Holmleigh Rd TQ7 ....145 D1
Holmsleigh Cross EX14 ..86 C5
Holmwood Ave PL9 .....255 E5
Holne Chase PL6 ....245 B7
Holne Ct EX4 ....176 E8
Holne Moor Cl TQ3 .....225 E7
Holne Rd TQ11 ....236 B6
Holne Rise EX2 ....178 B4
Holne Turn
Ashburton TQ13 ....130 E5
Holne Turn *continued*
Holne TQ13 ....130 B5
Holset Cross TQ8 ....148 D5
Holsome La TQ9 ....138 D7
Holstock Cross EX20 ....74 D3
Holsworthy Com Coll
EX22 ....164 C5
Holsworthy Hospl EX22 164 D6
Holsworthy Mus* EX22 164 C4
Holsworthy Prim Sch
EX22 ....164 C5
Holsworthy Rd EX20 ....93 D5
Holt The
19 Appledore EX39 ....15 A1
Honiton EX14 ....166 E7
Holtwood Dr PL21 ....237 A5
Holtwood Rd PL6 ....245 D6
Holway TA20 ....88 D8
Holwell Cl PL9 ....256 A5
Holwell La EX16 ....64 B5
Holwell Rd TQ5 ....230 B4
Holwill Dr EX38 ....159 D5
Holwill Tor Wlk TQ4 ....225 F3
Holy Cross RC Prim Sch
PL4 ....263 A3
Holy Moor Cross EX36 ...32 C1
Holy Moor La EX36 ....32 C1
Holyford La EX24 ....102 F3
Holyoake St TA21 ....160 C7
Holyrood Pl PL1 ....262 C2
Holyshute Cross EX14 ..166 D6
Holywell CE Prim Sch
EX31 ....27 D8
Holywell Cross EX36 .....19 F2
Holywell Pk EX21 ....73 D3
Home Cl Brixham TQ5 ...230 C3
Chillington TQ7 ....145 A1
Home Farm Cl Croyde EX33 7 E2
Kingston TQ7 ....142 C6
Home Farm Cross EX15 ..65 F4
Home Farm Ct TQ12 ...209 B2
Home Farm Rd
Fremington EX31 ....153 D5
Plymouth PL9 ....255 E8
Home Gate EX6 ....98 A3
Home La EX34 ....1 C3
Home Mdw TQ9 ....223 C5
Home Park (Plymouth Argyle
FC) PL2 ....248 C5
Home Park Ave PL3 .....248 E6
Home Park Rd PL12 .....243 A3
Home Pk Ashburton TQ13 130 F5
Plymouth PL2 ....247 F4
Home Sweet Home Terr
PL4 ....263 C2
Homebaye Ho 3 EX12 ..192 B4
Homebourne Ho TQ4 ...226 C5
Homeclose La EX13,TA20 .88 A8
Homeclyst Ho EX2 ....261 A1
Homecourt Ho EX4 ....261 A2
Homedown Cross EX37 ...28 F4
Homefield
Thurlestone TQ7 ....143 A1
Wellington TA21 ....160 E4
Homefield Cl EX11 ....169 E3
Homefield Cotts TQ1 ...220 D7
Homefield Rd EX1 ....177 F6
Homelace Ho EX14 ....166 C7
Homelands Pl TQ7 ....258 C6
Homelands Rd TQ7 ....258 C6
Homemeadows Ho
EX10 ....188 A5
Homepalms Ho 2 TQ1 .219 F6
Homer Cl EX31 ....18 A8
Homer Cres EX33 ....152 B7
Homer Ct EX33 ....152 B7
Homer Dr EX33 ....152 B7
Homer La Seaton EX12 ..191 F8
Seaton EX12 ....192 A6
Homer Park La S PL9 ...255 C5
Homer Pk Plymouth PL9 .255 C5
Saltash PL12 ....242 D3
Homer Rd EX33 ....152 B7
Homer Rise PL9 ....256 B7
Homers Cl TQ12 ....207 D6
Homers Cres TQ12 ....207 D6
Homers La TQ12 ....207 D6
Homershill Cross PL21 .137 B6
Homesleigh Rd EX14 .....86 A5
Homestead Rd TQ1 ....220 A8
Homestead Terr TQ1 ...220 A8
Hometeign Ho TQ12 .....207 D4
Hometor Ho EX8 ....202 A8
Homeyards The TQ14 ...210 A3
Homing Down Cross
EX20 ....75 A1
Honcray PL9 ....255 D8
Hone Cross EX16 ....34 F5
Honest Heart Cross EX15 66 A3
Honestone St EX39 .....157 A1
Honey Ditches Dr EX12 .191 F8
Honey La
Daccombe TQ1,TQ12 .....213 F5
Exeter EX1 ....174 F2
Woodbury Salterton EX5 ..184 D7
Honey Park Rd EX9 .....198 B2
Honey St EX39 ....157 A7
Honeybeetle Cross EX37 .29 A5
Honeychurch Moor Cross
EX20 ....76 F5
Honeycroft Cross EX22 ..54 A4
Honeylands Childrens Ctr
(Hospl) EX4 ....178 B7
Honeylands Dr EX4 .....178 A7
Honeylands Way EX4 ...178 A7
Honeymoor La EX16 .....48 E7
Honeysuckle Cl
2 Barnstaple EX31 .....154 B3
Honeysuckle Cl *continued*
Paignton TQ3 ....225 E8
Plymouth PL6 ....245 E7
Saltash PL12 ....242 D4
Tiverton EX16 ....161 F6
Honeysuckle Ct EX4 ...176 D8
Honeysuckle Dr EX14 ...85 C2
Honeywell TQ12 ....207 E6
Honeywell Cl EX32 .....155 B2
Honeywell La TQ13 .....122 C3
Honeywell Rd TQ12 .....207 E6
Honeywins Cross EX36 ..19 C2
Honicknowle Gn PL5 ...244 B2
Honicknowle La PL5 ...244 B1
Honicombe Cnr PL17 ...125 B5
**Honicombe Manor Holiday
Village** PL17 ....125 B5
Honiton Bottom Rd
EX14 ....166 C4
Honiton Bsns Pk EX14 ..166 B6
Honiton Com Coll EX14 166 C6
Honiton Cross EX36 .....29 F3
Honiton Hospl EX14 .....166 C5
Honiton La EX36 ....29 E3
Honiton Mus* EX14 .....166 C6
Honiton Prim Sch EX14 166 C6
Honiton Rd
Clyst Honiton EX5 ....179 C7
Cullompton EX15 ....163 E3
Exeter EX1 ....178 C5
Honiton Sta EX14 ....166 C5
Honiton Wlk PL5 ....244 B4
Honors Farm EX5 ....173 F8
Hooda Cl EX32 ....17 E1
Hoodown La TQ6 ....234 B4
Hooe Hill PL9 ....255 C5
Hooe La PL9 ....255 D3
Hooe Prim Sch PL9 .....255 B5
Hooe Rd PL9 ....255 C5
Hook Cross EX13 ....87 D7
**Hook Farm Cvn & Camping
Pk** DT7 ....260 A5
Hooker Cl EX9 ....197 F2
Hookhill La EX17 ....62 A3
Hookhills Dr TQ4 ....226 C1
Hookhills Gdns TQ4 ....229 B7
Hookhills Gr TQ4 ....226 C1
Hookhills Rd TQ4 ....226 B1
Hookmoor Cross PL21 ..137 E7
Hooks Cross TQ12 ....131 C7
Hooksbury Ave PL7 .....251 B3
Hookway EX17 ....80 D1
Hookway Cross EX5 .....80 D1
Hookway La EX16 ....63 B5
Hookwell Down La EX36 .30 A8
Hoop Cross EX15 ....83 B4
Hooper St PL11 ....247 C3
Hooperhayne Rd EX24 ..102 E5
Hoopern Ave EX4 ....173 D1
Hoopern La EX4 ....177 C8
Hoopern St EX4 ....261 B4
Hoopern Terr 4 EX7 ....204 D6
Hoopers Cross EX16 ....34 D3
Hoopers La PL18 ....125 C6
Hoopers Way EX38 .....159 F5
Hooperton Cross EX6 ....96 E3
Hooperton La EX6 ....96 E3
Hope By-Pass TQ7 .....147 B7
Hope Cl TQ9 ....223 F5
Hope Rd EX2 ....178 A5
Hope Wlk TQ9 ....223 F5
Hope's Cl TQ14 ....210 A6
Hopkins Ct 8 TQ12 .....207 C3
Hopkins La TQ12 ....207 C3
Hopperstyle EX31 ....154 B3
Hopton Cl PL6 ....248 F8
Hopton Dr EX38 ....159 F5
Horace Rd TQ2 ....213 F2
Hore Down Gate EX34 ....9 B6
Hore's Cross PL21 ....137 D7
Horestone Cross EX16 ...47 F4
Horn Cross
Kentisbeare EX15 ....65 F2
Plymouth PL9 ....255 E7
Horn Cross Rd PL9 .....255 F7
Horn Hill TQ6 ....233 F3
Horn La Brixton PL8 .....257 A5
Plymouth PL9 ....255 F7
Horn Lane Flats PL9 ...255 F7
Horn Rd EX15 ....65 E2
Hornapark Cl PL16 .....105 E3
Hornbeam Cl
Honiton EX14 ....166 A4
Tiverton EX16 ....161 F5
Hornbeam Gdns EX5 ....83 A7
Hornbeam Hollow 1
EX31 ....154 C2
Hornbrook Gdns PL6 ...244 D6
Hornby St 2 PL2 ....247 F4
Hornchurch La PL5 .....243 E4
Hornchurch Rd PL5 .....243 E5
Horne Park Ave 11
EX34 ....150 B5
Horne Park Rd EX34 ...150 B5
Horne Rd EX34 ....150 B5
Hornebrook Ave 8
EX34 ....150 B5
Horner Tongue TQ9 .....138 F5
Horner Turn Cross TQ9 .139 A5
Horns Pk TQ14 ....208 E7
Hornshayes Knap Cross
EX14 ....86 F7
Hornshayne Rd EX24 ...102 B5
Horrabridge Prim Sch
PL20 ....126 F4
Horridge La EX18 ....59 A8
Horry Mill La EX18 ....58 F6
Horsdon Rd EX16 ....161 F4
Horsdon Terr EX16 .....161 F4
Horse Hill EX17 ....60 F7
Horse Hill Cross EX22 ..38 F1
Horse La TQ14 ....210 B3
Horsecombe Cross TQ8 259 B7
Horseguards EX4 ....261 B4
Horsehill Cross EX17 ....60 F7
Horsepond Mdw EX36 ..158 C3
Horsepool St TQ5 ....230 B3
Horseshoe Bend TQ4 ..226 C2
Horseshoe Cl 19 TQ13 ..123 E6
Horsham La
Plymouth, Honicknowle
PL5 ....244 C2
Plymouth, Tamerton Foliot
PL5 ....244 C7
Horslears EX13 ....167 C4
Horswell Cl PL7 ....251 B5
Horton Cross EX22 .....38 C3
Horwood & Newton Tracey
Prim Sch EX31 ....27 A6
Horwood Cross EX39 ....26 D7
Horwood Sq 11 EX31 ...154 F5
Hosegood Way TQ12 ...207 D7
Hosford Cl PL9 ....256 A4
Hoskings Ct TQ11 ....236 B5
Hospital Hill EX7 ....204 D6
Hospital La
17 Ashburton TQ13 .....131 A5
Exeter EX1 ....178 C8
Hospital Rd PL4 ....263 B4
Hostle Park Rd EX34 ...150 C6
Hostle Pk EX34 ....150 C6
Hotham Pl PL1 ....262 A4
Hothill La
Ashprington TQ9 ....139 F6
Cornworthy TQ9 ....227 A4
Houghton La EX10 .....187 A5
Houldsworth Rd PL9 ...255 C7
Hound Tor Cl TQ4 ....229 B7
Houndbeare La
Aylesbeare EX5 ....99 E4
West Hill EX5 ....168 A2
Houndhead Cross TQ9 .216 D8
Houndiscombe Rd PL4 .248 E4
Hounster Dr PL10 ....252 D4
Hounster Hill PL10 .....252 D4
Housecraft Ctr 7 PL4 ..263 A2
Housman Cl PL5 ....244 D3
Hove Villas EX2 ....261 A1
How St PL4 ....263 A2
Howard Ave EX32 ....155 B4
Howard Cl Exeter EX4 ...176 F8
Okehampton EX20 ....170 D6
Plymouth PL5 ....243 F2
Saltash PL12 ....242 D3
Tavistock PL19 ....171 A5
Teignmouth TQ14 ....210 A7
Torquay TQ2 ....219 D6
Howard Cross EX6 ....96 D7
Howard Ct TQ14 ....210 A7
Howard La Hittisleigh EX6 .96 D7
Marhamchurch EX23 .....70 B8
Howard Rd Plymouth PL9 255 E8
Wellington TA21 ....160 D7
Howards Cl EX36 ....158 C2
Howards Way
Ivybridge PL21 ....237 A6
Newton Abbot TQ12 .....207 F4
Howarth Cl EX10 ....188 A8
Howden La EX16 ....161 B3
Howden Rd EX16 ....161 C3
Howell Rd Exeter EX4 ...177 A7
Exeter EX4 ....261 A4
Howton La TQ12 ....206 B5
Howton Rd TQ12 ....206 C6
Hoxton Rd TQ1 ....220 B5
Hoyle's Ct TQ3 ....225 F8
Hoyle's Rd TQ3 ....225 E8
Hoyles Rd TA21 ....160 E4
Hubbastone Rd EX39 ...157 C8
Huccaby Cl TQ5 ....229 F2
Huckham Barn Cross
TQ7 ....149 C7
Huckham La EX31 ....10 F3
Huckland Cross EX20 ....76 E4
Huddisford Cross EX39 ..38 D7
Hudley Mill Hill EX32 ....18 D3
Hudson Cross EX22 ....53 B4
Hue La EX33 ....8 F1
Hugh Squier Ave EX36 .158 D5
Hughball Cross EX19 ....76 A8
Hughes Ave EX32 ....155 B3
Huish Cleeve TA4 ....35 E7
Huish Cross TQ13 ....123 C6
Huishlane End EX6 ....97 F5
Hukeleyhead Cross EX16 34 D3
Hulham Rd EX8 ....196 B2
Hulk La EX5 ....81 F4
Humber Cl PL3 ....249 D6
Humber La TQ12,TQ14 ..207 F8
Hume Ave EX35 ....151 A5
Hummingbird Cl EX1 ...174 E1
Humphrey's Cross
TQ13 ....130 C4
Humphreys Rd TA21 ....160 E7
Humphries Pk EX8 ....196 D1
Humpy The EX7 ....204 C7
Hungerford Rd PL2 .....248 B5
Hungry Fox Est EX5 .....175 E3
Huniver's La EX17 ....165 C4
Hunivers Pl EX17 ....165 D4
Hunsdon Rd
Ivybridge PL21 ....237 A2
Lee Mill PL21 ....136 D6
Torquay TQ1 ....220 C4
Hunstone Cross EX36 ....19 B2
Huntacott Way TQ2 .....219 B8

Hunter Cl PL6 244 F2
Hunter La EX34 7 F6
Hunter's Hill EX15 51 E1
Hunter's Way EX15 51 E1
Hunters Cl PL21 237 B5
Hunters Ct TQ3 224 F7
Hunters Gate EX20 170 D6
Hunters Moon TQ9 222 F7
Hunters Tor Dr TQ4 229 B7
Hunters's Oak PL20 126 A2
Hunterswell Rd TQ12 207 A3
Hunterswood EX38 159 F5
Hunthay La EX13 167 B6
Huntingdon Gdns PL5 244 D4
Huntley Cl EX13 167 F7
Huntley La EX13 88 A8
Huntley Pl PL3 249 C4
Hunton Cl EX8 195 F5
Hunts Cross PL21 137 B1
Huntshaw Cross EX31 27 B1
Huntshaw Moor Cross EX38 26 F2
Hurdwick Rd PL19 171 A5
Hurrabrook Cl PL6 245 E2
Hurrabrook Gdns PL6 245 E2
Hurrell Cl PL6 244 D6
Hurrell Ct
Kingsbridge TQ7 258 C5
Plymouth PL3 249 C5
Hurrell Rd TQ7 258 C5
Hursley Bsns Pk PL6 241 D1
Hurst Ave EX2 178 B4
Hurst Cl PL9 255 F5
Hussey's La EX14 86 F6
Husseys Cross EX14 86 F6
Hutcherleigh Cross TQ9 139 B1
Hutcherleigh Turn TQ9 139 D1
Hutchings Cl PL6 244 D6
Hutchings Mead EX1 178 F8
Hutchings Way TQ14 209 D8
Hutgate Rd EX14 86 A4
Hutton Rd TQ3 219 A1
Huxford Cross EX37 44 F7
Huxford La EX37 44 F7
Huxham Cl PL6 249 A8
Huxham's Cross TQ9 215 E3
Huxham's Cross Est TQ9 215 E3
Huxley Cl PL7 250 F7
Huxley Vale TQ12 212 F3
Huxnor Cross TQ12 212 F2
Huxnor Rd TQ12 212 F3
Huxtable Hill TQ2 219 E4
Huxtable La EX32 18 C2
Huxton Cross TQ7 143 D3
Huxton Fork TQ7 143 D3
Hyacinth Terr TA21 160 C5
Hyde Park Jun & Inf Schs PL3 248 E5
Hyde Park Rd PL3 248 E5
Hyde Rd TQ4 226 B6
Hyfield Gdns TQ1 220 B4
Hyfield Pl 4 EX39 157 A1
Hylands Cl EX11 168 D3
Hylton Gdns EX4 176 F6
Hyne Town Rd TQ6 145 E5
Hynetown Rd TQ6 145 E5
Hynicombe La TA4 35 D6

I

Ibex Ct EX39 15 A1
Ice House La EX10 187 F7
Icy Pk TQ7 143 C6
Iddesleigh Cross EX19 57 E3
Iddesleigh Rd EX4 177 E8
Iddesleigh Terr 10 EX7 204 E6
Ide Fst Sch EX2 176 E1
Ide La EX2 177 A1
Idestone Brook Cross EX2 113 F7
Idestone Cross EX2 114 A7
Idewell Rd TQ2 214 B2
Idston Cross TQ7 143 D7
Ilbert Cotts PL7 250 E4
Ilbert Rd Kingsbridge TQ7 258 C5
Thurlestone TQ7 143 A1
Ilbert St PL1 262 B4
Ilex Cl Exeter EX4 174 B2
Shillingford St George EX2 114 C6
Ilfracombe CE Jun Sch EX34 150 C5
Ilfracombe Coll EX34 150 C5
Ilfracombe Inf Sch EX34 150 B5
Ilfracombe Mus★ EX34 150 B5
Ilfracombe Rd
Braunton EX33 152 D7
Ilfracombe EX34 8 F5
Ilkerton Hill EX35 151 A1
Ilsham CE Prim Sch TQ1 220 E5
Ilsham Cl TQ1 220 F5
Ilsham Cres TQ1 220 F4
Ilsham Ho TQ1 220 E5
Ilsham Marine Dr TQ1 221 A4
Ilsham Rd TQ1 220 F5
Ilsington CE Prim Sch TQ13 122 C3
Ilton Cross TQ7 259 A7
Ilton Way TQ7 258 D5
Immenstadt Dr TA21 160 D4
Imperial Bldgs TQ12 207 D8
Imperial Ct TQ1 220 C7
Imperial Mews 5 TQ12 207 C3
Imperial Rd EX8 201 F6
Imperial St EX4 176 F5
Improvement Pl 5 TA21 160 D5
Ince Cl PL11 246 F4
Inchcoulter EX8 202 C5
Inchkeith Rd PL6 244 F7
Incledon Hill EX33 8 A3
Ind Units EX34 3 A3
Indicombe La EX32 18 B2
Indio Rd TQ13 180 C6
Ingleside EX13 167 E6
Ingleside Ct EX9 198 A1
Ingra Rd PL3 249 A6
Ingra Tor Cl 2 PL20 126 F3
Ingra Wlk PL6 245 B8
Inner Ting Tong EX9 197 C3
Innerbrook Rd TQ2 219 E5
Innes Ho PL1 262 B3
Instaple Cross EX22 53 D6
Instow Ho 4 EX39 15 B1
Instow Prim Sch EX39 15 C2
Instow Signal Box Mus★ EX39 15 B1
Instow Wlk PL5 244 A3
Inswell Ct PL19 171 A6
Insworke Cl PL10 253 A6
Insworke Cres PL10 252 F6
Insworke Pl PL10 253 A6
International Ho TQ12 180 F2
Inverdene PL3 248 D5
Inverteign Cty Jun Sch TQ14 209 D8
Inverteign Dr TQ14 210 A5
Inwardleigh Cross EX20 75 D2
Iolanthe Dr EX4 174 A2
Iona Ave EX8 196 A2
Ipplepen Bsns Pk TQ12 217 D8
Ipplepen Cross TQ12 211 C6
Ipplepen Prim Sch TQ12 211 D1
Ipplepen Rd TQ3 218 C4
Ipswich Cl PL5 244 C4
Irene Way EX16 161 F6
Iris Ave EX2 261 A1
Irishcombe Gate EX36 46 B5
Irishcombe La EX36 46 C4
Iron Bridge EX4 261 A3
Iron Bridge Cross EX20 77 B3
Iron Letters Cross EX34 2 B1
Iron Mine La PL20 127 B3
Iron Post TA22 33 B5
Iron Shovel La EX36 31 A3
Irsha St EX39 15 A1
Irving Cl EX33 152 B6
Isaac Cl EX9 198 E7
Isaacs Rd TQ2 214 A2
Isabella Rd EX16 161 D5
Isambard Ct TQ2 214 B3
Isambard Par EX4 177 A7
Isca Rd Exeter EX2 261 A1
Exmouth EX8 202 C5
Isigny Rd TQ7 258 C5
Isis Cl EX14 166 E7
Island Quay TQ8 259 E5
Island St TQ8 259 E5
Island View TQ7 143 A2
Isleworth Rd EX4 176 F5
Iter Cnr EX17 78 C4
Iter Cross EX17 78 C4
Iter Pk EX17 78 C4
Itton Cross EX20 77 D2
Itton Moor La EX17 77 F2
Itton Rd EX17 77 E2
Ivanhoe Rd PL5 243 D2
Ivatt Rd TQ6 233 C3
Iveagh Ct EX4 176 F8
Ivy Cl Exeter EX2 178 A4
Sidmouth EX10 188 B7
Ivy Cotts PL18 125 C6
Ivy Cross TA21 51 D7
Ivy Ct 28 EX39 15 A1
Ivy Ho TA21 160 C6
Ivy La Dartmouth TQ6 233 F3
14 Teignmouth TQ14 210 B4
Ivy Tree Hill TQ12 209 A2
Ivybridge Com Coll PL21 237 D6
Ivybridge Sta PL21 237 F6
Ivycombe Hill TQ7 149 B5
Ivydale EX8 196 D3
Ivydale Rd PL4 248 F4
Ivydene Rd PL21 237 C5
Ivyhouse Cross PL16 91 A4

J

Jack Backs Cross EX17 79 F7
Jack Bears Ho 10 TQ4 226 B6
Jack's La St John PL11 252 B8
Torquay TQ2 213 F3
Jackets La EX39 156 F7
Jacketts EX9 198 E7
Jacketts Cotts EX9 198 E7
Jackman's La TQ9 222 F4
Jackman's Mdw PL10 253 A3
Jackmans Cl TQ9 222 E6
Jackmoor Cross
Brampford Speke EX5 81 C1
Newton St Cyres EX5 81 B1
Jackson Cl PL5 247 F8
Jackson Pl PL2 247 F4
Jackson Way PL12 242 E3
Jacob's Pool EX20 170 B5
Jacobs Field EX39 39 E8
Jacolind Wlk TQ5 230 D5
Jago Ave PL11 247 B3
James Ave TQ3 218 E1
James Cl PL9 256 B6
James La EX14 69 C2
James Lane Cross EX13 69 C2
James Owen Ct EX4 261 C4
James Pl PL4 262 C4
James Rd PL19 171 E2
James St Plymouth PL4 262 C4
Plymouth, Mount Wise PL1 247 E1
James's Week La EX18 59 E8
Jane Way's Grave EX17 61 B1
Jardine Pk EX2 177 C1
Jarmins Pit Cross EX15 66 A4
Jarvis Cl EX8 202 E7
Jasmine Cl EX16 161 F6
Jasmine Gdns
Plymouth, Chaddlewood PL7 251 B5
Plymouth, Glenholt PL6 245 E6
Jasmine Gr TQ3 225 E8
Jawbones Hill TQ6 233 E2
Jaycroft EX15 162 E4
Jays Cross PL15 105 B6
Jean Cres PL3 249 B6
Jedburgh Cres PL2 248 A8
Jeffery Cl PL6 244 D6
Jefford Ho EX4 173 A1
Jeffrey Cl EX39 22 E3
Jeffs Way EX13 167 E6
Jellicoe Rd PL5 244 E1
Jellicoe Vills TQ9 223 B5
Jenker's Hill EX33 8 B2
Jenkins Cl PL9 256 A5
Jennifer Cl EX2 177 E3
Jenns Cross EX22 53 D7
Jenny's Portion EX5 82 A6
Jennycliff La PL9 255 A6
Jennys Combe Cl PL9 255 F4
Jenwood Rd EX14 67 B1
Jephson Rd PL4 249 B3
Jericho St EX5 81 E5
Jerrard Cl EX14 166 C5
Jerrard Cres EX14 166 C5
Jesmond Rd EX1 177 E7
Jessops PL7 250 D7
Jesu St EX11 169 D3
Jetty Marsh Rd TQ12 207 B5
Jewel's Cross EX22 70 E6
Jewell Cres EX32 155 C6
JHTaylor Dr EX39 157 A7
Jingles La EX32 155 A4
Jinkin Ave PL4 263 B4
Joan Spry Cl EX16 46 E1
Jobble's La EX24 102 E4
Jocelyn Mead EX17 165 B6
Jocelyn Rd EX9 198 A2
Jockey Hill EX17 165 C6
Joeys Field EX36 30 F3
John Acres La TQ12 123 D3
John Gay Cl EX32 155 C4
John Gay Rd EX32 155 C4
John Grinter Way TA21 160 D4
John Howe Cl EX38 159 D5
John Kitto Com Coll PL5 244 B1
John La PL4 262 C4
John Levers Way EX4 176 F5
John Nash Dr EX7 204 C4
John Penrose Rd EX31 154 B2
John Smale Rd EX31 154 C4
John Sparke Ho 18 PL1 263 A2
John St Exeter EX1,EX4 261 A2
Plymouth PL1 247 E3
Tiverton EX16 161 C4
John Stocker Mid Sch EX4 176 F4
John's Terr 7 EX16 161 B4
Johnson Cl 2 PL20 125 E1
Johnson Pk PL18 125 D3
Johnstone Dr EX16 161 B5
Johnstone La EX36 30 D4
Jones's Hill EX33 7 E2
Jonida Cl TQ1 220 A7
Jordan Cl EX32 155 C3
Jordan Cross TQ13 121 A2
Jordan Dr TQ14 209 D8
Jordan La
Horrabridge PL20 126 F5
Walkhampton PL20 127 A6
Jordan Mdw 15 TQ13 131 A5
Jordan Orch TQ11 236 A5
Jordan St TQ11 236 A5
Jordons Brook TQ9 222 E6
Jose's Cross EX37 44 F8
Jose's La EX31 4 B5
Joslin Ct TQ12 207 D8
Joslin Rd EX14 166 B5
Joy St EX31 154 F5
Jubilee Cl
Dartmouth TQ6 233 C3
Exminster EX6 182 B4
2 Ilfracombe EX34 150 B5
Ivybridge PL21 237 F6
Okehampton EX20 170 B5
Saltash PL12 242 D2
Jubilee Ct Ashwater EX21 90 E6
Exeter EX4 261 A3
Torquay TQ1 220 B5
Jubilee Dr Exmouth EX8 196 C3
8 Hemyock EX15 67 B8
Jubilee Gdns
Cullompton EX15 163 C2
North Molton EX36 30 D8
Jubilee Gr EX8 195 F5
Jubilee Path EX22 164 C5
Jubilee Rd Appledore EX39 14 F1
Exeter EX1 177 E7
Malborough TQ7 147 F6
Newton Abbot TQ12 207 B2
Plymouth PL5 243 F3
Jubilee Rd *continued*
Totnes TQ9 223 E6
Jubilee St TQ7 143 C6
Jubilee Terr
Copplestone EX17 79 B5
Kingswear TQ6 234 B3
Paignton TQ3 226 A6
Plymouth PL4 249 B2
Julian Cotts PL21 136 D6
Julian Rd PL21 237 B5
Julian St PL4 263 C2
Julian Wlk PL6 245 E6
Jump Cl PL6 241 C1
Junction Rd EX17 78 C4
Juniper Cl Exeter EX4 174 B2
3 Honiton EX14 166 A4
3 Tiverton EX16 161 F6
Juniper Ct EX31 154 C3
Juniper Way PL7 251 B5
Junket St EX37 43 B7
Jupes Cl EX6 182 B3
Juries La EX38 159 D6
Jurston Cross TQ13 110 F4
Jurston La
Wellington TA21 160 E6
Wellington TA21 160 F5
Jury Cross TA22 33 E6
Jury Hill TA22 33 E6
Jury Pk EX36 158 B4
Jury Rd TA22 33 E6
Jurys Cnr TQ12 213 A4
Jurys Corner Cl TQ12 213 A4
Justment Cross EX17 77 F2

K

Kabale Cl EX16 161 A6
Kala Fair EX39 156 E7
Karen Cl EX39 157 D1
Katherines La EX11 169 E4
Kathleaven St PL5 243 D1
Kay Cl Exmouth EX8 202 C8
Plymouth PL7 250 F7
Keals Croft EX35 151 B5
Keat St PL2 247 E4
Keatings La TQ14 210 A5
Keaton Barns PL8 141 E6
Keaton La PL21 237 D1
Keaton Rd PL21 237 C4
Keats Cl Exmouth EX8 196 C4
Teignmouth TQ14 124 E1
Kedlestone Ave PL5 244 A3
Keep Cotts TQ4 224 B7
Keep Gdns The TQ6 233 E3
Keep La TQ6 233 E4
Keep The PL12 242 C2
Keepers Cross EX16 49 A2
Kellacott Cross PL16 105 F7
Kelland Cl TQ3 226 A5
Kelland Cnr EX6 98 A1
Kelland Cross EX17 60 C2
Kelland Hill EX17 60 C2
Kellands Row TQ7 258 D5
Kellaton Cross
Beesands TQ7 149 C6
East Allington TQ9 144 E7
Kellett Cl 10 TQ13 131 A5
Kellock Dr TQ9 223 B5
Kelly Cl Plymouth PL5 247 C7
Torquay TQ1 220 C2
Kelly Coll PL19 171 D7
Kelly Cross TQ13 122 D8
Kelly La EX16 62 E8
Kelvin Ave PL4 263 C4
Kelvin Ct Brixham TQ5 230 D5
Torquay TQ1 214 C1
Kelway Rd TA21 160 E7
Kemmings Cl TQ4 225 F1
Kemp's La EX12 192 D7
Kempe Cl PL2 247 F6
Kempland La EX18 45 B2
Kempley Rd EX20 170 B5
Kemps Way TA22 33 D6
Kempton Terr PL11 247 B2
Kemyell Pl PL2 247 E4
Kenbury Cres EX6 201 B6
Kenbury Dr EX2 181 C8
Kendal Pl PL5 244 E4
Kendall Cl EX4 261 C4
Kendall Ho EX14 166 C5
Kendlewood Cl TQ4 225 F3
Kenilworth TQ1 220 D3
Kenilworth Rd PL2 248 B7
Kenley Gdns PL5 243 F4
Kenmare Dr PL7 251 A5
Kenn CE Prim Sch EX6 181 B1
Kenn Cl PL5 244 B3
Kenn La Exeter EX6 181 F1
Exminster EX6 182 A2
Kennacott Cross EX21 72 B1
Kennaway Rd EX11 169 F4
Kennedy Way
Dunkeswell EX14 67 C2
Tiverton EX16 161 C5
Kennel Bridge Cross EX20 92 E8
Kennel Hill PL7 250 D4
Kennel Hill Cl PL7 250 C4
Kennel La Georgeham EX33 8 A2
Ivybridge PL21 237 B5
Kennels Rd TQ5 229 C4
Kennels The PL21 237 B6
Kennerland Cross EX39 38 E8
Kennerley Ave EX4 178 B8
Kennet Cl PL3 249 B6
Kenneth Ct TQ2 219 C8
Kennford Rd EX2 177 B3
Kennicot House King Edward VI Com Coll TQ9 223 B6
Kenniford Cross EX5 183 D8
Kennydown La EX18 59 B7
Kensall Cross EX36 20 B1
Kensey Cl TQ1 220 E6
Kensham Ave EX5 83 A6
Kensham Cl EX5 82 F6
Kensington Pl 8 PL4 248 F4
Kensington Rd PL4 263 B4
Kenson Hill EX5 82 B5
Kent Cl EX2 178 A4
Kent Rd Plymouth PL2 247 F5
Tatworth TA20 88 D8
Kent's Bglws TA20 88 D8
Kent's Cotts TA20 88 D8
Kent's La TQ1 220 E5
Kent's Orch TA20 88 D8
Kent's Rd TQ1 220 E5
Kentisbeare CE Prim Sch EX15 66 A3
Kentisbury Cty Prim Sch EX31 10 E6
Kentisbury Grange Cvn Pk EX31 10 E5
Kenton Brook Ct TQ2 219 B8
Kenton Hill EX6 194 E3
Kenton Mews EX6 194 D3
Kenton Pl EX2 177 C2
Kenton Prim Sch EX6 194 D3
Kents Cavern★ TQ1 220 E5
Kents Cl Tatworth TA20 88 C8
Uffculme EX15 66 A7
Kents La TA20 88 D8
Kenwith Dr TQ7 258 D5
Kenwith Rd EX39 156 F4
Kenwith Terr EX39 156 F3
Kenwith View EX39 156 D2
Kenwyn Rd TQ1 220 C6
Keppel Pl PL2 247 F4
Keppel St PL2 247 F4
Keppel Terr 8 PL2 247 F4
Ker St PL1 247 E1
Ker St Ope PL1 247 E2
Kernou Rd TQ4 226 C6
Kernow Cl PL11 246 E3
Kernow Ct PL11 246 E3
Kernstone Cross EX39 22 B2
Kerria Cl TQ3 225 E8
Kerries Ct TQ10 135 A2
Kerries La TQ10 135 A2
Kerries Rd TQ10 135 A2
Kersbrook La EX9 198 A3
Kerscott EX32 28 F8
Kerse Cross
Thurlestone TQ7 143 B2
Thurlestone, South Milton TQ7 143 C2
Kerse La TQ7 143 B2
Kerslake's Ct 9 EX14 166 C6
Kerswell Cross TQ13 124 A7
Kerswell La
Kingskerswell TQ12 213 A5
Molland EX36 31 C8
Kerswill Cross TQ9 135 D1
Kerswill Rd EX4 176 F4
Kestell Rd EX10 188 C4
Kestor Cl EX20 170 D5
Kestor Dr Exeter EX4 176 E8
Paignton TQ3 219 A1
Kestral Units PL5 244 A1
Kestrel Cl
Okehampton EX20 170 B6
Plymouth PL6 245 D8
Kestrel Way
Barnstaple EX32 155 E5
Exeter EX2 178 E5
Keswick Cres PL6 245 D2
Keverel Rd EX8 196 A1
Kew Ct EX2 178 C3
Kewbridge Cl EX39 157 B4
Keyberry TQ12 207 D1
Keyberry Pk TQ12 207 D1
Keyberry Rd TQ12 207 D1
Keyes Cl PL1 247 F2
Keyham Barton RC Prim Sch PL2 247 E6
Keyham Rd PL2 247 E4
Keyham St PL5 247 E8
Keyham Sta PL2 247 E6
Keymelford Cross EX17 79 C2
Keysfield Rd TQ4 226 C5
Khartoum Pl TQ7 258 C5
Khyber Cl PL11 247 A3
Kiddicott EX17 165 B5
Kidland La
Bishops Nympton EX36 31 E1
South Molton EX36 46 E8
Kidwelly Cl PL7 251 C4
Kiel Pl PL3 249 D5
Kigbeare Cross EX20 93 B6
Kilb Arran Rise EX4 177 A8
Kildere TQ7 258 C4
Killarney Springs Leisure Pk★ EX23 37 E1
Killatree Cross EX22 71 E7
Killerton Cl 2 TQ3 226 B7
Killerton Ho★ EX5 82 D3
Killigrew Ave PL12 242 D1
Killington Cross EX31 4 D2
Kilmorie TQ1 220 F3
Kilmorie Cl TQ1 220 F3
Kiln Cl Bovey Tracey TQ13 180 C5
Plymouth PL5 247 C8
Kiln Close La 5 EX39 15 B1

Kiln Cross TQ3 218 D3
Kiln Ho TQ7 258 C4
Kiln La
[1] Barnstaple EX32 155 A4
Branscombe EX12 190 B4
Combe Martin EX34 3 B2
Stokenham TQ7 145 B1
Kiln Orch TQ12 206 F3
Kiln Path TQ5 230 C4
Kiln Rd
Bovey Tracey TQ13 180 C5
Marldon TQ3 218 C3
Kilnford Rd TQ12 207 F7
Kilnwood Pk EX31 154 A3
Kilworthy TQ1 220 B8
Kilworthy Hill PL19 171 C6
Kilworthy Rd PL19 171 C6
Kimber Cross EX20 74 E2
Kimberlands EX20 74 E2
Kimberlay Terr EX39 157 A8
Kimberley Ct PL21 237 D5
Kimberley Rd EX2 261 B2
Kimberley Villas PL21 237 C4
Kimberly Dr PL6 245 B1
Kimbland Cross EX32 18 C5
Kinevor Cl EX34 7 F8
King Alfred Way EX10 186 E8
King Arthur's Rd EX4 174 A1
King Charles I Bsns Pk TQ12 180 E4
King Edward Rd
Axminster EX13 167 C5
Saltash PL12 242 F2
King Edward St
[12] Barnstaple EX32 154 F6
Exeter EX4 173 A1
King Edward Vi Com Coll TQ9 223 B7
King Henry's Rd EX2 177 E3
King St [12] Bideford EX39 157 A2
Brixham TQ5 230 D5
Colyton EX24 103 A5
Combe Martin EX34 3 A3
[16] Dawlish EX7 204 D6
Exeter EX1,EX4 261 A2
[8] Exmouth EX8 202 A6
Gunnislake PL18 125 D6
Honiton EX14 166 C6
Millbrook PL10 252 E5
Newton Abbot TQ12 207 C3
Plymouth PL1 262 B3
Silverton EX5 82 B6
South Molton EX36 158 C4
Tavistock PL19 171 B6
Tiverton EX16 161 C3
Torpoint PL11 247 C3
King William Ho EX4 261 B4
King William St EX4 261 B4
King's Ash Cross TQ3 225 E6
King's Ash Rd TQ3 225 E6
King's Cl EX32 155 C2
King's Cnr TA22 33 D6
King's Cres EX16 161 E4
King's Cross TQ13 122 E6
King's Dr The TQ2 219 F4
King's Gdns EX14 166 C6
King's La
Bishop's Tawton EX32 27 F7
Lynton EX31 4 B5
King's Mill Rd EX15 163 E5
King's Nympton Prim Sch EX37 44 E6
King's Nympton Sta EX37 44 C3
King's Quay TQ6 233 F4
King's Quay Ho TQ6 233 F4
King's Rd Exeter EX4 177 E8
Honiton EX14 166 D6
Kennford EX6 114 A4
Plymouth PL1 248 A2
King's Tamerton Rd PL5 243 F2
Kingdom Mews EX4 177 A7
Kingdom's Cnr EX16 63 C4
Kingdon Ent Pk EX39 25 D4
Kingfisher Cl
Plymouth PL6 245 E6
Torquay TQ2 213 D2
Kingfisher Ct EX4 174 D1
Kingfisher Dr
Barnstaple EX32 155 E4
Exeter EX4 173 D2
Kingfisher Gdns EX15 163 B2
Kingfisher Gn EX2 176 D3
Kings Ave
Ottery St Mary EX11 169 F4
Paignton TQ3 226 C7
Kings Coombe Dr [13] TQ12 123 F1
Kings Cotts
[6] Newton Abbot TQ12 207 C3
Salcombe TQ8 259 E5
Kings Ct Honiton EX14 166 C6
Kingsbridge TQ7 258 D3
[5] Kingskerswell TQ12 212 F4
Kingsteignton TQ12 207 E6
Plymouth PL1 248 A3
Kings Farm La EX19 58 F3
Kings La EX10 188 B3
Kings Mdw TQ12 212 F4
Kings Meadow Dr EX19 58 F3
Kings Orch TQ9 223 E5
Kings Pk EX18 44 E1
Kings Rd Barnstaple EX32 155 B6
Paignton TQ3 226 C7
Plymouth, Devonport PL1 247 F2
Plymouth, West Park PL5 243 F3
Kings Rydon Cl TQ9 227 F8
Kings Sch PL3 248 E6
Kings Sch The EX11 169 B3
Kings Terr EX14 166 C6
Kings Way EX20 106 E5
Kingsacre EX33 152 C6
Kingsacre Prim Sch EX33 152 C6
Kingsale Rd TQ8 259 C4
Kingsbridge Com Coll (Tressilian Campus) TQ7 258 C6
Kingsbridge Com Coll (Westville Campus) TQ7 258 C4
Kingsbridge Com Prim Sch TQ7 258 E6
Kingsbridge Hill TQ9 223 C4
Kingsbridge La TQ13 130 F4
Kingsbridge Rd TQ10 137 E8
Kingsbridgefork Cross TQ9 144 E5
Kingscott Hill EX38 42 B4
Kingsdale [16] TQ1 220 D4
Kingsdon Hill EX24 103 B5
Kingsdown Cl
Dawlish EX7 204 E7
Teignmouth TQ14 209 D7
Kingsdown Cres EX7 204 E7
Kingsdown Rd TQ14 209 D7
Kingsgate EX4 177 D8
Kingsgate Bsns Units [5] EX14 166 A4
Kingsgate Cl TQ2 214 B4
Kingsholme EX24 103 B3
Kingshurst Dr TQ3 226 B8
Kingskerswell CE Prim Sch TQ12 213 A5
Kingskerswell Cross TQ2 213 C3
Kingskerswell Rd
Newton Abbot TQ12 212 D7
Torquay TQ2 213 D3
Kingslade La EX10 187 B2
Kingslake Ct EX8 202 A8
Kingslake Rise EX8 202 A8
Kingsland Ct TQ4 225 E4
Kingsland Dr TQ4 225 E4
Kingsland Gardens Cl PL3 248 E6
Kingsleigh Manor TQ1 220 C5
Kingsley Ave
[10] Appledore EX39 15 A1
[8] Barnstaple EX32 154 F6
Exeter EX4 178 B8
Ilfracombe EX34 150 B3
Torpoint PL11 247 B2
Kingsley Cl PL21 136 D6
Kingsley Pk EX39 156 E7
Kingsley Rd
Bideford EX39 157 A3
Kingsbridge TQ7 258 C4
Plymouth PL4 248 E4
Westward Ho! EX39 156 C6
Kingsley St EX39 157 A2
Kingsley Terr
[10] Bideford EX39 157 A1
[8] Combe Martin EX34 3 A3
Kingsmead Dr EX38 159 E6
Kingsmead Ho TQ3 226 B7
Kingsmill Ind Est EX15 163 E5
Kingsmill Rd PL12 242 C5
Kingsmoor Cross EX21 73 E7
Kingsteignton Rd TQ12 207 C4
Kingstephen Cl EX4 261 B4
Kingston Ave [4] EX34 3 A3
Kingston Cl
Kingskerswell TQ12 213 A5
Plymouth PL7 251 A5
Kingston Dr PL7 251 B5
Kingston Gate Cross TQ9 216 A6
Kingston La TQ6 233 E3
Kingston Rd
Exmouth EX8 202 C7
Stoke Climsland PL17 115 C1
Kingston Workshops TQ9 216 A7
Kingswater Ct TQ5 230 C5
Kingsway Cawsand PL10 253 B2
Exeter EX2 177 F5
Lyme Regis DT7 260 E4
South Molton EX36 158 C3
Teignmouth TQ14 209 D7
Kingsway Ave TQ4 226 A1
Kingsway Cl TQ4 226 A1
Kingsway Ct TQ4 226 A1
Kingsway Dr TQ4 226 A1
Kingsway Gdns PL6 244 F3
Kingsway Pk TQ7 258 C4
Kingswear Cres PL6 245 B1
Kingswear Prim Sch TQ6 234 B3
Kingswear Rd TQ5 234 F8
Kingswear Sta TQ6 234 A3
Kingswood Cl EX4 176 E8
Kingswood Ct TQ4 226 C5
Kingswood Mdw EX22 164 D5
Kingswood Park Ave PL3 248 D6
Kingswood Rd PL18 125 D6
Kinlacey Ct TQ1 220 C4
Kinnaird Cres PL6 244 F7
Kinnard Cres PL6 244 F7
Kinnerton Ct EX4 176 F8
Kinnerton Way EX4 176 E8
Kinross Ave PL4 249 A4
Kinsale Rd PL5 243 F3
Kinscome Ct TQ11 236 C5
Kinsford Gate Cross TA24 19 D7
Kinsford Hill TA24 19 E7
Kinterbury Rd PL5 247 B8
Kinterbury St PL1 263 A2
Kinterbury Terr PL5 247 B8
Kintyre Cl TQ2 213 E2
Kinver Cl PL6 245 D4
Kipling Ct EX39 156 C6
Kipling Dr EX2 177 F4
Kipling Gdns PL5 244 D2
Kipling Terr EX39 156 C6
Kipscombe Cross EX35 6 A6
Kipscombe Hill EX31 11 D2
Kirby Cl EX13 167 D5
Kirkby Pl PL4 262 C4
Kirkby Terr PL4 262 C4
Kirkdale Gdns PL2 248 B7
Kirkella Rd PL20 127 A2
Kirkham Ct [1] TQ3 226 A7
Kirkham House Mus* TQ3 226 B6
Kirkham St [4] TQ3 226 B7
Kirkland Cl PL6 245 C7
Kirkstall Cl PL2 248 A8
Kirkstead Cl TQ2 219 E8
Kirkwall Rd PL5 244 E3
Kirton La EX16 47 E4
Kirton Pl PL3 249 B5
Kirtons Rd TQ12 214 B7
Kismeldon Cross EX22 39 B3
Kissing Gate Cross EX16 48 D5
Kit Hill Cres PL5 247 C8
Kitchadon Gate EX18 59 D4
Kitchadon Rd EX18 59 D3
Kitcott Cross EX36 45 F6
Kitcott Hill EX36 45 F6
Kitley View PL8 257 B5
Kitley Way PL5 243 D1
Kitridge La TA24 21 B7
Kits Cl TQ13 123 F6
Kitter Dr PL9 256 A5
Kitterford Cross PL21 137 F7
Kittersley Dr [10] TQ12 122 F1
Kitts TA21 160 D4
Kitts Cross EX10 187 A7
Kitts La EX10 187 B6
Kitwell St EX15 66 A7
Klondyke Rd EX20 170 C3
Knacker's Hole La TA3 68 D6
Knackershole La EX17 61 B2
Knap Cross PL21 136 C4
Knap Down La EX34 3 B4
Knapp Hill EX10 188 A5
Knapp House Holiday Camp EX39 157 B7
Knapp Park Rd TQ4 226 C2
Knapp's La EX10 100 D1
Knapps Cl PL9 256 C6
Knaves Ash Cross TQ9 217 A5
Kneela Hill EX21 74 A8
Kneele Gdns PL3 248 E8
Kneller Cl EX34 150 C4
Knick Knack La TQ5 230 C3
Knight's La EX13 88 A4
Knightacott Cross EX32 11 C2
Knighthayes Wlk EX6 181 F5
Knightley Rd EX2 177 E3
Knighton Cross TQ12 131 F8
Knighton Hill Bsns Ctr PL9 140 E8
Knighton Rd
Plymouth PL4 263 C3
Wembury PL9 140 D8
Knighton Terr [4] PL20 126 F5
Knights Cres EX2 178 D3
Knights Field Way EX39 157 A8
Knights Rd TA21 52 D8
Knightstone Down La EX17 61 C2
Knightstone La
Ottery St Mary EX11 169 F1
Ottery St Mary EX11 169 F3
Knightstone Rd EX11 169 F1
Knightswood EX15 163 C2
Knill Cross PL10 252 E5
Knockworthy Cross EX38 26 F1
Knoll Knap EX13 103 E4
Knoll The PL7 250 B6
Knowland Cl PL1 247 F3
Knowle Ave PL2 247 E6
Knowle Cl
Ashburton TQ13 130 E4
Cullompton EX15 163 A3
Honiton EX14 166 C6
Landkey EX32 17 B2
Knowle Cnr EX9 197 D1
Knowle Cross
Bovey Tracey TQ13 123 C8
Copplestone EX17 79 C4
Whimple EX5 99 E8
Knowle Ct TQ8 259 D5
Knowle Dr Exeter EX4 176 F7
Sidmouth EX10 188 A4
Knowle Fork TQ7 148 F4
Knowle Gdns
Combe Martin EX34 3 A3
Kingsbridge TQ7 258 C6
Sidmouth EX10 187 F4
Knowle Grange EX10 188 A4
Knowle Hill EX9 197 C2
Knowle Ho (Fire Service HQ) EX3 183 B6
Knowle House Cl TQ7 258 D6
Knowle La
Butterleigh EX15 64 F1
Copplestone EX17 79 C4
Knowle La *continued*
Drewsteignton EX6 96 D1
Knowle Prim Sch PL5 244 A4
Knowle Rd
Budleigh Salterton EX9 197 E1
Lustleigh TQ13 122 C8
Salcombe TQ8 259 D5
Knowle Terr PL20 127 B4
Knowle View EX20 170 D6
Knowles Cross TQ13 130 E4
Knowles Dr [22] EX24 103 A4
Knowles Hill Rd TQ12 207 B4
Knowles Hill Sch
Newton Abbot TQ12 207 A4
Newton Abbot TQ12 207 B4
Knowstone Cross EX16 47 D6
Knowstone Moor Cross EX36 47 B8
Kyl Cober Parc PL17 115 C1
Kynance Cl PL11 246 F4
Kynock Ind Est EX39 25 F4

L

Labbett's Cross EX18 60 C6
Laboon La EX18 59 C7
Laburnam Ct TQ12 212 B6
Laburnam Terr TQ12 212 B7
Laburnham Gr TQ9 223 A7
Laburnum Cl
Exmouth EX8 196 D3
[1] Honiton EX14 85 C2
Laburnum Cotts PL19 171 C6
Laburnum Dr
Barnstaple EX32 155 E3
[6] Wembury PL9 140 D8
Laburnum Rd Exeter EX2 177 F3
Newton Abbot TQ12 207 E1
Wellington TA21 160 E5
Laburnum Row [4] TQ2 219 F6
Laburnum St TQ2 219 F5
Laburnum Villas PL19 117 E6
Laburnum Way TQ9 144 E7
Lace Wlk EX14 166 C6
Lackaborough Ct EX2 181 A8
Lacy Rd TQ3 219 A1
Ladder La EX34 3 B3
Ladies Mile EX31 4 A4
Ladies' Mile EX32 155 A3
Ladram Rd EX9 199 A8
Lady Harriet Acland's Dr TA22 34 A8
Lady Meadow Terr TQ13 121 B2
Lady Modifords CE Prim Sch PL20 127 B4
Lady Park Rd TQ2 219 D3
Lady Seawards Prim Sch EX3 183 C6
Lady St TA22 33 D7
Lady Victoria's Dr TA22 33 E6
Ladymead EX10 187 F8
Ladysmith Ct PL4 263 C4
Ladysmith Fst Sch EX1 177 F7
Ladysmith Mid Sch EX1 177 F7
Ladysmith Rd Exeter EX1 177 F7
Plymouth PL4 249 B3
Ladywell Pl PL4 263 B3
Lag Hill EX17 62 F1
Lagge Hill Cross EX17 80 F8
Lagoon View EX31 153 A4
Lahteglos Cl PL21 137 C7
Laira Ave PL3 249 D4
Laira Bridge Rd PL4 249 B1
Laira Green Prim Sch PL3 249 C4
Laira Park Cres PL4 249 B4
Laira Park Pl PL4 249 B4
Laira Park Rd PL4 249 B4
Laira Pl PL4 263 C2
Laira St PL4 263 C3
Laity Wlk PL6 244 D6
Lake Ave TQ14 210 A7
Lake Cl EX14 166 D5
Lake Cross TQ9 131 D2
Lake La Ashreigney EX18 58 F7
Dousland PL20 127 B3
Newton St Cyres EX5 80 F2
Northlew EX20 74 D2
Stockleigh Pomeroy EX17 81 A7
Lake Mews PL10 252 E5
Lake Rd PL9 255 B6
Lake St TQ6 233 F3
Lake View EX17 165 E6
Lake View Cl PL5 244 B6
Lakelands Cl EX16 46 E1
Lakelands Dr EX4 176 F6
Lakenham Cotts EX39 156 E7
Lakenham Hill EX39 156 F7
Lakes Cl TQ5 230 A5
Lakes Cross EX20 57 A8
Lakes La EX4 98 F4
Lakes Rd TQ5 230 A4
Lakeside
Abbotskerswell TQ12 212 B6
Dawlish Warren EX7 201 A2
Salcombe TQ8 259 D5
Tavistock PL19 171 B6
Lakeside Ave EX2 182 B8
Lakeside Cl TQ13 180 C4
Lakeside Dr PL5 243 E5
Lakeview Dr PL5 244 B5
Lakewater Cross TQ9 131 E1
Lalebrick Rd PL9 255 B5
Lama Cross EX18 59 C4
Lamacraft Cl EX7 204 F8
Lamacraft Dr EX4 178 A7
Lamaton Pk EX36 158 D3
Lamb Park Cl [10] TQ12 123 F1
Lamb Pk Chagford TQ13 111 A6
Drewsteignton EX6 96 D1
Ilfracombe EX34 150 A4
Lamb The TQ9 223 B5
Lambert Cl EX7 204 F8
Lambert Cross EX20 75 A3
Lambert La EX6 96 F3
Lambert Rd PL5 244 B6
Lambert's La TQ14 209 D4
Lambhay Hill PL1 263 A1
Lambhay St PL1 263 A1
Lambpark Ct TA3 68 C6
Lambs Cl TQ7 143 A2
Lambscombe Cross EX36 31 A8
Lambscombe Hill EX36 31 A8
Lamejohns Field EX17 165 D6
Lamerhooe Cross PL19 116 A1
Lamerhooe Dr PL19 116 A1
Lamerton Cl PL5 244 B3
Lamerton Cross EX20 75 F2
Lammacott Cross EX17 78 E5
Lammacott La EX17 78 E6
Lammas La TQ3 226 A8
Lamorna Pk PL11 246 E4
Lampard-Vachell Sch The EX32 155 C3
Lamplough Rd EX8 196 A3
Lana Cotts EX22 89 F7
Lana Cross EX22 55 C1
Lanbridge Cross TQ9 222 F1
Lancaster Cl
Cullompton EX15 163 C5
Exeter EX2 178 B5
Lancaster Dr TQ4 226 A2
Lancaster Gdns PL5 244 D4
Lancaster Ho TQ4 226 C5
Lancelot Rd EX4 174 A2
Lancer Ct TA21 160 D6
Lancercombe La EX10 100 D3
Lanchitt Cross EX36 19 B2
Lancock St TA21 160 A5
Land Pk EX18 44 E1
Landacre La TA24 21 A7
Landboat Cotts EX17 62 F1
Landboat View EX17 62 F1
Landcroft La EX15 66 F4
Lander Rd PL12 242 F3
Landhayes Rd EX4 176 F5
Landkey Prim Sch EX32 17 B2
Landkey Rd EX32 155 C2
Landlord's Hill TA21 51 E7
Landmark Rd TQ8 259 B4
Landpath TQ7 143 A2
Landrake Cl PL5 247 C8
Lands Pk PL9 255 F7
Lands Rd Brixham TQ5 230 F6
Exeter EX4 174 D1
Landscore EX17 165 B5
Landscore Cl
Crediton EX17 165 B5
Teignmouth TQ14 210 B5
Landscore Prim Sch EX17 165 A5
Landscore Rd
[3] Exeter EX4 177 A5
Teignmouth TQ14 210 B5
Landscove CE Prim Sch TQ13 131 B1
Landsdowne Pk TQ9 223 E4
Landsend La EX17 78 E3
Landulph Cross PL12 238 F1
Landulph Gdns PL5 247 C8
Landuph Sch PL12 238 F1
Lane Cross EX22 53 F7
Lane End Cl [1] EX39 15 B1
Lane End Cross
Broadhembury EX14 84 E8
Broadhempston TQ13 131 D3
Halwill EX21 73 D3
Lamerton PL19 116 B2
Lane End Pk EX32 155 D4
Lane End Pool TQ9 227 B3
Lane End Rd EX39 15 B1
Lane Field Rd EX39 156 D2
Lane Head Cl EX33 7 E2
Lane The Dittisham TQ6 228 D2
Lutton PL21 133 B2
Lanehead Rd EX12 191 D5
Lanepark La EX39 37 A5
Lang Gdns PL18 125 D3
Lang Gr Plymouth PL9 256 C7
Tavistock PL19 171 D5
Lang Way TQ12 211 E2
Langaford La EX21 73 B2
Langage Cross PL7 251 F6
Langage Ind Est PL7 251 D4
Langage Pk PL7 251 C4
Langage Science Pk PL7 251 D5
Langaller Cl TQ13 180 B5
Langaller Hill TA22 33 D4
Langaller La TQ13 180 B4
Langarron Pk EX32 155 B5
Langaton Gdns EX1 174 F1
Langaton La EX1 175 A1
Langbrook Cross PL21 136 E3
Langdale Cl PL6 245 D1
Langdale Gdns PL6 245 D1
Langdon Cross PL21 137 F1
Langdon Ct PL9 256 B6
Langdon Down Way PL11 246 E3
Langdon Fields TQ5 229 B6
Langdon Hospl EX7 200 E2
Langdon La Dawlish EX7 204 C8
Galmpton TQ4,TQ5 229 B6

Langdon Rd
Bradworthy EX22 .38 E1
Dawlish EX7 .204 D8
Paignton TQ3 .219 C1
Langdons Way TA20 .88 C8
Langerwehe Way EX8 .201 F6
Langerwell Cl PL12 .242 C3
Langerwell La PL12 .242 C3
Langfield Terr 6 EX34 .150 C5
Langford Ave EX14 .166 D6
Langford Cres TQ2 .213 F3
Langford Cross EX17 .78 B4
Langford Gate PL21 .137 F8
Langford Gn EX15 .83 D5
Langford Rd
Honiton EX14 .166 D7
Honiton EX14 .166 E8
Langford EX5 .172 E7
Langham Cross EX19 .57 D6
Langham La EX17 .61 F2
Langham Levels PL21 .237 B6
Langham Pl PL4 .263 C3
Langham Way PL21 .237 C5
Langhams Cross TQ7 .143 A2
Langhill Rd PL3 .248 D5
Langland Hill EX17 .61 A4
Langland La EX11 .169 B7
Langlands Bsns Pk EX15 .65 F6
Langlands Cl TQ4 .225 E4
Langlands Cross EX14 .87 A6
Langlands Rd EX15 .163 A3
Langleigh La EX34 .150 A4
Langleigh Pk EX34 .150 A4
Langleigh Rd EX34 .150 A5
Langley Ave TQ5 .230 C4
Langley Cl Brixham TQ5 .230 C4
Plymouth PL6 .245 A7
Langley Com Inf Sch
PL6 .245 A6
Langley Cres PL6 .244 F7
Langley Cross EX37 .27 F3
Langley Gdns EX18 .44 E1
Langley La EX18 .44 E1
Langmead EX39 .157 E5
Langmead Cl PL6 .249 C8
Langmead Rd PL6 .249 C8
Langmoor La EX13 .88 D2
Langmore Cl PL6 .249 A7
Langridge Cross EX37 .27 F1
Langridge Rd TQ3 .225 E8
Langs Rd TQ3 .226 C8
Langsfield EX33 .7 D1
Langsford Rd PL19 .117 E3
Langston Cross PL21 .142 D7
Langstone Cl
Heathfield TQ12 .180 F2
Torquay TQ1 .220 D6
Langstone Cross TQ13 .121 E8
Langstone Dr EX8 .196 C1
Langstone Hill
Lustleigh TQ13 .121 E8
Moretonhampstead TQ13 .111 E1
Langstone Rd PL2 .248 C7
Langstone Terr PL2 .248 C7
Langton Rd 8 PL20 .126 F3
Langtree Com Prim Sch
EX38 .40 F2
Langwells Ct TQ9 .139 E1
Langworthys Barn TQ7 .143 E2
Lanherne EX7 .204 E6
Lanherne Sch EX7 .204 D6
Lanhydrock Cl TQ3 .225 D8
Lanhydrock Rd PL4 .249 B2
Lannacombe Gn TQ7 .149 C5
Lanscore La EX14 .101 A8
Lansdown Terr 2 EX32 .155 A6
Lansdowne EX2 .178 B4
Lansdowne La 2 TQ2 .219 F5
Lansdowne Pk EX39 .156 F8
Lansdowne Rd
Budleigh Salterton EX9 .197 D1
Plymouth PL6 .244 F2
1 Torquay TQ2 .219 F5
Lansdowne Terr
Bideford EX39 .156 F1
Exeter EX2 .261 B2
Lapford Com Prim Sch
EX17 .60 D3
Lapford Cross EX17 .60 C2
Lapford Sta EX17 .60 C2
Lapthorn Cl PL9 .255 C7
Lapwing Cl EX15 .163 A3
Larch Cl Exmouth EX8 .196 D3
Saltash PL12 .242 C3
Seaton EX12 .192 A8
Teignmouth TQ14 .210 B8
Larch Dr PL6 .245 E7
Larch Rd EX2 .176 F3
Larch Wlk TQ2 .219 C8
Larcombe End TQ9 .135 F1
Lark Cl EX4 .173 D1
Lark Hill PL2 .248 A6
Lark Rise
5 Barnstaple EX31 .154 A2
Newton Poppleford EX10 .186 E8
Larkbeare Ave EX5 .100 B8
Larkbeare Cross EX5 .100 B8
Larkbeare Rd EX2 .261 B1
Larkey La EX16 .63 D4
Larkhall Rise PL3 .249 B5
Larkham Cl PL7 .250 C6
Larkham La PL7 .250 C6
Larks Cl TQ14 .209 D4
Larks Rise EX15 .163 A2
Larkshayes Cross EX13 .86 E3
Larkshayes Droveway
EX13 .86 F3
Larkshayes Knap EX13 .86 F3
Larksmead Cl TQ12 .207 A1
Larksmead Way TQ12 .207 A1
Larkspur Gdns EX32 .155 E4
Larkstone Cres 3 EX34 150 D5
Larkstone Gdns EX34 .150 D5
Larkstone La EX34 .150 D6
Larkstone Terr EX34 .150 D6
Lashbrook EX5 .84 B2
Lashingcott Cross EX31 .27 B3
Lashingcott Lane End
EX31 .27 B2
Laskeys Heath 1 TQ12 .122 F1
Laskeys La EX10 .188 C4
Latch La EX38 .40 E2
Latches Wlk EX13 .167 D6
Latchgate Cross EX36 .31 F7
Latchgate Hill EX36 .31 F7
Latham Cl PL6 .249 A7
Latimer Cl PL7 .251 B5
Latimer Rd EX4 .178 A8
Latimer Wlk PL6 .244 E7
Lauder La EX31 .154 C1
Lauderdale 1 EX32 .155 B4
Lauderdale Dr EX32 .155 B4
Launceston Cl PL6 .245 B7
Launceston Head EX5 .83 C1
Launceston Rd EX20 .107 E8
Laura Ave TQ3 .226 B8
Laura Gr TQ3 .226 A8
Laurel Ave EX39 .156 E1
Laurel Bank EX14 .85 B4
Laurel Ct PL2 .248 A7
Laurel Dene PL2 .248 A7
Laurel Dr PL6 .245 E6
Laurel La TQ14 .209 D5
Laurel Rd Exeter EX2 .177 F3
1 Honiton EX14 .166 A4
Plymouth PL2 .248 A7
Laurel Rise EX8 .202 D8
Laurels The
Barnstaple EX31 .154 B2
Sidmouth EX10 .188 A5
Laureston Rd TQ12 .207 C2
Laurie Ave TQ12 .206 F4
Lauriston Cl TQ2 .220 A5
Lavender Cl TQ5 .230 A4
Lavender Cres TQ3 .218 D2
Lavington Cl PL7 .251 B5
Lavinia Dr PL7 .250 C5
Law Wlk PL6 .244 D6
Lawn Cl 2 Plymouth PL7 251 C5
Torquay TQ2 .213 F4
Lawn Dr TQ13 .123 E6
Lawn Gdns 16 TQ13 .123 E6
Lawn Hill 3 EX7 .204 E6
Lawn Rd EX8 .202 A7
Lawn Terr 22 EX7 .204 D6
Lawn The
2 Budleigh Salterton EX9 198 A1
Tavistock PL19 .171 D6
1 Wellington TA21 .160 D6
Lawn Vista EX10 .188 B5
Lawns End TQ14 .208 E8
Lawns The Plymouth PL5 .244 E1
Torpoint PL11 .247 A4
Lawrence Ave EX4 .177 A5
Lawrence Cl EX14 .84 D7
Lawrence Pl TQ2 .220 B4
Lawrence Rd PL9 .255 A6
Lawson Gr PL9 .255 C7
Laxton Ave EX1 .178 C6
Layne Cl EX6 .113 B4
Layne Fields EX6 .113 B4
Laywell Cl TQ5 .230 B2
Laywell Rd TQ5 .230 A3
Lazenby Rd EX16 .161 F3
Le Locle Cl EX10 .187 F8
Le Marchant Cl EX14 .67 B1
Le Molay-Littry Way
TQ13 .180 E7
Lea Combe EX13 .167 D5
Lea La EX9 .198 F7
Lea Mount TQ14 .209 A8
Lea Mount Cl EX7 .204 D5
Lea Mount Dr EX7 .204 D5
Lea Mount Rd EX7 .204 E5
Lea Rd Otterton EX9 .198 E7
Tiverton EX16 .161 F6
Torquay TQ2 .214 B3
Lea Side EX6 .112 E8
Lea Terr EX39 .15 A1
Lea The TQ14 .209 C7
Lea Vale Rd TQ12 .207 A3
Lea View EX15 .162 D5
Leaches La EX18 .60 B7
Leachway La EX2 .113 F7
Leachway Lane Cross
EX2 .113 F7
Leadengate Cl EX33 .7 E1
Leadengate Fields EX33 .7 D1
Leader La TQ3 .218 D2
Leaholes Ave EX20 .170 C5
Lealands TQ13 .180 C6
Leander Ct 17 TQ14 .210 B4
Leander Way PL5 .244 D2
Leanway PL12 .242 E2
Lear La EX13 .167 C4
Lear Pk EX15 .83 F5
Lears La 6 TQ13 .123 F6
Leary Cross EX32 .29 B8
Leas Rd EX9 .198 A1
Leas The EX34 .150 A3
Lease Cotts EX5 .82 D4
Lease Hill EX5 .82 E4
Leat Cl PL20 .127 B3
Leat Mdw
3 Liverton TQ12 .122 F1
Tiverton EX16 .161 B5
Leat Rd PL16 .105 F3
Leat St EX16 .161 B5
Leat View PL12 .242 B3
Leat Wlk Plymouth PL3 .248 E6
Roborough PL6 .241 D1
Leatfield Dr PL6 .244 F4
Leather Cl PL6 .244 E7
Leather Tor Cl 4 PL20 .126 F3
Leatside Exeter EX2 .261 A2
Roborough PL6 .241 C1
Leatside Ho TQ12 .207 A3
Leatway Gdns EX15 .163 B3
Leaves Yd PL3 .249 B7
Leaway Cotts EX16 .161 E4
Leaze Rd TQ12 .207 D8
Lebanon Cl EX4 .173 E1
Leburnick Cross PL15 .115 B8
Ledgate La Plymouth PL7 251 F8
Sparkwell PL7 .132 F1
Ledsgrove TQ12 .211 E2
Ledstone Cross TQ7 .144 B5
Lee Ave EX39 .25 F1
Lee Ball Cross EX31 .11 E3
Lee Ball Hill EX31 .11 D3
Lee Cl EX14 .166 B6
Lee Cross
Broadhempston TQ9 .131 E1
Great Torrington EX37 .42 F7
North Molton EX36 .30 B8
Woolacombe EX34 .1 C1
Lee Ct TQ5 .230 E4
Lee La
Bishops Nympton EX36 .31 F6
Dartmouth TQ6 .232 C7
Dunsford EX6 .112 E7
Lee Lane End TQ7 .148 F8
Lee Mill Hospl PL21 .136 C7
Lee Mill Ind Est PL21 .136 C6
Lee Pk TA21 .52 F7
Lee Rd EX35 .151 B5
Lee Terr 2 TQ13 .123 E6
Leechwell La TQ9 .223 C5
Leechwell St TQ9 .223 B5
Leecross Gate EX17 .61 A7
Leecross La EX5 .81 F8
Leeford La EX35 .6 B5
Lees Mdw EX5 .84 A2
Leeward La TQ2 .213 E3
Leeze Park Est EX20 .170 B4
Leggetts La DT7 .193 C7
Legion La PL8 .257 A5
Legion Way EX2 .177 B2
Legis Wlk PL6 .245 B8
Leicester Mead EX4 .176 E7
Leigh Cl PL21 .137 C8
Leigh Cross
Bittaford PL21 .137 D8
Bovey Tracey TQ13 .123 C7
Chulmleigh EX18 .59 C8
Doddiscombsleigh EX6 .113 B6
Kentisbeare EX15 .66 F6
Kingsbridge TQ7 .258 A8
Modbury PL21 .137 F3
South Brent TQ10 .135 A4
Zeal Monachorum EX17 .77 F7
Leigh Ct PL6 .249 A8
Leigh La Bittaford PL21 .137 C8
Combe Martin EX34 .3 C2
Roborough PL6 .241 D2
Leigh Rd Bideford EX39 .156 E1
Chulmleigh EX18 .44 D1
Combe Martin EX34 .3 B2
Leigh Villas EX18 .44 E1
Leigham Ct
7 Dawlish EX7 .204 E6
Plymouth PL1 .262 B2
Leigham Inf & Jun Schs
PL6 .245 E1
Leigham St PL1 .262 B1
Leigham Terr TQ7 .258 C5
Leigham Terrace La
PL1 .262 B2
Leighcott Cross EX17 .62 A2
Leighcott La EX17 .62 A2
Leighmoor Cross PL21 .137 F3
Leighon Rd TQ3 .226 C7
Leighton Rd PL3 .248 F8
Leighton Terr EX4 .261 B4
Leighty Water EX38 .42 A6
Leland Gr PL21 .237 D4
Lembury Rd TQ9 .225 A1
Lemon Pl TQ12 .207 C3
Lemon Rd TQ12 .207 C3
Lemonford La TQ12 .131 D7
Lenards Rd EX39 .156 F6
Lenda La TQ12 .122 C2
Lendon Way EX19 .58 F2
Lennard Rd 6 EX17 .165 C5
Lennox Ave EX10 .188 B4
Lentney Cl PL9 .140 A8
Lenton La EX37 .44 C6
Lenwood Ctry Club
EX39 .156 E5
Lenwood Pk EX39 .156 E4
Lenwood Rd EX39 .156 E5
Leofric Rd EX16 .161 D6
Leonard Moor Cross
EX15 .65 F8
Leonards Cl TQ7 .143 A1
Leonards Rd PL21 .237 D5
Lerwell Beech Tree Cross
EX37 .29 A5
Leslie Rd EX8 .202 A8
Lester Cl PL3 .249 B6
Lestock Cl EX8 .202 F7
Lethaby Rd EX32 .155 B6
Lethbridge Rd EX2 .178 B4
Lethbridge's & Davey's
Almshouses EX1 .261 C4
Lettaford Cross TQ13 .111 B3
Level The TQ6 .228 C2
Lever Cl EX39 .156 F8
Leverlake Cl EX16 .161 F6
Leverlake La EX16 .161 F7
Lewdon Cross EX6 .97 A5
Lewes Gdns PL5 .244 C4
Lewhaven Cl EX20 .106 E5
Lewis Ave EX16 .161 E4
Lewis Cres EX2 .178 D3
Lewis Ct 4 EX34 .150 B5
Leworthy Cross EX39 .39 B6
Leworthy Hill EX31 .11 D1
Leworthy Post EX32 .11 C1
Lewsley Cross EX13 .87 E4
Lewsley La EX13 .87 E4
Lewthorn Cross TQ13 .122 B3
Lewtrenchard Cty Prim Sch
EX20 .106 F5
Lexhayne La EX13 .103 A7
Ley Cl TQ12 .180 B1
Ley Cres TQ12 .180 B1
Ley Cross Ashreigney EX18 58 F8
Aveton Gifford PL21 .143 A8
Ermington PL21 .136 D4
Holsworthy Beacon EX22 .54 F3
North Molton EX36 .30 F8
Widecombe in the Moor
TQ13 .121 C6
Ley La Bere Ferrers PL20 .239 D6
Combe Martin EX31 .10 D6
Kingsteignton TQ12 .207 D8
Ley La Cross TQ12 .207 D8
Ley Meadow Dr EX31 .154 A3
Ley's Cross EX17 .62 E2
Ley's La EX31 .4 C1
Leyburn Gr TQ4 .226 A4
Leyfield Wlk EX7 .204 E7
Leyford Cl PL9 .140 D8
Leyland Cross EX22 .53 E8
Leypark Cl EX1 .178 C7
Leypark Cres EX1 .178 C7
Leypark Dr PL6 .245 E2
Leypark Rd EX1 .178 C7
Leypark Wlk PL6 .245 E2
Leys Rd TQ2 .219 D5
Leyton Ct EX15 .163 C3
Leywood EX14 .86 D7
Liberator Way EX14 .67 C1
Liberty Stile EX39 .22 C2
Libra Gdns EX34 .2 F4
Lichfield Ave TQ2 .214 A1
Lichfield Cl TQ5 .230 A4
Lichfield Dr TQ5 .230 A4
Lichfield Rd EX4 .176 D6
Lichgate Rd EX2 .181 C8
Lidburn Hill EX6 .97 E5
Lidford Tor Ave TQ4 .225 F3
Lidyates La DT7,EX13 .103 F3
Liffey Rise EX4 .176 E8
Lifton La EX19 .59 B3
Lifton Prim Sch PL16 .105 E4
Lifton Rd PL4 .263 C2
Liftondown Cross PL16 .105 C4
Light La TQ5 .229 B4
Lighthouse Cross EX39 .23 B3
Lightleigh Cross EX18 .44 F5
Lilac Cl PL9 .255 C5
Lilac Rd Exeter EX2 .177 F3
Tiverton EX16 .161 F5
Lilac Terr EX16 .161 D4
Lilian Cl EX17 .78 B4
Lillagey La EX9 .198 A6
Lillebonne Cl TA21 .160 F6
Lillicrap Ct EX20 .170 B5
Lillybrook La EX6 .98 A5
Lillycombe La TA3,EX15 .67 E8
Lily Cl EX39 .157 A7
Lily La EX5 .172 A8
Lily Mount EX4 .176 D8
Lilybridge EX39 .157 A7
Lilylake Cross EX24 .102 F7
Lime Ave TQ2 .219 F5
Lime Cl Broadclyst EX5 .175 C6
Tiverton EX16 .161 F5
Lime Cres EX15 .162 C4
Lime Gr Bideford EX39 .156 F2
Exminster EX6 .182 A5
Exmouth EX8 .196 C3
Kingsbridge TQ7 .258 C5
Lime Kiln La Exeter EX2 .178 A1
Uplyme DT7 .260 A6
Lime Kiln Rd EX16 .161 F3
Lime Rd EX16 .161 F5
Lime St TQ13 .111 F5
Lime Tree Cl EX2 .178 C3
Lime Tree Mead 1 EX16 .64 D7
Lime Tree Wlk TQ12 .207 E1
Lime Way EX12 .192 A7
Limegrove Rd EX4 .176 F5
Limehayes Rd EX20 .170 C5
Limekiln La EX31 .16 A6
Limer's Hill EX38 .159 B5
Limer's La EX36 .158 B2
Limer's Lane Cross
EX36 .158 B2
Limerick Pl PL4 .263 C3
Limers Cross
Chittlehampton EX37 .29 A4
Wolverstone EX14 .85 C7
Limers La Merton EX20 .57 A7
Northam EX39 .157 A5
Wolverstone EX14 .85 C7
Limes Cotts EX6 .182 A4
Limes The PL6 .244 F2
Limetree Cross EX16 .64 D6
Limetree Gr EX33 .152 C6
Limetree Rd PL3 .248 D7
Linacre La TQ12 .213 C6
Linacre Rd TQ2 .213 F4
Lincoln Ave PL4 .263 C4
Lincoln Cl Exmouth EX8 .196 E4
Feniton EX14 .84 D2
Lincoln Gn TQ2 .214 A1
Lincoln Rd EX4 .176 E6
Lincombe Cross
Diptford TQ9 .138 D8
Salcombe TQ8 .259 D7
Lincombe Dr TQ1 .220 E3
Lincombe Hill Rd TQ1 .220 E4
Linda Cl EX1 .178 B5
Linden Cl
Barnstaple EX31 .154 C3
Braunton EX33 .152 D6
Exmouth EX8 .196 D2
Great Torrington EX38 .159 C5
Linden Ct 2 TQ5 .230 C5
Linden Gdns EX31 .154 C3
Linden Hill TA21 .160 A6
Linden Rd
Cullompton EX15 .163 C4
Dawlish EX7 .204 D5
Linden Terr
Newton Abbot TQ12 .207 A3
Plymouth PL4 .263 C3
Lindisfarne Way TQ2 .213 E2
Lindridge Cl 5 TQ12 .123 E1
Lindridge Hill TQ12 .123 F1
Lindridge La 6 TQ12 .123 E1
Lindridge Pk TQ14 .124 B2
Lindridge Rd TQ1 .220 C8
Lindsay Rd TQ3 .219 A2
Lindthorpe Way TQ5 .230 B4
Liney Cross TQ11 .236 A6
Linfield Gdns EX4 .176 F4
Linhay Bsns Pk TQ13 .131 A5
Linhay Cl Brixham TQ5 .234 F8
Honiton EX14 .166 B3
Millmoor EX15 .51 E1
Linhay Dr EX31 .153 F6
Linhay Pk EX17 .80 A5
Linhey Cl TQ7 .258 D4
Link House Cl EX39 .156 C7
Link Rd EX20 .170 C6
Linkadells PL7 .250 D6
Linketty La PL7 .250 C5
Linketty La E PL6 .245 A1
Linketty La W PL6 .248 F8
Linkhay TA20 .88 D8
Linkhay Cl TA20 .88 D8
Links Cl
Churston Ferrers TQ5 .229 E6
Exmouth EX8 .202 C8
Links Ct TQ7 .143 A1
Links Rd EX9 .203 E8
Links The EX39 .156 E7
Linnet Cl EX4 .173 D2
Linnet Ct PL12 .242 C2
Linnet Dene EX15 .163 A2
Linscott Cres EX31 .153 A4
Linton Cl PL5 .244 C8
Linton La EX39 .37 B5
Linton Rd PL5 .244 C7
Linton Sq PL5 .244 C8
Lion Cl TQ7 .258 C5
Lion's Close Hill EX24 .103 A5
Lion's Rump EX32,EX36 .18 F1
Lions Mill EX31 .154 E7
Lippell Dr PL9 .255 E6
Lipson Ave PL4 .263 C4
Lipson Com Coll PL4 .249 C4
Lipson Ct PL4 .263 B3
Lipson Rd PL4 .263 B4
Lipson Terr PL4 .263 C4
Lipson Vale PL4 .249 A4
Lipson Vale Prim Sch
PL4 .249 A4
Lipstone Cres PL4 .263 C4
Lisa Cl EX2 .178 A4
Lisburne Cres 14 TQ1 .220 D4
Lisburne Pl 9 TQ1 .220 D4
Lisburne Sq TQ1 .220 D4
Liscawn Terr PL11 .247 B3
Liscombe Cl PL18 .125 D7
Lisham's Drain EX24 .103 A5
Lishaperhill Cross EX22 .53 B2
Liskeard Rd PL12 .242 B3
Lisson Gr PL4 .248 F4
Lister Cl PL7 .250 F6
Litchardon Cross EX31 .26 F8
Litchaton Cres PL7 .250 B7
Litchaton Cross
East Buckland EX32 .18 F1
North Molton EX36 .30 A8
Litchaton Hill
East Buckland EX36 .18 F1
North Molton EX36 .30 A8
Litchaton Way PL7 .250 B7
Litchdon La EX32 .154 F4
Litchdon St EX32 .155 A4
Litchfield Cl PL7 .251 B6
Litelbury Rd EX16 .64 D7
Littabourne EX31 .154 F7
Little Ash Gdns PL5 .243 B1
Little Ash Rd PL5 .243 B1
Little Barton 7 TQ12 .123 F1
Little Bicton Ct 18 EX8 .202 A6
Little Bicton Pl EX8 .202 A6
Little Bossell La TQ11 .236 B4
Little Bray Cross EX32 .18 C8
Little Butts PL9 .255 E6

Little Castle St EX4 ....261 B3
Little Chockenhole La
EX9 ....199 A8
Little Cl
Kingsteignton TQ12 ....207 E8
Ottery St Mary EX11 ....169 D3
Little Cross TQ13 ....130 A4
Little Dock La PL5 ....244 B2
Little Down La PL6 ....241 E3
Little Down Orch EX10 .186 D7
Little Esworthy La EX16 .48 A1
Little Fancy Cl PL6 ....245 C7
Little Field EX39 ....156 D2
Little Gate TQ7 ....143 F7
Little Gornhay La
Chevithorne EX16 ....49 D1
Tiverton EX15 ....64 D8
5 Tiverton EX16 ....161 F6
Little Hayes 12 TQ12 ....123 F1
Little Hayes La EX18 ....58 D8
Little Heath Cross EX16 .63 A6
Little Helstonbench Cross
TQ13 ....123 B6
Little Hill TQ8 ....259 C5
Little Hill Cl TQ12 ....123 F1
Little John's Cross Hill
EX2 ....176 E3
Little John's Wlk TQ13 .122 F6
Little Knowle EX9 ....197 F1
Little Knowle Ct EX9 ..197 F1
Little La Beer EX12 ....191 D4
Cawsand PL10 ....253 A2
Staddiscombe PL9 ....255 D3
Little Mdw EX8 ....196 E3
Little Mdws EX18 ....59 C4
Little Meadow Way
EX39 ....156 E2
Little Normans EX15 ....83 F6
Little Park Rd TQ3 ....226 A6
Little Point Cres PL10 ..252 F5
Little Queen St EX4 ....261 B3
Little Rack St 4 EX1 ..261 A2
Little Rackenford La
EX16 ....47 E5
Little Raddon Cross EX17 80 F6
Little Roborough TQ13 .130 F5
Little Silver Exeter EX4 .261 A4
Tiverton EX16 ....161 D3
Little Silver La
Exeter EX2 ....181 D5
Wellington TA21 ....160 D2
Little Toms EX15 ....65 A2
Little Torrington EX38 ..159 B1
Little Week Cl EX7 ....200 F1
Little Week Gdns EX7 ..200 F1
Little Week Rd EX7 ....200 F1
Little Wiveliscombe La
TA4 ....35 D6
Littleborough Cross
EX17 ....62 A5
Littlebray La EX32 ....18 E6
Littlebridge Mdw EX22 ..70 F5
Littledown Cl EX8 ....202 F7
Littledown La EX10 ....186 D7
Littlefield TQ14 ....208 E8
Littlefield Cl
Barnstaple EX32 ....155 D4
Torquay TQ2 ....213 D1
Littlefields EX12 ....192 A7
Littleford Cross EX22 ...53 E8
Littlegate Rd TQ3 ....226 B6
Littleham CE Prim Sch
EX8 ....202 F7
Littleham Cross EX8 ..202 D7
Littleham Rd EX8 ....202 E7
Littlehempston Cross
TQ9 ....216 F2
Littlejoy Rd TQ12 ....206 C4
Littlemead La EX8 ....196 B3
Littlemoor Cl EX31 ....153 A4
Littleton Pl PL2 ....247 F4
Littletown Rd EX14 ....166 B4
Littletown Villas EX14 ..166 C4
Littleway EX2 ....176 F3
Littleweek La EX7 ....200 F1
Littlewood Cl PL7 ....251 A4
Livarot Wlk EX36 ....158 B4
Livaton Cross EX20 ....95 D4
Livermead Hill TQ2 ....219 E2
Livermore Rd EX14 ....166 C5
Liverpool Hill EX4 ....176 E7
Liverton Bsns Pk EX8 ..196 F1
Liverton Cl EX8 ....202 E8
Liverton Ct TQ12 ....180 A1
Liverton Hill EX8 ....197 B1
Livery Dole Almshouses
EX2 ....177 E5
Livingshayes Rd EX5 ....82 C6
Livingstone Ave PL8 ....141 B8
Livingstone Rd TQ14 ....210 C6
Livonia Rd EX10 ....188 B6
Lixton Pk PL21 ....137 F1
Lizard Cl PL6 ....244 F7
Lizard Wlk PL6 ....245 A7
Lloyd Ave TQ2 ....219 D7
Lloyd Maunder Rd EX15 162 C5
Lloyds Cres EX1 ....178 C8
Lloyds Ct EX1 ....178 C8
Loatmead Cross EX22 ...38 B3
Lobbthorn Stile EX33 ....8 B1
Locarno Ave TQ3 ....219 D1
Locarno Rd EX4 ....176 F4
Lock La EX31 ....10 E4
Lock Lane Cross EX31 ..10 F3
Lock's Gate Cross
TQ13 ....129 F8
Lockeridge Rd PL20 ....125 E1
Lockfield Ct EX2 ....177 B1
Lockington Ave PL3 ....248 F7
Locks Cl Braunton EX33 .152 D5
Torquay TQ1 ....220 D7
Locks Hill TQ1 ....220 D7
Locks Wlk PL1 ....247 E1
Locksey's La EX12 ....190 D6
Locksley Cl Exeter EX2 .182 A8
Torquay TQ1 ....220 B7
Locksley Grange TQ1 ..220 A7
Lockyer Ave EX10 ....188 C8
Lockyer Cres EX16 ....161 A6
Lockyer Ct PL1 ....262 C2
Lockyer Mews PL19 ....171 C6
Lockyer Rd PL3 ....248 E5
Lockyer St PL1 ....262 C2
Lockyer Terr PL12 ....243 A3
Lockyers Quay PL4 ....263 B2
Loddiswell Butts TQ7 ..143 E8
Loddiswell Prim Cross
TQ7 ....143 F7
Lodge Cl TA21 ....160 D6
Lodge Cnr EX31 ....27 D8
Lodge Cross
Chulmleigh EX18 ....45 A1
Longdown EX6 ....98 E1
Lodge Gdns PL6 ....244 E3
Lodge Hill Exeter EX4 ..177 A8
Okehampton EX20 ....170 B5
Lodge La Axminster EX13 .88 B2
Bratton Fleming EX31 ....18 E8
Brixton PL8 ....256 F5
Shute EX13 ....103 A8
Lodge Rd EX16 ....161 E4
Lodge Trad Est EX5 ....175 E3
Lofoten Cl PL1 ....247 E2
Loftus Gdns PL5 ....243 C2
Logan Rd TQ3 ....226 C7
Logan Way EX15 ....67 B8
Lolesbury Cross PL8 ....136 A1
Lollabury Rd PL12 ....242 E3
Lombard Cl EX39 ....25 D4
London Ct The PL21 ....237 D5
London Inn Sq EX1 ....261 B3
Long Acre PL12 ....242 B4
Long Barton 5 TQ12 ....123 F1
Long Bridge Cross EX13 .87 B8
Long Copp EX9 ....198 A2
Long Cross
Dartmouth TQ6 ....233 C3
South Pool TQ7 ....148 F7
Long Cswy EX8 ....202 B6
Long Down Gdns PL6 ..245 E3
Long Drag EX15 ....65 E3
Long Entry DT7 ....260 E3
Long Hill EX12 ....191 D5
Long Holcombe Cross
EX36 ....20 A6
Long La Appledore EX39 ...14 F1
Ashford EX31 ....16 B6
Barnstaple EX31 ....154 A8
Calverleigh EX16 ....48 D2
Combe Martin EX31,EX34 ...3 D1
Dawlish EX7 ....200 B1
Exmouth EX8 ....202 C6
Georgeham EX33 ....8 B1
Newton Abbot TQ12 ....208 B1
Northam EX39 ....157 A8
Shaldon TQ14 ....209 C4
Tiverton EX16 ....161 A7
Wolverstone EX14 ....85 B8
Long Ley PL3 ....249 B6
Long Mdw Plymouth PL7 .250 D7
South Brent TQ10 ....134 F2
Long Meadow Dr EX32 .155 B6
Long Moor
Cullompton EX15 ....163 F6
Willand EX15 ....162 E1
Long Orch PL20 ....125 E1
Long Park Cl PL9 ....255 F5
Long Park Dr PL6 ....245 D7
Long Park Rd PL12 ....242 D2
Long Pk Ashburton TQ13 .131 A5
Modbury PL21 ....137 B3
Woodbury EX5 ....184 C3
Long Rd Paignton TQ4 ..225 D1
Saltash PL12 ....242 B4
Long Rowden PL3 ....248 E6
Long Rydon TQ9 ....227 F8
Long Terrace Cl 5 PL7 .251 C5
Long Walk Dr EX32 ....29 C6
Long Wools TQ4 ....229 D7
Long-Go La EX14 ....84 E8
Longacre PL7 ....250 B7
Longbridge Cl PL6 ....249 F6
Longbridge Meadow Trad Est
EX15 ....163 D4
Longbridge Rd
Plymouth, Laira PL3 ....249 C4
Plymouth, Longbridge PL6 .249 E7
Longbrook TQ7 ....145 A1
Longbrook Barton PL7 .250 D5
Longbrook Cl PL21 ....237 B5
Longbrook La EX8 ....195 F4
Longbrook Rd PL21 ....237 B5
Longbrook St Exeter EX4 261 B4
Plymouth PL7 ....250 F4
Longbrook Terr EX4 ....261 B4
Longcause PL7 ....250 F4
Longcause Com Specl Sch
PL7 ....250 F4
Longcombe Cross TQ9 .224 C5
Longcroft Ave TQ5 ....230 B3
Longcroft Dr TQ5 ....230 B3
Longdogs Cl EX11 ....169 E3
Longdogs La EX11 ....169 E3
Longdown Rd EX2,EX6 ..176 B3
Longdrag Hill EX16 ....161 A4
Longfield
11 Appledore EX39 ....15 A1
Lutton PL21 ....133 B1
Longfield Ave TQ12 ....207 F8
Longfield Cl
Braunton EX33 ....152 E5
Lutton PL21 ....133 B2
Longfield Dr TQ8 ....259 C5
Longfield Est EX6 ....201 A8
Longfield Pl PL4 ....263 B4
Longfield Villas PL9 ....255 D8
Longfields TQ7 ....258 A4
Longford Cross TQ12 ..207 E8
Longford Down Head
PL21 ....137 F6
Longford La TQ12 ....207 E8
Longford Pk TQ12 ....207 E8
Longforth Rd TA21 ....160 D6
Longland Cl EX32 ....17 B5
Longland Cross TQ9 ...227 C3
Longland La EX33 ....8 A2
Longlands Dawlish EX7 ..204 D6
Plymouth PL9 ....255 D8
Longlands Cross
Ashwater EX21 ....90 E6
Holsworthy EX22 ....71 F2
Longlands Dr PL9 ....140 A8
Longlands La PL12 ....242 B1
Longmead EX35 ....151 A5
Longmead Cl TA21 ....160 B8
Longmead Cotts TA21 ..160 B8
Longmead Rd TQ3 ....218 F1
Longmead Wlk TQ3 ....218 F1
Longmeadow Budlake EX5 82 E1
Tiverton EX16 ....161 D5
Woodbury EX5 ....184 C3
Longmeadow Cl PL7 ...250 E7
Longmeadow Rd
Lympstone EX8 ....195 F5
Saltash PL12 ....242 E3
Longmeadows EX17 ....165 D6
Longpark Hill TQ1 ....214 C6
Longstone Ave PL6 ....245 A6
Longstone Cross 1
TQ13 ....131 A5
Longstone Rd TQ4 ....225 E4
Longthorn Rd TQ13 ....124 B4
Longview Rd PL12 ....242 D3
Longview Terr PL3 ....249 B7
Longwood Cl PL7 ....251 A4
Longwood La TA21 ....51 C4
Longwool Mdw EX23 ....70 A6
Lonsdale Rd Exeter EX1 .178 B5
Newton Abbot TQ12 ....207 D2
Loo Cross TQ7 ....144 F1
Looe Rd EX4 ....177 A7
Looe St PL4 ....263 A2
Looseall La TA22 ....33 D8
Loosebeare Cross
Zeal Monachorum EX17 ....78 B8
Zeal Monachorum EX17 ....78 C8
Loosebeare La EX17 ....78 B8
Loosedon Cross EX19 ....58 B4
Looseland Cross EX16 ..47 D1
Looseleigh Cl PL6 ....245 A4
Looseleigh La PL6 ....244 F5
Looseleigh Pk PL6 ....244 E5
Lopes Cres EX20 ....170 C5
Lopes Dr PL6 ....241 C1
Lopes Rd Dousland PL20 .127 B3
Plymouth PL2 ....248 B6
Lopwell Cl PL6 ....244 F5
Loram Way EX2 ....181 C8
Lord Louis Cres PL9 ....254 F6
Lord Mamhead Homes
EX2 ....177 E4
Lords Meadow La 5
EX16 ....34 B1
Lords Pl TQ1 ....220 B6
Lords Way EX2 ....178 C4
Loretto Rd EX13 ....167 E5
Loring Rd TQ8 ....259 D4
Lorrie Dr TQ14 ....210 B6
Lorrimore Ave PL2 ....247 F5
Lotherton Cl PL7 ....251 B3
Loughboro Rd PL5 ....243 C1
Loughborough EX16 ....161 B5
Loughwood La EX13 ....87 B2
Louis Way EX14 ....67 C1
Louisa Gate TA22 ....33 F7
Louisa Pl EX8 ....202 A5
Louisa Terr EX8 ....202 A5
Louise Terr EX38 ....159 C5
Louvigny Cl EX14 ....84 E2
Louville Cl TQ4 ....226 C2
Lovacott Cross EX31 ...153 F2
Lovacott School Cross
EX31 ....27 A6
Love La Ashburton TQ13 .130 F4
Bickington TQ12 ....131 D7
Bideford EX39 ....156 E1
Colyton EX24 ....103 A4
Marldon TQ3 ....218 D4
Saltash PL12 ....242 E2
Love Lane Cl TQ3 ....218 D4
Lovelace Cres EX8 ....202 D8
Lovelace Gdns EX2 ....181 B8
Loveland Cross EX20 ....74 C1
Lovell Cl EX8 ....196 C3
Lovell Rd PL3 ....248 F6
Loventor La TQ3,TQ9 ...217 F3
Lover's La EX39 ....14 F1
Loveridge La TA20 ....88 D8
Lovering Cl EX8 ....196 C3
Loverings Ct 3 EX31 ...154 F5
Low Brook EX5 ....99 C5
Low Meml Ho 4 EX32 ....16 E1
Lower Albert St EX1 ...261 C3
Lower Aller La TQ13 ...122 E6
Lower Almshouses 2
EX31 ....154 F6
Lower Anderton Rd
PL10 ....252 F5
Lower Argyll Rd EX4 ...173 A2
Lower Audley Rd TQ2 ..219 F8
Lower Ave EX1 ....177 F6
Lower Biteford Cross
EX39 ....38 B6
Lower Blagdon Cross
TQ3 ....225 B6
Lower Blagdon La TQ3 .225 C6
Lower Brand La EX14 ..166 C4
Lower Brimley Cl 2
TQ14 ....210 C5
Lower Brimley Rd TQ14 210 C5
Lower Broad Oak Rd
EX11 ....168 E4
Lower Broad Path TQ9 .228 A7
Lower Broad Pk TQ6 ...233 D3
Lower Brook Mdw 2
EX10 ....101 B1
Lower Brook Pk PL21 ..237 A5
Lower Brook St 13
TQ14 ....210 C5
Lower Brookfield Cotts
TQ13 ....122 C8
Lower Budleigh EX9 ...198 B5
Lower Budleigh Mdw
TQ12 ....206 F3
Lower Bulkamore Cross
TQ10 ....135 E5
Lower Bulworthy Gate
EX16 ....47 D4
Lower Bulworthy La
EX16 ....47 D4
Lower Burston EX17 ....78 B5
Lower Burwood Rd
EX38 ....159 E5
Lower Cannon Rd
Bovey Tracey TQ12 ....123 B2
Heathfield TQ12 ....180 F2
Lower Church St
5 Barnstaple EX32 ....155 A4
Colyton EX24 ....103 A5
Lower Cl EX16 ....65 A7
Lower Claypark EX34 ....7 F7
Lower Cleave EX39 ....157 B5
Lower Cleve EX33 ....152 C7
Lower Cobbaton EX37 ...28 D5
Lower Collapark TQ9 ...223 B6
Lower Collins Rd TQ9 ..223 B6
Lower Compton Rd PL3 248 F5
Lower Congella Rd TQ1 220 C6
Lower Contour Rd TQ6 .234 B3
Lower Cookworthy Cross
PL16 ....106 A6
Lower Coombe La EX17 .79 B3
Lower Coombe Rd TQ12 207 F7
Lower Coombe St EX1 .261 A2
Lower Coombses TA20 ..88 D8
Lower Cotteylands
EX16 ....161 B3
Lower Court Rd PL8 ....140 F7
Lower Cross EX15 ....51 C1
Lower Cross Rd EX31 ..154 B4
Lower Dawlish Water Rd
EX7 ....204 A7
Lower Dean Cross EX31 ...3 F2
Lower Dean La EX34 ....3 B3
Lower Dr EX7 ....204 E8
Lower Duck St EX6 ....182 B3
Lower East St EX36 ....30 E8
Lower Ellacombe Church Rd
TQ1 ....220 C6
Lower Erith Rd TQ1 ....220 D4
Lower Fairview Rd TQ6 233 E3
Lower Farm Rd PL7 ....251 A4
Lower Farthings EX10 ..186 F8
Lower Fern Rd TQ12 ...212 F8
Lower Forches Cross
EX17 ....60 D4
Lower Fore St
3 Exmouth EX8 ....202 A6
Saltash PL12 ....243 A2
Lower Fowden TQ4 ....229 D6
Lower Foxmoor Rd
TA21 ....160 B5
Lower French Pk TQ12 .206 F3
Lower Fyldon Cross
EX36 ....19 D4
Lower Gaydon St 1
EX32 ....155 A5
Lower Green Cross TQ7 145 C4
Lower Griggs EX10 ....187 D7
Lower Gunstone EX39 ..157 A2
Lower Harrington La
EX4 ....174 E1
Lower Hill Barton Rd
EX1 ....178 C6
Lower Hollicombe Cotts
TQ3 ....219 D1
Lower Kelly PL18 ....125 D3
Lower King's Ave EX4 ..177 D8
Lower Kingsdown Rd
TQ14 ....209 D7
Lower Kinsman's Dale
TQ13 ....111 F5
Lower Knowle Rd TQ13 122 D7
Lower La Chulmleigh EX18 .59 C8
Dalwood EX13 ....87 B2
Ebford EX3 ....183 C4
6 Plymouth PL1 ....263 A2
Lower Ladram La EX9 ..199 A7
Lower Lodfin EX16 ....34 B2
Lower Lowton La EX6 ..112 E6
Lower Manor Rd TQ5 ..230 C5
Lower Marlpits Hill
EX14 ....166 D4
Lower Meadow Rise
EX7 ....204 C6
Lower Meddon St 9
EX39 ....157 A1
Lower Mill La EX15 ....163 C3
Lower Millhayes EX15 ...67 C8
Lower Moor EX32 ....155 D4
Lower Moor Way EX15 ..64 D8
Lower North St EX4 ....261 A3
Lower Northcote Rd
EX14 ....166 E7
Lower Park Dr PL9 ....255 F4
Lower Park Rd EX33 ....152 E5
Lower Penns Rd TQ3 ...219 C1
Lower Pk
2 Paignton TQ3 ....226 A7
Umberleigh EX37 ....28 D2
Lower Polsham Rd TQ3 226 C7
Lower Port View PL12 ..242 F2
Lower Preston TQ12 ...123 D1
Lower Preston Cross
TQ9 ....138 E2
Lower Raleigh Rd EX31 155 A7
Lower Rd EX5 ....184 B7
Lower Rea Rd TQ5 ....230 D5
Lower Ridings PL7 ....251 B7
Lower Row PL10 ....253 A2
Lower Saltram PL9 ....255 C7
Lower Shapter St EX3 ..182 F4
Lower Shirburn Rd TQ1 220 A7
Lower St Chagford TQ13 .111 A6
Dartmouth TQ6 ....233 F3
Dittisham TQ6 ....228 B3
Plymouth PL4 ....263 A3
West Alvington TQ7 ....258 A4
Lower St German's Rd
EX4 ....177 C8
Lower Summerlands
EX1 ....261 C3
Lower Tamar Terr PL18 .125 D7
Lower Terr EX22 ....38 E1
Lower Thurlow Rd TQ1 .220 A6
Lower Tidderson Cross
EX16 ....47 E4
Lower Town
Halberton EX16 ....65 A7
Malborough TQ7 ....147 E6
Sampford Peverell EX16 ...50 D1
Winkleigh EX19 ....58 F2
Woolfardisworthy EX39 ....38 F7
Lower Union La TQ2 ...220 B5
Lower Union Rd TQ7 ...258 C5
Lower Warberry Rd
TQ1 ....220 C4
Lower Warcombe Cross
TQ7 ....144 A6
Lower Warren Rd TQ7 .258 D3
Lower Way EX10 ....187 A8
Lower Wear Rd EX2 ....182 B8
Lower Westlake Rd
EX31 ....154 A2
Lower Wheathill EX10 ..188 B8
Lower Winsham Rd EX33 .8 D1
Lower Woodfield Rd
TQ1 ....220 C4
Lower Woodhayes Ct
EX5 ....99 E7
Lower Yalberton Rd
TQ4 ....225 C2
Lowerdale Turn TQ9 ....144 B8
Lowerdown TQ13 ....122 D5
Lowerside PL2 ....248 A8
Lowertown Cotts EX20 .107 A3
Lowery Cross PL20 ....127 C4
Loweswater Ho EX4 ....176 F6
Lowley Brook Ct TQ2 ..219 B8
Lowman Cross EX16 ....50 B1
Lowman Units EX16 ....64 D8
Lowman Way EX15 ....64 D8
Lowmoor Ind Est TA21 .160 B8
Lownard Cross TQ9 ....222 E8
Lowton Cross EX20 ....77 C7
Lowton La EX6 ....112 E6
Lowtrow Cross TA4 ....35 A8
Loxbury Rd TQ2 ....219 D4
Loxbury Rise TQ2 ....219 D5
Loxdown Rd EX39 ....41 A7
Loxhore Cross EX31 ....17 D7
Lucas Ave EX4 ....177 D8
Lucas La PL7 ....250 D6
Lucas Terr PL4 ....249 B2
Lucerne 1 TQ1 ....220 D4
Lucius St TQ2 ....219 F5
Luckhams La TQ7 ....147 E6
Lucky La EX2 ....261 B2
Lucombe Oaks EX5 ....179 B6
Ludbrook Gate PL21 ....137 C5
Ludlow Rd 2 PL3 ....248 E6
Ludwell La EX2 ....178 A3
Lugsmoor La EX10 ....189 E7
Lugworthy Cross EX21 ...91 B5
Luke St EX16 ....34 B1
Lulworth Cl TQ4 ....225 F2
Lulworth Dr PL6 ....245 B7
Lumley Cl EX6 ....194 E3
Lummaton Cross TQ2 ..214 A2
Lummaton Pl TQ2 ....214 B1
Lundy Cl Barnstaple EX32 155 C5
Plymouth PL6 ....244 F7
Lundy View EX39 ....156 E6
Lurley Cross EX16 ....48 E2
Luscombe Cl
Ipplepen TQ12 ....211 D1

Luscombe Cl *continued*
Ivybridge PL21 237 A4
Luscombe Cres TQ3 225 E6
Luscombe Cross TQ9 139 D8
Luscombe Hill
Dawlish EX7 204 A6
Teignmouth EX7 124 E3
Luscombe La TQ3 225 D8
Luscombe Rd TQ3 225 E6
Luscombe Terr 11 EX7 204 D6
Luson Cross PL8 136 C1
Lustleigh Cl EX2 181 C8
Lutehouse La EX19 58 E3
Lutsford Cross EX39 37 D6
Lutterburn St PL21 137 D6
Lutyens Dr TQ3 225 D7
Lutyens Fold PL19 116 A6
Luxmore Cl PL6 245 E1
Luxton Cl EX21 73 E3
Luxton La EX20 77 B8
Luxton Moor La EX20 59 A1
Luxton Rd TQ12 211 F8
Lwr Bull Ring EX15 163 C3
Lych Cl PL9 255 A6
Lyd Gdns PL19 171 D5
Lydacott Cross EX31 153 F3
Lydcot Wlk PL6 245 A1
Lyddicleave EX31 154 A3
Lyddon Cl TA21 160 D4
Lydford Castle★ EX20 107 E3
Lydford Cl PL21 237 D4
Lydford Gorge★ EX20 107 E3
Lydford Ho TQ12 207 D4
Lydford Park Rd PL3 248 D5
Lydgates Rd EX12 192 A6
Lydia Cl EX10 186 D8
Lydia Way PL4 263 B4
Lydiate La Lynton EX35 151 B5
Lynton EX35 5 A5
Lydon La TA4 35 D5
Lydwell Park Rd TQ1 220 E5
Lydwell Rd TQ1 220 D6
Lye La EX14 87 A8
Lym Cl DT7 260 E3
Lyme Bay Holiday Village
EX12 192 B5
Lyme Bay Rd TQ14 210 C7
Lyme Cl EX13 167 D5
Lyme Mews 5 EX12 192 B4
Lyme Rd Axminster EX13 167 E5
Uplyme DT7 104 B5
Lyme Regis Ind Est DT7 260 C4
Lyme Regis Marine
Aquarium★ DT7 260 D2
Lyme Regis Philpot Mus★
DT7 260 E3
Lyme St EX13 167 D6
Lyme View Cl TQ1 220 D7
Lyme View Rd TQ1 220 D7
Lymeborne Ave EX1 178 A6
Lymebourne Ave EX10 188 B6
Lymebourne La EX10 188 B6
Lymebourne Pk EX10 188 B6
Lymington Rd TQ1 220 A6
Lympne Ave PL5 243 F5
Lympstone CE Prim Sch
EX8 195 E5
Lympstone Commando Sta
EX8 195 C8
Lympstone Sta EX8 195 D5
Lyn Cross EX35 151 D2
Lyn Gr TQ12 212 F6
Lyn La EX35 151 D3
Lynbridge Ct 5 PL19 171 B5
Lynbridge Hill EX35 151 B3
Lynbridge Rd EX35 151 C4
Lynbro Rd EX31 154 F7
Lynch Cl EX5 81 E5
Lynch Head EX10 100 C1
Lyncombe Cl EX4 173 E1
Lyncombe Cres TQ1 220 E3
Lyncourt TQ1 220 D3
Lyndale Rd TQ12 207 D8
Lyndhurst Ave TQ12 213 A5
Lyndhurst Cl
Kingskerswell TQ12 213 A6
Plymouth PL2 248 C6
Lyndhurst Rd Exeter EX2 177 E5
Exmouth EX8 202 A8
Plymouth PL2 248 C6
Lyndon Ct PL12 242 D4
Lyndrick Rd PL3 248 E7
Lyneham Cross TQ13 123 D6
Lyngrove Ct TQ12 212 F6
Lynhayes EX13 87 C1
Lynher Dr PL12 242 F1
Lynher St PL5 243 D2
Lynhurst Ave EX31 154 C4
Lynmouth Ave TQ4 225 F2
Lynmouth Cl PL7 250 C7
Lynmouth Hill EX35 151 C5
Lynmouth St EX35 151 C6
Lynton & Exmoor Mus★
EX35 151 C5
Lynton & Lynmouth Cliff
Rlwy★ EX35 151 C6
Lynton CE Prim Sch
EX35 151 C5
Lynton Cross EX34 9 B6
Lynton YH★ EX35 151 C4
Lynway Lynton EX35 151 C4
Lynton EX35 151 C5
Lynway Ct TQ1 220 B6
Lynwood TQ12 206 F1
Lynwood Ave Exeter EX4 177 A5
Plymouth PL7 250 B6
Lyte La TQ7 144 C1
Lyte's Rd TQ5 230 D4
Lythe-Land Cross EX16 63 A6
Lytton Ho TQ2 220 A4

M

Mabel Pl TQ4 226 B5
Macadam Rd PL4 263 C1
Macandrew Wlk PL21 237 E6
Macaulay Cres PL5 244 C1
Macauley Cl EX14 166 E6
Macey St PL11 247 C3
Macey's Terr EX20 170 B6
Machine Cross TA22 33 F6
Mackenzie Pl PL5 243 C2
Mackenzie Way EX16 161 F4
Mackrell's Almshouses
TQ12 207 A2
Maclins Cl EX36 158 C4
Macwood Dr EX12 192 A6
Madagascar Cl EX8 202 E8
Maddacombe Cross
TQ12 212 C4
Maddacombe Rd TQ12 212 D4
Madden Rd PL1 247 F2
Maddock Cl PL7 251 A4
Maddock Dr PL7 251 B4
Maddocks Cross EX22 38 D2
Madeira Ct EX8 202 B5
Madeira Pl TQ2 220 A5
Madeira Rd PL1 263 A1
Madeira Villas EX8 202 A7
Madeira Wlk EX9 199 H2
Madeirs Villas 1 PL20 126 F5
Madford Cross EX15 67 C6
Madge Ct PL19 171 B6
Madge La PL19 171 B6
Madgeon La TA20 69 B8
Madges Cross
Aylesbeare EX5 99 E2
Rockbeare EX5 99 E6
Madicks Orch TQ9 227 F8
Madison Ave EX1 178 A6
Madison Cl EX5 173 F8
Madison Wharf EX8 201 E6
Madrepore Rd TQ1 220 B4
Maer Bay Ct EX8 202 B5
Maer La EX8 202 E5
Maer Rd EX8 202 C5
Maer Top Way EX31 155 A7
Maer Vale EX8 202 C6
Magdala Rd EX31 154 A3
Magdalen Bridge Ct 3
EX2 261 B2
Magdalen Court Sch
EX2 177 E5
Magdalen Gdns
Exeter EX2 177 E5
Plymouth PL7 250 F3
Magdalen Rd EX2 261 C2
Magdalen St EX1,EX2 261 B2
Magdalene Cl TQ9 223 C5
Magdalene Lawn 9
EX32 155 A6
Magdalene Rd TQ1 220 A6
Magnolia Ave
Exeter EX2 178 A3
Exmouth EX8 202 E8
Magnolia Cl
Barnstaple EX32 155 E4
3 Plymouth PL7 251 B5
Magnolia Ct EX16 161 E7
Magnolia Ho 10 EX8 202 A6
Magnolia Wlk 2 EX8 202 A6
Magpie Cres EX2 176 D3
Magpie Hill TQ13 130 C4
Maida Vale Terr PL4 248 F4
Maiden St 14 EX31 154 F5
Maidencombe Cross
TQ1 214 C6
Maidencombe Ho TQ1 214 C4
Maidenhayne La EX13 103 D6
Maidenhead Cross EX16 51 C2
Maidenway La TQ3 225 F8
Maidenway Rd TQ3 225 F8
Maidenwell Rd PL7 250 C5
Maidstone Pl PL5 243 E4
Main Ave TQ1 220 A8
Main Rd Exeter EX4 174 E2
Salcombe TQ8 259 C4
Main St TQ9 139 E1
Maine Cl EX39 156 D2
Maine Gdns PL2 247 F7
Mains Down La EX33 8 B4
Mainstone Ave PL4 263 C2
Maire Rd EX36 46 E5
Maitland Dr PL3 248 F8
Major Cross EX16 64 A2
Major Terr 2 EX12 192 A5
Major's Mdw EX20 170 C5
Majorfield Rd EX3 182 F5
Maker La PL10 253 B4
Maker Rd PL11 247 A2
Maker View PL3 248 B4
Malborough Gn TQ7 147 E6
Malborough Pk TQ7 147 F6
Malborough with South
Huish CE Prim Sch
TQ7 147 E6
Malden Cl EX10 188 B7
Malden La EX10 188 B8
Malden Rd EX10 188 C8
Malderek Ave TQ3 219 C1
Mallands Mdw TQ12 212 A7
Mallard Cl Plymouth PL7 250 F5
Torquay TQ2 213 D3
Mallard Rd EX2 178 E5
Mallet Rd PL21 237 A6
Malletts La EX32 155 A5
Mallingbrook Cross EX18 44 E1
Mallison Cl EX4 176 F8
Mallock Rd TQ2 219 E5
Mallocks Cl EX10 100 D2
Mallow Ct EX15 162 D5
Malmesbury Cl PL2 248 B8
Malory Cl PL5 244 D2
Malson La EX16 47 B4
Malston Cross TQ7 144 D4
Malt Field EX8 195 F5
Malt Mill TQ9 223 B6
Malthouse The
Noss Mayo PL8 141 A7
5 Totnes TQ9 223 D5
Malting Ct 4 EX7 204 E6
Maltings The
21 Appledore EX39 15 A1
Black Torrington EX21 74 A8
Crediton EX17 165 D5
East Prawle TQ7 149 B5
Exeter EX2 177 F5
Malvern Gdns EX2 178 A4
Malvern Rd EX10 188 B6
Malvern Way EX39 156 D2
Malvernleigh TQ1 220 B8
Mambury Cross EX22 39 D3
Mamhead Rd Exeter EX2 178 C4
Kenton EX6 194 C2
Mamhead View EX8 201 E6
Manadon Cl PL5 244 E1
Manadon Dr PL5 244 E1
Manadon Hill PL5,PL6 244 E1
Manadon Vale Prim Sch
PL5 248 E8
Manaton Cl EX2 181 C8
Manaton Ct EX2 181 C8
Manaton Tor Rd TQ3 218 F1
Manby Gdns PL5 243 F5
Manchester Rd EX8 201 F6
Manchester St EX8 201 F6
Mandrake Cl EX2 177 B1
Mandrake Rd EX2 177 A1
Manifold Gdns PL3 249 D5
Manitoba Gdns EX15 163 B3
Manley Cl 1 EX5 99 E8
Manleys La EX14 67 B2
Manna Ash Ct EX2 261 C1
Mannacott La EX31 4 C4
Mannacott Lane Head
EX31 4 C4
Mannamead Ave PL3 248 F5
Mannamead Rd PL3 248 F6
Manning Ave EX15 163 A2
Mannings Mdw TQ13 180 D7
Mannings Way EX31 154 F7
Manor Ave
Lyme Regis DT7 260 D4
Paignton TQ3 226 C8
Manor Bend TQ5 229 C5
Manor Bourne Rd
Down Thomas PL9 255 C1
Heybrook Bay PL9 140 A8
Manor Cl
Abbotskerswell TQ12 212 A7
Awliscombe EX14 85 C3
Barnstaple EX31 154 C3
Dawlish EX7 204 D6
Fremington EX31 153 E6
Ivybridge PL21 237 C5
Kentisbeare EX15 66 A3
Kingskerswell TQ12 213 A3
Sidmouth EX10 188 A5
Tavistock PL19 171 A6
Uffculme EX15 66 B8
Wrafton EX33 152 E4
1 Seaton EX12 192 A5
Manor Cotts
15 Newton Abbot TQ12 207 B3
Rackenford EX16 47 C6
Manor Court Barns TQ7 147 F8
Manor Cres
Honiton EX14 166 C4
Paignton TQ3 226 C8
Manor Ct Galmpton TQ5 229 A5
Kingskerswell TQ12 213 A3
Landkey EX32 17 B2
Seaton EX12 192 A5
8 South Brent TQ10 134 F3
Stoke Fleming TQ6 146 B7
Torquay TQ2 219 F6
Manor Dr Chagford TQ13 110 F6
Ivybridge PL21 237 C5
Kingskerswell TQ12 213 A3
Manor Farm PL20 127 B3
Manor Farm Cl TA20 88 C8
Manor Farm Mews EX5 99 E4
Manor Gdn TQ1 220 E3
Manor Gdns
Abbotskerswell TQ12 212 B6
Horrabridge PL20 126 E4
Kingskerswell TQ12 213 A3
Paignton TQ3 226 C8
Plymouth PL1 262 B2
Seaton EX12 192 B5
Manor Gn EX14 68 C2
Manor Ho TQ1 220 E3
Manor Ho The TQ9 223 C6
Manor La PL3 249 D5
Manor Mead TQ12 131 D7
Manor Mill Rd EX33 8 D1
Manor Park Cl PL7 250 F5
Manor Park Dr PL7 251 A4
Manor Pk Ashwater EX21 90 E6
Barnstaple EX31 154 C3
Bradworthy EX22 53 E8
Clyst St Mary EX5 179 A3
Dousland PL20 127 B3
Manor Pk *continued*
Kingsbridge TQ7 258 D6
Saltash PL12 242 D2
Manor Prim Sch PL21 237 C5
Manor Rd
Abbotskerswell TQ12 212 B7
Bishopsteignton TQ14 208 F8
Chagford TQ13 110 F6
Exeter EX4 177 A5
Landkey EX32 17 B2
Newton Abbot TQ12 206 F3
Paignton TQ3 226 C8
Plymouth PL9 255 E8
Seaton EX12 192 A5
Sidmouth EX10 188 A3
Tavistock PL19 171 B6
Torquay TQ1 220 C8
Manor St Dittisham TQ6 228 D2
Plymouth PL1 262 A3
Manor Terr Brixham TQ5 230 C5
Paignton TQ3 226 A5
Manor Vale Rd TQ5 229 C5
Manor View TQ12 207 A3
Manor Way
Ivybridge PL21 237 C5
Totnes TQ9 223 C6
Manorglade Ct 1 TQ1 220 D5
Mansbridge Rd TQ9 223 E5
Manscombe Cl TQ2 219 D3
Manscombe Rd TQ2 219 D3
Mansfield Rd EX4 177 E8
Mansfield Terr EX9 198 B2
Mansion House St TQ6 233 F3
Mansion King Edward VI Com
Coll The TQ9 223 C5
Mansion Terr 5 EX34 3 A3
Manston Cl PL5 243 E5
Manston Ct TQ1 220 C2
Manston Rd EX1 177 E7
Manston Terr EX2 177 E5
Manstone Ave EX10 188 A7
Manstone Cl EX10 188 B7
Manstone La EX10 188 B7
Manstone Mead EX10 188 B8
Manstone Workshops
EX10 188 B7
Manstree Cross EX2 114 A6
Manstree Rd EX2 114 B6
Manstree Terr EX2 114 C6
Mantle Gdns PL5 247 D8
Mantle St TA21 160 C5
Maple Ave PL11 247 A3
Maple Cl Brixham TQ5 230 A2
10 Chudleigh Knighton
TQ13 123 C4
7 Honiton EX14 85 C2
Kingsteignton TQ12 207 E6
Plymouth PL6 245 E6
Seaton EX12 192 A7
Tavistock PL19 171 C3
Willand EX15 162 C4
Maple Dr EX8 196 D3
Maple Gr
Barnstaple EX31 154 C3
Plymouth, Mutley PL4 248 D4
Plymouth, Plympton PL7 250 B5
Tiverton EX16 161 D4
Maple Rd Brixham TQ5 230 A2
Broadclyst EX5 175 D6
Exeter EX4 177 A5
Maple Way PL6 245 E7
Maple Wlk TQ2 219 C8
Mapledene Cl TQ9 227 F8
Maples Ct 6 EX32 154 F6
Mapleton Cl TQ12 206 F4
Marber Cross TQ7 149 A8
Marchant's Cross PL20 127 C1
Marchant's Way PL20 127 C2
Marcom Cl EX8 196 D3
Marcombe Rd TQ2 219 E5
Marcus Rd
Dunkeswell EX14 67 B2
Exmouth EX8 196 D1
Marder's Bequest DT7 260 E3
Mardle Way TQ11 236 B5
Mardon Cl PL6 245 D4
Mardon Cross EX6 112 E2
Mardon Hill EX4 173 B1
Mare Hill EX17 61 C5
Mare La Barnstaple EX31 9 B1
Beer EX12 191 B5
Marepark Cross TQ7 144 D3
Marepark Gate EX20 77 C7
Marett Rd PL5 243 F3
Margaret Cl
East Ogwell TQ12 206 F1
Kingsteignton TQ12 207 E7
Margaret Gdns TQ12 207 F2
Margaret Pk PL3 248 E8
Margaret Rd
East Ogwell TQ12 206 F1
Exeter EX4 173 E1
Kingsteignton TQ12 207 E7
Margaret St 4 EX8 202 A6
Margrove Terr 9 EX32 154 F6
Marguerite Cl TQ12 206 F4
Marguerite Rd EX16 161 F6
Marguerite Way TQ12 213 A4
Marhamchurch CE Prim Sch
EX23 70 A6
Mariansleigh Cross EX36 30 E1
Marina Cl TQ5 230 E5
Marina Ct Brixham TQ5 230 F6
Exmouth EX8 202 B5
Paignton TQ4 226 C5
23 Teignmouth TQ14 210 C4
Marina Dr TQ5 230 E5
Marina Rd Brixham TQ5 230 E4
Marina Rd *continued*
Plymouth PL5 243 F3
Marina Terr 7 PL4 248 F4
Marina Way 6 EX16 64 D7
Marine Cres EX12 192 A4
Marine Ct
Budleigh Salterton EX9 199 H2
Instow EX39 15 B1
Torpoint PL11 247 B2
Marine Dr
Bigbury-on-Sea TQ7 142 E3
Heybrook Bay PL9 140 A7
Paignton TQ3 226 C7
Torpoint PL11 247 B2
Woolacombe EX33,EX34 7 F5
Marine Gdns TQ3 226 C8
Marine Par
Appledore EX39 15 A1
Budleigh Salterton EX9 199 H2
Dawlish EX7 204 E5
Instow EX39 15 B1
Lyme Regis DT7 260 D2
Paignton TQ3 226 D8
Teignmouth TQ14 210 B3
Marine Pk TQ3 226 C7
Marine Pl
Ilfracombe EX34 150 B6
Seaton EX12 192 A4
Marine Rd PL9 255 B7
Marine Terr 16 TQ14 210 B4
Marine Way EX8 202 A8
Mariner's Way 33 EX39 15 A1
Mariners Ct
7 Brixham TQ5 230 D5
13 Dawlish EX7 204 E6
Mariners Way TQ3 218 F1
Marino The EX10 187 F3
Marions Way EX8 196 D2
Marist Way EX32 155 C2
Maristow Ave
Exmouth EX8 196 B2
Plymouth PL2 247 F5
Maristow Cl PL6 244 F5
Marjery Cross PL21 237 A2
Marjorie Kelly Way
PL21 237 D4
Marjory Wlk PL8 257 E3
Mark Twain Ho 1 EX4 178 C8
Mark's Cross EX6 176 B2
Marker Way EX14 166 C4
Markers EX15 66 A7
Markers Pk EX14 84 C4
Markers Rd EX15 66 A7
Market Ave PL1 262 B3
Market Cl
4 Bampton EX16 34 B1
Brushford TA22 33 E4
Buckfastleigh TQ11 236 B5
Plymouth PL1 248 A1
Market Pl Bideford EX39 157 A2
Burlescombe EX16 51 B3
Colyton EX24 103 A5
Sidmouth EX10 188 B3
Market Rd Plymouth PL7 250 D5
Tavistock PL19 171 C5
Market Sq
Axminster EX13 167 D6
Dartmouth TQ6 233 F3
Plymouth PL1 262 C3
2 Ilfracombe EX34 150 B6
Market St
2 Appledore EX39 15 A1
5 Barnstaple EX31 154 F5
8 Brixham TQ5 230 C5
Buckfastleigh TQ11 236 B5
Cawsand PL10 253 A2
Crediton EX17 165 C5
Dartmouth TQ6 233 F3
Exeter EX1,EX4 261 A2
Exmouth EX8 202 A6
Hatherleigh EX20 75 C7
Ilfracombe EX34 150 B6
Lynton EX35 151 C5
Newton Abbot TQ12 207 B3
North Tawton EX20 77 C4
Okehampton EX20 170 B5
Plymouth PL1 248 A1
Salcombe TQ8 259 E5
South Molton EX36 158 C4
Tavistock PL19 171 C5
Torquay TQ1 220 B5
Yealmpton PL8 257 F4
Market Way
7 Chudleigh TQ13 123 E6
Plymouth PL1 262 C3
Market Wlk 7 TQ12 207 B3
Markham Cross EX2 114 B8
Markham La Exeter EX2 181 B7
Ide EX2 114 C8
Markwood Pl EX14 166 D6
Marl Pk
Harbertonford TQ9 139 C7
Holne TQ13 130 A3
Marland Cross PL8 136 B1
Marland Sch EX38 56 B8
Marland Terr EX39 156 F1
Marlborough Ave TQ1 220 D5
Marlborough Cl
Exmouth EX8 196 E2
Ilfracombe EX34 150 B5
Musbury EX13 103 D5
Saltash PL12 242 F1
Marlborough Cross
EX5 179 D6

Marlborough Ct
Bideford EX39 .157 A3
Exeter, Alphington EX2 .181 C8
Exeter, Heavitree EX2 .177 E5
Marlborough Pk 7
EX34 .150 B5
Marlborough Pl TQ12 .207 A4
Marlborough Prim Sch
PL1 .247 E2
Marlborough Rd
Exeter EX2 .261 C2
Ilfracombe EX34 .150 C5
Musbury EX13 .103 D5
Plymouth PL4 .263 A4
Marlborough Row PL1 .247 E2
Marlborough St PL1 .247 E2
Marlborough Terr TQ13 .180 C7
Marlborough Way EX34 150 C4
Marlcombe Cross EX14 .85 A6
Marldon Ave TQ3 .226 A6
Marldon CE Prim Sch
TQ3 .218 D3
Marldon Cl PL5 .244 B3
Marldon Cross TQ3 .218 D2
Marldon Cross Hill TQ3 218 D3
Marldon Gr TQ3 .218 D3
Marldon La TQ3 .218 B4
Marldon Rd
Paignton TQ3 .225 F8
Torquay TQ2 .219 B7
Marldon Way TQ3 .218 E2
Marlen Ct EX39 .25 F4
Marles Cl EX14 .85 B4
Marles The EX8 .196 C2
Marley EX8 .196 C4
Marley Dr EX8 .196 D5
Marley Head TQ10 .135 C3
Marley Rd EX8 .196 C3
Marlow Cres PL16 .106 D1
Marlow Gdns PL9 .255 F5
Marlowe Cl TQ2 .219 D7
Marlpit Cl EX12 .191 F7
Marlpit Cross EX14 .87 A6
Marlpit La EX12 .192 A5
Marlpits La EX14 .166 C5
Marlpool Hill EX8 .202 B7
Marmora Terr EX12 .191 D5
Marnham Rd TQ1 .220 B7
Marpool Cres EX8 .202 C8
Marpool Hill EX8 .202 B7
Marpool Prim Sch EX8 .202 C8
Marridge Cross PL21 .137 F5
Marrowbone Slip PL4 .263 B2
Marryat Gdns PL5 .244 E1
Mars Hill Way EX35 .151 C5
Marsh Barton La EX5 .172 D8
Marsh Barton Rd EX2 .177 B3
Marsh Barton Trad Est
EX2 .177 C2
Marsh Cl PL6 .249 F6
Marsh Cross EX15 .83 E4
Marsh Dro EX13 .87 B2
Marsh End EX17 .165 F5
Marsh Green La EX5 .99 E5
Marsh Green Rd E EX2 .177 C2
Marsh Green Rd N EX2 .177 C2
Marsh Green Rd W EX2 177 C2
Marsh Hill Dulverton TA22 .33 C8
Tiverton EX16 .63 A4
Marsh La Bow EX17 .78 B5
Calstock PL18 .125 D3
Chudleigh TQ13 .123 F8
Clyst St George EX3 .183 B6
Crediton EX17 .165 E5
Instow EX39 .15 B1
Newton St Cyres EX5 .98 F8
North Molton EX36 .30 E6
Seaton EX12 .192 B7
South Molton EX36 .158 F7
Tiverton EX16 .63 A4
West Charleton TQ7 .144 C1
Marsh La Cross TQ13 .123 F8
Marsh Mill Ct EX5 .172 D7
Marsh Mills PL6 .249 F7
Marsh Mills Pk PL6 .249 F6
Marsh Mills Ret Pk PL6 249 E7
Marsh Rd Crediton EX17 .165 E5
Newton Abbot TQ12 .207 C3
Newton Abbot TQ12 .207 C4
Seaton EX12 .192 B5
Marshall Cl
Tavistock PL19 .171 D2
Tiverton EX16 .161 F3
Marshall Dr PL21 .237 D4
Marshall Rd
Plymouth PL7 .250 A5
Tavistock PL19 .171 D2
Marshalls Field PL21 .237 E5
Marshalls Mead EX19 .42 D1
Marshbridge Cross TA22 .33 C7
Marshclose Hill TA22 .21 E2
Marston Cl EX7 .204 F7
Mart The EX20 .170 B5
Martin La
Plymouth, Barbican PL4 .263 A2
Plymouth, Millbay PL1 .262 B2
Martin Rd EX32 .155 B5
Martin St PL1 .262 B2
Martin's La EX1,EX4 .261 B3
Martinhoe Cross EX31 .4 C3
Martins Bldgs 4 TA21 .160 D5
Martins Cl
Great Torrington EX38 .159 F5
Wellington TA21 .160 D5
Martins Rd EX8 .196 E2
Martlesham Pl PL5 .243 F4
Marwell Cross TQ7 .142 E6
Marwood Cross EX5 .99 B3
Marwood Ct EX38 .159 D5
Marwood La EX5 .99 C3
Marwood Prim Sch EX31 .9 D1
Marwood's Cross
TQ10 .134 D1
Mary Arches St EX4 .261 A3
Mary Cross PL21 .137 C3
Mary Dean Ave PL5 .244 C7
Mary Dean Cl PL5 .244 C7
Mary Dean's CE Prim Sch
PL5 .244 C7
Mary La 10 EX16 .34 B1
Mary Newman's Cottage*
PL12 .243 A2
Mary Rose Ho TQ1 .220 D7
Mary Seacole Rd PL1 .262 A3
Mary St TQ13 .180 D8
Mary Tavy Sch PL19 .117 E6
Maryfield Ave EX4 .177 D8
Maryland Gdns PL2 .247 F7
Marypole Rd EX4 .173 F1
Marypole Wlk EX4 .173 F1
Marythorne Rd 15 PL20 .125 E1
Masefield Ave EX31 .154 F7
Masefield Gdns PL5 .244 B1
Masefield Rd EX4 .178 C8
Masey Rd EX8 .202 D8
Mashford Ave TQ6 .233 C4
Masons Row PL18 .125 C6
Masterman Rd PL2 .247 F4
Matford Ave EX2 .177 E4
Matford La EX2 .261 C1
Matford Mews EX2 .181 D7
Matford Park Rd EX2 .181 D8
Matford Rd EX2 .177 E4
Mathews Cl EX14 .166 B4
Mathill Cl TQ5 .230 B3
Mathill Rd TQ5 .230 B3
Maton Cl PL21 .237 D4
Matthew's Ct EX15 .163 C3
Matthews Cross EX15 .66 B1
Matthews Ct EX4 .174 D2
Mattiscombe Cross TQ7 145 B1
Mattys Cross EX14 .68 A3
Maudlin Dr TQ14 .210 B8
Maudlin Rd TQ9 .223 C5
Maudlins La PL19 .171 A5
Maunder's Hill EX9 .198 E7
Maunsell Cl PL2 .247 F7
Maurice Ct PL7 .250 F4
Mawes Ct PL18 .125 A5
Maxstoke Ct 3 TQ1 .220 D5
Maxwell Rd PL4 .255 B8
May Terr Plymouth PL4 .263 B3
Sidmouth EX10 .188 B4
Maybank Rd PL4 .263 C3
Maybrook Dr PL12 .242 D2
Mayers Way PL9 .255 D6
Mayfair EX16 .64 E8
Mayfair Cres PL6 .245 B1
Mayfair Rd TQ12 .211 D2
Mayfield PL21 .237 A4
Mayfield Cres TQ12 .206 F3
Mayfield Dr EX8 .202 D6
Mayfield Rd
Exeter, Pinhoe EX4 .174 E1
Exeter, Wonford EX2 .178 A5
Mayfield Sch TQ3 .226 C7
Mayflower Ave
Exeter EX4 .173 D2
Newton Abbot TQ12 .207 F2
Mayflower Cl
18 Bere Alston PL20 .125 E1
Chittlehampton EX37 .28 F4
Dartmouth TQ6 .233 D4
Dawlish EX7 .204 E6
Plymouth PL9 .255 F7
Mayflower Ct TQ6 .233 F4
Mayflower Dr
6 Brixham TQ5 .230 C3
Plymouth PL2 .248 B5
Mayflower St PL1 .262 C3
Maynard Pk PL20 .125 E1
Maynard Sch for Girls
EX1 .261 C3
Maynarde Cl PL7 .251 B5
Mayne Cl EX20 .75 B7
Mayor's Ave TQ6 .233 F4
Maytree Cl EX21 .73 D3
Mazard Tree Hill
Bishops Nympton EX36 .31 C1
South Molton EX36 .46 C8
Mazzard Cl 9 EX32 .17 B2
Mead Cl Cullompton EX15 163 B2
Ivybridge PL21 .237 A6
Paignton TQ3 .226 C7
Mead Cnr EX39 .37 A4
Mead Cotts EX8 .202 F7
Mead Cross TQ13 .131 B6
Mead Dr TQ7 .143 A1
Mead La Paignton TQ3 .226 C7
Thurlestone TQ7 .143 A1
Mead Park Cl EX31 .16 A3
Mead Pk EX31 .16 A3
Mead Rd TQ2 .219 D2
Mead The Plymouth PL7 .250 D7
Silverton EX5 .82 B5
Mead View Rd EX14 .166 C5
Mead Way EX12 .192 A6
Meadcombe Rd TQ7 .143 A1
Meadfoot TQ7 .143 A1
Meadfoot Cl TQ1 .220 F4
Meadfoot Ct TQ1 .220 C3
Meadfoot Grange TQ1 .220 C3
Meadfoot La TQ1 .220 C3
Meadfoot Rd TQ1 .220 C3
Meadfoot Sea Rd TQ1 .220 D3
Meadfoot Terr PL4 .248 F5
Meadhurst Ct EX10 .188 A3
Meadow Ave EX12 .192 A6
Meadow Bank EX13 .87 D1
Meadow Brook PL19 .171 A4
Meadow Bsns Pk EX17 .165 F5
Meadow Cl
Bratton Fleming EX31 .18 A8
Budleigh Salterton EX9 .197 F1
Clyst St Mary EX5 .179 E3
Harberton TQ9 .222 D2
Ilfracombe EX34 .150 B4
Kingskerswell TQ12 .212 F6
Landkey EX32 .17 C1
Lympstone EX8 .195 F5
Newton Ferrers PL8 .141 A7
Ottery St Mary EX11 .169 E4
Plymouth PL7 .251 D4
Saltash PL12 .242 F3
Totnes TQ9 .223 F5
Meadow Cotts TQ6 .228 C2
Meadow Cres EX8 .203 A6
Meadow Ct Barns TQ7 .145 B1
Meadow Dr Brixton PL8 .257 A4
Newton Poppleford EX10 .186 F8
Saltash PL12 .242 D4
Meadow Gdns EX17 .165 D5
Meadow Halt TQ12 .207 A1
Meadow La Croyde EX33 .7 E2
Cullompton EX15 .163 C2
Instow EX39 .15 B1
Meadow Lea EX5 .82 B6
Meadow Park Dr EX37 .43 F3
Meadow Pk
Barnstaple EX31 .154 B2
Bideford EX39 .25 D4
Brixham TQ5 .230 B5
Dawlish EX7 .204 C7
Marldon TQ3 .218 D3
Molland EX36 .31 E7
Plymouth PL9 .255 C5
South Molton EX36 .158 C3
Willand EX15 .162 C4
Meadow Rd
Barnstaple EX31 .154 E7
Budleigh Salterton EX9 .197 F1
Seaton EX12 .192 A5
Torquay TQ2 .219 E3
Meadow Rise
Dawlish EX7 .204 C7
Plymouth PL7 .251 A4
Spreyton EX17 .96 A7
Teignmouth TQ14 .124 E1
Meadow St EX8 .202 A7
Meadow Vale EX20 .57 A7
Meadow View
2 Bampton EX16 .34 B1
Bishops Nympton EX36 .30 F2
East Ogwell TQ12 .206 F1
Hartland EX39 .22 E3
Holsworthy EX22 .164 C6
Lympstone EX8 .195 F5
Rackenford EX16 .47 D5
Uffculme EX15 .66 A7
Meadow View Cl EX10 .188 C5
Meadow View Rd PL7 .250 D5
Meadow Way
Colaton Raleigh EX10 .186 D3
Exeter EX2 .177 F5
Plymouth PL7 .250 D7
Meadowbrook Cl EX4 .176 E8
Meadowcroft Dr TQ12 .123 E1
Meadowfield Pl PL7 .251 B3
Meadowlands
Newton St Cyres EX5 .98 F8
Plymouth PL6 .245 D7
Meadows Cres EX14 .166 C5
Meadows The
Beer EX12 .191 D5
Kingsteignton TQ12 .207 F6
St Dominick PL12 .125 A2
Torpoint PL11 .246 E4
Yeoford EX17 .79 C2
Meadowside Ashford EX31 16 B6
Chillington TQ7 .145 A1
Newton Abbot TQ12 .207 A3
Plymouth PL9 .255 F7
Rockwell Green TA21 .160 B5
Meadowside Rd EX17 .80 B5
Meadowstone Cl EX38 .40 F5
Meadowsweet La 3
EX31 .154 B3
Meadowsweet Pk PL12 .242 C2
Meadowview Rd EX8 .196 E2
Meadowville Rd EX39 .157 A3
Meadway
Newton Abbot TQ12 .212 D8
Saltash PL12 .242 E1
Sidmouth EX10 .188 B6
Meadwood TQ1 .220 D3
Mear Top EX31 .154 F7
Measbury Moor Cross
EX18 .45 C5
Meatherel Cl PL21 .237 B4
Meavy Ave Plymouth PL5 .244 E2
Torquay TQ2 .219 B7
Meavy Bourne PL20 .127 A2
Meavy CE Prim Sch
PL20 .127 C2
Meavy La PL20 .127 A2
Meavy Villas PL20 .127 A2
Meavy Way Plymouth PL5 244 E2
Tavistock PL19 .171 D5
Medard Ho 13 EX32 .155 A5
Meddon Cross
Edistone EX39 .37 F5
Meddon Cross *continued*
Welcombe EX39 .37 F4
Meddon St EX39 .157 A1
Mede The Exeter EX4 .178 B8
Topsham EX3 .182 E5
Medland Cres PL6 .244 D6
Medland Cross EX6 .97 C6
Medland La EX6 .97 B6
Medway Pl PL3 .249 D6
Medway Rd TQ2 .214 B2
Meeches The EX16 .48 F2
Meeks Row PL18 .125 D6
Meerhay La DT6 .104 F6
Meetford Cross EX6 .97 F7
Meethe Gate Cross EX36 29 D2
Meethe Hill EX36 .29 D1
Meeting La EX8 .195 E6
Meeting St
Appledore EX39 .15 A1
Exmouth EX8 .202 A7
Melbourne Cotts PL1 .262 B3
Melbourne Ct
10 Exeter EX2 .261 B2
Torquay TQ1 .220 A6
Melbourne Gn 2 PL1 .262 B3
Melbourne Pl Exeter EX2 261 B2
Plymouth PL1 .262 B4
Melbourne St Exeter EX2 261 B2
Plymouth PL1 .262 B3
Tiverton EX16 .161 B4
Melbury Rd EX39 .39 E8
Melcot Cl TQ12 .207 E7
Meldon La EX20 .93 E3
Meldon Rd TQ13 .111 A6
Meldrum Cl EX7 .204 E6
Melhuish Cl EX16 .46 E1
Mellons Cl TQ12 .206 D4
Mellons Wlk TQ12 .206 D4
Mellows Mdw TQ12 .206 F3
Melrose Ave PL2 .248 C8
Melville La TQ1 .220 B4
Melville Pl 1 PL2 .248 A5
Melville Rd PL2 .248 A5
Melville St TQ1 .220 B4
Membury Cl EX1 .178 D6
Membury Com Sch EX13 87 D6
Membury Rd EX13 .87 E3
Memory Cross TQ13 .215 E8
Mena Park Cl
Paignton TQ4 .225 F2
Plymouth PL9 .256 B7
Mena Park Rd PL9 .256 B7
Mendip Rd TQ2 .219 D3
Merafield Cl PL7 .250 B5
Merafield Dr PL7 .250 C4
Merafield Farm Cotts
PL7 .250 B4
Merafield Rd PL7 .250 B4
Merafield Rise PL7 .250 C4
Mercer Ct EX2 .178 A2
Merchant's Gdn TQ7 .143 A1
Merchants Cnr EX17 .61 C1
Merchants House (Mus)*
PL1 .262 C2
Mere La 15 TQ14 .210 C5
Meredith Rd PL2 .248 C6
Meresyke EX8 .202 C6
Meriden TQ14 .210 C7
Meridian Ho PL4 .263 A3
Meridian Pl EX34 .150 B6
Merivale Cl TQ14 .210 C7
Merley Rd EX39 .156 B7
Merlin Bsns Pk EX5 .99 A4
Merlin Cl PL6 .245 E8
Merlin Cres EX4 .174 A1
Merlin Way TQ2 .213 D2
Mermaid Ct 6 EX1 .261 A2
Mermaid Yd EX1 .261 A2
Merrifield Cross
Bridgerule EX22 .70 E4
Slapton TQ7 .145 C6
Merrifield Rd TQ11 .130 C1
Merrion Ave EX8 .202 D6
Merritt Flats 4 TQ3 .226 A5
Merritt Rd TQ3 .226 A5
Merrivale Cl TQ2 .214 B4
Merrivale Rd Exeter EX4 .176 F4
Okehampton EX20 .170 E6
Plymouth, Ham PL2 .248 B7
Plymouth, Honicknowle
PL5 .244 B3
Merrivale View Rd PL20 127 B3
Merrow Down Dr EX12 .191 F8
Merrydale Cres EX31 .27 D6
Merryfield La EX6 .95 F2
Merryfield Rd EX39 .157 C1
Merryland Cl TQ3 .219 B2
Merryland Gdns TQ3 .219 B2
Merrylees Dr EX32 .155 C3
Merrymeet
Tedburn St Mary EX17 .97 F8
Whitestone EX4 .98 E4
Merryside Villas EX16 .61 E8
Merrythorn Rd EX31 .153 D5
Merrywood TQ12 .206 F1
Mersey Cl PL3 .249 D6
Meshaw Cross Rds EX36 .46 A5
Meshaw Moor Cross
EX36 .46 A5
Meshaw Rectory Cross
EX36 .46 A5
Metcombe Cross EX31 .9 C2
Metcombe La EX31 .9 B1
Metcombe Rise EX11 .100 C2
Metcombe Vale EX11 .100 C2
Meteor Wlk 2 EX32 .155 B5
Metherell Ave TQ5 .230 D3
Metherell Avenue Ind Est
TQ5 .230 C3
Metherell Cross EX21 .91 F8
Metherell Rd EX39 .156 F1
Metley Cross TQ12 .131 E5
Mettaford Cross EX39 .22 F3
Mews Ct 20 EX7 .204 E6
Mews Gdns TQ6 .233 F3
Mews The Bittaford PL21 .137 C8
Dawlish EX7 .204 E6
Exmouth EX8 .196 F3
Plymouth, Devonport PL1 .248 A3
Plymouth, Stonehouse PL1 262 A3
7 Teignmouth TQ14 .210 B4
Mewstone Ave PL9 .140 D8
Meyrick Rd TQ1 .220 C7
Mezidon-Canon Ave
EX14 .166 D5
Michael Rd PL3 .249 A5
Michelcombe La TQ13 .130 A4
Michigan Way
Exeter EX4 .173 C2
Plymouth PL3 .249 C6
Mid Churchway PL9 .256 A7
Middle Blagdon La TQ3 225 B6
Middle Budleigh Mdw
TQ12 .206 F3
Middle Combe Dr EX31 .154 A3
Middle Down Cl PL9 .256 A5
Middle Green Rd TA21 .160 E3
Middle Leigh PL8 .140 F7
Middle Lincombe Rd
TQ1 .220 D3
Middle Mill La EX15 .163 C3
Middle Park Terr TQ7 .143 B1
Middle Ramshill La TQ3 225 C7
Middle Rd PL9 .140 D8
Middle St Brixham TQ5 .230 C5
East Budleigh EX9 .198 B6
Teignmouth TQ14 .210 A3
Middle Warberry Rd
TQ1 .220 D5
Middle Westerland Cross
TQ3 .218 D1
Middleborough La EX33 .7 D3
Middlecombe La PL8 .140 F6
Middlecott Cross
Holemoor EX22 .73 B8
Virginstow EX21 .90 E4
Middlecott Hill EX32 .18 D3
Middlecott La EX17 .60 F2
Middlefield Rd PL6 .244 D6
Middlefield Cl PL12 .242 B2
Middlemead Rd EX16 .161 D5
Middlemoor Cross EX37 .43 C3
Middlemoor Police Training
Coll EX2 .178 D5
Middleton Rd EX39 .156 F3
Middleton Wlk PL5 .243 D4
Middletown La EX9 .198 B6
Middlewood Hill EX6 .201 A5
Midella Rd PL20 .127 A2
Midlands Cvn Pk EX31 .154 A8
Midvale Rd TQ4 .226 B5
Midway Exmouth EX8 .202 E8
Kingskerswell TQ12 .212 F6
Midway Cl EX2 .177 A1
Midway Terr EX2 .177 A1
Miers Cl PL5 .247 C8
Miglo Ind Est TQ4 .225 E3
Milber Com Inf Sch
TQ12 .207 F3
Milber Com Jun Sch
TQ12 .207 F3
Milber La TQ12 .213 B6
Milber Trad Est TQ12 .208 A1
Milbury Cl EX6 .182 B4
Milbury La EX6 .182 B4
Mildmay Cl EX4 .176 F7
Mildmay St PL4 .263 A4
Mile End Rd TQ12 .206 E5
Mile Gdns EX4 .173 F2
Mile La EX4 .174 A1
Milehouse Rd PL2 .248 A5
Miles Mitchell Ave PL6 .245 A1
Miles Mitchell Village
PL6 .245 A1
Milestone Cross TQ13 .123 F8
Milestone La TQ13 .123 F8
Milford Ave EX10 .188 B4
Milford Cl TQ14 .210 A5
Milford Cotts EX6 .181 B2
Milford Cross EX39 .22 B1
Milford La PL5 .244 B5
Milford Rd EX10 .188 B4
Military Rd
Millbrook PL10 .252 C3
Plymouth PL3 .249 E6
Rame PL10 .140 J2
Milizac Cl PL8 .257 E4
Milk Hill EX5 .81 D7
Milkaway La EX33 .7 E1
Milky Way Adventure Pk*
EX39 .23 E1
Mill Bottom La TQ12 .209 A3
Mill Bridge PL1 .262 A3
Mill Cl Lee Mill PL21 .136 D6
Newton Abbot TQ12 .206 F4
Mill Cotts
Okehampton EX20 .170 B5
Stoke Canon EX5 .173 F7
Mill Cres TQ6 .233 D4
Mill Cross
Bickington TQ12 .131 F7
Halwill EX21 .73 C1
Harberton TQ9 .222 C2
Rattery TQ10 .135 D4
Mill Dr EX2 .177 F1

Mill End 1 TQ12 123 F1
Mill Ford Sch PL5 243 F4
Mill Gn DT7 260 E3
Mill Head EX34 150 C6
Mill Hill Barnstaple EX31 16 A3
Fremington EX31 153 F5
Stoke Gabriel TQ9 227 F7
Witheridge EX16 61 F7
Mill Hill Ct TQ9 227 F7
Mill La Alfington EX11 84 F1
Aveton Gifford TQ7 143 C6
Axminster EX13 88 F3
Barnstaple EX31 154 E6
Berrynarbor EX34 2 D4
Bow EX17 78 B4
Branscombe EX12 190 D4
Bratton Fleming EX31 11 E3
Brayford EX32 18 F6
Brixham TQ5 230 A1
Burrington EX37 44 A2
Charmouth DT6 104 F6
Cheriton Fitzpaine EX17 62 E2
Clyst Honiton EX1 175 C1
Croyde EX33 7 E2
East Buckland EX32 18 E2
East Ogwell TQ12 206 D1
Exeter EX2 177 B1
Exton EX3 183 D2
Galmpton TQ5 229 A4
George Nympton EX36 30 A1
Loddiswell TQ7 138 C7
Lyme Regis DT7 260 E3
Newton Poppleford EX10 186 F6
North Tawton EX20 77 B4
North Whilborough TQ12 212 D2
North Whilborough TQ2 212 D1
Offwell EX14 86 B1
3 Paignton TQ3 226 B7
Sandford EX17 80 B5
Shirwell EX31 17 F8
South Molton EX36 45 F7
Stockland EX13 87 B7
Stoke Fleming TQ6 146 A7
Teignmouth TQ14 209 D7
Torpoint PL11 247 A2
Torquay TQ2 219 F5
Totnes TQ9 223 D5
Uplyme DT7 260 C5
Wambrook TA20 69 F2
Woolacombe EX34 7 F6
Wrafton EX33 152 F4
ill Lane Cotts EX20 77 B4
ill Leat Cotts EX17 78 B4
ill Mdw
9 Combe Martin EX34 3 A3
Ivybridge PL21 237 D5
ill Park Ind Est EX5 184 E8
ill Path TQ13 130 F4
ill Pk 2 TQ12 123 E1
ill Rd Barnstaple EX31 154 E5
Bradworthy EX22 38 E1
Exeter EX2 177 F1
Fremington EX31 153 E5
High Bickington EX37 43 B7
Landkey EX32 17 B1
Millbrook PL10 253 A5
Okehampton EX20 170 B4
Totnes TQ9 222 E8
ill Rise EX14 85 F8
ill St Bideford EX39 157 A2
Chagford TQ13 110 F6
Crediton EX17 165 D5
Great Torrington EX38 159 C4
Honiton EX14 166 B5
Kingsbridge TQ7 258 C5
Ottery St Mary EX11 169 C3
Sidmouth EX10 188 B4
South Molton EX36 158 D4
Uffculme EX15 66 B7
ill Steep Molland EX36 31 C8
Twitchen EX36 20 C1
ill Stream Ct EX11 169 D3
ill Stream Gdns
Halberton EX16 65 A7
Wellington TA21 160 B7
ill Tail TQ9 223 D5
ill The EX2 261 C1
ill View 9 TQ13 123 F6
ill View Gdns PL10 252 F5
ill View Rd PL10 252 F5
ill-Leat Gdns EX32 17 B2
ill-on-the-Mole EX36 158 E4
illand Cross EX20 75 B1
illards Hill 10 EX39 15 B1
illbarn Cross EX16 61 F8
illbay Rd PL1 262 A2
illbrook CE Sch PL10 252 E5
illbrook Cross EX13 167 E6
illbrook Dale EX13 167 E6
illbrook La EX2 177 F2
illbrook Park Rd TQ2 219 E5
illbrook Rd 2 TQ3 226 B6
illcombe Cnr TQ9 139 E1
illcombe La TQ9 224 C3
illcroft EX11 169 D3
illdale Cres EX14 166 B5
illen La TQ12 209 C2
illennium Way EX39 156 E7
iller Cl EX2 178 C4
iller Cres EX32 155 A5
iller Ct PL1 262 A2
iller Way Exminster EX6 181 F5
Plymouth PL6 245 E3
illers Brook EX33 7 E2
illers Way
Honiton EX14 166 B5
Tedburn St Mary EX6 97 F4
illetts Cl EX6 182 A4
Millgreen La EX13 87 D1
Millham La TA22 33 D6
Millhayes Cross EX14 86 F6
Millhayes Rd EX14 86 F6
Millhead Rd EX14 166 B5
Millhill PL19 116 F1
Millhouse Pk PL11 247 A2
Millmans Rd TQ3 218 D3
Millmoor Cross EX37 44 B2
Millmoor La EX10 186 F8
Millmoor Vale EX10 186 F8
Millpool Head PL10 252 E4
Millpool Rd PL10 253 A6
Mills Rd PL1 247 F2
Millsome La
Bondleigh EX18 77 C8
North Tawton EX18 59 D1
Millstream Mdw 4
TQ13 123 F6
Milltown Hill EX36 45 F7
Milltown La
Northlew EX20 74 E2
Sidmouth EX10 188 C6
Millway Bradninch EX5 82 F6
18 Chudleigh TQ13 123 E6
Millway Gdns EX5 82 F6
Millway Pl PL9 255 D8
Millwey Ave EX13 167 F7
Millwood TQ13 180 C4
Millwood Bsns Pk TQ12 207 E3
Millwood Dr PL6 245 E1
Millwood Terr EX37 28 C2
Milne Pl PL1 247 F3
Milsfords La EX5 81 E5
Milton Abbott Sch PL19 116 B5
Milton Cl Brixham TQ5 230 B2
Plymouth PL5 244 D2
Milton Cres Brixham TQ5 230 B2
Tavistock PL19 171 D5
Milton Ct
3 Newton Abbot TQ12 207 C2
Plymouth PL4 249 B1
Plymouth PL4 263 C2
Milton Fields TQ5 230 A2
Milton La TQ6 233 C2
Milton Pk TQ5 230 B2
Milton Pl EX39 156 F1
Milton Rd Exeter EX2 177 F3
6 Newton Abbot TQ12 207 B4
Milton St TQ5 230 A2
Milverton Rd TA21 160 B8
Mimosa Cl 2 EX16 161 F6
Minacre La TQ12 212 E1
Mincent Cl TQ2 214 A3
Mincent Hill TQ2 214 A3
Minchin La EX5 99 D2
Minchin Orch EX5 99 E2
Mincinglake Rd EX4 173 F1
Minden Rd 4 TQ14 210 B5
Minehead La TA22 34 A7
Miners Cl 11 TQ13 131 A5
Minerva Cl PL7 251 A6
Minerva Way TQ12 207 E3
Mines Rd Bideford EX39 157 C1
Bideford EX39 157 D1
Miniature Pony Ctr★
TQ13 111 B3
Minifie Rd EX14 166 B6
Minniemoor Cross EX31 4 B1
Minniemoor La EX31 4 C1
Minses Cl PL9 256 C7
Minster Rd EX6 182 B5
Mint Park Rd EX33 152 B7
Mirador Pl PL4 249 C3
Miranda Rd TQ3 225 F8
Mire La EX10 189 B7
Mirey La EX5 184 C3
Misterton Cl PL9 256 B8
Mitchell Ho EX4 177 D8
Mitchell St TA21 160 C7
Mitre Cl TQ14 208 E8
Mitre Ct 15 Plymouth PL1 263 A2
Tavistock PL19 171 A3
Mitre La EX4 261 A3
Moat Hill TQ9 223 C4
Mockham Down Gate
EX32 18 C7
Modbury Cl PL5 244 B3
Modbury Cross PL21 136 E2
Modbury Prim Sch
PL21 137 B2
Model Terr 2 EX39 157 A1
Modred Cl EX4 174 A1
Modyford Wlk PL20 126 C3
Mogworthy La EX16 47 D3
Mohun's Cl PL19 171 C4
Mohun's Pk PL19 171 C3
Mole Bridge La EX36 158 E4
Mole Ridge Way EX36 158 C5
Moles Cross TQ3 218 E7
Moles La
Kingskerswell TQ12 212 E1
Paignton TQ3 218 E8
Torquay TQ3 219 A7
Molesworth Rd
Plymouth, Plympton PL7 250 C6
Plymouth, Stoke PL1,PL3 248 A3
Molesworth Terr PL10 252 F5
Moll Tall's Cross PL7 136 A8
Molland Cross
Brayford EX36 19 B4
Chulmleigh EX18 45 E3
Molland Hill EX32,EX36 19 A5
Mollison Rd PL5 243 E2
Molyneaux Pl 10 PL1 247 F3
Monastery Rd TQ3 226 A6
Mondeville Way
Northam EX39 156 F6
Mondeville Way *continued*
8 Northam EX39 156 F7
Money Acre Cross EX24 101 E7
Money Acre Rd EX24 101 E7
Money Pit La EX13 69 D1
Monica Wlk PL4 263 B4
Monitor Cl EX2 261 A1
Monk's Rd EX4 177 F7
Monkerton Ct EX1 178 E8
Monkerton Dr EX1 178 E8
Monkey La EX10 186 E6
Monkleigh Mill La EX39 40 D8
Monkleigh Prim Sch
EX39 40 F7
Monkokehampton Cross
EX19 76 A8
Monks Cl EX39 26 A4
Monks Hill PL15 115 A4
Monks Orch TQ12 212 A6
Monks Way TQ13 180 C6
Monksbridge Rd TQ5 230 B3
Monksmead PL19 171 A4
Monkswell Rd EX4 177 E8
Monkton Rd EX14 166 E7
Monkton Wyld Cross
DT6 104 C7
Monkton Wyld La DT6 104 E7
Monmouth Ave EX3 182 F4
Monmouth Gdns PL5 244 C4
Monmouth Hill EX3 182 F4
Monmouth St
Lyme Regis DT7 260 E3
Topsham EX3 182 F4
Monmouth Way EX14 166 D5
Monro Mead 7 TQ12 122 F1
Mons Terr 10 TQ10 134 F3
Monshall EX19 57 E3
Mont Le Grand EX1 177 E6
Montacute Ave PL5 244 B2
Montagu Rd TQ7 258 C5
Montague Gdns EX9 197 E1
Montague Pl EX39 156 F1
Montague Rise EX4 261 B4
Montague Terr PL7 132 F4
Monterey TQ4 226 C1
Monterey Cl TQ2 219 E3
Monterey Gdns EX4 173 E1
Montery Pl 3 EX32 155 B3
Montesson Cl TQ3 225 D7
Montesson Rd TQ3 225 D7
Montgomery Cl
Ivybridge PL21 237 E5
Saltash PL12 242 D3
Montgomery Comb Sch
EX4 177 A5
Montpelier Ct
Exeter EX4 177 A7
Paignton TQ3 219 B1
Montpelier Jun & Inf Schs
PL2 248 B6
Montpelier Rd
Ilfracombe EX34 150 C6
Plymouth PL2 248 C7
Montpelier Terr 6
EX34 150 C6
Montpellier Rd
Exmouth EX8 202 A6
Torquay TQ1 220 B4
Monument Cl TA21 160 E4
Monument Rd TA21 160 E3
Monument St PL1 247 E1
Moon Hill Cl EX2 181 C8
Moon La Modbury PL21 137 B2
Plymouth PL4 263 A3
Moon St PL4 263 A3
Moon's Cross EX20 95 B5
Moonhayes Cross EX14 68 C4
Moonridge EX2 182 C7
Moor Cl TQ14 210 C7
Moor Cres PL20 128 A8
Moor Farm Cotts TQ8 148 F4
Moor Gate EX20 170 C1
Moor La Barnstaple EX31 9 C5
Bovey Tracey TQ13 180 C5
Braunton EX33 152 A5
Broadclyst EX5 175 C8
Brushford TA22 33 F4
Budlake EX5 82 E1
Budleigh Salterton EX9 197 F2
Churchinford TA3 68 D7
Croyde EX33 7 D2
Exeter EX2 178 F5
Hatherleigh EX20 75 D7
Molland EX36 31 E7
Newton Poppleford EX10 100 C1
Plymouth PL5 243 E1
Poltimore EX4 174 F7
Shobrooke EX17 80 E4
Staverton TQ9 216 B5
Torquay TQ2 214 B3
Yarnscombe EX31 27 E2
Zeal Monachorum EX17 78 B8
Moor Lane Cl TQ2 214 A3
Moor Lane Cross N EX36 31 E8
Moor Lea EX33 152 F5
Moor Park Cl EX33 7 D2
Moor Pk Chagford TQ13 111 A6
Honiton EX14 166 B3
Kingskerswell TQ12 212 F6
Moor Rd Ipplepen TQ12 211 E3
Staverton TQ9 216 B5
Moor View
Bovey Tracey TQ13 180 C5
Chudleigh TQ13 123 E6
Hatherleigh EX20 75 B6
Mary Tavy PL19 117 E6
Northlew EX20 74 E2
Plymouth, Keyham PL2 247 F5
Moor View *continued*
Plymouth, Laira PL3 249 C4
Torpoint PL11 247 B3
Witheridge EX16 62 E6
Moor View Cl EX10 187 F7
Moor View Terr
Plymouth PL4 248 E4
Yelverton PL20 127 A2
Moorcourt Cl EX10 187 F3
Moorcox Cross EX13 86 E2
Moorcroft Cl
Okehampton EX20 170 E5
Plymouth PL9 256 A7
Moore Cl TQ12 212 F8
Moore Ct EX17 165 C5
Mooredge La EX5 82 E1
Moorfield PL16 105 E4
Moorfield Ave 4 PL6 249 C7
Moorfield Cl EX8 202 C8
Moorfield Gdn TA24 21 C6
Moorfield Rd
Exmouth EX8 202 C8
St Giles on the Heath PL15 90 C1
Moorfields
Bittaford PL21 137 C8
19 Colyton EX24 103 A4
Moorfoot Cross TQ12 131 E3
Moorhaven EX9 197 F2
Moorhayes TQ13 180 D7
Moorhayes Bglws EX16 161 E5
Moorhayes Cross EX15 67 B6
Moorhayes Ct EX5 84 A1
Moorhayne Cross EX15 66 A2
Moorhouse La TA4 35 A8
Moorings Reach TQ5 230 D5
Moorings The
Braunton EX33 152 D6
Exmouth EX8 201 E6
Kingsbridge TQ7 258 D3
Paignton TQ4 226 C5
Moorland Ave
Denbury TQ12 211 A7
Plymouth PL7 250 F6
Moorland Cl
Bittaford PL21 137 C8
Yelverton PL20 241 D8
Moorland Ct PL20 126 F2
Moorland Dr PL7 250 E6
Moorland Gate
Bovey Tracey TQ12 123 B2
Roborough EX19 43 B3
Moorland Gdns PL7 250 F6
Moorland Rd PL7 250 E5
Moorland Terr EX38 159 B5
Moorland View
Buckfastleigh TQ11 236 A5
Lapford EX17 60 D3
Newton Abbot TQ12 208 A2
Plymouth, Derriford PL6 245 A5
Plymouth, Plymstock PL9 256 B7
Princetown PL20 128 A8
Saltash PL12 242 F4
South Molton EX36 46 D8
Moorland Way
Exeter EX4 176 F8
Gunnislake PL18 125 C5
Moorlands Tiverton EX16 161 E6
West Hill EX11 168 D5
Moorlands La PL12 242 C4
Moorlands Rd EX9 197 E1
Moorlands Trad Est
PL12 242 C4
Moormead EX9 197 F1
Moorpark EX8 202 C6
Moorpark Rd TQ12 212 F6
Moorplot La EX18 59 D3
Moors End TQ12 207 D8
Moors Pk TQ14 208 F7
Moorsend TQ12 206 E4
Moorshead Cross
Buckfastleigh TQ11 135 B6
Yealmpton PL21 136 D2
Moorside TQ7 147 E7
Moorstone Leat TQ4 226 C1
Moortown EX18 59 F8
Moortown Cross
Chulmleigh EX18 59 F8
Rackenford EX36 47 B8
Moorview
Broadhempston TQ13 131 B1
Marldon TQ3 218 D2
North Tawton EX20 77 C4
Moorview Cl EX4 173 D1
Moorview Dr TQ14 209 D8
Moorview End TQ3 218 D2
Moory Mdw EX34 2 F4
Moothill Cross TQ9 216 A6
Morchard Bishop CE Prim
Sch EX17 61 B2
Morchard Road Sta EX17 78 F8
Morecombe Cross EX21 73 A4
Moreton Ave
Bideford EX39 156 E1
Plymouth PL6 244 F1
Moreton Dr EX39 156 E2
Moreton Park Rd EX39 156 E1
Moreton Terr EX6 112 F5
Moretonhampstead General
Hopsl TQ13 111 F5
Moretonhampstead Prim Sch
TQ13 111 F5
Moretonhampstead Rd
TQ13 122 F6
Morgan Ave TQ2 220 A5
Morgan Ct EX8 202 A6
Morganhayes Cross
EX24 102 D4
Morgans Quay TQ14 210 B3
Morice Sq PL1 247 E2
Morice St PL1 247 E2
Morice Terr EX22 54 A6
Morice Town Prim Sch
PL2 247 E4
Morin Rd TQ3 226 C8
Morlaix Dr PL6 245 B4
Morleigh Cross TQ9 139 A3
Morleigh Green Cross
TQ9 139 A3
Morleigh Rd TQ9 139 C6
Morley Cl PL7 250 A5
Morley Ct PL1 262 B3
Morley Dr PL20 126 D2
Morley Rd EX4 177 E8
Morley View Rd PL7 250 C6
Mornacott Cross EX36 31 A4
Mornacott Rd EX36 31 A4
Morningside
Dawlish EX7 204 C4
Torquay TQ1 220 E5
Mornington Pk TA21 160 E5
Morrell's Cross EX16 34 B4
Morrell's La EX16 50 B6
Morris Cl EX20 75 B7
Morrish Pk PL9 255 F6
Morshead Rd PL6 244 F2
Mortain Rd PL12 242 D4
Mortehoe Station Rd EX34 1 B1
Mortimer Ave TQ3 226 B8
Mortimer Ct EX2 178 A2
Mortimers Cross EX15 66 B4
Mortimore Cl PL12 242 D2
Morton Cres EX8 201 F6
Morton Crescent Mews
EX8 201 F6
Morton Rd EX8 201 F6
Morton Way EX13 167 D4
Morven Dr EX8 196 A2
Morwell Gdns PL2 248 A6
Morwellham Quay★
PL19 125 E4
Morwenna Park Rd
EX39 156 F7
Morwenna Rd EX23 37 A1
Morwenna Terr 2 EX39 156 F7
Moses Cl PL6 244 E7
Moses Ct PL6 244 E7
Mosshayne La EX1,EX5 175 B2
Mossop Cl EX11 169 D3
Mostyn Ave PL4 249 A4
Mote Pk PL12 242 C3
Motehole Rd TQ12 211 D2
Mothecombe PL8 142 A6
Mothecombe Wlk PL6 245 E1
Mott's Cross EX15 84 A7
Mott's La EX15 84 A7
Moult Rd TQ8 259 B2
Moulton Cl PL7 251 B5
Mounson Hill EX6 97 C5
Mount Batten Waterside Pk★
PL9 254 F7
Mount Boone TQ6 233 F4
Mount Boone Hill TQ6 233 F4
Mount Boone La TQ6 233 F4
Mount Boone Way TQ6 233 E4
Mount Cl EX14 166 B5
Mount Edgcumbe Country
Pk★ PL10 253 E6
Mount Gould Ave PL4 249 B2
Mount Gould Cres PL4 249 B3
Mount Gould Hospl PL4 249 B3
Mount Gould Rd PL4 249 B3
Mount Gould Way PL4 249 B3
Mount Hermon Rd TQ1 220 B6
Mount House Sch PL19 171 E7
Mount Pleasant
Bideford, East-the-Water
EX39 157 C3
Bideford, Littleham EX39 25 D2
3 Bishop's Tawton EX32 16 E1
10 Chudleigh TQ13 123 F6
9 Crediton EX17 165 C5
Millbrook PL10 252 E5
Moretonhampstead TQ13 111 F4
Plymouth PL5 244 B2
Mount Pleasant Ave
EX8 196 B3
Mount Pleasant Cl
Kingsbridge TQ7 258 D6
Kingskerswell TQ12 213 A3
Mount Pleasant Ct EX8 196 B2
Mount Pleasant La 7
TQ14 210 A3
Mount Pleasant Mews
TQ5 230 C4
Mount Pleasant Rd
Brixham TQ5 230 C4
Dawlish Warren EX7 201 B1
Exeter EX4 177 E8
Kingskerswell TQ12 213 A3
Newton Abbot TQ12 207 C2
2 Torquay TQ1 220 B6
Mount Radford Cres
EX2 261 C2
Mount Raleigh Ave
EX39 156 F4
Mount Raleigh Dr EX39 156 E3
Mount Rd TQ5 230 D5
Mount Ridley Rd TQ6 234 C3
Mount Rise EX6 114 E4
Mount St
Plymouth, Mount Wise PL1 247 E1
Plymouth, Mutley PL4 263 A4
Mount Stone Rd PL1 254 A8

Mount Street Prim Sch PL4 . . . . .263 A4
Mount Tamar Cl PL5 . . .243 E2
Mount Tamar Sch PL5 . .243 E2
Mount Tavy Rd PL19 . . . .171 E6
Mount The
32 Appledore EX39 . . . . . . .15 A1
Brixham TQ5 . . . . .230 C6
Teignmouth TQ14 . . . . . . .210 B6
Torquay TQ2 . . . . .213 F4
Totnes TQ9 . . . . .223 C4
Mount View
18 Colyton EX24 . . . . .103 A4
Feniton EX14 . . . . .84 E2
Mount View Cotts EX32 .155 F2
Mount View Terr 2 TQ9 . . . . .223 C5
Mount Wear Sq EX2 . . .182 C8
Mount Wise Ct PL1 . . . .247 F1
Mount Wise Prim Sch PL1 . . . . .247 E1
Mountain Cl EX8 . . . . . . .202 F8
Mountain Hill EX8 . . . . .197 A1
Mountbatten Cl
Exmouth EX8 . . . . .196 D2
Plymouth PL9 . . . . .255 D6
Mountbatten Rd EX16 . . .161 C5
Mountbatten Way PL9 . .255 E6
Mounter's Hill TA20 . . . . .69 E2
Mounthill Cotts TQ12 . . .122 F1
Mounthill La EX13 . . . . .103 E5
Mounticombe Cross EX18 . . . . .45 C1
Mounticombe La EX18 . . .45 C1
Mourne Villas PL9 . . . . .255 F8
Mouse Hole La EX14 . . . .84 C4
Mouseberry Cross EX17 .46 A4
Mouseberry La TQ13 . . .124 B4
Mousehole Cross EX14 . .84 D5
Mowbars Hayes EX13 . . .87 A3
Mowbray Ave EX4 . . . . . .261 B4
Mowbray Ct EX2 . . . . . . .178 A5
Mowhay Mdw PL11 . . . .252 B8
Mowhay Rd
Plymouth PL5 . . . . .243 F1
Plymouth PL5 . . . . .244 A2
Mowlish La EX6 . . . . . . .200 B7
Mowstead Pk EX33 . . . . .152 B7
Mowstead Rd EX33 . . . .152 B7
Moxeys Cl EX17 . . . . .62 E1
Moyses La EX20 . . . . . . .170 B4
Moyses Mdw EX20 . . . . .170 A4
Mrs Ethelston's Prim Sch DT7 . . . . .260 A5
Mucky La EX19 . . . . .57 D6
Mudbank La EX8 . . . . . .202 A8
Muddy La
East Buckland EX32 . . . . . .18 E2
Ottery St Mary EX11 . . . . .101 B7
Mudford Gate EX16 . . . . .62 E7
Mudgate Cross EX36 . . . .20 D3
Mudge La TQ12 . . . . . . .217 E6
Mudge Way PL7 . . . . . . .250 E5
Mudges Terr PL18 . . . . .125 D6
Mudhouse Cross EX19 . . .58 B7
Mudstone La TQ5 . . . . . .230 E3
Mulberry Cl Exeter EX1 . .178 B6
Paignton TQ3 . . . . .225 E6
Plymouth PL6 . . . . .245 E7
Willand EX15 . . . . .162 D4
Mulberry Gr PL19 . . . . . .171 C2
Mulberry Rd PL12 . . . . . .242 E1
Mulberry St 3 TQ14 . . .210 B4
Mulberry Way EX31 . . . .154 B2
Mulgrave St PL1 . . . . . . .262 C2
Mullacott Cross EX34 . . . . . .1 E1
Mullet Ave PL3 . . . . .249 C4
Mullet Cl PL3 . . . . .249 C4
Mullet Rd PL3 . . . . .249 C4
Mullion Cl PL11 . . . . . . .246 F4
Munro Ave PL8 . . . . .141 B8
Murchington Cross TQ13 . . . . .110 E7
Murdock Rd PL11 . . . . . .246 F3
Murley Cl EX17 . . . . .165 A6
Murley Cres TQ14 . . . . . .208 E8
Murley Grange TQ14 . . .208 E8
Musbury Prim Sch EX13 . . . . .103 D5
Musbury Rd EX13 . . . . . .167 C4
Museum Ct TQ7 . . . . . . .258 C6
Museum Rd TQ1 . . . . . . .220 C4
Musgrave Row EX4 . . . .261 B3
Musgraves TA22 . . . . .33 E6
Musket Rd TQ12 . . . . . . .180 F2
Mutley Ct PL4 . . . . .263 A4
Mutley Plain PL4 . . . . . .248 E4
Mutley Plain La PL4 . . . .248 E4
Mutley Rd PL3 . . . . .248 E5
Muttersmoor Rd EX10 . . .187 E5
Mutton La EX2 . . . . .181 C8
Muxworthy La EX32 . . . . .19 A8
Mylor Cl PL2 . . . . .248 D8
Myra Ct 27 EX39 . . . . .15 A1
Myrtle Cl Exeter EX2 . . . .177 B1
Yelverton PL20 . . . . .127 B3
Myrtle Cottage Rd EX39 157 B8
Myrtle Farm View EX33 . . .7 E2
Myrtle Gdns EX39 . . . . . .157 A2
Myrtle Gr EX39 . . . . .157 A2
Myrtle Hill TQ14 . . . . . . .210 C5
Myrtle La TA21 . . . . .51 E7
Myrtle Rd EX4 . . . . .176 E4
Myrtle Row Exmouth EX8 202 A6
4 Torquay TQ1 . . . . .220 B5
Myrtle St 17 EX39 . . . . . . .15 A1
Myrtles Ct PL12 . . . . . . .242 D4
Myrtleville PL2 . . . . .248 A6

N

Nadder Bottom EX4 . . . .176 B8
Nadder La
Nadderwater EX4 . . . . . . .176 B8
South Molton EX36 . . . . . .158 B4
Nadder Park Rd EX4 . . .176 D5
Nadrid Cross EX36 . . . . . .30 A8
Nadrid East Cross EX36 . .30 A8
Naish's La EX13 . . . . .87 B3
Nancarrows PL12 . . . . . .242 C2
Nap La EX18 . . . . .44 C1
Nap View EX14 . . . . .85 B4
Napier St PL1 . . . . .247 F3
Napier Terr Exeter EX4 . .261 A3
Plymouth PL4 . . . . .248 E4
Naps La EX10 . . . . .186 C5
Narfords La TA20 . . . . . . .69 F1
Narracott La
Hollocombe EX18 . . . . .58 E7
South Molton EX36 . . . . . .158 A2
Narratons Rd EX20 . . . . . .93 E6
Narrow La
Copplestone EX17 . . . . . . .79 C4
Saltash PL12 . . . . .242 C7
Tiverton EX16 . . . . .161 C2
Narrowmoor Cross TQ7 144 D4
Naseby Dr TQ12 . . . . . . .180 F2
Nash Cl PL7 . . . . .251 A5
Nash Gdns EX7 . . . . .204 D4
Nash La DT6 . . . . .88 H2
Nasmith Cl EX8 . . . . .196 D1
Natcott La EX39 . . . . .22 F2
National Marine Aquarium★ PL4 . . . . .263 A2
National Shire Horse Ctr The★ PL8 . . . . .136 B2
Nats La Cornwood PL21 . .133 D1
Sparkwell PL21 . . . . .136 C8
Natson Mill La EX17 . . . . .78 B4
Nattadon Rd TQ13 . . . . . .111 A6
Natty Cross EX38 . . . . . . .43 A5
Neadon La EX6 . . . . .112 F5
Neal Cl PL7 . . . . .251 B4
Neath Rd PL4 . . . . .263 C4
Needlewood Cl EX11 . . .168 C3
Neet Way EX22 . . . . .164 C6
Neilgate Cnr TQ13 . . . . .131 A3
Nelson Ave PL1 . . . . .247 F3
Nelson Cl Staverton TQ9 .216 A5
Teignmouth TQ14 . . . . . . .210 A6
Topsham EX3 . . . . .182 E5
Torquay TQ1 . . . . .220 D2
Nelson Dr Exmouth EX8 . .202 E8
Westward Ho! EX39 . . . . .156 C7
Nelson Gdns 5 PL1 . . . .247 F3
Nelson Pl TQ12 . . . . .207 B5
Nelson Rd Brixham TQ5 . .230 C5
Dartmouth TQ6 . . . . .233 C3
Exeter EX4 . . . . .177 A5
Westward Ho! EX39 . . . . .156 C7
Nelson St PL4 . . . . .263 A4
Nelson Terr
Plymouth PL6 . . . . .245 E6
Westward Ho! EX39 . . . . .156 C7
Neopardy Cross
Yeoford, Neopardy EX17 . . .79 D2
Yeoford, Winstode EX17 . . .79 D1
Nepean St 1 PL2 . . . . . .247 F5
Neptune Ct 3 EX1 . . . . .261 A2
Ness Dr TQ14 . . . . .210 B2
Ness View Rd TQ14 . . . .210 C8
Neswick St PL1 . . . . .262 B3
Neswick Street Ope PL1 . . . . .262 A3
Nether Mdw TQ3 . . . . . . .218 D3
Nethercott Cross
Ashwater EX21 . . . . .90 C7
Oakford EX16 . . . . .48 C8
Nethercott Hill EX16 . . . .48 C7
Nethercott La EX17,EX20 .95 F6
Nethercott Rd EX33 . . . . . .8 C2
Netherham Cross EX33 . . .8 A2
Netherhams Hill EX33 . . . .8 A2
Netherleigh Rd TQ1 . . . .220 B7
Netherton Cross EX34 . . . .3 A4
Netherton Est PL20 . . . . .126 D3
Netherton La EX34 . . . . . . .3 A4
Netley Rd TQ12 . . . . . . .207 B4
Nettacott Cross EX5 . . . . .81 B2
Nettleford Hill EX16 . . . . .46 F5
Nettlehayes PL9 . . . . . . .256 D7
Netton Cl PL9 . . . . .256 B6
Nevada Cl PL3 . . . . .249 D6
Neville Rd
Newton Abbot TQ12 . . . . .207 A4
Okehampton EX20 . . . . . .170 C5
New Barn Hill PL7 . . . . .250 F3
New Barnstaple Rd EX34 . . . . .150 E3
New Bldgs Bampton EX16 .34 C1
8 Barnstaple EX32 . . . . .155 A6
Broadclyst EX5 . . . . .175 C7
Chittlehampton EX37 . . . . . .28 F3
Doddiscombsleigh EX6 . . .113 D5
3 Exeter EX4 . . . . .177 D8
Fremington EX31 . . . . . . .153 E5
Thurlestone TQ7 . . . . .143 C1
New Bridge Cross EX31 . .27 E7
New Bridge St EX4 . . . . .261 A2
New Cotts Exmouth EX8 .202 F7
Gunnislake PL18 . . . . .125 D6
New Cross
Avonwick TQ10 . . . . .135 C2
Kingsteignton TQ12 . . . . . .123 E1
New Cut Beer EX12 . . . . .191 D5
Crediton EX17 . . . . .165 B5
New England Hill PL7 . .136 B5
New England Rd PL7 . . .136 B5
New Esplanade Ct TQ4 .226 C6
New Est EX5 . . . . .81 A2
New Exeter Rd TQ13 . . . .123 F7
New Exeter St TQ13 . . . .123 E6
New George St PL1 . . . .262 C3
New Inn Cross 5 EX5 . . .99 E8
New Inn Ct
Cullompton EX15 . . . . . . .163 C3
6 Holsworthy EX22 . . . . . .164 C4
New La Bampton EX16 . . . .33 F2
Broadhempston TQ9 . . . . .131 E1
Ottery St Mary EX11 . . . . .169 E4
Staverton TQ9 . . . . .215 F5
Tatworth TA20 . . . . .88 C8
New Launceston Rd PL19 . . . . .171 A5
New London PL20 . . . . . .128 B8
New Mdw PL21 . . . . .237 B6
New Mill Ind Est PL21 . .137 B2
New North Rd
Exeter EX4 . . . . .261 A4
Exmouth EX8 . . . . .202 A7
New Park (Cvn Site) TQ13 . . . . .180 C4
New Park Cl TQ5 . . . . . . .230 D4
New Park Cres TQ12 . . .207 D8
New Park Rd
Kingsteignton TQ12 . . . . .207 D8
Lee Mill PL7,PL21 . . . . . . .136 B6
Paignton TQ3 . . . . .225 F7
Plymouth PL7 . . . . .251 A4
New Passage Hill PL1 . .247 E3
New Path EX17 . . . . .97 C7
New Pk Bridford EX6 . . . .112 F5
Horrabridge PL20 . . . . . . .126 F4
New Quay La TQ5 . . . . .230 D5
New Quay St
Appledore EX39 . . . . .15 A1
Teignmouth TQ14 . . . . . . .210 B4
New Rd Barnstaple EX32 .155 A4
Beer EX12 . . . . .191 D6
Bere Alston PL20 . . . . . . .125 E2
Bickleigh PL6,PL7 . . . . . . .132 A5
Bideford EX39 . . . . .157 A1
Bishop's Tawton EX32 . . . . .16 E1
Brendon EX35 . . . . .6 D4
Brixham TQ5 . . . . .230 B4
Buckfastleigh TQ11 . . . . . .236 B5
Cawsand PL10 . . . . .253 A1
Cawsand, Kingsand PL10 .253 B2
Chard Junction TA20 . . . . . .88 F8
Clyst St Lawrence EX5 . . . .83 B3
Great Torrington EX38 . . .159 D4
Instow EX39 . . . . .15 C1
Lifton PL16 . . . . .105 F4
Loddiswell TQ7 . . . . .143 F7
Lutton PL21 . . . . .133 B2
Merton EX20 . . . . .57 A6
Modbury PL21 . . . . .137 B2
Morchard Bishop EX17 . . . . .61 B2
Okehampton EX20 . . . . . .170 A3
Roborough PL6 . . . . .241 D2
Saltash PL12 . . . . .242 E3
South Molton EX36 . . . . . .158 D4
Starcross EX6 . . . . .201 A8
Stoke Fleming TQ6 . . . . . .146 B7
Stoke Gabriel TQ9 . . . . . . .227 F7
Teignmouth TQ14 . . . . . . .210 C7
Totnes TQ9 . . . . .223 D6
Upottery EX14 . . . . .68 B1
Waterrow TA21 . . . . .35 F4
West Hill EX5 . . . . .168 B5
Wilmington EX14 . . . . .86 D2
Yealmpton PL8 . . . . .136 A2
New Road Cl PL10 . . . . .253 A2
New Road Cross
Milton Damerel EX22 . . . . . .54 D3
Okehampton EX20 . . . . .93 F5
South Molton EX36 . . . . . . .46 D6
Wilmington EX14 . . . . .86 D1
New Road Est EX20 . . . . .93 F8
New Row 8 EX39 . . . . . .157 A2
New Sch The EX6 . . . . . .182 A5
New Sidmouth Rd EX24 102 F4
New St 6 Appledore EX39 .15 A1
13 Bideford EX39 . . . . . . .157 A2
Chagford TQ13 . . . . .111 A6
Chulmleigh EX18 . . . . .44 E1
Cullompton EX15 . . . . .163 B3
Exmouth EX8 . . . . .202 A7
Great Torrington EX38 . . .159 C5
Honiton EX14 . . . . .166 C6
Merton EX20 . . . . .57 A6
Millbrook PL10 . . . . .252 E5
Moretonhampstead TQ13 . .111 F5
Ottery St Mary EX11 . . . . .169 E4
Paignton TQ3 . . . . .226 B6
Plymouth PL1 . . . . .263 A2
Sidmouth EX10 . . . . .188 B3
New Valley Rd EX4 . . . . .176 F7
New Village Cross EX17 . .59 F2
New Way EX5 . . . . .184 C6
New Way Est EX14 . . . . . .67 B2
New Wlk TQ9 . . . . .223 D5
New Wood Cl PL6 . . . . . .245 E8
New Zealand Ho PL3 . . . .248 B4
Newacott Cross EX22 . . . .70 E5
Newberry Cl EX34 . . . . .2 E4
Newberry Cotts EX33 . . . . .8 A2
Newberry Hill EX34 . . . . . . .2 F4
Newberry Rd
Combe Martin EX34 . . . . .2 F4
Georgeham EX33 . . . . .8 A2
Newberry's Patch TA3 . . .68 D7
Newbery Cl
Axminster EX13 . . . . .167 E6
Colyton EX24 . . . . .103 A4
Newbery Comm Ctr EX5 .99 A4
Newbridge Cross
Bishop's Tawton EX32 . . . . .27 F7
Cowley EX5 . . . . .172 D6
Newbridge Cswy EX31, EX32 . . . . .27 E7
Newbridge Hill
Cowley EX5 . . . . .172 E6
Gunnislake PL18 . . . . .125 D6
Holne TQ13 . . . . .130 A6
Witheridge EX16 . . . . .46 D1
Newbuilding's Hill EX17 .63 A3
Newbuildings Cross EX17 . . . . .79 D6
Newbury Cl PL5 . . . . . . .244 B4
Newbury Dr TQ13 . . . . . .180 E7
Newcastle Gdns PL5 . . .244 B5
Newcombe Cl EX20 . . . .170 D5
Newcombe St EX1 . . . . .178 A6
Newcombe Street Gdns EX1 . . . . .178 A6
Newcombe Terr EX1 . . . .177 F6
Newcombes 5 EX17 . . . .165 C5
Newcomen Rd TQ6 . . . .233 F3
Newcot Cross EX15 . . . . .67 D5
Newcourt Rd
Silverton EX5 . . . . .82 B5
Topsham EX3 . . . . .182 E7
Newcross Pk 10 TQ12 . . .123 E1
Newfoundland Cl EX4 . .173 E2
Newfoundland Way 13 TQ12 . . . . .207 B3
Newgate Cross TA22 . . . .33 D7
Newhay Cl EX7 . . . . .204 C6
Newhay Cross TQ12 . . . .211 C1
Newhayes TQ12 . . . . . . .211 C1
Newhayes Cl EX2 . . . . . .177 A2
Newhouse Hill EX16 . . . . .46 E2
Newhouse La
Chipstable TA4 . . . . .35 E6
Hittisleigh EX6 . . . . .96 D5
Newland Cotts EX32 . . . . .17 C1
Newland Cross
King's Nympton EX37 . . . . .44 C8
North Tawton EX20 . . . . . . .77 B3
Rackenford EX16 . . . . .47 B2
Newlands Dawlish EX7 . . .204 E7
Honiton EX14 . . . . .166 C6
Newlands Ave EX8 . . . . .202 D8
Newlands Cl Exeter EX2 .177 A2
Landkey EX32 . . . . .17 C2
Sidmouth EX10 . . . . .188 B8
Newlands Cross PL21 . .237 D3
Newlands Pk EX12 . . . . .192 A6
Newlands Rd EX10 . . . . .188 B8
Newlane End TQ9 . . . . .215 F5
Newman Cres TQ9 . . . . .222 F8
Newman Ct EX4 . . . . . . .176 E5
Newman Rd Exeter EX4 .176 F5
Plymouth PL5 . . . . .243 E2
Saltash PL12 . . . . .242 F3
Newnhall Ind Est PL7 . . .250 F7
Newnham Cross EX37 . . .44 C4
Newnham Ind Est PL7 . .250 F6
Newnham La EX18,EX37 . .44 C4
Newnham Rd PL7 . . . . . .250 F7
Newnham Way PL7 . . . .250 F6
Newport Com Sch EX32 155 B3
Newport Rd
Barnstaple EX32 . . . . .155 A3
Exeter EX2 . . . . .182 C7
Newport St
Dartmouth TQ6 . . . . .233 F3
Millbrook PL10 . . . . .252 E5
Plymouth PL1 . . . . .248 A1
Tiverton EX16 . . . . .161 D4
Newport Terr
Barnstaple EX32 . . . . .155 A3
7 Bideford EX39 . . . . . . .157 B1
Newtake Rd PL19 . . . . . .171 E2
Newtake Rise TQ12 . . . .207 F2
Newte's Hill EX16 . . . . . . .64 D5
Newton Abbot & GWR Mus★ TQ12 . . . . .207 C3
Newton Abbot Hospl TQ12 . . . . .207 C3
Newton Abbot Sta TQ12 . . . . .207 D3
Newton Ave PL5 . . . . . . .243 E2
Newton Cl Exeter EX1 . . .261 C3
Newton Ferrers PL8 . . . . .141 A7
Newton Cross
Blackawton TQ9 . . . . .145 B7
Denbury TQ12 . . . . .211 B6
Hartland EX39 . . . . .22 C2
Zeal Monachorum EX17 . . . .77 F7
Newton Ct PL8 . . . . .140 F7
Newton Ferrers CE Prim Sch PL8 . . . . .140 F7
Newton Fst Sch EX1 . . .261 C3
Newton Gdns PL5 . . . . . .243 F2
Newton Hall TQ12 . . . . .207 C2
Newton Hill
Daccombe TQ12 . . . . .213 F6
Newton Ferrers PL8 . . . . .140 F7
Newton Ho EX5 . . . . .80 F1
Newton La EX17 . . . . .77 F7
Newton Poppleford Prim Sch EX10 . . . . .186 F8
Newton Rd
Bideford EX39 . . . . .157 A3
Newton Rd *continued*
Bishopsteignton TQ14 . . . .208 D
Bovey Tracey TQ13 . . . . . .180 C
Bovey Tracey, Heathfield TQ13 . . . . .180 E
Kingskerswell TQ12 . . . . .213 A
Kingsteignton TQ12 . . . . .207 D
Salcombe TQ8 . . . . .259 D
Torquay TQ2 . . . . .213 D
Newton Sch EX38 . . . . . . .55 C
Newton Sq 8 EX16 . . . . . .34 B
Newton St Cyres Prim Sch EX5 . . . . .172 A
Newton St Cyres Sta EX5 81 A
Newton St Petrock Cross EX38 . . . . .40 B
Newtons Orch EX13 . . . . .87 C
Newtown Cornwood PL21 133 C
Sidmouth EX10 . . . . .188 B
Newtown Cross EX36 . . . .31 A
Newtown La EX36 . . . . . . .31 A
Nibbys Cross EX15 . . . . . .66 B
Nicholas Cl TA22 . . . . .33 E
Nicholas Mdw PL17 . . . .125 E
Nicholas Rd EX1 . . . . . . .178 A
Nichols Nymett Cross EX20 . . . . .77 F
Nichols Nymett La EX20 .77 F
Nichols Nymett Moors Cross EX20 . . . . .77 F
Nicholson Rd
Plymouth PL5 . . . . .244 E
Torquay TQ2 . . . . .213 D
Nick Reed's La EX15 . . . .52 D
Nightingale Cl
Plymouth PL9 . . . . .256 C
Torquay TQ2 . . . . .213 E
Nightingale Lawns EX15 . . . . .163 A
Nilch Pk PL12 . . . . .242 C
Nilgala Cl EX39 . . . . .156 E
Nine Ash Cross EX16 . . . .49 D
Nine Milestone Cross PL21 . . . . .137 D
Nine Oaks Aylesbeare EX5 .99 C
Dousland PL20 . . . . .127 C
Nirvana Cl PL21 . . . . . . .237 C
No Hill Pl TQ9 . . . . .131 E
No Man's Land EX33 . . . . .8 E
No Mans Chaple EX5 . . . .81 D
No Place Hill TQ9 . . . . . .131 E
Noelle Dr TQ12 . . . . .207 A
Noland Pk TQ10 . . . . . . .135 A
Nomandsland Cross EX16 . . . . .62 E
Nomansland EX17 . . . . . .80 D
Nook The PL19 . . . . .171 D
Norcombe Ct EX12 192
Norden La TQ7 258
Nordon Cross TQ12 131
Norfolk Cl PL3 249
Norfolk Rd PL3 249
Norfolk Terr 23 EX32 . . .155
Norleigh Cross EX20 75
Norley Rd EX33 8
Norman Cl Exmouth EX8 .196
Newton Abbot TQ12 206
Norman Dr EX15 163
Norman Lockyer Obsy★ EX10 188
Norman Rd TQ3 226
Norman Terr EX39 157
Normand y Way EX36 . .158
Normandy Cl EX8 196
Normandy Hill PL5 243
Normandy Rd EX1 177
Normandy Way
Plymouth PL5 243
Salcombe TQ8 259
Normans Cleave EX35 . .151
Norns La TQ6 145
Norsworthy's Grave EX17 97
North Ave Bideford EX39 .157
Exeter EX1 177
Lyme Regis DT7 260
North Boundary Rd TQ5 230
North Buckland Hill EX33 .8
North Combe Cross EX16 48
North Combe Rd EX14 . . .86
North Coombe La EX16 . .47
North Devon Coll EX31 .154
North Devon Cottage Rd EX16 161
North Devon District Hospl EX31 155
North Devon Maritime Mus★ EX39 15
North Devon Mus★ EX32 154
North Dimson PL18 125
North Down Cres PL2 . .247
North Down Cross EX17 .79
North Down Gdns PL2 . .247
North Down Rd
Braunton EX33 152
Plymouth PL2 248
North East St EX39 157
North Emb TQ6 233
North End Cl TQ12 211
North Ford Rd TQ6 233
North Furzeham Rd TQ5 230
North Gate Ct EX4 261
North Gn 2 EX32 155
North Grange EX2 178
North Hayne Cross EX36 .31
North Heasley Cross EX36 19

North Hill PL4 ...263 A4
North Hill Cl TQ5 ...230 B5
North Hill La
Morchard Bishop EX17 ...61 B3
Stockland EX14 ...86 F8
North Huish Cross TQ10 138 B8
North La Ashford EX31 ...16 A6
Barnstaple, Bickington EX31 ...154 A4
Barnstaple, Middle Marwood EX31 ...9 B3
Barnstaple, Whiddon EX31 ...9 D2
Bratton Fleming EX31 ...11 F4
North Lawn Ct EX1 ...177 F6
North Lodge Cl EX7 ...204 C5
North Molton Cross EX36 ...30 D8
North Molton Prim Sch EX36 ...30 D8
North Moor Cross EX22 .38 C3
North Morte Rd EX34 ...7 F8
North Park Almshouses EX2 ...261 C2
North Park Cnr TQ9 ...139 C6
North Park Rd
Exeter EX4 ...173 B1
Tedburn St Mary EX6 ...97 F4
North Park Villas PL12 .242 C4
North Prospect Prim Sch PL2 ...248 A7
North Prospect Rd PL2 .248 A6
North Rd
Barnstaple EX31 ...155 A7
Bideford EX39 ...157 A2
Bradworthy EX22 ...38 E1
Hartland EX39 ...22 D3
High Bickington EX37 ...43 B7
Holsworthy EX22 ...164 D5
Lee Mill PL21 ...136 C7
Lifton PL16 ...105 F4
Okehampton EX20 ...170 C7
Saltash PL12 ...242 F3
South Molton EX36 ...158 C5
Torpoint PL11 ...247 B3
Yelverton PL20 ...126 F3
North Rd E PL4 ...262 C4
North Rd W PL1 ...262 B4
North Road Ind Est EX20 ...170 C6
North Rocks Rd TQ4 ...229 C7
North St Ashburton TQ13 .130 F5
Axminster EX13 ...167 D6
Braunton EX33 ...152 D6
Chagford TQ13 ...111 A6
Crediton EX17 ...165 C5
Denbury TQ12 ...211 A7
Dolton EX19 ...57 F7
Exeter EX4 ...261 A3
Exeter, Heavitree EX1 ...177 F6
Exmouth EX8 ...202 A7
Hartland EX39 ...22 D3
Ipplepen TQ12 ...211 D2
North Tawton EX20 ...77 C4
Northam EX39 ...157 A7
Okehampton EX20 ...170 B5
Ottery St Mary EX11 ...169 E4
Plymouth PL4 ...263 A3
Sheepwash EX21 ...56 C1
South Molton EX36 ...158 C5
Tavistock PL19 ...171 C5
Topsham EX3 ...182 F4
Wellington TA21 ...160 D6
Witheridge EX16 ...46 E1
North Street [2] TQ9 ...223 C6
North Tawton Prim Sch EX20 ...77 C4
North Terr EX31 ...154 A4
North Thorne La EX31 ...11 A4
North View Ave EX39 ...156 F3
North View Hill EX39 ...156 F3
North View Rd TQ5 ...230 D5
North Walk Hill EX35 ...151 C6
North Weald Gdns PL5 .243 E5
North Wlk
Barnstaple EX31 ...154 F5
Lynton EX35 ...151 B6
Northam Burrows Ctry Pk★ EX39 ...14 E1
Northam Rd EX39 ...156 F3
Northampton Cl PL5 ...244 B5
Northams Mdw EX20 ...170 A4
Northay Cross EX13 ...88 H3
Northay La
Axminster EX13 ...88 G3
Combe St Nicholas TA20 ...69 E6
Northbeer Cross EX17 ...96 A8
Northbeer La EX17 ...95 F8
Northclose Rd EX18 ...59 D2
Northcombe La TA22 ...33 E7
Northcote EX14 ...166 C6
Northcote Cross EX37 ...43 E4
Northcote Hill EX14 ...166 F7
Northcote La
Honiton EX14 ...166 B6
Witheridge EX16 ...62 F8
Northcote Rd EX14 ...166 E7
Northcott Gdns EX39 ...157 A7
Northcott Terr [9] EX22 .164 C4
Northdene EX39 ...156 E4
Northdown Dr EX39 ...156 F3
Northdown La EX36 ...45 F6
Northdown Rd
Bideford EX39 ...156 F2
Thorverton EX5 ...81 F7
Northern La
Branscombe EX12 ...190 B5
Sidmouth EX10 ...189 E8
Northernhay [15] TQ12 ...207 C3
Northernhay Pl EX4 ...261 B3
Northernhay Sq EX4 ...261 A3
Northernhay St EX4 ...261 A3
Northesk St PL2 ...248 A4
Northfield EX13 ...103 D5
Northfield La EX31 ...154 F7
Northfield Pk EX31 ...154 F7
Northfield Rd
Bideford EX39 ...157 C1
Georgeham EX33 ...8 B2
Ilfracombe EX34 ...150 B6
Okehampton EX20 ...170 B5
Northfield Terr [1] EX34 .150 B6
Northfields EX13 ...103 D5
Northfields Ind Est TQ5 230 B5
Northfields La TQ5 ...230 B5
Northgate EX39 ...22 D3
Northgate La EX14 ...86 A3
Northground La EX10 ...101 D1
Northland Cnr EX31 ...11 D2
Northland Cross EX36 ...19 A1
Northleat Ave TQ3 ...225 E5
Northleigh Cross
Barnstaple EX32 ...17 C6
Northleigh EX24 ...102 B7
Northleigh Hill Rd
Honiton EX14 ...166 E3
Offwell EX14 ...86 A1
Northleigh Rd EX24 ...102 D6
Northlew & Ashbury CE Prim Sch EX20 ...74 E2
Northlew Rd EX20 ...93 D6
Northlieigh Hill Rd EX14 102 B8
Northmoor Rd TA22 ...33 D7
Northmostown Ct EX10 .187 A7
Northolt Ave PL5 ...243 D4
Northridge Cross EX5 ...98 E7
Northridge La EX5 ...98 E7
Northside TA21 ...160 B5
Northumberland Pl TQ14 ...210 B4
Northumberland St PL5 247 E8
Northumberland Terr PL1 ...262 B1
Northview Rd EX9 ...203 F8
Northville Pk TQ7 ...258 C6
Northville Rd TQ7 ...258 C6
Northways La PL21 ...137 D7
Northwood Cross EX17 ...61 B3
Northwood La
Buckfast TQ11 ...236 C8
Buckland Brewer EX39 ...40 C7
Morchard Bishop EX17 ...61 B3
Northwoods TQ13 ...180 C4
Norton Ave PL4 ...263 C4
Norton Cross TQ6 ...233 A3
Norton View TQ6 ...233 C3
Nortons Cross EX5 ...81 A2
Norwich Ave PL5 ...244 B5
Norwich Cl EX8 ...196 D4
Norwich Rd EX4 ...176 F6
Norwood Ave EX2 ...261 C1
Norwood Ho EX4 ...261 B4
Norwood Rd EX16 ...161 D6
Notre Dame Cl PL6 ...244 F5
Notre Dame Ho PL1 ...262 B3
Notre Dame RC Sch PL6 ...244 F5
Notte St PL1 ...262 C2
Nottiston Cross EX31 ...16 A1
Novorossisk Rd PL6 ...245 E2
Nower Rd EX13 ...87 C3
Nowers La TA21 ...160 C3
Nurseries Cl Exton EX3 ...183 C1
Topsham EX3 ...182 E4
Nursery Cl Exmouth EX8 .202 C8
Paignton TQ3 ...226 A5
Plymouth PL5 ...244 B7
Nursery End EX31 ...154 F7
Nursery Mews EX8 ...202 C8
Nursery Rd TQ12 ...207 E7
Nursey Cl EX16 ...49 B2
Nut Bush Cnr TQ2 ...219 B7
Nut Bush La TQ2 ...219 C6
Nut Tree Ct TQ5 ...230 B2
Nut Tree Orch TQ5 ...230 B2
Nutaberry Hill EX39 ...157 B1
Nutbrook EX8 ...196 B1
Nutcombe Hill EX34 ...3 C2
Nuttaberry Bglws EX39 ...25 F4
Nutwell Rd EX8 ...195 E7
Nymet Ave EX17 ...78 C4
Nymet Bridge Cross EX17 ...60 B4
Nymet Villas EX37 ...44 E6
Nymetwood Cross EX6 ...96 D8
Nymphayes La EX17 ...78 C8
Nynehead Rd TA21 ...160 F8

O

Oak Apple Cl PL12 ...242 D4
Oak Cl Exeter EX4 ...174 E1
Exminster EX6 ...182 A4
Kingsteignton TQ12 ...207 F6
Ottery St Mary EX11 ...169 D3
Shillingford Abbot EX2 ...181 A6
Silverton EX5 ...82 C6
Tiverton EX16 ...161 D5
Oak Cottage Cross EX22 .72 E2
Oak Cres EX15 ...162 C4
Oak Cross Bondleigh EX18 .77 D8
Inwardleigh EX20 ...75 C1
Oak Ct Holsworthy EX22 .164 C5
Lee Mill PL21 ...136 D6
Oak Dr Cullompton EX15 .163 C5
Plymouth PL6 ...244 F3
Oak End Ct TQ3 ...218 D2
Oak Gdns PL21 ...237 E5
Oak Hill
Budleigh Salterton EX9 ...198 C6
Dawlish EX7 ...204 C5
East Budleigh EX9 ...198 B6
Oak Hill Cross Rd
Dawlish EX7 ...204 C4
Teignmouth TQ14 ...210 D8
Oak La East Anstey TA22 ...32 E6
Thorverton EX17 ...81 A4
Whitstone EX22 ...70 E1
Oak Park Ave TQ2 ...219 D8
Oak Park Cl TQ2 ...219 D8
Oak Park Rd Dawlish EX7 204 E7
Newton Abbot TQ12 ...206 F4
Oak Pl TQ12 ...207 D3
Oak Rd Exeter EX4 ...176 F4
Okehampton EX20 ...170 C6
Tavistock PL19 ...171 C2
West Hill EX11 ...168 C2
Oak Ridge PL16 ...105 E4
Oak Tree Ct PL6 ...244 F1
Oak Tree Dr
Barnstaple EX32 ...155 E4
Newton Abbot TQ12 ...212 F8
Oak Tree Gdns EX34 ...150 B5
Oak Tree Gr [8] TQ14 ...210 A3
Oak Tree La PL19 ...171 C3
Oak Tree Pk
Plymouth PL6 ...245 D6
Sticklepath EX20 ...95 A5
Oak Tree Pl EX2 ...181 C8
Oak Units EX17 ...165 F5
Oak View EX14 ...166 A3
Oakapple Cl PL7 ...250 B7
Oakbank TQ13 ...180 C4
Oakcroft Rd PL2 ...248 B6
Oakdale Ave EX32 ...17 E1
Oakdene Rise PL9 ...255 F6
Oaken Ground TA21 ...160 B5
Oaken Hill
Great Torrington EX31 ...42 E8
Yarnscombe EX31 ...27 D1
Oakery Cres PL20 ...128 B8
Oakey Orch PL17 ...125 A4
Oakfield Cl PL7 ...251 C6
Oakfield Pk TA21 ...160 E4
Oakfield Pl PL4 ...249 B1
Oakfield Rd Exeter EX4 ...177 A5
Hatherleigh EX20 ...75 C7
Plymouth PL7 ...250 C6
Oakfield St EX1 ...177 F5
Oakfield Terr EX39 ...157 A7
Oakfield Terrace Rd PL4 ...249 B1
Oakford TQ12 ...207 D7
Oakford Cl EX36 ...30 D8
Oakford Cross
Kingsteignton TQ12 ...207 D7
North Molton EX36 ...30 C8
Oakford Villas EX36 ...30 D8
Oakham Rd PL5 ...244 B5
Oakhayes Rd EX5 ...184 B3
Oakhays EX36 ...158 D4
Oakhill Rd TQ1 ...219 F6
Oakhill Rise [3] EX31 ...154 C3
Oakland Ave EX31 ...154 D4
Oakland Dr EX7 ...204 D5
Oakland Park Sch EX7 .204 C5
Oakland Pk S EX31 ...154 B4
Oakland Rd TQ12 ...207 F2
Oakland Wlk EX7 ...204 D5
Oaklands Bideford EX39 ...25 D4
Petrockstow EX20 ...56 F4
Tavistock PL19 ...171 D2
Oaklands Cl
Buckfastleigh TQ11 ...236 A5
Plymouth PL6 ...245 D7
Seaton EX12 ...192 A8
Oaklands Cvn Pk EX20 .170 A6
Oaklands Dr
Okehampton EX20 ...170 B6
Saltash PL12 ...242 C3
Oaklands Gn PL12 ...242 D3
Oaklands Pk
Buckfastleigh TQ11 ...236 A5
Okehampton EX20 ...170 A5
Oaklands Rd TQ11 ...236 A6
Oaklawn Ct TQ1 ...219 F7
Oaklawn Terr TQ1 ...219 F7
Oaklea Honiton EX14 ...166 B6
Tiverton EX16 ...161 D6
Oaklea Cl TQ7 ...258 C4
Oaklea Cres EX31 ...153 D5
Oaklea Pk TQ12 ...123 A1
Oakleaf Cl EX21 ...73 E2
Oakleigh Rd
Barnstaple EX32 ...155 A4
Exmouth EX8 ...202 B7
Oakley Cl Exeter EX1 ...174 E1
Teignmouth TQ14 ...210 B7
Oakpark Cross PL21 ...137 E6
Oakpark La EX7 ...124 E6
Oakridge EX2 ...181 A8
Oaks The
Bovey Tracey TQ13 ...180 E7
[4] Hemyock EX15 ...67 B8
Mary Tavy PL19 ...117 E6
Newton Abbot TQ12 ...212 F8
Yeoford EX17 ...79 C1
Oaktree Cl
Broadclyst EX5 ...175 D6
Exmouth EX8 ...196 B3
Ivybridge PL21 ...237 A5
Upottery EX14 ...68 C2
Oakwell Cl EX38 ...159 E5
Oakwood Cl
Barnstaple EX31 ...154 C2
Dartmouth TQ6 ...233 C3
Plymouth PL6 ...245 D7
Oakwood Ct EX36 ...158 D4
Oakwood Dr PL21 ...137 B3
Oakwood Pk TQ7 ...143 E7
Oakwood Rise EX8 ...196 E3
Oakymead Pk TQ12 ...207 D6
Oates Rd PL2 ...248 B5
Oatlands Ave EX32 ...155 A1
Oatlands Dr TQ4 ...226 A4
Oberon Rd EX1 ...178 E7
Occombe Cross TQ3 ...218 F3
Occombe Valley Rd TQ3 ...219 A2
Ocean Ct PL1 ...253 F8
Ocean Pk EX39 ...156 B7
Ocean St PL2 ...247 E6
Ocean View Cres TQ5 ...230 A1
Ocean View Dr TQ5 ...230 A1
Ochil Cl EX39 ...26 A4
Octagon St PL1 ...262 B3
Octagon The PL1 ...262 B2
Octon Gr TQ1 ...219 E7
Odam Cross EX36 ...45 E7
Odam Moor Cross EX36 .45 E5
Oddicombe Beach Hill TQ1 ...220 D8
Oddicombe Cliff Rly★ TQ1 ...220 D8
Odle Hill TQ12 ...212 A6
Odlehill Gr TQ12 ...212 A6
Odun Rd [22] EX39 ...15 A1
Offwell CE Prim Sch EX14 ...86 B2
Offwell Turn EX24 ...102 B8
Ogwell Cross TQ12 ...207 A1
Ogwell End Dr TQ12 ...206 F2
Ogwell Mill Rd TQ12 ...206 E3
Ogwell Rd TQ12 ...206 F1
Oilmill Cross EX5 ...179 C2
Oilmill La
Clyst St George EX5 ...183 D8
Clyst St Mary EX5 ...179 C1
Oke Tor Cl TQ3 ...219 A2
Okefield Ave EX17 ...165 C6
Okefield Rd EX17 ...165 C6
Okefield Ridge EX17 ...165 C6
Okehampton & District Hospl EX20 ...170 C5
Okehampton Castle★ EX20 ...170 A3
Okehampton Cl PL7 ...251 B4
Okehampton Coll EX20 .170 B4
Okehampton Mus of Dartmoor Life★ EX20 .170 B5
Okehampton Pl [8] EX4 .177 A5
Okehampton Prim Sch EX20 ...170 B5
Okehampton Rd EX4 ...177 A5
Okehampton St EX4 ...177 A5
Okehampton Sta EX20 ...170 C3
Okehampton Way PL21 .237 D4
Oketor Cl EX20 ...170 D5
Okewill Cross EX31 ...10 A2
Okewood Ct EX8 ...202 B5
Olands Rd TA21 ...160 D6
Olchard La TQ12,TQ13 ...124 A4
Old Abbey Ct EX2 ...177 E2
Old Bakery Cl EX4 ...176 F7
Old Bakery Cotts PL8 ...257 F4
Old Bakery The EX8 ...202 B8
Old Barn Cl EX5 ...173 F8
Old Barnstaple Rd
Bideford EX39 ...157 D2
Braunton EX31 ...15 F7
Ilfracombe EX34 ...150 D2
Old Beer Rd EX12 ...191 E6
Old Bell Hill EX16 ...47 D5
Old Berrynarbor Rd EX34 ...150 F5
Old Bideford Rd
Barnstaple EX31 ...154 B2
Barnstaple EX31 ...154 C3
Old Blundell's EX16 ...161 D3
Old Bridge Rd EX15 ...83 F6
Old Bridwell EX15 ...65 F7
Old Butterleigh Rd EX5 ...82 B6
Old Bystock Dr EX8 ...196 E3
Old Canal Cl EX23 ...70 A6
Old Chapel Gdns EX19 ...58 F3
Old Chapel Way PL10 ...252 F6
Old Chard Rd EX14 ...86 C6
Old Cider Works La TQ12 ...212 A7
Old Cider Works The TQ12 ...212 A7
Old Coach Rd EX5 ...175 C6
Old Coast Rd EX34 ...2 E4
Old Coastguard PL9 ...140 E7
Old Coastguard Sta EX12 ...192 D5
Old Corn Mill (Hele Mill) The★ EX34 ...150 E5
Old Dairy The PL3 ...249 B6
Old Dawlish Rd EX6 ...181 C2
Old Ebford La EX3 ...183 C4
Old Exeter Rd
Bishop's Tawton EX32 ...16 E1
Chudleigh TQ13 ...123 F8
Chudleigh TQ13,EX6 ...114 A2
Newton Abbot TQ12 ...207 B4
Tavistock PL19 ...171 D7
Old Exeter St TQ13 ...123 E6
Old Farm Rd PL5 ...247 C8
Old Farm Way EX7 ...204 D4
Old Ferry Rd PL12 ...243 A3
Old Fore St EX10 ...188 B3
Old Foundry The PL19 ...171 D6
Old Gatehouse Rd EX7 .204 E7
Old George St PL1 ...262 C2
Old Greystone Hill PL15, PL19 ...115 D6
Old Hill Bickington TQ12 .131 D7
Cullompton EX15 ...163 D2
Old Ide La EX2 ...176 E2
Old Laira Rd PL3 ...249 C4
Old Launceston Rd PL19 ...171 B6
Old Laundry The PL1 ...262 A3
Old Lyme Hill DT6 ...104 F4
Old Lyme Rd DT6 ...104 F4
Old Manor Cl TQ13 ...130 E5
Old Manor Ct [20] EX7 ...204 D6
Old Manor Gdns EX24 ...103 B3
Old Market Cl EX2 ...177 B3
Old Market Dr EX39 ...38 F8
Old Market Field EX16 ...46 E1
Old Matford La EX6,EX2 .181 E6
Old Mill Cl EX2 ...261 C1
Old Mill Ct PL7 ...250 E5
Old Mill Ind Est EX5 ...173 E7
Old Mill La TQ6 ...233 C4
Old Mill Rd TQ2 ...219 E3
Old Mill The EX15 ...66 E8
Old Mine La PL18 ...125 B6
Old Newton Rd
Bovey Tracey TQ13 ...180 E4
Kingskerswell TQ12 ...212 E5
Old Nursery Dr EX4 ...178 B8
Old Orchard Cl EX23 ...70 A6
Old Orchard The EX20 ...74 E2
Old Paignton La TQ2 ...219 D2
Old Paignton Rd TQ2 ...219 D3
Old Park Rd Exeter EX4 .261 B4
Plymouth PL3 ...248 D6
Old Pavilion Cl EX2 ...178 C4
Old Pinn La EX1 ...174 E1
Old Plymouth Rd PL3 ...249 E5
Old Priory PL7 ...250 D5
Old Priory Jun Sch PL7 250 D5
Old Quarry Rd PL20 ...126 D3
Old Quay La [8] EX39 ...15 B1
Old Quay St TQ14 ...210 B4
Old Rd Brixton PL8 ...257 A5
Galmpton TQ5 ...229 B5
Harbertonford TQ9 ...139 C7
Lutton PL21 ...133 B2
Okehampton EX20 ...170 A4
Stoke Fleming TQ6 ...146 B7
Tiverton EX16 ...161 E4
Old Rectory Cl EX39 ...15 C2
Old Rectory Cross TQ13 110 C7
Old Rectory Gdns
Morchard Bishop EX17 ...61 B2
Thurlestone TQ7 ...143 A2
Old Rectory La
Ashwater EX21 ...90 E6
Bratton Fleming EX31 ...18 A8
Old Rydon Cl EX2 ...178 E2
Old Rydon La EX2 ...178 D1
Old Rydon Ley EX2 ...178 D2
Old Sawmill The EX10 ...186 C4
Old School Cl EX16 ...161 B4
Old School Ct
[6] Hemyock EX15 ...67 B8
[5] Honiton EX14 ...166 C6
Old School La EX31 ...153 E5
Old School Rd
Barnstaple EX32 ...155 C2
Plymouth PL5 ...247 C8
Old Sidmouth Rd EX24 .103 A4
Old Smithy Cotts EX39 ...37 B4
Old Station Rd
Barnstaple EX32 ...155 B4
Horrabridge PL20 ...126 F4
Old Station The PL20 ...126 E4
Old Sticklepath Hill EX31 ...154 E3
Old Stone Cl EX39 ...156 B6
Old Tannery Bsns Pk The [4] PL4 ...263 A4
Old Teignmouth Rd EX7 ...204 D4
Old Tinhay PL16 ...105 F4
Old Tiverton Rd
Bampton EX16 ...34 C1
Crediton EX17 ...165 E6
Exeter EX4 ...177 D8
Old Torquay Rd TQ3 ...226 C8
Old Torrington Rd EX31 154 D2
Old Torwood Rd TQ1 ...220 D4
Old Totnes Rd
Ashburton TQ13 ...130 F4
Buckfastleigh TQ11 ...236 C5
Newton Abbot TQ12 ...207 A1
Old Town EX39 ...157 A1
Old Town Hill TQ12, TQ13 ...122 C2
Old Town St
Dawlish EX7 ...204 D6
Plymouth PL1 ...262 C3
Old Vicarage Cl EX2 ...176 D1
Old Vicarage Gdn DT7 ...260 D3
Old Vicarage Rd EX2 ...177 A4
Old Walls Hill TQ14 ...124 D1
Old Warleigh La PL5 ...244 B7
Old Way Chipstable TA4 ...35 D6
Chudleigh TQ13 ...123 E6
Old Wharf The PL9 ...255 C7
Old Widdicombe La TQ3 ...225 D6

Old Widdicombe Rd TQ3 225 C7
Old Widdicome La TQ3 225 B8
Old Woodlands Rd PL5 244 D3
Old Woods Hill TQ2 219 E7
Old Woods Trad Est TQ2 219 E8
Old's View EX4 177 A7
Oldaway La EX5 172 C7
Oldaway Tongue TQ7 143 E1
Oldbarn Cross TQ12 212 A7
Oldbarn La EX16 33 E1
Oldberry La TA22 33 D6
Oldborough Cross EX17 61 B1
Oldborough La EX17 61 B1
Olde Ct EX22 164 C3
Oldenburg Pk TQ3 226 C7
Oldfields EX8 202 C6
Oldhouse La TQ7 142 F7
Oldlands Cl PL6 245 B6
Oldridge Rd EX4 98 B6
Oldridge View EX6 97 F5
Oldshute La TA22 33 C7
Oldstone Cross TQ9 139 F2
Oldway Mansion★ TQ3 226 B8
Oldway Pk TA21 160 F4
Oldway Prim Sch TQ3 226 B7
Oldway Rd
East Anstey TA22 32 F5
Paignton TQ3 226 B8
Wellington TA21 160 E4
Olga Terr EX8 195 F5
Olive Gdns EX7 201 B2
Olive Gr EX7 201 B2
Oliver Rd EX32 155 B5
Olivia Ct PL4 263 B4
Omega Ctr The EX2 178 E5
Once Upon A Time Childrens Theme Pk★ EX34 8 C6
One End St 4 EX39 15 A1
Onslow Rd Plymouth PL2 248 C7
Salcombe TQ8 259 D5
Ora Cl EX33 7 E2
Ora La EX33 7 E2
Ora Stone Pk EX33 7 E1
Orange Gr TQ2 214 A2
Orange Moor Cross EX18 44 F3
Orbec Ave TQ12 207 F7
Orchard Ave PL6 249 B7
Orchard Cl
Ashprington TQ9 139 F7
Barnstaple EX31 154 C3
Beesands TQ7 149 D7
Braunton EX33 152 C6
8 Brixham TQ5 230 C3
7 Chudleigh TQ13 123 F6
Colyford EX24 103 B3
7 Combe Martin EX34 3 A3
Dawlish EX7 204 D6
Denbury TQ12 211 A6
East Budleigh EX9 198 B6
East Ogwell TQ12 206 D1
Exeter EX1 174 F1
Exmouth EX8 196 B1
Exmouth, Littleham EX8 203 A6
Frogmore TQ7 144 E1
Galmpton TQ5 229 C5
Kingsteignton TQ12 207 F7
Kingsteignton, Sandygate TQ12 123 E2
Lympstone EX8 195 E5
Newton Poppleford EX10 186 D8
Okehampton EX20 170 B4
Ottery St Mary EX11 169 E3
3 Plymouth PL7 251 C5
Rockwell Green TA21 160 A5
Sandford EX17 80 A5
Shaldon TQ14 209 D5
Sidmouth EX10 187 F3
St Giles on the Heath PL15 90 C1
Talaton EX5 84 A2
Tavistock PL19 126 A8
Uffculme EX15 66 A7
Upton Pyne EX5 173 A7
Whitford EX13 103 B6
Wilmington EX14 86 C2
Woodbury EX5 184 C3
Yealmpton PL8 257 F3
Orchard Cotts
Holbeton PL8 136 D1
Lamerton PL19 116 F3
Newton Tracey EX31 27 A6
Orchard Cres PL9 255 C7
Orchard Cross EX17 60 D3
Orchard Ct
1 Crediton EX17 165 C5
Exeter EX1 178 E6
Ivybridge PL21 237 B5
Lamerton PL19 116 E3
Wellington TA21 160 E6
3 Whimple EX5 99 E8
Orchard Dr
Ipplepen TQ12 211 D2
2 Kingskerswell TQ12 212 F4
Otterton EX9 198 E7
Orchard Gate EX19 57 F7
Orchard Gdns
Bideford EX39 157 A4
Broadclyst EX5 175 D6
14 Dawlish EX7 204 D6
Exeter EX4 176 F4
10 Teignmouth TQ14 210 C4
West Buckland TA21 52 F7
Orchard Gr Brixham TQ5 230 C3
Croyde EX33 7 E1
Orchard Hill
Bideford EX39 157 A4
Exeter EX2 176 F3
Yealmpton PL8 136 B3
Orchard Ho
8 Chudleigh TQ13 123 E6
1 Teignmouth TQ14 210 C4
Orchard Ind Est's TQ7 258 C5
Orchard La Silverton EX5 82 B6
Starcross EX6 201 A4
Orchard Leigh EX16 161 C3
Orchard Mdw TQ13 111 A6
Orchard Pk
Dartington TQ9 222 F8
Dittisham TQ6 228 C3
Orchard Pl 3 TQ1 220 A7
Orchard Rd
Ashburton TQ13 130 F4
Barnstaple EX32 155 B3
1 Ilfracombe EX34 150 C5
Knowle EX33 8 D1
Plymouth PL2 248 B7
4 Torquay, Ellacombe TQ1 220 B6
Torquay, Hele TQ2 213 F1
Wrafton EX33 152 E3
Orchard Rise EX39 157 A4
Orchard Terr
Abbotskerswell TQ12 212 B7
Barnstaple EX32 155 B2
3 Bovey Tracey TQ13 180 D8
Buckfastleigh TQ11 236 B5
Chagford TQ13 111 A6
Crediton EX17 165 B5
Kingskerswell TQ12 212 F5
Totnes TQ9 223 C5
Tuckenhay TQ9 139 F6
Orchard The
Abbotskerswell TQ12 212 B6
Avonwick TQ10 135 B1
Barnstaple EX31 154 A3
Bishopsteignton TQ14 208 F8
Gunnislake PL18 125 D6
Holcombe EX7 210 E8
Holywell Lake TA21 51 E7
Honiton EX14 166 B5
Kilmington EX13 87 D1
Seaton EX12 192 A5
Tipton St John EX10 100 D2
Totnes TQ9 223 C5
Yealmpton PL8 257 F3
Orchard Vale Com Sch EX32 155 E4
Orchard View
Frogmore TQ7 144 E1
Halberton EX16 65 B7
Orchard Way
1 Bovey Tracey TQ13 180 D8
Chillington TQ7 145 A1
Cullompton EX15 163 B2
Honiton EX14 166 D6
Kenton EX6 194 D3
Lapford EX17 60 D3
Stoke Gabriel TQ9 227 F8
Tiverton EX16 161 B3
Topsham EX3 182 E5
Uffculme EX15 66 A7
Willand EX15 162 D4
Orchard Waye TQ9 223 B5
Orchardon La EX33 8 B1
Orchards The
Galmpton TQ5 229 B5
Landkey EX32 17 B2
Swimbridge EX32 28 E8
Orchardside EX10 188 B7
Orchardton Terr PL9 255 F5
Orchid Ave
Ivybridge PL21 237 A6
Kingsteignton TQ12 207 E7
Orchid Cl 7 EX16 161 F6
Orchid Vale 14 TQ12 123 F1
Orcombe Ct EX8 202 D8
Ordnance St PL1 247 E2
Ordulf Rd PL19 171 A5
Oregon Way PL3 249 D6
Oreston Prim Sch PL9 255 C7
Oreston Rd PL9 255 C8
Orestone Cross TQ2 213 D3
Orestone Dr TQ1 214 C6
Orestone La TQ2,TQ12 213 E3
Orient Rd TQ3 226 D8
Oriole Dr EX4 173 D1
Orkney Cl TQ2 213 E2
Orkney Mews EX16 161 D6
Orleigh Ave TQ12 207 B5
Orleigh Cl EX39 40 C7
Orleigh Ct EX39 25 C1
Orleigh Pk TQ12 207 B5
Orley Rd TQ12 211 B2
Orplington Ct EX16 65 B7
Orstone Cross EX32 18 E3
Orway Ash Cross EX15 66 B2
Orway Cross EX15 66 C1
Orwell Garth EX4 178 C8
Osbern Rd TQ3 219 A2
Osborn Cl TQ12 211 D2
Osborne Cl EX39 156 D2
Osborne La EX39 156 D2
Osborne Rd
Ilfracombe EX34 150 A5
Plymouth PL3 248 A3
Osborne St TQ12 207 D3
Osborne Villas 2 PL3 248 A3
Osmond Lodge TQ4 226 C5
Osmond's La 11 TQ14 210 B4
Osney Ave TQ4 226 B4
Osney Cres TQ4 226 B4
Osney Gdns TQ4 226 B4
Osprey Dr TQ2 213 D3
Osprey Gdns PL9 256 C7
Osprey Rd EX2 178 F6
Oswald Browning Way 4 EX31 155 A7
Otter Cl
Okehampton EX20 170 D6
Tipton St John EX10 100 D3
West Hill EX11 168 D4
Otter Ct Bickington TQ12 131 F8
Budleigh Salterton EX9 198 C1
Exeter EX2 181 C8
Otter Estuary Nature Reserve★ EX9 198 D1
Otter Rd TQ2 219 C7
Otter Reach EX10 186 F8
Otter Vale Cl EX14 68 C1
Otter Way EX32 155 D4
Otterbourne Ct EX9 198 B1
Otters The EX16 49 B2
Otterton CE Prim Sch EX9 198 E7
Otterton Mill★ EX9 198 D7
Ottervale Rd EX9 198 C1
Ottery Cotts PL19 116 E2
Ottery La EX10 101 A1
Ottery Moor Ind Est EX14 166 B6
Ottery Moor La EX14 166 A6
Ottery Park Ind Est PL19 116 E2
Ottery St EX9 198 F8
Ottery St Mary Hospl EX11 169 C3
Ottery St Mary Prim Sch EX11 169 E3
Our Lady & St Patrick's RC Prim Sch TQ14 210 A6
Our Lady's RC Prim Sch EX32 155 B5
Oussaborough La EX34 8 C6
Outer Ting Tong EX9 197 B3
Outland Rd PL2 248 C7
Oval Gn EX2 178 C3
Overbeck's Mus & Gdn★ TQ8 259 B1
Overbrook EX7 204 D6
Overcliff Ct EX7 204 E7
Overclose TQ3 225 F8
Overcott La EX36 46 D8
Overdale Cl TQ2 213 F4
Overdale Rd PL2 248 A7
Overgang TQ5 230 D5
Overgang Rd TQ5 230 C6
Overland Ct EX4 174 E2
Overlangs TQ7 142 C6
Overseas Est TQ6 146 B6
Overton Cl DT7 260 E5
Overton Gdns PL3 248 F5
Owen St TA21 160 C6
Owlaborough La EX36 32 B2
Owlacombe Cross TQ12 131 A7
Ox Hill La EX24 102 F4
Oxenham Cross EX20 95 C5
Oxenham Gn TQ2 219 D6
Oxenpark Gate EX6 112 F5
Oxenpark La
Berrynarbor EX34 2 C3
Ilfracombe EX34 2 C2
Morchard Bishop EX17 61 C1
Stockleigh Pomeroy EX17 80 F7
Oxford Ave PL3 248 E5
Oxford Cl EX8 196 E4
Oxford Cross EX33 8 A3
Oxford Ct TQ2 213 F1
Oxford Gdns PL3 248 E5
Oxford Gr EX34 150 B6
Oxford La TQ5 230 A4
Oxford Pk EX34 150 B5
Oxford Pl PL1 262 C3
Oxford Rd EX4 261 C4
Oxford St Dartmouth TQ6 233 F3
Exeter EX2 177 A4
Plymouth PL1 262 B3
Oxford Terr
Crediton EX17 165 D5
4 Plymouth PL1 262 B3
Sandford EX17 80 A5
Oxham Cross EX36 45 D8
Oxlea Cl TQ1 220 E4
Oxlea Rd TQ1 220 E4
Oxman's Cotts EX39 157 E6
Oxmon's La EX39 157 A7
Oyster Bend TQ4 226 C2
Oyster Cl TQ4 226 C2
Ozone Terr DT7 260 D2

P

Paccombe Pool La EX10 189 C7
Pacehayne La
Dalwood EX13 87 A1
Shute EX13 103 A8
Packhall La TQ5 230 A2
Packhorse Cl EX10 188 D8
Packington St PL2 248 A4
Packs Cl TQ9 139 C7
Padacre Rd TQ2 214 A4
Paddock Cl Plymouth PL9 255 E5
Saltash PL12 242 D4
Seaton EX12 191 F7
Paddock Dr PL21 237 D4
Paddock The
Brixham TQ5 230 B4
Dawlish EX7 204 E7
Dolton EX19 57 F7
Paddock The *continued*
Dulverton TA22 33 D6
Torquay TQ1 214 B1
Paddocks The
Abbotskerswell TQ12 212 B7
Honiton EX14 166 A2
Membury EX13 87 D6
Totnes TQ9 223 D6
Wellington TA21 160 E5
Paddons Coombe 9 TQ12 123 F1
Paddons La TQ14 210 A7
Pafford Ave TQ2 214 B2
Pafford Cl TQ2 214 A2
Page's Cross EX16 62 F7
Paige Adams Rd TQ9 223 B6
Paiges Farm PL9 255 C1
Paiges La 8 EX31 154 F5
Paignton & Dartmouth Rly★ TQ4 226 C2
Paignton & Dartmouth Steam Rly★ TQ5 229 C5
Paignton & District Hospl TQ3 226 B6
Paignton (Queen's Park) Sta TQ4 226 B6
Paignton Com Coll
Paignton TQ3 225 E5
Paignton TQ4 225 D4
Paignton Rd TQ9 228 A
Paignton Sta TQ4 226 B6
Paignton Zoological & Botanical Gdns★ TQ4 225 F4
Pail Pk EX33 8 D1
Painsford Cross TQ9 139 D7
Painter's Cross EX13 102 F7
Painters Ct EX2 261 A1
Painton Water EX39 37 D8
Paizen La EX12 191 B6
Palace Ave TQ3 226 B6
Palace Gate EX1 261 B2
Palace Mdw TQ13 123 E6
Palace Pl TQ3 226 B6
Palace St PL1 263 A2
Palatine Cl TQ1 220 B5
Pale Gate Cl EX14 166 D7
Palegate Cross TQ7 258 A8
Palermo 10 TQ1 220 D4
Palermo Rd TQ1 220 C7
Palfrey's La EX16 49 C5
Palk Cl TQ14 209 D5
Palk St TQ2 220 B4
Palm Cl EX8 196 D3
Palm Cross PL21 137 B2
Palm Ct EX7 201 A2
Palm Rd TQ2 220 A5
Palmer Ct EX9 198 A1
Palmer's La EX5 99 E5
Palmers Cl EX33 152 D5
Palmers Ct EX38 159 E5
Palmerston Dr EX4 176 E7
Palmerston Pk EX16 161 B2
Palmerston St PL1 262 A4
Palms The 2 TQ1 220 D4
Pamela Rd EX1 177 F7
Pankhurst Cl EX8 202 E7
Panney The EX4 178 A7
Pannier Mkt
Great Torrington EX38 159 D5
Tavistock PL19 171 C5
Panorama TQ2 219 E2
Panson Cross PL15 90 B3
Papermakers La PL21 237 E6
Parade Chudleigh TQ13 123 E6
Exmouth EX8 202 A7
Plymouth PL1 263 A2
Parade Bsns Pk 4 PL19 171 B4
Parade Ope PL1 263 A2
Parade Rd PL5 244 A3
Parade The
Chardstock EX13 88 A7
Millbrook PL10 252 E5
Milton Abbot PL19 116 A6
Paradise Glen TQ14 210 B6
Paradise Lawn EX36 158 D4
Paradise Pk EX22 70 E1
Paradise Pl 1 TQ5 230 D5
Paradise Rd
Plymouth PL1 248 A2
Teignmouth TQ14 210 C6
Paradise Wlk TQ4 226 C4
Paramore Way EX36 158 C4
Parehayne La EX24 102 E7
Parely Hill TQ13 110 F6
Paris Rd TQ3 226 C8
Paris St EX1 261 B3
Park Ave
Barnstaple EX31 154 C4
Bideford EX39 157 A3
Brixham TQ5 230 B3
Plymouth, Devonport PL1 247 E3
Plymouth, Plymstock PL9 255 D7
Westward Ho! EX39 156 C7
Park Bglws EX16 51 B3
Park Cl Clyst Hydon EX15 83 D4
Fremington EX31 153 E5
Holsworthy EX22 164 C6
Ivybridge PL21 237 C5
Plymouth PL7 250 B7
Silverton EX5 82 C5
Tiverton EX16 161 D5
Woodbury EX5 184 C2
Park Com Sch The EX32 155 A3
Park Cotts PL21 137 D6
Park Cres
Combe Martin EX34 3 A3
Plymouth PL9 255 C7
Park Cross EX17 62 C3
Park Ct Brixham TQ5 230 E5
Chillaton PL16 106 D1
Ilfracombe EX34 150 B4
Park Field Terr EX12 190 D4
Park Five Bsns Ctr EX2 178 E4
Park Gate EX37 28 D2
Park Gdns EX35 151 B5
Park Hall TQ1 220 B3
Park Hill
Teignmouth TQ14 210 B5
Tiverton EX16 161 C5
Park Hill Rd EX34 150 B5
Park La Barnstaple EX32 155 A3
8 Bere Alston PL20 125 E1
Bideford EX39 157 A3
Blackawton TQ9 139 E1
Budleigh Salterton EX9 197 F1
Chittlehampton EX37 43 F8
Combe Martin EX34 3 A3
Combe St Nicholas TA20 69 F6
Dunkeswell EX14 67 C4
Exeter EX4 174 E4
Exmouth EX8 202 A8
Filleigh EX32 29 D7
Otterton EX9 198 E6
Plymouth PL9 255 C7
Sparkwell PL7 132 C1
Torquay TQ1 220 B3
Wellington TA21 160 C1
Wellington, Chelston TA21 52 E7
Whitford EX13 103 B6
Witheridge EX16 62 D6
Park Lane Cotts EX32 29 D7
Park Manor EX39 38 F8
Park Meadow Cl EX17 60 D3
Park Mews TQ5 230 E5
Park Mill Cross EX17 59 F3
Park Mill La EX18 59 F8
Park Pl
Exeter, Heavitree EX1 177 F6
Exeter, Mount Radford EX2 261 C2
Winkleigh EX19 58 F2
Park Place La 9 PL3 248 A4
Park Rd Beer EX12 191 C5
Crediton EX17 165 D4
Dartington TQ9 216 B2
Dawlish EX7 204 D6
Exeter EX1 177 E7
Exmouth EX8 202 A8
Hatherleigh EX20 75 C7
Kingskerswell TQ12 212 F5
Lapford EX17 60 D3
Lifton PL16 105 E3
Plymouth PL3 249 A6
Silverton EX5 82 C5
St Dominick PL12 125 A2
Tiverton EX16 161 D5
Torpoint PL11 247 B3
Torquay TQ1 214 B1
Park Rise Dawlish EX7 204 D4
Salcombe TQ8 259 C4
Park Row EX20 170 B5
Park Sch TQ9 216 C3
Park St Crediton EX17 165 D5
Ivybridge PL21 237 C4
Lynton EX35 151 B5
Plymouth PL3 248 A4
Tiverton EX16 161 D5
Willand EX15 162 C5
Park Street Mews PL21 237 C4
Park Street Ope PL3 248 A4
Park Terr
21 Barnstaple EX32 155 A4
Ivybridge PL21 237 C4
Park View Axminster EX13 88 A3
Beaford EX19 42 D1
Holsworthy EX22 71 D5
Kenton EX6 194 F3
Newton Abbot TQ12 212 F8
Plymouth PL4 263 C3
Park View Cl 18 EX34 3 A3
Park View Cotts
Great Torrington EX38 42 B6
Kingston TQ7 142 C6
Park View Rd EX32 155 A6
Park View Terr
Okehampton EX20 170 C3
Westward Ho! EX39 156 C7
Park Way Exmouth EX8 202 C8
Woodbury EX5 184 C2
Park Wood Rise PL16 105 E4
Parkelands TQ13 180 C7
Parker Cl Plymouth PL7 250 B5
Wellington TA21 160 E6
Parker Rd
Bigbury-on-Sea TQ7 142 E3
Plymouth PL2 248 B6
Parker's Gn PL18 125 C6
Parker's Rd EX6 201 A8
Parkers Cl TQ9 223 D4
Parkers Cross La EX1 174 F2
Parkers Farm Holiday Pk TQ13 131 C6
Parkers Hollow EX31 154 B3
Parkers Way TQ9 223 D4
Parkes Rd EX38 159 F5
Parkesway PL12 242 D2
Parkfield TQ7 143 A2
Parkfield Cl
Marldon TQ3 218 D3
Totnes TQ9 223 F5
Parkfield Cross TQ13 131 A3
Parkfield Dr PL6 245 F1
Parkfield Rd
Topsham EX3 182 F5
Torquay TQ1 219 F7

Parkfield Wlk TQ7 143 A2
Parkham Cross EX39 24 F1
Parkham Glade TQ5 230 C4
Parkham La TQ5 230 C4
Parkham Prim Sch EX39 39 E8
Parkham Rd TQ5 230 C4
Parkham Twrs 6 TQ5 230 C4
Parkhayes EX5 184 C7
Parkhill Cotts PL21 136 F4
Parkhill Ho TQ12 211 F3
Parkhill Rd TQ1 220 C3
Parkhouse Rd EX2 176 F3
Parkhurst Rd TQ1 219 F7
Parkland Dr EX2 178 C3
Parklands
Barnstaple EX31 154 C3
12 Hemyock EX15 67 B8
Okehampton EX20 170 B3
South Molton EX36 158 B3
Totnes TQ9 223 C6
Parklands Cl EX36 158 B3
Parklands Rd TA21 160 D7
Parklands Way TQ13 180 C4
Parks Villas EX33 152 D5
Parkside Ivybridge PL21 237 E5
Plymouth PL2 247 F5
Salcombe TQ8 259 D5
Parkside Com Tech Coll
PL10 247 E3
Parkside Cres EX1 174 F3
Parkside Ct EX2 261 B2
Parkside Dr EX8 196 E3
Parkside Rd Exeter EX1 174 F3
Paignton TQ4 226 C6
Parkside Villas TQ1 220 C7
Parkstone La PL7 250 F6
Parkway Exeter EX2 176 F3
Ilfracombe EX34 150 B3
Parkway Ct PL6 249 E7
Parkway Ind Est The
PL6 249 E7
Parkway Rd TQ13 123 E6
Parkway The PL3,PL5,
PL6 244 B1
Parkwood Cl PL6 241 B2
Parkwood Ct PL19 171 D6
Parkwood Rd
Tavistock PL19 171 D6
Tavistock PL19 171 E7
Parkyns Cross EX19 43 B4
Parliament Ct 7 EX34 150 C6
Parliament St EX17 165 C5
Parnell Cl PL6 249 A8
Parr Cl EX1 261 C4
Parr La PL4 263 B2
Parr St Exeter EX1 261 C4
Plymouth PL4 263 B2
Parr's La TQ13 123 E6
Parracombe CE Prim Sch
EX31 4 C1
Parracombe La EX31 4 D2
Parracombe Lane Head
EX31 4 D2
Parricks La EX13 88 D3
Parrocks La TA20 88 C8
Parson Cl EX8 196 C2
Parson St TQ14 210 B5
Parson's Cl EX15 66 A3
Parsonage Cross
Chulmleigh EX18 44 F2
Dartington TQ9 215 F2
Germansweek EX21 91 D5
Staverton TQ9 216 E3
West Putford EX22 39 B2
Woodbury EX5 184 C3
Parsonage Ct PL16 105 E4
Parsonage Hill EX36 31 A3
Parsonage La
Awliscombe EX14 85 C1
Combe Martin EX31 10 E5
George Nympton EX36 29 F2
Hittisleigh EX6 96 C6
Honiton EX14 166 D5
Moreleigh TQ9 139 A3
Silverton EX5 82 B6
South Molton EX36 158 C5
Staverton TQ9 216 E4
Ugborough PL21 137 D6
Parsonage Lane Cross
EX32 18 B2
Parsonage Lane End
PL21 137 D6
Parsonage Rd PL8 141 A7
Parsonage St EX5 83 A7
Parsonage Way EX5 184 C4
Parsons Cl
Newton Poppleford EX10 186 D8
Plymouth PL9 256 A4
Parsons La EX5 99 B5
Parthia Pl EX8 196 E1
Partridge Cross EX16 63 A8
Partridge Hill EX36 45 D7
Partridge La EX16 63 A8
Partridge Rd EX8 196 C2
Partwayes PL19 116 E3
Pasley St PL2 247 E4
Pasley St E PL2 247 F4
Passage Rd PL8 140 F6
Passmore Rd EX5 82 F6
Pasture Cross TQ9 144 F8
Pastures The EX20 92 A2
Patchacott Cross
Bratton Clovelly EX21 92 A8
Northlew EX21 74 B1
Patchel Cross EX20 56 F3
Patches Rd EX16 161 B4
Paternoster La TQ12 211 C2
Paternoster Row
9 Barnstaple EX31 154 F5
Ottery St Mary EX11 169 D4
Path Field Cl EX32 18 B2
Path The 23 EX39 15 A1
Pathdown La EX33 7 F2
Pathfield EX38 159 F5
Pathfield Cl EX31 154 A3
Pathfield Lawn EX31 154 E6
Pathfield Sch EX31 154 E6
Pathfields Croyde EX33 7 E2
Totnes TQ9 223 D5
Uffculme EX15 66 A7
Pathfields Cl TQ9 223 D5
Pathfields Ind Est EX36 158 D6
Pathwhorlands EX10 188 A6
Patna Pl PL1 262 B4
Patricia Cl EX4 173 C2
Pattard Cross EX39 22 D4
Patterdale Cl PL6 245 D3
Patterdale Wlk PL6 245 D3
Patterson's Cross
EX11 169 D8
Patteson Cl EX11 100 F8
Patteson Dr EX11 169 F4
Pattinson Cl PL6 245 E2
Pattinson Dr PL6 245 F2
Paul St EX4 261 A3
Paullet EX16 50 C1
Pauntley Gdn EX10 187 F3
Paviland Grange 6 PL1 248 A3
Pavilion Pl EX2 261 B2
Pavington Cross EX37 43 E3
Pavor Rd TQ2 214 B2
Paws Rd EX37 43 B7
Payne Ct EX4 178 B8
Payne's Cotts EX14 85 C3
Paynsford Mews 2
TQ12 207 B4
Paynsford Rd 1 TQ12 207 B4
Paynter Wlk 5 PL7 251 B5
Payton Rd
Holywell Lake TA21 51 F7
Rockwell Green TA21 160 A5
Peacegate Cross EX20 76 E4
Peacehay La TA21 51 E4
Peacock Ave PL11 247 A3
Peacock Cl PL7 250 F7
Peacock La PL4 263 A2
Peacock Pl EX6 201 A8
Peacocks Cl TA21 52 F7
Peadhill La EX16 49 D2
Peak Cnr EX16 62 E7
Peak Cross TQ9 222 F3
Peak Hill Rd EX10 187 E3
Peak Tor Ave TQ1 220 C2
Peakfield Cross Ways
EX5 82 E6
Pear Dr EX15 162 D4
Pear Tree Cotts PL8 257 A5
Pear Tree Way 5 EX32 17 B2
Peard Rd EX16 64 D6
Peards Down Cl EX32 155 D4
Pearmain Cl EX15 162 D4
Pearn Cotts 2 PL3 248 F6
Pearn Gdns PL3 249 A7
Pearn Rd PL3 249 A7
Pearn Ridge PL3 249 A7
Pearse Cl EX20 75 B7
Pearson Ave 3 PL4 248 F4
Pearson Cl EX22 164 C5
Pearson Rd PL4 248 F4
Peartree Cl EX6 194 E3
Peartree Cross
Ashburton TQ13 130 E4
Denbury TQ12 211 A7
Peaseditch TQ5 230 D3
Peasland Rd TQ2 214 A4
Peaslands Rd EX10 188 A5
Peaspark Cross TQ7 144 D3
Peazen Flats EX12 191 C6
Pebble Ct TQ4 226 B4
Pebbleridge Rd EX39 156 C8
Pecorama Pleasure Gdns*
EX12 191 B5
Pedlerspool La EX17 165 E7
Peek La PL21 137 C8
Peek Mead DT7 193 F7
Peek Moor Cross EX22 90 B4
Peeks Ave PL9 255 F7
Peel Row 3 EX4 178 C8
Peel St PL1 248 A1
Peep La 4 EX17 165 D5
Pegasus Ct Exeter EX1 177 F6
Paignton TQ3 226 B8
Pegwell La TQ14 209 B3
Pellew Arc 5 TQ14 210 B4
Pellew Ho 6 TQ14 210 B4
Pellew Pl PL2 247 F4
Pellew Way TQ14 210 A7
Pellinore Rd EX4 174 A1
Pembrey Wlk PL5 243 E4
Pembroke La PL1 247 E1
Pembroke Lodge 12
EX34 150 B5
Pembroke Pk TQ3 218 E3
Pembroke Rd
Paignton TQ3 225 E7
Torquay TQ1 220 B5
Pembroke St
Plymouth PL1 247 E1
Plymouth PL1 247 F1
Pemros Rd PL5 243 C1
Pen-y-dre EX15 163 C4
Pencair Ave PL11 246 E2
Pencepool Cotts EX15 83 F6
Pencepool Orch EX15 83 F6
Pencombe Rocks EX31 4 C1
Pencorse Rd TQ2 219 F8
Pencreber Rd 3 PL20 126 F4
Pencross View 1 EX15 67 B8
Pendarves TQ9 222 D2
Pendeen Cl PL6 244 F6
Pendeen Cres PL6 245 A6
Pendeen Pk TQ7 145 A1
Pendennis Cl
Plymouth PL3 248 F8
Torpoint PL11 246 F3
Pendennis Rd TQ2 219 F8
Pendilly Ave PL11 246 F2
Pendragon Rd EX4 174 A2
Penfield Gdns 1 EX7 204 D6
Pengelly Cl PL11 246 F5
Pengelly Hill PL11 247 A5
Pengelly Pk PL11 246 F5
Pengilly Way EX39 22 E3
Penhale Dr EX22 164 B5
Penhayes Rd EX6 194 E3
Penhill Chalets TQ6 146 B7
Penhill Cross EX6 113 F5
Penhill La TQ5 234 E8
Peninsular Pk PL12 242 C4
Penlee EX9 199 G2
Penlee Cotts PL10 140 J2
Penlee Gdns PL3 248 A4
Penlee Pk PL11 246 E4
Penlee Pl 4 PL4 248 F4
Penlee Rd PL3 248 A4
Penlee Way PL3 248 A4
Penleonard Cl EX2 177 E5
Penn Cross DT6 260 F7
Penn Ho TQ12 207 E2
Penn Inn Cl TQ12 207 E2
Penn La TQ5 230 D3
Penn Mdws TQ5 230 D3
Pennant Ho EX8 201 E6
Pennant Way PL21 136 D6
Pennball Cross TQ9 217 B3
Pennine Dr TQ4 225 D4
Pennington Cl EX17 79 A5
Pennsland La TQ13 130 F7
Pennsylvania Cl EX4 177 D8
Pennsylvania Cres EX4 177 C8
Pennsylvania Pk EX4 173 D1
Pennsylvania Rd
Exeter EX4 173 C3
Torquay TQ1 220 B5
Penny Cl Exminster EX6 182 A4
Wellington TA21 160 D7
Penny Plot DT7 260 C4
Penny Thorn Cross EX14 85 E7
Penny's Hill TQ1 219 F7
Penny's La PL9 256 D6
Penny's Terr EX13 167 D5
Pennyacre Rd TQ14 210 C6
Pennycomequick Hill
PL1,PL3 262 B4
Pennycross Cl PL2 248 D8
Pennycross Park Rd
PL2 248 C7
Pennycross Prim Sch
PL2 248 C8
Pennywell Cl TQ13 131 B1
Pennywell Farm & Wildlife
Ctr* TQ11 135 E6
Penpethy Cl TQ5 230 B4
Penpethy Rd TQ5 230 B5
Penrith Cl PL6 245 D3
Penrith Gdns PL6 245 D3
Penrith Wlk PL6 245 D3
Penrose Almshouses 4
EX32 155 A4
Penrose St PL1 262 B3
Penrose Terr 7 EX1 261 A6
Penrose Villas 5 PL4 248 F4
Penroses Terr EX22 164 C4
Penryn Pl 4 TQ14 210 A3
Pens La EX15 67 B7
Penscombe Cross PL15 115 A6
Penshurst Rd TQ12 207 B1
Pensilva Pk TQ5 230 C2
Penson Cross EX20 59 B1
Penson La Bondleigh EX20 77 B8
North Tawton EX20 59 B1
Penswell Cross TQ10 135 E4
Pentamar St PL2 247 E4
Pentgrove Ct EX8 202 D7
Pentice La EX34 3 A3
Pentillie Rd
Bere Alston PL20 125 E1
Plymouth PL4 248 E4
Pentillis Cres PL4 248 D4
Pentire Rd PL11 246 F3
Pentland Cl PL6 244 F7
Penton Cl EX17 165 D6
Penton La EX17 165 D5
Penton Rise EX17 165 D6
Pentridge Ave TQ2 219 C2
Pentyre Ct PL4 263 C4
Pentyre Terr PL4 263 C4
Penwill Way TQ4 226 A4
Peoples Park Rd EX17 165 C6
Pepper La
Kingswear TQ6 234 E4
Plymouth PL9 256 D7
Pepper St PL19 171 C6
Pepper's Cnr EX9 198 F7
Pepperdon Hall La
TQ13 112 B3
Peppery La TQ14 209 D5
Pepys Pl PL5 244 E1
Perceval Rd EX4 174 A2
Perches Cl PL8 141 B7
Percy Cross EX14 67 B2
Percy Rd EX2 177 B3
Percy St PL5 243 D1
Percy Terr PL4 249 A4
Peregrine Cl TQ2 213 D3
Perinville Cl TQ1 220 E6
Perinville Rd TQ1 220 D7
Periwinkle Dr
Barnstaple EX31 154 B3
Plymouth PL7 251 C5
Perkins Cross EX5 99 C1
Perranporth Cl PL5 243 E4
Perriam's Pl EX9 199 G2
Perridge Cl EX2 176 E3
Perridge Cross EX6 98 E1
Perriman's Row EX8 202 A7
Perriton Cross EX5 99 E8
Perros Cl TQ14 209 D8
Perry Cross TQ12 206 D7
Perry Hill EX17 80 E8
Perry La
Doddiscombsleigh EX6 113 D5
Newton Abbot TQ12 206 D6
Perry New Rd TA22 33 F4
Perry Rd EX4 177 B8
Perry St TA20 88 D8
Perryman Cl PL7 250 E7
Perryman's Hill EX17 79 F7
Perrys Gdns EX11 168 D4
Perseverance Cotts 1
PL7 250 E7
Perth Cl EX4 173 E2
Peryam Cres EX2 178 A4
Peryn Rd PL19 171 A5
Peter Hopper's Hill PL5 240 C2
Peter St EX5 82 F7
Peter's Cl PL9 256 C7
Peter's Gn EX17 61 A1
Peter's Park La PL5 243 E1
Peterborough Rd EX4 176 E7
Peterclose Rd EX16 161 F3
Peters Cres TQ3 218 D3
Peters Park Cl PL5 243 E1
Petersfield Cl PL3 249 B6
Petertavy Cross PL19 117 E3
Pethertons EX16 65 A7
Pethick Cl PL6 244 D6
Pethill Cl PL6 245 F2
Pethybridge TQ13 122 B8
Petit Well La TQ1 214 B1
Petitor Mews TQ1 214 B1
Petitor Rd TQ1 214 C1
Petrel Cl TQ2 213 C3
Petticoat La EX13 167 A6
Petton Cross EX16 35 A3
Peverell Park Rd PL3 248 D6
Peverell Terr PL3 248 D5
Pew Tor Cl
Tavistock PL19 171 E5
3 Yelverton PL20 126 F3
Phear Ave EX8 202 B7
Philham Cross EX39 22 D1
Philham La EX39 22 D1
Philham Water EX39 22 D1
Philip Ave EX31 154 D2
Philip Cl PL9 256 A6
Philip Gdns PL9 255 F6
Philip Ho EX1 178 E6
Philip Rd EX4 177 F8
Philips La 1 EX33 152 D5
Phillimore St 3 PL2 247 F4
Phillipps Ave EX8 196 B1
Phillips Sq EX14 166 B6
Phoenix Cl 9 PL20 126 F4
Phoenix La EX16 161 D3
Phoenix Pl TQ7 258 C5
Phoenix St PL1 262 A2
Piazza Terr EX2 261 B1
Pick Pie Dr PL6 245 E8
Picket Head Hill TQ14 210 A2
Pidgeley Rd EX7 204 F8
Pidgeon's La EX13 104 B7
Pidland La EX16 47 F1
Pidsley Hill EX17 79 F7
Pidsley La EX17 79 F8
Piece Hill EX6 97 E4
Piend La EX17 62 B1
Pier Head EX8 201 E6
Pier La PL10 253 A1
Pier St PL1 262 B1
Piermont Pl EX7 204 E6
Pig La EX13 167 D6
Piggy La EX39 156 F7
Pigs Leg Cross EX20 108 A8
Pigspark Cross TQ13 131 A5
Pike Rd PL3 249 D5
Pike's Mead EX20 170 B4
Pikes Hill EX6 97 E3
Pilemoor La EX16 48 E3
Pilemore Cross EX16 48 E4
Piley La TA21 51 D8
Pilgrim Cl PL2 248 B6
Pilgrim Ct 11 PL20 125 E1
Pilgrim Dr PL20 125 E1
Pilgrim Prim Sch PL1 262 B3
Pill Gdns EX33 152 D5
Pill La Barnstaple EX32 155 A2
Barnstaple, Chestwood
EX32 155 A1
Saltash PL12 242 E4
Pill Lawn EX32 155 A2
Pill Rd EX39 157 A2
Pilland Way EX31 154 D6
Pillar Ave TQ5 230 B5
Pillar Cl TQ5 230 B5
Pillar Cres TQ5 230 B5
Pillar Ct TQ5 230 B5
Pillar Flats TQ5 230 B5
Pillar Wlk PL6 244 E7
Pillavins La EX36 158 F6
Pilliven Cross EX16 46 F2
Pilliven La EX16 47 A2
Pillmere Dr PL12 242 D4
Pillory Hill PL8 140 F6
Pilmuir Ave TQ2 219 E5
Pilton Cswy EX32 154 F6
Pilton Inf Sch EX31 154 F6
Pilton La EX1 178 D8
Pilton Lawn EX31 154 F6
Pilton Quay EX31 154 F6
Pilton Sch & Com Coll
EX31 154 E7
Pilton St EX31 154 F6
Pimlico TQ1 220 B5
Pimm Rd TQ3 225 E7
Pin La PL1 263 A2
Pinaster Cl EX14 166 E5
Pinbrook Mews EX4 174 C2
Pinbrook Rd EX4 174 D1
Pinbrook Units EX4 174 D1
Pinces Gdns EX2 177 A3
Pinces Rd EX2 177 A3
Pinch Hill EX23 70 A7
Pinder Ct PL19 171 B5
Pine Ave EX4 176 F7
Pine Cl Brixham TQ5 230 B2
Ilfracombe EX34 150 E4
Teignmouth TQ14 210 D7
Tiverton EX16 161 B4
Pine Ct TQ1 220 D5
Pine Gdns EX14 166 D6
Pine Gr EX14 166 D6
Pine Park Rd EX14 166 D5
Pine Ridge DT7 260 E5
Pine Tree Cl EX7 201 B2
Pine View PL18 125 D6
Pine View Ave TQ1 220 C6
Pine View Cl
Exmouth EX8 196 F2
Halwill Junction EX21 73 E3
Pine View Gdns TQ1 220 C6
Pine View Rd TQ1 220 C6
Pine Wlk DT7 260 D2
Pinefields Cl EX11 168 E3
Pinehurst Way PL21 237 A6
Pineridge Cl EX4 176 F4
Pines Cl EX39 22 E3
Pines Rd Exmouth EX8 196 D3
Paignton TQ3 225 F8
Pines The Exeter EX4 176 F7
Honiton EX14 166 D5
Pinewood Cl
Dawlish EX7 205 A8
Plymouth PL7 250 F6
Pinewood Dr PL6 245 E7
Pinewood La EX4 174 B2
Pinewood Rd TQ12 207 E2
Pinhay Hollow DT7 104 B2
Pinhey's Cross TQ9 144 F5
Pinhoe Bridge Halt Sta
EX1 178 A7
Pinhoe CE Comb Sch
EX4 174 E1
Pinhoe Rd EX4 178 B8
Pinhoe Sta EX1 174 E1
Pinhoe Trad Est EX4 174 D1
Pinksmoor La TA21 51 E7
Pinkworthy Cross EX16 48 C8
Pinkworthy Hill EX16 48 B7
Pinn Hill EX1 174 F2
Pinn La Exeter EX1 178 F8
Otterton EX10 187 B2
Pinn Lane Cnr EX10 187 A1
Pinn Valley Rd EX1 174 F1
Pinnbridge Ct EX1 178 E8
Pinncourt La EX1 174 F2
Pinnex Moor Rd EX16 161 E6
Pins Pk EX22 164 C5
Pinslow Cross PL15 105 B8
Pinwood La EX4 174 B1
Pinwood Meadow Dr
EX4 174 B2
Pioneer Cotts EX12 191 D5
Pioneer Terr TQ11 236 A5
Pipehouse La TQ13 123 C4
Pipers Cross TQ7 142 C7
Pipers Pl EX14 68 C2
Pippin Cl EX1 178 C6
Pippins Field EX15 66 A7
Pippins The PL21 237 A5
Piscombe La EX9 198 F7
Pit Hill EX34 2 D4
Pitchingstone Cross
TQ7 147 C7
Pitcombe La TA4 35 B5
Pitfield Cl EX15 162 D3
Pitham La EX11 169 F7
Pitland Cnr PL19 117 B4
Pitland La TQ12 213 E6
Pitlands La EX15 67 A8
Pitley Cross TQ13 131 A5
Pitley Rd TQ13 131 B5
Pitman's La PL21 133 C2
Pits La PL10 140 H2
Pitsham La TA4 34 E6
Pitson La EX10 187 A5
Pitt Ave 12 EX39 15 A1
Pitt Cres TQ4 224 B7
Pitt Cross EX39 22 C4
Pitt Ct 8 Appledore EX39 15 A1
Loddiswell TQ7 143 F7
Pitt Hill Appledore EX39 157 B8
Crediton EX17 79 F3
Kenton EX6 194 D3
Shebbear EX21 55 D4
Pitt Hill Rd TQ12 206 F4

Pitt Ho TQ13 123 D5
Pitt La Bideford EX39 157 A2
Bow EX17 78 B5
Butterleigh EX16 64 C4
Cadbury EX5 81 C8
Chevithorne EX16 49 D2
Huish Champflower TA4 35 E8
North Molton EX36 30 F8
Thorverton EX5 81 F7
Waterrow TA4 35 F5
Pitton Cross EX6 96 E5
Pitts Cnr EX16 63 D4
Pitts Ct EX2 261 C1
Pixey Plain EX36 31 B3
Pixie Dell EX33 152 B7
Pixie La EX33 152 C6
Pixon La PL19 171 B4
Pixon Trad Est 2 PL19 171 B4
Pixton Cross EX19 58 B2
Pixton Way TA22 33 E6
Place Cross
Ashburton TQ13 131 A6
Okehampton EX20 93 E5
Place de Brest PL1 262 C3
Place La TQ13 131 A5
Plainfield La EX16 63 C7
Plainmoor Rd 2 TQ1 220 B7
Plains The TQ9 223 D5
Plaistow Cl PL5 243 E2
Plaistow Cres PL5 243 E2
Plaistow Hill Inf Sch PL5 243 E2
Plant World Gdns* TQ12 213 C7
Plantagenet Dr EX15 163 C6
Plantation Cl TQ12 207 F1
Plantation Terr EX7 204 E6
Plantation Way
Torquay TQ2 213 C2
Totnes TQ9 222 F6
Plassey Cl EX4 173 D2
Plaston Gn EX6 112 D5
Plat The TQ6 145 E5
Platt Cl TQ8 259 B4
Platway La TQ14 209 D5
Play Cross TQ13 130 A4
Playmoor Dr EX1 174 F1
Pleasant Terr 1 TQ3 226 A6
Pleasure Hill Cl PL9 255 D8
Plintona View PL7 250 E7
Ploudal Rd EX15 163 B2
Plougastel Dr PL12 242 E3
Plough Gn PL12 242 C3
Ploughman Way PL8 136 A2
Plover Rise PL21 237 B5
Plum Way EX15 162 D4
Plume Of Feathers Cl EX11 169 E4
Plumer Rd PL6 244 F2
Plumper's Cross EX38 41 A7
Plumtree Dr EX2 178 B4
Plumtree La EX5 99 E7
Plym Cl TQ2 219 B7
Plym Cres PL19 171 D5
Plym St PL4 263 A3
Plym Valley Rly* PL7 250 A7
Plym View Prim Sch PL3 249 D6
Plymbridge Gdns PL7 250 C7
Plymbridge La PL6 245 B4
Plymbridge Rd
Plymouth, Estover PL6 245 E5
Plymouth, Plympton PL7 250 C7
Plymouth PL6 245 A4
Plymouth City Airport PL6 245 C5
Plymouth Coll PL4 248 E4
Plymouth Coll of Art & Design PL4 263 A3
Plymouth Coll of Art & Design (Sutton Annexe) PL4 263 A3
Plymouth Coll of F Ed PL1 248 A2
Plymouth Coll of F Ed (Annexe) PL1 262 C4
Plymouth Coll Prep Sch PL3 248 E6
Plymouth Dome Discovery Ctr* PL1 262 C1
Plymouth High Sch for Girls PL4 263 A4
Plymouth Hill PL20 128 A8
Plymouth International Bsns Pk PL6 245 A3
Plymouth Nuffield Hospl The PL6 245 B4
Plymouth Pavilions PL1 262 B2
Plymouth Rd
Buckfastleigh TQ11 236 A3
Buckfastleigh TQ11 236 B4
Kingsbridge TQ7 258 C6
Plymouth PL7 250 B6
South Brent TQ10 134 F2
Tavistock PL19 171 B4
Totnes TQ9 223 B5
Plymouth Road Ind Est PL19 171 C3
Plymouth Sta PL1,PL4 262 C4
Plympton Cross TQ7 147 F5
Plympton Hill PL7 250 F3
Plympton Hospl PL7 250 D5
Plympton St Mary CE Inf Sch PL7 250 D5
Plympton St Maurice Prim Sch PL7 250 F3
Plymstock Rd PL9 255 D7
Plymstock Sch PL9 255 F8
Plymtree CE Prim Sch EX15 83 F5
Plymtree Dr PL7 250 C7
Poadmarsh Cross EX36 31 D1
Poadmarsh Hill
Bishops Nympton EX36 30 F1
Bishops Nympton, Rose Hill EX36 31 D1
Pocklington Rise PL7 250 E5
Pocombe Hill EX2 176 D3
Pod La EX13 87 F4
Pode Dr PL7 251 B4
Point In View Cotts EX8 196 B3
Point Terr EX8 201 E6
Pole Rue La TA20 69 F6
Polehouse La EX2 176 E1
Poles Hill EX31 154 E7
Poleshill La EX31 154 D7
Polhearne La TQ5 230 B3
Polhearne Way TQ5 230 B3
Pollard Cl Plymouth PL9 255 B5
Saltash PL12 242 B2
Pollard's La TA21 52 F7
Pollards The EX32 155 C3
Pollards Way PL12 242 E3
Pollyblank Rd 2 TQ12 207 B3
Pollybrook EX5 184 C2
Polmer Mews EX9 199 G2
Polruan Terr PL1 262 A3
Polsham Pk TQ3 226 B7
Polsloe Rd EX1 177 E6
Polson Hill EX17 61 A2
Poltimore Cl EX36 158 D4
Poltimore Cross EX4 174 E6
Poltimore Ct EX4 174 F7
Poltimore Lawn EX32 155 B6
Poltimore Rd
Farway EX24 101 F7
Offwell EX14 102 A8
South Molton EX36 158 D4
Poltimore Sq EX4 261 B4
Polwhele Rd 14 EX16 64 D7
Polywell EX39 14 F1
Polzeath Gdns PL2 248 D8
Pomeroy Ave TQ5 230 A5
Pomeroy Pl 8 TQ12 122 F1
Pomeroy Rd
Newton Abbot TQ12 207 B3
Tiverton EX16 64 E8
Pomphlett Cl PL9 255 D8
Pomphlett Farm Ind Est PL9 249 E1
Pomphlett Gdns PL9 255 D8
Pomphlett Prim Sch PL9 255 E8
Pomphlett Rd PL9 255 E8
Pond Hill EX16 65 A7
Pond La TA21 51 D3
Pondfield Rd PL12 242 B3
Ponsford Cross EX15 65 A2
Ponsford La EX15 65 A2
Ponsonby Rd PL3 248 B4
Pooks La TQ13 130 F5
Pool Anthony Dr EX16 64 E8
Pool Cross EX20 107 F8
Pool Hill Ashbrittle TA21 35 E1
Bridestowe EX20 107 F8
Pool La Burrington EX37 44 A4
Chittlehampton EX37 29 A1
Woolacombe EX34 1 B1
Pool Pk TQ10 135 A3
Poole Cross TQ12 211 A1
Poole Hill TA22 33 B5
Poole Park Rd PL5 247 C8
Poole's Ct DT7 260 E3
Pooley Cross TQ7 143 E4
Poolmill Cross TQ13 112 E1
Pools Weir TQ12 214 B8
Pop La EX13,TA20 88 B8
Pope's La Lapford EX17 60 C3
Rockwell Green TA21 160 B4
Popes Cl EX17 165 C6
Popes La EX24 103 A3
Popham Cross EX36 19 A3
Popham Flats TA21 160 D6
Popham La EX36 19 A3
Poplar Cl Brixham TQ5 229 F2
Exeter EX2 177 A3
Exmouth EX8 196 D3
Newton Abbot TQ12 213 A8
Plymouth PL7 251 B5
Poplar Dr TQ7 258 C5
Poplar Mount EX13 167 D6
Poplar Row EX9 199 H2
Poplar Terr EX37 43 C7
Poplar Tree Cnr EX12 192 A8
Poplar Tree Dr EX12 192 A7
Poplars Dr TQ3 218 D2
Poplars The
7 Chudleigh Knighton TQ13 123 C4
Exeter EX4 174 E2
Poppy Cl EX4 176 D8
Porch EX13 88 A3
Pork Hill PL19 117 F1
Porlock Way TQ4 225 F2
Porsham Cl PL6 241 B1
Porsham La PL5 244 E8
Porspoder Pl PL10 253 A2
Port Cross
Bishops Nympton EX36 31 B4
Bratton Fleming EX31 10 F5
Port Hill EX31 10 F5
Port La
Bishops Nympton EX36 31 C4
Chillington TQ7 145 A1
Dulverton TA22 34 A5
Wotter PL7 132 C4
Port Lane Cl TQ7 144 F1
Port Mer Cl EX8 196 E3
Port Rd EX6 200 D4
Portal Pl PL21 237 B5
Portbridge Cross TQ9 215 F8
Portchester Hts EX4 261 C4
Porteous Cl PL1 247 F3
Porter Way PL12 242 C3
Porter's La EX8 195 E8
Portford Cross EX31 27 E3
Portford La TQ10 135 A2
Portgate Cross EX36 30 B8
Portland Ave
Exmouth EX8 202 B6
Teignmouth TQ14 210 C7
Portland Bldgs 6 EX32 155 A6
Portland Ct
19 Barnstaple EX32 155 A4
Lyme Regis DT7 260 C3
9 Plymouth PL1 247 F3
Torquay TQ1 220 D7
Portland La
Kilmington EX13 103 C8
Meavy PL20 127 D2
Portland Pk EX34 150 C6
Portland Pl E PL4 263 A4
Portland Rd
Plymouth PL1 247 F3
Torquay TQ1 220 D7
Portland Sq
Plymouth PL4 262 C4
Plymouth PL4 263 A4
Portland Square La N PL4 263 A4
Portland St
Barnstaple EX32 155 B3
Exeter EX1 177 E6
Ilfracombe EX34 150 C6
Portland Villas PL4 262 C4
Portledge Pl EX39 25 A3
Portlemore Cl TQ7 147 E6
Portlemore Gdns TQ7 147 E6
Portmarsh La EX32 155 A4
Portsmouth Arms Cross EX18 60 B7
Portsmouth Arms Sta EX37 43 F6
Portway EX15 66 C7
Portway Cl PL9 256 D7
Possession Cross EX37 28 E7
Post Box Cross
Bondleigh EX20 76 F6
Cheriton Fitzpaine EX17 63 B3
Post Cl TA21 160 E4
Post Cross EX15 65 F2
Post Cross Bsns Pk EX15 65 F2
Post Hill EX16 64 E8
Post La Brendon EX35 6 C4
Upton TA4 34 E7
Post Office La
Cheriton Fitzpaine EX17 62 F1
Tatworth TA20 88 C8
Post Office St EX1 261 B3
Potacre St EX38 159 D5
Potem's Cross
Atherington EX37 28 A1
Yarnscombe EX37 27 F1
Potshop Cross EX17 79 D2
Potter's Cross TA4 35 C7
Potters Cl EX11 168 D5
Potters Hill TQ1 220 B5
Potters Stile EX14 67 B1
Potters Way PL7 250 D5
Potters Yd TQ12 180 B1
Potterswell EX31 154 B3
Pottery Cl
Bovey Tracey TQ13 180 C5
Honiton EX14 166 D6
Pottery Ct TQ6 233 D4
Pottery Est PL10 252 E6
Pottery La EX31 153 A4
Pottery Mews TQ3 218 D3
Pottery Rd
Bovey Tracey TQ13 180 C5
Kingsteignton TQ12 207 D6
Plymouth PL1 247 D3
Pottery Units TQ12 207 D4
Pottington Bsns Pk EX31 154 C6
Pottington Dr EX31 154 E6
Pottington Ind Est EX31 154 D5
Pottington Rd EX31 154 E6
Pottles Cl EX6 182 B3
Poultney Cl PL7 251 A5
Pouncers Cross EX18 60 E6
Pound Cl Burrington EX37 43 F3
Sidbury EX10 101 B2
Topsham EX3 182 E6
Pound Cnr
Clyst Honiton EX5 179 E7
Whitestone EX4 98 C5
Pound Cross EX5 99 B5
Pound Down Cnr EX4 98 D5
Pound Field TQ9 227 F8
Pound Gate EX6 112 F5
Pound Hill Axmouth EX12 192 D7
Holcombe Rogus TA21 51 A5
Pound La Bridford EX6 113 A5
Buckland St Mary TA20 69 D8
Colaton Raleigh EX10 186 C5
13 Combe Martin EX34 3 A3
Exmouth EX8 196 C1
High Bickington EX37 43 C8
Pound La *continued*
Kingskerswell TQ12 212 F4
Nadderwater EX4 98 F4
Raymond's Hill DT6 104 D8
Shaldon TQ14 209 C5
Stoke Climsland PL17 115 C1
5 Teignmouth TQ14 210 C4
Topsham EX3 182 E6
Uplyme DT7 260 B5
Upottery EX14 68 C1
Woodbury EX5 184 C3
Yarcombe EX14 69 B2
Pound Lane End EX37 43 D8
Pound Lane Trad Est EX8 196 C1
Pound Mdw
Great Torrington EX38 42 B7
Hatherleigh EX20 75 C7
Parkham EX39 39 E8
Pound Pk EX20 170 D6
Pound Pl TQ13 180 D8
Pound Rd Axminster EX13 88 F2
Crapstone PL20 126 E3
Lyme Regis DT7 260 D3
Pound Sq EX15 163 C2
Pound St Exmouth EX8 202 A6
Lyme Regis DT7 260 D3
Moretonhampstead TQ13 111 F4
Plymouth PL1 254 A8
Pound Terr 3 TA21 160 D5
Pound's Cross PL6 240 E5
Poundfield Cl EX31 153 F5
Poundhouse Cross TQ6 146 B8
Pounds Hill EX17 165 D6
Pounds Park Rd
1 Bere Alston PL20 125 E1
Plymouth PL3 248 D7
Pounds Pk PL12 242 F3
Poundsclose TA22 33 E4
Poundsgate Cl TQ5 230 E4
Poundshill Cross EX17 165 D6
Poundsland EX5 175 C6
Poundstone Ct TQ8 259 D4
Poundwell Mdws PL21 137 B2
Poundwell St PL21 137 B2
Powderham Castle* EX6 194 F4
Powderham Cl
Newton Abbot TQ12 207 B2
Topsham EX3 182 E6
Powderham Cres EX4 177 D8
Powderham Ct 21 TQ14 210 C4
Powderham Rd
Exeter EX2 177 A4
Newton Abbot TQ12 207 B2
Plymouth PL3 248 F7
Torquay TQ2 213 F1
Powderham Terr
Newton Abbot TQ12 207 B2
Teignmouth TQ14 210 C4
Powderham Wlk EX6 181 F5
Powell Cl EX12 192 A6
Powells Way EX14 67 C1
Powis Gdns PL5 244 B2
Powisland Dr PL6 245 A5
Powlesland La EX17 95 E6
Powys Ho EX10 188 A4
Poyers EX33 152 E4
Pratt's La TQ7 143 B7
Precinct The TQ7 258 D6
Premier Pl EX2 261 C2
Prescot Rd EX4 176 E5
Prescott Rd EX15 51 D1
Prestbury Pk 4 TQ2 219 F5
Preston Barns TQ9 222 D1
Preston Cross
Loddiswell TQ7 138 E3
West Alvington TQ7 143 E2
Preston Down Ave TQ3 219 B2
Preston Down Rd TQ3 219 B2
Preston Fork TQ9 138 E2
Preston Gate EX31 10 E6
Preston La EX17 80 D7
Preston Prim Sch TQ2 219 D2
Preston St EX1 261 A2
Prestonbury Cl PL6 245 B7
Prestor EX13 167 E5
Pretoria Rd EX1 177 F7
Pretoria Terr EX34 150 A3
Pretty Top
Great Torrington EX20 41 F1
Petrockstow EX20 56 F8
Priddis Cl EX8 196 C3
Priddles La TA20 69 F8
Prideaux Cl PL12 242 C5
Prideaux Cres EX16 161 D6
Prideaux La TQ6 145 F6
Prideaux Rd PL21 237 E6
Prideax Mdw EX38 159 F5
Pridham La PL2 248 D7
Pridhams Way EX6 182 A4
Priest Hill EX15 66 A3
Priesthood Terr PL10 252 E5
Priestley Ave Exeter EX4 178 B8
Plymouth PL5 243 E2
Prigg Mdw TQ13 130 F4
Primley Cross TQ3 225 F5
Primley Ct TQ3 225 E5
Primley Gdns EX10 188 C7
Primley Mead EX10 188 C7
Primley Paddock EX10 188 B7
Primley Pk TQ3 225 F5
Primley Pk E TQ3 226 A5
Primley Rd EX10 188 B7
Primrose Ave EX32 155 E4
Primrose Cl
Chillington TQ7 144 F1
Ivybridge PL21 237 D5
Primrose Cl *continued*
Kingsteignton TQ12 207 E7
6 Tiverton EX16 161 F6
Torpoint PL11 246 E4
Primrose Gdns PL19 171 E4
Primrose La EX39 157 B8
Primrose Lawn EX4 176 D8
Primrose Mdw PL21 237 A6
Primrose Way
Crediton EX17 165 E6
Kingskerswell TQ12 212 F6
Launceston PL15 105 A2
Seaton EX12 192 B7
Primrose Wlk PL12 242 D4
Prince Charles Cl EX8 196 E1
Prince Charles Ct TQ2 214 A3
Prince Charles Rd EX4 177 F8
Prince Charles Way EX12 192 A8
Prince Maurice Ct PL4 263 B3
Prince Maurice Rd PL4 248 F4
Prince Of Wales Dr
Dartmouth TQ6 233 F4
Exmouth EX8 196 E1
Prince Of Wales Rd
Crediton EX17 165 C6
Exeter EX4 177 B8
Kingsbridge TQ7 258 C5
Prince Rock Prim Sch PL4 249 B2
Prince Rupert Way TQ12 123 B2
Prince St TQ12 207 C3
Prince William Ct 1 TQ5 230 C4
Prince William Quay TQ5 230 D5
Prince's Sq EX2 177 A3
Prince's St E EX2 177 A3
Prince's St N EX2 177 A4
Prince's St S EX2 177 A3
Prince's St W EX2 177 A4
Princes Point TQ1 220 C3
Princes Rd Plymouth PL6 245 E6
Torquay TQ1 220 B5
Princes Rd E TQ1 220 C5
Princes Rd W TQ1 220 B5
Princes St
15 Dawlish EX7 204 D6
Exmouth EX8 202 A6
Paignton TQ3 226 B6
Plymouth PL1 247 E2
Torquay TQ1 220 D7
Princess Ave
Ilfracombe EX34 150 C5
Plymouth, Plymstock PL9 255 E6
Plymouth, West Park PL5 244 A3
Princess Cotts TQ12 213 C6
Princess Cres PL9 255 E6
Princess Elizabeth Terr EX20 107 F8
Princess Rd
Kingskerswell TQ12 213 A4
Kingsteignton TQ12 207 D8
Princess St
Barnstaple EX32 155 A6
Plymouth PL1 262 C2
Princess Street Ope PL1 262 C2
Princess Way PL1 262 C2
Princesshay EX1 261 B3
Princetown Prim Sch PL20 128 A8
Priorton Hill EX17 80 B7
Priorton La EX17 80 B7
Priory Bovey Tracey TQ13 180 C8
Wellington TA21 160 E6
Priory Ave
Kingskerswell TQ12 213 A5
Totnes TQ9 223 C6
Priory Cl Barnstaple EX31 154 F7
East Budleigh EX9 198 B7
Ivybridge PL21 237 B5
Tavistock PL19 171 D3
Priory Ct 3 Totnes TQ9 223 C6
Wellington TA21 160 E7
Priory Dr Plymouth PL7 250 D5
Totnes TQ9 223 C6
Priory Gdns
Barnstaple EX31 154 F7
1 Dawlish EX7 204 E6
Exeter EX4 261 A2
Tavistock PL19 171 D3
Totnes TQ9 223 C6
Wellington TA21 160 E6
Priory Gn EX4 178 A7
Priory High Sch EX2 177 E2
Priory Hill
2 Dawlish EX7 204 E6
Totnes TQ9 223 C6
Priory La EX6 113 B4
Priory Lawn Terr PL3 249 A6
Priory Mill PL7 250 D5
Priory Park Rd 12 EX7 204 D6
Priory RC Prim Sch TQ1 220 B8
Priory Rd
Abbotskerswell TQ12 212 C7
Barnstaple EX31 154 F7
Dawlish EX7 204 E6
Exeter EX4 177 E8
Plymouth PL3 249 A6
Tiverton EX16 161 F6
Torquay TQ1 220 B8
Priory Ridge PL7 250 D5
Priory St TQ6 234 A2
Priory The
Abbotskerswell TQ12 212 C7

Priory The *continued*
Modbury PL21 137 B2
Priory View TQ9 227 B4
Priory Wall Cross EX15 66 B2
Prisam La EX20 75 E2
Prisam Lane Cross EX20 75 F2
Priscott Way TQ12 207 E6
Prispen Dr EX5 82 B6
Prispen Ho EX5 82 B6
Prispen View EX5 82 B6
Prixford EX31 16 C7
Promenade
Ilfracombe EX34 150 B6
Kingsbridge TQ7 258 D5
Paignton TQ3 226 D8
Paignton, Goodrington TQ4 226 C4
Promenade The PL1 262 C1
Prospect EX7 204 E6
Prospect Cnr EX31 27 A7
Prospect Cres EX15 66 A7
Prospect Gdns EX4 177 E7
Prospect Hill
Okehampton EX20 170 B4
Slapton TQ7 145 C4
Prospect La PL12 242 C3
Prospect Pk EX4 177 D8
Prospect Pl
Barnstaple EX32 155 B3
Exeter EX4 177 A4
Ottery St Mary EX11 169 D3
Plymouth PL1 262 B2
5 Tiverton EX16 161 B4
Prospect Rd 3 TQ5 230 C5
Prospect Row PL1 247 E1
Prospect St PL4 263 A3
Prospect Terr
Gunnislake PL18 125 D6
Gunnislake, St Ann's Chapel PL18 125 B5
Newton Abbot TQ12 207 C3
Prospect Way EX17 60 D3
Prospect Wlk PL12 242 C3
Prouse Cres PL2 248 C8
Prouse Rise PL12 242 E2
Providence Pl
Calstock PL18 125 D3
Plymouth PL1 248 A3
Providence Row 15 EX39 157 A2
Providence St PL4 263 A4
Prowse La
Cheriton Fitzpaine EX17 80 C8
Lapford EX17 60 D3
Prowse's La EX16 63 E1
Prowses EX15 67 B8
Prynne Cl PL1 262 B3
Puckridge Rd EX4 174 D2
Puddavens Terr TQ9 223 A8
Pudleylake Rd
Axminster EX13 167 B1
Musbury EX13 103 E6
Puffin Way EX2 176 D3
Pugsley Rd 9 EX16 64 D7
Pulborough Farm Cvn Pk EX20 107 F4
Pulchrass St 11 EX32 155 A4
Pullen's Row EX16 46 E1
Pulleys Cl TQ7 143 C6
Pulling Rd EX4 174 D2
Pullins Terr 10 TQ13 123 E6
Pump La EX39 156 A2
Pump St 4 Brixham TQ5 230 D5
Newton St Cyres EX5 172 A8
Punchards Down TQ9 222 F6
Purbeck Ave TQ2 219 D2
Purcell Cl EX2 178 C5
Purcombe Cross TQ13 131 D3
Purlbridge Cross EX24 102 D6
Purzebrook Cl EX13 167 D5
Pusehill Rd EX39 156 B5
Putsborough Cl EX33 8 A2
Putsborough Rd EX33 7 F3
Putshole La EX38 40 E1
Putson Cross EX16 64 E8
Putts Cnr EX10 101 C7
Pye Cnr
Brampford Speke EX5 81 D1
Cullompton EX15 163 C3
Kennford EX6 181 B2
Pye La TA20 88 E8
Pykes Down PL21 237 F4
Pyles Thorne TA21 160 F4
Pyles Thorne Cl TA21 160 E5
Pyles Thorne Rd TA21 160 E4
Pym St Plymouth PL1 247 F3
Tavistock PL19 171 C6
Pyne Gdns EX5 173 A7
Pyne Meadow Cross EX18 44 D3
Pynes Cl
Cheriton Fitzpaine EX17 62 E1
East Budleigh EX9 198 B6
Pynes Hill EX2 178 C2
Pynes Hill Bsns Pk EX2 178 C3
Pynes Inf Sch EX39 156 F1
Pynes La EX39 156 E1
Pynes Wlk EX39 25 E4
Pynsent Ct 4 TQ13 123 E6
Pytte Gdns EX3 183 C7
Pyworthy CE Prim Sch EX22 71 D5

Q

Quadrangle The EX4 177 C8
Quadrant The EX2 261 C2
Quagmire La EX22 164 C7
Quant Pk PL19 171 C6
Quantock Rd TA21 160 D7
Quantocks EX33 152 B6
Quantocks Rd TQ2 219 C3
Quarries La EX37 43 C7
Quarries The EX4 176 D4
Quarry Cl Bideford EX39 156 E2
Totnes TQ9 222 F6
Quarry Cotts Beer EX12 191 B5
Plymouth PL1 262 A3
Plymouth, Honicknowle PL5 244 B2
Quarry Foot Cross EX17 79 C4
Quarry Gdns TQ3 226 A7
Quarry La Beer EX12 191 B5
Down St Mary EX17 78 F6
Exeter EX2 178 C4
Gunnislake PL18 125 C6
Silverton EX5 82 B5
Thorverton EX5 81 D4
Quarry Park Ave PL9 255 D7
Quarry Park Rd
Exeter EX2 178 C4
Plymouth, Peverell PL3 248 D5
Plymouth, Plymstock PL9 255 D7
Quarry Rd EX37 43 B7
Quarry St PL11 247 C3
Quarryfields EX20 170 C6
Quarter Mile La EX5 99 D3
Quarterdeck The PL1 254 A8
Quartley Hill EX16 34 E4
Quay Hill EX1,EX2 261 A2
Quay La Instow EX39 15 B1
Lympstone EX8 195 D4
Quay Rd
Newton Abbot TQ12 207 D3
Plymouth PL1 263 A2
Teignmouth TQ14 210 B4
Quay Terr TQ12 207 D3
Quay The Appledore EX39 15 A1
Ashprington TQ9 139 F7
Bideford EX39 157 A2
Brixham TQ5 230 D5
Dartmouth TQ6 233 F3
Dittisham TQ6 228 D2
Exeter EX2 261 B2
Ilfracombe EX34 150 C6
Plymouth PL9 255 C7
Quayfield Rd EX34 150 C6
Quayside 6 PL19 171 B5
Quaywest Waterpark★ TQ4 226 C3
Queen Anne's Ct 12 EX31 154 F5
Queen Annes 14 EX39 157 A2
Queen Annes Copse TQ12 206 F1
Queen Dart Cross EX16 47 B4
Queen Dart Hill EX16 47 B3
Queen Elizabeth Ave TQ6 233 E4
Queen Elizabeth Ct EX39 156 C6
Queen Elizabeth Dr
Crediton EX17 165 A6
Paignton TQ3 225 E6
Queen Elizabeth's Com Coll EX17 165 B6
Queen Elizabeth's Lower Sch EX17 165 B5
Queen La 7 EX7 204 D6
Queen Sq EX15 163 C3
Queen St
Barnstaple EX32 155 A5
Bideford EX39 157 A2
Budleigh Salterton EX9 199 G2
9 Colyton EX24 103 A4
Dawlish EX7 204 D6
Exeter EX4 261 A3
11 Exmouth EX8 202 A6
Honiton EX14 166 C6
Lynton EX35 151 C5
Newton Abbot TQ12 207 D3
Northlew EX20 74 E2
Plymouth PL1 247 D2
Seaton EX12 192 A5
South Molton EX36 158 C4
12 Teignmouth TQ14 210 B4
Tiverton EX16 161 C3
Torquay TQ1 220 B5
Winkleigh EX19 58 F3
Queen's Ave EX34 150 C5
Queen's Cres
Brixham TQ5 230 D3
Exeter EX4 261 B4
Queen's Ct 12 EX8 202 A6
Queen's Dr EX8 202 C5
Queen's Dr The EX4 177 B8
Queen's Gate
Plymouth, Lipson PL4 263 B4
Plymouth, Stoke PL3 262 A4
Queen's Gate Mews PL4 263 B4
Queen's Gate Villas PL4 263 B4
Queen's Gate Villas Rd PL4 263 B4
Queen's Ho 4 EX32 155 A5
Queen's Park Rd TQ4 226 C6
Queen's Pk EX22 55 C1
Queen's Rd Brixham TQ5 230 C6
Budleigh Salterton EX9 197 F2
Moretonhampstead TQ13 111 F5
Paignton TQ4 226 C6
Plymouth PL4 263 B4
Queen's Sq 8 EX24 103 A4
Queen's Terr EX4 261 A4
Queen's Terr
Great Torrington EX38 159 B5
4 Totnes TQ9 223 C6
Queens Cl
Kingsteignton TQ12 207 F8
Plymouth PL6 245 E6
Queens Pk EX17 80 D4
Queens Rd Exeter EX2 261 A1
Plymouth PL5 243 F3
Wellington TA21 160 E4
Queens Wlk DT7 260 E4
Queenshaye EX20 95 A5
Queensland Dr EX4 173 E2
Queensway
Newton Abbot TQ12 207 E2
Tiverton EX16 161 F5
Torquay TQ2 219 D6
Queensway Cl TQ2 219 E7
Queensway Cres TQ2 219 E7
Queensway Ho TQ12 207 E2
Queensway Rc Sch TQ2 219 D7
Quentin Ave TQ5 230 B2
Questant La EX10 188 C6
Quicks Wlk EX38 159 F5
Quilletts The TQ7 147 E6
Quince Cross
South Molton EX36 46 B8
Spreyton EX17 96 C7
Quince Hill EX36 31 A1
Quince Honey Farm★ EX36 158 C5
Quinnel Ho 7 TQ14 210 B5
Quinta Cl TQ1 220 C6
Quinta Ct TQ1 220 C7
Quinta Rd TQ1 220 D6
Quintet Cl EX1 178 C5
Quirk Hill EX16 63 D7
Quoditch Cross EX21 73 B1
Quoitgate Cross EX22 38 D3

R

Rack Park Cl EX38 159 C5
Rack Park Rd TQ7 258 D5
Rack St EX1 261 A2
Rackclose La EX4 261 A2
Rackenford CE Prim Sch EX16 47 D5
Rackenford Cross EX16 47 D5
Rackenford Rd
Tiverton EX16 161 A6
Witheridge EX16 46 E1
Rackfield TA21 160 A5
Rackfield Ct EX32 154 F6
Rackleigh La EX17 46 A2
Rackmead EX37 28 F4
Radcliffe Cl PL6 244 E6
Radcliffe Ct TQ3 226 C7
Raddenstile Ct EX8 202 B6
Raddenstile La EX8 202 B6
Raddick La PL20 127 F5
Raddicombe Cl TQ5 234 F8
Raddicombe Dr TQ5 234 F8
Raddicombe Farm TQ5 234 F8
Raddon Cross EX17 81 A5
Raddon Down Cross EX17 79 D4
Raddon Hill EX17 81 A6
Raddon Top EX17 81 A6
Radford Ave PL4 249 B1
Radford Ho 11 TQ4 226 B6
Radford La PL10 252 D4
Radford Park Dr PL9 255 D6
Radford Park Rd PL9 255 D6
Radford Rd Exeter EX2 261 C2
Plymouth PL1 262 B1
Radford View PL9 255 D6
Radford Way EX20 170 E6
Radfords Orch TQ9 131 E1
Radish La EX12 102 A2
Radley Cross EX36 30 D2
Radnidge La EX16 32 D4
Radnor Hall PL4 263 A3
Radnor Pl Exeter EX2 261 C2
Plymouth PL4 263 A3
Radnor St PL4 263 A3
Radsbury La EX35 5 B3
Radway EX10 188 B4
Radway Ct TQ14 209 A8
Radway Gdns TQ14 209 A8
Radway Hill TQ14 209 A8
Radway La EX9 187 B1
Radway St TQ14 209 A8
Radworth Terr TQ9 223 C6
Rag La Aylesbeare EX5 99 D4
Copplestone EX17 79 A2
Yarcombe EX14 69 A2
Ragg La EX9 199 G2
Ragged La EX18 44 B1
Raglan Ct PL1 247 F2
Raglan Gdns PL1 247 F2
Raglan Rd PL1 247 F2
Raglans EX2 181 C8
Railway Cotts
Holsworthy EX22 164 C3
6 Plymouth, Ford PL2 247 F5
Plymouth, Plymstock PL9 255 D7
Tavistock PL19 171 B6
Railway Terr
3 Bideford EX39 157 B1
Broadclyst EX5 175 E3
Rainbow Ct TQ2 219 E7
Rainbow La TA3 67 F8
Raisey La TA20 69 F7
Rake Cnr TQ7 143 F6
Rakeham Hill EX38 41 B6
Rakelane Cross TQ7 143 F6
Raleigh Ave TQ2 219 D6
Raleigh Cl
Dartmouth TQ6 233 C3
Sidmouth EX10 188 B7
South Molton EX36 158 C4
Raleigh Cotts 3 EX31 155 A7
Raleigh Ct
Budleigh Salterton EX9 198 B2
Plymouth PL7 251 B6
Torquay TQ2 219 D6
Raleigh Dr TQ4 226 B2
Raleigh Hill
Bideford, Raleigh Hill EX39 156 E4
Bideford, Silford EX39 156 D5
Raleigh Hts EX31 154 F7
Raleigh Lawn EX31 154 F7
Raleigh Mdw EX31 155 A7
Raleigh Pk EX36 158 C4
Raleigh Rd
Barnstaple EX32 154 F6
Budleigh Salterton EX9 198 B2
Dartmouth TQ6 233 E4
Exeter EX1 261 C2
Exmouth EX8 202 A6
Ivybridge PL21 237 A6
Newton Abbot TQ12 207 F3
Ottery St Mary EX11 169 E4
Salcombe TQ8 259 D4
Teignmouth TQ14 210 A8
Raleigh St PL1 262 B3
Raleigh View EX39 157 A3
Ralph Cl EX33 152 B6
Ralph Rd EX33 152 B6
Ralph's Ct PL19 171 B5
Ramage Cl PL6 245 F3
Rame Cotts PL10 140 H2
Rame La Cawsand PL10 252 F1
Rame PL10 140 H2
Ramehead Cotts PL10 140 H1
Ramehead La PL10 140 H2
Ramillies Ave PL5 244 A4
Ramsey La
Runnington TA21 51 F8
Sampford Courtenay EX20 76 F3
Ramshill Cross TQ3 225 E8
Ramshill Rd TQ3 225 E8
Rance Dr EX8 196 E3
Randolph Ct TQ12 207 A4
Randwick Park Rd PL9 255 D7
Ranelagh Rd EX20 170 A5
Rangers Cl TQ11 236 B4
Ranscombe Cl TQ5 230 E5
Ranscombe Ct 9 TQ5 230 D5
Ranscombe Rd TQ5 230 D5
Ransum Way PL19 171 B4
Raphael Cl PL9 256 B5
Raphael Dr PL9 256 A6
Rapscott Cross EX36 18 F1
Rapscott Hill EX36 18 F1
Rashleigh Ave
Plymouth PL7 250 F7
Saltash PL12 242 D1
Rashleigh La EX18 59 D7
Ratcliffe Sch EX7 204 C4
Rathmore Rd TQ2 219 F4
Ratshole Gate EX24 102 E5
Ratsloe Cross EX4 174 D8
Rattenbury Cotts EX12 191 C6
Rattenbury Cross EX19 76 A8
Rattle St TQ13 113 D1
Ravelin Gdns 4 EX32 155 B5
Ravelin Manor Rd EX32 155 B5
Raven Cl EX4 173 C1
Ravensbourne La TQ6 146 B7
Ravensbury Dr TQ6 234 A2
Rawlin Cl PL6 249 C8
Rawlyn Rd TQ2 219 E4
Rawnsley La EX34 7 F6
Rayer Rd 13 EX16 64 D7
Raymond Way PL7 250 D6
Rayners EX6 181 A2
Raynham Rd PL3 248 B4
Rea Barn Cl TQ5 230 D4
Rea Barn Rd TQ5 230 D4
Rea Dr TQ5 230 D5
Read Cl EX8 196 C1
Reading Wlk PL5 244 C4
Recreation Rd PL2 248 C7
Recreation Way PL7 132 F4
Rectory Cl Filleigh EX32 29 B6
9 Whimple EX5 99 E8
Willand EX15 162 D4
Wrafton EX33 152 F4
Rectory Close Cross EX33 152 F3
Rectory Cross TQ10 138 A7
Rectory Dr EX2 181 B8
Rectory Hill
Berrynarbor EX34 2 D3
Cheriton Fitzpaine EX17 62 E1
Rectory La Parkham EX39 39 E8
Stoke Fleming TQ6 146 B7
Yelland EX39 15 C2
Rectory Pk EX39 156 F2
Rectory Rd Ashbrittle TA21 50 F8
Bridestowe EX20 107 F8
Combe Martin EX34 3 A3
Dolton EX19 57 F7
East Ogwell TQ12 211 E8
Morchard Bishop EX17 61 A2
Plymouth PL1 248 A2
Rectory Rise EX20 56 F4
Red Brook Cl TQ4 226 C1
Red Cross Colyton EX24 102 F6
Raymond's Hill EX13 104 C7
Silverton EX5 82 C5
Red Cross Hill EX17 165 E6
Red Devon Ct PL21 137 B2
Red Gate
King's Nympton EX37 44 E8
Winkleigh EX19 58 D2
Red House Cl 9 TQ13 123 C4
Red La Churchinford TA3 68 C7
Hatherleigh EX20 75 C7
Hemyock EX15 52 E3
Raymond's Hill EX13 104 C6
Red Lion Hill PL8 257 B5
Red Lion La EX1,EX4 261 C4
Red Lion Pl 2 EX7 204 D6
Red Lion Yd EX20 170 B5
Red Post Cross
Burrington EX37 43 F4
Totnes TQ9 217 C4
Red Rock EX5 81 E2
Red Rock Rd EX5 81 D1
Redavon Rise TQ2 219 B8
Redburn Cl TQ3 226 A7
Redburn Rd TQ3 226 A7
Redcliff Ct EX9 199 G2
Redcliffe Rd TQ1 214 C1
Reddacleave Kiln Cross TQ11 135 A6
Reddaway Dr EX6 182 A4
Reddenhill Rd TQ1 220 C7
Reddicliff Cl PL9 255 E5
Reddicliff Rd PL9 255 D5
Reddington Rd PL3 249 B7
Redford Cross TQ7 258 A8
Redford Mdw TQ7 258 C5
Redford Way TQ7 258 C5
Redgate Cl TQ1 220 D6
Redhill Cl PL5 243 E4
Redhill Cotts EX11 169 F6
Redhills
Budleigh Salterton EX9 199 G2
Exeter EX4 176 E6
Redhills Cl EX4 176 E6
Redhills Comb Com Sch The EX4 176 F5
Redlake TQ9 222 F8
Redlake Cross TQ9 222 F8
Redland Cross EX18 58 F7
Redland Rd EX31 153 F5
Redlands EX16 161 F4
Redlands Cl EX4 178 A8
Redlands Ct TQ3 225 F7
Redlands The EX10 188 A3
Redlane Cross DT7 104 C6
Redlap Cross TQ6 146 C8
Redlap Rd TQ6 146 C8
Redmoor Cl PL19 171 A7
Redoubt Hill TQ6 234 B3
Redpost Cross
North Tawton EX20 76 F5
Sampford Courtenay EX20 76 E5
Redruth Cl PL5 244 A5
Redside Terr EX5 172 E5
Redstart Cl TQ12 206 F1
Redvers Gr PL7 250 E4
Redvers Rd EX4 177 A5
Redwalls Mdw TQ6 233 E4
Redwell La TQ3 225 F8
Redwell Rd TQ3 225 F8
Redwing Dr PL6 245 D8
Redwood Cl
Bovey Tracey TQ13 180 C4
Exmouth EX8 196 D3
10 Hemyock EX15 67 B8
4 Honiton EX14 85 C2
Redwood Dr PL7 251 B5
Redwood Rd EX10 188 C5
Redwoods TQ13 180 C5
Redyeates Cross EX17 63 A2
Reed Mdw EX20 75 C7
Reed Vale TQ14 210 A5
Reed's Cross
Barnstaple EX31 9 E4
Uffculme EX15 66 C6
Reeds Pl EX15 163 C3
Reedsdown Cross EX17 79 F6
Reedy Hill EX6 112 F8
Reeveacre Cross TQ9 216 D5
Reeves Cl 3 TQ9 223 D5
Reeves Rd The TQ2 219 D5
Reform St 3 EX31 154 F6
Regal Ct PL12 242 F2
Regency Cres EX8 202 C6
Regent Cl
Barnstaple EX31 154 C2
Fremington EX31 153 F5
Torquay TQ2 219 E8
Regent Pl EX34 150 B6
Regent Sq EX1 177 F5
Regent St Dawlish EX7 204 D6
Exeter EX2 177 A3
Plymouth PL4 263 A3
18 Teignmouth TQ14 210 C4
Regent's Pk EX1 177 E6
Regents Gate EX8 202 B6
Regents Gdns 6 TQ14 210 C4
Reigate Rd PL9 255 E8
Reme Dr EX14 85 C2
Rena Hobson Ct EX16 161 F3
Rendells Mdw TQ13 180 E7
Rendle St PL1 262 B3
Rendlesham Gdns PL6 245 E3
Rennes Dr EX4 173 C1
Rennes Ho EX1 178 B7
Renney Rd
Down Thomas PL9 255 C1
Heybrook Bay PL9 140 B8
Rennie Ave PL5 243 C1
Rennie Rd 2 EX16 64 D7

Renoir Cl PL9 256 A6
Renown St PL2 247 E6
Rensey La EX17 60 C4
Renton La TQ7 142 E7
Research Way PL6 245 C4
Reservoir Cres PL9 256 B7
Reservoir Cross PL16 91 A4
Reservoir La 1 PL3 248 F6
Reservoir Rd
Plymouth, Hartley PL3 248 F6
Plymouth, Plymstock PL9 256 B7
Reservoir Way PL9 256 B7
Resolution Ho PL4 263 B3
Rest Hill TQ12 131 D7
Restland La EX20 94 F7
Restormel Rd PL4 262 C4
Restormel Terr PL4 262 C4
Retail Park Cl EX2 177 B3
Retreat Cl TQ7 258 C5
Retreat Dr The EX3 182 D6
Retreat Rd EX3 182 E6
Retreat The PL3 249 B7
Revel Rd PL3 249 A6
Revell Park Rd PL7 250 D6
Revelstoke Rd PL8 140 F6
Revill Ind Units EX5 99 A4
Rew Cross
Ashburton TQ13 130 F5
Newton St Cyres EX5 81 A2
Rew Rd TQ13 130 F5
Rew's Cl EX34 2 F4
Rewdown Cross TQ13 130 F6
Rewe Barton EX5 82 A2
Rewe Cross EX5 82 A2
Rewe Ct EX5 82 B3
Rewe La EX5 99 D6
Rewes Cross EX5 82 F2
Rewlea Cross TQ13 130 F6
Rewles Cotts TQ13 130 F5
Rews Cross EX36 19 C2
Rews Mdw EX1 174 F1
Rews Park Dr EX1 174 F1
Rexon Cross PL16 106 B7
Rexona Cl EX2 177 A2
Reynell Ave TQ12 207 F3
Reynell Rd TQ12 211 F8
Reynolds Cl EX4 174 D1
Reynolds Gr PL5 247 C8
Reynolds Rd PL7 250 C6
Rheola Gdns PL6 245 D3
Rhodanthe Rd TQ3 219 B1
Rhode La DT7 260 C6
Rhodes Cl PL7 250 E7
Rhododendron Ave
Barnstaple EX31 154 D3
Dunkeswell EX14 67 B1
Rhude Cross EX22 53 D2
Rhydda Bank Cross EX31 4 A5
Rhyll Gate Cross TA22 32 E7
Ribble Gdns PL3 249 D7
Ribston Ave EX1 178 C6
Rices Mews EX2 177 A4
Richard Cl EX39 25 E4
Richards Cl Dawlish EX7 204 D5
Exmouth EX8 196 D2
Wellington TA21 160 C8
Richards Row PL3 248 F7
Richards Terr PL10 252 E5
Richardson Dr PL8 141 B8
Richmond Ave EX34 150 A5
Richmond Cl
Sampford Peverell EX16 50 D1
Torquay TQ1 221 A4
Richmond Ct
14 Dawlish EX7 204 E6
Paignton TQ3 226 B7
Richmond Gn EX39 14 F1
Richmond Hill TQ12 213 A5
Richmond Pk EX39 156 F7
Richmond Pl 15 EX7 204 E6
Richmond Rd
Appledore EX39 15 A1
Exeter EX4 261 A3
Exmouth EX8 202 D7
Ilfracombe EX34 150 A4
Plymouth PL6 245 A2
Richmond St EX32 155 A5
Richmond Terr
9 Appledore EX39 15 A1
Buckland Monachorum PL20 126 C3
Kingsbridge TQ7 258 D6
Richmond Wlk
10 Barnstaple EX32 155 A6
Plymouth PL1 247 F1
Rickards Gn EX39 156 B2
Rickham Cross TQ8 148 D4
Riddell Ave EX32 154 F6
Riddistone Cross EX20 77 A8
Riddistone La EX20 77 A8
Ride The PL7,PL9 249 D2
Ridge Cross
Chillington TQ7 149 B8
Plymouth PL9 256 A3
Wilmington EX14 86 E4
Ridge Hill Berrynarbor EX34 2 E3
Combe Martin EX34 3 A2
Dartmouth TQ6 233 F4
Ridge Ho PL4 249 A4
Ridge La Chudleigh TQ13 124 B7
Cornworthy TQ9 139 F4
Paignton TQ3 218 F8
Tiverton EX16 63 F8
Wilmington EX14 86 C3
Ridge Lane Cross TQ9 139 E4
Ridge Park Ave PL4 248 D4
Ridge Park Rd PL7 250 F5
Ridge Pk PL7 250 E5
Ridge Rd
Combeinteignhead TQ12 208 D2
Maidencombe TQ1,TQ12 214 B7
Modbury PL21 137 B4
Plymouth PL7 250 E3
Stokeinteignhead TQ12 209 A1
Ugborough PL21 137 D7
West Anstey TA22 32 D7
Ridge Way EX6 194 E2
Ridgeleish Ct 10 EX14 166 C6
Ridgemark Cl TQ5 230 E5
Ridges The TQ6 233 D1
Ridgeway Exeter EX4 173 A3
Honiton EX14 166 B4
Ottery St Mary EX11 169 E4
Plymouth PL7 250 D5
Plymouth PL7 250 F5
Saltash PL12 242 D1
Sidbury EX10 101 B2
Ridgeway Ave EX39 156 E7
Ridgeway Cl
Newton Abbot TQ12 207 F1
Sidbury EX10 101 B2
Westward Ho! EX39 156 D7
Ridgeway Ct EX39 156 D7
Ridgeway Dr EX39 156 D7
Ridgeway Gdns EX11 169 E4
Ridgeway Gn EX37 43 B7
Ridgeway Hill TQ3 218 D6
Ridgeway Hts 15 TQ1 220 D4
Ridgeway La
Awliscombe EX14 85 A5
Coffinswell TQ12 213 D6
Shillingford EX16 34 D2
Ridgeway Mead EX10 187 F7
Ridgeway Rd
Newton Abbot TQ12 207 F1
Torquay TQ1 220 D4
Torquay TQ1 220 E4
Ridgeway Sch PL7 250 E5
Ridgeway's Cross EX17 79 E6
Ridgewood Cross EX15 67 D8
Ridgewood La EX15 67 D8
Ridgey Cross TQ13 130 B4
Ridgway Cross EX36 20 E1
Ridgway Ct EX13 167 D5
Ridgway La EX24 102 F4
Riding Cross EX37 29 A4
Ridings The EX3 183 C4
Ridley Hill TQ6 234 A3
Rifford Rd EX2 178 B4
Rifton La EX16 48 B4
Riga Terr PL3 249 C4
Rigdale Cl PL6 249 A7
Riggles Cross EX14 68 A3
Rill Cnr EX5 99 D3
Rill La EX9 199 H2
Rillage La TQ2 219 F6
Ring Hill EX20 95 C5
Ringdown La EX15 52 F2
Ringhill Cross EX20 95 D5
Ringmore Cl TQ14 209 D5
Ringmore Dr TQ7 142 E3
Ringmore Rd
Shaldon TQ14 209 D5
Teignmouth TQ14 210 A3
Ringmore Way PL5 244 B3
Ringrona TQ8 259 B2
Ringslade Cl TQ12 206 F5
Ringslade Rd TQ12 206 F5
Ringswell Ave EX1 178 C6
Ringswell Cross TQ9 216 E6
Riphay Cross TA22 33 E3
Ripon Cl EX4 176 E6
Rippon Cl Brixham TQ5 229 F2
17 Tiverton EX16 64 D7
Riscombe Hill EX5 98 F8
Risdon Ave PL4 249 B1
Rising Sun EX13 87 A3
Ritson La TQ9 139 D3
Rivenford La EX5,EX17 81 C3
River Cl EX5 173 F8
River Ct Saltash PL12 242 D5
Tavistock PL19 171 D6
River Dart Country Pk★
TQ13 130 D5
River Dr EX15 163 D3
River Exe Ctry Pk★ EX2 181 F8
River Front EX3 183 C2
River Mdws EX2 177 C3
River Pk PL21 137 A4
River Tamar Way EX22 164 C6
River Valley Rd 13 TQ13 123 C4
River View
Barnstaple EX32 155 C2
Brushford TA22 33 F3
Gunnislake PL18 125 B5
Plymouth PL4 249 B1
Saltash PL12 242 F3
River View Cl
12 Chudleigh Knighton TQ13 123 C4
20 Colyton EX24 103 A4
River View Commercial Ctr
EX31 154 D6
River View Dr 21 EX24 103 A4
River View La PL4 249 B1
River View Terr EX6 182 B3
Riverbank Cotts EX39 157 B4
Riverdale
Harbertonford TQ9 139 C7
Seaton EX12 192 B7
Riverdale Cl EX12 192 B7
Riverford Cl PL6 245 D7
Rivermead EX15 163 C2
Rivermead Ave EX8 196 A3
Rivermead Rd EX2 177 D3
Rivers Cl PL21 237 E5
Rivers The PL12 242 E1
Rivers Wlk EX2 182 C7
Riversdale Ave EX34 150 A6
Riverside
Kingsbridge TQ7 258 D4
Teignmouth TQ14 210 A3
Totnes TQ9 223 B7
Wellington TA21 160 B7
Riverside Apartments
EX36 158 E4
Riverside Bsns Pk PL1 247 E3
Riverside Cl
Bideford EX39 157 B4
Honiton EX14 166 B6
1 Horrabridge PL20 126 F4
Riverside Cott PL12 242 C1
Riverside Cross EX17 62 A3
Riverside Ct
Bideford EX39 157 B4
Dartmouth TQ6 233 F3
Exeter EX2 261 B2
Newton Abbot TQ12 207 D4
Riverside Mews PL12 243 A3
Riverside Pl PL1 247 D2
Riverside Rd
Barnstaple EX31 154 C6
Dittisham TQ6 228 C3
Lynmouth EX35 151 C6
Sidmouth EX10 188 B3
Topsham EX3 182 E6
Riverside Rd E PL8 140 F6
Riverside Rd W PL8 140 F6
Riverside Terr TQ9 223 D5
Riverside Units EX31 154 C6
Riverside View EX11 169 D3
Riverside Way EX12 192 C5
Riverside Wlk
Plymouth PL5 244 B6
Yealmpton PL8 136 A2
Riverside Workshops
EX12 192 C5
Riversmeet EX39 15 A1
Rivervale Cl TQ13 110 F6
Riverview Dr EX4 176 F8
Riverview Pl TQ7 258 C5
Riviera Terr Dawlish EX7 204 F7
Exminster EX6 182 B3
Riviera The Paignton TQ4 226 B5
Torquay TQ1 220 B3
Riviera Way TQ2 213 D1
Rixafer Rd TQ13 124 B4
Rixdale Rd TQ13 124 C4
Rixey La EX17 61 B2
Rixeypark Cnr TQ13 123 D3
Roach Hill EX36 31 F7
Roach La EX5 82 C6
Roachill Cross EX36 32 C1
Road Down Cross EX6 96 F7
Road End Cross EX14 87 A8
Road Pk TQ13 123 B7
Roadway Cnr EX34 8 A5
Robartes Ct EX2 261 C2
Robeclave Cl PL7 251 C6
Robers Rd TQ12 207 D8
Robert Adams Cl PL7 250 B5
Robert Way EX10 186 F8
Roberts Ave PL11 247 B3
Roberts Cl
Cullompton EX15 163 B2
Torquay TQ2 214 B2
Roberts Rd Exeter EX2 261 B2
Plymouth PL5 247 D8
Roberts Way TQ12 206 F4
Robin Cl EX15 163 B2
Robin Dr PL15 105 A2
Robins Field TQ7 144 F1
Robins Hill EX39 156 E4
Robins Way PL9 255 E8
Robinson's Row TQ8 259 E4
Roborough Ave PL6 245 B5
Roborough Cl PL6 245 B5
Roborough Down La
PL6 241 F5
Roborough Gdns 3
TQ13 131 A5
Roborough La
Ashburton TQ13 130 F5
Plymouth PL5 244 D8
Roborough Rd EX31 155 A8
Roborough Terr TQ13 130 F5
Robyns Cl PL7 251 B5
Roche Gdn EX2 182 A8
Rochester Rd 5 PL4 248 E4
Rochford Cres PL5 243 F5
Rock Ave
Barnstaple EX32 155 A3
Lynton EX35 151 B5
Rock Cl TQ4 229 C7
Rock Cross EX17 97 B7
Rock End Ave TQ1 220 C2
Rock Gdns
Barnstaple EX32 155 A3
Plymouth PL9 249 D1
Rock Head EX37 28 C2
Rock Hill
Aveton Gifford TQ7 143 C6
Berrynarbor EX34 2 D3
Braunton EX33 152 D6
Chulmleigh EX18 59 E8
Georgeham EX33 8 A2
Knowle EX34 8 F4
Umberleigh EX37 28 C2
Rock House La TQ1 214 C5
Rock La
Cheriton Bishop EX17 97 B7
Rock La *continued*
Chudleigh TQ13 123 F8
14 Combe Martin EX34 3 A3
Offwell EX14 86 C1
Rock Lodge Pk EX35 151 B5
Rock Park Terr 22 EX32 155 A4
Rock Pk
4 Ashburton TQ13 131 A5
Dartmouth TQ6 233 D4
Rock Rd Chudleigh TQ13 123 E5
Torquay TQ2 220 B4
Rock Terr PL7 250 D4
Rock The EX31 154 F7
Rock View EX16 65 B7
Rockbeare CE Prim Sch
EX5 99 B5
Rockbeare Hill EX5 168 A5
Rockdale Rd PL8 136 A2
Rockerhayne Cross
EX24 102 D7
Rockey La EX20 74 E2
Rockfield 5 EX16 161 C3
Rockfield Ave PL6 244 F6
Rockfield Cl TQ14 210 D7
Rockfield Cotts
Exeter EX4 176 F8
Holywell Lake TA21 51 F7
Rockfield Rd EX34 7 F7
Rockhill PL5 244 C7
Rockingham Rd PL3 249 A5
Rocklands TQ13 123 E5
Rockley La EX32 11 F1
Rockmount Terr 6
EX39 157 A2
Rockpark Cross TQ13 131 A5
Rocks The EX39 156 B6
Rockshead Hill EX32 18 F3
Rockville Pk PL9 255 E8
Rockwell Green Prim Sch
TA21 160 B5
Rockwood Rd PL6 245 E8
Rocky Hill PL19 171 B5
Rocky La
Abbotsham EX39 156 A3
Buckfastleigh TQ11 236 A3
Combe Martin EX34 3 A4
Teignmouth TQ14 210 A6
Rocky Park Ave PL9 255 E8
Rocky Park Rd PL9 255 E8
Rocombe Cl TQ2 213 F4
Rocombe Cross
Daccombe TQ12 213 F6
Raymond's Hill EX13 104 C6
Rocombe Hill TQ12 213 F7
Rodda Cl PL18 125 D7
Roddick Way 8 PL7 251 C5
Rodgements Cross EX18 59 E8
Rodgemont's La EX18 59 F8
Rodgemonts Cross EX18 59 F8
Rodgers Ind Est TQ4 225 D3
Rodney Cl
Dartmouth TQ6 233 D3
Exmouth EX8 203 A7
Rodney St PL5 247 D8
Rods La PL19 117 E6
Rodway Cross EX14 87 A6
Roeselare Ave PL11 247 A3
Roeselare Cl PL11 247 A3
Rogada Ct TQ5 230 D3
Rogate Dr PL6 245 D4
Rogate Wlk PL6 245 D4
Rogers Cl EX16 161 E6
Rogers Dr PL12 242 D4
Roland Bailey Gdns
PL19 171 A6
Rolle Barton EX9 198 D7
Rolle Cotts EX9 197 E2
Rolle Ct EX38 159 C5
Rolle Rd
Budleigh Salterton EX9 199 G2
Exmouth EX8 202 A6
Great Torrington EX38 159 A5
Rolle St Barnstaple EX31 154 F6
Exmouth EX8 202 A6
Rolle The EX9 199 G2
Rolle Villas EX8 202 A6
Rolle's Quay EX31 154 F5
Rolles Terr EX39 40 C7
Rollestone Cres EX4 173 E2
Rollis Park Cl PL9 255 C8
Rollis Park Rd PL9 255 C8
Rolston Cl PL6 244 D6
Romaleyn Gdns TQ4 226 B4
Roman Rd Feniton EX5 84 C2
Kilmington EX13 87 C1
Lyme Regis DT7 260 D4
Plymouth PL5 243 E2
Roman Way
Honiton EX14 166 E7
Plymouth PL5 243 E2
Seaton EX12 192 A6
Romans Way EX16 161 F6
Romansleigh Cross EX36 45 C7
Romansleigh Ridge EX18 45 C5
Romilly Gdns PL7 250 B5
Romney Cl PL5 244 B1
Romsey Dr EX2 177 E5
Ronald Terr PL2 247 F5
Roncombe Cnr EX24 101 E5
Roncombe Gate EX24 101 E5
Roncombe Hill EX10 101 E5
Ronsdale Cl PL9 255 D8
Rook La PL21 133 C3
Rook Lane End PL21 133 C3
Rookbear La EX31 9 E2
Rookery Hill EX16 48 C8
Rookery La DT7 260 C8
Rookery Terr TA21 160 C5
Rooklands Ave TQ2 219 E6
Rooks Cl EX31 154 B3
Rooks Cross EX31 27 D3
Rooks Farm Rd EX31 153 A4
Rooks Nest EX31 153 E5
Rooks Way EX16 161 E6
Rookswood La EX5 99 C5
Rookwood Cl EX14 166 B5
Rookwood Ho EX14 166 B6
Room Hill Rd TA24 21 D7
Roope Cl PL5 247 C7
Rooty Cross EX31 27 A7
Rope Wlk
2 Teignmouth TQ14 210 B5
Wellington TA21 160 C4
Roper Ave PL9 255 D8
Roper's La EX9 198 E7
Roperidge Cross PL21 137 F6
Ropers Ct EX9 198 E7
Ropery Rd EX34 150 C6
Ropewalk Bideford EX39 157 A2
Kingsbridge TQ7 258 C4
Ropewalk Hill TQ5 230 C5
Ropewalk Ho EX8 201 E6
Rorkes Cl PL5 243 E2
Roscoff Cl EX38 159 E5
Rose & Crown Hill EX17 80 A5
Rose Acre Terr TQ5 230 D4
Rose Cl EX16 161 F6
Rose Cotts Beer EX12 191 D5
8 Bishop's Tawton EX32 16 E1
Plymouth PL6 249 B8
Rose Dene TQ2 213 F2
Rose Duryard EX4 173 A1
Rose Gdns PL6 245 E6
Rose Hill
Kingskerswell TQ12 212 F4
Wembury PL9 140 D7
Rose Hill Cl 3 TQ12 212 F4
Rose Hill Terr PL17 125 D3
Rose La EX32 155 C3
Rose Mary Ho 9 EX15 67 B8
Rose Moor Rd EX38 159 E5
Rose Terr PL18 125 B5
Rosea Bridge La EX34 3 A4
Rosebank Cres EX4 173 E1
Rosebarn Ave EX4 173 D1
Rosebarn La EX4 173 E1
Rosebery Ave PL4 263 C4
Rosebery La PL4 263 C4
Rosebery Rd Exeter EX4 177 E8
Exmouth EX8 202 A7
Plymouth PL4 263 C4
Rosedale Ave PL2 248 D7
Rosedown Ave PL2 248 A7
Rosehill Cl TQ1 220 C5
Rosehill Gdns TQ12 212 F4
Rosehill Rd TQ1 220 C5
Rosehip Cl PL6 245 E7
Roseland Ave EX1 178 A6
Roseland Cres EX1 178 A6
Roseland Cross EX22 54 C8
Roseland Dr EX1 178 A5
Roseland Sq TQ12 207 E7
Roselands EX10 188 A4
Roselands Dr TQ4 225 F2
Roselands Prim Sch
TQ4 225 F2
Roselands Rd TQ4 226 B2
Rosemary Ave TQ12 206 F4
Rosemary Ct TQ3 226 C8
Rosemary Gdns TQ3 225 F8
Rosemary La
Colyton EX24 103 A5
Dulverton TA22 33 D6
Holne TQ11 130 A3
Musbury EX13 103 D5
Rosemary St EX4 176 F5
Rosemarylane Cross
EX15 52 D1
Rosemont 8 TQ1 220 D4
Rosemont Ct EX2 177 B1
Rosemoor Gdn★ EX38 159 D2
Rosemoor Rd EX38 159 E5
Rosemount TQ4 226 C5
Rosemount Cl EX14 166 B5
Rosemount Ct TQ8 259 D5
Rosemount La EX14 166 B5
Rosery Rd TQ2 219 E5
Rosevean Ct 8 PL3 248 F6
Rosevean Gdns PL3 248 F6
Rosevean Ho 7 PL3 248 F6
Roseveare Cl PL9 256 A8
Roseville St TQ6 233 F3
Rosewarne Ave TQ12 207 F2
Roseway EX8 202 F8
Rosewell Cl EX14 166 D7
Rosewood Cl PL9 255 F5
Rosewood Cres EX5 179 E2
Rosewood Gr EX31 154 C3
Rosewood Terr 5 EX4 177 D8
Rospeath Cres PL2 248 D8
Ross Cl EX1 174 F1
Ross St PL2 247 E4
Rossall Dr TQ3 226 A5
Rosse Rd EX16 161 D6
Rosshayne La EX14 68 F5
Rosslyn Park Rd PL3 248 D5
Rosyl Ave EX7 204 C3
Rothbury Cl PL6 245 E4
Rothbury Gdns PL6 245 D4
Rotherfold TQ9 223 B5
Rothesay Gdns PL5 244 D3
Rothlin TQ1 220 C7
Rougemont EX13 167 D5
Rougemont Ave TQ2 213 D1
Rougemont Cl PL3 249 B7
Rougemont Ct EX6 181 F4

Round Berry Dr TQ8 259 C4
Round Cross TQ11 236 B6
Roundball Cl EX14 166 C4
Roundball La EX14 166 B2
Roundham Ave TQ4 226 D5
Roundham Cres TQ4 226 D5
Roundham Gdns TQ4 226 D4
Roundham Ho TQ4 226 C5
Roundham Rd TQ4 226 C5
Roundhead Rd TQ12 180 F3
Roundhill EX16 161 B3
Roundhill Cl EX4 173 A3
Roundhill Rd TQ2 219 D2
Roundhouse La EX8 196 B2
Roundings The TQ5 229 B5
Roundmoors Cl TQ12 213 A3
Roundsleys La PL19 117 E6
Roundtable Meet EX4 174 B1
Roundway The TQ12 212 F6
Rousdown Rd TQ2 219 E4
Row La PL5 243 E2
Row The EX36 30 A2
Row Tor Cl EX20 170 D5
Rowan Cl
East Ogwell TQ12 206 F1
2 Honiton EX14 85 C2
Plymouth PL7 251 B5
Tavistock PL19 171 C3
Tiverton EX16 161 F5
Rowan Ct PL12 242 C2
Rowan Dr EX12 192 A8
Rowan Pk 2 EX31 154 C2
Rowan Way Brixham TQ5 230 A2
Exeter EX4 176 F7
Plymouth PL6 245 E7
Rowans EX17 78 B7
Rowans The PL16 105 E4
Rowantree Rd TQ12 207 E1
Rowbrook Cl TQ4 225 E3
Rowcliffe Cotts TA21 50 F8
Rowcroft Cl EX14 166 B5
Rowcroft Rd TQ3 226 C8
Rowden Cross
Salcombe TQ7 148 A8
Teignmouth TQ14 124 C1
Widecombe in the Moor
TQ13 121 A3
Rowden Ct PL8 141 A6
Rowden St PL3 248 E5
Rowdens Ho The TQ14 210 D6
Rowdens Rd TQ2 219 F5
Rowdens The TQ14 210 C6
Rowdon Brook EX6 112 F5
Rowdown Cl PL7 251 D4
Rowe Cl TA21 160 A4
Rowe St
Plymouth PL1,PL4 262 C3
Torpoint PL11 247 B3
Rowells Mead 4 TQ12 122 F1
Rowes Orch EX15 162 C3
Rowhorne Rd EX4 176 C8
Rowland Cl PL9 255 E5
Rowley Cross EX31 4 D1
Rowley Rd TQ1 214 C1
Rowlstone Cl EX8 196 C3
Rows La Bampton EX16 34 A1
19 Combe Martin EX34 3 A3
Rowse Gdns PL18 125 D3
Rowsell's La TQ9 223 D5
Rowtry Cross EX20 76 F5
Royal Albert Meml Mus★
EX4 261 A3
Royal Ave The EX8 201 F7
Royal Charter Pk EX18 44 E1
Royal Cl EX2 181 B7
Royal Ct Princetown PL20 128 A8
Torquay TQ1 220 D7
Royal Devon & Exeter Hospl
(Heavitree) EX1 177 E6
Royal Devon & Exeter Hospl
(Wonford) EX2 177 F4
Royal Eye Infmy PL4 248 E4
Royal Navy Ave PL2 247 F6
Royal Oak Cross EX14 86 E6
Royal Par PL1 262 C2
Royal Pines TQ1 220 E3
Royal Way EX6 201 B8
Royal West of England Sch
for the Deaf EX2 261 C1
Royal William Rd PL1 254 A8
Royston Ct 4 EX1 178 C8
Royston Rd
Bideford EX39 156 F1
Churchinford TA3 68 D7
Rozel TQ1 220 D3
Rubby Cross EX6 97 E5
Ruckamore Rd TQ2 219 E5
Ruckham La EX16 62 F6
Rudda Bldgs 4 EX16 161 B4
Rudolf Steiner Sch TQ9 215 C3
Rudyard Way EX39 156 B6
Rudyerd Wlk PL3 249 D6
Rue de Courseulles sur Mer
TQ6 233 F4
Rue St Pierre PL21 237 E5
Rufford Cl PL2 248 A7
Rugby Rd EX4 177 A4
Ruggadon La TQ13 123 D8
Ruggaton La EX34 2 D2
Rule Cross EX23 37 B2
Rull Cross EX16 48 C5
Rull Hill Oakford EX16 48 C5
West Worlington EX17 61 B8
Rull La EX15 163 B6
Rumbelow Rd EX16 161 E6
Rumsam Gdns EX32 155 C2
Rumsam Rd EX32 155 B2
Rumsams Cl EX32 155 B2
Runaway La PL21 137 A2
Rundle Rd TQ12 207 C4
Runnacleave Rd EX34 150 B6
Runnymede Ct PL6 245 E2
Rupert Price Way TQ12 123 B2
Rupertswood EX34 150 C6
Rupertswood Terr 2
EX34 150 C6
Rus Cotts EX17 165 A5
Rush Park Terr PL18 125 C7
Rush Way TQ9 223 F5
Rushcott Cl EX31 153 A4
Rushcott Cross EX31 27 B7
Rushforth Pl EX4 176 E8
Rushlade Cl TQ4 225 F2
Ruskin Cres PL5 244 D2
Rusper Cl EX15 83 F6
Russel Cl EX32 17 C1
Russel La EX15 65 A1
Russell Ave PL3 248 F7
Russell Cl
East Budleigh EX9 198 B6
Gunnislake PL18 125 D7
Plymouth PL9 256 B7
Saltash PL12 242 C3
Russell Court Gdns
PL19 171 B6
Russell Ct Plymouth PL1 262 C2
Saltash PL12 242 C3
Tavistock PL19 171 B6
Russell Dr EX9 198 B6
Russell Pl PL1 262 B4
Russell St Exeter EX1 261 C3
Sidmouth EX10 188 B3
Tavistock PL19 171 C5
Russell Terr EX4 261 A4
Russell Way EX2 178 D2
Russet Ave EX1 178 C6
Russet Cl EX15 66 A7
Russet Wood PL5 243 F4
Russets La TQ11 236 C5
Ruston Hill EX17 61 A6
Rutger Pl PL1 262 A4
Rutherford St EX2 178 A4
Ruthven Cl PL6 248 F8
Rutland Rd PL4 248 F4
Rutt's Cross EX14 84 E2
Ruxhill La EX31 10 D5
Ryall's Cnr Beaford EX20 42 A1
Merton EX20 57 A8
Ryalls Ct EX12 192 A5
Rydal Cl PL6 245 D2
Rydal Mews EX4 176 F5
Ryde Cl TQ2 214 A2
Ryder Cl 16 EX16 64 D7
Ryder Rd PL2 247 F4
Rydon Acres
Kingsteignton TQ12 207 E8
Stoke Gabriel TQ9 227 F8
Rydon Ave TQ12 207 E8
Rydon Cross
Denbury TQ12 211 D6
Stoke Gabriel TQ9 227 F8
Rydon Est TQ12 207 E8
Rydon Ind Est TQ12 207 D6
Rydon La
Abbotskerswell TQ12 212 C6
Exeter EX2 178 C3
Exton EX3,EX5 183 E2
Holsworthy EX22 71 E7
Payhembury EX14 84 B4
Rydon Prim Sch TQ12 207 E8
Rydon Rd
Holsworthy EX22 164 B5
Kingsteignton TQ12 207 E8
Rydonball Cross TQ12 211 F7
Rydons TQ5 230 A4
Rye Hill PL12 242 C2
Rye La TQ7 144 B5
Rye Park Cl EX19 42 D1
Rye Pk Beaford EX19 42 D1
Monkton EX14 86 C5
Ryeland Cl PL9 140 D8
Ryll Cl EX8 202 B7
Ryll Court Dr EX8 202 B7
Ryll Gr EX8 202 B7

S

Sabre Cl TQ12 180 E3
Sabre Wlk 1 EX32 155 B5
Sackery TQ12 208 D4
Sacred Heart RC Prim Sch
TQ3 226 B7
Saddle The TQ4 226 C2
Saddlers Cl EX6 96 F3
Saddlers Way EX20 170 D6
Sadler Cl EX8 202 E8
Saffron Ct TQ7 258 D5
Saffron Pk TQ7 258 D5
Sage Gr EX16 161 F4
Sage Park Rd EX33 152 B7
Sages Lea EX5 184 C6
Sailmakers Ct EX8 201 E6
Saint Luke's Campus
EX1 177 E6
Saint Luke's Coll EX1 177 E6
St Agnes La TQ2 219 E3
St Albans Cl EX4 176 E6
St Albans Pk PL20 127 A2
St Albans Rd TQ1 220 C7
St Andrew St
Millbrook PL10 252 E5
Plymouth PL1 262 C2
Tiverton EX16 161 C3
St Andrew's CE Prim Sch
PL20 126 C3
St Andrew's CE Prim Sch
PL1 262 B2
St Andrew's Cl
Calstock PL18 125 D3
Feniton EX14 84 D2
Kennford EX6 114 E4
Yarnscombe EX31 27 E2
St Andrew's Cross 1
PL1 263 A2
St Andrew's Est EX15 163 B4
St Andrew's Pl PL10 253 A1
St Andrew's Rd
Cowley EX4 172 F2
Exmouth EX8 201 F6
St Andrew's Sch EX13 88 A7
St Andrew's Sq EX24 103 A5
St Andrew's St PL10 253 A1
St Andrews Cl
Ashburton TQ13 130 F4
12 Bere Alston PL20 125 E1
Cullompton EX15 163 C3
Saltash PL12 242 C2
Sutcombe EX22 54 A6
St Andrews Ct TQ2 219 C8
St Andrews Dr EX13 167 F7
St Andrews Ho EX8 201 F6
St Andrews Mdw DT7 260 D4
St Andrews Orch EX24 103 A5
St Andrews Prim Sch
EX15 163 B3
St Andrews Rd
Cullompton EX15 163 C3
Fremington EX31 153 D6
Paignton TQ4 226 C5
Tavistock PL19 171 D2
St Anne's Chapel Mus★
EX31 154 F5
St Anne's Rd Exeter EX1 177 E7
Plymouth PL6 245 D6
Saltash PL12 242 E3
Torquay TQ1 220 D7
St Annes EX6 194 D3
St Annes Cl EX22 70 E1
St Annes Ct TQ12 207 B3
St Annes Well Brewery
EX4 261 A3
St Annes Well Mews
EX4 261 A3
St Anthony's Cl EX11 169 E4
St Aubyn Ave PL2 247 F5
St Aubyn Rd PL1 247 E3
St Aubyn St PL1 247 E2
St Aubyn Terr PL7 132 F4
St Aubyn's Villas EX16 161 F3
St Augustines Cl TQ2 214 A3
St Austin Cl PL21 237 B5
St Austin's Priory Private Sch
PL21 136 D7
St Barnabas Hospl PL12 242 F2
St Barnabas Terr PL1 262 A4
St Bartholomew Way
TQ12 206 D1
St Bernard's Cl
Buckfast TQ11 236 B7
Exeter EX2 261 C1
St Bernards Sch TQ12 207 C2
St Boniface Cl PL2 248 C7
St Boniface Dr PL2 248 C7
St Boniface Prim Sch
PL1 262 B3
St Boniface Rd EX17 165 A5
St Boniface's RC Coll
PL5 244 E1
St Brannock's Hill EX33 152 D7
St Brannock's Park Rd
EX34 150 B4
St Brannock's Rd EX34 150 B4
St Brannock's Well Cl
EX33 152 D7
St Briac Way EX8 196 E3
St Bridget Ave PL6 244 F1
St Budeaux Cl EX11 169 E3
St Budeaux Ferry Rd Sta
PL5 247 D8
St Budeaux Foundation Jun
Sch PL5 243 F2
St Catherine's Rd TQ1 220 B8
St Catherines Pk PL8 141 A7
St Clement's Terr TQ9 222 D2
St Clements Ct TQ6 233 D4
St Columba Cl TQ12 207 E8
St Cyres Rd EX14 166 B6
St David's CE Fst Sch
EX4 261 A3
St David's Dr EX13 167 F7
St David's Hill EX4 177 A7
St David's Rd PL19 171 E5
St David's Sta EX4 177 A7
St David's Terr EX4 261 A3
St Davids 12 EX39 157 A1
St Davids Cl EX13 167 F7
St Davids Rd TQ14 210 C8
St Dominic's Cl TQ1 220 B8
St Dominick CE Sch
PL12 125 A2
St Dunstan's Abbey Sch
PL1 262 A3
St Dunstan's Rd TQ8 259 C4
St Dunstan's Terr PL4 263 C3
St Edmund's Rd TQ1 220 B7
St Edmunds Rd TQ7 258 C6
St Edmunds wlk TQ7 258 C6
St Edward Gdns PL6 245 B1
St Edward's CE Prim Sch
PL6 245 C1
St Efride's Rd TQ2 219 F5
St Elizabeth Cl PL7 250 F3
St Elmo Ct TQ8 259 C3
St Erth Rd PL2 248 D7
St Eval Pl PL5 243 E4
St Francis Ct PL5 244 B3
St Gabriel's Ave PL3 248 D5
St George's Ave PL2 248 C7
St George's CE Inf Sch
EX39 156 F8
St George's CE Prim Sch
PL1 262 A1
St George's Rd
Barnstaple EX32 155 A6
Saltash PL12 242 E3
Torquay TQ1 220 C7
St George's Terr 1
EX32 155 A6
St George's Terr
Plymouth PL2 247 F4
Shillingford St George EX2 114 C6
St George's View EX15 163 B4
St George's Way EX16 161 C3
St George's Well EX15 163 C4
St George's Well Ave
EX15 163 B4
St Georges Ave EX13 167 F7
St Georges Cl PL21 137 B2
St Georges Cres TQ1 220 C7
St Georges Ct 1 PL2 247 F4
St Georges Hill DT7 260 C4
St Georges Rd PL12 242 D3
St German's Rd EX4 177 C8
St Giles on the Heath Prim
Sch PL15 90 C1
St Gregorys Ct EX12 192 A6
St Helen's CE Prim Sch
EX39 156 A1
St Helen's Cl EX33 7 E2
St Helens EX39 156 A2
St Helens Wlk PL5 244 C5
St Hilary Terr PL4 263 C3
St Hill Cl EX2 177 A2
St Ida's Cl EX2 176 D1
St Ives Ct 3 TQ1 220 A6
St Jame's Prec 15
TQ14 210 B5
St James Cl Exeter EX4 261 C4
Landkey EX32 17 C1
Parkham EX39 39 E8
St James Ct
Plymouth PL1 262 B2
Torpoint PL11 247 B3
St James High Sch EX4 174 B1
St James Pl TQ1 220 D7
St James Rd
Torpoint PL11 247 B2
Torquay TQ1 220 A7
St James St EX20 170 B5
St James Terr EX4 261 C4
St James' Ho 16 TQ14 210 B5
St James' Park (Exeter City
AFC) EX4 261 C4
St James' Park Halt
EX4 261 C4
St James' Pl E PL1 262 B2
St James' Pl W PL1 262 B2
St James' Rd EX4 261 C4
St James's Pl EX34 150 C6
St Joeseph's RC Prim Sch
TQ12 207 A4
St John the Baptist RC Prim
Sch TQ6 233 C2
St John's Bridge Rd
PL4 263 B2
St John's CE Prim Sch
TQ9 223 E5
St John's CE Prim Sch
TA21 160 E6
St John's Cl
Bishopsteignton TQ14 208 F7
Bovey Tracey TQ13 180 C6
Honiton EX14 166 C6
Ivybridge PL21 237 B5
Millbrook PL10 252 E5
St John's Cotts TQ13 180 C6
St John's Ct 3 TQ3 226 B6
St John's Dr
Bradworthy EX22 53 E8
Plymouth PL9 255 B6
St John's La
Barnstaple EX32 155 C3
Bovey Tracey TQ13 180 C7
St John's Pl TQ1 220 B4
St John's Rd Exeter EX1 177 E7
Exmouth EX8 196 E2
Exmouth EX8 196 F4
Horrabridge PL20 126 F4
Ivybridge PL21 237 B5
Millbrook PL10 252 F6
Plymouth PL4 263 B2
Plymouth, Turnchapel PL9 255 A6
St John's Sch EX10 187 F5
St John's St PL4 263 B2
St John's Terr TQ9 223 B6
St John's Villas EX2 177 F5
St Johns PL19 171 C5
St Johns Ave PL19 171 C5
St Johns Cl
16 Colyton EX24 103 A4
Plymouth PL6 245 D4
Wellington TA21 160 E6
St Johns Ct EX22 53 E8
St Johns Farm Mews
EX8 196 F3
St Johns La PL11 252 B8
St Johns RC Prim Sch
EX16 161 B4
St Johns Rd PL4 263 C2
St Johns St TQ12 207 D4
St Joseph's Cl PL6 244 F1
St Joseph's RC Prim Sch
Exmouth EX8 202 B7
Plymouth PL1 247 E2
St Jude's Rd PL4 263 B2
St Julian's Cotts PL10 253 E7
St Katharine's Rd TQ2 219 E6
St Katherine's Cl EX31 153 A5
St Katherine's Way TQ9 223 C5
St Katherines Rd EX4 178 A8
St Katherne's Mews 5
TQ9 223 C5
St Keverne Pl PL2 248 D8
St Keyes Cl 10 EX32 17 B2
St Kitts Cl TQ2 213 F2
St Lawrence Cl 12 EX16 64 D7
St Lawrence Cres EX1 178 D6
St Lawrence Dr EX17 165 B5
St Lawrence La TQ13 130 F4
St Lawrence Mews PL4 263 A4
St Lawrence Rd PL4 263 A4
St Lawrence's Gn EX17 165 B5
St Leo Pl PL2 247 E4
St Leonard's Ave EX2 261 B1
St Leonard's Cl 16 TQ12 207 B3
St Leonard's Pl EX2 261 C2
St Leonard's Rd
Exeter EX2 261 C2
Newton Abbot TQ12 207 B3
Plymouth PL4 263 C2
St Leonards Cl EX14 166 A5
St Levan Rd PL2 247 F5
St Loyd's Ct EX2 178 A4
St Loye's Coll EX2 177 F2
St Loye's Terr EX2 178 A4
St Loyes Rd EX2 178 A5
St Luke's CE High Sch
EX1 178 C6
St Luke's Cl TQ12 207 F1
St Luke's Pk TQ2 220 A4
St Luke's Rd
Kingskerswell TQ12 212 E8
Torquay TQ2 220 A4
St Luke's Rd N TQ2 220 B4
St Luke's Rd S TQ2 220 A4
St Malo Cl EX8 196 E3
St Marco Gdns TQ7 258 D6
St Margaret Clitherow RC
Prim Sch TQ5 230 B3
St Margaret's Ave TQ1 220 B7
St Margaret's CE Jun Sch
EX39 156 E7
St Margaret's Cl TQ1 220 B8
St Margaret's Ct 7
EX39 156 F7
St Margaret's Prim Sch
TQ1 220 B8
St Margaret's Rd TQ1 220 B8
St Margaret's Sch EX2 177 E5
St Margaret's View EX8 203 A7
St Margarets Cl EX15 67 B8
St Margarets Ct EX3 182 E5
St Margarets Gdn 1
EX31 154 F6
St Margarets La TA20 88 C8
St Margarets Rd PL7 250 B7
St Margarets Terr EX3 182 F5
St Mark's Prim Sch
EX23 37 B2
St Mark's Rd
Honiton EX14 166 A4
Torquay TQ1 220 D3
St Marks 21 EX7 204 E6
St Marks Ave EX1 177 F7
St Marks Rd PL6 245 D5
St Martin's Ave PL3 248 D7
St Martin's Cl EX17 78 C4
St Martin's La EX17 165 B6
St Martin's Mews TQ1 220 C8
St Martins Cl EX10 188 B6
St Martins Ct TQ2 213 F1
St Martins Rd EX23 70 A8
St Marwenne Cl EX23 70 A6
St Mary St PL1 262 A2
St Mary Steps Terr 8
EX1 261 A2
St Mary's CE Prim Sch
Bideford EX39 157 A4
Brixton PL8 257 A4
St Mary's Cl
Axminster EX13 167 F5
Brixham TQ5 230 B2
Great Torrington EX38 159 B4
St Mary's Cotts EX7 200 F4
St Mary's Ct
Torquay TQ1 214 B1
4 Newton Abbot TQ12 207 B3
Paignton TQ3 226 A6
St Mary's Flats 7
EX39 157 A1
St Mary's La DT7 104 B6
St Mary's Pk TQ4 225 C4
St Mary's RC Prim Sch
EX13 167 E5
St Mary's RC Prim Sch
TQ11 236 C7
St Mary's Rd
Barnstaple EX32 155 A6
Brixham TQ5 230 D2
Croyde EX33 7 E2
Newton Abbot TQ12 207 B2
Plymouth PL7 250 C6
Teignmouth TQ14 210 A7
St Marychurch CE Prim Sch
TQ1 214 B1

St Marychurch Rd
Newton Abbot TQ12 .....207 F1
Torquay, Plainmoor TQ1 ..220 B6
Torquay, St Marychurch TQ1 ....214 C1
St Maryhaye PL19 ......171 A5
St Marys Cl
Abbotskerswell TQ12 ....212 A6
17 Chudleigh TQ13 ......123 E6
Plymouth PL7 ....250 D5
St Marys Ct
Plymouth PL7 ....250 D5
Teignmouth TQ14 ....210 C5
St Marys Pk EX11 ......169 F3
St Marys View
Silverton EX5 ....82 B5
West Hill EX11 ....168 E5
St Matthew's Rd TQ2 ..219 D4
St Matthews Cl EX1 ....177 E6
St Matthews Wlk EX1 ..261 C3
St Matthias Church Rd TQ1 ....220 E5
St Maurice Mews PL7 ..250 E4
St Maurice Rd PL7 .....250 F3
St Maurice View PL7 ...251 B4
St Mawes Dr TQ4 ......229 B8
St Mawes Terr 8 PL2 ..247 F5
St Michael Ave PL2 ....247 F5
St Michael's TQ2 ......219 E6
St Michael's Bsns Ctr DT7 ....260 E3
St Michael's CE Mid Sch EX1 ....177 F6
St Michael's CE Prim Sch TQ12 ....207 E7
St Michael's Cl
Clyst Honiton EX5 ....179 D8
Exeter EX2 ....177 B1
Plymouth PL1 ....247 E1
Torquay TQ1 ....219 E6
St Michael's Ct
Paignton TQ4 ....226 A4
7 Plymouth PL1 ....247 F3
St Michael's Hill EX5 ..179 D8
St Michael's Prim Sch DT7 ....260 E4
St Michael's Rd
Newton Abbot TQ12 .....207 D1
Paignton TQ4 ....226 B5
Torquay TQ1 ....219 E7
St Michael's Terr
Plymouth PL4 ....262 C4
8 Plymouth, Devonport PL1 ....247 F3
St Michael's Terr 2 TQ1 ....220 B5
St Michaels DT7 ....260 E4
St Michaels Cl
Launceston PL15 ....105 B1
Otterton EX9 ....198 E7
St Michaels Rd
Kingsteignton TQ12 .....207 D6
Teignmouth TQ14 ....210 C7
St Michaels Sch EX31 ...27 D8
St Michaels Terr 5 TQ10 ....134 F2
St Michaels View EX21 ...55 E4
St Modwen Rd PL6 .....249 F7
St Nazaire App PL1 ....247 F2
St Nazaire Cl PL1 .....247 E2
St Nicholas CE Jun Sch EX10 ....188 A7
St Nicholas RC Comb Sch EX2 ....261 C1
St Olave's Cl EX4 .....261 A3
St Pancras Ave PL2 ....248 D8
St Paul St Plymouth PL1 .254 A8
Tiverton EX16 ....161 C4
St Paul's Cres TQ1 .....220 B7
St Paul's Ct 13 TQ12 ...207 C3
St Paul's RC Prim Sch PL5 ....243 D1
St Paul's Rd
Honiton EX14 ....166 A5
12 Newton Abbot TQ12 ...207 C3
Paignton TQ3 ....219 D1
Torquay TQ1 ....220 B7
St Paul's Sq EX16 ......161 C3
St Pauls Cl
Bovey Tracey TQ13 ......180 D7
Plymouth PL3 ....249 C5
St Peter Cl PL7 ....250 F4
St Peter St EX16 ......161 C4
St Peter's Cath EX1 ....261 B3
St Peter's CE High Sch EX2 ....178 C5
St Peter's CE Jun Sch PL19 ....171 D5
St Peter's Cl TQ13 .....180 E8
St Peter's Hill 5 TQ5 ..230 D5
St Peter's Prim Sch EX9 ....197 F2
St Peter's Quay TQ9 ...223 D4
St Peter's RC Prim Sch PL5 ....244 B5
St Peter's Rd EX14 .....166 A5
St Peter's Sch EX8 .....196 A6
St Peters CE Prim Sch PL1 ....262 B3
St Peters Cl Torquay TQ2 219 D6
West Buckland EX32 ......18 B2
St Peters Ct PL1 ....262 A3
St Peters Mount EX4 ...176 D7
St Peters Rd
Fremington EX31 ....153 D5

St Peters Rd *continued*
Holsworthy EX22 ....164 B5
Plymouth PL5 ....244 C2
St Peters Terr 2 EX34 ..150 C5
St Peters Way
Ivybridge PL21 ....237 E3
Ivybridge PL21 ....237 E5
St Peters Well La EX22 ...53 E8
St Petrock's Cl EX2 ....261 C2
St Phillips Ct EX4 ......176 F4
St Rumon's CE Inf Sch PL19 ....171 C6
St Saviour's Way EX17 .165 B5
St Saviours Rd EX11 ...169 D3
St Scholastica's Abbey TQ14 ....210 D7
St Sevan Way EX8 .....196 E3
St Sidwell's Ave EX4 ...261 C4
St Sidwell's CE Comb Sch EX4 ....261 C4
St Sidwell's Ct EX4 ....261 B4
St Simon's La PL4 .....249 B3
St Stephen Rd PL7 .....250 F3
St Stephen St PL1 .....247 F1
St Stephen's Hill PL12 .242 C1
St Stephen's Pl PL7 ....250 E5
St Stephen's Rd PL12 ..242 E2
St Stephens Com Prim Sch PL12 ....242 E2
St Swithin's Gdns EX17 ..80 A5
St Teresa Ho PL4 ......263 A3
St Teresa's Cl EX39 ....156 F7
St Teresa's Ct 9 EX39 ..156 F7
St Therese's Ct PL1 ....247 F2
St Thomas Cl
Bovey Tracey TQ13 ......180 E7
Plymouth PL7 ....250 F3
St Thomas Ct EX4 .....177 A4
St Thomas Fst Sch EX2 .177 A4
St Thomas Sh Ctr EX4 ..177 A4
St Vincent Ct TQ1 .....220 C3
St Vincent St PL2 .....247 E4
St Vincent's Rd TQ1 ....219 F7
St Vincents Cl TQ1 .....219 F6
St Werburgh Cl PL9 ....140 D7
St Wilfrid's Sch EX4 ....261 A3
Salamanca St PL11 .....247 B3
Salcombe CE Prim Sch TQ8 ....259 C5
Salcombe Ct EX10 .....188 C4
Salcombe Hill Cl EX10 ..188 B4
Salcombe Hill Rd EX10 .188 C4
Salcombe Lawn EX10 ..188 B4
Salcombe Rd
Malborough TQ7,TQ8 .....147 F6
Sidmouth EX10 ....188 B4
Salcombe The TQ8 .....259 E4
Salem Almshouses 7 EX32 ....155 A4
Salem Pl 12 TQ12 ......207 B3
Salem St 8 EX32 ......155 A4
Salisbury Ave
Feniton EX14 ....84 D2
Torquay TQ2 ....213 F1
Salisbury Cl EX14 ....84 D2
Salisbury Ope PL3 .....248 B5
Salisbury Rd Exeter EX4 .177 E8
Exmouth EX8 ....202 A7
Newton Abbot TQ12 .....207 D4
Plymouth PL4 ....263 C4
Salisbury Road Jun Sch PL4 ....263 C3
Salisbury Terr
Kilmington EX13 ....87 C1
9 Teignmouth TQ14 .....210 C5
Sallicombe Rd EX24 ....101 F6
Salmonhutch Cotts EX17 ....165 B3
Salmonpool La EX2 ....177 E3
Salston Barton EX11 ...169 C2
Salston Ride EX11 .....169 B2
Salt Mill PL12 ....242 F4
Salt Wood La EX34 ......2 F3
Saltash Bsns Pk PL12 ..242 C4
Saltash Coll PL12 ......242 D2
Saltash Com Sch PL12 ..242 E1
Saltash Ctr (Coll of F Ed) PL12 ....242 D2
Saltash Ind Est PL12 ...242 D4
Saltash Parkway Ind Est PL12 ....242 B4
Saltash Rd Plymouth PL3 262 C4
Plymouth, Keyham PL2 ...247 E6
Saltash Sta PL12 ....243 A2
Saltburn Rd PL5 ....243 C1
Salter's Cross EX10 ....187 D6
Salter's La EX24 ....103 A4
Salter's Rd EX2 ....178 A4
Saltern Rd TQ4 ....226 C1
Salterns Terr EX39 .....157 B2
Salters Ct EX2 ....178 A4
Salters Mdw EX10 ......188 B5
Salterton Rd
Budleigh Salterton EX8, EX9 ....197 B1
Exmouth EX8 ....202 C7
Salterton Workshops 1 EX9 ....198 A1
Salting Hill EX9 ....199 J2
Saltings The
Seaton EX12 ....192 B7
Shaldon TQ14 ....209 D5
Saltmer Cl EX34 ....150 A2
Saltram Ho★ PL7 ....250 A4
Saltram Terr
Lee Moor PL7 ....132 F4
Plymouth PL7 ....250 E5
Saltways La EX10 ......100 F1

Salty La TQ14 ....209 D5
Salway Cl EX15 ....163 B3
Salway Gdns EX13 ......167 F5
Samara Bsns Pk TQ12 ..180 F3
Sampford Arundel Com Prim Sch TA21 ....51 E5
Sampford Cross EX20 ....76 F3
Sampford Gdns PL20 ...127 A5
Sampford Peverell CE Prim Sch EX16 ....50 C1
Sampford Terr 7 PL20 ..126 F5
Sampson Cl PL18 ....125 A6
Sampson Cross EX37 ....44 E8
Sampson's Hill EX2 .....114 C6
Sampsons La EX1 ......177 E7
San Remo Terr EX7 ....204 F7
Sanctuary Cl EX32 ......16 E1
Sanctuary La
Hatherleigh EX20 ....75 C7
Woodbury Salterton EX5 ..185 B7
Sanctuary Rd EX22 .....164 C4
Sand Down La EX5 .....172 A8
Sand Hill PL18 ....125 D6
Sand La Calstock PL18 ..125 D3
Totnes TQ9 ....224 A8
Sand Pit Hill La EX24 ...102 F4
Sandaway La EX34 ....2 F4
Sandclose La EX36 ......31 D7
Sanders Cl EX5 ....175 D6
Sanders Cross EX22 .....54 C8
Sanders La 7 EX32 ......16 E1
Sanders Rd Bow EX17 ....78 C4
Brixham TQ5 ....230 A5
Exeter EX4 ....174 E1
Sanders' La EX22 ....164 C5
Sandersfield EX15 ....83 F6
Sanderspool Cross TQ10 ....135 A2
Sandford Ash La EX17 ...79 A7
Sandford Cl EX32 ......155 D1
Sandford Cross EX20 ....77 E4
Sandford La EX20 ....77 F3
Sandford Orleigh TQ12 .207 B5
Sandford Rd PL9 ....255 F8
Sandford Sch EX17 ......80 A5
Sandford View TQ12 ...207 B4
Sandford Wlk EX1 .....261 C3
Sandfords EX6 ....181 B1
Sandfords Gdns EX38 ..159 B4
Sandgate La EX11 .....100 D4
Sandheap Cross TQ7 ...143 C2
Sandhill Cross TQ13 ....111 E5
Sandhill St EX11 ....169 E4
Sandhills TQ8 ....259 C3
Sandhills Rd TQ8 ......259 C3
Sandhole Cross EX39 ....37 A8
Sandick Cross EX32 ......17 F2
Sandon Wlk PL6 ....245 A1
Sandown Rd TQ4 ....225 F2
Sandpark La EX31 ....10 D5
Sandpark Rd EX18 ....59 D2
Sandpath Rd TQ12 .....207 E6
Sandpiper Ct EX4 ......174 D1
Sandpiper Dr EX3 ......183 C2
Sandpiper Gn EX2 ......176 D3
Sandpit Hill EX24 ....101 E6
Sandquay Rd TQ6 ......233 F5
Sandringham Dr TQ3 ...219 B2
Sandringham Gdns TQ3 219 C1
Sandringham Rd TQ12 .207 E3
Sands Ct Paignton TQ4 ..226 B5
Seaton EX12 ....191 F7
Sands Gate Cross TQ13 ..95 F1
Sands Rd Paignton TQ4 ..226 C5
Slapton TQ7 ....145 D3
Sanduck Cross TQ13 ...112 A2
Sandy Cross EX9 ......198 A8
Sandy La
Brampford Speke EX5 .....81 E1
Braunton EX33 ....15 A6
Broadclyst EX5 ....175 D5
Chittlehampton EX37 .....29 A5
Croyde EX33 ....7 E2
Ivybridge PL21 ....237 D5
Kingsbridge TQ7,TQ9 ....144 B5
Staverton TQ9 ....216 A6
Woolacombe EX34 ....1 A1
Sandy Rd PL7 ....251 C4
Sandy Way EX33 ....7 E1
Sandy's La EX14 ....68 C2
Sandygate Bsns Pk TQ12 ....123 E1
Sandygate Mill TQ12 ...123 E1
Sandylane Cross EX38 ...41 A2
Sandymere Rd EX39 ....156 F7
Sandymoor Cross EX22 ..72 E1
Sandypark La EX32 ......18 E3
Sandyway Cross EX36 ....20 D4
Sandyways Cross TQ13 .111 C7
Sanford Rd TQ2 ....219 E5
Sango Ct PL10 ....252 F6
Sango Rd PL11 ....247 A2
Sannerville Way EX6 ...182 B5
Sanson Cl EX5 ....173 F8
Sarah Cl PL20 ....125 E1
Sargent Cl EX1 ....178 C6
Sargents Mdw EX23 .....37 A1
Sarlsdown Rd EX8 .....202 D7
Sarum Cl PL3 ....248 F7
Satterleigh Cross EX37 ..29 C1
Saturday's La TQ12 ....212 F1
Saundercroft Rd EX5 ....99 B7
Saunders Way
Cullompton EX15 ....163 E4
West Charleton TQ7 .....144 C1
Saunders Wlk PL6 .....244 D6
Saunton Beach Villas EX33 ....14 E8

Saunton Cl EX33 ....152 C6
Saunton Rd EX33 ......152 B6
Savage Rd PL5 ....247 D7
Savery Cl PL21 ....237 E6
Savile Rd EX4 ....176 F5
Savoy Hill EX4 ....174 A2
Sawmill La EX9 ....197 F7
Sawmills Way 3 EX14 ..166 C5
Sawpit La TQ9 ....222 F7
Sawrey St PL1 ....262 A2
Sawyer Dr TQ14 ....124 E1
Sawyers Mill EX16 ....34 E2
Saxon Ave EX4 ....174 F2
Saxon Hts 2 TQ5 ......230 C4
Saxon Mdw TQ3 ....225 C5
Saxon Rd EX1 ....177 F6
Saxon Way EX15 ....163 C6
Saxons Croft EX32 .....155 C3
Scabbacombe La TQ6 ..235 A6
Scadsbury La EX20 ......75 A4
Scalders La PL21 ......137 C2
Scalwell La EX12 ....192 A7
Scalwell Mead EX12 ...192 A7
Scalwell Pk EX12 ......192 A7
Scarborough Pl TQ2 ...219 F5
Scarborough Rd TQ2 ...219 F5
Scarhill Cross EX20 .....95 D4
Scarsdale EX8 ....202 C5
Scattor View EX6 ......112 F5
School Cl Bampton EX16 ..34 B1
Fremington EX31 ....153 E5
Plymouth PL7 ....250 D7
Shobrooke EX17 ....80 E4
Tavistock PL19 ....171 D5
School Cnr EX39 ....22 E3
School Cotts TQ12 .....207 A8
School Ct TQ6 ....233 D3
School Dr PL6 ....245 D7
School Hill
Cockwood EX6 ....201 B6
6 Dawlish EX7 ....204 D6
Lympstone EX8 ....195 E5
Stoke Gabriel TQ9 ....227 F7
School La
6 Bishop's Tawton EX32 ..16 E1
Blackawton TQ9 ....139 E1
Broadclyst EX5 ....175 C7
Chilsworthy EX22 ....53 E1
5 Colyton EX24 ....103 A4
Exeter EX2 ....178 A1
Exmouth EX8 ....196 C1
Great Torrington EX38 ...159 C5
Hartland EX39 ....22 E3
Honiton EX14 ....166 C6
Newton Poppleford EX10 .186 F8
Plymouth PL7 ....250 E4
Rousdon DT7 ....193 F7
Tatworth TA20 ....88 C8
Tedburn St Mary EX6 .....97 F4
3 Teignmouth TQ14 .....210 A3
Thorverton EX5 ....81 E4
West Hill EX11 ....168 E5
School Rd
Ermington PL21 ....136 F4
Exeter EX2 ....177 A4
Kingskerswell TQ12 .....212 F4
Lydford EX20 ....107 F4
Newton Abbot TQ12 .....207 C3
Silverton EX5 ....82 B5
Stoke Fleming TQ6 ......146 A7
Teigngrace TQ12 ....206 F8
Whitchurch PL19 ....171 D2
School St 9 EX10 ......101 B1
School Way EX20 ......170 B5
Schooners Ct EX8 ......201 E6
Scobhill Rd EX35 ....5 E3
Sconner Rd PL11 ....247 A3
Score Farm Cvn Pk EX33 ....152 C5
Score View EX34 ....150 C3
Scoresby Cl TQ2 ....214 B3
Scotchmead EX5 ....99 D3
Scott Ave
18 Appledore EX39 ....15 A1
Exeter EX2 ....177 F3
Plymouth PL5 ....247 C8
Scott Dr EX8 ....196 B2
Scott Hospl PL2 ....248 A6
Scott Rd PL2 ....248 B6
Scott's Cl TQ7 ....143 E4
Scott's Hill TA4 ....35 E8
Scott's La
Raymond's Hill EX13 .....104 C7
Wellington TA21 ....160 E6
Scottleigh TQ2 ....219 F3
Scouse Cross EX13 ......88 E2
Scouse La EX13 ....88 E2
Scrapton La TA20 ....69 F5
Scratch Face La EX2 ...176 C2
Scratchface La
Bideford EX39 ....25 D4
Bideford, Littleham EX39 ..25 F2
Buckland Brewer EX39 ....40 B6
Thorverton EX17 ....81 B6
Screechers Hill TQ13 ...130 F5
Scurfield Cl EX33 ......152 D7
Sea Hill Beer EX12 ......191 E5
Seaton EX12 ....192 A4
Sea Lawn Terr EX7 .....204 F7
Sea Trout Mews TQ9 ...216 A5
Sea View PL18 ....125 B5
Sea View Ave PL4 ......263 C4
Sea View Dr 7 PL9 .....140 D8
Sea View Gdns TQ7 .....147 B7
Sea View Rd EX39 ......156 F7
Sea View Terr
Beer EX12 ....191 D5
Brixham TQ5 ....230 C6

Sea View Terr *continued*
Plymouth PL4 ....263 B4
Sidmouth EX10 ....188 A5
Thurlestone TQ7 ....143 A2
Seabourne Ct TQ4 .....226 C4
Seabrook Ave EX2 ......182 C7
Seacroft Rd PL5 ....243 C2
Seafield Ave EX8 ......196 A2
Seafield La EX10 ....188 A3
Seafield Rd Seaton EX12 192 A5
Sidmouth EX10 ....188 A4
Seaforth Lodge EX12 ...191 F6
Sealands EX34 ....8 C6
Seale Cl TQ6 ....233 D4
Seale-Hayne (Univ of Plymouth) TQ12 ......206 B7
Seapoint 15 TQ14 ....210 B4
Searle St EX17 ....165 C5
Searle Terr EX39 ....157 A7
Seashore Ctr★ TQ4 ....226 C4
Seaside EX34 ....2 F4
Seaton EX12 ....192 B5
Seaton & District Electric Tramway★ EX12 ....192 C7
Seaton & District Hospl EX12 ....192 A6
Seaton Ave PL4 ....248 E4
Seaton Bsns Pk PL6 .....245 B3
Seaton Cl TQ1 ....220 D7
Seaton Down Cl EX12 ..191 F8
Seaton Down Hill EX12 .191 F8
Seaton Down Rd EX12 .192 A5
Seaton La PL4 ....248 E4
Seaton Orch PL7 ....136 A8
Seaton Pl PL2 ....247 F5
Seaton Prim Sch EX12 .192 A6
Seaton Rd
Branscombe EX12,EX24 ..102 A2
Colyford EX24 ....103 A3
Farway EX24 ....101 E5
Musbury EX13 ....103 D5
Seaton EX24 ....192 B8
Seaton Way PL20 ......126 D2
Seaview TQ7 ....149 A3
Seaview Cres TQ3 .....219 C1
Seaview Rd
Thurlestone TQ7 ....143 A2
Uplyme DT7 ....104 B4
Seaward Cl EX12 ....190 E4
Seaway Cl TQ2 ....219 E3
Seaway Cres TQ3 ......226 D8
Seaway Ct TQ5 ....230 B4
Seaway Gdns TQ3 .....226 D8
Seaway La
Tipton St John EX10 .....100 D2
Torquay TQ2 ....219 E3
Seaway Rd TQ3 ....226 D8
Seckerleigh Cross EX16 .64 E5
Seckington Cross EX19 ..58 E4
Secmaton La EX7 ......200 E1
Secmaton Rise EX7 ....200 E1
Second Ave
Axminster EX13 ....167 F7
Dawlish EX7 ....204 C5
Exeter, Countess Wear EX2 ....182 D7
Exeter, Heavitree EX1 ....177 F6
Plymouth, Billacombe PL9 .250 A1
Plymouth, Devonport PL1 .248 A2
Plymouth, Weston Mill PL2 247 E7
Teignmouth TQ14 ....210 A5
Torquay TQ1 ....220 A8
Second Dr
Teignmouth TQ14 ....210 B5
Teignmouth TQ14 ....210 D6
Second Field La EX33 ..152 C6
Sector Hill EX13 ....88 B1
Sector La EX13 ....167 F5
Sedemuda Cl EX10 .....188 A8
Sedemuda Rd EX10 ....187 F8
Sedge Cl PL21 ....237 D4
Sedgeclaire Cl EX1 .....174 F1
Sedgewell Cross EX21 ...55 F4
Sedley Way PL5 ....244 D3
Sefton Ave PL4 ....249 B3
Sefton Cl PL4 ....263 C4
Sefton Ct 23 EX7 ....204 E6
Segrave Rd PL2 ....248 B6
Selcombe Cross TQ9 ...144 E4
Seldons Cl PL21 ....137 D6
Selkirk Pl PL5 ....244 E2
Sellbed Cross TA24 ......21 A8
Seller's Grave EX24 ....103 A4
Seller's Wood Hill EX12 190 E6
Sellick Ave TQ5 ....230 D3
Selsden Cl PL9 ....256 C6
Senate Ct EX8 ....196 E1
Senate Way EX8 ....196 E1
Sendall's Way PL6 .....244 F4
Sennen Cl PL11 ....246 F4
Sennen Pl PL2 ....247 E5
Sentry Cnr EX39 ....157 C1
Sentry Cross EX31 ......18 A8
Sentry La
Bishop's Tawton EX32 .....16 F1
Huntsham EX16 ....49 E6
Sentrys Orch EX6 ......182 B3
Sercombes Gdns EX6 ..201 B8
Serge Ct EX2 ....261 A2
Serpell Cl PL6 ....244 E6
Serstone Cross EX17 ....78 C5
Sessland La
North Tawton EX17 ....77 E1
Spreyton EX17 ....95 D8
Sett Cl TQ13 ....180 D7
Seven Acre Cross EX36 ..31 E6
Seven Acre La
Braunton EX33 ....152 E5

Seven Acre La *continued*
Bridford EX6 .....112 F5
Seven Acres Pk EX33 .....152 E5
Seven Ash Cross EX34 .....3 C1
Seven Brethren Ind Est
EX31 .....154 F3
Seven Crosses EX16 .....63 F6
Seven Crosses Rd EX16 161 A3
Seven Hills Ho TQ2 .....220 A5
Seven Stars La PL5 .....244 C6
Seven Stones Cross
TQ7 .....142 E8
Seven Thorns EX35 .....6 D5
Seven Trees Ct PL4 .....263 B4
Seventh St 14 EX32 .....154 F6
Severn Pl PL3 .....249 C5
Severn Rd TQ2 .....219 B7
Sewell Ct PL3 .....248 E5
Sexton's Cross EX6 .....113 E6
Seymour Ave PL4 .....263 B4
Seymour Bglws EX34 .....1 A1
Seymour Ct Exmouth EX8 196 B2
9 Totnes TQ9 .....223 D5
Seymour Dr
Dartmouth TQ6 .....233 C3
Plymouth PL3 .....248 F5
Torquay TQ2 .....214 B4
Seymour Mews PL4 .....263 C4
Seymour Pk PL3 .....249 A5
Seymour Pl TQ9 .....223 D5
Seymour Rd
Exmouth EX8 .....196 B2
Newton Abbot TQ12 .....207 C4
Plymouth, Mannamead
PL3 .....248 F5
Plymouth, Plympton PL7 .....250 C6
Seymour St
Plymouth PL4 .....263 A3
Wellington TA21 .....160 C6
Seymour Terr EX16 .....161 C4
Seymour Villas EX34 .....1 A1
Shackel Cross TA3 .....67 E8
Shackhayes EX34 .....3 A4
Shackleton Cl EX8 .....196 B2
Shadrack Cross TQ9 .....217 B3
Shady La TQ6 .....146 B7
Shadycombe Ct TQ8 .....259 D5
Shadycombe Rd TQ8 .....259 D5
Shaftesbury Cl 22 EX7 .....204 E6
Shaftesbury Cotts PL4 .....263 A4
Shaftesbury Ct 3 PL4 .....263 A4
Shaftesbury Rd
Exeter EX2 .....177 A4
4 Ilfracombe EX34 .....150 C5
Shaftsborough La EX34 .....1 C1
Shaftsbury Pl 9 TQ9 .....223 C5
Shakespeare Cl
Tiverton EX16 .....161 D6
Torquay TQ2 .....219 D6
Shakespeare Rd
Exeter EX2 .....177 F3
Plymouth PL5 .....244 C2
Shakespeare Way EX8 .....196 C4
Shaldon Cres PL5 .....244 B3
Shaldon Prim Sch TQ14 210 A3
Shaldon Rd
Combeinteignhead TQ12 .....208 F5
Newton Abbot TQ12 .....207 F2
Shalford Terr EX13 .....103 B6
Shallowford Cl PL6 .....249 C8
Shallowford Rd PL6 .....249 C8
Shamble Way EX35 .....151 E2
Shameface La TQ13 .....123 B7
Shamel's End EX16 .....64 E7
Shand Pk EX13 .....167 C5
Shapcott La EX36 .....32 C2
Shapcott Wood Hill EX36 31 F2
Shapland Pl EX16 .....161 C2
Shapley Tor Cl TQ5 .....230 A2
Shapley Way TQ12 .....180 C1
Shapleys Gdns PL9 .....256 A5
Shapters Rd PL4 .....263 C2
Shapters Way PL4 .....255 B8
Shaptor Cross TQ13 .....122 F8
Shaptor View TQ13 .....180 B5
Sharland La EX17 .....78 F8
Sharland's La EX33 .....152 C6
Sharlands Rd EX23 .....70 A6
Sharon Way PL6 .....245 A5
Sharp Rock EX34 .....7 F7
Sharper La TQ14 .....209 C3
Sharpham Dr TQ9 .....223 D4
Sharpitor Cl TQ3 .....218 F1
Sharpitor Row PL20 .....127 B4
Sharpland La EX33 .....7 E3
Sharps Cl TQ12 .....123 B2
Sharps Crest TQ12 .....123 B2
Sharps Ct EX8 .....201 F6
Sharrose Rd PL9 .....255 B5
Shaugh Prior Prim Sch
PL7 .....132 C6
Shaw Way PL9 .....255 A7
Sheafhayne Cross EX14 .....69 B4
Shearford La EX31 .....154 F8
Shearman Ct 10 EX2 .....261 A2
Shearwater Dr TQ2 .....213 D3
Shearwood Cl PL7 .....250 C6
Shebbear Coll EX21 .....55 E4
Shebbear Cross EX38 .....41 A2
Shebbear Sch EX21 .....55 E4
Shedden Hill Rd TQ2 .....220 A4
Sheepstor Rd PL6 .....245 D1
Sheepwash Cross EX36 .....31 C6
Sheepwash Hill EX36 .....31 C6
Sheilds The EX34 .....150 C4
Sheldon Cross EX14 .....66 F2
Sheldon's La TA22 .....33 A7
Shell Cl PL6 .....245 E1
Shell La EX16 .....47 F1
Shell's La TA20 .....69 D3
Shelley Ave
Tavistock PL19 .....171 D5
Torquay TQ1 .....220 B8
Shelley Cl EX2 .....177 A2
Shelley Ct EX8 .....201 E6
Shelley Way PL5 .....243 D1
Shells La EX24 .....103 A3
Shelly Ct EX20 .....95 B4
Shelly Rd Exmouth EX8 .....201 E6
South Zeal EX20 .....95 B4
Shelly Reach EX8 .....201 F6
Shelston Tor Dr TQ4 .....225 F3
Shepherd Cl TQ3 .....225 E5
Shepherd's La
Hemyock EX15 .....52 F1
Plymouth PL4 .....263 B2
Shepherds La
Colaton Raleigh EX10 .....186 E4
Teignmouth TQ14 .....124 E1
Shepherds Mdw
Abbotsham EX39 .....156 A2
Beaford EX19 .....42 D1
Sheplegh Ct TQ9 .....145 B8
Sheppard's Knap EX13 .....87 A2
Sheppard's Row EX8 .....202 A7
Sheppards Rd EX4 .....173 D2
Sheppaton La EX18,EX19,
EX37 .....43 B2
Sherborne Cl PL9 .....256 C6
Sherborne Rd TQ12 .....207 B3
Sherbourne La DT7 .....260 E3
Sherbrook Cl EX9 .....203 F8
Sherbrook Hill EX9 .....203 F8
Shercroft Cl EX5 .....175 E2
Sherford Cres
Plymouth, Elburton PL9 .....256 C7
Plymouth, West Park PL5 .....244 A3
Sherford Cross TQ7 .....145 A3
Sherford Down Cross
TQ7 .....144 D3
Sherford Down Rd TQ7 .....144 E3
Sherford Rd PL9 .....256 D7
Sherford Wlk PL9 .....256 E7
Sheridan Rd Exeter EX4 .....178 C8
Plymouth PL5 .....244 C1
Sherman Ho EX11 .....169 E3
Sherracombe Cross
EX36 .....19 C6
Sherratt's Oak EX31 .....155 B7
Sherrell Pk PL20 .....125 E1
Sherril Cl PL9 .....255 F4
Sherwell Cl
Dawlish Warren EX7 .....201 A2
Staverton TQ9 .....216 A5
Sherwell Ct TQ11 .....236 B5
Sherwell Hill TQ2 .....219 E5
Sherwell La
Plymouth PL4 .....263 A4
Torquay TQ2 .....219 E5
Sherwell Park Rd TQ2 .....219 E5
Sherwell Rise S TQ2 .....219 D5
Sherwell Valley Prim Sch
TQ2 .....219 C7
Sherwell Valley Rd TQ2 219 D6
Sherwill Cl PL21 .....237 A6
Sherwill La TQ9 .....216 A5
Sherwood Cl EX2 .....177 F5
Sherwood Cross EX14 .....84 D2
Sherwood Dr EX8 .....196 E3
Sherwood Gn EX38 .....42 E7
Shetland Cl TQ2 .....213 E2
Shewte Cross TQ13 .....122 D5
Shields The EX34 .....150 C4
Shieling Rd EX31 .....16 A3
Shiers Orch EX9 .....197 F8
Shillands EX16 .....161 B5
Shillingate Cl EX7 .....204 C4
Shillingford Fst Sch
EX16 .....34 F3
Shillingford La EX6 .....181 A3
Shillingford Rd EX2 .....181 A7
Shilston Gate PL21 .....137 D4
Shilstone Cross EX32 .....28 C5
Shilstone La TQ13 .....113 C1
Shindle Pk TQ7 .....144 F1
Shinners Cotts TQ6 .....228 C2
Ship La EX5 .....179 D8
Shiphay Ave TQ2 .....219 D7
Shiphay Com Prim Sch
TQ2 .....219 C8
Shiphay La TQ2 .....219 D7
Shiphay Manor Dr TQ2 .....219 D7
Shiphay Park Rd TQ2 .....219 D8
Shipley Cl TQ10 .....135 A3
Shipley Rd EX14 .....166 E6
Shipley Wlk PL6 .....245 A1
Shipney La TQ13 .....124 A7
Shirburn Rd
Plymouth PL6 .....249 B8
Torquay TQ1 .....220 A7
Shire Cl Honiton EX14 .....166 A5
Paignton TQ4 .....229 B8
Shire Horse Ctr The★
EX34 .....150 A1
Shire La DT7 .....260 B3
Shirley Cl EX8 .....196 D4
Shirley Cnr EX17 .....79 B5
Shirley Gdns PL5 .....244 C1
Shirley Twrs TQ1 .....220 C3
Shirwell Cross
Barnstaple EX31 .....16 E6
Shirwell EX31 .....17 B8
Shirwell Prim Sch EX31 .....17 B8
Shirwell Rd EX31 .....17 A7
Shoalgate Cross EX20 .....94 F8
Shobbrook Hill TQ12 .....206 E4
Shobrook La EX17 .....78 F7
Shobrooke Cross EX17 .....80 D4
Shoot's La EX14 .....67 A3
Shooting La EX18 .....60 B7
Shooting Marsh Stile
EX2 .....261 A1
Shoots Barn Cross EX14 .....84 D3
Shop Cotts PL7 .....132 F4
Shore Head EX14 .....86 F5
Shoreland Cross EX18 .....44 F5
Shorelands Rd EX31 .....154 D3
Shorelands Way
Barnstaple EX31 .....154 D3
Northam EX39 .....156 E7
Shoreline The EX12 .....192 C4
Shoresgate Cross EX19 .....76 F8
Shorland Cl EX7 .....204 F8
Shorneywell TQ7 .....145 A1
Short Cl EX39 .....156 D2
Short Cotts PL11 .....247 A3
Short Cross TQ9 .....139 B3
Short La Halwell TQ9 .....139 B3
Shaldon TQ14 .....209 C4
Short Park Rd PL3 .....248 D5
Shorta Cross TQ7 .....143 C7
Shortacombe Cnr EX31 .....10 A5
Shortacombe Dr EX33 .....152 B7
Shorter Cross TQ9 .....135 D2
Shortlands
Budleigh Salterton EX9 .....197 F8
Holsworthy EX22 .....71 D5
Shortlands La EX15 .....163 B3
Shortlands Rd EX15 .....163 B3
Shortmoor Cross EX14 .....86 E6
Shorton Rd TQ3 .....226 A8
Shorton Valley Rd TQ3 .....219 A1
Shortridge Cl
Honiton EX14 .....166 C4
Witheridge EX16 .....46 E1
Shortridge Mead 1
EX16 .....161 B4
Shorts Way TQ9 .....222 E6
Shortwood Cl EX9 .....197 F2
Shortwood Cres PL9 .....256 A7
Shovelpiece La EX32 .....19 A7
Shrewsbury Ave TQ2 .....214 A1
Shrewsbury Rd PL5 .....244 C4
Shrinkhill La EX16 .....161 D3
Shrubbery Cl EX32 .....155 C3
Shrubbery La EX14 .....86 E6
Shrubbery The EX20 .....76 C5
Shubbery The EX13 .....167 D5
Shute TQ7 .....147 E6
Shute Barton★ EX13 .....103 B8
Shute Cross
Newton St Cyres EX17 .....81 B2
South Brent TQ10 .....134 E1
Shute Ct TQ14 .....209 A8
Shute Hill
Bishopsteignton TQ14 .....209 A8
Malborough TQ7 .....147 E6
Teignmouth TQ14 .....210 C5
Shute Hill Cres 10 TQ14 210 C5
Shute La Combe Martin EX34 3 A4
Denbury TQ12 .....211 A6
Huish Champflower TA4 .....35 C8
Moretonhampstead TQ13 .....111 F5
Winkleigh EX19 .....58 F2
Shute Meadow St 2
EX8 .....202 A7
Shute Park Rd PL9 .....255 F6
Shute Pk TQ7 .....147 E6
Shute Prim Sch EX13 .....103 B8
Shute Rd Kilmington EX13 .....87 C1
Shute EX13 .....103 A7
Totnes TQ9 .....223 D5
Shute Row TA21 .....160 E5
Shute Wood EX18 .....58 F6
Shuteleigh TA21 .....160 E5
Shutes Mead EX11 .....169 E4
Shutscombe Hill EX32 .....18 E5
Shutter Water Rd
Westwood EX15 .....83 C1
Whimple EX5 .....99 C8
Shuttern Cl EX5 .....172 A8
Shutterton Ind Est EX7 .....200 F1
Shutterton La EX7 .....201 A3
Sicklemans Cl TQ7 .....144 C1
Sid La EX10 .....188 C5
Sid Park Rd EX10 .....188 B5
Sid Rd EX10 .....188 C6
Sid Vale Cl 10 EX10 .....101 B1
Sidborough Hill EX17 .....61 B1
Sidbury CE Prim Sch
EX10 .....101 C2
Sidcliffe EX10 .....188 C6
Siddalls Gdns EX16 .....161 E5
Siddals Gdns EX16 .....161 E4
Side Wood La EX36 .....32 A1
Sideling Cl EX2 .....114 A6
Sideling Fields EX16 .....161 F2
Sidford Cross 7 EX10 .....101 B1
Sidford Rd EX10 .....188 B7
Sidgard Rd EX10 .....188 C6
Sidholme Cotts EX10 .....188 A5
Siding Cross TQ10 .....137 E8
Sidings The
Braunton EX33 .....152 D6
Kingsbridge TQ7 .....258 C5
Sidleigh EX10 .....188 C5
Sidmount Gdns EX10 .....188 A5
Sidmouth Coll EX10 .....188 C7
Sidmouth Inf Sch EX10 .....188 B7
Sidmouth Int Sch EX10 .....188 B4
Sidmouth Junc Cross
EX14 .....84 D2
Sidmouth Rd
Bradninch EX5 .....83 B5
Sidmouth Rd *continued*
Clyst St Mary EX2,EX5 .....179 A3
Colyton EX24 .....103 A4
Exeter EX2 .....178 D5
Exeter EX2 .....178 E4
Honiton EX14 .....166 A3
Lyme Regis DT7 .....260 C3
Ottery St Mary EX11 .....169 E2
Sidney Ct 3 EX7 .....204 D6
Sidvale Ct 12 EX10 .....101 B1
Sidwell St EX4 .....261 C4
Sigford Cross TQ13 .....122 B2
Sign of the Owl Cross
TQ10 .....137 E8
Signal Ct EX33 .....152 D5
Signal Terr EX31 .....154 F4
Signals The EX14 .....84 D2
Signpost La EX17 .....80 A7
Silbury Terr EX17 .....165 C5
Silcombe Cross EX36 .....30 F3
Silcombe Hill EX36 .....30 E4
Silford Cross EX39 .....156 D5
Silford Rd EX39 .....156 E5
Silvan Dr EX33 .....152 E7
Silver Birch Cl
Exeter EX2 .....178 A3
Plymouth PL6 .....245 C7
Silver Birch Ct 5 EX31 .....154 C2
Silver Bridge Cl TQ4 .....229 C8
Silver Head Hill TQ9 .....216 F1
Silver La Exeter EX4 .....261 C4
Rockbeare EX5 .....99 C5
Silver Lea EX13 .....87 C1
Silver St
3 Appledore EX39 .....15 A1
Axminster EX13 .....167 D5
11 Bampton EX16 .....34 B1
6 Barnstaple EX32 .....155 A5
Bere Ferrers PL20 .....240 A3
Berrynarbor EX34 .....2 E3
Bideford EX39 .....157 A1
Braunton EX33 .....152 D7
Buckfastleigh TQ11 .....236 B5
Colyton EX24 .....103 A5
Culmstock EX15 .....66 D8
Honiton EX14 .....166 C6
Ipplepen TQ12 .....211 C1
Kentisbeare EX15 .....66 A3
Kilmington EX13 .....87 C1
Lydford EX20 .....107 F3
Lyme Regis DT7 .....260 D3
Ottery St Mary EX11 .....169 D4
Saltash PL12 .....243 A2
Thorverton EX5 .....81 E4
Tiverton EX16 .....161 D4
West Buckland TA21 .....52 F7
Willand EX15 .....162 D4
Silver Stream Way PL8 .....257 B5
Silver Terr Exeter EX4 .....261 A3
Millbrook PL10 .....253 A6
Silverdale Exmouth EX8 .....196 E3
Silverton EX5 .....82 B6
Silverdale Cl TA22 .....33 E4
Silverhill Bldgs TQ12 .....212 D8
Silverhills Rd TQ12 .....212 D8
Silvers The EX3 .....178 F2
Silverston CE Prim Sch
EX5 .....82 B6
Silverton Rd EX2 .....181 D8
Silverway EX17 .....80 E4
Silverwell Pk PL21 .....137 C2
Silverwood Ave TQ12 .....207 E1
Silworthy Cross EX22 .....38 F2
Simcoe Pl EX15 .....67 B8
Simcoe Way EX14 .....67 B1
Simey Cl EX4 .....176 F7
Simmonds Pl EX15 .....163 E4
Simmons Cl EX20 .....170 C5
Simmons Way EX20 .....170 C5
Simms Hill TQ12,TQ13 .....122 C2
Simon Cl PL9 .....255 E6
Simons Cross EX13 .....87 E4
Sinai Hill EX35 .....151 C5
Sing's La EX33 .....152 D5
Singer Cl TQ3 .....226 A5
Singmore Rd TQ3 .....218 E2
Sir Alex Wlk EX3 .....182 E5
Sir John Hunt Com Coll
PL5 .....244 D4
Sir Robert's Path EX31 .....4 D5
Siskin Chase EX15 .....163 A2
Sithney St PL5 .....243 C1
Sivell Mews EX2 .....177 F5
Sivell Pl EX2 .....177 F5
Six Acre Cross EX35 .....5 A4
Six Acre La EX35 .....5 A5
Six Mile Hill
Doddiscombsleigh EX6 .....113 A8
Tedburn St Mary EX6 .....98 A5
Skardale Gdns PL6 .....249 D8
Skardon Pl PL4 .....263 A4
Skern Cl EX39 .....156 F8
Skern Way EX39 .....156 F8
Skerries Rd PL6 .....244 F7
Skinnard La PL18 .....125 C5
Skinner Cl EX16 .....161 B4
Skirhead La EX34 .....3 B3
Skye Cl TQ2 .....213 E2
Skylark Rise PL6 .....245 E8
Skylark Spinney 3
EX31 .....154 A2
Skyways Bsns Pk EX5 .....99 A4
Slade EX39 .....156 E2
Slade Cl
Ottery St Mary EX11 .....169 F4
Plymouth PL9 .....256 A5
Slade Cross
Kingsbridge TQ7 .....144 B6
Slade Cross *continued*
Lustleigh TQ13 .....122 D8
North Tawton EX20 .....77 D5
Slade La
Abbotskerswell TQ12 .....212 B6
Combe Martin EX31 .....3 E1
Galmpton TQ5 .....229 B5
Hawkridge TA22 .....21 D1
Sidmouth EX10 .....189 C7
West Anstey EX36 .....32 B6
Slade Lane Cross EX34 .....3 E1
Slade Rd
Ilfracombe EX34 .....150 A3
Ottery St Mary EX11 .....169 F3
Slade Valley Rd EX34 .....150 A3
Sladnor Park Rd TQ1 .....214 C5
Sladnor Pk TQ1 .....214 C5
Slanns Mdw TQ12 .....207 D6
Slappers Hill TQ4,TQ5 .....234 E7
Slatelands Cl PL7 .....251 B3
Slattenslade La EX31 .....4 D5
Sleap Hill EX9 .....198 C7
Sleepy La TQ3 .....219 A1
Sletchcott Cross EX37 .....44 E8
Slew Hill EX34 .....2 C2
Slewhill Cross EX20 .....95 B5
Slewton Cres EX5 .....99 E8
Slipper Stone Dr PL21 .....237 A6
Slipperstone TQ9 .....139 A7
Slipperstone Cross TQ9 216 C7
Slipperstone La TQ9 .....216 C7
Slittercombe La EX6 .....194 E3
Sloe La 4 EX32 .....17 B2
Slough La
Bishops Nympton EX36 .....30 F3
Upottery EX14 .....68 C5
Small La Broadclyst EX5 .....175 D7
Burlescombe EX16 .....51 B2
Rattery TQ10 .....135 D3
Smallack Cl PL6 .....244 F2
Smallack Dr PL6 .....244 F2
Smallacombe Dross
TQ10 .....135 D6
Smallacombe Hill EX16,
EX36 .....32 D4
Smallacombe La EX36 .....31 F8
Smallacombe Rd EX16 .....161 B4
Smallacott Hill EX6 .....97 D3
Smallcombe Cross TQ3 .....225 E8
Smallcombe Rd TQ3 .....225 E8
Smalldon La TQ2 .....214 B3
Smallridge Cl PL9 .....255 F5
Smallridge Rd EX13 .....87 F4
Smallwell La
Ashprington TQ9 .....139 E7
Marldon TQ3 .....218 C3
Smardon Ave TQ5 .....230 A5
Smardon Cl TQ5 .....230 A5
Smeathy La EX15 .....52 F3
Smeaton Sq PL3 .....249 D6
Smiter's Pit La EX13 .....87 A1
Smith Field Rd EX2 .....181 A8
Smith Hill TQ14 .....208 F8
Smith St TQ6 .....233 F3
Smith's La
Calverleigh EX16 .....48 E4
Hollocombe EX18 .....58 E6
Smithay Mdws EX6 .....113 B4
Smithfield Dr PL12 .....242 B3
Smithfields TQ9 .....223 A6
Smiths Ct EX2 .....261 A1
Smiths Way PL12 .....242 B3
Smithy Cl PL12 .....242 C4
Smockpark La PL9 .....140 B8
Smokey Cross TQ13 .....122 B3
Smugglers' La EX7 .....210 F8
Smythen Cross EX34 .....9 E6
Smythen St EX1,EX4 .....261 A2
Smythes Cross EX15 .....67 F7
Snell Dr PL12 .....242 B3
Snodbrook Cross EX10 .....101 C1
Snowberry Cl TQ1 .....219 F7
Snowdonia Cl TQ4 .....225 D4
Snowdrop Cl 2 EX14 .....166 A4
Snowdrop Cres PL15 .....105 A2
Snowdrop Mews EX4 .....176 D8
Snows EX17 .....80 B5
Snydles La EX37 .....44 B6
Sog's La EX10 .....100 C2
Solar Cres EX4 .....176 F4
Soldon Cross EX22 .....53 E5
Solland Cross EX20 .....76 D4
Solland La EX20 .....76 D4
Soloman Dr EX39 .....157 A1
Solsbro Rd TQ2 .....219 E4
Solways DT7 .....260 C5
Somerfields DT7 .....260 C3
Somerlea EX15 .....162 D5
Somers Rd DT7 .....260 C3
Somerset Ave EX4 .....176 E4
Somerset Cotts 7 PL3 .....248 A4
Somerset Ct
10 Brixham TQ5 .....230 C5
17 Totnes TQ9 .....223 D5
Somerset Pl
16 Barnstaple EX31 .....154 F5
Plymouth PL3 .....248 A4
10 Teignmouth TQ14 .....210 B4
Totnes TQ9 .....223 D5
Somerset Place La 8
PL3 .....248 A4
Somerslea EX21 .....73 E2
Somerthing La EX33 .....7 E1
Somerville Cl
Exmouth EX8 .....196 D1

Somerville Cl *continued*
Willand EX15 162 C5
Somerville Pk EX15 162 C4
Somerville Rd EX15 162 C5
Sommers' Cres EX34 150 C6
Soper Rd TQ14 210 A7
Soper Wlk TQ14 210 A7
Soper's Hill PL5 240 E1
Sophia Way TQ12 207 A2
Sorley Green Cross TQ7 143 F5
Sorley La TQ7 143 F5
Sorley Tunnel Adventure Farm* TQ7 143 F5
Sorrell Ct TQ12 207 D7
Sorrento TQ1 220 C5
South Ave Bideford EX39 157 D1
Exeter EX1 177 E6
Lyme Regis DT7 260 D4
South Bank Dr EX39 156 F2
South Brent Prim Sch TQ10 135 A3
South Brent Rd TQ7 143 E7
South Burrow Rd 10 EX34 150 B5
South Church La EX20 170 A4
South Common La EX13 88 A5
South Dartmoor Com Coll TQ13 131 A5
South Dartmoor Com Coll Sixth Form Ctr TQ13 131 A6
South Dean Cnr EX31 4 A5
South Dean La EX31 4 A5
South Devon Coll TQ1 219 F6
South Devon Rly*
Buckfastleigh TQ11 236 E4
* Staverton TQ9 215 D4
South Down Cross EX19 76 C7
South Down Farm TQ7 147 E5
South Down La EX36 31 E6
South Down Rd
Beer EX12 191 D5
Plymouth PL2 248 B6
South Downs Rd EX7 204 D4
South Dr EX38 159 B5
South Emb TQ6 233 F3
South End Cl 6 EX33 152 D5
South Farm Rd EX9 198 C3
South Ford Rd TQ6 233 F3
South Furzeham Rd TQ5 230 C5
South Gate EX2 261 B2
South Gn 4 EX32 155 B4
South Grange EX2 178 D3
South Hams Bsns Pk TQ7 143 E4
South Hams Hospl TQ7 258 C6
South Hayes Copse EX32 17 B2
South Hayne Cross EX36 31 B4
South Hele Cross EX16 35 C1
South Hill
Plymouth, Hooe PL9 255 C5
Plymouth, Stoke PL1 248 A3
South Hill Rd TQ1 220 C4
South La
Bratton Fleming EX31 11 F3
Braunton EX33 15 E8
Hartland EX39 22 E2
Lynton EX35 5 F5
South Lawn Exeter EX2 261 C2
Sidmouth EX10 188 C8
South Lawn Terr EX1 177 F6
South Lea EX33 152 E5
South Lea Cl EX33 152 E5
South Lee Cross EX36 30 B7
South Ley Cross EX31 3 D1
South Milton St PL4 263 C2
South Molton Com Coll EX36 158 C3
South Molton Com Hospl EX36 158 C4
South Molton Inf Sch EX36 158 C5
South Molton Mus* EX36 158 C4
South Molton Rd EX16 34 B1
South Molton St EX18 44 E1
South Molton United CE Jun Sch EX36 158 C5
South Moor La EX17 59 E1
South Par EX9 199 H2
South Parks Rd TQ2 213 F2
South Pk
Barnstaple EX32 155 B3
Braunton EX33 152 F5
Woolfardisworthy EX39 38 F7
South Rd
16 Appledore EX39 15 A1
Newton Abbot TQ12 207 B2
South Sands TQ4 226 C2
South Sq 10 EX24 103 A4
South St Axminster EX13 167 D5
Barnstaple EX32 155 B2
Barnstaple EX32 155 B3
Braunton EX33 152 D5
Colyton EX24 103 A4
Denbury TQ12 211 A6
Dolton EX19 57 F7
Exeter EX1 261 B2
Exmouth EX8 202 A6
Great Torrington EX38 159 C5
Hatherleigh EX20 75 C7
Holcombe Rogus TA21 50 F5
Sheepwash EX21 56 C1
South Molton EX36 158 C4
Torquay TQ2 219 F6
South St *continued*
Totnes TQ9 223 C5
Wellington TA21 160 E5
Winkleigh EX19 58 F3
Woolacombe EX34 7 F6
South Tawton Prim Sch EX20 95 B4
South Trelawny Prim Sch PL2 248 A8
South View
Abbotskerswell TQ12 212 B6
Ashford EX31 16 C7
Barnstaple EX31 154 D7
Bideford EX39 156 F2
Bovey Tracey TQ13 180 D7
Braunton EX33 152 D4
5 Hemyock EX15 67 B8
10 Horrabridge PL20 126 F4
Ilfracombe EX34 1 E3
Lydford EX20 107 F4
Mary Tavy PL19 117 E6
Plymouth, Crownhill PL5 244 E2
Plymouth, Elburton PL9 256 B6
Westleigh EX16 51 A3
South View Cl
Braunton EX33 152 D4
Plymouth PL7 250 D7
Willand EX15 162 D5
South View Est EX15 162 D5
South View Pk PL7 250 D7
South View Rd EX15 162 D5
South View Terr
Exeter EX4 177 D8
Exminster EX6 182 B4
Plymouth PL4 263 C3
Sidmouth EX10 188 A5
South Yeo Cross
Cheriton Fitzpaine EX17 62 E3
Northlew EX20 74 F2
South Yeo Hill EX17 62 E3
Southay Cross TA20 69 D4
Southay La TA20 69 C4
Southbank TQ12 207 C4
Southbrook Cl 2 TQ13 180 C8
Southbrook La
Bovey Tracey TQ13 180 B8
1 Bovey Tracey TQ13 180 C8
Otterton EX10 187 B1
Rockbeare EX5 99 C7
Southbrook Rd
Bovey Tracey TQ13 180 C8
Exeter EX2 178 A2
Southbrook Sch EX2 178 A2
Southcombe Cross
Hittisleigh EX6 96 F4
Widecombe in the Moor TQ13 121 B3
Southcombe Hill EX6 96 F4
Southcombe St TQ13 111 A6
Southcoombe Terr EX12 192 E7
Southcote La EX14 86 C4
Southcote Orch TQ9 223 E5
Southcott Cross
Chawleigh EX18 60 A6
Langtree EX38 40 F3
Okehampton EX20 93 C5
Okehampton EX20 93 E5
Southcott Rd EX39 156 F4
Southdown Ave TQ5 230 B2
Southdown Cl
Beer EX12 191 D5
Brixham TQ5 230 B2
Southdown Cross
Brixham TQ5 230 B1
Burlescombe EX16 51 B2
South Molton EX36 46 A5
Southdown Hill
Brixham TQ5 230 B2
Copplestone EX17 79 D7
South Molton EX36 45 F6
Southdown Ho 5 TQ13 180 D8
Southdown La EX37 43 D3
Southdown Rd
Brixham TQ5 230 B1
Millbrook PL10 253 A6
Southdown Terr PL10 253 A6
Southella Rd PL20 127 A2
Southern Cl
Plymouth PL2 247 F7
Torquay TQ2 214 A4
Southern Rd EX8 202 A8
Southern Terr PL4 248 F4
Southern Wood EX8 196 E2
Southernhay
Newton Abbot TQ12 207 C2
Winkleigh EX19 58 F2
Southernhay E EX1 261 B3
Southernhay Gdns EX1 261 B3
Southernhay W EX1 261 B3
Southerns Cross EX13 103 D5
Southernway PL9 256 A8
Southey Cres TQ12 213 A3
Southey Dr TQ12 213 A3
Southey La
Kingskerswell TQ12 213 A3
Sampford Courtenay EX20 76 F3
Southfied Rise TQ3 226 A7
Southfield Saltash PL12 242 C3
West Alvington TQ7 258 A4
Southfield Ave TQ3 226 A8
Southfield Cl TQ3 226 A8
Southfield Dr EX17 165 B6
Southfield Rd
Bideford EX39 157 C1
Paignton TQ3 226 A7
Southfield Way EX16 161 B4
Southfields EX22 70 F5
Southford La TQ9 216 A4
Southgate Ave PL9 255 E4
Southgate Cl PL9 255 E4
Southgate Ct 7 EX2 261 B2
Southland Park Cres 8 PL9 140 D8
Southland Park Rd PL9 140 D8
Southlands EX33 152 E4
Southlands Rd TQ2 220 A5
Southlea EX39 156 E6
Southleigh Hill Cross EX24 102 B3
Southleigh Rd EX24 102 E5
Southley Rd EX36 158 C4
Southmead Prim Sch EX33 152 E4
Southport Ave EX4 176 E5
Southside Ope 14 PL1 263 A2
Southside St PL1 263 A2
Southtown
Dartmouth TQ6 233 F2
Kenton EX6 194 F3
Southview PL10 253 A6
Southview Rd TQ3 226 A7
Southville Gdns TQ7 258 D3
Southway Sidmouth EX10 188 C4
Tedburn St Mary EX6 97 F4
Southway Ave TQ2 213 F1
Southway Com Coll PL6 244 F6
Southway Dr PL6 244 E6
Southway La
Plymouth, Southway PL6 245 B6
Plymouth, Tamerton Foliot PL6 244 C6
Southway Prim Sch PL6 244 E6
Southwell Rd PL6 244 E1
Southwood Cross EX5 99 C4
Southwood Ct TQ1 220 C5
Southwood Dr EX39 157 A3
Southwood Mdws EX39 40 C7
Sovereign Cl EX8 196 E1
Sovereign Ct PL7 250 C5
Sovereign Mews TQ2 214 B2
Sowden La
Barnstaple EX32 155 B5
Lympstone EX8 195 E4
Sowden Pk EX32 155 C4
Sowton Ind Est EX2 178 E5
Sowton La EX5 179 B6
Spa Ct TQ1 220 C4
Space Pl EX2 177 C1
Spanish Lane End TQ9 139 A5
Spanishlake Cross EX6 113 C6
Sparhanger Cross EX35 5 B3
Sparhanger La EX35 5 B3
Sparkatown La PL20 127 B3
Sparke Cl PL7 251 B4
Sparks Barn Rd TQ4 226 B4
Sparkwell CE Prim Sch PL7 251 F8
Sparrow La TA24 21 C7
Sparrow Pk TQ7 147 F6
Sparrow Rd TQ9 223 B5
Speakers Rd PL21 237 E5
Speares The PL12 242 B2
Spearfield Cl EX36 158 D4
Spears La TA21 35 F4
Speedwell Cl
Barnstaple EX32 155 E3
Brixham TQ5 230 C3
Millbrook PL10 252 F5
Speedwell Cres PL6 249 B7
Speedwell Units TQ6 233 C3
Speedwell Wlk PL6 249 B7
Spekes Cross EX18 59 C4
Spence Combe Cross EX17 79 D4
Spence Cross EX14 84 D4
Spence La DT6 104 F7
Spencer Cl EX8 196 E2
Spencer Ct EX11 169 D3
Spencer Dr EX16 161 F3
Spencer Gdns PL12 242 F1
Spencer Rd
Newton Abbot TQ12 207 C2
Paignton TQ3 225 E7
Plymouth PL9 255 E8
Spenser Ave EX2 177 F3
Speranza Gr 17 TQ14 210 B5
Spestos La EX17 78 C1
Spicer Cl EX15 163 B2
Spicer Rd EX1 261 C3
Spicers Rd TQ13,EX6 114 A1
Spider's La EX8 196 C3
Spinaker Quay PL9 254 F7
Spindlebury EX15 163 A2
Spindlewood Cl EX14 166 C3
Spinney Cl EX2 178 C4
Spinney The
Ivybridge PL21 237 A5
Plymouth PL7 251 A4
Uffculme EX15 66 A8
Spinning Bath Gdns EX17 165 C4
Spinning La EX13 104 B8
Spire Ct PL3 249 B5
Spire Hill Pk PL12 242 C2
Spire Lake Cl EX36 30 F3
Spire's Cross EX20 77 A3
Spirelake Cross EX17 79 C8
Spirelake Hill EX17 79 C8
Spitfire Wlk EX32 155 C5
Spithead TQ6 233 F3
Spitlar Cross EX20 95 C6
Spittis Pk TQ6 234 B3
Spittle Cross EX18 44 D4
Spittles La DT7 260 E4
Spitup La EX10 187 E7
Splatford Dr EX15 163 C5
Splatts Cross EX19 76 C7
Splitwell Cross EX17 62 B2
Spreacombe Gdns EX33 8 C4
Spreyton Cross EX17 96 A7
Spreyton Prim Sch EX17 96 A7
Spring Cl
Newton Abbot TQ12 206 E4
Northam EX39 156 E6
Spring Field EX39 22 D3
Spring Gdns EX11 169 E3
Spring Head Rd DT7 260 B6
Spring Hill PL19 171 B5
Spring Pk PL6 245 E7
Spring Rd PL9 140 B8
Springdale Cl TQ5 230 C2
Springfield
Dunkeswell EX14 67 C2
Membury EX13 87 D6
Springfield Ave
Barnstaple EX32 155 B3
Plymouth PL9 256 B6
Springfield Cl PL9 256 B7
Springfield Cres
Fremington EX31 153 F6
Northam EX39 156 F7
Springfield Dr
Kingsbridge TQ7 258 C5
Plymouth PL3 248 A4
Tiverton EX16 161 B4
Springfield Gdns EX7 200 F1
Springfield La PL9 256 B7
Springfield Pk EX20 107 F8
Springfield Rd
Barnstaple EX31 154 B3
Exeter EX4 177 D8
Exmouth EX8 196 B1
Honiton EX14 166 F5
Ilfracombe EX34 150 B6
Offwell EX14 86 A3
Plymouth PL9 256 B6
South Brent TQ10 134 F3
Torquay TQ1 220 B7
Wellington TA21 160 C7
Woolacombe EX34 8 A6
Springfield Rise PL9 256 B7
Springfield Terr
1 Bideford EX39 157 B1
11 Combe Martin EX34 3 A3
3 Northam EX39 156 F7
Tatworth TA20 88 D8
Westward Ho! EX39 156 C7
Springfields EX24 103 A3
Springhead Cross EX12 193 A6
Springhead La EX13 87 C1
Springhill PL2 248 C8
Springhill Down Hill EX16 47 D4
Springhill Gdns DT7 260 D4
Springhill Gn PL2 248 C8
Springhill Rd TQ9 223 E5
Springwood Cl
Ivybridge PL21 237 E5
Plymouth PL7 251 A3
Spruce Cl Exeter EX4 174 B2
Exmouth EX8 196 D3
Spruce Gdns PL7 251 B5
Spruce Pk EX17 165 C4
Spruce Way TQ3 225 E8
Spry La PL16 106 A4
Sprys Shop Cross EX21 72 D2
Sprytown Cross PL16 106 B4
Sprywood Cross EX21 56 A1
Spur Cross EX39 22 E2
Spurway Gdns EX34 3 B3
Spurway Hill EX16 48 A7
Spurway Hill Cross EX16 48 A8
Spurway Rd EX16 161 F3
Square 5 EX22 164 C4
Square The
Barnstaple EX32 154 F4
Beer EX12 191 D5
16 Bere Alston PL20 125 E1
10 Bishop's Tawton EX32 16 E1
Braunton EX33 152 D6
Bridestowe EX20 107 F8
Cawsand PL10 253 A1
Chagford TQ13 111 A6
Chittlehampton EX37 28 F4
Chulmleigh EX18 44 E1
Ermington PL21 136 F4
Exeter EX4 176 F8
Galmpton TQ7 147 B6
Gunnislake PL18 125 D6
Hartland EX39 22 D3
Kingswear TQ6 234 A3
Lutton PL21 133 B2
Moretonhampstead TQ13 111 F5
North Molton EX36 30 D8
North Tawton EX20 77 C4
6 Northam EX39 156 F7
Petrockstow EX20 56 F4
Plymouth, Hooe PL9 255 B6
Plymouth, Stonehouse PL1 248 A2
Rockbeare EX5 99 C5
Saltash PL12 242 C3
Sandford EX17 80 A5
7 Seaton EX12 192 A5
Shebbear EX21 55 D4
Sheepwash EX21 56 C1
South Molton EX36 158 C4
Uffculme EX15 66 A7
Ugborough PL21 137 D6
8 Whimple EX5 99 E8
Witheridge EX16 46 E1
Square's Quay TQ7 258 C4
Squire's La EX12 192 C5
Squires Cl EX32 155 B2
Squires Cotts PL20 128 B8
Squires' La Shebbear EX21 55 D6
Shebbear EX21 55 D7
Squirrel Ct TA21 160 D5
Stabb Cl TQ4 226 A1
Stabb Dr TQ4 226 A1
Stabdon La EX20 59 C1
Stable La TQ1 214 B1
Stables The TQ9 223 D6
Stadbury Cross EX14 86 B5
Stadbury La EX14 86 C5
Staddens Lea La TQ2 219 C6
Staddiscombe Rd PL9 255 F4
Staddon Cl
Braunton EX33 152 C6
Exeter EX4 178 B7
Staddon Court Cotts PL9 140 B8
Staddon Cres PL9 255 E6
Staddon Cross EX22 72 C6
Staddon Gate EX20 77 D5
Staddon Gdns TQ2 214 B2
Staddon Gn PL9 255 D6
Staddon La PL9 255 B4
Staddon Moor Cross EX20 77 D5
Staddon Park Rd PL9 255 E6
Staddon Rd
Appledore EX39 15 A1
Holsworthy EX22 164 F3
Tedburn St Mary EX6 97 E2
Staddon Terrace La PL1 262 B4
Staddonhill Rd TA24 21 F8
Staddons View TQ13 180 C8
Stadium Dr TQ12 213 A2
Staffick Cl EX6 194 E3
Stafford Cross EX24 102 D2
Stafford Ct 1 TQ9 223 E5
Stafford Hill EX14 84 F8
Stafford La EX24 103 A3
Stafford Rd Dolton EX19 57 F7
Exeter EX4 176 F5
Paignton TQ4 226 C5
Stafford Way EX19 57 F7
Stag Cnr EX15 162 E1
Stag La
Plymouth, Elburton PL9 256 B8
Plymouth, Plympton PL9 250 B1
Stag Mill Cross EX16 50 B3
Staggers La EX33 152 E3
Stags Wood Dr EX21 73 E2
Stakes Hill TQ7 143 A5
Stallards Braunton EX33 152 C7
Wellington TA21 160 C3
Stamford Cl PL9 255 A6
Stamford Fort Cotts PL9 255 A6
Stamford La PL9 255 A6
Stammery Hill EX13 88 C1
Stamps Hill PL8 257 A6
Stamps The PL17 125 A5
Stanborough Cross PL9 256 C7
Stanborough Rd PL9 256 B7
Stanbridge Pk EX39 156 D2
Stanbury Ave PL6 244 F1
Stanbury Cl PL15 90 C1
Stanbury Copse EX34 150 A4
Stanbury Cross
Holsworthy EX22 164 D6
Morwenstow EX23 36 F1
Stanbury Ct EX17 165 C5
Stanbury Rd Knowle EX33 8 D1
Torquay TQ2 219 C7
Stanbury's Orch EX6 96 F3
Stancombe Cross TQ7 144 E4
Standard Ct PL19 117 E6
Standarhay Cl PL9 256 C7
Standarhay Villas PL9 256 C7
Stanfield TQ1 220 E5
Stanford Rd EX2 178 C5
Stang La EX34 8 F5
Stangray Ave PL4 248 D4
Stanhope Cl EX22 164 C5
Stanhope Dr EX10 188 B6
Stanhope Rd PL5 243 C1
Stanhope Sq 7 EX22 164 C4
Stanhope Terr EX39 157 A3
Stani Forth Dr PL21 237 D4
Stanley Gdns TQ3 226 A7
Stanley Mews EX9 198 A1
Stanley Pl PL4 249 B2
Stanley Rd TQ1 220 C8
Stanley Sq EX3 182 F4
Stanley St 9 TQ14 210 B4
Stanley Wlk EX8 196 D4
Stanmore Rise EX7 204 E7
Stanmore Tor TQ3 226 A5
Stannary Bridge Rd PL19 171 D6
Stannary Cl PL21 237 E5
Stannary Pl TQ13 111 A6
Stansfeld Ave TQ3 226 A6
Stant Way TA20 69 F6
Stantaway Hill TQ1 219 F7
Stantaway Pk TQ1 219 F7
Stanton Ct TQ7 138 A1
Stantor La TQ3 218 F5
Stantyway Cross EX9 198 F6
Stantyway Ct EX9 198 E7
Stantyway Rd EX9 198 F5
Stanwell Dr EX39 156 C6
Stanwell Hill EX39 156 C6
Stanwey EX1 178 A5
Staplake La EX6 201 A7
Staplake Rd EX6 195 B1
Staplake Rise EX6 195 A1
Staple Back La EX19 57 E5

Staple Cl PL6 241 C1
Staple Cross EX19 57 F5
Staple Orch TQ9 222 F8
Stapleback Cross EX19 57 E5
Stapledon La TQ13 130 F5
Stapleford Gdns PL5 243 F5
Staplegate EX16 50 A3
Staplehill Rd
Liverton TQ12 122 F1
Newton Abbot TQ12 206 B8
Staples Mdw TA20 88 D8
Staples Mews 4 EX8 202 A7
Staples Terr DT7 260 E4
Stapleton Cl TQ4 225 E3
Star Barton La EX5 172 D4
Star Cross EX13 87 E6
Star Pk PL18 125 D6
Starcombe La EX10 101 D4
Starcross Prim Sch EX6 201 A8
Starcross Sta EX6 201 B8
Starkey Cl 10 EX16 64 D7
Starlings Roost EX15 163 A2
Starpitten Gr TQ2 214 B3
Starpitten La W TQ2 214 A2
Starre Cl EX12 192 A7
Start Ave Chillington TQ7 145 A1
Teignmouth TQ14 210 C7
Start Bay Pk TQ6 145 F6
Start Cross TQ12 211 A7
Starved Oak Cross EX5 81 D1
Station App TQ10 134 F3
Station Bsns Pk TQ14 210 C5
Station Cl EX33 152 D5
Station Cotts
Bittaford TQ10 137 E8
Brandis Corner EX22 73 A5
Station Cross
Bittaford TQ10 137 E8
Crediton EX17 165 E4
Station Ct TQ13 180 C7
Station Fields EX21 73 E2
Station Hill
Bideford EX39 157 B1
Bratton Fleming EX31 11 A1
Brixham TQ5 230 C5
Great Torrington EX38 159 A6
Lynton EX35 151 B4
Swimbridge EX32 17 E1
Station La Calstock PL18 125 D3
Paignton TQ4 226 B5
Station Rd Bampton EX16 34 B1
Barnstaple EX31 154 F4
Bere Alston PL20 125 E1
Bere Ferrers PL20 239 E3
Bovey Tracey TQ13 180 C7
Bow EX17 78 B3
Bratton Fleming EX31 18 A8
Braunton EX33 152 D5
Bridestowe EX20 107 F7
Broadclyst EX5 175 E3
Buckfastleigh TQ11 236 C5
Budleigh Salterton EX9 198 A1
Burlescombe EX16 51 B3
Chard Junction TA20 88 D8
Chulmleigh EX18 44 C3
Colyton EX24 103 A5
Cullompton EX15 163 C4
17 Dawlish EX7 204 E6
Exeter, Pinhoe EX1 174 E1
Exeter, St David's EX4 177 A8
Exminster EX6 182 D3
Exton EX3 183 C1
Feniton EX14 84 D2
Gunnislake PL18 125 C6
Halwill Junction EX21 73 E2
Hele EX5 82 F5
Hemyock EX15 67 B8
Holsworthy EX22 164 C4
Horrabridge PL20 126 F4
Ide EX2 176 D1
Ilfracombe EX34 150 A4
Ivybridge PL21 237 D6
Lifton PL16 105 F4
Lydford EX20 108 A6
Mary Tavy PL19 117 E6
Meeth EX20 57 C2
Moretonhampstead TQ13 111 F4
Newton Abbot TQ12 207 D3
Newton Poppleford EX10 186 F8
Newton St Cyres EX5 81 A1
North Brentor PL19 117 C8
Northlew EX20 74 E1
Okehampton EX20 170 B4
Plymouth, Elburton PL9 256 C7
Plymouth, Keyham PL2 247 E5
Plymouth, Plympton PL7 250 E5
Plymouth, Tamerton Foliot PL5 244 A6
Princetown PL20 128 A8
Saltash PL12 243 A2
Sidmouth EX10 188 A4
7 South Brent TQ10 134 F3
South Molton EX36 158 D5
3 Teignmouth TQ14 210 C4
Tiverton EX16 161 D4
Topsham EX3 182 F5
Totnes TQ9 223 C6
Wellington TA21 160 C7
Willand EX15 162 C5
Woolacombe EX34 8 A6
Yelverton PL20 127 A2
Yeoford EX17 79 C1
Station Road Ind Est EX15 67 B8
Station View PL19 117 C8
Station Yard Ind Est TQ7 258 C5
Staverton Cotts TQ13 130 F4
Staverton Sta★ TQ9 215 E4
Stawley Prim Sch TA21 51 B8
Ste Honorine Du Fay Cl EX32 28 E8
Steamer Quay Rd TQ9 223 D4
Steamer Quay Wharf 11 TQ9 223 D5
Steartfield Rd TQ3 226 C7
Steddaford Ct EX20 95 A5
Steed Cl TQ4 229 A8
Steel Cl EX14 166 D6
Steep Head EX36 19 B1
Steep Hill TQ1 214 D6
Steep La Landkey EX32 17 D2
Upton TA22 34 C8
Steeperton Cl EX20 170 D5
Steeple Cl PL9 255 F4
Steeple Dr EX2 181 B8
Steer Park Rd PL7 251 C5
Steer Point Cotts PL8 256 F2
Steer Point Rd PL8 257 A4
Stefan Cl PL9 255 B5
Stella Maris Ct EX39 157 A2
Stella Rd TQ3 219 A1
Stenlake Pl PL4 249 B2
Stenlake Terr PL4 249 B2
Stentaway Cl PL9 255 F8
Stentaway Dr PL9 256 A8
Stentaway La EX33 7 E2
Stentaway Rd PL9 255 F8
Stentiford Hill TQ7 258 D7
Stentiford Hill Rd TQ1 220 B5
Stentiford La TQ13 122 D4
Stepcote Hill EX1 261 A2
Steppes Mdw TQ12 207 A2
Steppingstone Cross EX33 8 D1
Stepps Cross EX12 192 E7
Stepps La EX12,DT7 193 A5
Steps Cl EX1 174 F1
Steps Cross TQ2 214 B3
Steps Cross Specl Sch TQ2 214 B3
Steps La TQ2 214 B3
Stepstone La EX33 8 D1
Steven's Cross EX10 188 D8
Steven's Cross Cl EX10 188 E8
Stevens La EX10 188 A7
Stevenstone Ct EX38 42 A6
Stevenstone Rd EX8 202 D7
Stewart Cl EX8 196 E1
Stibb La PL21 136 D7
Stickle Path EX16 35 C1
Sticklepath Ct EX31 154 E3
Sticklepath Hill EX31 154 E4
Sticklepath Prim Sch
Barnstaple EX31 154 C3
Okehampton EX20 94 F5
Sticklepath Terr EX31 154 F4
Stidson Cross TQ10 135 B3
Stidston La TQ10 135 A3
Stile Ct EX15 163 B2
Stile La DT7 260 D3
Stile Orch TQ7 143 F7
Stillman Ct 8 PL4 263 A2
Stillman St PL4 263 A2
Stiniel Cross TQ13 111 A4
Stintway La EX10 187 E5
Stirling Ct PL5 243 C1
Stirling Rd PL5 243 C1
Stitchill Rd TQ1 220 C4
Stitworthy Cross EX39 23 C1
Stoat Pk EX32 155 D4
Stoats Cl EX36 158 C2
Stoats Mews EX20 77 C4
Stock Hill EX35 151 A1
Stock La EX12 192 A5
Stock Rd EX35 5 B3
Stockadon La EX17 63 A1
Stocker Rd EX4 173 B1
Stockeydown La EX17 79 E2
Stockham Hill TA22 33 E8
Stockland CE Prim Sch EX14 87 A7
Stockland Head Cross EX15 84 B7
Stockland Hill EX14 86 E6
Stockleigh Cross
Cheriton Fitzpaine EX17 62 C1
Stockleigh Pomeroy EX17 80 F6
Stockman La TA20 88 C7
Stockmeadow Gdns TQ14 209 A7
Stockstyle La EX13 88 A8
Stockton Ave EX7 204 E6
Stockton Hill EX7 204 D6
Stockton La 8 EX7 204 D6
Stockton Rd EX7 204 D6
Stockwell Cross EX5 82 D5
Stoford La TA21 52 F7
Stoggy La PL7 251 A6
Stoke Canon CE Prim Sch EX5 173 F8
Stoke Climsland Prim Sch PL17 115 B1
Stoke Cross PL8 141 B5
Stoke Damerel Bsns Ctr 5 PL3 248 A4
Stoke Damerel Com Coll PL3 248 B4
Stoke Damerel Prim Sch PL1 248 A3
Stoke Fleming Prim Sch TQ6 146 A7
Stoke Gabriel Prim Sch TQ9 227 F7
Stoke Gabriel Rd
Galmpton TQ5 229 A5
Paignton TQ5 228 E6
Stoke Hill Exeter EX4 173 E2
Stoke Canon EX5 173 F6
Stoke Gabriel TQ9 227 F7
Stoke Hill Cres EX4 173 E1
Stoke Hill Fst Sch EX4 173 E1
Stoke Hill La PL20 126 E2
Stoke Hill Mid Sch EX4 173 E1
Stoke House Gdns TQ6 146 B7
Stoke Lyne EX8 196 C1
Stoke Meadow Cl EX4 173 E2
Stoke Rd
Higher Gabwell TQ1,TQ12 214 C7
Noss Mayo PL8 141 A6
Paignton, Higher Yalberton TQ4 225 C3
Paignton, Waddeton TQ5 228 F6
Plymouth PL1 262 A3
Stoke Canon EX4,EX5 173 D5
Stoke Valley Rd EX4 173 D2
Stoke Woods Forest Wlks★ EX4,EX5 173 B4
Stokeinteignhead Prim Sch TQ12 209 B1
Stokelake TQ13 123 D5
Stokenham Area Prim Sch TQ7 145 B1
Stokenham Cross TQ7 145 B1
Stokes La PL1 263 A2
Stokes Mead EX5 184 D3
Stokingway Cl PL9 255 E5
Stone Ash La EX17 61 C3
Stone Barton Cl PL7 250 C6
Stone Barton Rd PL7 250 C6
Stone Cl EX14 166 B4
Stone Cross
Chagford TQ13 96 A1
Lifton PL16 105 E5
Meeth EX20 57 C4
Molland EX36 31 F7
North Tawton EX20 77 E4
West Buckland EX32 18 A4
Widecombe in the Moor TQ13 121 B1
Stone La Lympstone EX8 195 E5
Thorverton EX5 81 F7
Stone Lane Ret Pk EX2 177 B3
Stone Moor Cross EX18 45 C1
Stone Pk TQ4 229 D6
Stone's Hill EX17 80 A7
Stoneacre Cl TQ5 230 C3
Stonebarrow La EX13 88 F2
Stoneborough Cnr EX9 198 B1
Stoneborough Ct EX9 198 B1
Stoneborough La EX9 198 B1
Stonecombe Hill EX31 10 C6
Stonehall Flats PL1 248 A1
Stonehanger Ct TQ8 259 D4
Stonehedge Cl PL21 237 D4
Stonehouse Bridge PL1 248 A1
Stonehouse St PL1 262 A2
Stoneland Cross EX16 47 F4
Stoneland La EX16 47 F5
Stonelands EX6 96 F3
Stonelands Ct EX7 204 C6
Stonelands Mews EX7 204 C6
Stonelands Pk EX7 204 C6
Stonelands Terr EX7 204 C6
Stoneleigh
Sidmouth EX10 189 C7
Wellington TA21 160 B8
Stoneleigh Cl TQ12 206 F4
Stoneleigh Dr TQ2 219 D3
Stoneman's Hill TQ12 212 B7
Stonemans La EX38 159 C5
Stonemoor Cross EX38 56 B7
Stonemoor La EX36 31 F7
Stonepark TQ13 130 F4
Stonepark Cres TQ13 130 F4
Stoneridge La TA4 35 D5
Stones Cl
8 Kingsteignton TQ12 123 F1
Modbury PL21 137 C2
Stoneshill Cross EX17 80 A7
Stonewall La EX17 165 C6
Stoney La Bradninch EX5 82 F7
Honiton EX14 166 D2
Stoney Lane Cross EX16 50 B3
Stoney Lane Hill EX16 48 C2
Stoney Park La EX20 170 A4
Stoneyford Pk EX9 198 B1
Stoneyhill TQ12 212 B3
Stoneyhouse La EX14 86 D1
Stoneylands EX5 99 C5
Stoneylane Hill EX16 48 B3
Stoneywell 3 EX39 15 B1
Stoning Cross EX20 75 C7
Stony Close La EX12 192 E5
Stony Cnr EX34 3 D3
Stony Hill Cross EX36 31 A3
Stony La Axminster EX13 167 E6
Gunnislake PL18 125 D6
Hawkridge TA22 21 E3
Landkey EX32 17 B1
Lympstone EX8 195 F8
Parracombe EX31 4 D1
Swimbridge EX32 28 B8
Woodbury Salterton EX5 184 C6
Stony La End EX32 17 B1
Stonybridge Cross EX36 30 B8
Stonybridge Hill EX36 30 B8
Stonypark La EX17 165 B5
Stoodleigh Cross
Calverleigh EX16 48 B4
West Buckland EX32 18 B2
Stoodleigh Moor Cross EX16 48 D6
Stoodley Knowle Convent Sch TQ1 220 F5
Stooke Bridge Rd EX15 83 C1
Stooks Cl EX5 81 E1
Stoop Cross TQ9 131 E1
Stooper's Hill TA20 69 F6
Stopford Pl PL1 247 F3
Stopgate Cross
Stopgate EX14 68 F4
Zeal Monachorum EX17 78 C8
Stormsdown Cotts TQ12 131 B7
Storridge La EX13 88 B6
Storrs Cl TQ13 180 C8
Stott Cl PL3 249 D5
Stour Cl PL3 249 D6
Stourscombe Wood PL15 105 A2
Stout Cross EX14 68 F5
Stovar Long La EX12 191 D6
Stover Country Pk★ TQ12 123 B2
Stover Ct EX4 261 C4
Stover Sch TQ12 123 B1
Stowe Gdns PL5 244 B2
Stowe La EX20 76 C4
Stowell La TA20 88 D8
Stowford Bsns Pk PL21 237 D4
Stowford Cl PL20 127 B3
Stowford Cross
Bradworthy EX22 53 C8
Bratton Fleming EX31 11 C3
Chittlehampton EX37 29 A5
Cobbaton EX37 28 E5
Halwill EX21 91 D8
South Molton EX36 19 B2
West Putford EX22 39 E2
Stowford Gate EX10 187 E8
Stowford Hill EX17 61 A7
Stowford Hts EX12 191 F8
Stowford Prim Sch PL21 237 E5
Stowford Rise EX10 187 F8
Straightway Head EX5 100 A7
Strand Teignmouth TQ14 210 A3
Topsham EX3 182 F4
Torquay TQ1 220 B4
Strand Cl EX31 16 B6
Strand Ct
1 Bideford EX39 157 A2
Topsham EX3 182 F4
Strand Hill EX7 204 E6
Strand La EX31 16 B6
Strand Ringmore TQ14 209 C5
Strand St PL1 254 A8
Strand The
Barnstaple EX32 154 F5
Bideford EX39 157 A2
3 Brixham TQ5 230 D5
Culmstock EX15 66 E8
Dawlish EX7 204 E6
Exmouth EX8 202 A6
Ilfracombe EX34 150 C6
Lympstone EX8 195 D5
Starcross EX6 201 B7
Strand View EX3 182 F4
Strashleigh View PL21 136 D6
Stratford Ave EX4 178 C8
Strathculm Rd EX5 82 F5
Stratton Wlk PL2 248 D8
Strawberry Ave EX2 181 C8
Strawberry Hill EX8 195 F5
Strawberry La EX7 204 C3
Strawberry Terr TQ12 207 E8
Stray Pk PL8 257 F4
Straypark Cnr EX35 5 E4
Stream Ct EX2 261 A1
Streamcombe La TA22 33 B5
Streamers Mdws EX14 166 C5
Streams La EX31 9 B2
Streatham Dr EX4 177 B8
Streatham Rise EX4 177 A8
Street Ash La TA20 69 F8
Street The
Kilmington EX13 87 C1
Musbury EX13 103 D5
Strete Ralegh EX5 168 A8
Strode Rd
Buckfastleigh TQ11 236 B4
Plymouth PL7 250 F6
Stroma Cl PL6 244 F7
Strongs Hill Cross EX21 73 F1
Stroud Park Rd PL2 248 C7
Stroxworthy Cross EX39 38 F6
Stuart Cres EX15 163 C6
Stuart Ct EX7 204 D4
Stuart Rd Exeter EX1 177 F6
Plymouth PL3 262 A4
Stuart Road Prim Sch PL1 262 A4
Stubbing Cross EX24 102 C5
Stubbins Cross TQ12 211 D7
Stubborn Cross EX16 62 C7
Stuckeridge Cross EX16 48 D8
Stucley Rd EX39 156 E1
Studd Dr EX32 29 C7
Studhayes Cross EX13 87 C1
Studhayes Rd EX13 87 B2
Studley Ho 4 EX14 166 C5
Studley Rd TQ1 220 A7
Stumpy Cross
Shobrooke EX17 80 F4
Silverton EX5 82 B4
Stumpypost Cross TQ7 144 B6
Sturcombe Ave TQ4 225 F3
Sturdee Rd PL2 248 A5
Sturges Rd EX8 202 D8
Sturt Cotts EX17 78 E7
Sturtlebury La TQ7 143 F5
Style Cl EX32 155 B2
Suddon's Cross EX24 102 B6
Suddon's La EX24 102 B6
Sugar Mill Bsns Pk PL9 249 C1
Sullivan Rd EX2 178 C5
Summer Cl Exeter EX4 178 B8
Exmouth EX8 202 E8
13 Hemyock EX15 67 B8
Summer La
Bovey Tracey TQ13 123 C2
Brixham TQ5 230 B2
Exeter EX4 174 B1
Exmouth EX8 196 B4
Northlew EX20 74 F2
Ottery St Mary EX11 100 F8
Summer Well La EX34 9 A5
Summercourt Way TQ5 230 A2
Summerfield
Sidmouth EX10 188 B8
Woodbury EX5 184 C4
Summerfield Ave TA21 52 D8
Summerfield Ct
Ivybridge PL21 237 A5
Paignton TQ4 226 C5
Summerfield Rd TQ2 219 E8
Summerfield Way TA21 52 D8
Summerfields PL12 242 D1
Summerhayes EX7 204 D4
Summerhill Cl 17 TQ12 122 F1
Summerhill Cres 16 TQ12 122 F1
Summerhill Cross TQ13 130 E4
Summerhill Rd
15 Liverton TQ12 122 F1
Lyme Regis DT7 260 E4
Summerland EX14 166 C5
Summerland Ave EX7 204 D7
Summerland Cl EX7 204 D6
Summerland Cotts
10 Newton Abbot TQ12 207 C3
Ottery St Mary EX11 100 F8
Summerland Ct 11 TQ12 207 C3
Summerland Pl 12 EX32 155 A4
Summerland St
Barnstaple EX32 155 A5
Exeter EX1,EX4 261 C4
Summerland Terr 1 EX34 3 A3
Summerlands TQ12 123 A1
Summerlands Cl
Brixham TQ5 230 A2
Plymouth PL7 251 C5
Summerlands Ct
Brixham TQ5 230 A2
14 Liverton TQ12 122 F1
Summerlands Gdns PL7 251 C5
Summermoor La EX37 28 E6
Summers Cl PL6 249 B7
Summers Moor Cross EX19 58 F1
Summersby Cl EX12 192 A6
Summerville Cross EX39 37 F6
Summerway EX4 178 C8
Summerway Mid Sch EX4 178 C8
Summerwell La EX16 62 D4
Sumner Rd PL21 137 C7
Sun Ct 9 TQ12 207 B3
Sun Valley Cl TQ5 230 C5
Sunbury Hill TQ1 220 A6
Sunbury Rd TQ4 226 B5
Sunbury Terr 2 TQ1 220 A6
Suncrest Cl TQ2 213 F3
Sunderland Cl PL9 255 A6
Sunflower Rd EX32 155 A5
Sunhill Ave EX3 182 F6
Sunhill La EX3 182 F6
Sunningbrook Rd EX16 161 E5
Sunningdale EX39 157 A3
Sunningdale Rd PL12 242 C2
Sunny Bank EX32 155 B4
Sunny Cl TQ12 207 F3
Sunny Ct EX16 161 D4
Sunny Dene PL5 243 D1
Sunny Gdns TQ1 220 A6
Sunny Hill EX11 169 E4
Sunny Hollow TQ12 211 D8
Sunny View EX19 58 F3
Sunnybank EX6 194 E3
Sunnyfield EX5 175 C7
Sunnylands Cross EX13 87 A2
Sunnylands Way EX7 210 F8
Sunnymead EX17 79 B5
Sunnymead Terr 8 TQ9 223 C5
Sunnymoor Cl EX1 174 F2
Sunnyside
Awliscombe EX14 85 C4
9 Bideford EX39 157 B1
2 Braunton EX33 152 D5
Burlescombe EX16 51 C2
Combe Martin EX34 3 A3
Great Torrington EX38 42 B5
Woolfardisworthy EX39 38 F8
Sunnyside Cotts 16 EX34 3 A3
Sunnyside La EX31 4 D1
Sunnyside Rd
Kingskerswell TQ12 213 A4
Plymouth PL4 249 B2
Woolacombe EX34 7 F6
Sunset Ho 1 EX12 192 A4
Sunset Hts EX32 155 A5
Sunway Cl PL19 171 A6
Sunwell La PL11 252 A8
Sunwine Pl EX8 202 B6
Surbiton Cres EX4 176 F4

Surf Bay Cvn Pk EX39 . . 156 D8
Surridge La TQ2 . . . . 220 A5
Sussex Cl Exeter EX4 . . . . 176 E4
Torquay TQ2 . . . . 214 A3
Sussex Pl PL1 . . . . 262 C2
Sussex Rd PL2 . . . . 247 F5
Sussex St PL1 . . . . 262 C2
Sussex Terr 5 PL2 . . . . . 247 F5
Sutcliffe Cl TQ9 . . . . 222 F7
Sutcombe Com Prim Sch EX22 . . . . 54 A6
Sutherland Cl TQ12 . . . . 212 F8
Sutherland Dr TQ2 . . . . . 214 B2
Sutherland Rd
Plymouth PL4 . . . . 263 A4
Torquay TQ1 . . . . 220 C5
Sutton Cl Dawlish EX7 . . . 204 D7
Torquay TQ2 . . . . 213 F4
Sutton Cross
Moretonhampstead TQ13 . 111 E5
Thurlestone TQ7 . . . . 143 D1
Sutton Ct PL1 . . . . 247 F1
Sutton Mews 22 PL4 . . . 263 A2
Sutton Rd PL4 . . . . 263 B2
Suttons Cross EX14 . . . . . 86 D1
Swaddicott Cross EX21 . . 56 C2
Swaindale Rd 3 PL3 . . . 248 E6
Swains TA21 . . . . 160 D4
Swains Ct EX3 . . . . 182 E5
Swains La TA21 . . . . 160 D4
Swains Rd EX9 . . . . 198 B1
Swale Cl Plymouth PL3 . . 249 B6
Torquay TQ2 . . . . 214 A3
Swallerton Gate TQ13 . . 121 D6
Swallow Cl EX32 . . . . 155 E4
Swallow Dr EX2 . . . . 176 D3
Swallow Field EX31 . . . . . 154 A2
Swallow Units EX2 . . . . . 177 D1
Swallow Way EX15 . . . . . 163 B2
Swallowfield Rd EX2 . . . . 178 B2
Swallowfield Rise TQ2 . 213 C2
Swallowfields TQ9 . . . . . 223 B7
Swallows Acre EX7 . . . . . 204 E7
Swallows End PL9 . . . . . 255 E8
Swallowtree Cross EX6 . . 96 C7
Swan Cl PL10 . . . . 253 A6
Swan Ct Dartmouth TQ6 . . 233 E3
Exeter EX2 . . . . 261 B1
Swan Gdns PL7 . . . . 250 F5
Swan Hill Rd EX24 . . . . . 103 A3
Swan Rd EX6 . . . . 201 A8
Swan Units EX2 . . . . 178 E5
Swan Yd Exeter EX4 . . . . . 177 A5
11 Honiton EX14 . . . . 166 C6
Swanaford Rd EX6 . . . . . 112 F7
Swanborough Rd TQ12 . 208 A2
Swannaton La
Crediton EX17 . . . . 79 E8
Morchard Bishop EX17 . . . . 61 E1
Swannaton Rd TQ6 . . . . 233 F1
Swannywell Hill EX17 . . . 78 F8
Swanswood Gdns EX39 . 156 D7
Swedwell La TQ2 . . . . . 214 A4
Swedwell Rd TQ2 . . . . . 214 A4
Sweetbriar Cl EX7 . . . . . 204 C3
Sweetbriar La EX7 . . . . . 204 C3
Sweetbrier La EX1 . . . . . 178 B6
Swiddacombe La EX36 . . 32 C7
Swift Gdns PL5 . . . . 244 C2
Swift Ind Est TQ12 . . . . . 207 D6
Swimbridge CE Prim Sch EX32 . . . . 17 D1
Swinburne Gdns PL5 . . . 244 C1
Swincombe Dr TQ3 . . . . 225 F6
Swincombe La EX31 . . . . . 11 F4
Swing Gate EX6 . . . . 194 A4
Swing Gate Cross EX37 . . 29 A2
Swingate Cross EX22 . . . . 90 B8
Swiss Cl EX8 . . . . 196 B3
Sycamore Ave
Dawlish Warren EX7 . . . . 201 A2
Plymouth PL4 . . . . 263 C2
Tavistock PL19 . . . . 171 C2
Sycamore Cl
Broadclyst EX5 . . . . 175 D6
Exeter EX1 . . . . 178 B5
Exmouth EX8 . . . . 196 E2
Exmouth EX8 . . . . 196 F2
Honiton EX14 . . . . 166 A4
Paignton TQ4 . . . . 229 D7
Willand EX15 . . . . 162 C4
Sycamore Dr
Plymouth PL6 . . . . 245 C7
Torpoint PL11 . . . . 247 A3
Sycamore Rd
Saltash PL12 . . . . 242 B3
Tiverton EX16 . . . . 161 E5
Sycamore Way
Brixham TQ5 . . . . 230 A2
Plymouth PL6 . . . . 245 E6
Sydenham Cross PL19 . . 116 A2
Sydenham La EX16 . . . . . 47 E6
Sydney Cl PL7 . . . . 250 E4
Sydney Rd Exeter EX2 . . . 177 A4
Torpoint PL11 . . . . 247 B3
Sydney St PL1 . . . . 262 B4
Sylvan Ave EX4 . . . . 173 D1
Sylvan Cl EX8 . . . . 196 A2
Sylvan Ct EX8 . . . . 196 A2
Sylvan Rd Exeter EX4 . . . 173 D1
Wellington TA21 . . . . 160 E5
Sylvania Dr EX4 . . . . 173 E2
Symons Rd PL12 . . . . . . 242 F2
Synagogue Pl EX4 . . . . . 261 A3
Syncock's Cross EX39 . . 157 F3

T

Tabernacle Ct 9 EX1 . . 261 A2
Tackbear Rd EX22,EX23 . . 70 D4
Tacket Ct TQ7 . . . . 258 C4
Taddiford Est EX4 . . . . . . 177 A8
Taddiford Rd EX4 . . . . . . 177 A8
Tadworthy Rd EX39 . . . . 156 E7
Tail Cnr EX17 . . . . 79 D7
Tailyour Rd PL6 . . . . 244 F2
Talbot Gdns PL5 . . . . 247 D7
Talbot Rd DT7 . . . . 260 D5
Tale Common Head Cross EX14 . . . . 84 B4
Taleford Cl EX11 . . . . 169 C7
Taleford Villas EX11 . . . . 169 C7
Talewater Cross EX5 . . . . 84 C2
Tallow Wood Cl TQ3 . . . 225 E6
Tamar Ave Plymouth PL2 . 247 E5
Tavistock PL19 . . . . 171 D5
Torquay TQ2 . . . . 219 B7
Tamar Bridge PL5 . . . . . 243 A2
Tamar Cl 17 PL20 . . . . . . 125 E1
Tamar Cotts PL19 . . . . . . 116 A1
Tamar Rd EX31 . . . . 15 E5
Tamar St Plymouth PL1 . . 247 E3
Saltash PL12 . . . . 243 A2
Torpoint PL11 . . . . 247 C3
Tamar Terr
Calstock PL17 . . . . 125 D3
Saltash PL12 . . . . 243 A2
Tamar Valley Donkey Pk* PL18 . . . . 125 A5
Tamar View
Milton Abbot PL19 . . . . . . 116 A6
St Dominick PL12 . . . . 125 A2
Tamar View Ind Est PL12 . . . . 242 D5
Tamar Villas PL9 . . . . 255 D7
Tamar Way PL18 . . . . 125 D6
Tamar Wharf PL1 . . . . . . 247 E3
Tamar's Dr EX15 . . . . 162 C4
Tamarind EX15 . . . . 162 C4
Tamarisk Cl EX4 . . . . 174 B2
Tamarside Com Coll PL5 . . . . 243 E1
Tamerton Ave PL5 . . . . . 243 D1
Tamerton Cl PL5 . . . . . . 244 A6
Tamerton Foliot Rd PL6 . . . . 244 D5
Tamerton Rd PL6 . . . . . . 241 B2
Tamerton Vale Prim Sch PL6 . . . . 244 C6
Tan La EX2 . . . . 177 B3
Tangmere Ave PL5 . . . . . 243 E5
Tanner's Hill TA4 . . . . 35 E7
Tanners Cl EX15 . . . . 163 B2
Tanners Rd Landkey EX32 . 17 C2
Paignton TQ4 . . . . 226 C4
Tannery Flats 4 EX17 . . . 165 C5
Tanpits Cross TQ7 . . . . . 145 A1
Tanpits Mdw TQ7 . . . . . . 145 A1
Tanworth Ho TQ7 . . . . . . 143 A1
Tanyard La TQ12 . . . . 217 F6
Tanyards Ct 6 EX12 . . . . 192 A5
Tape La EX14 . . . . 85 B3
Tapfield Cross TQ7 . . . . . 142 F4
Tapley Gdns TQ14 . . . . . 209 A8
Tapp's La PL8 . . . . 257 B5
Tappers Cl EX3 . . . . 182 F5
Tappers Knapp DT7 . . . . 260 B5
Taps Cl EX6 . . . . 182 B4
Tapson Dr PL9 . . . . 255 A6
Tarbet Ave EX1 . . . . 177 F7
Tarka Cl EX20 . . . . 170 D6
Tarr Stps* TA22 . . . . 21 E3
Tarr's Ave TQ12 . . . . 207 E7
Tarraway Rd TQ3 . . . . . . 219 D1
Tarrs End TQ12 . . . . 207 E7
Tarrs La TQ12 . . . . 207 E7
Tatworth Prim Sch TA20 . 88 C8
Tatworth St TA20 . . . . 88 C8
Taunton Ave PL5 . . . . . . 244 B5
Taunton Cl EX2 . . . . 177 A3
Taunton Cross EX13 . . . . . 87 A1
Taunton Ct 2 TQ9 . . . . . 223 D5
Taunton Pl PL5 . . . . 244 B5
Taunton Rd TA21 . . . . . . 160 E7
Tavern Gdns EX39 . . . . . . 26 B1
Tavis Rd TQ3 . . . . 225 F8
Tavistock Coll PL19 . . . . 171 A3
Tavistock Cross PL20 . . . 125 F2
Tavistock General PL19 . 171 B5
Tavistock Mus* PL19 . . 171 C6
Tavistock Pl
Paignton TQ4 . . . . 229 B8
Plymouth PL4 . . . . 263 A3
Tavistock Prim Sch PL19 . . . . 171 B4
Tavistock Rd Exeter EX4 . 177 A7
Launceston PL15 . . . . 105 A2
Okehampton EX20 . . . . 93 E4
Plymouth PL6 . . . . 245 B5
Plymouth, Manadon PL5 . . 244 E1
Princetown PL20 . . . . 128 A8
Yelverton PL20 . . . . 126 F3
Tavy Ave TQ2 . . . . 219 B8
Tavy Pl PL4 . . . . 248 F4
Tavy Rd Saltash PL12 . . . 243 A3
Tavistock PL19 . . . . 171 D5
Taw Bridge Cross EX20 . . 77 B4
Taw Cl PL3 . . . . 249 D6
Taw Cres EX31 . . . . 15 E5
Taw Ct 14 EX32 . . . . 155 A4
Taw Green Cross EX20 . . 95 B7
Taw Meadow Cres EX31 153 F6
Taw Mills La EX18 . . . . . . 59 C1
Taw Rd EX31 . . . . 15 E5
Taw Vale EX32 . . . . 154 F4
Taw Vale Ave EX20 . . . . . . 77 B4
Taw Vale Cl EX20 . . . . 77 B4
Taw View
1 Bishop's Tawton EX32 . . 16 E1
Fremington EX31 . . . . 153 F6
Tawgreen La EX18 . . . . . . 59 C1
Tawgreen Rd EX20 . . . . . . 59 C1
Tawmoor Cross EX20 . . . . 95 C7
Tawny Cl TQ3 . . . . 226 C8
Tawton La EX20 . . . . 95 B4
Tay Gdns PL3 . . . . 249 D7
Taylor Cl Dawlish EX7 . . . 204 D5
Ottery St Mary EX11 . . . . . 169 B4
Saltash PL12 . . . . 242 C3
Taylor Rd PL12 . . . . 242 C4
Taylor Sq PL19 . . . . 171 B6
Taylor's Cross EX17 . . . . . 62 E3
Taylor's Hill EX16,EX17 . . . 62 E4
Taylor's La EX37 . . . . 43 D6
Taylors Ct EX16 . . . . 161 E7
Taylors Field EX20 . . . . . . 77 C4
Taylors Newtake 2 TQ12 . . . . 122 F1
TDC Units EX22 . . . . 164 C6
Teal Cl TQ2 . . . . 213 C2
Teats Hill Flats PL4 . . . . 263 B1
Teats Hill Rd PL4 . . . . . . 263 B1
Teazle Ct EX2 . . . . 261 A2
Tedburn Rd EX4 . . . . 176 B5
Tedburn St Mary Prim Sch EX6 . . . . 97 F5
Tedburrow La EX15 . . . . . 67 A8
Tedders Cl 3 EX15 . . . . . . 67 B8
Tedstone La EX8 . . . . 196 A7
Tees Cl PL3 . . . . 249 C7
Teign Cl TQ14 . . . . 208 E8
Teign Ct
Bishopsteignton TQ14 . . . . 209 A8
Stokeinteignhead TQ12 . . . 209 B1
Teign La Chudleigh TQ13 . 123 D7
Trusham TQ13 . . . . 113 D1
Teign Rd
Newton Abbot TQ12 . . . . . 207 D4
Plymouth PL3 . . . . 249 B6
Teign Sch TQ12 . . . . 207 D8
Teign St TQ14 . . . . 210 B4
Teign Terr EX6 . . . . 113 B5
Teign View TQ13 . . . . 123 C4
Teign View Pl 13 TQ14 . . 210 B4
Teign Village TQ13 . . . . . 123 B7
Teignbridge Bsns Ctr TQ12 . . . . 180 F3
Teignbridge Crossing LC TQ12 . . . . 207 A7
Teignbridge Gate TQ12 . 207 A7
Teigncombe Ct EX6 . . . . 113 B4
Teignharvey Rd TQ12 . . . 209 A3
Teignholt Cross EX6 . . . . 96 D7
Teignmouth Com Coll TQ14 . . . . 210 B5
Teignmouth Hill EX7 . . . 204 E5
Teignmouth Hospl TQ14 . . . . 210 A5
Teignmouth Inverteign Inf Sch TQ14 . . . . 209 D8
Teignmouth Mus* TQ14 . . . . 210 C4
Teignmouth Rd
Bishopsteignton TQ14 . . . . 209 B7
Holcombe EX7 . . . . 210 E7
Kingsteignton TQ12,TQ14 . 208 B6
Shaldon TQ1,TQ14 . . . . . . 210 A1
Torquay TQ1 . . . . 220 A8
Torquay, Maidencombe TQ1 . . . . 214 C6
Teignmouth Sta TQ14 . . 210 C5
Teignview Rd TQ14 . . . . 208 F8
Tekoa Bldgs EX2 . . . . . . 177 C1
Telegraph Cross PL21 . . 136 D4
Telegraph Hill EX6 . . . . . 114 D2
Telegraph La EX5,EX11 . . 168 B6
Telegraph View TQ12 . . . 180 B1
Telegraph Wharf PL1 . . . 254 A8
Telford Cres PL5 . . . . 243 F2
Telford Rd EX4 . . . . 177 A7
Temeraire Rd PL5 . . . . . . 244 D2
Temperance Pl 6 TQ5 . . 230 D5
Temperance St TQ2 . . . . 220 A5
Templar Way
Bovey Tracey TQ12 . . . . . . 123 C1
Newton Abbot TQ12 . . . . . 206 F8
Temple Cres EX16 . . . . . . 161 F4
Temple Gdns EX10 . . . . . 188 B5
Temple Rd EX2 . . . . 261 B2
Temple St EX10 . . . . 188 B5
Templer Rd TQ3 . . . . 219 A3
Templer's Way 11 TQ12 . 123 E1
Templers Rd TQ12 . . . . . 207 D4
Templeton Cross EX16 . . . 48 A1
Templeton La EX16 . . . . . . 47 F1
Ten Acre Gate EX13 . . . . . 87 E7
Tenby Rd PL5 . . . . 243 C1
Tencery Orch EX14 . . . . . . 67 C2
Teneriffe TQ1 . . . . 220 C5
Tennacott Hts EX39 . . . . . 26 A4
Tennacott La EX39 . . . . . . 26 B4
Tennyson Ave EX2 . . . . . 177 F3
Tennyson Cl TQ1 . . . . . . 220 A8
Tennyson Gdns PL5 . . . . 244 B1
Tennyson Way EX8 . . . . . 196 C4
Tern Gdns PL7 . . . . 250 F5
Terra Nova Gn PL2 . . . . . 248 B5
Terrace The
Braunton EX33 . . . . 152 D6
Harrowbarrow PL17 . . . . . 125 A5
Torquay TQ1 . . . . 220 B4
Terris Cross EX20 . . . . 76 A6
Tewkesbury Cl PL2 . . . . . 248 A8
Tews La
Barnstaple, Bickington EX31 . . . . 154 A3
Barnstaple, Roundswell EX31 . . . . 154 A2
Tewsley Cl EX31 . . . . 154 A3
Thackeray Gdns PL5 . . . 244 B1
Thackeray Rd EX4 . . . . . 178 C8
Thames Gdns PL3 . . . . . 249 D5
Thanckes Cl PL11 . . . . . . 247 A3
Thanckes Dr PL11 . . . . . . 247 A4
Thatcher Ave TQ1 . . . . . . 221 A4
Thatcher Dr TQ14 . . . . . . 210 C8
Thatcher Hts TQ1 . . . . . . 220 F3
Thatcher's La EX5 . . . . 81 E6
Thatcher's Lane End EX5 81 E5
Theatre La 13 EX31 . . . . . 154 F5
Theatre Ope PL1 . . . . 247 F1
Theatre Royal PL1 . . . . . 262 C2
Thelbridge Cross EX17 . . 61 D6
Thelbridge Hill EX17 . . . . 61 C7
Therlow Rd PL3 . . . . 249 B6
Thetford Gdns PL6 . . . . . 249 D8
Third Ave Dawlish EX7 . . . 204 D5
Exeter, Countess Wear EX2 . . . . 182 C7
Exeter, Heavitree EX1 . . . . 177 F6
Plymouth, Billacombe PL9 . 250 A1
Plymouth, Camels Head PL2 . . . . 247 E7
Plymouth, Stoke PL1 . . . . 248 A2
Teignmouth TQ14 . . . . 210 A5
Torquay TQ1 . . . . 220 A8
Third Dr TQ14 . . . . 210 B5
Thirlmere Gdns PL6 . . . . 244 F4
Thistle Cl PL6 . . . . 245 E7
Thomas Bassett Rd EX24 . . . . 103 A3
Thomas Cl EX8 . . . . 196 C4
Thomas Newcomen Ct TQ6 . . . . 233 C3
Thomas's Cross EX6 . . . . 112 F8
Thompson Rd EX1 . . . . . 178 A7
Thorn Cl Exeter EX1 . . . . 178 B6
Newton Abbot TQ12 . . . . . 206 E4
Thorn Cnr EX18 . . . . 77 E8
Thorn Cross
Bovey Tracey TQ13 . . . . . . 180 C5
Chagford TQ13 . . . . 110 E5
Slapton TQ7 . . . . 145 C6
Thorn Cross Way TA21 . . 50 D8
Thorn Hill EX16 . . . . 63 B6
Thorn La Membury EX13 . . 87 D7
Saltash PL12 . . . . 242 C3
Thorn Moor Cross PL15 105 E7
Thorn Orch TQ12 . . . . . . 211 E2
Thorn Pk PL3 . . . . 248 F5
Thorn Villas TQ12 . . . . . . 208 E3
Thornberry Ave EX1 . . . . 178 B6
Thornbury Cross
Sampford Courtenay EX20 . . 76 E4
Shebbear EX22 . . . . 55 A3
Thornbury Mill EX22 . . . . 55 A4
Thornbury Park Ave PL3 . . . . 248 D6
Thornbury Prim Sch PL6 . . . . 245 D4
Thornbury Rd PL6 . . . . . 245 E4
Thorncliff Cl TQ1 . . . . . . 220 E5
Thorndale Cts EX4 . . . . . 176 D8
Thorndon Cross EX22 . . . 71 E5
Thorne Cotts EX11 . . . . . 169 B3
Thorne Cross EX6 . . . . 96 E4
Thorne Farm Way EX11 169 C3
Thorne La Bow EX17 . . . . . 78 D3
Spreyton EX17 . . . . 96 D8
Thorne Moor Cross EX6 . 96 E4
Thorne Park Rd TQ2 . . . 219 D5
Thorne Pk EX34 . . . . 8 F5
Thornemoor La EX17 . . . . 78 D2
Thornes Cross EX16 . . . . . 64 E5
Thornes Mdw EX2 . . . . . 114 A6
Thornes Terr EX36 . . . . . 158 C4
Thorney Cross EX21 . . . . . 90 E7
Thornfield Cl
Exmouth EX8 . . . . 196 A2
Seaton EX12 . . . . 192 A7
Thornham Chapel Cross EX17 . . . . 46 B1
Thornham La EX17 . . . . . . 46 B1
Thornhedges Cross EX17 80 B5
Thornhedges La EX17 . . . 80 B5
Thornhill Rd PL3 . . . . 248 E6
Thornhill Way PL3 . . . . . 248 E6
Thornhillhead EX39 . . . . . 40 B3
Thorning St TQ8 . . . . 259 E5
Thornlea Ave EX31 . . . . . 153 D5
Thornley Dr TQ14 . . . . . . 210 A5
Thornpark Cross EX32 . . . 18 C6
Thornpark Rise EX1 . . . . 178 B6
Thorns Cross TQ13 . . . . . 111 C4
Thornton Ave PL4 . . . . . . 263 B4
Thornton Hill EX4 . . . . . . 261 B4
Thorntree Bsns Units EX8 . . . . 196 F1
Thornville Terr PL9 . . . . 255 C7
Thornyville Cl PL9 . . . . . 255 C8
Thornyville Dr PL9 . . . . . 255 D8
Thornyville Villas PL9 . . 255 C8
Thorpe Ave EX8 . . . . 196 B3
Thorverton CE Prim Sch EX5 . . . . 81 E4
Three Ash Cross EX14 . . . 87 B5
Three Close La EX33 . . . . . 8 E2
Three Corner Cross EX36 45 C5
Three Corner Pl EX2 . . . 181 C8
Three Corners Cross EX14 . . . . 85 A6
Three Cross Ways EX19 . 58 D2
Three Crossways
Chulmleigh EX18 . . . . 44 E1
Zeal Monachorum EX17 . . . 78 A6
Three Elms Cross EX15 . . 83 D3
Three Firs EX15 . . . . 83 D4
Three Gate Cross
Cheriton Bishop EX17 . . . . . 97 B6
Yeoford EX17 . . . . 79 D2
Three Gates Cross
Dulverton TA22 . . . . 33 C6
Huntsham EX16 . . . . 49 E6
Yarnscombe EX31 . . . . 27 D1
Three Gates Hill EX16 . . . 49 E6
Three Hammers Cross EX17 . . . . 61 A6
Three Lane End EX22 . . . . 38 E1
Three Limbed Oak EX5 . . 81 D3
Three Mariners Cross EX14 . . . . 86 C6
Three Sycamores Cross EX24 . . . . 102 F6
Three Tree La TQ14 . . . . 124 C2
Three Ways EX31 . . . . 18 A8
Threefoot Stool EX6 . . . . 98 A3
Threshers EX17 . . . . 165 A5
Threwstones Cl EX16 . . . 161 E5
Thriverton Cross EX22 . . . 39 B1
Throgmorton Ho 1 TQ9 . . . . 223 D5
Throwcombe Cross EX16 48 A6
Throwcombe La EX16 . . . 48 A6
Thrushel Cl TQ5 . . . . 230 A2
Thuborough Cross EX22 . 54 A4
Thurlescombe Cross EX16 . . . . 64 E6
Thurlestone Gdns TQ6 . . 233 E3
Thurlestone Rd 5 TQ12 207 B4
Thurlestone Rock TQ7 . . 147 B8
Thurlestone Wlk PL6 . . . 249 D8
Thurlow Cl EX17 . . . . 165 A5
Thurlow Hill TQ1 . . . . . . 220 A6
Thurlow Pk TQ1 . . . . 220 A6
Thurlow Rd Exeter EX4 . . 177 E7
Torquay TQ1 . . . . 220 A6
Tichfield Gdns TQ3 . . . . 225 F7
Tick La EX6 . . . . 113 E5
Ticklemore St TQ9 . . . . . 223 D5
Tidcombe Cl 11 EX16 . . . . 64 D7
Tidcombe La EX16 . . . . . . 64 D7
Tidderson Cross EX16 . . . 47 F4
Tidderson La EX16 . . . . . . 47 E3
Tiddy Cl PL19 . . . . 171 B3
Tideford Cross TQ9 . . . . 227 A1
Tidlake La EX36 . . . . 45 C8
Tidwell Cl EX9 . . . . 198 A2
Tidwell La EX9 . . . . 198 B5
Tidwell Rd EX9 . . . . 198 A2
Tigley Cross TQ9 . . . . . . 135 F3
Tilery EX14 . . . . 69 A3
Tillard Cl PL7 . . . . 251 C5
Tilly Cl PL9 . . . . 255 F4
Timber Hill DT7 . . . . 260 E5
Timber Terr TQ12 . . . . . . 212 F4
Timber Vale Cvn Pk DT7 . . . . 260 E5
Timbers Cl TQ11 . . . . 236 A3
Timbers Rd TQ11 . . . . . . 236 A3
Timewell Hill EX16 . . . . . . 34 C4
Timridge La EX6 . . . . 113 E6
Tin La PL4 . . . . 263 A2
Tincombe PL12 . . . . 242 C2
Tinhay Cross PL16 . . . . . 105 F4
Tinhay Mill Ind Est PL16 105 F4
Tinker's Cross EX18 . . . . . 59 A5
Tinkers Wood Ct 4 TQ5 . . . . 230 C4
Tinkley La TQ13 . . . . 123 C8
Tinpit Hill EX5 . . . . 98 F7
Tintagel Cl Exeter EX4 . . 174 A2
Torquay TQ2 . . . . 219 F8
Tintagel Cres PL2 . . . . . . 248 C8
Tintern Ave PL4 . . . . 263 C2
Tip Hill EX11 . . . . 169 D3
Tipleyhill Cross TQ12 . . . 122 D2
Tipleyhill La TQ12,TQ13 . 122 D3
Tippacott La EX35 . . . . 6 A4
Tipple Cross PL15 . . . . . 105 B6
Tipton Cross EX11 . . . . . 168 B2
Tipton La EX11 . . . . 168 E7
Tipton St John CE Prim Sch EX10 . . . . 100 C2
Tipton Vale EX11 . . . . . . 100 C3
Titchen's La
Calverleigh EX16 . . . . 48 B1
Tiverton EX16 . . . . 63 B8
Titching Park La EX34 . . . . 9 B5
Titham Hill EX16 . . . . 47 C6
Tithe Barn Cross EX15 . . . 51 D2
Tithe Rd PL7 . . . . 250 B7
Tithebarn Copse EX1 . . . 178 F8
Tithebarn La EX1 . . . . . . 179 A8
Titterton Cross EX20 . . . . 77 D7
Tiverton Castle* EX16 . . 161 C4
Tiverton Cl PL6 . . . . 245 B8
Tiverton Craft Ctr* EX16 . . . . 161 C4
Tiverton High Sch EX16 161 C5
Tiverton Parkway Sta EX16 . . . . 65 E8
Tiverton Rd Bampton EX16 49 B8
Cullompton EX15 . . . . 163 B3
Silverton EX5 . . . . 82 B6
Tiverton Way EX16 . . . . . 161 F5
Tiveton Mus* EX16 . . . . 161 C3
Toadpit La EX11 . . . . 168 E6

Tobruk Rd PL12 242 E3
Toby Cross PL21 137 D6
Toby La EX5 184 E5
Tod Moor Cross PL21 237 A1
Tolchers TQ9 222 F8
Tolcis Cross EX13 87 D3
Toll Bar Cross EX18 44 E3
Tollards Rd EX2 178 B2
Tollbar Cl PL21 237 F5
Tollbar Cross EX31 17 B8
Tolleys EX17 165 E5
Tollit Gdn 12 TQ9 223 D5
Tollox Pl PL3 249 B4
Tolman Cres EX12 192 B6
Tom Maddock Gdns PL21 237 E4
Tom Sanders Cl EX34 3 A3
Tom's La EX39 25 A3
Tombstone La EX16 63 D8
Tomhead Cross EX4 98 B6
Tomouth Cres 14 EX39 15 A1
Tomouth Rd EX39 15 A1
Tomouth Sq 15 EX39 15 A1
Tomouth Terr 13 EX39 15 A1
Tomsclose La EX18 59 C2
Tone Hill TA21 160 B8
Tonedale Bsns Pk TA21 160 B7
Tongue End Cross EX20 94 E5
Tongue Gate EX36 45 E7
Tongue Gate Hill EX36 45 E7
Tongue Lake La EX37 44 E5
Tonyfield Wood Cross EX17 60 B4
Top Cliff TQ14 209 D5
Top Of The Town Ctyd PL12 242 F2
Topcliff Rd TQ14 209 D5
Topsham Mus★ EX3 182 F4
Topsham Rd EX2 178 A1
Topsham Sch The EX3 182 E5
Topsham Sta EX3 182 F5
Tor Church Rd TQ2 220 A5
Tor Cl Exeter EX4 174 A1
Paignton TQ4 229 B7
Plymouth, Hartley PL3 248 E7
Plymouth, Marsh Mills PL3 249 F5
Tor Dale 1 TQ1 220 A6
Tor Down EX20 94 D5
Tor Gdns TQ12 206 D1
Tor Haven TQ2 220 B4
Tor Hill Rd TQ2 220 A5
Tor La PL12 242 B1
Tor Lane End TQ9 144 C7
Tor Mare Ct TQ2 219 E4
Tor Park Rd
Paignton TQ4 225 D3
Torquay TQ2 219 F6
Tor Rd PL3 248 E7
Tor Vale TQ1 219 F6
Tor View
Buckfastleigh TQ11 236 A4
8 Horrabridge PL20 126 F4
Tor View Ave TQ12 207 F2
Tor View Gdns TQ3 226 A6
Torbay Ct TQ5 230 E5
Torbay Hospl TQ2 219 D8
Torbay Hospl Annexe TQ2 213 D1
Torbay Rd Paignton TQ4 226 C6
Torquay TQ2 219 F3
Torbay Trad Est TQ5 230 C4
Torbridge Cl PL12 242 D2
Torbridge Rd
7 Horrabridge PL20 126 F4
Plymouth PL7 250 E6
Torbryan Cl PL6 249 E8
Torbryan Hill TQ12 211 A3
Torches Cnr EX19 42 D1
Tordown Gn EX32 17 F2
Torland Rd PL3 248 E7
Toronto Ho EX4 177 E8
Toronto Rd EX4 261 C4
Torpeek Cross PL21 137 C7
Torpoint Com Sch PL11 247 A4
Torpoint Inf Sch PL11 247 B3
Torquay Boy's Gram Sch TQ2 219 D7
Torquay Com Coll TQ2 219 F8
Torquay Gram Sch for Girls TQ1 219 D7
Torquay Mus★ TQ1 220 C4
Torquay Rd
Kingskerswell TQ12 213 A3
Newton Abbot TQ12 207 C3
Newton Abbot, Milber TQ12 212 E8
Paignton TQ3 226 C8
Teignmouth TQ14 210 A3
Torquay Sta TQ2 219 F4
Torr Bridge Pk PL8 136 A2
Torr Cres PL3 248 E7
Torr Hill PL8 257 F4
Torr La East Allington TQ9 144 B7
Plymouth PL3 248 E7
Yealmpton PL8 136 A2
Torr Rd PL3 248 E7
Torr View Ave PL3 248 D7
Torre Cl PL21 237 F5
Torre Cty Prim Sch TQ1 219 E7
Torre Sta TQ2 219 E6
Torridge Ave TQ2 219 B7
Torridge Cl
12 Bideford EX39 157 B1
Plymouth PL7 251 A6
Torridge Hill EX39 157 A1
Torridge Mount EX39 157 B1
Torridge Pl 13 EX39 157 B1
Torridge Rd
Appledore EX39 15 A1
Braunton EX31 15 E5
Plymouth PL7 250 F6
Torridge St EX39 157 B1
Torridge View EX38 159 B5
Torridge View Bglws EX38 159 B5
Torridge Way
Holsworthy EX22 164 C6
Plymouth PL3 249 C5
Torrington 1646★ EX38 159 C4
Torrington Cottage Hospl EX38 159 D5
Torrington Cross EX37 29 C4
Torrington La EX39 157 B1
Torrington Pl EX6 194 D3
Torrington Rd EX19 58 E3
Torrington St 10 EX39 157 B1
Torrs Pk EX34 150 A5
Torrs Walk Ave EX34 150 A6
Tors Pk EX35 151 D5
Tors Rd Lynmouth EX35 151 D5
Okehampton EX20 170 B3
Tors The TQ12 212 F4
Tors View EX39 156 B6
Torver Cl PL6 245 D2
Torview Flats 6 TQ13 180 D8
Torwood Cl TQ1 220 C3
Torwood Ct 4 TQ1 220 D4
Torwood Gardens Rd TQ1 220 C4
Torwood Ho 4 TQ1 220 D4
Torwood Mount 6 TQ1 220 D4
Torwood St TQ1 220 C4
Tory Brook Ave PL7 250 E6
Tory Brook Ct PL7 250 E6
Tory Way PL7 250 D6
Tosberry Cross EX39 37 E8
Tothill Ave PL4 263 B3
Tothill Ct 2 TQ14 210 A3
Tothill Rd PL4 263 B3
Totnes Castle★ TQ9 223 B6
Totnes Cl PL7 251 B4
Totnes Com Hospl TQ9 223 C6
Totnes Cross TQ9 139 C3
Totnes Down Hill TQ9 223 D3
Totnes Mus★ TQ9 223 C5
Totnes Rd
Buckfastleigh TQ11 236 D5
Ipplepen TQ12 211 F5
Marldon TQ3 218 C1
Paignton TQ3,TQ4 225 F5
9 South Brent TQ10 134 F3
Strete TQ6 145 F5
Torquay TQ2 219 C4
Totnes Riverside Sta★ TQ9 223 C7
Totnes Sta TQ9 223 C6
Tottons Ct EX2 181 A8
Touts Ct EX36 158 D4
Towell La EX19 42 D2
Tower Cross EX14 86 A3
Tower Ct
Dunchideock EX6 114 A5
Saltash PL12 242 C2
Tower Gdns EX17 165 C6
Tower Hill
Cheriton Fitzpaine EX17 62 E1
Holcombe Rogus TA21 50 D5
Tower Hill Cross EX17 62 E1
Tower Hill Rd PL15 90 D1
Tower Ho PL1 247 E1
Tower House Sch TQ4 226 B5
Tower La PL21 137 C8
Tower Moor EX37 28 F6
Tower Pk EX36 158 C3
Tower Rd Honiton EX14 166 F4
Offwell EX14 86 A3
Paignton TQ3 226 B6
Tower St
5 Bideford EX39 157 A1
13 Exmouth EX8 202 A6
Northam EX39 156 F7
Tower View
Broadclyst EX5 175 C5
Saltash PL12 242 D1
Tower Way EX14 67 B1
Tower Wlk EX2 181 C8
Towerfield EX3 182 E7
Towerfield Dr PL6 245 C8
Towerhill La TQ13 124 B4
Towers Cl PL6 245 F2
Town Cl TQ6 233 E3
Town Ct EX13 87 A3
Town End EX5 175 D7
Town End Cross EX20 76 C5
Town Farm Bldgs EX14 85 B1
Town Farm Cl
6 Honiton EX14 166 B6
6 Horrabridge PL20 126 F4
Town Farm Cotts TQ9 139 E1
Town Farm Ct EX33 152 C6
Town Farm La TQ13 124 B4
Town Hall Pl 4 TQ13 180 D8
Town Hill Broadclyst EX5 175 C7
Culmstock EX15 66 E8
Ermington PL21 136 F3
Staverton TQ9 216 A5
West Anstey EX36 32 C6
Town La
Bratton Fleming EX31 11 E3
Rackenford EX16 47 D4
Woodbury EX5 184 C3
Town Living Cross EX20 76 B5
Town Mdw
Great Torrington EX38 41 D3
Town Mdw *continued*
Ilsington TQ13 122 C3
Town Mdws EX39 38 E8
Town Mill Gdns PL19 171 C6
Town Mills EX7 204 C6
Town Moor Cross EX17 46 B1
Town Moor Hill EX17 46 B1
Town Pk Crediton EX17 165 B5
Great Torrington EX38 159 C5
Loddiswell TQ7 143 E7
West Alvington TQ7 258 B4
Town Rd TQ7 148 F3
Town Tree Hill 18 EX7 204 D6
Town View EX17 165 C5
Town Wlk EX32 155 B4
Town's End Cross TQ7 145 C3
Town's La TQ7 143 E7
Townfield EX6 182 A4
Townlands Bradninch EX5 82 F6
Willand EX15 162 D3
Townliving Cross EX36 30 E1
Townsend EX12 191 C6
Townsend Ave EX12 192 A6
Townsend Cl TQ7 258 A4
Townsend Cross
Malborough TQ7 147 F6
Winkleigh EX19 58 E2
Townsend Hill TQ12 211 C3
Townsend Rd
Seaton EX12 192 A5
West Alvington TQ7 258 A4
Townshend Ave PL2 247 E5
Townstal Cres TQ6 233 D4
Townstal Hill TQ6 233 E3
Townstal Pathfields TQ6 233 D3
Townstal Rd TQ6 233 D3
Tracey Almshouses 7 TQ13 180 D8
Tracey Ct PL1 262 B3
Tracey Vale TQ13 180 C6
Tracey View 2 EX14 166 B6
Traceys Ave EX12 191 F8
Trackfordmoor Cross TA22 33 B3
Trafalgar Cl
Newton Abbot TQ12 207 B5
Plymouth PL5 247 D8
Trafalgar Ct EX3 182 E5
Trafalgar Gdns EX32 155 A3
Trafalgar Lawn EX32 155 A3
Trafalgar Pl
4 Bideford EX39 156 F1
Exeter EX4 261 C4
3 Plymouth PL1 247 F3
Trafalgar Place La PL1 247 F3
Trafalgar Rd EX8 195 E6
Trafalgar St PL4 263 A3
Trafalgar Terr TQ5 230 C6
Trafford Mews EX2 178 C3
Trago Mills L Pk★ TQ12 123 A1
Traine Brake PL9 256 C1
Traine Rd PL9 140 D8
Traine Terr PL21 137 C2
Traine Villas PL21 137 C3
Tramway Rd PL6 245 E7
Tramways TQ1 220 B7
Transit Way PL5 244 C3
Travershes Cl EX8 196 B1
Traylane EX37 28 B1
Treable La EX6 96 B3
Treago Gdns PL6 245 C8
Treasbeare La EX5 99 A5
Trebblepark Rd TQ7 258 C6
Treburley Cl PL15 115 A4
Treburley Ind Est PL15 115 A4
Treby Rd PL7 250 F4
Trecott Cross EX20 76 F3
Tree Cl EX32 17 F4
Treefield EX31 18 A8
Treefield Wlk EX32 155 D4
Treefields TQ5 230 B4
Treesdale Cl TQ3 225 F6
Trefusis Gdns PL3 249 A4
Trefusis Pl EX8 202 A5
Trefusis Terr
Exmouth EX8 202 A5
Merton EX20 57 A7
Millbrook PL10 252 E6
Trefusis Way EX9 198 B6
Tregenna Cl PL7 251 C4
Tregoning Rd PL11 246 F2
Trehill La PL10 140 H2
Trehill Rd PL21 237 E5
Trekenner Prim Sch PL15 115 A5
Trelawney Ave PL5 243 D1
Trelawney Cl PL11 246 E3
Trelawney Pl PL5 243 D1
Trelawney Rd
Plymouth PL3 248 D5
Saltash PL12 242 E2
Trelawney Rise PL11 246 E3
Trelawney Way PL11 246 E3
Trelawny Rd
Plymouth PL7 250 C6
Tavistock PL19 171 C6
Trelissick Cl TQ3 225 D7
Trelissick Rd TQ3 225 D7
Treloweth Cl PL2 248 D8
Tremaine Cl EX14 166 D6
Trematon Ave TQ1 220 A5
Trematon Cl PL11 246 E4
Trematon Dr PL21 237 E5
Trematon Terr PL4 248 E4
Tremayne Rise PL19 171 B5
Tremere Ct 20 EX32 155 A4
Tremlett Gr TQ12 211 D2
Tremletts Cl EX6 97 F5
Trencher La PL10 252 D2
Trenchfirs Cnr TQ9 139 E2
Trendlewood Rd PL6 245 D7
Trengrouse Ave PL11 246 F3
Treninnow & Wiggle Chalets PL10 252 C2
Trennaway Cross EX6 96 C1
Trenode Ave EX34 2 F4
Trent Cl Bideford EX39 26 A4
Plymouth PL3 249 B6
Trentbridge Sq EX2 178 C4
Trentham Cl
Paignton TQ3 225 E8
Plymouth PL6 245 B6
Trentishoe Hill EX31 4 A5
Trentishoe La EX31 4 A5
Trentworthy Cross EX22 38 B2
Trescote Way EX20 92 F1
Tresilian Cotts EX3 182 F3
Tresilian Gdns EX3 182 F4
Tresillian Gdns EX4 177 E8
Tresillian St PL4 263 C2
Tresluggan Rd PL5 243 D1
Treston Cl EX7 204 E7
Trethewey Gdns PL7 132 D4
Tretower Cl PL6 244 F5
Trevanna Rd TQ7 258 C4
Trevannion Cl PL6 249 A8
Trevelyan Rd EX12 192 C4
Trevendon PL17 115 B1
Treveneague Gdns PL2 248 D8
Trevenn Dr TQ12 213 A3
Trevenor Gdns PL21 137 C3
Treverbyn Cl PL7 250 D6
Treverbyn Rd PL7 250 D6
Trevessa Cl PL2 248 D8
Trevethan Pk PL20 239 F4
Trevithick Ave PL11 246 F4
Trevithick Rd PL5 243 E2
Trevol Bsns Pk PL11 246 D3
Trevol Pl PL11 246 E3
Trevol Rd PL11 246 E3
Trevone Gdns PL2 248 D8
Trevorder Cl PL11 246 F2
Trevorder Rd PL11 246 F2
Trevose Way PL3 249 C6
Trewithy Dr PL6 244 F1
Trews Weir Reach EX2 261 C1
Trewyn Pk EX22 164 B5
Trewyn Rd EX22 164 B6
Triangle Pl 15 TQ14 210 C4
Triangle The 16 TQ14 210 C4
Trickey Cl EX16 161 F5
Tridley Foot Cross EX17 61 F4
Tridley Foot Hill EX17 61 F3
Trigger's Hill EX19 42 D3
Trill Cross EX13 103 E6
Trill La Axminster EX13 167 C2
Musbury EX13 103 E6
Trimstone Cnr EX34 8 F5
Trimstone Cross EX34 8 E6
Trimstone La
Ilfracombe EX34 8 E5
Woolacombe EX34 8 D6
Trinfield Ave EX8 196 B1
Trinity Cl
Bere Alston PL20 125 E1
1 Teignmouth TQ14 210 B6
Wellington TA21 160 C5
Trinity Cross EX5 83 A8
Trinity Ct
Westward Ho! EX39 156 B6
Sidmouth EX10 188 B3
Trinity Gdns EX34 150 A5
Trinity Hill TQ1 220 C3
Trinity Hill Rd
Axminster EX13 167 F1
Raymond's Hill EX13 104 B7
Uplyme EX13 104 A5
Trinity Pl 15 EX32 155 A4
Trinity Rd EX8 201 E6
Trinity Row TA21 160 C5
Trinity Sch TQ14 210 B7
Trinity Sq EX13 167 D6
Trinity St EX32 155 A4
Trinity Way PL19 171 A4
Trinnaman Cl PL21 237 D4
Trinnicks Orch PL21 137 D6
Tristan Cl EX4 174 A2
Tristford Cross TQ9 223 A4
Tristford Rd TQ9 222 D2
Trittencott Cross EX36 46 A8
Troarn Way 21 TQ13 123 E6
Trobridge Cross EX17 165 D2
Trojan Ind Pk TQ4 225 E3
Trood La EX2 181 D7
Trough La TQ13 123 A6
Trouville 12 EX32 155 A5
Trow Hill EX10 188 D8
Trowbridge Cl PL5 244 C4
Trowell La TA4 35 E4
Truckham La EX34 3 D2
Trumlands Rd TQ1 214 B1
Trumpers Cl PL21 237 A6
Trumps Cross EX16 50 E3
Trumps Orch EX15 163 A4
Truro Ave TQ2 214 A1
Truro Dr Exeter EX4 176 F7
Exmouth EX8 196 D4
Plymouth PL5 244 A5
Trusham Cross TQ13 113 D1
Trusham Rd EX2 177 C2
Tub Cnr EX5 99 C7
Tucker Cl PL5 247 F8
Tucker Ct EX14 166 C6
Tucker's Hill PL21 133 C1
Tucker's Hill Head PL21 133 C2
Tucker's Moor Cross EX16 32 F3
Tuckers Cl EX17 165 A5
Tuckers Maltings★ TQ12 207 D4
Tuckers Mdw EX17 165 A5
Tuckers Pk
Bradworthy EX22 38 E1
Buckland Brewer EX39 40 B7
Tuckfield Cl EX2 178 A4
Tucking Mill La EX36 158 E3
Tuckmill Cross EX14 84 C4
Tudor Cl Northam EX39 156 F6
Paignton TQ4 226 A2
Plymouth PL9 255 E5
Tudor Ct Exeter EX4 261 A2
Saltash PL12 243 A2
Tudor Dr EX31 154 D2
Tudor Gr EX15 163 C5
Tudor Rd TQ12 207 B3
Tudor St EX4 261 A2
Tuffery Ct EX4 177 F8
Tugela Terr EX5 179 A3
Tully Gdns EX10 188 B7
Tuly St EX31 154 F5
Tumbles The EX20 76 C5
Tumbling Field La EX16 161 D3
Tumbling Fields EX16 161 D3
Tumbly Hill TQ7 258 D4
Tunnaford Cross TQ13 110 E4
Tunnel La EX14 166 F8
Tuns La EX5 82 B5
Tunworth Ct 1 EX1 261 A2
Tuplins TQ12 207 E8
Turbill Gdns 4 PL7 251 B5
Turbury Cross EX14 85 A8
Turk's Head La EX14 166 A6
Turkey La EX5 99 E5
Turlake Ho EX5 172 F5
Turlake Mews EX5 172 F5
Turner Ave EX8 202 B7
Turner Cl EX10 186 F7
Turner's La DT6 88 H2
Turners Cres EX39 22 E3
Turnpike Halberton EX16 65 C8
Honiton EX14 166 D6
Sampford Peverell EX16 50 C1
Turnpike Cl Clovelly EX39 23 D3
Whiddon Down EX20 95 F3
Turnpike Cross EX34 8 C6
Turnpike Rd EX20 95 F3
Turnquay PL9 255 C7
Turret Gr PL4 248 F4
Tute's La EX34 3 B4
Tuxton Cl PL7 251 C3
Tweed Cl EX14 166 C4
Tween Moor Cross EX17 60 F6
Tweenaway Ct TQ4 225 E4
Tweenaways TQ11 236 A4
Tweenaways Cross TQ4 225 E4
Tweenways TQ12 207 D7
Twelve Acre Post TA22 33 A4
Twelve Milestone Hill EX17 79 D7
Twelve Oaks Cross EX18 58 E6
Twickenham Rd TQ12 208 A1
Twinaway La EX2 114 B8
Twindle Beer TQ13 123 E6
Twiscombe Cnr EX4 98 D5
Twiscombe La EX4 98 C6
Twisted Oak EX6 97 D5
Twistgates La EX14 68 D4
Twitchen Ball Cnr EX36 20 C3
Twitchen Cross
Great Torrington EX38 26 F2
Ilfracombe EX34 8 E6
Twitchen Gate EX31 11 F3
Twitchen La
Bratton Fleming EX31 10 F4
Burrington EX37 43 F3
Two Acre Cl TQ3 225 E6
Two Bridges Rd
Princetown PL20 128 B8
Sidford EX10 101 B1
Two Crosses
Doddiscombsleigh EX6 113 A8
Yealmpton PL8 136 A1
Two Gate Cross EX37 44 A4
Two Gates Cross EX16 47 E5
Two Hills Pk PL12 242 C2
Two Mile Oak Cross TQ12 211 F5
Two Moors Prim Sch EX16 161 E5
Two Post Cross
Spreyton EX17 95 D7
Witheridge EX16 62 E7
Two Post La EX17 95 D7
Two Rivers Ind Est EX31 154 E6
Two Stone La EX6 114 C5
Two Trees Rd EX31 153 D5
Twoacre Ct EX2 181 A8
Twyford Pl Tiverton EX16 161 D4
Wellington TA21 160 D5
Tyes Orch EX15 83 F5
Tylney Cl PL6 245 B6
Tyndale Cl PL5 244 B1
Tyrrell Hosp (Private) EX34 150 B5
Tyrrell Mead EX10 188 B7
Tyrrell Rd EX16 161 B4
Tytheing Cl EX5 172 A8
Tything Wlk 4 PL3 248 E6

U

Uffculme Ct EX15 66 A7
Uffculme Prim Sch EX15 66 A7
Uffculme Rd
Culmstock EX15 66 D8
Uffculme EX15 66 A7
Willand EX15 162 E6
Uffculme Sch EX15 66 A7
Ugborough Prim Sch PL21 137 D6
Ugborough Rd PL21 137 C7
Ugbrooke Ho* TQ13 123 F5
Uggaton Cross EX14 84 D5
Ullcombe La EX14 68 C4
Ullswater Cres PL6 244 E4
Ullswater Ct EX4 176 F5
Umber Cl EX34 2 F4
Umberleigh Prim Sch EX37 28 D2
Umberleigh Sta EX37 28 C2
Umberside 17 EX34 3 A3
Under La
Bovey Tracey TQ13 180 A5
Holsworthy EX22 164 C3
Sidbury EX10 101 C1
Under Minnow Rd EX31 154 E7
Under Rd Bridgerule EX22 70 F5
Gunnislake PL18 125 D6
Under Way TQ12 213 A6
Undercliff TQ6 233 F4
Undercliff Rd PL9 255 B7
Underdown EX6 114 A4
Underdown Cotts EX39 23 D3
Underdown La EX20 76 D4
Underfleet The EX12 192 B5
Underground Passages Mus* EX4 261 B3
Underhay PL8 257 E4
Underheath 4 TQ1 220 D5
Underhill EX8 195 E5
Underhill Cl EX8 195 E4
Underhill Cres EX8 195 E4
Underhill Rd
Plymouth PL3 248 A4
Torquay TQ2 219 E3
Underhill Terr EX3 182 F5
Underhill Villas 1 PL3 248 A3
Underidge Cl TQ3 225 E6
Underidge Dr TQ3 225 E6
Underidge Rd TQ3 225 E6
Underlane Boyton PL15 89 D3
Marhamchurch EX23 70 A6
Plymouth, Plympton PL7 250 C5
Plymouth, Plymstock PL9 255 E6
Underleat Cl 3 TQ13 123 F6
Underleys EX12 191 C5
Undertown PL21 137 D6
Underways PL20 125 E1
Underwood Cl EX7 204 D4
Underwood Rd PL7 250 D4
Unicorn Cl PL7 250 B6
Union Cl EX39 156 F1
Union Hill EX17 78 E7
Union La 9 TQ5 230 C5
Union Pl PL1 262 A2
Union Rd Crediton EX17 165 C5
Exeter EX4 177 D8
Union Sq TQ1 220 B5
Union St Dartmouth TQ6 233 F3
Dulverton TA22 33 D6
Exeter EX2 177 A4
5 Exmouth EX8 202 A6
Newton Abbot TQ12 207 C3
Plymouth PL1 262 A2
Salcombe TQ8 259 E5
Torquay TQ2 220 A5
Union Terr
Barnstaple EX32 155 A4
Barnstaple, Bickington EX31 154 A4
Crediton EX17 165 C5
Unity Cl PL6 245 D5
Univ of Exeter EX4 177 B8
Univ of Plymouth
Exeter EX2 177 E2
Plymouth PL1,PL4 262 C3
Univ of Plymouth (Cookworthy Bldg) PL4 263 A3
Univ of Plymouth Bsns Sch PL4 262 C4
Univ of Plymouth Faculty of Art & Education
Exeter EX2 177 E2
Exeter EX4 261 A3
Univ of Plymouth Faculty of Arts & Education EX8 202 B6
Univ of Plymouth The Hoe Ctr PL1 262 C2
Upcott Ave EX31 154 C6
Upcott Cross
Cobbaton EX32 28 C5
Halwill EX21 91 D8
Holsworthy EX22 72 D7
Iddesleigh EX19 57 F4
St Giles on the Heath PL16 90 E1
Welcombe EX39 37 C5
West Buckland EX32 18 C3
Upcott Gate EX18 59 B3
Upcott Hill
Barnstaple EX31 154 D8
Bideford EX39 25 F4
Upcott Hill *continued*
Okehampton EX20 170 A6
Upcott La Thorverton EX5 81 E6
West Buckland EX32 18 C3
Upcott Mead Rd EX16 161 B4
Upcott Valley EX20 170 A6
Upexe La EX5 82 B5
Upham Cross EX17 63 A3
Upham La EX5 99 C1
Uphay La EX13 167 B8
Uphill Cl PL21 237 E5
Upland Chase EX14 166 B3
Upland Dr PL6 245 A5
Upland Gdns PL9 140 D8
Uplands Saltash PL12 242 E1
Tavistock PL19 171 A4
Uplands Dr EX4 174 A1
Uplands Rd TQ3 219 A2
Uplands Terr EX22 164 C3
Uplowman CE Prim Sch EX16 50 B2
Uplowman Rd
Chevithorne EX16 49 F1
Tiverton EX16 64 E8
Uplyme Rd DT7 260 C4
Uplyme Road Ind Est DT7 260 C4
Upottery Prim Sch EX14 68 C2
Uppacott Cnr EX31 27 D8
Uppacott Cross
Moretonhampstead TQ13 111 D7
South Molton EX36 45 F8
Uppaton La PL21 133 D1
Upper Braddons Hill Rd TQ1 220 C4
Upper Church St 9 EX8 202 A6
Upper Churston Rise EX12 191 E8
Upper Claypark EX34 7 F7
Upper Cockington La TQ2 219 C7
Upper Headland Park Rd TQ3 219 C1
Upper Hermosa Rd 1 TQ14 210 B5
Upper Highfield EX10 188 A5
Upper Knollys Terrace La PL3 248 C4
Upper Longlands EX7 204 D7
Upper Manor Rd TQ3 226 B8
Upper Morin Rd TQ3 226 C7
Upper Paul St EX4 261 A3
Upper Penns Rd TQ3 219 C1
Upper Ridings PL7 251 B7
Upper Stoneborough La EX9 198 A1
Upper Torrs EX34 1 E4
Upper West Terr EX9 198 A1
Upper Westhill Rd DT7 260 C3
Upper Wood La TQ6 234 B3
Upperton La PL6 241 F3
Upperton Rd EX6 97 D1
Uppincott Hill EX5 63 C1
Uppincott La EX5 81 C8
Upright Villas 3 EX33 152 D5
Upton Cl PL3 249 B7
Upton Cross
Payhembury EX14 84 D5
Thurlestone TQ7 143 D2
Upton Hill TQ1 220 A6
Upton Hill Rd TQ5 230 C2
Upton Manor Ct TQ5 230 C2
Upton Manor Pk TQ5 230 C2
Upton Manor Rd TQ5 230 C2
Upton Pyne Cross EX5 172 E4
Upton Pyne Hill EX5 172 F6
Upton Rd
11 Bideford EX39 157 B1
Torquay TQ1 219 F6
Upton St James CE Prim Sch TQ1 220 A7
Usticke La EX34 3 B3
Uton Steep Cross EX17 165 B1
Uxbridge Dr PL5 243 E4

V

Vaagso Cl PL1 247 E2
Vachell Cres EX2 178 D5
Vale Cl Barnstaple EX32 155 A6
Galmpton TQ5 229 B5
Vale La EX13 167 D6
Vale Rd Exmouth EX8 202 D7
Kingskerswell TQ12 213 A5
Newton Abbot TQ12 207 D1
Valentines TA22 33 E6
Vales Rd EX9 198 B1
Valiant Ave PL5 244 A4
Valletort Flats PL1 248 A2
Valletort Ho PL1 262 C3
Valletort La PL1 248 A3
Valletort Pk TQ5 230 A4
Valletort Pl PL1 248 A2
Valletort Rd PL1,PL3 248 A3
Valley Cl Barnstaple EX32 155 B5
Teignmouth TQ14 124 E1
Valley Dr PL9 140 D8
Valley La 6 EX34 3 A3
Valley of Rocks The* EX35 5 A6
Valley Park Cl EX4 173 D2
Valley Path TQ12 206 E4
Valley Rd
Clyst St Mary EX5 179 E3
Exeter EX4 176 F7
Plymouth PL7 250 B5
Valley Rd *continued*
Saltash PL12 242 E2
Valley View
Axminster EX13 167 E5
Bampton EX16 34 B3
Bideford EX39 156 D2
Chagford TQ13 111 A6
Farway EX24 101 F6
Landkey EX32 17 C1
Millmoor EX15 51 E1
Plymouth PL6 245 D7
Seaton EX12 192 A6
Shebbear EX21 55 E4
Valley View Cl
Plymouth PL3 249 B6
Seaton EX12 192 B6
Torquay TQ1 219 F7
Valley View Rd PL3 249 B7
Valley Way EX8 196 E3
Valley Wlk PL6 245 E6
Valleyside TQ7 143 A2
Van Buren Pl EX2 178 D3
Van Post EX16 49 D6
Vanehill Rd TQ1 220 C3
Vanguard Cl PL5 244 D1
Vanpost Hill EX16 49 D5
Vansittart Dr EX8 196 C3
Vansittart Rd TQ2 219 F6
Vapron Rd PL3 248 F6
Varco Sq EX2 178 C4
Varian Ct 4 TQ9 223 E5
Varley Ct EX16 161 E6
Vauban Pl PL2 247 F4
Vaughan Cl PL2 248 C7
Vaughan Par TQ2 220 B4
Vaughan Rd Exeter EX1 178 B6
Torquay TQ2 220 B3
Vaughan Rise EX1 178 B6
Vauxhall Ct 11 PL4 263 A2
Vauxhall St PL4 263 A2
Vauxhall Street Flats 19 PL4 263 A2
Vavasours Slip TQ6 233 F4
Veale Cl EX20 75 B6
Vealenia Terr TQ13 130 F4
Veales Rd TQ7 258 C4
Veasypark PL9 140 D8
Veille La TQ2 219 C8
Veitch Gdns EX2 181 B8
Velator Cl EX33 152 D4
Velator Dr EX33 152 D4
Velator Lane Ave EX33 152 D5
Velator Rd EX33 152 D4
Vellacott La EX34 3 C3
Vellaford Cross EX20 75 E7
Velland Ave TQ2 213 F4
Vellator Way EX33 152 D4
Velwell Rd EX4 261 A4
Venborough Cl EX12 191 F8
Venbridge Hill EX6 97 B4
Venford Cl TQ4 229 B8
Venford Hill
East Anstey TA22 32 E8
Hawkridge TA22 21 D1
Venford Villas EX36 30 D4
Venhay Cross EX36 46 D6
Venlake DT7 260 A5
Venlake Cl DT7 260 A5
Venlake End DT7 260 A5
Venlake Mdw DT7 260 A5
Venlock Cl EX32 155 D4
Venmore Orch EX5 184 B2
Venn Cl Instow EX39 15 C2
6 Plymouth PL3 248 E6
Stoke Fleming TQ6 146 B7
Venn Cotts EX39 15 C2
Venn Cres PL3 248 E6
Venn Cross
Barnstaple EX32 155 D1
Broadhempston TQ12 131 D4
East Allington TQ9 144 E5
Stoke Fleming TQ6 146 B8
Ugborough PL21 137 E7
Waterrow TA4 35 D3
West Putford EX22 39 D3
Venn Ct Brixton PL8 257 A4
Plymouth PL3 248 E6
Venn Dr PL8 257 A4
Venn Gdns PL3 248 E7
Venn Gr PL3 248 E6
Venn Hill
Copplestone EX17 79 B8
Milton Abbot PL19 116 A6
Venn La
Cheriton Fitzpaine EX17 63 A1
Dartmouth TQ6 233 B1
Plymouth PL2,PL3 248 C6
Stoke Fleming TQ6 146 A8
Venn La End EX32 17 B1
Venn Ottery Rd EX10 186 E8
Venn Pk TQ6 146 B8
Venn Rd EX32 155 C1
Venn Way Plymouth PL3 248 E7
Stoke Fleming TQ6 146 B7
Venny Bridge EX4 174 D1
Ventiford Cotts TQ12 123 C2
Vention La EX33 7 E3
Vention Rd EX33 7 E3
Venton Cross
Highampton EX21 74 E6
Totnes TQ9 135 F3
Venton Dr EX39 156 D7
Venture Ct TQ12 207 A3
Verbena Terr TQ14 209 D5
Vermont Gdns PL2 247 F7
Verna Pl PL5 243 D2
Verna Rd PL5 243 E2
Verney St EX1 261 C4
Vernhill Cross PL7 132 E3
Vernon Cl TQ1 220 C2
Vernon Rd EX8 196 D2
Vernons La 25 EX39 15 A1
Verona Ct 3 EX32 155 A6
Verwill La EX34 3 D3
Vestry Dr EX2 181 B8
Viaduct View EX22 164 C4
Vial's Cnr EX16 48 D5
Vicarage Ball TQ9 222 C2
Vicarage Cl Brixham TQ5 230 C5
Hartland EX39 22 D3
Stoke Gabriel TQ9 227 F7
Vicarage Gdns
Dawlish EX7 204 C6
Milton Abbot PL19 116 A6
Plymouth PL5 243 B1
Vicarage Gr TQ9 227 F8
Vicarage Hill
Cornwood PL21 133 D3
Dartmouth TQ6 233 E3
Dulverton TA22 33 D6
Holbeton PL8 136 D1
Kingsteignton TQ12 207 F7
Marldon TQ3 218 E3
Torquay TQ2 219 D4
Vicarage La
15 Chudleigh TQ13 123 E6
Exeter EX4 174 E2
Longdown EX6 98 E1
South Tawton EX20 95 B5
Strete TQ6 145 F6
Vicarage Lawn EX32 155 A5
Vicarage Rd
Abbotskerswell TQ12 212 B6
Blackawton TQ9 139 E1
Brixham TQ5 230 C2
Cockwood EX6 201 B6
East Budleigh EX9 198 B6
Landkey EX32 17 B2
Marldon TQ3 218 E2
Okehampton EX20 170 A5
Plymouth PL7 250 C6
Sidmouth EX10 188 B4
South Brent TQ10 134 F3
Stoke Gabriel TQ9 227 F8
Torpoint PL11 247 B2
Torquay TQ2 219 D4
Vicarage St
Barnstaple EX32 155 A5
Colyton EX24 103 A5
Vicary Cl TQ12 207 A3
Vickers Ground EX39 156 F8
Vickery Cl EX15 163 B3
Vicrage Hill TQ5 230 C5
Victor La EX1 178 A5
Victor St EX1 178 A5
Victoria Ave PL1 262 A4
Victoria Cl
5 Barnstaple EX32 155 B4
Kenton EX6 194 D3
Willand EX15 162 D4
Victoria Cottage Hospl EX10 188 B4
Victoria Cotts
2 Holsworthy EX22 164 C4
Lee Mill PL21 136 D6
North Tawton EX20 77 C4
Plymouth PL6 249 B8
Victoria Cres EX17 165 D6
Victoria Ct
Dartmouth TQ6 233 D3
4 Totnes TQ9 223 C5
Victoria Gdns 1 EX39 157 A1
Victoria Gr EX39 157 A1
Victoria Hill EX22 164 C5
Victoria Hts TQ6 233 D3
Victoria La PL12 242 F2
Victoria Lawn EX32 155 B4
Victoria Par TQ1 220 B3
Victoria Park Rd
Exeter EX2 177 E5
Torquay TQ1 220 B7
Victoria Pl
Axminster EX13 167 D6
Brixham TQ5 230 C6
Budleigh Salterton EX9 199 G2
Chardstock EX13 88 A7
Dartmouth TQ6 233 F3
6 Exmouth EX8 202 A6
Newton Abbot TQ12 207 C3
Plymouth PL1 262 A2
Plymouth, Devonport PL2 247 F4
Victoria Rd
Barnstaple EX32 155 A4
Barnstaple EX32 155 B4
Black Torrington EX21 74 A8
Brixham TQ5 230 F6
Dartmouth TQ6 233 E3
1 Exeter EX4 177 D8
Exmouth EX8 201 F6
Hatherleigh EX20 75 C7
Ilfracombe EX34 150 B5
Plymouth PL5 243 D2
Saltash PL12 242 F2
Sidmouth EX10 188 B4
Topsham EX3 182 F5
Torquay TQ1 220 B6
Victoria Road Prim Sch PL5 243 D1
Victoria Sh Ctr TQ4 226 C6
Victoria Sq
3 Holsworthy EX22 164 C4
Paignton TQ4 226 C6
Victoria St
Barnstaple EX32 155 B4
Combe Martin EX34 3 B3
Exeter EX4 177 D8
Victoria St *continued*
Holsworthy EX22 164 C4
Okehampton EX20 170 C5
Paignton TQ4 226 B6
Torpoint PL11 247 B3
Totnes TQ9 223 C5
Wellington TA21 160 D6
Victoria Terr
Barnstaple EX32 155 A4
2 Bovey Tracey TQ13 180 D8
3 Brixham TQ5 230 C4
Honiton EX14 166 B6
Kingsteignton TQ12 207 E7
Ottery St Mary EX11 169 C3
Plymouth PL4 262 C4
Tiverton EX16 161 B4
Victoria Way EX8 201 F6
Victory Rd
Dartmouth TQ6 233 D3
North Tamerton EX22 89 D8
Victory St PL2 247 E6
Vieux Cl EX9 198 E7
View Rd DT7 260 D3
Vigo Mews PL19 171 C6
Vigobridge Rd PL19 171 C6
Villa Cl EX32 155 B2
Villa Rd EX38 159 C5
Village Cl EX8 202 F7
Village Cross
Coldridge EX17 59 F2
Loddiswell TQ7 143 E7
Morchard Bishop EX17 61 B2
Village Cross Rd TQ7 143 E7
Village Dr PL6 241 C1
Village Farm Cl EX23 70 A6
Village La EX14 86 B1
Village Rd Christow EX6 113 B3
Marldon TQ3 218 D3
Woodbury Salterton EX5 184 C6
Village St 9 EX32 16 E1
Village The PL20 126 C3
Village Way PL19 117 F4
Villiers Ave TQ12 207 F2
Villiers Cl PL9 255 D7
Vincent Way PL12 242 F2
Vincents Rd TQ7 258 D5
Vine Cl EX2 261 C2
Vine Cres PL2 248 B6
Vine Gdns PL2 248 B6
Vine Pas EX14 166 C6
Vine Rd TQ2 219 F6
Vine St EX19 58 F2
Vinery La PL7,PL9 250 E1
Vinery The TQ1 220 B4
Viney Cross EX14 86 B6
Viney La Monkton EX14 86 C7
Upottery EX14 68 C1
Viney Lane Cross EX14 86 B5
Vineyard TQ9 223 A8
Vineyard Hill TQ9 223 A8
Vineyard La EX13 167 C7
Vineyard Terr TQ9 144 D7
Vineyards The EX22 164 C5
Vineycroft La EX10 188 F7
Vinivers Cross TQ8 148 F4
Vinnicombes Rd EX5 173 F8
Vinstone Way PL5 243 D1
Violet Dr PL6 245 E8
Violet La PL19 171 E6
Virginia Cl EX39 157 A1
Virginia Gdns PL2 247 F7
Virginia Lodge 12 TQ1 220 D4
Vision Hill Rd EX9 198 B2
Visitors Hill EX16 63 D4
Vittery Cl TQ5 230 B5
Vix Ct TQ5 230 B5
Vixen Tor Cl
Okehampton EX20 170 E5
Yelverton PL20 126 F3
Vognacott Cross EX22 53 F3
Voscombe Cross EX31 26 F7
Voulsdon Cross EX20 92 A4
Voysey Hill EX17 62 F1
Vuefield Hill EX2 176 E3
Vulscombe Cross EX16 63 A6
Vulscombe La EX16 63 B6
Vyvyan Ct EX1 178 A5

W

Wadbrook Cross EX13 88 C4
Waddens Cross EX24 102 D4
Wadderly Hill EX17 79 F7
Waddeton Cl TQ4 225 F1
Waddeton Ind Est TQ4 225 F1
Waddeton Rd
Paignton TQ4 225 F1
Stoke Gabriel TQ5 228 D6
Waddington Cross EX36 31 A3
Waddington La EX18 45 A5
Waddles Down Cross EX4 98 E5
Waddon Cl PL7 250 E7
Waddons Cross TQ9 216 C6
Wade Cl EX8 202 E8
Wadham Cross
Knowstone EX36 32 A2
West Anstey EX36 32 A4
Wadham Hill EX36 32 A2
Wadham Ho EX4 173 A1
Wadham Terr 6 PL2 248 A5
Waggon Hill PL7 251 A4
Waggoners Way EX4 177 A8
Waggs Plot EX13 88 B4
Waie Cotts EX17 78 C6
Waie Cross EX17 78 B6
Wain La TQ12 207 A4

Wain Pk PL7 250 F4
Wake St PL4 262 B4
Wakefield Ave PL5 243 E1
Wakehams Cl PL21 137 C2
Walborough CE Prim Sch TQ12 207 C3
Walcot Cl PL6 245 E3
Walcott Way EX14 67 C1
Walden Rd EX14 67 C1
Waldon Cl PL7 251 B6
Waldon Ct TQ2 220 B4
Waldon Ho TQ2 220 B4
Waldon Point TQ2 220 B4
Waldon Way EX22 164 C6
Waldons Cross EX19 57 F1
Waldron's Cross TA21 35 E1
Walk La EX36 30 F6
Walker Terr PL1 262 B1
Walkers Gate TA21 160 D5
Walkham Bsns Pk PL5 244 B1
Walkham Cl PL19 171 D5
Walkham Mdws PL20 126 F4
Walkham Rise TQ2 219 B8
Walkham Terr 5 PL20 126 F5
Walkhampton Rd PL20 126 F4
Walkhampton Wlk PL6 245 E1
Wall Park Cl TQ5 230 E5
Wall Park Rd TQ5 230 E5
Wall Pk TQ9 222 F6
Wallace Ave Dawlish EX7 204 E7
Exeter EX4 178 B8
Torquay TQ2 219 C8
Wallace La
Kingsbridge TQ7 258 B3
Lynton EX35 5 A3
Wallace Rd PL7 251 A4
Wallaford Rd TQ11 135 C8
Walland Cross EX32 18 E3
Wallaton Cross TQ9 145 A7
Wallfield Rd TQ13 180 B5
Wallingford Rd TQ7 258 D6
Wallis Gr TQ14 209 A8
Wallon Cross TQ13 110 F7
Wallpark Cl PL7 250 F7
Walls Cl EX8 196 D2
Walls Hill Rd TQ1 220 D7
Walnut Cl Exminster EX6 182 A4
Plymouth PL7 251 B5
Totnes TQ9 223 B6
Walnut Ct Brixham TQ5 230 D4
Torquay TQ2 219 E4
Walnut Dr Crediton EX17 165 D6
Plymouth PL7 251 C5
Tiverton EX16 161 F5
Walnut Gdns PL7 251 C5
Walnut Gr EX8 202 C7
Walnut La TQ2 219 E4
Walnut Rd Exeter EX2 177 F2
Honiton EX14 166 A4
Torquay TQ2 219 E4
Walnut Way EX32 155 D4
Walpole Cl EX4 174 C1
Walreddon Cl PL19 171 B4
Walshams EX14 87 A7
Walsingham Ct PL7 251 B6
Walson Cross EX17 78 D3
Walson La EX19 76 E7
Walson Rd EX17 78 D3
Waltacre PL8 257 F3
Walter Daw Fst Sch EX2 178 B4
Walters Rd PL5 243 C2
Waltham Pl PL2 248 A8
Waltham Rd TQ12 207 A3
Waltham Way PL21 237 E4
Walton Cres PL5 244 C1
Walton Rd EX2 178 C5
Walton Way EX32 155 C5
Wandle Pl PL3 249 D5
Wanstead Gr PL5 244 A2
Wantage Gdns PL1 262 A3
Warberry CE Prim Sch TQ1 220 C5
Warberry Rd W TQ1 220 B5
Warberry Vale 3 TQ1 220 B6
Warboro Terr EX6 201 B8
Warborough Hill EX6 194 E3
Warborough Rd TQ5 229 C6
Warbrightsleigh Hill EX16 48 B7
Warbro Ct 1 TQ1 220 B7
Warbro Rd TQ1 220 C7
Warburton Gdns PL5 243 C1
Warcombe La EX34 1 B2
Ward La EX19 59 A2
Ward Pl PL3 249 B5
Wardens Cl EX37 43 B7
Wardleworth Way TA21 160 C7
Wardlow Cl PL6 248 F8
Wardlow Gdns PL6 248 F8
Wardrew Rd EX4 176 F5
Wards Cross EX5 99 C8
Ware Cl TQ12 207 F7
Ware Cliff Chalets DT7 260 D2
Ware Cross
Kingsteignton TQ12 207 F7
Ugborough PL21 137 D6
Ware La DT7 260 B2
Warecroft Rd TQ12 207 F7
Warecross Gdns TQ12 207 F7
Warefield Rd TQ3 226 C7
Wareham Cross EX13 88 E1
Wareham Rd EX13 88 E2
Waresfoot Dr EX17 165 B6
Warfelton Cres PL12 242 E2
Warfelton Gdns PL12 242 E2
Warfelton Terr PL12 242 E2
Warfield Villas EX34 150 C5
Warfleet Creek Rd TQ6 234 A1
Warfleet Rd TQ6 234 A2
Waring Bowen Ct EX2 177 F1
Waring Rd PL6 244 D7
Warkidons Way EX5 185 A5
Warkleigh Cross EX37 29 B1
Warland TQ9 223 C5
Warleigh Ave PL2 247 E5
Warleigh Cres PL6 244 F5
Warleigh La PL2 247 E5
Warleigh Rd 1 PL4 248 E4
Warm Hill TQ13 123 B7
Warmwell Rd PL5 243 E4
Warne La PL19 117 E6
Warneford Gdns EX8 196 E2
Warnicombe La EX16 64 D6
Warran La PL19 171 C3
Warraton Cl PL12 242 D3
Warraton Gn PL12 242 D3
Warraton La PL12 242 D3
Warraton Rd PL12 242 D3
Warren Cl
Great Torrington EX38 159 C5
Wembury PL9 140 D7
West Hill EX11 168 D4
Warren Cotts PL9 140 E6
Warren Cross EX16 161 B7
Warren Dr EX9 198 B2
Warren Hill TQ2 220 B4
Warren La
Dartington TQ9 216 B3
Exeter EX4 261 B4
Farway EX24 102 A7
Great Torrington EX38 159 C5
Lee Mill PL21 136 D6
Plymouth PL5 244 A8
Wembury PL9 140 E7
Warren Pk Plymouth PL6 245 D7
West Hill EX11 168 D4
Warren Rd
Bigbury-on-Sea TQ7 142 E3
Dawlish EX7 205 A8
Kingsbridge TQ7 258 E3
Mary Tavy PL19 117 E6
Thurlestone TQ7 143 A1
Torquay TQ2 220 B4
Warren St Plymouth PL2 247 E4
Rockwell Green TA21 160 A4
Warren The TQ12 206 F3
Warren View EX39 156 E2
Warrens Mead EX10 188 D8
Warspite Gdns PL5 244 D2
Warton Cl PL5 244 D3
Warwick Ave Exeter EX1 178 C5
Plymouth PL5 244 D3
Warwick Cl Feniton EX14 84 E2
Torquay TQ1 220 E7
Warwick Orchard Cl PL5 244 B3
Warwick Rd EX1 178 C6
Warwick Terr 7 EX32 154 F6
Warwick Way EX4 178 C8
Wasdale Cl PL6 245 D2
Wasdale Gdns PL6 245 D2
Wash Cross TQ11 215 B8
Washabrook La TQ7 258 E6
Washabrook Way TQ7 258 E5
Washbourne Cl
Brixham TQ5 230 E5
Plymouth PL1 247 E3
Washbourne Cross TQ9 139 D6
Washbrook View EX11 169 E4
Washfield La
Calverleigh EX16 48 F2
Tiverton EX16 161 B7
Washford Pyne Cross EX17 61 E4
Washington Cl TQ3 219 B1
Wastor Cross PL21 142 D7
Wastor Pk PL21 142 D7
Watch The TQ7 143 A2
Watching Place Cross TQ13 111 B3
Watcombe Heights Rd TQ1 214 C4
Watcombe Prim Sch TQ2 214 B3
Water Bridge Cross EX17 78 F6
Water Cotts TQ13 121 F7
Water Gate EX2 261 B2
Water La
Barnstaple EX32 155 B3
Bow EX17 78 C4
Combe Martin EX34 3 A3
Cornworthy TQ9 227 A3
Exeter EX2 177 C3
Kingskerswell TQ12 213 A4
Sidmouth EX10 188 B5
Tiverton EX16 161 D4
Torquay TQ2 219 C8
Water Lane Cl 2 EX32 155 B3
Water Lane End TQ9 215 B3
Water Mdw EX15 163 C2
Water Park Rd EX39 156 D2
Water Terr 10 EX34 3 A3
Water Turn TQ13 130 E5
Waterbeer St EX4 261 A3
Waterdale Farm TQ12 213 A4
Waterford Cross TQ9 131 E1
Waterford La EX13 103 C5
Watergate Cotts PL9 140 D8
Watergate Cross EX20 107 E6
Waterhaynes La TA20 68 F8
Waterhead Cl TQ6 234 B4
Waterhead Terr TQ6 234 B4
Waterhouse Cross EX17 62 E1
Waterhouse Hill EX20 74 F1
Waterhouse La EX13, EX14 87 C6
Watering Ct EX9 198 E7
Waterlake La EX31 16 A7
Waterlake Rd TA20 88 C8
Waterlears Cross TQ7 147 D8
Waterleat Ave
Honiton EX14 166 D5
Paignton TQ3 225 E6
Waterleat Cl TQ3 225 F5
Waterleat Ct TQ3 225 F5
Waterleat Rd TQ3 225 E5
Waterloo Cl PL1 248 A2
Waterloo Cross EX15 65 F8
Waterloo Ct PL1 248 A2
Waterloo Hill EX16 47 B6
Waterloo Rd Exeter EX2 177 A3
Holsworthy EX22 164 D5
Kingsbridge TQ7 258 D6
Torquay TQ1 220 B6
Wellington TA21 160 C6
Waterloo St
Plymouth PL4 263 A4
Plymouth, Stoke PL1 248 A3
14 Teignmouth TQ14 210 C4
Waterloo Terr 1 EX39 156 F1
Waterloo Yard Flats PL1 248 A2
Watermead TA20 88 D8
Watermill Ct 5 TQ5 230 C4
Watermore Ct EX4 177 E7
Watermouth Castle★ EX34 2 D3
Watermouth Rd EX34 150 E6
Waterpool Rd TQ6 233 E2
Waterside Exeter EX2 261 A1
Kingsbridge TQ7 258 D4
Waterside Ho
Ivybridge PL21 237 C4
8 Totnes TQ9 223 D5
Waterside Rd TQ4 226 C1
Waterslade Dr PL21 237 F4
Waterslade La EX5 179 E8
Watersmeet★ EX35 5 E5
Watersmeet Ho★ EX35 5 E5
Watersmeet Rd EX35 151 E4
Waterstream Sq 5 TQ13 123 F6
Waterwell La TQ12 213 C8
Waterworks La TQ14 209 D4
Watery La Axminster EX13 88 A3
Barnstaple, Beara EX31 9 A1
Barnstaple, Whiddon EX31 9 C1
Braunton EX33 152 F5
Budlake EX5 82 E3
Colyton EX13,EX24 103 A6
Combe Martin EX34 3 A3
Croyde EX33 7 E2
Great Torrington EX38 159 E5
Great Torrington, Taddiport EX38 159 B4
Milton Combe PL6 240 D6
Thorverton EX5 81 F3
Tiverton EX16 161 E5
Woodbury EX5 184 B4
Watkins Way TQ3 225 D7
Watson Gdns PL4 263 B3
Watson Pl PL4 263 B2
Watts Park Rd PL2 248 C7
Watts Rd PL19 171 B5
Watts' Rd PL4 263 C3
Waveney Gdns PL5 244 C3
Waverley Ave EX4 261 B4
Waverley Rd
Exmouth EX8 202 A8
Kingsbridge TQ7 258 C4
Newton Abbot TQ12 207 B4
Plymouth PL5 243 D2
Wavish Pk PL11 246 E3
Way Cnr EX16 63 A5
Way Cross EX20 107 D8
Way Down Cross TQ13 110 F8
Way La EX6 98 B5
Way's La EX15 163 C2
Waybrook Cotts EX2 181 B7
Waybrook Cres EX2 181 C8
Waybrook La EX2 181 B6
Waycott Wlk PL6 244 D6
Waye Cross TQ13 110 E5
Wayfaring EX32 155 D3
Wayland Ave EX2 261 C1
Wayside Brixham TQ5 230 A4
Ivybridge PL21 237 C4
Wayside Cl TQ5 230 A4
Wayside Cres EX1 178 B7
Waytown Cross TQ9 131 D2
Wear Barton Rd EX2 182 B7
Wear Cl EX2 182 C7
Wearde Rd PL12 242 E1
Weatherdon Dr PL21 237 F5
Weatherill Rd EX14 166 C4
Weaver Cross EX15 83 E6
Weaver Ct TQ2 219 B8
Weaver La EX15 83 E7
Weavers Ct EX2 261 A2
Weavers Way TQ12 213 A4
Weavers Wlk EX15 163 B2
Webber Cl TQ12 211 F8
Webbers CE Prim Sch TA21 50 F5
Webbers Cl
Wellington TA21 160 E4
Whimple EX5 99 E8
Webbers Way
Dartington TQ9 222 F8
Willand EX15 162 D4
Webbers Yard Est TQ9 222 E8
Webberton Cross EX2 113 F6
Webbery Cross EX39 26 D4
Webbery Moor Cross EX36 31 A3
Webble Green Cross EX13 87 C8
Webland La TQ10 135 C3
Webley Rd EX2 176 F3
Weddicott Cross TQ13 111 A4
Wedding Well La EX33 8 F1
Weech Cl EX7 204 C6
Weech Rd EX7 204 C6
Week Cross
Bishop's Tawton EX31 27 F6
Burrington EX37 43 C5
Chulmleigh EX18 45 D3
Moretonhampstead TQ13 111 C4
South Zeal EX20 95 B3
Witheridge EX16 62 D6
Zeal Monachorum EX17 78 C7
Week La
Dawlish Warren EX7 201 A1
High Bickington EX37 43 D5
Week Lane End EX31 27 F5
Week Park Cross EX37 43 C5
Weekaborough Dr TQ3 218 D2
Weekaborough Oak Cross TQ12 217 E4
Weeke Cross PL21 137 D4
Weeke Hill TQ6 146 C8
Weekes Mdw TA21 51 E6
Weeksland Rd TQ2 219 C6
Weekstone Cross EX22 71 B8
Weir Cl PL6 245 F2
Weir Gdns PL6 245 F2
Weir Head Cotts TA22 33 D7
Weir Rd PL6 245 F2
Weirfield Ho EX2 261 B1
Weirfield Rd EX2 261 B1
Weirfields TQ9 223 C6
Weirford La EX20 76 F4
Weirside Pl EX2 261 B1
Weirside Way EX32 155 B6
Welbeck Ave PL4 262 C4
Welch's La EX31 15 C2
Welcombe Cross EX39 37 E4
Welcome St EX2 261 A1
Weld Park Ave 1 EX34 150 D5
Well Cross PL21 137 E6
Well Gdns PL1 262 B3
Well Hill TQ7 147 E6
Well Hill Cl TQ7 147 E6
Well La EX39 37 B5
Well Mead EX13 87 C1
Well Oak Pk EX2 177 F3
Well Park Flats EX38 159 D5
Well Park Rd
Great Torrington EX38 159 D5
Torpoint PL11 247 B3
Well Spring Cl EX39 22 E3
Well St Exeter EX4 261 C4
Great Torrington EX38 159 D5
Paignton TQ3 226 B6
Starcross EX6 201 B8
Well The TA21 160 B5
Welland Gdns PL3 249 C5
Wellands Cl EX15 66 B7
Wellands Cross EX13 87 D4
Wellbrook Gn EX16 161 B4
Wellbrook St EX16 161 C4
Wellbrook Terr
8 Tiverton EX16 161 B4
11 Bideford EX39 157 A1
Wellclose Rd EX33 152 D5
Welle House Gdns TQ7 258 D6
Wellesley Park Prim Sch TA21 160 E4
Wellesley Pk TA21 160 D4
Wellesley Rd TQ1 220 B6
Wellesley Way TA3 68 D7
Wellfield Cl PL7 251 C5
Wellfield Hill EX13,DT6 88 H2
Wellhay Cl PL9 256 C6
Welling Cl TA20 88 C8
Wellings Cl TA20 88 C8
Wellington Cottage Hospl TA21 160 D5
Wellington Hill TA21 160 F2
Wellington Jun Sch TA21 160 E5
Wellington Mus TA21 160 D6
Wellington Pl 1 TQ1 220 B6
Wellington Rd
Exeter EX2 177 A3
Torquay TQ1 220 B6
Wellington Sch TA21 160 E5
Wellington Sq 14 TQ10 134 F3
Wellington St
Plymouth PL4 263 A4
Plymouth, Stoke PL1 248 A3
13 Teignmouth TQ14 210 C4
Torpoint PL11 247 B3
Wellpark Cl EX4 176 F6
Wellpark Rd PL18 125 C5
Wells Ave EX14 84 E2
Wells Cl EX8 196 E4
Wells Ct PL10 252 E4
Wells St EX32 154 F5
Wellsbourne Pk PL3 249 A6
Wellsprings La EX20 76 F3
Wellstones Cl PL21 237 E4
Wellswood Ave TQ1 220 E5
Wellswood Gdns
Exeter EX4 176 E5
Torquay TQ1 220 E5
Wellswood Manor 2 TQ1 220 D5
Wellswood Path TQ1 220 D5
Wellswood Pk TQ1 220 D5
Welman Rd PL10 252 F6
Welsbere La EX17 62 C3
Welsford Ave PL2 247 F5
Welstor Cross TQ13 130 D7
Wembury Dr TQ2 214 B2
Wembury Marine Ctr★ PL9 140 C7
Wembury Mdw 1 PL9 140 D8
Wembury Park Rd PL3 248 D6
Wembury Prim Sch PL9 140 D8
Wembury Rd
Plymouth PL9 256 A4
Wembury PL9 140 E8
Wembworthy Down La EX18 59 C4
Wendover Way EX2 178 B2
Wenlock Gdns PL2 248 B8
Wensum Cl PL7 251 A4
Wentwood Gdns PL6 245 E3
Wentwood Pl PL6 245 E3
Wentworth Gdns EX4 176 E4
Wentworth Pl PL4 249 B2
Wentworth Rd TQ12 180 F3
Wentworth Way PL12 242 C2
Wesley Ave PL3 248 E5
Wesley Cl
3 Tiverton EX16 64 D7
Torquay TQ2 214 A3
Wesley Ct PL11 247 C3
Wesley La PL12 242 F2
Wesley Mews TQ2 214 A2
Wesley Pl
Plymouth, Mutley PL3 248 E5
1 Plymouth, Stoke PL2 248 A4
Wesley Rd PL12 242 F2
Wesley Terr TQ12 211 D2
Wesley View TQ12 211 D2
Wesley Way EX2 181 B8
Wessex Cl EX3 182 D6
Wessex Est EX4 177 A7
Wessiters EX12 192 A5
West & East Putford Prim Sch EX22 39 C2
West Acres EX12 191 F7
West Alvington Butts TQ7 143 E2
West Alvington CE Prim Sch TQ7 258 A4
West Alvington Hill TQ7 258 C5
West Anstey School Cross EX36 32 C5
West Ave
Barnstaple EX31 154 D3
Exeter EX4 177 C8
4 Tavistock PL19 171 B5
West Ball Hill EX39 22 D3
West Barton La EX20 76 E4
West Beckon Cl EX23 37 A1
West Brushford La EX18 59 C2
West Buckeridge TQ14 210 B6
West Buckland Com Prim Sch TA21 52 F7
West Buckland Cross EX32 18 B2
West Buckland Rd TA21 52 D7
West Buckland Sch EX32 18 C2
West Burridge Cross EX18 60 E7
West Challacombe La EX34 3 A4
West Charleton Ct TQ7 144 C1
West Cl EX13 167 C5
West Cliff EX7 204 E6
West Cliff Cl EX7 204 D5
West Cliff Park Dr EX7 204 D5
West Cliff Rd EX7 204 D6
West Cliff Terr 2 EX12 192 A4
West Coombe La TA4 35 D8
West Cotts TA24 13 A2
West Country Amb Trust HQ EX2 178 F5
West Croft Jun Sch EX39 156 F1
West Croft Rd EX22 164 B4
West Cross EX33 152 D6
West Devon Bsns Pk PL19 171 B3
West Down EX16 65 A6
West Down Hill EX33,EX34 8 F4
West Down La EX8 203 A6
West Down Prim Sch EX34 8 F5
West Down Rd PL2 248 B6
West Down View EX8 203 B6
West Efford La EX17 81 A4
West Emlett La EX17 61 E3
West End EX16 48 D5
West End Cross EX16 48 D5
West End La EX16 48 D5
West End Rd
Bradninch EX5 82 F6
Buckfastleigh TQ11 236 B4
West End Terr
Ashburton TQ13 130 F4
Denbury TQ12 211 A6
South Molton EX36 158 C4
West Exe N EX16 161 C4
West Exe S EX16 161 C3
West Exe Tech Coll EX2 177 A2
West Field Rd EX6 182 B3
West Ford Dr TA21 160 A5
West Garth Ct EX4 172 F2
West Garth Rd EX4 173 A3
West Grove Rd EX2 261 C2

West Hill
Budleigh Salterton EX9 203 F8
Heybrook Bay PL9 140 A7
Heybrook Bay PL9 140 B7
West Hill Ct EX9 203 F8
West Hill La
Braunton EX33 152 C6
Budleigh Salterton EX9 197 F1
Parracombe EX31 4 B2
West Hill Prim Sch EX11 168 D4
West Hill Rd
Lyme Regis DT7 260 D3
Plymouth PL4 248 F4
West Hill EX11 168 D4
West Hoe Rd PL1 262 B1
West La
Bratton Fleming EX31 11 D4
Dolton EX19 57 E6
Knowle EX33 8 C2
Lapford EX17 60 C3
Paignton TQ3 225 A6
West Leigh Cross TQ9 135 F1
West Lyn Rd EX35 151 C2
West Malling Ave PL5 243 E5
West Manley La EX16 64 E7
West Meadow Cl EX33 152 B7
West Meadow Rd EX33 152 A7
West Mill Cross TQ11 236 B4
West Molland La EX36 31 D7
West Moor Cl EX39 156 F8
West Moor Way EX39 156 F8
West Mount TQ12 207 D1
West of England Sch for Children with Little or no Sight EX2 178 B1
West Ogwell Cross TQ12 211 C8
West Pafford Ave TQ2 214 B3
West Park Dr PL7 251 C5
West Park Hill PL7 251 B7
West Park Prim Sch PL5 244 A2
West Park Rd EX10 188 A5
West Pk Braunton EX33 152 C6
Galmpton TQ7 147 B7
South Molton EX36 158 B4
Stoke Fleming TQ6 146 B8
West Point (County Showground) EX5 179 C3
West Pugsley Cross EX37 29 A2
West Rd Roborough EX19 42 F4
Sheepwash EX21 56 C1
Woolacombe EX34 7 F6
West Spurway La EX16 48 A8
West St Ashburton TQ13 130 F4
Axminster EX13 167 D5
Bampton EX16 34 B1
Bishops Nympton EX36 30 F2
Bishopsteignton TQ14 208 F8
Denbury TQ12 211 A6
Exeter EX1,EX4 261 A2
Hartland EX39 22 D3
Millbrook PL10 252 E5
Okehampton EX20 170 B5
South Molton EX36 158 C4
Tavistock PL19 171 B5
Witheridge EX16 46 E1
West Terr
Budleigh Salterton EX9 198 A1
Churston Ferrers TQ5 229 E4
Exeter EX1 177 F6
West Town Cross EX39 38 E8
West Town Mdw TQ14 208 E8
West Town Rd EX5 98 F8
West Ugworthy Cross EX22 53 E3
West Underleys EX12 191 C5
West View Beer EX12 191 D5
Holsworthy EX22 164 C5
Tavistock PL19 171 E2
West View Ave EX39 157 B2
West View Cl TQ12 206 F1
West View Rd
5 Bere Alston PL20 125 E1
Marldon TQ3 218 D2
Okehampton EX20 170 C5
West View Terr
Exeter EX4 261 A2
3 Honiton EX14 166 B6
Lympstone EX8 195 F5
West Waters La EX31 4 D5
West Yelland EX31 15 C2
West Yeo Cross EX16 46 C2
West Yeo Moor Hill EX16 46 C3
Westabrook Ave TQ13 130 F5
Westabrook Cl TQ13 130 F5
Westabrook Dr TQ13 130 F5
Westacombe EX31 27 B8
Westacott Cross
Inwardleigh EX20 75 C3
North Tawton EX20 77 E5
South Molton EX36 45 E8
Westacott La
Coldridge EX17 59 E2
East Buckland EX32 18 D2
North Tawton EX20 77 E5
Westacott Mdw EX32 155 E3
Westacott Rd EX32 155 E4
Westaway EX31 153 E5
Westaway Cl EX31 155 A7
Westaway Plain EX31 155 A8
Westaway Rd 6 EX24 103 A4
Westbourne Gr EX34 150 A5
Westbourne Rd
Plymouth PL3 248 D5
Torquay TQ1 220 A7
Westbourne Terr
Budleigh Salterton EX9 203 F8
Saltash PL12 242 F3
Westward Ho! EX39 156 C7
Westbridge Cl EX20 170 B5
Westbridge Cotts PL19 171 B4
Westbrigde Ind Est 3 PL19 171 B4
Westbrook Ave TQ14 210 A5
Westbrook Cl EX4 178 B8
Westbury Cl PL5 244 B4
Westcliff Rd DT6 104 F4
Westcliff Sch EX7 204 C5
Westclyst EX1 175 A3
Westcombe EX2 181 B8
Westcombe Cres PL9 255 D5
Westcombe La EX39 156 F2
Westcombes EX13 88 B7
Westcots Dr EX19 58 F2
Westcott Cl PL6 249 A8
Westcott Cross EX14 66 F2
Westcott La
Aylesbeare EX5 99 D4
Barnstaple EX31 9 A1
Witheridge EX16 61 E7
Westcott Rd 15 EX16 64 D7
Westcott Way EX14 166 D6
Westcountry Cl PL2 247 F7
Westcroft Ct 3 EX39 156 F1
Westcroft Rd PL5 243 D1
Westcroyde EX33 7 D1
Westella Rd PL20 127 A2
Westentown TQ7 142 C6
Wester-Moor Cl 6 EX31 154 A2
Wester-Moor Dr EX31 154 A2
Wester-Moor Way EX31 154 A2
Westeria Terr PL2 248 C7
Westerland TQ6 234 B3
Westerland Gn TQ3 218 D2
Westerland La TQ3 218 D2
Western App PL1 262 B2
Western Ave
Appledore EX39 15 A1
Exeter EX2 182 D7
Western Bsns Pk TQ4 225 F2
Western By-Pass TQ9 223 B5
Western Bye-Pass TQ9 223 B6
Western College Rd PL4 248 F5
Western Cotts EX20 107 E1
Western Dr
Newton Abbot TQ12 206 F4
Plymouth PL3 249 B4
Starcross EX6 201 B8
Western Gardens Rd EX34 3 A3
Western Ho EX7 204 E7
Western Pl 4 EX24 103 A4
Western Rd
Ashburton TQ13 130 F4
Crediton EX17 165 A6
Exeter EX4 177 A5
Holsworthy EX22 164 C4
Ivybridge PL21 237 C4
Newton Abbot TQ12 207 C3
Torquay TQ1 214 B1
Western Rise EX34 8 A6
Western Terr
Barnstaple EX31 154 E5
Ilfracombe EX34 150 A4
Totnes TQ9 223 B6
Western Units TQ13 180 D5
Western Villas EX17 165 B5
Western Way Exeter EX1 261 A2
Exeter EX1,EX2 261 C3
Western Way Ind Est EX15 163 C4
Western Wood Way PL7 251 D5
Westernlea EX17 165 A5
Westfield Bradninch EX5 82 F6
Plymouth PL7 251 A6
Westfield Ave
Barnstaple EX31 154 D4
Plymouth PL9 255 C6
Westfield Cl
Brixham TQ5 230 B3
Budleigh Salterton EX9 198 A1
Westfield Rd
Budleigh Salterton EX9 198 A1
Tiverton EX16 161 C3
Westfield Terr 8 EX16 161 C3
Westford Cl TA21 160 A5
Westgate EX17 60 D3
Westhampnett Pl PL5 243 F4
Westhay Cross EX13 88 F3
Westhayes Cvn Pk DT7 193 D8
Westhays Cl PL9 255 F4
Westhead Rd PL10 140 H2
Westhill Ave TQ1 220 B7
Westhill Avenue Cl TQ1 220 B7
Westhill Cres TQ3 226 B7
Westhill Rd
Paignton TQ3 226 A7
Torquay TQ1 220 B8
Westhill Terr TQ12 213 A4
Westholme TQ1 220 C5
Westlake Cl PL11 246 F3
Westlake Rd PL9 140 A8
Westlake Rise PL9 140 A8
Westland La EX16 62 C6
Westlands Exmouth EX8 202 C6
Wrafton EX33 152 E4
Westlands La TQ1 220 B7
Westlands Lwr Sch TQ1 220 B8
Westlands Upper Sch TQ1 220 C7
Westleat Ave TQ3 225 F6
Westleigh La EX34 3 C2
Westmead Cl EX33 152 C6
Westminster Cl
Exmouth EX8 196 D3
Feniton EX14 84 D2
Westminster Rd EX4 176 E6
Westminster Villas EX34 150 D5
Westmoor Cl PL7 251 C6
Westmoor Pk PL19 171 C4
Weston Cl Brixham TQ5 230 C3
Broadhembury EX14 84 D7
Weston Cross
Awliscombe EX14 85 C3
Sidmouth EX10 189 D8
Weston La
Awliscombe EX14 85 B4
Totnes TQ9 223 E4
Weston Mill Com Prim Sch PL2 247 E7
Weston Mill Dr PL5 247 F8
Weston Mill Hill PL5 243 F1
Weston Mill La PL5 244 A1
Weston Mill Rd PL5 243 E1
Weston Park Rd PL3 248 D6
Weston Rd TQ9 223 D5
Westonfields TQ9 223 E5
Westover Cl
Brixham TQ5 230 D4
Ivybridge PL21 237 B5
Westover Hill DT6 104 F5
Westover Ind Est PL21 237 C4
Westover La PL21 237 B4
Westown Rd EX2 176 C1
Westridge Cross EX16 63 C4
Westview Cl EX5 99 E8
Westward Cl TQ9 223 C5
Westward Dr EX8 202 B7
Westward View TQ12 208 A2
Westwater Hill EX6 97 E5
Westway Cross EX16 61 F8
Westways PL9 255 B5
Westwood Ave PL6 245 C6
Westwood Cl EX17 165 A5
Westwood Cotts EX6 98 E2
Westwood Hill EX6 201 A5
Westwood La EX6 176 B4
Westwood Rd
Crediton EX17 165 A5
East Ogwell TQ12 212 A8
Westwood Units EX2 177 D1
Westwood Way EX12 192 B7
Westworthy Cross EX20 77 E6
Westyard La EX18 58 E8
Wet La Christow EX6 113 B4
15 Combe Martin EX34 3 A3
Wethered Cl EX16 161 C3
Weycroft Ave EX13 167 F7
Weycroft Cl EX1 178 D6
Weymouth Pk TQ7 147 B7
Whalley La DT7 260 B4
Wharf Cotts TA21 160 B8
Wharf Rd TQ12 207 D4
Whatley La TA20 69 A7
Wheadon Cross EX16 46 D4
Wheal Betsy* PL19 117 F8
Wheal Maria Cotts PL19 116 B1
Wheal Rd PL19 117 E6
Wheat Pk TQ9 138 D8
Wheatclose Cross EX36 20 D2
Wheatcombe Ct TQ2 214 B3
Wheatfield Cl EX15 163 B2
Wheatland Cross EX16 48 D6
Wheatland La EX16 48 C6
Wheatlands Rd TQ4 226 B4
Wheatley Cl EX4 176 E5
Wheatley Ct 5 EX1 261 A2
Wheatly La EX31 4 B2
Wheatridge PL7 250 B7
Wheatridge La TQ2 219 E2
Wheatsheaf Way EX2 177 A1
Wheel Cross EX34 2 F1
Wheel La EX34 2 F1
Wheelbarrow La EX15 67 C8
Wheelers Cross EX22 39 B1
Wheelwright Ct PL20 127 B4
Whelmstone Cross EX17 78 E3
Whetcombe Cross PL21 137 F6
Whey Cross EX37 28 D3
Whidborne Ave TQ1 221 A4
Whidborne Cl TQ1 220 F3
Whiddon Cross TQ12 212 B4
Whiddon Dr EX32 155 D3
Whiddon La
Barnstaple EX31 9 D1
Ide EX2 114 A8
Whiddon Rd TQ12 212 B4
Whiddon Valley Ind Est EX32 155 D3
Whidley La EX6 112 E8
Whilborough Rd TQ12 212 E2
Whimble Hill EX22 164 D3
Whimple Prim Sch EX5 99 E8
Whimple St PL1 262 C2
Whimple Sta EX5 99 E8
Whin Bank Rd PL5 244 E2
Whippenscott Hill EX36 46 B8
Whipple's Cross PL21 136 E4
Whipton Barton Ho EX1 178 B7
Whipton Barton Mid Sch EX1 178 B7
Whipton Barton Rd EX1 178 C7
Whipton First Sch EX1 178 B7
Whipton Hospl EX1 178 C7
Whipton La EX1 178 A6
Whipton Rd EX4 178 A8
Whipton Village Rd EX4 178 B8
Whistley Down PL20 126 E2
Whistley Hill TQ13 131 A4
Whistley Hill Cross TQ13 131 A4
Whitby Cres PL6 245 A1
Whitby Rd PL6 245 A1
Whitchurch Ave EX2 178 B4
Whitchurch Prim Sch PL19 171 D2
Whitchurch Rd
Horrabridge PL20 126 F5
Tavistock PL19 171 C3
Whitcott Hill EX36 31 A8
White Ash La TA20 69 D5
White Cl TQ3 219 B2
White Cross
Aylesbeare EX5 99 C1
Cheriton Fitzpaine EX17 62 F1
Malborough TQ7 147 E6
Ottery St Mary EX11 100 F3
White Cross Ct PL4 263 A3
White Cross Hill EX17 62 F1
White Cross Rd EX5 184 D6
White Ct 11 EX7 204 E6
White Down Cross EX16 64 E5
White Farm La EX11 168 D3
White Gate EX24 102 E3
White Gates Cross TQ13 110 F7
White Hart La TA21 160 D6
White Heather Terr TQ13 180 D8
White Hill Dro TA20 69 F5
White La PL1 263 A2
White Ladies TQ6 146 B7
White Lodge EX9 198 B1
White Pk TQ9 139 A3
White Post EX36 20 F2
White Rock Prim Sch TQ4 229 A8
White St EX3 182 F4
White Tor Cl EX20 170 E5
White's La EX38 159 C5
Whiteabury Cross TQ13 111 C7
Whitear Cl TQ14 124 E1
Whitear's Way TQ12 207 E7
Whitebeam Cl
Exeter EX4 174 B2
Paignton TQ3 225 E7
Whitebeam Gr EX14 67 B1
Whitebear Cross EX22 54 F6
Whiteborough La
Chudleigh TQ13 123 D8
Trusham TQ13 113 D1
Whitebridge EX14 166 C5
Whitebridges EX14 166 B4
Whitebrook Terr TA21 50 F5
Whitechapel La EX36 30 F6
Whitecleave Cross EX37 43 F2
Whitedown Cross EX15 67 E4
Whitefield EX14 86 C3
Whitefield Cross EX36 32 D3
Whitefield Hill EX31 9 E2
Whitefield La EX32 19 A6
Whitefield Terr PL4 263 B4
Whiteford Rd PL3 248 E6
Whitefriars La PL4 263 B3
Whitegates EX34 2 F4
Whitehall Cl EX36 158 C3
Whitehall Dr
9 Bere Alston PL20 125 E1
Plymouth PL9 256 B7
Whitehall La EX3 182 F8
Whitehall Manor TQ7 143 E4
Whitehayes Cl EX14 86 D2
Whiteheads Cross TQ11 135 C7
Whitehill Cl TQ12 207 B5
Whitehill Cotts TQ12 206 F5
Whitehill Cross PL15 105 B6
Whitehill Gdns PL7 132 F4
Whitehill La TQ9,TQ9 228 B8
Whitehill Rd TQ12 207 A5
Whitehorse La EX39 157 A8
Whitehouse Cl 2 EX39 15 B1
Whitehouse Cross EX39 156 B3
Whitehouse La EX18 58 D5
Whiteland Head EX20 57 B8
Whiteley Ave TQ9 222 F6
Whiteley Cross PL21 137 B5
Whitemoor Cross PL8 142 A8
Whitemoor Hill EX32 16 E1
Whitemoor La EX5,EX17 81 C8
Whiterocks Pk PL18 125 A6
Whites Cotts EX20 95 B4
Whites La EX31 154 F7
Whiteside Cl EX2 178 C4
Whitestaunton Cross TA20 69 E5
Whitestone Cross TQ7 145 C5
Whitestone La EX33 8 D1
Whitethorn Cl
Honiton EX14 166 C4
Sidmouth EX10 187 F8
Whitethorn Pk EX4 173 C3
Whiteway Cl 6 EX5 99 E8
Whiteway Dr EX1 178 B6
Whiteway La TQ1 214 D8
Whiteway Rd TQ12 207 D7
Whitford Rd
Kilmington EX13 103 D8
Musbury EX13 103 D7
Whitham Pk PL19 171 C4
Whitleigh Ave PL5 244 E2
Whitleigh Cotts PL5 244 E2
Whitleigh Ct PL5 244 D4
Whitleigh Gn PL5 244 C4
Whitleigh Prim Sch PL5 244 D4
Whitleigh Villas PL5 244 E2
Whitleigh Way PL5 244 C4
Whitley Cross TQ7 143 C3
Whitley Rd Farway EX24 101 F7
Paignton TQ4 226 A4
Whitley Rocks EX36 31 C7
Whitlow Copse EX2 178 C4
Whitman Cl EX8 196 C4
Whitmore La PL21 137 C4
Whitmore Way EX14 166 A4
Whitnage La EX16 50 C2
Whitnole Cross EX16 48 A5
Whitnole La EX16 48 A4
Whitsam Cross PL20 125 D1
Whitsford Cross EX32 18 C4
Whitsley Cross EX19,EX38 42 C4
Whitson Cross PL5 244 C7
Whitsoncross La PL5 244 C7
Whitstone Cty Prim Sch EX22 70 E1
Whitstone Head Sch EX22 70 E1
Whitstone La
Bovey Tracey TQ13 180 C8
South Molton EX36 46 B5
Whitstone Rd TQ4 226 B5
Whittingham Rd
Ilfracombe EX34 150 C5
Yealmpton PL8 141 B8
Whittington St PL3 262 B4
Whitton Ct EX10 187 F7
Whitwell La EX24 103 A3
Whity Cross PL12 242 A4
Whitycombe Way EX4 176 D8
White Stones EX8 202 C6
Whympston Cross PL21 137 D1
Wicaford Cross EX36 31 A2
Wicaford La EX36 31 A2
Wick Cross EX14 85 F7
Wicket The EX2 178 C3
Wickington La EX20 95 B7
Widdicombe Cross TQ3 218 E5
Widdicombe Dr PL21 237 D4
Widecombe in the Moor Prim Sch TQ13 121 B3
Widecombe Way EX4 173 E1
Widegate Nursery PL9 256 D8
Widend Camping Pk TQ3 225 A8
Widepost La EX13 167 C5
Widewell La PL6 245 C7
Widewell Prim Sch PL6 245 B7
Widewell Rd PL6 245 B7
Widey Court Prim Sch PL6 244 F1
Widey Cross PL6 244 F1
Widey Ct PL6 244 F1
Widey Hill PL8 141 A7
Widey La PL6 244 F1
Widey View PL3 248 F6
Widgery Dr EX36 158 C4
Widgery Rd EX4 178 A8
Widworthy Ct EX14 86 C2
Wigford Cross TQ7 138 C1
Wigley Cross EX31 16 C8
Wilbarn Rd TQ3 226 C7
Wilburton Cross PL21 136 C3
Wilbury Way EX7 204 F7
Wilcocks Rd EX4 174 D1
Wilcombe Cross EX32 18 E4
Wilcove La PL11 246 E5
Wilder Pk EX34 150 B5
Wilder Rd EX34 150 B6
Wilderness La EX14 84 D6
Wilderness Rd PL3 248 E5
Wildmoor La TA21 52 F6
Wildner Top EX35 4 F4
Wildwoods Cres TQ12 207 F4
Wilford Rd EX2 178 B5
Wilingcott Cross EX34 8 C6
Wilkey Cl EX32 155 C4
Wilkinson Rd PL5 247 D8
Willake Rd TQ12 213 A5
Willand Moor Mews EX15 162 E5
Willand Moor Rd EX15 162 E5
Willand Old Village EX15 162 C3
Willand Rd
Braunton EX33 152 C6
Cullompton EX15 163 C4
Willand EX15 162 B6
Willand Sch EX15 162 D4
Willas Rd PL16 105 E4
Willcocks Cl 6 TA21 160 D5
Willet St 3 EX39 157 A2
Willeys Ave EX2 261 A1
Willeys Ct EX2 261 A1
Willhay La EX13 167 D7
Willhayes Cross EX6 113 E6
Willhayes Hill EX6 113 E6
Willhayes Pk EX13 167 D6
Willhays Cl 15 TQ12 123 F1
William Evans Cl PL6 244 D5
William St EX16 161 D4
Williams Ave Exeter EX2 261 A1
Plymouth PL4 249 B1
Williams Cl Dawlish EX7 204 C5
Wrafton EX33 152 E4
Williams Ct EX31 154 C2
Williamson Cl EX33 152 D4
Williamson Way EX36 158 C4
Willicombe Rd TQ3 226 A5
Willing Cross TQ10 135 F5
Willing Gate TQ10 135 E5
Willingcott Hill EX34 8 D4

Willis Ct [1] TQ1 ....220 A7
Willis's Cross TQ12 ....122 D2
Willmott Cl EX8 ....196 E1
Willoughby Cl EX8 .....196 C3
Willoughby Rd TQ1 ....220 C6
Willow Ave Exmouth EX8 .196 B3
Torquay TQ2 ....214 A3
Willow Cl
Ilfracombe EX34 ....150 E4
Newton Abbot TQ12 .....213 A8
Plymouth PL3 ....249 E5
Seaton EX12 ....192 A8
Stoke Canon EX5 ....173 F8
Willow Cotts PL7 ......250 D4
Willow Ct
Buckfastleigh TQ11 ......236 B5
Exeter EX2 ....178 A4
Plymouth PL6 ....249 E7
Willow Gdns EX5 ......175 C6
Willow Gn PL12 ....242 D2
Willow Gr Bideford EX39 ..25 D4
Stibb Cross EX38 ....40 D1
Willow La
Cornworthy TQ9 ....227 B3
★ Hemyock EX15 ....52 F2
Willow Rd PL19 ....171 C3
Willow St [2] TQ14 ......210 B4
Willow Tree Cl EX20 ....170 C5
Willow Tree Rd EX32 ...155 B2
Willow Way EX7 ....201 A2
Willow Wlk
Crediton EX17 ....165 E6
[2] Exeter EX4 ....177 D8
Honiton EX14 ....166 B4
Plymouth PL6 ....245 D5
Willoway Gr EX33 ......152 C6
Willoway La EX33 ......152 C7
Willoways Cl EX33 .....152 C6
Willowbank Prim Sch
EX15 ....163 B3
Willowbrook Sch EX4 ..174 B1
Willowby Pk PL20 ......127 A2
Willowdale Cl [1] EX14 ..166 B6
Willowfield EX33 ......152 C7
Willowpark La TQ12 ....213 C4
Willows Cl TQ7 ....144 E1
Willows The
Chilsworthy EX22 ....53 E1
Shillingford St George EX2 114 C6
Torquay TQ2 ....213 D2
Wills Ave TQ3 ....219 C1
Wills Cl PL6 ....244 E7
Wills Rd TQ9 ....223 D6
Willsdown Rd EX2 .....181 C8
Willshere Rd EX32 .....155 C4
Willsland Cl EX6 ....194 D3
Wilmington La EX13,EX14 86 E2
Wilminstone Ind Est
PL19 ....171 E7
Wilmot Gdns PL5 ......244 D3
Wilncote Lodge [4] TQ1 .220 A6
Wilsham Cross EX35 ......6 A5
Wilsham La EX35 ....5 F5
Wilson Cres PL2 ....248 B5
Wilson La Rackenford EX16 47 B4
Witheridge EX17 ....46 B1
Wilton Cl TQ12 ....212 B6
Wilton Rd Paignton TQ3 ..219 B2
Plymouth PL1 ....248 A3
Wilton St PL1 ....262 A4
Wilton Way
Abbotskerswell TQ12 ....212 B6
Exeter EX1 ....178 D6
Wiltown La EX15 ....52 F3
Wiltshier Cl EX5 ....175 C7
Wiltshire Cl Exeter EX4 ..176 E4
Plymouth PL4 ....248 F4
Wilway La TA22 ....33 C6
Wimble Cross EX22 ....164 D3
Winchester Ave
Exeter EX4 ....176 F7
Torquay TQ2 ....213 F1
Winchester Cl EX14 .....84 D2
Winchester Dr EX8 .....196 D4
Winchester Gdns PL5 ..244 A5
Wind Whistle Cross EX15 66 C1
Windabout Cross EX39 ..39 B7
Windard Terr EX20 ......93 B1
Windball Hill TA22 ......33 B7
Windbow La EX16 ....48 D3
Windeatt Sq [4] TQ9 ....223 D5
Windermere Cl EX4 ....176 F6
Windermere Cres PL6 ..244 F4
Windermere Rd TQ1 ...220 C6
Windford Hill EX31 ......10 D4
Windjammer Ct EX8 ....201 E6
Windmill Ave TQ3 .....219 A1
Windmill Cl TQ5 ....230 D4
Windmill Cross EX31 ....27 A3
Windmill Ct [9] TQ5 ....230 C4
Windmill Gdns TQ3 ....219 A1
Windmill Hill
Brixham TQ5 ....230 D4
Saltash PL12 ....242 E2
Windmill La
North Whilborough TQ12 ..212 D1
Northam EX39 ....157 B7
Paignton TQ3 ....218 F1
West Hill EX11 ....168 D5
Windmill Rd
Brixham TQ5 ....230 D4
Holsworthy EX22 ....164 D4
Paignton TQ3 ....219 A1
Windmilland Cross EX21 .74 A6
Windout La EX6 ....97 E3
Windrush Rise EX11 ....169 D3
Windsor Ave TQ12 .....207 F3
Windsor Cl
Cullompton EX15 ....163 C6
Exeter EX4 ....177 A7
Ivybridge PL21 ....237 E4
Newton Abbot TQ12 .....207 C2
Torquay TQ1 ....220 B6
Windsor Ct
Ilfracombe EX34 ....150 B5
Kingsbridge TQ7 ....258 D5
Windsor Dr EX7 ....200 E2
Windsor La PL12 ......242 E2
Windsor Mead EX10 ...101 A1
Windsor Pl PL1 ....262 C2
Windsor Rd
Barnstaple EX31 ....154 E7
Dartmouth TQ6 ....233 C3
Kingsbridge TQ7 ....258 D5
Northam EX39 ....156 F7
Plymouth PL3 ....249 B7
Torquay TQ1 ....220 C6
Windsor Sq EX8 ....202 A7
Windsor Terr DT7 ......260 D4
Windsor Villas PL1 .....262 C2
Windthorn Cross TQ12 .218 A7
Windthorn La TQ3,TQ12 .218 B7
Windward La EX7 ......210 F8
Windward Rd TQ2 .....213 E3
Windway Hill TA4 ....34 D6
Windwhistle Cross EX5 ..81 C8
Windwhistle La EX16 ....49 B8
Windy Ash Cross EX32 ...16 F1
Windy Ash Hill EX32 ...155 C1
Windy Cnr TQ4 ....229 B6
Windy Cross Ashford EX31 16 A6
Chulmleigh EX18 ....44 E1
Doddiscombsleigh EX6 ...113 E7
Great Torrington EX38 ...159 C5
Holsworthy Beacon EX22 ...54 F2
Windypost Cross EX35 .151 C2
Wingfield TQ7 ....143 A1
Wingfield Cl [3] EX16 ..161 C3
Wingfield Rd PL3 ......262 A4
Wingfield Way PL3 .....262 A4
Winham La EX15 ....83 B6
Winifred Baker Ct [5]
PL4 ....263 A4
Winifred Cliff Ct [1] EX16 .34 B1
Winkleigh Cl EX2 ......177 A2
Winkleigh Moor Cross
EX19 ....58 C7
Winkleigh Prim Sch
EX19 ....58 F2
Winneford La EX14 ......85 C3
Winner Hill Rd TQ3 ....226 A6
Winner St TQ3 ....226 A6
Winnicott Cl PL6 ....244 E7
Winnings Way TQ1 .....220 D7
Winnow Cl PL9 ....255 F4
Winsbeer La
Rockwell Green TA21 ....160 A6
Runnington TA21 ....51 F8
Winsbury Ct PL6 ....245 A1
Winscott Cross
Holsworthy EX21 ....72 A4
Newton St Cyres EX5 .....81 B1
Winsford Rd TQ2 ......219 C3
Winsham Cross
Knowle EX33 ....8 D1
Knowle EX33 ....8 E2
Winsham Rd EX33 ....8 D1
Winslade Cl TQ7 ....144 E1
Winslade Park Ave EX5 .179 B2
Winslade Rd EX10 .....188 B6
Winslake Mdw EX6 ......97 F4
Winsland Ave TQ9 .....222 E6
Winson Cross EX37 ......29 A4
Winsor Cross PL8 ......136 C4
Winstanley Wlk PL3 ....249 D6
Winstitchen Cross TA24 .13 C2
Winstitchen La TA24 ....13 C2
Winston Ave PL4 ....262 C4
Winston Cl TQ12 ....207 E7
Winston Ct TQ14 ....210 C6
Winston Ho EX36 ....158 C5
Winston Pk EX36 ....158 C5
Winston Rd EX8 ....196 E2
Winstone Ave TQ2 .....214 A1
Winstone La PL8 ....257 B4
Winsu Ave TQ3 ....226 A8
Winswood EX17 ....165 D4
Winsworthy EX39 ....23 D3
Winter Gdn TQ2 ....220 B4
Winter's La EX11 ......169 D3
Winterbourne Rd TQ14 .210 C5
Winterland La EX22 ....164 D2
Winters Cross TA4 ......35 C8
Wiriga Way EX16 ....46 E1
Wishings Rd TQ5 ......230 D3
Wiston Cross EX36 ......32 D2
Witch La EX14 ....86 F8
Witcombe La EX6 ......194 D3
Witham Gdns PL3 .....249 C5
Witheby EX10 ....187 F3
Withecombe Cross
TQ13 ....110 F8
Withen Cross EX5 ....99 C1
Withen La EX5 ....99 D2
Witherdon Cross EX21 ...91 D5
Witheridge CE Prim Sch
EX16 ....46 E1
Witheridge Mill Cross
EX16 ....46 E2
Witheridge Moor Cross
(East) EX16 ....47 E1
Witheridge Moor Cross
(West) EX16 ....47 D1
Witheridge Pl EX34 ....150 E5
Withleigh Cross EX16 ...63 C8
Withleigh La EX16 ......63 D7
Withnoe La PL10 ....252 B6
Withy Bed La EX5 ....99 E3
Withy Cl EX16 ....161 F3
Withy Cross EX38 ....42 E6
Withy La EX15 ....52 B1
Withy The EX5 ....99 E8
Withycombe Park Dr
EX8 ....196 E2
Withycombe Raleigh CE Prim
Sch EX8 ....196 C1
Withycombe Rd EX8 ...202 B8
Withycombe Village Rd
EX8 ....202 B8
Withygate La EX32 ......19 A5
Withypool Cross
Hawkridge TA22 ....21 C2
Twitchen EX36 ....20 E4
Withywell La EX33 ....7 E1
Withywine La TA22 .....34 C5
Wixon Cross EX18 ......45 B3
Wixon La EX18 ....45 B3
Woburn Cl TQ3 ....225 D7
Woburn Terr PL9 ......255 C7
Wolborough Cl TQ12 ...207 C2
Wolborough Gdns
Brixham TQ5 ....230 E6
Newton Abbot TQ12 .....207 C2
Wolborough Hill Sch
TQ12 ....207 B2
Wolborough St TQ12 ...207 B3
Wolford Cross EX14 .....85 B8
Wollaton Cross PL8 ....257 A6
Wollaton Gr PL5 ....243 F3
Wolrige Ave PL7 ....251 B5
Wolrige Way PL7 ......251 A5
Wolsdon Pl PL1 ....262 A3
Wolsdon St PL1 ....262 B3
Wolseley Bsns Pk [2]
PL2 ....248 A5
Wolseley Cl PL2 ....248 A5
Wolseley Rd
Plymouth, Camels Head
PL5 ....247 F6
Plymouth, St Budeaux PL5 243 C1
Wolseley Road Flats
PL2 ....247 F6
Wolston Cl TQ5 ....230 B6
Wolverstone Cross EX14 .85 A8
Wolverstone Hill EX14 ...85 A7
Wolverton Dr TQ12 ....207 D7
Wolverwood Cl PL7 ....251 C3
Wolverwood La PL7 ....251 B3
Wombwell Cres PL2 ....247 E7
Wonders Cnr EX38 ......40 D2
Wonford Rd EX2 ....261 C2
Wonford St EX2 ....178 A4
Wonnacott's Rd EX20 ..170 C5
Wonton Cross TQ9 .....135 D2
Wood Acre PL12 ....242 B4
Wood Cl Christow EX6 ..113 B4
Saltash PL12 ....242 B3
Wood Cnr EX6 ....97 C2
Wood Cotts TQ12 ......180 C1
Wood Cross EX14 ....86 C6
Wood La
Abbotskerswell TQ12 ....212 A5
Ashreigney EX18 ....43 D1
Broadhembury EX14 ......84 E7
Christow EX6 ....113 B4
Combe Martin EX34 ....3 B2
Exmouth EX8 ....196 D1
Ilfracombe EX34 ....8 F4
Kingswear TQ6 ....234 B3
Monkton EX14 ....86 C6
Morchard Bishop EX17 ....61 A2
Slapton TQ7 ....145 D4
Thorverton EX17 ....81 B4
West Alvington TQ7 .....258 A4
Wood Park La EX34 ......2 D3
Wood Pk Ivybridge PL21 .237 D6
Plymouth PL6 ....132 A2
Wood Rock EX36 ....32 C5
Wood View TQ12 ......207 A3
Wood Way EX35 ....6 D4
Wood's Cross EX36 ......32 C5
Wooda Rd EX39 ....157 C8
Woodacott Cross EX22 ..54 E2
Woodah Rd EX4 ....176 F5
Woodbine Cotts PL7 ...250 E4
Woodbine Pl [4] EX12 ..192 A5
Woodbine Terr EX4 ....261 A4
Woodbridge La
Bondleigh EX18 ....77 D8
Farway EX24 ....102 B6
North Tawton EX17 ......59 E1
Woodbrook Rd TQ9 ....223 E5
Woodburn Cl PL21 .....237 B5
Woodburn Cross EX16 ...32 F2
Woodburn Hill EX16 .....32 F2
Woodburn Water Cross
EX16 ....32 F1
Woodbury CE Prim Sch
EX5 ....184 C3
Woodbury Ct EX8 ......202 C6
Woodbury Gdns PL5 ...244 A3
Woodbury La EX13 ....167 E3
Woodbury Pk EX13 ....167 C4
Woodbury Rd EX3,EX5 ..183 E5
Woodbury Salterton CE Prim
Sch EX5 ....184 C7
Woodbury View
Exeter EX2 ....177 A2
Broadclyst EX5 ....175 D6
Woodbury Way EX13 ...167 D4
Woodchurch PL20 .....126 E3
Woodcock Cl PL10 .....253 A6
Woodcock Way EX13 ....88 B7
Woodcote Ct EX5 ......184 C3
Woodcourt Rd TQ9 ....139 C7
Woodcroft Cross EX19 ...76 D7
Woodcroft La EX19 ......76 D8
Woodcroft Mdws TA20 ...69 B7
Woodend Rd
Plymouth PL6 ....245 D7
Torquay TQ1 ....220 D4
Wooder Wharf [13] EX39 .157 A1
Woodfield Cl EX8 ......196 E2
Woodfield Cres PL21 ...237 E4
Woodfield Ct TQ1 ......220 D3
Woodfield Prim Sch
PL5 ....244 C5
Woodfields EX12 ....192 A7
Woodford Ave PL7 .....250 A7
Woodford Cl PL7 ....250 A7
Woodford Cres PL7 ....250 A6
Woodford Gn PL7 ......250 B6
Woodford Inf Sch PL7 ..250 B6
Woodford Jun Sch PL7 .250 B7
Woodford Rd PL6 ......245 D6
Woodhaye Cl [2] TQ10 ..134 F2
Woodhaye Gdns [5] TQ1 220 D4
Woodhaye Terr [1] TQ10 .134 F2
Woodhead Cross
Branscombe EX12 ....190 E7
Totnes TQ9 ....217 D4
Woodhead La
Tiverton EX16 ....63 A7
Totnes TQ9 ....217 E4
Woodhey Rd PL2 ....248 A7
Woodhill View EX14 ....166 B4
Woodhouse Cl TQ7 ....258 C4
Woodhouse Cross TQ13 122 D3
Woodhouse Fields DT7 .104 B4
Woodhouse La
Axminster EX13 ....88 D1
Uplyme DT7 ....104 B4
Woodhouse Rd EX13 ....88 D1
Woodhuish La TQ5,TQ6 .235 B7
Woodland Ave
Kingskerswell TQ12 ......212 F5
Plymouth PL9 ....256 A8
Teignmouth TQ14 ....210 D7
Woodland Bsns Pk TQ2 219 E8
Woodland Cl
Barnstaple EX32 ....155 E4
Denbury TQ12 ....131 F3
Ivybridge PL21 ....237 B5
Staverton TQ9 ....216 A4
Torquay TQ2 ....219 E8
Woodland Cotts PL21 ..237 A5
Woodland Cross EX31 ...27 B4
Woodland Ct
[10] Barnstaple EX32 .....155 A4
Ivybridge PL21 ....237 A5
Paignton TQ3 ....226 B7
Woodland Dr PL7 ......250 B4
Woodland Hill EX17 ....97 B8
Woodland La TQ9 .....227 D4
Woodland Mews EX5 ..175 D6
Woodland Pk
Northam EX39 ....157 A5
Paignton TQ3 ....226 B7
Woodland Rd
Ashburton TQ13 ....130 F4
Broadclyst EX5 ....175 C6
Denbury TQ12 ....211 A6
Exeter EX1 ....178 D7
Harbertonford TQ9 ......139 C7
Ivybridge PL21 ....237 B5
Ivybridge, Lee Mill PL21 ..136 D7
Plymouth PL7 ....250 C6
Torquay TQ2 ....219 E8
Woodland Terr
Ivybridge PL21 ....237 B4
Kingswear TQ6 ....234 A3
Plymouth PL4 ....263 B4
Woodland Way
Gunnislake PL18 ....125 D7
Torpoint PL11 ....246 F3
Woodland Way Cl PL18 .125 C6
Woodlandhead Cross
EX17 ....97 B7
Woodlands
Budleigh Salterton EX9 ...203 E8
Churchstow TQ7 ....143 E4
Combe Martin EX34 ....2 F4
Dousland PL20 ....127 B3
Halwill EX21 ....73 D3
Kingsteignton TQ12 ......123 E2
Newton St Cyres EX5 .....98 F8
Plymouth PL9 ....255 F6
Sidmouth EX10 ....188 A4
Wellington TA21 ....160 F3
Whimple EX5 ....99 F8
Woodlands Bsns Pk
EX16 ....51 C3
Woodlands Cl
Churchstow TQ7 ....143 E4
Offwell EX14 ....86 B2
Teignmouth TQ14 ....210 C5
Woodlands Ct
Exmouth EX8 ....196 B3
Plymouth PL5 ....244 A3
Woodlands Dr EX8 .....196 B3
Woodlands End PL6 ...245 D5
Woodlands Gdns [5]
TQ12 ....207 F2
Woodlands La PL6 .....245 F1
Woodlands Leisure Pk★
TQ9 ....139 F3
Woodlands Park Prim Sch
PL21 ....237 A5
Woodlands Rd TQ12 ...207 F2
Woodlands Sch PL5 ....244 B4
Woodlands Way EX5 ...179 E3
Woodlands Wlk TQ13 ..180 C4
Woodlark La [2] EX31 ..154 A2
Woodleigh Cl EX4 .....173 A3
Woodleigh Cross EX19 ..42 B3
Woodleigh Pk TQ14 ....210 B2
Woodleigh Rd TQ12 ...206 F3
Woodley Cross EX5 .....98 F8
Woodley La EX5 ....98 E8
Woodleys Dr EX10 .....186 D8
Woodman's Cnr PL20 ..127 A3
Woodmans Cres [2]
EX14 ....166 C5
Woodmans Orch EX5 ....84 A2
Woodmead Rd
Axminster EX13 ....167 C5
Lyme Regis DT7 ....260 D3
Woodmere Way TQ12 ..207 E6
Woodmill Hospl EX15 ..163 C1
Woodovis Holiday Pk
PL19 ....116 D1
Woodpark Cross EX17 ..61 A8
Woodpark La
Molland EX36 ....31 E6
Paignton TQ3 ....218 E8
Woodpecker Way EX6 ...97 B4
Woodplace La EX16 .....62 F8
Woodridge Cross EX19 ..57 E6
Woodroffe Sch The
DT7 ....260 C4
Woods Cross EX36 ......31 D6
Woods The TQ1 ....220 E3
Woodside
Crapstone PL20 ....126 E2
Plymouth PL4 ....263 B4
Woodside Ave PL9 .....255 C6
Woodside Cl PL21 .....237 D4
Woodside Ct PL7 ......250 E4
Woodside Dr TQ1 ......220 C4
Woodside La PL4 ......263 B4
Woodside Wlk EX14 ...166 D6
Woodstock Gdns PL5 ..243 D1
Woodstock Rd EX2 ....178 A5
Woodview Pk PL9 .....256 A6
Woodview Rd TQ4 .....225 E1
Woodville EX31 ....154 C3
Woodville Ave PL20 ...128 A8
Woodville Cl
Barnstaple EX31 ....154 C4
Plymouth PL2 ....247 F7
Woodville Cross EX23 ...36 F1
Woodville Rd Exeter EX2 177 B3
Exmouth EX8 ....202 A8
Morwenstow EX23 ....36 F1
Plymouth PL2 ....247 F6
Torquay TQ1 ....220 C6
Woodward Rd EX16 ....161 B2
Woodwater La
Exeter EX2 ....178 B4
Exeter EX2 ....178 C3
Woodway PL9 ....256 A7
Woodway Cl TQ14 .....210 C7
Woodway Dr TQ14 ....210 C6
Woodway Rd TQ14 ....210 C6
Woodway St TQ13 .....123 E6
Woolacombe Cross
PL20 ....125 F1
Woolacombe Ct EX34 ....8 A6
Woolacombe Prim Sch
EX34 ....8 A6
Woolacombe Rd PL20 ..125 F1
Woolacombe Rise EX34 ..8 B6
Woolacombe Sands Cvn Pk
EX34 ....8 A6
Woolacombe Station Rd
EX34 ....8 B6
Woolaway Ave EX6 ....182 B4
Woolbarn Lawn EX32 ..155 D4
Woolbrook Cl EX10 ...188 A6
Woolbrook Mdws EX10 .188 A7
Woolbrook Mead EX10 .187 F7
Woolbrook Pk EX10 ...188 A7
Woolbrook Rd EX10 ...188 A7
Woolbrook Rise EX10 ..188 A7
Woolcombe La
Ivybridge PL21 ....237 D4
Sidmouth EX10 ....188 B5
Woolcott Way EX15 ...163 B2
Woolfardisworthy Cross
Cheriton Fitzpaine EX17 ...62 A3
Clovelly EX39 ....23 D2
Woolfardisworthy West Prim
Sch EX39 ....38 F7
Woolhanger's La EX34 ...2 E3
Woollcombe Ave PL7 ..250 F4
Woolms Mdw PL21 ....237 A4
Woolpit La TA24 ....21 B7
Woolsery Ave EX4 .....178 B8
Woolsery Cl EX4 ......178 B8
Woolsery Gr EX4 ......178 B8
Woolster Ct [9] PL4 ....263 A2
Woolwell Cres PL6 ....245 C8
Woolwell Dr PL6 ......245 C7
Woolwell Rd PL6 ......245 D7
Wootton Cross EX13 ....88 F1
Worcester Cres EX15 ..162 D4
Worden Cross
Milton Damerel EX22 .....54 E6
Sutcombe EX22 ....54 C8
Wordland Cross EX17 ...80 F8
Wordsworth Ave EX31 ..154 F7
Wordsworth Cl
Exmouth EX8 ....196 C4
Torquay TQ2 ....219 E6
Wordsworth Cres PL2 ..247 F7
Wordsworth Rd PL2 ...247 F7

Worham's La EX13 ......86 F2
Works The EX16 ......161 C4
World of Country Life★
EX8 ....203 B6
Worlington Cross EX39 ..15 C1
Worlington Hill EX39 ....15 C1
Wormsworthy Hill EX16 .48 D6
Worth La Hele EX5 ....82 E5
Withypool TA22,TA24 ......21 C4
Worth Rd EX34 ....150 C5
Worthele Cl PL21 ......237 A4
Worthele Cross PL21 ...237 B1
Worthy La EX16 ....47 C6
Wotton Cross TQ12 ....131 E4
Wotton La EX8 ....196 B5
Wotton Pound EX8 .....196 A5
Wotton Way TQ9 ....131 E1
Wrafton Rd EX33 ......152 E4
Wragcombe La TA21 ....52 A4
Wrangaton Rd Pl21,
TQ10 ....137 D8
Wrangcombe Rd TA21 ...52 A4
Wrangway Rd EX15 .....52 A3
Wrangworthy Cross EX39 39 E4
Wreford's Cl EX4 ....173 A3
Wreford's Dr EX4 ......173 A3
Wreford's La Exeter EX4 .173 A3
Exeter EX4 ....173 B3
Wreford's Link EX4 ....173 A3
Wren Cl Honiton EX14 ...166 B4
Northam EX39 ....157 A6
Wren Ct [10] TQ5 ....230 C4
Wren Gdns PL7 ....250 C6
Wren Hill TQ5 ....230 C4
Wren Pk TQ2 ....213 D2
Wrens Gate PL9 ....255 E8
Wrentham Bsns Ctr
EX4 ....177 D8
Wrentham Est EX4 .....177 D8
Wrenwell Cross TQ12 ..131 F3
Wressing View EX15 .....66 A3
Wrey Ave EX31 ....154 D4
Wright Cl PL1 ....247 E3
Wright Dr EX17 ....79 A5
Wright's La Exmouth EX8 196 F6
Torquay TQ1 ....220 A7
Wrights La PL8 ....140 F7
Wrigwell Cross TQ12 ..211 E1
Wrigwell La TQ12 ......217 F8
Wrinkleberry La EX39 ...23 D3
Wroxall Grange TQ1 ...220 C4
Wulphere Cl EX14 ....67 B1
Wyatts La PL19 ....171 B6
Wych Ct EX13 ....88 E3
Wychall Orch EX12 .....192 A6
Wychall Pk EX12 ....192 A7
Wychwood Cl EX7 .....204 E7
Wycliffe Rd PL3 ....249 B4
Wye Gdns PL3 ....249 D7
Wyke Cross EX17 ....80 F2
Wyke Hill EX17 ....80 F2
Wyke La EX13 ....167 D2
Wyke Moor Cross EX20 ..95 C8
Wyke Rd EX13 ....167 D3
Wykeham Dr PL2 ......248 A7
Wykes Rd EX1 ....177 F7
Wynards EX2 ....261 B2
Wynards Cl EX9 ....198 B6
Wynards La [2] EX2 .....261 B2
Wynards Rd EX9 ....198 B6
Wyndham Ave EX1 .....177 F6
Wyndham La PL1 ......262 A3
Wyndham Rd EX5 ....82 B6
Wyndham Sq PL1 ......262 A3
Wyndham St E PL1 .....262 B3
Wyndham St W PL1 ....262 B3
Wynford Rd EX4 ....173 F1
Wyoming Cl PL3 ....249 C6
Wyre Cl TQ4 ....226 A2
Wytch Gn EX13 ....88 E3
Wythburn Gdns PL6 ....245 D3

Y

Yalberton Ind Est TQ4 ..225 D3
Yalberton Ind Management
Units TQ4 ....225 E3
Yalberton Rd TQ4 ......225 D3
Yalberton Tor Ind Est
TQ4 ....225 D3
Yalland Cross TQ10 .....134 F5
Yallop Way EX14 ....166 B4
Yanhey Hill EX16 ....32 E4
Yannon Dr TQ14 ....210 B5
Yannon La TQ12 ....212 E5
Yannon Terr TQ14 ......210 B6
Yannons The TQ14 ......210 B6
Yapham Cross EX39 .....23 A4
Yard Cross EX14 ....86 B7
Yard Down Cross EX36 ..19 C6
Yard Downs La EX5 .....82 D6
Yard Hill TQ13 ....111 D2
Yard La EX36 ....46 B8
Yarda Wlk PL8 ....257 A4
Yardbury Hill Rd EX24 ..102 E7
Yarde Cl EX10 ....188 B7
Yarde Cotts EX38 ....41 D1
Yarde Cross EX32 ....18 A4
Yarde Gate Cross EX36 ..19 B5
Yarde Hill Orch EX10 ...188 B7
Yarde Mead EX10 ......188 B7
Yarde Medieval Farmhouse★
TQ7 ....147 F7
Yarde's Grave Cross
TQ9 ....222 F7
Yardelands EX10 ....188 B7
Yardelands Cl EX10 ....188 B7
Yardewells Cross EX36 ..19 B5
Yardleigh Cross EX13 ....88 D4
Yardley Gdns PL6 ......245 E3
Yards La TQ5 ....230 C2
Yarmleigh La EX17 ......79 E7
Yarnacott Cnr EX32 .....17 E1
Yarnapitts Cross TQ13 ..110 E7
Yarrow Mead PL9 ......256 D7
Yawl Cres DT7 ....104 B5
Yawl Cross DT7 ....104 B6
Yawl Hill DT7 ....104 C6
Yawl La DT7 ....104 B5
Yealm Gr TQ2 ....219 C7
Yealm Pk PL8 ....257 E4
Yealm Rd PL8 ....140 F6
Yealm View Rd PL8 .....141 A6
Yealmbury Hill PL8 .....257 F4
Yealmpstone Cl PL7 ....251 B4
Yealmpstone Dr PL7 ...251 B3
Yealmpstone Farm Prim Sch
PL7 ....251 B3
Yealmpton Prim Sch
PL8 ....257 E4
Yearlstone Vineyard★
EX16 ....63 F3
Yearnor Mill La TA24 .....6 F5
Yeats Cl PL5 ....244 C2
Yeatt Cross TQ12 ....131 F3
Yellaford Way [1] EX31 ..154 B3
Yelland Bglws TQ10 ....135 E5
Yelland Cross
Bratton Fleming EX31 .....11 D4
Rattery TQ10 ....135 E5
Yelland EX31 ....153 A5
Yelland Rd EX31 ....153 C5
Yellands Pk TQ7 ....142 C6
Yellaton La EX34 ....3 B1
Yellow Moor La EX19 ....58 F1
Yellow Tor Ct PL12 .....242 C2
Yellow Tor La PL12 .....242 C2
Yellowtor Rd PL12 .....242 B2
Yelverton Bsns Pk PL20 126 E2
Yelverton Cl PL5 ....243 E4
Yelverton Paperweight Mus★
PL20 ....126 F2
Yelverton Terr
Tavistock PL19 ....171 D6
Yelverton PL20 ....127 A2
Yendacott La EX17 ......81 B3
Yeo Cl PL3 ....249 B5
Yeo Dr [20] EX39 ....15 A1
Yeo Gate EX36 ....31 C4
Yeo La Molland EX36 .....31 C5
North Tawton EX20 ....77 B5
Yeo Mill Cross EX36 .....32 C5
Yeo Pk PL8 ....136 A3
Yeo Rd Braunton EX31 ....15 E5
Zeal Monachorum EX17 ...78 D7
Yeo Vale Cross EX17 .....60 C2
Yeo Vale Cross Ind Est
EX17 ....60 C2
Yeo Vale Ho [4] EX32 ....154 F6
Yeo Vale Rd EX32 ......154 F6
Yeo Valley Prim Sch
EX32 ....155 A6
Yeoford Com Prim Sch
EX17 ....79 C1
Yeoford Mdws EX17 .....79 C1
Yeoford Sta EX17 ....79 C1
Yeoford Way EX2 ......181 D8
Yeoland La
Swimbridge EX32 ....17 F1
Yelverton PL20 ....126 F1
Yeolands The TQ9 ......227 F8
Yeolland La PL21 ......237 D5
Yeolland Pk PL21 ......237 E5
Yeomadon Cross EX22 ...71 D4
Yeomans Way PL7 .....251 A4
Yeotown Cross EX37 ....44 C8
Yerris Rd EX15 ....65 F2
Yetsonais Cross TQ9 ...144 D8
Yettington Rd EX9 .....198 A7
Yew Cl Brixham TQ5 .....229 F2
Honiton EX14 ....166 A4
Yew Tree Cl Exeter EX4 ..173 E1
Exmouth EX8 ....196 C3
Yew Tree Dr TQ12 ......207 E6
Yew Wood Cross EX15 ...66 A4
Yewdale Gdns PL6 .....245 D2
Yolhey La TQ12 ....212 C5
Yon St TQ12 ....212 F4
Yonder Cl EX11 ....169 E3
Yonder Cnr EX11 ....169 E3
Yonder Mdw TQ9 ......227 F8
Yonder Mount EX13 ....103 D5
Yonder St
Ottery St Mary EX11 .....169 E3
Plymouth PL9 ....255 B6
York Cl Axminster EX13 ..167 E6
Exmouth EX8 ....196 E2
Feniton EX14 ....84 D2
York Cres Feniton EX14 ..84 D2
Torquay TQ1 ....220 C8
York Gdns TQ4 ....226 B4
York Pl Bideford EX39 ...157 A3
Cullompton EX15 ....163 C5
Plymouth PL2 ....247 F4
York Rd Exeter EX4 .....261 C4
Paignton TQ4 ....226 B4
Plymouth PL5 ....247 E8
Seaton EX12 ....192 A5
Torpoint PL11 ....247 B3
Torquay TQ1 ....220 C8
York St Plymouth PL1 ....247 E2
York St *continued*
Sidmouth EX10 ....188 B3
York Terr
[7] Plymouth PL2 ....247 F5
Sidmouth EX10 ....188 B3
York Villas TQ1 ....220 C8
Yorke Rd TQ6 ....233 D3
Youings Dr EX31 ....155 A7
Youlden La EX20 ....95 C7
Youldon Moor Cross
EX22 ....53 E4
Youldon Way PL20 .....126 F4
Youldons Cl TQ9 ....139 C7
Youlston Cl EX31 ....17 A7
Youltree Cross EX39 .....22 E4
Young's Park Rd TQ4 ..226 C4
Youngaton Rd EX39 ....156 C7

Z

Zeal Cross EX6 ....112 F8
Zeal Rd Dunsford EX6 ...112 F8
Tedburn St Mary EX6 ......97 F1
Zealley Est TQ12 ....207 E6
Zempson Cross TQ10 ...135 B5
Zephyr Cres EX32 ......155 B5
Zeth Hill La PL21 ......136 D8
Zion Pl Dartmouth TQ6 ...233 F4
Ivybridge PL21 ....237 C5
Zion Rd [3] TQ2 ....219 F5
Zion St PL1 ....262 C2

Using the Ordnance Survey National Grid

Any feature in this atlas can be given a unique reference to help you find the same feature on other Ordnance Survey maps of the area, or to help someone else locate you if they do not have a Street Atlas.

The grid squares in this atlas match the Ordnance Survey National Grid and are at 500 metre intervals. The small figures at the bottom and sides of every other grid line are the National Grid kilometre values (**00** to **99** km) and are repeated across the country every 100 km (see left).

To give a unique National Grid reference you need to locate where in the country you are. The country is divided into 100 km squares with each square given a unique two-letter reference. Use the administrative map to determine in which 100 km square a particular page of this atlas falls.

The bold letters and numbers between each grid line (**A** to **F**, **1** to **8**) are for use within a specific Street Atlas only, and when used with the page number, are a convenient way of referencing these grid squares.

Example *The railway bridge over DARLEY GREEN RD in grid square B1*

Step 1: Identify the two-letter reference, in this example the page is in **SP**

Step 2: Identify the 1 km square in which the railway bridge falls. Use the figures in the southwest corner of this square: Eastings **17**, Northings **74**. This gives a unique reference: **SP 17 74**, accurate to 1 km.

Step 3: To give a more precise reference accurate to 100 m you need to estimate how many tenths along and how many tenths up this 1 km square the feature is (to help with this the 1 km square is divided into four 500 m squares). This makes the bridge about **8** tenths along and about **1** tenth up from the southwest corner.

This gives a unique reference: **SP 178 741**, accurate to 100 m.

Eastings (read from left to right along the bottom) come before Northings (read from bottom to top). If you have trouble remembering say to yourself "Along the hall, THEN up the stairs"!

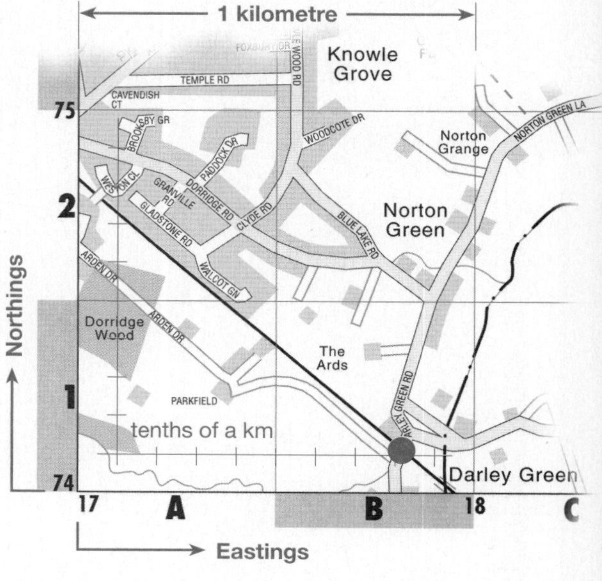

Notes

Addresses

Name and Address	Telephone	Page	Grid reference

Name and Address	Telephone	Page	Grid reference

Street Atlases from Philip's

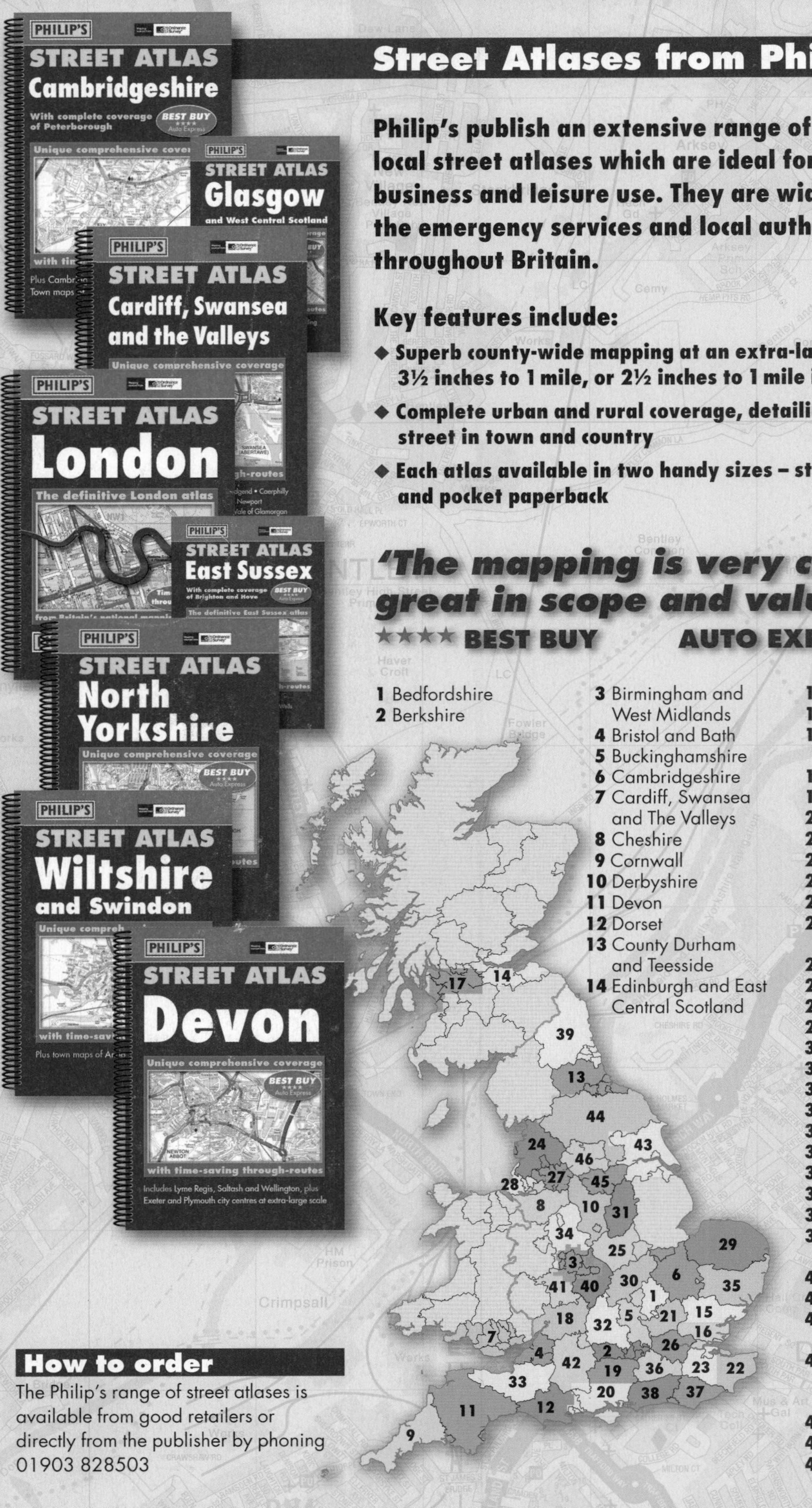

Philip's publish an extensive range of regional and local street atlases which are ideal for motoring, business and leisure use. They are widely used by the emergency services and local authorities throughout Britain.

Key features include:

- **Superb county-wide mapping at an extra-large scale of 3½ inches to 1 mile, or 2½ inches to 1 mile in pocket editions**
- **Complete urban and rural coverage, detailing every named street in town and country**
- **Each atlas available in two handy sizes – standard spiral and pocket paperback**

'The mapping is very clear... great in scope and value'

★★★★ BEST BUY AUTO EXPRESS

1 Bedfordshire
2 Berkshire
3 Birmingham and West Midlands
4 Bristol and Bath
5 Buckinghamshire
6 Cambridgeshire
7 Cardiff, Swansea and The Valleys
8 Cheshire
9 Cornwall
10 Derbyshire
11 Devon
12 Dorset
13 County Durham and Teesside
14 Edinburgh and East Central Scotland
15 North Essex
16 South Essex
17 Glasgow and West Central Scotland
18 Gloucestershire
19 North Hampshire
20 South Hampshire
21 Hertfordshire
22 East Kent
23 West Kent
24 Lancashire
25 Leicestershire and Rutland
26 London
27 Greater Manchester
28 Merseyside
29 Norfolk
30 Northamptonshire
31 Nottinghamshire
32 Oxfordshire
33 Somerset
34 Staffordshire
35 Suffolk
36 Surrey
37 East Sussex
38 West Sussex
39 Tyne and Wear and Northumberland
40 Warwickshire
41 Worcestershire
42 Wiltshire and Swindon
43 East Yorkshire and Northern Lincolnshire
44 North Yorkshire
45 South Yorkshire
46 West Yorkshire

How to order

The Philip's range of street atlases is available from good retailers or directly from the publisher by phoning 01903 828503